Lifespan
Development
Second Canadian Edition

Lifespan
Second Canadian Edition
Development

Helen Bee

Denise Boyd
Houston Community College System

Paul Johnson
Confederation College of Applied Arts and Technology

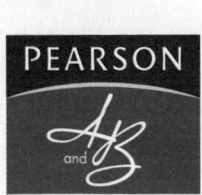

PEARSON

Toronto

Library and Archives Canada Cataloguing in Publication

Bee, Helen L., 1939–
    Lifespan development / Helen Bee, Denise Boyd, Paul Johnson.—2nd
Canadian ed.

Includes bibliographical references and index.
ISBN 0-205-43198-4

    1. Developmental psychology—Textbooks. I. Boyd, Denise Roberts
II. Johnson, Paul A. III. Title.

BF713.B437 2005   155   C2005-900264-6

ISBN 0-205-43198-4

Vice President, Editorial Director: Michael J. Young
Acquisitions Editor: Ky Pruesse
Executive Marketing Manager: Judith Allen
Senior Developmental Editor: Joel Gladstone
Production Editor: Avivah Wargon
Copy Editor: Ann McInnis
Proofreader: Gilda Mekler
Production Manager: Wendy Moran
Manufacturing Coordinator: Susan Johnson
Page Layout: Carolyn E. Sebestyen
Permissions and Photo Research: Lisa Brant
Art Director: Julia Hall
Interior Design: Julia Hall
Cover Design: Miguel Acevedo
Cover Image: Getty Images / Photographer's Choice / Eddie Soloway

5 6 7 8   10 09 08 07

Statistics Canada information is used with the permission of the Minister of Industry, as Minister responsible for Statistics Canada. Information on the availability of the wide range of data from Statistics Canada can be obtained from Statistics Canada's Regional Offices, its World Wide Web site at http://www.statcan.ca and its toll-free access number, 1-800-263-1136.

Printed and bound in the USA.

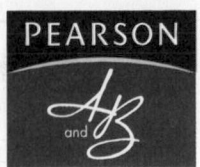

This book is dedicated to my husband, Jerry Boyd, in appreciation for the help and support he provided to me while I was preparing the fourth edition of *Lifespan Development*.

Denise Boyd

To my best friend, my wife, Bonnie Johnson, and our two daughters, Jessica and Alexandra.

Paul Johnson

BRIEF CONTENTS

LIST OF FEATURES

NO EASY ANSWERS

POLICY QUESTIONS

CONTENTS

UNIT 2   INFANCY AND EARLY CHILDHOOD

4   PHYSICAL AND COGNITIVE DEVELOPMENT IN INFANCY   95

5   SOCIAL AND PERSONALITY DEVELOPMENT IN INFANCY   129

UNIT 3   MIDDLE CHILDHOOD AND ADOLESCENCE

8   PHYSICAL AND COGNITIVE DEVELOPMENT IN MIDDLE CHILDHOOD   235

9   SOCIAL AND PERSONALITY DEVELOPMENT IN MIDDLE CHILDHOOD   265

TO THE STUDENT

Welcome to the second Canadian edition of *Lifespan Development*. As you begin your study of human development across the lifespan from the Canadian perspective, it is important that you know what an incredibly fascinating, complex, and indispensable field of study it is. To convey this richness, *Lifespan Development* covers a great deal of information. Thus, you may discover the study of human development to be one of the most information-intensive learning experiences of your academic career. Fortunately, this book includes a number of features that will help you manage and sort out all this information in a meaningful and rewarding manner.

HOW TO WORK WITH THIS BOOK

A textbook isn't like a magazine or a novel. You should keep in mind that the goal of working with a textbook is to understand and remember the information in it so that you can apply it effectively in your professional and personal life. To work with this book most effectively, take advantage of its structural and pedagogical features:

Chapter Outlines. Before you read each chapter, read over the outline at its beginning. More information will stick in your mind if you have an idea of what to expect.

Preview Questions. The introduction to each chapter ends with a list of questions to keep in mind as you read. Be sure to read the questions before continuing with the rest of the chapter. Like the chapter outline, the questions create a set of mental "hooks" on which to hang the information in the chapter.

Headings and Subheadings. The preview questions correspond to the chapter's major headings. Think of these headings and their subheadings as a way of organizing the information that follows into categories. This will help to structure the information in your mind and will make it easier to recall and use the information when you need it. Taking notes on your reading and arranging them according to the book's headings will help even more. To give yourself the best chance of creating organized memory networks, stop reading between major sections, reflect back on what you have read, and review your written notes.

Before Going On. To help you review, the book includes a feature called *Before Going On* at the end of each major section. You should stop reading and

try to answer the questions in this feature when you come to it. If you can't answer the questions, go back and review the section. You will know what parts of the text to review because each question corresponds to a subheading. Once you've completed this process, take a break before you begin another major section.

Marginal Glossary. Key terms are defined in the margin near where they are first used in the text. As you come to each boldface term in the text, stop and read its definition in the margin. Then go back and reread the sentence that introduced the key term.

Critical Thinking Questions. These questions encourage you to relate material in the book to your own experiences. They can also help you remember the information in the text, because linking new information to things you already know is a highly effective memory strategy.

Make the Connection. Each chapter includes a question titled *Make the Connection*. Thinking about these questions will help you integrate information across chapters.

Themed Essays. There are four kinds of themed essays throughout the book. "No Easy Answers" help you understand the complexities involved in trying to apply developmental theories and research to real-life problems. "Development in the Information Age" essays will inform you about how various information media have affected perceptions of development and how such media may influence the developmental process itself. "Research Report" essays recount the findings of important studies, and essays entitled "The Real World" offer practical advice on parenting, teaching, caregiving, and other aspects of daily life to which developmental psychology is relevant.

Developmental Psychology in Your Career. As you learn about lifespan development, it is important to keep asking yourself, "What can I do with what I know?" This feature will help you make the connection between facts and theory and how this information can best be applied to your career.

Policy Questions. Discussions of Canadian social policy issues relevant to human development appear at the end of each unit. For example, the policy question at the end of Unit 1 addresses the legal questions surrounding the rights of a pregnant woman versus the status and well-being of her fetus. These discussions will provide you with insight into how the findings of developmental research may be used to influence policy changes in the real world. They may also serve as starting points for group discussions and research projects.

Key Terms. Key terms are listed alphabetically at the end of each chapter, in addition to being defined in the margin. When you finish a chapter, try to recall the definition of each term. Page numbers are listed for all the terms, so you can easily look back in the chapter if you can't remember a definition.

Chapter Summaries. Looking over the chapter summary can also help you assess how much of the information you remember.

The task of understanding and remembering the information in a developmental psychology textbook may seem quite challenging. However, when you finish reading this book, you will have a better understanding of yourself and of other people. So, all your hard work will be well worth the effort.

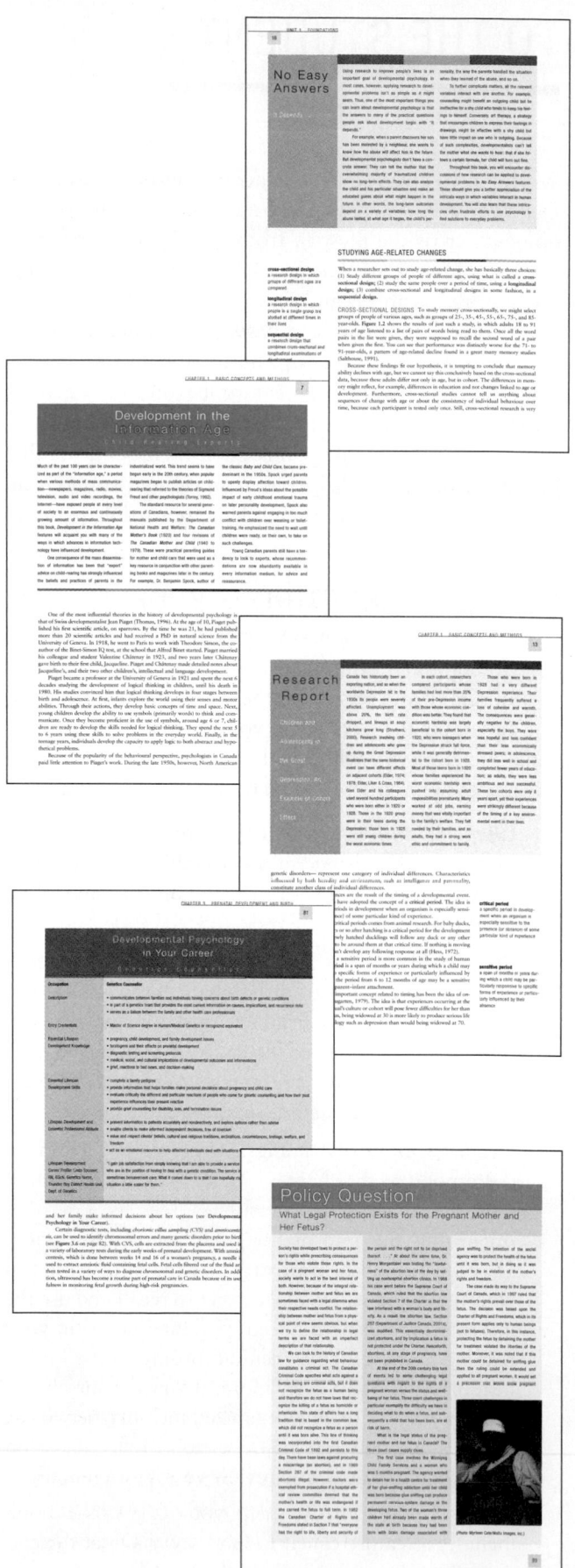

TO THE INSTRUCTOR

The foremost goal in preparing the second Canadian edition of Helen Bee's well-established developmental textbook was to take a concise, research-based, field-proven, student- and teacher-friendly textbook and overlay it with an extensive range of up-to-date Canadian research and issues. This Canadian focus should help your students become more fully engaged and ready to understand and remember the developmental psychology content as they recognize the Canadian celebrities, cities, current events, and cultural and social issues illustrated throughout the textbook.

The outcome of this endeavour is the second Canadian edition of *Lifespan Development*, with over 300 new Canadian references for a total of over 700 Canadian references infused into every possible content area of the textbook. Canadian students may at first experience "reverse culture shock" as they read about the many influential Canadian researchers working in Canadian institutions and how their research contributes to a uniquely Canadian perspective. Moreover, students will be pleased to find that the text is written in standard Canadian English and includes metric conversions. In addition, several Canadian research projects, such as the Canadian Perinatal Surveillance System (CPSS), the National Longitudinal Survey of Children and Youth (NLSCY), and the General Social Survey (GSS), are highlighted throughout the textbook.

The other goals of the second Canadian edition of *Lifespan Development* are the same as those articulated by Helen Bee in her earlier editions:

- To find that difficult but essential balance of theory, research, and practical application.
- To make the study of human development relevant not just for psychologists but also for students in the various fields in which this information is needed, including nursing, medicine, social work, education, and many others.
- To keep all discussions as current as possible, so that students can encounter the very latest thinking and the most recent research.
- To write in as personal and direct a way as possible, so that the book is more like a conversation than a traditional text, without sacrificing either theoretical clarity or rigour of research.

STRUCTURAL ELEMENTS OF THE SECOND CANADIAN EDITION

The second Canadian edition of *Lifespan Development* includes up-to-date theories and research, as detailed below.

ORGANIZATION The chapters are organized into five units:

Unit 1: Foundations (Chapters 1–3)

Unit 2: Infancy and Early Childhood (Chapters 4–7)

Unit 3: Middle Childhood and Adolescence (Chapters 8–11)

Unit 4: Early and Middle Adulthood (Chapters 12–15)

Unit 5: Late Adulthood and the End of Life (Chapters 16–18)

HISTORY OF DEVELOPMENTAL PSYCHOLOGY

Chapter 1 (Basic Concepts and Methods) includes a special section on the brief history of the roots of psychology in Canada and how these set the stage for modern developmental psychology.

STREAMLINED PRESENTATION OF RESEARCH METHODS
A substantial effort has been made to present research information as clearly and concisely as possible.

EVALUATION OF THEORIES Chapter 2, "Theories of Development," cautions students against thinking of theories as either "true" or "false." Instead, students are urged to compare theories as developmentalists do, in terms of their underlying epistemological assumptions and overall usefulness (heuristic value, ability to be tested, and so on).

BIOLOGICAL THEORIES Biological theories are given prominent emphasis in this second Canadian edition. For example, Chapter 2 includes a section on evolutionary and biological theories. The discussion of Piaget's sensorimotor stage in Chapter 4 touches on recent theories that object permanence may be inborn rather than learned. Chapter 13 discusses evolutionary theories of mate selection, and Chapter 16 includes an extensive examination of biological theories of aging.

INFORMATION-PROCESSING AND OTHER COGNITIVE THEORIES

The discussion of newer cognitive theories has been expanded further in this second Canadian edition. For example, there is ample explanation of the memory system in Chapter 2. In addition, Canadian-based information-processing alternatives to Piaget's stages are presented in Chapters 6, 8, and 10. Social-cognitive theories of social and personality development are also thoroughly discussed.

PREGNANCY AND PRENATAL DEVELOPMENT

The second Canadian edition of *Lifespan Development* presents substantial coverage of prenatal development, reflecting rapidly expanding knowledge about this period of development within a Canadian context. The coverage of pregnancy includes a discussion of the pregnant woman's experience and a comprehensive table outlining the major events, discomforts, prenatal care priorities, and possible complications for each trimester. New tables outline fetal development and dangers. In addition, the text provides a week-by-week description of the major milestones of prenatal development. There is also a preliminary section on prenatal behaviour and assessment.

BRAIN DEVELOPMENT

Each chapter on physical and cognitive development includes a section on the brain and nervous system, which highlights updated brain imaging research on neurobiological changes across the lifespan. The goal in including this information for every age period was to convey the idea that the brain changes with age and that it influences, or is influenced by, behaviour throughout the lifespan.

HEALTH PROMOTION AND WELLNESS

In Chapter 2 there is a new discussion of wellness in context of systems theory. Each subsequent chapter on physical development includes a section that discusses the major concerns and health care needs of that age period.

MENTAL HEALTH

The second Canadian edition of *Lifespan Development* includes elemental coverage of atypical development, such as post-traumatic stress disorder (Chapter 6), attention deficit hyperactivity disorder (Chapter 8), problem gambling in Canadian youth (Policy Question, Unit 3), and personality disorders (Chapter 12).

MORAL DEVELOPMENT

In this Canadian edition, moral development is discussed in both Chapter 9 (Social and Personality Development in Middle Childhood) and Chapter 11 (Social and Personality Development in Adolescence). The coverage of moral development includes emotions and behaviour as well as cognition.

EDUCATION

The chapters on cognitive development in early childhood, middle childhood, adolescence, and early adulthood (Chapters 6, 8, 10, and 12, respectively) contain a great deal of new and explicitly Canadian information about schooling and education. The early childhood chapter includes Canadian-based research on the psychological foundations of literacy learning. The middle childhood chapter includes expanded discussions of literacy learning, schooling and cognitive development, and children with disabilities from a solidly Canadian outlook. The adolescence chapter discusses emerging research on the transitions from elementary to high school. In addition, this chapter covers the issue of employment and Canadian teens. The early adulthood chapter offers extensive discussion of issues surrounding post-secondary education.

CANADIAN SOCIAL POLICY

At least one *Policy Question* feature follows each unit in this second Canadian edition. The features discuss the following questions:

Unit 1: What Legal Protection Exists for the Pregnant Mother and Her Fetus?

Unit 2: How Should We Discipline Our Children? What Are the Effects of Childhood Poverty in Canada?

Unit 3: What Can Be Done About Gambling Among Canadian Youth?

Unit 4: What Is the Changing Status of Canadian Couples?

Unit 5: Do People Have a Right to Die?

The first goal of these discussions is to acquaint students with a few Canadian social and political issues related to topics discussed in the text. The second goal is to encourage students to find out how these issues are being dealt with where they live. Each Policy Question feature ends with a list of suggestions that should help students find out more about the issue. The hope is that students will gain an understanding of the implications of developmental psychology for social policy as well as of the impact of social policies on human development.

CONNECTING CONTENT TO CAREERS

A new feature of the second Canadian edition, *Developmental Psychology in Your Career*, will encourage your students to appreciate the relevancy of lifespan development facts and theory to many career paths. Your students are presented with brief descriptions of the *essential* knowledge, skills, and professional attitudes that human service, education, and health specialists are expected to demonstrate. Some of the careers profiled include genetics counsellor, kindergarten teacher, and gerontological specialist.

PEDAGOGY

The second Canadian edition of *Lifespan Development* includes several important pedagogical features:

Marginal Glossary. Each boldface term mentioned in the text is defined in the margin.

Before Going On. At the end of each major section, this feature encourages students to stop reading and test their recall of various pieces of information before continuing.

Make the Connection. These questions encourage students to look back at previously discussed theories or data and relate them to information in the current chapter.

Critical Thinking. Critical thinking questions throughout each chapter focus on relationships between the information in the text and students' personal experiences.

Key Terms. All boldface terms in a chapter are also listed at the end of the chapter in alphabetical order with page references.

Chapter Summaries. Each chapter ends with a summary organized by major chapter headings, with each point under each heading corresponding to a specific subheading in the chapter. This organization allows students to assess systematically how well they remember the chapter material and to know exactly where to look back in the chapter for information they may want to review.

THEMED ESSAYS

The second Canadian edition of *Lifespan Development* includes four kinds of thought-provoking themed essays.

NO EASY ANSWERS The *No Easy Answers* essays introduce students to the idea that there are many questions for which developmental psychologists cannot provide definitive answers. For example, the essay in Chapter 3 deals with the issue of pregnancy in women with epilepsy. A woman with epilepsy must decide between two risks: possible birth defects in her baby caused by her anticonvulsant medication, or the many complications that can accompany epileptic seizures during pregnancy. Either path she chooses carries risk.

Developmentalists can't tell a woman with epilepsy that if she does x, y, or z, her baby will turn out fine.

These discussions were developed in order to help students understand that psychology is not a science that can offer straightforward recipes for perfect behavioural outcomes. The hope is that, by reading these discussions, students will become more sensitive to the complexity of human development and more tolerant of the ambiguities inherent in the behavioural and social sciences.

DEVELOPMENT IN THE INFORMATION AGE In the first three chapters, the *Development in the Information Age* essay discussions focus students' attention on how various information media have shaped the Canadian public's understanding of development. For example, the essay in Chapter 3 discusses how the news media sensationalize multiple births and, as a result, often obscure the real risks inherent in multiple pregnancies. In subsequent chapters, *Development in the Information Age* essays present ideas and research about how information technology may shape development itself. For example, the essay in Chapter 4 considers what babies actually learn from television, Chapter 11 deals with the social aspects of electronic communication and Canadian youth, and Chapter 17 deals with older Canadians in a technical world.

RESEARCH REPORT *Research Report* essays provide detailed accounts of specific, predominantly Canadian research studies. For example, Chapter 2 discusses the Type 2 diabetes epidemic in a northern Canadian community. Chapter 4 features two reports based on Canadian research into language acquisition and word learning, and early gestural "language" in the children of deaf parents. Chapter 6 presents a comprehensive Canadian study of early long-term memories in children.

THE REAL WORLD *The Real World* essays explore practical applications of developmental theory and research. The focus of each of these essays has been indicated by the addition of subheadings such as *Parenting, Teaching, Caregiving, Aging,* or *Working.* For example, the essay in Chapter 4 is titled *The Real World: Parenting,* and provides Canadian nutrition recommendations for infants from birth to one year. The subheadings let students know what kind of practical information they can expect in each essay.

SUPPLEMENTS FOR THE INSTRUCTOR

INSTRUCTOR'S RESOURCE CD-ROM The Instructor's Resource CD-ROM (0205457681) includes the following supplements:

- **Instructor's Resource Manual.** The *Instructor's Manual* has been thoroughly revised. Each chapter includes the following sections:

  - Chapter Preview
  - Learning Goals
  - Extensive Teaching Notes, which include the Learning Objectives, cross-referenced in the student *Study Guide*
  - Lecture Enhancement notes
  - Instructor Resources, including suggested videos, transparency and handout masters, and references to the full-colour transparency acetates found in the Allyn & Bacon Human Development Transparency Set (0205346391)

- **Test Item File.** This test bank contains almost 2000 questions, including multiple choice, true/false, short answer, and essay questions. It is offered in both Microsoft Word and TestGen formats (see below).

- **TestGen.** The Pearson TestGen is a special computerized version of the Test Item File that enables instructors to view and edit the existing questions, add questions, generate tests, and print the tests in a variety of formats. Powerful search and sort functions make it easy to locate questions and arrange them in any order desired. TestGen also enables instructors to administer tests on a local area network, have the tests graded electronically, and have the results prepared in electronic or printed reports.

- **PowerPoint Presentations.** These PowerPoint slides cover the key concepts in each chapter of the text.

- **Image Library.** The Figures and Tables presented in the text are provided electronically for instructors to create their own in-class slide presentations.

- **Videos.** Over 40 video clips help reinforce topics covered in the text.

Some of these resources can also be downloaded from a password-protected location on Pearson Education Canada's online catalogue (**vig.pearsoned.ca**). Simply search for the text, and then click on "Instructor" go to "Resources" in the left-hand menu. Contact your local sales representative for further information.

SUPPLEMENTS FOR THE STUDENT

STUDY GUIDE The *Study Guide*, revised for the second Canadian edition of *Lifespan Development*, offers students a rich and highly structured learning tool. Each chapter of the *Study Guide* includes the following sections:

- Overview of the chapter
- Learning Goals
- Guided Study Questions, which form the bulk of the *Study Guide*, including Learning Objectives cross-referenced in the *Instructor's Manual*
- Critical Reflection Exercises
- Practice Questions, similar in format to those found in the *Test Bank* and accompanied by an answer key
- Research Projects, updated for the second edition

WEBSITE—OPEN ACCESS The *Lifespan Development* Companion Website at **www.pearsoned.ca/bee** is worth exploring. It can be accessed using the Student Access Kit, included free with every new text. It offers a wide range of resources to both instructors and students that is organized in several ways—by chapter, chronologically, and topically.

Students will find practice tests *for every chapter*, featuring Grade Tracker and Study Plan capability, plus interesting learning activities, over 40 video clips with questions (requires QuickTime), links to websites, summaries of classic research, glossary terms, and more. The Companion Website is available 24/7.

Individual Student Access Kits are available separately from your campus bookstore.

ACKNOWLEDGMENTS

Preparing this second Canadian edition of *Lifespan Development* was made possible only with the considerable coordinated efforts of many people who each played a vital role in the process.

I am very grateful to Bonnie Johnson and Jennifer Muir, for their indispensable feedback on the preliminary drafts; to Jessica Johnson, for her discerning research assistance; and to Marge Roberts, for timely research material acquisition.

I have also had the good fortune to be able to collaborate with the good-spirited people on the Pearson Education Canada editorial team. They demonstrated the epitome of professionalism. In particular, I wish to express my gratitude to Ky Pruesse, Acquisitions Editor; Martina van de Velde and Joel Gladstone, Senior Developmental Editors; Avivah Wargon, Production Editor; Ann McInnis, Copy Editor; and Judith Allen, Executive Marketing Manager. Thank you all—you are a remarkable team to work with.

I heartily thank the dozens of fellow Canadian Psychological Association members who generously responded to my DPNet call for Canadian references. Your timely replies, letters, and reprints made it possible for me to include much important research from a variety of researchers across the country.

In closing, I would like to thank the many colleagues who served as reviewers for their valuable comments and suggestions on this Canadian edition:

Rachel Birnbaum, King's College,
    University of Western Ontario
Judith Grad, Concordia University
Dr. Serena Patterson, North Island College
Madeleine Poynter, Conestoga College
Tulsie A. Raghubir-Mamuzelos, Mohawk College
Dr. Rhonda Snow, University College of the Fraser Valley
Lorraine Storry Mockford,
    Nova Scotia Community College

Paul Johnson
Confederation College of Applied Arts and Technology

A Great Way to Learn and Instruct Online

The Pearson Education Canada Companion Website is easy to navigate and is organized to correspond to the chapters in this textbook. Whether you are a student in the classroom or a distance learner you will discover helpful resources for in-depth study and research that empower you in your quest for greater knowledge and maximize your potential for success in the course.

[www.pearsoned.ca/bee]

PEARSON
Jump to...   http://www.pearsoned.ca/bee   ⬍   Home   Search   Help   Profile   Companion Website

Home >

Companion Website

Lifespan Development, Second Canadian Edition, by Bee, Boyd, and Johnson

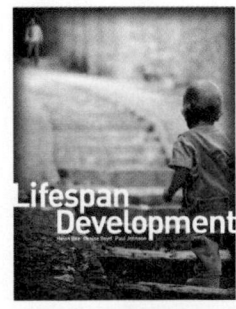

Student Resources

The modules in this section provide students with tools for learning course material. These modules include:

- Learning Activities
- Weblinks
- Classic Research
- Glossary
- In the News
- Video and Questions
- Learning Objectives
- Multiple Choice Test
- True and False Test
- Essay Questions

In the quiz modules students can send answers to the grader and receive instant feedback on their progress through the Results Reporter. Coaching comments and references to the textbook may be provided to ensure that students take advantage of all available resources to enhance their learning experience.

Lifespan

Second Canadian Edition

Development

Wayne R. Bilenduke/Getty Images

BASIC CONCEPTS AND METHODS

We are all observers of human development. For example, at family gatherings, we comment on the changes we notice in our relatives:

He's grown so much since the last time I saw him.

She's turned into such a beautiful young lady.

His hair's turning grey—the hair he has left, that is.

Grandma seems frailer than last year.

At the same time, we notice the things about people that appear to remain the same:

Aunt Frieda's as witty as ever.

I don't understand how someone could go through so much and still be so cheerful, but he's always had a lot of faith.

We also view people in light of the expectations of our culture for their age group:

Is he going to college after he graduates this year?

I wonder when those two are going to start a family of their own. They've been married for 3 years now.

We even theorize about why our relatives behave the way they do:

They've never tried to control that child. No wonder he's such a brat.

She was born with the gift of the gab.

Scientists who study human development do precisely the same things. Their goal, however, is to produce observations and explanations that can be applied to as wide a range of human beings and in as many contexts as possible. To accomplish this goal, they study both change and stability. In addition, they examine the impact of cultural expectations on individual development. They make predictions about development and use scientific methods to test them. Finally, most hope that their findings can be used to positively influence the development of individual human beings.

In this chapter, you will learn how the science of developmental psychology came into being. You will also learn how modern psychologists differ from the early pioneers with respect to a variety of issues. In addition, when you finish reading the chapter, you will be acquainted with the research designs and methods used by developmentalists. While you read, keep the following questions in mind:

- What were the contributions of early philosophers and behavioural scientists to developmental psychology?

- How do today's psychologists think about issues that have to do with nature and nurture and age-related change?

- What research designs and methods do developmentalists use to study change across the human lifespan?

THE SCIENTIFIC STUDY OF HUMAN DEVELOPMENT

developmental psychology
the scientific study of age-related changes in our bodies, behaviour, thinking, emotions, social relationships, and personalities

The field of **developmental psychology** is the scientific study of age-related changes in our bodies, behaviour, thinking, emotions, social relationships, and personalities. Long before the scientific method was used to study development, though, philosophers offered a variety of explanations for differences they observed in individuals of different ages. Their ideas continue to influence the field today, and many Western beliefs about human development are based on them.

PHILOSOPHICAL ROOTS

Philosophers who attempted to explain human development were especially interested in understanding why babies, who seem to start life so similarly, grow up to be adults who differ widely in intelligence, personality, and other characteristics. Of particular concern to most was the problem of explaining how and why some people grow up to be productive citizens while others become threats to the community. Expressed more simply, why do some of us grow up to be "good" and others "bad"?

In one way or another, most philosophers have approached this question by trying to determine whether factors inside people (such as intelligence) or outside of them (such as family environment) make them good or bad. Three ideas about the interaction of internal and external factors have been especially important in Western thinking about human development.

For centuries, the Christian doctrine of *original sin* has influenced Western world views on human development. This doctrine teaches that all humans are born with a selfish and stubborn nature because of the sin of Adam and Eve in the Garden of Eden. Even when people do good works, this doctrine says, they do so for selfish reasons. For example, a man may give money to charity so that others will admire him.

The ideas of 18th-century Swiss philosopher Jean-Jacques Rousseau have also influenced Western views on human development. Rousseau claimed that all humans have *innate goodness*. This view asserts that all human beings are naturally good and seek out experiences that help them grow (Ozman & Craver, 1986). Rousseau believed that, just as an acorn contains everything necessary to make an oak tree, children have within themselves everything they need to grow up to be competent and moral adults. Like acorns, children need only nutrition and protection to reach their full potential. For Rousseau, the goal of human development is to achieve one's inborn potential. "Good" behaviour results from growing up in an environment that doesn't interfere with the individual's attempts to do so. In contrast, "bad" behaviour is learned from others or happens when a person experiences frustration in his efforts to express the innate goodness with which he was born. Therefore, like the original sin view, the innate goodness perspective suggests that development involves a struggle between internal and external factors.

In contrast to both of these perspectives, 17th-century English philosopher John Locke proposed that the mind of a child is a *blank slate*. Locke said, "I imagine the minds of children as easily turned, this or that way, as water" (Ozman & Craver, 1986, p. 62). The blank slate view suggests that adults can mould children into whatever they want them to be. Therefore, differences among adults can be explained in terms of differences in their childhood environments. Thus, from this perspective, development—whether its results are good or bad—takes place because of external, environmental factors acting on a person, whose only relevant internal characteristic is the capacity to respond.

> ## Critical Thinking
>
> Other cultures and religions have different ways of viewing the process of development. How do the original sin, innate goodness, and blank slate views compare with your own beliefs? How do you think your own culture and religion have contributed to these beliefs?

THE STUDY OF HUMAN DEVELOPMENT BECOMES A SCIENCE

Philosophy can provide a framework for ideas about human development. However, in the 19th century, people who wanted to better understand development began to turn to science. By 1930, the foundations of modern developmental psychology had been established (see **Table 1.1**) and had begun to influence everyday child-rearing practices (see **The Real World**).

Charles Darwin and other evolutionists believed they could understand the development of the human species by studying child development. Many, including Darwin, kept detailed records of their own children's early development (called *baby biographies*), in the hope of finding evidence to support the theory of evolution (Charlesworth, 1992). These were the first organized studies of human development.

Darwin's theory of evolution is the source of many important ideas in modern developmental psychology. For example, the concept of developmental stages comes from evolutionary theory. However, critics of baby biographies claimed that studying children for the purpose of proving a theory might cause observers to misinterpret or ignore important information.

G. Stanley Hall of Clark University wanted to find more objective ways to study development. He used questionnaires and interviews to study large numbers of children. His 1891 article titled "The Contents of Children's Minds on Entering School" represented the first scientific study of child development (White, 1992).

Hall agreed with Darwin that the milestones of childhood were similar to those that had taken place in the development of the human species. He thought that developmentalists should identify **norms**, average ages at which milestones are reached. Norms, Hall said, could be used to learn about the evolution of the species as well as to track the development of individual children.

In 1904, Hall published *Adolescence: Its Psychology and Its Relations to Physiology, Anthropology, Sociology, Sex, Crime, Religion and Education*. This book introduced the idea that adolescence is a unique developmental period. Hall also arranged for Sigmund Freud, a Viennese physician who was unknown in Canada and the United States at the time, to lecture at Clark University in 1909, thereby introducing North Americans to one of the most important theories in developmental psychology.

By the time Freud accepted Hall's invitation to lecture in the United States, he had been studying hysterical disorders for more than 20 years. Hysterical disorders are physical problems, like blindness, for which doctors can't find a medical cause. Freud thought that these problems were caused by experiences patients couldn't remember. He hypnotized patients to help them remember, and he studied the dreams they reported. He also asked patients to tell him everything they could remember about specific periods

norms
average ages at which developmental milestones are reached

TABLE 1.1	Milestones in the History of Modern Developmental Psychology
1875–1900	Darwin and others publish baby biographies based on evolutionary theory.
1891	Hall publishes first scientific study of children.
1890–1900	Freud begins publishing and lecturing in Europe about his psychosexual theory.
1904	Hall publishes book on adolescence.
1913	Watson publishes his behaviourist theory.
1925	Gesell publishes his views on maturation.
1921–1930	Piaget publishes several books about his theory of cognitive development.

The Real World
Toys: More Than Just Playthings
Toys as Tools for Development

Today, a vital element of children's development is centred on playing with toys—"If play is the child's work then toys are the child's tools, and appropriate toys can help children do their work well" (Keep Kids Healthy, 2003). Accordingly, it is important to design toys that promote the development of the child (Auerback, 1998). With this in mind, many toys are now designed to promote children's

- *physical development*—improving muscle control and eye–hand coordination

- *cognitive development*—understanding about spatial and temporal relationships and fostering reasoning ability through creative expression and problem-solving

- *emotional development*—acting out inner thoughts, feelings, and fantasies in a safe manner and learning persistence and mastery

- *social development*—learning to share with others, practising social and cultural values and rules through make-believe

The Developmental Science Behind Toys

In Canada, the Canadian Toy Testing Council (CTTC) (2004) is responsible for conducting ongoing research to ensure the value and appropriateness of toys. Age-appropriate means that a toy not only matches a child's capabilities; it also captures a child's interest. "No matter how promising, if a toy is not fun, it will gather dust" (CTTC, n.d.). Toy testing results come from many sources including toy manufacturers' in-house facilities, nursery schools, college and university child centres, parents, teachers, child development specialists, psychologists, physicians, and marketing experts. This research helps identify what parents and

children want in toys and it also considers safety, performance, appeal, usefulness, durability, age-appropriateness, and potential improvements.

At each stage of development a child faces new challenges and different risks (Canadian Child Care Federation [CCCF], 2001). The Canadian and international toy industries have developed age-appropriate recommendations so that toys challenge and stimulate based on a child's chronological age, as well as physical size, skill level, temperament, and maturity. Toys that are beneath or beyond a child's capabilities may discourage the child from developing further interests.

The research that goes into toy design and manufacture is represented by the information contained on toy product labels. The label provides important guidelines for parents when making toy selections (Health Canada, 2003a). For instance: babies tend to put things into their mouths and are therefore at high risk for choking on small toys or toy parts; riding toys for toddlers pose a risk because children at this age do not have well developed coordination and this can result in a child running into objects or falling down stairs; and projectile toys, although appealing to young children, can cause a variety of injuries, especially eye injuries (CCCF, 2001). As a result, toys are labelled with suitable age

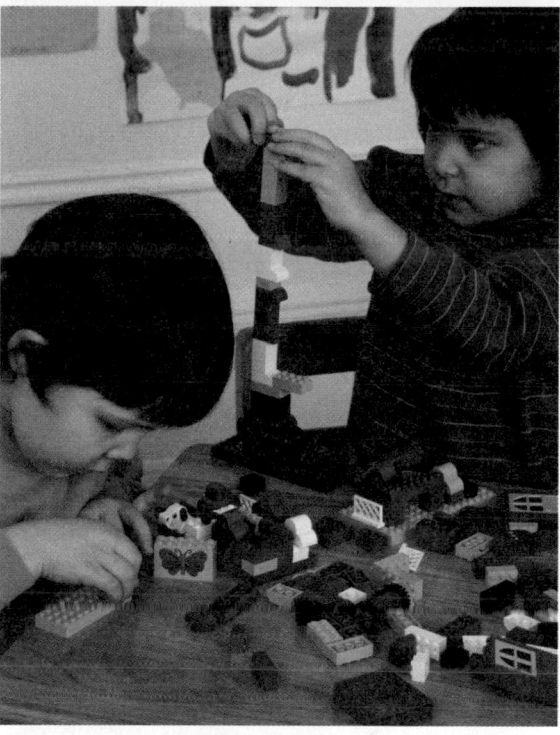

LEGO, the "automatic building brick," was invented by a Danish carpenter in 1949. Its name means "play well." Almost 103 million combinations are possible with just six of the basic eight-stud bricks (Weincek, 1987). Arguably, LEGO can be considered the perfect toy, in that it fosters development in the four key areas of growth—physical, cognitive, emotional, and social. This may account for why children, parents, and early childhood educators around the world have embraced LEGO and why toy experts deemed it the "Toy of the Century" (British Association of Toy Retailers, n.d.; Chen & Carvell, 1999).
(*Photo:* Laura Dwight/CORBIS/MAGMA)

ranges—"recommended for children from 18 months to 3 years." In many instances, toy labels may also carry a safety warning—"choking hazard—this toy contains small parts and is not intended for children under the age of 3." At any age, parental supervision is important and toys meant for older children should be kept away from smaller children (CCCF, 2001).

of their lives, without censoring anything. These methods led to the development of modern psychotherapy.

Many of Freud's patients had memories of sexual feelings and behaviour in childhood. This led Freud to believe that sexual feelings are important in personality development. Based on his patients' childhood memories, Freud proposed stages of personality development, which you will read about later in this book.

When Freud began publishing his theory in the early 1890s, people were shocked by it. Eventually, his views changed the way people thought about sexuality and the role of early childhood experiences in development. In addition, his theory introduced many new ideas, such as the existence of the unconscious mind. For these reasons, Freud's theory continues to be influential in modern developmental psychology (Emde, 1992).

Psychologist John Watson offered ideas about child development very different from those of Hall and Freud. Watson coined a new term, **behaviourism**, to refer to his point of view (Watson, 1913). Behaviourism defines development in terms of behaviour changes caused by environmental influences. Watson believed that, through manipulation of the environment, children could be trained to be or do anything (Jones, 1924; Watson, 1930). As Watson put it,

> Give me a dozen healthy infants, well-formed, and my own specified world to bring them up in and I'll guarantee to take any one at random and train him to become any type of specialist I might select—doctor, lawyer, merchant, chief, and yes, even beggarman and thief, regardless of his talents, penchants, abilities, vocations, and race of his ancestors. (1930, p. 104)

In a famous study known as the "Little Albert" experiment, Watson conditioned a baby boy to fear white rats (Watson & Rayner, 1920). As the baby played with a rat, Watson made banging sounds that frightened him. Over time, the baby came to associate the rat with the noises. He cried and tried to escape from the room whenever the rat was present. (Note that the purposeful conditioning of intense fears in Little Albert raises some serious ethical concerns that are discussed later in this chapter, under Research Ethics.) Based on the Little Albert study and several others, Watson claimed that all developmental changes are the result of learning (Watson, 1928).

Watson's views came to dominate American developmental psychology almost as soon as he published them. He also wrote popular books and magazine articles on child-rearing (see **Development in the Information Age**). Although Watson's theories are considered extreme by modern developmental psychologists, when they were first introduced they helped developmentalists better understand the role of environmental influences in development. Thus, Watson's ideas led to the development of modern learning theories, and the learning principles Watson used in the Little Albert experiment continue to be important in the treatment of children's fears.

Arnold Gesell studied and wrote about development in the same era as Watson, but his views were very different. Gesell's research suggested the existence of a genetically programmed sequential pattern of change (Gesell, 1925; Thelen & Adolph, 1992). Gesell used the term **maturation** to describe such a pattern of change. He thought that maturational-determined development occurred regardless of practice, training, or effort. For example, infants don't have to be taught how to walk—they begin to do so on their own once they reach a certain age. Because of his strong belief that many important developmental changes are determined by maturation, Gesell spent decades studying children and developing norms. He pioneered the use of movie cameras and one-way observation devices to study children's behaviour. Gesell's findings became the basis for many tests that are used today to determine whether individual children are developing normally.

---

behaviourism
the view that defines development in terms of behaviour changes caused by environmental influences

Make the Connection

Review philosopher John Locke's blank slate idea. How does Watson's view, quoted in the text, compare with it?

maturation
the gradual unfolding of genetically programmed sequential patterns of changes

Development in the
Information Age
Child-Rearing Experts

Much of the past 100 years can be characterized as part of the "information age," a period when various methods of mass communication—newspapers, magazines, radio, movies, television, audio and video recordings, the Internet—have exposed people at every level of society to an enormous and continuously growing amount of information. Throughout this book, *Development in the Information Age* features will acquaint you with many of the ways in which advances in information technology have influenced development.

One consequence of the mass dissemination of information has been that "expert" advice on child-rearing has strongly influenced the beliefs and practices of parents in the industrialized world. This trend seems to have begun early in the 20th century, when popular magazines began to publish articles on child-rearing that referred to the theories of Sigmund Freud and other psychologists (Torrey, 1992).

The standard resource for several generations of Canadians, however, remained the manuals published by the Department of National Health and Welfare: *The Canadian Mother's Book* (1920) and four revisions of *The Canadian Mother and Child* (1940 to 1979). These were practical parenting guides for mother and child care that were used as a key resource in conjunction with other parenting books and magazines later in the century. For example, Dr. Benjamin Spock, author of the classic *Baby and Child Care*, became predominant in the 1950s. Spock urged parents to openly display affection toward children. Influenced by Freud's ideas about the possible impact of early childhood emotional trauma on later personality development, Spock also warned parents against engaging in too much conflict with children over weaning or toilet-training. He emphasized the need to wait until children were ready, on their own, to take on such challenges.

Young Canadian parents still have a tendency to look to experts, whose recommendations are now abundantly available in every information medium, for advice and reassurance.

One of the most influential theories in the history of developmental psychology is that of Swiss developmentalist Jean Piaget (Thomas, 1996). At the age of 10, Piaget published his first scientific article, on sparrows. By the time he was 21, he had published more than 20 scientific articles and had received a PhD in natural science from the University of Geneva. In 1918, he went to Paris to work with Theodore Simon, the co-author of the Binet-Simon IQ test, at the school that Alfred Binet started. Piaget married his colleague and student Valentine Châtenay in 1923, and two years later Châtenay gave birth to their first child, Jacqueline. Piaget and Châtenay made detailed notes about Jacqueline's, and their two other children's, intellectual and language development.

Piaget became a professor at the University of Geneva in 1921 and spent the next 6 decades studying the development of logical thinking in children, until his death in 1980. His studies convinced him that logical thinking develops in four stages between birth and adolescence. At first, infants explore the world using their senses and motor abilities. Through their actions, they develop basic concepts of time and space. Next, young children develop the ability to use symbols (primarily words) to think and communicate. Once they become proficient in the use of symbols, around age 6 or 7, children are ready to develop the skills needed for logical thinking. They spend the next 5 to 6 years using these skills to solve problems in the everyday world. Finally, in the teenage years, individuals develop the capacity to apply logic to both abstract and hypothetical problems.

Because of the popularity of the behavioural perspective, psychologists in Canada paid little attention to Piaget's work. During the late 1950s, however, North American developmentalists "discovered" Piaget. From then on, developmental psychologists in Canada and the United States began to focus on children's thinking more than on how environmental stimuli influence their behaviour.

The stages Piaget described and the theory he proposed to explain them became the foundation of modern cognitive-developmental psychology. Consequently, you will be reading a great deal more about them in later chapters. Although many developmentalists disagree with Piaget's theoretical explanations, a vast body of research, including numerous cross-cultural studies, supports the existence of the sequence of cognitive development that Piaget observed in his research (Mishra, 1997).

A BRIEF HISTORY OF THE ROOTS OF PSYCHOLOGY IN CANADA

The first psychology course in Canada was taught at Dalhousie University in 1838. Later, in the 1850s, prescientific psychology courses were offered at McGill University in Montreal and the University of Toronto. In these early years psychology was not considered a distinct discipline but rather a branch of mental and moral philosophy (Wright & Myers, 1982). It wasn't until 1889 that modern scientific psychology came to Canada. James M. Baldwin began lecturing in the fall of that year at the University of Toronto and set up a small psychophysical laboratory (Hoff, 1992).

In the 1920s funding became available for child-related and family research, and in 1925 William Blatz opened the St. George's School for Child Study in Toronto. Blatz is regarded as "the founder and leader of child study in Canada" (Wright & Myers, 1982). St. George's was later renamed the Institute of Child Study and is now incorporated into the Ontario Institute for Studies in Education (OISE). Blatz is also known for his 3 years of work with the Dionne quintuplets, beginning in 1935.

Prior to World War II, there was no formal organization of practising psychologists in Canada. The impetus for creating a psychological organization came from the threat of war in Europe. In June of 1938 psychologists were deliberating how they could provide their services for the war effort. From these discussions, E.A. Bott of the University of Toronto, George Humphry of Queen's University, and Roy Liddy of the University of Western Ontario founded the Canadian Psychological Association in 1939. Also present during these early discussions were Mary Wright and Mary Salter (later Ainsworth). Mary Wright, an assistant to Mary Salter Ainsworth, became the first woman president of the Canadian Psychological Association in 1969 (Wright, 1993). Mary Salter Ainsworth, whose work on infant attachment you will encounter in **Chapter 5**, established the theoretical and empirical framework through which developmentalists continue to view infant–caregiver relations.

Canadian psychologists were very active during World War II, especially in Britain, where they focused on personnel selection, recruitment and training methods, morale issues, and all aspects of public opinion. Important strides in early education came about at that time because of the major evacuation of children in Britain away from urban centres. Canadian psychologists were empowered to generate solutions to the ensuing child-care problems. William Blatz was called on to establish a nursery school teachers' training school in Birmingham (Ferguson, 1993). The school was staffed by Canadian child psychologists.

Another early contributor to the Canadian Psychological Association was Donald O. Hebb, who was the first editor of the *Bulletin of the Canadian Psychological Association* (which later became the *Canadian Journal of Psychology*). Hebb, an internationally renowned pioneer in the

In the early days of psychology, female psychologists seldom received credit for their accomplishments because of societal attitudes toward women. Mary Salter Ainsworth was one of the earliest female psychologists to be recognized in Canada, and part of a group of psychologists actively involved in the creation of the Canadian Psychological Association.
(*Photo:* Courtesy of the Estate of Mary Salter Ainsworth; Robert S. Marvin)

field of experimental psychology at McGill, was president of the CPA in 1953 and the American Psychological Association in 1960. Noel Mailloux, another academic who helped organize the Canadian Psychological Association, is credited with establishing the study of modern psychology in French Canada (Ferguson, 1993). He founded the Institut de Psychologie in 1942 at the Université de Montréal (Wright & Myers, 1982).

In 1981 the Developmental Section of the Canadian Psychological Association was established. Its goal is to facilitate communication among developmental psychologists in terms of research, teaching, and practice. At present, the Developmental Section provides a forum for collaboration and the sharing of expertise for over 340 members.

Before Going On

- Summarize the original sin, innate goodness, and blank slate views of human development.
- List the contributions of Darwin, Hall, Freud, Watson, and Piaget to developmental psychology.

CONTEMPORARY DEVELOPMENTAL PSYCHOLOGY

Developmental psychology has changed considerably since the early days. For one thing, developmentalists have come to understand that inborn characteristics interact with environmental factors in complex ways. For another, the pioneers thought of change almost exclusively in terms of norms, whereas today's developmentalists view norms as representing only one way to measure change. Finally, the term *development* now encompasses the entire human lifespan rather than just childhood and adolescence.

NATURE AND NURTURE INTERACTIONS IN DEVELOPMENT

You may have noticed that some early developmentalists, such as Watson and Gesell, thought of change as resulting from *either* forces outside the person (Watson's learning) *or* forces inside the person (Gesell's maturation). The debate about the relative contributions of biological processes and experiential factors is known as the **nature–nurture controversy**. In struggling with this important issue, psychologists have moved away from either/or approaches like those of Watson and Gesell toward more subtle ways of looking at both types of influences. Today many theorists have adopted an **interactionist model** that considers development to be the result of complex reciprocal interactions between multiple personal and environment factors.

One of the newer ideas on the nature side is the concept of *inborn biases*. The basic notion is that children are born with tendencies to respond in certain ways. Some of these inborn biases are shared by virtually all children. For instance, from the earliest days of life, babies seem to listen more to the beginnings and ends of sentences than to the middle (Slobin, 1985). Babies also come equipped with a set of apparently instinctive behaviours that entice others to care for them, including crying, snuggling, and, very soon after birth, smiling.

nature–nurture controversy
the debate about the relative contributions of biological process and experiential factors to development

interactionist model
the theory that development results from complex reciprocal interactions between multiple personal and environment factors

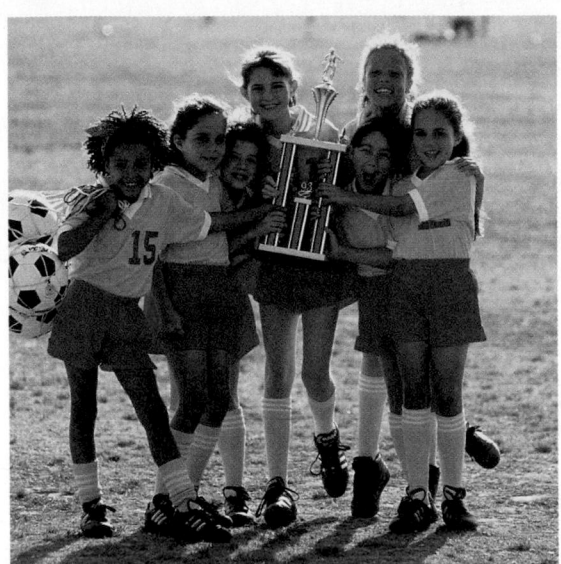

If the concept of internal models is correct, then what matters about this team's victory is not the experience of success itself but rather how each girl interprets it.
(*Photo:* Frank Siteman/Getty Images)

Other inborn biases may vary from one individual to another. Even in the early days of life, for example, some infants are relatively easy to soothe when they become distressed, while others are more difficult to manage. Whether these inborn patterns are coded in the genes, are created by variations in the prenatal environment, or arise through some combination of the two, the basic point is that a baby is not a blank slate at birth. Babies seem to start life prepared to seek out and react to particular kinds of experiences.

Thinking on the nurture side of the issue is also more complex than in the past. For example, modern developmentalists have accepted the concept of *internal models of experience.* There are two key elements to this concept. The first is the idea that the effect of some experiences depends not on any objective properties of the experience but rather on the individual's *interpretation* of it, the meaning the individual attaches to that experience. For instance, suppose a friend says to you, "Your new haircut looks great; it's a lot nicer when it's short like that." Your friend intends to pay you a compliment, but you also hear an implied criticism ("Your hair used to look awful"), so your reactions, your feelings, and even your relationship with your friend are affected by how you interpret the comment—not by what your friend meant or by the objective qualities of the remark.

The second key element of the internal models concept is that interpretations of experience are not random or governed by temporary moods but rather are organized into *models,* which can be thought of as organized sets of assumptions or expectations about oneself or others. For example, if you regularly hear criticism in other people's comments, you may have an internal model whose basic assumption is something like this: "I usually do things wrong, so other people criticize me."

Another important facet of current thinking about environmental influences is a growing emphasis on the importance of looking beyond a child's immediate family for explanations of development. According to this view, we must understand the *ecology,* or the *context,* in which the child is growing: his neighbourhood and school, the occupations of his parents and their level of satisfaction in these occupations, his parents' relationships with each other and their own families, and so on (e.g., Bronfenbrenner, 1979, 1989). For example, a child growing up in a poverty-stricken, inner-city neighbourhood, where drugs and violence are a part of everyday life, is coping with a set of problems radically different from those of a child in a relatively safe and more affluent neighbourhood.

A good example of research that examines such a larger system of influences is Gerald Patterson's work on the origins of delinquency (Patterson, Capaldi, & Bank, 1991; Patterson, DeBarsyshe, & Ramsey, 1989). His studies show that parents who use poor discipline techniques and poor monitoring are more likely to have noncompliant children. Once established, such a behaviour pattern has repercussions in other areas of the child's life, leading to both rejection by peers and difficulty in school. These problems, in turn, are likely to push the young person toward delinquency (Dishion, Patterson, Stoolmiller, & Skinner, 1991; Vuchinich, Bank, & Patterson, 1992). So a pattern that began in the family is maintained and exacerbated by interactions with peers and with the school system. **Figure 1.1** shows Patterson's conception of how these various components fit together. Clearly, such models enhance our understanding of how the environment influences development.

A similarly interactionist model is implicit in the ideas of *vulnerability* and *resilience* (Garmezy, 1993; Masten, Best, & Garmezy, 1990; Moen & Erickson, 1995; Rutter, 1993; Werner, 1995; Willms, 2002a). According to this view, each child is born with

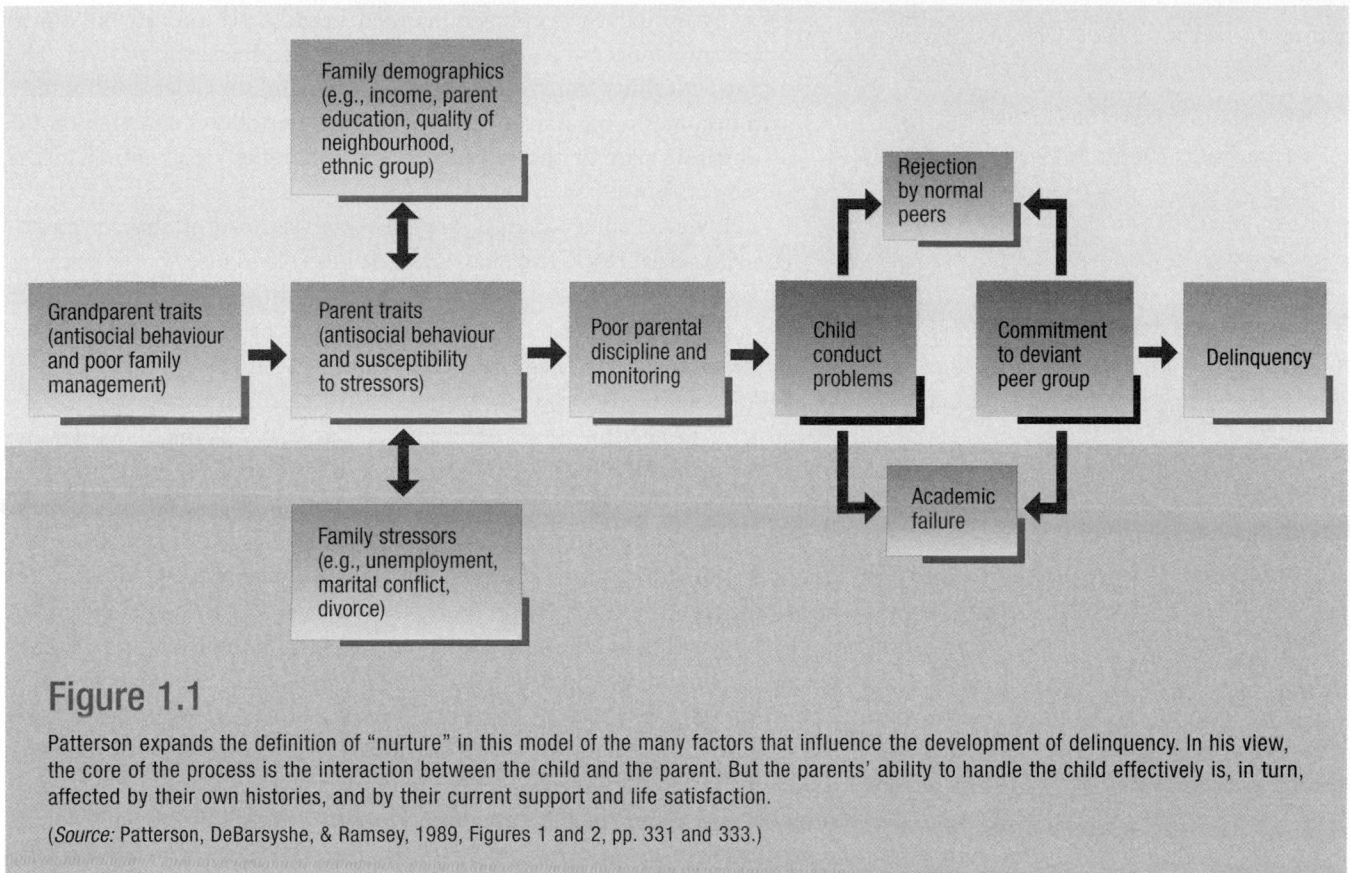

Figure 1.1

Patterson expands the definition of "nurture" in this model of the many factors that influence the development of delinquency. In his view, the core of the process is the interaction between the child and the parent. But the parents' ability to handle the child effectively is, in turn, affected by their own histories, and by their current support and life satisfaction.

(*Source:* Patterson, DeBarsyshe, & Ramsey, 1989, Figures 1 and 2, pp. 331 and 333.)

certain vulnerabilities, such as a tendency toward emotional irritability or alcoholism, a physical abnormality, or an allergy. Each child is also born with some protective factors, such as high intelligence, good physical coordination, an easy temperament, or a lovely smile, that tend to make her more resilient in the face of stress. These vulnerabilities and protective factors then interact with the child's environment so that the same environment can have quite different effects, depending on the qualities the child brings to the interaction.

Studies of Canadian children have shown that a combination of a highly vulnerable child and a poor or unsupportive environment produces by far the most negative outcome (Schonert-Reichl, 2000; Willms, 2002b). Either of these two negative conditions alone—a vulnerable child or a poor environment—can be overcome. A resilient child in a poor environment may do quite well, since she can find and take advantage of all the stimulation and opportunities available; similarly, a vulnerable child may do quite well in a highly supportive environment in which parents help the child overcome or cope with her vulnerabilities.

UNIVERSALS, CONTEXTS, AND INDIVIDUAL DIFFERENCES

In addition to their views on individuals and the environment, present-day developmental psychologists' views on change itself are more complex than those of the field's pioneers. Contemporary developmentalists study three very different types of age-related changes: universal changes, group-specific changes, and individual differences. *Universal changes* are common to every individual in a species and are linked to specific

Critical Thinking

How do expectations of 20-year-olds differ from expectations of 70-year-olds in your culture?

social clock

a set of age norms that defines a sequence of life experiences that is considered normal in a given culture and that all individuals in that culture are expected to follow

ageism

a prejudicial view of older adults that characterizes them in negative ways

cohort

a group of individuals who share the same historical experiences at the same times in their lives

The biological clock obviously constrains the social clock to some extent at least. Virtually every culture emphasizes family formation in early adulthood because that is, in fact, the optimal biological time for child-bearing.

(*Photos:* Alan Oddie/PhotoEdit)

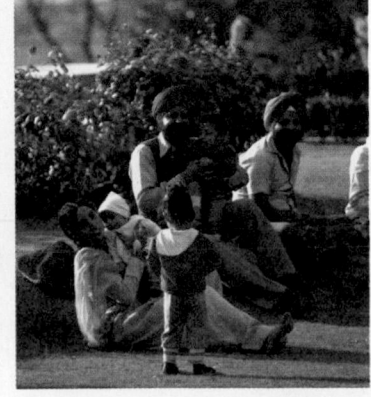

ages. Some universal changes happen because we are all biological organisms subject to a genetically programmed maturing process. The infant who shifts from crawling to walking and the older adult whose skin becomes progressively more wrinkled are following a plan that is an intrinsic part of the physical body, most likely something in the genetic code itself.

However, some changes are universal because of shared experiences. A social clock also shapes all (or most) lives into shared patterns of change (Helson, Mitchell, & Moane, 1984). In each culture, the **social clock,** or a set of *age norms,* defines a sequence of normal life experiences, such as the right time to start school, the appropriate timing of marriage and child-bearing, and the expected time of retirement.

Age norms can lead to **ageism**—a set of prejudicial attitudes about older adults, analogous to sexism or racism (Palmore, 1990). In Canadian society, for example, conventional wisdom states that job performance will decline in older adults. As a result, many older adults are denied opportunities to work because employers believe that they are less capable of carrying out required job functions than younger adults. Thus, social expectations about the appropriate age for retirement work together with ageism to shape individual lives, resulting in a pattern in which most people retire or significantly reduce their working hours in later adulthood.

Group-specific changes are shared by all individuals who grow up together in a particular group. One of the most important groups to which we all belong is our culture. The term *culture* has no commonly agreed-on definition, but in essence it describes some system of meanings and customs, including values, attitudes, goals, laws, beliefs, moral guidelines, and physical artifacts of various kinds, such as tools, forms of dwellings, and the like. Furthermore, to be called a culture, a system of meanings and customs must be shared by some identifiable group, whether that group is a subsection of some population or a larger unit, and must be transmitted from one generation of that group to the next (Betancourt & Lopez, 1993; Cole, 1992). Culture shapes not only the development of individuals, but also our ideas about what normal development is.

For example, researchers interested in middle and late adulthood often study retirement: why people retire, how retirement affects their health, and so on. But their findings do not apply to older adults in nonindustrialized cultures, where adults gradually shift from one kind of work to another as they get older rather than giving up work altogether and entering a new phase of life called "retirement." Consequently, developmentalists must be aware that retirement-related phenomena do not constitute universal changes. Instead, they represent developmental experiences that are culturally specific.

Equally important as a source of variation in life experience are historical forces, which affect each generation somewhat differently. Social scientists use the word **cohort** to describe groups of individuals who are born within some fairly narrow span of years and thus share the same historical experiences at the same time in their lives. Within any given culture, successive cohorts may have quite different life experiences (see **Research Report** on page 13).

Individual differences are changes resulting from unique, unshared events. One clearly unshared event in each person's life is conception; the combination of genes each individual receives at conception is unique. Thus, genetic differences—including physical characteristics such as body type and hair colour as well as

Research Report

Children and Adolescents in the Great Depression: An Example of Cohort Effect

Canada has historically been an exporting nation, and so when the worldwide Depression hit in the 1930s its people were severely affected. Unemployment was above 20%, the birth rate dropped, and lineups at soup kitchens grew long (Struthers, 2000). Research involving children and adolescents who grew up during the Great Depression illustrates that the same historical event can have different effects on adjacent cohorts (Elder, 1974; 1978; Elder, Liker & Cross, 1984). Glen Elder and his colleagues used several hundred participants who were born either in 1920 or 1928. Those in the 1920 group were in their teens during the Depression; those born in 1928 were still young children during the worst economic times.

In each cohort, researchers compared participants whose families had lost more than 35% of their pre-Depression income with those whose economic condition was better. They found that economic hardship was largely beneficial to the cohort born in 1920, who were teenagers when the Depression struck full force, while it was generally detrimental to the cohort born in 1928. Most of those teens born in 1920 whose families experienced the worst economic hardship were pushed into assuming adult responsibilities prematurely. Many worked at odd jobs, earning money that was vitally important to the family's welfare. They felt needed by their families, and as adults, they had a strong work ethic and commitment to family.

Those who were born in 1928 had a very different Depression experience. Their families frequently suffered a loss of cohesion and warmth. The consequences were generally negative for the children, especially the boys. They were less hopeful and less confident than their less economically stressed peers; in adolescence, they did less well in school and completed fewer years of education; as adults, they were less ambitious and less successful. These two cohorts were only 8 years apart, yet their experiences were strikingly different because of the timing of a key environmental event in their lives.

genetic disorders— represent one category of individual differences. Characteristics influenced by both heredity and environment, such as intelligence and personality, constitute another class of individual differences.

Other individual differences are the result of the timing of a developmental event. Child development theorists have adopted the concept of a **critical period**. The idea is that there may be specific periods in development when an organism is especially sensitive to the presence (or absence) of some particular kind of experience.

Most knowledge about critical periods comes from animal research. For baby ducks, for instance, the first 15 hours or so after hatching is a critical period for the development of a following response. Newly hatched ducklings will follow any duck or any other moving object that happens to be around them at that critical time. If nothing is moving at that critical point, they don't develop any following response at all (Hess, 1972).

The broader concept of a sensitive period is more common in the study of human development. A **sensitive period** is a span of months or years during which a child may be particularly responsive to specific forms of experience or particularly influenced by their absence. For example, the period from 6 to 12 months of age may be a sensitive period for the formation of parent–infant attachment.

In studies of adults, one important concept related to timing has been the idea of *on-time* and *off-time* events (Neugarten, 1979). The idea is that experiences occurring at the expected times for an individual's culture or cohort will pose fewer difficulties for her than will off-time experiences. Thus, being widowed at 30 is more likely to produce serious life disruption or forms of pathology such as depression than would being widowed at 70.

critical period
a specific period in development when an organism is especially sensitive to the presence (or absence) of some particular kind of experience

sensitive period
a span of months or years during which a child may be particularly responsive to specific forms of experience or particularly influenced by their absence

atypical development
development that deviates from the typical developmental pathway in a way that is harmful to the individual

Atypical development is another kind of individual change. **Atypical development** (also known as *abnormal behaviour, psychopathology, pathological behaviour,* and *maladaptive development*) refers to deviation from a typical, or "normal," developmental pathway in a direction that is harmful to an individual. Examples of atypical development include developmental delay, mental illness, and behavioural problems such as extreme aggressiveness in children and compulsive gambling in adults.

THE LIFESPAN PERSPECTIVE

Until quite recently, psychologists thought of adulthood as a long period of stability followed by a short span of unstable years immediately preceding death. This view has changed because, for one thing, it has become common for adults to go through major life changes, such as divorce and career shifts. As a result, several theorists, whose ideas you will encounter later in this book, have proposed stage models of development that include adult phases. Stage models view development as comprising periods of stability punctuated by periods of transition throughout the lifespan.

Another important factor that has affected developmental perspectives on adulthood is the significant increase in life expectancy that has occurred in the industrialized world. The life expectancy of a Canadian born in 1921 was 59 years for a male and 61 years for a female. A Canadian male born today can expect to live to age 77.2 and a female to 82.1 (Statistics Canada, 2004a). As a result, older adults now constitute a larger proportion of the population than ever before. In fact, adults over the age of 85 are one of the most rapidly growing age groups in Canada, and their numbers are expected to increase fivefold over the next 50 years (Health Canada, 2001a). Thus, the characteristics and needs of older adults are increasingly influencing many disciplines, including developmental psychology.

As interest in the entire lifespan has grown, developmental psychology has become more *interdisciplinary*. Psychologists, who are primarily interested in individuals, have learned that research in other sciences can greatly enhance their understanding of human development. Anthropologists provide information about culture, and sociologists explain the influence of race, socioeconomic status, and other social factors on individual development. Advances in biology are especially critical to an understanding of the physiological foundations of human behaviour.

lifespan perspective
the current view of developmentalists that changes happen throughout the entire human lifespan and that changes must be interpreted in light of the culture and context in which they occur; thus, interdisciplinary research is critical to understanding human development

The changes outlined above have led to the adoption of a lifespan perspective. The **lifespan perspective** maintains that important changes occur during every period of development and that these changes must be interpreted in terms of the cultures and contexts in which they occur (Baltes, Reese, & Lipsitt, 1980). Thus, understanding change in adulthood has become just as important as understanding change in childhood, and input from many disciplines is necessary to fully explain human development.

Before Going On

- How do contemporary developmental psychologists view the two sides of the nature–nurture controversy?
- What are the three kinds of change contemporary developmentalists study?
- What is the lifespan perspective?

RESEARCH DESIGNS AND METHODS

The easiest way to understand research methods is to look at a specific question and the alternative ways we might answer it. For example, older adults frequently complain that they have more trouble remembering people's names than they did when they were younger. Suppose we wanted to find out whether memory really declines with age. How would we go about answering this question?

RELATING GOALS TO METHODS

Developmental psychology uses the scientific method to achieve four goals: *to describe, to explain, to predict, and to influence* human development from conception to death. To describe development is simply to state what happens. A descriptive statement such as "Older adults make more memory errors than young and middle-aged adults" is an example of this first goal of developmental psychology. To meet this goal, all we would have to do is measure memory function in adults of various ages.

Explaining development involves telling why a particular event occurs. To generate explanations, developmentalists rely on *theories*—sets of statements that propose general principles of development. Students often say that they hate reading about theories; what they want are the facts. However, theories are important because they help us look at facts from different perspectives. For example, "Older adults make more memory mistakes because of changes in the brain that happen as people get older" is a statement that attempts to explain the fact of age-related memory decline from a biological perspective. Alternatively, we could explain memory decline from an experiential perspective and hypothesize that memory function declines with age because older adults don't get as much memory practice as younger adults do.

Useful theories produce predictions, or *hypotheses,* that researchers can test, such as "If changes in the brain cause declines in memory function, then elderly adults whose brains show the most change should also make the greatest number of memory errors." To test this hypothesis about changes in the brain and memory, we would have to measure some aspects of brain structure or function as well as memory function. Then we would have to find a way to relate one to the other. Alternatively, we could test the experiential explanation by comparing the memories of older adults who presumably get the most memory practice, such as those who are still working, with the memories of those who get less practice. If the working adults do better on tests of memory, the experiential perspective gains support. Moreover, if both the biological and the experiential hypotheses are supported by research, we have far more insight into age-related memory decline than we would have from either kind of hypothesis alone. In this way, theories add tremendous depth to psychologists' understanding of the facts of human development and provide them with information they can use to influence it.

Let's say, for example, that an older adult is diagnosed with a condition that can affect the brain, such as high blood pressure. If we know that brain function and memory are related, we can use tests of memory to make judgments about how much the person's medical condition may have already influenced his brain. At the same time, because we know that experience affects memory as well, we may be able to provide him with training that will help prevent memory problems from developing or worsening (see **No Easy Answers** on page 16).

No Easy Answers

It Depends . . .

Using research to improve people's lives is an important goal of developmental psychology. In most cases, however, applying research to developmental problems isn't as simple as it might seem. Thus, one of the most important things you can learn about developmental psychology is that the answers to many of the practical questions people ask about development begin with "It depends."

For example, when a parent discovers her son has been molested by a neighbour, she wants to know how the abuse will affect him in the future. But developmental psychologists don't have a concrete answer. They can tell the mother that the overwhelming majority of traumatized children show no long-term effects. They can also analyze the child and his particular situation and make an educated guess about what might happen in the future. In other words, the long-term outcomes depend on a variety of variables: how long the abuse lasted, at what age it began, the child's per-

sonality, the way the parents handled the situation when they learned of the abuse, and so on.

To further complicate matters, all the relevant variables interact with one another. For example, counselling might benefit an outgoing child but be ineffective for a shy child who tends to keep his feelings to himself. Conversely, art therapy, a strategy that encourages children to express their feelings in drawings, might be effective with a shy child but have little impact on one who is outgoing. Because of such complexities, developmentalists can't tell the mother what she wants to hear: that if she follows a certain formula, her child will turn out fine.

Throughout this book, you will encounter discussions of how research can be applied to developmental problems in *No Easy Answers* features. These should give you a better appreciation of the intricate ways in which variables interact in human development. You will also learn that these intricacies often frustrate efforts to use psychology to find solutions to everyday problems.

STUDYING AGE-RELATED CHANGES

cross-sectional design
a research design in which groups of different ages are compared

longitudinal design
a research design in which people in a single group are studied at different times in their lives

sequential design
a research design that combines cross-sectional and longitudinal examinations of development

When a researcher sets out to study age-related change, she has basically three choices: (1) Study different groups of people of different ages, using what is called a **cross-sectional design;** (2) study the same people over a period of time, using a **longitudinal design;** (3) combine cross-sectional and longitudinal designs in some fashion, in a **sequential design.**

CROSS-SECTIONAL DESIGNS To study memory cross-sectionally, we might select groups of people of various ages, such as groups of 25-, 35-, 45-, 55-, 65-, 75-, and 85-year-olds. **Figure 1.2** shows the results of just such a study, in which adults 18 to 91 years of age listened to a list of pairs of words being read to them. Once all the word pairs in the list were given, they were supposed to recall the second word of a pair when given the first. You can see that performance was distinctly worse for the 71- to 91-year-olds, a pattern of age-related decline found in a great many memory studies (Salthouse, 1991).

Because these findings fit our hypothesis, it is tempting to conclude that memory ability declines with age, but we cannot say this conclusively based on the cross-sectional data, because these adults differ not only in age, but in cohort. The differences in memory might reflect, for example, differences in education and not changes linked to age or development. Furthermore, cross-sectional studies cannot tell us anything about sequences of change with age or about the consistency of individual behaviour over time, because each participant is tested only once. Still, cross-sectional research is very useful because it can be done relatively quickly and can reveal possible age differences or age changes.

LONGITUDINAL DESIGNS Longitudinal designs seem to solve the problems presented by cross-sectional designs, because they follow the same individuals over a period of time. For example, to examine our hypothesis on memory decline, we could test a group first at age 25, then at 35, again at 45, and so on. Such studies allow psychologists to look at sequences of change and at individual consistency or inconsistency over time. And because longitudinal studies compare performance by the same people at different ages, they get around some aspects of the cohort problem.

Some longitudinal studies are relatively short. McMaster University psychologists Daphne Maurer and Terri Lewis studied babies who had their sight restored after cataract surgery. Each baby had his or her sight tested soon after surgery and for several months thereafter (1993).

Other studies are relatively open-ended. Jane Ledingham and Alex Swartzman initiated the ongoing Concordia Longitudinal Project in 1976. They studied children living in low-income, inner-city neighbourhoods in Montreal. These children are now in their 20s and 30s and are still part of the study that now includes their offspring. One interesting finding was that at-risk mothers who displayed aggression and withdrawal in childhood grew up to have children who were at high risk of serious psychosocial and health problems (see **Figure 1.3** on page 18). This suggests significant intergenerational risk, but one mediating factor was the level of education of the mother. A higher level of education predicted better outcomes (Serbin, Cooperman, Peters, Lehoux, Stack, & Schwartzman, 1998).

Some longitudinal studies are of a delimited length. For example, the TLC3 national project was instituted in seven centres across Canada in 1997 for a time span of 5 years. The plan is to determine what kind of child-care activities across a variety of child-care settings will predict intellectual, emotional, and social well-being in economically disadvantaged preschool children (Hincks-Dellcrest Institute Foundation, 2001).

Despite their importance, longitudinal designs have several drawbacks and limitations. They can be time consuming, and it can be difficult to maintain contact with subjects over a long period of time. Some participants drop out; others die or move away. As a general rule, the healthiest and best educated are most likely to stick it out, and that fact biases the results, particularly if the study covers the final decades of life. Each succeeding set of test results comes from proportionately more and more healthy adults, which may make it look as if there is less change, or less decline, than actually exists.

Some longitudinal studies typically involve giving each participant the same tests over and over again. Over time, people learn how to take the tests. Such *practice effects* may distort the measurement of any underlying developmental changes.

Figure 1.2

In this study, adults of various ages listened to an experimenter reading a series of pairs of words. The participant's task was to try to repeat back the second word of a pair when given the first. The scores shown here are the average number of words each age group could repeat back.

(*Source:* Uttl, Graf, & Richter, 2002. Reprinted with permission from Elsevier.)

Critical Thinking

Suppose a cross-sectional study of sex-role attitudes reveals that adults between ages 20 and 50 have the most egalitarian attitudes, while teenagers and adults over 50 have more traditional attitudes. How might cohort differences influence your interpretation of these results?

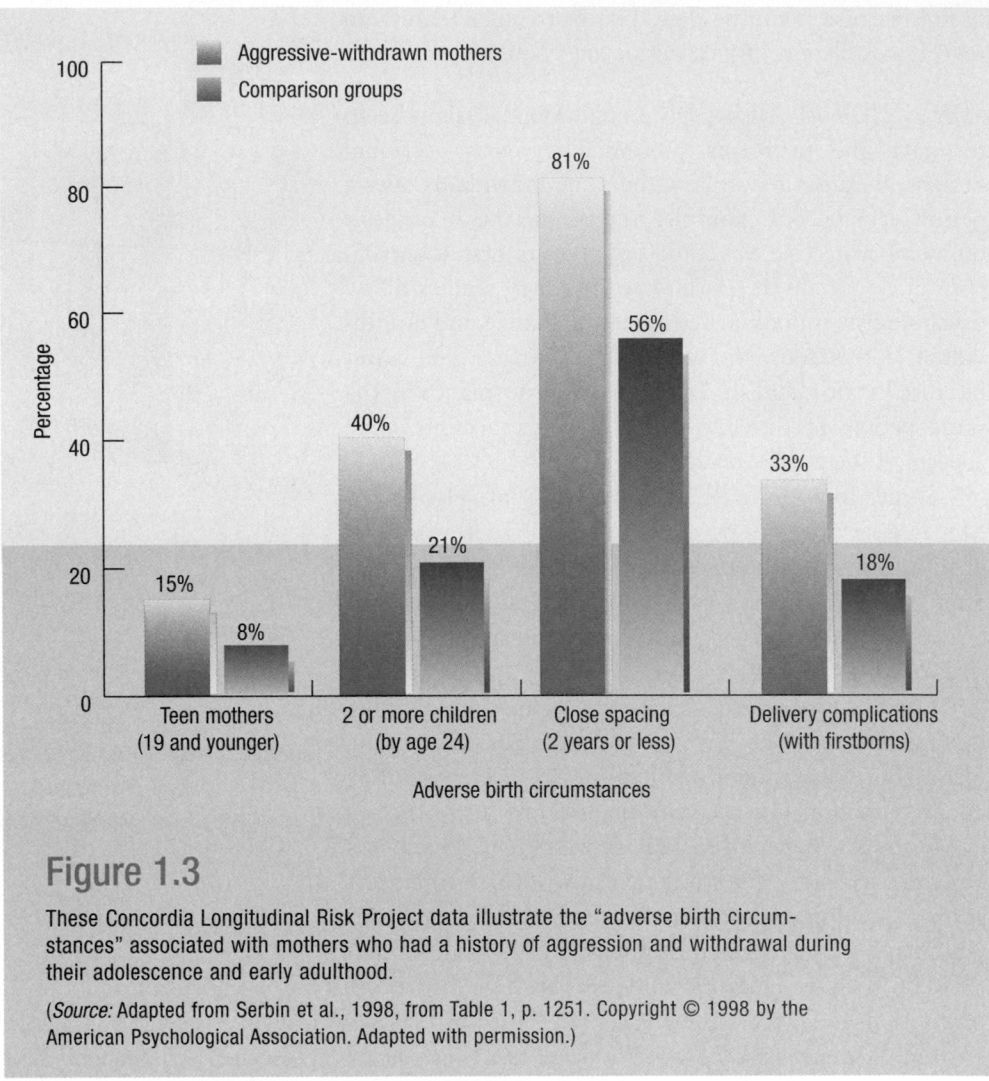

Figure 1.3

These Concordia Longitudinal Risk Project data illustrate the "adverse birth circum-stances" associated with mothers who had a history of aggression and withdrawal during their adolescence and early adulthood.

(*Source:* Adapted from Serbin et al., 1998, from Table 1, p. 1251. Copyright © 1998 by the American Psychological Association. Adapted with permission.)

Longitudinal studies don't completely get around the cohort problem either. Longitudinal studies that were conducted decades ago may offer useful information, but they may be contaminated by factors that are unique to that group of subjects at that particular time. Each generation experiences unique cultural, social, economic, and historical conditions that may not apply to subjects living at other times.

SEQUENTIAL DESIGNS One way to avoid the shortcomings of both cross-sectional and longitudinal designs is to use a sequential design. To study our memory hypothesis using a sequential design, we would begin with at least two age groups. One group might include 25- to 30-year-olds, and the other 30- to 35-year-olds. We would then test each group several times over a number of years, as illustrated in **Figure 1.4**. In a sequential study, each testing point beyond the initial one allows researchers to make two types of comparisons. Age-group comparisons provide them with the same kind of information as a cross-sectional study. Comparison of each group with itself at an earlier testing point allows the researchers to collect longitudinal evidence at the same time.

Sequential designs also allow for comparisons of cohorts. For example, notice in **Figure 1.4** that Group A is 30 to 35 years old at testing point 1, and Group B is 30 to 35 years old at testing point 2. Likewise, Group A is 35 to 40 at point 2, and their counterparts in Group B are this age at point 3. If same-age comparisons of the two groups reveal that their memory performance is different, researchers have evidence that, for some reason, the two cohorts differ. Conversely, if the groups perform similarly, investigators can conclude that their respective performances represent developmental characteristics rather than cohort effects. Moreover, if both groups demonstrate similar age-related patterns of change over time, researchers can conclude that the developmental pattern is not specific to any particular cohort. Finding the same developmental pattern in two cohorts provides psychologists with stronger evidence than either cross-sectional or longitudinal data alone.

Group	Age at testing point 1	Age at testing point 2	Age at testing point 3
A	30 to 35	35 to 40	40 to 45
B	25 to 30	30 to 35	35 to 40

Figure 1.4

This grid represents a design for a sequential study of memory function.

In 1994 Human Resources Development Canada (HRDC, 1996) embarked upon an ambitious sequential design study: the National Longitudinal Survey of Children and Youth (NLSCY). The NLSCY measures how social and environmental factors influence a child's physical, social, intellectual, emotional, and behavioural development. Beginning with an initial base of almost 23 000 children aged 0 to 11 years, the NLSCY was designed to collect data every 2 years (1 cycle) until the cohort reaches age 25 in 2018. A new sample of newborns and 1-year-old children is added, and will continue to be added, at each subsequent 2-year cycle. By 2001, the NLSCY had included about 27 000 Canadian children from birth to 17 years of age (Statistics Canada, 2004b). Interim results from this study will be examined in later chapters.

IDENTIFYING RELATIONSHIPS BETWEEN VARIABLES

After deciding what design to use, the researcher interested in age and memory ability must decide how to go about finding relationships between *variables*. To developmentalists, variables are characteristics that vary from person to person, such as physical size, intelligence, and personality. When two or more variables vary together, there is some kind of relationship between them. The hypothesis that memory declines with age involves two variables, memory and age, and suggests a relationship between them. There are several ways of identifying such relationships.

CASE STUDIES AND NATURALISTIC OBSERVATION Case studies are in-depth examinations of single individuals. To test the hypothesis about memory and age, we could use a case study comparing one individual's scores on tests of memory in early and late adulthood. Such a study might tell us a lot about the stability or instability of memory in the individual studied, but we wouldn't know if our findings applied to others.

Still, case studies are extremely useful in making decisions about individuals. For example, to find out whether a child is mentally retarded, a psychologist would conduct an extensive case study involving tests, interviews of the child's parents, behavioural observations, and so on. Case studies are also frequently the basis of important hypotheses about unusual developmental events, such as head injuries and strokes.

When psychologists use **naturalistic observation** as a research method, they observe people in their normal environments. For instance, to find out more about memory in older adults, a researcher could observe them in their homes or workplaces. Such studies provide developmentalists with information about psychological processes in everyday contexts.

case study
an in-depth examination of a single individual

naturalistic observation
the process of studying people in their normal environments

A unique variation on standard observation techniques was conducted by Debra Pepler and Wendy Craig of York University. They used video camera and wireless microphone technology to observe aggression in children. They videotaped children in an unstructured, free-play setting of a school playground where there were minimal constraints on the children's interactions. This was an effective method of collecting data on children from 6 to 10 years old. Moreover, it was particularly sensitive to cues of aggression that would otherwise be difficult to detect. The authors suggest that remote video recording in a natural setting offers a useful alternative means for studying child interactions (1995).

The weakness of naturalistic observation, however, is *observer bias*. For example, if the researcher who is observing teenagers is convinced that most of them have poor table manners, he is likely to ignore any behaviour that goes against this view. Because of observer bias, naturalistic observation studies often use "blind" observers who don't know what the research is about. In most cases, for the sake of accuracy, researchers use two or more observers so that the observations of each observer can be checked against those of the other(s). The measure for this is procedure is known as *inter-rater reliability*.

Like case studies, naturalistic observation studies are limited in the extent to which the results can be generalized. In addition, naturalistic observation studies are very time-consuming. They must be repeated in a variety of settings so that researchers can be sure people's behaviour reflects development and not the influences of a specific environment.

correlation

a relationship between two variables that can be expressed as a number ranging from −1.00 to +1.00

CORRELATIONS   A **correlation** is a relationship between two variables that can be expressed as a number ranging from −1.00 to +1.00. A zero correlation indicates that there is no relationship between those variables. A positive correlation means that high scores on one variable are usually accompanied by high scores on the other. The closer a positive correlation is to +1.00, the stronger the relationship between the variables. Two variables that change in opposite directions result in a negative correlation, and the nearer the correlation to −1.00, the more strongly the two are connected.

To understand positive and negative correlations, think about the relationship between temperature and the use of air conditioners and heaters here in Canada. Temperature and air conditioner use are positively correlated. As the temperature climbs, the number of air conditioners in use goes up. Conversely, temperature and heater use are negatively correlated. As the temperature decreases, the number of heaters in use goes up.

Naturalistic observation refers to the research method used by psychologists who observe and study people in their natural, everyday environments.
(*Photo:* David Young-Wolff/PhotoEdit)

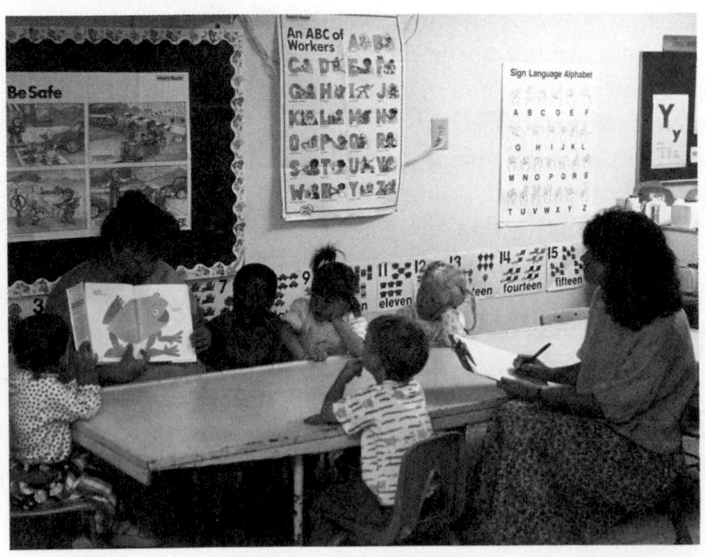

If we wanted to know whether age is related to memory, we could use a correlation. All that would be necessary would be to administer memory tests to adults of varying ages and calculate the correlation between test scores and ages. If there is a positive correlation between age and the number of memory errors people make—if older people make more errors—then we could say that our hypothesis has been supported. Conversely, if there is a negative correlation—if older people make fewer errors—then we would have to conclude that our hypothesis has not been supported.

Useful as they are, though, correlations have a major limitation: They do not indicate *causal* relationships. For example, even a high positive correlation between memory errors and age would only tell us that memory performance and age are connected in some way. It wouldn't tell us what caused the connection. It might be that younger adults understand the test instructions better. In order to identify a cause, we have to carry out experiments.

EXPERIMENTS An **experiment** is a study that tests a causal hypothesis. Suppose, for example, that we think age differences in memory are caused by older adults' failure to use memory techniques such as repeating a list mentally in order to remember it. We could test this hypothesis by providing memory technique training to one group of older adults and no training to another group. If the trained adults got higher scores on memory tests than they did before training, and the no-training group showed no change, we could claim support for our hypothesis.

A key feature of an experiment is that participants are assigned *randomly* to one of two or more groups. In other words, chance determines which group each participant is placed in. When participants are randomly assigned to groups, the groups have equal amounts of variation with respect to characteristics such as intelligence, personality traits, height, weight, health status, and so on. Consequently, none of these variables can affect the outcome of the experiment.

Participants in the **experimental group** receive the treatment the experimenter thinks will produce a particular effect, while those in the **control group** receive either no special treatment or a neutral treatment. The presumed causal element in the experiment is called the **independent variable**, and the characteristic or behaviour that the independent variable is expected to affect is called the **dependent variable**.

In a memory technique training experiment like the one suggested above, the group that receives the memory training is the experimental group, and the one that receives no instruction is the control group. Memory technique training is the variable that we, the experimenters, think will cause differences in memory function, so it is the independent variable. Performance on memory tests is the variable we are using to measure the effect of the memory technique training. Therefore, performance on memory tests is the dependent variable.

Experiments are essential for understanding many aspects of development. But two special problems in studying child or adult development limit the use of experiments: First, many of the questions researchers want to answer have to do with the effects of particular unpleasant or stressful experiences on individuals—abuse, prenatal influences of alcohol or tobacco, low birth weight, poverty, unemployment, widowhood. For obvious ethical reasons, researchers cannot manipulate these variables. For example, they cannot ask one set of pregnant women to have two alcoholic drinks a day and others to have none. To study the effects of such experiences, they must rely on nonexperimental methods, such as correlations.

Second, the independent variable developmentalists are often most interested in is age itself, and researchers cannot assign participants randomly to age groups. They can compare 4-year-olds and 6-year-olds in their approach to some particular task, such as searching for a lost object, but the children differ in a host of ways other than their ages. Older children have had more and different experiences. Thus, unlike psychologists studying other aspects of behaviour, developmental psychologists cannot systematically manipulate many of the variables they are most interested in.

To get around this problem, researchers can use any one of a series of strategies, sometimes called *quasi-experiments,* in which they compare groups without assigning the participants randomly. Cross-sectional studies are a form of quasi-experiment. So are studies in which researchers compare members of naturally occurring groups that differ in some dimension of interest, such as children whose parents choose to place them in day-care programs and children whose parents keep them at home.

> ## Critical Thinking
>
> Researchers have found a positive correlation between a mother's age at the birth of her child and the child's later IQ: Very young mothers have children with lower IQs. How many different explanations of this correlation can you think of?

experiment
a study that tests a causal hypothesis

experimental group
the group in an experiment that receives the treatment the experimenter thinks will produce a particular effect

control group
a group in an experiment that receives either no special treatment or a neutral treatment

independent variable
the presumed causal element in an experiment

dependent variable
the characteristic or behaviour that is expected to be affected by the independent variable

Such comparisons have built-in problems, because groups that differ in one way are likely to differ in other ways as well. Parents who send their children to private schools may be wealthier and have different social values compared with parents who keep their children in public schools. If researchers found that the two groups of children differ on a specific academic measure, is it because they have spent their school days in different environments or because of other differences in their families? Researchers can make such comparisons a bit easier if they select comparison groups that are matched on those variables the researchers think might matter, such as income, marital status, or religion. But a quasi-experiment, by its very nature, will always yield more ambiguous results than will a fully controlled experiment.

CROSS-CULTURAL RESEARCH

Increasingly common in developmental psychology are studies comparing cultures or contexts, a task that researchers approach in several ways. One method of study, borrowed from the field of anthropology, is **ethnography**. The ethnographic method creates a detailed description of a single culture or context based on extensive observation. Often the observer lives in the culture or context for a period of time, perhaps as long as several years. Each ethnographic study is intended to stand alone, although it is sometimes possible to combine information from several different studies to see whether similar developmental patterns exist in the various cultures or contexts.

Alternatively, investigators may attempt to compare two or more cultures directly, by testing children or adults in each of the cultures with the same or comparable measures. Sometimes this involves comparing groups from different countries. Sometimes the comparisons are between subcultures within the same country; for example, increasingly common in Canada is research involving comparisons of children or adults living in different ethnic groups or communities, such as First Nations, South Asian, Caribbean, and European Canadians (Statistics Canada, 2000a). This is important in Canada because in 1971 our nation was the first in the world to make multiculturalism an official policy; the Canadian Multicultural Act was passed in 1988 (Canadian Heritage, 2001a).

Cross-cultural research is important to developmental psychology for two reasons. First, developmentalists want to identify universal changes, that is, predictable events or processes experienced by individuals in all cultures. Developmentalists don't want to make a general statement about development—such as "Memory declines with age"—if the phenomenon in question happens only in certain cultures. Without cross-cultural research, it is impossible to know whether studies involving North Americans and Europeans apply to people in other parts of the world.

Second, one of the goals of developmental psychology is to produce findings that can be used to improve people's lives. Cross-cultural research is critical to this goal as well. For example, developmentalists know that children in cultures that emphasize the community more than the individual are more cooperative than children in more individualistic cultures. However, to use this information to help all children learn to cooperate, they need to know exactly how adults in such cultures teach their children to be cooperative. Cross-cultural research helps developmentalists identify specific variables that explain cultural differences.

ethnography
a detailed description of a single culture or context

research ethics
the guidelines researchers follow to protect the rights of animals used in research and people who participate in studies

RESEARCH ETHICS

Research ethics are the guidelines researchers follow to protect the rights of animals used in research and humans who participate in studies. Ethical guidelines are published by professional organizations such as the Canadian Psychological Association. Universities, private foundations, and government agencies have review committees that make sure all research sponsored by the institution is ethical. Guidelines for animal research include the requirement that animals be protected from unnecessary pain and suffering. Further, researchers must demonstrate that the potential benefits of their studies to either human or animal populations will be greater than any potential harm to animal subjects.

The Canadian Psychological Association (2000) has published ethical standards for practitioners, researchers, and scientists that include the following principles: respect for the dignity of persons, responsible caring, integrity in relationships, and responsibility to society. These ethical standards address the following major concerns:

PROTECTION FROM HARM It is unethical to do research that may cause participants permanent physical or psychological harm. Moreover, if the possibility of temporary harm exists, researchers must provide participants with some way of repairing the damage. For example, if the study will remind subjects of unpleasant experiences, like rape, researchers must provide them with counselling.

INFORMED CONSENT Researchers must inform participants of any possible harm and have them sign a consent form stating that they are aware of the risks of participating. In order for children to participate in studies, their parents must give permission after the researcher has informed them of possible risks. Children older than 7 must also give their own consent. If the research takes place in a school or day-care centre, an administrator representing the institution must consent. In addition, both children and adults have the right to discontinue participation in a study at any time. Researchers are obligated to explain this right to children in language they can understand.

CONFIDENTIALITY Participants have the right to confidentiality. Researchers must keep the identities of participants confidential and must report their data in such a way that no particular piece of information can be associated with any specific participant. The exception to confidentiality is when children reveal to researchers that they have been abused in any way by an adult. In Canada, citizens are required to report suspected cases of child abuse.

KNOWLEDGE OF RESULTS Participants, their parents, and the administrators of institutions in which research takes place have a right to a written summary of a study's results.

DECEPTION If deception has been a necessary part of a study, participants have the right to be informed about the deception as soon as the study is over.

Before Going On

- Discuss the pros and cons of cross-sectional, longitudinal, and sequential research designs.
- How do developmentalists use case studies, naturalistic observation, correlations, and experiments to identify relationships between variables?
- Why is cross-cultural research important to developmental psychology?
- List the ethical standards used by researchers to protect the rights of research participants.

Summary

The Study of Human Development

- The philosophical concepts of original sin, innate goodness, and the blank slate have influenced Western ideas about human development.

- Darwin studied child development to gain insight into evolution. G. Stanley Hall published the first scientific study of children, introduced the concepts of norms and adolescence, and brought Freud to America. Freud based his psychoanalytic theory on sexual themes in the childhood memories of his emotionally disturbed patients. Watson convinced American psychologists and parents that most changes in childhood are due to learning. Piaget identified stages of cognitive development.

Contemporary Developmental Psychology

- Historically, developmentalists have argued about nature versus nurture, but now they believe that every developmental change is a product of both.

- Contemporary developmental psychologists study three kinds of changes: universal, group-specific, and individual.

- Today's developmentalists recognize that change happens throughout the lifespan.

Research Designs and Methods

- Developmental psychologists use scientific methods to describe, explain, and predict age-related changes and individual differences. Most also want to use research results to improve people's lives.

- In cross-sectional studies, separate age groups are each tested once. In longitudinal designs, the same individuals are tested repeatedly over time. Sequential designs combine cross-sectional and longitudinal comparisons.

- Case studies and naturalistic observation provide a lot of important information, but it usually isn't generalizable to other individuals or groups. Correlational studies measure relationships between variables. They can be done quickly, and the information they yield is more generalizable than that from case studies or naturalistic observation. To test causal hypotheses, it is necessary to use experimental designs in which participants are assigned randomly to experimental or control groups.

- Cross-cultural research helps developmentalists identify universal factors and cultural variables that affect development.

- Ethical principles governing psychological research include protection from harm, informed consent, confidentiality, knowledge of results, and protection from deception.

Key Terms

ageism (p. 12)

atypical development (p. 14)

behaviourism (p. 6)

case study (p. 19)

cohort (p. 12)

control group (p. 21)

correlation (p. 20)

critical period (p. 13)

cross-sectional design (p. 16)

dependent variable (p. 21)

developmental psychology (p. 2)

ethnography (p. 22)

experiment (p. 21)

experimental group (p. 21)

independent variable (p. 21)

interactionist model (p. 9)

lifespan perspective (p. 14)

longitudinal design (p. 16)

maturation (p. 6)

naturalistic observation (p. 19)

nature–nurture controversy (p. 9)

norms (p. 4)

research ethics (p. 22)

sensitive period (p. 13)

sequential design (p. 16)

social clock (p. 12)

Weblinks

Canadian Psychological Association: A History
www.cpa.ca/history/history.html
The Canadian Psychological Association presents a number of articles describing its
developing role in Canada, from the late 19th century to the present.

The Human Nature Daily Review
www.human-nature.com/nibbs
This site contains articles and commentary on psychological issues and trends, press
releases and breaking news, links to databases of research material, and reviews of
current publications.

The Great Depression in Canada
www.yesnet.yk.ca/schools/projects/canadianhistory/depression/depression.html
This student site presents an overview of the causes and effects of the Great
Depression, as well as the roles of the political and social organizations that developed in Canada as a result.

Canadian Toy Testing Council
www.toy-testing.org/
The Canadian Toy Testing Council website publishes an annual rating report of the
value and age-appropriateness of toys sold in Canada.

A Century of Motherhood in Canada
www.todaysparent.com/lifeasparent/motherhood/article.jsp?content=1249501
"From Pablum to the Pill, from maternity wear to Mr. Dressup." This article, by
Ann Douglas, "looks at some of the most memorable moments in the history of
Canadian parenthood."

David J. Sams, Stock Boston

CHAPTER 2

THEORIES OF DEVELOPMENT

Every parent knows it's a constant struggle to keep babies from putting everything in their mouths. Whether it's an attractive toy or a dead insect they encounter while crawling across the living room floor, infants seem to be driven to use their mouths to explore. Have you ever wondered why? An inborn drive to explore the environment may be responsible, or babies may find the physical sensation of mouthing an object highly pleasurable. Perhaps babies use their mouths more than toddlers and preschoolers do because they don't yet have the ability to fully control other parts of their bodies. Clearly, there are many possible explanations.

As you learned in **Chapter 1,** developmental psychologists use theories to formulate *hypotheses,* or testable answers, to such "why" questions. For this reason, you'll be reading about theories in every chapter of this book. To help you make sense of all these theories, this chapter will introduce you to five influential families of theories that have quite different ways of answering questions about development. Theories in these families will come up again and again as you make your way through this book. This chapter will also acquaint you with a few current theoretical trends in the field of developmental psychology, and you will learn how developmental psychologists compare theories. As you read, keep the following questions in mind:

- How do the theories of Freud and Erikson explain developmental change?

- How do the theories of Pavlov, Skinner, and Bandura explain developmental change?

- How do Piaget's theory, the information-processing approach, and Vygotsky's theory explain developmental change?

- What kinds of evolutionary and systems theories have recently captured the attention of developmental psychologists?

- What criteria do psychologists use to compare one theory with another?

PSYCHOANALYTIC THEORIES

One theoretical approach to explaining babies' fascination with mouthing objects might suggest that infants derive more physical pleasure from mouthing objects than from manipulating them with other parts of their bodies. Such an approach would most likely belong to the family of **psychoanalytic theories,** a school of thought that originated with Sigmund Freud. Psychoanalytic theorists believe that developmental change happens because internal drives and emotions influence behaviour.

FREUD'S PSYCHOSEXUAL THEORY

Although much of Freud's formal theory remains contentious, his ideas still influence our understanding of personality development. One of Freud's most distinctive concepts is the idea that behaviour is governed by both conscious and unconscious processes. The most basic of these unconscious processes is an internal drive for physical pleasure that Freud called the **libido.** He believed the libido to be the motivating force behind most behaviour.

Freud also argued that personality has three parts. The **id** contains the libido and operates at an unconscious level; the id is a person's basic sexual and aggressive impulses, which are present at birth. The **ego,** the conscious, thinking part of personality, develops

psychoanalytic theories
theories proposing that developmental change happens because of the influence of internal drives and emotions on behaviour

libido
in Freud's theory, an instinctual drive for physical pleasure present at birth and forming the motivating force behind virtually all human behaviour

id
in Freud's theory, the part of the personality that comprises a person's basic sexual and aggressive impulses; it contains the libido and motivates a person to seek pleasure and avoid pain

ego
according to Freud, the thinking element of personality

superego
Freud's term for the part of personality that is the moral judge

defence mechanisms
strategies for reducing anxiety, such as repression, denial, or projection, proposed by Freud

psychosexual stages
Freud's five stages of personality development through which children move in a fixed sequence determined by maturation; the libido is centred in a different body part in each stage

in the first 2 to 3 years of life. One of the ego's jobs is to keep the needs of the id satisfied. For instance, when a person is hungry, it is the id that demands food immediately, and the ego is supposed to find a way to obtain it. The **superego**, the portion of the personality that acts as a moral judge, contains the rules of society and develops near the end of early childhood, at about age 6. Once the superego develops, the ego's task becomes more complex. It must satisfy the id without violating the superego's rules.

The ego is responsible for keeping the three components of personality in balance. According to Freud, a person experiences tension when any of the three components is in conflict with another. For example, if a person is hungry, the id may motivate her to do anything to find food, but the ego—her conscious self—may be unable to find any. Alternatively, food may be available, but the ego may have to violate one of the superego's moral rules to get it. In such cases, the ego may generate **defence mechanisms,** ways of thinking about a situation that reduce anxiety (see **Table 2.1**). Without defence mechanisms, Freud thought, the degree of tension within the personality would become intolerable, leading to mental illness or suicide.

Freud proposed a series of **psychosexual stages** through which a child moves in a fixed sequence determined by maturation. In each stage, the libido is centred on a different part of the body. In the infant, the mouth is the focus of the drive for physical pleasure; the stage is therefore called the *oral stage*. As maturation progresses, the libido

TABLE 2.1	Common Defence Mechanisms	
Mechanism	**Definition**	**Example**
Denial	Behaving as if a problem doesn't exist	A pregnant woman fails to get prenatal care because she convinces herself she can't possibly be pregnant, even though she has all the symptoms.
Repression	Pushing the memory of something unpleasant into the unconscious	A child "forgets" about a troublesome bully on the bus as soon as he gets home safely from school every day.
Projection	Seeing one's own behaviour or beliefs in others, whether they are actually present or not	A woman complains about her boss to a co-worker and comes away from the conversation believing that the co-worker shares her dislike of the boss, even though the co-worker made no comment on what she said.
Regression	Behaving in a way that is inappropriate for one's age	A toilet-trained 2-year-old starts wetting the bed every night after a new baby arrives.
Displacement	Directing emotion to an object (or a person) other than the one that provoked it	An elderly adult suffers a stroke, becomes physically impaired, and expresses her frustration through verbal abuse of the hospital staff.
Rationalization	Creating an explanation to justify an action or to deal with a disappointment	A man stealing money from his employer says to himself "They won't give me a raise, so I deserve whatever I can take."

becomes focused on the anus (hence, the *anal stage*), and later on the genitals (the *phallic stage* and, after a period of dormancy called the *latency stage*, the *genital stage*).

Optimum development, according to Freud, requires an environment that will satisfy the unique needs of each period. For example, the infant needs sufficient opportunity for oral stimulation. An inadequate early environment will result in *fixation*, characterized by behaviours that reflect unresolved problems and unmet needs. Thus, emphasis on the formative role of early experiences is a hallmark of psychoanalytic theories.

ERIKSON'S PSYCHOSOCIAL THEORY

Apart from Freud, Erik Erikson is the psychoanalytic theorist who has had the greatest influence on the study of development (Erikson, 1950, 1959, 1980b, 1982; Erikson, Erikson, & Kivnick, 1986; Evans, 1969). Erikson, like many of Freud's other early followers, accepted many of Freud's ideas, but later went on to expand on them. For instance, Erikson claimed that development results from the interaction between internal drives and cultural demands; thus, his theory refers to **psychosocial stages** rather than to psycho*sexual* ones. Furthermore, Erikson thought that development continued through the entire lifespan.

In Erikson's view, to achieve a healthy personality, an individual must successfully resolve a psychosocial crisis at each of the eight stages of development, as summarized in **Table 2.2**. Each crisis is defined by a pair of opposing possibilities, such as trust versus mistrust or integrity versus despair. Successful resolution of a crisis results in the development of the characteristic on the positive side of the dichotomy. A healthy resolution, however, does not mean moving totally to the positive side. For example, an infant needs to have experienced some mistrust in order to learn to identify people who are not trustworthy. But healthy development requires a favourable ratio of positive to negative. Of the eight stages described in **Table 2.2**, four have been the focus of the greatest amount of theorizing and research: trust in infancy, identity in adolescence, intimacy in early adulthood, and generativity in middle adulthood.

Erikson believed that the behaviour of the major caregiver (usually the mother) is critical to the child's resolution of the first life crisis: *trust versus mistrust*. To ensure successful resolution of this crisis, the caregiver must be consistently loving and must respond to the child predictably and reliably. Infants whose early care has been erratic or harsh may develop mistrust. In either case, the child carries this aspect of personality throughout her development, and it affects the resolution of later tasks.

Erikson's description of the central adolescent dilemma, *identity versus role confusion*, has been particularly influential. He argued that, in order to arrive at a mature sexual and occupational identity, every adolescent must examine his identity and the roles he must occupy. He must achieve an integrated sense of self, of what he wants to do and be, and of his appropriate sexual role. The risk is that the adolescent will suffer from confusion arising from the profusion of roles opening up to him at this age.

In the first of the three adult stages, the young adult builds on the identity established in adolescence to confront the crisis of *intimacy versus isolation*. Erikson defined intimacy as "the ability to fuse your identity with someone else's without fear that you're going to lose something yourself" (Erikson, in Evans, 1969). Many young people, Erikson thought, make the mistake of thinking they will find their identity in a relationship, but in his view it is only those who have already formed (or are well on the way to forming) a clear identity who can successfully enter this fusion of identities that

psychosocial stages
Erikson's eight stages, or crises, of personality development in which inner instincts interact with outer cultural and social demands to shape personality

Critical Thinking

In which of Erikson's psychosocial stages would you place yourself? Does Erikson's description of this stage correspond to the challenges and concerns you are confronting?

TABLE 2.2   Erikson's Psychosocial Stages

Approximate Ages	Stage	Positive Characteristics Gained and Typical Activities
Birth to 1 year	Trust versus mistrust	Hope; trust in primary caregiver and in one's own ability to make things happen (secure attachment to caregiver is key)
1 to 3	Autonomy versus shame and doubt	Will; new physical skills lead to demand for more choices, most often seen as saying "no" to care-givers; child learns self-care skills such as toileting
3 to 6	Initiative versus guilt	Purpose; ability to organize activities around some goal; more assertiveness and aggressiveness (harsh parental criticism may lead to guilt)
6 to 12	Industry versus inferiority	Competence; cultural skills and norms, including school skills and tool use (failure to master these leads to sense of inferiority)
12 to 18	Identity versus role confusion	Fidelity; a unified and consistent sense of self that integrates pubertal changes into a mature sexual identity, assumes adult social and occupational roles, and establishes personal values and attitudes
18 to 30	Intimacy versus isolation	Love; person develops intimate relationships beyond adolescent love; many become parents
30 to old age	Generativity versus stagnation	Care; people rear children, focus on occupational achievement or creativity, and train the next genera-tion; turn outward from the self toward others
Old age	Integrity versus despair	Wisdom; person conducts a life review, integrates earlier stages and comes to terms with basic iden-tity; develops self-acceptance

he called *intimacy*. Young adults whose identities are weak or unformed will remain in shallow relationships and will experience a sense of isolation or loneliness.

The middle adulthood crisis is *generativity versus stagnation*, which is "primarily the concern in establishing and guiding the next generation" (Erikson, 1963, p. 267). The rearing of children is the most obvious way to achieve a sense of generativity, but it is not the only way. Doing creative work, giving service to an organization or to soci-ety, or serving as a mentor to younger colleagues can help the midlife adult achieve a sense of generativity. Failing that, the self-absorbed, nongenerative adult may feel a sense of stagnation.

The key idea underlying Erikson's theory is that each new crisis is thrust on the developing person because of changes in social demands that accompany changes in age. The fourth stage of industry versus inferiority, for example, begins when the child starts school and must learn to read and write. If the child fails to read and write at grade level, she is often still able to advance with her same-aged peers. As the child enters the higher grade levels lacking the essential reading and writing skills, she may experience an increasing sense of inferiority. This evolving negative self-image may adversely affect the child's transition to the next stage of psychosocial development—the formation of a healthy identity. Thus, childhood crises set the stage for those of adolescence and adulthood.

EVALUATION OF PSYCHOANALYTIC THEORIES

Psychoanalytic theories such as Freud's and Erikson's, summarized in **Table 2.3**, have several attractive aspects. Most centrally, they highlight the importance of the child's earliest relationships with caregivers. Furthermore, they suggest that the child's needs change with age, so that parents and other caregivers must constantly adapt to the changing child. One of the implications of this is that we should not think of "good parenting" as an unchanging quality. Some people may be very good at meeting the needs of an infant but less capable of dealing with teenagers' identity struggles. The child's eventual personality and her overall mental health thus depend on the interaction pattern that develops in a particular family. The idea of changing needs is an extremely attractive element of these theories, because more and more of the research in developmental psychology is moving developmentalists toward just such a conception of the process.

Psychoanalytic theory has also given psychologists a number of helpful concepts, such as the unconscious, the ego, and identity, which have become a part of everyday language as well as theory. Moreover, psychologists are taking a fresh look at Freud's ideas about the importance of defence mechanisms in coping with anxiety (Cramer, 2000). Freud is also usually credited with the invention of psychotherapy, which is still practised today. An additional strength of the psychoanalytic perspective is the emphasis on continued development during adulthood found in Erikson's theory. His ideas have provided a framework for a great deal of new research and theorizing about adult development.

The major weakness of psychoanalytic theories is the fuzziness of many of their concepts. For example, how could researchers detect the presence of the id, ego, superego, and so on? Without more precise definitions, it is extremely difficult to test these theories, despite their provocative explanations of development.

TABLE 2.3	Psychoanalytic Theories		
		Evaluation	
Theory	**Main Idea**	**Strengths**	**Weaknesses**
Freud's Psychosexual Theory	Personality develops in five stages from birth to adolescence; in each stage, the need for physical pleasure is focused on a different part of the body.	Emphasizes importance of experiences in infancy and early childhood; provides psychological explanations for mental illness	Sexual feelings are not as important in personality development as Freud claimed.
Erikson's Psychosocial Theory	Personality develops through eight life crises across the entire lifespan; a person finishes each crisis with either a good or a poor resolution.	Helps explain the role of culture in personality development; important in lifespan psychology; useful description of major themes of personality development at different ages	Describing each period in terms of a single crisis is probably an oversimplification.

THE HUMANISTIC ALTERNATIVE

In addition to criticizing the fuzziness of some psychoanalytic concepts, psychologists have taken issue with the psychoanalytic emphasis on atypical development. Some have proposed alternative theories that focus on the positive aspects of development while accepting the psychoanalytic assumption that behaviour is motivated by internal drives and emotions. These *humanistic theories* share Jean-Jacques Rousseau's basic premise of *innate goodness* (refer back to Chapter 1), and they begin with the optimistic assumption that the most important internal drive is each individual's motivation to achieve his or her full potential. A key figure in the humanistic tradition is Abraham Maslow (1968, 1970a, 1970b, 1971), who used the term *self-actualization* to describe this ultimate goal of human life.

Maslow's greatest interest was in the development of motives, or needs, which he divided into two subsets: deficiency motives and being motives. *Deficiency motives* involve drives to maintain physical or emotional homeostasis (inner balance), such as the drive to get enough to eat or drink, the sexual drive, or even the drive to obtain sufficient love or respect from others. *Being motives* involve the desire to understand, to give to others, and to grow—that is, to achieve self-actualization. In general, the satisfaction of deficiency motives prevents or cures illness or re-creates homeostasis. In contrast, the satisfaction of being motives produces a general sense of well-being. The

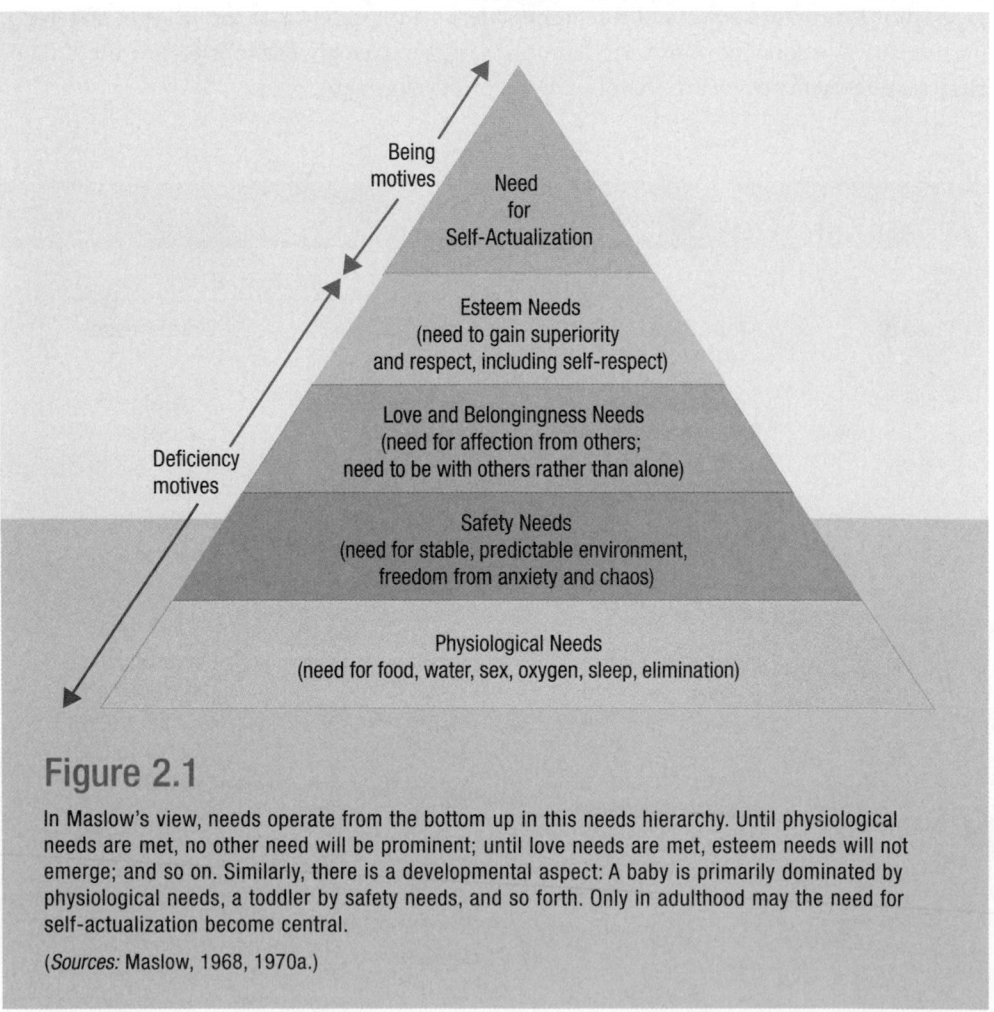

Figure 2.1

In Maslow's view, needs operate from the bottom up in this needs hierarchy. Until physiological needs are met, no other need will be prominent; until love needs are met, esteem needs will not emerge; and so on. Similarly, there is a developmental aspect: A baby is primarily dominated by physiological needs, a toddler by safety needs, and so forth. Only in adulthood may the need for self-actualization become central.

(*Sources:* Maslow, 1968, 1970a.)

distinction is like the "difference between fending off threat or attack, and positive triumph and achievement" (Maslow, 1968, p. 32).

Maslow described these various needs or motives in his famous needs hierarchy, shown in **Figure 2.1**. He argued that the various needs must be met in order from the bottom up. For example, only when physiological needs are met do safety needs come to the fore; only when love and esteem needs are met can the need for self-actualization become dominant. For that reason, Maslow thought that being motives were likely to be significant only in adulthood, and only in those individuals who had found stable ways to satisfy both love and esteem needs. In this sense, Maslow's theory sounds very similar to Erikson's stages of intimacy and generativity.

Another prominent humanistic psychologist, Carl Rogers, talked about the capacity of each individual to become a "fully functioning person," without guilt or seriously distorting defences (Rogers, 1961). In this idea, we see an assumption that it is never too late—not only can adults overcome early conditioning or the residue of unresolved dilemmas, but they are motivated to try to do just that.

The inherent optimism in humanistic theories makes them very appealing. However, as is true of psychoanalytic theories, humanistic models like Maslow's are stated in broad, rather imprecise terms. They have appealed to a great many people because they seem to resonate with some aspects of everyday experience. But they are difficult to test empirically because the propositions are not stated clearly enough.

Before Going On

- In Freud's view, how do the id, ego, and superego work together to keep the personality functioning?

- How do Erikson's stages differ from Freud's?

- Name at least two strengths and two weaknesses of psychoanalytic theory.

- What are the major ideas of Maslow's and Rogers's humanistic theories?

LEARNING THEORIES

In general, **learning theories** assert that development results from an accumulation of experiences. Learning theories are aligned with the philosophy of John Locke who, as you recall from **Chapter 1**, said that children are born with neither good nor bad tendencies, but their behaviour is shaped, for better or worse, by their environment. Thus, in contrast to psychoanalysts, learning theorists would say that infants repeat the behaviour of putting objects in their mouths because they find the sensations it produces rewarding. Alternatively, when they put something in their mouths that tastes bad, infants learn not to mouth such an object again.

learning theories
theories that assert that development results from an accumulation of experiences

PAVLOV'S CLASSICAL CONDITIONING

Classical conditioning is the acquisition of new signals for existing responses. Each incidence of learning begins with a biologically programmed stimulus-response connection, or *reflex*. For example, salivation happens naturally when you put food in your mouth.

classical conditioning
learning that results from the association of stimuli

In classical conditioning terms, the food is the *unconditioned (unlearned, natural) stimulus;* salivating is an *unconditioned (unlearned, natural) response.*

Stimuli presented just before or at the same time as the unconditioned stimulus are those that are likely to be associated with it. For example, most foods have odours, and to get to your mouth, food has to pass near your nose. Thus, you usually smell food before you taste it. Food odours eventually become *conditioned (learned) stimuli* that elicit salivation. In effect, they act as a signal to your salivary glands that food is coming. Once the connection between food odours and salivation is established, smelling food triggers the salivation response even when you do not actually eat the food. When a response occurs reliably in connection with a conditioned stimulus in this way, it is known as a *conditioned (learned) response.*

Classical conditioning is of interest in the study of development because of the role it plays in the acquisition of emotional responses. For example, things or people that are present when you feel good will become conditioned stimuli for pleasant feelings, while those associated with uncomfortable feelings may become conditioned stimuli for a sense of unease. Classical conditioning is especially important in infancy. Because a child's mother or father is present so often when nice things happen, such as when the child feels warm, comfortable, and cuddled, the mother and father usually serve as conditioned stimuli for pleasant feelings, a fact that makes it possible for the parents' presence to comfort a child.

SKINNER'S OPERANT CONDITIONING

operant conditioning
learning to repeat or stop behaviours because of their consequences

reinforcement
any immediate consequence that follows a behaviour and increases the likelihood that the behaviour will be repeated

punishment
any immediate consequence that follows a behaviour and decreases the likelihood that the behaviour will be repeated

Another type of learning is **operant conditioning,** a term coined by B.F. Skinner, the most famous proponent of this theory (Skinner, 1953, 1980). Operant conditioning involves learning to repeat or stop behaviours because of the consequences they bring about. **Reinforcement** is any immediate consequence that follows a behaviour that increases the likelihood that the behaviour will be repeated. **Punishment** is any immediate consequence that follows a behaviour that decreases the likelihood that the behaviour will be repeated.

Positive reinforcement entails adding a consequence (usually something pleasant) that follows a behaviour and increases the chances that the behaviour will occur again. Some kinds of pleasant consequences, such as attention, serve as reinforcers for most people most of the time. But strictly speaking, reinforcement is defined by its effect; we don't know something is reinforcing unless we see that its presence increases the probability of some behaviour.

Laboratory research involving animals was important in the development of Skinner's operant conditioning theory. (*Photo:* Ken Hayman/Black Star)

Negative reinforcement entails the taking away of a condition (usually something unpleasant) following a behaviour and increases the chances that the behaviour will occur again. For example, coughing is an unpleasant experience for most of us, and taking a dose of cough medicine usually stops it. As a result, the next time we begin to cough, we reach for the cough syrup because the behaviour of consuming a spoonful of cough syrup is reinforced by the cessation of coughing. In other words, we make the unpleasant experience of coughing go away when we engage in the behaviour of swallowing cough syrup. Thus, the behaviour of taking cough syrup is learned through negative reinforcement.

Definitions and simple examples of positive and negative reinforcement may be misleading when it comes to understanding how the two operate in real-life contexts. For example, most people understand that paying attention to a preschooler's whining is likely to increase it. This is a case of positive reinforcement—a child's whining is reinforced whenever a parent shows attention. At the same time, however, a parent learns to attend to a whining preschooler because whining is irritating, and responding to it usually makes it stop. As a result, the parent's behaviour of responding to whining is negatively reinforced by its consequence—namely, that the child *stops* whining. In this case of negative reinforcement, parental attention is reinforced if the child stops whining.

There are two general forms of punishment but, in contrast to both kinds of reinforcement, both forms of punishment stop a behaviour. Sometimes punishments involve eliminating nice things, for example, taking away TV privileges. This is referred to as *negative punishment* and entails taking away a condition (usually something pleasant) that follows a behaviour and decreases the chances that the behaviour will occur again. Negative punishment can be considered a type of **extinction**, which is the gradual elimination of a behaviour through repeated nonreinforcement. If a teacher succeeds in eliminating a student's undesirable behaviour by ignoring it, the behaviour is said to have been *extinguished*.

However, punishment may also involve unpleasant things such as scolding. A *positive punishment* entails adding a consequence (usually something unpleasant) that follows a behaviour and decreases the chances that the behaviour will occur again. Like reinforcement, however, punishment is defined by its effect. Consequences that do not stop behaviour can't be properly called punishments.

Such examples illustrate the complex manner in which reinforcements and punishments operate in the real world. In laboratory settings, operant conditioning researchers usually work with only one participant or animal subject at a time; they needn't worry about the social consequences of behaviours or consequences. They can also control the situation so that a particular behaviour is reinforced every time it occurs. In the real world, *partial reinforcement*—reinforcement of a behaviour on some occasions but not others—is more common (see **The Real World**). Studies of partial reinforcement show that people take longer to learn a new behaviour under partial reinforcement conditions; once established, however, such behaviours are very resistant to extinction.

Shaping is the reinforcement of intermediate steps until an individual learns a complex behaviour. For example, you wouldn't start learning to play tennis by challenging a skilled player to a match. Instead, you would first learn to hold the racquet properly. Next, you would learn the basic strokes and practise hitting balls hit or thrown to you by an instructor. Next, you would learn to serve. Finally, you would put all your skills together and play an actual match. All along the way, you would be encouraged by the sense of satisfaction gained from accomplishing each step toward the goal.

BANDURA'S SOCIAL-COGNITIVE THEORY

Learning theorist Albert Bandura was born and raised in Alberta and graduated with a bachelor's degree in psychology from the University of British Columbia in 1949 and a PhD from the University of Iowa in 1952. His ideas are more influential among developmental psychologists than those of the conditioning theorists, as he contends that learning does not always require reinforcement (1977a, 1982a, 1989, 2001). Learning may also occur as a result of watching someone else perform some action and experience reinforcement or punishment. Learning of this type, called **observational learning, or modelling**, is involved in a wide range of behaviours. Children learn to hit by watching other people in real life and on television. Adults learn job skills by observing or being shown them by others.

Critical Thinking

Describe instances in your everyday life when your behaviour is affected by classical or operant conditioning or when you use these principles to affect others' behaviour.

extinction
the gradual elimination of a behaviour through repeated nonreinforcement

shaping
the reinforcement of intermediate steps until an individual learns a complex behaviour

observational learning, or modelling
learning that results from seeing a model reinforced or punished for a behaviour

Robert Munsch, the Canadian author and story-teller, has been delighting families for more than a generation. In one of his stories, *Thomas' Snowsuit*, he tells a humorous tale about a boy named Thomas who refuses to wear his new snowsuit with an unbending "NNNNNO," much to the exasperation of his mother, teacher, and school principal (Munsch, 1985). First, Thomas' mother tries to get him to wear his new snowsuit by cajoling and then jumping up and down, but Thomas still refuses. Only after an enormous tussle is Thomas wrestled into his snowsuit. Later at school, Thomas again refuses to put his snowsuit on and go out for recess and no amount of cajoling or jumping up and down by his teacher or principal encourages Thomas to comply. The situation worsens as everybody's clothes get switched in the ensuing confusion. However, as soon as Thomas hears his friends' calling for him to come out and play he gets into his snowsuit in a flash leaving the teacher and principal frustrated and inadvertently dressed in each other's clothes. This story illustrates that when it comes to dealing with children it is easy to create unintended consequences if you do not apply effective behaviour management strategies.

Let's consider some common real-life situations. For example, suppose your 3-year-old daughter repeatedly demands your attention while you are fixing dinner. Because you don't want to reinforce this behaviour, you ignore her the first six or eight times she calls you or tugs at your clothes. But after the ninth or tenth repetition, with her voice getting whinier each time, you can't stand it any longer and finally say something like "All right! What do you want?" Since you have ignored most of her demands, you might think you have not been reinforcing them. But what you have actually done is create a *partial reinforcement schedule*. By responding to every ninth or tenth demand, you have in essence, taught her that persistent whining will eventually be rewarded with attention. This intermittent pattern of reinforcement helps create behaviour that is very hard to extinguish. So your daughter may continue to be overly demanding for a very long time.

Another thing we know about reinforcement is that, when two people interact, they mutually *shape* each other's behaviour—for better or for worse. For example, if a child begins to holler at his mother to fetch his school lunch bag before he goes out the door, and the mother complies, two things happen. First, the mother has just strengthened the child's hollering behaviour through positive reinforcement by giving him what he wanted when he hollered; in this case, the school lunch bag. Second, the child has just strengthened the mother's obliging behaviour through nega-tive reinforcement by taking away something the mother finds distressing; in this case, hollering. We would predict that the next time the boy wants something from his mother, he is more likely to holler and, unfortunately, his mother is more likely to comply if the boy stops hollering once his mother gets him what he wants. As you can see, we can easily and inadvertently set up reciprocal patterns of reinforcement and expectations that can benefit one person, but disadvantage the other. Moreover, once such a pattern of reciprocal parent–child interaction is established, it can be very difficult to break, especially if you are not aware of the reinforcing sequence of events.

If such situations are all too familiar to you, it may pay to keep careful records for a while, noting each incident and your response. Then see whether you can figure out which principles are really at work and how you might change the pattern.

(*Artwork:* Michael Martchenko. © *Thomas' Snowsuit* by Michael Martchenko, 1985. Used with permission of Annick Press)

If only Thomas's mother, teacher, and principal had read Skinner!

Modelling is an important source of learning for both children and adults. What behaviours have you learned by watching and copying others?
(*Photos: left,* Kathy Sloane, 1992, Photo Researchers; *right,* Richard Sobel/Stock Boston)

Furthermore, what a person learns from observing others is influenced by processes such as attention and memory. Maturation is important as well: A 4-year-old probably won't learn geometry from watching his high-school-age sister do her homework. Bandura also suggests that what an observer learns from a particular model is influenced by his own goals, expectations about what kinds of consequences are likely if he adopts the model's behaviour, and judgments of his own performance.

Bandura (1977a, 1986) also put forth the idea of **reciprocal determinism,** a process of human development based upon the interaction of three factors: *personal* (cognitive abilities, physical characteristics, beliefs, attitudes, and expectations), *behavioural* (physical-motor and verbal actions), and *environmental* (other people and physical surroundings)(see **The Real World**). Bandura's *reciprocal determinism model* forms a triangle of bidirectional influence as depicted in **Figure 2.2.** From this perspective, we are not only affected by our circumstances, but we are also able to exert influence over our situation, which in turn affects our expectations about how much influence we have over future events. In the case of children, they are actively involved in shaping the very environments that influence their behaviour and personality development.

With respect to personal factors, Bandura (1997a, b) has placed particular emphasis on a concept he called **self-efficacy**—the belief in one's own capacity to cause an intended event to occur (a topic we will cover in later chapters). People who have a strong sense of self-efficacy have higher expectations for success and will put forth more effort and persistence when faced with a challenge. Conversely, a person with low self-efficacy has a lower expectation for success, which is associated with acquiescence or avoidance when confronted with a difficult task.

reciprocal determinism
a process of human development based upon the interaction of personal, behavioural, and environmental factors

self-efficacy
the belief in one's own capacity to cause an intended event to occur or to perform a task

EVALUATION OF LEARNING THEORIES

Several implications of learning theories, summarized in **Table 2.4,** are worth emphasizing. First, learning theories can explain both consistency and changes in behaviour. If

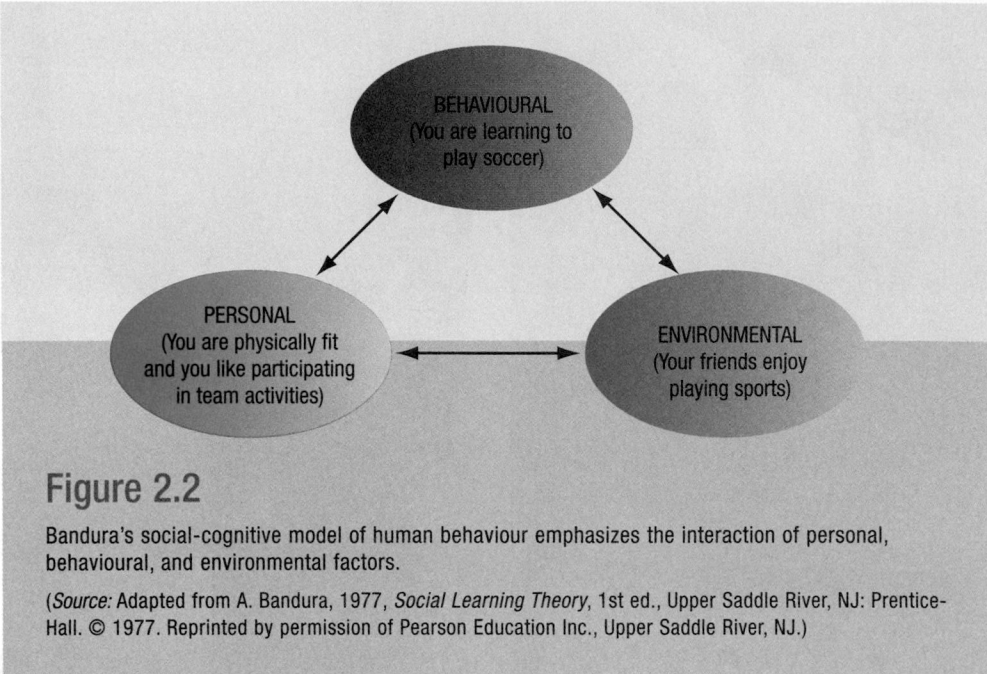

Figure 2.2

Bandura's social-cognitive model of human behaviour emphasizes the interaction of personal, behavioural, and environmental factors.

(*Source:* Adapted from A. Bandura, 1977, *Social Learning Theory*, 1st ed., Upper Saddle River, NJ: Prentice-Hall. © 1977. Reprinted by permission of Pearson Education Inc., Upper Saddle River, NJ.)

TABLE 2.4   Learning Theories

Theory	Main Idea	Evaluation	
		Strengths	**Weaknesses**
Pavlov's Classical Conditioning	Learning happens when neutral stimuli become so strongly associated with natural stimuli that they elicit the same response.	Useful in explaining how emotional responses such as phobias are learned	Explanation of behaviour change is too limited to serve as comprehensive theory of human development.
Skinner's Operant Conditioning Theory	Development involves behaviour changes that are shaped by reinforcement and punishment.	Basis of many useful strategies for managing and changing human behaviour	Humans are not as passive as Skinner claimed; the theory ignores hereditary and cognitive, emotional, and social factors in development.
Bandura's Social-Cognitive Theory	People learn from models; what they learn from a model depends on how they interpret the situation cognitively and emotionally.	Helps explain how models influence behaviour; explains more about development than other learning theories because of addition of cognitive and emotional factors	Does not provide an overall picture of development.

a child is friendly and smiling both at home and at school, learning theorists would explain the child's behaviour by saying that the child is being reinforced for that behaviour in both settings. It is equally possible to explain why a child is happy at home but miserable at school. We need only hypothesize that the home environment reinforces cheerful behaviour but the school setting does not.

Learning theorists also tend to be optimistic about the possibility of change. Children's behaviour can change if the reinforcement system, or their beliefs about themselves, change. So, problem behaviour can be modified.

The great strength of learning theories is that they seem to give an accurate picture of the way in which many behaviours are learned. It is clear that both children and adults learn through conditioning and modelling. Furthermore, Bandura's addition of mental elements to learning theory adds further strength, since it allows an integration of learning models and other approaches.

However, the traditional learning theorists' approach is not really developmental; it doesn't tell us much about change over a lifespan, either in childhood or adulthood. In comparison, Bandura's variation on learning theory does—it tells us how a child's level of cognitive development affects his or her impressions and reactions to the environment. In turn, the child's perception directs her behaviour in particular situations (Bandura, 1991, 1997a; Bandura & Schunk, 1981; Schunk, 1983). Thus, learning theories help developmentalists understand how specific behaviours are acquired, while social-cognitive theory contributes to an understanding of age-related change.

Before Going On

- What is classical conditioning?

- How does operant conditioning cause learning?

- What concepts does Bandura add to learning theories to make them more useful?

- What are the strengths and weaknesses of learning theories as an explanation of human development?

COGNITIVE THEORIES

The group of theories known as **cognitive theories** emphasize mental aspects of development such as logic and memory. A cognitive theorist might propose that babies use their senses, including the sense of taste, to build mental pictures of the world around them. Thus, infants mouth everything in their environment until they have learned all they can from this behaviour, then they move on to a more mature way of interacting with the world.

cognitive theories
theories that emphasize mental processes in development, such as logic and memory

PIAGET'S COGNITIVE-DEVELOPMENTAL THEORY

For Jean Piaget, as you should remember from **Chapter 1**, the central question of interest in developmental psychology was "How does thinking develop?" (Piaget, 1952, 1970, 1977; Piaget & Inhelder, 1969). He was struck by the fact that all children seem to go through the same sequence of discoveries about their world, making the same

Piaget based many of his ideas on naturalistic observations of children of different ages on playgrounds and in schools.
(*Photo:* Judith Behling Ford)

scheme
in Piaget's theory, an internal cognitive structure that provides an individual with a procedure to use in a specific circumstance

assimilation
the process of using a scheme to make sense of an event or experience

accommodation
changing a scheme as a result of some new information

equilibration
the process of balancing assimilation and accommodation to create schemes that fit the environment

Critical Thinking

Describe three or four examples of assimilation and accommodation in your everyday life.

mistakes and arriving at the same solutions. For example, all 3- and 4-year-olds seem to think that if water is poured from a short, wide glass into a taller, narrower one, there is then more water, because the water level is higher in the narrow glass than it was in the wide glass. In contrast, most 7-year-olds realize that the amount of water has not changed. To explain such age differences, Piaget proposed several concepts that continue to guide developmental research.

A pivotal idea in Piaget's model is that of a **scheme**, an internal cognitive structure that provides an individual with a procedure to follow in a specific circumstance. For example, when you pick up a ball, you use your picking-up scheme. To throw it to someone, you use your looking scheme, your aiming scheme, and your throwing scheme. Piaget proposed that each of us begins life with a small repertoire of sensory and motor schemes, such as looking, tasting, touching, hearing, and reaching. As we use each scheme, it becomes better adapted to the world; in other words, it works better.

We possess mental schemes as well, most of which develop in childhood and adolescence. Mental schemes allow us to use symbols and think logically. Piaget proposed three processes to explain how children get from built-in schemes such as looking and touching to the complex mental schemes used in childhood, adolescence, and adulthood.

Assimilation is the process of using schemes to make sense of experiences. Piaget would say that a baby who grasps a toy is *assimilating* it to his grasping scheme. The complementary process is **accommodation**, which involves changing the scheme as a result of some new information acquired through assimilation. When the baby grasps a square object for the first time, he will accommodate his grasping scheme; so the next time he reaches for a square object, his hand will be more appropriately bent to grasp it. Thus, the process of accommodation is the key to developmental change. Through accommodation, we improve our skills and reorganize our ways of thinking.

Equilibration is the process of balancing assimilation and accommodation to create schemes that fit the environment. To illustrate, think about infants' tendency to put things in their mouths. In Piaget's terms, they assimilate objects to their mouthing scheme. As they mouth each object, their mouthing scheme changes to include the instructions "*Do* mouth this" or "*Don't* mouth this." The accommodation is based on mouthing experiences. A pacifier feels good in the mouth, but a dead insect has an unpleasant texture. So, eventually, the mouthing scheme says it's okay to put a pacifier in the mouth, but it's not okay to mouth a dead insect. In this way, an infant's mouthing scheme attains a better fit with the real world.

Piaget's research suggested to him that logical thinking evolves in four stages. During the *sensorimotor stage,* from birth to 18 months, infants use their sensory and motor schemes to act on the world around them. In the *preoperational stage,* from 18 months to about age 6, youngsters acquire symbolic schemes, such as language and fantasy, that they use in thinking and communicating. Next comes the *concrete operational stage,* during which 6- to 12-year-olds begin to think logically and become capable of solving problems such as the one illustrated in **Figure 2.3**. The last phase is the *formal operational stage,* in which adolescents learn to think logically about abstract ideas and hypothetical situations.

Table 2.5 describes these stages more fully; you will read about each of them in detail later in the book. For now, it is important to understand that in Piaget's view, each stage grows out of the one that precedes it, and each involves a major restructuring of the child's way of thinking. It's also important to know that research has confirmed Piaget's belief that the sequence of the stages is fixed.

However, children progress through them at different rates. In addition, some individuals do not attain the formal operational stage in adolescence or even in adulthood. Consequently, the ages associated with the stages are approximations.

INFORMATION-PROCESSING THEORY

The goal of **information-processing theory** is to explain how the mind manages information (Klahr, 1992). Information-processing theorists use the computer as a model of human thinking. Consequently, they focus on what happens to information as it enters the mind (*input*), is transformed by mental programs (*throughput*), and is used to perform actions (*output*).

Theorizing about and studying memory processes are central to information-processing theory. This theory breaks memory down into the subprocesses of encoding, storage, and retrieval. *Encoding* is organizing information to be stored in memory. For example, you may be encoding the information in this chapter by relating it to your own childhood. *Storage* is keeping information, and *retrieval* is getting information out of memory. As information flows through these memory processes we use mental strategies to manipulate information so that we can complete mental operations, solve everyday problems, and learn new tasks.

Most memory research assumes that the human memory is made up of multiple components. The idea is that information moves through these components in an organized way (see **Figure 2.4** on page 42). The process of understanding a spoken word serves as a good example.

First, you hear the word when the sounds enter your *sensory memory*. Your experiences with language allow you to recognize the pattern of sounds as a word. Next, the word moves into your *short-term memory*, the component of the memory system where all information is processed. Thus, short-term memory is often called *working memory*. Knowledge of the word's meaning is then called up out of *long-term memory*, the component of the system where information is permanently stored, and placed in short-term memory, where it is linked to the word's sounds to enable you to understand the word.

Each memory component manages information differently. Information flows through the sensory memory in a constant stream. Bits of information that are not attended to drop out quickly. The short-term memory is extremely limited in capacity —it can contain only about seven items at a time. However, information can be retained in short-term memory as long as it is processed in some way—as you do when you repeat your grocery list to yourself on the way to the store.

Long-term memory is unlimited in capacity, and information is often organized and stored in terms of meaningful associations. For example, suppose you read a sentence such as "Bill wrote a letter to his brother." When you think about the sentence later, you might mistakenly recall that it contained the word *pen*. This happens because information about the process of writing and the tools used to do it are stored together in long-term memory.

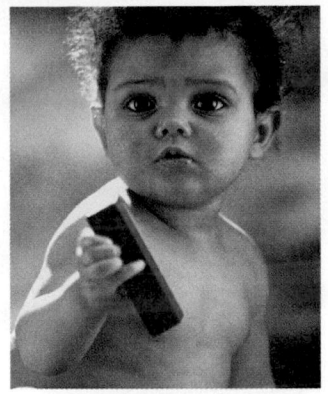

Using Piaget's terminology, we would say this infant is assimilating the object to her grasping scheme. What scheme is being accommodated at the same time as she adapts her grasping scheme? (*Photo:* Getty Images)

information-processing theory
theoretical perspectives that use the computer as a model to explain how the mind manages information

Figure 2.3

In one of the problems Piaget devised, a child is shown two clay balls of equal size and asked if they both contain the same amount of clay. Next, the researcher rolls one ball into a sausage shape and asks the child if the two shapes still contain the same amount of clay. A preoperational child will say that one now contains more clay than the other and will base his answer on their appearance: "The sausage has more because it's longer now." A concrete operational thinker will say that the two still contain the same amount of material because no clay was added or taken away from either.
(*Photo:* Will Hart)

TABLE 2.5		Piaget's Cognitive-Developmental Stages
Approximate Ages	**Stage**	**Description**
Birth to 18 months	Sensorimotor	The baby understands the world through her senses and her motor actions; she begins to use simple symbols, such as single words and pretend play, near the end of this period.
18 months to 6 years	Preoperational	By age 2, the child can use symbols both to think and to communicate; he develops the abilities to take others' points of view, classify objects, and use simple logic by the end of this stage.
6 to 12	Concrete operational	The child's logic takes a great leap forward with the development of new internal operations, such as conservation and class inclusion, but is still tied to the known world; by the end of the period, he can reason about simple "what if" questions.
12+	Formal operational	The child begins to manipulate ideas as well as objects; she thinks hypothetically and, by adulthood, can easily manage a variety of "what if" questions; she greatly improves her ability to organize ideas and objects mentally.

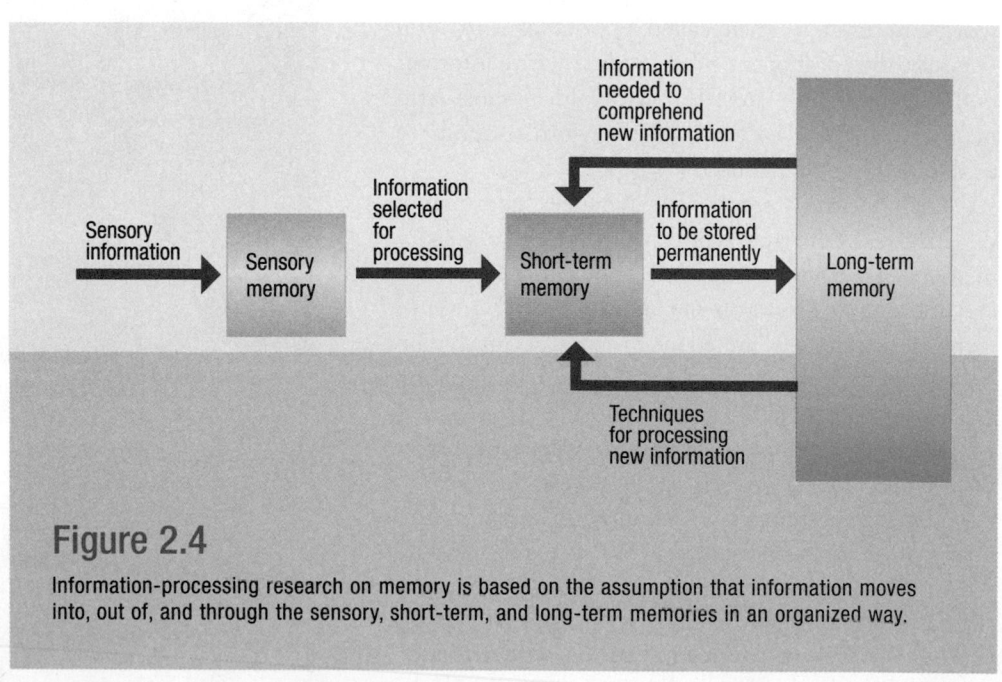

Figure 2.4

Information-processing research on memory is based on the assumption that information moves into, out of, and through the sensory, short-term, and long-term memories in an organized way.

York University psychologist Juan Pascual-Leone established neo-Piagetian theories by using information-processing theory to explain Piaget's stages (1987). Another leading theorist, Robbie Case, who was centred at the Ontario Institute for Studies in Education until his death at age 55 in May 2000, argued that **neo-Piagetian theories** expand on Piaget's theory rather than contradict it (Case, 1985; 1997). According to neo-Piagetians, older children and adults can solve complex problems like those in Piaget's research because they can hold more pieces of information in their short-term memories at the same time than younger children can. To solve the problem in **Figure 2.3**, for example, a child must be able to think about the appearance of the two balls of clay before one was rolled into a sausage shape and their appearance afterward in her working memory at the same time. She must also think about how the transformation was carried out. Neo-Piagetians maintain that children are incapable of performing all of this mental work in short-term memory until after age 6 or 7 (Case, 1985; 1997).

VYGOTSKY'S SOCIOCULTURAL THEORY

Following the Bolshevik revolution of 1917, the new Soviet government hired Russian psychologist Lev Vygotsky, among others, to create a school system that would serve the ends of the new communist regime (Vygotsky, 1978). His death in 1938 and the historical events that followed—World War II and the Cold War—resulted in his work remaining largely unknown outside the Soviet Union for decades. Recently, however, developmentalists have become interested in his views on the influence of cultural forces on individual development (Thomas, 1996).

Vygotsky's **sociocultural theory** asserts that complex forms of thinking have their origins in social interactions rather than in the child's private explorations, as Piaget thought. According to Vygotsky, children's learning of new cognitive skills is guided by an adult (or a more skilled child, such as an older sibling), who structures the child's learning experience, a process Vygotsky called **scaffolding**. To create an appropriate scaffold, the adult must gain and keep the child's attention, model the best strategy, and adapt the whole process to the child's developmental level, or **zone of proximal development** (Landry, Garner, Swank, & Baldwin, 1996; Rogoff, 1990). Vygotsky used this term to signify tasks that are too hard for the child to do alone but that he can manage with guidance. For example, parents of a beginning reader provide a scaffold when they help him sound out new words.

EVALUATION OF COGNITIVE THEORIES

Research based on cognitive theories, especially the work of Piaget, has demonstrated that simplistic views, such as those of the conditioning theorists, cannot explain the development of the complex phenomenon that is logical thinking. Moreover, Piaget's research findings have been replicated in virtually every culture and in every cohort of children since his work was first published in the 1920s. Thus, not only did he formulate a theory that forced psychologists to think about child development in a new way, but he also provided a set of findings that were impossible to ignore

neo-Piagetian theory
an approach that uses information-processing principles to explain the developmental stages identified by Piaget

sociocultural theory
Vygotsky's view that complex forms of thinking have their origins in social interactions rather than in an individual's private explorations

scaffolding
a process in which the learning of new cognitive skills is guided by someone who is more skilled

zone of proximal development
signifies tasks that are too hard for a child to do alone but that can be managed with guidance

Critical Thinking

How is scaffolding involved when a parent helps a child with homework?

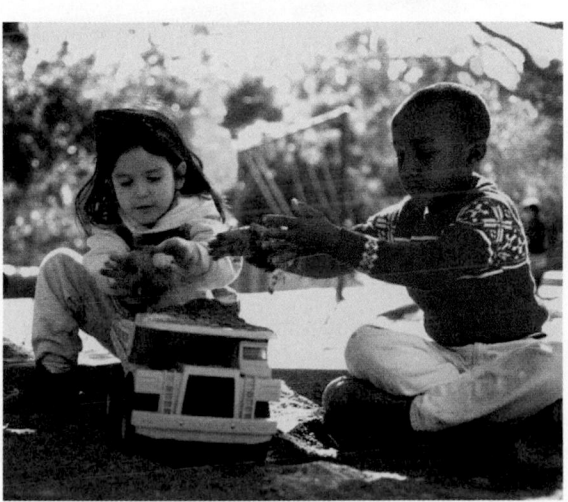

Developmental psychologist Lev Vygotsky hypothesized that social interactions among children are critical to both cognitive and social development.
(*Photo:* David Young-Wolff/PhotoEdit)

and difficult to explain. In addition, he developed innovative methods of studying children's thinking that continue to be important today.

Nevertheless, Piaget turned out to be wrong about some of the ages at which children develop particular skills. As you will see in later chapters, researchers have found that children develop some intellectual skills at earlier ages than Piaget's findings suggested. Furthermore, Piaget was probably wrong about the generality of the stages themselves. Most 8-year-olds, for example, show concrete operational thinking on some tasks but not on others, and they are more likely to show complex thinking on familiar tasks than on unfamiliar ones. Thus, the whole process seems to be a great deal less stage-like than Piaget proposed. Not surprisingly, most information-processing theorists have abandoned the stage model of cognitive development in favour of a continuous model in which they believe cognitive development takes place continuously and gradually over time. Their focus is on the incremental changes that take place in a specific mental process, such as analytic problem-solving skills, rather than on global cognitive skills.

Vygotsky's ideas have important educational applications. Like Piaget's, Vygotsky's theory suggests the importance of opportunities for active exploration. But assisted discovery would play a greater role in a Vygotskian than in a Piagetian classroom; the teacher would provide the scaffolding for children's discovery, through questions, demonstrations, and explanations (Tharp & Gallimore, 1988). To be effective, the assisted discovery processes would have to be within the zone of proximal development of each child.

Critics of information-processing theory point out that human thinking is more complex than that of a computer. For example, University of Waterloo cognitive scientist Paul Thagard (1996, 2002) suggests that information is processed through a complex network of mental rules that simultaneously shape and are shaped by the

TABLE 2.6   Cognitive Theories

Theory	Main Idea	Evaluation	
		Strengths	**Weaknesses**
Piaget's Theory of Cognitive Development	Reasoning develops in four universal stages from birth through adolescence; in each stage, the child builds a different kind of scheme.	Helps explain how children of different ages think about and act on the world.	Stage concept may cause adults to underestimate children's reasoning abilities; there may be additional stages in adulthood.
Information-Processing Theory	The computer is used as a model for human cognitive functioning; encoding, storage, and retrieval processes change with age, causing changes in memory function; these changes happen because of both brain maturation and practice.	Helps explain how much information people of different ages can manage at one time and how they process it; provides a useful framework for studying individual differences in people of the same age.	Human information-processing is much more complex than that of a computer; the theory doesn't provide an overall picture of development.
Vygotsky's Sociocultural Theory	Cognitive development is strengthened through social interactions that involve speaking during guided problem-solving tasks.	Stresses the importance of sociocultural interaction for cognitive development.	Verbal instructions may not benefit cognitive development in some cultures.

information. This explains how we do not just passively react to environmental forces, but actively respond to and alter our environment. Critics also point out that much information-processing research involves artificial memory tasks such as learning lists of words. Therefore, they say, research based on the information-processing approach doesn't always fully describe how memory works in the real world.

Piagetians claim that information-processing theory emphasizes explanations of single cognitive tasks at the expense of a comprehensive picture of development. Finally, critics of cognitive theories in general say that these theories ignore the role of other important cognitive functions such as emotions, imagination, and creativity in development (Thagard, 2002). In addition, cognitive theories underplay the effect of our physical and social surroundings on development (Thagard, 1996). The cognitive theories are summarized in **Table 2.6**.

Before Going On

- What did Piaget discover about the development of logical thinking in children, and how did he explain it?

- What is the focus of information-processing theory?

- How did Vygotsky use the concepts of scaffolding and the zone of proximal development to explain cognitive development?

- List some contributions and criticism of cognitive theories.

EVOLUTIONARY AND BIOLOGICAL THEORIES

These theories propose that the genetic and physiological processes that underlie human behaviour changed gradually over time through a process of genetic mutation and natural selection. By analogy, evolutionary theory is used to explain cognitive and, by extension, social and cultural behaviour.

NATIVISM, ETHOLOGY, BEHAVIOUR GENETICS, AND SOCIOBIOLOGY

NATIVISM **Nativism** is the view that humans possess unique genetic traits that will be manifested in all members of the species, regardless of differences in their environments. Nativist theory is supported when developmentalists identify behaviours that appear early in life, develop in almost all individuals in every culture, and do not exist in other species. For example, all healthy children learn language early in life without any specific instruction from adults, and, to date, scientists have found no evidence of grammatical language in nonhuman species.

ETHOLOGY **Ethology** emphasizes genetically determined survival behaviours that are assumed to have evolved through natural selection. For example, nests are necessary for the survival of young birds. Therefore, ethologists say, evolution has equipped birds with nest-building genes.

nativism
the view that human beings possess unique genetic traits that will be manifested in all members of the species, regardless of differences in environments

ethology
a perspective on development that emphasizes genetically determined survival behaviours presumed to have evolved through natural selection

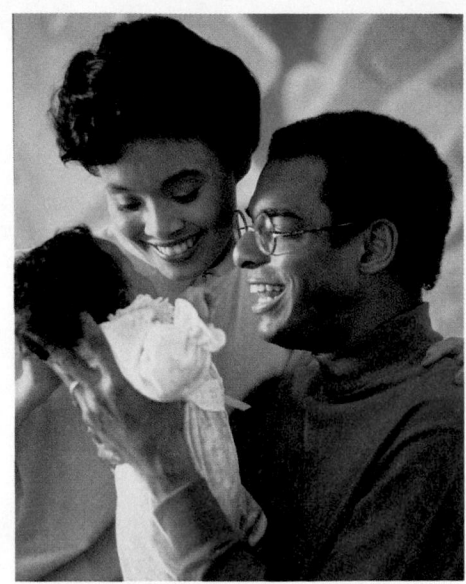

Ethologists assert that the first 2 years of life are a critical period for the establishment of relationships between infants and caregivers.
(*Photo:* Getty Images)

behaviour genetics
the study of the role of heredity in individual differences

sociobiology
the study of society using the methods and concepts of biology; when used by developmentalists, an approach that emphasizes genes that aid group survival

evolutionary psychology
the view that genetically inherited cognitive and social characteristics have evolved through natural selection

Similarly, ethologists believe that emotional relationships are necessary to the survival of human infants (Bowlby, 1969, 1980). They claim that evolution has produced genes that cause humans to form these relationships. For example, most people feel irritated when they hear a newborn crying. Ethologists say the baby is genetically programmed to cry in a certain way, and adults are genetically programmed to get irritated when they hear it. The caretaker responds to a crying baby's needs in order to remove the irritating stimulus of the noise. As the caretaker and infant interact, an emotional bond is created between them. Thus, genes for crying in an irritating manner increase infants' chances of survival.

BEHAVIOUR GENETICS A related area of study, **behaviour genetics** focuses on the effect of heredity on individual differences. Traits or behaviours are believed to be influenced by genes when those of related people, such as children and their parents, are more similar than those of unrelated people. Behaviour geneticists have shown that heredity affects a broad range of traits and behaviours, including intelligence, shyness, and aggressiveness.

SOCIOBIOLOGY **Sociobiology** is the study of society using the methods and concepts of biological science. When applied to human development, sociobiology emphasizes genes that aid group survival. Sociobiologists claim that individual humans have the best chance for survival when they live in groups. Therefore, they claim, evolution has provided humans with genetic programming that helps us cooperate.

To support their views, sociobiologists look for social rules and behaviours that exist in all cultures. For example, every society has laws against murder. Sociobiologists believe that humans are genetically programmed to create rules based on respect for other people's lives. Evolution has selected these genes, they claim, because people need to respect each other's lives and to be able to cooperate.

EVOLUTIONARY PSYCHOLOGY

Evolutionary psychology is the study of how genetically inherited cognitive and social characteristics have evolved through natural selection. Accordingly, cognitive abilities that underlie social relations and interactions are a major focus. Evolutionary psychology is an interdisciplinary approach to explaining human behaviour that involves biology, anthropology, cognitive science, and neuroscience (Cosmides & Tooby, 2000).

Harvard psychologist Steven Pinker (1997, 2002), a Canadian from Montreal, has been a leading advocate of evolutionary psychology (EP). His basic premise is that, through a process of biological evolution, the mind, like the body, has been shaped by natural selection to serve adaptive functions and promote survival. Moreover, Pinker (2002) contends that we have "hard-wired" inherited patterns of thinking and feeling shaped over time by the demands made upon the species for survival. Today, this "human nature," as he calls it, affects every aspect of our lives from child-rearing practices, to the formation of our political views, to our taste in art and music.

EVOLUTIONARY DEVELOPMENTAL PSYCHOLOGY

Contrary to what philosopher John Locke thought about infants (refer to **Chapter 1**), a newborn's mind is not a "blank slate," say the proponents of this view. Rather, the mind has been genetically programmed with a predisposition to learn and develop in certain ways—it has a readiness to learn language or recognize human faces, for instance (Bjorklund & Pellegrini, 2002; Pinker, 2002).

Evolutionary developmental psychology theorists suggest that although nature (genes) and nurture (environment) interact in determining individual intelligence, personality, and social behaviour (Bjorklund & Pellegrini, 2002), the cognitive abilities that help infants and children adapt and survive are different from those that adults require to adapt and survive. For example: infants need to form attachments; adults contend with mating; once children arrive, adults are faced with parenting; and later, with grandchildren, they contend with grandparenting (Buss, 1999).

evolutionary developmental psychology
the view that genetically inherited cognitive and social characteristics that promote survival and adaptation appear at different times across the lifespan

EVALUATION OF EVOLUTIONARY AND BIOLOGICAL THEORIES

Critics of evolutionary theories claim that they underestimate the impact of the environment and place too much emphasis on heredity. For example, it is true that children learn all languages in the same way. However, environmental factors, including characteristics of different languages, affect the rate at which children learn language. Moreover, when describing social behaviour, critics say that societies have similar rules because, over many generations, people have learned which rules work. When social rules no longer work, say critics, people invent new ones. Both the new rules and the reasons for them are passed on from one generation to the next through language, not genes.

Another major concern is that these theories are difficult to prove. How could a researcher test the idea that infants attach to caregivers because attachment has survival value that has evolved over time? Furthermore, even if there is a strong biological basis for specific cognitive strategies or social behaviours, they can still be modified by experience and learning. The **Research Report** illustrates how a gene variation, which may have aided adaptation for generations, can suddenly give rise to an epidemic when lifestyle behaviours are altered.

Research Report

Type 2 Diabetes

Epidemic in a

Remote

Community

Prior to the middle of the last century, Type 2 diabetes was rare among Aboriginal populations (Health Canada, 1999a). By the 1970s, however, research suggested that an epidemic might be emerging. Two decades later this was confirmed (Young, Reading, Elias, & O'Neil, 2000). Today in Canada, Type 2 diabetes is three times as prevalent among First Nations people as in the general population, and the incidence rate is escalating. It is estimated that one-quarter of all First Nations people will have

the disease within 20 years (Health Canada, 1999a).

Type 2 diabetes generally has a later life onset and carries with it serious health and social ramifications. It leads to conditions such as heart disease, blindness, kidney failure, and gangrene (Young et al., 2000), and is a leading cause of death and disability among First Nations people (Health Canada, 1999a).

Dr. Robert Hegele and his research team at the John P. Robarts Research Institute in

London, Ontario, discovered a strong genetic effect related to a single gene variant. This genetic mutation was discovered in the Oji-Cree, who reside on the Sandy Lake Reserve in Northern Ontario. The adults of the community were found to have a high incidence of the G319S mutation, which affects the structure of a specific liver protein. The incidence of Type 2 diabetes was found to be five times higher than it is in the general Canadian population. This is the third highest rate in the world

(Continued)

(Hegele, Cao, Harris, Hanley, & Zinman, 1999).

The Type 2 diabetes epidemic demonstrates how we can study the interaction between genes and behaviour, and suggests that a genetic susceptibility interacts with multiple environmental factors. The sudden increase in the incidence of the disease may be related to a significant change in lifestyle. For instance, the Oji-Cree's traditional low-carbohydrate diet has been replaced by a "junk food" and high "fatty" content

diet coupled with a more sedentary level of physical activity. This modern lifestyle encourages obesity of the mid-body area in Oji-Cree who have the G319S mutation, and this is connected to a higher risk of diabetes (Hegele et al., 1999; Young et al., 2000).

This new understanding of the interplay between genetics and environment has led to a complex health care initiative. Community-wide prevention and health education programs that actively involve Oji-Cree resi-

dents and demonstrate an appreciation for their language and cultural concerns begin in Grade 3. The focus is on healthy lifestyle practices that include a balanced diet and physical exercise. Moreover, a screening program for detecting diabetes and a lifestyle support program for those who are living with the disease were both established in order to decrease the severity of its effects. (Health Canada, 1999a; John P. Robarts Research Institute, 1999).

Before Going On

- What kind of behaviours interest proponents of nativism, ethology, behaviour genetics, and sociobiology?
- What human characteristics do evolutionary theorists say have been shaped by a process of natural selection?

SYSTEMS THEORY

systems approach
the view that personal factors together with external factors form a dynamic integrated system

holism
the view that the whole is greater than the sum of its parts

wellness
a measure of holistic optimal health

bioecological systems theory
Bronfenbrenner's theory that explains development in terms of relationships between individuals and their environments, or interconnected contexts

The **systems approach** to human development takes into consideration the ever-changing (dynamic) interaction of personal factors with external factors. Personal factors may include biophysical, spiritual, intellectual, emotional, behavioural, and interpersonal aspects of functioning. External factors typically include the physical environment and social and cultural influences. A basic tenet of systems theory is that of holism. **Holism** maintains that the "whole" is primary and often greater than the sum of its parts. By way of example, consider that a loaf of bread is more than the sum of its ingredients—wheat flour, yeast, and water. A person develops in relation to changes in any part of the whole dynamic system. From this perspective, growth is the result of a reorganization of the system as it adjusts to change. When adjustment is adaptive it promotes a high level of holistic health called **wellness**, but when it is maladaptive it can lead to disorder or dysfunction.

BRONFENBRENNER'S BIOECOLOGICAL SYSTEMS THEORY

One systems approach that has gained prominence in developmental psychology is Bronfenbrenner's **bioecological systems theory**, which explains development in terms of

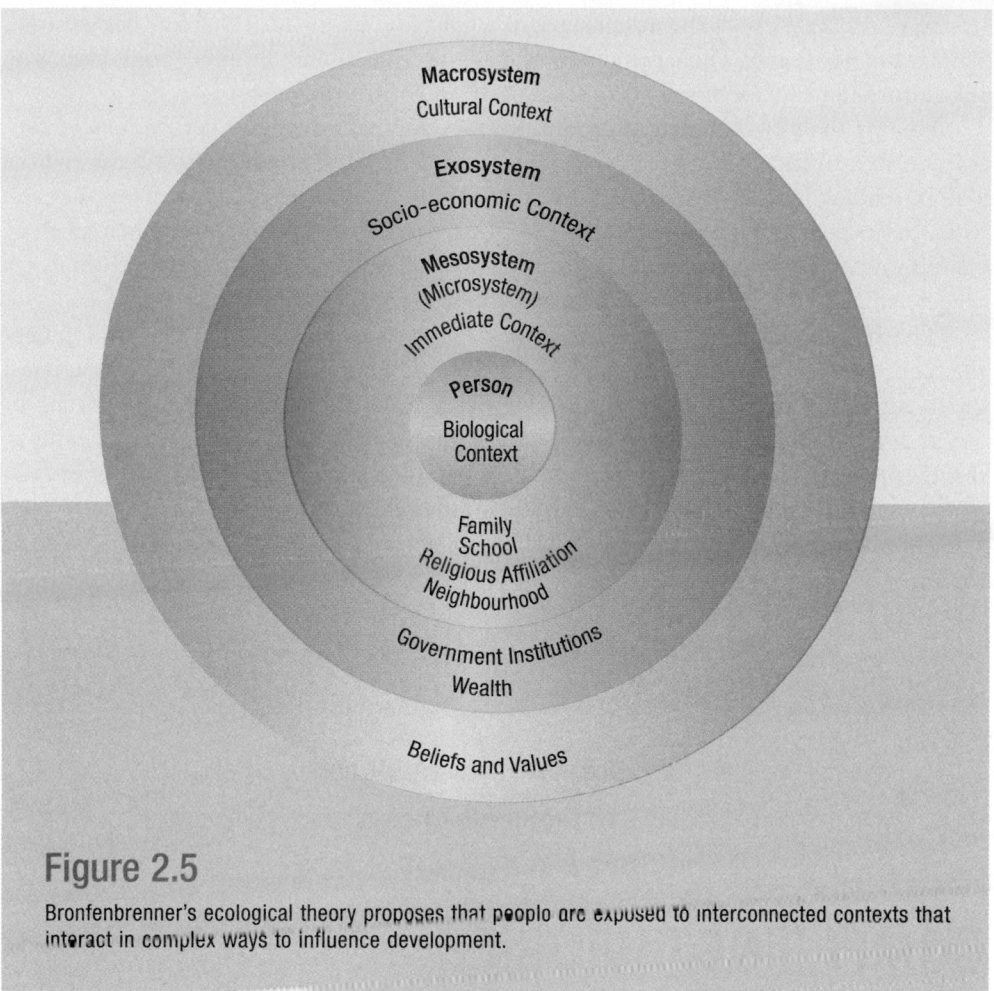

Figure 2.5

Bronfenbrenner's ecological theory proposes that people are exposed to interconnected contexts that interact in complex ways to influence development.

relationships between people and their environments, or *contexts,* as Bronfenbrenner calls them (Bronfenbrenner, 1979, 1993). Bronfenbrenner attempts to classify the individual and contextual variables that affect development and to specify how they interact.

According to Bronfenbrenner, the contexts of development are like circles within circles (see **Figure 2.5**). The outermost circle, the *macrosystem* (or the cultural context), contains the values and beliefs of the culture in which a child is growing up. For example, Canadians' beliefs about the importance of education exist in the cultural context.

The next level, the *exosystem* (the socioeconomic context), includes the institutions of the culture that affect children's development indirectly. For example, funding for education exists in the socioeconomic context. The citizens of a specific nation may strongly believe that all children should be educated (cultural context), but their ability to provide universal education may be limited by the country's wealth (socioeconomic context).

The *microsystem* (or the immediate context) includes those variables to which people are exposed directly, such as their families, schools, religious institutions, and neighbourhoods. The *mesosystem* is made up of the interconnections between these components. For example, the specific school a child attends and her own family are part of the microsystem. Her parents' involvement in her school and the response of the school to their involvement are part of the mesosystem. Thus, the culture a child is born into may strongly value quality education. Moreover, her nation's economy may provide ample funds for schooling. However, her own education will be more strongly affected by the particular school she attends and the connections, or lack thereof, between her school and her family. Thus, the child's immediate context may be either consistent with the cultural and socioeconomic contexts or at odds with them.

Finally, the child's genetic makeup and developmental stage—her *biological context*—also influence her development. For example, a student who hasn't mastered the skill of reading isn't likely to benefit from an enriched literature program. Thus, her culture, the socioeconomic situation, the school she attends, and her own family may all be geared toward providing a quality education. However, her ability to benefit from it will be determined by the degree to which her education fits her individual needs.

The bioecological systems theory provides a way of thinking about development that captures the complexity of individual and contextual variables. To date, its greatest contribution to developmental psychology has been its emphasis on the need for research examining interactions among these variables (Thomas, 1996). For example, this theory has helped developmentalists understand that studies of infant day care can't just compare infants in day care with infants in home care. Such studies must also consider family variables, such as parents' educational level, and day-care variables, such as the ratio of caretakers to infants.

Before Going On

- From the systems theory perspective, what causes healthy development?
- What is the main idea of Bronfenbrenner's bioecological systems theory?

COMPARING THEORIES

After learning about theories, students usually want to know which one is right. However, developmentalists don't think of theories in terms of right or wrong but, instead, compare theories on the basis of their assumptions and how useful they are in promoting understanding of development.

ASSUMPTIONS ABOUT DEVELOPMENT

When we say that a theory assumes something about development, we mean that it holds some general perspective to be true. We can think of a theory's assumptions in terms of its answers to three questions about development.

One question addresses the *active or passive* issue: *Is a person active in shaping his own development, or is he a passive recipient of environmental influences?* Theories that claim a person's actions on the environment are the most important determinants of development are on the active side. Cognitive theories, for example, typically view development this way. In contrast, theories on the passive side, such as those of Pavlov and Skinner, maintain that development results from the environment acting on the individual. A third view, as depicted by Bandura and Bronfenbrenner, argues that a person both shapes and, reciprocally, is shaped by his or her environment.

As you learned in **Chapter 1**, the *nature versus nurture* question—*How do nature and nurture interact to produce development?*—is one of the most important in developmental psychology. All developmental theories, while admitting that both nature and nurture are involved in development, make assumptions about their relative importance. Theories claiming that biology contributes more to development than environment does are on the nature side of the question. Those that view environmental influences as most important are on the nurture side. Other theories assume that nature and nurture are equally important, and that it is impossible to say which contributes more to development.

Developmental theories also differ on the *continuity versus stages* issue. Here, the question is *Does development happen continuously or in stages?* Theories that do not refer to stages assert that development is a gradual, cumulative process. Stage theories, on the other hand, emphasize that development is a series of distinct, qualitative changes more than uninterrupted growth. They claim that development happens in leaps from lower to higher steps.

For the five major families of theories you have read about in this chapter, **Table 2.7** lists the assumptions each makes regarding these issues. Because each theory is based on different assumptions, each takes a different approach to studying development. Consequently, research derived from each theory tells us something different about development. Moreover, a theory's assumptions shape the way it is applied in the real world.

For example, a teacher who approaches instruction from the cognitive perspective would create a classroom in which children could experiment to some degree on their

Critical Thinking

What personal assumptions about human development do you have? What evidence do you have to support them?

TABLE 2.7   How Theories Answer Essential Questions About Development

Theories	Active or Passive?	Nature or Nurture?	Continuous or Stages?
Psychoanalytic Theories			
Psychosexual Theory	Both	Both	Stages
Psychosocial Theory	Both	Both	Stages
Humanistic	Active	Both	Continuous
Learning Theories			
Classical Conditioning	Passive	Nurture	Continuous
Operant Conditioning	Passive	Nurture	Continuous
Social-Cognitive Theory	Both	Both	Continuous
Cognitive Theories			
Cognitive Developmental Theory	Active	Both	Stages
Information-Processing Theory	Active	Both	Continuous
Vygotsky's Sociocultural Theory	Active	Both	Continuous
Evolutionary and Biological Theory			
Nativism, Ethology, Behaviour Genetics, and Sociobiology	Active	Nature	Both
Evolutionary Psychology	Active	Nature	Both
Evolutionary Developmental Psychology	Active	Nature	Both
Systems Theory			
Bioecological Systems Theory	Both	Both	Both

own. He would also recognize that children differ in ability, interests, developmental level, and other internal characteristics. He would believe that structuring the educational environment is important, but would assume that what each student ultimately learns will be determined by his own actions on the environment.

Alternatively, a teacher who adopts the learning perspective would guide and reinforce children's learning very carefully. Such a teacher would place little importance on ability differences among children. Instead, she would try to accomplish the same instructional goals for all children through proper manipulation of the environment.

Before Going On

- **What assumptions do the five families of theories make about development?**

Developmental Psychology in Your Career

Introduction

As you recall from **Chapter 1**, the science of psychology has four main goals: to describe, explain, predict, and influence positive change in human behaviour. This chapter gave you a look at the tools that researchers use to gather information to accurately *describe* human development. Then in **Chapter 2** we described the major theories that help us to better *explain* human development. We use scientific methods to test our theories and to *predict* developmental outcomes. Finally, the ultimate goal of this knowledge is to *influence* or control human development.

This fourth goal is accomplished by a wide array of specialists, each having a unique set of knowledge, skills, and professional attitudes that are suited to promoting positive development. Sometimes these professionals focus on a relatively narrow slice of the lifespan, e.g., prenatal development. Others require a wide focus, e.g., physical fitness throughout the lifespan. Regardless of their particular professional focus, they need to consider the "big picture" of development—to know how someone reached her present condition, to know how someone compares to her cohort, to know what can be done to positively influence the person's future development, and to have an idea of what a "well" person will look like in the future. Accordingly, professionals in human development need a wide breadth of knowledge about human development in order to make judgments about a person's current status, what factors influenced their development, and what can be done to improve the person's quality of life in the short and long term. This background knowledge enables professionals to apply appropriate methods of evaluation, support, and sometimes intervention. Thirdly, each professional specialty has a set of professional standards that stipulate codes for ethical decision-making, conduct, and responsibilities; that have expectations about the quality of communication with clients, patients, and other professionals; and generally, that encourage interest, initiative, and effort from the beginning to the end of one's career.

Throughout this book, you will be exposed to descriptions of the *essential knowledge, skills, and professional attitudes* that specific human development specialists are expected to demonstrate. We will highlight a range of careers within the fields of human service, education, and health.

Summary

Psychoanalytic Theories

- Freud emphasized that behaviour is governed by both conscious and unconscious motives and that the personality develops in steps: The id is present at birth; the ego and the superego develop in childhood. Freud also proposed psychosexual stages: the oral, anal, phallic, latency, and genital stages.

- Erikson emphasized social forces more than unconscious drives as motives for development. He proposed that personality develops in eight psychosocial stages over the course of the lifespan: trust versus mistrust; autonomy versus shame and doubt; initiative versus guilt; industry versus inferiority; identity versus role confusion; intimacy versus isolation; generativity versus stagnation; and integrity versus despair.

- Psychoanalytic concepts, such as the unconscious and identity, have contributed to psychologists' understanding of development. However, these theories propose many ideas that are difficult to test.

- Humanistic theorist Abraham Maslow suggested that individuals are motivated to fulfill inner needs in order to ultimately attain self-actualization.

Learning Theories

- Classical conditioning—learning through association of stimuli—helps explain the acquisition of emotional responses.

- Operant conditioning involves learning to repeat or stop behaviours because of their consequences. However, consequences often affect behaviour in complex ways in the real world.

- Bandura's social-cognitive theory places more emphasis on mental elements than other learning theories and assumes a more active role for the individual.

- Learning theories provide useful explanations of how behaviours are acquired but fall short of a truly comprehensive picture of human development.

Cognitive Theories

- Piaget focused on the development of logical thinking. He discovered that such thinking develops across four childhood and adolescent stages: the sensorimotor, preoperational, concrete operational, and formal operational stages. He proposed that movement from one stage to another is the result of changes in mental frameworks called *schemes*.

- Information-processing theory uses the computer as a model to explain intellectual processes such as memory and problem-solving. It suggests that there are both age differences and individual differences in the efficiency with which humans use their information-processing systems.

- Research has confirmed the sequence of skill development Piaget proposed but suggests that young children are more capable of logical thinking than he believed. Information-processing theory has been important in explaining Piaget's findings and memory processes.

- Vygotsky's sociocultural theory has become important to developmentalists' attempts to explain how culture affects development.

Evolutionary and Biological Theories

- Biological theories such as nativism, ethology, behaviour genetics, and sociobiology have gained popularity as developmentalists have sought to better understand the role of physiological processes in development.

- Evolutionary psychology is the view that through a process of biological evolution, the mind, like the body, has been shaped by natural selection to serve adaptive functions and promote survival.

- Evolutionary developmental psychology theorists suggest that heredity and the environment interact in determining the cognitive abilities that promote survival and adaptation at different times across the lifespan.

Systems Theory

- Systems theory considers the reciprocal interactions of personal and external factors in development.

- Bronfenbrenner's bioecological systems theory has helped developmental psychologists categorize environmental factors and think about the ways in which they influence individuals.

Comparing Theories

- Theories vary in how they answer three basic questions about development: Are individuals active or passive in their own development? How do nature and nurture interact to produce development? Does development happen continuously or in stages?

- Useful theories allow psychologists to devise hypotheses to test their validity, are heuristically valuable, provide practical solutions to problems, and explain the facts of development.

Key Terms

accommodation (p. 40)

assimilation (p. 40)

behaviour genetics (p. 46)

bioecological systems (p. 48)

classical conditioning (p. 33)

cognitive theories (p. 39)

defence mechanisms (p. 28)

ego (p. 27)

equilibration (p. 40)

ethology (p. 45)

evolutionary developmental psychology (p. 47)

evolutionary psychology (p. 46)

extinction (p. 35)

holism (p. 48)

id (p. 27)

information-processing theory (p. 41)

learning theories (p. 33)

libido (p. 27)

nativism (p. 45)

neo-Piagetian theory (p. 43)

observational learning, modelling (p. 35)

operant conditioning (p. 34)

Weblinks

The Journal of Theories and Issues in Human Development
http://labweb.education.wisc.edu/edpsy725/documents/freud/frout.html
"The Outline Paper of Theories and Issues in Human Development—Psychoanalysis Theory" by Wei-Fen Lin contextualizes and compares Freud's theory of psychoanalysis with those of other leading psychologists.

Recovery Canada—The Wellness Network
www.vansondesign.com/RecoveryCanada/SexualAbuse/Library/repressedmemory.html
The Sexual Abuse Reading Centre offers questions and answers about repressed memory. This self-help support network presents information and support within a theme of healing and wellness for those struggling with life-affecting challenges, such as illness, abuse, or stress.

Classics in the History of Psychology
http://psychclassics.yorku.ca/
This electronic resource, developed by Christopher D. Green of York University, is home to copies of hundreds of original documents from historically significant psychological theorists.

Canadian Psychological Association: History and Philosophy of Psychology Section
www.cpa.ca/hpp/
This electronic resource has links to hundreds of documents, journals, books, and other history and philosophy of psychology websites.

CHAPTER 3

A. Scott/Masterfile

PRENATAL DEVELOPMENT AND BIRTH

Like any good story, human development has a beginning, a middle, and an end. Genes and chromosomes passed on to the new individual at the moment of conception and the prenatal environment of the first months set the stage for all that is to follow. From conception to birth, prenatal development follows a truly amazing course that begins with a single cell and ends with a crying, but curious, newborn making his or her debut in the outside world.

Throughout pregnancy, most parents speculate about the baby's inherited characteristics, confident that all will be well. ("Will she be tall like her father?" "Will he be musically talented like his mother?") However, for those few parents-to-be whose babies are affected by a variety of agents that can cause birth defects or whose children are born too soon or too small, pregnancy and birth can bring more anxiety than joy. Nevertheless, it's important to keep in mind that, in many of these cases, there are ways of limiting the damage.

In this chapter, you will learn about the beginning of the developmental process: conception, prenatal development, and birth. As you read, keep the following questions in mind:

- How does conception happen, and what rules govern the transmission of genetic traits from parent to child?

- What are the milestones of pregnancy and prenatal development? How does prenatal development for males and females differ? What have researchers learned about prenatal behaviour?

- What are the potential negative effects of genetic disorders, chromosomal errors, diseases, drugs, and other factors on prenatal development?

- What are the stages in the birth process, from labour to delivery? What choices do parents in the industrialized world have to make regarding birth? What can go wrong during birth?

CONCEPTION AND GENETICS

The first step in the development of an individual human being happens at conception, when each of us receives a combination of genes that will shape our experiences throughout the rest of our lives.

THE PROCESS OF CONCEPTION

CONCEPTION Ordinarily, a woman produces one *ovum* (egg cell) per month from one of her two ovaries, roughly midway between menstrual periods. If the ovum is not fertilized, it travels from the ovary down the *fallopian tube* toward the *uterus*, where it gradually disintegrates and is expelled as part of the menstrual fluid. However, if a couple has intercourse during the crucial few days when the ovum is in the fallopian tube, one of the millions of sperm ejaculated as part of each male orgasm may travel the full distance through the woman's vagina, cervix, uterus, and fallopian tube and penetrate the wall of the ovum.

As you probably know, every cell in the human body contains 23 pairs of **chromosomes**, or strings of genetic material. However, sperm and ovum, collectively called **gametes**, contain 23 single (unpaired) chromosomes.

chromosomes
strings of genetic material in the nuclei of cells

gametes
cells that unite at conception (ova in females; sperm in males)

zygote
single cell created when sperm and ovum unite

At conception, chromosomes in the ovum and the sperm combine to form 23 pairs in an entirely new cell called a **zygote**. Twenty-two of these pairs of chromosomes, called *autosomes,* contain most of the genetic information for the new individual. The twenty-third pair, the *sex chromosomes,* determine the sex. One of the two sex chromosomes, the X *chromosome,* is one of the largest chromosomes in the body and carries a large number of genes. The other, the Y *chromosome,* is quite small and contains only a few genes. Zygotes containing two X chromosomes develop into females, and those containing one X and one Y chromosome develop into males. Since the cells in a woman's body contain only X chromosomes, all her ova carry X chromosomes. Half of a man's sperm contain X chromosomes; the other half contain Y chromosomes. Consequently, the sex of the new individual is determined by the sex chromosome in the sperm.

deoxyribonucleic acid (DNA)
chemical material that makes up chromosomes and genes

genes
pieces of genetic material that control or influence traits

Chromosomes are composed of molecules of **deoxyribonucleic acid (DNA)**. Each chromosome can be further subdivided into segments, called **genes**, each of which influences a particular feature or developmental pattern. A gene controlling some specific characteristic always appears in the same place (the *locus*) on the same chromosome in every individual of the same species. For example, the locus of the gene that determines whether a person's blood is type A, B, or O is on chromosome 9.

TWINS In most cases, human infants are conceived and born one at a time. However, in about 2.7 out of every 100 births in Canada, more than one baby is born, usually twins (Health Canada, 2003b). Roughly two-thirds of twins are *fraternal twins,* or twins that come from two sets of ova and sperm. Such twins, also called *dizygotic twins* (meaning that they originate from two zygotes), are no more alike genetically than any other pair of siblings, and need not even be of the same sex.

The remaining one-third of twins are *identical twins (monozygotic,* or arising from one zygote). Identical twins result when a single zygote, for unknown reasons, separates into two parts, each of which develops into a separate individual. Because identical twins develop from the same zygote, they have identical genes. Research involving identical twins is one of the major investigative strategies in the field of behaviour genetics (see the **Research Report**).

Over the past decade, the annual number of multiple births has increased almost 29% in Canada (Health Canada, 2003b). Furthermore, births of triplets, quadruplets, and quintuplets have increased almost 400% (National Center for Health Statistics [NCHS], 1999). One reason for the increase is that the number of women over 35 giving birth for the first time has grown. As women get older, they are more likely to conceive fraternal twins. Another reason for the increased frequency of multiple births is the growing number of women who are using fertility drugs. These drugs stimulate the ovaries in ways that may result in the simultaneous production of more than one ovum.

assisted human reproduction (AHR)
"any activity undertaken for the purpose of facilitating human reproduction" (Health Canada, 2001b)

ASSISTED HUMAN REPRODUCTION In Canada, new legislation now regulates **assisted human reproduction (AHR)** and related research. The Act, Bill-C6, protects the health and safety of Canadians undergoing AHR treatment and the children born from such procedures (Communication Canada, 2004).

Fertility drugs are one of many AHR procedures available to couples who have trouble conceiving. Another is *in vitro fertilization* (IVF), popularly known as the "test-tube baby" method. (*In vitro* is Latin for "in glass.") This technique involves uniting an ovum and a sperm in a laboratory dish and implanting the resulting embryo in a woman's uterus. The egg can come from the woman who will carry the child or from a donor. Likewise, sperm can be from the woman's partner or a donor.

Typically, IVF laboratories create numerous embryos, which are then frozen, or *cryopreserved,* prior to being implanted. Cryopreservation increases the likelihood that implantation of an IVF embryo will result in a live birth (Schieve et al., 1999).

Research Report

Twins in Genetic Research

Researchers interested in the role of heredity in human development have been comparing identical and fraternal twins since the earliest days of developmental psychology. The logic is this: If identical twins (whose genes are exactly the same) who are raised apart are more similar than fraternal twins or non-twin siblings (whose genes are similar, but not identical) who are raised together, heredity must be important in the trait being studied. For example, the numbers below are correlations based on several studies of twins' intelligence test scores (Bouchard & McGue, 1981, p. 1056, Fig. 1). Recall from **Chapter 1** that the closer to 1.00 a correlation is, the stronger the relationship.

Identical twins reared together	.85
Identical twins reared apart	.67
Fraternal twins reared together	.58
Non-twin siblings reared apart	.24

As you can see, intelligence test scores are more strongly correlated in identical twins than in fraternal twins or non-twin siblings, even when the identical twins are raised in different families. Such findings are taken to be evidence for the heritability of intelligence.

Developmentalists have also studied the heritability of other human traits such as attitudes. Canadian researchers from the universities of Western Ontario and British Columbia surveyed 195 pairs of identical and 141 pairs of fraternal adult twins and found that about 35% of the difference in attitudes could be attributed to genetic factors. Measures of how strongly twins favoured various issues, activities, and social settings revealed that twins' attitudes about abortion on demand, roller coaster rides, playing organized sports, and the death penalty for murder yielded a high genetic influence (Olson, Vernon, Aitken Harris, & Jang, 2001).

Taken together, the findings of these studies point to strong genetic components in both intelligence and attitudes. However, what these studies reveal about environment may be even more significant. If psychological characteristics such as intelligence and attitudes were determined solely by heredity, identical twins would be exactly alike, and researchers would find correlations of +1.00. The correlations that twin researchers have found are less than +1.00, even for identical twins who grow up in the same home. Moreover, the correlations for identical twins raised apart are lower than those for identical twins raised together.

To see the point more clearly, think about blood type. An individual's blood type is determined by the genes. Thus, identical twins always have the same blood type; that is, there is a correlation of +1.00, a perfect correlation, between the blood types of identical twins. Identical twin studies offer strong evidence that psychological traits, though clearly influenced by heredity, are not determined by the genes to the same extent as physical traits such as blood type.

Developmentalists have addressed concerns about the possible effects of cryopreservation on children's development in several studies. Both comparative (IVF infants and children versus non-IVF ones) and longitudinal studies have failed to find any significant effects of the procedure (Levy-Shiff et al., 1998; van Balen, 1998).

However, IVF is not a highly successful procedure. For one thing, the older a woman is, the lower the probability that she will be able to achieve a successful IVF pregnancy. Roughly 35% of 20- to 29-year-old women undergoing IVF achieve a live birth, but only about 13% of IVF procedures involving women over age 40 are successful (Schieve et al., 1999). The failure of IVF treatment can lead to depression (Weaver, Clifford, Hay, & Robinson, 1997). Even with successful IVF procedures, women sometimes remain emotionally detached from their fetuses for fear of losing them. However, once an IVF baby is born, some studies suggest that parents are more likely to express emotional warmth toward her or him than parents who conceive naturally (Eugster & Vingerhoets, 1999).

Multiple births are more frequent among women who become pregnant using IVF because doctors typically implant several embryos at once in order to increase the likelihood of at least one live birth. In order to reduce the chance of multiple births (which can place both mother and babies at risk), most European nations limit the number of embryos that can be simultaneously implanted to three (Schieve et al., 1999).

Another technique, *artificial insemination,* is both more successful and less likely to result in multiple births. In artificial insemination, sperm are injected directly into a woman's uterus, usually during the part of her menstrual cycle when she is most likely to conceive. The procedure can employ the sperm of a woman's partner or that of a donor. This method is most often used by couples in which the male partner has a low sperm count or by fertile women who want to conceive without a male partner. However, like blood transfusions, artificial insemination procedures carry some risk of infection.

Assisted human reproductive techniques have been somewhat controversial. For example, if donated ova and sperm were provided by anonymous donors it would be impossible to determine the genetic heritage of children conceived through these donations. The Canadian AHR legislation addresses this concern by setting up an information registry that will contain nonidentifying medical information about the sperm and egg donors. This will allow children of donated sperm and ova to have access to their medical histories (Communication Canada, 2004).

GENOTYPES, PHENOTYPES, AND PATTERNS OF INHERITANCE

genotype
the unique genetic blueprint of each individual

phenotype
an individual's particular set of observed characteristics

At conception, the genes from the father contained in the sperm and those from the mother in the ovum combine to create a unique genetic blueprint—the **genotype**—that characterizes the new individual. The **phenotype** is the individual's whole set of actual characteristics. One way to remember the distinction is that the phenotype can be identified by directly observing the individual. For example, you can easily see that a woman has brown eyes, which are part of her phenotype. Her genotype, though, can't be so easily determined. In many cases, you have to know her parents' and offsprings' eye colour to find out whether she carries genes for another eye colour, because complex rules govern the way genotypes influence phenotypes.

dominant-recessive pattern
pattern of inheritance in which a single dominant gene influences a person's phenotype but two recessive genes are necessary to produce an associated trait

DOMINANT AND RECESSIVE GENES The simplest genetic rule is the **dominant-recessive pattern**, in which a single dominant gene strongly influences phenotype. (**Table 3.1** lists several normal phenotypical traits and indicates whether they arise from dominant or recessive genes.) People whose chromosomes carry either two dominant or two recessive genes are referred to as *homozygous.* Those with one dominant and one recessive gene are said to be *heterozygous.*

If a child receives a single dominant gene for a trait from one parent, the child's phenotype will include the trait determined by that gene. In contrast, a child's phenotype will include a recessive trait only if she inherits a recessive gene from both parents. For example, geneticists have found that the curliness of hair is controlled by a single pair of genes (see **Figure 3.1**). The gene for curly hair is dominant; therefore, if a man has curly hair, his genotype includes at least one gene for curly hair and at least half of his sperm carry this gene. Conversely, straight hair is recessive, so a straight-haired man's genotype must include two straight-hair genes for his phenotype to include straight hair. Geneticists also know that the only kind of hair type a straight-haired father can pass on to his children is straight hair, because all his sperm carry recessive, straight-hair genes.

TABLE 3.1   Genetic Sources of Normal Traits

Dominant Genes	Recessive Genes	Polygenic (many genes)
Freckles	Flat feet	Height
Coarse hair	Thin lips	Body type
Dimples	Rh-negative blood	Eye colour
Curly hair	Fine hair	Skin colour
Nearsightedness	Red hair	Personality
Broad lips	Blond hair	
Rh-positive blood	Type O blood	
Types A and B blood		
Dark hair		

(*Source:* Tortora & Grabowski, 1993.)

Figure 3.1

Examples of how the recessive gene for straight hair passes from parents to children.

In addition, human geneticists have learned that both dominant and recessive genes differ in *expressivity,* meaning that the degree to which any gene influences phenotypes varies from person to person. For example, all individuals who have the gene for curly hair don't have equally curly hair. So, even when a child receives a dominant gene for curly hair from her father, the amount and type of curl in her hair probably won't be exactly the same as his.

Blood type is also determined by a dominant-recessive pattern of inheritance. Because a person must have two recessive genes to have type O blood, the genotype of every person who has this type is clear. However, the genotype of people with type A or B blood is not obvious because types A and B are dominant. Thus, when a person's phenotype includes either type A or type B blood, one of the person's blood type genes must be for that type, but the other could be for some other type. However, if a type A father and a type B mother produce a child with type O, each of them carries a gene for type O, because the child must receive one such gene from each parent to have the type O phenotype.

Figure 3.2 illustrates the possible blood types of the offspring of a heterozygous type A father and a heterozygous type B mother. Notice that type AB is one of the possible phenotypes. This can happen because the genes for types A and B are *co-dominant* when they are together; each exerts an equal influence on the phenotype. As you can see, even the simplest pattern of inheritance can get fairly complicated.

polygenic inheritance

pattern of inheritance in which many genes influence a trait

POLYGENIC AND MULTIFACTORIAL INHERITANCE With **polygenic inheritance,** many genes influence the phenotype. There are many polygenic traits in which the dominant-recessive pattern is also at work. For example, geneticists believe that children get three genes for skin colour from each parent (Tortora & Grabowski, 1993). Dark skin is dominant over light skin, but the skin colours also blend together. Thus, when one parent is dark-skinned and the other is fair-skinned, the child will have skin that is somewhere between the two. The dark-skinned parent's dominant genes will ensure that the child will be darker than the fair parent, but the fair-skinned parent's genes will prevent the child from having skin as dark as that of the dark-skinned parent.

Eye colour is another polygenic trait with a dominant-recessive pattern (Tortora & Grabowski, 1993). Scientists don't know for sure how many genes influence eye colour. They do know, however, that these genes don't cause specific colours. Instead, they cause the coloured part of the eye to be dark or light. Dark colours (black, brown, hazel, and green) are dominant over light colours (blue and grey). However, blended colours are also possible. People whose chromosomes carry a combination of genes for green, blue, and grey eyes can have blue-grey, green-blue, or blue-green eyes. Likewise, genes that cause different shades of brown can combine their effects to make children's eye colour phenotypes different from those of their brown-eyed parents.

Many genes influence height, and they are not subject to a dominant-recessive pattern of inheritance. Most geneticists believe that each height gene has a small influence over a child's size (Tanner, 1990). Thus, a child's height will be the sum of the effects of all of these genes.

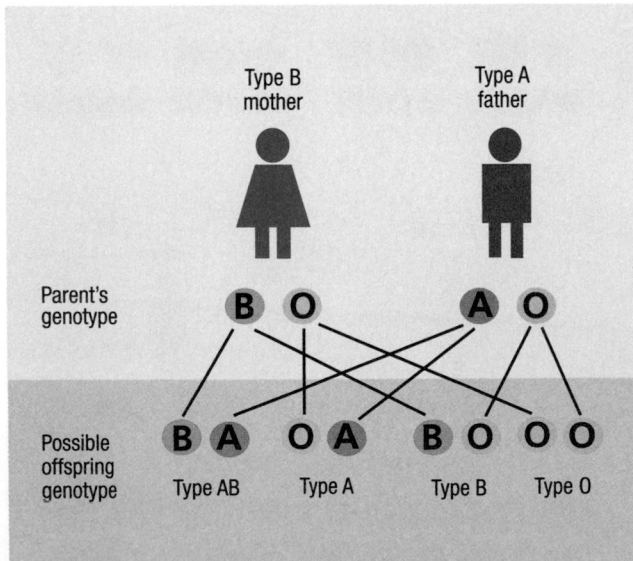

Figure 3.2

Possible blood types of offspring of a type B heterozygote and a type A heterozygote.

Height, like most polygenic traits, is also a result of **multifactorial inheritance**—that is, it is affected by both genes and environment. For this reason, doctors use a child's height as a measure of his general health (Sulkes, 1998; Tanner, 1990). If a child is ill, poorly nourished, or emotionally neglected, he may be smaller than others his age. Thus, when a child is shorter than 97% of his age-mates, doctors try to determine if he is short because of his genes or because something is causing him to grow poorly (Tanner, 1990).

MITOCHONDRIAL INHERITANCE Scientists have discovered some additional principles of genetic inheritance. In *mitochondrial inheritance,* children inherit genes that are carried in structures called *mitochondria,* which are found in the fluid that surrounds the nucleus of the ovum before it is fertilized. Consequently, mitochondrial genes are passed only from mother to child. Geneticists have learned that several serious disorders, including some types of blindness, are transmitted in this way. In most such cases, the mother herself is unaffected by the harmful genes (Amato, 1998).

multifactorial inheritance
inheritance affected by both genes and the environment

Before Going On

- Explain the process by which gametes from a woman and a man unite to form a zygote. What are the characteristics of the new cell?

- Explain the dominant-recessive, polygenic, multifactorial, and mitochondrial patterns of inheritance.

PREGNANCY AND PRENATAL DEVELOPMENT

Pregnancy is a physical condition in which a woman's body is nurturing a developing embryo or fetus. *Prenatal development,* or *gestation,* is the process that transforms a zygote into a newborn. Thus, the process that ends with the birth of a baby involves two sets of experiences: those of the pregnant woman, and those of the developing zygote, embryo, and fetus.

THE MOTHER'S EXPERIENCE

Pregnancy is customarily divided into *trimesters,* three periods of 3 months each (see **Table 3.2** on page 64).

FIRST TRIMESTER Pregnancy begins when the zygote implants itself in the lining of the woman's uterus (also called the *womb*). The zygote then sends out chemical messages that cause the woman's menstrual periods to stop. Some of these chemicals are excreted in her urine, making it possible to diagnose pregnancy within a few days after conception. Other chemicals cause physical changes, such as breast enlargement.

The *cervix* (the narrow, lower portion of the uterus, which extends into the vagina) thickens and secretes mucus that serves as a barrier to

During the second trimester of pregnancy, ultrasound tests allow doctors to identify the fetus's sex, to diagnose fetal deformities and growth problems, and to determine the fetus's position in the uterus. (*Photo:* PhotoDisc, Inc.)

protect the developing embryo from harmful organisms that might enter the womb through the vagina. The uterus begins to shift position and put pressure on the woman's bladder, causing her to urinate more often. This and other symptoms, like fatigue and breast tenderness, may interfere with sleep. Another common early symptom of preg-

TABLE 3.2   Pregnancy Summary

Trimester	Events	Discomforts	Prenatal Care	Serious Problems
First trimester: From first day of last menstrual period (LMP) to 12 weeks	Missed period Breast enlargement Abdominal thickening	Nausea Frequent urination Breast soreness Insomnia Fatigue	Confirmation of pregnancy Calculation of due date Blood and urine tests (and other tests if needed) Monthly doctor visits to monitor vital functions, uterine growth, weight gain, sugar and protein in urine	Ectopic pregnancy Abnormal urine or blood tests Increased blood pressure Malnutrition Bleeding Miscarriage
Second trimester: From 12 weeks after LMP to 24 weeks after LMP	Weight gain "Showing" Fetal movements felt Increased appetite	Varicose veins Frequent urination	Monthly doctor visits continue Ultrasound to measure fetal growth and locate placenta	Gestational diabetes Excessive weight gain Increased blood pressure Rh incompatibility of mother and fetus Miscarriage 13 to 20 weeks Premature labour 21+ weeks
Third trimester: From 25 weeks after LMP to beginning of labour	Weight gain Breast discharge	Swelling of extremities Indigestion Hemorrhoids Insomnia Diminished sex drive Difficulty moving around Hot flashes Fatigue Backache Leg cramps Stretch marks False labour	Weekly visits beginning at 32nd week Ultrasound to assess position of fetus Treatment of Rh incompatibility if needed Pelvic exams to check for cervical dilation	Increased blood pressure Bleeding Premature labour Bladder infection

(*Source:* Hobbs & Ferth, 1993; Kliegman, 1998; Tortora & Grabowski, 1993.)

nancy is *morning sickness*—feelings of nausea, often accompanied by vomiting, that usually occur in the morning.

Prenatal care during the first trimester is critical to prevent birth defects, because all of the baby's organs form during the first 8 weeks. Early prenatal care can identify maternal conditions, such as sexually transmitted diseases, that may threaten prenatal development. Doctors and nurses can also urge women to abstain from drugs and alcohol early in prenatal development, when such behaviour changes may prevent birth defects.

Early prenatal care can also be important to the pregnant woman's health. For example, in a small number of cases, a zygote implants in one of the fallopian tubes instead of in the uterus, a condition called *ectopic pregnancy*. Early surgical removal of the zygote is critical to the woman's future ability to have children.

About 15% of pregnancies end in miscarriage, or *spontaneous abortion*. From the woman's point of view, an early miscarriage is similar to a menstrual period, although feelings of discomfort and blood loss are usually greater. Medical care is always necessary after a miscarriage because the woman's body may fail to completely expel the embryo.

SECOND TRIMESTER During the second trimester of pregnancy, from the end of week 12 through week 24, morning sickness usually disappears, resulting in increases in appetite. The pregnant woman gains weight, and the uterus expands to accommodate a fetus that is growing rapidly. Consequently, the woman begins to "show" sometime during the second trimester. She also begins to feel the fetus's movements, usually at some point between the 16th and 18th weeks.

At monthly clinic visits, doctors monitor both the mother's and the baby's vital functions and keep track of the growth of the baby in the womb. Ultrasound tests are usually performed, and the sex of the baby can be determined after about the 13th week. Monthly urine tests check for *gestational diabetes,* a kind of diabetes that happens only during pregnancy. A woman who has any kind of diabetes, including gestational diabetes, has to be carefully monitored during the second trimester because her baby may grow too rapidly, leading to premature labour or a baby that is too large for vaginal delivery.

The risk of miscarriage drops in the second trimester. However, a few fetuses die between the 13th and 20th weeks of pregnancy. In addition, premature labour after the 21st week can result in delivery of a living, but extremely small, baby. A small percentage of such infants survive, but most have significant health problems.

THIRD TRIMESTER At 25 weeks, the pregnant woman enters her third trimester. Weight gain and abdominal enlargement are the main experiences of this period. In addition, the woman's breasts may begin to secrete a substance called *colostrum* in preparation for nursing.

Most women begin to feel more emotionally connected to the fetus during the third trimester. Individual differences in fetal behaviour, such as hiccupping or thumb-sucking, sometimes become obvious during the last weeks of pregnancy. These behaviours may be observed during ultrasound tests that produce increasingly clear images of the fetus. In addition, most women notice that the fetus has regular periods of activity and rest.

Monthly prenatal doctor visits continue in the third trimester until week 32, when most women begin visiting the doctor's office or clinic once a week. Monitoring of blood pressure is especially important, as some women develop a life-threatening condition called *toxemia of pregnancy* during the third trimester.

Critical Thinking

Why do you think most women become emotionally attached to the fetus during the third trimester?

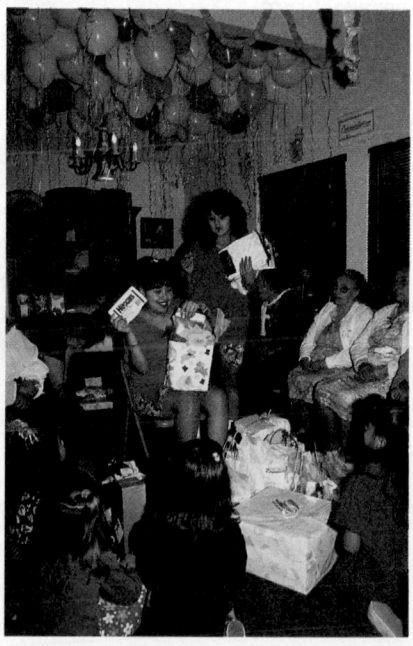

Supportive partners, friends, and relatives can help third-trimester mothers-to-be to maintain positive attitudes and balance negative emotions that often accompany their feelings of physical awkwardness against the anticipated joy of birth.
(*Photo:* Michael Newman/PhotoEdit)

This condition is signalled by a sudden increase in blood pressure and can cause a pregnant woman to have a stroke.

PRENATAL DEVELOPMENT

In contrast to the trimesters of pregnancy, the three stages of prenatal development are defined by specific developmental milestones and are not of equal length. Moreover, the entire process follows two developmental patterns that you can see at work in the photographs in **Table 3.3**. With the **cephalocaudal pattern**, development proceeds from the head down. For example, the brain is formed before the reproductive organs. With the **proximodistal pattern**, development happens in an orderly way from the centre of the body outward to the extremities. In other words, structures closer to the centre of the body, such as the rib cage, develop before the fingers and toes.

cephalocaudal pattern
growth that proceeds from the head downward

proximodistal pattern
growth that proceeds from the middle of the body outward

germinal stage
the first stage of prenatal development, beginning at conception and ending at implantation (approximately 2 weeks)

THE GERMINAL STAGE The first 2 weeks of gestation, from conception to implantation, constitute the **germinal stage**. During this stage, cells specialize into those that will become the fetus's body and those that will become the structures needed to support its development. Over the first 2 days, the single-celled zygote becomes 4-celled as it drifts down the fallopian tube. On the 3rd day, cell division begins to happen rapidly, and by the 4th day, the zygote contains dozens of cells.

On day 5, the cells become a hollow, fluid-filled ball called a *blastocyst*. Inside the blastocyst, cells that will eventually become the embryo begin to clump together. On day 6 or 7, the blastocyst comes into contact with the uterine wall, and by the 12th day, it is completely buried in the uterine tissue. Some of the cells of the blastocyst's outer wall combine with cells of the uterine lining to begin creating the **placenta**, an organ that allows oxygen, nutrients, and other substances to be transferred between the mother's and baby's blood. The placenta's specialized structures bring the mother's and baby's blood close to one another without allowing them to mix.

placenta
specialized organ that allows substances to be transferred from mother to embryo and from embryo to mother, without their blood mixing

Like the zygote, the placenta secretes chemical messages (hormones) that stop the mother's menstrual periods and keep the placenta connected to the uterus. Other placental hormones allow the bones of the woman's pelvis to become more flexible, induce breast changes, and increase the mother's metabolic rate. At the same time, the blastocyst's inner cells begin to specialize. One group of cells will become the **umbilical cord**, the organ that connects the embryo to the placenta. Vessels in the umbilical cord carry blood from the baby to the mother and back again. Other cells will form the *yolk sac*, a structure that produces blood cells until the embryo's blood-cell-producing organs are formed. Still others will become the **amnion**, a fluid-filled sac in which the baby floats until just before it is born. By the 12th day, the cells that will become the embryo's body are also formed.

umbilical cord
organ that connects the embryo to the placenta

amnion
fluid-filled sac in which the fetus floats until just before it is born

embryonic stage
the second stage of prenatal development, from week 2 through week 8, during which the embryo's organ systems form

THE EMBRYONIC STAGE The **embryonic stage** begins at implantation, approximately 2 weeks after conception, and continues until the end of week 8. By the time many women first suspect a pregnancy, usually 3 weeks after conception, the embryo's cells are starting to specialize and come together to form the foundations of all the body's organs. For example, the cells of the nervous system, the **neurons**, form a structure called the *neural tube*, from which the brain and spinal cord will develop. A primitive heart and the forerunners of the kidneys also develop during week 3, along with three sacs that will become the digestive system.

neurons
specialized cells of the nervous system

In week 4, the end of the embryo's neural tube swells to form the brain. Spots that will become the eyes appear on the embryo's head, and its heart begins to beat. The backbone and ribs become visible as bone and muscle cells move into place. The face starts to take shape, and the endocrine system begins to develop.

TABLE 3.3   Milestones in Prenatal Development

Stage/Time Frame	Milestones	
Germinal Stage Day 1: Conception	Sperm and ovum unite, forming a zygote containing genetic instructions for the development of a new and unique human being. (Photo: P. Motta & J. Van Blerkom, Photo Researchers)	
Days 10 to 14: Implantation	The zygote burrows into the lining of the uterus. Specialized cells that will become the placenta, umbilical cord, and embryo are already formed. (Photo: Lennart Nilsson/Albert Bonniers Forlag AB)	
Embryonic Stage Weeks 3 to 8: Organogenesis	All of the embryo's organ systems form during the 6-week period following implantation. (Photo: Petit Format/Nestlé/Science Source Library, Photo Researchers)	

Fetal Stage
Weeks 9 to 38: Growth and Organ Refinement

The fetus grows from 2.5 cm and 7 grams to a length of about 51 cm and a weight of 3.2 kg. By week 12, most fetuses can be identified as male or female. Changes in the brain and lungs make viability possible by week 24; optimum development requires an additional 14 to 16 weeks in the womb. Most neurons form by week 28, and connections among them begin to develop shortly thereafter. In the last 8 weeks, the fetus can hear and smell, is sensitive to touch, and responds to light. Learning is also possible.

(Photo: Petit Format/Nestlé/Science Source Library, Photo Researchers)

(Photo: James Stevenson/Science Source Library, Photo Researchers)

(Photo: Petit Format/Nestlé/Science Source Library, Photo Researchers)

(*Sources:* Kliegman, 1998; Tortora & Grabowski, 1993.)

gonads
sex glands (ovaries in females; testes in males)

By week 5, the embryo is about 6.5 millimetres long, 10 000 times larger than the zygote. Its arms and legs are developing rapidly. Five fingers are visible on each hand. Its eyes have corneas and lenses, and its lungs are beginning to develop.

In week 6, the embryo's brain begins to produce patterns of electrical activity. It moves in response to stimuli, and the **gonads**, or sex glands (ovaries in females and testes in males), develop. At first, the gonads of male and female embryos are identical. However, between the 4th and 6th weeks, genes on the Y chromosome cause the male embryo to produce the male hormone *testosterone*. The testosterone causes the gonads to become testes. In the absence of testosterone, the gonads develop into ovaries.

During week 7, a male embryo begins to develop a penis. Also, by this time, both male and female embryos begin to move spontaneously (Joseph, 2000). They have visible skeletons and fully developed limbs. The bones are beginning to harden and the muscles are maturing; by this point, the embryo can maintain a semi-upright posture. The eyelids seal shut to protect the developing eyes. The ears are completely formed, and X-rays can detect tooth buds in the jawbones.

During the last week of the embryonic stage, week 8, the liver and spleen begin to function. These organs allow the embryo to make and filter its own blood cells. Its heart is well developed and efficiently pumps blood to every part of the body. The embryo's movements increase as the electrical activity in its brain becomes more organized. Connections between the brain and the rest of the body are also well established. The embryo's digestive and urinary systems are functioning. By the end of week 8, **organogenesis**, the technical term for organ development, is complete.

organogenesis
process of organ development

THE FETAL STAGE The final phase is the **fetal stage**, beginning at the end of week 8 and continuing until birth. The fetus grows from a weight of about 7 grams and a length of 2.5 centimetres to a baby weighing about 3.2 kilograms and having a length of about 51 centimetres, who is ready to be born. In addition, this stage involves refinements of the organ systems, especially the lungs and brain, that are essential to life outside the womb.

fetal stage
the third stage of prenatal development, from week 9 to birth, during which growth and organ refinement take place

During week 9, the fetus develops fingerprints and can grasp objects that come into contact with the palms of its hands. By week 11, the muscles in its face respond reflexively to stimuli in ways that look like facial expressions. The 9-week fetus also swallows amniotic fluid and urinates. Neurons are rapidly multiplying in the fetus's brain, spinal cord, and peripheral nervous system.

By the end of week 12, the facial profile of the fetus is almost identical to that of a full-term baby. The genitals are clearly visible, making it possible to identify the sex using ultrasound. The fetus has definable, though irregular, periods of activity and rest. The lungs rhythmically expand and contract as the fetus "breathes" amniotic fluid through the nose.

Hair follicles begin to form in the 13th week. The fetus also begins to be able to hear its mother's voice and loud, external noises between the 13th and 15th weeks. Major brain structures are beginning to take shape, as the **glial cells** needed to support the neurons develop. By the 16th week, the umbilical cord is transporting 340 litres of fluid per day. The fetus is 20.4 to 25.4 centimetres long and weighs about 170 grams.

glial cells
specialized cells in the brain that support neurons

In approximately week 17 or week 18, the mother begins to feel the fetus moving. The heartbeat can be detected with a stethoscope, and the fetus grows an additional 5 centimetres. A fine hair, *lanugo*, covers the body, and some fetuses already have hair on the head.

In the 19th and 20th weeks, the fetus becomes much more responsive to stimuli. For example, when a light is introduced into the womb, the fetus covers its eyes with its hands (Nilsson & Hamberger, 1990). The fetus also develops eyebrows and fingernails. By week 20, the mother's family members or friends may be able to hear the baby's heartbeat by pressing an ear against her rapidly enlarging abdomen.

By week 21, the fetus is covered with an oily, cheese-like substance, *vernix*, that protects its skin from harsh chemicals in the amniotic fluid. At approximately week 22, the lungs begin producing a substance called *surfactant*, which is necessary for the exchange of oxygen and carbon dioxide in the blood.

By the end of week 23, a small number of babies have attained **viability**, the ability to live outside the womb (Moore & Persaud, 1993). However, most babies born this early die, and those who do survive struggle for many months. Remaining in the womb just 1 week longer, until the end of week 24, greatly increases a baby's chances of survival. The extra week probably allows time for lung function to become more efficient. In addition, most brain structures are completely developed by the end of the 24th week. For these reasons, most experts accept 24 weeks as the average age of viability.

viability
ability of the fetus to survive outside the womb

At the end of week 25, the fetus is 35.5 to 38 centimetres long and weighs 0.9 kilograms. It responds to its mother's voice, and its eyelids reopen sometime between weeks 26 and 27. The 28-week-old fetus has regular periods of rest and activity. A fetus born at this time has a good chance of survival, though most babies born this early have significant health problems.

As week 29 begins, the fetus is growing very rapidly. Neurons in the brain are beginning to form connections, a process that will continue across the entire lifespan (see **Figure 3.3**). The fetus is 40.6 to 43.2 centimetres long and weighs 1.8 kilograms. In weeks 30 and 31, it begins to acquire antibodies from the mother's blood that will provide protection against many illnesses for several weeks after birth. By week 32, the fetus is getting very crowded in the uterus and is beginning to put on layers of fat in preparation for life outside the womb.

In weeks 33 and 34, the approximately 45.7 centimetre-long, 2.7-kilogram fetus undergoes the final preparations for birth. The fetus reverses position so that its head, which had been toward the top of the uterus, is at the bottom of the uterus; the womb is now so crowded that the fetus has to remain in one position (the "fetal" position) all the time. Important changes that will allow the baby to breathe efficiently after birth take place in the lungs. By week 35, the fetus is spending more and more time at rest (DiPietro, Hodgson, Costigan, & Johnson, 1996).

By the time the fetus reaches week 36, it has virtually a 100% chance of survival. All organs are fully functional. *Engagement*—the movement of the head into the lower neck of the uterus—happens at the end of the 36th week. At 37 weeks, the fetus is considered full-term. Most fetuses are 48.3 to 53.3 centimetres long and weigh 2.7 to 4.1 kilograms. At this point, pressure from the baby's head on the cervix may cause it to begin to open. In addition, the placenta may begin to deteriorate in preparation for expulsion from the uterus following the baby's birth.

SEX DIFFERENCES

Because prenatal development is strongly influenced by maturational codes that are the same for both males and females, there are only a few sex differences in prenatal development. One fairly well-documented difference is that male fetuses, on average, are more physically active (DiPietro, Hodgson, Costigan, & Johnson, 1996;

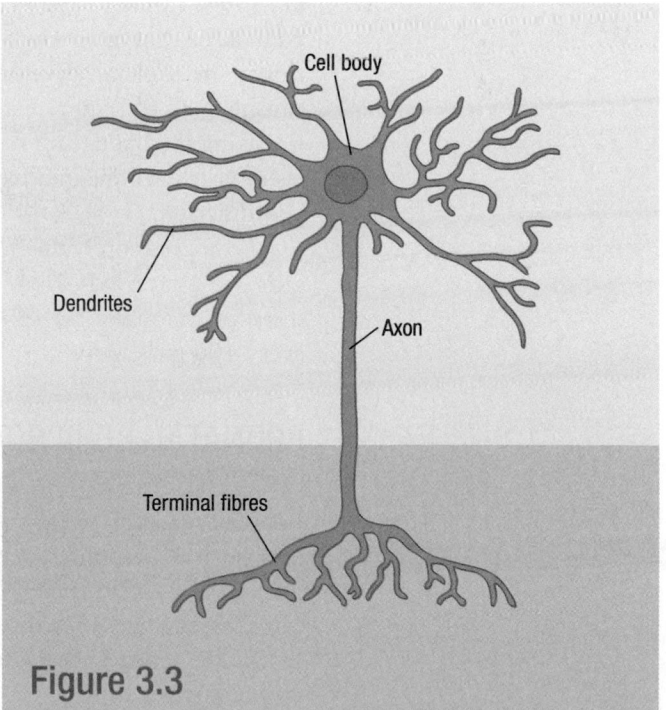

Figure 3.3

The structure of a single developed neuron. The cell bodies are the first to be developed, primarily between weeks 12 and 24. Axons and dendrites develop later, especially during the final 12 weeks, and continue to increase in size and complexity for several years after birth.

DiPietro, Hodgson, Costigan, Hilton, & Johnson, 1996). Further, activity level is fairly stable from the fetal stage through childhood (Accardo et al., 1997). This means that the sex differences in children's activity level you'll read about in later chapters probably begin in the womb.

Sometime between 4 and 8 weeks after conception, the male embryo begins to secrete the male hormone *testosterone*. If this hormone is not secreted or is secreted in inadequate amounts, the embryo will be "demasculinized," even to the extent of developing female genitalia. Female embryos do not appear to secrete any equivalent hormone. However, the presence of male hormone at the critical time (from a drug the mother takes or from a genetic disease called *congenital adrenal hyperplasia*) acts to "masculinize" the female fetus, sometimes resulting in genitalia that appear to be male. Some research even suggests that prenatal masculinization of female fetuses leads to "tomboyish" childhood behaviour, such as rough-and-tumble play (Collaer & Hines, 1995).

In addition, male fetuses secrete small amounts of testosterone into the amniotic fluid. If a male shares the womb with a female fraternal twin, she is likely to swallow the secreted testosterone. Although the research is fairly new, studies suggest that these girls have some neurological characteristics that are more similar to the average male than to the average female (McFadden, 1998).

Subtle sex differences in prenatal brain development probably contribute to different patterns of growth hormone secretions in adolescence as well. Researchers have linked prenatal hormones to sex differences in the dominance of the right and left hemispheres of the brain, physical aggression, and connections between brain and motor patterns (Pressman et al., 1998; Todd, Swarzenski, Rossi, & Visconti, 1995).

Developmentalists aren't sure why, but female fetuses appear to be more sensitive to external stimulation and to advance more rapidly in skeletal development (Groome et al., 1999; Tanner, 1990). Female infants are about 1 to 2 weeks ahead in bone development at birth, even though newborn boys are typically longer and heavier. Female superiority in skeletal development persists through childhood and early adolescence, causing girls to acquire many coordinated movements and motor skills, especially those involving the hands and wrists, earlier than boys. The gap between the sexes gets wider every year until the mid-teens, when boys catch up and surpass girls in general physical coordination.

Boys are more vulnerable to all kinds of prenatal problems. Many more boys than girls are conceived—from 120 to 150 male embryos to every 100 female ones—but more of the males are spontaneously aborted. At birth, there are about 105 boys for every 100 girls. Boys are also more likely to have birth defects (Tanner, 1990).

PRENATAL BEHAVIOUR

Centuries before scientists began to study prenatal development, pregnant women noticed fetal responses to music and other sounds. However, in recent years, developmentalists have learned a great deal about how such stimuli affect the fetus. For one thing, researchers have discovered that the fetus responds to sounds and vibrations with heart rate changes, head turns, and body movements as early as the 25th week of gestation (Joseph, 2000).

Research also suggests that the fetus can distinguish between familiar and novel stimuli by the 32nd or 33rd week (Sandman, Wadhwa, Hetrick, Porto, & Peeke, 1997). In one study, pregnant women recited a short children's rhyme out loud each day from week 33 through week 37. In week 38 researchers played a recording of either the rhyme the mother had been reciting or a different rhyme and measured the fetal heart rate. Fetal heart rates dropped during the familiar rhyme, but not during the unfamiliar one, suggesting that the fetuses had learned the sound patterns of the rhyme recited by their mothers (DeCasper, Lecaneut, Busnel, Granier-DeFerre, & Maugeais, 1994). In another study, researchers from Queen's University and Zhejiang University in China exposed full-term fetuses to either their mother's voice or to the voice of a female stranger via loudspeaker. In both cases the same poem was read to each fetus. The fetuses demonstrated a significantly different heart rate pattern in response to the poem read by their mother (heart rate increase) than to that read by a stranger (heart rate decrease), suggesting that fetuses can remember and recognize their mother's voice (Kisilevsky, et al., 2003). The ability to learn in this way seems to emerge between 24 and 38 weeks, along with changes in the nervous system that allow the fetal brain to gain greater control of physical movements (Pressman et al., 1998).

Evidence for fetal learning also comes from studies in which newborns appear to remember stimuli to which they were exposed prenatally: their mother's heartbeats, the odour of the amniotic fluid, and stories or pieces of music they heard in the womb (Righetti, 1996; Schaal, Marlier, & Soussignan, 1998). For example, in a classic study of prenatal learning, pregnant women read Dr. Seuss's children's story *The Cat in the Hat* out loud each day for the final 6 weeks of their pregnancies. After the infants were born, they were allowed to suck on special pacifiers that turned a variety of sounds off and on. Each kind of sound required a special type of sucking. Researchers found that the babies quickly adapted their sucking patterns in order to listen to the familiar story, but did not increase their sucking in order to listen to an unfamiliar story (DeCasper & Spence, 1986). In other words, babies preferred the sound of the story they had heard *in utero* (in the womb).

Developmentalists are trying to find out how, or whether, prenatal learning affects later development. In one study, pregnant women wore waistbands equipped with speakers through which they exposed their fetuses to an average of 70 hours of classical music between 28 weeks and birth (Lafuente et al., 1997). By age 6 months, the babies who had heard the music were more advanced than control infants in many motor and cognitive skills. Of course, the exact meaning of this result is difficult to assess, but it does suggest that the prenatal sensory environment may be important in later development.

Stable individual differences in behaviour are also identifiable in fetuses. You have already read about the sex difference in activity level. As is true of most sex differences, however, the range of individual differences within each gender is far greater than the difference in *average* activity levels between male and female fetuses. Longitudinal studies have shown that very active fetuses, both males and females, tend to become children who are very active. Moreover, these children are more likely to be labelled "hyperactive" by parents and teachers. In contrast, fetuses who are less active than average are more likely to be intellectually delayed (Accardo et al., 1997).

Before Going On

- Describe a woman's experiences during the three trimesters of pregnancy.
- Outline the milestones of the germinal, embryonic, and fetal stages of prenatal development.
- How do male and female fetuses differ?
- What do developmentalists know about prenatal behaviour?

PROBLEMS IN PRENATAL DEVELOPMENT

congenital anomaly
an abnormality present at birth

Prenatal development is not immune to outside influences, as you'll see in this section. Keep in mind that most of the problems you'll read about are very rare, many are preventable, and many need not have permanent consequences for the child. In Canada, 2–3% of babies are born with a serious **congenital anomaly**—an abnormal structure, function, or body metabolism present at birth that results in physical or mental disability or death (Health Canada, 2002a).

GENETIC DISORDERS

Many disorders appear to be transmitted through the operation of dominant and recessive genes (see **Table 3.4**). *Autosomal disorders* are caused by genes located on the autosomes (chromosomes other than sex chromosomes). The genes that cause *sex-linked* disorders are found on the X chromosome.

AUTOSOMAL DISORDERS Most disorders caused by recessive genes are diagnosed in infancy or early childhood. For example, a recessive gene causes a baby to have problems digesting the amino acid phenylalanine. Toxins build up in the baby's brain and cause developmental delay. This condition, called *phenylketonuria (PKU)*, is found in about 1 in every 10 000 babies (Nicholson, 1998). If a baby consumes no foods containing phenylalanine, however, he will not become intellectually delayed. Milk is one of the foods PKU babies can't have, so early diagnosis is critical. For this reason, there is universal screening for PKU soon after birth in all Canadian provinces.

Like many recessive disorders, PKU is associated with ethnicity. Caucasian babies are more likely to have the disorder than infants in other groups. Similarly, West African and African American infants are more likely to suffer from *sickle-cell disease,* a recessive disorder that causes red blood cell deformities (Scott, 1998). In sickle-cell disease, the blood can't carry enough oxygen to keep the body's tissues healthy. Few children with sickle-cell disease live past the age of 20, and most who survive to adulthood die before they are 40 (Scott, 1998).

TABLE 3.4	Some Genetic Disorders	
Autosomal Dominant Disorders	**Autosomal Recessive Disorders**	**Sex-Linked Recessive Disorders**
Huntington's disease	Phenylketonuria	Hemophilia
High blood pressure	Sickle-cell disease	Fragile-X syndrome
Extra fingers	Cystic fibrosis	Red-green colour blindness
Migraine headaches	Tay-Sachs disease	Missing front teeth
Schizophrenia	Kidney cysts in infants	Night blindness
	Albinism	Some types of muscular dystrophy
		Some types of diabetes

(*Sources:* **Amato,** 1998; **Tortora & Grabowski,** 1993.)

About 1 in every 3000 babies born to couples of Eastern European Jewish ancestry suffers from another recessive disorder, *Tay-Sachs disease.* Another group that is at risk for the disease is French Canadians in the Gaspé region of Quebec (Triggs-Raine, Richard, Wasel, Prence, & Natowicz, 1995). They carry the gene for a severe form of Tay-Sachs disease at a rate 10 times that of the general population (Myerowitz & Hogikyan, 1987). A baby with Tay-Sachs is likely to be severely intellectually delayed and blind. Very few survive past the age of 3 (Painter & Bergman, 1998).

Disorders caused by dominant genes, such as *Huntington's disease,* are usually not diagnosed until adulthood (Amato, 1998). This disorder causes the brain to deteriorate and affects both psychological and motor functions. The risk of Huntington's in Canada is one in 10 000 and the child of a parent with Huntington's has a 50% chance of developing the disease (Huntington Society of Canada, 2001). There is now a blood test to identify the Huntington's gene. Thus, people who have a parent with this disease can now make better decisions about their own child-bearing, as well as prepare themselves to live with a serious disorder when they get older.

SEX-LINKED DISORDERS Most sex-linked disorders are caused by recessive genes (see **Figure 3.4**). One fairly common sex-linked recessive disorder is *red-green colour blindness.* People with this disorder have difficulty distinguishing between the colours red and green when these colours are adjacent. About 7 to 8% of men and 0.5% of women have this disorder. Most learn ways of compensating for the disorder and thus live perfectly normal lives.

A more serious sex-linked recessive disorder is *hemophilia.* The blood of people with hemophilia lacks the chemical components that cause blood to clot. Thus, when a person with hemophilia bleeds, the bleeding doesn't stop naturally. Approximately 1 in 5000 baby boys is born with this disorder, which is almost unknown in girls (Scott, 1998)

About 1 in every 1500 males and 1 in every 2500 females have a sex-linked disorder called *fragile-X syndrome* (Amato, 1998). A person with this disorder has an X chromosome with a "fragile," or damaged, spot. Fragile-X syndrome can cause developmental delay that becomes progressively worse as a child gets older (Adesman, 1996). In fact, experts estimate that 5–7% of all developmentally delayed males have fragile-X syndrome (Zigler & Hodapp, 1991).

CHROMOSOMAL ERRORS

A variety of problems can be caused by a child having too many or too few chromosomes, a condition referred to as a *chromosomal error,* or *chromosomal anomaly.* Like genetic disorders, these are distinguished by whether they involve autosomes or sex chromosomes.

TRISOMIES A *trisomy* is a condition in which a child has three copies of a specific autosome. The most common is *trisomy 21,* or *Down syndrome,* in which the child has three copies of chromosome 21. The number of infants born with this anomaly has remained fairly constant in Canada averaging just over 1.3 in 1000 births (Health Canada, 2002a). These children are intellectually delayed and have distinctive facial features, smaller brains, and often other physical abnormalities such as heart defects (Haier et al., 1995).

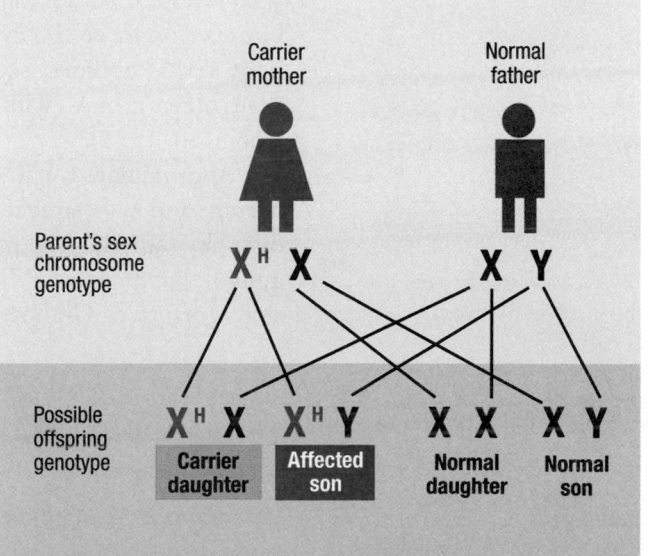

Figure 3.4

Compare this pattern of sex-linked transmission of a recessive disease (hemophilia) with the pattern shown in **Figure 3.2**.

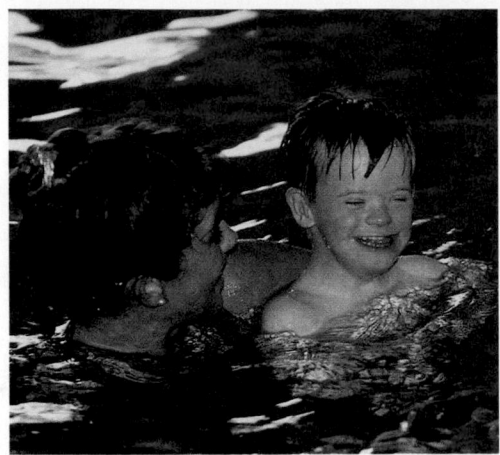

This child shows the distinctive facial features of a child with Down syndrome.
(*Photo:* Mark Richards/PhotoEdit)

The risk of bearing a child with trisomy 21 is greatest for mothers over 35. Among Canadian women aged 35 to 39, the rate of Down syndrome is about 1 in 350 births. Among women 40 to 45, it climbs to 1 in 150 births and for women above age 45, Down syndrome is present in almost one quarter of all births (Health Canada, 2002a). These figures underestimate the true rates by 15% to 24% because they exclude spontaneous abortions and terminated pregnancies (Benn & Egan, 2000).

Scientists have identified children with trisomies in the 13th and 18th pairs of chromosomes as well (Amato, 1998). These disorders have more severe effects than trisomy 21. Few trisomy 13 or trisomy 18 children live past the age of 1 year. As with trisomy 21, the chances of having a child with one of these disorders increase with a woman's age.

SEX-CHROMOSOME ANOMALIES A second class of anomalies is associated with the sex chromosomes. The most common is an XXY pattern, called *Klinefelter's syndrome,* that occurs in 1 or 2 out of every 1000 males (Amato, 1998). Affected boys usually look normal but have underdeveloped testes and, as adults, very low sperm production. Most are not intellectually delayed, but many have language and learning disabilities. At puberty, these boys experience both male and female changes. For example, their penises enlarge and their breasts develop.

A single-X pattern (X0), called *Turner's syndrome,* may also occur. Individuals with Turner's syndrome are anatomically female but show stunted growth and are usually sterile. Without hormone therapy, they do not menstruate or develop breasts at puberty. About one quarter have serious heart defects (Amato, 1998). These girls also show an imbalance in their cognitive skills: They often perform particularly poorly on tests that measure spatial ability but usually perform at or above normal levels on tests of verbal skill (Golombok & Fivush, 1994).

Neither Kleinfelter's nor Turner's syndrome is associated with the mother's age. However, older mothers are more likely to produce normal-appearing girls with an extra X chromosome and boys with an extra Y chromosome (Amato, 1998). Females with an XXX pattern, about 1 in every 1000 female births, are usually of normal size but develop more slowly than their peers (Amato, 1998). Many, though not all, have poor verbal abilities, score low on intelligence tests, and do more poorly in school than other groups with sex chromosome anomalies (Bender, Harmon, Linden, & Robinson, 1995).

Approximately 1 in 1000 boys has an extra Y chromosome. Most are taller than average and have large teeth. They usually experience normal puberty, and they have no difficulty fathering children (Amato, 1998). Developmentalists now know that it is only a myth that an extra Y chromosome causes below-average intelligence and high aggression (Tortora & Grabowski, 1993).

TERATOGENS: MATERNAL DISEASES

teratogens
substances such as viruses and drugs that can cause birth defects

Deviations in prenatal development can result from exposure to **teratogens**, agents that cause damage to an embryo or fetus. The general rule is that each organ system is most vulnerable to harm when it is developing most rapidly (Moore & Persaud, 1993). Because most organ systems develop most rapidly during the first 8 weeks of gestation, this is the period when exposure to teratogens carries the greatest risk (see **Figure 3.5**). Because of space limitations, we will discuss only a few of the most significant teratogens. **Table 3.5** (page 76) lists several others.

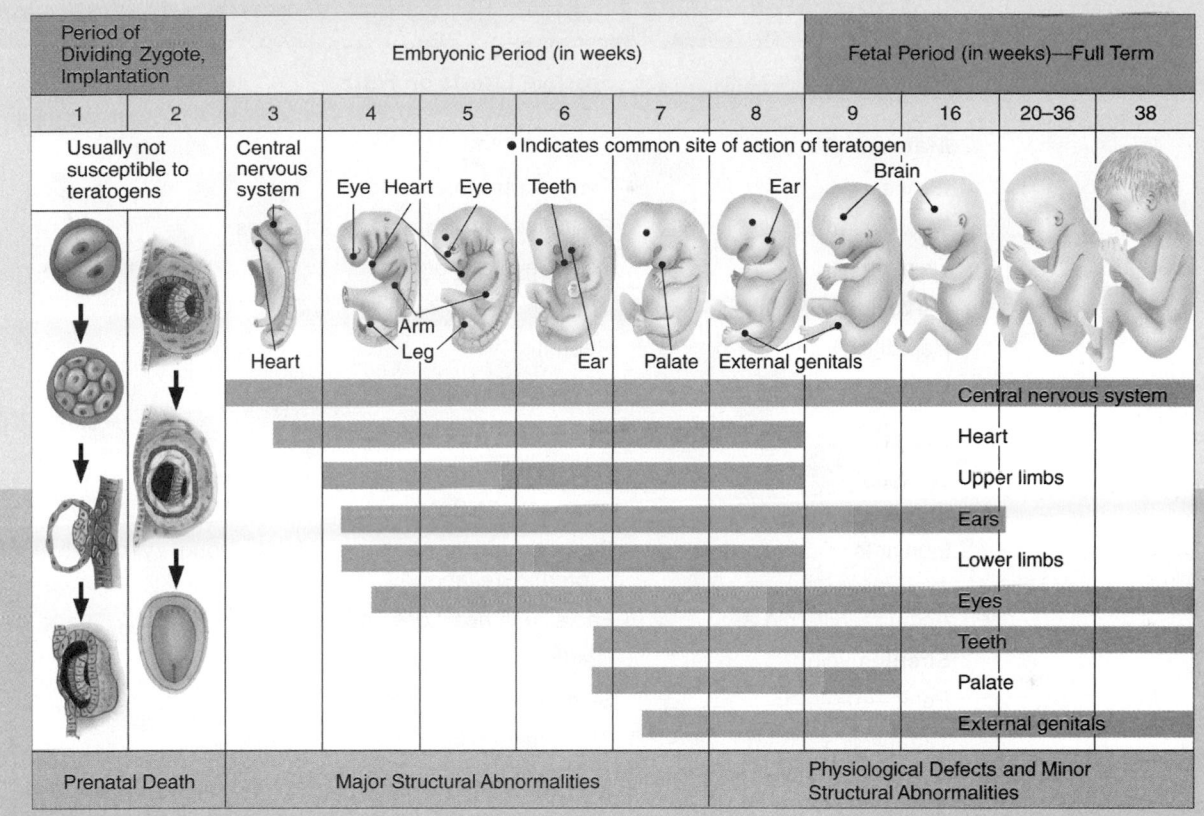

Period of Dividing Zygote, Implantation		Embryonic Period (in weeks)						Fetal Period (in weeks)—Full Term			
1	2	3	4	5	6	7	8	9	16	20–36	38

Usually not susceptible to teratogens

Central nervous system

Eye Heart Eye   Teeth   Ear   Brain

Heart   Arm   Leg   Ear   Palate   External genitals

● Indicates common site of action of teratogen

| | | | | | | | | | Central nervous system |
| Heart |
| Upper limbs |
| Ears |
| Lower limbs |
| Eyes |
| Teeth |
| Palate |
| External genitals |

| Prenatal Death | Major Structural Abnormalities | Physiological Defects and Minor Structural Abnormalities |

Figure 3.5

Sensitivity to teratogens peaks during the first eight weeks of gestation, although damage can occur throughout the prenatal period.

Source: K.L. Moore & T.V.N. Persaud, 1998, *Before We Are Born*, 5th ed., Philadelphia: Saunders, p. 156. Reprinted with permission from Elsevier.)

Several viruses pass through the placental filters and attack the embryo or fetus directly. For example, *rubella*, or *German measles*, causes a short-lived mild reaction in adults but may be deadly to a fetus. Most infants exposed to rubella in the first 4 to 5 weeks show some abnormality (Moore & Persaud, 1993). Deafness, cataracts, and heart defects are the most common ones.

HIV, the virus that causes AIDS, is one of many sexually transmitted organisms that can be passed directly from mother to fetus. The virus may cross the placenta and enter the fetus's bloodstream, or the infant may contract the virus in the birth canal during delivery, or the virus can be passed through the breast milk after delivery. Seventy-eight percent of Canadian children (aged 0 to 14) with AIDS acquired the virus through these means. The rate of HIV infection among pregnant women in Canada's provinces is about 3 to 4 per 10 000 (Health Canada, 2001c). Transmission appears to be more likely when the mother has AIDS than when she is HIV-positive but not yet ill (Abrams et al., 1995). In addition, Canadian researchers have demonstrated that HIV-positive pregnant women who take the drug AZT have a markedly lower risk of transmitting the disease to their children (Forbes, Money, Remple, et al., 2000; King, Singer, Forbes et al., 2000).

Infants who acquire HIV from their mothers typically become ill within the first 2 years of life (Prince, 1998). The virus weakens children's immune systems, allowing a host of other infectious agents, such as the bacteria that cause pneumonia and meningitis, to attack their bodies. Even children who remain symptom-free must restrict their exposure to viruses and bacteria. For example, HIV-positive children cannot be

TABLE 3.5 Some Important Teratogens and Their Effects

Teratogens	Possible Effects on Fetus
Maternal Diseases	
Cancer	Fetal or placental tumour
Toxoplasmosis	Brain swelling, spinal abnormalities
Chicken pox	Scars, eye damage
Parvovirus	Anemia
Hepatitis B	Hepatitis
Chlamydia	Conjunctivitis, pneumonia
Drugs	
Warfarin	Underdeveloped nasal tissue, abnormal long bone growth, CNS defects
Inhalants	Problems similar to those of fetal alcohol syndrome; premature labour
Accutane/vitamin A	Facial, ear, heart deformities
Streptomycin	Deafness
Penicillin	Skin disorders
Tetracycline	Tooth deformities
Diet pills	Low birth weight

(*Sources:* **Amato, 1998; Kliegman, 1998; Martinez, 2002**).

Critical Thinking

Given the new findings about the benefits of AZT, do you think all pregnant women should be required to be tested for HIV infection so that those who test positive can be given AZT?

immunized with vaccines that utilize live viruses, such as the polio vaccine (Prince, 1998).

Other sexually transmitted diseases (STDs), including *syphilis, genital herpes,* and *gonorrhea,* cause a variety of birth defects. Unlike most teratogens, the bacterium that causes syphilis is most harmful during the last 26 weeks of prenatal development and causes eye, ear, and brain defects. Genital herpes is usually passed from mother to infant during birth. One third of infected babies die, and another 25–30% suffer blindness or brain damage. Thus, doctors usually advise surgical delivery for the babies of women who have herpes. Gonorrhea, which can cause the infant to be blind, is also usually transmitted during birth. For this reason, doctors usually treat the eyes of newborns with a special ointment that prevents damage from gonorrhea.

TERATOGENS: DRUGS

Sorting out the effects of drugs (prescription and nonprescription, legal and illegal) on prenatal development has proven to be an immensely challenging task because many pregnant women take multiple drugs. Other factors, such as maternal stress, lack of social support, or poverty and poor prenatal care, also often accompany illegal drug use (Johnson, Nusbaum, Bejarano, & Rosen, 1999). Nevertheless, there are several drugs that seem to affect infant development, independent of other variables.

TOBACCO Infants of mothers who smoke are on average about 225 grams lighter at birth than infants of nonsmoking mothers, and lower birth weight has a variety of potential negative consequences (Floyd, Rimer, Giovino, Mullen, & Sullivan, 1993; Fourn, Ducic, & Seguin, 1999). For instance, the rate of miscarriage, stillbirth, and neonatal death is higher in smokers. In Canada, 23.7% of women smoked during pregnancy, and of those, 84.1% smoked throughout their pregnancy (Connor & McIntyre, 1998). Younger women are more likely to smoke during pregnancy than older women although, overall, smoking during pregnancy is on the decrease in Canada (Health Canada, 2003b).

Children with fetal alcohol syndrome have distinctive features.
(*Photo:* © 2000 George Steinmetz)

ALCOHOL Researchers have also documented the effects of alcohol on prenatal development. In fact, recent studies show that alcohol can even adversely affect an ovum prior to ovulation or during its journey down the fallopian tube to the uterus. Likewise, a zygote can be affected by alcohol even before it has been implanted in the uterine lining (Kaufman, 1997).

Mothers who are heavy drinkers or alcoholics are at significant risk of delivering infants with *fetal alcohol syndrome (FAS)*. These children are generally smaller than normal, with smaller brains. They frequently have heart defects and hearing losses, and their faces are distinctive, with a somewhat flattened nose and often an unusually long space between nose and mouth (Church, Eldis, Blakley, & Bawle, 1997). As children, adolescents, and adults, they are shorter than normal and have smaller heads, and their intelligence test scores indicate mild developmental delay. FAS children who are not intellectually delayed often have learning and behaviour difficulties (Mattson & Riley, 1999; Mattson, Riley, Gramling, Delis, & Jones, 1998; Meyer, 1998; Uecker & Nadel, 1996).

In Canada 17–25% of women reported consuming alcohol at some point during their pregnancy, but only 7–9% admitted to drinking throughout their pregnancy (Health Canada, 1998a). Although the overall alcohol consumption rate is coming down, older Canadian women are still more likely to consume alcohol during pregnancy than younger women (Health Canada, 2003b). Unfortunately, even moderate drinking by a pregnant woman may cause her child to have learning and behavioural difficulties in childhood and adolescence (Larroque & Kaminski, 1998; Sampson et al., 1997). Binge drinking, even once during pregnancy, is also associated with a variety of problems (Olson, Sampson, Barr, Streissguth, & Bookstein, 1992; Streissguth, Barr, & Sampson, 1990). In the face of this evidence, the safest course for pregnant women is to drink no alcohol at all.

HEROIN AND COCAINE Heroin can cause miscarriage, premature labour, and early death (Brockington, 1996). Further, 60–80% of babies born to heroin-addicted women are addicted to heroin as well. Addicted babies have high-pitched cries and suffer from withdrawal symptoms, such as irritability, uncontrollable tremors, vomiting, convulsions, and sleep problems. These symptoms may last as long as 4 months.

Use of cocaine by pregnant women, in either powder or "crack" form, is linked to many kinds of developmental problems in their children (Chatlos, 1997). However, most cocaine-using pregnant women are poor and abuse multiple substances, making it difficult to separate the effects of cocaine from those of poverty and other drugs. Some studies suggest that cocaine alone has no long-term effects on cognitive or social development (Kilbride, Castor, Hoffman, & Fuger, 2000; Phelps, Wallace, & Bontrager, 1997; Richardson, Conroy, & Day, 1996). However, other research has demonstrated that prenatal exposure to cocaine, especially when women use it several times a week, leads to a variety of developmental problems in infants (Brown, Bakeman, Coles, Sexson, & Demi, 1998; Madison, Johnson, Seikel, Arnold, & Schultheis, 1998; Schuler

& Nair, 1999). Still other studies indicate that cocaine-exposed infants' problems may seem to be minimal when the children are assessed individually in researchers' laboratories. However, in complex environments such as school classrooms, their difficulties become more apparent (Betancourt et al., 1999).

OTHER HARMFUL INFLUENCES ON PRENATAL DEVELOPMENT

Other factors that can adversely affect prenatal development include the mother's diet, her age, and her mental and physical health, as well as environmental factors such as pollution and radiation.

DIET Some specific nutrients are vital to prenatal development. One is folic acid, a B vitamin found in beans, spinach, and other foods. Inadequate amounts of this nutrient are linked to neural tube defects, such as *spina bifida* (Daly, Kirke, Molloy, Weir, & Scott, 1995). The potential negative effects of insufficient folic acid occur in the very earliest weeks of pregnancy, before a woman may know she is pregnant. Canada now has regulations that indicate that flour must be enriched with folic acid, thereby lowering the risk of a folic deficiency (Health Canada, 1998b).

It is also important for a pregnant woman to take in sufficient overall calories and protein to prevent malnutrition. A woman who experiences malnutrition during pregnancy, particularly during the final 3 months, has an increased risk of delivering a low-birth-weight infant (under 2500 grams) who will have intellectual difficulties in childhood (Mutch, Leyland, & McGee, 1993). In addition, researchers have recently identified prenatal malnutrition, along with a variety of obstetrical complications, as an important risk factor in the development of mental illnesses in adulthood (Neugebauer, Hoek, & Susser, 1999; Susser, & Lin, 1992).

The impact of maternal malnutrition appears to be greatest on the developing nervous system—a pattern found in studies of both humans and other mammals. For example, rats whose caloric intake has been substantially restricted during the fetal and early postnatal periods show a pattern described as *brain stunting,* in which both the weight and volume of the brain are reduced. They also develop fewer dendrites and show less rich synaptic formation (Pollitt & Gorman, 1994).

Canadian weight-gain guidelines suggest that the average woman should gain 11.5 to 16.0 kilograms during pregnancy. Women who have a low **body mass index (BMI)** (BMI is a ratio of weight to height) should gain more weight than those who have a higher BMI (indicates obesity). Generally, if a woman follows the Health Canada (2002b) guide *Nutrition for a Healthy Pregnancy: National Guidelines for the Childbearing Years* from early in her pregnancy, she will likely maintain the necessary degree of weight gain.

AGE One intriguing trend in the industrialized world is that more women postpone first pregnancy until their late 20s or early 30s. Between 1981 and 1997 the proportion of live births to women 30 years of age and older nearly doubled from 23.7% to 44.5% (Health Canada, 2000a). One effect of this trend, as you have already learned, is that the number of multiple births each year has increased dramatically.

Mothers over 30 are at increased risk for several kinds of problems, including miscarriage, complications of pregnancy such as high blood pressure, and death during pregnancy or delivery (Berkowitz, Skovron, Lapinski, & Berkowitz, 1990; McFalls, 1990). These effects of age seem to be exacerbated if the mother has not had adequate prenatal care or has poor health habits. For example, the negative effects of maternal smoking on birth weight are considerably greater among women over 35 than among younger women (Wen et al., 1990).

body mass index (BMI)
a body composition ratio of weight to height that is an estimate of under- or overweight

Whether the infants born to these older mothers also face higher risks is not so clear. Infants born to older mothers appear to be only slightly more likely to weigh less than 2.5 kilograms at birth, a difference that may be entirely explained by the different rates of multiple births between younger and older women (Berkowitz et al., 1990; Cnattingius, Berendes, & Forman, 1993; NCHS, 1999). Babies of older mothers are also no more likely to have birth defects—aside from the well-established risk of chromosomal anomalies such as trisomy 21 (Baird, Sadovnick, & Yee, 1991). However, researchers in Sweden, where mothers of all ages receive good prenatal care, have found higher rates of late-pregnancy miscarriage and infant mortality for older mothers, especially for first births to mothers over 35 (Cnattingius et al., 1993). Given these varying results, the experts have been unable to reach a clear conclusion about risks for babies born to older mothers.

At the other end of the age continuum, there is also disagreement about how to interpret the findings regarding very young mothers. When simply comparing the rates of problems seen in teenage mothers with those among mothers in their 20s, almost all researchers find higher rates among the teens. However, teenage mothers are also more likely to be poor and less likely to receive adequate prenatal care, so it is very hard to sort out the causal factors.

CHRONIC ILLNESSES Chronic illnesses, whether emotional or physical, can also affect prenatal development. For example, long-term severe depression and other mood disorders can lead to slow fetal growth and premature labour (Weinstock, 1999). Moreover, developmentalists have learned that depressed mothers are less likely to feel attached to their fetuses. At least one study suggested that infants whose mothers do not develop a prenatal attachment to them are less socially responsive than other infants of the same age (Oates, 1998).

Conditions such as heart disease, diabetes, lupus, hormone imbalances, and epilepsy can also affect prenatal development negatively (Kliegman, 1998; McAllister et al., 1997; Sandman, Wadhwa, Chicz-DeMet, Porto, & Garite, 1999). In fact, one of the most important goals of the new specialty of *fetal-maternal medicine* is to manage the pregnancies of women who have such conditions in ways that will support the health of both mother and fetus. For example, pregnancy often makes it impossible for a diabetic woman to keep her blood sugar levels under control. In turn, erratic blood sugar levels may damage the fetus's nervous system or cause it to grow too rapidly (Allen & Kisilevsky, 1999; Kliegman, 1998). To prevent such complications, a fetal-maternal specialist must find a diet, a medication, or a combination of the two that will stabilize the mother's blood sugar but will not harm the fetus. Similarly, fetal-maternal specialists help women who have epilepsy balance their own need for anticonvulsant medication against possible harm to the fetus (see **No Easy Answers**).

MATERNAL EMOTIONS Some psychologists have suggested that maternal emotions can affect prenatal development. Their rationale is that stressful psychological states such as anxiety and depression lead to changes in body chemistry. In a pregnant woman, these changes result in both qualitative and quantitative differences in the hormones and other chemicals to which the fetus is exposed.

One fairly consistent finding is that the fetuses of severely distressed mothers tend to grow more slowly than others (Paarlberg, Vingerhoets, Passchier, Dekker, & van Geign, 1995). Developmentalists do not really know whether this effect results directly from emotion-related hormones or is an indirect effect of the mother's emotional state. A stressed or depressed mother may eat less, or her weakened immune system may limit her ability to fight off viruses and bacteria—either of these situations may retard fetal growth. Consequently, many psychologists suggest that providing stressed and/or

No Easy Answers

Pregnancy, Epilepsy,

and Anticonvulsant

Drugs

Epilepsy is a chronic neurological disorder that causes seizures. To control the seizures, most people with epilepsy take anticonvulsant drugs. However, epileptic women who want to bear children face a dilemma that can be agonizing.

In about 30% of epileptics, seizures increase in both severity and frequency during pregnancy. The physical trauma associated with seizures can rupture the placenta and, in rare cases, cause fatal bleeding in the fetus's brain. However, brain and spinal cord defects happen more frequently in fetuses exposed to anticonvulsant drugs. In addition, a recent study found an extraordinarily high rate of transsexualism among adults who had been prenatally exposed to anticonvulsants (Dessens et al., 1999).

Balancing the risks of medication against those of seizures, most physicians think it's bet-ter to try to manage the effects of the medicines through proper dosage than to risk uncontrolled seizures during pregnancy. They point out that the risks of medication and methods for minimizing them are better known and more predictable than those of epileptic seizures (American Association of Family Physicians, 1998). However, pregnancy changes the way an epileptic woman's body responds to anticonvulsant medication. In most cases, many adjustments in dosage and type of medication are required before the right combination is found. For some women, nothing works. Therefore, even though doctors can advise them of the various probabilities, epileptic women often have to make child-bearing decisions without really knowing what the outcome will be.

depressed pregnant women with social support and counselling may lead to improvements in both maternal and fetal health (Brockington, 1996).

mutagens
agents that damage cellular DNA

MUTAGENS **Mutagens** are agents that damage genetic material in normal cells. Although mutagens are present throughout the environment, exposure to some types is capable of altering the DNA of any human cells including gametes (egg or sperm cells). Exposure to mutagens, such as radiation or biological and chemical toxins, can interfere with both conception and the normal development of the embryo and fetus. For example, if gametes are exposed to high levels of X-rays infertility can result, but if conception does occur the resulting genetic mutation can lead to a failure to implant or a miscarriage. In other instances sperm or eggs that were exposed to mutagens may result in offspring that have chromosomal or genetic anomalies or who are carriers of recessive gene disorders (Edwards, n.d.; Mutagens, 1995).

Mutagens contribute to birth defects because they cause genetic damage and the mutagenic changes are passed along when the affected cells reproduce. Teratogens contribute to birth defects because they cause cellular damage, but they leave the genetic material of the cell unaffected. Someone who has a congenital disorder caused by a teratogenic agent will not pass the disorder on to his or her offspring, but if a person's congenital anomaly was caused by a mutagen then the resulting genetic mutation can be passed on to future generations (Edwards, n.d.; Prasad, Cole, & Hasse, 2004).

FETAL ASSESSMENT AND TREATMENT

Genetic counsellors assist women who are at risk of bearing a child with a congenital defect to understand potential outcomes and choices. Preconception and first trimester screening procedures assay the potential for developmental complications and determine if prenatal diagnostic testing is warranted or even desired. If diagnostic tests are performed and they detect abnormal results, then a genetics counsellor can help the mother

Developmental Psychology in Your Career

Genetics Counsellor

Occupation	Genetics Counsellor
Description	• communicates between families and individuals having concerns about birth defects or genetic conditions • is part of a genetics team that provides the most current information on causes, implications, and recurrence risks • serves as a liaison between the family and other health care professionals
Entry Credentials	• Master of Science degree in Human/Medical Genetics or recognized equivalent
Essential Lifespan Development Knowledge	• pregnancy, child development, and family development issues • teratogens and their effects on prenatal development • diagnostic testing and screening protocols • medical, social, and cultural implications of developmental outcomes and interventions • grief, reactions to bad news, and decision-making
Essential Lifespan Development Skills	• complete a family pedigree • provide information that helps families make personal decisions about pregnancy and child care • evaluate critically the different and particular reactions of people who come for genetic counselling and how their past experience influences their present reaction • provide grief counselling for disability, loss, and termination issues
Lifespan Development and Essential Professional Attitude	• present information to patients accurately and nondirectively, and explore options rather than advise • enable clients to make informed independent decisions, free of coercion • value and respect clients' beliefs, cultural and religious traditions, inclinations, circumstances, feelings, welfare, and freedom • act as an emotional resource to help affected individuals deal with situations they face
Lifespan Development Career Profile: Linda Spooner, RN, BScN, Genetics Nurse, Thunder Bay District Health Unit, Dept. of Genetics	"I gain job satisfaction from simply knowing that I am able to provide a service to individuals and their families who are in the position of having to deal with a genetic condition. The service includes a great deal of support and sometimes bereavement care. What it comes down to is that I can hopefully make a difficult, almost unbearable, situation a little easier for them." May 10, 2004

and her family make informed decisions about her options (see **Developmental Psychology in Your Career**).

Certain diagnostic tests, including *chorionic villus sampling (CVS)* and *amniocentesis,* can be used to identify chromosomal errors and many genetic disorders prior to birth (see **Figure 3.6** on page 82). With CVS, cells are extracted from the placenta and used in a variety of laboratory tests during the early weeks of prenatal development. With amniocentesis, which is done between weeks 14 and 16 of a woman's pregnancy, a needle is used to extract amniotic fluid containing fetal cells. Fetal cells filtered out of the fluid are then tested in a variety of ways to diagnose chromosomal and genetic disorders. In addition, ultrasound has become a routine part of prenatal care in Canada because of its usefulness in monitoring fetal growth during high-risk pregnancies.

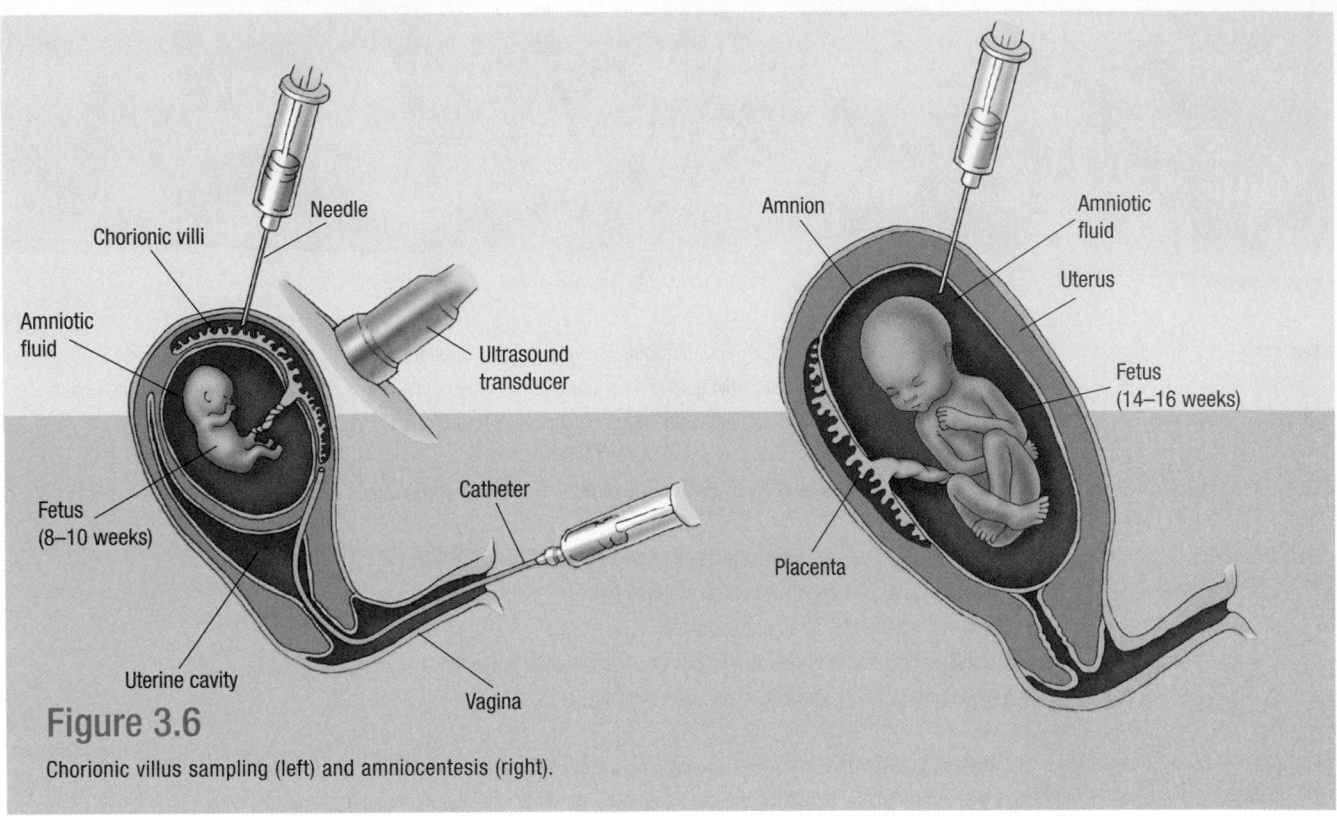

Figure 3.6

Chorionic villus sampling (left) and amniocentesis (right).

There are also many laboratory tests that use maternal blood, urine, and/or samples of amniotic fluid to help health care providers monitor fetal development. For example, the presence of a substance called *alpha-fetoprotein* in a pregnant woman's blood is associated with a number of prenatal defects, including abnormalities in the brain and spinal cord. Doctors can also use a laboratory test to assess the maturity of fetal lungs (Kliegman, 1998). This test is critical when doctors advise early delivery of a baby because of the mother's health.

Fetoscopy involves insertion of a tiny camera into the womb to directly observe fetal development. Fetoscopy makes it possible for doctors to correct some kinds of defects surgically (Kliegman, 1998). Likewise, fetoscopy has made such techniques as fetal blood transfusions and bone marrow transplants possible. Specialists also use fetoscopy to take samples of blood from the umbilical cord. Laboratory tests performed on fetal blood samples can assess fetal organ function, diagnose genetic and chromosomal disorders, and detect fetal infections (D'Alton & DeCherney, 1993). For example, fetal blood tests can help doctors identify a bacterial infection that is causing a fetus to grow too slowly. Once diagnosed, the infection can be treated by injecting antibiotics into the amniotic fluid (so that they will be swallowed by the fetus) or into the umbilical cord (Kliegman, 1998).

Researchers have examined how prenatal diagnosis affects parents-to-be. Compared with parents of 1-year-olds with disabilities who did not know about the problems prior to birth, parents whose infants' difficulties were diagnosed prenatally report greater feelings of stress and depression (Hunfeld et al., 1999). However, specialists in fetal medicine suggest that the negative emotional effects of prenatal diagnosis can be moderated by providing parents-to-be with counselling and specific information about treatment at the time the diagnosis is made, rather than waiting until after the birth.

Before Going On

- Briefly describe the genetic disorders presented in this section: PKU, sickle-cell disease, Tay-Sachs disease, Huntington's disease, red-green colour blindness, hemophilia, and fragile-X syndrome.

- What is a trisomy, and which type is most common?

- Which sex chromosome anomalies are the most serious?

- List the risks associated with the teratogenic diseases.

- What are the potential adverse effects of smoking, drinking, and drug use on prenatal development?

- What additional maternal factors influence prenatal development?

- What options are available to women with high risk pregnancies?

BIRTH AND THE NEONATE

Once gestation is complete, the fetus must be born—an event that holds some pain for the mother as well as a good deal of joy for most parents.

BIRTH CHOICES

In most places around the world, tradition dictates how babies are delivered. However, in industrialized countries, especially in Canada, hospital deliveries became routine in the second half of the 20th century. Today, though, parents in such societies have several choices as to who will attend their baby's birth, whether medication will be used to manage the physical discomforts of labour and delivery, and where the birth will take place.

BIRTH ATTENDANTS—MIDWIVES Midwifery is a regulated health care profession in most provinces in Canada. Midwife practice involves assessing, supervising, and caring for women prior to and during pregnancy, labour, and the postpartum period. A midwife is licensed to conduct deliveries and to care for the newborn infant. To become a midwife

In the developing world, tradition determines where a baby is born and who attends its birth. Hospital deliveries are common in Canada, but many hospitals offer parents the option of delivering their babies in nonsurgical settings such as the birthing room pictured on the right. (*Photos: left,* Sean Sprague/Stock Boston; *right,* © Margaret Miller, 1992/Photo Researchers)

in Canada, one must attend a midwifery education program at a recognized institution. Degree programs are offered in Ontario at McMaster University in Hamilton, Ryerson Polytechnic University in Toronto, and Laurentian University in Sudbury. As well, the University of British Columbia is expected to have its first graduating class in 2005.

DRUGS DURING LABOUR AND DELIVERY One key decision for expectant mothers concerns whether to use drugs during labour and delivery. *Analgesics* may be given during labour to reduce pain. *Sedatives* or *tranquillizers* can be administered to reduce anxiety. *Anaesthesia,* when used, is usually given later in labour to block pain, either totally (using general anaesthesia) or in certain portions of the body (using local anaesthesia).

Studying the causal links between drug use during labour and delivery and the baby's later behaviour or development has proven to be difficult. First, it's clear that nearly all drugs given during labour pass through the placenta, enter the fetal bloodstream, and may remain there for several days. Not surprisingly, then, infants whose mothers have received any type of drug are typically slightly more sluggish, gain a little less weight, and spend more time sleeping in the first few weeks than do infants of nondrugged mothers (Maurer & Maurer, 1988).

Second, there are no consistently observed effects from analgesics and tranquillizers beyond the first few days, and only hints from a few studies of long-term effects of anaesthesia (Rosenblith, 1992). Given such inconclusive findings, only one specific piece of advice seems warranted: If you are a new mother who receives medication during childbirth, bear in mind that your baby is also drugged, and that this will affect her behaviour in the first few days. If you allow for this effect and realize that it will wear off, your long-term relationship with your child is likely to be unaffected.

Nevertheless, many women choose to avoid drugs altogether. The general term *natural childbirth* is commonly used to refer to this particular choice. This approach is also often called the *Lamaze method,* after the physician who popularized the notion of natural childbirth and devised a variety of pain management techniques. In natural childbirth, women rely on psychological and behavioural methods of pain management rather than on pain-relieving drugs.

Natural childbirth involves several components. First, a woman selects someone, typically the baby's father or another supportive person, to serve as a labour coach. *Prepared childbirth classes* psychologically prepare the woman and her labour coach for the experience of labour and delivery. For example, they learn to use the term *contraction* instead of *pain.* Further, believing that her baby will benefit from natural childbirth provides the woman with the motivation she needs to endure labour without the aid of pain-relieving medication. Finally, relaxation and breathing techniques provide her with behavioural responses to contractions that serve to replace the negative emotions that typically result from physical discomfort. Aided by her coach, the woman focuses attention on her breathing rather than on the pain.

THE LOCATION OF BIRTH Another choice parents must make is where the baby is to be born. In most of the industrialized world, women deliver their babies in specialized maternity clinics. However, in Canada there are four alternatives in most communities:

- A traditional hospital maternity unit

- A birth centre or birthing room located within a hospital, which provides a more homelike setting for labour and delivery and often allows family members to be present throughout

- A free-standing birth centre, like a hospital birth centre except that it is located apart from the hospital, with delivery typically attended by a midwife rather than (or in addition to) a physician

- The mother's home

Most babies in Canada are born in hospitals. Thus, much of what researchers know about out-of-hospital births comes from studies in Europe. For example, in the Netherlands, a third of all deliveries occur at home (Eskes, 1992). Home deliveries are encouraged for uncomplicated pregnancies during which the woman has received good prenatal care. When these conditions are met, with a trained birth attendant present at delivery, the rate of delivery complications or infant problems is no higher than for hospital deliveries.

Many fathers take prenatal classes like this one so that they can provide support to their partners during labour.

(*Photo:* Joseph Nettis/Stock Boston)

THE PHYSICAL PROCESS OF BIRTH

Labour is typically divided into three stages. Stage 1 covers the period during which two important processes occur: dilation and effacement. The cervix (the opening at the bottom of the uterus) must open up like the lens of a camera (*dilation*) and also flatten out (*effacement*). At the time of actual delivery, the cervix must normally be dilated to about 10 centimetres.

Customarily, stage 1 is itself divided into phases. In the *early* (or *latent*) phase, contractions are relatively far apart and typically not too uncomfortable. In the *active* phase, which begins when the cervix is 3 to 4 centimetres dilated and continues until dilation has reached 8 centimetres, contractions are closer together and more intense. The last 2 centimetres of dilation are achieved during a phase usually called *transition*. It is this phase, when contractions are closely spaced and strong, that women typically find the most painful. Fortunately, transition is also ordinarily the shortest phase.

Figure 3.7 shows the typical length of these various phases of labour for first births and later births. What the figure does not convey is the wide individual variability that exists. Among women delivering a first child, stage 1 may last as few as 3 hours or as many as 20 (Biswas & Craigo, 1994; Kilpatrick & Laros, 1989).

At the end of the transition phase, the mother will normally have the urge to help the infant emerge by "pushing." When the birth attendant (physician or midwife) is sure the cervix is fully dilated, she or he will encourage this pushing, and stage 2 of labour, the actual delivery, begins. The baby's head moves past the stretched cervix, into the birth canal, and finally out of the mother's body. Most women find this part of labour markedly less distressing than the transition phase because at this point they can assist the delivery process by pushing. Stage 2 typically lasts less than an hour and rarely takes longer than 2 hours. Stage 3, also typically quite brief, is the delivery of the placenta (also called the *afterbirth*) and other material from the uterus.

Most infants are delivered head first, facing toward the mother's spine; 3% to 4%, however, are oriented differently, either feet first or bottom first (called *breech* presentations) (Brown, Karrison, & Cibils, 1994). In Canada today, infants in breech

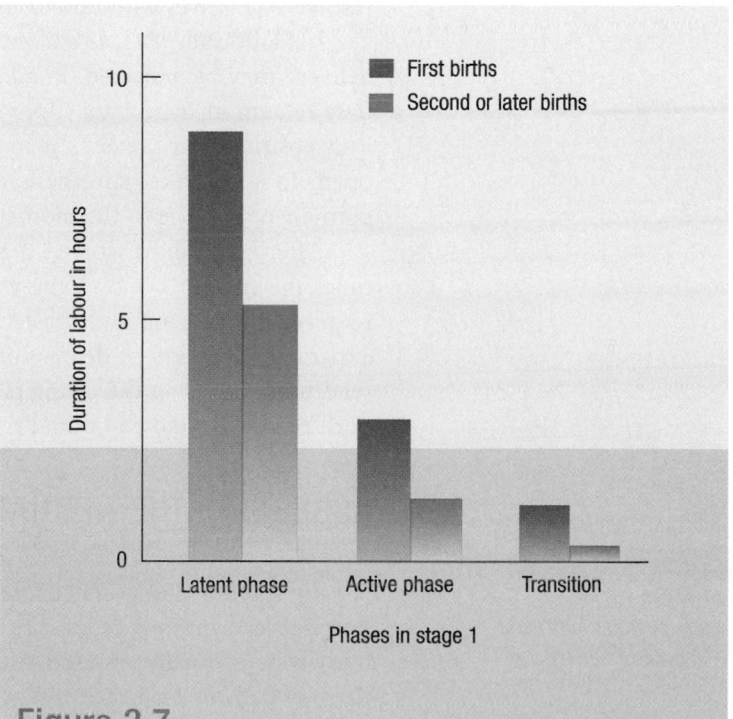

Figure 3.7

Typical pattern of the stages of labour for first births and subsequent births.

(*Source:* Based on Biswas & Craigo, 1994, from Figures 10–16, p. 216 and 10–17, p. 217.)

positions are nearly all delivered through an abdominal incision (a *Caesarean section*) rather than vaginally.

Though most physicians agree that a breech presentation requires a Caesarean delivery, the procedure itself is somewhat controversial. Critics argue that the operation is often performed unnecessarily. There are concerns about possible increased risk due to complications and the increased health care cost arising from unnecessary Caesarean sections. In the late 1960s, only about 5% of babies in Canada were delivered by Caesarean section. By 2001 the frequency of surgical delivery had risen above 21% (Health Canada, 2003b), among the highest in the world. The Society of Obstetricians and Gynecologists of Canada (SOGC) does not promote caesarean section on demand and recommends that the decision to have an elective caesarean delivery be based on an informed discussion about risks and benefits between a woman and her doctor. (SOGC, 2004).

BIRTH COMPLICATIONS During the process of birth, some babies go into *fetal distress,* signalled by a sudden change in heart rate. In most cases, doctors don't know why a baby experiences fetal distress. However, one cause of distress is pressure on the umbilical cord. For example, if the cord becomes lodged between the baby's head and the cervix, each contraction will push the baby's head against the cord. The collapsed blood vessels can no longer carry blood to and from the baby. When this happens, the baby experiences **anoxia**, or oxygen deprivation. Anoxia can result in death or brain damage, but doctors can prevent long-term effects by acting quickly to surgically deliver infants who experience distress (Handley-Derry et al., 1997).

anoxia
oxygen deprivation experienced by a fetus during labour and/or delivery

Infants may also dislocate their shoulders or hips during birth. Some experience fractures, and in others, nerves that control facial muscles are compressed, causing temporary paralysis on one side of the face. Such complications are usually not serious and resolve themselves with little or no treatment.

If a labouring woman's blood pressure suddenly increases or decreases, a Caesarean delivery may be indicated. In addition, some women's labour progresses so slowly that they remain in stage 1 for more than 24 hours. This can happen if the infant's head is in a position that prevents it from exerting enough pressure on the cervix to force it open. In such cases, surgery is often indicated, because continuing labour can cause permanent damage to the mother's body.

After birth, most women require a period of a month or so to recover. During this time, the mother's body experiences a variety of hormonal changes, including those required for nursing and for returning to the normal menstrual cycle. A few women experience a period of depression after giving birth (a potential problem that you will read more about in the chapters on early adulthood). However, most recover quickly, both physically and emotionally, from the ordeal of pregnancy and birth.

ASSESSING THE NEONATE

neonate
baby between birth and 1 month of age

A baby is referred to as a **neonate** for the first month of life. The health of babies born in hospitals and birthing centres, as well as most who are delivered at home by professional midwives, is usually assessed with the *Apgar scale* (Apgar, 1953). The baby receives a score of 0, 1, or 2 on each of five criteria, listed in **Table 3.6**. A maximum score of 10 is fairly unusual immediately after birth, because most infants are still somewhat blue in the fingers and toes at that stage. At a second assessment, usually 5 minutes after birth, however, 85–90% of infants score 9 or 10. Any score of 7 or better indicates that the baby is in no danger. A score of 4, 5, or 6 usually means that the baby needs help establishing normal breathing patterns; a score of 3 or below indicates a baby in critical condition.

TABLE 3.6	The Apgar Scale		
	Score Assigned		
Aspect Observed	**0**	**1**	**2**
Heart rate	Absent	< 100 beats per minute	> 100 beats per minute
Respiratory rate	No breathing	Weak cry and shallow breathing	Good cry and regular breathing
Muscle tone	Flaccid	Some flexion of extremities	Well flexed extremities
Response to stimulation of feet	None	Some motion	Crying
Colour	Blue; pale	Body pink, extremities blue	Completely pink

(*Source:* Francis, Self, & Horowitz, 1987, pp. 731–732.)

Standard screening procedures across Canada have been expanded to include the detection of rare metabolic disorders in newborns (Dyack, 2004). New *tandem mass spectrometry* technology is capable of running multiple tests at the same time in an efficient and cost effective way. This means that inborn metabolic errors can now be detected presymptomatically, which allows for early treatment measures and better outcomes for infants and their families.

Health professionals often use the *Brazelton Neonatal Behavioral Assessment Scale* to track a newborn's development over about the first 2 weeks following birth (Brazelton & Nugent, 1995). A health professional examines the neonate's responses to stimuli, reflexes, muscle tone, alertness, cuddliness, and ability to quiet or soothe herself after being upset. Scores on this test can be helpful in identifying children who may have significant neurological problems.

A new device, the *Nipissing District Developmental Screen* (NDDS), is a comprehensive Canadian screening tool that assists professionals and parents to identify various aspects of a child's development that may require early intervention. The NDDS can be used with children aged 1 month to 6 years to screen for problems in any of these critical areas: vision, hearing, speech, language, communication, gross motor, fine motor, cognitive, social/emotional, and self-help. This culturally sensitive tool is now being used in many jurisdictions across Canada and is available in English, French, Spanish, and Chinese. (**NDDS** webpage: **http://www.ndds.ca**).

Critical Thinking

New technology developed at Toronto's Hospital for Sick Children can screen a newborn's first bowel movement (meconium) for telltale signs that a mother drank too much alcohol during her pregnancy, thus putting her baby at risk for *Fetal Alcohol Spectrum Disorder* (FASD). Early detection can aid early intervention, but detractors say universal automatic testing is a violation of a mother's rights and comes too late to prevent harm to the baby. What are some key pros and cons of standard meconium testing for both mother and baby?

LBW infants' chances of survival are better when they receive care in a neonatal intensive care unit. (*Photo:* Susan Leavines/Photo Researchers)

LOW BIRTH WEIGHT

Classification of a neonate's weight is another important factor in assessment. All neonates below 2500 grams are classified as having **low birth weight (LBW)**. The proportion of LBW infants is relatively stable in Canada, ranging between 5.4 and 5.7% of newborns, but hospitalization rates are higher for LBW infants and the incidence of illness and mortality is also elevated (Canadian Institute of Child Health, 2000a).

low birth weight (LBW)
newborn weight below 2500 grams

Most LBW infants are *preterm*, or born before the 38th week of gestation. However, it is possible for an infant to have completed 38 weeks or more of gestation and still be an LBW baby. In addition, some preterm babies weigh the right amount for their gestational age, while others are smaller than expected. These *small-for-date* neonates appear to have suffered from retarded fetal growth and, as a group, have poorer prognoses than do infants who weigh an appropriate amount for their gestational age.

LBW infants display markedly lower levels of responsiveness at birth and in the early months of life. Those born more than 6 weeks early also often suffer from *respiratory distress syndrome* (also referred to as *hyaline membrane disease*). Their poorly developed lungs cause serious breathing difficulties. In 1990, physicians began treating this problem by administering surfactant (the chemical that makes it possible for the lungs to exchange oxygen and carbon dioxide in the blood) to preterm neonates, a therapy that has reduced the rate of death among very-low-birth-weight infants by about 30% (Corbet, Long, Schumacher, Gerdes, & Cotton, 1995; Schwartz, Anastasia, Scanlon, & Kellogg, 1994).

The Real World
Parenting
Singing to Your Newborn

Singing to newborns is a behaviour that has been found everywhere in the world, and has been a serious interest of Canadian researchers Sandra Trehub and Tonya Bergeson of the University of Toronto and Laurel Trainor and her colleagues at McMaster University. Just as they do when speaking to a newborn or an older infant, both mothers and fathers sing to infants with a unique singing style that includes a high-pitched tone and exaggerated rhythms (Bergeson & Trehub, 1999; Trainor, Clark, Huntley, & Adams, 1997; Trehub et al., 1997). Remarkably, researchers have found that newborns as young as 2 days old can distinguish among videotaped adults who are singing to babies, to other adults, or to no audience (Masataka, 1999). These findings suggest that the characteristics of the infant-directed singing style, as well as the ability to recognize it, may be inborn.

Researchers have identified two universal categories of songs for newborns: lullabies and playsongs. Songs of even tempo that are composed of smoothly connected notes are classified as lullabies. A good example in English is

"Rock-a-Bye Baby." Songs that feature sharp disconnections between notes, often accompanied by gestures, are playsongs. The English song "The Itsy-Bitsy Spider" is such a song.

Lullabies and playsongs elicit different responses from infants. Babies respond to lullabies by turning their attention toward themselves and playing with their hands or sucking their thumbs (Rock, Trainor, & Addison, 1999). In contrast, they display externally directed responses to playsongs. Infants listening to playsongs wriggle, smile, and behave in ways that seem to encourage adults to continue singing (Rock et al., 1999). Adults seem to have an intuitive understanding of infants' responses to the two types of songs and can easily determine which type of song a videotaped baby is hearing (Rock et al., 1999). Thus, it isn't surprising that parents the world over use the two types of songs to regulate infant behaviour. Lullabies help calm them, and playsongs entertain them.

However, being sung to may make important contributions to babies' development as well. One study found that preterm newborns in

a neonatal intensive care nursery who were sung to three times a day for 20 minutes over a 4-day period ate more, gained weight faster, and were discharged from the hospital earlier than infants who were not sung to (Coleman, Pratt, Stoddard, Gerstmann, & Abel, 1997). Remarkably, too, the physiological functioning of babies who were sung to (as measured by variables such as oxygen saturation levels in their bloodstreams) was superior.

Some developmentalists speculate that singing to infants is linked to language development because important milestones in singing and speech—the first songs and the first words—appear at the same time (Chen-Hafteck, 1997). Others theorize that stimulation of the part of the brain used to perceive songs may enhance intellectual development. However, the greatest effect of parents' singing and babies' reactions to it may be communication of a mutual "I love you" message that helps to establish a lasting emotional bond between parent and child (Bergeson & Trehub, 1999).

Development in the Information Age

The Youngest Celebrities

The Information Age was just beginning when Elzire Dionne, a Canadian housewife, gave birth to five identical girls in 1934. The doctor who delivered the babies notified the local newspaper, whose reporters telegraphed the information to news agencies around the world. The Dionne quintuplets became instant celebrities. Well-wishers overwhelmed them with letters and gifts. Publicity-seeking manufacturers sent them diapers, clothes, toys, and baby food.

Today, it takes more than five babies to capture public attention. Births of quadruplets and quintuplets, though certainly not commonplace, rate only a few local headlines. However, the McCaughey septuplets, born in 1997, and the Chukwu octuplets, born in 1998, became international sensations. In fact, when the octuplets' mother was hospitalized during the last 2 months of her pregnancy, the hospital staff spent almost as much time managing the horde of reporters that hovered near the labour and delivery unit 24 hours a day as they did taking care of Nkem Chukwu, the babies' mother (Hellinghausen, 1999).

Health care professionals worry that the media attention given to multiple births obscures the more typical outcomes of pregnancies involving multiple fetuses (McCullough, 1998). In most cases, they say, pregnancies involving more than three fetuses end in prenatal or neonatal death of all of them. They also fear that the rosy portrait of multiple births painted in the press may cause couples to seek fertility-drug treatment to deliberately pursue such births.

Reproductive specialists are also concerned about the possibility that the news media so strongly link fertility drugs with multiple births that infertile couples may forgo such treatment because they think such a birth is always the outcome. Even with fertility drugs, experts say, multiple pregnancy is still the exception rather than the rule. In addition, reproductive specialists do everything possible to avoid multiple pregnancy because of its inherent risks.

(Photo: CORBIS)

The majority of LBW babies who weigh more than 1500 grams and who are not small-for-date catch up to their normal peers within the first few years of life. But those below 1500 grams remain smaller than normal and have significantly higher rates of long-term health problems, lower intelligence test scores, and more problems in school (Breslau et al., 1994; Hack et al., 1994). In fact, 40–50% of such babies show some kind of significant problem later.

An LBW neonate's general health also makes a difference. For example, LBW babies who experience bleeding in the brain immediately after birth are more likely to have later problems (Bendersky & Lewis, 1994). The economic circumstances of an LBW infant's family matter as well. Children in low-income families are more likely to suffer from long-term effects of low birth weight, such as attention problems, than are those who grow up in more affluent homes (Breslau & Chilcoat, 2000).

Boys are more likely than girls to show long-term effects of low birth weight. In fact, one recent study involving more than 700 6-year-olds found a higher rate of learning disabilities and other problems in LBW boys than among their normal-birth-weight (NBW) peers (Johnson & Breslau, 2000). By contrast, LBW girls did not differ at all from their NBW counterparts. The difference between LBW and NBW boys persisted when they were examined again at age 11.

Critical Thinking

What three pieces of advice would you give a pregnant friend after reading this chapter?

Before Going On

- What happens in each of the three stages of labour?

- What choices do most mothers in Canada have with respect to birth attendants, drugs to relieve pain, and birth location? What are some of the complications that can happen during birth?

- Explain how neonates are assessed, and list the risks of low birth weight.

Summary

Conception and Genetics

- At conception, the 23 chromosomes from the sperm join with the 23 chromosomes from the ovum to make up the set of 46 that will be reproduced in each cell of the new individual.

- Geneticists distinguish between the genotype (the pattern of inherited genes) and the phenotype (the individual's observable characteristics). Genes are transmitted from parents to children according to complex rules that include the dominant-recessive pattern, the polygenic pattern, and multifactorial inheritance.

Pregnancy and Prenatal Development

- Pregnancy is divided into three approximately equal trimesters.

- Prenatal development occurs in three stages of unequal length (germinal, embryonic, fetal) that are marked by specific developmental milestones.

- During the embryonic period, an XY embryo secretes the hormone testosterone, which stimulates the growth of male genitalia and shifts the brain into a "male" pattern. Boys are more active, develop more slowly skeletally, are bigger at birth, and are more vulnerable to most forms of prenatal stress.

- The fetus is responsive to stimuli and appears to learn in the womb. Prenatal temperamental differences (for example, activity level) persist into infancy and childhood, and some aspects of the prenatal sensory environment may be important to future development.

Problems in Prenatal Development

- Genes for specific diseases can cause a variety of disorders at conception.

- Abnormal numbers of chromosomes or damage to chromosomes causes a number of serious disorders, including Down syndrome.

- Some diseases contracted by the mother may cause abnormalities or disease in the child. These include rubella, AIDS, syphilis, gonorrhea, and genital herpes.

- Drugs such as alcohol and nicotine appear to have harmful effects on the developing fetus; effects of drugs depend on the timing of exposure and the dosage.

- If the mother suffers from poor nutrition, her fetus faces increased risks of stillbirth, low birth weight, and death during the first year of life. Older mothers and very young mothers also run increased risks, as do their infants. Long-term, severe depression or chronic physical illnesses in the mother may also increase the risk of complications of pregnancy or difficulties in the infant.

- Several methods of prenatal diagnosis and treatment of birth defects or fetal abnormalities have become available in recent years.

Birth and the Neonate

- Most babies are delivered by physicians in Canada. In uncomplicated low-risk pregnancies, delivery at home or in a birthing centre is as safe as hospital delivery.

- The normal birth process has three parts: dilation and effacement, delivery, and placental delivery. Most drugs given to the mother during delivery pass through to the infant's bloodstream and have short-term effects on infant responsiveness and feeding patterns.

- Doctors, nurses, and midwives use the Apgar scale to assess a neonate's health immediately after birth.

- Neonates weighing less than 2500 grams are designated as having low birth weight. The lower the weight, the greater the risk of significant lasting problems, such as low intelligence test scores or learning disabilities.

Key Terms

assisted human reproduction (AHR) (p. 58)

amnion (p. 00)

anoxia (p. 86)

body mass index (BMI) (p. 78)

cephalocaudal pattern (p. 66)

chromosomes (p. 57)

congenital anomaly (p. 72)

deoxyribonucleic acid (DNA) (p. 58)

dominant-recessive pattern (p. 60)

embryonic stage (p. 66)

fetal stage (p. 68)

gametes (p. 57)

genes (p. 58)

genotype (p. 60)

germinal stage (p. 66)

glial cells (p. 68)

gonads (p. 68)

low birth weight (LBW) (p. 87)

multifactorial inheritance (p. 63)

mutagens (p. 80)

neonate (p. 86)

neurons (p. 66)

organogenesis (p. 68)

phenotype (p. 60)

placenta (p. 66)

polygenic inheritance (p. 62)

proximodistal pattern (p. 66)

teratogens (p. 74)

umbilical cord (p. 66)

viability (p. 69)

zygote (p. 58)

Weblinks

Multiple Births/Naissances multiples Canada
www.multiplebirthscanada.org/english/index.php
This site seeks to improve the quality of life for multiple birth individuals and their families in Canada through an extensive network of local chapters, health care professionals, and organizations. MBC provides national support, education, research and advocacy to those with a personal or professional interest in multiple birth issues.

Society of Obstetricians and Gynaecologists of Canada
www.sogc.org/multiple/index_e.shtml
SOGC provides clinical practice guidelines, information on continuing professional development, discussions of women's health issues, and links to other valuable health resources.

Childbirth.Org
www.childbirth.org
Childbirth.org offers a wide variety of information on pregnancy, childbirth, and postpartum issues, including online consultations with pre- and postnatal care professionals.

Motherisk
www.motherisk.org/
A Canadian source for information about the safety or risk of teratogens and mutagens during pregnancy and lactation.

Nutrition for a Healthy Pregnancy: National Guidelines for the Childbearing Years
www.hc-sc.gc.ca/hpfb-dgpsa/onpp-bppn/national_guidelines_entire_e.html
These Health Canada guidelines provide evidence-based, nutrition-related information for women during the preconception and prenatal periods.

Policy Question

What Legal Protection Exists for the Pregnant Mother and Her Fetus?

Society has developed laws to protect a person's rights while prescribing consequences for those who violate those rights. In the case of a pregnant woman and her fetus, society wants to act in the best interest of both. However, because of the integral relationship between mother and fetus we are sometimes faced with a legal dilemma when their respective needs conflict. The relationship between mother and fetus from a physical point of view seems obvious, but when we try to define the relationship in legal terms we are faced with an imperfect description of that relationship.

We can look to the history of Canadian law for guidance regarding what behaviour constitutes a criminal act. The Canadian Criminal Code specifies what acts against a human being are criminal acts, but it does not recognize the fetus as a human being and therefore we do not have laws that recognize the killing of a fetus as homicide or infanticide. This state of affairs has a long tradition that is based in the common law, which did not recognize a fetus as a person until it was born alive. This line of thinking was incorporated into the first Canadian Criminal Code of 1892 and persists to this day. There have been laws against procuring a miscarriage (an abortion), and in 1969 Section 287 of the criminal code made abortions illegal. However, doctors were exempted from prosecution if a hospital ethical review committee deemed that the mother's health or life was endangered if she carried the fetus to full term. In 1982 the Canadian Charter of Rights and Freedoms stated in Section 7 that "everyone has the right to life, liberty and security of

the person and the right not to be deprived thereof. . . ." At about the same time, Dr. Henry Morgentaler was testing the "lawfulness" of the abortion law of the day by setting up nonhospital abortion clinics. In 1988 his case went before the Supreme Court of Canada, which ruled that the abortion law violated Section 7 of the Charter in that the law interfered with a woman's body and liberty. As a result the abortion law, Section 287 (Department of Justice Canada, 2001a), was modified. This essentially decriminalized abortions, and by implication a fetus is not protected under the Charter. Henceforth, abortions, at any stage of pregnancy, have not been prohibited in Canada.

At the end of the 20th century this turn of events led to some challenging legal questions with regard to the rights of a pregnant woman versus the status and well-being of her fetus. Three court challenges in particular exemplify the difficulty we have in deciding what to do when a fetus, and subsequently a child that has been born, are at risk of harm.

What is the legal status of the pregnant mother and her fetus in Canada? The three court cases supply clues.

The first case involves the Winnipeg Child Family Services and a woman who was 5 months pregnant. The agency wanted to detain her in a health centre for treatment of her glue-sniffing addiction until her child was born because glue sniffing can produce permanent nervous-system damage in the developing fetus. Two of the woman's three children had already been made wards of the state at birth because they had been born with brain damage associated with

glue sniffing. The intention of the social agency was to protect the health of the fetus until it was born, but in doing so it was judged to be in violation of the mother's rights and freedom.

The case made its way to the Supreme Court of Canada, which in 1997 ruled that the mother's rights prevail over those of the fetus. The decision was based upon the Charter of Rights and Freedoms, which in its present form applies only to human beings (not to fetuses). Therefore, in this instance, protecting the fetus by detaining the mother for treatment violated the liberties of the mother. Moreover, it was noted that if this mother could be detained for sniffing glue then the ruling could be extended and applied to all pregnant women. It would set a precedent that would allow pregnant

(*Photo:* Myrleen Cate/MaXx Images, Inc.)

women to be scrutinized and incarcerated for lifestyle choices that allegedly cause harm to the fetus. This leads to questions about who would set the standard for appropriate maternal behaviour. The judgment in this case reaffirmed that a fetus has no legal rights (although a fetus does retain a moral right to be treated well).

The second case, Dobson v. Dobson, involves a New Brunswick woman who was 27 weeks pregnant. She had been driving on a snow-covered road when she lost control and collided with a pickup truck. The child, a boy, was later delivered by Caesarean section and has permanent mental and physical problems attributable to the accident. The mother's father was suing her for negligence on behalf of the boy. There was already a legal precedent that permits legal action to be taken by a child born alive against a third party for injuries that the child incurred while in the womb. For example, children of mothers who took thalidomide for morning sickness in the 1950s were able to receive compensation from the manufacturer of the drug. The drug caused birth defects such as missing or deformed limbs, which limited the children's ability to have a full life. The courts were asked to decide if the mother in Dobson v. Dobson could be sued as if she were a third party to the case. The New Brunswick Courts ruled that the boy was indeed entitled to compensation. An appeal of this ruling was sent to the Supreme Court in 1999 and was overturned on several grounds. It was noted that the relationship between a mother and her fetus is unlike any other.

Mother and fetus are essentially one until birth. Therefore no analogy can be made between the role of the mother and that of a third party in terms of any damage committed upon the fetus. Furthermore, there is no practical way to determine what standard of care a pregnant mother should have to live up to in caring for her fetus that wouldn't violate her privacy and autonomy.

The third case concerns Brenda Drummond, an Ontario woman who was charged with attempted murder and failing to provide the necessities of life. The woman apparently kept her pregnancy hidden from co-workers and her husband, and late in her pregnancy she fired a pellet through her vagina into the head of her full-term fetus. The boy was born 2 days later and over the following week his health deteriorated to a critical level. A brain scan was taken and revealed a pellet lodged in his skull. An operation removed the pellet and the boy recovered, but the mother didn't explain what had happened until after the operation.

In an Ontario Provincial Court the judge ruled that at the time of the shooting the fetus could not be legally considered a victim separate from its mother. Thus, because the fetus has no separate rights in law, no crime was committed and the case was dismissed. However, the mother was then charged with the lesser offence of failing to provide the necessities of life for her newborn child when she failed to inform the doctors that she had shot her son, thereby allowing his health to be dangerously compromised. She pleaded guilty to this charge and was given a suspended sentence.

YOUR TURN

- What do you think the result would be if the outcome of the court decision were different in each case? For instance, what problems do you foresee if pregnant women could be forced into treatment, or what may happen if children could sue their mothers for damages that were sustained prenatally?

- Describe a hypothetical legal standard of conduct for pregnant women.

- If Canadian laws were changed to protect the fetus from a mother's potentially damaging behaviour, how do you think the laws should address the following concerns? How would the rights of Canadian mothers be affected? What lifestyle behaviours of the mother would be considered harmful to the fetus? Who would decide how much protection is sufficient? How would you enforce such a law?

- In what ways would forcing a woman to seek treatment do more harm than good?

- To what extent do you think society is at least indirectly responsible for harm to the fetus?

David Young-Wolff/PhotoEdit

CHAPTER 4

PHYSICAL AND COGNITIVE DEVELOPMENT IN INFANCY

One of the most fascinating features of babies' behaviour is their "busyness." They seem to be constantly on the go, manipulating objects with their hands, looking at them, feeling them, tasting them, and making sounds with them. At times, such activities seem purposeless, but they provide just the kind of skill practice and information infants need for both physical and cognitive development. Considering the energy it takes to keep up with infants' level of activity, it's little wonder their parents seem to be exhausted much of the time.

In this chapter, you will read about the processes through which a relatively unskilled newborn becomes a 2-year-old who can move about efficiently, formulate goals and plans, and use words. You will also learn about important variations across individuals and groups. While you read, keep the following questions in mind:

- What changes occur in infants' bodies, and how can their health be maintained?
- How do babies think, learn, and remember?
- How does language begin to develop?
- Can individual differences in intelligence be identified in infancy, and is development different for preterm babies, boys and girls, and infants in different cultures?

PHYSICAL CHANGES

Babies grow 25 to 30 centimetres and triple their body weight in the first year of life. By age 2 for girls and about 2 $\frac{1}{2}$ for boys, toddlers are half as tall as they will be as adults. This means a 2- to 2 $\frac{1}{2}$-year-old's adult height can be reliably predicted by doubling his or her current height. But 2-year-olds have proportionately much larger heads than do adults—which they need to hold their nearly full-sized brains.

THE BRAIN AND THE NERVOUS SYSTEM

The body's systems grow and develop at different rates and at different times. The reproductive system, for instance, is completely formed at birth but doesn't grow or change much until puberty. In contrast, the brain and nervous system develop rapidly during the first 2 years. **Figure 4.1** shows the main structures of the brain. At birth, the midbrain and the medulla are the most fully developed. These two parts, both in the lower part of the skull and connected to the spinal cord, regulate vital functions such as heartbeat and respiration, as well as attention, sleeping, waking, elimination, and movement of the head and neck—all actions a newborn can perform at least moderately well. The least-developed part of the brain at birth is the cortex, the convoluted grey matter that wraps around the midbrain and is involved in perception, body movement, thinking, and language.

SYNAPTIC DEVELOPMENT You'll recall from **Chapter 3** that all brain structures are composed of two basic types of cells: neurons and glial cells. Virtually all of a person's full complement of both types of cells are already present at birth. The developmental process after birth primarily involves the creation of **synapses**, or connections between neurons. Synapse development results from growth of both dendrites and axons (look back at **Figure 3.3** on page 69). *Synaptogenesis*, the creation of synapses, occurs rapidly in the cortex during the first 2 years after birth, resulting in a tripling of the overall weight of the brain during that period (Nowakowski, 1987). However, brain development is not entirely smooth and continuous. An initial burst of synapse formation in

synapses
connections between neurons

about the first year after birth is followed by **synaptic pruning** in each area of the brain, as redundant pathways and connections are eliminated and the "wiring circuitry" is made more efficient (Huttenlocher, 1994).

For example, early in development, each muscle cell seems to develop synaptic connections with several motor neurons (nerve cells that carry impulses to muscles) in the spinal cord. But after the pruning process has occurred, each muscle fibre is connected to only one neuron. Some neurophysiologists have suggested that the initial surge of synapse formation follows a built-in pattern (Greenough, Black, & Wallace, 1987). The organism seems to be programmed to create certain kinds of neural connections and makes an abundance of them, creating redundant pathways. According to this argument, the pruning that takes place beginning at around 18 months is a response to experience and results in selective retention of the most efficient pathways. Putting it briefly, "Experience does not create tracings on a blank tablet; rather, experience erases some of them" (Bertenthal & Campos, 1987). However, neurophysiologists point out that some synapses are formed entirely as a result of experience, and that synaptogenesis continues throughout our lives as we learn new skills (Johnson, 2001).

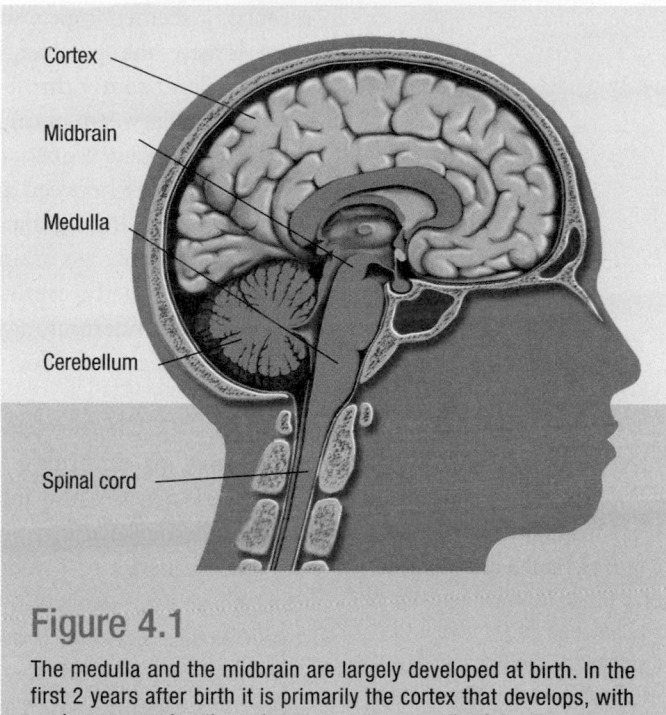

Figure 4.1

The medulla and the midbrain are largely developed at birth. In the first 2 years after birth it is primarily the cortex that develops, with each neuron going through an enormous growth of dendrites and a vast increase in synapses.

Interestingly, pruning does not occur at the same time in all parts of the brain. For example, synapses in the portions of the brain that have to do with language comprehension and production achieve their maximum density when a child is about 3 years old. In contrast, the part of the cortex devoted to vision is maximally dense when an infant is 4 months old, and rapid pruning occurs thereafter (Huttenlocher, 1994).

One of the most intriguing points about this pattern of development is that the combination of the early surge of synaptic growth and the later pruning means that a 1-year-old actually has denser dendrites and synapses than an adult does—a piece of information that has surprised many psychologists. Even at age 4, when the early burst of pruning has occurred in all areas of the brain, a child's synaptic density is about twice that of an adult. Pruning continues in spurts throughout childhood and adolescence.

Developmentalists draw several important implications from information about neurological development. First, they conclude that a kind of "programmed plasticity" is built into the human organism. **Plasticity** refers to the brain's remarkable ability to reorganize itself, to make the "wiring circuitry" more efficient—it allows uncommitted neurons to form new connections and to use compensatory pathways following some injury (Johnson, 1998, 2001). But this plasticity is greater in infancy than it is later. Perhaps paradoxically, the period of greatest plasticity is also the period in which the child may be most vulnerable to major deficits—just as a fetus is most vulnerable to teratogens during the time of most rapid growth of any body system. Thus, a young infant needs sufficient stimulation and order in his environment to maximize the early period of rapid growth and plasticity (de Haan, Luciana, Maslone, Matheny, & Richards, 1994). A really inadequate diet or a serious lack of stimulation in the early months may thus have subtle but long-range effects on the child's later cognitive progress.

Second, new information about the continuation of the pruning process throughout childhood and adolescence and into adulthood has forced developmental psychologists to change their ideas about the links between brain development and behaviour. If the brain is almost completely organized by age 2, as most developmentalists believed until

synaptic pruning
process by which unused or unnecessary neural pathways and connections are eliminated

plasticity
ability of the brain to reorganize neural pathways and connections

recently, it seemed logical to assume that whatever developments occurred after that age were largely the product of experience. But researchers now know that the brain changes significantly throughout the entire human lifespan and that there is a two-way interaction between brain development and input from the environment (Johnson, 2001). These facts reopen all the questions about brain–behaviour connections. Is there a language spurt between ages 2 and 3 because that is when the relevant portion of the brain is undergoing significant reorganization? Or does the spurt in language behaviour induce changes in the brain? Researchers do not yet have enough data to answer such questions, but the theoretical climate has definitely shifted toward greater interest in the neurological underpinnings of development across the lifespan and away from the assumption that brain development is complete very early in life.

MYELINIZATION Another crucial process in the development of neurons is the creation of sheaths, or coverings, around individual axons, which insulate them from one another electrically and improve their conductivity. These sheaths are made of a substance called *myelin*; the process of developing the sheath is called **myelinization**.

The sequence of myelinization follows both cephalocaudal and proximodistal patterns (these were defined in **Chapter 3**). Thus, nerves serving muscle cells in the hands are myelinized earlier than those serving the feet. Myelinization is most rapid during the first 2 years after birth, but it continues at a slower pace throughout childhood and adolescence. For example, the parts of the brain that govern motor movements are not fully myelinized until a child is about 6 years old (Todd, Swarzenski, Rossi, & Visconti, 1995).

Other structures take even longer to become myelinized. For example, the **reticular formation** is the part of the brain responsible for keeping your attention on what you're doing and for helping you sort out important and unimportant information. Myelinization of the reticular formation begins in infancy but continues in spurts across childhood and adolescence. In fact, the process isn't complete until a person is in her mid-20s (Spreen, Risser, & Edgell, 1995). Consequently, during the first 2 years, infants improve their ability to focus on a task. Likewise, a 12-year-old is much better at concentrating than an infant but is still fairly inefficient when compared with an adult.

REFLEXES, SENSORY ABILITIES, AND BEHAVIOURAL STATES

Changes in the brain result in predictable changes in babies' reflexes, sensory capacities, and patterns of waking and sleeping. In fact, such changes, or their lack, can be important indicators of nervous system health.

REFLEXES Humans are born with many **adaptive reflexes** that help them survive. Some, such as automatically sucking any object that enters the mouth, disappear in infancy or childhood. Others protect us against harmful stimuli over the whole lifespan. These include withdrawal from a painful stimulus and the opening and closing of the pupil of the eye in response to variations in brightness. Weak or absent adaptive reflexes in neonates suggest that the brain is not functioning properly and that the baby requires additional assessment.

The purposes of **primitive reflexes**, so called because they are controlled by the less sophisticated parts of the brain (the medulla and the midbrain), are less clear. For example, if you make a loud noise or startle a baby in some other way, you'll see her throw her arms outward and arch her back, a pattern that is part of the *Moro*, or *startle, reflex*. Stroke the bottom of her foot and she will splay out her toes and then curl them in, a reaction called the *Babinski reflex*. By about 6 months of age, primitive reflexes begin to disappear. If such reflexes persist past about 6 months, the baby may have some kind of neurological problem.

myelinization
a process in the development of neurons in which sheaths of a substance called myelin gradually cover individual axons and electrically insulate them from one another, which improves the conductivity of the nerve

reticular formation
the part of the brain that regulates attention

adaptive reflexes
reflexes such as sucking that help newborns survive; some adaptive reflexes persist throughout life

primitive reflexes
reflexes controlled by primitive parts of the brain; these reflexes disappear by about 6 months of age

Although primitive infant reflexes disappear with age, stimulation of reflexes may facilitate later motor development. For instance, University of Toronto psychologist Philip Zelazo has found that infants who were encouraged to exercise the stepping reflex were more likely to spontaneously display the stepping movements and began walking at an earlier age (Zelazo et al., 1993; Zelazo, Zelazo, & Kolb, 1972).

SENSORY ABILITIES **Visual acuity**, the ability to see details from various distances, is fairly poor in newborns compared with adults. However, if objects are positioned within 20 to 25 centimetres of a baby's eyes, he can focus on them. Newborns can also track slowly moving objects with their eyes, and they learn to recognize their mothers' faces soon after birth. Moreover, researchers have recently discovered that measures of visual development in early infancy, like changes in adaptive and primitive reflexes, are correlated with mental development at 18 months (Birch, Garfield, Hoffman, Uauy, & Birch, 2000). Consequently, a slow rate of visual development in the first 4 months may mean that a baby is suffering from some kind of general developmental problem.

Babies respond to the same four categories of tastes (sweet, sour, bitter, and salty) as adults do. In addition, they can identify familiar body odours and can even discriminate their mother's smell from the smell of another woman (Porter, Making, Davis, & Christensen, 1992). Likewise, they display sensitivity to temperature by increasing physical activity in a cold room and to touch by becoming calmer when stroked and crying in protest when pricked with a needle by a nurse drawing blood for a laboratory test.

BEHAVIOURAL STATES Researchers have described five different states of sleep and wakefulness in neonates, referred to as **states of consciousness** and summarized in **Table 4.1.** Most infants move through these states in the same sequence: from deep sleep to lighter sleep and then to alert wakefulness and fussing. After they are fed, they become drowsy and drop back into deep sleep. The cycle repeats itself about every 2 hours.

Neonates sleep as much as 90% of the time, as much in the daytime as at night (Whitney & Thoman, 1994). By 6 or 8 weeks of age, the total amount of sleep per day has dropped somewhat and signs of day/night sleep rhythms (called *circadian rhythms*) become evident. Babies of this age begin to sleep through two or three 2-hour cycles in sequence without coming to full wakefulness, and are thus often said to have started to

This 4-week-old baby is using the inborn adaptive reflex of sucking. (*Photo:* Getty Images)

visual acuity
the ability to see details at a distance

states of consciousness
different states of sleep and wakefulness in infants

TABLE 4.1	The Basic States of Infant Sleep and Wakefulness
State	**Characteristics**
Deep sleep	Eyes closed, regular breathing, no movement except occasional startles
Active sleep	Eyes closed, irregular breathing, small twitches, no gross body movement
Quiet awake	Eyes open, no major body movement, regular breathing
Active awake	Eyes open, movements of the head, limbs, and trunk, irregular breathing
Crying, fussing	Eyes partly or entirely closed, vigorous diffuse movement with crying or fussing sounds

(*Sources:* Based on the work of Hutt, Leonard, & Prechtl, 1969; Parmelee, Wenner, & Schulz, 1964; Prechtl & Beintema, 1964.)

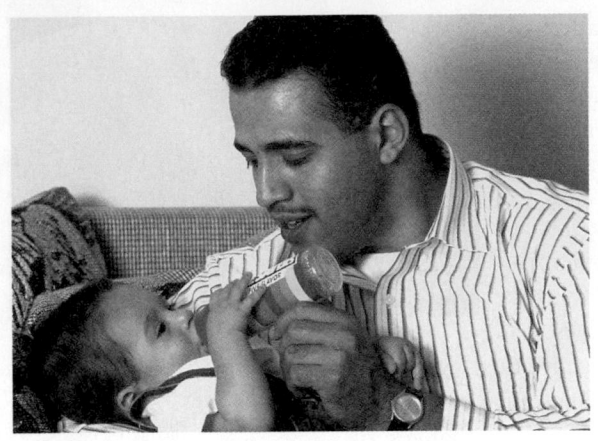

Newborns are quite nearsighted, so they can focus very well at about 25 to 80 centimetres, just the distance between a parent's face and the baby's eyes when the baby is held for feeding.

(*Photo:* Jonathan Nourok/PhotoEdit)

Critical Thinking

What advice would you give to parents who believe that picking up a baby when she cries will "spoil" her?

colic

an infant behaviour pattern involving intense daily bouts of crying, totalling 3 or more hours a day

"sleep through the night." By 6 months, babies are still sleeping a bit over 14 hours per day, but sleep is more regular and predictable. Most have clear nighttime sleep patterns and nap during the day at more predictable times.

Of course, babies vary a lot around these averages. Of the 6-week-old babies in one study, there was one who slept 22 hours per day and another who slept only 8.8 hours per day (Bamford et al., 1990). (Now, *that* must have been one tired set of parents!) And some babies do not develop a long nighttime sleep period until late in the first year of life. Moreover, cultural beliefs play an important role in parents' responses to infants' sleep patterns. For example, North American parents typically see a newborn's erratic sleep cycle as a behaviour problem that requires "fixing" through parental intervention (Harkness, 1998). As a result, they focus a great deal of attention on trying to force babies to sleep through the night. In contrast, European parents are more likely to regard newborns' patterns of sleeping as manifestations of normal development and tend to expect babies to acquire stable sleeping patterns naturally, without parental intervention, during the first 2 years.

Infants have a whole repertoire of cry sounds, with different cries for pain, anger, or hunger. The basic cry, which often signals hunger, is usually a rhythmical pattern: cry, silence, breath, cry, silence, breath, with a kind of whistling sound often accompanying the in-breath. An anger cry is typically louder and more intense, and the pain cry normally has a very abrupt onset—unlike the other two kinds of cries, which usually begin with whimpering or moaning.

Cross-cultural studies suggest that crying increases in frequency over the first 6 weeks and then tapers off (St. James-Roberts, Bowyer, Varghese, & Sawdon, 1994). Moreover, parents across a variety of cultures use very similar techniques to soothe crying infants. Most babies stop crying when they are picked up, held, and talked or sung to. Getting a baby to suck on a pacifier also usually helps. Parents sometimes worry that picking up a crying baby will lead to even more crying. But research suggests that prompt attention to a crying baby in the first 3 months actually leads to less crying later in infancy (Sulkes, 1998).

McGill University Professor of Pediatrics Paul Roumeliotis (2001) estimates that up to 20% of infants suffer from **colic**, a pattern involving intense bouts of crying for no immediately apparent reason such as hunger or a wet diaper, totalling 3 or more hours a day. Typically, colic appears at about 2 weeks of age and then disappears spontaneously at 3 to 4 months. The crying is generally worst in late afternoon or early evening.

Although neither psychologists nor physicians know why colic begins, or why it stops without any intervention, dietary needs have often been blamed as the culprit. To test this common belief, University of Western Ontario medical researchers tracked the feeding patterns of 856 mother-infant pairs of which almost one in four of the infants were rated as colicky (Clifford, Campbell, Speechley, & Gorodzinsky, 2002). They found that there was no significant difference in colic ratings regardless of whether an infant was exclusively breastfed, bottle formula-fed, or fed by a combination of breast milk and nonhuman milk. This study suggests that changing an infant's diet or early weaning is generally uncalled for. It is a difficult pattern to live with, but the good news is that it does go away.

On average, neonates are awake and alert for a total of only 2 to 3 hours each day, and this time is unevenly distributed over a 24-hour period. In other words, the baby may be awake for 15 minutes at 6:00 a.m., another 30 minutes at 1:00 p.m., another 20 minutes at 4:00 p.m. and so on. Over the first 6 months, advances in neurological development enable infants to remain awake and alert for longer periods of time as their patterns of sleeping, crying, and eating become more regular.

OTHER BODY SYSTEMS AND MOTOR SKILLS

Like behavioural states, the acquisition of motor skills also depends on brain development. Substantial changes in other body systems—bones, muscles, and so on—are required as well.

BONES During infancy, bones change in size, number, and composition. Increases in the lengths of the body's long bones—those in the legs and arms—underlie increases in height (Tanner, 1990). Changes in the number and density of bones in particular parts of the body are responsible for improvements in coordinated movement.

For example, at birth, the wrist contains a single mass of cartilage; by 1 year of age, the cartilage has developed into three separate bones. The progressive separation of the wrist bones is one of the factors behind gains in manipulative skills over the first 2 years. Wrist bones continue to differentiate over the next several years until eventually, in adolescence, the wrist has nine separate bones (Tanner, 1990).

The process of bone hardening, called *ossification*, occurs steadily, beginning in the last weeks of prenatal development and continuing through puberty. Bones in different parts of the body harden in a sequence that follows the typical proximodistal and cephalocaudal patterns. Motor development depends on ossification to a large extent. Standing, for example, is impossible if an infant's leg bones are too soft, no matter how well developed the muscles and nervous system are.

MUSCLES The body's full complement of muscle fibres is present at birth, although the fibres are initially small and have a high ratio of water to muscle (Tanner, 1990). In addition, a newborn's muscles contain a fairly high proportion of fat. By 1 year of age, the water content of an infant's muscles is equal to that of an adult, and the ratio of fat to muscle tissue has begun to decline (Tershakovec & Stallings, 1998). Changes in muscle composition lead to increases in strength that enable 1-year-olds to walk, run, jump, climb, and so on.

LUNGS AND HEART The lungs also grow rapidly and become more efficient during the first 2 years (Kercsmar, 1998). Improvements in lung efficiency, together with the increasing strength of heart muscles, give a 2-year-old greater *stamina*, or ability to maintain activity, than a newborn. Consequently, by the end of infancy, children are capable of engaging in fairly long periods of sustained motor activity without rest (often exhausting their parents in the process!).

MOTOR SKILLS Changes in all of the body's systems are responsible for the impressive array of motor skills children acquire in the first 2 years. Developmentalists typically divide these skills into three rough groups: *locomotor skills, nonlocomotor skills*, and *manipulative skills* (Malina, 1982). **Table 4.2** (page 102) summarizes developments in each of these three areas over the first 18 months; it is based primarily on two large studies, one in the United States and one in the Netherlands. The U.S. study involved 381 babies tested by their pediatricians at regular visits during the first 2 years of life (Capute et al., 1984). The Dutch study included 555 babies who had been tested repeatedly for their first 5 years (Den Ouden, Rijken, Brand, Verloove-Vanhorick, & Ruys, 1991). The milestones identified in these two studies were highly similar in sequence, as were the ages at which babies passed each test.

TABLE 4.2	Milestones of Motor Development in the First 2 Years		
Age (in months)	Locomotor Skills	Nonlocomotor Skills	Manipulative Skills
1	Stepping reflex	Lifts head slightly; follows slowly moving objects with eyes	Holds object if placed in hand
2–3		Lifts head up to 90-degree angle when lying on stomach	Begins to swipe at objects in sight
4–6	Rolls over; sits with support; moves on hands and knees ("creeps")	Holds head erect while in sitting position	Reaches for and grasps objects
7–9	Sits without support; crawls		Transfers objects from one hand to the other
10–12	Pulls self up and walks grasping furniture; then walks alone	Squats and stoops	Shows some signs of hand preference; grasps a spoon across palm but has poor aim when moving food to mouth
13–18	Walks backward, sideways; runs (14–20 mos.)	Rolls ball to adult	Stacks two blocks; puts objects into small container and dumps them out

(*Sources:* Capute et al., 1984; Den Ouden et al., 1991.)

Canadian norms are currently being developed as part of University of Manitoba psychologist Warren Eaton's ongoing *Infant Milestone Study*. About 200 babies are being tracked to determine week-to-week changes as they progress toward motor skills milestones. Although the timing of the first time a baby sits, crawls, and walks is variable, the researchers have so far observed a seasonal trend whereby babies born in the spring reach crawling and walking milestones at a younger age (Eaton, 2003).

EXPLAINING MOTOR SKILL DEVELOPMENT The sequence of motor skill development is virtually the same for all children, even those with serious physical or mental handicaps. Intellectually delayed children, for example, move through the various motor milestones more slowly than normal children do, but they do so in the same sequence. Furthermore, motor skill development follows the cephalocaudal and proximodistal patterns. Whenever developmentalists find such consistencies, maturation of some kind seems an obvious explanation (Thelen, 1995).

However, a classic early study of children raised in Iranian orphanages demonstrated that babies who were routinely placed on their backs in cribs learned to walk eventually, but they did so about a year later than babies in less restrictive settings (Dennis, 1960). In contrast, early studies seemed to show that extra practice in such basic skills as sitting and crawling didn't speed up babies' development at all. However, more recent research contradicts this conclusion, including one study showing that very young babies who are given more practice sitting are able to sit upright longer than those without such practice (Zelazo, Zelazo, Cohen, & Zelazo, 1993). Consequently, developmentalists are fairly

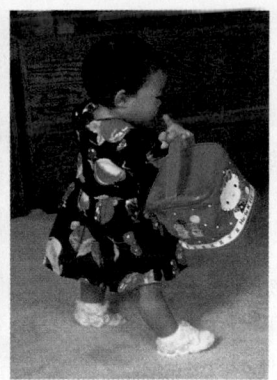

The striking improvements in motor development in the early months are easy to illustrate. Between 6 and 12 months of age, babies progress from sitting alone, to crawling, to walking.
(*Photos: left and right*, © Myrleen Ferguson Cate/PhotoEdit; *centre*, Laura Dwight/PhotoEdit)

certain that severely restricting a baby's movement slows down acquisition of motor skills, but they are less sure about the effects of more typical restrictions, such as keeping babies in playpens for short periods of time, or of motor skills practice.

HEALTH PROMOTION AND WELLNESS

Babies depend on the adults in their environments to help them stay healthy. Specifically, they need the right foods in the right amounts, and they need regular medical care.

NUTRITION After several decades of extensive research in many countries, experts agree that, for most infants, breast-feeding is substantially superior nutritionally to bottle-feeding. The Canadian Paediatric Society, the Dietitians of Canada, and Health Canada (Health Canada, 2000a) recommend that breastfeeding should be the sole source of infant nutrition for at least the first 4 months of life (see **The Real World**). Breast milk provides the infant with important antibodies against many kinds of diseases, especially gastrointestinal and upper respiratory infections (Cunningham, Jelliffe, & Jelliffe, 1991). Human breast milk also appears to promote the growth of the nerves and intestinal tract and to contribute to more rapid weight and size gain, and may improve immune system functioning over the long term (Prentice, 1994).

However, Canadian experts caution that breastfeeding is not recommended for all babies (Newman & Pittman, 2003). For example, small amounts of some prescription medications may be passed along to the nursling when breastfed, and these drugs can negatively affect infant behaviour and development (Hale, 2004). Consequently, breast-feeding mothers who are taking any medication should consult their primary care practitioner to determine if safer alternatives are available or whether to stop breast-feeding altogether. In such cases, babies can be fed high-quality infant formula.

Malnutrition in infancy can seriously impair a baby's brain because the nervous system is the most rapidly developing body system during the first 2 years of life. **Macronutrient** malnutrition results from a diet that contains too few calories. Macronutrient malnutrition is the world's leading cause of death of children under the age of 5 (Tershakovec & Stallings, 1998).

When the calorie deficit is severe, a disease called *marasmus* results. Infants with marasmus weigh less than 60% of what they should at their age, and many suffer permanent neurological damage from the disease. Most also suffer from parasitic infections that lead to chronic diarrhea. This condition makes it very difficult to treat marasmus by simply increasing an infant's intake of calories. However, a program of dietary supplementation with formula combined with intravenous feedings and treatment for parasites can reverse marasmus (Tershakovec & Stallings, 1998).

macronutrients
large amounts of carbohydrates, fats, and proteins that are needed for energy and for body- and brain-building elements

The Real World

Parenting
Nutrition from Birth to One Year

In Canada, 82% of mothers initiate breastfeeding of their babies (Health Canada, 2003b), up from just 38% in 1963 (McNally, Hendricks & Horowitz, 1985). However, there is a wide disparity in breastfeeding trends across Canada. Mothers in the western provinces have the highest rates, while mothers in Quebec and the Maritime provinces have had the lowest rates since the 1960s (Health Canada, 1998d, 2003b; Statistics Canada, 2001a). Moreover, breastfeeding practices vary greatly between and within Canadian subcultures. For instance, there is a tendency for recent immigrant mothers to bottle-feed regardless of what the dominant feeding practice was in their home country (Health Canada, 1997a). This tendency is believed to be reflective of the newcomer's perception that formula feeding is the preferred method of feeding infants in Canada and is considered a sign of adaptation to what they perceive as Canadian culture. Within any given subculture, a mother's breastfeeding pattern has more in common with the health beliefs of women from the same socioeconomic status (SES) than with the beliefs of her subculture (Masi, 1988). Women who are older, better educated, have higher incomes and are not single parents are more likely to initiate and maintain breastfeeding (Girard, 2004; Health Canada, 2003b).

Health care experts recommend exclusive breastfeeding for 4 or more months (Canadian Paediatric Society, 2004b; Health Canada, 2003b). However, about 40% of mothers stop breastfeeding their infants by 3 months of age even though breastfeeding may continue, with the introduction of solid foods, to beyond 2 years. Infants between 4 and 6 months are ready to try new foods, and this helps meet the infant's increasing nutritional needs. The first foods should include iron-fortified infant cereal followed by puréed vegetables, fruits, and lastly meat or meat substitutes. A gradual introduction of new foods allows for better identification of possible allergic reactions. By 1 year of age the baby should have a wide variety of foods based on **Canada's Food Guide to Healthy Eating** (Health Canada, 2001d).

Some infants' diets contain almost enough calories, but not enough protein. Diets of this type lead to a disease called *kwashiorkor*, which is common in countries where infants are weaned too early to low-protein foods. Kwashiorkor-like symptoms are also seen in children who are chronically ill because of their bodies' inability to use the protein from the foods they eat. Like marasmus, kwashiorkor can lead to a variety of health problems as well as permanent brain damage (Tershakovec & Stallings, 1998).

A small proportion of infants in North America have feeding problems, such as a poorly developed sucking reflex, that place them at risk for macronutrient malnutrition (Wright & Birks, 2000). However, most nutritional problems in industrialized societies involve **micronutrient** malnutrition, a deficiency of certain vitamins and/or minerals. The exception is Canada, which is a world leader in food fortification. Micronutrients have been added to our food supply for about 50 years (Lotfi, 2001). Specifically, vitamin D has been added to fluid milk since the 1960s, essentially eliminating childhood rickets; iodine is added to table salt, which has eliminated endemic goiter, and vitamin A is added to low-fat milk and butter substitutes like margarine (Health Canada, 1999c). Canada is also a leader in promoting and distributing three essential micronutrients—vitamin A, iodine, and iron—throughout developing countries (CIDA, 2000). As a result, for example, George Beaton, professor emeritus of the University of Toronto and a world-renowned pioneer in the study of human nutrition requirements, found that mortality rates can be reduced by 23% by supplying young children living in at-risk countries with vitamin A (Beaton et al., 1993).

micronutrients
essential vitamins and minerals that are needed in small amounts to regulate physical and mental processes

HEALTH CARE AND IMMUNIZATIONS Infants need frequent medical checkups. Much of *well baby care* may seem routine, but it is extremely important to development.

For example, during routine visits to the doctor's office or health clinic, babies' motor skills are usually assessed. An infant whose motor development is less advanced than expected for his age may require additional screening for developmental problems such as mental retardation (Sulkes, 1998).

One of the most important elements of well baby care is vaccination of the infant against a variety of diseases. Although immunizations later in childhood provide good protection, the *Canadian Immunization Guide* (6th Edition) recommends that routine immunization should commence at 2 months of age and continue through childhood and adolescence (Health Canada, 2002c). Even adults need occasional "booster" shots to maintain immunity.

At the beginning of the last century infectious diseases were a leading cause of childhood death, but have since been virtually eradicated. This was the result of mass vaccination programs (Trovato, 1991). At present, Canadian children typically receive vaccinations at two months of age for DTaP (diphtheria, tetanus, pertussis [acellular]), IPV (inactivated poliovirus vaccine), Hib (haemophilus influenzae type b), PC (pneumococcal conjugate vaccine), and MC (meningococcal conjugate vaccine). Vacinations for MMR (measles, mumps, and rubella), Hep B (hepatitis B vaccine), and V (varicella) are administered around an infant's first birthday (Health Canada, 2002c).

However, the public can easily become complacent about immunizations (CDC, National Immunization Program, 1999). For example, declines in whooping cough immunizations during the late 1980s and early 1990s led to outbreaks of this serious illness in Canada (Trovato, 1991). Thus, it is important to remember that diseases such as measles will remain rare only as long as parents are diligent in having their children immunized.

ILLNESSES IN THE FIRST 2 YEARS The average baby has seven respiratory illnesses in the first year of life. Interestingly, research in a number of countries shows that babies in day-care centres have about twice as many infections as those reared entirely at home, with those in small-group day care falling somewhere in between, presumably because babies cared for in group settings are exposed to a wider range of germs and viruses (Collet et al., 1994; Hurwitz, Gunn, Pinsky, & Schonberger, 1991). In general, the more people a baby is exposed to, the more often she is likely to be sick.

Neuropsychologists have suggested that the timing of respiratory illnesses that can lead to ear infections is important. Many note that infants who have chronic ear infections are more likely than their peers to have learning disabilities and language deficits during the school years. These psychologists hypothesize that, because ear infections temporarily impair hearing, they may compromise the development of brain areas that are essential for language learning during the first 2 years of life (Spreen, Risser, & Edgell, 1995). Thus, most pediatricians emphasize the need for effective hygiene practices in day-care centres, such as periodic disinfection of all toys, as well as prompt treatment of infants' respiratory infections.

INFANT MORTALITY IN CANADA

About half of infant deaths in Canada occur in the neonate and the rest between 4 weeks and 1 year of age. Over the past century Canada's rate of infant mortality has shown a dramatic rate of decline—from 134 in 1901 to 27.3 in the 1960s to just 5.1 per 1000 live births in 2000 (Health Canada, 1998c, 2003b; Wilkins, Houle, Berthelot, & Ross, 2000). Even though regional disparities in infant mortality rates across Canada have diminished significantly, income disparity stubbornly remains a problem—lower-income families experience higher infant mortality rates than middle- and upper-income groups (see **Figure 4.2** on page 106).

Canada's Food Guide to Healthy Eating
guidelines for a balanced and healthy diet based on the four major food groups: grain products, vegetables and fruits, milk products, and meat and alternatives

Make the Connection

Formulate an idea about how an infant's suffering a series of ear infections might affect the social environment that supports language development. Do you think it's possible for ear infections in infancy to affect language development for social as well as neurological reasons?

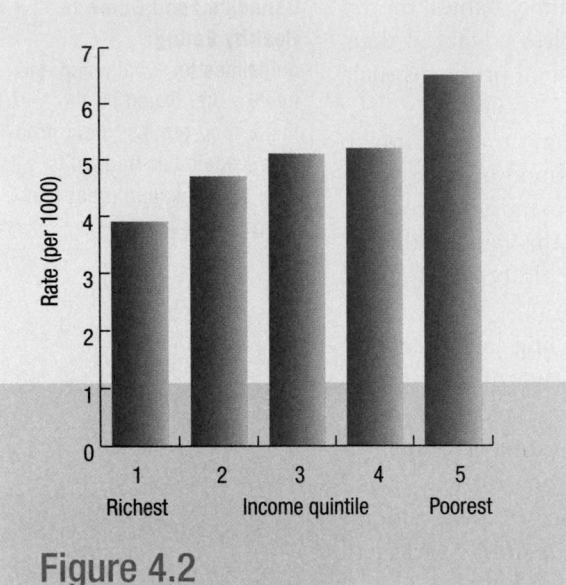

Figure 4.2

Infant mortality by income quintile, urban Canada, 1996.

(*Source:* Adapted from the article "Health status of children," in Statistics Canada, 1999, *Health Reports 11*(3), Catalogue no. 82-003 [as cited in Wilkins, Houle, Berthelot, & Ross, [2000].)

**sudden infant death
syndrome (SIDS)**
the sudden and unexpected
death of an apparently healthy
infant

SUDDEN INFANT DEATH SYNDROME Sudden Infant Death Syndrome (SIDS) is the term associated with the sudden and unexpected death of an apparently healthy infant. In Canada, SIDS is the leading cause of death for post-neonatal children aged 28 days to one year (over 29% of deaths) (Health Canada, 2003b). SIDS deaths occur worldwide, although for unexplained reasons the rates vary greatly from country to country. For example, SIDS rates are particularly high in Australia and New Zealand and particularly low in Japan and Sweden (Hoffman & Hillman, 1992). The rate of SIDS in Canada has declined from 12 per 1000 in 1980 to 0.5 per 1000 in the late 1990s (Health Canada, 1999d). However, there are significant differences in the incidence of SIDS across Canada, with lower rates in British Columbia, Quebec, and Ontario. Rates for First Nations infants are three times the national average.

Researchers have not yet uncovered the underlying cause(s) of SIDS, but there are some factors that are associated with higher risk. Some of the key factors are:

- sleeping in a prone position (on their front) (Paediatrics & Child Health, 1999) or on their side (Fleming et al., 1996)

- smoking by mothers during pregnancy or by anyone in the home after the infant's birth. Babies exposed to such smoke are about four times as likely to die of SIDS as babies with no smoking exposure (Klonoff-Cohen et al., 1995; Schoendorf & Kiely, 1992; Taylor & Danderson, 1995)

- quilts, duvets, pillows, soft toys, and crib bumpers that may cover the infant's head (Henderson-Smart, Ponsonby & Murphy, 1998)

- sex (the incidence is higher for male babies) (Dwyer & Ponsonby, 1992)

- income (the incidence is higher in low-income families) (Dwyer & Ponsonby, 1992)

Autopsies of SIDS babies have revealed that their brains often show signs of delayed maturation. Myelinization seems to have been progressing at a particularly slow rate in many such infants' brains. Because myelinization depends on dietary fat intake, some researchers suggest that low-fat diets, either consumed by the mother during the final weeks of pregnancy or fed to the infant after birth, may be a factor in many SIDS deaths (Saugstad, 1997). Studies linking poverty to SIDS may also indicate that inadequate nutrition plays a role in these deaths (Bambang, Spencer, Logan, & Gill, 2000).

Before Going On

- What important changes in the brain take place in infancy?
- How do babies' states of consciousness change?
- How do other body systems change during infancy, and what is the typical pattern of motor skill development in the first 2 years?
- What are the nutritional and health care needs of infants?
- What factors have been found to be associated with higher risk for SIDS?

COGNITIVE CHANGES

Changes in cognitive skills over the first 2 years are highly consistent across environments (see **Development in the Information Age**). Two-year-olds are still a long way from cognitive maturity, but they have taken several important steps toward that goal.

PERCEPTION

Recent evidence suggests that very young infants can make remarkably fine discriminations among sounds, sights, and tactile sensations, and that they attend to and respond to patterns.

WHAT BABIES LOOK AT From the first days of life, babies have poor *visual acuity*—roughly 40 times poorer than normal-sighted adults (Maurer & Lewis, 2001). Despite this extreme nearsightedness, babies scan the world around them—not very smoothly or skilfully, to be sure, but nonetheless regularly, even in the dark (Haith, 1980). A baby keeps moving his eyes until they come to a sharp contrast between light and dark, which typically signals the edge of some object. Having found an edge, the baby stops searching and moves his eyes back and forth across and around the edge. These looking strategies change at about 2 months of age, when attention shifts from *where* an object is to *what* an object is.

Several studies on infant perception suggest that many abilities and preferences are inborn. For example, infants appear to discriminate between attractive and unattractive

Development in the Information Age
What Do Babies Really Learn from Watching Television?

Television is a part of most babies' daily routine. Parents often assume that exposing babies to intellectual stimulation via television, especially programs produced specifically for infants, will enhance their cognitive development (Harkness, 1998). A research review by Wendy Josephson for Child & Family Canada (Josephson, 1995) states that 3-month-old infants pay minimal attention to television. By 10 months of age, however, infants can imitate what they see on television and point at familiar characters on shows that they watch regularly. Parents should be concerned about what infants are exposed to because later television viewing patterns are becoming established at this age. For instance, if left unmonitored, toddlers prefer to watch fast-paced programs, such as cartoons, which often have violent content.

Studies have shown that infants and young children readily acquire the information presented in programs such as *Sesame Street* and *Blue's Clues*, especially if they watch the same program repeatedly (Crawley, Anderson, Wilder, Williams, & Santomero, 1999). However, it also seems clear that extraordinary amounts of intellectual stimulation contribute little or nothing to basic developmental processes such as the acquisition of object permanence (Bruer, 1999). Moreover, research suggests that ordinary infant toys such as rattles and balls—and even common household items like pots and pans—are just as useful in an infant's attempts to learn about the world as TV programs or videos. Thus, many developmentalists suggest that the main thing babies learn from watching television is the behaviour of watching television.

faces in the same way adults do. Babies as young as 2 months will look longer at a face that adults rate as attractive than at one adults judge to be less attractive, without regard to the face's race, sex, or other variables (Langlois, Ritter, Roggman, & Vaughn, 1991; Langlois et al., 1987).

In addition, babies as young as 3 or 4 months attend to relationships among objects, or among features of objects. For example, suppose you show babies a series of drawings, one at a time, each of which shows a small object above a larger object of the same shape—like the ones in the top row of **Figure 4.3**. After seeing a series of such pictures, babies **habituate**, or decrease their attention because the stimulus has become familiar. Once habituation has occurred, you can present a picture that illustrates the opposite pattern, like the one shown at the bottom of **Figure 4.3**. What you will find is that babies 3 and 4 months old will show renewed interest in this different pattern; this indicates that the baby's original habituation was not to the specific stimuli but to a pattern (Caron & Caron, 1981).

Appropriate visual stimulation in infancy is crucial to the later development of visual perception. For instance, McMaster University psychologists Daphne Maurer, Terri Lewis, and their colleagues have studied infants who are born with cataracts on their eyes. Infants who have cataracts have clouded vision and can only see light and dark. In a longitudinal study, the researchers examined people aged 9 through 21, who, when they were between 2 and 6 months of age, had had cataracts removed and were then fitted with corrective lenses that gave them normal vision. When these individuals were examined years later they were found to have subtle visual abnormalities. For instance, they did not develop the ability to distinguish the relative position of facial features in the same way as sighted people do (Le Grand, Mondloch, Maurer, & Brent, 2001). In related studies it was found that infants who had a cataract in only one eye had, surprisingly, poorer visual acuity than infants who had cataracts in both eyes unless the unaffected eye was covered with a patch for an extensive period following corrective surgery (Maurer & Lewis, 2001). In general, although not all visual processes are affected in the same ways by early deprivation of visual stimulation, there is a critical period of time in early infancy when an infant needs a specific quality of visual stimulation in order to develop normal visual perception (Lewis, et al., 2002; Le Grand, et al., 2001).

Depth perception, the ability to judge how far away an object is, develops slowly over the first year. A complex visual skill, depth perception requires that the baby integrate visual information from both eyes at the same time. One reason why this skill takes a while to develop is that the baby's movements provide her with experiential information about distance and depth as she moves toward and away from objects. Thus, babies' depth perception improves as they gain motor skills. Research suggests that babies possess some degree of depth perception fairly early, as young as 3 months of age, but don't really use information from both eyes in a coordinated way until they are about 7 months old (Bornstein, 1992; Yonas & Owsley, 1987).

INTERSENSORY INTEGRATION AND CROSS-MODAL PERCEPTION If you think about the way you use perceptual information, you'll quickly realize that, ordinarily, you perceive complex combinations of sound, sight, touch, and smell. Psychologists have been interested in knowing how early an infant can integrate information from several senses, so that she knows, for example, which mouth movements go with which sounds, a skill called **intersensory integration**. As with all perceptual abilities, debate centres on the question of whether such skill is inborn or learned.

Research suggests that intersensory integration isn't completely inborn. Some studies indicate that infants younger than 4 months have some ability to coordinate sensory information. However, in most investigations, younger infants do not consistently demonstrate this skill (Lewkowicz, 1994).

habituate
to decrease one's attention because a stimulus has become familiar

depth perception
ability to judge the relative distances of objects

intersensory integration
coordination of information from two or more senses, such as knowing which mouth movements go with which sounds

By contrast, intersensory integration is common in older babies. Recent research by University of British Columbia psychologists Michelle Patterson and Janet Werker found that, by age 4½ months, infants could associate lip movements with sounds of specific parts of speech (1999). For instance, infants in Patterson and Werker's study spent more time watching lip movements that corresponded to vowel sounds they were listening to rather than lip movements of unrelated vowel sounds. This shows that infants appear to have some understanding of the link between the language sound and the language lip movement—knowledge they could only acquire through intersensory integration.

Moreover, intersensory integration appears to be important in infant learning. One group of researchers found that babies who habituated to a combined auditory-visual stimulus were better able to recognize a new stimulus than infants who habituated to either the auditory or the visual stimulus alone (Bahrick & Lickliter, 2000). For example, suppose you played a videotape of someone singing for one baby, played the videotape without the sound for another, and played an audio recording of the song for a third. Research suggests that the first baby, the one who both saw the singer and heard the song, would recognize a change in either the singer (visual stimulus) or the song (auditory stimulus) more quickly than either of the other two infants.

Figure 4.3

In Caron and Caron's study, babies were first habituated to a series of pictures, each of which displayed the same pattern, like those in the upper row. Then they were tested either on more of the same, or on a picture with a reverse pattern, like the one on the bottom. Babies 3 and 4 months old showed renewed interest in the test stimulus, which indicates that they noticed the pattern and saw that it had changed.

Evidence suggests that **cross-modal perception**, the ability to perceive something via one sense and transfer the information to another sense, is probably inborn. For example, if you give a baby a nubby round pacifier and let the baby suck on it, you can test for cross-modal perception by showing the baby pictures of a nubby sphere and a smooth sphere. If the baby looks longer at the nubby sphere, that would suggest cross-modal perception. In one study of this type, developmentalists demonstrated cross-modal perception in infants as young as 12 hours old (Kaye & Bower, 1994). Clearly, these newborns were too young to have learned to combine information from different senses.

cross-modal perception
transfer of information from one sense to another, as when an infant can recognize by feel a toy he has seen but never felt before

PIAGET'S VIEW OF THE FIRST 2 YEARS

Recall from **Chapter 2** that Piaget assumed that a baby *assimilates* incoming information to the limited array of schemes she is born with—looking, listening, sucking, grasping—and *accommodates* those schemes based on her experiences. He called this form of thinking *sensorimotor intelligence*. Thus, the **sensorimotor stage** is the period during which infants develop and refine sensorimotor intelligence.

SENSORIMOTOR STAGE In Piaget's view, the newborn is entirely tied to the immediate present, responding to whatever stimuli are available. She forgets events from one encounter to the next and does not appear to plan. This gradually changes, across six substages during the first 18 months, as the baby comes to understand that objects continue to exist even when they are out of sight (Piaget & Inhelder, 1969) (see **Table 4.3** on page 110).

sensorimotor stage
Piaget's first stage of development, in which infants use information from their senses and motor actions to learn about the world

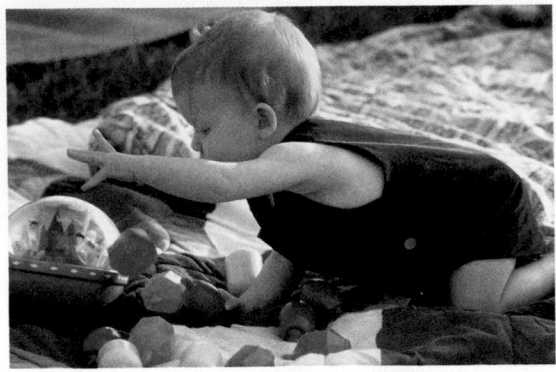

Over the first few months, babies learn to make perceptual judgments based on depth. Among other things, this helps them determine if they are near enough to an object to grasp it.
(*Photo:* Laima Druskis/Stock Boston)

Each substage represents a definite advance over the one that came before. Substage 2 is marked by the beginning of the coordinations between looking and listening, between reaching and looking, and between reaching and sucking that are such central features of the 2-month-old's means of exploring the world. The technique that distinguishes substage 2, *primary circular reactions*, refers to the many simple repetitive actions seen at this time, each organized around the infant's own body. For example, the baby may accidentally suck her thumb one day, find it pleasurable, and repeat the action.

In substage 3, the baby repeats some action in order to trigger a reaction outside her own body, a *secondary circular reaction*. The baby coos and Mom smiles, so the baby coos again to get Mom to smile again. These initial connections between body actions and external consequences seem to be simple, almost mechanical, links between stimuli and responses. However, in substage 4, the baby shows the beginnings of understanding causal connections, at which point she moves into exploratory high gear.

In substage 5, exploration of the environment becomes more focused, with the emergence of *tertiary circular reactions*. In this pattern, the baby doesn't merely repeat the

TABLE 4.3	Substages of Piaget's Sensorimotor Stage		
Substage	**Age (in months)**	**Primary Technique**	**Characteristics**
1	0–1	Reflexes	Use of built-in schemes or reflexes such as sucking or looking. Primitive schemes begin to change through very small steps of accommodation. Limited imitation, no ability to integrate information from several senses.
2	1–4	Primary circular reactions	Further accommodation of basic schemes, as the baby practises them endlessly—grasping, listening, looking, sucking. Beginning coordination of schemes from different senses, so that the baby now looks toward a sound and sucks on anything he can reach and bring to his mouth. But the baby does not yet link his body actions to results outside of his body.
3	4–8	Secondary circular reactions	The baby becomes much more aware of events outside his own body and makes them happen again in a kind of trial-and-error learning. Scientists are unsure whether babies this young understand the causal links yet, however. Imitation may occur, but only of schemes already in the baby's repertoire. Beginning understanding of the "object concept" can also be detected in this period.
4	8–12	Coordination of secondary schemes	Clear intentional means–ends behaviour. The baby not only goes after what she wants, she may combine two schemes to do so, such as moving a pillow aside to reach a toy. Imitation of novel behaviour occurs, as does transfer of information from one sense to the other (cross-modal perception).
5	12–18	Tertiary circular reactions	"Experimentation" begins, in which the infant tries out new ways of playing with or manipulating objects. Very active, very purposeful trial-and-error exploration.
6	18–24	Beginning of mental representation	Development of use of symbols to represent object or events. The child understands that the symbol is separate from the object. Deferred imitation can only occur after this point because it requires ability to represent internally the event to be imitated.

original behaviour but tries out variations. She may try out variations. She may try out many sounds or facial expressions to see if they will trigger Mom's smile, or she may try dropping a toy from several heights to see if it makes different sounds or lands in different places. At this stage, the baby's behaviour has a purposeful, experimental quality. Nonetheless, Piaget thought that the baby still does not have mental symbols to stand for objects in this substage.

The ability to manipulate mental symbols, such as words or images, marks substage 6, which lasts from roughly 18 months to 24 months of age. This new capacity also allows the infant to generate solutions to problems simply by thinking about them, without the trial-and-error behaviour typical of substage 5. For example, a 24-month-old who knows there are cookies in the cookie jar can figure out how to get one. Furthermore, she can find a way to overcome just about any obstacle placed in her path (Bauer, Schwade, Wewerka, & Delaney, 1999). Suppose, for example, parents respond to a toddler's climbing on the kitchen counter in pursuit of a cookie by moving the cookie jar to the top of the refrigerator. The toddler's response, thanks to the advances of substage 6, will likely be to find a way to climb to the top of the refrigerator. Thus, changes in cognition are probably behind the common impression of parents and other caregivers that 18- to 24-month-olds cannot be left unsupervised, even for very short periods of time.

THE OBJECT CONCEPT You know that this book continues to exist even when you are unable to see it—an understanding that Piaget called **object permanence**. Piaget thought that babies acquired this understanding gradually during the sensorimotor period. According to his observations, replicated frequently by later researchers, the first sign that a baby is developing object permanence comes at about 2 months of age (in substage 2). Suppose you show a toy to a child of this age, then put a screen in front of the toy and remove the toy. When you then remove the screen, the baby shows some indication of surprise, as if he knows that something should still be there. The child thus seems to have a rudimentary expectation about the permanence of an object. But infants of this age show no signs of searching for a toy that has fallen over the side of the crib or that has disappeared beneath a blanket or behind a screen.

In substage 3, however (at about 6 to 8 months), babies will look over the edge of the crib for dropped toys or on the floor for food that was spilled. (In fact, babies of this age may drive their parents nuts playing "dropsy" from the high chair.) Infants this age will also search for partially hidden objects. If you put a baby's favourite toy under a cloth but leave part of it sticking out, the infant will reach for the toy, which indicates that in some sense he "recognizes" that the whole object is there even though he can see only part of it. But if you cover the toy completely with the cloth or put it behind a screen, the infant will stop looking at it and will not reach for it, even if he has seen you put the cloth over it.

This behaviour changes again between 8 and 12 months, in substage 4. Infants of this age will reach for or search for a toy that has been covered completely by a cloth or hidden by a screen. Thus, by 12 months, most infants appear to grasp the basic fact that objects continue to exist even when they are no longer visible.

IMITATION Piaget thought that as early as the first few months of life, infants could imitate actions they could see themselves make, such as hand gestures. But he thought that they could not imitate other people's facial gestures until substage 4 (8 to 12 months). This second form of imitation seems to require some kind of cross-modal perception, combining the visual cues of seeing the other's face with the *kinesthetic cues* (perceptions of muscle motion) from one's own facial movements. Piaget also argued that imitation of any action that wasn't already in the child's repertoire did not occur until about 1 year, and that **deferred imitation**—a child's imitation of some action at a later time—was possible only in substage 6, since deferred imitation requires some kind of internal representation.

object permanence
the understanding that objects continue to exist when they can't be seen

deferred imitation
imitation by an infant of an action seen earlier

CHALLENGES TO PIAGET'S VIEW

Computer- and other advanced technology-aided research suggests that very young babies have more understanding of object permanence than Piaget supposed. For example, in a series of studies, researchers have shown that babies as young as $3^1/_2$ or 4 months show clear signs of object permanence if a visual response rather than a reaching response is used to test it (Baillargeon, 1987, 1994; Baillargeon & DeVos, 1991; Baillargeon, Spelke, & Wasserman, 1985).

Similarly, another series of experiments demonstrated that 2- and 3-month-olds are remarkably aware of the kinds of movements objects are capable of—even when the objects are out of sight (Spelke, 1991). Infants expect objects to continue to move on their initial trajectories and show surprise if the objects appear somewhere else. They also seem to have some awareness that solid objects cannot pass through other solid objects.

Findings like these reopened the debate about Piaget's description of the development of object permanence. More generally, they sparked renewed discussion of the nature-versus-nurture issue (e.g., Diamond, 1991; Fischer & Bidell, 1991; Karmiloff-Smith, 1991). Piaget assumed that a baby came equipped with a repertoire of sensori-motor schemes, but his most fundamental theoretical proposal was that the child constructed an understanding of the world based on experience. In contrast, later research suggests that the development of object permanence is more a process of elaboration than discovery. Newborns may have considerable awareness of objects as separate entities that follow certain rules. Certainly, all the research on the perception of patterns suggests that babies pay far more attention to relationships between events than Piaget's model supposed. Indeed, the research on babies' preferences for attractive faces suggests that there may be built-in preferences for particular patterns. Still, no one would argue that a baby comes equipped with a full-fledged knowledge of objects or a well-developed ability to experiment with the world.

With respect to imitation, Piaget's proposed sequence has been supported. Imitation of someone else's hand movement or an action with an object seems to improve steadily, starting at 1 or 2 months of age; imitation of two-part actions develops much later, perhaps around 15 to 18 months (Poulson, Nunes, & Warren, 1989). Yet there are two important exceptions to this general confirmation of Piaget's theory: Infants imitate some facial gestures in the first weeks of life, and deferred imitation seems to occur earlier than Piaget proposed.

Several researchers have found that newborn babies will imitate certain facial gestures, particularly tongue protrusion (Anisfeld, 1991). This seems to happen only if the model sits there with his tongue out looking at the baby for a fairly long period of time, perhaps as long as a minute. But the fact that newborns imitate at all is striking—although it is entirely consistent with the observation that quite young babies are capable of tactile/visual cross-modal perception.

Studies of deferred imitation also support Piaget. However, at least one study showed that babies as young as 9 months can defer their imitation for as long as 24 hours (Meltzoff, 1988). By 14 months, toddlers can recall and imitate someone's actions as much as 2 days later (Hanna & Meltzoff, 1993).

These findings are significant for several reasons. First, they make it clear that infants can and do learn specific behaviours through modelling, even when they have no chance to imitate the behaviour immediately. In addition, these results suggest that babies may be more skilful than Piaget thought, and more abilities than he suggested may be built in from the beginning. However, the findings leave open deeper questions about the relative contributions of nature and experience to the developmental process.

LEARNING

From the first moments following birth, babies are capable of learning in a variety of ways.

CONDITIONING Learning of emotional responses through classical conditioning processes may begin as early as the first week of life. Thus, the mere presence of Mom or Dad or another favoured person may trigger a sense of comfort or "feeling good." Such early learning may contribute to the child's attachment to the parent.

Newborns also clearly learn by operant conditioning. Both the sucking response and head turning have been successfully increased by the use of reinforcements such as sweet liquids or the sound of the mother's voice or heartbeat (Moon & Fifer, 1990). At the least, the fact that conditioning of this kind can take place means that whatever neurological wiring is needed for operant learning is present at birth. Results like these also tell developmentalists something about the sorts of reinforcements that are effective with very young children; it is surely highly significant for the whole process of mother–infant interaction that the mother's voice is an effective reinforcer for virtually all babies.

> ## Critical Thinking
>
> Can you think of other examples of classically conditioned emotional responses that might develop in early infancy?

HABITUATION AND DISHABITUATION As you learned earlier in this chapter, *habituation* is the process of getting used to a stimulus. Its opposite is **dishabituation**, or learning to respond to a familiar stimulus as if it were new. Both habituation and dishabituation are well developed by 10 weeks of age. For example, an infant will stop showing a startle reaction (Moro reflex) to a loud sound after the first few presentations, but will again show the startle reaction if the sound is changed somewhat. Such habituation and dishabituation are not voluntary processes; they are entirely automatic. But in order for them to work, the newborn must be equipped with the capacity to recognize familiar experiences. That is, she must have, or must develop, schemes of some kind.

dishabituation
learning to respond to a familiar stimulus as if it were new

The existence of these processes in the newborn has an added benefit for researchers: It has enabled them to figure out what an infant perceives as being "the same" or "different." If a baby is habituated to some specific stimulus, such as a sound or a picture, the experimenter can then present slight variations on the original stimulus to see the point at which dishabituation occurs. In this way, researchers have begun to get a picture of how the newborn baby or young infant experiences the world around him.

SCHEMATIC LEARNING Studies of a third type of infant learning, sometimes referred to as *schematic learning*, are based on both Piaget's theory and the information-processing approach. **Schematic learning** is the organizing of experiences into expectancies, or "known" combinations. These expectancies, often called *schemas*, are built up over many exposures to particular experiences. Once formed, they help the baby to distinguish between the familiar and the unfamiliar.

schematic learning
organization of experiences into expectancies, called schemas, which enable infants to distinguish between familiar and unfamiliar stimuli

One kind of schematic learning involves categories. Research suggests that by 7 months of age, and perhaps even earlier, infants actively use categories to process information (Pauen, 2000). For example, a 7-month-old is likely to habituate to a sequence of ten animal pictures and, if the next picture is another animal, will not show surprise or look at it any longer than the first ten. If, however, researchers show the baby a picture of a human after ten animals, the baby will look surprised and gaze at the picture longer. The same thing is likely to happen if researchers show an infant several pictures of humans and then switch to an animal picture. Such findings suggest that infants build and use categories as they take in information.

MEMORY

Researchers have used an ingenious variation of an operant conditioning procedure to demonstrate that babies as young as 3 months of age can remember specific objects and their own actions with those objects over periods as long as a week (Bhatt & Rovee-Collier, 1996; Gerhardstein, Liu, & Rovee-Collier, 1998; Hayne & Rovee-Collier, 1995; Rovee-Collier, 1993). A researcher first hangs an attractive mobile over a baby's crib and watches to see how the baby responds, noting how often he kicks his legs while looking at the mobile. After 3 minutes of this "baseline" observation, a string is used to connect the mobile to the baby's leg, so that each time the baby kicks his leg, the mobile moves. Babies quickly learn to kick repeatedly in order to make this interesting action occur. Within 3 to 6 minutes, 3-month-olds double or triple their kick rates, clearly showing that learning has occurred. The researcher next tests the baby's memory of this learning by coming back some days later and hanging the same mobile over the crib but not attaching the string to the baby's foot. The crucial issue is whether the baby kicks rapidly at the mere sight of the mobile. If the baby remembers the previous occasion, he should kick at a higher rate than he did when he first saw the mobile, which is precisely what 3-month-old babies do, even after a delay of as long as a week.

Such findings demonstrate that the young infant is more cognitively sophisticated than developmentalists (and Piaget) had supposed. At the same time, these studies support Piaget's view that infants show systematic gains in the ability to remember over the months of infancy. Two-month-olds can remember their kicking action for only 1 day, 3-month-olds can remember for over a week, and 6-month-olds can remember longer than 2 weeks.

However, early infant memories are strongly tied to the specific context in which the original experience occurred. Even 6-month-olds do not recognize or remember the mobile if the context is changed even slightly, for example, by hanging a different cloth around the crib in which the child was originally tested. Thus, babies do remember more than Piaget believed, but their memories are highly specific. With age, their memories become less and less tied to specific cues or contexts.

Before Going On

- Describe the development of the senses in the first 2 years of life.
- How do infants combine information from two or more senses?
- Outline the important milestones of Piaget's sensorimotor stage.
- What are some recent challenges offered to Piaget's explanation of infant cognitive development?
- How do infants learn through classical conditioning, operant conditioning, habituation, and schematic learning?
- Describe infants' ability to remember.

THE BEGINNINGS OF LANGUAGE

Most of us think of "language" as beginning when the baby uses her first words, at about 12 months of age, but all sorts of important developments precede the first words.

THEORETICAL PERSPECTIVES

In the late 1950s, B.F. Skinner, the scientist who formulated operant conditioning theory, suggested a *behaviourist* explanation of language development. He claimed that language development begins with babbling. While babbling, babies accidentally make sounds that somewhat resemble real words as spoken by their parents. Parents hear the word-like sounds and respond to them with praise and encouragement, which serve as reinforcers. Thus, word-like babbling becomes more frequent, while utterances that do not resemble words gradually disappear from babies' vocalizations. Skinner further hypothesized that parents and others respond to grammatical uses of words and do not respond to non-grammatical ones. As a result, correct grammar is reinforced and becomes more frequent, but incorrect grammar is extinguished through nonreinforcement.

At first glance, Skinner's theory might appear to make sense. However, systematic examination of the interactions between infants and parents reveals that adults do not reinforce babies' vocalizations in this manner. Instead, parents and others respond to *all* of a baby's vocalizations, and even sometimes imitate them—a consequence that, according to operant conditioning theory, should prolong babbling rather than lead to the development of grammatical language. Skinner's mistake was that his theory was not based on observations of language development but rather on his assumption that the principles of operant conditioning underlie all human learning and development.

Linguist Noam Chomsky strongly criticized Skinner's theory (Chomsky, 1959). The cornerstone of Chomsky's argument was the universal observation of field linguists that children make rule-governed rather than random grammatical errors when learning language. For example, almost all 3-year-old English-speaking children *overregularize* the past tense of verbs. That is, they create the past tense for every verb by adding *-ed* to the present tense. Consequently, they say such things as, "Yesterday, we goed to the store," or "I breaked my cookie." In response to correction, they often regularize the correction itself by saying, "Yesterday we wented to the store," or "I broked my cookie."

Chomsky argued that the only possible explanation for such errors was that children acquire grammar rules before they master the exceptions to them. Further, Chomsky proposed a *nativist* explanation for language development: Children's comprehension and production of language are guided by an innate language processor that he called the **language acquisition device (LAD)**, which contains the basic grammatical structure of all human language. In effect, the LAD tells infants what characteristics of language to look for in the stream of speech to which they are exposed. For example, newborns actively segment the sounds of natural human speech into vowel and consonant categories. Chomsky identified this phenomenon as an example of the LAD's action on the phonological (sound) data contained in spoken language. Simply put, the LAD tells babies that there are two basic types of sounds—consonants and vowels—and enables them to properly divide the speech they hear into the two categories so that they can analyze and learn the sounds that are specific to the language they are hearing. Chomsky further supported the existence of the LAD with evidence compiled over hundreds of years by field linguists, which demonstrated that all human languages have the same grammatical forms. He also argued that the LAD is species-specific—that is, non-human species do not have one, and therefore, cannot learn grammatical language.

language acquisition device (LAD)
an innate language processor, theorized by Chomsky, that contains the basic grammatical structure of all human language

SPEECH PERCEPTION

Babies as young as 1 month can discriminate between simple speech sounds like *pa* and *ba* (Jusczyk, 1995). By 6 months old, they can discriminate between two-syllable "words" like *bada* and *baga* and can even respond to a syllable that is hidden inside a string of other syllables (as in *tibati* or *kobako*) (Fernald & Kuhl, 1987; Goodsitt, Morse, Ver Hoeve, & Cowan, 1984; Morse & Cowan, 1982). Even more remarkable, it doesn't seem to matter what voice quality is used to produce the sound. By 2 or 3 months of age, babies respond to individual sounds in the same way, whether the sounds are spoken by male or female, children's or adult voices (Marean, Werner, & Kuhl, 1992).

Also striking is the finding that babies are actually better than adults at discriminating some kinds of speech sounds. Each language uses only a subset of all possible speech sounds. Japanese, for example, does not use the *l* sound that appears in English; Spanish distinguishes between the *d* and *t* sounds differently than English does. It turns out that up to about 6 months of age, babies can accurately discriminate among all sounds that appear in any language, including sounds they do not hear in the language spoken to them. At about 6 months of age, they begin to lose the ability to distinguish pairs of vowels that do not occur in the language they are hearing; by age 1, the ability to discriminate nonheard consonant contrasts begins to fade (Polka & Werker, 1994) (see **Research Report**).

SOUNDS, GESTURES, AND WORD MEANINGS

The ability to discriminate among sounds arises early but is not accompanied by much skill in producing sounds. From birth to about 1 month of age, the most common sound an infant makes is a cry, although she also produces other fussing, gurgling, and satisfied sounds. This sound repertoire expands at about 1 or 2 months, when the baby begins to make some laughing and cooing vowel sounds. Sounds like this are usually signals of pleasure and may show quite a lot of variation in tone, running up and down in volume or pitch.

Consonant sounds appear at about 6 or 7 months, frequently combined with vowel sounds to make a kind of syllable. Babies of this age seem to play with these sounds, often repeating the same sound over and over (such as *babababababa* or *dahdahdah*). This sound pattern is called *babbling*, and it makes up about half of babies' noncrying sounds from about 6 to 12 months of age (Mitchell & Kent, 1990).

Any parent can tell you that babbling is a delight to listen to. It also seems to be an important part of the preparation for spoken language. For one thing, infants' babbling gradually acquires some of what linguists call the *intonational pattern* of the language they are hearing—a process one developmental psychologist refers to as "learning the tune before the words" (Bates, O'Connell, & Shore, 1987). At the very least, infants do seem to develop at least two such "tunes" in their babbling. Babbling with a rising intonation at the end of a string of sounds seems to signal a desire for a response; a falling intonation requires no response.

The left side of the brain controls the right side of the body and, in most people, the left brain is also home to our language capacity (see **Chapter 6** for more details on brain specialization). With these facts in mind, McGill University psychologists studied the mouth movements of 5- to 12-month-olds to see if babies display a right mouth bias when babbling similar to the right mouth asymmetry seen in adults when they talk. Indeed the researchers, Holowka & Petitto (2002), found that babies differentially used right mouth openings when babbling, but not when engaging in nonlanguage mouthing activity such as chewing or crying. This suggests that babbling is not just generic oral-motor behaviour, but it is related to the beginnings of language production.

Another important thing about babbling is that when babies first start babbling, they typically babble all kinds of sounds, including some that are not part of the language they are hearing. But at about 9 or 10 months, their sound repertoire gradually begins to narrow down to the set of sounds they are listening to, with the nonheard

Research Report

Early Gestural "Language" in the Children of Deaf Parents

For scientists who want to understand language development, deaf children of deaf parents are a particularly interesting group to study. The children do not hear oral language, but many are exposed to sign language. Do these children show the same early steps in language development as hearing children do, only using gestural language?

The answer seems to be yes. At McGill University, Dr. Laura-Ann Petitto found that deaf children show a kind of "sign babbling" between about 7 and 11 months of age, much as hearing children babble sounds in these same months. Then, at 8 or 9 months, deaf children begin using simple gestures, such as pointing, which is just about the age when such gestures emerge in hearing babies of hearing parents. At about 12 months of age, deaf babies seem to display their first referential signs—that is, gestures that appear to stand for some object or event—such as signalling that they want a drink by making a motion of bringing a cup to the mouth (Petitto & Marrentette, 1991; Petitto, 1988).

Researchers have also studied an equally interesting group: hearing children of deaf parents. In one such study 6-, 10-, and 12-month-old babies who were only exposed to sign language, but heard no spoken language, displayed a pattern of rhythmic hand movements ("silent babbling") that was distinctly different from babies who heard spoken language. While babies who were exposed to spoken language babbled, they didn't display the same pattern of hand gestures (Petitto, Holowka, Sergio, Levy, & Ostry, 2004). In another study, babies were exposed to sign language from their parents and to hearing language from their contacts with others in their world, including teachers, other relatives, playmates, and even people on television. In a small sample of nine such babies, the first sign appeared at an average age of 8 months, the first referential sign at 12.6 months, and the first spoken word at 12.2 months (Folven & Bonvillian, 1991). What is striking here is that the first referential signs and the first spoken words appear at nearly the same time, and that the spoken words appear at a completely normal time, despite the fact that these children of deaf parents hear comparatively little spoken language.

This marked similarity in the sequence and timing of the steps of early language in deaf and hearing children provides strong support for the argument that babies are somehow "primed" to learn language in some form, whether spoken or gestural.

But how do babies separate a single word from the constant flow of speech to which they are exposed? Many linguists have proposed that a child can cope with the monumentally complex task of word learning only because he applies some built-in biases or constraints (Baldwin, 1995; Golinkoff, Mervis, & Hirsh-Pasek, 1994; Jusczyk & Hohne 1997; Markman, 1992; Waxman & Kosowski, 1990). For example, the child may have a built-in assumption that words refer to objects or actions but not both.

These little girls probably haven't yet spoken their first words, but chances are they already understand quite a few. Receptive language usually develops before expressive language. (*Photo:* Michael Newman/PhotoEdit)

stress, such as in the word "gar*age*." Thus, when English-learning infants hear a stressed syllable, they may assume that a new word is beginning. This strategy would help them single out a very large number of individual English words.

All of this information reveals a whole series of changes that seem to converge by 9 or 10 months: the beginning of meaningful gestures, the drift of babbling toward the heard language sounds, imitative gestural games, and the first comprehension of individual words. It is as if the child now understands something about the process of communication and is intending to communicate to adults.

THE FIRST WORDS

expressive language
the ability to produce spoken language

Expressive language, the ability to produce as well as understand and respond to words, typically appears at about 12 or 13 months (Fenson et al., 1994). The baby's first word is an event that parents eagerly await, but it's fairly easy to miss. A word, as linguists usually define it, is any sound or set of sounds that is used consistently to refer to some thing, action, or quality. This means that a child who uses *ba* consistently to refer to her bottle is using a word even though it isn't considered a word in English.

Often, a child's earliest words are used in specific situations and in the presence of many cues. The child may say "bow-wow" or "doggie" only in response to such promptings as "How does the doggie go?" or "What's that?" Typically, this early word learning is very slow, requiring many repetitions for each word. In the first 6 months of word usage, children may learn as few as 30 words. Most linguists have concluded that this earliest word-use phase involves learning each word as something connected to a set of specific contexts. What the child has apparently not yet grasped is that words are symbolic—that they refer to objects or events.

Very young children often combine a single word with a gesture to create a "two-word meaning" before they use two words together in their speech. For example, a child may point to his father's shoe and say "Daddy," as if to convey "Daddy's shoe" (Bates et al., 1987). In such cases, meaning is conveyed by the use of gesture and body language combined with a word. Linguists call these word-and-gesture combinations **holophrases**, and children use them frequently between 12 and 18 months of age.

holophrases
"phrases" or "sentences" consisting of words and gestures, used by infants in the second year of life

naming explosion
a period between 16 and 24 months of age when most children rapidly begin to add new words to their vocabularies

Between 16 and 24 months, after the early period of very slow word learning, most children begin to add new words rapidly, as if they had figured out that things have names. Developmentalists refer to this period as the **naming explosion**. In this period, children seem to learn new words with very few repetitions, and they generalize these words to many more situations. According to one large cross-sectional study based on mothers' reports, the average 16-month-old has a speaking vocabulary of about 50 words; for a 24-month-old the total has grown to about 320 words (Fenson et al., 1994).

For most children, the naming explosion is not a steady, gradual process; instead, vocabulary "spurts" begin at about the time that the child has acquired 50 words. This pattern, observed by several researchers, is illustrated in **Figure 4.4**, which shows the vocabulary growth curves of six children studied longitudinally (Bloom, 1993; Goldfield & Reznick, 1990). Not all children show precisely this pattern, but a rapid increase over a period of a few months is typical.

Most observers agree that the bulk of new words learned during this early period of rapid vocabulary growth are names for things or people: "ball," "car," "milk," "doggie," "he." Action words tend to appear later (Gleitman & Gleitman, 1992). One study involving a large group of children suggested that as many as two-thirds of the words children knew by age 2 were nouns, and only 8.5% were verbs (Fenson et al., 1994). It appears that infants lack the ability to

Critical Thinking

Think of contrasting "nature" and "nurture" explanations for expressive and referential styles.

consistently associate words with actions until about 18 months of age (Casasola & Cohen, 2000). Recent cross-linguistic research also suggests that compared with Korean-speaking parents, English-speaking parents emphasize nouns more than verbs in speaking and reading to infants (Choi, 2000). Thus, the pattern of learning nouns before verbs may be influenced by the characteristics of the language being learned as well as by the behaviour of mature speakers as they speak to infants. Indeed, the noun-before-verb pattern does not hold even for all English-speaking children. Some toddlers use what developmentalists call an *expressive style* (Nelson, 1973; Shore, 1995; Thal & Bates, 1990). For these children, most early words are linked to social relationships rather than to objects. They often learn pronouns ("you," "me") early and use many more of what Nelson calls "personal-social" words, such as "no," "yes," "want," or "please." Their early vocabulary may also include some multiword strings, such as "love you" or "do it" or "go away." This is in sharp contrast to children who use a *referential style,* that is, children whose early vocabulary is made up predominantly of nouns or pronouns.

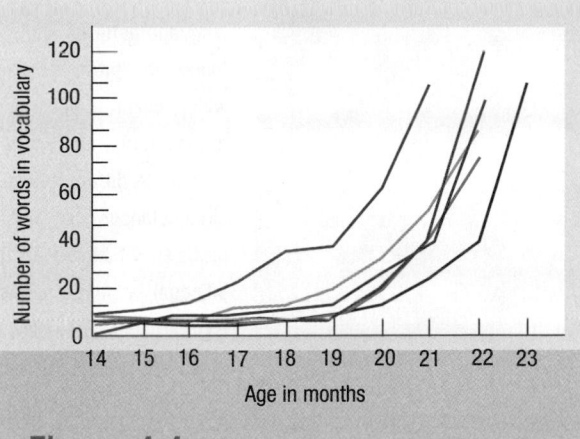

Figure 4.4

Each of the lines in this figure represents the vocabulary growth of one of the children studied longitudinally by Goldfield and Reznick. The six children shown here each acquired new words in the most common pattern: slow initial growth followed by a fairly rapid spurt.

(*Source:* Goldfield & Reznick, 1990, Figure 3, p. 177.)

No Easy Answers

One Language

or Two?

Canada's population consists of the world's most diverse cultural, ethnic, and linguistic peoples (Canadian Heritage, 2001). Almost 18% of Canadians are fluent in English and French and, due to recent immigration trends, about 1 in 6 Canadians speaks one of 100 other languages (Statistics Canada, 2002a). However, most children of immigrants never acquire native proficiency in their parents' language (Pease-Alvarez, 1993). Many immigrant parents believe that teaching children their language will undermine the children's future educational and economic success—even though knowing two languages is clearly a social and economic benefit for an adult. The research suggests that there are cognitive advantages and disadvantages to growing up bilingual.

On the positive side are the findings of Canadian researchers Elena Nicoladis of the University of Alberta and Fred Genesee of McGill University. They conducted a longitudinal study of infants raised in English/French bilingual homes and found that at about 2 years of age infants would start to speak in the mother's dominant language with the mother and, differentially, speak the father's dominant language with the father (1996). They also noted that, unlike monolingual children who resist the idea that there can be more than one word for the same object, bilingual children had no difficulty using two translation terms for the same object.

Canadian researcher Ellen Bialystok and her colleagues at York University have found that, in preschool and school-age children, bilingualism is associated with a clear advantage in metalinguistic ability, the capacity to think about language (Bialystok, Shenfield, & Codd, 2000; Mohanty & Perregaux, 1997). In addition, most bilingual children display greater ability than monolingual children to focus attention on both language tasks (Bialystok & Majumder, 1998) and nonlanguage tasks (Bialystok, 1999). These advantages enable bilingual children to more easily grasp the connection between sounds and symbols in the beginning stages of learning to read (Bialystok, 1997; Oller, Cobo-Lewis, & Eilers, 1998).

On the downside, Nicoladis and Genesee (1997) contend that inconsistent exposure to a second language can lead to both uncertain language patterns and levels of competence. They found that "there are a variety of circumstances in which children become bilingual—from parents, grandparents, child-care workers, or peer groups who speak different languages, and these different circumstances can influence a bilingual child's proficiency." Moreover, they express the need for bilingual language norms so that speech specialists can accurately determine when and if a child may need special intervention.

Pettito and Holowka (2002) found that the earlier a child is exposed to two languages the better—early exposure promotes higher levels of language competence and mastery. Moreover, bilingual children who are equally fluent in both languages encounter few, if any, learning problems in school (Vuorenkoski, Kuure, Moilanen, & Peninkilampi, 2000). However, most children do not attain equal fluency in both languages. As a result, they tend to think more slowly in the language in which they have the lesser fluency (Chincotta & Underwood, 1997). Thus, if the language in which they are less fluent is the language they are taught in at school, they are at risk for learning problems

(Anderson, 1998; Thorn & Gathercole, 1999). Therefore, parents who choose bilingualism should probably take into account whether they will be able to help their children become fluent in both languages. In **Chapter 8** you will discover factors that contribute to bilingual proficiency when considering French immersion programs.

Whatever the cognitive advantages or disadvantages, children who speak their immigrant parents' language appear to develop a stronger sense of attachment to their parents' culture of origin (Buriel, Perez, DeMent, Chavez, & Moran, 1998). Additionally, teaching children about a parent's culture of origin seems to help them acquire the language (Wright, Taylor, & Macarthur, 2000). Finally, the advantages in adulthood of being bilingual are substantial and may outweigh any disadvantages experienced in childhood. Thus, bilingual parents should weigh the various advantages and disadvantages of bilingualism and consider their long-term parenting goals in order to reach an informed decision about the kind of linguistic environment to provide for their babies.

Before Going On

- Briefly explain the behaviourist and nativist theories of language development.
- Describe infants' ability to perceive speech sounds.
- How do infants use sounds and gestures to communicate?
- What are the first words used, and what kinds of words do most infants learn first?

INDIVIDUAL AND GROUP DIFFERENCES

We've already touched on several kinds of differences among babies that affect their physical and cognitive development in the first few years: diet, feeding experience, and opportunities for exploration. Let's consider several others.

INDIVIDUAL DIFFERENCES IN INTELLIGENCE

Psychologists have developed various infant intelligence tests. One such test is the widely used Bayley Scales of Infant Development, which measures primarily sensory and motor skills (Bayley, 1969, revised 1993). For example, 3-month-old infants are challenged to reach for a dangling ring; older babies are observed as they attempt to put cubes in a cup (9 months). Some more clearly cognitive items are also included; for example, uncovering a toy hidden by a cloth is a test item used with 8-month-old infants to measure an aspect of object permanence.

Bayley's test has proven to be helpful in identifying infants and toddlers with serious developmental delays (Sulkes, 1998). But as more general predictive tools for forecasting later IQ or school performance, it has not been nearly as useful as many had hoped; it appears that what is being measured on typical infant intelligence tests is not the same as what is tapped by the commonly used childhood or adult intelligence tests (Colombo, 1993).

Recent research has indicated that habituation tasks have high potential as measures of infant intelligence. For example, if a baby is shown an object or a picture over and over, how many exposures does it take before the infant stops showing interest? The speed with which such habituation/recognition takes place may reveal something about the efficiency of the baby's perceptual/cognitive system and its neurological underpinnings. And if such efficiency lies behind some of the characteristics that psychologists call "intelligence," then individual differences in rate of habituation in the early months of life may predict later intelligence test scores.

That is exactly what researchers have found in studies over the past 15 years. Babies who habituate quickly (that is, who rapidly become uninterested when shown the same object repeatedly) when they are 4 or 5 months old are likely to have higher intelligence test scores at later ages; slower infant habituation is associated with subsequent lower test scores and poorer language skills. The average correlation is in the range of .45 to .50 (Rose & Feldman, 1995; Slater, 1995). This is certainly not perfect correlation, but it is remarkably high compared with the correlation between conventional tests of infant intelligence and later IQ tests. Moreover, results like these underline the importance of examining speed and efficiency in information-processing skills in any effort to understand individual differences in cognitive abilities in early infancy (Rose, Feldman, & Janowsky, 2001).

PRETERM AND LOW-BIRTH-WEIGHT INFANTS

Infants born live before 37 weeks of gestation are considered preterm. The Canadian preterm rate of 7.6 per 100 live births in 2000 has been steadily increasing since 1981. Although preterm rates are significantly higher for multiple birth infants, singleton births still account for more than 80% of all preterm births (see **Figure 4.5**) (Health Canada, 2000a, 2003b).

Infants born before 32 weeks of gestation may not have adaptive reflexes that are sufficiently developed to enable them to survive. Sucking and swallowing, for example, are extremely difficult for these tiny infants. Consequently, many preterm infants must be fed intravenously or through a tube inserted into the esophagus or stomach (Kliegman, 1998). Preterm babies are also at higher risk for neurological impairment, respiratory difficulties, infections, and for neonatal and infant mortality (Berkowitz & Papiernik, 1993).

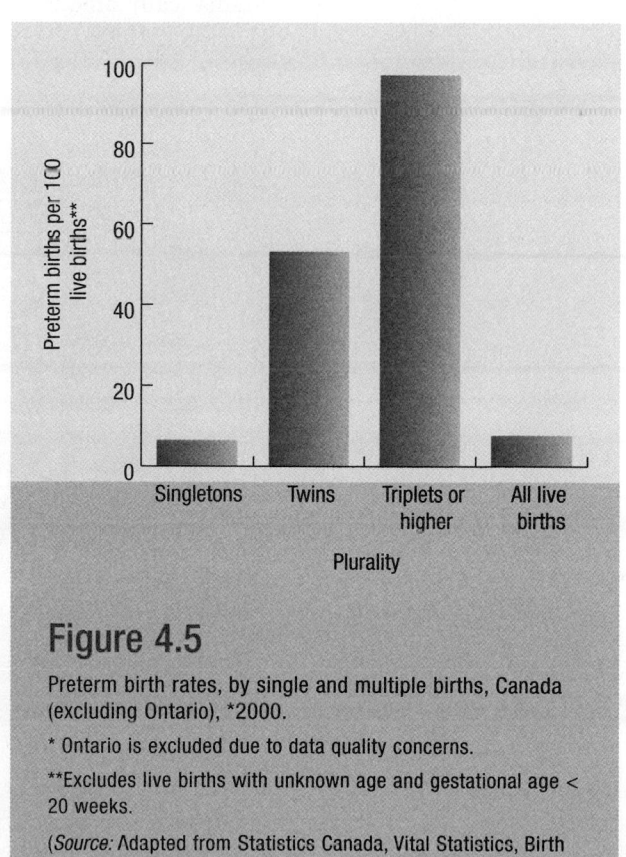

Figure 4.5

Preterm birth rates, by single and multiple births, Canada (excluding Ontario), *2000.

* Ontario is excluded due to data quality concerns.

**Excludes live births with unknown age and gestational age < 20 weeks.

(*Source:* Adapted from Statistics Canada, Vital Statistics, Birth Database, 2000.)

Once preterm infants can be fed orally, breast milk is often not the best food for them. For one thing, premature infants require diets supplemented with amino acids and fats that full-term infants' bodies can manufacture on their own (Guesry, 1998; Kliegman, 1998). In most cases, preterm babies are fed a combination of breast milk and specially formulated substitutes that contain exactly the proteins, fats, vitamins, and minerals their bodies need.

Preterm and low-birth-weight babies (weighing less than 2.5 kilograms at birth) also move more slowly from one developmental milestone to the next. This is what researchers would expect, of course, because the preterm baby is, in fact, maturationally younger than the full-term baby. If a correction is made for the baby's gestational age, most (but not all) of the difference in physical development disappears. Parents of preterms need to keep this in mind when they compare their babies' progress with that of full-term babies. By age 2 or 3, the physically normal preterm will catch up to his peers, but in the early months he is definitely behind.

POST-TERM INFANTS

Infants born after 42 or more weeks of gestation are referred to as post-term. Of concern is that post-term babies are at higher risk for fetal and neonatal mortality (Hilder, Costeloe, & Thilaganathan, 1998). Fortunately, the rate of post-term live birth deliveries in Canada has decreased by 75% between 1991 and 2000 to a low 1.2%. This decrease can be attributed in part to the effective use of ultrasound dating and the practice of inducing post-term pregnancies. However, the rates of post-term deliveries vary dramatically among the provinces and territories of Canada (see **Figure 4.6**) (Health Canada, 2003b).

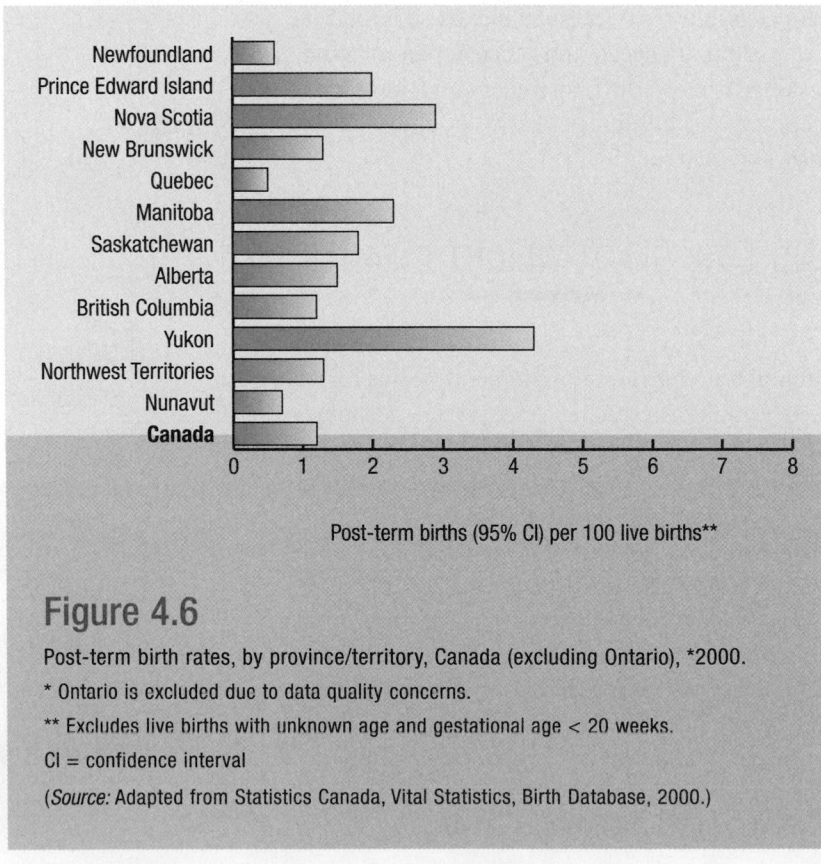

Post-term births (95% CI) per 100 live births**

Figure 4.6

Post-term birth rates, by province/territory, Canada (excluding Ontario), *2000.

* Ontario is excluded due to data quality concerns.

** Excludes live births with unknown age and gestational age < 20 weeks.

CI = confidence interval

(*Source:* Adapted from Statistics Canada, Vital Statistics, Birth Database, 2000.)

Developmental Psychology in Your Career

Neonatal Intensive Care Nurse

Occupation	Neonatal Intensive Care Nurse
Description	• plan and provide care to critically ill neonates from birth to transfer and/or discharge • provide care and information to families of high-risk neonates
Credentials	• Registered Nurse with neonatal intensive care nursing certificate
Essential Lifespan Development Knowledge	• perinatal risk factors • disorders of growth and development • diagnostic and screening tests • impact of sick newborn on family dynamics and functioning
Essential Lifespan Development Skills	• conduct developmental physiological and behavioural assessments • integrate developmental care in the nursery • conduct discharge planning for infant and family adaptation
Essential Lifespan Development Professional Attitude	• present accurate information to parents about developmental issues facing acutely ill infants • act as an emotional resource as parents deal with ethical decisions • use evidence-based approaches to care
Lifespan Development Career Profile: Anne Scott, Neonatal Intensive Care Nurse, Thunder Bay Regional Health Sciences Centre	"The field of neonatology has made great strides over the past 25 years. During my career I have seen advancements such as neonatal developmental care; infants as young as 24 weeks mentally and physically intact; pain management for babies; and many new medications that improve the medical outcome of these precious little individuals. Some premature babies may be in the hospital as long as 4–6 months. Friendships develop between nurses and parents, and often babies come back to visit us as toddlers, students, and even as teenagers." February 23, 2005

BOYS AND GIRLS

As is always true when sex differences are considered, discussions of variations in averages can obscure the fact that boys and girls develop in highly similar ways. Nevertheless, there are a few important differences between averages for male infants and those for female infants. Just as they were prenatally, girls continue to be ahead in some aspects of physical maturity during infancy. For example, the separate bones of the wrist appear earlier in girls than in boys (Tanner, 1990). This means that female infants may have a slight advantage in the development of manipulative skills such as self-feeding. In addition, boys are more likely to suffer from developmental delays, are less healthy, and have higher mortality rates (Halpern, 1997; MacDorman & Atkinson, 1999).

University of Montreal researchers found that boys are typically more physically active, but some investigators report no difference at all (Cossette, Malcuit, & Pomerleau, 1991). However, both in human and primate studies, male infants display a clear preference for rough-and-tumble play even during the first few months of life (Brown & Dixson, 2000; Humphreys & Smith, 1987). Likewise, differences between boys and girls in physical aggression are already evident near the end of the second year, a finding that has been replicated in studies of many cultures (Maccoby & Jacklin, 1974; Whiting & Edwards, 1988).

Most studies suggest that cognitive development is virtually identical for boys and girls in infancy, with one important exception. Girls acquire language somewhat more rapidly than boys do (Halpern, 1997). However, a Norwegian study involving approximately 200 children suggested that boys may be more cognitively vulnerable to the effects of impoverished environments. Researchers found that boys' intelligence test scores at age 5 were more strongly correlated with environmental conditions they had experienced in infancy (such as access to developmentally appropriate toys) than were the scores of girls of that age (Andersson, Sonnander, & Sommerfelt, 1998).

Before Going On

- How do psychologists measure intelligence in infancy? What is the best predictor of future IQ test score?

- How do preterm babies differ from full-term infants in physical and cognitive development?

- In what ways do boys and girls develop differently in the first 2 years?

Summary

Physical Changes

- Changes in the nervous system are extremely rapid in the first 2 years. In most parts of the brain, development of dendrites and synapses reaches its first peaks between 12 and 24 months, after which "pruning" of synapses occurs. Myelinization of nerve fibres also occurs rapidly in the first 2 years.

- Adaptive reflexes include such essential responses as sucking; primitive reflexes include the Moro and Babinski reflexes, which disappear within a few months. At birth, a baby's vision and other senses function, but are limited in some ways; they improve substantially across the first year. Babies move through a series of states of consciousness in a cycle that lasts about 2 hours.

- During infancy, bones increase in number and density; muscle fibres become larger and contain less water. Stamina improves as the lungs grow and the heart gets stronger. Motor skills rapidly improve in the first 2 years, as the baby moves from creeping to crawling to walking to running and becomes able to grasp objects.

- The Canadian Paediatric Society recommends breast-feeding, which has been shown to be better for a baby nutritionally. Babies need regular checkups and a variety of immunizations.

- Poverty seems a likely explanation for why some Canadian babies are more likely than average to die in the first year of life, but the relationship between low income and infant mortality is complex.

- SIDS is the leading cause of death for post-neonatal children aged 28 days to one year. Several factors have been found to be associated with higher risk for SIDS.

Cognitive Changes

- In the first weeks of life, infants appear to be intent on locating objects; after about 2 months, they seem intent on identifying objects, so their method of scanning changes. Babies also show cross-modal perception as early as a few weeks of age.

- Television viewing patterns are becoming established at 10 months of age. Parents should be concerned because toddlers prefer to watch fast-paced programs, such as cartoons, which often have violent content.

- Piaget described the sensorimotor stage as a period of six substages in which an infant with a small repertoire of basic schemes moves toward symbolic representation. The most important cognitive milestone of this stage is object permanence.

- More recent research suggests that Piaget underestimated infants' capabilities as well as the degree to which some concepts may be "wired into" the brain.

- Babies are able to learn by both classical and operant conditioning within the first few weeks of life.

- Infants as young as 3 to 4 months show signs of remembering specific experiences over periods as long as a few days to a week, a sign that they must have some ability to form internal representations, well before Piaget proposed they could.

The Beginnings of Language

- Behaviourist theories of language development claim that infants learn language through parental reinforcement of word-like sounds and correct grammar. Nativists point out that parents seldom reinforce babies in this way. Instead, they say, babies have an innate language processor that helps them learn the rules of language.

- Babies can discriminate among speech sounds in their first weeks. Between 6 and 12 months of age, babies lose the ability to respond to subtle differences in speech sounds to which they are not exposed.

- As babies give up their sensitivity to speech sound distinctions, they begin to pay more attention to word meaning at about 14 months of age.

- Babies' earliest sounds are cries, followed by cooing at about 2 months, then by babbling at about 6 months. At 9 months, babies typically use meaningful gestures and can understand a small vocabulary of spoken words.

- A baby's first spoken words, usually names for objects or people, typically occur at about 1 year, after which toddlers add words slowly for a few months and then rapidly during the naming explosion.

- Canada has a large minority of bilingual children. Research shows that for most children, knowing more than one language has many advantages.

Individual and Group Differences

- Infant intelligence tests are not strongly correlated with later measures of intelligence. However, basic information-processing skills in infancy, such as rate of habituation at 4 months, are correlated with later intelligence test scores.

- Preterm infants lag behind their full-term peers in achieving the milestones of development, but they normally catch up within a few years.

- Girls are physically more advanced than boys and acquire language more rapidly. Most studies find boys to be more active and to prefer rough-and-tumble play.

Key Terms

adaptive reflexes (p. 98)

Canada's Food Guide to Healthy Eating (p. 104)

colic (p. 100)

cross-modal perception (p. 109)

deferred imitation (p. 111)

depth perception (p. 108)

dishabituation (p. 113)

expressive language (p. 120)

grammatical words (p. 118)

habituate (p. 108)

holophrases (p. 120)

intersensory integration (p. 108)

language acquisition device (LAD) (p. 115)

lexical words (p. 118)

macronutients (p. 103)

micronutrients (p. 104)

myelinization (p. 98)

naming explosion (p. 120)

object permanence (p. 111)

plasticity (p. 97)

primitive reflexes (p. 98)

receptive language (p. 118)

reticular formation (p. 98)

schematic learning (p. 113)

sensorimotor stage (p. 109)

states of consciousness (p. 99)

sudden infant death syndrome (SIDS) (p. 106)

synapses (p. 96)

synaptic pruning (p. 97)

visual acuity (p. 99)

Weblinks

A Parent's Guide to Early Brain Development
www.iamyourchild.org/
As part of the *I Am Your Child* public engagement campaign, this site aims to raise awareness about the importance of the first three years of life. Brain Facts contextualizes recent early development findings and how they affect parents and children.

Centres of Excellence for the Children's Well-Being—Health Canada
www.hc-sc.gc.ca/dca-dea/allchildren_touslesenfants/centres_main_e.html
The Centres program is the federal government's first contribution to the National Children's Agenda (NCA). It provides advanced knowledge on key issues of children's health, including child welfare, communities, early childhood development, special needs, and youth engagement.

National Longitudinal Survey of Children and Youth—Human Resources and Development Canada
www11.hrdc-drhc.gc.ca/pls/edd/NLSCY.html
The Applied Research branch of HRDC offers reports, key data summaries, slide presentations, and related publications pertaining to child-related research, based on data from the NLSCY.

Zero to Three
www.zerotothree.org/
Resources for parents and professionals covering the first years of life.

DeVore/Anthro-Photo

CHAPTER 5

SOCIAL AND PERSONALITY DEVELOPMENT IN INFANCY

During infancy, there is more physical closeness, or proximity, between parents and child than in any other period. Proximity is pleasurable for both parents and babies, but it is also practical. For one thing, a mother or father usually has to carry out other duties while simultaneously caring for a baby. Keeping young infants close by helps because they aren't sufficiently mobile to move to the parent when they need care. Once infants become mobile, they can get themselves into all kinds of trouble. Thus, with older babies, one of the goals of maintaining proximity is to protectively restrict their movements.

Practical considerations aside, caregiver–infant proximity contributes to the development of a strong emotional bond. In many parts of the world, mothers carry their babies with them most of the time in some kind of sling or wrap—as the Masai mother is doing in the photo on the previous page. This system is not only practical but also keeps the caregiver and baby in close physical contact, a factor that seems to promote the development of a secure, affectionate relationship between them. In addition, physical closeness allows parents and babies to interact by exchanging smiles, frowns, or silly faces. Likewise, when parents and babies are close to each other, the parents can easily teach infants the names of objects in the environment.

In industrialized societies, a variety of devices such as strollers allow caregivers to easily transport babies just about anywhere an adult can go. You might think that a stroller would restrict contact between caregiver and infant. However, if you observe parents and their stroller-bound infants at a shopping mall or park, you will see babies taken out of their strollers to be fed and put back in for naps. You will also notice that parents wheel infants to places they think the babies will find interesting—such as a pet store window where kittens are frolicking—and converse with the babies about what they see: "Look at the kitties. Aren't they cute?" Thus, baby slings such as those used by the Masai may look very different from the industrialized world's strollers, but both help caregivers and infants form relationships.

Developmentalists of diverse theoretical orientations agree that the formation of a strong emotional connection to a primary caregiver early in life is critical to healthy child development and has important implications across the entire human lifespan. In this chapter, you will learn how such relationships develop. In addition, you will read about inborn biases concerning social interaction that infants bring with them into the world, as well as how their perceptions of themselves develop over the first 2 years. The chapter will also address the effects of nonparental care and a variety of other variables on infant development. As you read, keep the following questions in mind:

Every culture devises ways of transporting infants that protect them and keep them close to their caregivers.
(*Photo:* Getty Images)

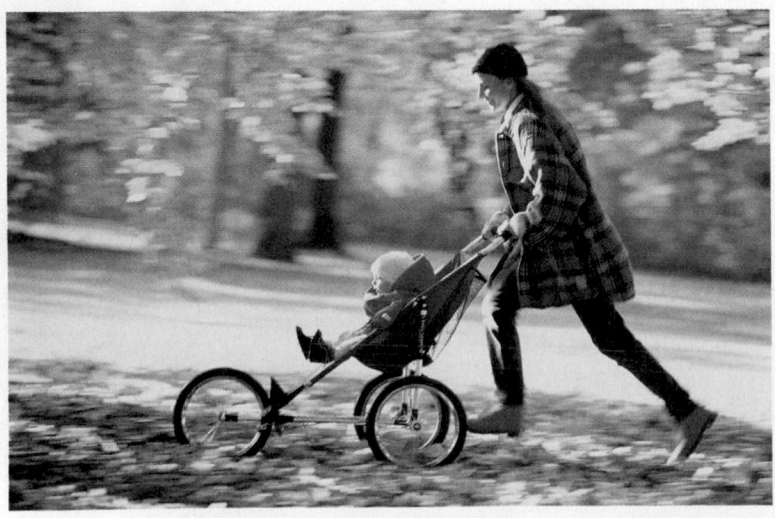

- What are the major theoretical perspectives that inform research on infants' social and personality development?

- How does the parent–infant relationship develop?

- Do infants come into the world with inborn traits? How do infants develop their self-concepts?

- How does nonparental care affect infant development?

- What are some important individual and group differences in infant social and personality development?

THEORIES OF SOCIAL AND PERSONALITY DEVELOPMENT

Psychologists have used all the theoretical perspectives you learned about in **Chapter 2** to formulate hypotheses about infant social and personality development. However, the two most influential perspectives on these issues are the psychoanalytic and the ethological perspectives.

PSYCHOANALYTIC PERSPECTIVES

You may remember from **Chapter 2** that Freud proposed a series of psychosexual stages that extend from birth through adolescence, during which individuals attempt to satisfy certain basic drives in different ways. In the first stage, from birth to age 2, infants derive satisfaction through the mouth. Therefore, Freud named this stage the oral stage. He further believed that the weaning process should be managed in such a way that the infant's need to suck is neither frustrated nor overgratified. The consequences of either, Freud claimed, would be fixation at this stage of development. As a result of fixation, the infant would carry with her into adulthood a need to use her mouth to attain physical gratification of her instinctual drives. Fixation would manifest itself, in Freud's view, in oral behaviours such as nail-biting and swearing.

Freud also emphasized the symbiotic relationship between the mother and young infant, in which the two behave as if they were one. He believed that the infant did not understand herself to be separate from her mother. Thus, another result of a gratifying nursing period followed by a balanced weaning process, Freud thought, was the infant's development of a sense of both attachment to and separation from the mother.

Erikson went beyond Freud's view. Nursing and weaning are important, he conceded, but they are only one aspect of the overall social environment. Erikson claimed that responding to the infant's other needs by talking to him, comforting him, and so on, was just as important. He proposed that the first 2 years comprise a period during which the infant learns to trust the world around him or becomes cynical about the social environment's ability to meet his needs—the trust versus mistrust stage.

One of the best-known studies in developmental psychology demonstrated that Erikson's view of infant development was more accurate than Freud's (Harlow & Zimmerman, 1959). In this study, infant monkeys were separated from their mothers at birth. The experimenters placed two different kinds of "surrogate" mothers in their cages. The monkeys received all their feedings from a wire mother with a nursing bottle attached. The other mother was covered with soft terrycloth. The researchers found that the monkeys approached the wire mother only when hungry. Most of the time, they cuddled against the cloth mother and ran to it whenever they were frightened or stressed. Subsequent studies with human infants correlating maternal feeding practices with infant adjustment suggested that the infant's social relationships are not based solely on either nursing or weaning practices (Schaffer & Emerson, 1964).

ETHOLOGICAL PERSPECTIVES

The strongest theoretical influence in modern-day studies of infant–parent relationships is an ethological approach known as **attachment theory**, based originally on the work of John Bowlby (1969, 1973, 1980, 1988a, 1988b). Bowlby argued that "the propensity to make strong emotional bonds to particular individuals [is] a basic component of

Freud asserted that infant weaning practices were central to the attachment process.
(*Photo:* Felicia Martinez/PhotoEdit)

attachment theory
the view that the ability and need to form an attachment relationship early in life are genetic characteristics of all human beings

Harlow's ingenious research demonstrated that infant monkeys became attached to a terrycloth covered "mother" and would cling to it rather than to a wire mother that provided them with food.
(*Photo:* © Martin Rogers/Woodfin Camp and Associates)

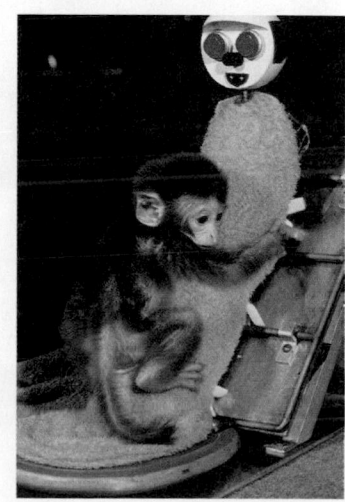

Make the Connection

Choose one of the theoretical perspectives in **Chapter 2** not discussed here and think about how it would colour hypotheses about infants' social and personality development. For example, how would B.F. Skinner apply operant conditioning principles to explain the development of parent–infant relationships in the first 2 years?

Critical Thinking

Think about your own relationships. In Bowlby's and Ainsworth's terms, which are attachments and which are affectional bonds?

affectional bond
the emotional tie to an infant experienced by a parent

attachment
the emotional tie to a parent experienced by an infant, from which the child derives security

reactive attachment disorder
a disorder that appears to prevent a child from forming close social relationships

human nature, already present in germinal form in the neonate" (1988a, p. 3). Such relationships have survival value, because they ensure that the infant will be nurtured. They are built and maintained by instinctive behaviours that create and sustain proximity between parent and child.

The writings of Ainsworth (described in **Chapter 1** in A Brief History of the Roots of Psychology in Canada) and Bowlby draw a distinction between different types of affectionate human relationships (Ainsworth, Blehar, Waters, & Wall, 1978). An **affectional bond** is defined as "a relatively long-enduring tie in which the partner is important as a unique individual and is interchangeable with none other. In an affectional bond, there is a desire to maintain closeness to the partner" (Bowlby, 1989, p. 711). An **attachment** is a type of affectional bond in which a person's sense of security is bound up in the relationship. When you are attached, you feel a special sense of security and comfort in the presence of the other, and you can use the other as a "safe base" from which to explore the rest of the world.

Ethologists believe that the first 2 years of life constitute a sensitive period for attachment in human infants. They claim that infants who fail to form a close relationship with a primary caregiver are at risk for future social and personality problems. Studies of infants whose life circumstances do not permit them to engage in extended contact with a single caregiver— such as children who are brought up in orphanages or who are hospitalized for long periods during infancy—seem to confirm ethologists' view (DeAngelis, 1997; Fahrenfort, Jacobs, Miedema, & Schweizer, 1996).

For example, children who are adopted after spending more than 2 years in an orphanage are more likely to suffer from a disorder known as **reactive attachment disorder** than those who are adopted in infancy (DeAngelis, 1997). Children with reactive attachment disorder seem to be unable to form close emotional relationships with anyone, including foster and adoptive parents. Long-term institutional care is also associated with cognitive deficits (Castle et al., 1999). Even children whose institutional care does not extend beyond the first 2 years are more likely to display developmental delays and emotional difficulties the later in infancy they are adopted (De Angelis, 1997); see **No Easy Answers**.

No Easy Answers

Adoption and Development

Most people who adopt a child assume that if they provide enough love and support, the child will develop both cognitively and emotionally pretty much the way their biological child would. By now, you should know enough about human development to realize that it just isn't that simple. For one thing, many aspects of temperament and personality are inherited. Therefore, an adopted child is more likely than a biological child to be different from his parents in these traits, which may give rise to problems. For example, if two extremely shy parents adopt a child who is very outgoing, the parents may view the child's behaviour as difficult or even "disturbed" in some way, rather than just different from theirs.

Adoptive parents also need to take into account the child's circumstances prior to the adoption in order to form a realistic set of expectations. Children adopted before the age of 6 months, who have no history of institutionalization or abuse, are generally indistinguishable from nonadopted children in security of attachment, cognitive development, and social adjustment (Kirchner, 1998). This is true whether adoptive parents and children are of the same or different races and/or nationalities (Juffer & Rosenboom, 1997).

However, in special circumstances the outcomes are more equivocal. For instance, researchers from Simon Fraser University have been studying Romanian Orphans (RO) who were adopted by Canadian families early in the 1990s. The infants had been raised in Romanian orphanages, where they experienced extreme deprivation, understimulation, malnourishment, and only minimal custodial care. Elinor Ames's (1997) research team found that the infants who had lived in the Romanian orphanages for more than 4 months before being adopted by British Columbian families tended to have more psychological and motor-behaviour problems than nonadopted children. Moreover, the more months an infant had lived in the Romanian orphanage the more serious his or her difficulties were.

Lucy Le Mare has continued the project and last assessed the RO when they were 10 years old (Le Mare, Warford, & Fernyhough, 2001; Le Mare, Fernyhough, & Warford, 2001). Her team found that there was considerable variability between individuals, but as a group the RO continued to show significantly more difficulties than comparable Canadian-born or early-adopted Romanian children. In particular, RO children had lower average IQs and academic achievement, and more difficulties with attention, learning, and peer relationships. Despite these challenges, the RO children were just as well liked as any other child and the adoption experience has continued to be mutually rewarding for both the RO children and their adoptive families.

Accordingly, there are a few important facts that parents who adopt high-risk children should keep in mind. First, these children are better off developmentally than their peers who remain institutionalized or who are returned to biological parents who abused and/or neglected them (Bohman & Sigvardsson, 1990). Further, despite increased risks, the large majority of adopted children are indistinguishable from nonadopted children in social behaviour and emotional functioning by the time they reach late adolescence or adulthood (Brand & Brinich, 1999; Cederblad Hook, Irhammar, & Mercke, 1999).

Second, the task of raising high-risk children can be made more manageable with parent training (Juffer, Hoksbergen, Riksen-Walraven, & Kohnstamm, 1997). Thus, adoptive parents should take advantage of any training offered by the institutions through which the adoption was arranged. If none is available, they should look for training elsewhere, perhaps at a local community college.

Finally, at the first sign of difficulty, adoptive parents should seek help from a social worker or psychologist who specializes in treating children. In fact, many developmentalists recommend that agencies that place high-risk children in adoptive or long-term foster families should routinely provide them with postadoption therapeutic services (Mainemer et al., 1998; Minty, 1999; Smith et al., 1998). Therapists can help with everyday tasks such as toilet-training and teach parents strategies for dealing with behaviour that reflects severe emotional disturbance, such as self-injury.

Before Going On

- How do Freud's and Erikson's views of personality development in the first 2 years differ?
- What is attachment theory, and what evidence is there to suggest that the first 2 years are a critical period for forming an attachment?

ATTACHMENT

Somehow, in the midst of endless diaper changes, food preparation, baths, and periods of exhaustion that exceed anything they have ever experienced before, the overwhelming majority of parents manage to respond to their infants in ways that foster the development of a close relationship. To understand the early relationship between parent and infant, it is important to look at both sides of the equation—at the development of both the parents' bond to the child and the child's attachment to the parents.

THE PARENTS' ATTACHMENT TO THE INFANT

Contact between parent and infant immediately after birth does not appear to be either necessary or sufficient for the formation of a stable long-term affectional bond between either mother or father and child (Wong, 1993). What is essential in the formation of that bond is the opportunity for parent and infant to develop a mutual, interlocking pattern of attachment behaviours, called **synchrony**.

synchrony
a mutual, interlocking pattern of attachment behaviours shared by a parent and child

Synchrony is like a conversation. The baby signals his needs by crying or smiling; he responds to being held by quieting or snuggling; he looks at the parents when they look at him. The parents, in their turn, enter into the interaction with their own repertoire of caregiving behaviours. One of the most intriguing things about this process is that we all seem to know how to engage in this particular conversation and do it in very similar ways. In the presence of a young infant, most adults will automatically display a distinctive pattern of interactive behaviours, including smiling, raised eyebrows, and very wide-open eyes. And we all seem to use our voices in special ways with babies. Parents all over the world use a characteristic high-pitched and lilting voice when speaking to an infant and specific intonation patterns to signal different meanings. For example, one study found that Chinese, German, and American mothers all tended to use a rising voice inflection when they wanted their babies to become involved in the interaction and a falling intonation when they wanted to soothe their babies (Papousek & Papousek, 1991).

Critical Thinking

Listen to yourself speak the next time you interact with a baby. Do you speak in a higher, more lilting voice? Do your intonation patterns match the ones described in the Papousek study?

Even though adults can perform all these attachment behaviours with many infants, they do not form a bond with every baby they coo at in a restaurant or the grocery store. For an adult, the critical ingredient for the formation of a bond seems to be the opportunity to develop real synchrony—to practise the conversation until the participants follow each other's lead smoothly and pleasurably. For example, research suggests that an imitative conversation style, a pattern in which mother imitates baby's vocalizations and vice versa, may be an important component of parent–infant synchrony (Masur & Rodemaker, 1999). Such interactions require time and many rehearsals, and some parents (and infants) become more skilful at them than others. In general, the smoother and more predictable the process becomes, the more satisfying it seems to be to the parents and the stronger the attachment relationship becomes. Moreover, the degree of synchrony in parent–infant interactions seems to contribute to cognitive development as well. Developmentalists have found that 6- to 8-month-old infants whose interactions with their parents are highly synchronous tend to have larger vocabularies at age 2 and higher intelligence test scores at age 3 than their counterparts whose interactions are less synchronous (Saxon, Colombo, Robinson, & Frick, 2000).

The father's bond with the infant, like the mother's, seems to depend more on the development of synchrony than on contact immediately after birth. Aiding the development of such mutuality is the fact that fathers seem to have the same repertoire of attachment behaviours as do mothers. In the early weeks of the baby's life, fathers touch, talk to, and cuddle their babies in the same ways that mothers do (Parke & Tinsley, 1981).

After the first weeks of the baby's life, however, signs of a kind of specialization of parental behaviours begin to emerge. Fathers spend more time playing with the baby, with more physical roughhousing; mothers spend more time in routine caregiving and also talk to and smile at the baby more (Walker, Messinger, Fogel, & Karns, 1992). This does not mean that fathers have a weaker affectional bond with the infant; it simply means that fathers and mothers use different attachment behaviours in interacting with their infants. For instance, Canadian researchers found that fathers can be as sensitive to the needs of their child as the mother. However, fathers are less consistent than mothers in responding to infant cues; sometimes reacting and sometimes not (Harrison, Magill-Evans, & Benzies, 1999). It has also been found that fathers who reported that they felt accepted during their childhood were more responsive to their offspring. Moreover, if the father's current level of marital satisfaction was high he was more responsive to his child's needs, regardless of his perception of his own childhood experiences (Onyskiw, Harrison, & Magill-Evans, 1997).

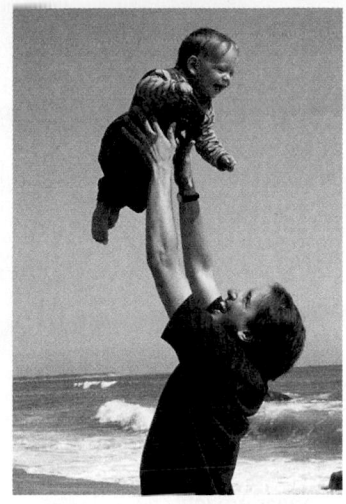

Fathers engage in physical play with infants more often than mothers do.
(*Photo:* © Lynne J. Weinstein/Woodfin Camp and Associates)

THE INFANT'S ATTACHMENT TO THE PARENTS

Like the parent's bond to the baby, the baby's attachment emerges gradually and is based on her ability to discriminate between her parents and other people. As you learned in **Chapters 3** and **4**, an infant can recognize her mother's voice prior to birth. By the time the baby is a few days old, she recognizes her mother by sight and smell as well (Cernoch & Porter, 1985; Walton, Bower, & Bower, 1992). Thus, the cognitive foundation for attachment is in place within days after birth.

Bowlby suggested three phases in the development of the infant's attachment (Bowlby, 1969). Bowlby thought that in the first phase, known as nonfocused orienting and signalling, the baby uses a set of innate behaviour patterns that orient her toward others and signal her needs. Ainsworth described these as "proximity promoting" behaviours—they bring people closer. In the newborn's repertoire, these behaviours include crying, making eye contact, clinging, cuddling, and responding to caregiving efforts by being soothed. At this stage, there is little evidence of an attachment. As Ainsworth says, "These attachment behaviours are simply emitted, rather than being directed toward any specific person" (1989, p. 710). Nonetheless, the roots of attachment are to be found in this phase. The baby is building up expectancies and schemas and fine-tuning her ability to discriminate Mom and Dad from others.

By 3 months of age, the baby enters the focus on one or more figures phase and begins to aim her attachment behaviours somewhat more narrowly. She may smile more at the people who regularly take care of her and may not smile readily at a stranger. Yet despite the change, Bowlby and Ainsworth have argued that the infant does not yet have a full-blown attachment. The child still favours a number of people with her "proximity promoting" behaviours, and no one person has yet become the "safe base." Children in this phase show no special anxiety at being separated from their parents and no fear of strangers.

In phase 3, secure base behaviour, the 6-month-old changes her attachment behaviour. Because the 6- to 7-month-old begins to be able to move about the world more freely by creeping and crawling, she can move toward a parent as well as enticing the parent to come to her. Her attachment behaviours therefore shift from mostly

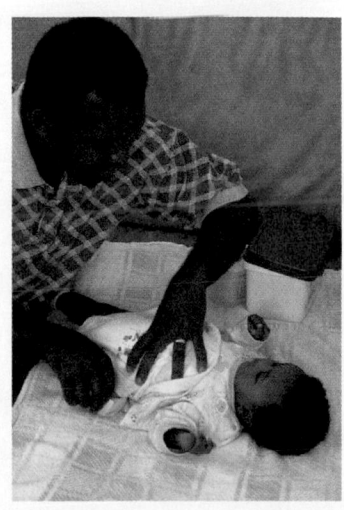

Dads like this one, who get involved with the day-to-day care of their babies, seem to develop stronger attachment relationships with their babies.
(*Photo:* Laura Dwight/PhotoEdit)

"come here" signals (proximity promoting) to what Ainsworth called "proximity seeking" behaviours—which might be thought of as "go there" behaviours. A child of this age also uses the "most important" person as a safe base from which to explore the world around her—one of the key signs that an attachment exists.

Not all infants have a single attachment figure, even at this stage. Some may show strong attachment to both parents or to a parent and another caregiver, such as a babysitter or a grandparent. But even these babies, when under stress, usually show a preference for one of their favoured persons over the others.

ATTACHMENT BEHAVIOURS Once the child has developed a clear attachment, at about 6 to 8 months of age, several related behaviours also begin appearing. Stranger anxiety and separation anxiety, attachment behaviours that are rare before 5 or 6 months, rise in frequency until about 12 to 16 months, and then decline. Infants express **stranger anxiety** with behaviours such as clinging to their mothers when strangers are present. **Separation anxiety** is evident when infants cry or protest being separated from the mother. The research findings are not altogether consistent, but fear of strangers apparently emerges first. Separation anxiety starts a bit later but continues to be visible for a longer period. Such an increase in fear and anxiety has been observed in children from a number of different cultures, and in both home-reared children and children in day care.

Another attachment behaviour is **social referencing** (Walden, 1991). By roughly 10 months, infants use cues from the facial expressions of their attachment figures to help them figure out what to do in novel situations, such as when a stranger comes to visit. Babies this age will first look at Mom's or Dad's face to check for the adult's emotional expression. If Mom looks pleased or happy, the baby is likely to explore a new toy with more ease or to accept a stranger with less fuss. If Mom looks concerned or frightened, the baby responds to those cues and reacts to the novel situation with equivalent fear or concern.

From the age of 7 to 8 months, when strong attachments are first seen, infants prefer either the father or the mother to a stranger. When both the father and the mother are available, an infant will smile at or approach either or both, except when he is frightened or under stress. When that happens, especially between 8 and 24 months of age, the child typically turns to the mother rather than the father (Lamb, 1981).

stranger anxiety
expressions of discomfort, such as clinging to the mother, in the presence of strangers

separation anxiety
expressions of discomfort, such as crying, when separated from an attachment figure

social referencing
an infant's use of others' facial expressions as a guide to his or her own emotions

VARIATIONS IN ATTACHMENT QUALITY

Virtually all babies seem to go through the three phases of attachment first identified by Bowlby, but the quality of the attachments they form differs from one infant to the next.

INTERNAL MODELS In Bowlby's terminology, infants create different internal models of their relationships with parents and other key adults. These models include such elements as the child's confidence (or lack of it) that the attachment figure will be available or reliable, the child's expectation of rebuff or affection, and the child's sense of assurance that the other is really a safe base for exploration. The internal model begins to be formed late in the child's first year of life and becomes increasingly elaborated and better established through the first 4 or 5 years. By age 5, most children have a clear internal models of the mother (or other primary caregiver), a self model, and a model of relationships. Once formed, such models shape and explain experiences and affect memory and attention. Children notice and remember experiences that fit their models and miss or forget experiences that don't match. As Piaget might say, a child more readily assimilates data that fit the model. More importantly, the model affects the child's behaviour: The child tends to re-create, in each new relationship, the pattern with which he is familiar.

SECURE AND INSECURE ATTACHMENTS Variations in the quality of the first attachment relationship are now almost universally described using Ainsworth's category system (Ainsworth et al., 1978). The Ainsworth system distinguishes between secure attachment and two types of insecure attachment, which psychologists assess using a procedure called the Strange Situation.

The Strange Situation consists of a series of eight episodes played out in a laboratory setting, typically with children between 12 and 18 months of age. The child is observed in each of the following situations:

- With the mother
- With the mother and a stranger
- Alone with the stranger
- Completely alone for a few minutes
- Reunited with the mother
- Alone again
- With the stranger again
- Reunited with the mother

Ainsworth suggested that children's reactions in these situations—particularly to the reunion episodes—showed attachment of one of three types: **secure attachment, avoidant attachment,** and **ambivalent attachment.** A fourth type, **disorganized/disoriented attachment,** includes attachment reactions that do not readily fit into the other two insecure patterns (Main & Solomon, 1990).

Whether a child cries when he is separated from his mother is not a helpful indicator of the security of his attachment. Some securely attached infants cry then, others do not: the same is true of insecurely attached infants. It is the entire pattern of the child's response to the Strange Situation that is critical, not any one response. These attachment types have been observed in studies in many different countries, and secure attachment is the most common pattern in every country.

David Pederson and Greg Moran (1996) of the University of Western Ontario have refined the measurement of attachment. Unlike the Strange Situation, which is laboratory-based, mother–infant interactions are observed in the more natural and convenient surroundings of the home environment. By using either method, it was determined that in a secure type of relationship, mothers were more sensitive to their infant's needs and their infant tended to be less fussy and preferred physical contact with the mother (Pederson & Moran, 1996; Pederson, Gleason, Moran, & Bento, 1998).

ORIGINS OF SECURE AND INSECURE ATTACHMENTS Studies of parent–child interactions suggest that one crucial ingredient for secure attachment is emotional availability on the part of the primary caregiver (Biringen, 2000). An emotionally available caregiver is one who is able and willing to form an emotional attachment to the infant. For example, economically or emotionally distressed parents may be so distracted by their own problems that they can't invest emotion in the parent–infant relationship. Such parents may be able to meet the baby's physical needs but unable to respond emotionally.

Contingent responsiveness is another key ingredient of secure attachment (Isabella, 1995; Pederson & Moran, 1995; Pederson et al., 1990; Seifer, Schiller, Sameroff, Resnick, & Riordan, 1996). Parents who demonstrate **contingent responsiveness** are sensitive to the child's cues and respond appropriately. They smile when the baby smiles, talk to the baby when he vocalizes, pick him up when he cries, and so on (Ainsworth & Marvin, 1995). Infants of parents who display contingent responsiveness in the early

secure attachment
a pattern of attachment in which an infant readily separates from the parent, seeks proximity when stressed, and uses the parent as a safe base for exploration

avoidant attachment
a pattern of attachment in which an infant avoids contact with the parent and shows no preference for the parent over other people

ambivalent attachment
a pattern of attachment in which the infant shows little exploratory behaviour, is greatly upset when separated from the mother, and is not reassured by her return or efforts to comfort him

disorganized/disoriented attachment
a pattern of attachment in which an infant seems confused or apprehensive and shows contradictory behaviour, such as moving toward the mother while looking away from her

contingent responsiveness
being sensitive to the child's verbal and nonverbal cues and responding appropriately

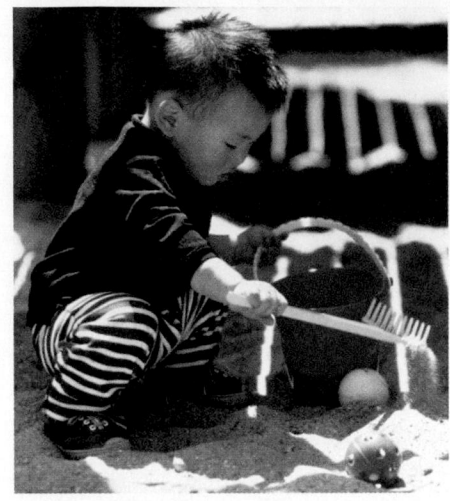

Whether a child cries when he is separated from his mother is not a helpful indicator of the security of his attachment. Some securely attached infants cry when separated from their mothers; others do not. The same is true of insecurely attached infants.

(*Photo:* Elizabeth Halton/Firstlight.ca)

months are more likely to be securely attached at age 12 months (Heinicke et al., 2000).

A low level of parental responsiveness thus appears to be an ingredient in any type of insecure attachment. However, each of the several subvarieties of insecure attachment is affected by additional distinct factors. For example, if the mother rejects the infant or regularly withdraws from contact with her, the baby is more likely to show an avoidant pattern of attachment, although the pattern also seems to occur when the mother is overly intrusive or overly stimulating toward the infant (Isabella, 1995). An ambivalent pattern is more common when the primary caregiver is inconsistently or unreliably available to the child. A disorganized/disoriented pattern seems especially likely when the child has been abused, and in families in which either parent had some unresolved trauma in his or her own childhood, such as abuse or a parent's early death (Cassidy & Berlin, 1994; Main & Hesse, 1990).

STABILITY OF ATTACHMENT CLASSIFICATION Researchers have found that the quality of a child's attachment can be either consistent or changeable. It seems that, when a child's family environment or life circumstances are reasonably consistent, the security or insecurity of her attachment also seems to remain consistent, even over many years (Hamilton, 1995; Wartner, Grossman, Fremmer-Bombik, & Suess, 1994). However, when a child's circumstances change in some major way—such as when the parents divorce or the family moves—the security of the child's attachment may change as well, either from secure to insecure, or the reverse. For example, in one important study, developmentalists followed one group of middle-class white children from age 1 to age 21 (Waters, Treboux, Crowell, Merrick, & Albersheim, 1995). Those whose attachment classification changed over this long interval had nearly all experienced some major upheaval, such as the death of a parent, physical or sexual abuse, or a serious illness.

The fact that the security of a child's attachment can change over time does not refute the notion of attachment as arising from an internal model. Bowlby suggested that for the first 2 or 3 years, the particular pattern of attachment a child shows is in some sense a property of each specific relationship. For example, studies of toddlers' attachments to mothers and fathers show that about 30% of the children are securely attached to one parent and insecurely attached to the other, with both possible combinations equally likely (Fox, Kimmerly, & Schafer, 1991). It is the quality of each relationship that determines the security of the child's attachment to that specific adult. If the relationship changes markedly, the security of attachment may change, too. But, Bowlby argued, by age 4 or 5, the internal model becomes more a property of the child, more generalized across relationships, and thus more resistant to change. At that point, the child tends to impose the model on new relationships, including relationships with teachers or peers.

LONG-TERM CONSEQUENCES OF ATTACHMENT QUALITY

Ainsworth's classification system has proven to be extremely helpful in predicting a remarkably wide range of other behaviours in infants, children, adolescents, and adults. Dozens of studies show that children rated as securely attached to their mothers in infancy are later more sociable, more positive in their behaviour toward friends and siblings, less clinging and dependent on teachers, less aggressive and disruptive, more empathetic, and more emotionally mature in their interactions in school and other settings outside the home (e.g., Carlson & Sroufe, 1995; Jacobsen, Husa, Fendrich, Kruesi, & Ziegenhain, 1997).

Adolescents who were rated as securely attached in infancy or who are classed as secure on the basis of interviews in adolescence are also more socially skilled, have more intimate friendships, are more likely to be rated as leaders, and have higher self-esteem and better grades (Black & McCartney, 1995; Jacobsen & Hofmann, 1997; Lieberman, Doyle, & Markiewicz, 1995; Ostoja, McCrone, Lehn, Reed, & Sroufe, 1995). Those with insecure attachments—particularly those with avoidant attachments—not only have less positive and supportive friendships in adolescence, but are also more likely to become sexually active early and to practise riskier sex (O'Beirne & Moore, 1995; Sroufe, Carlson, & Schulman, 1993; Urban, Carlson, Egeland, & Sroufe, 1991).

Quality of attachment in infancy also predicts sociability through early, middle, and late adulthood (Van Lange, DeBruin, Otten, & Joireman, 1997). Moreover, one study found a link between attachment history and sexual dysfunction in adult males (Kinzl, Mangweth, Traweger, & Biebl, 1996). In fact, that investigation found that quality of attachment in infancy predicted sexual dysfunction in adulthood better than a history of sexual abuse did.

Developmentalists have also begun to examine the question of whether an adult's internal model of attachment affects his or her parenting behaviours (Crittenden, Partridge, & Claussen, 1991). To answer this question, psychologists have devised an interview that allows them to classify the security or insecurity of an adult's attachment to his or her parents (Main & Hesse, 1990). In this interview, adults are asked about their childhood experiences and their current relationship with their parents. For example, one question asks the adult to choose five adjectives to describe her relationship with each parent and to say why she chose each adjective. On the basis of the interview, the adult's internal model of attachment is assigned to one of three categories.

Adults in the *secure/autonomous/balanced* category value attachment relations and see their early experiences as influential, but they are objective in describing both good and bad qualities of their parents. They speak coherently about early experiences and have thought about what motivated their parents' behaviour. Those in the *dismissing/detached* category minimize the importance or the effects of early experiences. Many of these adults idealize their parents, perhaps even denying the existence of any negative experiences, and emphasize their own personal strengths. *Preoccupied/enmeshed* adults often talk about inconsistent or role-reversed parenting. These individuals are still engrossed in their relationships with their parents, still actively struggling to please them or still very angry at them. They are confused and ambivalent, but still engaged.

When researchers study the security of attachment displayed by the children of adults in each of these three categories, the expected patterns emerge strongly. Adults with secure attachment to their own parents are much more likely to have infants or toddlers with secure attachment. Those with dismissing attachment are more likely to have infants with avoidant attachment; adults with preoccupied attachment are more likely to have infants with ambivalent attachment. Across 20 studies, the typical finding was that three-quarters of the mother–infant pairs shared the same attachment category (van IJzendoorn, 1995). Researchers have even found marked consistency across three generations of Canadian grandmothers, young mothers, and infants (Benoit & Parker, 1994).

Clearly, a mother's (or other primary caregiver's) behaviour toward her child varies as a function of her own internal model of attachment. Mothers who are themselves securely attached are more responsive and sensitive in their behaviour toward their infants or young children (Hammond, Landry, Swank, & Smith, 2000; van IJzendoorn, 1995). For example, securely attached mothers are more likely to prepare their children ahead of time for an anticipated separation (Crowell & Feldman, 1988). These mothers

Critical Thinking

What could be done to break the cycle of insecure attachment that can be perpetuated from generation to generation? What kind of external interventions would be required?

also have less anxiety themselves about the separation and are most physically responsive to the child at reunion. Preoccupied mothers tend to be more anxious about separating from their children and to prepare them less well than secure mothers do. Dismissing mothers also prepare the child very little, but leave without difficulty and remain physically distant from their children after they are reunited.

Mothers with dismissing or preoccupied internal models also appear to interpret children's behaviour very differently than the secure mothers do. For example, in one study, a mother observed her crying child through the observation window and said, "See, she isn't upset about being left." At reunion, she said to the child, "Why are you crying? I didn't leave" (Crowell & Feldman, 1988, p. 604). Thus, the mother's own internal model not only affects her actual behaviour but affects the meaning she ascribes to the child's behaviour, both of which will affect the child's developing model of attachment.

Examinations of the long-term consequences of quality of attachment suggest that both psychoanalysts and ethologists are correct in their assumption that the attachment relationship becomes the foundation for future social relationships. Certainly, it appears to be critical to the relationship most similar to it—the relationship an individual ultimately develops with her or his own child.

Before Going On

- Describe the effects of synchrony on parent–infant relations.
- What are the three phases of attachment and the behaviours that are associated with them?
- Define the four types of attachment and discuss their origins and stability.
- What are the long-term consequences of attachment quality?

PERSONALITY, TEMPERAMENT, AND SELF-CONCEPT

personality
a pattern of responding to people and objects in the environment

Psychologists typically use the word **personality** to describe patterns in the way children and adults relate to the people and objects in the world around them. Individual differences in personality appear to develop throughout childhood and adolescence, based on a basic set of behavioural and emotional predispositions present at birth (McCrae, Costa, Ostendord, & Angleitner, 2000). These predispositions are usually referred to as **temperament** (Rothbart, Ahadi, & Evans, 2000).

temperament
inborn predispositions such as activity level that form the foundations of personality

DIMENSIONS OF TEMPERAMENT

Psychologists who study infant temperament have yet to agree on a basic set of temperament dimensions. One influential early theory, proposed by Thomas and Chess, listed nine dimensions: activity level, rhythmicity, approach/withdrawal, adaptability to new experience, threshold of responsiveness, intensity of reaction, quality of mood (positive or negative), distractibility, and persistence (Thomas & Chess, 1977). Thomas and Chess further proposed that variations in these nine qualities tended to cluster into three types, which they called the **easy child**, the **difficult child**, and the **slow-to-warm-up child**. In contrast, Buss and Plomin have argued for three basic temperament dimensions: *activity level*, *emotionality*, and *sociability* (Buss, 1989; Buss & Plomin, 1984, 1986). The questionnaire they devised to measure these three dimensions has been widely used by researchers studying infants, children, and adults.

Despite such disagreements, a few key dimensions are now appearing in lists compiled by many researchers who study infant temperament (Ahadi & Rothbart, 1994; Belsky, Hsieh, & Crnic, 1996; Kagan, 1994; Martin, Wisenbaker, & Huttunen, 1994). Activity level refers to an infant's tendency to either move often and vigorously or remain passive or immobile. Inhibition—a tendency to respond with fear or withdrawal to new people, new situations, new objects—is the flip side of approach. Negative emotionality is a tendency to respond to frustrating circumstances with anger, fussing, loudness, or irritability. Finally, effortful control/task persistence is an ability to stay focused, to manage attention and effort.

ORIGINS AND STABILITY OF TEMPERAMENT

Because temperamental differences appear so early in life, even during the prenatal period (see **Chapter 3**), it may seem that genes are entirely responsible for them. However, research suggests that both nature and nurture contribute to individual differences in temperament.

HEREDITY Clear, strong evidence, both from studies of adult personality and from studies of children's temperament, supports the assertion that temperamental differences are inborn (Caspi, 1998; Goldsmith, Lemery, Buss, & Campos, 1999). Studies of twins in many countries show that identical twins are more alike in their temperament than are fraternal twins (Rose, 1995). For example, one group of researchers studied 100 pairs of identical twins and 100 pairs of fraternal twins at both 14 and 20 months. At each age, the children's temperaments were rated by their mothers using the Buss and Plomin categories. In addition, each child's level of behavioural inhibition was measured by observing how the child reacted to strange toys and a strange adult in a special laboratory playroom. Did the child approach the novel toys quickly and eagerly or hang back or seem fearful? Did the child approach the strange adult or remain close to the mother? The correlations between temperament scores on all four of these dimensions were consistently higher for identical than for fraternal twins, indicating a strong genetic effect (Emde et al., 1992; Plomin et al., 1993).

Many temperament theorists take the argument a step further and trace the basic differences in behaviour to variations in underlying physiological patterns (e.g., Gunnar, 1994; Rothbart, Derryberry, & Posner, 1994). For example, Jerome Kagan has suggested that differences in behavioural inhibition are based on differing thresholds for arousal in the parts of the brain that control responses to uncertainty—the amygdala and the hypothalamus (Kagan, 1994; Kagan, Reznick, & Snidman, 1990; Kagan, Snidman, & Arcus, 1993). Arousal of these parts of the brain leads to increases in muscle tension and heart rate. Shy or inhibited children are thought to have a low threshold for such a reaction. That is, they more readily become tense and alert in the presence of uncertainty, perhaps even interpreting a wider range of situations as uncertain. What we inherit, then, according to this view, is not "shyness" or some equivalent, but a tendency for the brain to react in particular ways (Davidson, 1994).

Critical Thinking

How would you describe your own temperament as a child? Is your adult personality similar to the temperament you displayed in childhood?

easy temperament
These babies have predictable routines and they approach and adjust quickly and easily to new experiences. They react mildly to discomfort and are generally cheerful.

difficult temperament
These active babies have uneven routines and adapt reluctantly to new experiences. They react with intensity and often negatively, and once upset, they are difficult to soothe.

slow-to-warm-up temperament
These inactive babies turn away from and adjust slowly to unfamiliar people and new experiences. They display mild signs of negativity and discomfort.

niche-picking
the process of selecting experiences on the basis of temperament

ENVIRONMENT The child's experiences play a crucial role in personality development as well. A number of temperament–environment interactions tend to strengthen built-in qualities. For one thing, people of all ages choose their experiences, a process Sandra Scarr refers to as **niche-picking** (Scarr & McCartney, 1983). Our choices reflect our temperaments. For example, highly sociable children seek out contact with others; children low on the activity dimension are more likely to choose sedentary activities such as puzzles or board games than baseball.

Similarly, temperament may affect how a child interprets a given experience—a factor that helps to account for the fact that two children in the same family may experience the family's patterns of interaction and situation quite differently. Imagine, for example, a family that moves often, such as a military family. If one child in this family has a strong built-in pattern of behavioural inhibition, the myriad changes and new experiences will trigger repetitive fear responses. This child comes to anticipate each new move with dread and is likely to interpret his family life as highly stressful. A second child in the same family, with a more strongly approach-oriented temperament, will find the many moves stimulating and energizing and is likely to think of his childhood in a much more positive light.

A third environmental factor that tends to reinforce built-in temperamental patterns is the tendency of parents and others to respond quite differently to children, depending on the children's temperaments. The sociable child, who may smile often, is likely to elicit more smiles and more positive interactions with parents, simply because she has reinforced their behaviour by her positive temperament. Buss and Plomin have proposed the general argument that children in the middle range on temperament dimensions typically adapt to their environment, while those children whose temperaments are extreme—for example, extremely difficult children—force their environments to adapt to them (Buss & Plomin, 1984). Parents of difficult children, for example, may adapt to the children's negativity by punishing them more and providing them with less support and stimulation than do parents of more adaptable children (Luster, Boger, & Hannan, 1993).

However, although it is borne out by observations of children, Buss and Plomin's proposal doesn't convey the additional complexities of personality development. First of all, sensitive and responsive parents can moderate the more extreme forms of infant or child temperament. For example, a series of investigations involving a group of highly inhibited toddlers who differed in the security of their attachment to their mothers revealed that insecurely attached and inhibited toddlers showed the usual physiological responses to challenging or novel situations. In contrast, securely attached and inhibited toddlers showed no such indications of physiological arousal in the face of novelty or challenge (Colton et al., 1992; Gunnar, 1994; Nachmias, 1993). Thus, the secure attachment appears to have modified a basic physiological/temperamental style. Over time, secure attachment may shift the child's personality pattern away from extreme inhibition or shyness. Such findings suggest that, while many forces in the environment reinforce children's basic temperaments, other forces can push them toward new patterns or enable them to control temperamental extremes.

Most researchers who study temperament in infants assume that these dispositions persist through childhood and into adulthood. No one proposes that initial temperamental dispositions remain unchanged by experience. However, if temperament patterns create a kind of "bias" toward particular behaviours, there should be a fair amount of stability of temperament over time. Such stability ought to show itself in the form of at least modest correlations between measures of a given temperamental dimension at different ages.

Although the results of research are somewhat mixed, there is growing evidence of consistency in temperamental ratings over rather long periods of infancy and childhood. For example, Australian researchers studying a group of 450 children found that mothers' reports of children's irritability, cooperation/manageability, inflexibility, rhythmicity, persistence, and tendency to approach rather than avoid contact were all quite consistent from infancy through age 8 (Pedlow, Sanson, Prior, & Oberklaid, 1993). Similarly, in an American longitudinal study of a group of children from age 1 through 12, psychologists found strong consistency in parents' reports of their children's overall "difficultness" as well as approach versus withdrawal, positive versus negative mood, and activity level (Guerin & Gottfried, 1994a, 1994b). Other research suggests that temperamental differences are stable from the preschool years into adulthood (Caspi, 2000).

Researchers have also found considerable consistency at various ages in Kagan's measure of inhibition, which is based on direct observation of the child's behaviour rather than on the mother's ratings of the child's temperament. In one study, for example, children who had been classified as inhibited at 4 months were less socially responsive to both adults and children at age 2 than uninhibited peers (Young, Fox & Zahn-Waxler, 1999). In Kagan's own longitudinal study, half of the children who had shown high levels of crying and motor activity in response to a novel situation when they were 4 months old were still classified as highly inhibited at age 8, and three-fourths of those rated as uninhibited at 4 months remained in that category 8 years later (Kagan et al., 1993).

Thus, babies who approach the world around them with some eagerness and with a positive attitude continue to be more positive as children; babies who show a high level of behavioural inhibition are quite likely to continue to show such "shyness" at later ages. Similarly, cranky, or temperamentally difficult, babies continue to show many of the same temperamental qualities 10 years later (Kagan et al., 1993).

TEMPERAMENT AND ATTACHMENT

The general timing of the development of attachment behaviours is the same for virtually all children. However, the emotional intensity of the attachment relationship varies considerably from child to child. For example, infants differ widely in how much fear they show toward strangers or in novel situations. Some of this difference may reflect basic temperamental variations (Kagan, 1994). Heightened fearfulness may also be a temporary response to some upheaval or stress in the child's life, such as the family's recent move or a parent's changing jobs. Whatever the origin of such variations in fearfulness, heightened fearfulness does eventually disappear in most toddlers, typically by the middle of the second year.

Individual differences in infant temperament may also be related to security of attachment. Generally speaking, easy infants, as defined by Thomas and Chess, are more likely to be securely attached than babies in those theorists' other two categories (Goldsmith & Alansky, 1987; Seifer et al., 1996; Vaughn et al., 1992). The relationship makes sense if you think about the traits of difficult infants and slow-to-warm-up ones. Difficult infants actively resist comfort; consequently, synchrony may lead a parent to make less effort to establish a nurturing relationship with a difficult infant. Likewise, slow-to-warm-up babies are less responsive to parental behaviours directed toward them. Once again, synchrony causes the parents of these unresponsive infants to reduce the frequency of behaviours directed toward them. The result is that the kind of give-and-take relationships that most easy infants experience with their parents never develop for babies who are difficult or slow to warm up (Kagan, 1989).

It's important to remember, however, that a correlation is just a correlation—it is certainly not the case that all easy infants develop secure attachment or that all babies of the other two temperament categories are insecurely attached. In fact, the majority of infants in all three temperament categories are securely attached (van IJzendoorn, Goldberg, Kroonenberg, & Frenkel, 1992). In addition, if infant temperament dictated attachment quality, researchers wouldn't expect to see infants who are securely attached to one parent but insecurely attached to the other. In reality, this is a very common research finding (e.g., Goossens & van IJzendoorn, 1990).

For these reasons, developmentalists propose that it is not temperament, per se, that influences attachment. Rather, it is the **goodness of fit** between an infant's temperament and his or her environment (Thomas & Chess, 1977). For example, if the parents of an irritable baby boy are good at tolerating his irritability and persist in establishing a synchronous relationship with him, then his irritability doesn't lead to the development of an insecure attachment.

SELF-CONCEPT

During the same months when a baby is creating an internal model of attachment and expressing her own unique temperament, she is also developing an internal model of self. Freud suggested that the infant needed to develop a sense of separateness from her mother before she could form a sense of self. Piaget emphasized that the infant's understanding of the basic concept of object permanence was a necessary precursor for the child's attaining self-permanence. Both of these aspects of early self-development reappear in current descriptions of the emergence of the sense of self (Lewis, 1990, 1991).

More recently, Canadian researchers have demonstrated that an infant's capacity to differentiate objects emerges well before object permanence is achieved. For instance, an infant can discriminate between objects and people by 2 months (Legerstee, Pomerleau, Malcuit, & Feider, 1987). An infant can also differentiate between images of itself, other infants, and dolls between 5 and 8 months of age (Legerstee, Anderson, & Schaffer, 1998).

THE SUBJECTIVE SELF The child's first task is to figure out that he is separate from others and that this separate self endures over time and space. Developmentalists call this aspect of the self-concept the **subjective self**, or sometimes the existential self, because the key awareness seems to be "I exist." The roots of this understanding lie in the myriad everyday interactions the baby has with the objects and people in his world that lead him to understand during the first 2 to 3 months of life that he can have effects on things (Lewis, 1991). For example, when the child touches a mobile, it moves; when he cries, someone responds; when he smiles, his mother smiles back. Through this process, the baby separates self from everything else and a sense of "I" begins to emerge.

By the time the infant has constructed a fairly complete understanding of object permanence, at about 8 to 12 months, the subjective self has fully emerged. Just as he is figuring out that Mom and Dad continue to exist when they are out of sight, he is figuring out—at least in some preliminary way—that he exists separately and has some permanence.

THE OBJECTIVE SELF The second major task is for the toddler to come to understand that she is also an object in the world (Lewis, 1991). Just as a ball has properties—roundness, the ability to roll, a certain feel in the hand—so the "self" also has qualities or properties, such as gender, size, a name, or qualities such as shyness or boldness, coordination or clumsiness. It is this self-awareness that is the hallmark of the second aspect of identity, the **objective self**, sometimes called the **categorical self**, because once the child achieves self-awareness the process of defining the self involves placing oneself in a whole series of categories.

It has not been easy to determine just when a child has developed the initial self-awareness that delineates the formation of the objective self. The most commonly used procedure involves a mirror. First, the baby is placed in front of a mirror, just to see how she behaves. Most infants between about 9 and 12 months old will look at their own

goodness of fit
the degree to which an infant's temperament is adaptable to his or her environment, and vice versa

subjective self
an infant's awareness that she or he is a separate person who endures through time and space and can act on the environment

objective (categorical) self
the toddler's understanding that she or he is defined by various categories such as gender or qualities such as shyness

images, make faces, or try to interact with the baby in the mirror in some way. After allowing this free exploration for a time, the experimenter, while pretending to wipe the baby's face with a cloth, puts a spot of rouge on the baby's nose, and then lets the baby look in the mirror again. The crucial test of self-recognition, and thus of awareness of the self, is whether the baby reaches for the spot on her own nose, rather than the nose on the face in the mirror.

The results of a classic study using this procedure are graphed in **Figure 5.1**. As you can see, few of the 9- to 12-month-old children in this study touched their own noses, but three-quarters of the children aged 21 months showed that level of self-recognition, a result confirmed in a variety of other research studies, including studies in Europe (Asendorpf, Warkentin, & Baudonniere, 1996; Lewis & Brooks, 1978). **Figure 5.1** also shows the rate at which children refer to themselves by name when they are shown a picture of themselves, which is another commonly used measure of self-awareness. You can see that this development occurs at almost exactly the same time as self-recognition in a mirror. Both are present by about the middle of the second year of life, a finding confirmed by other investigators (Bullock & Lütkenhaus, 1990). At this point, toddlers begin to show a newly proprietary attitude ("Mine!") toward toys or other treasured objects.

Research examining the development of self-awareness suggests that the "terrible twos" is a rather unfortunate term that can lead to misunderstanding of young children's behaviour. Instead of applying negative labels to behaviour that is assumed to represent wilful defiance, parents and other caregivers should understand the self-oriented behaviour of 2-year-olds as an outgrowth of self-awareness. Such understanding may not make it any easier to live with a 2-year-old, but it can lead to more positive interactions between parents and child.

As self-awareness develops, infants begin to refer to themselves by name and, near the end of the second year, to label themselves as boys or girls. In addition, infants recognize that they belong to the "child" category. They also use categorical terms such as "good" and "big" to describe themselves. For example, a girl might say "good girl" when she obeys her parent or "big girl" when she is successful at a task like using the toilet (Stipek, Gralinski, & Kopp, 1990).

In Bowlby's language, a child apparently creates an internal model of self, just as he creates an internal model of relationships. He first learns that he exists separately and that he has effects on the world. Then he begins to understand that he is also an object in the world, with properties including gender and age. The internal model of self, or the self-scheme, as it is often labelled, is not developed fully at age 2. But the toddler is already building up an image of himself, his qualities, and his abilities. Like the internal model of attachment, this self-model, or self-scheme, affects the choices the toddler makes—such as choosing to play with other children of the same gender—and influences the way he interprets experiences. Thus, the internal model is strengthened and tends to endure.

THE EMOTIONAL SELF Development of the emotional self begins when the baby learns to identify changes in emotion expressed in others' faces. Before about 2 months of age, babies seem to look mostly at the edges of adults' faces (the hairline and

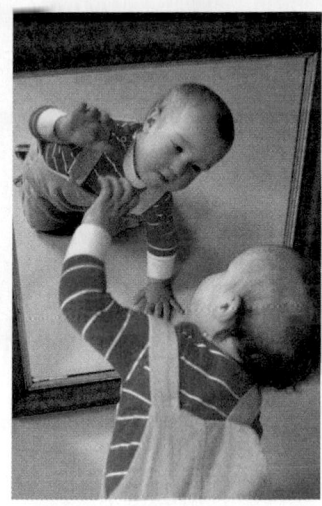

Research that has examined babies' ability to recognize themselves suggests that self-awareness develops in the middle of the second year. (*Photo:* Ray Ellis/Photo Researchers)

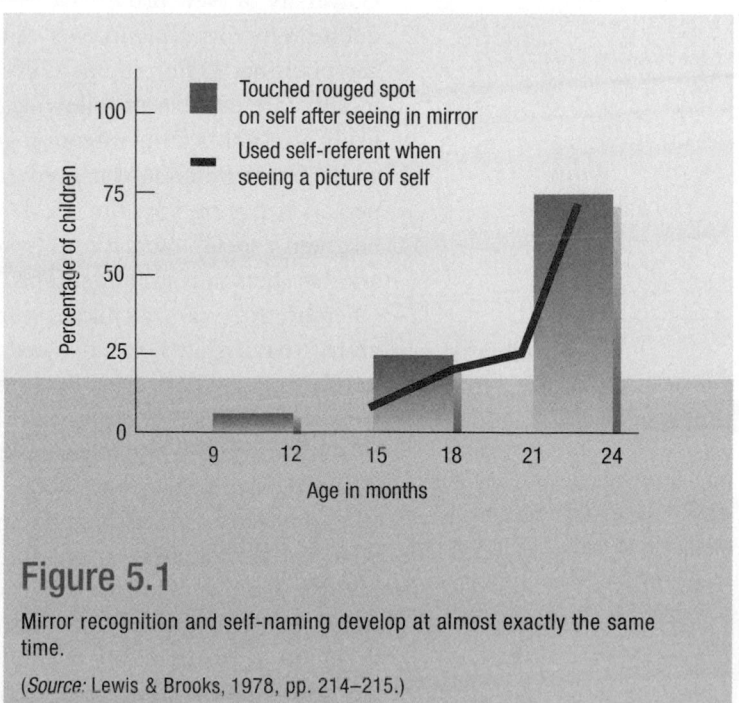

Figure 5.1

Mirror recognition and self-naming develop at almost exactly the same time.

(*Source:* Lewis & Brooks, 1978, pp. 214–215.)

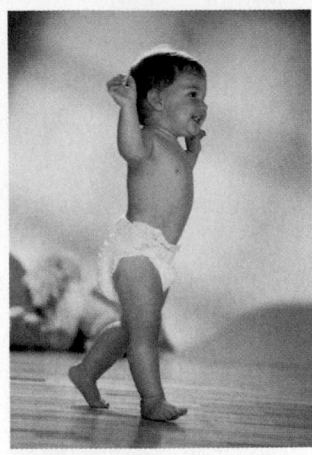

This baby's emotional reaction is best described as joy or delight rather than pride; her sense of self is not yet well-enough developed that she can feel pride in learning to walk.
(*Photo:* Getty Images)

the chin); after 2 months, they seem to look more at the features nearer the centre, particularly the eyes. At this point, infants begin to respond differently to various emotional expressions. For example, when her mother expresses happiness, a 10-week-old baby looks happy and interested and gazes at the mother. When the mother expresses sadness, the baby shows increased mouth movements or looks away. When the mother expresses anger, some babies cry; others display a "frozen" look (Haviland & Lelwica, 1987). These responses seem to be not merely imitation, but rather responses to the parent's specific emotions.

By 5 to 7 months, babies respond differently to strangers' faces that display different emotions as well as to voices speaking with varying emotional tones (Balaban, 1995). They can tell the difference between happy and sad voices and can distinguish happy, surprised, angry, fearful, interested, and sad faces (Soken & Pick, 1999; Walker-Andrews & Lennon, 1991). Near the end of the first year, infants react to another infant's neutral facial expression by actively trying to elicit an emotional expression from that child (Striano & Rochat, 1999). Just as adults often work at getting a baby to smile at them, babies seem to be following the same sort of script by 8 to 10 months of age.

As the infant's understanding of self advances, it is matched by parallel progressions in expression of emotions. At birth, infants have different facial expressions for interest, pain, and disgust, and an expression that conveys enjoyment develops very quickly. By the time a baby is 2 to 3 months old, adult observers can also distinguish expressions of anger and sadness, with expressions of fear appearing by 6 or 7 months (Izard et al., 1995; Izard & Harris, 1995). However, it is only in the middle of the second year of life, at about the same time that a child shows self-recognition in the mirror, that such self-conscious emotional expressions as embarrassment, pride, or shame emerge—all of which involve some aspect of self-evaluation (Lewis, Allesandri, & Sullivan, 1992; Lewis, Sullivan, Stanger, & Weiss, 1989; Mascolo & Fischer, 1995).

AWARENESS OF THE INTENTIONS OF OTHERS Developmentalists have also begun to examine the question of when an infant becomes aware that other people have separate intentions or "internal mental states" (D'Entremont, Hains, & Muir, 1997). University of New Brunswick psychologist Barbara D'Entremont has been studying this question by observing infants' reactions to an adult's gaze and by studying a child's finger pointing. D'Entremont (2000) contends that, although infants between 3 and 6 months are capable of following the direction of gaze of another person, this is more likely a response to an attention-getting cue than true social communication. In another study, finger pointing was used as a measure of an infant's awareness of what another person is paying attention to. It was discovered that 1-year-olds point as a means to heighten "social interaction," whereas 2-year-olds can point in an attempt to redirect another person's attention. This implies there is an age-related shift in development whereby, at 2 years, a child now has the capacity to appreciate that other people are not always paying attention to what she is paying attention to and that she can redirect another person's attention by pointing. This capability to pay attention to both another person's intentions and an object at the same time is a form of **joint attention** and it is related to later language, intellectual, behavioural, and emotional adjustment (D'Entremont & Hartung, 2003; Moore & D'Entremont, 2001).

Some theorists, such as Jeremy Carpendale of Simon Fraser University and others (Carpendale & Lewis, in press), propose that *joint attention* is a good example of the infant's dawning awareness that other people have separate mental states—an understanding that another person has a "mind of his own." The point being that the infant is beginning to appreciate the import of paying attention to another person's intentions. According to this perspective, an infant begins to construct an understanding of mental states and the social world primarily within the context of her social interactions with

joint attention
when two people are focusing their attention on an object and each is aware that the other is attending to that same object

others (we will revisit this idea later in **Chapter 6**). Both joint attention and secure emotional attachment have been linked to mother–infant social interactions early in life (D'Entremont & Hartung, 2003).

Before Going On

- What is the difference between personality and temperament?

- On which dimensions of temperament do most developmentalists agree?

- Discuss the roles of heredity and environment in the formation of temperament.

- Is temperament consistent over time?

- How do the subjective self, the objective self, and the emotional self develop during the first 2 years?

- What are some ways to measure joint attention between a parent and child?

EFFECTS OF NONPARENTAL CARE

In virtually every industrialized country in the world, women have entered the workforce in great numbers over the past few decades. In Canada, the change has been particularly rapid and massive. In 1967, only 17% of Canadian mothers with preschool children were in the labour force; by 1997, 65% of such women were working outside the home. This complements other Canadian employment trends. For instance, **Figure 5.2** shows how employment rates have doubled over the past 25 years for both dual income and single parent families with children under the age of 6 years (HRDC, 2003a). More recently however, following changes in 2000 to the Federal *Employment Insurance Act* that extended the duration of benefit payments for parental leave, more mothers and about 5% of fathers are now staying home from work during the first year to care for their infants (HRDC, 2003a, 2004a; Johnson, Lero, & Rooney, 2001).

Still, many children are in some form of nonparent care before their first birthday. Moreover, about 40% of Canadian children under the age of 5 are cared for by someone other than a parent on a regular basis (Cleveland & Hyatt, 1997). A closer look at the data as illustrated in **Figure 5.3** reveals that arrangements for child care differ based on income level —children from lower income families are more likely to be cared for by a relative, but higher income families are more likely to have their children cared for by a nonrelative (HRDC, 2003a). The key question for psychologists is, what effect does such nonparental care have on infants and young children?

DIFFICULTIES IN STUDYING NONPARENTAL CARE

It might seem that the effect on infant development of this trend toward nonparental care could easily be determined by comparing babies receiving nonparental care with those cared for by their parents. However, both "nonparental care" and "parental care" are really complex interactions among numerous variables rather than single factors whose effects can be studied independently. Thus, interpretation of research on nonparental care has to take into account a variety of issues.

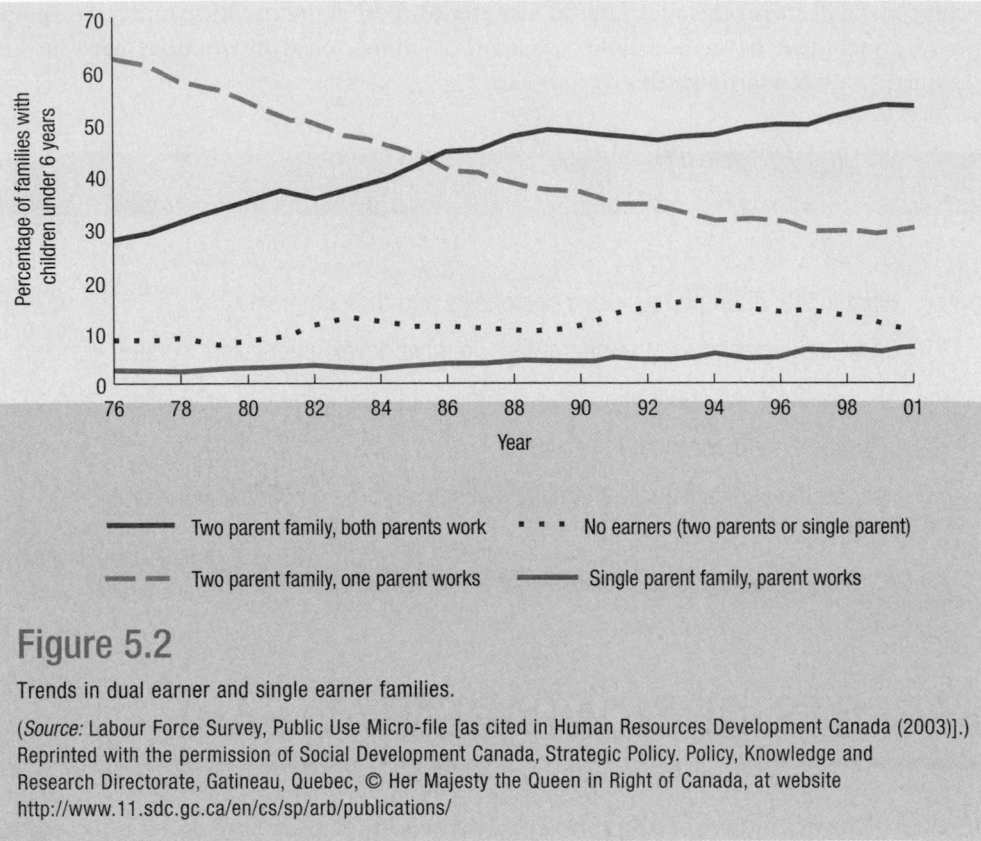

Figure 5.2

Trends in dual earner and single earner families.

(*Source:* Labour Force Survey, Public Use Micro-file [as cited in Human Resources Development Canada (2003)].) Reprinted with the permission of Social Development Canada, Strategic Policy. Policy, Knowledge and Research Directorate, Gatineau, Quebec, © Her Majesty the Queen in Right of Canada, at website http://www.11.sdc.gc.ca/en/cs/sp/arb/publications/

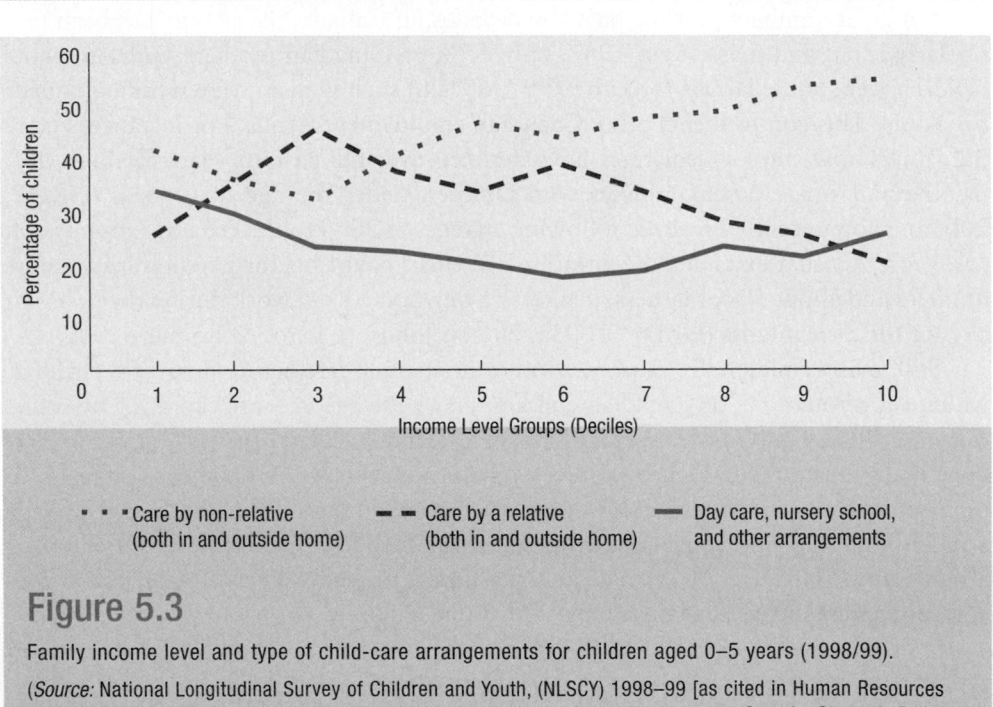

Figure 5.3

Family income level and type of child-care arrangements for children aged 0–5 years (1998/99).

(*Source:* National Longitudinal Survey of Children and Youth, (NLSCY) 1998–99 [as cited in Human Resources Development Canada (2003)].) Reprinted with the permission of Social Development Canada, Strategic Policy. Policy, Knowledge and Research Directorate, Gatineau, Quebec, © Her Majesty the Queen in Right of Canada, at website http://www.11.sdc.gc.ca/en/cs/sp/arb/publications/

First, an enormous range of different care arrangements are all lumped under the general title of "nonparental care." Infants who are cared for by grandparents in their own homes as well as those who are enrolled in day-care centres receive nonparental care. In addition, infants enter these care arrangements at different ages, and they remain in them for varying lengths of time. Some have the same nonparental caregiver over many years; others shift often from one care setting to another. Moreover, nonparental care varies widely in quality.

Furthermore, even distinguishing among the various types of care arrangements does not begin to convey the numerous hybrid solutions parents arrive at in seeking alternative care for their children (Clarke-Stewart, Gruber, & Fitzgerald, 1994). For example, in one national survey, between a quarter and a third of employed mothers reported that their children were in some type of combined care, such as family day care some of the time and care by a relative part of the time (Folk & Yi, 1994). (In family day care a person takes care of other parents' children in her own home.) The majority of researchers have studied only children in day-care centres. It is not known whether these findings will generalize to children in family day care or to children who are given at-home care by someone other than a parent. Moreover, it's not clear whether the results of these studies apply to other cultures.

The majority of infants in North America now experience at least some nonparental care.
(*Photo:* Lawrence Migdale/Photo Researchers)

Nonparental day care of children is now a part of the Canadian way of life. The most common pattern—especially for infants and toddlers—is for a child to be cared for in an unregulated setting outside the home (Kohen & Hertzman, 1998). The second most prevalent type of nonparental child care is provided in regulated licensed day-care centres. For instance, almost 1.4 million Canadian children were in a paid child-care service but only about one-third of those children were in licensed centres (Canadian Child Care Federation, 1998a).

Families who place their children in nonparental care are different in a whole host of ways from those who care for their children primarily at home. How can researchers be sure that effects attributed to nonparental care are not instead the result of these other family differences? Mothers also differ in their attitudes toward the care arrangements they have made. Some mothers with children in nonparental care would far rather be at home taking care of their children; others are happy to be working. Similarly, some mothers who are at home full-time would rather be working and some are delighted to be at home. Some studies suggest that children show more positive reactions to their situations when the mother is satisfied with her situation, whether she is working or at home (DeMeis, Hock, & McBride, 1986; Greenberger & Goldberg, 1989). For example, Canadian researchers found that when there is congruency between a mother's employment preference and her employment decision, she was less depressed and more stable care was provided (McKim, Cramer, Stuart, & O'Conner, 1999).

Most of the research on nonparental versus parental care has not taken these complexities into account. Researchers have frequently compared children "in day care" with those "reared at home" and assumed that any differences between the two groups were attributable to the day-care experience. Recent studies are often better, but clear answers to even the most basic questions about the impact of nonparental care on children's development are still not available. Research that measures the principal factors within the variety of Canadian nonparental day-care settings is needed. However, studying alternative forms of child care, such as care provided by relatives or in a home setting, is difficult because of its "private nature" (Conner & Brink, 1999).

EFFECTS ON COGNITIVE DEVELOPMENT AND PEER RELATIONS

There is a good deal of evidence that high-quality, cognitively enriched day care has beneficial effects on many children's overall cognitive development. This effect is particularly strong for children from poor families, who show significant and lasting gains in

Developmental Psychology
in Your Career

Early Childhood Educator

Occupation	Early Childhood Educator
Description	• develop and maintain warm, caring, responsive relationships with children • protect and promote the psychological and physical safety, health, and well-being of each child through appropriate environments • use observations to access children's skills, abilities, interest, and needs • plan and implement daily experiences that support and promote physical, emotional, social, communication, cognitive, ethical and creative development for both the individual child and groups of children • establish supportive, collaborative relationships with each child's family and professionals (program and community)
Entry Credentials	• 2-year Early Childhood Education college diploma
Essential Lifespan Development Knowledge	• developmental principles and theories • stages, milestones, and variations of children's skills, abilities, and interests • principles of learning through play
Essential Lifespan Development Skills	• plan and adopt curriculum for developmentally appropriate experiences including storytelling and discussion, music, artwork, dramatics, and physical activity • facilitate developmentally appropriate interactions • guide and assist children in developmentally appropriate eating, dressing, and toileting habits • implement a program that incorporates child-directed activities, care routines and transitions • observe, record, and assess children's behaviour
Lifespan Development and Essential Professional Attitude	• demonstrate positive interactions with children, families, and other child-care staff and community professionals • demonstrate sensitivity to fairness, equity, and diversity • ensure confidentiality • demonstrate commitment to life-long learning
Lifespan Development Career Profile: Karen Chandler, Professor, Early Childhood Development, George Brown College	"In addition to providing stimulating programs for young children and creating safe, healthy learning environments, the Early Childhood Educator faces increased expectations that she or he will address broader family and social issues such as child poverty; offer inclusive environments to children with special needs with inadequate resources; and respect the values of families from diverse backgrounds. Greater emphasis is also being placed on school readiness. Career opportunities for ECE graduates in education and health have increased." January 17, 2005

IQ and later school performance after attending highly enriched day care throughout infancy and early childhood (Campbell & Ramey, 1994; Ramey, 1993). Even middle-class children show some cognitive benefit when they are in high-quality day care (Peisner-Feinberg, 1995).

When researchers have looked at the impact of day care on children's personalities, they have found that most children in day care are more sociable and more popular and have better peer-play skills than their counterparts reared primarily at home (Andersson, 1989, 1992; Scarr & Eisenberg, 1993). However, at least one researcher has reported finding links between day care and behaviour problems at school age (Kim, 1997). Many others find day-care attendance linked to subsequent heightened aggression with peers and lower compliance with teachers and parents.

For example, in one very well-designed large study, developmentalists found that kindergarteners who had spent the most time in day care—in infancy, toddlerhood, or the preschool years—were more aggressive and less popular with their peers at school age than were children who had been reared entirely at home or who had spent fewer years in day care (Bates et al., 1994). Interestingly, the age at which children entered nonparental care—that is, the timing of that care—was less important than the total length of time in nonparental care. Of course, a child's level of aggressiveness in elementary school is influenced by a wide variety of things, including temperament and the effectiveness of the parents' disciplinary techniques, but the fact that day care is implicated in this equation certainly sounds a cautionary note.

Confusing, isn't it? By some measures, children who have been in day care seem to be more socially competent; by other measures, they seem less so. One possible resolution is to look again at the relative quality of care at home versus day care. Some studies have found that what seems to be critical for the child's level of aggression is whether the child spends his daytime hours in an organized, well-structured situation or in a messy, unstimulating one—the unstructured and messy setting is the problem, whether it is at home or in day care (Clarke-Stewart et al., 1994; Field, 1991). If this argument holds, then it is not being in day care itself that leads to later social problems, but the quality of the child's daily experiences.

EFFECTS ON ATTACHMENT

Can an infant or toddler develop a secure attachment to her mother and father if she is repeatedly separated from them? This question has been at the centre of a hot debate. Until the mid-1980s, most psychologists believed that infant day care had no negative effect on attachment. But then developmental psychologist Jay Belsky sounded an alarm (Belsky, 1985, 1992; Belsky & Rovine, 1988). Combining data from several studies, he concluded that there was a heightened risk of an insecure attachment for infants who enter day care before their first birthday.

Critical Thinking

How do you think the way you were cared for (at home or not, by a parent or by another adult) influenced your development?

However, recent Canadian studies show different outcomes. In one study, for instance, Douglas Symons (1998) of Acadia University found that "women who returned to employment outside the home after six months postpartum had infants display higher levels of secure-based behaviour than women who returned before six months or those who were not employed" (p. 10). This is consistent with the findings of McKim et al. (1999), who have shown that out-of-home day care can help compensate for the negative effects of an insecure mother–infant relationship.

The present controversy focuses on how to interpret inconsistencies in day-care research. Some developmentalists argue that there are so many variables affecting attachment that it is impossible to draw any clear conclusion (e.g., Roggman, Langlois, Hubbs-Tait, & Rieser-Danner, 1994). For one thing, mothers who work are different in some ways from mothers who do not: More are single mothers; more find child care onerous.

Developmental psychologist Sandra Scarr, a leading day-care researcher, has suggested that the kind of day care parents choose is an extension of their own characteristics and parenting styles (Scarr, 1997). For example, poorly educated parents may choose day-care arrangements that do not emphasize infant learning. Similarly, parents whose focus is on intellectual development may not place a high priority on the

The Real World
Parenting
Choosing a Day-Care Centre

You may be wondering what criteria a parent can use to identify a high-quality day-care setting. Of course, it's important to realize that the "fit" between an infant and her day-care setting is what really matters. Some babies do well no matter where they are cared for or by whom. Others, perhaps those with more difficult temperaments, seem to have problems adjusting to even the best of settings. Consequently, parents can't really judge the quality of a given setting until their babies have spent some time in it. Nevertheless, there are a few general characteristics common to good-quality day-care settings.

The Canadian Child Care Federation (1998a) suggests that the following characteristics should be considered for both centre and home day care:

- warm, friendly, patient, capable caregivers who are trained in child development, first aid, and CPR
- stable, committed, experienced caregivers (low turnover rate)
- a variety of activities that are enjoyable and support healthy development
- daily routines that are predictable but flexible
- relaxed, caring, stimulating environment
- written program policies and plans

- a variety of toys, equipment, and learning materials at the child's level
- space for active and quiet activities, indoor and outdoor play, and rest
- nutritious meals and snacks
- cultural sensitivity
- regular communication between parent and caregiver
- compatible child-rearing philosophy and goals
- mutual respect and trust
- access to community resources and supports

(*Sources:* Canadian Child Care Federation, 1998a; Co-ordinated Access for Child Care, 2001.)

emotional aspects of a particular day-care arrangement. Thus, Scarr claims, day-care effects are likely to be parenting effects in disguise.

The confusion inherent in the mixed findings on nonparental care serves to underline the importance of the quality of child care. A general conclusion that can be drawn is that good-quality care is generally linked with positive or neutral outcomes, while inconsistent or poor-quality care can be actively detrimental to the child. Beyond that, all psychologists can tell parents at this point is that the debate about the effects of nonparental care on children is still an open one (see **The Real World**).

Before Going On

- Why is it difficult to study the effects of nonparental care on development?
- What might be the effects of nonparental care on cognitive development?
- Do children who experience nonparental care develop personalities different from those of children who are cared for at home in infancy?
- What does research suggest about the potential risks of nonparental care with respect to attachment?

INDIVIDUAL AND GROUP DIFFERENCES

You have already learned that a parent's own internal model of attachment can influence how she or he interacts with an infant. Other variables can also affect infant social and personality development.

CAREGIVER CHARACTERISTICS AND ATTACHMENT

One caregiver variable that predicts attachment quality is age. Adolescent mothers are more likely than older mothers to describe their babies as "difficult" and to be less responsive to them (Miller, Eisenberg, Fabes, & Shell, 1996). Not surprisingly, at school age, children of teen mothers experience emotional difficulties more often than their peers. However, studies suggest that training in child development along with specific instruction on how to interpret an infant's behaviour may change this pattern (Culp, Culp, Blankemeyer, & Passmark, 1998; Stockman & Budd, 1997).

Depression is another caregiver characteristic that appears to be related to attachment quality (Murray et al., 1999; Teti, Gelfand, Messinger, & Isabella, 1995). In fact, when mothers are depressed, babies' own facial expressions and behaviours suggest that they feel depressed as well. They smile less, show more sad and angry facial expressions, and seem to be less organized in motor activity and attention (Hart, Jones, Field, & Lundy, 1999).

However, not all depressed mothers interact with their babies in the same way. Some are withdrawn and detached; they look at, touch, or talk to their babies less often than nondepressed mothers do and are less affectionate toward them (Field, 1995; Hart et al., 1999). Children of such mothers are less likely to form a secure attachment with the mother. They are also at higher risk for later behaviour problems, including either heightened aggression or withdrawal (Cummings & Davies, 1994; Murray et al., 1999; Teti et al., 1995). Other depressed mothers are overly involved with their infants, often interrupting and overstimulating them. Babies seem to respond to this kind of treatment by withdrawing from both their mothers and others in their environments (Hart et al., 1999). Still other depressed mothers overreact and respond angrily to babies' undesirable behaviours. Infants of these depressed mothers are more likely than others to display aggressive behaviour in early childhood (O'Leary, Slep, & Reid, 1999).

Of course, there are many depressed mothers who are just as sensitive and responsive to their babies' needs as those who do not suffer from depression. Infants whose depressed mothers exhibit sensitive parenting behaviours are less likely to display long-term negative effects than are infants with less sensitive depressed mothers (NICHD Early Child Care Research Network, 1999). Further, training can increase the frequency of parents' sensitive behaviours and, as a result, lead to changes in infants' attachment status (van den Boom, 1994, 1995).

As you learned earlier in this chapter, parents who were abused in childhood may have problems forming attachments to their infants (Cassidy & Berlin, 1994; Main & Hesse, 1990). In some cases, these parents fall into the interactional pattern that they themselves experienced with their own parents—namely, an abusive relationship. This may happen when parents adapt poorly to their baby's temperament and become frustrated with their inability to manage the infant effectively.

Stressful living conditions may also contribute to the development of an abusive relationship. Infant abuse is more common in large families, in single-parent households,

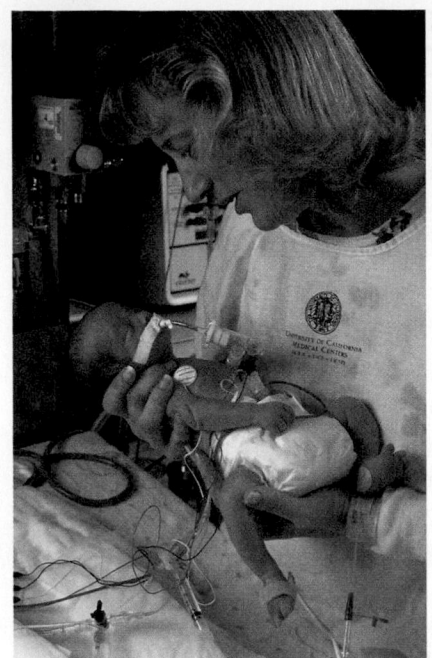

Preterm babies may be less responsive to parents than full-term infants.

(*Photo:* Jonathan Nourok/PhotoEdit)

in families living in poverty or in extremely crowded conditions, and in families in which substance abuse is a problem (Garbarino & Sherman, 1980; Pianta, Egeland, & Erickson, 1989; Sack, Mason, & Higgins, 1985). Even these adverse conditions can be surmounted, though, if the parents have adequate emotional support, either from each other or from other adults.

PRETERM AND LOW-BIRTH-WEIGHT INFANTS

For the most part, preterm and low-birth-weight (LBW) babies seem to differ little in attachment pattern from full-term infants (Pederson & Moran, 1996; Wintgens et al., 1998). However, preterm and LBW infants who are very ill, especially those who hover between life and death for many weeks after birth or who have physical deformities, are at significantly greater risk for developing insecure attachments than those who are healthy. This risk arises because parents distance themselves both physically and emotionally from babies who might not live and those who are deformed (Clark & Miles, 1999; Feldman, Weller, Leckman, Kuint, & Eidelman, 1999; Moehn & Rossetti, 1996; Weiss, 1998).

Preterm infants also may display temperamental characteristics that place them at risk for insecure attachment. For example, most are less responsive than full-term infants, and their parents more often become frustrated in attempts to engage them in synchronous social interactions (Lester, Hoffman, & Brazelton, 1985). As a result, these infants are more likely to be insecurely attached and more likely to be abused than are full-term babies (Brockington, 1996; Mangelsdorf et al., 1996).

To further complicate the picture, the insecure attachment itself is an additional risk factor for preterm and LBW infants (Heidt-Kozisek, Pipp-Siegel, Easterbrooks, & Harmon, 1997). Those who are both very ill and insecurely attached to parents in infancy are more likely to suffer from developmental problems later in childhood (Andersson & Sommerfelt, 1999; Wintgens et al., 1998). Consequently, health care professionals have devised training programs to help parents establish close relationships with preterm and LBW infants in the early days of their lives and throughout the preschool and grade school years (Brooks-Gunn, Klebanov, Liaw, & Spiler, 1993; McCarton et al., 1997).

EFFECTS OF GENDER

It is clear that parents treat boys and girls differently beginning in infancy. Some of these differences depend on both the parent's and the baby's sex. For example, parents sing more expressively to same-sex than to opposite-sex infants (Trehub, Hill, & Kamenetsky, 1997). Likewise, mothers maintain more physical and visual contact with infant daughters than with sons (Lindahl & Heimann, 1997). Differences such as these may contribute in some way to the formation of same-sex alliances between parents and children that may be important later in childhood.

Both mothers and fathers demonstrate other kinds of variations in their interactions with boys and girls. For example, temperamental differences between boys and girls are much smaller than the differences perceived by parents and other adults. In one classic study, researchers found that adults viewing a videotape of an infant interpreted the baby's behaviour differently depending on the gender label experimenters provided. Participants who were told the baby was a girl inter-preted a particular behaviour as expressing "fear." Amazingly, participants who believed the infant was a boy labelled the same behaviour "anger" (Condry & Condry, 1976). More recently, University of Montreal researchers employing this technique have suggested that the current cohort of adults is somewhat less likely to stereotype infant behaviour in this way, although, like their counterparts in the 1970s, they attend to and comment on motor activity more when they believe an infant under observation is a boy (Pomerleau, Malcuit, Turgeon, & Cossette, 1997).

Critical Thinking

Make a list of your own personality characteristics. How many of them relate to your gender?

Thus, temperamental stereotyping may affect the quality of the parent–infant rela-tionship. For example, a parent of a calm, quiet girl may view her activity level as a sign of "girlness" and respond to her behaviour with acceptance and approval. At the same time, parents of a very active boy may tolerate his activity level, or even encour-age it, because they regard it as evidence of masculinity. But what about parents of active girls and quiet boys? A parent whose infant girl is very active may work hard to teach her to be less active because of concerns about the sex-appropriateness of her activity level. Likewise, parents of quiet boys may push them to be more active. In the process, such parents may develop a rejecting, disapproving attitude toward their chil-dren that generalizes to all aspects of their relationships with them. In this way, stereo-typically based ways of responding to infants can lead to differences in quality of attachment.

Research on another dimension of temperament—emotionality—provides another example of gender effects. Most studies have found that even in infancy, girls use gestures and language to express emotions more often than boys do (Kuebli, Butler, & Fivush, 1995). Similarly, girls are more responsive to others' facial expres-sions (McClure, 2000). These differences often lead to the perception that girls are more emotionally sensitive. However, studies of actual behaviour reveal that boys are just as affectionate and empathetic as girls during infancy (Melson, Peet, & Sparks, 1991; Zahn-Waxler, Radke-Yarrow, Wagner, & Chapman, 1992). Nevertheless, a par-ent's perception of an infant's emotional sensitivity affects how the parent responds to the child. Not surprisingly, then, parents initiate conversations about emotions and emotion-provoking events more often with girls than with boys (Kuebli et al., 1995). But which comes first, girls' greater emotional expressivity or parents' greater will-ingness to discuss emotions with them? Likewise, are boys less expressive because par-ents don't frame conversations with them in ways that encourage emotional expression?

Stereotypes notwithstanding, some sex differences in social behaviour are quite striking even in infancy. For example, if you observe 2-year-olds playing freely in a room stocked with a wide range of attractive toys, girls are more likely to play with dolls. Boys of this age more often choose to play with guns, toy trucks, or tools (O'Brien, 1992). Psychologists call this behavioural difference **sex-typing**, which is formally defined as the manifestation or adoption of culturally defined sex-appropri-ate behaviour.

However, the question "which comes first?" arises here, too. Do boys and girls have different play preferences because of inborn differences or because their parents, siblings, and others encourage them to behave differently? Clearly, infants' behaviour and their parents' reactions to that behaviour are difficult variables to separate. Thus, most developmental psychologists believe that parents' stereotypical reactions to male and female infants contribute just as much to the development of sex differences in behaviour and personality as any inborn gender-based differences (Halpern, 1997).

sex-typing
the manifestation or adoption of culturally defined sex-appropriate behaviour

Before Going On

- What variables might affect parents' ability to establish a good fit between their behaviour and an infant's behaviour?

- How do preterm and LBW infants differ from healthy babies in temperament and attachment?

- How do developmentalists explain sex differences in infants' social and personality development?

Summary

Theories of Social and Personality Development

- Freud suggested that individual differences in personality originated in the nursing and weaning practices of infants' mothers. Erikson emphasized the roles of both mothers and fathers, as well as other adults in the infant's environment, in providing for all the infant's needs, thereby instilling a sense of trust concerning the social world.

- Ethologists hypothesize that attachment is the foundation of later personality and social development. They further suggest that the first 2 years of life are a sensitive, or critical, period for the development of attachment.

Attachment

- For parents to form a strong attachment relationship with an infant, what is most crucial is the development of synchrony, a set of mutually reinforcing and interlocking behaviours that characterize most interactions between parent and infant. Fathers as well as mothers form strong bonds with their infants, but fathers show more physically playful behaviours with their children than do mothers.

- Bowlby proposed that the child's attachment to a caregiver develops in three phases, beginning with rather indiscriminate aiming of attachment behaviours toward anyone within reach, through a focus on one or more figures, and finally to "secure base behaviour," beginning at about 6 months of age, which signals the presence of a clear attachment.

- Children differ in the security of their first attachments, and thus in the internal models of relationships that they develop. The secure infant uses the parent as a safe base for exploration and can be readily consoled by the parent.

- The security of the initial attachment is reasonably stable, and, later in childhood, securely attached children appear to be more socially skilful, more curious and persistent in approaching new tasks, and more mature. The internal model of attachment that individuals develop in infancy affects how they parent their own babies.

Personality, Temperament, and Self-Concept

- Temperament theorists generally agree on the following basic temperamental dimensions: activity level, approach/positive emotionality, inhibition, negative emotionality, and effortful control/task persistence.

- There is strong evidence that temperamental differences have a genetic component, and that they are at least somewhat stable over infancy and childhood. However, temperament is not totally determined by heredity or ongoing physiological processes. A child's built-in temperament does shape the child's interactions with the world and affect others' responses to the child.

- Infant temperament may affect security of attachment. However, it is more likely that the goodness of fit between an infant's temperament and the ways his environment responds to him is the real basis of correlations between temperament and attachment.

- The infant also begins to develop a sense of self, including the awareness of a separate self and the understanding of self-permanence (which may be collectively called the subjective self) and awareness of herself as an object in the world (the objective self). In addition, the infant begins to develop awareness that other people have separate thoughts and intentions. An emotional self also develops in the first year. The range of emotions babies experience as well as their ability to make use of information about emotions, such as facial expressions, increases dramatically over the first year.

Effects of Nonparental Care

- Comparing parental with nonparental care is difficult because there are so many types of nonparental care arrangements.

- Day care often has positive effects on the cognitive development of less advantaged children and also some benefit for middle-class children.

- The impact of day care on children's social relationships is unclear. Some studies show children who spend more time in day care to be more aggressive; others show them to be more socially skilful.

- Some studies show a small difference in security of attachment between children in day care and those reared at home; others suggest that home-care and day-care children do not differ with respect to attachment.

Individual and Group Differences

- Caregiver characteristics such as age, emotional state, and a history of abuse can affect infants' attachment quality.

- Preterm and LBW infants are at greater risk for developing insecure attachments, perhaps because of their temperamental differences from full-term babies or because of frustrations parents experience in attempting to achieve synchrony with them.

- Perceived temperamental differences between boys and girls may affect attachment. Most developmentalists believe that gender differences in infant social development are affected both by biological factors and by parents' beliefs about the differences between boys and girls.

Key Terms

affectional bond (p. 132)

attachment (p. 132)

ambivalent attachment (p. 137)

attachment theory (p. 131)

avoidant attachment (p. 137)

contingent responsiveness (p. 137)

difficult temperament (p. 141)

disorganized/disoriented attachment (p. 137)

easy temperament (p. 141)

goodness of fit (p. 144)

joint attention (p. 146)

niche-picking (p. 142)

objective (categorical) self (p. 144)

personality (p. 140)

reactive attachment disorder (p. 132)

secure attachment (p. 137)

separation anxiety (p. 136)

sex-typing (p. 155)

slow-to-warm-up temperament (p. 141)

social referencing (p. 136)

stranger anxiety (p. 136)

subjective self (p. 144)

synchrony (p. 134)

temperament (p. 140)

 # Weblinks

Adoption: What to Expect at Different Ages
www.adopting.org/expect.html
Adopting.org provides assistance, information, and support for adopted children and their families, as well as those seeking to adopt. This website includes frequently asked questions and a support forum.

Adoption Council of Canada
www.adoption.ca/
The Adoption Council of Canada is a charitable organization that provides information and support for adopted children and their families, as well as those seeking to adopt. The Council's website includes frequently asked questions and a support forum.

The Well-Being of Canada's Young Children: Government of Canada Reports
www.socialunion.ca/ecd_e.html
Annual reports provide a description of the physical environment (including food, air, water, and soil) and the family environment in which young Canadian children are growing up and the impact it has on their well-being.

Invest in Kids
www.investinkids.ca/
This Canadian charitable organization promotes the healthy social, emotional, and intellectual development of children aged 0 to 5 by strengthening the parenting skills, knowledge, and confidence of Canadians to ensure the best possible start for all of our children.

© Jacques Cheney/Woodfin Camp and Associates

CHAPTER 6

PHYSICAL AND COGNITIVE DEVELOPMENT IN EARLY CHILDHOOD

Watch a 2-year-old playing near her mom or dad and you'll notice that she glances at her parent regularly, as if checking to make sure the safe base is still there. Her play is dominated by sensory explorations of objects; she seems motivated to touch and manipulate everything in her environment. In contrast to infants, however, most 2-year-olds have added a new dimension to sensorimotor play—the idea that objects have names. Consequently, almost every object manipulation is accompanied by an important question for nearby adults: "Whazit?" (What is it?) A few years later, by about age 4, sophisticated forms of pretending, such as "dress-up," become the preferred modes of play.

Profound changes in the physical and cognitive domains underlie these shifts in play behaviour. In the years from 2 to 6, the period known as *early childhood*, the child changes from a dependent toddler, able to communicate only in very primitive ways, to a remarkably competent, communicative, social creature, ready to begin school.

In this chapter, you will learn about the subtle physical changes and a number of advances in cognitive and language development that happen during early childhood. Furthermore, after reading the chapter, you should have a better understanding of the issues involved in intelligence testing. While you read, keep the following questions in mind:

- What important physical and motor changes happen during early childhood?
- How did Piaget characterize this period, and what does recent research suggest about his theory?
- How does children's language change during the early childhood years?
- What are the strengths and weaknesses of IQ tests?

PHYSICAL CHANGES

Chapter 4 chronicled the many rapid changes in the infant's body. The physical changes between ages 2 and 6 are less dramatic.

GROWTH AND MOTOR DEVELOPMENT

Changes in height and weight happen far more slowly in the preschool years than in infancy. Each year, the child adds about 5 to 8 centimetres in height and 2.7 kilograms in weight. At the same time, the young child makes steady progress in motor development. The changes are not as dramatic as the beginning of walking, but they enable the child to acquire skills that markedly increase his independence and exploratory ability.

University of Manitoba developmentalists, using stringent motor-behaviour assessment techniques, have recently uncovered some intriguing findings about children's activity levels and behavioural self-control. The researchers discovered that children who exhibited higher motor activity levels demonstrated a significantly better ability to control or inhibit their behaviour, allowing for successful task achievement. They suggest that children's extraneous motor activity is an important form of purposeful, exploratory behaviour especially in children less than $5^{1}/_{2}$ years of age (Campbell, Eaton, & McKeen, 2002). The researchers also found that children's motor activity levels increase linearly with age and tend to peak between 7 and 9 years of age—later than previously thought (Eaton, 1994; Eaton, McKeen, & Campbell, 2001).

Table 6.1 lists the major locomotor, nonlocomotor, and manipulative skills that emerge in these preschool years. What is most striking are the impressive gains the child makes in large-muscle skills. By age 5 or 6, children are running, jumping, hopping, galloping, climbing, and skipping. They can ride a tricycle; some can ride a two-wheeled bike. The degree of confidence with which the 5-year-old uses her body for these movements is impressive, particularly in contrast to the somewhat unsteady movements of the 18-month-old.

Manipulative skills also improve in these years, but not to the same level of confidence. Three-year-olds can indeed pick up Cheerios, and 5-year-olds can thread beads on a string. But even at age 5 or 6, children are not highly skilled at such fine-motor tasks as using a pencil or crayon or cutting accurately with scissors. When a young child uses a crayon or a pencil, he uses his whole body—the tongue is moving and the whole arm and back are involved in the writing or drawing motion. This is important for teachers to understand; it is the rare kindergartner who is really skilled at such fine-motor tasks.

THE BRAIN AND NERVOUS SYSTEM

Brain growth, synapse formation, and myelinization continue in early childhood, although at a pace slower than in infancy. However, the slower rate of growth should not be taken to mean that brain development is nearly complete. Indeed, a number of important neurological milestones happen between the ages of 2 and 6. It is likely that these milestones represent the neurological underpinnings of the remarkable advances in thinking and language that occur during this period.

TABLE 6.1	Milestones of Motor Development		
Age	**Locomotor Skills**	**Nonlocomotor Skills**	**Manipulative Skills**
18–24 months	Runs (20 months); walks well (24 months); climbs stairs with both feet on each step	Pushes and pulls boxes or wheeled toys; unscrews lid on a jar	Shows clear hand preference; stacks four to six blocks; turns pages one at a time; picks up things without overbalancing
2–3	Runs easily; climbs on furniture unaided	Hauls and shoves big toys around obstacles	Picks up small objects; throws small ball while standing
3–4	Walks upstairs one foot per step; skips on two feet; walks on tiptoe	Pedals and steers tricycle; walks in any direction pulling large toys	Catches large ball between outstretched arms; cuts paper with scissors; holds pencil between thumb and fingers
4–5	Walks up and down stairs one foot per step; stands, runs, and walks on tiptoe		Strikes ball with bat; kicks and catches ball; threads beads on a string; grasps pencil properly
5–6	Skips on alternate feet; walks on a line; slides, swings		Plays ball games well; threads needle and sews large stitches

(*Sources:* Connolly & Daigleish, 1989; The Diagram Group, 1977; Fagard & Jacquet, 1989; Mathew & Cook, 1990; Thomas, 1990.)

corpus callosum
the membrane that connects the right and left hemispheres of the cerebral cortex

lateralization
the process through which brain functions are divided between the two hemispheres of the cerebral cortex

LATERALIZATION The **corpus callosum**, the brain structure through which the left and right sides of the cerebral cortex communicate, grows and matures more during the early childhood years than in any other period of life. The growth of this structure accompanies the functional specialization of the left and right hemispheres of the cerebral cortex. This process is called **lateralization**.

Figure 6.1 illustrates how brain functions are lateralized in 95% of humans, a pattern known as *left-brain dominance*. In a small proportion of the remaining 5%, the functions are reversed, a pattern called *right-brain dominance*. However, most people who are not left-brain dominant have a pattern known as *mixed dominance*, with some functions following the typical pattern and others reversed.

Neuroscientists suspect that our genes dictate which functions will be lateralized and which will not be, because some degree of lateralization is already present in the human fetus (de LaCoste, Horvath, & Woodward, 1991). For example, both fetuses and adults turn their heads in order to be able to listen to language with the right ear. Because sounds entering the right ear are routed to the left side of the brain for interpretation, such findings suggest that language is already lateralized in most fetuses. Full lateralization of language function, though, doesn't happen until near the end of the early childhood period (Spreen, Risser, & Edgell, 1995).

Critical Thinking

Ask your friends, relatives, and fellow students to estimate the age at which brain development is complete. How do you think people's assumptions about the completeness or incompleteness of brain development affect their attitudes and behaviour toward children?

EXPERIENCE AND BRAIN MATURATION It appears that the experience of learning and using language, not simply genetically programmed maturation of the brain, is the impetus behind hemispheric specialization. Young children whose language skills are the most advanced also show the strongest degree of lateralization (Mills, Coffey-Corina, & Neville, 1994). Neuroscientists have not determined whether some children advance rapidly in language acquisition *because* their brains are lateralizing at a faster pace. It seems that the reverse is just as likely to be true—namely, that some children's brains are lateralizing language function more rapidly because they are learning language faster.

Studies of deaf children who are learning sign language also suggest that experience contributes to brain development (Mills et al., 1994). These children use the same area of the brain to process sign meanings as hearing children use for spoken word meanings. Likewise, deaf children's sign vocabularies grow at about the same rate as those of children learning spoken language.

However, deaf children's processing of the grammar of sign language happens in an entirely different area of the brain from that used by hearing children to understand the structure of spoken language. In addition, deaf children acquire grammatical knowledge at a slower pace. These results suggest that some aspects of brain development are linked more to the kinds of linguistic stimuli to which the brain is exposed (in other words, to experience) than to a rigid genetic plan.

Figure 6.1

Brain functions are lateralized, as shown in the figure. Generally, the left hemisphere specializes in logical sequential processes, such as language and computation, and in the coordination of complex movement. The right hemisphere is associated with holistic simultaneous processes that involve complex perceptual and visual-spatial functions, such as the detection and expression of emotions and nonverbal behaviour. Neurologists think that the basic outline of lateralization is genetically determined, whereas the specific timing of the lateralization of each function is determined by an interaction of genes and experiences.

THE RETICULAR FORMATION AND THE HIPPOCAMPUS Myelinization of the neurons of the reticular formation, which you will remember from **Chapter 4** is the brain structure that regulates attention and concentration, is another important milestone of early childhood brain development. Neurons in other parts of the brain, such as the *hippocampus*, are also myelinated during this period (Tanner, 1990). The **hippocampus** is involved in the transfer of information to long-term memory. Maturation of this brain structure probably accounts for improvements in memory function across the preschool years (Rolls, 2000).

HANDEDNESS **Handedness**, the tendency to rely primarily on the right or left hand, is another neurological milestone of the 2- to 6-year-old period (Tanner, 1990). Scientists used to assume that right-handedness increased among humans along with literacy. The idea was that parents and teachers encouraged children to use their right hands when teaching them how to write. In this way, right-handedness became a custom that was passed on from one generation to the next through instruction.

By examining skeletons that predate the invention of writing, archaeologists have determined that the proportions of right- and left-handers were about the same in illiterate ancient populations as among modern humans (83% right-handed, 14% left-handed, and 3% ambidextrous) (Steele & Mayes, 1995). These findings suggest that the prevalence of right-handedness is likely to be the result of genetic inheritance. Moreover, geneticists at the National Cancer Institute (NCI) have recently identified a dominant gene for right-handedness, which they believe to be so common in the human population that most people receive a copy of it from both parents (Talan, 1998).

Studies relating brain lateralization to handedness suggest that a common neurological process may be involved in both. About 96% of right-handers possess the typical pattern of left-brain dominance (Pujol, Deus, Losilla, & Capdevila, 1999). However, only 75% of left-handers are left brain dominant. About 1% have complete right-brain dominance, and the rest have a mixed pattern of dominance (Pujol et al., 1999). The prevalence of mixed dominance among left-handers may explain the frequent finding of higher rates of learning disabilities and mental disorders among them (Grouios, Sakadami, Poderi, & Alevriadou, 1999; Hernandez, Camacho-Rosales, Nieto, & Barroso, 1997; Tanner, 1990).

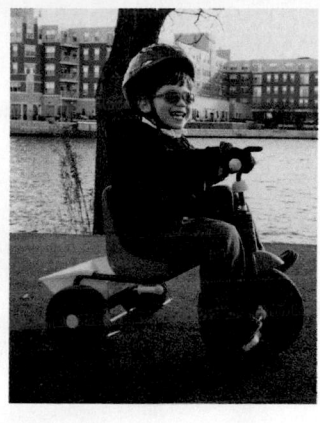

By age 3, most preschoolers can ride a tricycle.
(*Photo:* Courtesy of Erik Skagestad)

hippocampus
a seahorse-shaped brain structure that is essential for the formation of memories

handedness
a strong preference for using one hand or the other that develops between 3 and 5 years of age

HEALTH PROMOTION AND WELLNESS

Young children continue to require periodic medical check-ups as well as a variety of immunizations. Just as they do with infants, doctors monitor preschoolers' growth and motor development. At the same time, doctors and nurses often serve as parents' first source of help with children who have sensory or developmental disabilities that were not diagnosed in infancy (Sulkes, 1998).

Because children grow more slowly during the early childhood years, they may seem to eat less than when they were babies. Moreover, food aversions often develop during the preschool years. For example, a child who loved carrots as an infant may refuse to eat them at age 2 or 3. Consequently, conflicts between young children and their parents often focus on eating behaviour (Wong, 1993).

Nutritionists point out that it is important that parents not become so concerned about the quantity of food a child consumes that they cater to his preferences for sweets and other high-calorie or high-fat foods (Wong, 1993). Although obesity in early childhood is rare, many children acquire eating habits during these years that lead to later weight problems. Nutritionists recommend

Immunizing young children against a variety of diseases is an important goal of routine health care for this age group.
(*Photo:* Corbis Sygma)

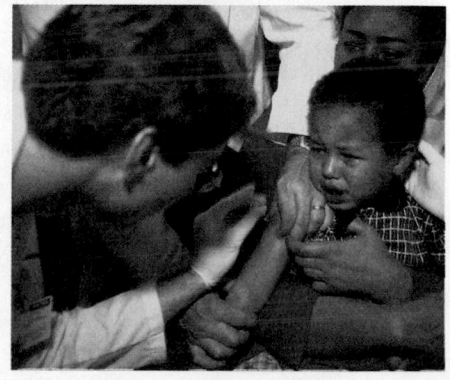

keeping a variety of nutritious foods on hand and allowing a child's appetite to be a good guide to how much food he should eat. Of course, this approach only works if young children's access to sweets and other attractive, but nonnutritious, foods is limited.

Research Report

Unintentional

Injuries in

Canadian

Preschoolers

It shouldn't be assumed that children can easily recall safety rules (4- to 6-year-olds could recite fewer than half of their home safety rules). In one recent study of 4- to 6-year-olds and their parents, Barbara Morrongiello of the University of Guelph found that a child's knowledge of home safety rules was not significantly related to the incidence of injuries. Moreover, parents should not assume that any knowledge of the rules children possess will protect them. Parents need to ensure that their children can demonstrate that they can act in ways that are consistent with the rules. For instance, researchers have found that parents who practised greater levels of protective supervision and whose children were more compliant with respect to home safety rules had children who experienced lower rates of injury (Morrongiello, Midgett, & Shields, 2001).

Later studies have shown that being within easy reach of the child was the only technique that lowered risk-taking behaviour and resulted in fewer injuries in young children (Morrongiello & House, 2004; Saluja, et al., 2004).

Morrongiello and Rennie (1998) examined cognitive fac-

tors that may contribute to a higher risk of injury in boys. They found that boys express greater optimism about their activities and believe that they are less susceptible to injury than their peers. This sense of optimism increases with age in both boys and girls. By age 6, boys believe that they will not get hurt and any injury they may incur will not be severe. They attribute injuries to bad luck rather than a dangerous choice of activity. Parents expect that boys are more likely to be injured than girls, yet they are less likely to intervene in their sons' activities with safety precautions. Conversely, parents see girls as more vulnerable than boys and therefore make their daughters more aware of the potential for harm, although their risk of injury is lower than it is for boys. Parents also assume that boys are natural risk takers, which may foster risk-taking behaviour as boys are allowed to engage in situations that put them at greater risk for injury.

Another aspect of how cognitive factors affect the rates of injury was found in a study that looked at mothers' differing expectations of risk for different clusters of home injuries. Burns, cuts, and falls were considered

less severe and therefore resulted in lower levels of precautionary behaviours by mothers than other more severe injuries such as drowning, poisoning, and suffocation/strangulation/choking (Morrongiello & Kiriakou, 2004). Accordingly, mothers were less motivated to engage in precautionary measures for less severe types of potential injuries.

Morrongiello and Dawber (1999) investigated socialization factors that contribute to higher rates of injury in boys. They discovered that both mothers and fathers are similar in their interactions with their children, treating boys differently than girls. Both parents put more pressure on their sons, beginning as young as 3 years, to play independently with less supervision and more freedom to roam. By contrast, parents will intervene and support their daughters when they are using play equipment. Furthermore, boys receive more encouragement and direct instructions while girls receive more verbal cautions about safety and possible injury. These differences in parental interaction were evident regardless of the fact that their sons and daughters were all equally physically capable of performing various activities.

Parents should also keep in mind that young children eat only about half as much food as adults, and, unlike adults, many don't consume the majority of their daily calories at regular meals (Wong, 1993). Nutritionists suggest that concerned parents keep a daily record of what their children are actually eating for a week. In most cases, parents will find that children are consuming plenty of food.

Another danger for young children is accidents. In any given year, about 5 in 1000 children aged 1 to 4 years in Canada have an accident that requires hospitalization (Public Health Agency of Canada, 1999). Fortunately, relatively few of these injuries result in death (less than 1 per 10 000 population) (Health Canada, 2000b). Boys are more likely than girls to be injured; more than half of all injuries are likely to happen at home; and most injuries occur between the months of April and October, and most often in the afternoon hours (Statistics Canada, 1995a; Statistics Canada, 1994a).

Each year, about one-half of 1 percent of Canadian children aged 1 to 4 years have an unintentional injury that requires hospitalization. (*Photo:* Comstock)

CHILD MALTREATMENT IN CANADA

Child maltreatment includes physical abuse, sexual abuse, neglect, and emotional maltreatment (Health Canada, 2001e). In the Canadian Incidence Study of Reported Child Abuse and Neglect (CIS), nationwide statistics were gathered to determine the incidence of child maltreatment in Canada, based on 7672 cases from 51 sites in all provinces and territories (Health Canada, 2001f). Overall there were 21.52 investigations of child maltreatment per 1000 children, of which almost half were substantiated. The most common forms of substantiated cases were physical abuse related to inappropriate punishment (69%) and other forms of physical abuse including shaking, choking, and burning (31%); sexual abuse including touching and fondling of genitals (68%) and attempted and completed sexual activity (35%); neglect involving a failure to supervise leading to physical harm (48%) and physical neglect (19%), and emotional maltreatment involving exposure to family violence (58%) and emotional abuse (34%). Of all the reported cases of child maltreatment, about 25% involved more than one category. The most common combinations included neglect along with emotional maltreatment, followed by physical abuse combined with emotional maltreatment.

Biological parents account for the largest portion of alleged maltreatment. Mothers (61%) followed by fathers (38%) are implicated most often. Stepfathers/common-law partners (9%) or stepmothers/common-law partners (3%) are included in the next largest group of people investigated. About 6% of alleged maltreatment involves non-relative perpetrators (Health Canada, 2001f).

One useful model for explaining abuse classifies its causes into four broad categories: sociocultural factors, characteristics of the child, characteristics of the abuser, and family stresses (Bittner & Newberger, 1981). The main idea of this model is that episodes of abuse are typically precipitated by everyday interactions between parents and children—for example, when a parent reprimands a young child for spilling a glass of milk. At the time of the episode, several causal factors work together to produce abusive responses in parents. Thus, what differentiates abusive from nonabusive parents, according to this model, is the presence of a number of risk factors that shape how they respond to the ordinary stresses of parenting.

Sociocultural factors include personal or cultural values that regard physical abuse of children as morally acceptable. Parents are more likely to be abusive if they believe that there are few, if any, moral limits on what they can do to their children physically. Sociologists suggest that such beliefs stem from cultural traditions that regard children as property rather than human beings with individual rights (Mooney, Knox, & Schacht, 2000a, 2000b). Moreover, parents who live in communities where others share and act on these beliefs are more likely to be abusive.

Several characteristics of children or parents may set the stage for child abuse. For example, children with physical or mental disabilities or those who have difficult temperaments are more likely to be abused than others (Sulkes, 1998). Indeed, one recent Canadian study found that a child with developmental delay is about 4.4 times as likely as the average Canadian child to be maltreated (Brown & Fudge Schormans, 2004). Parents who are depressed, lack parenting skills and knowledge, have a history of abuse themselves, or are substance abusers are more likely to abuse or neglect their children (Emery & Laumann-Billings, 1998). In addition, mothers' live-in male partners who are not biologically related to the children in a household are more likely than biological fathers to be abusers (Daly & Wilson, 1996). Family stressors include factors such as poverty, unemployment, and interparental conflict (Sulkes, 1998). Keep in mind that no single factor produces abuse; but the presence of several of these variables in a particular family significantly increases the chances that the children will experience abuse.

Some children who are frequently or severely abused develop *post-traumatic stress disorder (PTSD)* (Margolin & Gordis, 2000; Morrissette, 1999; Perry, 2001). This disorder involves extreme levels of anxiety, flashback memories of episodes of abuse, nightmares, and other sleep disturbances. Abused children are also more likely than nonabused peers to exhibit poor school performance in middle childhood, to develop substance abuse problems in adolescence, and to exhibit slower rates of brain growth (Glaser, 2000; Malinosky-Rummell & Hansen, 1993; Rogosch, Cicchetti, & Aber, 1995) (See the **Research Report** below.)

amygdala
an almond-shaped brain structure that plays a key role in the regulation of defensive emotions like fear and anger

functional magnetic resonance imaging (fMRI)
is a form of *Magnetic Resonance Imaging* (MRI) that records what regions of the brain are active during specific mental activities

Research Report

Traumatic Events

and

Neurobiological

and Functional

Changes in the

Brain

Bruce Perry, Director of Provincial Programs in Children's Mental Health for Alberta, contends that traumatic experiences from early childhood affect long-term behaviour (Perry, 2002; Perry, Pollard, Blakely, Baker, & Vigilante, 1995). His ideas are supported by recent neurological studies that have found that severe maltreatment during childhood (physical, sexual, and/or emotional abuse) is related to molecular and neurobiological damage in the emotional and memory areas of the brain that are still growing (Teicher, 2002). In particular, brain imaging studies of adults who were traumatized as children have revealed reductions in the size of the *hippocampus*, where memory processing takes place, and the **amygdala**, which regulates negative emotions. Atypical left/right cerebral hemisphere functioning was also found.

This complements the research of Ruth Lanius, of the University of Western Ontario, who has been using a brain imaging technique called **functional magnetic resonance imaging (fMRI)** to see if people who experience traumatic life events use different regions of the brain when they recall the events. Lanius and others (Lanius et al., 2003, 2004) compared the brain functioning of people who developed PTSD to those who did not, in the aftermath of comparably traumatic events. When subjects were prompted to recall their traumatic event, e.g., a horrific auto accident or sexual assault, those with PTSD showed arousal in the right brain areas whereas those who did not develop PTSD experienced heightened activation in the left brain. As you recall from Figure 6.1, the right brain generally deals with nonverbal information, which may help to explain why people who have PTSD react so strongly to memories that are perceptually vivid and visceral in nature. In comparison, the left brain is better at processing verbal information, which may account for why people who do not develop PTSD recall a less emotionally laden, narrative memory of traumatic events. To what extent traumatic life events either cause these disparities in brain functioning or somehow trigger a predisposition to process emotionally charged information in atypical ways remains unclear.

Preventing abuse begins with education. Informing parents about the potential consequences of some physical acts, such as the link between shaking an infant and brain damage, may help. In addition, parents need to know that injuring children is a crime, even if the intention is to discipline them. Parenting classes, perhaps as a required part of high school curricula, can help inform parents or future parents about principles of child development and appropriate methods of discipline (Mooney et al., 2000).

Another approach to prevention of abuse involves identification of families at risk. Physicians, nurses, and other professionals who routinely interact with parents of infants and young children have a particularly important role to play in this kind of prevention. Parents who seem to have problems attaching to their children can sometimes be identified during medical office visits. These parents can be referred to parenting classes or to social workers for help. Similarly, parents may ask doctors or nurses how to discipline their children. Such questions provide professionals with opportunities to discuss which practices are appropriate and which are not.

Finally, children who are abused must be protected from further injury. This can be accomplished through vigorous enforcement of existing child abuse laws. As noted, health professionals must report suspected abuse. However, ordinary citizens are also bound by mandatory reporting laws in all provinces and territories except the Yukon, which requests that all concerns be reported. Any person who has reasonable grounds to suspect abuse or neglect of a child or youth has a duty to report the abuse or neglect to the local child protection agency. Once abuse is reported, steps must be taken to protect injured children from suspected abusers.

Before Going On

- What are the major milestones of growth and motor development between ages 2 and 6?

- What important changes happen in the brain during these years?

- How do young children's nutritional and health care needs differ from those of infants?

- What factors can contribute to abuse and neglect, and how does abuse affect children's development?

COGNITIVE CHANGES

The changes in thinking that happen during the early childhood years are staggering. At the beginning of the period, children are just beginning to learn how to accomplish goals. By the time they reach age 5 or 6, they are proficient at manipulating symbols and can make accurate judgments about others' thoughts, feelings, and behaviour.

PIAGET'S PREOPERATIONAL STAGE

According to Piaget, the 18- to 24-month-old child begins to use symbols—images or words or actions that stand for something else—and enters the **preoperational stage**.

preoperational stage
Piaget's second stage of cognitive development, during which children become proficient in the use of symbols in thinking and communicating but still have difficulty thinking logically

During this stage, children become proficient at using symbols for thinking and communicating but still have difficulty thinking logically. At age 2 or 3, children begin to pretend in their play (Walker-Andrews & Kahana-Kalman, 1999). A broom may become a horse, or a block may become a train. Cross-cultural research suggests that this kind of object use by 2- to 3-year-olds in pretend play is universal (Haight et al., 1999). In fact, observing children at play can provide parents or teachers with a good idea about their levels of cognitive development (see **Table 6.2**). Young children also show signs of increasing proficiency at symbol use in their growing ability to understand models, maps, and graphic symbols such as letters (Callaghan, 1999; DeLoache, 1995).

Although young children are remarkably good at using symbols, their reasoning about the world is often flawed. For example, Piaget described the preoperational child's tendency to look at things entirely from her own point of view, a characteristic Piaget called **egocentrism** (Piaget, 1954). This term does not suggest that the young child is a self-centred egomaniac. It simply means that she assumes that everyone sees the world as she does. For example, while riding in the back seat of a car, a 3- or 4-year-old may suddenly call out "Look at that, Mom!"—not realizing that Mom can't see the object she's talking about. Moreover, the child doesn't realize that the car's motion prevents Mom from ever seeing the object in question. As a result, the youngster may become frustrated in her attempts to communicate with her mother about what she saw.

egocentrism

the young child's belief that everyone sees and experiences the world the way she does

TABLE 6.2   Children's Play and Cognitive Development

Types of Play	Description
Sensorimotor Play	A 12-month-old child spends most of her playtime exploring and manipulating objects. She puts things in her mouth, shakes them, and moves them along the floor.
Constructive Play	By age 2 children also begin to use objects to build or construct things. Building a tower with blocks, drawing a picture, and digging in sand are typical activities at this stage.
First Pretend Play	The first instances of such pretending are usually simple, like pretending to drink from a toy cup. The toy is used for its actual or typical purpose (a cup is for drinking), and the actions are still oriented to the self, but some pretending is involved. Between 15 and 21 months, the recipient of the pretend action becomes another person or a toy. The child is still using objects for their usual purposes, but now he is using the toy cup with a stuffed bear instead of using it himself.
Substitute Pretend Play	Between 2 and 3 years of age, children begin to use objects to stand for something altogether different. Children this age may use a broom as a horse or make "trucks" out of blocks.
Sociodramatic Play	Sometime in the preschool years children also begin to play parts or take roles. For example, in playing house, participants fill roles such as "mommy," "daddy," "sister," "brother," and "baby." At first, children simply take up these roles; later, they name the various roles and may give each other explicit instructions about the right way to pretend a particular role. Interestingly, at about the same age, a great many children seem to create imaginary companions (Taylor, Cartwright, & Carlson, 1993).
Rule-Governed Play	By age 5 or 6, children begin to prefer rule-governed pretending and formal games. For example, children of this age use rules such as "Whoever is smallest has to be the baby" when playing "house" and play simple games such as Red Rover and Red Light, Green Light. Younger children play these games as well, but 5- and 6-year-olds better understand their rules and will follow them for longer periods of time.

At ages 2 to 3, children begin to pretend in their play, using one object to stand in for something else, as the child in the photo on the left is doing. During the preschool years, children will also begin to play parts or take roles. In playing house, for example (as the children in the photo on the right are doing), participants fill roles such as "mommy," "daddy," "sister," "brother," and "baby."
(*Photos: left*, Courtesy of Jerry and Denise Boyd. Used with permission; *right*, © D. Young-Wolff/PhotoEdit)

Figure 6.2 on page 170 illustrates a classic experiment in which most young children demonstrate this kind of egocentrism. The child is shown a three-dimensional scene with mountains of different sizes and colours. From a set of drawings, she picks out the one that shows the scene the way she sees it. Most preschoolers can do this without much difficulty. Then the examiner asks the child to pick out the drawing that shows how someone else sees the scene, such as a doll or the examiner. At this point, most preschoolers choose the drawing that shows their own view of the mountains (Flavell, Everett, Croft, & Flavell, 1981; Gzesh & Surber, 1985).

Piaget also pointed out that the preschool aged child's thinking is guided by the appearance of objects—a theme that still dominates the research on children of this age. In Piaget's work, this theme is evident in some of the most famous of his studies, those on conservation, which you read about in **Chapter 2. Conservation** is the understanding that matter can change in appearance without changing in quantity. Children rarely show any type of conservation before age 5. They think that spreading out the pennies in a row means that there are now more pennies, or that pouring water from a short, wide glass into a taller, thinner glass means that there is now more water. From their point of view, the spread-out row of pennies *looks* like more, so it must be more. Likewise, the liquid rises to a higher level in the thinner glass, so there must be more. Children younger than 5 disregard the fact that the number of pennies or the quantity of liquid has not changed.

conservation
the understanding that matter can change in appearance without changing in quantity

CHALLENGES TO PIAGET'S VIEW

Studies of conservation have generally confirmed Piaget's observations (e.g., Ciancio et al., 1999; Gelman, 1972; Sophian, 1995; Wellman, 1982). Although younger children can demonstrate some understanding of conservation if the task is made very simple, most children cannot consistently solve conservation and other kinds of logical problems until at least age 5. However, evidence suggests that preschoolers are a great deal more cognitively sophisticated than Piaget thought.

EGOCENTRISM AND PERSPECTIVE TAKING Despite their egocentrism, children as young as 2 and 3 appear to have at least some ability to understand that another person sees things or experiences things differently than they do. For example, children this

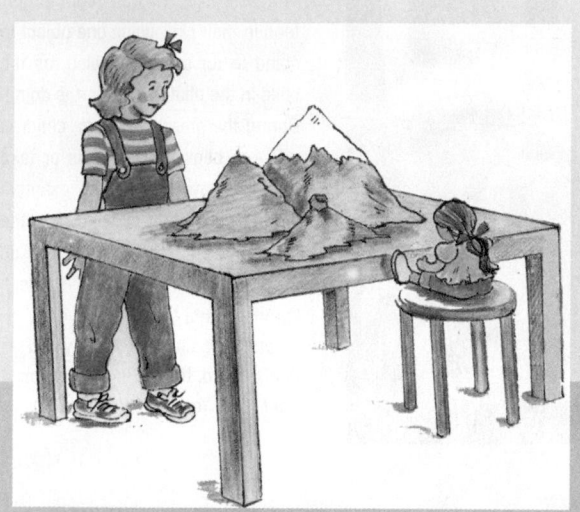

Figure 6.2

The experimental situation shown here is similar to one Piaget used to study egocentrism in children. The child is asked to pick out a picture that shows how the mountains look to her, and then to pick out a picture that shows how the mountains look to the doll.

false belief principle

an understanding that enables a child to look at a situation from another person's point of view and determine what kind of information will cause that person to have a false belief

This young child is able to adapt his speech to the needs of his younger sibling, one of many indications that preschoolers are less egocentric than Piaget thought. (*Photo:* TROIS/EXPLORER/Photo Researchers, Inc.)

age adapt their speech or their play to the demands of a companion. They play differently with older and younger playmates and talk differently to a younger or handicapped child (Brownell, 1990; Guralnik & Paul-Brown, 1984).

However, such understanding is clearly not perfect at this young age. Developmental psychologist John Flavell has proposed two levels of perspective-taking ability. At level 1, the child knows that other people experience things differently. At level 2, the child develops a whole series of complex rules for figuring out precisely what the other person sees or experiences (Flavell, Green, & Flavell, 1990). At 2 and 3 years old, children have level 1 knowledge but not level 2; level 2 knowledge begins to be evident in 4- and 5-year-olds.

For example, a child of 4 or 5 understands that another person feels sad if she fails or happy if she succeeds. The preschool child also begins to figure out that unpleasant emotions occur in situations in which there is a gap between desire and reality. Sadness, for example, normally occurs when someone loses something that is valued or fails to acquire some desired object (Harris, 1989).

Studies of preschoolers' understanding of emotion have also challenged Piaget's description of the young child's egocentrism. For example, between 2 and 6, children learn to regulate or modulate their expressions of emotion to conform to others' expectations (Dunn, 1994). In addition, preschool children use emotional expressions such as crying or smiling to get things they want. These behaviours are obviously based at least in part on a growing awareness that other people judge your feelings by what they see you expressing. These behaviours wouldn't occur if children were completely incapable of looking at their own behaviour from another person's perspective, as Piaget's assertions about egocentrism would suggest.

APPEARANCE AND REALITY The young child's movement away from egocentrism seems to be part of a much broader change in her understanding of appearance and reality. Flavell has studied this understanding in a variety of ways (Flavell, Green, & Flavell, 1989; Flavell, Green, Wahl, & Flavell, 1987). In the most famous Flavell procedure, the experimenter shows the child a sponge that has been painted to look like a rock. Three-year-olds will say either that the object looks like a sponge and is a sponge or that it looks like a rock and is a rock. But 4- and 5-year-olds can distinguish between appearance and reality; they realize that the item looks like a rock but is a sponge (Flavell, 1986). Thus, the older children understand that the same object can be represented differently, depending on one's point of view.

Using similar materials, investigators have also asked when a child can first grasp the **false belief principle**. Individuals who understand this principle can look at a problem or situation from another person's point of view and discern what kind of information would cause that person to believe something that isn't true. For example, after a child has felt the sponge/rock and has answered questions about what it looks like and what it "really" is, a researcher can ask something like this: "John [a playmate of the child] hasn't touched this, he hasn't squeezed it. If John just sees it over here like this, what will he think it is? Will he think it's a rock or will he think it's a sponge?" (Gopnik & Astington, 1988, p. 35). Most 3-year-olds think John will believe the object is a sponge because it is a sponge. By contrast, 4- and 5-year-olds realize that, because John hasn't felt the sponge, he will have a false belief that it is a rock. Some studies show that 3-year-olds can perform more accurately if they are given a hint or clue. For example, if experimenters tell them that a "naughty" person is trying to fool John, more of them will say that he will falsely think the sponge is a rock (Bowler, Briskman, & Grice, 1999). But the child of 4 or 5 more consistently understands that someone else can believe something that isn't true and act on that belief.

A recent study by Phillip Zelazo and Janet Boseovski (2001) of the University of Toronto helps to clarify the boundaries of the false belief principle. The researchers introduced mnemonic cues that challenged false beliefs in young children. Specifically, they videotaped children during a "representational change task." Children in this situation were shown common objects and asked what they expected would be inside. For example, they were shown a box of Smarties and they guessed that there would be Smarties inside. Then the actual contents of the Smarties box, a piece of string, was revealed to the children. This example illustrates that children had held a false belief about the actual contents. When the children were later asked what they had thought had been in the box originally most 3-year-olds denied their original (false) belief and said that they thought there had been string in the Smarties box. Even after the videotape was played to them showing that they originally said Smarties would be inside, the 3-year-olds persisted in saying that they had thought string would be inside. By comparison, most 4-and 5-year-olds acknowledged that they had originally been incorrect about the contents.

THEORIES OF MIND

Evidence like that described in the previous section has led a number of theorists to propose that the 4- or 5-year-old has developed a new and quite sophisticated **theory of mind**, or a set of ideas that explains other people's ideas, beliefs, desires, and behaviour (e.g., Astington & Gopnik, 1991; Gopnik & Wellman, 1994; Harris, 1989).

theory of mind
a set of ideas constructed by a child or adult to explain other people's ideas, beliefs, desires, and behaviour

UNDERSTANDING THOUGHTS, DESIRES, AND BELIEFS The theory of mind does not spring forth full-blown at age 4. Toddlers as young as 18 months have some beginning understanding of the fact that people (but not inanimate objects) operate with goals and intentions (Meltzoff, 1995). For instance, in a study by Joan Peskin (1992) of the Ontario Institute for Studies in Education, the use of deception by 3- to 5-year-olds was investigated. Unlike previous theory of mind studies that utilized hidden identities or objects, Peskin created a more competitive situation in which children could acquire highly desirable stickers. However, in order to obtain the stickers a child would have to hide his true feelings about the desired sticker lest a "bad puppet" choose it first. For a child to be able to hide his feelings he would first need to understand that he had to influence another person's mental state. The results revealed that although 3-year-olds could use physical means to acquire the desirable sticker (including physical blocking and loud protestations), they failed to conceal their true desire for the sticker and thus lost it to the "bad puppet." The 3-year-olds in this study were not able to misinform or withhold information even if it meant that the "bad puppet" would repeatedly end up with the sticker that the child preferred. Therefore, it appears that 3-year-olds lack the capacity to appreciate that someone may misrepresent a situation because they cannot grasp the concept of deceit. In comparison, 4- to 5-year-olds in this situation were able to understand the state of

Critical Thinking

Consider your own theory of mind. What assumptions do you make about the way other people's behaviour is affected by their beliefs, feelings, or ideas? You operate on the basis of such a theory all the time, but can you articulate it?

mind of others, and could accordingly conceal information that allowed them to succeed in obtaining the desired stickers.

Between the ages of 3 and 5 years, children understand some aspects of the link between people's thinking or feeling and their behaviour. Still, there is much that the 4- or 5-year-old doesn't yet grasp about other people's thinking. The child of this age understands that other people think, but does not yet understand that other people can think about him. The 4-year-old understands "I know that you know." But he does not yet fully understand that this process is reciprocal, namely, "You know that I know."

Furthermore, it is not until about age 6 that most children realize that knowledge can be derived through inference. For example, researchers in one study showed 4- and 6-year-olds two toys of different colours (Pillow, 1999). Next, they placed the toys in separate opaque containers. They then opened one of the containers and showed the toy to a puppet. When asked whether the puppet now knew which colour toy was in each container, only the 6-year-olds said yes.

Understanding of the reciprocal nature of thought seems to develop between ages 5 and 7 for most children. This would seem to be a particularly important understanding, because it is probably necessary for the creation of genuinely reciprocal friendships, which begin to emerge in the elementary school years (Sullivan, Zaitchik, & Tager-Flusberg, 1994). In fact, the rate at which an individual preschooler develops a theory of mind is a good predictor of her social skills both later in early childhood and during the school years (Moore, Barresi, & Thompson, 1998; Watson, Nixon, Wilson, & Capage, 1999).

INFLUENCES ON THE DEVELOPMENT OF A THEORY OF MIND Developmentalists have found that a child's theory of mind is correlated with his performance on Piaget's tasks as well as on more recently developed problems designed to assess egocentrism and appearance/reality (Melot & Houde, 1998; Yirmiya & Shulman, 1996). In addition, pretend play seems to contribute to theory of mind development. Shared pretense with other children, in particular, is strongly related to theory of mind (Dockett & Smith, 1995; Schwebel, Rosen, & Singer, 1999). Furthermore, children whose parents discuss emotion-provoking past events with them develop a theory of mind more rapidly than do their peers who do not have such conversations (Welch-Ross, 1997).

Language skills—such as knowledge of words like *want*, *need*, *think*, or *remember*, which express feelings, desires, and thoughts—are also related to theory of mind development (Astington & Jenkins, 1995). Indeed, some level of language facility may be a necessary condition for the development of a theory of mind. Developmentalists have found that children in this age range simply do not succeed at false-belief tasks until they have reached a certain threshold of general language skill (Astington & Jenkins, 1999; Jenkins & Astington, 1996; Watson et al., 1999).

Further support for the same point comes from the finding that children with disabilities that affect language development, such as congenital deafness or mental retardation, develop a theory of mind more slowly than others (Peterson & Siegal, 1995; Sicotte & Stemberger, 1999). Research has also demonstrated that, for children with mental disabilities, progress toward a fully developed theory of mind is better predicted by language skills than by type of disability (Bauminger & Kasari, 1999; Peterson & Siegal, 1999; Yirmiya, Eriel, Shaked, & Solomonica-Levi, 1998; Yirmiya, Solomonica-Levi, Shulman, & Pilowsky, 1996).

ALTERNATIVE THEORIES OF EARLY CHILDHOOD THINKING

In recent years, a number of interesting theoretical approaches have attempted to explain both Piaget's original results and the more recent findings that contradict them.

INFORMATION-PROCESSING THEORIES One set of alternative proposals is based on the information-processing model. As you may remember from **Chapter 2**, Robbie Case explained age differences in cognitive development as a function of changes in children's use of their short-term memories (Case, 1985, 1992). Case used the term **short-term storage space (STSS)** to refer to the child's working memory. According to Case, there is a limit on how many schemes can be attended to in STSS. He referred to the maximum number of schemes that may be put into STSS at one time as operational efficiency. Improvements in operational efficiency occur through both practice (doing tasks that require memory use, such as learning the alphabet) and brain maturation as the child gets older. Thus, a 7-year-old is better able to handle the processing demands of conservation tasks than is a 4-year-old because of improvements in **operational efficiency** of the STSS.

A good example of the function of STSS may be found by examining *matrix classification*, a task Piaget often used with both young and school-aged children (see **Figure 6.3**). Matrix classification requires the child to place a given stimulus in two categories at the same time. Young children fail such tasks, according to neo-Piagetian theory, because they begin by processing the stimulus according to one dimension (either shape or colour) and then either fail to realize that it is necessary to reprocess it along the second dimension or forget to do so.

However, researchers have trained young children to perform correctly on such problems by using a two-step strategy. The children are taught to think of a red triangle, for example, in terms of shape first and colour second. Typically, instruction involves a number of training tasks in which researchers remind children repeatedly to remember to reclassify stimuli with respect to the second variable. According to Case, both children's failure prior to instruction and the type of strategy training to which they respond illustrate the constraints imposed on problem-solving by the limited operational efficiency of the younger child's STSS. There is only room for one scheme at a time in the child's STSS, either shape or colour. The training studies show that younger children *can* learn to perform correctly, but their approach is qualitatively different from that of older children. The older child's more efficient STSS allows her to think about shape and colour at the same time and, therefore, perform successfully without any training.

Young children can solve simple perceptual matching problems like the ones described above, but run into difficulty when they are instructed to solve problems that require higher-level abstract flexible thinking. Sophie Jacques, now at Dalhousie University, and her colleagues developed the *Flexible Item Selection Task (FIST)* to measure abstraction and cognitive flexibility (Jacques & Zelazo, 2001). The FIST involves a card-sorting technique to measure if a child can match objects on cards that vary on two of four dimensions (shape, colour, size, and number, as illustrated in **Figure 6.4** on page 174). A child is presented with three cards at once and first instructed to pick two cards that match on one of the four dimensions, e.g., size (a measure of abstract mental ability), and then to pick two cards that match on a different dimension, e.g., shape (a measure of cognitive flexibility—a child has to be able to consider each object on multiple categories). The researchers found that 2-year-olds were unable to grasp the instructions; 3-year-olds

short-term storage space (STSS)
neo-Piagetian theorist Robbie Case's term for the working memory

operational efficiency
a neo-Piagetian term that refers to the maximum number of schemes that can be processed in working memory at one time

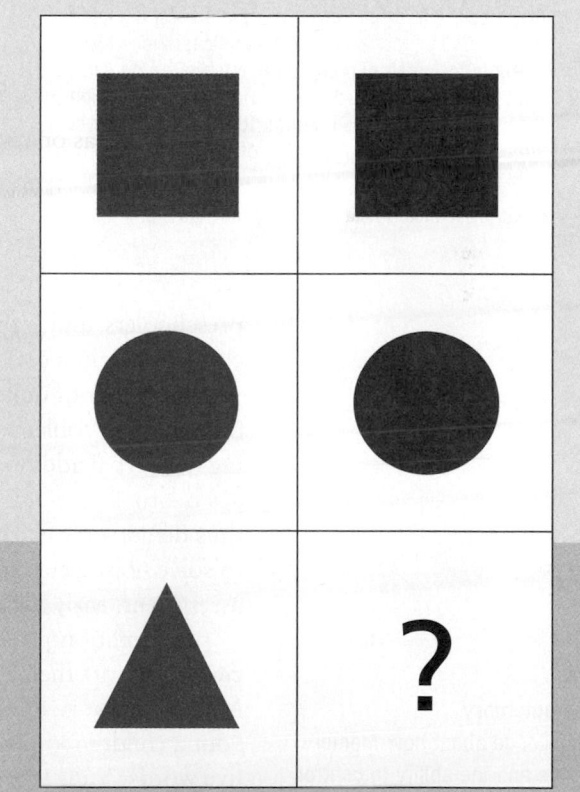

Figure 6.3

Neo-Piagetians have used Piaget's matrix classification task in strategy training studies with young children. Before training, most preschoolers say that a blue triangle or red circle belongs in the box with the question mark. After learning a two-step strategy in which they are taught to classify each object first by shape and then by colour, children understand that a red triangle is the figure that is needed to complete the matrix.

Figure 6.4

On the Flexible Item Selection Task (FIST) children are presented with three cards with pictures of objects that vary on two of four possible dimensions. A child is required to match two cards on one dimension and then to match two cards using a different dimension. By age 5 years children can perform both tasks, which suggests that they are capable of abstraction and cognitive flexibility.

(*Source:* Jacques & Zelazo, 2001, from Figure 2, p. 578.)

could understand the instructions, but had difficulty matching cards on even one dimension. This reflects an underdeveloped abstract reasoning ability in these younger children. By comparison, 4-year-olds could match objects on one dimension, but struggled with matching objects on a second dimension, suggesting that although they are capable of abstracting relevant information to solve a problem, they lack the cognitive flexibility to switch between abstract dimensions. However, the 5-year-olds were able to match cards on one or more dimensions. It seems that, even though children as young as 3 years of age can match objects based on concrete perceptual categories, they have a hard time matching objects based on abstract categories required on the FIST. Moreover, it isn't until a child reaches the age of 5 that she demonstrates the ability to show both cognitive abstraction and flexibility.

Jeffrey Bisanz and his colleagues at the University of Alberta have been studying how information-processing capacities affect the development of arithmetic skills in preschoolers. These researchers have been trying to understand what children know about arithmetic prior to formal schooling in terms of the cognitive interplay between arithmetic procedures, concepts, and facts (J. Bisanz, personal communication, July 30, 2001). One problem with testing 4-year-olds' ability to do arithmetic is that they do not have the cognitive ability to use words and symbols to solve number problems. To compensate for their lack of cognitive ability, Klein and Bisanz (2000) developed a novel method of studying arithmetic skills in preschoolers, using poker chips in lieu of numbers for counting. When the researchers studied preschoolers under these new testing procedures, they observed some interesting outcomes. First, in a two-term problem (e.g., a + b) the "representational set size," the maximum number of units of information that must be held in working memory at the same time during problem solution, is a major constraint on the preschooler's success in solving nonverbal addition and subtraction problems. Second, in a three-term problem (e.g., a + b – b) 4-year-olds can spontaneously invent shortcuts to solve this type of problem, thus demonstrating that even at this young age children can apply arithmetic principles to solve nonverbal tasks. Findings such as these may eventually lead to new methods of assessment, early identification, and instruction in the early years.

Information-processing theorists also maintain that children's ability to make efficient use of their memory system is influenced by other cognitive processes. **Metamemory** is knowledge about and control of memory processes. For example, young children know that it takes longer to memorize a list of ten words than a list of five words (Kail, 1990). However, between the ages of 2 and 6, children aren't very good at coming up with strategies to apply to more difficult memory tasks. Thus, they can't perform as well as older children on tasks, like those of Piaget, that call for efficient use of the memory system.

Metacognition is knowledge about and control of thought processes. For example, a child listening to a story may realize he has forgotten the main character's name and ask the reader what it is. Both knowing that the character's name has been forgotten and knowing that the character's name will make the story easier to understand are forms of metacognition. Moreover, metacognitive processes enable the child to generate a strategy, such as asking the reader, that will solve the problem.

metamemory

knowledge about how memory works and the ability to control and reflect on one's own memory function

metacognition

knowledge about how the mind thinks and the ability to control and reflect on one's own thought processes

Children's metamemory and metacognition improve during the early childhood period. Between age 3 and age 5, for example, children figure out that in order to tell whether a sponge painted like a rock is really a sponge or a rock, a person needs to touch or hold it. Just looking at it doesn't give someone enough information (Flavell, 1993; O'Neill, Astington, & Flavell, 1992). Thus, by about age 4 or 5, children seem to have some beginning grasp of these processes, but they still have a long way to go. As a result, their ability to solve complex problems such as those Piaget used is limited compared with that of older children.

VYGOTSKY'S SOCIOCULTURAL THEORY In **Chapter 2** you learned that psychologists' interest in Russian psychologist Lev Vygotsky's views on development has grown recently. Vygotsky's theory differs from both Piagetian and information-processing theory in its emphasis on the role of social factors in cognitive development. For example, two preschoolers working on a puzzle together discuss where the pieces belong. After a number of such dialogues, the participants internalize the discussion. It then becomes a model for an internal conversation the child uses to guide himself through the puzzle-solving process. In this way, Vygotsky suggested, solutions to problems are socially generated and learned. Vygotsky did not deny that individual learning takes place. Rather, he suggested that group learning processes are central to cognitive development. Consequently, from Vygotsky's perspective, social interaction is required for cognitive development (Thomas, 1996).

Chapter 2 described two important general principles of Vygotsky's theory: *the zone of proximal development* and *scaffolding*. Vygotsky also proposed specific stages of cognitive development from birth to age 7. Each stage represents a step toward the child's internalization of the ways of thinking used by the adults around him.

In the first period, called the *primitive stage*, the infant possesses mental processes that are similar to those of lower animals. He learns primarily through conditioning, until language begins to develop in the second year. At that point, he enters the *naive psychology stage*, in which he learns to use language to communicate but still does not understand its symbolic character. For example, he doesn't realize that any collection of sounds could stand for the object "chair" as long as everyone agreed—that is, if all English speakers agreed to substitute the word *blek* for *chair*, we could do so because we would all understand what *blek* meant.

Once the child begins to appreciate the symbolic function of language, near the end of the third year of life, he enters the *egocentric speech stage*. In this stage, he uses language as a guide to solving problems. In effect, he tells himself how to do things. For example, a 3-year-old walking down a flight of stairs might say "Be careful" to himself. Such a statement would be the result of his internalization of statements made to him by adults and older children.

Piaget recognized the existence and importance of egocentric speech. However, he believed that such speech disappeared as the child approached the end of the preoperational stage. In contrast, Vygotsky claimed that egocentric speech becomes completely internalized at age 6 or 7, when children enter the final period of cognitive development, the *ingrowth stage*. Thus, he suggested that the logical thinking Piaget ascribed to older children resulted from their internalization of speech routines they had acquired from older children and adults in the social world rather than from schemes children constructed for themselves through interaction with the physical world.

At present, there is insufficient evidence to either support or contradict most of Vygotsky's ideas (Thomas, 1996). However, some intriguing research on children's construction of theory of mind during social interactions lends weight to Vygotsky's major propositions. It seems that children in pairs and groups do produce more sophisticated ideas than individual children who work on problems alone. However, the sophistication

infantile amnesia
the inability of adults and older children to remember more than a few events that took place before 3 years of age

of a group's ideas appears to depend on the presence of at least one fairly advanced individual child in the group (Tan-Niam et al., 1998). Thus, Vygotsky's theory may ignore the important contributions of individual thought to group interaction.

By integrating the individualistic "theory of mind" approach (that stemmed from a Piagetian tradition) with Vygotskys' "social interaction" approach, contemporary theorists are attempting to overcome some serious theoretical dilemmas, such as which set of cognitive abilities develops first and which is foremost. The suggestion is that cognitive abilities develop in unison—the child's emerging understanding of the mind helps him interact better with others and in turn his social interactions reinforce his understanding of thoughts, desires, and beliefs. In essence, "concepts about the mind are not just passed on from the social group, nor are they completely formed by individual child-theorists" (Carpendale & Lewis, in press, p. 12). It is only through his interactions with others that a child develops a personal understanding of mind that is distinct from his understanding of the minds of others and which is separate from his understanding of objects in the real world.

Before Going On

- List the characteristics of children's thought during Piaget's preoperational stage.
- How has recent research on topics such as egocentrism and perspective taking, appearance and reality, and nonverbal arithmetic, challenged Piaget's view of this period?
- What is a theory of mind, and how does it develop?
- How do the information-processing and sociocultural theories explain the changes in children's thinking that happen between age 2 and age 6?

CHANGES IN LANGUAGE

By age 2½, the average child has a vocabulary of about 600 words; by age 5 or 6, that number has risen to roughly 15 000 words (Pinker, 1994). By age 3, most children have acquired all the basic tools needed to form sentences and make conversation (Bloom, 1991).

FIRST SENTENCES

inflections
grammatical markers attached to words to indicate tense, gender, number, and the like, such as the use of the ending -ed to mark the past tense of a verb in English

You may recall that toddlers combine single words with gestures to create *holophrases* (see **Chapter 4**). The first two-word sentences usually appear near the end of the second year of life. Research suggests that sentences appear when a child has reached a threshold vocabulary of around 100 to 200 words rather than at any particular age (Fenson et al., 1994).

The first sentences have several distinguishing features. They are short—generally two or three words—and they are simple. Nouns, verbs, and adjectives are usually included, but virtually all grammatical markers (which linguists call **inflections**) are missing. When they first use sentences, children learning English, for example, do not normally use the -s ending for plurals or put the -ed ending on verbs to make the past tense.

Research Report

Early Long-Term

Memories in

Children

In early childhood, memory improves considerably for both one-time events and everyday experiences. However, adults and older children rarely remember more than a few events that took place before 3 years of age. This is referred to as **infantile amnesia**. New research suggests that infantile amnesia seems to be a variable condition that may yield to significant life events that occur before the 2nd birthday (Peterson, 2002). Carol Peterson at Memorial University of Newfoundland has been studying children's memory for highly stressful life events to determine how these significant life events add to our "autobiographical memory," through which we eventually come to define ourselves (C. Peterson, personal communication, August 13, 2001; Peterson, 2002).

In a series of studies, Peterson and her colleagues measured long-term narrative memory for a traumatic injury and its subsequent hospital Emergency Room (ER) treatment. Examples of traumatic injuries included lacerations requiring suturing, bone fractures, second-degree burns, dog bites, crushed fingers requiring drainage, and so forth. Children from 13 months to 13 years of age at the time of the injury were interviewed following hospital ER treatment. Parents and other relevant people were also interviewed in order to establish a standard by which to measure the completeness and accuracy

of each child's recollections of the event.

In one study, Peterson and Rideout (1998) interviewed children from three younger age groups, 13 to 18, 20 to 25, and 26 to 34 months of age, about their injuries. Only the latter group of children had sufficient language skills, at the time, to describe their injury experiences. All the children were visited again 6 months, 1 year, $1^1/_2$ years, and 2 years after the original injury and interview. The youngest children remembered only fragments or nothing at all about their injuries. In comparison, children in the intermediate age range, who were mostly preverbal at the time of their injury, could verbally recall some details of the injury experience. Most children in the eldest group accurately recalled the events of their injury even after 2 years had elapsed. It was suggested that recall for children under 25 months at the time of the event is hampered by poor language skills at the time of their injury and thus poor narrative comprehension of the event.

Two 5-year follow-up studies were conducted on these youngsters as well as on an older sample of children. For example, when re-interviewed 5 years later none of the children who were 13 to 25 months of age at the time of the original injury and ER treatment were able to recall any of the events (Peterson & Parsons, in press). In comparison, Peterson and Whalen (2001) re-interviewed

another group of children who had been 2 to 13 years of age at the time of their injury and hospital ER treatment. They found that the children who were injured at 2 years of age had difficulty remembering details of the ER experience. However, contrary to the predictions of infantile amnesia, they were able to recall many details about their injury. Older children found it easier to describe the details of both the injury and the hospital ER events with a greater degree of accuracy. The researchers discovered that, in general, older children had excellent recall for the essential elements of their injury 5 years later. Surprisingly, even 2-year-olds recalled more than half of the central elements of their injury with 70% accuracy. It seems that several factors facilitate the long-term narrative memory of early life events, including the child's ability to verbally describe the event, the emotional impact it had at the time, the importance of the event to the child, the distinctiveness and uniqueness of the event, and the age of a child when it occurred.

An adjunct to this memory research is the examination of the method of inquiry that was used to interview the children. This is important for child interview methods in general and for forensic situations in particular because the interview technique itself can result in variable outcomes when using children's eye-witness testimony (Peterson

& Biggs, 1997; Peterson, Dowdon, & Tobin, 1999; Peterson & Grant, 2001; Peterson, Moores, & White, 2001; Peterson & Whalen, 2001). Facts that are reported across subsequent interviews can be deemed accurate as long as the interview format and questions remain consistent and there are different interviewers for each interview. However, new information that is not recalled until at least 6 months after an event is less accurate for children under 9 years of age. Moreover, a yes/no type of questioning produces the least accurate responses from children, since young children have the tendency to say "yes" whether it's true or not (Peterson & Grant, 2001). In summary, if an event was vivid and distinct, and the interviewer avoids yes/no questions and misleading questions and suggestions, children as young as 2 years of age are capable of giving reliable testimony when proper interview protocols by trained interviewers are followed (Peterson, 2002).

These 2- to 3-year-olds probably speak to each other in short sentences that include uninflected nouns and verbs.
(*Photo:* Will Faller)

It is also clear that, even at this earliest stage, children create sentences following rules—not adult rules, to be sure, but rules nonetheless. They focus on certain types of words and put them together in particular orders. They also manage to convey a variety of different meanings with their simple sentences. For example, young children frequently use a sentence made up of two nouns, such as "Mommy sock" or "sweater chair" (Bloom, 1973). The child who says "Mommy sock" may mean either "This is mommy's sock" or "Mommy is putting a sock on my foot" (Bloom, 1973). Thus, to understand what a child means by a two-word sentence, it is necessary to know the context in which the statement is made.

THE GRAMMAR EXPLOSION

Just as the vocabulary explosion you read about in **Chapter 4** begins slowly, so the grammar explosion of the 2- to 6-year-old period starts with several months of simple sentences such as "Mommy sock." You can get some feeling for these changes from **Table 6.3**, which lists some of the sentences spoken by a little boy named Daniel (Ingram, 1981). The left-hand column lists some of Daniel's sentences at about 21 months of age, when he was still using the simplest forms; the right-hand column lists some of his sentences only 2½ months later (aged 23 months), when he had shifted into higher gear.

INFLECTIONS Daniel obviously did not add all the inflections at once. The sentences in the right-hand column of **Table 6.3** include only a few, such as *-s* for plural. The beginning of negative constructions is apparent in "No book," and the beginning of the question form shows in "Where going?" Within each language community, children seem to add inflections and more complex word orders in fairly predictable sequences.

In a classic early study, Roger Brown found that the earliest inflection used among children learning English is typically *-ing* added to a verb, as in "I playing" or "Doggie running," expressions that are common in the speech of 2½- to 3-year-olds (Brown, 1973). Over the next year or so come (in order) prepositions such as "on" and "in," the plural *-s* on nouns, irregular past tenses (such as "broke" or "ran"), possessives, articles

TABLE 6.3	Examples of Daniel's Sentences at Two Ages	
Early Simple Sentences (aged 21 months)	**More Complex Sentences (aged 23 months)**
A bottle	A little boat
Broke it	Doggies here
Here bottle	Give you the book
Hi Daddy	It's a boy
Horse doggie	It's a robot
What that?	Little box there
Kitty cat	No book
Poor Daddy	Oh cars
That monkey	That flowers
Want bottle	Where going?

(*Source:* Reprinted by permission of the publisher. Ingram, 1981, Tables 6 and 7, pp. 133–345. Copyright © 1981 by Elsevier Science Publishing Co., Inc.)

("a" and "the" in English), the -*s* added to third-person verbs such as "He wants," regular past tenses such as "played" and "wanted," and various forms of auxiliary verbs, as in "I *am* going."

QUESTIONS AND NEGATIVES There are also predictable sequences in the child's developing use of questions and negatives. In each case, the child seems to go through periods when he creates types of sentences that he has not heard adults use, but that are consistent with the particular set of rules he is using. For example, in the development of questions there is a point at which the child can put a *Wh-* word ("who," "what," "when," "where," "why") at the front end of a sentence, but doesn't yet put the auxiliary verb in the right place, as in "Where you are going now?" Similarly, in the development of negatives, children go through a stage in which they put in *not* or *n't* or *no* but omit the auxiliary verb, as in "I not crying."

OVERREGULARIZATION Another intriguing phenomenon is **overregularization**, or overgeneralization. No language is perfectly regular; every language includes some irregularly conjugated verbs or unusual forms of plurals. What 3- to 4-year-olds do is apply the basic rule to all these irregular instances, thus making the language more regular than it really is (Maratsos, 2000). In English, this is especially clear in children's creation of past tenses such as "wented," "blowed," and "sitted" or plurals such as "teeths" and "blockses" (Fenson et al., 1994).

Such overregularizations illustrate yet again that language development is a rule-governed process that cannot be explained by imitation theories. Children show that they are using rules when they create word forms (such as "wented") they have not heard. Clearly, children cannot have learned these words by imitation. Instead, their presence in children's speech suggests that children actively infer and use language rules.

COMPLEX SENTENCE After children have figured out inflections and the basic sentence forms using negatives and questions, they soon begin to create remarkably complex sentences, using a conjunction such as "and" or "but" to combine two ideas or

overregularization
attachment of regular inflections to irregular words, such as the substitution of *goed* for *went*

using embedded clauses. Here are some examples from children aged 30 to 48 months (de Villiers & de Villiers, 1992, p. 379):

> I didn't catch it but Teddy did!
> I'm gonna sit on the one you're sitting on.
> Where did you say you put my doll?
> Those are punk rockers, aren't they?

When you remember that only about 18 months earlier these children were using sentences little more complex than "See doggie," you can appreciate how far they have come in a short time.

PHONOLOGICAL AWARENESS

phonological awareness
children's understanding of the sound patterns of the language they are acquiring

Certain aspects of early childhood language development, such as rate of vocabulary growth, predict how easily a child will learn to read and write when she enters school (Wood & Terrell, 1998). However, one specific component of early childhood language development, **phonological awareness**, seems to be especially important. Phonological awareness is a child's sensitivity to the sound patterns that are specific to the language being acquired. It also includes the child's knowledge of that particular language's system for representing sounds with letters. Researchers measure English-speaking children's phonological awareness with questions like these: "What would *bat* be if you took away the *b*? What would *bat* be if you took away the *b* and put *r* there instead?"

A child doesn't have to acquire phonological awareness in early childhood. It can be learned in elementary school through formal instruction (Ball, 1997; Bus & van IJzendoorn, 1999). However, numerous studies have shown that the greater a child's phonological awareness *before* he enters school, the faster he learns to read (Christensen, 1997; Gilbertson & Bramlett, 1998; Schatschneider, Francis, Foorman, Fletcher, & Mehta, 1999; Wood & Terrell, 1998). In addition, phonological awareness in the early childhood years is related to rate of literacy learning in languages as varied as English, Punjabi, and Chinese (Chiappe & Siegel, 1999; Ho & Bryant, 1997; Huang & Hanley, 1997; McBride-Chang & Ho, 2000).

Phonological awareness appears to develop primarily through word play. For example, among English-speaking children, learning and reciting nursery rhymes contributes to phonological awareness (Bryant, MacLean, & Bradley, 1990; Bryant, MacLean, Bradley, & Crossland, 1990; Layton, Deeny, Tall, & Upton, 1996). For Japanese children, a game called *shiritori*, in which one person says a word and another comes up with a word that begins with its ending sound, helps children develop these skills (Norboru, 1997; Serpell & Hatano, 1997). Educators have also found that using such games to teach phonological awareness skills to preschoolers is just as effective as more formal methods such as flash cards and worksheets (Brennan & Ireson, 1997). *Shared*, or *dialogic*, *reading* has also been found to contribute to growth in phonological awareness (Burgess, 1997).

invented spelling
a strategy young children with good phonological awareness skills use when they write

Preschoolers with good phonological awareness skills—those who have learned a few basic sound–letter connections informally, from their parents or from educational TV programs or videos—often use a strategy called **invented spelling** when they attempt to write (see **Figure 6.5**). In spite of the many errors they make, children who use invented spelling strategies before receiving school-based instruction in reading and writing are more likely to become good spellers and readers later in childhood (McBride-Chang, 1998). Thus, the evidence suggests that one of the best ways parents and preschool teachers can help young children prepare for formal instruction in reading is to engage them in activities that encourage word play and invented spelling.

Figure 6.5

Translation: A snake came to visit our class. A 5-year-old used a strategy called "invented spelling" to write this sentence about a snake's visit (hopefully accompanied by an animal handler!) to her kindergarten class. Invented spelling requires a high level of phonological awareness. Research suggests that children who have well-developed phonological awareness skills by the time they reach kindergarten learn to read more quickly.

(Courtesy of Jerry and Denise Boyd. Used with permission.)

receptive vocabulary
the words that are understood when heard

expressive vocabulary
the words whose meaning is used correctly when speaking

The Real World

Teaching
Strengthening Language Skills in Preschoolers

Both the quantity and quality of reading experiences that young children have influence their language and reading development (M. Sénéchal, personal communication, July 14, 2001). Researchers at Monique Sénéchal's language lab at Carlton University have been investigating how young children develop language skills, especially in relation to such natural experiences as storybook reading. An early study found that when parents change their communication style when reading to infants between 9 and 18 months of age it can help language development. Nine-month-old infants vocalized more when parents talked about a picture book they were reading than when parents simply read a story to their infant (Sénéchal, Cornell, & Broda, 1995). Although reading a storybook just once to a child improves her **receptive vocabulary** (Sénéchal & Cornell, 1993), it was found that children who were read the same book three times did much better in later development of both receptive and **expressive vocabulary** (Sénéchal, 1997). Moreover, when children were asked questions about what was being read, their expressive vocabulary increased even more than their receptive vocabulary. It appears that children who actively participate in story-reading by answering questions comprehend and produce more words than do children who passively listen (Sénéchal, Thomas, & Monker, 1995).

It is important to encourage children to begin preparation for independent reading during the preschool years, and is especially important to intervene early when children show a delay in vocabulary development. A variety of formal reading experiences (e.g., teaching letter names and sounding-out words) and informal storybook reading early in a child's life contribute in unique ways to reading performance later on. It seems that both formal and informal parental involvement in reading experiences contribute to children's reading skill by the end of Grade 1. Moreover, a child's reading fluency in Grade 1 predicted a child's vocabulary and listening comprehension in Grade 3 (Sénéchal & LeFevre, 1998, 2002; Sénéchal, LeFevre, Thomas, and Daley, 1998).

As a means of assessing the effects of language skill development intervention for disadvantaged preschoolers, Hargrave and Sénéchal (2000) studied techniques that could be applied in the preschool day-care settings to improve the acquisition of vocabulary for children with poor vocabularies. They studied preschoolers in a standard day-care reading situation where there was a ratio of eight children to every teacher. Children were divided into two groups. One group experienced the standard story-reading situation in which the teacher reads the story and the children listen. The other group was exposed to a "dialogic-reading" intervention.

In the dialogic-reading situation teachers were trained to actively involve the children. The teacher helped the child become the teller of the story while the teacher became the audience and listened and questioned the child. Dialogic reading included the following techniques: asking "wh" questions (i.e., what, where, when, why, who, which, and how), asking open-ended questions, and expanding on what the child said (Arnold, Lonigan, Whitehurst, & Epstein, 1994). These techniques were designed to teach vocabulary and to encourage children to provide more complete descriptions of what they see.

Another part of the procedure involved the parents. Parents of children in the dialogic-reading group received the same training as the teachers. In addition, the parents were encouraged to read to their children at home.

All the children were assessed before and after the dialogic reading intervention. A comparison of the children's vocabulary scores showed that the children in the dialogic-reading group demonstrated significantly higher expressive vocabulary scores than children in the regular reading group. The children in the dialogic-reading group were on average 13 months behind in their expressive vocabulary before the intervention but advanced to the point where they were just 4 months behind after just 4 weeks of intervention.

Tips for Dialogic Reading

- Repeat what a child says. Let a child know that his or her answer is correct by restating it: "Yes, that is an elephant."

- Follow answers with questions. When a child names an object, ask a question about it. For example: "What colour is the car?" "Where is the ball hidden?" "Why do we use soap?" or "Who works in the hospital?"

- Help a child as needed. If a child is not able to answer your question, provide a correct answer and ask him or her to repeat what you have said.

- Expand what a child says. When a child says something about a picture, praise him or her and add a little to what's been said. For example, if your child says "Doggy bark" you might say, "Yes, the dog is barking at the kitty." In this way, you model correct grammar and provide a new piece of information. Later you might ask a question about this new information: "Who's the dog barking at?"

- Follow a child's interests. If a child shows an interest in a picture either by talking about it or pointing to it, follow up immediately by asking questions.

- Adapt to a child's "growing linguistic abilities." A child who is adept at naming colours should be encouraged to talk about some other aspects of the story.

- Praise and encourage. Tell a child when he or she is doing well by saying things like: "Good answer!" or "That's right. Are you ever brilliant!"

- Have fun. Try to keep reading times fun and like a game. One way to do this is to switch between asking questions and just plain reading. For example, you could read one page and then have a child tell you about the next page.

- Try to read with a child once a day. Pick a time when a child is interested in sharing a book with you. Before bed is a good time for many children and parents. Even 5 to 10 minutes can make a difference.

(Source: Adapted from Arnold, Lonigan, Whitehurst, & Epstein, 1994. Copyright © 1994 by the American Psychological Association. Adapted with permission.)

INDIVIDUAL AND CROSS-LINGUISTIC VARIATIONS

Longitudinal studies suggest that individual rates of language development vary greatly. Some children begin using individual words at 8 months, others do not do so until 18 months; some do not use two-word sentences until they are 3 years old or more (e.g., Blake, 1994; Bloom, 1991; Brown, 1973). Cross-cultural studies have produced similar findings (e.g., Fenson et al., 1994).

Researchers affiliated with the University of Montreal compared children from various socioeconomic levels and found that several factors influence language and cognitive development in children up to 3 years of age (Lacroix, Pomerleau, Malcuit, Séguin, & Lamarre, 2001). For instance, children of both teenage mothers and mothers of lower socioeconomic status displayed inferior levels of language and cognitive development. They also found that a child's language expression and comprehension were related to the duration of a mother's vocalization when her infant was at 6 and

Developmental Psychology in Your Career

Kindergarten Teacher

Occupation	Kindergarten Teacher
Description	• plan and deliver a program that meets the specific expectations for children's learning outlined in approved curriculum • lead students in activities that engender growth in the areas of language, mathematics, science and technology, personal and social development, and the arts • identify students with special learning needs and prepare and implement remedial programs • assess and evaluate students' progress and discuss with parents and school officials
Entry Credentials	• A post-bachelor's degree in education and a provincial/territorial teaching certificate
Essential Lifespan Development Knowledge	• human development principles and theories • principles of education and learning • cognitive, psychomotor, and social developmental norms • educational assessment methods
Essential Lifespan Development Skills	• creative, experiential teaching methods, including storytelling and discussion, music, artwork, school concerts, field trips, and sporting activities, to direct and promote holistic student development • academic teaching methods to promote literacy, numeracy, and general knowledge • student behaviour management • observation and evaluation of students' cognitive, psychomotor, and social development
Lifespan Development and Essential Professional Attitude	• enjoy working with young children • demonstrate sensitivity to fairness, equity, and diversity • value a stimulating and safe environment • demonstrate positive interactions with parents, other school staff, and community professionals • ensure confidentiality
Lifespan Development Career Profile: Bonnie Johnson, Kindergarten Teacher, Balsam Street School, Lakehead Public Schools	"At this age there is rapid growth in all areas of development and each day brings new surprises and heart-warming moments. It is very fulfilling, exciting, and rewarding to be responsible for some of the growth, but also to see children in open-ended activities that allow them to direct some of their own learning. "Learning in the early years prepares the foundation for future learning and, for vulnerable children in particular, a teacher may be the only reliable and nurturing adult in the child's life. It is fascinating to see how unique and special each child is before they grow older and begin to conform and become more like their peers." June 21, 2004

18 months of age. Another factor that was related to language and cognitive development was the number of linguistic and social toys available to the child.

The timing of complex speech predicts later intelligence test scores only for those few late talkers who also have poor receptive language. This group appears to remain behind in language development and perhaps in cognitive development more generally (Bates, 1993). Variations in speed of language acquisition seem to have some genetic basis, but they are also at least partly a response to differences in the richness of the child's language environment (Mather & Black, 1984; Plomin & DeFries, 1985).

Studies of speakers of a wide variety of languages, including Turkish, Serbo-Croatian, Hungarian, Hebrew, Japanese, a New Guinean language called Kaluli, German, and Italian, have revealed important similarities in young children's language development (Maitel, Dromi, Sagi, & Bornstein, 2000). For example, the prelinguistic phase seems to be identical in all language communities. All babies coo, then babble; all babies understand language before they can speak it; babies in all cultures begin to use their first words at about 12 months.

Moreover, a one-word phase always seems to precede a two-word phase in every language, with the latter beginning at about 18 months. Likewise, in all languages studied so far, prepositions describing locations are added in essentially the same order. Children learn words for "in," "on," "under," and "beside" first. Then they learn the words for "front" and "back" (Slobin, 1985). Finally, children everywhere seem to pay more attention to the ends of words than the beginnings, so they learn suffixes before they learn prefixes.

Before Going On

- Describe children's first sentences.
- What happens during the grammar explosion?
- What is phonological awareness, and why is it important?
- Describe individual and cross-cultural differences in language development.

DIFFERENCES IN INTELLIGENCE

Psychologists have constructed intelligence tests that can be used beginning in early childhood and that are correlated both with later test scores and with important variables such as school performance. However, the widespread use of these tests has led to an ongoing debate about the origins of score differences and the degree to which they can be modified.

MEASURING INTELLIGENCE

An important assumption in studying differences in intelligence is that these differences can be measured. Thus, it's important to understand something about the tests psychologists use to measure intelligence as well as the meaning and stability of the scores the tests generate.

THE FIRST TESTS The first modern intelligence test was published in 1905 in France by Alfred Binet and Theodore Simon (Binet & Simon, 1905). From the beginning, the test had a practical purpose—to identify children who might have difficulty in school. For this reason, the tasks Binet and Simon devised for the test were very much like some school tasks, including measures of vocabulary, comprehension of facts and relationships, and mathematical and verbal reasoning. For example, could the child describe the difference between wood and glass? Could the young child identify his nose, his ear, his head? Could he tell which of two weights was heavier?

Lewis Terman and his associates at Stanford University modified and extended many of Binet's original tasks when they translated and revised the test for use in the United States (Terman, 1916; Terman & Merrill, 1937). The Stanford-Binet, the name by which the test is still known, initially described a child's performance in terms of a score called an **intelligence quotient**, later shortened to **IQ**. This score was computed by comparing the child's chronological age (in years and months) with his mental age, defined as the level of questions he could answer correctly. For example, a child who could solve the problems for a 6-year-old but not those for a 7-year-old would have a mental age of 6. The formula used to calculate the IQ was

intelligence quotient (IQ) the ratio of mental age to chronological age; also, a general term for any kind of score derived from an intelligence test

$$\text{mental age/chronological age} \times 100 = \text{IQ}$$

This formula results in an IQ above 100 for children whose mental age is higher than their chronological age and an IQ below 100 for children whose mental age is below their chronological age.

This system for calculating IQ is no longer used. Instead, IQ scores for the Stanford-Binet and all other intelligence tests are now based on a direct comparison of a child's performance with the average performance of a large group of other children of the same age. But the scoring is arranged so that an IQ of 100 is still average.

As you can see in **Figure 6.6**, about two-thirds of all children achieve scores between 85 and 115; roughly 96% of scores fall between 70 and 130. Children who score above 130 are often called gifted; those who score below 70 are referred to by such terms as intellectually delayed or as having a development disability. A child classified as having

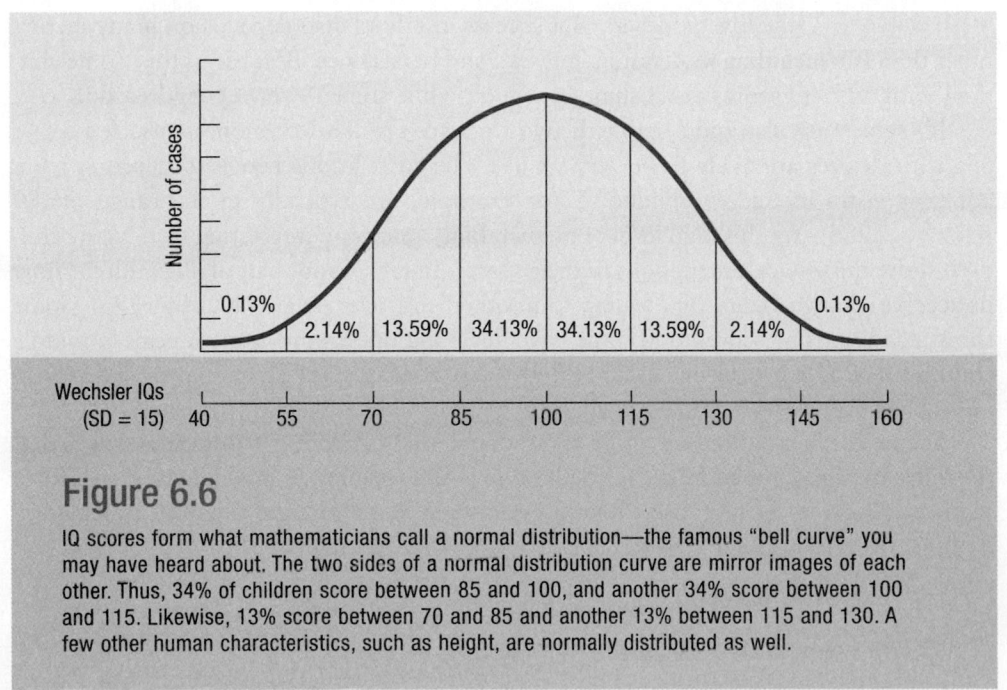

Figure 6.6

IQ scores form what mathematicians call a normal distribution—the famous "bell curve" you may have heard about. The two sides of a normal distribution curve are mirror images of each other. Thus, 34% of children score between 85 and 100, and another 34% score between 100 and 115. Likewise, 13% score between 70 and 85 and another 13% between 115 and 130. A few other human characteristics, such as height, are normally distributed as well.

a developmental disability will also tend to have problems with "adaptive behaviour," such as an inability to dress or feed himself, a problem getting along with others, or a significant problem adapting to the demands of a regular school classroom. Some children with IQ scores in this low range are able to function in a regular schoolroom and should not be labelled retarded.

MODERN INTELLIGENCE TESTS The test used most frequently by psychologists today is the fourth revision of the Wechsler Intelligence Scales for Children, called the WISC-IV, the most recent version of a test originally developed by David Wechsler (Wechsler, 2003). On this fourth edition of the WISC, the child is tested with ten core and five supplemental subtests of different types of problems, each ranging from very easy to very hard. The 15 subtests are categorized into four new indices. The *verbal comprehension index* contains measures for verbal reasoning, comprehension, and the ability to express ideas in words; the *perceptual reasoning index* involves visual non-verbal tasks in the measurement of **fluid reasoning**—the ability to manipulate and use information in a reasoning process; the *working memory index* taps into short-term memory processes such as the ability to briefly hold onto and pay attention to information in the mind long enough to accurately perform some kind of mental operation or manipulation; and the *processing speed index* is a measure of visual selective attention and speed of mental processing. The four indices are based on recent neurocognitive models of information-processing and can be used to indicate learning disabilities and attentional disorders in children (see **Chapter 8** for details on these conditions). A Full Scale IQ is derived from the scores on the subtests of the four indices. An updated supplement is available that provides norms for Canadian children.

fluid reasoning
ability to manipulate and use information in a reasoning process

Critical Thinking

In your opinion, how does having a higher IQ make a child more resilient? For example, in what specific ways might the life of a brighter child living in a slum be different from the life of a less-bright child in the same environment?

STABILITY AND PREDICTIVE VALUE OF IQ SCORES The correlation between a child's test score and her current or future grades in school is about .50 to .60 (Brody, 1992; Carver, 1990; Neisser et al., 1996). This is a strong, but by no means perfect, correlation. It indicates that on the whole, children with high IQ scores will be among the high achievers in school, and those who score low will be among the low achievers. But success in school also depends on many factors other than IQ, including motivation, interest, and persistence. Because of this, some children with high IQ scores don't shine in school, while some lower-IQ children do.

IQ scores are also quite stable. If two tests are given a few months or a few years apart, the scores are likely to be very similar. The correlations between IQ scores from adjacent years in middle childhood, for example, are typically in the range of .80 (Honzik, 1986). Yet this high level of predictability masks an interesting fact: Many children show quite wide fluctuations in their scores. In fact, about half of all children show noticeable changes from one testing to another and over time (McCall, 1993). Some show steadily rising scores, and some have declining ones; some show a peak in middle childhood and then a decline in adolescence. In rare cases, the shifts may cover a range as large as 40 points.

Such wide fluctuations are more common in young children. The general rule is that the older the child, the more stable the IQ score—although even in older children, scores may still fluctuate in response to major stresses such as parental divorce, a change of schools, or the birth of a sibling.

LIMITATIONS OF IQ TESTS Before moving on to the question of the possible origins of differences in IQ, it is important to emphasize a few key limitations of IQ tests and the scores derived from them. IQ tests do not measure underlying competence. An IQ score cannot tell you (or a teacher, or anyone else) that your child has some specific, fixed, underlying capacity. Traditional IQ tests also do not measure a whole host of skills that are likely to be highly significant for getting along in the world. Originally, IQ tests were designed to measure only the specific range of skills that are needed for success in school. This they do quite well. What they do *not* do is indicate anything about a particular person's creativity, insight, street-smarts, ability to read social cues, or understanding of spatial relationships (Gardner, 1983; Sternberg & Wagner, 1993).

ORIGINS OF INDIVIDUAL DIFFERENCES IN INTELLIGENCE

You will not be surprised to discover that arguments about the origins of individual differences in IQ nearly always boil down to a dispute about nature versus nurture.

EVIDENCE FOR HEREDITY Both twin studies and studies of adopted children show strong hereditary influences on IQ, as you already know from the **Research Report** in **Chapter 3**. Identical twins are more like each other in IQ than are fraternal twins, and the IQs of adopted children are better predicted from the IQs of their natural parents than from those of their adoptive parents (Brody, 1992; Loehlin, Horn, & Willerman, 1994; Scarr, Weinberg, & Waldman, 1993). These are precisely the findings researchers would expect if a strong genetic element were at work.

EVIDENCE FOR ENVIRONMENT Adoption studies also provide some strong support for an environmental influence on IQ scores, because the IQ scores of adopted children are clearly affected by the environment in which they have grown up. The clearest evidence for this comes from a study of 38 French children, all adopted in infancy (Capron & Duyme, 1989). Roughly half the children had been born to better-educated parents from a higher social class, while the other half had been born to working-class or poverty-level parents. Some of the children in each group had then been adopted by parents in a higher social class, while the others grew up in poorer families. The effect of rearing conditions was evident in that the children reared in upper-class homes had IQs 15 to 16 points higher than those reared in lower-class families, regardless of the social class level or education of the birth parents. A genetic effect was evident in that the children born to upper-class parents had higher IQs than those from lower-class families, no matter what kind of environment they were reared in.

When developmentalists observe how individual families interact with their infants or young children and then follow the children over time to see which ones later have high or low IQs, they begin to get some sense of the kinds of specific family interactions that foster higher scores. For one thing, parents of higher IQ children provide them with an interesting and complex physical environment, including play materials that are appropriate for the child's age and developmental level (Bradley et al., 1989; Pianta & Egeland, 1994). They also respond warmly and appropriately to the child's behaviour, smiling when the child smiles, answering the child's questions, and in myriad ways reacting to the child's cues (Barnard et al., 1989; Lewis, 1993).

Parents of higher-IQ children also talk to them often, using language that is descriptively rich and accurate (Hart & Risley, 1995; Sigman et al., 1988). And when they play with or interact with their children, they operate in what Vygotsky referred to as the *zone of proximal development* (described in **Chapter 2**), aiming their conversation, their questions, and their assistance at a level that is just above the level the children could manage on their own, thus helping the children to master new skills (Landry et al., 1996).

In addition, parents who appear to foster intellectual development try to avoid being excessively restrictive, punitive, or controlling, instead giving children room to explore,

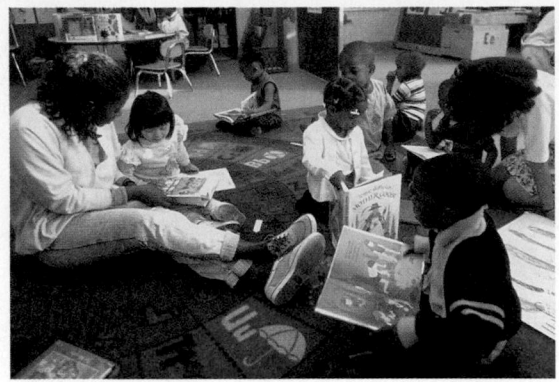

Children who attend enrichment programs typically do not show lasting gains in IQ, but they are more likely to succeed in school. (*Photo:* Paul Conklin/PhotoEdit)

and even opportunities to make mistakes (Bradley et al., 1989; Olson, Bates, & Kaskie, 1992). In a similar vein, these parents ask questions rather than giving commands (Hart & Risley, 1995). Most also expect their children to do well and to develop rapidly. They emphasize and press for school achievement (Entwisle & Alexander, 1990).

Evidence of intergenerational influences comes from a recent analysis of the Concordia Longitudinal Risk Project (see **Chapter 1**), which looked at the intellectual functioning of offspring of mothers who were themselves high-risk children (Saltaris, et al., 2004). In particular, Saltaris and her colleagues found that mothers who had a history of aggression in childhood were less likely to provide effective intellectual stimulation for their own preschool-age children. These mothers displayed less constructive feedback during problem-solving activities and less effective teaching strategies. This in turn puts the early cognitive development of their offspring at risk.

Home environments and family interactions are not the only sources of environmental influence. Programs like Head Start are based squarely on the assumption that it is possible to modify the trajectory of a child's intellectual development, especially if the intervention occurs early enough (Ramey & Ramey, 1998) (see **Development in the Information Age**). Children in enriched preschool programs normally show a gain of about 10 IQ points while enrolled in them, but this IQ gain typically fades and then disappears within the first few years of school (Zigler & Styfco, 1993).

When the enrichment program is begun in infancy rather than at age 3 or 4, even IQ scores remain elevated after the intervention has ended (Ramey & Ramey, 1998). One very well-designed and meticulously reported infancy intervention was called the Abecedarian project (Campbell & Ramey, 1994; Ramey, 1993; Ramey & Campbell, 1987). Infants from poverty-level families whose mothers had low IQs were randomly assigned either to a special day-care program or to a control group that received nutritional supplements and medical care but no special enriched day care. The special day-care program began when the infants were 6 to 12 weeks old and lasted until they began kindergarten.

Figure 6.7 graphs the average IQ scores of the children in each of these two groups from age 2 to age 12. You can see that the IQs of the children who had been enrolled in the special program were higher at every age. Fully 44% of the control group children had IQ scores classified as borderline or developmentally delayed (scores below 85), compared with only 12.8% of the children who had been in the special program. In addition, the enriched day-care group had significantly higher scores on both reading and mathematics tests at age 12 and were only half as likely to have repeated a grade (Ramey, 1992, 1993).

Figure 6.7

In Ramey's study, children from poverty-level families were randomly assigned in infancy to an experimental group that received special day care or to a control group, with the intervention lasting until age 5. At kindergarten, both groups entered public school. The difference in IQ between the experimental and control groups remained statistically significant even at age 12, seven years after the intervention had ended.

(*Source:* Ramey & Campbell, 1987, Figure 3, p. 135, with additional data from Ramey, 1983, Figure 2, p. 29.)

Development in the
Information Age
Computers and Early Childhood Learning

Chapter 4 explored the issue of videos for babies and pointed out that they serve to introduce infants to a culturally important medium but do not necessarily enhance cognitive development. A similar question can be asked about the trend toward increasing computer use by 2- to 6-year-olds: Is the computer an effective medium for teaching young children intellectual skills? If so, then preschool programs might be more effective if computer access were part of the curriculum.

Computer programs have been used to teach prereading and mathematics skills to preschoolers from a variety of backgrounds (Boone, Higgins, Notari, & Stump, 1996; Elliot & Hall, 1997). Playing computer games also appears to improve children's fine-motor skills and reaction times (Yuji, 1996). Further, children who have access to computers at home during early childhood are more successful in the early school years (Weinberger, 1996).

However, important questions remain to be answered. First, computers are a great deal more expensive than traditional materials, so it's important to examine their effectiveness compared with other media. Comparison studies have often shown no differences between the skills of computer-trained children and those of peers who were taught with less expensive media, unless those learning with computers spent a significant amount of time using educational software (Johnston, 1996). Second, preschoolers who spend a lot of time using a computer at home or at school learn to use software more quickly than other children, but they do not learn the material presented in the software any more rapidly or with any greater degree of accuracy (Yuji, 1996). Third, home studies show that parents who make computers available to young children also provide them with a lot of books and educational toys. They also have more knowledge about early childhood development than parents who do not provide computers. Thus, it is impossible to say whether the home computer has any independent effect on young children's acquisition of intellectual skills (Weinberger, 1996). Finally, most of the research on computer learning in early childhood has involved 5- to 6-year-old kindergarteners. Results of these studies may not be applicable to 2- to 4-year-olds.

Early childhood educators view the computer as a means of providing children with additional learning opportunities rather than as a replacement for traditional activities (Driscoll & Nagel, 1999). They point out that preschoolers can probably learn a great deal from well-designed educational software, but they still need to play with other children. They also benefit from three-dimensional physical interactions, such as playing with blocks, sand, and fingerpaints. In addition, an interactive computer storybook may be both fun and educational for a child, but it can't replace the human interaction that takes place when a parent or teacher reads a story to a child.

Two programs in Canada that target high-risk children are Aboriginal Head Start and High/Scope. First, Health Canada (2002c) sponsors several hundred Aboriginal Head Start programs for First Nations, Inuit, Métis, and other Aboriginal children. This early intervention program provides young Aboriginal children with a half-day preschool experience that prepares them for their school years by focusing on the following: education and school readiness, Aboriginal culture and language, parental involvement, health promotion, nutrition, and social support. Second, High/Scope, a preschool program that has shown long-term success in high-risk children in the United States, now has two centres in Canada—one at Sheridan College and the other in Moncton. One High/Scope study followed children of poverty into adulthood. The results showed significant differences between those at-risk children who were in the program and those who were not. Children who went through the program had better school readiness skills, spent less time in special education programs, had superior high-school graduations rates, had higher employment income, and had lower rates of criminal arrests (Schweinhart, 2003).

reaction range
a range between upper and lower boundaries for traits such as intelligence, which is established by one's genes; one's environment determines where, within those limits, one will be

COMBINING THE INFORMATION Virtually all psychologists would agree that heredity is a highly important influence on IQ scores. Studies around the world consistently yield estimates that roughly half the variation in IQ within a given population is due to heredity (Neisser et al., 1996; Plomin & Rende, 1991; Rogers, Rowe, & May, 1994). The remaining half is clearly due to environment or to interactions between environment and heredity.

One useful way to think about this interaction is to use the concept of **reaction range**, a range between some upper and lower boundary of functioning established by one's genetic heritage; exactly where a child will fall within those boundaries is determined by environment. Some developmental psychologists estimate that the reaction range for IQ is about 20 to 25 points (Weinberg, 1989). That is, given a specific genetic heritage, a child's actual IQ test performance may vary as much as 20 or 25 points, depending on the richness or poverty of the environment in which he grows up. When the child's environment is changed for the better, the child moves closer to the upper end of his reaction range. When the environment becomes worse, the child's effective intellectual performance falls toward the lower end of his reaction range. Thus, even though intelligence as measured on an IQ test is highly heritable and falls within the reaction range, the absolute IQ score is determined by environment.

Before Going On

- Briefly describe the history, usefulness, and limitations of IQ tests.
- What kinds of evidence support the nature and nurture explanations for differences in IQ?

Summary

Physical Changes

- Physical development is slower from age 2 to age 6 than it is in infancy, but it nevertheless progresses steadily. Motor skills continue to improve gradually, with marked improvement in large-muscle skills (running, jumping, galloping) and slower advances in small-muscle (fine-motor) skills. Motor activity levels increase through early childhood, and higher activity levels have been associated with improved behavioural control that facilitates meaningful exploratory behaviour.

- Significant changes in brain lateralization occur in early childhood. Handedness is weakly related to brain lateralization, but the association between the two is poorly understood.

- Slower rates of growth contribute to declines in appetite.

- Unintentional injuries are a major cause of harm and death for preschoolers. Parenting, cognitive, and social factors affect injury rates.

- Certain characteristics of both children and parents increase the risk of child maltreatment. Long-term consequences of abuse and neglect can include a variety of emotional problems and can result in changes in brain structure and function.

Cognitive Changes

- Piaget marked the beginning of the preoperational period at about 18 to 24 months, at the point when the child begins to use mental symbols. Despite this advance, the preschool child still lacks many sophisticated cognitive skills. In Piaget's view, such children are still egocentric, lack understanding of conservation, and are often fooled by appearances.

- Research challenging Piaget's findings makes it clear that young children are less egocentric than Piaget thought. By age 4, they can distinguish between appearance and reality in a variety of tasks.

- By the end of early childhood, children have a well-developed theory of mind. They understand that other people's actions are based on their thoughts and beliefs.

- Information-processing theory explains early childhood cognitive development in terms of limitations on young children's memory systems. Four-year-olds are capable of successfully solving nonverbal math operations. Vygotsky's sociocultural theory asserts that children's thinking is shaped by social interaction through the medium of language.

Changes in Language

- Language develops at a rapid pace from age 2 to age 4, beginning with simple two-word sentences.

- After 24 months of age children are capable of forming long-term narrative memories for significant life events.

- During the grammar explosion (ages 3 to 4), children make large advances in grammatical fluency.

- Development of an awareness of the sound patterns of a particular language during early childhood is important in learning to read during the school years. Children seem to acquire this skill through word play and dialogic reading.

- There are individual differences in the rate of language development. Cross-linguistic studies have shown both similarities and differences in language development among children in different groups.

Differences in Intelligence

- Scores on early childhood intelligence tests are predictive of later school performance and are at least moderately consistent over time.

- Differences in IQ have been attributed to both heredity and environment. Twin and adoption studies make it clear that at least half the variation in IQ scores is due to genetic differences; the remainder is attributable to environment and the interaction of heredity and environment.

- Several kinds of differences in IQ or other test scores have been found consistently. Such differences seem most appropriately attributed to environmental variation, rather than to genetics.

Key Terms

amygdala (p. 166)

corpus callosum (p. 162)

conservation (p. 169)

egocentrism (p. 168)

expressive vocabulary (p. 181)

false belief principle (p. 170)

fluid reasoning (p. 186)

functional magnetic resonance imaging
  (fMRI) (p. 166)

handedness (p. 163)

hippocampus (p. 163)

infantile amnesia (p. 176)

inflections (p. 176)

intelligence quotient (IQ) (p. 185)

invented spelling (p. 180)

lateralization (p. 162)

metacognition (p. 174)

metamemory (p. 174)

operational efficiency (p. 173)

overregularization (p. 179)

phonological awareness (p. 180)

preoperational stage (p. 167)

reaction range (p. 190)

receptive vocabulary (p. 181)

short-term storage space (STSS) (p. 173)

theory of mind (p. 171)

Weblinks

Government of Canada Initiatives to Protect Children
http://canada.justice.gc.ca/en/news/nr/2000/doc_25111.html
The Department of Justice outlines its various initiatives to improve the welfare of
Canada's children, such as preventing child abuse and neglect, prenatal nutrition
and health and safety programs, and action plans for those living in high-risk
communities.

**"Early Childhood: Theories, Research and Implications for Bilingual Education" by
Thomas D. Yawkey and Joseph O. Prewitt-Diaz**
www.ncela.gwu.edu/pubs/symposia/first/early.htm#early
This article presents an overview of early childhood theories and research studies, as
well as various theoretical frameworks, and their implications for practitioners and
researchers.

**Scientific American Quarterly—"Intelligence Considered: What Does It Mean to
Have Brainpower? A Search for a Definition of Intelligence" by Philip Yam**
www.psych.utoronto.ca/~reingold/courses/intelligence/cache/1198yam.html
This paper investigates the complex levels that comprise "intelligence" and the
means by which they can be defined and assessed.

Smartrisk
www.smartrisk.ca/Default.aspx?dd=1
A nonprofit organization that is dedicated to helping reduce the risk due to injury
for Canadians of all ages. Website features articles, news, discussion, and links suitable for researchers, teachers, and the general public.

Electronic Child Health Network
www.echn.ca/hsc/chn-echn.nsf/pages/main
This Canadian nonprofit organization is dedicated to communicating relevant, accurate, and up-to-date health, safety, and wellness information among parents, children, and health care providers.

© 1998 Aaron Haupt/Stock Boston

CHAPTER 7

SOCIAL AND PERSONALITY DEVELOPMENT IN EARLY CHILDHOOD

If you asked a random sample of adults to tell you the most important characteristics of children between the ages of 2 and 6, the first thing on the list would probably be their rapidly changing social abilities during these years. Nay-saying, oppositional toddlers who spend most of their play time alone become skilled, cooperative playmates by age 5 or 6. Certainly, the huge improvements in language skills are a crucial ingredient in this transition. But the most obvious thing about 5-year-olds is how socially "grown up" they seem compared with toddlers.

This chapter will introduce you to two very different theoretical approaches to understanding both social and personality development during the early childhood years. You will also learn about preschoolers' relationships with parents and peers. You will read about important changes in personality, self-concept, and gender understanding that take place during this period. Finally, you will become familiar with how a variety of contexts influence young children's development. As you read, keep the following questions in mind:

- How do the psychoanalytic and social-cognitive perspectives differ in their explanations of social and personality development during early childhood?

- In what ways do family relationships change during the early childhood period?

- What does research reveal about the effects of various family structures and divorce?

- How do preschoolers relate to peers?

- What important changes in personality and self-concept happen during early childhood?

- How does the child's understanding of gender and gender roles develop?

THEORIES OF SOCIAL AND PERSONALITY DEVELOPMENT

Freud and Erikson's psychoanalytic perspective offered key insights into the emotional components of development in the early childhood years. Modern theorists have focused on the role of cognition. Each point of view contributes something to scientists' understanding of early childhood.

PSYCHOANALYTIC PERSPECTIVES

Freud's theory of stages of personality development emphasized psychosexual stages of maturation (as described in **Chapter 2**), whereas Erikson placed the emphasis for development somewhat differently. Erikson emphasized the importance of internal drives and culture in his psychosocial stages of development. Accordingly, both of the stages Erickson identified in the preschool period (see **Table 2.2**, page 30) are triggered by children's growing physical, cognitive, and social skills. The stage Erikson called *autonomy versus shame and doubt,* for example, is centred on the toddler's new mobility and the accompanying desire for autonomy. The stage of *initiative versus guilt* is ushered in by new cognitive skills, particularly the preschooler's ability to plan, which accentuates his wish to take the initiative.

Both Freud and Erikson believed that the key to healthy development during this period is striking a balance between the child's emerging skills and desire for autonomy and the parents' need to protect the child and control the child's behaviour. Thus, the parents' task changes rather dramatically after infancy. In the early months of life, the parents' primary task is to provide enough warmth, predictability, and responsiveness to foster a secure attachment and to support basic physiological needs. But once the child becomes physically, linguistically, and cognitively more independent, the need to control becomes a central aspect of the parents' task. Too much control and the child will not have sufficient opportunity to explore; too little control and the child will become unmanageable and fail to learn the social skills he will need to get along with peers as well as adults.

Neither Freud nor Erikson talked much about the role of the child's peers in development, but a number of other theorists have emphasized the vital significance of such encounters. Hartup suggests that each child needs experience in different kinds of relationships (Hartup, 1996). First, each child needs an attachment to someone who has greater knowledge and social power, such as a parent, a teacher, or even an older sibling. Such relationships are complementary rather than reciprocal. The bond may be extremely powerful in both directions, but the actual behaviours the two individuals show toward each other are not the same. For example, a parent makes a sandwich for a child's lunch far more often than the reverse.

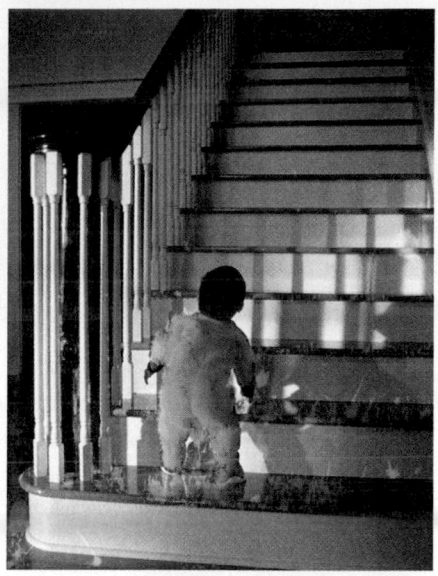

According to Erikson, young children need an opportunity to develop autonomy and show initiative within the bounds of parental guidance and direction.
(*Photo:* John Olson/Firstlight.ca)

Second, children need reciprocal relationships with others, such as same-age peers or near-age siblings, whose knowledge and social power are equal to their own. In reciprocal relationships, partners demonstrate the same behaviour toward each other and often work together to accomplish a task. Thus, two children may work together to make sandwiches for lunch.

Hartup's point is that these two kinds of relationships serve different functions for the child, and that a child needs both in order to develop effective social skills. Attachment relationships are necessary to provide the child with protection and security. In these relationships, children create basic internal working models and learn fundamental social skills. But in reciprocal relationships—in friendships and in peer groups—children practise social behaviour and acquire those social skills that can only be learned in a relationship between equals: cooperation, competition, and intimacy.

SOCIAL-COGNITIVE PERSPECTIVES

The emphasis on peer relations proposed by Hartup and others has been important in turning developmentalists' attention toward the contribution of cognitive skills to changes in social and personality development. In contrast to the psychoanalytic tradition, **social-cognitive theory** assumes that social and emotional changes in the child are the result of, or at least are facilitated by, the enormous growth in cognitive abilities that happens during the preschool years (Macrae & Bodenhausen, 2000). Over the past three decades, psychologists have devoted a great deal of theoretical and empirical attention to determining just how the two domains are connected.

social-cognitive theory
the theoretical perspective that asserts that social and personality development in early childhood are related to improvements in the cognitive domain

PERSON PERCEPTION Preschoolers' emerging capacity for forming meaningful categories manifests itself in the social domain as a set of ideas and behaviours that psychologists call **person perception**, or the ability to classify others (see **The Real World**). For example, by kindergarten age, children make judgments very similar to those of adults when asked to identify the most intelligent child in their class or play group (Droege & Stipek, 1993). Moreover, they describe their peers in terms of traits such as "grumpy" and "mean" (Yuill, 1997). They also make statements about other people's patterns of behaviour—"Grandma always lets me pick the cereal at the grocery store."

person perception
the ability to classify others according to categories such as age and gender

The Real World

Learning

Storybooks and Learning to Classify Personality

You might be familiar with the saying "You are what you read." In the previous chapter, Carole Peterson described how our earliest childhood experiences can be woven into the fabric of our self-concept. For instance, when you were a youngster some children's books probably helped you learn about colours, animals, various aspects of your home and neighbourhood, and what other people were like. Have you ever wondered in what way the characters in your childhood storybooks helped to shape your understanding and expectations of others?

The Canadian author of your textbook has at times mused about where his interest in the study of psychology originated. Perhaps it is related to some of his earliest memories of listening to songs and stories on vinyl records. One particular source of early exposure to psychology may have been from the raspy-voiced narration of "Winnie-the-Pooh" stories. This possibility became evident after he read a whimsical article by Sarah Shea and her colleagues at Dalhousie University entitled "Pathology in the Hundred Acre Wood: A Neurodevelopmental Perspective on A.A. Milne" published by the *Canadian Medical Association Journal* (Shea, Gordon, Hawkins, Kawchuk, & Smith, 2000). They contend that "somewhere at the top of the Hundred Acre Wood, a little boy and his bear play. On the surface it is an innocent world, but on closer examination. . . we find a forest where neurodevelopmental and psychosocial problems go unrecognized and untreated." It seems that the characters of the A.A. Milne stories display a wide range of serious emotional conditions. Pooh, for instance, arguably suffers from both Attention Deficit Hyperactivity Disorder (ADHD), Inattentive type, and possibly Obsessive Compulsive Disorder (OCD) related to his "obsessive fixation on honey" and "his repetitive counting behaviours." Piglet, who is characteristically "anxious, blushing [and] flustered. . . suffers from Generalized Anxiety Disorder." Eeyore, who displays "chronic negativism, low energy and anhe(haw)donia. . . would benefit greatly from an antidepressant [and individual therapy.]" As for Owl, he is "obviously bright, but dyslexic." They also considered Tigger's character closely and described him as "gregarious and affectionate, but he has a recurrent pattern of risk-taking behaviours. . . in a context of obvious hyperactivity and impulsivity."

In light of Shea et al.'s analysis of A.A. Milne's storybook characters, an alternative subtitle for the series of stories could have been *My First Psychology Book*. It may lead you to wonder if exposure to these stories could serve to shape an understanding of emotion and personality in early childhood. Research is needed to determine if there is any significant connection between exposure to these stories and later interest in the study of psychology.

(*Source:* "Pathology in the Hundred Acre Wood: A neurodevelopmental perspective on A.A. Milne". Reprinted from *CMAJ* 12 December 2000 163(12), page(s) 1557–1559 by permission of the publisher. © 2000 Canadian Medical Association [**www.cma.ca/cmaj/index.asp**].)

Critical Thinking

Think of as many explanations as you can for the fact that children begin to prefer to play with same-sex peers as early as age 3 or 4.

They use these observations to classify others into groups such as "people I like" and "people I don't like."

However, young children's observations and categorizations of people are far less consistent than those of older children. A playmate they judge to be "nice" one day may be referred to as "mean" the next. Developmentalists have found that young children's judgments about others are inconsistent because they tend to base them on their most recent interactions with those individuals (Ruble & Dweck, 1995). In other words, a 4-year-old girl describes one of her playmates as "nice" on Monday because she shares a cookie, but as "mean" on Tuesday because she refuses to share a candy bar. Or, the child declares "I don't like Grandma any more because she made me go to bed early."

Preschoolers also categorize others on the basis of observable characteristics such as age and gender. They talk about "big kids" (school-age children) and "little kids" (their age mates), and seem to know that they fit in best with the latter. Self-segregation by gender—a topic you'll read more about later in the chapter—begins as early as age 2.

UNDERSTANDING RULE CATEGORIES According to social-cognitive theorists, young children also use classification skills to take another important step in social development when they begin to understand the difference between *social conventions* and *moral rules* (Turiel, 1983). A social convention is a rule that serves to regulate behaviour but has no moral implications. For example, in Canada, shaking hands with others when you meet them is a social convention. Moral rules are regulations based on an individual's or a society's fundamental sense of right and wrong. Most of us would feel differently about eliminating laws against stealing than we would about switching from driving on the right to the left side of the street, because laws against stealing are based on a moral principle—we believe it is morally wrong for one person to take another's property.

Researchers have found that children begin to respond differently to violations of social conventions and moral rules between ages 2 and 3 (Smetana, Schlagman, & Adams, 1993). For example, they view taking another child's toy without permission as a more serious violation of rules than forgetting to say "thank you." They also say, just as adults would in response to similar questions, that stealing and physical violence are wrong, even if their particular family or preschool has no explicit rule against them. This kind of understanding seems to develop both as a consequence of preschoolers' increasing capacity for classification and as a result of adults' tendency to emphasize moral transgressions more than social-convention violations when punishing children (Nucci & Smetana, 1996).

UNDERSTANDING OTHERS' INTENTIONS Would you feel differently about a person who deliberately scratched your car paint with a key than you would about someone who accidentally scratched it while washing your car for you? Chances are you would be far more forgiving of the person who unintentionally scratched your car paint, because we tend to base our judgments of others' behaviour and our responses to them on what we perceive to be their intentions. Working from his assumptions about young children's egocentrism, Piaget suggested that young children are incapable of such discriminations.

However, more recent research has demonstrated that young children do understand intentions to some degree. For one thing, it's quite common for preschoolers to say "It was an accident. . . I didn't mean to do it" when they are punished. Such protests suggest that children understand that intentional wrongdoing is punished more severely than unintentional transgressions of the rules.

Several studies suggest that children can make judgments about actors' intentions both when faced with abstract problems and when personally motivated by a desire to avoid punishment. For example, in a classic study, 3-year-olds listened to stories about children playing ball (Nelson, 1980). Pictures were used to convey information about intentions (see **Figure 7.1**). The children were more likely to label as "bad" or "naughty" the child who intended to harm a playmate than the child who accidentally hit another child in the head with the ball. However, the children's judgments were also influenced by outcomes. In other words, they were more likely to say a child who wanted to hurt his playmate was "good" if he failed to hit the child with the ball. These results suggest that children know more about intentions than Piaget thought, but that they are still limited in their ability to base judgments entirely on intentions.

Figure 7.1

Pictures like these have been used to assess young children's understanding of an actor's intentions

Before Going On

- How do the theories of Freud, Erikson, and social-cognitive theorists differ in their emphasis on children's families and peers?

- What are the findings of social-cognitive theorists with respect to preschoolers' skills in person perception, understanding of rules, and understanding of others' intentions?

FAMILY RELATIONSHIPS

Despite changing views concerning the various influences on early childhood development, psychologists agree that family relationships constitute one of the most, if not the most, influential factors in early childhood development. These relationships reflect both continuity and change, in that the preschooler is no less attached to her family than the infant but, at the same time, is struggling to establish independence.

ATTACHMENT

You'll remember from **Chapter 5** that by 12 months of age, a baby has normally established a clear attachment to at least one caregiver. By age 2 or 3, the attachment is just as strong, but many attachment behaviours have become less visible. Three-year-olds still want to sit on Mom's or Dad's lap; they are still likely to seek some closeness when Mom returns from an absence. But when she is not afraid or under stress, the 3-year-old is able to wander farther and farther from her safe base without apparent distress. She can also deal with her potential anxiety due to separation by creating shared plans with the parents. For example, a parent might say "I'll be home after your naptime," to which the child may respond "Can we watch a movie then?" (Crittenden, 1992).

Attachment quality also predicts behaviour during the preschool years. Children who are securely attached to parents experience fewer behaviour problems. Specifically, those who are insecurely attached display more anger and aggression toward both peers and adults in social settings such as day care and preschool (DeMulder, Denham, Schmidt, & Mitchell, 2000). For example, in a longitudinal study by University of Montreal researchers, Ellen Moss et al. (1999) reported that children between 3 and 5 years of age with mixed-ambivalent attachment are especially prone to displaying outward-focused behavioural problems.

For most children, the attachment relationship, whether secure or not, seems to change at about age 4. Bowlby described this new stage, or level, as a *goal-corrected partnership*. Just as the first attachment probably requires the baby to understand that his mother will continue to exist when she isn't there, so the preschooler grasps that the *relationship* continues to exist even when the partners are apart. Also at about age 4, the child's internal model of attachment appears to generalize. Bowlby argued that the child's model becomes less a specific property of an individual relationship and more a general property of all the child's social relationships. Thus, it's not surprising that 4- and 5-year-olds who are securely attached to their parents are more likely than their insecurely attached peers to have positive relationships with their preschool teachers (DeMulder et al., 2000).

At the same time, advances in the internal working model lead to new conflicts. In contrast to infants, 2-year-olds realize that they are independent contributors to the parent–child relationship. This heightened sense of autonomy brings them into more and more situations in which parents want one thing and children another. However, contrary to popular stereotypes, 2-year-olds actually comply with parents' requests more often than not. They are more likely to comply with safety requests ("Don't touch that, it's hot!") or with prohibitions about care of objects ("Don't tear up the book") than they are with requests to delay ("I can't talk to you now, I'm on the phone") or with instructions about self-care ("Please wash your hands now"). On the whole, however, children of this age comply fairly readily (Gralinski & Kopp, 1993). When they resist, it is most likely to be passive resistance—simply not doing what is asked rather than saying "no."

PARENTING STYLES

Families vary in their responses to preschoolers' increasing demands for independence. Psychologists have struggled over the years to identify the best ways of describing the many dimensions along which families may vary. An early conceptualization was offered by developmentalist Diana Baumrind, who focused on four aspects of family functioning: (1) warmth or nurturance; (2) clarity and consistency of rules; (3) level of expectations, which she describes in terms of "maturity demands"; and (4) communication between parent and child (Baumrind, 1972).

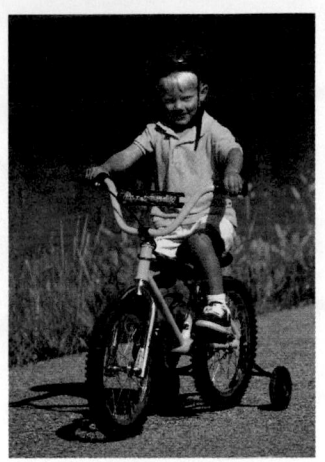

Off he goes, into greater independence. A child this age, especially one with secure attachment, is far more confident about being at a distance from his safe base. (*Photo:* Corbis Digital Stock)

Make the Connection

What effect do you think a child's increasingly complex theory of mind (see **Chapter 6**) has on the child's relationship with her parents?

Children with nurturant and warm parents are more securely attached in the first two years of life than those with more rejecting parents. They also have higher self-esteem and are more empathetic, more altruistic, and more responsive to others' hurts or sufferings. They have higher IQs, are more compliant in preschool and elementary school, do better in school, and are less likely to show delinquent behaviour in adolescence or criminal behaviour in adulthood (Maccoby, 1980; Maughan, Pickles, & Quinton, 1995; Simons, Robertson, & Downs, 1989; Stormshak et al., 2000). Even children from high-risk families (such as low-income, low-parental-education, or dysfunctional families) are less likely to have problems if they are raised in a positive and nurturing environment (Chao & Willms, 1998; Human Resources Development Canada & Statistics Canada, 1996).

A study of Canadian families by Landy and Tam (1996) found that positive and supportive parenting practices reduced the incidence of problems, especially for children in high-risk family situations (such as low income, family dysfunction, or parental depression). In a later study Landy and Tam (1998) found that in children 2 to 3 years of age, the likelihood of problems (such as emotional disorder, aggressive behaviour, and hyperactivity) increased significantly with hostile parenting practices. Positive parenting practices tended to have a buffering effect, showing a reduction in these problems by 25% to 52%.

The degree and clarity of the parents' control over the child are also significant. Parents with clear rules, consistently applied, have children who are much less likely to be defiant or noncompliant. Results from the second cycle of the National Longitudinal Survey of Children and Youth (NLSCY) (Statistics Canada, 1998) showed that children living in a high-risk family where they are exposed to consistent interactions with parents had fewer behavioural problems. In fact, Landy and Tam (1998) found that the rates of aggressive behaviour and hyperactivity in children of families with consistent parenting styles were less than half the rates found in other families.

Another important factor is the form of control the parents use. The most optimal outcomes for the child occur when the parents are not overly restrictive, explain things to the child, and avoid the use of physical punishments. Children whose parents have high expectations (high "maturity demands" in Baumrind's [1971] language) also fare better. Such children have higher self-esteem and show more generosity and altruism toward others.

Finally, open and regular communication between parent and child has been linked to more positive outcomes. Listening to the child is as important as talking to him. Ideally, parents need to convey to the child that what the child has to say is worth listening to, that his ideas are important and should be considered in family decisions. Children of such parents have been found to be more emotionally and socially mature (Baumrind, 1971; Bell & Bell, 1982).

While each of these characteristics of families may be significant individually, they do not occur in isolation but in combinations and patterns. In her early research, Baumrind identified three patterns, or styles, of parenting (Baumrind, 1967). The **permissive parenting style** is high in nurturance but low in maturity demands, control, and communication. The **authoritarian parenting style** is high in control and maturity demands but low in nurturance and communication. The **authoritative parenting style** is high in all four dimensions: nurturance, communication, clarity and consistency, and maturity demands.

Eleanor Maccoby and John Martin have proposed a variation of Baumrind's category system, shown in **Figure 7.2** (Maccoby & Martin, 1983). They categorize families on two dimensions: the degree of demand or control, and the amount of acceptance versus rejection. The intersection of these two dimensions creates four types, three of which correspond quite closely to Baumrind's authoritarian, authoritative, and permissive

permissive parenting style
a style of parenting that is high in nurturance and low in maturity demands, control, and communication

authoritarian parenting style
a style of parenting that is low in nurturance and communication, but high in control and maturity demands

authoritative parenting style
a style of parenting that is high in nurturance, maturity demands, control, and communication

types. Maccoby and Martin's conceptualization adds a fourth type, the **uninvolved parenting style.**

uninvolved parenting style
a style of parenting that is low in nurturance, maturity demands, control, and communication

THE AUTHORITARIAN TYPE Children growing up in authoritarian families—with high levels of demand and control but relatively low levels of warmth and communication—do less well in school, have lower self-esteem, and are typically less skilled with peers than are children from other types of families. Some of these children appear subdued; others may show high aggressiveness or other indications of being rebellious or "out of control."

THE PERMISSIVE TYPE Children growing up with indulgent or permissive parents also show some negative outcomes. Researchers have found that these children do slightly worse in school during adolescence and are likely to be both more aggressive (particularly if the parents are specifically permissive toward aggressiveness) and somewhat immature in their behaviour with peers and in school. They are less likely to take responsibility and are less independent.

THE AUTHORITATIVE TYPE The most consistently positive outcomes have been associated with an authoritative pattern in which the parents are high in both control and acceptance—setting clear limits but also responding to the child's individual needs. Children reared in such families typically show higher self-esteem and are more independent, but are also more likely to comply with parental requests and may show more altruistic behaviour as well. They are self-confident and achievement-oriented in school and get better grades than do children whose parents have other parenting styles.

Critical Thinking

Why do you think children of permissive parents are less independent than those from authoritative families?

THE UNINVOLVED TYPE The most consistently negative outcomes are associated with the fourth pattern, the uninvolved or neglecting parenting style. You may remember from the discussion of secure and insecure attachments in **Chapter 5** that one of the family characteristics often found in infants rated as insecure/avoidant is the "psychological unavailability" of the mother. The mother may be depressed or may be overwhelmed by other problems in her life and may simply have not made any deep emotional connection with the child. Likewise, a parent may be distracted from parenting by more attractive activities. Whatever the reason, such children continue to show disturbances in their social relationships for many years. In adolescence, for example, youngsters from neglecting families are more impulsive and antisocial, less competent with their peers, and much less achievement oriented in school.

Chao and Willms (1998, 2002) analyzed the key dimensions of Canadian parenting practices from the first cycle of the NLSCY and found that the largest portion of parents (about one-third) were authoritative. The authoritative parents scored above average on all measures of key parenting practices. About one-quarter of the parents were authoritarian and another one-quarter were permissive. A fourth category, similar to uninvolved parenting style, included the remaining 15% of parents who scored low on all key measures of positive parenting. McCain and Mustard (1999) reported that almost half of the children who were raised with this parenting style experienced

Figure 7.2

Maccoby and Martin expanded on Baumrind's categories in this two-dimensional category system.

(*Source:* Adapted from Maccoby & Martin, 1983, Figure 2, p. 39.)

behavioural problems. In comparison, only one in five children of authoritative parents had behavioural problems.

PARENTING AND CHILD DISCIPLINE The Canadian Paediatric Society (CPS) describes discipline in this way:

> The word discipline means to impart knowledge and skill—to teach. However, it is often equated with punishment and control. There is a great deal of controversy about the appropriate ways to discipline children, and parents are often confused about effective ways to set limits and instil self-control in their child. [The goal of] effective and positive discipline is about teaching and guiding children, not just forcing them to obey. (Canadian Paediatric Society 2004a, p. 37)

Through instruction and practice, parents, teachers and other significant adults help socialize a child in such a way that she has the knowledge, skills and attitudes required to become a well-functioning person. The purpose of **discipline**, whether physical, mental, or moral, is to develop self-control, moral character, and proper conduct.

There are two key problems that make it hard to establish what constitutes effective discipline. For one thing, it is difficult to establish the deleterious or beneficial effects of various forms of discipline. For example, is physical punishment, such as spanking or washing a child's mouth out with soap, any better or worse than nonphysical corrections like a verbal reprimand, reasoning with an explanation of consequences, or a **time-out** away from sources of attention or enjoyment? Yet if nonphysical interventions were found to be at least as effective as physical punishment, then it would be hard to justify the continued use of physical intervention because of its potential to cause pain and harm.

The second issue concerns the intensity and frequency of discipline. First, there is no established, clear delineation between mild, moderate, and severe discipline. Second, regardless of the type of discipline, any corrective measure that is too extreme or too frequent can easily cross the line into child abuse that can contribute to detrimental physical and emotional outcomes in children (Baumrind, Larzelere, & Cowan, 2002; Kazdin & Benjet, 2003; Larzelere, 2003). In fact, punishment is the leading reason given by perpetrators in substantiated cases of child maltreatment in Canada (Trocmé, Durrant, Ensom, & Marwah, 2004). Although research has yet to provide unequivocal answers to address these issues (Baumrind, 2003; Kazdin & Benjet, 2003), Canadian child-care advocates agree that physical interventions are not appropriate. Instead, they advocate the use of minimal nonphysical interventions in the context of a loving family relationship; and they encourage parents to be proactive by improving parenting skills and anticipating and limiting situations that will require intervention (Canadian Paediatric Society, 2004a; Canadian Psychological Association, 2004; Children's Hospital of Eastern Ontario, 2003; Durrant, 2004; Durrant & Ensom, 2004).

Another area of complexity is evident in the interaction between parenting style and child temperament. For example, authoritative parents often use **inductive discipline**, a discipline strategy in which parents explain to children why a punished behaviour is wrong (Hoffman, 1970). Inductive discipline helps most preschoolers gain control of their behaviour and learn to look at situations from perspectives other than their own. Likewise, the majority of preschool-aged children of parents who respond to demonstrations of poor self-control, such as temper tantrums, by asserting their social and physical power—as often happens when parents physically punish children—have poorer self-control than preschoolers whose parents use inductive discipline (Kochanska, 1997b; Kochanska, Murray, Jacques, Koenig, & Vandegeest, 1996).

However, research on inductive discipline suggests that it is not equally effective for all children. Those who have difficult temperaments or who are physically active and who seem to enjoy risk-taking—such as children who like to climb on top of furniture

discipline
training, whether physical, mental, or moral, that develops self-control, moral character, and proper conduct

time-out
removing the child from the situation and from attention and rewards for a short period of time, typically one minute for every year of the child's age, in order to stop unwanted behaviour

inductive discipline
a discipline strategy in which parents explain to children why a punished behaviour is wrong

and jump off—seem to have a greater need for firm discipline and to benefit less from inductive discipline than do their peers whose temperamental make-up is different (Kochanska, 1997a). In fact, assumptions about the superiority of inductive discipline, as well as authoritative parenting in general, have been criticized by developmentalists who claim that correlations between discipline strategy and child behaviour may arise simply because parents adapt their techniques to their children's behaviour. Thus, parents of poorly behaved children may be more punitive or authoritarian because they have discovered that this is the kind of parenting their children respond to. In a broader context, corrective intervention for any persistent, severe problem, whether it be for inappropriate behaviour, assistance with homework, a medical condition that requires hospitalization, or a psychological situation such as suicide risk or delinquency, will demand more intensive intervention, which increases the likelihood of detrimental outcomes (Larzelere, Kuhn, & Johnson, 2004).

Canadian researchers have been measuring four dimensions of parent–child interactions in the NLSCY that complement Baumrind's classification of parenting styles. The four dimensions include the following types of interactions: *hostile/ineffective* (e.g., parents manipulate through the use of sarcasm or "put-downs" and/or mix anger with punishment); *punitive/aversive* (e.g., parents intimidate by shouting at their child and/or they use physical punishment); *consistent* (e.g., parents ensure compliance with directives and/or "follow through" with consequences after giving a warning); and *positive* (e.g., parents engage in mutually satisfying activities with their child and/or have fun together). An analysis of parent–child interactions over the course of two cycles of the NLSCY revealed that the hostile/ineffective parenting style resulted in persistent behavioural problems at a rate nine times higher than what was exhibited in children who were not exposed to that pattern of parenting. Moreover, hostile/ineffective parenting interactions had a stronger negative effect on a child's behaviour than either income level or family structure (Statistics Canada, 1998a).

ETHNICITY, SOCIOECONOMIC STATUS, AND PARENTING STYLES

When we consider cultural and social influences in relation to parenting styles, we find that the research reveals some complex patterns. For example, studies in which children provide information about their parents' style as well as those in which researchers conduct direct observation of parents have consistently found that, in general, Asian American parents display an authoritarian style (Chao, 1994; Wang & Phinney, 1998). The finding that Asian American children score higher than their white counterparts on almost all measures of cognitive competence argues against the assumption that authoritative parenting is best. In fact, developmentalists have found a link between Asian American children's achievement and authoritarian parenting— that is, parents who have the most authoritarian parenting style have the highest-scoring children (Wang & Phinney, 1998). Moreover, the authoritarian parenting style was not associated with any negative outcomes in Asian American children, which is not what would be predicted from Baumrind's model. Another example of a parenting style that did not fit Baumrind's prediction of the superiority of the authoritative parenting style for all cultures was reported by Johnson and Cremo (1995). They studied Aboriginal child-rearing practices in Canada and described parenting characteristics that are similar to the permissive style, but found no association with negative outcomes in Aboriginal children. These studies suggest that parenting style may be dependent upon the cultural context in which parents and children live, so that as the cultural context changes the best corresponding type of parenting style changes with it.

Make the Connection

Recall Bronfenbrenner's ecological theory, described in **Chapter 2**. Why is it important to have consistency between a child's immediate context (microsystem) and his or her culture (macrosystem)?

Other important aspects of the macrosystem to consider include the effect of socio-economic status (SES) on child development. First, SES factors such as low family income and low level of parental education are risk factors that are associated with an increase in a child's vulnerability to problems (Landy & Tam, 1998) (see **Figure 7.3**). However, several Canadian studies have shown that parenting style is a better predictor of poor outcomes in a child. In particular, the hostile/ineffective parenting style has been shown to be the strongest predictor of behaviour problems in children. At the same time, researchers have found that even when a child was being raised in a high-risk family situation (i.e., low income, parental depression, or family dysfunction), a positive and consistent parenting style acted as a protective factor against these social disadvantages that increase vulnerability for a child (Chao & Willms, 1998, 2002; Landy & Tam, 1998; Miller, Jenkins, & Keating, 2002; Ross, Roberts, & Scott, 1998; Statistics Canada, 1998a).

Second, it was found that good parenting practices are common in all SES levels, and that hostile/ineffective parenting practices also cross all income levels (Chao & Willms, 1998, 2002). In a recent study by Brock University psychologist Tanya Martini and others, mothers who held authoritarian beliefs reported that they were less likely to control their hostile emotions in situations where their child was expressing negative emotions. This was true regardless if the mother was from the lower or middle class (Martini, Root, & Jenkins, in press). All the same, children raised in families in the lower SES are more likely to experience a greater number of risk factors and this, coupled with hostile or ineffective parenting practices, resulted in proportionally higher levels of vulnerability (see **Figure 7.4**). Overall, however, the majority of children being

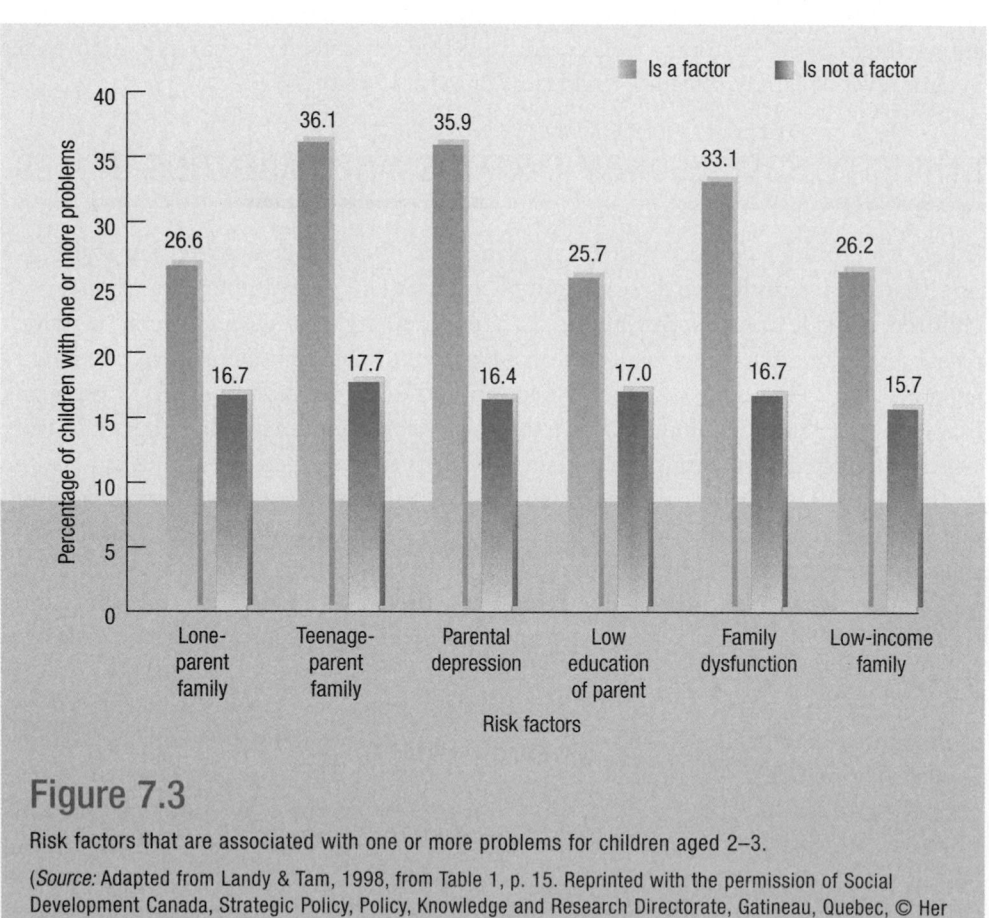

Figure 7.3

Risk factors that are associated with one or more problems for children aged 2–3.

(*Source:* Adapted from Landy & Tam, 1998, from Table 1, p. 15. Reprinted with the permission of Social Development Canada, Strategic Policy, Policy, Knowledge and Research Directorate, Gatineau, Quebec, © Her Majesty the Queen in Right of Canada, at website http://www.11.sdc.gc.ca/en/cs/sp/arb/publications/)

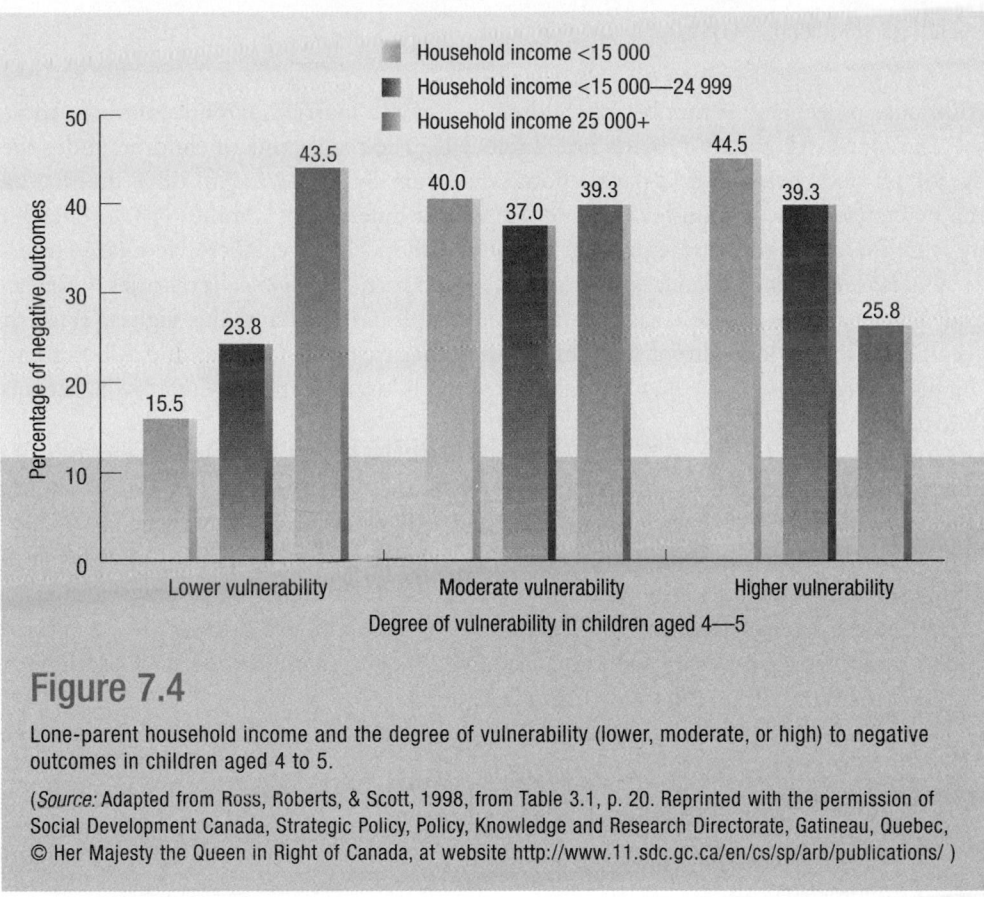

Figure 7.4

Lone-parent household income and the degree of vulnerability (lower, moderate, or high) to negative outcomes in children aged 4 to 5.

(*Source:* Adapted from Ross, Roberts, & Scott, 1998, from Table 3.1, p. 20. Reprinted with the permission of Social Development Canada, Strategic Policy, Policy, Knowledge and Research Directorate, Gatineau, Quebec, © Her Majesty the Queen in Right of Canada, at website http://www.11.sdc.gc.ca/en/cs/sp/arb/publications/)

raised in low-income families are faring well (Ross, Roberts, & Scott, 1998). Therefore, even though low SES is associated with increased vulnerability, effective parenting goes a long way toward compensating for any negative influence associated with the consequences of low SES. The problem remains, however, that a low SES parent may be less capable of providing effective parenting (refer to the Policy Question on poverty in Canada at the end of this chapter).

Before Going On

- How does attachment change during the early childhood years?
- How do parents differ in their approaches to parenting, and how do these differences affect children's development?
- Why are nonphysical discipline methods preferred?
- How are ethnicity and socioeconomic status related to parenting style?

FAMILY STRUCTURE AND DIVORCE

To better understand human development, it is important to examine how the structure of children's families may influence their development.

FAMILY STRUCTURE

Although in decline, the number of children living with married parents continues to be the dominant structure in Canada (see **Table 7.1**). The percentage of children under the age of 15 years living in two-parent homes fell from 84% in 1981 to 68% in 2001 as the percentage of common-law (3% to 13%) and lone-parent families (13% to 19%) increased over the same time period (Turcotte, 2003). However, there were large inter-provincial/territorial differences. For instance, Nunavut, Northwest Territories, Quebec, and Yukon had the lowest rates of married-couple families and the highest rates of common-law and lone-parent families. At the other extreme, Ontario and Alberta had the highest rates of married-couple families with children (Statistics Canada, 2002b).

DIVERSITY IN TWO-PARENT AND LONE-PARENT FAMILIES The number of two-parent blended families in Canada has risen to 12%. The blended two-parent family consists of stepfamilies that were created when a divorced or never-married single biological parent married another single parent or a nonparent. Half of Canadian stepfamilies comprise children living with the biological mother and a stepfather; 10% consist of the biological father and a stepmother; and 40% are blended, i.e., a mix of children that both parents brought into the family (8%) or combined with children born to the new union (32%) (Statistics Canada, 2002c).

TABLE 7.1	Living Arrangements of Children Under the Age of 15 (by province/territory, Canada, 2001)		
	Living with married parents	**Living with common-law parents**	**Living with a lone parent[1]**
	%	%	%
Canada	68.4	12.8	18.8
Newfoundland and Labrador	70.7	10.3	18.9
Prince Edward Island	73.2	8.6	18.2
Nova Scotia	68.0	9.9	22.2
New Brunswick	67.4	12.7	19.9
Quebec	52.1	28.5	19.4
Ontario	75.4	7.3	17.3
Manitoba	70.0	8.8	21.3
Saskatchewan	68.1	9.4	22.5
Alberta	74.0	8.8	17.1
British Columbia	71.5	8.0	20.5
Yukon	52.9	19.8	27.3
Northwest Territories	50.7	25.8	23.5
Nunavut	46.8	30.8	22.3

[1]Also includes about 1% or less of children with no parents, e.g., living with another relative or foster family.

(*Source:* Statistics Canada (2002b). Adapted from Statistics Canada, 2002, *Profile of Canadian families and households: Diversification continues, 2001 Census,* Catalogue no. 96F0030, October 22, available at http://www.12.statcan.ca/english/census01/products/analytic/companion/fam/childfam.cfm)

Twenty-seven percent of school-aged children live in a lone-parent family, which represents a 35% increase between 1990 and 1999 (Canadian Council on Social Development, 2001a). The largest proportion of lone-parent families consists of separated or divorced parents, followed by never-married parents, and a very small proportion of widowed parents. Mothers are five times as likely to be the head of the lone-parent household, and about one-quarter of the mothers are never-married (Ambert, 1998). Other lone parents, especially unmarried teenagers, are likely to live with their own parents (Jorgenson, 1993). Consequently, we find that lone-parent households are no more alike than are two-parent households.

FAMILY STRUCTURE EFFECTS Most children being raised in lone-parent families are doing fairly well by all measures, but there is a subset of these families in which children are more vulnerable to a range of problems (Ross, Roberts, & Scott, 1998). Landy and Tam (1998) found that the impact of lone parenthood had different outcomes depending on the age of the child. For instance, lone parenthood was not related to any specific problem outcome in children aged 2 or 3. However, for children aged 4 to 11, lone parenthood was associated with double the rates of emotional disorder, conduct disorder, hyperactivity, repeating a grade, relationship problems, and having any one or more of these problems. Not surprisingly, lone parents reported experiencing high levels of chronic stress in comparison with two-parent families (see **Figure 7.5**). Moreover, almost half of the female lone-parent families reported experiencing high levels of chronic stress (Health Canada, 1999e).

OTHER TYPES OF FAMILY STRUCTURES In contrast to the amount of research comparing two-parent and lone-parent families, there are relatively few studies of the effects of other kinds of family structures. For example, research on custodial grandparenting tends to focus on the effects of the parenting experience on aging adults. Consequently, researchers know that grandparents' responses to children's problems are quite similar to those of parents (Daly & Glenwick, 2000). However, the stresses of parenting combined with the physical effects of aging are likely to cause older adults to feel more anxious and depressed than younger adults in similar situations (Burton, 1992; Jendrek, 1993). In short, developmentalists know something about how parenting affects older adults but very little about how children raised by grandparents fare.

An exception is the research on gay and lesbian parenting. Concerns about children's sex-role identity and sexual orientation have dominated this research (Bailey, Brobow, Wolfe, & Mikach, 1995). Canada's 2001 census estimates that there are 3000 same-sex couples raising children today (Ambert, 2003a). Studies have generally shown that children raised by gay and lesbian parents develop sex-role identities in the same way as children of heterosexual parents. They are also just as likely to be heterosexual (Golombok & Tasker, 1996).

To help answer general questions about cognitive and social development among the children of gay and lesbian parents, researchers have conducted comprehensive reviews of the small number of studies that have been done. Such

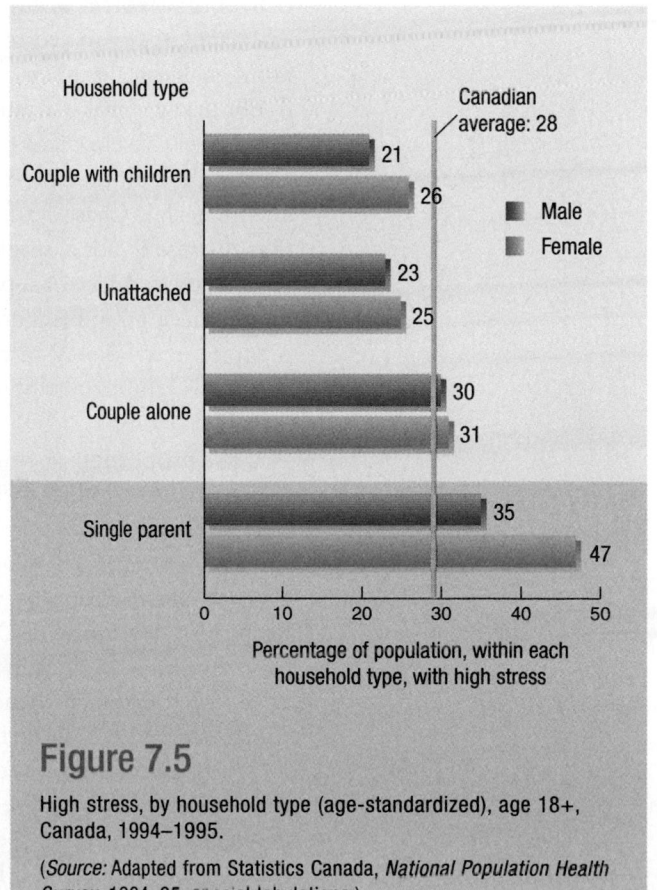

Figure 7.5

High stress, by household type (age-standardized), age 18+, Canada, 1994–1995.

(*Source:* Adapted from Statistics Canada, *National Population Health Survey,* 1994–95, special tabulations.)

reviews have examined a wide variety of studies of gay and lesbian parenting, including case studies, correlational studies, and comparisons of children in gay and lesbian families with those being raised by heterosexual parents. These reviews have typically found that the majority of studies suggest that children raised by gay and lesbian parents do not differ from those raised by heterosexuals (Fitzgerald, 1999; Patterson, 1997). However, most of the gay and lesbian participants in these studies have been raising their own biological children, who were conceived while the parents were involved in heterosexual relationships. Very few studies have involved children who have been raised exclusively by openly gay or lesbian parents, and fewer still have compared children of gay or lesbian parents with partners to those raised by single gays or lesbians.

One recent study involved 80 school-aged children who had been conceived by artificial insemination (Chan, Raboy, & Patterson, 1998). Researchers compared these children across four types of family structures: lesbian couples, single lesbian mothers, heterosexual couples, and single heterosexual mothers. The study found no differences in either cognitive or social development among them. However, they did find that the same variables—parenting stress, parental conflict, parental affection—predicted developmental outcomes in all four groups. These findings, much like those of research contrasting two-parent and lone-parent families, suggest that children's development depends more on how parents interact with them than on any particular family configuration.

DIVORCE

The number of divorces in Canada has steadily declined from the all-time peak in 1987; half of all divorces occur within the first 14 years of marriage and one-quarter of all marriages are dissolved by the fourth anniversary (Statistics Canada, 2004c). For many families divorce happens during the prime child-rearing period, and there can be little doubt that divorce is traumatic for children. It's important to note, however, that some of the negative effects of divorce are due to factors that were present *before* the divorce, such as difficult temperament in the child or excessive marital conflict between the parents (Cherlin, Chase-Lansdale, & McRae, 1998). It's also important to keep in mind that divorce is not a single variable; children are probably affected by a multitude of divorce-related factors—parental conflict, poverty, disruptions of daily routine, and so on (Hetherington, Bridges, & Insabella, 1998). For this reason, children whose parents separate or who stay in conflict-ridden marriages may experience many of the same effects as children whose parents actually divorce (Ingoldsby, Shaw, Owens, & Winslow, 1999).

The proportion of children living in post-divorce/separation versus two-parent custody that were found to be experiencing emotional or behavioural problems can be seen in **Figure 7.6**. Most children in either living arrangement are doing well; although children living in post-divorce/separation situations have a higher prevalence of problems in most areas except unsocial behaviour (low prosocial behaviour) (Human Resources Development Canada, 2001a). In the first few years after a divorce, children typically show declines in school performance and show more aggressive, defiant, negative, or depressed behaviour (Furstenberg & Cherlin, 1991; Hetherington & Clingempeel, 1992; Morrison & Cherlin, 1995; Pagani, Boulerice, Tremblay, & Vitaro, 1997). By adolescence, the children of divorced parents are more likely than their peers to become sexually active at an early age, to experiment with drugs and alcohol, and to engage in criminal behaviour (Wallerstein & Lewis, 1998). Children living in step-parent families also have higher rates of delinquency, more behaviour problems in school, and lower grades than do those in intact families (Lee et al., 1994; Pagani et al., 1997).

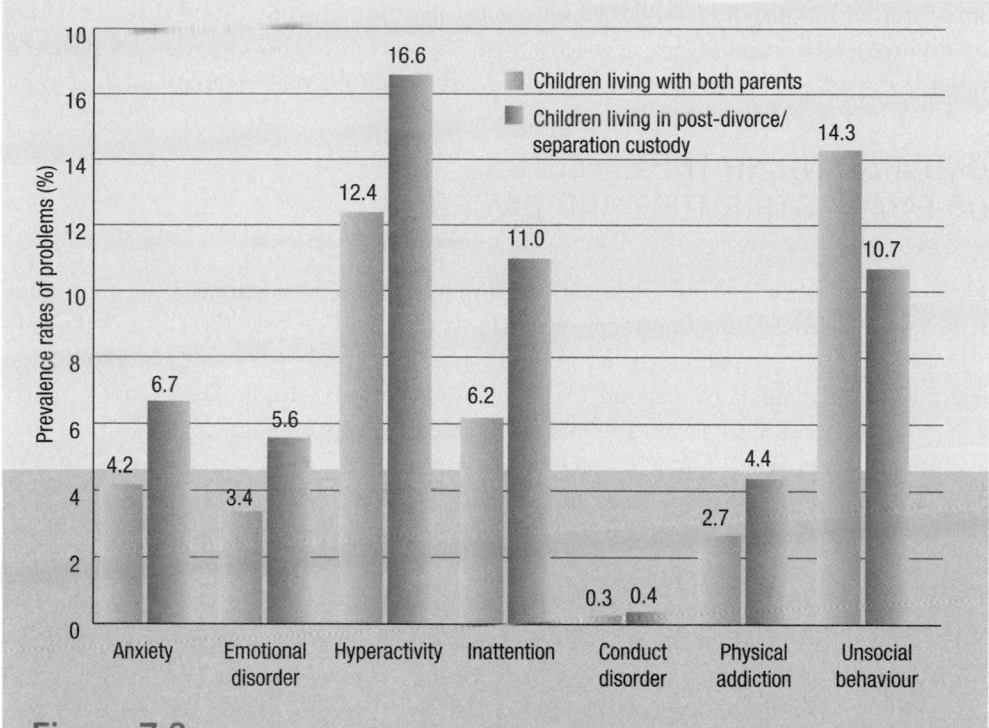

Figure 7.6

The proportion of children with emotional or behavioural problems, comparing those living with both parents with those in post-divorce/separation custody.

(*Source:* Human Resources Development Canada, 2001a. Reprinted with the permission of Social Development Canada, Strategic Policy, Policy, Knowledge and Research Directorate, Gatineau, Quebec, © Her Majesty the Queen in Right of Canada, at website http://www.11.sdc.go.ca/en/cs/sp/arb/publications/)

Many single parents manage to overcome substantial obstacles to give their children the support and supervision they need.
(*Photos: top,* John Fortunato/Getty Images; *bottom,* Cindy Charles/PhotoEdit)

The negative effects of divorce seem to persist for many years. For example, about 92% of adult Canadians who had lived in an intact two-parent family from birth to age 15 reported that they had had a very happy childhood. In comparison, only 72% of adult Canadians who had experienced disruption before the age of 15 due to a change in family structure reported that they believe they had been very happy children (Williams, 2001). Moreover, children whose parents divorce have a higher risk of mental health problems in adulthood (Chase-Lansdale, Cherlin, & Kiernan, 1995; Cherlin, Chase-Lansdale, & McRae, 1998; Wallerstein & Lewis, 1998). Many young adults whose parents are divorced lack the financial resources and emotional support necessary to succeed in post-secondary education; a majority report that they struggle with fears of intimacy in relationships; and they are more likely to rely upon social assistance income (Ambert, 1998; Wallerstein & Lewis, 1998). Not surprisingly, adults whose parents divorced are themselves more likely to divorce (Ambert, 1998).

As a general rule, these negative effects are more pronounced for boys than for girls. However, some researchers have found that the effects are delayed in girls, making it more difficult to associate the effects with the divorce. Consequently, longitudinal studies often find that girls show equal or even greater negative effects (Amato, 1993; Hetherington, 1991a, 1991b). Age differences in the severity of the reaction have been found in

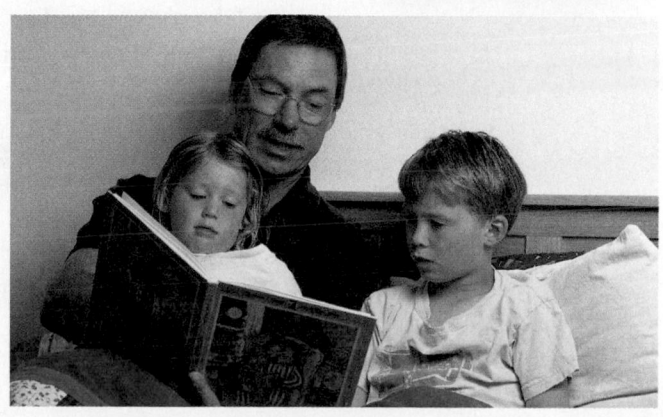

some studies but not others. For example, one longitudinal study found that the effects of divorce were most severe in a group of 12-year-olds who experienced parental divorce in early childhood rather than during their school years (Pagani et al., 1997).

UNDERSTANDING THE EFFECTS OF FAMILY STRUCTURE AND DIVORCE

How are we to understand these various findings? First, lone parenthood or divorce reduces the financial and emotional resources available to support the child. With only one parent, the household typically has only one income and only one adult to respond to the child's emotional needs. Data from Canada indicate that a woman's income drops an average of 50% in the first year after a divorce while a man's drops by 25% (Finnie, 2000). Remarriage does indeed add a second adult to the family system, which alleviates these problems to some degree, but it adds others (Hetherington et al., 1999).

Second, any family transition involves upheaval. Both adults and children adapt slowly and with difficulty to the subtraction or addition of new adults to the family system (Hetherington & Stanley-Hagan, 1995). The period of maximum disruption appears to last several years, during which the parents often find it difficult to monitor their children and maintain control over them.

Perhaps most importantly, lone parenthood, divorce, and step-parenthood all increase the likelihood that the family climate or style will shift away from authoritative parenting. This shift is not uncommon in the first few years after a divorce, when the custodial parent (usually the mother) is distracted or depressed and less able to manage warm control; it occurs in stepfamilies as well, where rates of authoritative parenting are lower than in intact families.

Remember, authoritarian or neglectful parenting is linked to poor outcomes whether it is triggered by a divorce, a stressful remarriage, the father's loss of a job, or any other stress (Goldberg, 1990). Ultimately, it is the parenting style, rather than any particular type of disruption, that is significant for the child (see **No Easy Answers**). After all, three-quarters of children reared in lone-parent or step-parent families finish high school, and roughly half of those high school graduates go on to attend college (McLanahan & Sandefur, 1994).

Many families construct a social network called an **extended family**, a family structure that includes parents, grandparents, aunts, uncles, cousins, and so on. Extended families seem to serve a protective function for children who are growing up in lone-parent homes (Wilson, 1995). Grandmothers, for example, appear to be important sources of emotional warmth for the children of teenaged mothers (Coley & Chase-Lansdale, 1998). Further, extended family members often help single and divorced mothers with financial and emotional support as well as with child care.

Critical Thinking

How important was your own extended family to you and your parent(s) during your early childhood years?

extended family
a social network of grandparents, aunts, uncles, cousins, and so on

Before Going On

- How is family structure related to children's development?

- How does divorce affect children's behaviour in early childhood and in later years?

- What are some possible reasons for the relationship between family structure and development?

No Easy Answers

When Divorce Is

Unavoidable

Most parents know that divorce is traumatic for children and do their best to avoid it. However, as we all know, there are situations in which there is no alternative. In such cases, parents often turn to counsellors and psychologists for advice on how to prevent the negative effects of divorce. Like so many other important challenges, helping a child overcome the trauma of divorce is not one for which there is a simple, or even a complex, formula parents can follow.

It's important for divorcing parents to realize that they cannot eliminate all the short-term disruptive effects of this event on children. However, there are some specific things they can do that are likely to soften or lessen the effects:

- Try to keep the number of separate changes the child has to cope with to a minimum. If at all possible, keep the children in the same school or day-care setting and in the same house or apartment.

- If the children are teenagers, consider having each child live with the parent of the same gender. The data are not totally consistent, but it looks as if this may be a less stressful arrangement (Lee et al., 1994).

- The custodial parent should help children stay in touch with the noncustodial parent. Likewise, the noncustodial parent should maintain as much contact as possible with the children, calling and seeing them regularly, attending school functions, and so on.

- Keep the open conflict to a minimum. Most of all, try not to fight in front of the children. Open conflict has negative effects on children whether the parents are divorced or not (Amato, 1993; Coiro, 1995; Insabella, 1995). Thus, divorce is not the only culprit; divorce combined with open conflict between the adults has worse effects.

- Parents should not use the children as go-betweens or talk disparagingly about their ex-spouses to them. Children who feel caught in the middle between the two parents are more likely to show various kinds of negative symptoms, such as depression or behaviour problems (Buchanan, Maccoby, & Dornbusch, 1991).

- Divorced parents should not expect their children to provide them with emotional support. Parents should maintain their own network of support, and use that network liberally. They should stay in touch with friends, seek out others in the same situation, join a support group.

In the midst of the emotional upheaval that accompanies divorce, these are not easy prescriptions to follow. However, if divorcing parents are able to do so, their children will probably suffer less.

PEER RELATIONSHIPS

The child's family experience is undeniably a central influence on emerging personality and social relationships, particularly in early childhood when a good portion of the time is still spent with parents and siblings. But over the years from 2 to 6, relationships with non-sibling peers become increasingly important—this is the critical period when brain development and function is most sensitive to social skills development (McCain & Mustard, 1999).

RELATING TO PEERS THROUGH PLAY

At every age, children are likely to spend at least some of their time playing alone—a pattern known as *solitary play*. However, children first begin to show some positive interest in playing with others as early as 6 months of age. If you place two babies that age on the floor facing each other, they will look at each other, touch, pull each other's hair, imitate each other's actions, and smile at each other.

By 14 to 18 months, two or more children play together with toys—sometimes cooperating, but more often simply playing side by side with different toys. Developmentalists refer to this as *parallel play*. Toddlers this age express interest in one another and gaze at or make noises at one another. However, it isn't until around 18 months that children engage in *associative play*. In associative play, toddlers pursue their own activities but also engage in spontaneous, though short-lived, social interactions. For example, one toddler may put down a toy to spend a few minutes chasing another toddler, or one may imitate another's action with a toy.

By 3 or 4, children begin to engage in *cooperative play*, a pattern in which several children work together to accomplish a goal. Cooperative play can be either constructive or symbolic. A group of children may cooperate to build a city out of blocks, or they may assign roles such as "mommy," "daddy," and "baby" to one another to play house.

As you learned in **Chapter 6**, play is related to cognitive development. Play is also related to the development of **social skills**, a set of behaviours that usually leads to being accepted as a play partner or friend by others. For example, many researchers have focused on the social skill of *group entry*. Children who are skilled in group entry spend time observing others to find out what they're doing and then try to become a part of it. Children who have poor group-entry skills try to gain acceptance through aggressive behaviour or by interrupting the group. Developmentalists have found that children with poor group-entry skills are often rejected by peers (Fantuzzo, Coolahan, & Mendez, 1998). Peer rejection, in turn, is an important factor in future social development.

According to recent studies, there appear to be sex differences in the reasons for and consequences of poor group-entry skills. For example, one study found that 3-year-old girls with poorly developed group-entry skills spent more time in parallel play than in cooperative play (Sims, Hutchins, & Taylor, 1997). In contrast, girls with better group-entry skills engaged in more cooperative than parallel play. Thus, the unskilled 3-year-old girls' patterns of play placed them at risk for future developmental problems, because age-appropriate play experience in the preschool years is related to social development later in childhood (Howes & Matheson, 1992; Maguire & Dunn, 1997).

The same study found that 3-year-old boys with poor group-entry skills tended to be aggressive and were often actively rejected by peers. They typically responded to rejection by becoming even more aggressive and disruptive (Sims, Hutchins, & Taylor, 1997). Thus, the boys in this study seemed to be caught in a cycle: Aggressive behaviour led to peer rejection, which, in turn, led to more aggression. This pattern may place boys at risk for developing an internal working model of relationships that includes aggressive behaviour and, as a result, lead them to routinely respond aggressively to others in social situations.

Because of the risks associated with poor social skills, developmentalists have turned their attention to social-skills training as a preventive measure. For example, in one study, socially withdrawn 4- and 5-year-olds were taught specific verbal phrases to use when trying to gain acceptance by a group of peers (Doctoroff, 1997). In addition, their socially accepted peers were taught to remind the trained children to use their new skills. For the most part, social-skills interventions like this one lead to immediate gains in social acceptance. However, the degree to which early childhood social-skills training can prevent later social difficulties is unknown at present.

social skills
a set of behaviours that usually lead to being accepted as a play partner or friend by peers

AGGRESSION

Aggressive interactions are common during the early childhood period. Researchers at Queen's University have reported that a large number of young children between the ages of 4 and 6 bully other children. Parents reported that 14.9% of boys and 9.4% of girls bullied others. Moreover, bullying was frequently found to be associated with a variety of other antisocial activities (Craig, Peters, & Konarski, 1998). The most common definition of **aggression** is behaviour apparently intended to injure another person or damage an object. The emphasis on intentionality helps separate true aggression from rough-and-tumble play in which children sometimes accidentally hurt one another. Every young child shows at least some aggressive behaviour, but the form and frequency of aggression changes over the preschool years and beyond, as you can see in **Figure 7.7**. Hildy Ross of the University of Waterloo and her colleagues have found that overt aggression is fairly common in preschoolers, with an average of 6.4 conflicts per hour between siblings (Perlman & Ross, 1997; Martin & Ross, 1995). Taking a closer look, Richard Tremblay (2000) of the University of Montreal found that overt aggression, e.g., direct confrontation such as hitting or name calling, peaks with toddlers and declines during the preschool years. However, relational aggression, e.g., indirect harm such as gossiping or telling others to exclude someone, begins to increase throughout the preschool years to the age of 11. Tremblay also reported a familial effect, whereby siblings living within the same household exhibit relatively equivalent levels of aggression toward each other (Tremblay et al., 1996).

aggression
behaviour intended to harm another person or an object

Critical Thinking

Think about the groups you belong to. Do they have clear dominance hierarchies? Now imagine a group of adults coming together for the first time. Within a few weeks, a pecking order will emerge. What might determine that order? How might a dominant person establish dominance?

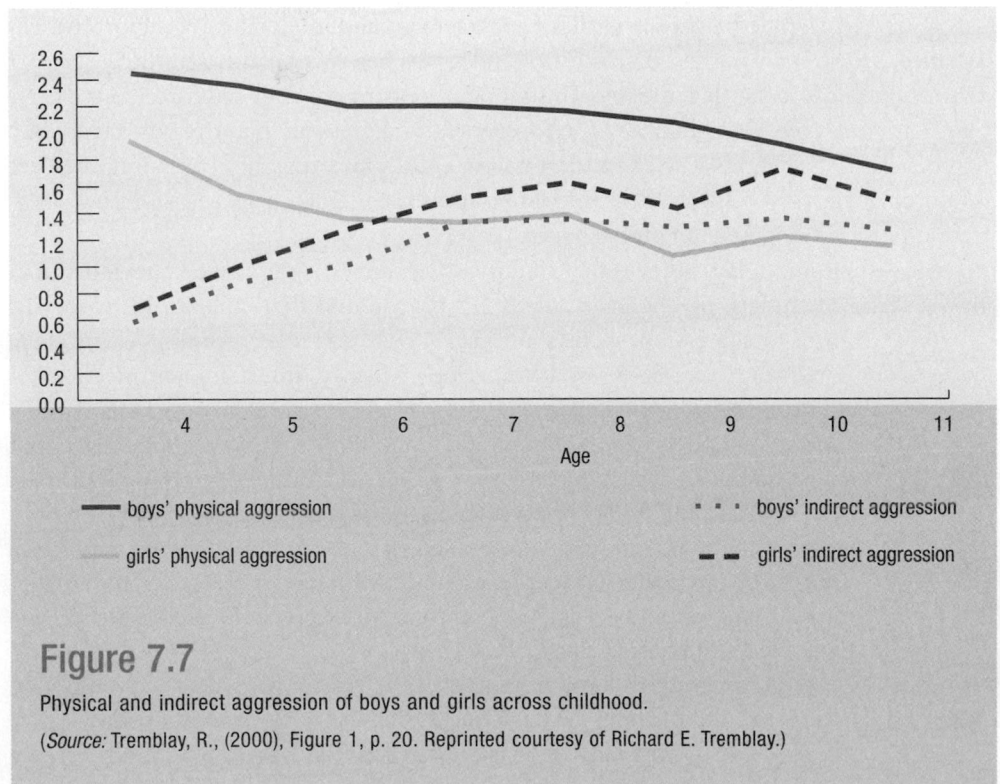

Figure 7.7

Physical and indirect aggression of boys and girls across childhood.

(*Source:* Tremblay, R., (2000), Figure 1, p. 20. Reprinted courtesy of Richard E. Tremblay.)

When 2- or 3-year-old children are upset or frustrated, they are most likely to throw things or hit each other. As their verbal skills improve, however, they shift away from such overt physical aggression toward greater use of verbal aggression, such as taunting or name calling, just as their defiance of their parents shifts from physical to verbal strategies.

The decline in physical aggression over these years also undoubtedly reflects the preschooler's declining egocentrism and increasing understanding of other children's thoughts and feelings. Yet another factor in the decline of physical aggression is the emergence of *dominance hierarchies*. Janet Strayer of Simon Fraser University found that, as early as age 3 or 4, groups of children arrange themselves in well-understood *pecking orders* of leaders and followers (Strayer, 1980). They know who will win a fight and who will lose one, which children they dare attack and which ones they must submit to—knowledge that serves to reduce the actual amount of physical aggression.

A second change in the quality of aggression during the preschool years is a shift from *instrumental aggression* to *hostile aggression*. **Instrumental aggression** is aimed at gaining or damaging some object; the purpose of **hostile aggression** is to hurt another person or gain an advantage. Thus, when 3-year-old Leah pushes aside her playmate Shania in the sandbox and grabs Shania's bucket, she is showing instrumental aggression. When Shania responds by getting angry at Leah and calling her a dummy, she is displaying hostile aggression.

Psychologists have suggested several key factors in aggressive behaviour. For example, one early group of American psychologists argued that aggression is always preceded by frustration, and that frustration is always followed by aggression (Dollard, Doob, Miller, Mowrer, & Sears, 1939). The frustration-aggression hypothesis turned out to be too broadly stated; not all frustration leads to aggression, but frustration does make aggression more likely. Toddlers and preschoolers are often frustrated—because they cannot always do what they want, and because they cannot express their needs clearly—and they often express that frustration through aggression. As the child acquires greater ability to communicate, plan, and organize her activities, her frustration level declines, and overt aggression drops.

Other developmentalists argue that reinforcement and modelling are important. For instance, when Leah pushes Shania away and grabs her toy, Leah is reinforced for her aggression because she gets the toy. This straightforward effect of reinforcement clearly plays a vital role in children's development of aggressive patterns of behaviour. Moreover, when parents give in to their young child's tantrums or aggression, they are reinforcing the very behaviour they deplore, and they thereby help to establish a long-lasting pattern of aggression and defiance.

Modelling, too, plays a key role in children's learning of aggressive behaviours. In a classic series of studies, psychologist Albert Bandura found that children learn specific forms of aggression, such as hitting, by watching other people perform them (Bandura, Ross, & Ross, 1961, 1963). Clearly, entertainment media offer children many opportunities to observe aggressive behaviour, but real-life aggressive models may be more influential. For example, children learn that aggression is an acceptable way of solving problems by watching their parents, siblings, and others behave aggressively. Recent analysis of the NLSCY revealed that children who are exposed to violence in the home are twice as likely to be physically aggressive, commit delinquent acts, and exhibit higher rates of emotional disorders as children not exposed to such violence (see **Figure 7.8**) (Statistics Canada, 2001b).

Other researchers are interested in the relationship between childhood aggression and the family environment. For example, in another study of the NLSCY data, a strong link was found between harsh, punitive parenting practices and aggressive behaviour in children. Children living in punitive

instrumental aggression

aggression used to gain an advantage or control of objects, territory, or rights

hostile aggression

aggression used to hurt another person physically or emotionally

Developmentalists distinguish between true aggression (intentional harm) and the accidental injuries that often occur during normal rough-and-tumble play.

(*Photo:* Steve/Mary Skjold/MaXx Images Inc.)

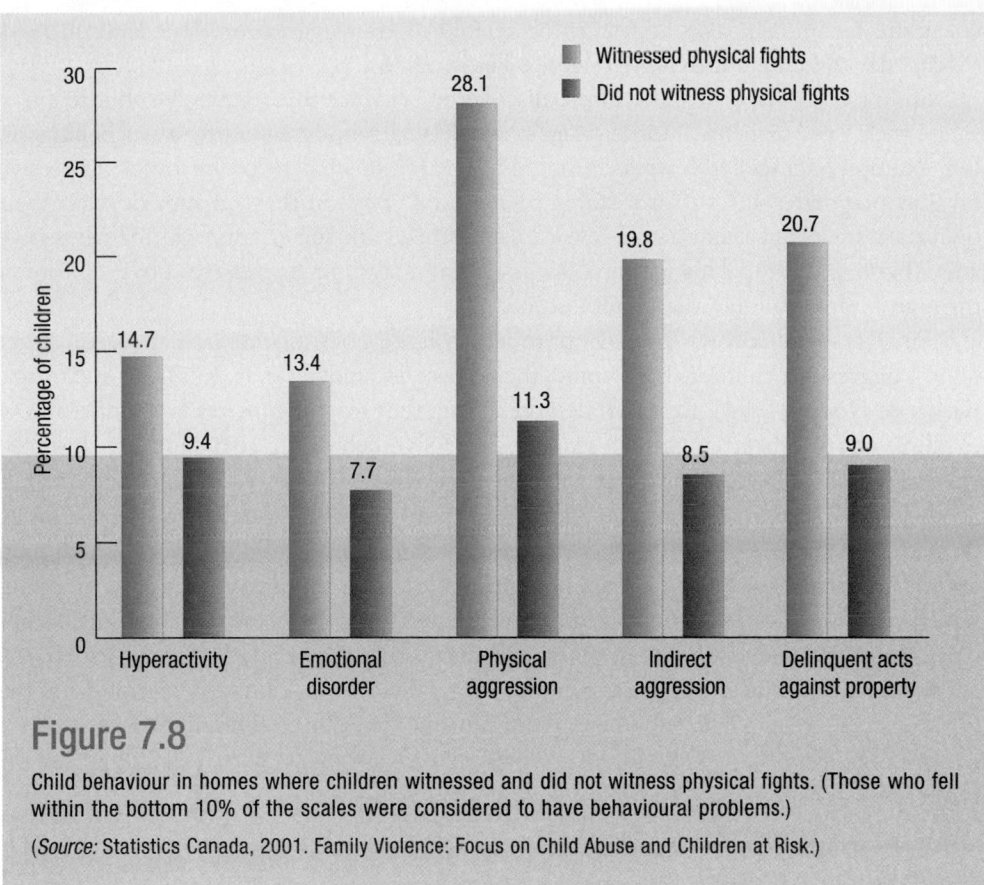

Figure 7.8

Child behaviour in homes where children witnessed and did not witness physical fights. (Those who fell within the bottom 10% of the scales were considered to have behavioural problems.)

(*Source:* Statistics Canada, 2001. Family Violence: Focus on Child Abuse and Children at Risk.)

environments at age 2 to 3 years were rated as significantly more aggressive then children living in nonpunitive families. These cohorts were reassessed at age 8 to 9 years and, as was true at the earlier age, a punitive parental environment predicted levels of aggression in children (Thomas, 2004). This finding held true for both genders, for all family income levels, and in all regions of Canada. Moreover, in cases where the punitive parenting behaviour increased or decreased over time, so did the levels of child aggression. It's important to note, however, that the underlying causal relationship between punitive parenting and child aggression in this study is not known.

Whatever the cause, Canadian researchers using data from the NLSCY found that aggressive behaviour tends to run in families (Baillargeon, Tremblay, & Willms, 2002). For example, a second-born child is three to four times more likely to be aggressive if the first-born child is aggressive. The odds are even greater for a third-born child—they are more than 10 times as likely to be aggressive if one or both elder siblings are aggressive.

Fortunately for these and other families, most children become less aggressive during the preschool years. There are a few children, however, whose aggressive behaviour pattern in early childhood becomes quite literally a way of life, a finding that has been supported by cross-cultural research (Hart, Olsen, Robinson, & Mandleco, 1997; Henry, Caspi, Moffitt, & Silva, 1996; Newman, Caspi, Moffitt, & Silva, 1997). Researchers have searched for causes of this kind of aggression, which some psychologists refer to as *trait aggression,* to distinguish it from developmentally normal forms of aggression.

Some psychologists looking for a genetic basis for trait aggression have produced some supportive data (Plomin, 1990). Others suggest that trait aggression is associated with being raised in an aggressive environment, such as an abusive family (Dodge, 1993). Family factors other than abuse, such as lack of affection and the use of coercive discipline techniques, also appear to be related to trait aggression, especially in boys (McFayden-Ketchumm, Bates, Dodge, & Pettit, 1996).

Still other developmentalists have discovered evidence that aggressive children may shape their environments in order to gain continuing reinforcement for their behaviour. For example, aggressive boys as young as 4 years old tend to prefer other aggressive boys as playmates and to form stable peer groups. Boys in these groups develop their own patterns of interaction and reward each other with social approval for aggressive acts (Farver, 1996). This pattern of association among aggressive boys continues through middle childhood and adolescence.

Finally, social-cognitivists have produced a large body of research suggesting that highly aggressive children lag behind their peers in understanding others' intentions (Crick & Dodge, 1994). Research demonstrating that teaching aggressive children how to think about others' intentions reduces aggressive behaviour also supports this conclusion (Crick & Dodge, 1996). Specifically, these studies suggest that aggressive school-aged children seem to reason more like 2- to 3-year-olds about intentions. For example, they are likely to perceive a playground incident (say, one child accidentally tripping another during a soccer game) as an intentional act that requires retaliation. Training, which also includes anger management techniques, helps aggressive school-aged children acquire an understanding of others' intentions that most children learn between the ages of 3 and 5. Thus, trait aggression may originate in some kind of deviation from the typical social-cognitive developmental path during the early childhood period.

PROSOCIAL BEHAVIOUR AND FRIENDSHIPS

prosocial behaviour
behaviour intended to help
another person

At the other end of the spectrum of peer relationships is a set of behaviours psychologists call **prosocial behaviour**. Like aggression, prosocial behaviour is intentional and voluntary, but its purpose is to help another person in some way (Eisenberg, 1992). In everyday language, such behaviour is called *altruism*, and it changes with age, just as other aspects of peer behaviour change.

DEVELOPMENT OF PROSOCIAL BEHAVIOUR
Altruistic behaviours first become evident in children of about 2 or 3 years of age—at about the same time as real interest in playing with other children arises. They will offer to help another child who is hurt, share a toy, or try to comfort another person (Marcus, 1986; Zahn-Waxler & Radke-Yarrow, 1982; Zahn-Waxler et al., 1992). As you read in **Chapter 6**, children this young are only beginning to understand that others feel differently than they do, but they obviously understand enough about the emotions of others to respond in supportive and sympathetic ways when they see other children or adults hurt or sad.

Some other kinds of prosocial behaviour, such as taking turns, also seem to increase with age. If you give children an opportunity to donate some treat to another child who is described as needy, older children donate more than younger children do. Helpfulness, too, seems to increase with age through adolescence. But not all prosocial behaviours show this pattern. Comforting another child, for example, seems to be more common among preschoolers and children in early elementary grades than among older children (Eisenberg, 1992).

Children vary a lot in the amount of altruistic behaviour they show, and young children who show relatively more empathy and altruism are also those who regulate their own emotions well. They show positive emotions readily and negative emotions less often (Eisenberg et al., 1996). These variations among children's level of empathy or altruism seem to be related to specific kinds of child rearing. In addition, longitudinal studies indicate that children who display higher levels of prosocial behaviour in the preschool years continue to demonstrate higher levels of such behaviour in adulthood (Eisenberg et al., 1999).

THE ROLE OF EMPATHY ON PROSOCIAL BEHAVIOUR William Roberts of the University College of the Cariboo in Kamloops, British Columbia, and Janet Strayer of Simon Fraser University have been studying prosocial behaviour in children. In one study they found that, in general, girls were more prosocial than boys. In boys, level of empathy predicted cooperative, helpful, and responsible behaviours (Roberts & Strayer, 1996). In a later study they reported that empathy in specific situations was also an important predictor of interpersonal closeness for both genders. For instance, when a child expressed a high level of empathy with a person portrayed in an emotion-laden video vignette he or she tended to decrease the personal distance with that character. This relationship between personal distance and empathy was generally stronger in girls but increased with age in both genders (Strayer & Roberts, 1997).

Following-up on their earlier research, Strayer and Roberts (2004) conducted a comprehensive analysis of the interactive pathways associated with a child's level of empathy. They looked at how child factors, such as age and several emotional qualities (i.e., ability to take the perspective or role of others, emotional insight, and emotional expressiveness), interact with emotional characteristics and practices of parents (i.e., level of empathy and emotional expressiveness, encouragement of their child's emotional expressiveness, warmth, and control). Taken together, the links between child and parent characteristics predicted two-thirds of children's empathy. The researchers also found that children's anger plays an important role in the development of empathy, a finding that requires further investigation.

PARENTAL INFLUENCES ON PROSOCIAL BEHAVIOUR Research suggests that parental behaviour contributes to the development of prosocial behaviour (Eisenberg, 1992). Specifically, parents of altruistic children create a loving and warm family climate. If such warmth is combined with clear explanations and rules about what to do as well as what not to do, the children are even more likely to behave altruistically. Such parents also often explain the consequences of the child's action in terms of its effects on others— for example, "If you hit Susan, it will hurt her." Stating rules or guidelines positively rather than negatively also appears to be important; for example, "It's always good to be helpful to other people" is more effective guidance than "Don't be so selfish!"

Providing prosocial *attributions*—positive statements about the underlying cause for helpful behaviour—is also useful. For example, a parent might praise a child by saying "You're such a helpful child!" or "You certainly do a lot of nice things for other people." Having heard such statements often during early childhood helps children incorporate them into their self-concepts later in childhood. In this way, parents may help create a generalized, internalized pattern of altruistic behaviour in the child.

Parents of altruistic children also look for opportunities for them to do helpful things. For example, they allow children to help cook, take care of pets, make toys to give away, teach younger siblings, and so forth. Finally, parental modelling of thoughtful and generous behaviour—that is, parents demonstrating consistency between what they say and what they do—is another contributing factor.

FRIENDSHIPS Beginning at about 18 months, a few toddlers show early hints of playmate preferences or individual friendships (Howes, 1983, 1987). However, by age 3, about 20% of children have a stable playmate. By 4, more than half spend 30% or more of their time with one other child (Hinde, Titmus, Easton, & Tamplin, 1985). Thus, one important change in social behaviour during early childhood is the formation of stable friendships.

To be sure, these early peer interactions are still quite primitive. However, it is noteworthy that preschool friend pairs nonetheless show more mutual liking, more reciprocity, more extended interactions, more positive and less negative behaviour, and more supportiveness in a novel situation than do nonfriend pairs at this same age—all signs that these relationships are more than merely passing fancies. Moreover, having had a friend in early childhood is related to social competence during the elementary school years (Maguire & Dunn, 1997).

Before Going On

- What are the various kinds of play observed among preschoolers?
- What is the difference between instrumental aggression and hostile aggression, and which is more prevalent in early childhood?
- How does empathy contribute to prosocial behaviour?
- How does prosocial behaviour change during early childhood, and how can parents and teachers encourage its development?
- What are the characteristic patterns of friendship found in younger and older preschoolers?

PERSONALITY AND SELF-CONCEPT

As young children gain more understanding of the social environment, their temperaments ripen into true personalities. At the same time, their self-concepts become more complex, allowing them to exercise greater control over their own behaviour.

FROM TEMPERAMENT TO PERSONALITY

As you learned in **Chapter 5**, a child's temperament—whether he is "easy," "difficult," or "inhibited"—is reasonably stable over infancy, toddlerhood, and later ages (Novosad & Thoman, 1999; Ruben, Nelson, Hastings, & Asendorpt, 1999). By preschool, a link between difficultness of temperament and both concurrent and future behaviour problems becomes evident: 3- or 4-year-olds with difficult temperaments are more likely to show heightened aggressiveness, delinquency, or other forms of behaviour problems in school, as teenagers, and as adults (Bates, 1989; Caspi, Henry, McGee, Moffitt, & Silva, 1995; Chess & Thomas, 1984). Likewise, shy preschoolers are at risk of developing emotional difficulties later in childhood (Sanson et al., 1996; Schwartz, Snidman, & Kagan, 1996).

You should also remember from **Chapter 5** that psychologists distinguish between temperament and personality, and most believe that inborn infant temperament constitutes the foundation of personality in later childhood and adulthood. It seems likely that the processes through which temperament becomes modified into personality begin during the early childhood years. For example, preschoolers with difficult temperaments learn that the behaviours

Children with difficult temperaments may show heightened aggressiveness or other behavioural problems in school—but when such behaviour results in peer rejection, they may be motivated to change their behaviour in order to gain social acceptance.
(*Photo:* Chris Cole/Getty Images)

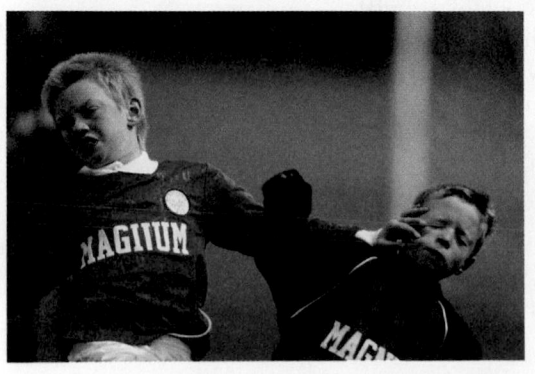

associated with difficultness, such as complaining, often result in peer rejection. As a result, many of them change their behaviour to gain social acceptance. Thus, personality represents the combination of the temperament with which children are probably born and the knowledge they gain about temperament-related behaviour during childhood (McCrae, Costa, Ostendord, & Angleitner, 2000; Svrakic, Svrakic, & Cloninger, 1996). As a result, correlations between infant temperament and later measures of personality, though still strong, tend to decline over childhood and adolescence (Shaw, Ryst, & Steiner, 1996).

The transition from temperament to personality is also influenced by parental responses to the young child's temperament. If the parents reject the difficult or shy child, the child is likely to emerge from the preschool years with a personality that puts him at risk for developing serious problems in social relationships, and he may suffer from cognitive deficits as well (Bates, 1989; Fish, Stifter, & Belsky, 1991).

> ## Critical Thinking
>
> If parents received a description of their child's temperament at birth (sort of like the owner's manual you get with new appliances), do you think it would help them be better parents? Conversely, do you think it would cause them to be overly tolerant of temperamental characteristics that might need to be modified for the child's own benefit, such as irritability?

SELF-CONCEPT

The 18- to 24-month-old is beginning to develop categorical and emotional selves. Between 2 and 6, the child continues to develop these two aspects of the self and adds to them a *social self*. Gender differences also begin to appear in self-concept during the preschool years. For instance, Brock University researcher Sandra Bosacki (2001b) conducted a longitudinal study of the self-concept-related dimensions of self-knowledge, emotional understanding, and gender typed play in children aged 3 to 4. She found that girls scored higher than boys in their cognitive ability to solve false-belief tasks (as described in **Chapter 6**), their ability to understand emotions within themselves and in others, and their perceived level of self-control in social situations. Familiarity with the dimensions of preschoolers' self-concepts helps parents, teachers, and others better understand many aspects of their social behaviour.

THE CATEGORICAL SELF   By the end of the preschool period, a child can give you quite a full description of herself on a whole range of dimensions. Still, these early self-concepts remain highly concrete. The self-concept of a preschool child tends to focus on her own visible characteristics—whether she's a boy or girl, what she looks like, what or whom she plays with, where she lives, what she is good at—rather than on more enduring inner qualities.

As you learned earlier in this chapter, categories are also important in young children's perceptions of others—big kids, little kids, boys, girls, and so on. Preschoolers prefer playmates of their own age and gender. Consequently, the categorical self seems to be as much an internal working model for social relationships as for the self.

THE EMOTIONAL SELF   In a Canadian study of children's emotional knowledge, Bosacki and Moore (in press) found that preschool girls scored higher than boys in the ability to correctly label emotions and understand complex emotions. Both girls and boys were found to be better at understanding their own emotions as opposed to the emotions of others. Preschool children also demonstrated the ability to conceptualize complex emotions, such as pride, before they could understand them, e.g., knowing why a specific situation would lead to a sense of pride. In general, preschool children with better vocabularies were better able to label and explain emotions.

Development of the emotional self during the early childhood years also centres on the acquisition of emotional control. Recent research has shown that the degree to which young children can control emotion-related behaviour, such as finding a way to cheer themselves up when they are sad, is linked to important variables later in life. For instance, self-control in early childhood is related to children's ability to obey moral rules and to think about right and wrong during the school years (Kochanska, Murray, & Coy, 1997).

The process of acquiring emotional control is one in which control shifts slowly from the parents to the child. Here again, the child's temperament is a factor. For example, preschoolers who have consistently exhibited difficult behaviour since infancy are more likely to have self-control problems in early childhood (Schmitz et al., 1999). Similarly, preschoolers who were born prematurely or who were delayed in language development in the second year of life experience more difficulties with self-control during early childhood (Carson, Klee, & Perry, 1998; Schothorst & van Engeland, 1996).

However, parents' age-based expectations and parenting behaviours are also important. For instance, most parents know it is unreasonable to expect toddlers to wait for long periods of time, so they provide external control by, for example, reminding toddlers of prohibitions and repeating requests. Over the years from 3 to 6, children gradually internalize parental standards and expectations and take on more of the control task for themselves. For example, if you were to observe parents and children in a doctor's waiting room, you would see that parents of bored toddlers often physically direct and redirect their behaviour. A parent of a 2-year-old might be seen taking the child onto his lap and reading to her. In contrast, you would notice that older preschoolers look for things to do on their own. They are more likely to find a book or magazine that looks interesting and ask a parent to read it to them or look at it by themselves. In response to such evidences of emotional maturity, parents expect more control from older preschoolers and use verbal instructions, rather than physical control, to help them manage their behaviour.

THE SOCIAL SELF Another facet of the child's emerging sense of self is an increasing awareness of herself as a player in the social game. By age 2, the toddler has already learned a variety of social "scripts"—routines of play or interaction with others. The toddler now begins to develop some implicit understanding of her own roles in these scripts (Case, 1991). So she may begin to think of herself as a "helper" in some situations, or as "the boss" when she is telling some other child what to do.

You can see this clearly in children's sociodramatic play, as they begin to take explicit roles: "I'll be the daddy and you be the mommy," or "I'm the boss." As part of the same process, the young child also gradually understands her place in the network of family roles. She has sisters, brothers, father, mother, and so forth.

The development of social role scripts helps young children become more independent. For example, assuming the "student" role provides a preschooler with a prescription for appropriate behaviour in the school situation. Students listen when the teacher speaks to the class, get out materials and put them away at certain times, help their classmates in various ways, and so on. Once a preschooler is familiar with and adopts the student role, he can follow the role script and is no longer dependent on the teacher to tell him what to do every minute of the day.

However, not all children make a social adjustment to school in the same way. Carlton University psychologists Robert Coplan and Kavita Prakash (2003) looked at three patterns of child-teacher interactions and found that children rated as more aggressive initiated more interactions with teachers; shy and anxious children received, but didn't initiate interactions with teachers; and a third group of children who were

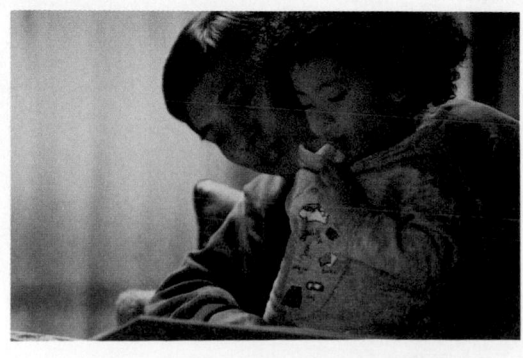

While bored toddlers often need to have their attention physically redirected to keep them occupied, by preschool age, most children are able to look for things to do on their own, like looking at a magazine or asking a parent to read to them. (*Photo:* Andy Sacks/Getty Images)

rated as more sociable, and less solitary, spent the least amount of time interacting with teachers as they spent more time interacting with other students and exploring learning opportunities in the classroom. A closer look at shy students found that their quietness may be due to either social disinterest (a nonfearful preference for solitude) or to conflicted shyness (an approach-avoidance conflict—their desire to interact with others is accompanied by fear or anxiety) (Coplan, Prakash, O'Neil, & Armer, 2004). Moreover, it seems that children's shyness is related to social anxiety rather than a lack of ability to verbally express themselves (Coplan & Armer, in press).

Before Going On

- Is temperament stable in early childhood? If not, how does it change?
- What changes take place in the young child's categorical, emotional, and social selves during the preschool years?

THE GENDER CONCEPT AND SEX ROLES

One of the most fascinating aspects of the preschool child's emerging sense of self is the development of a sense of gender. The child has several related tasks. On the cognitive side, she must learn the nature of the gender category itself—that boyness or girlness is permanent and unchanged by such things as modifications in clothing or hair length. This understanding is usually called the **gender concept**. On the social side, she has to learn what behaviours go with being a boy or a girl; that is, she must learn the **sex role** appropriate for her gender.

gender concept
understanding of gender, gender-related behaviour, and sex roles

sex roles
behaviour expected for males and females in a given culture

EXPLAINING GENDER CONCEPT AND SEX-ROLE DEVELOPMENT

Social learning theorists have emphasized the role of parents in shaping children's sex-role behaviour and attitudes (Bandura, 1977a; Mischel, 1966, 1970). Parents do seem to reinforce sex-typed activities in children as young as 18 months, not only by buying different kinds of toys for boys and girls, but by responding more positively when their sons play with blocks or trucks or when their daughters play with dolls (Fagot & Hagan, 1991; Lytton & Romney, 1991). Such differential reinforcement is particularly clear with boys, especially from fathers (Siegal, 1987). Some evidence also suggests that toddlers whose parents are more consistent in rewarding sex-typed toy choice or play behaviour and whose mothers favour traditional family sex roles learn accurate gender labels earlier than do toddlers whose parents are less focused on the gender-appropriateness of the child's play (Fagot & Leinbach, 1989; Fagot, Leinbach, & O'Boyle, 1992).

Still, helpful as it is, a social-learning explanation is probably not sufficient. In particular, parents differentially reinforce boys' and girls' behaviour less than you'd expect, and probably not enough to account for the very early and robust discrimination children seem to make on the basis of gender. Even young children whose parents seem to treat their sons and daughters in highly similar ways nonetheless learn gender labels and prefer same-sex playmates.

gender constancy theory
Kohlberg's assertion that children must understand that gender is a permanent characteristic before they can adopt appropriate sex roles

gender constancy
the understanding that gender is a component of the self that is not altered by external appearance

gender schema theory
an information-processing approach to gender concept development that asserts that people use a schema for each gender to process information about themselves and others

A second alternative, social-cognitive theory, suggests that children's understanding of gender is linked to gender-related behaviour. For example, one such view, based strongly on Piagetian theory, is Lawrence Kohlberg's suggestion that the crucial aspect of the process is the child's understanding of the gender concept (Kohlberg, 1966; Kohlberg & Ullian, 1974). Once the child realizes that he is a boy or she is a girl forever, he or she becomes highly motivated to learn how to behave in the way that is expected or appropriate for that gender. Specifically, Kohlberg's **gender constancy theory** predicts that systematic same-sex imitation will become evident only after the child has shown full gender constancy. **Gender constancy** is the understanding that gender is an innate characteristic that can't be changed. Most studies designed to test this hypothesis have supported Kohlberg. Children do seem to become much more sensitive to same-sex models after they understand gender constancy (Frey & Ruble, 1992). Kohlberg's theory allows developmentalists to make highly reliable predictions about the development of children's knowledge about gender and sex roles.

However, gender constancy theory is less accurate in predicting behaviour. Specifically, it can't explain the obvious fact that children show clearly different sex-role behaviour, such as toy preferences, long before they have achieved full understanding of the gender concept. A newer social-cognitive theory derived from the information-processing approach is usually called *gender schema theory* (Martin, 1991; Martin & Halverson, 1981). This approach includes many of Kohlberg's ideas about how gender constancy develops, but it does a better job of predicting behaviour.

You'll remember from **Chapter 6** that a great deal of *schematic* learning happens in early childhood. A schema is a mental pattern or model that is used to process information. Just as the self-concept can be thought of as a schema, so the child's understanding of gender can be seen in the same way. According to **gender schema theory**, the gender schema begins to develop as soon as the child notices the differences between male and female, knows his own gender, and can label the two groups with some consistency—all of which happens by age 2 or 3. Perhaps because gender is clearly an either/or category, children seem to understand very early that this is a key distinction, so the category serves as a kind of magnet for new information. Once the child has established even a primitive gender schema, a great many experiences can be assimilated to it. Thus, as soon as this schema begins to be formed, children may begin to show preference for same-sex playmates or for gender-stereotyped activities (Martin & Little, 1990).

Preschoolers first learn some broad distinctions about what kinds of activities or behaviour "go with" each gender, both by observing other children and through the reinforcements they receive from parents. They also learn a few gender *scripts*—whole sequences of events that are normally associated with a given gender, such as "fixing dinner" or "building with tools"—just as they learn other social scripts at about this age (Levy & Fivush, 1993). Then, between ages 4 and 6, the child learns a more subtle and complex set of associations for his own gender—what children of his own gender like and don't like, how they play, how they talk, what kinds of people they associate with. Only between the ages of 8 and 10 does the child develop an equivalently complex view of the opposite gender (Martin, Wood, & Little, 1990).

The key difference between this theory and Kohlberg's gender constancy theory is that gender schema theory asserts that the child need not understand that gender is permanent to form an initial gender schema. When they do begin to understand gender constancy, at about 5 or 6, children develop a more elaborate rule, or schema, of "what people who are like me do" and treat this rule the same way they treat other rules—as an absolute. Later, the child's application of the gender rule becomes more flexible. She knows, for example, that most boys don't play with dolls, but that they can do so if they like.

THE GENDER CONCEPT

Children seem to develop gender constancy in three steps. First comes **gender identity**, which is simply a child's ability to label his or her own sex correctly and to identify other people as men or women, boys or girls. By 9 to 12 months, babies already treat male and female faces as if they were different categories (Fagot & Leinbach, 1993). Within the next year, they begin to learn the verbal labels that go with these categories. By age 2, most children correctly label themselves as boys or girls and, within 6 to 12 months, most can correctly label others as well.

Accurate labelling, though, does not signify complete understanding. The second step is **gender stability**, which is the understanding that you stay the same gender throughout life. Researchers have measured this by asking children such questions as "When you were a little baby, were you a little girl or a little boy?" or "When you grow up, will you be a mommy or a daddy?" Most children understand the stability of gender by about age 4 (Slaby & Frey, 1975) (see **Figure 7.9**).

The final step is the development of true gender constancy, the recognition that someone stays the same gender even though he may appear to change by wearing different clothes or changing his hair length. For example, boys don't change into girls by wearing dresses. It may seem odd that a child who understands that he will stay the same gender throughout life (gender stability) can nonetheless be confused about the effect of changes in dress or appearance on gender. But numerous studies, including studies of children growing up in other cultures such as Kenya, Nepal, Belize, and Samoa, show that children go through this sequence (Munroe, Shimmin, & Munroe, 1984).

The underlying logic of this sequence may be a bit clearer if you think of a parallel between gender constancy and the concept of conservation. Conservation involves recognition that an object remains the same in some fundamental way even though it changes externally. Gender constancy is thus a kind of "conservation of gender," and is not typically understood until about 5 or 6, when children understand other conservations (Marcus & Overton, 1978).

SEX-ROLE KNOWLEDGE

Figuring out your gender and understanding that it stays constant are only part of the story. Learning what goes with being a boy or a girl in a given culture is also a vital part of the child's task. Researchers have studied this in two ways—by asking children what boys and girls (or men and women) like to do and what they are like (which is an inquiry about gender stereotypes), and by asking children if it is okay for boys to play with dolls or girls to climb trees or to do equivalent cross-sex things (an inquiry about roles).

In every culture, adults have clear sex-role stereotypes. Indeed, the content of those stereotypes is remarkably similar in cultures around the world. Psychologists who have studied gender stereotypes in many different countries, including non-Western countries such as Thailand, Pakistan, and Nigeria, find that the most clearly stereotyped traits are weakness, gentleness,

gender identity
the ability to correctly label oneself and others as male or female

gender stability
the understanding that gender is a stable, life-long characteristic

Figure 7.9

In describing this self-portrait, the 5-year-old artist said, "This is how I will look when I get married to a boy. I am under a rainbow, so beautiful with a bride hat, a belt, and a purse." The girl knows she will always be female and associates gender with externals such as clothing (gender stability). She is also already quite knowledgeable about gender-role expectations.

(Courtesy of Jerry and Denise Boyd. Used with permission.)

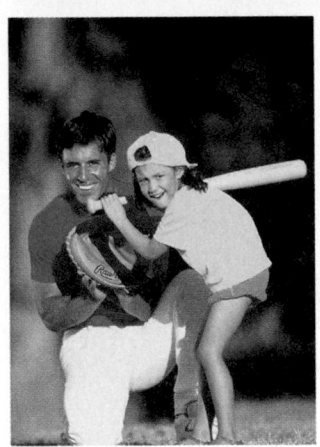

As their gender concept develops, children change their views about whether it is acceptable for boys to play with dolls or for girls to play sports such as baseball.
(*Photos: top,* Mary Kay Denny/ PhotoEdit; *bottom,* SUNSTAR/Photo Researchers, Inc.)

appreciativeness, and soft-heartedness for women, and aggression, strength, cruelty, and coarseness for men (Williams & Best, 1990). In most cultures, men are also seen as competent, skilful, assertive, and able to get things done, while women are seen as warm and expressive, tactful, quiet, gentle, aware of others' feelings, and lacking in competence, independence, and logic (Williams & Best, 1990).

A large study of Canadian children shows that these stereotyped ideas develop early (Serbin, Powlishta, & Gulko, 1993). It would not be uncommon to hear a 3-year-old say "Mommies use the stove, and daddies use the grill." A 4-year-old might define gender roles in terms of competencies: "Daddies are better at fixing things, but mommies are better at tying bows and decorating." Even 2-year-olds already associate certain activities and possessions with men and women depending on the adult activities they are most often and consistently exposed to in the home. For example, toddlers of both genders can associate feeding a baby, applying make-up, and dresses with women and, to a lesser extent, cars and hammering with men (Serbin, Poulin-Dubois, & Eichstedt, 2002). By age 3 or 4, children can assign stereotypic occupations, toys, and activities to each gender. By age 5, children begin to associate certain personality traits, such as assertiveness and nurturance, with males or females (Martin, 1993; Serbin, Powlishta, & Gulko, 1993).

Studies of children's ideas about how men and women (or boys and girls) ought to behave add an interesting further element. For example, in an early study, a psychologist told a story to children aged 4 to 9 about a little boy named George who liked to play with dolls (Damon, 1977). George's parents told him that only little girls play with dolls; little boys shouldn't. The children were then asked questions about the story, such as "Why do people tell George not to play with dolls?" or "Is there a rule that boys shouldn't play with dolls?"

Four-year-olds in this study thought it was okay for George to play with dolls. There was no rule against it and he should do it if he wanted to. Six-year-olds, in contrast, thought it was wrong for George to play with dolls. By about age 9, children had differentiated between what boys and girls usually do, and what is "wrong." One boy said, for example, that breaking windows was wrong and bad, but that playing with dolls was not bad in the same way: "Breaking windows you're not supposed to do. And if you play with dolls, well you can, but boys usually don't."

What this study appeared to reveal is that the 5- to 6-year-old, having figured out that gender is permanent, is searching for a rule about how boys and girls behave (Martin & Halverson, 1981). The child picks up information from watching adults, from television, from listening to the labels that are attached to different activities (e.g., "Boys don't cry"). Initially, children treat these as absolute, moral rules. Later, they understand that these are social conventions; at this point, sex-role concepts become more flexible and stereotyping declines somewhat (Katz & Ksansnak, 1994).

SEX-TYPED BEHAVIOUR

sex-typed behaviour
different patterns of behaviour exhibited by boys and girls

The final element in the development of sex roles is the actual behaviour children show with those of the same and the opposite sex. An unexpected finding is that **sex-typed behaviour**, or different patterns of behaviour among girls and boys, develops earlier than ideas about sex roles. By 18 to 24 months, children begin to show some preference for sex-stereotyped toys, such as dolls for girls or trucks or building blocks for boys, which is some months before they can consistently identify their own gender (O'Brien, 1992). By age 3, children begin to show a preference for same-sex friends and are much more sociable with playmates of the same sex—at a time when they do not yet have a concept of gender stability (Maccoby, 1988, 1990; Maccoby & Jacklin, 1987) (see **Figure 7.10**).

Not only are preschoolers' friendships and peer interactions increasingly sex-segregated, but it is also clear that boy–boy interactions and girl–girl interactions differ in quality, even in these early years. One important part of same-sex interactions seems to involve instruction and modelling of sex-appropriate behaviour. In other words, older boys teach younger boys how to be "masculine," and older girls teach younger girls how to be "feminine" (Danby & Baker, 1998).

However, these "lessons" in sex-typed behaviour are fairly subtle. Eleanor Maccoby, one of the leading theorists in this area, describes the girls' pattern as an *enabling style* (Maccoby, 1990). Enabling includes such behaviours as supporting the friend, expressing agreement, and making suggestions. All these behaviours tend to foster a greater equality and intimacy in the relationship and keep the interaction going. In contrast, boys are more likely to show what Maccoby calls a *constricting, or restrictive, style.* "A restrictive style is one that tends to derail the interaction—to inhibit the partner or cause the partner to withdraw, thus shortening the interaction or bringing it to an end" (1990, p. 517). Contradicting, interrupting, boasting, and other forms of self-display are all aspects of this style.

Critical Thinking

What do you think happens when opposite-sex adults interact in some nonromantic encounter? Is the interaction style some combination of enabling and constricting, or does one style dominate?

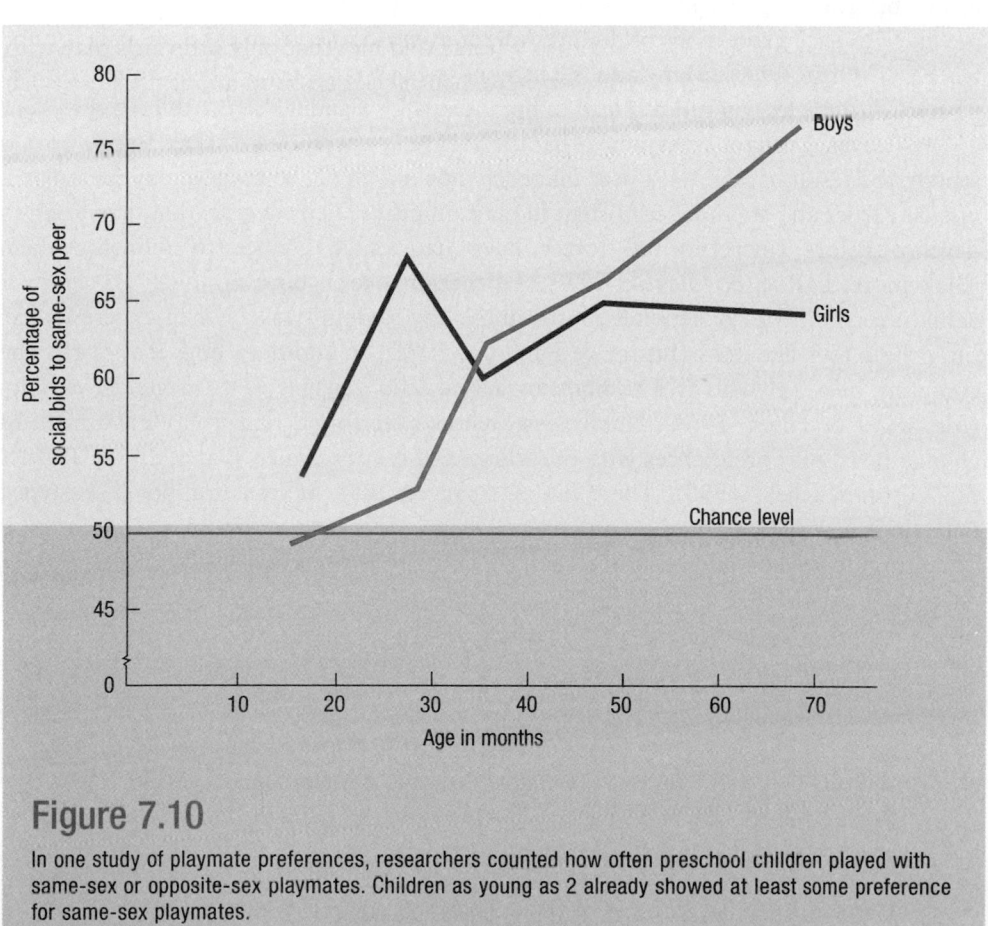

Figure 7.10

In one study of playmate preferences, researchers counted how often preschool children played with same-sex or opposite-sex playmates. Children as young as 2 already showed at least some preference for same-sex playmates.

(*Source:* La Freniere, Strayer, & Gautier, 1984, Figure 1, p. 1961. Copyright by the Society for Research in Child Development, Inc.)

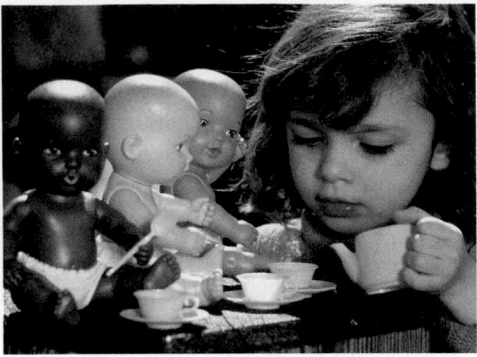

Play may provide children with opportunities to learn about gender-role expectations.
(*Photos: left,* Harry Wilks/Stock Boston; *right,* Sue Ann Miller/Getty Images)

cross-gender behaviour
behaviour that is atypical for one's own sex but typical for the opposite sex

These two patterns begin to be visible in the preschool years. For example, beginning as early as age 3, boys and girls use quite different strategies in their attempts to influence each other's behaviour (Maccoby, 1990). Girls generally ask questions or make requests; boys are much more likely to make demands or phrase things using imperatives ("Give me that!"). The really intriguing finding is that even at this early age, boys simply don't respond to the girls' enabling style. Thus, playing with boys yields little positive reinforcement for girls, and they begin to avoid such interactions and band together.

Another kind of learning opportunity happens when children exhibit **cross-gender behaviour**, behaviour that is atypical in their culture for their gender. For example, *tomboyishness,* girls' preference for activities that are more typical for boys, is a kind of cross-gender behaviour. Generally, tomboyishness is tolerated by adults and peers (Sandnabba & Ahlberg, 1999). Not surprisingly, then, cross-gender behaviour is far more common among girls than boys (Etaugh & Liss, 1992). Tomboyishness does not appear to interfere with the development of a "feminine" personality in adulthood, and it may allow girls to acquire positive characteristics such as assertiveness (Burn, O'Neil, & Nederend, 1996).

In contrast, both peers and adults actively discourage boys from engaging in cross-gender behaviour. Specifically, boys who play with dolls or behave in an effeminate manner are likely to elicit expressions of disapproval, or even ridicule, from children, parents, and teachers (Martin, 1990). Many adults' reactions to boys' cross-gender behaviour appear to be related to the fear that it may lead to homosexuality (Sandnabba & Ahlberg, 1999).

However, it cannot be assumed that the prevalence of sex-typed play among boys is strictly the result of adult and peer influence. For one thing, sex-typed play preferences appear earlier and are more consistent in male infants, which suggests that they begin to develop before environmental forces have had much chance to influence them (Blakemore, LaRue, & Olejnik, 1979). Further, by age 3, boys are likely to show an actual aversion to girls' activities, for example, by saying "yuck" when experimenters offer them toys like dolls (Bussey & Bandura, 1992). In addition, boys may prefer the company of a girl who is a tomboy to a boy who engages in cross-gender activity (Alexander & Hines, 1994). Finally, researchers have found that it is very difficult to change boys' play preferences with modelling and reinforcement (Paley, 1986; Weisner & Wilson-Mitchell, 1990). These findings suggest that, at least for boys, sex-typed behaviour is part of a complex process of identity development and not just the result of cultural modelling and reinforcement.

Before Going On

- How do the major theoretical orientations explain gender concept and sex-role development?
- Describe the development of gender identity, gender stability, and gender constancy.
- What are the characteristics of young children's sex-role knowledge?
- How is the behaviour of young children sex-typed?

Summary

Theories of Social and Personality Development

- Freud and Erikson each described stages of personality development during the preschool years. Erikson described two stages in which autonomy and initiative are developed. Both theories, but especially Freud's, place primary importance on the parent–child relationship. More recent psychoanalytic approaches emphasize the importance of relationships with peers and siblings.

- Social-cognitive theorists assert that advances in social and personality development are associated with cognitive development. Three topics of interest to such theorists are person perception, understanding of others' intentions, and understanding of different kinds of rules.

Family Relationships

- The young child's attachment to the parent(s) remains strong, but except in stressful situations, attachment behaviours become less visible as the child gets older. Preschoolers refuse or defy parental influence attempts more than infants do. Outright defiance, however, declines from age 2 to age 6. Both these changes are clearly linked to the child's language and cognitive gains.

- Authoritative parenting, which combines warmth, clear rules, and communication with high maturity demands, is associated with the most positive outcomes for children. Most child development experts recommend minimal nonphysical forms of child discipline.

- Ethnicity and socioeconomic class are linked to parenting style. Studies of parenting style and developmental outcomes in ethnic groups suggest that, in some situations, authoritative parenting may not be the best style. Good parenting practices are common in all SES levels, but when children of lower SES are exposed to inadequate parenting practices they become more vulnerable to a wide range of problems.

Family Structure and Divorce

- Family structure affects early childhood social and personality development. Data from Canadian studies suggest that many lone-parent families experience high levels of stress, yet only a portion of these children have an elevated risk of a range of problems.

- Following a divorce, children typically show disrupted behaviour for several years. Parenting styles also change, becoming less authoritative. However, many effects of divorce on children are associated with problems that existed before the marriage ended.

- To understand the influence of family structure on development, a number of variables, such as poverty, associated with differences in family structure must be taken into account. However, these variables alone are insufficient to explain differences in children that are correlated with variations in family makeup.

Peer Relationships

- Play with peers is evident before age 2 and becomes increasingly important through the preschool years.

- Physical aggression toward peers increases and then declines during these years, while verbal aggression increases among older preschoolers. Some children develop a pattern of aggressive behaviour that continues to cause problems for them throughout childhood and adolescence.

- Children as young as 2 show empathy and prosocial behaviour toward others, and this behaviour seems to become more common as the child's ability to take another's perspective increases. Stable friendships develop between children in this age range.

Personality and Self-Concept

- During early childhood, children's temperaments are modified by social experiences both within and outside of the family to form their personalities.

- The preschooler continues to define himself along a series of objective dimensions but does not yet have a global sense of self. Children make major strides in self-control and in their understanding of their own social roles in the preschool years, as parents gradually turn over the job of control to the child.

The Gender Concept and Sex Roles

- Social learning explanations are persuasive but ignore the role of cognitive development. Social-cognitive theories better explain and predict gender-related understanding and behaviour.

- Between ages 2 and 6, most children move through a series of steps in their understanding of gender constancy: first, labelling their own and others' gender; then, understanding the stability of gender; and, finally, at about age 5 or 6, comprehending the constancy of gender.

- Beginning at about age 2, children begin to learn what is appropriate behaviour for their gender. By age 5 or 6, most children have developed fairly rigid rules about what boys or girls are supposed to do and be.

- Children display sex-typed behaviour as early as 18 to 24 months of age. Some theorists think children play in gender-segregated groups because same-sex peers help them learn about sex-appropriate behaviour.

Key Terms

aggression (p. 213)	gender constancy theory (p. 222)
authoritarian parenting style (p. 200)	gender identity (p. 223)
authoritative parenting style (p. 200)	gender schema theory (p. 222)
cross-gender behaviour (p. 226)	gender stability (p. 223)
discipline (p. 202)	hostile aggression (p. 214)
extended family (p. 210)	inductive discipline (p. 202)
gender concept (p. 221)	instrumental aggression (p. 214)
gender constancy (p. 222)	permissive parenting style (p. 200)

person perception (p. 195)

prosocial behaviour (p. 216)

sex roles (p. 221)

sex-typed behaviour (p. 224)

social skills (p. 212)

social-cognitive theory (p. 195)

time-out (p. 202)

uninvolved parenting style (p. 201)

Weblinks

Improving the Odds: Healthy Child Development
www.beststart.org/resources/hlthy_chld_dev/pdf/HCD_complete.pdf
This toolkit was developed by a multidisciplinary healthcare team to help physicians
and primary health care providers promote healthy child development in families
and the community. It includes sections on risk factors, parenting, and effective
strategies for healthy growth and development in children.

Effective discipline for children
www.cps.ca/english/statements/PP/pp04-01.htm
This Canadian Paediatric Society position paper discusses goals, developmental considerations, and forms of discipline.

**"What Does Research Say About Early Childhood Education?" by S. Bredekamp,
R.A. Knuth, L.G. Kunesh, and D.D. Shulman**
www.ncrel.org/sdrs/areas/stw_esys/5erly_ch.htm
This article discusses the need for early childhood curriculum and assessment guidelines, as well as theoretical principles of child development and learning. It is accompanied by a multimedia list of resources and a glossary of key terminology.

Campaign 2000: End Child Poverty in Canada
www.campaign2000.ca
Campaign 2000 is a national public education movement to build awareness and
support for the 1989 all-party House of Commons resolution to end child poverty
in Canada. It seeks to encourage the federal and provincial governments to improve
social policies relating to child benefits, social housing, child care, community services, and other relevant policy areas. There is access to the annual report card on
child poverty.

Roots of Empathy
www.rootsofempathy.org
Roots of Empathy, a not-for-profit organization, delivers an "innovative classroom-
based parenting program that aims to reduce aggression through the fostering of
empathy and emotional literacy. The program reaches children aged 3 to 14 years."

Policy Question

How Should We Discipline Our Children?

Although most Canadian parents would agree that disciplining their offspring is an important, yet arduous, task, many parents disagree about the best ways to discipline. Even the term *discipline* can be interpreted variously by parents. For some it is a means to assure conformity while for others, it can be a form of punishment, a corrective tool, or a method of shaping desirable behaviour. Proponents of physical discipline generally argue that it serves a useful purpose and does no lasting harm while opponents say it does no good and it is associated with negative outcomes.

THE RESEARCH IS EQUIVOCAL

One retrospective health study by McMaster University researchers looked at a large sample of adults in Ontario (MacMillan, et al., 1999). Their analysis revealed a significant relationship between the reported frequency of being slapped and/or spanked during childhood and prevalence of psychiatric disorders later in life; the higher the reported frequency of being slapped or spanked the greater the lifetime prevalence of anxiety disorders, alcohol abuse or dependence, externalizing behaviours such as drug dependence and antisocial behaviours, and, to a lesser extent, major depression. However, in a literature review of 38 studies, Robert Larzelere could find no evidence that nonabusive spanking causes any notable detrimental outcomes in children (Larzelere, 2000). In comparison, an often cited report that analyzed 88 studies of corporal punishment and behavioural out-

comes in children by Elizabeth Gershoff found that physical punishment was associated with aggression and misconduct in children (Gershoff, 2002). Both Larzele and Gershoff agree on one point; that punishment does have one desirable effect—it elicits immediate compliance from children. Unfortunately, much of the research to date has methodological problems that preclude any causal inferences about the longer-term outcomes of nonabusive physical punishments, such as mild spanking. As well, the cause-and-effect research needed to provide some decisive answers raises serious ethical concerns and alternatively, correlational studies require more rigorous delineation of the variables being studied (Baumrind, 2003; Baumrind, Larzelere, & Cowan, 2002; Lee, 2004).

THE LEGAL LIMITS OF PHYSICAL DISCIPLINE IN CANADA

Physical discipline is a contentious issue and several recent high profile court cases have brought the issue to the forefront of public awareness. Two cases, in particular, involved the use of corporal punishment to discipline children in the context of the moral belief that "sparing the rod would spoil the child." One case involved 78-year-old Lucille Poulin, a former nun and leader of a P.E.I. cult-like commune, who frequently and routinely beat children

with a wooden paddle as a form of discipline. She was found guilty of assaulting five children and was sentenced to eight months in jail. In another case, the Children's Aid Society removed seven children from a family home in Aylmer, Ontario, where parents, who were members of a tight-knit religious congregation, regularly "spanked" their children with objects such as paddles and switches. The children were eventually returned to their parents' care under supervised court orders to refrain from using corporal punishment. It is clear from these examples that even "well-intentioned" physical punishment can be considered physical abuse by current Canadian standards.

In January 2004, Canada's highest court ruled that physical force can be applied within "reasonable limits" as a form of discipline. The law permits parents, teachers, and caregivers to use minor corrective force if it "is part of a genuine effort to educate the child, poses no reasonable risk of harm that is more than transitory and trifling, and is reasonable under the circumstances"

Lucille Poulin with supporters during her trial. (*Photo:* Andrew Vaughan/CP Photo Archive)

(Department of Justice Canada, 2004, p. 1), but it disallows hitting a child with objects or delivering blows or slaps to the face or head. In addition, the use of physical punishment on children under the age of 2 years or over 12 is prohibited. In its final ruling, the court tried to strike a balance between the needs of parents and the rights of children; the judges made it clear that they do not endorse or advocate the use of corporal punishment, such as spanking, but they also don't want to criminalize parents for any and every physical intervention.

University of Manitoba child psychologist Joan Durrant (2004) contends that the Supreme Court's decision affects both parents and child and family professionals alike. She points out that, even though physical discipline is becoming socially unacceptable in Canada, the law still excuses some degree of it. This raises the question: how is a parent to distinguish between physical punishment and physical abuse? How shall child welfare professionals advise parents about what is an acceptable degree and circumstance for physical discipline? For instance, is one spank or two appropriate? Is a tap on the bum or back of the hand permitted? Is it okay to spank with an open hand so long as it leaves no marks or bruising? How calm do parents have to be before they punish? Can you wash a child's mouth out with soap? What about forcing a child to remain motionless in an awkward stance? These are difficult questions to address. One answer is for professionals to provide a clear message to parents that physical punishment as a form of discipline is not appropriate (Durrant, 2004) and alternate forms of effective discipline are available. This approach has been endorsed in policy statements by the Canadian Psychological Association (2004), the Canadian Paediatric Society (2004a), and other child care organizations. Moreover, over 130 Canadian organizations have signed the "Joint Statement on Physical Punishment of Children and Youth" which states, in part, that "the physical punishment of children and youth plays no useful role in their upbringing and poses only risks to their development. Parents should be strongly encouraged to develop alternative and positive approaches to discipline" (Children's Hospital of Eastern Ontario, 2003, executive summary).

WHAT PARENTS THINK ABOUT PHYSICAL DISCIPLINE

The fact remains that until recently the use of physical punishment by parents was a fairly common and accepted form of discipline. Leger Marketing (2002) found that only 26 percent of adults acknowledged that they never received light physical punishment like a slap. Another study found that only one in five Ontario adults could not recall being slapped or spanked as a child (MacMillan, et al., 1999). Even today, about half of Canadian parents admit that they or their spouse have used, or do use, light physical discipline, like a slap or spanking, on their children (Focus on the Family Canada, 2002; Leger Marketing, 2002). Moreover, although most parents don't condone the use of physical discipline such as spanking, 70% to 83% agree that it should not be a criminal offence for parents to spank their children (Ipsos-Reid/CTV/Globe and Mail, 1999; Leger Marketing, 2002).

YOUR TURN

- What methods of physical discipline do parents employ besides spanking?
- Delineate between acceptable and unacceptable physical discipline.
- Justify why physical discipline should or should not be banned, as it now is in 11 countries around the world.
- What effective nonphysical discipline methods can be used by parents, teachers, and child caregivers alike?
- Explain the danger of doling out discipline when you are angry or frustrated.

What Are the Effects of Childhood Poverty in Canada?

Almost one in five children under the age of 18 live in poverty in Canada—a figure that has remained constant since the 1990s (Canadian Council on Social Development [CCSD], 2001, 2003a; Health Canada, 1999e). Moreover, the child poverty rate in Canada has increased by 28% since 1989 (McClelland, 2001, September 17) and continues to be higher than in many other industrialized countries in the world (CCSD, 2001a). By way of contrast, the poverty rate for children in Sweden is less than 2% (McLoyd, 1998).

Poverty in Canada is not equally distributed across various ages, ethnic groups, and family structures. Those with the lowest incomes became poorer, and toward the late 1990s, despite the robust Canadian economy at the time, about 10–12% of families experienced persistent poverty (CCSD, 2000a, 2001, 2003a). Persistent poverty leads to conditions in which the disadvantages experienced by young children are sustained over time, and any developmental problems they may have are not likely to readily improve (O'Conner & Jenkins, 2000). The families of the working poor (the next lowest 10% of the population) managed slightly better, but continued to merely cycle in and out of poverty during the economic recovery (Jackson, 2001). With respect to age, about 25% of children under the age of 6 and 22% of children 6 to 14 years of age lived in poverty. Poverty rates for Aboriginal children were more than twice the rate for non-Aboriginal children (CCSD, 2003b). The rate of poverty in lone-parent families has dropped slightly, but remains high at 46% compared with 16% in all families (CCSD, 2003a).

THE EFFECTS OF POVERTY ON FAMILIES AND CHILDREN

Low family income is strongly associated with poorer health, social problems, and lower educational achievement for children (Health Canada, 1999f). The children of low-income families have higher rates of birth defects and early disabilities; they suffer poorer overall health during the first 5 months of life and have higher rates of hospital admission; they recover less readily from early problems; and they are more often ill and undernourished throughout their childhood years (Klerman, 1991; Séguin, Xu, Potvin, Zunzunegui, & Frohlich, 2003). In addition, research shows that as children of low-income families enter school they have higher levels of truancy, lower grades, and 40% higher levels of indirect aggression (Ross, 1998b). In addition, they are more likely to experience hyperactivity, show delayed literacy and math development, have friends who are in trouble, and have lower rates of participation in sports (Ross, 1998a).

Children living in low-income families are also more likely to experience hunger. Although children constitute only 25% of the population, 39% of those using food banks are under age 18 (CCSD, 2001). Specifically, children of the working poor, children of lone-parent families, children of Aboriginal heritage, and children whose families are on social assistance are two to eight times more likely to go hungry than other Canadian children (McIntyre, Walsh, & Conner, 2001). As a result these groups of Canadian children are at risk for malnourishment, which is associated with higher rates of both illness and mortality (Health Canada, 1999f).

It's not poverty per se but the negative consequences it creates that puts children at greater risk. Among many other things, poverty reduces options for parents. Children of low-income families have less access to health benefits, child care, safe environments, and recreational and physical activities (CCSD, 2001). Low-income families have little access to services not covered by government health plans, e.g., dental care, mental health counselling, and

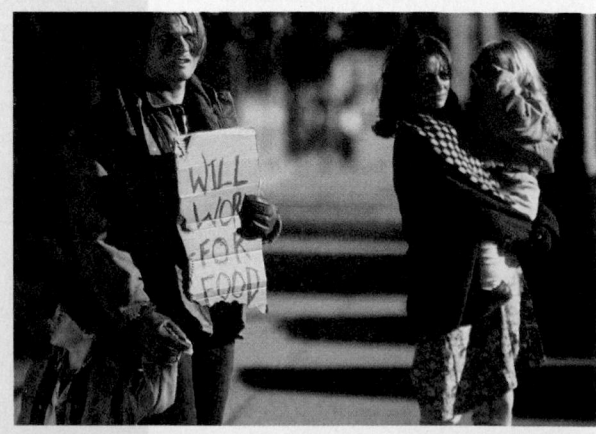

(*Photo:* Bruce Ayres/Getty Images)

prescription drugs (Health Canada, 1000f). When a low-income mother works, she is likely to have fewer choices of affordable child care. Her children spend more time in poor-quality care and shift more frequently from one care arrangement to another. Low-income families also live in smaller and less-than-adequate housing, often in decaying neighbourhoods with high rates of violence, and many such families move frequently, which means their children change schools often. The parents are less likely to feel that they have adequate social support, and the children often lack a stable group of playmates (Dodge, Pettit, & Bates, 1994). Parents in these circumstances also tend to be less involved in their children's schools (Griffith, 1998). Overall, the poor live in more chaotic environments, are more highly stressed, and have fewer psychological and social resources than those who are more economically secure (Brooks-Gunn, 1995; McLoyd & Wilson, 1991).

Parents living in poverty also tend to treat their children differently than do working-class or middle-class parents. They talk to them less, provide fewer age-appropriate toys, spend less time with them in intellectually stimulating activities, explain things less often and less fully, are less nurturing, and are stricter and more physical in their discipline (Dodge et al., 1994; Sampson & Laub, 1994). A portion of this pattern of parental behaviour is undoubtedly a response to the extraordinary stresses and special demands of living in poverty—a point buttressed by the repeated observation that parents who are poor but who nonetheless feel that they have enough social support are much less likely to be harshly punitive or unsupportive of their children (Hashima & Amato, 1994; Taylor & Roberts, 1995).

Some of the differences in child-rearing patterns between low-income and high-income parents may also result from straightforward modelling of the way the parents themselves were reared, and some may be a product of ignorance of children's needs. Lower-income parents with relatively more education, for example, typically talk to their children more, are more responsive, and provide more intellectual stimulation than do equally poor parents with lower levels of education (Kelley, Sanches-Hucles, & Walker, 1993). But whatever the cause, nearly all children reared in poverty experience physical conditions and interactions with their parents that differ from the experiences of children from high-income families.

THE ROLE OF STRESS

Most children from low-income families develop along the same lines as their more economically secure peers. To help sort out differences between poor children who do well and those who do not, developmentalists think of poverty in terms of accumulated stresses (McLoyd, 1998). For example, for a child growing up in poverty, perhaps urban poverty especially, the chances of experiencing such multiple stressors are very high indeed. A growing body of evidence shows that the effect of living in a concentrated pocket of poverty is an intensification of all the ill effects of family poverty (Klebanov, Brooks-Gunn, Hofferth, & Duncan, 1995; Kupersmidt, Griesler, DeRosier, Patterson, & Davis, 1995). When the whole neighbourhood is poor, parents have fewer other resources to rely on and children have more violent adult models and fewer supportive ones; rates of child abuse rise, along with rates of aggression and delinquency in children (Coulton, Korbin, Su, & Chow, 1995). When the whole neighbourhood also lacks what sociologists call connectedness and stability—when the adults do not collaborate to monitor the children and do not provide practical or emotional support to one another—the effects are still worse (Wilson, 1995).

IMPETUS FOR CHANGE

In recent years there has been an upsurge in interest in the importance of early childhood development and how social policy plays a

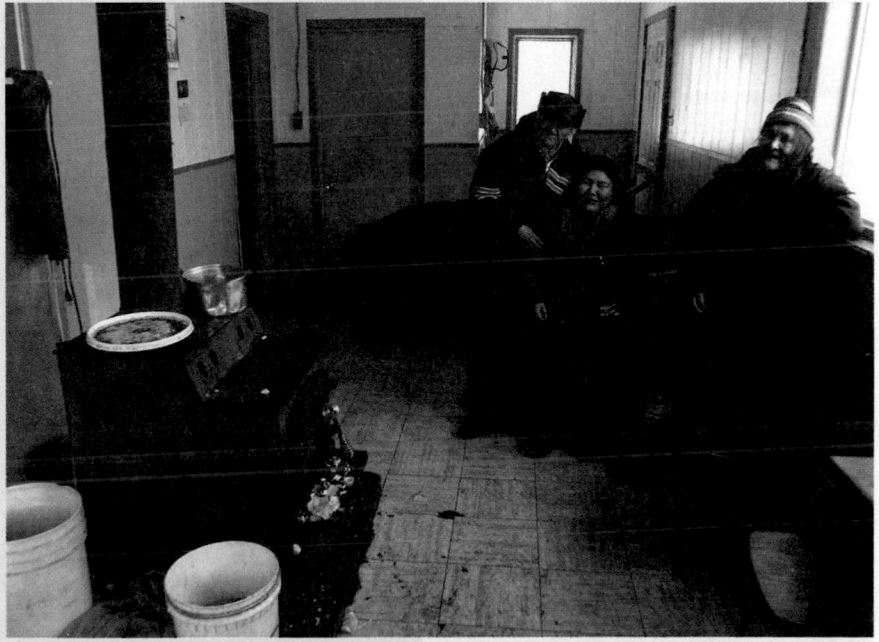

(*Photo:* Ryan Remiorz/CP Photo Archive)

role (Comley & Mousmanis, 2004). In 1999 Dr. Fraser Mustard, who received the F.N.G. Starr Award, the Canadian Medical Association's highest honour (CMA, 2001, August 3), and the Honourable Margaret McCain, former new Brunswick Lieutenant-Governor, co-authored a report for the Ontario government entitled "Early Years Study—Reversing the Real Brain Drain." The report emphasizes the impact of nutrition and stimulation on the rapidly developing neural connections within the brain during the first years of life and how these effects persist throughout life. Moreover, the pattern for growth and development later in life is mostly set within the first 3 years of life and thus has an effect on a child's readiness to learn. By age 6, most of the neurological changes that are precursors to lifelong learning, behaviour, and health are complete. Therefore, conditions that contribute to poor neurological development early in life lead to a lifelong disadvantage that is very difficult to reverse and ultimately affects both the individual and Canadian society. The authors of the report call for radical changes in how society supports its young children in all walks of life (McCain & Mustard, 1999, 2002).

SOCIAL POLICY ISSUES

There are many different contentious points of view concerning the issues surrounding poverty (CCSD, 2000a; Jackson, 2001; Ross, 1998a). One primary issue is how we should define low income itself. Some argue that if you give parents more money they will just squander it on nonessentials, and therefore the poverty line should be drawn at the point where the basic necessities are all that can be provided. This, however, fails to address just what constitutes a basic necessity. Some argue that physical needs such as food and shelter are the only needs that require attention. Others suggest that those needs beyond the physical (such as recreation, an intellectually stimulating environment, health care, etc.), if ignored, can lead to long-term outcomes that can carry a major economic cost in the future. They question the wisdom of cutting back on social support to save money today only to create even more difficult and expensive problems in the next generation of adults. Still others argue that Canada is a developed, industrialized nation that values safety, health, civility, and economic and cultural prosperity, and that we who live in such a fair and just society should embrace the ideal that all children should have an equal chance at becoming successful adults.

Generally, as family incomes increase the children's chances for success increase, but there is no income level below which a child is destined to fail or above which a child is guaranteed to succeed. In addition, it is not just a matter of improving incomes in order to increase the likelihood of a child's successful transition to adulthood; what is also required is the creation of pathways of opportunity, e.g., fair access to public services, education, health care, and recreation. The question of what level of income combined with what level of public support is needed in order to adequately prepare all Canadian children to meet tomorrow's challenges remains to be answered.

At present there exists a patchwork of social programs to deal with the negative consequences of poverty in general and inadequate early childhood support in particular. Some current initiatives include: (1) the National Child Benefit (NCB) program, which aims to prevent and reduce the depth of child poverty by providing equalized levels of income support, benefits, and services for children across Canada; (2) the Child Tax Benefit (CTB), which provides relief in the form of tax rebates for the low-est-income families; (3) the Canadian Prenatal Nutrition Program (CPNP) and Community Action Program for Children (CAPC), both of which target the needs of children under 6 years of age; and (4) the on-reserve Aboriginal Head Start (AHS) program. The federal government is also moving forward with "Foundations: A National Early Learning and Child Care Program," a high-quality national early learning and child care program based on four principles: *Quality* (safe, regulated facilities with qualified staff); *Universality* (open to all preschool children); *Accessibility* (affordable for all parents); and *Developmental* (includes development and learning components) (Liberal Party of Canada, 2004). Quebec leads the way in North America with an early learning and care program that meets these standards.

YOUR TURN

- What are some common perceptions that people have about low-income Canadians and their children?

- In what ways do misconceptions about the poor impede their chances of climbing the ladder out of poverty?

- Discuss who is responsible for defining the limits of poverty and justify who should pay for the cost of reducing poverty.

- Explain in what ways it is more than just low family income that creates unfair opportunities for children living in poverty.

- Why should we care about disadvantaged children? Describe how helping all Canadian children to thrive and have the readiness and opportunity to reach their potential can benefit all of society.

© Jose Azel/Woodfin Camp and Associates

CHAPTER 8

PHYSICAL AND COGNITIVE DEVELOPMENT IN MIDDLE CHILDHOOD

Throughout the industrialized world, as well as in most developing areas, the years of middle childhood are devoted to formal education. Indeed, the first day of school is considered to be one of the most important transition points in a child's life. In Canada, parents mark the occasion in a variety of ways—with new clothes, fresh school supplies, and carefully selected backpacks and lunch boxes. Some families take pictures of their children's first ride on the school bus or first classroom. All these ways of recognizing this important milestone say to children that this day is unique, and they begin to think of themselves as "big kids" who are engaged in the serious business of going to school, rather than "little kids" who spend most of their time playing.

As important as middle childhood is, however, researchers often pay little attention to these years, as if they were somehow insignificant. Far less research has been done on children in this age group than on either preschoolers or adolescents. Yet it is clear that major cognitive advances occur between the ages of 6 and 12 and that patterns and habits established during this time will affect not only adolescent experience, but also adulthood.

In this chapter, we will explore the many physical changes, including those in the brain, that happen between 6 and 12. You will also learn how children's linguistic abilities expand significantly during these years, and how children acquire the developmental foundation of adult logic and memory. We will examine the influence of formal education on a variety of developmental processes and explore some factors that shape academic achievement. As you read the chapter, keep the following questions in mind:

- How are sex differences in physical activities linked to the development of various body systems in middle childhood? How does the brain change during these years?

- What are the milestones in the development of linguistic, cognitive, and memory skills that mark the 6- to 12-year-old period?

- How does schooling influence development?

- What kinds of individual and group differences are related to development and school achievement?

PHYSICAL CHANGES

Although they are more difficult to observe directly, the physical changes of middle childhood are just as impressive as those of early childhood.

GROWTH AND MOTOR DEVELOPMENT

Between 6 and 12, children grow 5 to 8 centimetres and add about 2.75 kilograms each year. Large-muscle coordination continues to improve, and children become increasingly adept at skills like bike riding; both strength and speed also increase. Hand–eye coordination improves as well (Thomas, Yan, & Stelmach, 2000). As a result, school-aged children perform more skilfully in activities requiring coordination of vision with body movements, such as shooting a basketball or playing a musical instrument.

Perhaps even more significant is the school-aged child's improving fine-motor coordination. Improvements in fine-motor coordination make writing possible, as well as the playing of most musical instruments, drawing, cutting, and many other tasks and activities. Such accomplished uses of the hands are made possible by maturation of the wrist, which, as you may recall from earlier chapters, occurs more rapidly in girls than in boys (Tanner, 1990).

Girls in this age range are ahead of boys in their overall rate of growth as well. By 12, girls have attained about 94% of their adult height, while boys have reached only 84% of theirs (Tanner, 1990). Girls also have slightly more body fat and slightly less muscle tissue than boys. Sex differences in skeletal and muscular maturation cause girls to be better coordinated but slower and somewhat weaker than boys. Thus, girls outperform boys in activities requiring coordinated movement, and boys do better when strength and speed are advantages. Still, the overall sex differences in joint maturation, strength, and speed are small at this age.

When school-aged boys and girls participate in co-ed sports, boys' superior speed and strength is balanced by girls' advantage in coordination.
(*Photo:* Cindy Charles/PhotoEdit)

THE BRAIN AND NERVOUS SYSTEM

Two major growth spurts happen in the brain during middle childhood (Spreen, Risser, & Edgell, 1995). In most healthy children, the first takes place between ages 6 and 8, and the second between ages 10 and 12. Both spurts involve development of new synapses as well as increases in the thickness of the cerebral cortex.

The primary sites of brain growth during the first spurt are the sensory and motor areas. Growth in these areas may be linked to the striking improvements in fine-motor skills and eye–hand coordination that usually occur between 6 and 8. During the second spurt of brain growth, the frontal lobes of the cerebral cortex become the focus of developmental processes (Van der Molen & Molenaar, 1994). Predictably, the areas of the brain that govern logic and planning, two cognitive functions that improve dramatically during this period, are located primarily in the frontal lobes.

Myelinization also continues through middle childhood. Of particular importance is the continued myelinization of the reticular formation and of the nerves that link the reticular formation to the frontal lobes. These connections are essential if the child is to be able to take full advantage of improvements in frontal lobe functions because, as you may recall, the reticular formation controls attention. It is well documented that the ability to control attention increases significantly during middle childhood (Lin, Hsiao & Chen, 1999).

It seems likely that myelinization allows the linkages between the frontal lobes and the reticular formation to work together so that 6- to 12-year-olds are able to develop a particular kind of concentration called *selective attention*. **Selective attention** is the ability to focus cognitive activity on the important elements of a problem or situation. For example, suppose your psychology instructor, who usually copies tests on white paper, gives you a test printed on blue paper. You won't spend a lot of time thinking about why the test is blue instead of white; this is an irrelevant detail. Instead, your selective attention skills will prompt you to ignore the colour of the paper and focus on the test questions. In contrast, some younger elementary school children might be so distracted by the unusual colour of the test paper that their test performance is affected. As the nerves connecting the reticular formation and the frontal lobes become more fully myelinated between ages 6 and 12, children begin to function more like adults in the presence of such distractions.

The neurons of the **association areas**—parts of the brain where sensory, motor, and intellectual functions are linked—are myelinized to some degree by the time children enter middle childhood. However, from 6 to 12, the nerve cells in these areas achieve nearly complete myelinization. Neuroscientists believe that this advance in the

selective attention
the ability to focus cognitive activity on the important elements of a problem or situation

association areas
parts of the brain where sensory, motor, and intellectual functions are linked

myelinization process contributes to increases in information-processing speed. For example, suppose you were to ask a 6-year-old and a 12-year-old to identify pictures of common items—a bicycle, an apple, a desk, a dog—as rapidly as possible. Both children would know the items' names, but the 12-year-old would be able to produce the names of the items much more rapidly than the 6-year-old. Such increases in processing speed probably contribute to improvements in memory function, which you'll read about later in the chapter (Kail, 1990).

Another important advance in middle childhood occurs in the right cerebral hemisphere, with the lateralization of spatial perception, the ability to identify and act on relationships between objects in space. For example, when you imagine how a room would look with a different arrangement of furniture, you are using **spatial perception**. Perception of objects such as faces actually lateralizes before age 6. However, complex spatial perception, such as map-reading, isn't strongly lateralized until about age 8.

A behavioural test of the lateralization of spatial perception often used by neuroscientists involves **relative right-left orientation**, the ability to identify right and left from multiple perspectives. Such a test usually shows that most children younger than 8 know the difference between their own right and left. Typically, though, only children older than 8 understand the difference between statements like "It's on *your* right" and "It's on *my* right." Lateralization of spatial perception may also be related to the increased efficiency with which older children learn math concepts and problem-solving strategies. In addition, it is somewhat correlated to performance on Piaget's conservation tasks (Van der Molen & Molenaar, 1994).

However, the development of spatial perception is more than just a physiological process. Developmentalists know this because this function lateralizes much more slowly in blind children than in those who have sight. Thus, it appears that visual experience plays an important role in this aspect of brain development.

Furthermore, some researchers propose that differences in visual experiences explain sex differences in spatial perception and the related function of **spatial cognition**, the ability to infer rules from and make predictions about the movement of objects in space. For example, when you are driving on a two-lane road, and you make a judgment about whether you have enough room to pass a car ahead of you, you are using spatial cognition. From an early age, boys score much higher than girls, on average, on such spatial tasks (Halpern, 1986; Voyer, Voyer, & Bryden, 1995). Some researchers suggest that boys' play preferences, such as their greater interest in constructive activities such as building with blocks, help them develop more acute spatial perception and cognition (see **Development in the Information Age**).

spatial perception
the ability to identify and act on relationships between objects in space

relative right-left orientation
the ability to identify right and left from multiple perspectives

spatial cognition
the ability to infer rules from and make predictions about the movement of objects in space

HEALTH PROMOTION AND WELLNESS

Generally speaking, most school-aged children are very healthy. However, they continue to benefit from regular medical care. For one thing, children's immunization history should be reviewed to ensure that optimal vaccination coverage has been achieved. It is also recommended that children age 5 to 13 years be vaccinated for Hepatitis B if it was missed during infancy (Health Canada, 2002d). In addition, some school-aged children have undiagnosed health problems, such as vision or hearing problems. Another common childhood problem is sleep disturbance. About one-quarter of children from Grades 6 to 10 have difficulty falling asleep more than once a week and by Grade 9 about one-third report that they are tired most mornings (Health Canada, 2001g).

Although the rate of unintentional injury-related deaths has declined steadily since the 1980s, unintentional injury remains the most common cause of death in children between 5 and 14 years of age (36.5%) (Health Canada, 1999g, 2000b). The injury-

Development in the
Information Age
The Effects of Video Games

Anthropologists propose that video games are one of the many tools industrialized societies can use to teach children the technological and intellectual skills they need as adults (Greenfield, 1994). But like any device we invent, it can have beneficial or damaging effects depending upon its use.

Several studies suggest that playing video games has a plus side—video gaming can help boys and, more importantly, girls feel more comfortable with technology; promote team-work and interpersonal skills when played with others; enhance self-efficacy, self-esteem, and self-confidence through game mastery; foster visual-spatial skills, eye–hand coordination, and fine motor skills; facilitate reading, math, and problem-solving skills; and, in the case of educationally based video games, increase knowledge in various subjects, such as health, history, or science (Atwood, 2004; Chapman, 2004; Greenfield, Brannon, & Lohr, 1994; Kline, 1998; Lieberman,1997; Media Awareness Network, 2004a).

Despite the positive effects that video gaming can have on learning and development, a strong case has been made that playing video games has a darker side. For one, there is some cause for alarm over the amount of time children spend playing video games at the expense of other activities. Communications psychologist Stephen Kline of Simon Fraser University has been investigating the patterns and risks of video gaming. To begin with, he found that almost three-quarters of school-aged children have access to a video game console in the home, and video gaming takes time away from other activities, such as home-work, physical activity, and family and peer interactions. Even in the morning, before school, 15.5% of boys, but no girls, reported

that they played video games. Kline also found that the majority of parents had rules about video game usage time, but only about one-third of the parents actually monitored or restricted the length of playing time. Of even greater concern, 9 out of 10 children did not have rules about the content of their video games (Kline, 2003). Experts warn us about the adverse effects that video game content can have on personality development and behaviour—especially games with themes of violence, and gender and racial stereotyping (Funk, Buchman, Jenks, & Bechtoldt, 2002; Kline, 1998, 2003; Media Awareness Network, 2004b).

Violent video games appear to be part of a larger set of influences linking preferences for violent stimuli to aggressive behaviour. The more violent television programs children watch, the more violent the video games they prefer, and the more aggressively they behave toward peers (Mediascope, 1999). This finding holds for both boys and girls; most girls aren't interested in violent games, but those who are tend to be more physically aggressive than average. In particular, researchers have demonstrated that playing violent video games leads to increased physiological arousal; increased aggressive cognitions, emotions, and behaviours; decreased proso-cial behaviours; and is associated with long-term increases in such behaviours (Anderson, 2004; Anderson, et al., in press; Anderson & Bushman, 2001; Anderson & Dill, 2000, Gentile & Anderson, 2003; Gentile, Lynch, Linder, & Walsh, 2004). The negative outcomes are even more pronounced for those youth who are "addicted" to playing video games (e.g., those who averaged about 3

hours of video play time a day) (Hauge & Gentile, 2003). Consequently, parents who observe that aggressive and violent themes characterize most of their children's leisure-time interests as well as their interactions with peers should worry about their children playing video games with violent content (Funk, Buchman, Myers, & Jenks, 2000; Gentile, Walsh, Ellison, Fox, Cameron, 2004).

Alas, themes of aggression and power dominate the genre, and more than 75% of video games involve violence (Funk & Buchman, 1999). Unfortunately, the very quali-ties that make video games beneficial teaching tools also make them prime for the building up of aggressive thoughts, feelings, and behaviour. What's more, the engaging, interac-tive, and reinforcing nature of video games has the potential to be more detrimental than the violence that is transmitted via the relatively more passive medium of television (Gentile & Anderson, 2003). Ironically, in Canada, where television and movie content is highly regu-lated by the Canadian Radio-television and Telecommunications Commission (CRTC), the video gaming industry remains relatively unchecked (Kline, 2002).

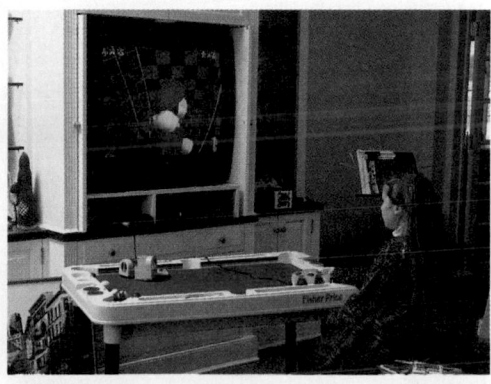

(*Photo:* Ken Lax/Photo Researchers)

related mortality rate increases with age and is higher for males than females in all age categories. About half of the fatal injuries were due to motor vehicle crashes (Health Canada, 1999h). The majority of nonfatal unintentional injuries are caused by falls, followed by those caused by participation in sports (Pless & Millar, 2000). One activity that has seen a recent rise in the number of injuries in children is the use of the unpowered scooter, and in 2001 Health Canada and Transport Canada released a safety advisory concerning the use of scooters (Health Canada, 2001h). Recent statistics have shown that children between 8 and 13 years of age experienced most injuries (76.4%), and that about two-thirds of the injured were male (Canadian Hospitals Injury Reporting and Prevention Program [CHIRPP], 2001).

Aside from unintentional injury, another significant health risk of the middle childhood period concerns body weight. The *body mass index* (BMI) is a measure that estimates a child's proportion of body fat. Using the BMI allows health care providers to more easily distinguish between children who are overweight and those who are obese. A child whose BMI is above the 85th percentile for his sex and age is generally considered **over-weight**, while a child who is above the 95th percentile is classified as **obese**. Using the 1981 weight-growth charts as a standard, between 1981 and 1996, the incidence of overweight increased in Canada by 92% in boys and 57% in girls, and obesity more than doubled to 13.5% for boys and 11.8% for girls (Tremblay & Willms, 2000).

The longer a child remains overweight, the more likely the child is to remain obese into the adult years (National Center for Health Statistics [NCHS], 2000). Only a fifth of overweight babies become overweight adults, but half of those who were overweight in elementary school continue to be overweight in adulthood (Serdula et al., 1993). In addition, more than half of obese children have one or more risk factors, such as elevated levels of cholesterol or high blood pressure, that predispose them to heart disease later in life (National Center for Chronic Disease Prevention and Health Promotion [NCCDPHP], 2000).

As you might suspect, overeating or eating too much of the wrong foods contributes to obesity in children, just as it does in adults (NCCDPHP, 2000). However, both twin and adoption studies suggest that obesity probably results from an interaction between a genetic predisposition for obesity and environmental factors that promote overeating or low levels of activity (Stunkard, Harris, Pedersen, & McClearn, 1990). Whatever the genetic contribution might be, the pattern of decrease in physical activity and increase in the consumption of high-calorie convenience foods has led to the current epidemic of obesity in today's Canadian children (Andersen, 2000).

It's important to keep in mind, though, that weight-loss diets for children can be fairly risky. As they are still growing, the nutritional needs of obese children differ from those of obese adults (Tershakovec & Stallings, 1998). Consequently, obese children require special diets developed and supervised by nutritional experts. Furthermore, increasing the amount of exercise children get is just as important as changing their eating habits (NCCDPHP, 2000).

Cycle 3 of the National Longitudinal Study of Children and Youth (NLSCY) revealed that participation in physical activities increases from age 4 and peaks between ages 10 and 13, with about 92% of children participating in some type of physical activity. At all ages, boys are more involved with sports than girls, whereas girls tend to participate more in the arts and music, and clubs or groups (Statistics Canada, 2001c). With the cutbacks in education funding for physical education and after-school sports programs across Canada, there has been less impetus for children to remain physically active as they get older. For instance, both the Canadian Association for Health, Physical Education, Recreation and Dance (CAHPERD)

overweight

having increased body weight in relation to height, as compared to a standard of desirable weight

obese

having an excessive amount of body fat in relation to lean body mass

An overweight child not only has different kinds of encounters with his peers, but is also more likely to be fat as an adult, with accompanying increased health risks. (*Photo:* Tony Freeman/PhotoEdit)

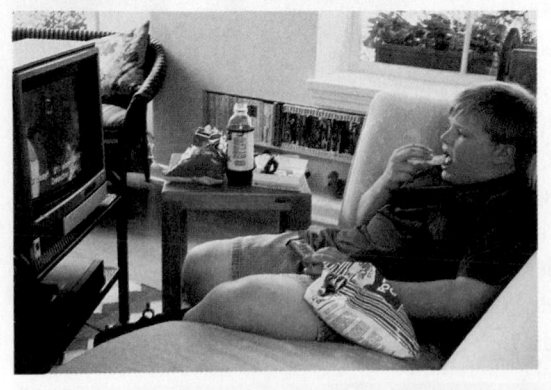

and the Canadian Medical Association (CMA) recommend that children from kindergarten through Grade 12 should have 30 minutes a day of compulsory physical activity, but studies have shown that schools average only 60 minutes a week (Andersen, 2000). A recent analysis of the NLSCY found that physical activity was especially important for overweight/obese children—an inactive overweight/obese student was more likely to become active and remain active later in childhood if he or she averaged at least 18 minutes of physical education a day (Pérez, 2003). Not only does a lack of physical exercise contribute to overweight and poorer health in general, it has also been linked to delayed vocabulary development, lower levels of prosocial behaviour, and lower levels of self-esteem in children (Statistics Canada, 2001c).

Fear of developing an unattractive body may become a significant problem for some children. Serious eating disorders (which you'll read about in detail in **Chapter 10**) don't become common until well into adolescence. However, most 6- to 12-year-olds are quite knowledgeable about weight-loss diets and products (Kostanski & Gullone, 1999). Moreover, research suggests that children as young as 7 years of age sometimes express dissatisfaction with their weight or physical appearance, and some begin dieting as early as age 9 (Kostanski & Gullone, 1999; NCHS, 1996; Nutter, 1997). In addition, weight concerns increase among both boys and girls across the 6- to 12-year-old period (Gardner, Friedman, & Jackson, 1999). Therefore, it is important to help children develop good eating habits without overemphasizing physical appearance to the extent that children develop patterns of dieting that can threaten their later mental and physical health.

Before Going On

- Describe the physical growth of 6- to 12-year-olds.
- List the changes in brain growth, myelinization, and lateralization that happen between 6 and 12.
- What are the two most important health hazards for 6- to 12-year-olds?

COGNITIVE CHANGES

Along with impressive gains in physical development, children acquire some of the important hallmarks of mature thinking between ages 6 and 12.

LANGUAGE

By age 5 or 6, virtually all children have mastered the basic grammar and pronunciation of their first language, but children of this age still have a fair distance to go before reaching adult levels of fluency. During middle childhood, children become skilled at managing the finer points of grammar (Prat-Sala, Shillcock, & Sorace, 2000; Ragnarsdottir, Simonsen, & Plunkett, 1999). For example, by the end of middle childhood, most children understand various ways of saying something about the past, such as "I went," "I was going," "I have gone," "I had gone," "I had been going," and so on. Moreover, they correctly use such tenses in their own speech. Across the middle childhood years, children also learn how to maintain the topic of conversation, how to create unambiguous sentences, and how to speak politely or persuasively (Anglin, 1993).

Between 6 and 12, children also continue to add new vocabulary at a fairly astonishing rate of from 5000 to 10 000 words per year. This estimate comes from several careful studies by developmental psychologist Jeremy Anglin of the University of Waterloo, who estimates children's total vocabularies by testing them on a sample of words drawn at random from a large dictionary (Anglin, 1993, 1995). **Figure 8.1** shows Anglin's estimates for Grades 1, 3, and 5. Anglin found that the largest gain between Grades 3 and 5 occurs in knowledge of the type of words he calls *derived words*—words that have a basic root to which some prefix or suffix is added, such as "happily" or "unwanted."

Anglin argues that at age 8 or 9 the child shifts to a new level of understanding of the structure of language, figuring out relationships between whole categories of words, such as between adjectives and adverbs ("happy" and "happily," "sad" and "sadly"), between adjectives and nouns ("happy" and "happiness"), and the like. Once he grasps these relationships, the child can understand and create a whole class of new words, and his vocabulary thereafter increases rapidly.

PIAGET'S CONCRETE OPERATIONAL STAGE

concrete operations
a set of mental schemes, including reversibility, addition, subtraction, multiplication, division, and serial ordering, that enable children to understand relations among objects

inductive logic
a type of reasoning in which general principles are inferred from specific experiences

deductive logic
a type of reasoning based on hypothetical premises that requires predicting a specific outcome from a general principle

From Piaget's perspective, a great leap forward occurs when the school-aged child discovers or develops a set of immensely powerful schemes that Piaget called *concrete operations*. By **concrete operations**, Piaget meant mental processes such as reversibility, addition, subtraction, multiplication, division, and serial ordering. Each of these is a kind of general rule about objects and their relationships. The school-aged child understands the rule that adding makes something more and subtracting makes it less; she understands that objects can belong to more than one category at once and that categories have logical relationships.

Of all the operations, Piaget thought the most critical was *reversibility*—the understanding that both physical actions and mental operations can be reversed. The clay sausage in a conservation experiment can be made back into a ball; the water can be poured back into the shorter, wider glass. This understanding of the basic reversibility of actions lies behind many of the gains made during the middle childhood period. For example, if a child has mastered reversibility, then knowing that A is larger than B also tells him that B is smaller than A. The ability to understand hierarchies of classes (such as Rover, spaniel, dog, and animal) also rests on this ability to move both ways in thinking about relationships.

Piaget also proposed that during this stage the child develops the ability to use **inductive logic**. She can go from a specific experience to a general principle. For example, she can make assumptions based on specific facts, such as that her friend's parents live in a mansion and have servants working for them; therefore her friend's parents are wealthy.

Elementary school children are fairly good observational scientists, and they enjoy activities such as cataloguing rock samples, counting species of trees or birds, and figuring out the nesting habits of guinea pigs. But they are not yet good at **deductive logic** based on hypothetical premises, which requires starting with a general principle and then predicting some outcome or observation—like going from a

Figure 8.1

Anglin's estimates of the total vocabulary of children in Grades 1, 3, and 5.

(*Source:* Anglin, 1995, from Figure 6, p. 7.)

theory to a hypothesis. For example, children have a general idea of what a fish is from its shape and habitat; a fish is long and sleek and lives under water. If you ask a child to determine whether a whale is classified as a fish or a mammal, he may incorrectly classify a whale as a fish because children at this age struggle with the concept that a whale is not a fish even though it has some outward characteristics of a fish. This kind of task is difficult for 6- to 12-year-olds because they must imagine things they have not experienced. The concrete-operations child is good at dealing with things she can see and manipulate or can imagine seeing or manipulating—that is, she is good with *concrete* things; she does not do well with manipulating ideas, abstract concepts, or possibilities. Thus, as the example above illustrates, children respond to deductive problems by generating ideas that are essentially copies of the things they already know about in the concrete world.

DIRECT TESTS OF PIAGET'S VIEW

Piaget understood that it took children some years to apply their new cognitive skills to all kinds of problems, a phenomenon he called *horizontal decalage*. (The French word *decalage* means "a shift.")

HORIZONTAL DECALAGE Researchers have generally found that Piaget was right in his assertion that concrete operational schemes are acquired gradually across the 6- to 12-year-old period. Studies of conservation, for example, consistently show that children grasp conservation of mass or substance by about age 7. That is, they understand that the amount of clay is the same whether it is in a pancake or a ball or some other shape. They generally understand conservation of weight at about age 8, but they don't understand conservation of volume until age 11 (Tomlinson-Keasey, Eisert, Kahle, Hardy-Brown, & Keasey, 1979).

Studies of classification skills show that at about age 7 or 8 the child first grasps the principle of **class inclusion,** the understanding that subordinate classes are included in larger, superordinate classes. Bananas are included in the class of fruit, and fruit is included in the class of food, and so forth. Preschool children understand that bananas are also fruit, but they do not yet fully understand the relationship between the classes.

class inclusion
the understanding that subordinate classes are included in larger, superordinate classes

A good illustration of all these changes comes from an early longitudinal study of concrete operations tasks conducted by Carol Tomlinson-Keasey and her colleagues (Tomlinson-Keasey et al., 1979). They followed a group of 38 children from kindergarten through Grade 3, testing them with five traditional concrete operations tasks each year: conservation of mass, conservation of weight, conservation of volume, class inclusion, and hierarchical classification. You can see from **Figure 8.2** on page 244 that the children got better at all five tasks over the 3-year period, with a spurt between the end of kindergarten and the beginning of Grade 1 (at about the age Piaget thought that concrete operations really arose) and another spurt during Grade 2.

CONCRETE OPERATIONS AS RULES FOR PROBLEM-SOLVING Other psychologists have conceptualized performance on concrete operational tasks in terms of rules for problem solving. For example, Robert Siegler's approach is a kind of cross between Piagetian theory and information-processing theory. He argues that cognitive development consists of acquiring a set of basic rules that are then applied to a broader and broader range of problems on the basis of experience. There are no stages, only sequences. Siegler proposes that problem-solving rules emerge from experience—from repeated trial and error and experimentation (Siegler, 1994).

Some of Siegler's own early work on the development of rules illustrates how they may be acquired (Siegler, 1976, 1978, 1981). In one test, Siegler used a balance scale

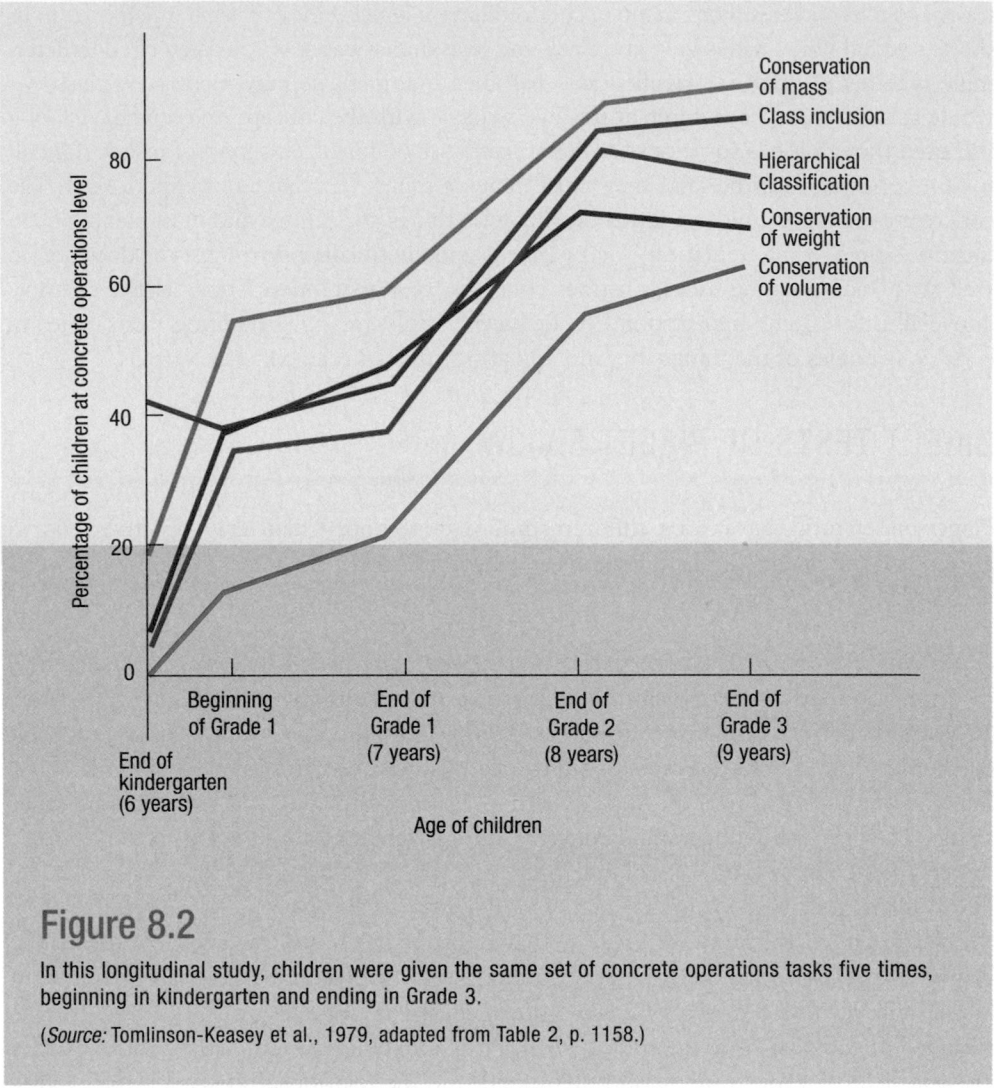

Figure 8.2

In this longitudinal study, children were given the same set of concrete operations tasks five times, beginning in kindergarten and ending in Grade 3.

(*Source:* Tomlinson-Keasey et al., 1979, adapted from Table 2, p. 1158.)

with a series of pegs on either side of the centre, like the one in **Figure 8.3**. The child is asked to predict which way the balance will fall, depending on the location and number of disk-shaped weights placed on the pegs. A complete solution requires the child to take into account both the number of disks on each side and the specific location of the disks.

Children do not develop such a complete solution immediately. Instead, Siegler suggests that they develop four rules, in this order: Rule I is basically a preoperational rule, taking into account only one dimension, the number of weights. Children using this rule will predict that the side with more disks will go down, no matter which peg they are placed on. Rule II is a transitional rule. The child still judges on the basis of number, except when the same number of weights appears on each side; in that case the child takes distance from the fulcrum (point of balance) into account. Rule III is basically a concrete operational rule; the child tries to take both distance and weight into account simultaneously, except that when the information is conflicting (such as when the side with weights closer to the fulcrum has more weights), the child simply guesses. Rule IV involves the understanding of the actual formula for calculating the combined effect of weight and distance for each side of the balance.

Siegler has found that virtually all children perform on this and similar tasks as if they were following one or another of these rules, and that the rules seem to develop in the given order. Very young children behave as if they don't have a rule (they guess or behave randomly); when they do seem to begin using a rule, it is always Rule I that comes first. But progression from one rule to the next depends heavily on experience. If children are given practice with the balance scale so that they can make predictions and then check which way the balance actually falls, many rapidly develop the next rules in the sequence.

Thus, Siegler is attempting to describe a logical sequence children follow, not unlike the basic sequence of stages that Piaget describes—but Siegler's research shows that a particular child's position in the sequence depends not so much on age as on the child's specific experience with a given set of material. In Piaget's terminology, this is rather like saying that when accommodation of some scheme occurs, it always occurs in a particular sequence, but the rate at which the child moves through that sequence depends on experience.

Figure 8.3

This balance scale is similar to what Siegler used in his experiments.

ADVANCES IN INFORMATION-PROCESSING SKILLS

As they progress through the middle childhood years, children are able to remember longer and longer lists of numbers, letters, or words, as illustrated in **Figure 8.4** on page 246. In fact, children's memories function so well that their testimony about events they have witnessed is usually accurate enough to be regarded as reliable in judicial proceedings (recall the Research Report in **Chapter 6**, which focused on Carole Peterson's studies of "Early Long-term Memories in Children"). Investigations of improvements in information processing skills such as memory provide developmentalists with a way of looking at cognitive development that is distinct from Piaget's theory.

PROCESSING EFFICIENCY **Processing efficiency**, the ability to make efficient use of short-term memory capacity, increases steadily with age, a change that most developmentalists now see as the basis for cognitive development (Case, 1985; Halford, Maybery, O'Hare, & Grant, 1994; Kuhn, 1992). The best evidence that cognitive processing becomes more efficient is that it gets steadily faster with age. Robert Kail has found virtually the same exponential increase in processing speed with age for a wide variety of tasks, including perceptual-motor tasks such as tapping in response to a stimulus (for example, pressing a button when you hear a buzzer) and cognitive tasks such as mental addition (Kail, 1991; Kail & Hall, 1994). He has found virtually identical patterns of speed increases in studies in cross-cultural studies.

AUTOMATICITY One of the most important ways in which processing efficiency grows in middle childhood is through the acquisition of **automaticity**, or the ability to recall information from long-term memory without using short-term memory capacity. For example, when children can respond "49" to the question "How much is 7 times 7?" without thinking about it, they have achieved automaticity with respect to that particular piece of information.

Automaticity is critical to efficient information-processing because it frees up short-term memory space for more complex processing. Thus, the child who knows "7 times 7" automatically can use that fact in a complex multiplication or division problem without giving up any of the short-term memory space he is using to solve the problem. As a result, he is better able to concentrate on the "big picture" instead of expending effort trying to recall a simple multiplication fact. Not surprisingly, researchers have found

processing efficiency
the ability to make efficient use of short-term memory capacity

automaticity
the ability to recall information from long-term memory without using short-term memory capacity

Experience with a teeter-totter, like this boy is getting, may be one source of knowledge about how balance scales work.
(*Photo:* Myrleen Ferguson/PhotoEdit)

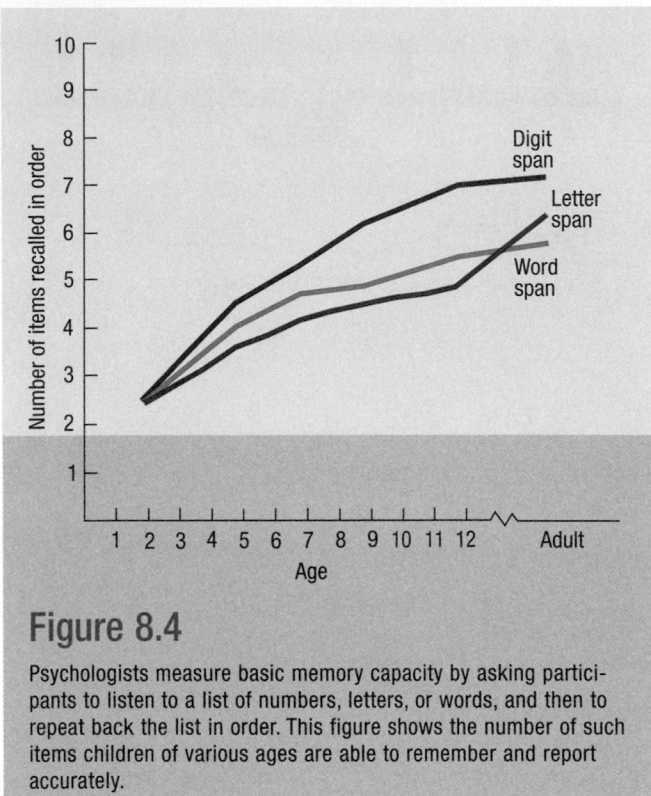

Figure 8.4

Psychologists measure basic memory capacity by asking participants to listen to a list of numbers, letters, or words, and then to repeat back the list in order. This figure shows the number of such items children of various ages are able to remember and report accurately.

(*Source:* Dempster, 1981, from Figures 1, 2, and 3, pp. 66, 67, 68.)

executive processes

information-processing skills that involve devising and carrying out strategies for remembering and solving problems

memory strategies

learned methods for remembering information

Unless they are rank novices, these school-aged chess players will remember a series of chess moves or an arrangement of chess pieces far better than adults who don't play chess.

(*Photo:* Elena Rooraid/PhotoEdit)

that elementary school children who have *automatized* basic math facts in this way learn complex computational skills more rapidly (Jensen & Whang, 1994).

Automaticity is achieved primarily through practice. For example, when babies first learn to walk, they must focus all their mental effort on the act of walking. After a few weeks of practice, walking becomes automatic, and they can think about chasing the family cat or retrieving a ball that has rolled away. Likewise, adults can think about the grocery list while driving to the supermarket, because driving skills and the routes they routinely use to get from place to place are automatized. Thus, automaticity is important to information processing throughout the lifespan. It is in middle childhood, however, that children seem to begin automatizing large quantities of information and skills at a fairly rapid rate.

EXECUTIVE AND STRATEGIC PROCESSES If you tried to recall a list of everyday items (chair, pencil, spaghetti, tree. . .), you might consciously consider the various alternative strategies for remembering and then select the best one. You could also explain some things about how your mind works, such as which kinds of mental tasks you find most difficult. These are examples of *metacognition*—knowing about knowing or thinking about thinking—a set of skills first mentioned in **Chapter 6**. Metacognition is part of a large group of skills known as **executive processes**—information-processing skills that allow a person to devise and carry out alternative strategies for remembering and solving problems. Executive processes are based on a basic understanding of how the mind works. Such skills improve a great deal during middle childhood. For example, 10-year-olds are more likely than 8-year-olds to understand that attending to a story requires effort (Parault & Schwanenflugel, 2000).

One of the advantages of having good metacognitive and executive processing skills is that they help the individual devise methods for remembering information, or **memory strategies**. Although many people possess their own unique methods for remembering, **Table 8.1** lists a few common memory strategies. For the most part, these memory techniques first appear between the ages of 6 and 12.

EXPERTISE There is a great deal of research showing that the amount of knowledge a person possesses makes a huge difference in how efficiently her information-processing system works. Children and adults who know a lot about a topic (dinosaurs, baseball cards, mathematics, or whatever it may be) categorize information about that topic in highly complex and hierarchical ways. They are also better at remembering and logically analyzing new information on that topic (Ni, 1998).

Even typical age differences in strategy use or memory ability disappear when the younger group has more expertise than the older. For example, psychologist Michelene Chi, in her now-classic early study, showed that expert chess players could remember the placement of chess pieces on a board much more quickly and accurately than novice chess players, even when the expert chess players were children and the novices were adults (Chi, 1978).

However, using advanced information-processing skills in their areas of expertise doesn't seem to help children's general memory and reasoning

TABLE 8.1	Some Common Information-Processing Strategies Used in Remembering

Strategy	Description
Rehearsal	Either mental or vocal repetition; may occur in children as young as 2 years under some conditions, and is common in older children and adults.
Organization	Grouping ideas, objects, or words into clusters to help in remembering them, such as "all animals," or "the ingredients in the lasagna recipe," or "the chess pieces involved in the move called castling." This strategy is more easily applied to something a person has experience with or particular knowledge about. Two-year-olds use primitive clustering strategies.
Elaboration	Finding shared meaning or a common referent for two or more things that need to be remembered.
Mnemonic	A device to assist memory; the phrase for the notes of the lines on the musical staff ("Every Good Boy Does Fine") is a mnemonic.
Systematic Searching	"Scanning" one's memory for the whole domain in which a piece of information might be found. Three- and 4-year-old children can begin to do this when they search for actual objects in the real world, but they are not good at doing this in memory. So search strategies may first be learned in the external world and then applied to inner searches.

(*Source:* Flavell, 1985.)

abilities (Ericsson & Crutcher, 1990). For this reason, many information-processing psychologists, such as the Canadian researcher Corinne Zimmerman, now believe that an individual's information-processing skills may depend entirely on the quantity and quality of relevant information stored in long-term memory. Thus, they say, to be able to learn scientific reasoning skills, for example, children must first acquire a body of knowledge about scientific topics (Zimmerman, 2000). To paraphrase developmental psychologist John Flavell, expertise makes any of us, including children, look very smart; lack of expertise makes us look very stupid (Flavell, 1986).

Before Going On

- Describe vocabulary growth and other advances in language that happen during the middle childhood years.

- What cognitive advantages do children gain as they move through Piaget's concrete operational stage?

- What is horizontal decalage, and how does Siegler explain concrete operational thinking?

- Explain the contributions of processing efficiency, automaticity, metacognition and strategic processes, and expertise to the development of information-processing skills.

SCHOOLING

As you learned at the beginning of this chapter, children all over the world begin school at age 6 or 7. Thus, an examination of the influence of this near-universal experience is important to understanding middle childhood.

LITERACY

In the industrialized world, *literacy,* the ability to read and write, is the focus of education in the 6- to 12-year-old period. As you learned in **Chapter 6,** the skills children bring to school from their early childhood experiences may influence early reading as much as formal instruction (Crone & Whitehurst, 1999). Especially significant among these skills is the set known as *phonological awareness.* Across the early elementary years, phonological awareness skills continue to increase (Shu, Anderson, & Wu, 2000). Thus, children who lack such expertise at the start of school are likely to fall behind unless some systematic effort is made by teachers to provide them with a base of phonological knowledge (Torgesen et al., 1999). However, all beginning readers, both those who have high levels of phonological awareness and those who know less about sounds and symbols, seem to benefit from specific instruction in sound–letter correspondences (Adams & Henry, 1997).

> ### Critical Thinking
>
> How do you think your elementary school experiences affected the rest of your life?

It also appears that beginning readers gain a significant advantage when they achieve automaticity with respect to identifying sound–symbol connections (Samuels & Flor, 1997). Thus, they need plenty of opportunities to practise translating written language into spoken words. For this reason, reading experts suggest that reading out loud is critical to success in the early years (Adams, 1990).

Once children have mastered the basic reading process, they are capable of learning about meaningful word parts, such as prefixes and suffixes, which then helps them to become more efficient readers and better understand what they read (Adams & Henry, 1997). At the same time, instruction in comprehension strategies, such as identifying the purpose of a particular text, also helps (Pressley & Wharton-McDonald, 1997). Of course, all along the way, children need to be exposed to good literature, both in their own reading and in what teachers and parents read to them.

Some of the strategies used to teach reading also help children learn writing, the other component of literacy. For example, instruction in sound–symbol connections helps children learn to spell as well as to read. Of course, good writing is far more than just spelling; it requires instruction and practice, just as reading does. Specifically, children need to learn about writing techniques such as outlining and paragraph development to become good writers. They also need to learn about language mechanics, such as grammar and appropriate uses of words, as well as how to edit their own and others' written work (Graham & Harris, 1997).

Despite educators' best efforts, many children fall behind their classmates in literacy during the early school years. In general, reading researchers have found that poor readers have problems with sound–letter combinations (Gonzalez & Valle, 2000; Mayringer & Wimmer, 2000). Thus, many children who have reading difficulties benefit from highly specific phonics approaches that provide a great deal of practice in translating letters into sounds and vice versa (Berninger et al., 1999).

However, curriculum flexibility is also important in programs for poor readers. Some do not improve when exposed to phonics approaches. In fact, programs that combine sound–letter and comprehension training, such as the Reading Recovery program, have proven to be highly successful in helping poor readers catch up, especially when the programs are implemented in the early elementary years (Klein & Swartz, 1996). Consequently, teachers need to be able to assess the effectiveness of whatever approach they are using and change it to fit the needs of individual students.

SCHOOLING AND COGNITIVE DEVELOPMENT

Studies across a variety of cultures—in Mexico, Peru, Colombia, Liberia, Zambia, Nigeria, Uganda, Hong Kong, and many other countries—have led to the conclusion that school experiences are indeed linked to the emergence of some advanced cognitive skills. For example, children who do not attend school proceed through Piaget's concrete operational stage at a much slower rate (Mishra, 1997). It's important to note, too, that most of these studies compared children who differed only in schooling; the children were of the same ethnicity and were similar in socioeconomic status.

You might think that rate of cognitive development doesn't matter, so long as everyone gets to the same place developmentally. However, longitudinal studies show that the rate of progression through the concrete operational stage predicts how well children will reason in adolescence and adulthood (Bradmetz, 1999). Thus, the cognitive-developmental advantage that a 6- to 12-year-old gains by attending school is one that probably lasts a lifetime.

Unschooled children are also less proficient at generalizing a learned concept or principle to some new setting. A good illustration comes from studies of South American street vendors, most of whom are of elementary school age. These children can carry out monetary calculations with lightning speed and impressive accuracy, yet they have trouble translating their mental calculations into written mathematical problems (Schliemann, Carraher, & Ceci, 1997). It seems that the "language" of mathematics that children learn in school helps them acquire number knowledge in a far more abstract way than children whose calculation skills originate exclusively from a practical context. Thus, attending school helps children learn to think—precisely what it is intended to do.

MEASURING AND PREDICTING ACHIEVEMENT

Canada lacks a single education system, since each province and territory is entitled to establish its own formal curriculum and school organization. Nonetheless, there has been some harmonization across the nation. For instance, Grades 6 and 10 have a common educational structure and content from province to province. Another initiative to harmonize education has been the creation of the Council of Ministers of Education, Canada (CMEC). The CMEC has been working on the development of a common Canadian curriculum and national testing standards with measurable outcomes for English, Math, and Science at Grades 3, 6, and 9 (Health Canada, 2001g).

Children's experiences in school are similar the world over. The similarities help explain why cognitive-developmental research involving 6- to 12-year-olds yields pretty much the same results in all cultures where children attend school. (*Photos, left to right:* A. Ramey/ Woodfin Camp and Associates; Tim Davis, Photo Researchers; S. Noorani, Woodfin Camp and Associates)

achievement test

a test designed to assess specific information learned in school

assessment

formal and informal methods of gathering information that can be used for programming to improve student learning. There are no grades or marks associated with assessment.

evaluation

the process of assigning a grade or mark to a student's performance, representing the student's highest, most consistent level of achievement over time

Standardized **achievement tests** are designed to assess specific information learned in school, using items like those in **Table 8.2.** Scores are based on comparison of an individual child's performance with those of other children in the same grade across Canada. Critics of achievement tests point out that although these tests are intended to measure what children learn in school, they are actually very similar to IQ tests. For example, suppose an achievement test contains the math problem "4 × 4." Bright children who have not yet learned multiplication may reason their way to the correct answer of 16. Others may answer correctly because they have learned it in school. Still others may know the answer because they learned to multiply from their parents. Thus, critics suggest that comprehensive portfolios of children's school work may be better indicators of actual school learning than standardized achievement tests (Neill, 1998). In comparison to achievement measures, educators conducting a student **assessment** will use a variety of formal and informal assessment tools to gather information that can be used to improve student learning at a developmentally appropriate level. Assessment is an ongoing process, and students are encouraged to be involved in the assessment process and in finding ways to improve.

In Canada, the trend is toward evaluating a student in terms of age-appropriate provincial or territorial standards. Accordingly, educators make an **evaluation** by calculating each student's highest, most consistent level of performance for each subject in order to assign a grade or level at any given point. This approach can offer a student a more valid measure of his achievement in terms of his own performance against the provincial standard rather than comparing his performance with that of his peers in the classroom (R. Windsor, personal communication, October 4, 2001). In contrast, the old model of evaluation served primarily to differentiate students based solely on their grade averages, and to "ultimately determine who [would] be eligible to attend post-secondary education and reap the status and economic rewards that typically result" (Health Canada: Trends in the Health of Canadian Youth, 2001g, p. 14).

Unlike in previous decades, intellectual assessment in Canadian schools is no longer routinely used to assess students. Intelligence testing (using tools like the WISC described in **Chapter 6**) is now primarily used to identify a student as exceptional in preparation for special educational programming support (R. Windsor, personal

---

TABLE 8.2	Some Sample Items from a Junior-Grade-Level Achievement Test

Vocabulary	**Reference Skills**	**Mathematics Computation**		
jolly old man	Which of these words	79	149	62
1. angry	would be first in ABC	+ 14	− 87	× 3
2. fat	order?			
3. merry	1. pair	**Mathematics**		
4. sorry	2. point			
	3. paint	What does the 3 in 13		
Language Expression	4. polish	stand for?		
Who wants ___ books?		1. 3 ones		
1. that	**Spelling**	2. 13 ones		
2. these	Jason took the *cleanest*	3. 3 tens		
3. them	glass.	4. 13 tens		
4. this	right ___ wrong ___			

(*Source:* From *Comprehensive Tests of Basic Skills*, Form S. Reprinted by permission of the publisher, CTB/McGraw-Hill, Del Monte Research Park, Monterey, CA 93940. Copyright © 1973 by McGraw-Hill, Inc. All rights reserved. Printed in the USA.)

No Easy Answers

IQ Testing in the

Schools

Although IQ tests are still a part of the process used to identify students with exceptionalities, they remain controversial. First, as you may remember from earlier discussions, IQ tests do not measure all the facets of a child's functioning that may be relevant. For example, intelligence tests do not measure other critical aspects of success in the classroom, such as motivation, attitude, and how well one gets along with others.

Second, there is the problem of the **self-ful-filling prophecy** that an IQ test score may foster. If a child is labelled a "slow learner" or "below average," his beliefs about his intellectual ability and his chances of being successful in school may start to lower. Lower expectations can lead to lowered effort and thus lower academic performance.

Labelling a child based on an IQ score can also have an effect on the expectations of others. Furthermore, once a child is labelled as "having" a particular IQ, that label tends to be difficult to remove. In a series of famous studies, psychologist Robert Rosenthal showed that a teacher's belief about a given student's ability and potential has a small but significant effect on her behaviour toward that student and on the student's eventual achievement (Rosenthal, 1994).

Another limitation of IQ tests is that they are biased in such a way that some minority groups of children are more likely to score high or low, even though their underlying ability is the same. The tests may contain items that are not equally familiar to all cultural groups, and thus can place those who are of other cultures at a disadvantage. In Canada, for instance, IQ tests have not been standardized on Aboriginal children (Darou, 1992). Many Aboriginal children score below average on verbal tests of IQ and average and above on nonverbal tests (Common & Frost, 1988).

Despite all the deficiencies of IQ test scores, they do accomplish the goal of predicting academic achievement and success in school. Educational success in our society is essential for helping a child acquire the basic skills needed to cope with the complexities of life in a technologically advanced country such as Canada. However, most developmentalists caution against using a single IQ test as the sole basis for making decisions about special education plans for a child, especially in the early elementary grades, when IQ test scores are not as reliable as they are later in childhood and in adolescence.

communication, October 4, 2001). In fact, some developmentalists say that the problem with relying on IQ tests to predict achievement is that they fail to provide a complete picture of mental abilities (see **No Easy Answers**). For example, psychologist Howard Gardner proposed a theory of *multiple intelligences* (Gardner, 1983). This theory claims there are eight types of intelligence:

self-fulfilling prophecy
when an expectation or belief causes a person to act in a way that is consistent with the expectations

- *Linguistic*—the ability to use language effectively. People who are good writers or speakers, who learn languages easily, or who possess a lot of knowledge about language possess greater than average linguistic intelligence.

- *Logical/mathematical*—facility with numbers and logical problem solving. Logical/mathematical intelligence enables individuals to learn math and to generate logical solutions to various kinds of problems.

- *Musical*—the ability to appreciate and produce music. Musicians, singers, composers, and conductors possess musical intelligence.

- *Spatial*—the ability to appreciate spatial relationships. Spatial intelligence is involved in the production and appreciation of works of art such as paintings and sculptures.

- *Bodily kinesthetic*—the ability to move in a coordinated way, combined with a sense of one's body in space. Professional athletes and top-notch amateur ones must possess high levels of this kind of intelligence.

- *Naturalist*—the ability to make fine discriminations among the flora and fauna of the natural world or the patterns and designs of human artifacts.

- *Interpersonal*—sensitivity to the behaviour, moods, and needs of others. "Helping" professionals—counsellors, social workers, clergy, and the like—usually need to have relatively high levels of interpersonal intelligence.

- *Intrapersonal*—the ability to understand oneself. People who are good at identifying their own strengths and choosing goals accordingly have high levels of intrapersonal intelligence.

Gardner's theory is based on observations of people with brain damage, mental retardation, and other severe mental handicaps. He points out that brain damage usually causes disruption of functioning in very specific mental abilities rather than a general decline in intelligence. He also notes that many individuals with mental deficits have remarkable talents. For example, some are gifted in music, while others can perform complex mathematical computations without using a calculator or pencil and paper.

Robert Sternberg's *triarchic theory of intelligence* proposes three components of human intelligence (Sternberg, 1988). *Contextual intelligence* has to do with knowing the right behaviour for a specific situation. For example, the South American street children you read about earlier (who are good at doing practical calculations but perform poorly on more abstract math problems) are highly "intelligent" in their daily context. However, in the school context, they appear to lack intellectual ability.

Experiential intelligence, according to Sternberg, is measured by IQ tests. It involves learning to give specific responses without thinking about them. For example, you can probably respond without thinking to the question "How much is 7 times 7?" IQ tests contain many such questions.

Componential intelligence is a person's ability to come up with effective strategies. To Sternberg, this is the most important component of intelligence. He claims that intelligence tests put more emphasis on "correctness" of answers than on the quality of the strategies people use to arrive at them.

In general, Sternberg says, IQ tests measure how familiar a child is with "school" culture. Thus, children whose cultural background does not include formal schooling perform poorly because they are unfamiliar with the context of the test. Unfortunately, their poor performance is often mistakenly interpreted to mean that they lack intelligence. Sternberg believes that intelligence tests should measure all three components of intelligence, and he has produced some research evidence suggesting that testing procedures based on his theory yield better predictions of performance than do conventional IQ tests (Sternberg, Wagner, Williams, & Horvath, 1995).

Both Gardner's and Sternberg's theories have become important in helping educators understand the weaknesses of IQ tests. Moreover, psychologist Daniel Goleman's theory of *emotional intelligence* has also added to scientists' understanding of intelligence and achievement (Goleman, 1995). Emotional intelligence has three components: awareness of one's own emotions, the ability to express one's emotions appropriately, and the capacity to channel emotions into the pursuit of worthwhile goals. Without emotional intelligence, Goleman claims, it is impossible to achieve one's intellectual potential. Indeed, research on the relationship between self-control (the third component of emotional intelligence) in early childhood and achievement in adolescence suggests that Goleman's view is correct. Children's ability to exercise control over their emotions in early childhood is strongly related to measures of academic achievement in high school (Shoda, Mischel, & Peake, 1990).

SCHOOL QUALITY, PARENT INVOLVEMENT, AND HOMESCHOOLING

Several factors shape achievement, but the quality of the school a child attends, along with the degree to which his or her parents are involved in the school, are among the most important. Some parents believe they can provide their children with a better education by teaching them at home.

EFFECTIVE SCHOOLS Researchers interested in possible effects of good and poor schools have most often approached the problem by identifying unusually *effective* schools (Good & Weinstein, 1986; Reynolds, 1992; Rutter, 1983). In this research, an effective school is defined as one in which pupils show one or more of the following characteristics at higher rates than would be predicted, given the kind of families or neighbourhoods the pupils come from:

- High scores on standardized tests
- Good school attendance
- Low rates of disruptive classroom behaviour and delinquency
- A high rate of later college attendance
- High self-esteem

Some schools seem to achieve these good outcomes year after year, so the effect is not just chance variation. When these successful schools are compared with others in similar neighbourhoods that have less impressive track records, certain common themes emerge. Interestingly, the characteristics of effective schools are similar to those of the authoritative parenting style. For example, effective schools have clear goals and rules, good control, good communication, and high nurturance. The same seems to be true of effective teachers: It is the "authoritative" teachers whose students do best academically. Such teachers have high expectations for their students and make sure that virtually all the students in their classes complete the year's normal work (MacIver, Reuman, & Main, 1995).

But as with any system, the quality of the whole school is more than the sum of the qualities of the teachers or classrooms. Each school also has an overall climate, or *ethos*, that affects its students. The most positive school climate is created when the principal provides clear and strong leadership, is dedicated to effective teaching, and gives concrete assistance to such teaching and when goals are widely shared.

PARENT INVOLVEMENT Canadian parents have typically been very involved in their children's education. For example, teachers have reported that two-thirds of their students had parents who were "very involved" in their children's education (Health Canada, 1999i). When parents come to parent–teacher conferences, attend school events, and get involved in supervising children's homework, children are more strongly motivated, feel more competent, and adapt better to school. They learn to read more readily, get better grades throughout elementary school, and stay in school for more years (Brody, Stoneman, & Flor, 1995; Grolnick & Slowiaczek, 1994; Reynolds & Bezruczko, 1993). The effects of parent involvement are similar for both poor and middle-class children, which indicates that the effect is not just a social class difference in disguise (Luster & McAdoo, 1996; Pianta, Steinberg, & Rollins, 1995; Reynolds & Bezruczko, 1993).

One of the characteristics of academically successful children is that their parents supervise their homework, as this father is doing. (*Photo:* Getty Images)

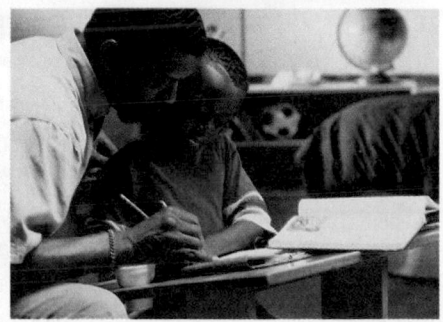

HOMESCHOOLING Most parents homeschool because they believe the dominant culture and its educational institutions are hostile to their religious beliefs. For example, many homeschooling parents don't want their children to learn about evolution or other ideas they feel will undermine the religious values they want their children to learn. Some want to protect their children from negative peer influences or school-based crime.

A few parents who have children with disabilities prefer teaching them at home to having them receive special-education services from local schools. The one-on-one teaching these children get at home often helps them achieve more than their disabled peers in public schools (Ensign, 1998). In addition, children with disabilities who are homeschooled don't have to deal with teasing from peers.

Research on homeschooling is sparse. Homeschooling advocates point to a small number of studies showing that homeschooled children are socially competent and emotionally well-adjusted and score above average on standardized achievement tests (Ray, 1999). However, opponents of homeschooling, a group that includes most professional educators, claim that comparisons of homeschooling and public education are misleading. They note that researchers have studied only homeschooled children whose families volunteer to participate in research studies. In contrast, most public school achievement test data are based on representative samples or on populations of entire schools.

Before Going On

- List the components of good literacy instruction.

- How do schooled and unschooled children differ in cognitive development?

- Describe the purpose and content of standardized achievement tests.

- What are the characteristics of effective schools, how does parent involvement affect children's academic achievement, and what are the issues surrounding homeschooling?

INDIVIDUAL AND GROUP DIFFERENCES

There are a number of individual and group variables that are associated with school performance (see **Table 8.3**). Various disabilities and attention problems are correlated with achievement in some way, as are language proficiency, sex, and culture. Canadian educators are now moving away from the use of labels for learning problems and instead place emphasis on a child's academic strengths and style of processing information in order to increase the likelihood of her school success (see **The Real World**).

LEARNING DISABILITIES

learning disability
a disorder in which a child has difficulty mastering a specific academic skill, even though she possesses normal intelligence and no physical or sensory handicaps

Some children are born with or develop differences that may significantly interfere with their education unless they receive some kind of special instruction. For instance, 10–15% of the Canadian population may experience learning problems that are a continuation of learning disabilities from early childhood (Learning Disabilities Association of Canada [LDAC], 2000). The **learning disability** concept itself is still controversial, but is generally associated with a difficulty in attaining a specific academic skill despite possessing average to above-average intelligence that is not due primarily to physical or scars, or congenital tumours, may develop in the brain during prenatal life. The growing brain compensates for these problems by "rewiring" around the problem areas. These rewirings, in turn, may scramble normal information-processing pathways just enough to make reading or calculation or some other specific task very difficult (Farnham-Diggory, 1992). There is also some evidence that learning disabilities, especially dyslexia, may have a genetic basis (Fiedorowicz et al., 1999, 2002; Gallagher, Frith, & Snowling, 2000).

When reading is the problem skill, the term **dyslexia** is often used (even though, technically speaking, *dyslexia* refers to a total absence of reading). Most children with reading disabilities can read, but not as well as others their age. Moreover, it appears that their skill deficits are specific to reading—such as an inability to automatize sound–letter correspondences—rather than the result of a general cognitive dysfunction (Wimmer, Mayringer, & Landerl, 1998).

School can be a discouraging and frustrating place for a child with a learning disability.
(*Photo:* Michael Newman/PhotoEdit)

ATTENTION-DEFICIT HYPERACTIVITY DISORDER

Some children experience learning difficulties that don't seem to fit the typical special education categories. For example, it is estimated that 5–10% of Canadian school children have a mental disorder called **attention-deficit hyperactivity disorder (ADHD)** (Romano, Baillargeon, & Tremblay, 2002). Children with ADHD are more physically active and/or less attentive than their peers. These characteristics often lead to both academic and behavioural problems in school. Therefore, ADHD is considered to be a mental disorder that may cause a child to develop school problems.

The cause of ADHD is unknown. However, some developmentalists suggest that children with ADHD are neurologically different from their peers. Specifically, some have asserted that children with ADHD have functional deficits in the right hemisphere of the brain (Sandson, Bachna, & Morin, 2000). Indeed, some type of biological factor does seem to be involved, as children who were born at 24 to 31 weeks of gestation are four to six times as likely to suffer from the symptoms of ADHD than their peers who were full-term infants (Barlow & Lewandowski, 2000). Other developmentalists hypothesize that children with ADHD require more sensory stimulation than their peers; thus, they move around more in order to get the stimulation they need (Antrop, Roeyers, Van Oost, & Buysse, 2000).

Psychologists are fairly sure that diet, environmental toxins, or brain damage is not the cause of ADHD, despite what some promoters of "cures" claim (Spreen, Risser, & Edgell, 1995). At present, most experts believe that each individual case of ADHD is caused by a complex interaction of factors that are unique to the specific child. These factors may include genetics, temperament, parenting styles, peer relations, the type and quality of school a child attends, and stressors in the child's life such as poverty, family instability, and parental mental illness.

Researchers at the Ontario Institute for Studies in Education (OISE) have been investigating the association between sleep problems and ADHD. They determined that one of the challenges of studying the relationship between ADHD and sleep problems is that both conditions are intertwined with multiple other conditions. Common to anxiety disorders, depressive disorders, and ADHD is a difficulty in falling asleep and/or staying asleep (Corkum, Moldofsky, Hogg-Johnson, Humphries, & Tannock, 1999). However, despite the difficulties of studying ADHD and sleep problems, there are some consistent findings. For example, ADHD children display more movements in their sleep when compared with children without the disorder (Corkum, Tannock, & Moldofsky,

dyslexia
problems in reading or the inability to read

attention-deficit hyperactivity disorder (ADHD)
a mental disorder that causes children to have difficulty attending to and completing tasks

true sleep
the number of minutes of sleep time excluding all periods of wakefulness, which can be distinguished by electroencephalograph (EEG) activity

1998). ADHD children also display instability in sleep onset, sleep duration, and **true sleep** (the number of minutes of sleep time excluding all periods of wakefulness, which can be distinguished by electroencephalograph [EEG] activity), and therefore it may be important to determine the impact that a disturbed sleep has on daytime behaviour (Gruber, Sadeh, & Raviv, 2000). For instance, sleep-deprived children may display hyperactivity, lack of coordination, and learning difficulty, all signs that could be mistaken for ADHD (Divgi, 2000). Low levels of true sleep time have been accurately predicted from teacher-reported behavioural symptoms such as attention and social problems (Aronen, Paavonen, Fjällberg, Soininen, & Törrönen, 2000).

On many kinds of attention tasks, ADHD children do not differ at all from normal children. They seem to vary from their normal peers in activity level, the ability to sustain attention (especially with boring and repetitive tasks), and the ability to control impulses. However, the degree of hyperactivity that ADHD children exhibit is unrelated to their performance on attention tasks. That is, a child can be very physically active and still be good at controlling his attention. Likewise, a child can be very calm yet have little ability to sustain attention. For this reason, there are now two types of ADHD: (1) the hyperactive/impulsive type, in which a high activity level is the main problem; and (2) the inattentive type, in which an inability to sustain attention is the major difficulty (American Psychiatric Association, 2000).

Most children with ADHD are successful in learning academic skills (Chadwick et al., 1999). However, their hyperactivity and/or inattentiveness often cause other kinds of problems. For one thing, children with both types of ADHD usually produce school work that is messy and filled with errors, causing them to get poor grades (Cahn et al., 1996). They may be disruptive in class and are often rejected by other children.

By the time their children are diagnosed with ADHD, usually upon entering school, many parents have lost confidence in their ability to control them (Barkley, 1990). Some cope with their difficult child by being extremely permissive. Others use commands and threats—"Go clean your room right now or I'll whip you with a belt." Thus, parent training can be useful in helping parents cope with children who have ADHD.

Make the Connection

Now that you know more about learning disabilities, look back at **Chapter 3** and review the prenatal factors, such as maternal smoking, that increase the likelihood that a child will suffer from such problems.

The goal of such parenting programs is to help parents regain a sense of control (Barkley, 1990). For example, experts recommend that teachers provide parents with daily reports of their children's work in the various school subjects—language, math, social studies, and so on. Parents can then use the information to enforce a standing rule that the child must have completed all school work before watching television or doing other desired activities. Such approaches, when applied consistently, can help parents of children with ADHD manage their children's difficulties, as well as their own emotional reactions, more effectively.

Many children with ADHD take stimulant medications, such as methylphenidate (Ritalin). About 70% of those who do are calmer and can concentrate better. However, some studies show that many children's "response to the medication" may actually be due to changes in expectations on the part of their teachers and parents—sort of a self-fulfilling prophecy (Spreen, Risser, & Edgell, 1995). In addition, studies suggest that the concentration skills of children with ADHD can be improved with training. For example, one study found that the attention skills of a group of children with ADHD were similar to those of a control group of children without attention difficulties following an intensive 18-week training program (Semrud-Clikeman et al., 1999).

It's also important to note that medication doesn't always improve the grades of children with ADHD. Rather, for the most part, it seems that stimulant medications reduce such children's activity levels, help them control their impulses, and somewhat improve their social behaviour. These effects usually result in improvements in classroom behaviour and peer acceptance. Medications such as methylphenidate have the greatest effect on school grades among children whose ADHD symptoms are so severe

Developmental Psychology in Your Career

Developmental Services Worker/Educational Assistant

Occupation	**Developmental Services Worker/Educational Assistant**
Description	• work with an educational team of teachers, counsellors, educational professionals, and families in a variety of educational settings • under the direction of a teacher, provide instructional, behavioural, physical/medical support to help students with exceptionalities maximize their learning potential
Entry Credentials	• 2-year Developmental Services Worker, Educational Assistant, or Teaching Assistant college diploma or a 1-year post-diploma/degree Educational Assistant college certificate
Essential Lifespan Development Knowledge	• developmental/educational principles and theories • exceptionalities including pervasive developmental disorders, developmental disabilities, learning disabilities, attention-deficit and disruptive behaviour disorders, childhood mental disorders, and physical disabilities • behavioural management and crisis intervention techniques
Essential Lifespan Development Skills	• assist students who have severe intellectual, sensory, emotional, social, behavioural, and/or medical difficulties to attain realistic and achievable goals • assist with educational remediation interventions • apply developmentally appropriate intervention strategies for life and/or living skills development • observe, record, and track students' behaviour and progress
Lifespan Development and Essential Professional Attitude	• interact in a professional manner with students, families, and other educational staff and community professionals • ensure confidentiality • be safety-conscious to maintain a safe work environment
Lifespan Development Career Profile: Dr. Danielle Renaud, Professor, Developmental Services Worker Program, Human Services Division, Fanshawe College, London, Ontario, and private consultant	"The role of an EA has evolved tremendously over the past few years to be more academically oriented and comprehensive than ever before. EAs need to know a great deal about child development, as well as about developmental and learning disabilities, in order to be of appropriate assistance to those students with whom they work. Since most EAs work one-to-one or with small groups, a thorough knowledge and understanding of each child's abilities, potential, and needs is essential." September 29, 2004
Lifespan Development Career Profile: Carol Prechotko, BA, BEd, Professor, Developmental Services Worker Program, Cambrian College	"Job opportunities and demand for Developmental Services Workers have expanded over the last 25 years. Developmental Services Workers utilize knowledge and skills in human development, community inclusion, and social skills training, and principles of learning and behaviour change. This knowledge base is useful in a variety of community settings for children and adults with developmental disabilities such as specialized residential and day program settings, supported employment, and in the school system as educational assistants." October 21, 2004

that they interfere with actual learning (Spreen, Risser, & Edgell, 1995). For this reason, the use of stimulant medications for children who have mild or moderate ADHD symptoms is controversial. Furthermore, Canadian pediatricians caution that there is a lack of evidence about the long-term effectiveness of stimulant medications beyond four weeks of treatment (Schachter, Pham, King, Langford, & Moher. 2001).

SECOND-LANGUAGE LEARNERS

Worldwide patterns of population growth and movement have led to tremendous increases in the number of children attending school in Canada, the United States, Great Britain, and Australia. Educators in English-speaking countries use the term *Limited English Proficient* (LEP) to refer to non-English-speaking children—either immigrant children or native-born children. There are analogous language challenges for educators in those parts of Canada where French is the dominant language but children are not proficient in French.

Historically, Canada has been host to waves of immigrants from all parts of the world. Most recently, immigrant children under age 15 have arrived from Asia and the Pacific Region (44%) and Africa and the Middle East (22%). Of these children, 5 in 10 landed in Ontario, 2 in 10 in British Columbia, and slightly more than 1 in 10 in Quebec. More than two-thirds of the children were unable to speak either official language when they arrived (BC Stats, 1998; Canadian Council on Social Development [CCSD], 1999a). This has resulted in abnormally high levels of official language deficiency in children in our school system, especially in these three provinces. In the Lower Mainland school districts of British Columbia, for instance, ESL enrolment has more than tripled since 1990, and a large majority of these new students are unfamiliar with both the Roman alphabet and Western cultural practices (British Columbia Ministry of Education, 2001). In the Toronto District School Board (the largest school board in Canada and one of the largest in North America), 41% of the students in elementary schools have a language other than English as their first language. This problem is compounded by the fact that there are more than 80 languages from all over the world represented in the Board's schools (Toronto District School Board, 2001).

Bilingual education is a logistical challenge for most school districts that include LEP children. For one thing, if a school system has only a handful of students who speak a particular language, it is not financially feasible to establish a separate curriculum for them. In addition, it may be impossible to find bilingual teachers for children whose language is spoken by very few people outside their country of origin. For these reasons, most LEP students are enrolled in **English-as-a-second-language (ESL) programs**, or if they intend to learn the French language, they are enrolled in French-as-a-second-language (FSL) programs (Canadian Parents for French [CPF], 2001). In ESL programs, children spend part of the day in classes to learn English and part in academic classes that are conducted entirely in English.

Research has shown that no particular approach to second-language learners is more successful than any other (Mohanty & Perregaux, 1997). There is some indication that programs that include a home-based component, such as those that encourage parents to learn the new language along with their children, may be especially effective (Koskinen et al., 2000). But it seems that any structured program, whether bilingual education or ESL, fosters higher achievement among non-English-speaking children than simply integrating them into English-only classes, an approach called *submersion*. Although most children in submersion programs eventually catch up to their English-speaking peers, many educators believe that instruction that supports children's home language and culture as well as their English-language skills enhances their overall development (Cushner, McClelland, & Safford, 1992).

bilingual education
an approach to second-language education in which children receive instruction in two different languages

English-as-a-second-language (ESL) program
an approach to second-language education in which children attend English classes for part of the day and receive most of their academic instruction in English

With respect to achievement, LEP students' performance in school is very similar to that of English-speaking children (NCES, 1997b). In fact, in American schools, native-born English-speaking children are more likely to fail one or more grades than children whose home language is either Asian or European. An exception is Spanish-speaking children, who fail in American schools at about the same rate as English speakers. Thus, there is no evidence that a child who enters school with limited English skills has any greater risk of failure than native-born students.

A cautionary note is necessary, however: An LEP student does not have an increased risk of failure as long as the school provides some kind of transition to English-only instruction and school officials take care to administer all standardized tests in the language with which the child is most familiar (Cushner, McClelland, & Safford, 1992). Providing a transition to English-only instruction is necessary to optimize the LEP child's potential for achievement. Testing children in their native language ensures that non-English-speaking children will not be misclassified as developmentally delayed or learning disabled because of their limited English skills.

BILINGUAL EDUCATION

Most Canadians have one of Canada's official languages, either English (59.2%) or French (23.3%), as their first language (Statistics Canada, 2000a). Since its experimental roots at St. Lambert in Quebec in 1965, French Immersion programs have become a successful fixture of our Canadian education system and a model for teaching a second language throughout the world (Lambert & Tucker; 1972; Safty, 1995). Children enrolled in early French Immersion programs are taught exclusively in French from kindergarten through to Grade 2 within the classroom. Starting in Grade 3, subjects taught in English are incrementally introduced every year until they receive instruction in both languages approximately equally in the senior grades.

Although initially there is some delay in English language development, by the later grades French Immersion students' English skills are indistinguishable from those of students taught in English (Holobow, Genesee, & Lambert, 1991). By age 15 French Immersion students of both genders have significantly higher reading achievement scores than their nonimmersion counterparts (Allen, 2004). In addition, French Immersion students achieve high proficiency in the French language (Harley & Jean, 1999). Ellen Bialystok (1999) of York University found that early immersion education not only facilitated both spoken and written language skills but also aspects of thinking, such as improved selective attention on nonlanguage tasks.

The process of learning to read, write, and speak a second language instils an appreciation for another culture; provides an alternative way to think about and value the world; and encourages children to become more objective and open-minded (Canadian Heritage, 1999). With more than 60 nonofficial languages spoken in Canada, heritage language programs are available in order to help families pass on their language and culture of origin (Settlement.org, 2001). Inherent in federal, provincial, and territorial legislation and policy is the recognition that heritage languages are fundamental to the preservation of the multicultural nature of our country. There is a particular need to preserve the languages of Canadian Aboriginal peoples, since their culture is based on oral tradition and is expressed most fully through their primary heritage language. Historically, more than 60 Aboriginal languages were spoken in Canada, but most are either lost or endangered because there are so few people left who can speak these languages (Kirkness, 1999). Heritage language education needs to consist of formal, structured programs designed to increase students' knowledge of these languages.

SEX DIFFERENCES IN ACHIEVEMENT

Comparisons of IQ test scores for boys and girls do not reveal consistent differences. It is only when the total scores are broken down into several separate skills that some serious and perplexing patterns of sex differences emerge. Recent studies from across Canada show that girls outperform boys in reading and writing (HRDC, 2001b) and in math (although it has been commonly thought that boys were superior in math) on provincial standards tests. Additionally, while girls surpass the provincial standards, boys mostly fail to even meet them (Fine, 2000a; Fine, 2000b). The question of where such differences come from remains unanswered. So far, environmental explanations have proven to be more useful than biological theories, particularly in relation to language skills. Some argue that in the early grades boys lack role models with whom they can identify, since most teachers at that level are females. Others suggest that the reading material for boys does not match their interests.

Before Going On

- Describe the controversy surrounding the term "learning disability."
- How does attention-deficit hyperactivity disorder affect a child's development?
- What is the difference between a bilingual and an ESL program? Is one approach more effective than the other?
- How do developmentalists explain sex differences in math achievement?

Summary

Physical Changes

- Physical development from age 6 to age 12 is steady and slow. Sex differences in bone and skeletal maturation may lead boys and girls to pursue different activities.
- Major brain growth spurts occur in 6- to 8-year-olds and in 10- to 12-year-olds. Neurological development leads to improvements in selective attention, information-processing speed, and spatial perception.
- School-aged children require regular medical check-ups. Accidental injuries and obesity are the most prevalent health problems of this age group.

Cognitive Changes

- Language development continues in middle childhood, with vocabulary growth, improvements in grammar, and understanding of the social uses of language.
- Piaget proposed that a major change in the child's thinking occurs at about age 6, when the child begins to understand powerful operations such as reversibility, addition, and serial ordering. The child also learns to use inductive logic, but does not yet use deductive logic.

- Research on this period confirms many of Piaget's descriptions of sequences of development but calls into question Piaget's basic concept of stages. The "operations" he observed may actually be rules for solving specific types of problems.

- Most information-processing theorists conclude that there are no age-related changes in children's information-processing capacity, but there are clearly improvements in speed and efficiency.

Schooling

- To become literate, children need specific instruction in sound–symbol correspondences, word parts, and other aspects of written language. They also need to be exposed to good literature and to have lots of opportunities to practise their reading and writing skills.

- School has a significant effect in fostering the 6- to 12-year-old's shift to a more abstract or strategic form of thinking. Children who lack school experience show less skill of this type.

- School progress in children with exceptionalities is sometimes assessed with both IQ tests and achievement tests. Both types of tests may ignore important aspects of intellectual functioning.

- Successful or effective schools have many of the same qualities seen in authoritative families: clear rules, good control, good communication, and nurturance. Parent involvement is also important. Some parents choose to educate their children at home, but opponents say that there is insufficient research on the cognitive and social effects of homeschooling.

Individual and Group Differences

- Canadian school children with exceptionalities receive special education services while remaining integrated within the classroom.

- Many children with attention-deficit hyperactivity disorder have problems in school but do not fit well into traditional special education categories.

- Children with limited English perform as well as English-speaking peers when they receive specific kinds of support in school.

- There are no sex differences in overall IQ scores, but girls do somewhat better on reading, writing, and math tasks. There is as yet no clear agreement on how to explain such differences.

Key Terms

achievement test (p. 250)

assessment (p. 250)

association areas (p. 237)

attention-deficit hyperactivity disorder (ADHD) (p. 257)

automaticity (p. 245)

bilingual education (p. 260)

class inclusion (p. 243)

concrete operations (p. 242)

deductive logic (p. 242)

dyslexia (p. 257)

English-as-a-second-language (ESL) program (p. 260)

evaluation (p. 250)

exceptional child (p. 255)

executive processes (p. 246)

Individual Education Plan (IEP) (p. 255)

inductive logic (p. 242)

learning disability (p. 254)

memory strategies (p. 246)

modified program (p. 255)

obese (p. 240)

overweight (p. 240)

processing efficiency (p. 245)

program accommodation (p. 255)

relative right-left orientation (p. 238)

selective attention (p. 237)

self-fulfilling prophecy (p. 251)

spatial cognition (p. 238)

spatial perception (p. 238)

true sleep (p. 258)

Weblinks

Children and Youth Obesity
www.centre4activeliving.ca/Education/Resources/CYObesity.html
This Alberta Centre for Active Living webpage has links to a variety of websites that focus on childhood obesity.

"Video Games and Violence" by Derrick Janushewski and Myna Truong
http://socserv2.socsci.mcmaster.ca/soc/courses/stpp4C03/ClassEssay/videogames.htm
This article examines degrees of violence in video and computer games, outlines the limiting conditions on violent effects, and presents policies and recommendations for game regulation.

Canada's School Net
www.schoolnet.ca/
This Industry Canada website has over 7000 links to information and communications technologies resources for teachers, students, and parents alike.

Autism Society of Canada
http://autismsocietycanada.ca/
A primary source for Canadian information about autism spectrum disorders, support services, and resources.

Learning Disabilities Association of Canada
www.ldac-taac.ca/
Canada's central repository for the latest information about learning disabilities, practical solutions, and extensive resources and supports.

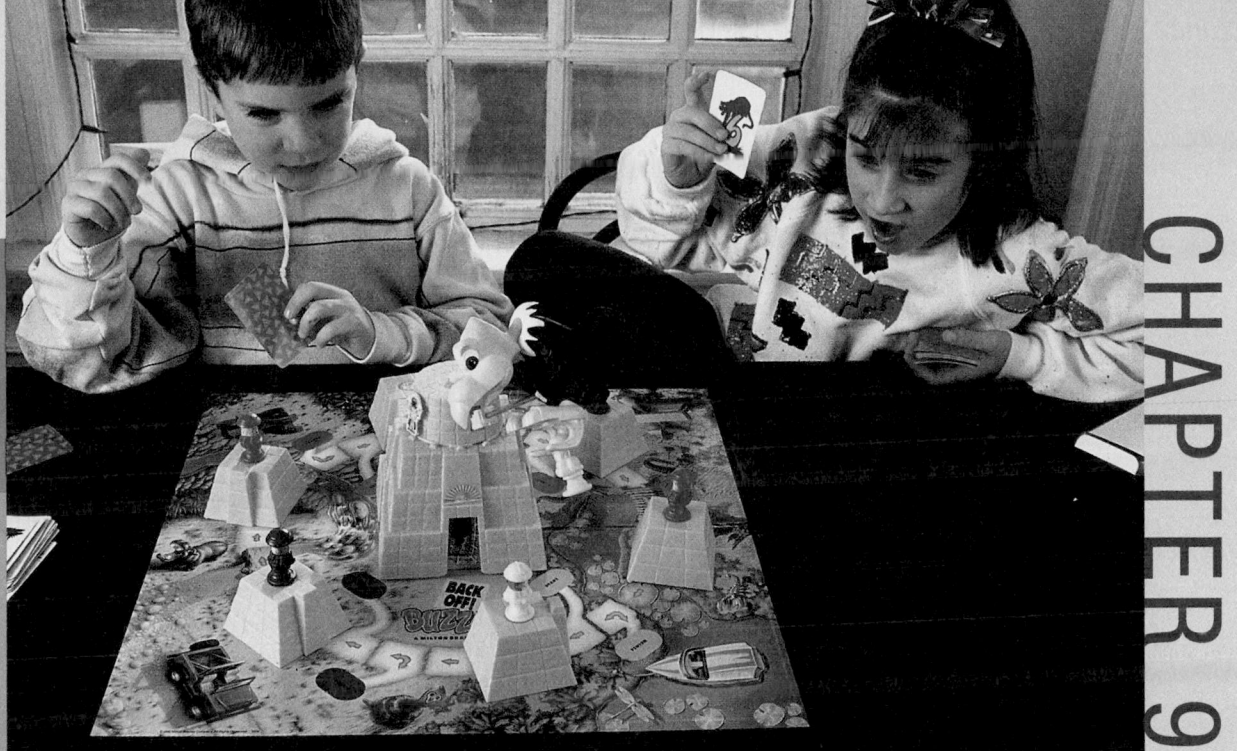

John Collett/Stock Boston

CHAPTER 9

SOCIAL AND PERSONALITY DEVELOPMENT IN MIDDLE CHILDHOOD

One mother who also happened to be a student in a developmental psychology graduate program had gotten into the habit of trying out research tasks on her 7-year-old daughter, Allison, before using them in actual research. One morning, she asked the girl what she wanted to wear to school. Allison answered, "Do you really want to know, or is this just another one of your studies?" Like most 6- to 12-year-olds, Allison wanted her mother to think of her as an individual, not just another 7-year-old. Children of this age are beginning to realize that they are unique, and they want their uniqueness to be recognized by parents and others.

At the same time, children of this age want to fit into the social world in a meaningful way. Every culture in the world has a *society of childhood*, in which children make up their own social rules that differ from those of adult society. For example, in most Canadian school lunchrooms, food trading is common. A child who refuses to trade may be seen as "stuck-up." But adults who try to talk co-workers into trading lunches are likely to be thought of as pushy or somewhat odd. Such comparisons show that children practise social competence by making up their own social rules rather than simply copying those that exist in the adult world. Creating and enforcing such rules helps children learn to look at things from other people's points of view and to cooperate.

In this chapter, you will read more about the psychoanalytic and social-cognitive approaches to social and personality development. You will also learn about the three dimensions of moral development—emotions, reasoning, and behaviour—that are the focus of theory and research. As in earlier chapters covering social and personality development, we will explore social relations, personality, and self-concept. We will also discuss how variables such as after-school care, poverty, and television influence the 6- to 12-year-old's development. As you read, keep the following questions in mind:

- What major points do psychoanalytic and social-cognitive theorists make about social and personality development in middle childhood? How do the major theories explain the three dimensions of moral development?
- How do 6- to 12-year-olds relate to parents, siblings, and peers?
- How do personality and self-concept change in middle childhood?
- What are the characteristics of school-aged children who care for themselves after school or who live in poverty? How does television influence development?

THEORIES OF SOCIAL AND PERSONALITY DEVELOPMENT

As you should remember from previous chapters, psychoanalytic theorists explain social and emotional development in terms of a struggle between internal drives and cultural demands. You should also recall that social-cognitive theorists have a very different view: The child's growing understanding of the world provides the impetus for social and emotional development.

PSYCHOANALYTIC PERSPECTIVES

latency stage
the fourth of Freud's psychosexual stages, during which 6- to 12-year-olds' libido is dormant while they establish relationships with same-sex peers

Freud believed that children between age 6 and age 12 repress sexual desires in order to concentrate on developing friendships with members of the same sex and learning academic and social skills. Freud called this period of development the **latency stage**. From

Freud's perspective, the important thing about school aged children's social behaviour is their preference for same-sex friends.

According to Erikson, children between 6 and 12 face a psychosocial crisis that he called the **industry versus inferiority stage**, during which they develop a sense of their own competence through the achievement of culturally defined learning goals (see **Table 2.2** on page 30). The psychosocial task of the 6- to 12-year-old is development of industry, or the willingness to work to accomplish goals. To develop industry, the child must be able to achieve the goals her culture sets for all children her age. In most countries, 6- to 12-year-olds must learn to read and write. If they fail to do so, Erikson's view claims they will enter adolescence and adulthood with feelings of inferiority.

Research suggests that Erikson was right about the link between school experiences and an emerging sense of competence. It seems that most 6- to 12-year-olds gradually develop a view of their own competence as they succeed or fail at academic tasks such as reading and arithmetic (Chapman & Tunmer, 1997; Skaalvik & Valas, 1999). Thus, their self-assessments and actual achievements are strongly correlated; that is, those who are most successful judge themselves to be highly competent, while those who have difficulty perceive themselves as less competent.

industry versus inferiority stage
the fourth of Erikson's psychosocial stages, during which children develop a sense of their own competence through mastery of culturally defined learning tasks

Critical Thinking

Think back to your own elementary school experiences. Do you think you gained a sense of industry or inferiority from them? How did they affect your subsequent development?

SOCIAL-COGNITIVE PERSPECTIVES

As you read in **Chapter 8**, the school-aged child can understand conservation in part because he can ignore the appearance of change and focus on the underlying continuity. Similarly, a number of early ground-breaking social-cognitive studies demonstrated that the child of this age looks beyond appearances and searches for deeper consistencies that will help him to interpret both his own and other people's behaviour.

Like their understanding of the physical world, 6- to 12-year-olds' descriptions of other people move from the concrete to the abstract. If you ask a 6- or 7-year-old to describe others, he will focus almost exclusively on external features—what the person looks like, where he lives, what he does. This description by a 7-year-old boy, taken from a classic study of social-cognitive development, is typical:

> He is very tall. He has dark brown hair, he goes to our school. I don't think he has any brothers or sisters. He is in our class. Today he has a dark orange [sweater] and gray trousers and brown shoes. (Livesley & Bromley, 1973, p. 213)

When young children do use internal or evaluative terms to describe people, they are likely to use quite global ones, such as "nice" or "mean," "good" or "bad." Further, young children do not seem to see these qualities as lasting or general traits of the individual, applicable in all situations or over time (Rholes & Ruble, 1984). In other words, the 6- or 7-year-old has not yet developed a concept that might be called "conservation of personality."

Beginning at about age 7 or 8, a rather dramatic shift occurs in children's descriptions of others. The child begins to focus more on the inner traits or qualities of another person and to assume that those traits will be visible in many situations (Gnepp & Chilamkurti, 1988). Children this age still describe others' physical features, but their descriptions are now used as examples of more general points about internal qualities. You can see the change when you compare the 7-year-old's description given above with this description by a child nearly 10 years old:

> He smells very much and is very nasty. He has no sense of humor and is very dull. He is always fighting and he is cruel. He does silly things and is very stupid. He has brown

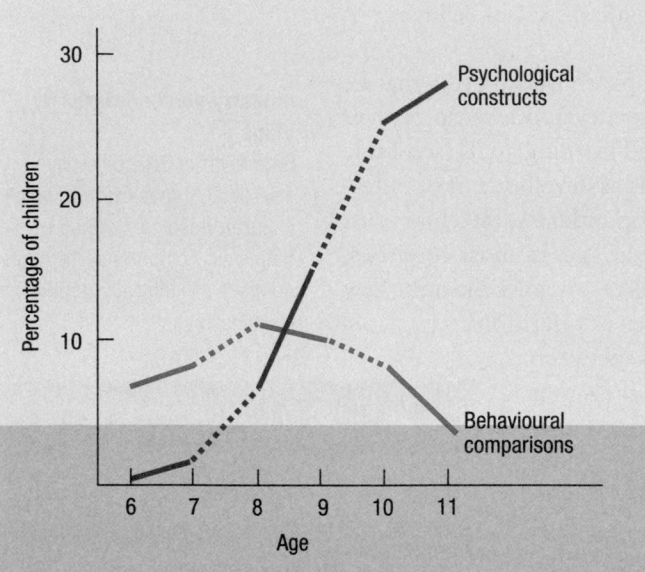

Figure 9.1

These data from Barenboim's study show the change in children's descriptions of their peers during the years of middle childhood. The solid lines represent longitudinal data, the dashed lines cross-sectional comparisons.

(*Source:* Barenboim, 1981, Figure 1, p. 134.)

hair and cruel eyes. He is sulky and 11 years old and has lots of sisters. I think he is the most horrible boy in the class. He has a croaky voice and always chews his pencil and picks his teeth and I think he is disgusting. (Livesley & Bromley, 1973, p. 217)

This description still includes many external physical features but goes beyond such concrete surface qualities to the level of personality traits, such as lack of humour and cruelty.

The movement from externals to internals in descriptions of others is well documented by research. For example, in one important early study, researchers asked 6-, 8-, and 10-year-olds to describe three other children; a year later, they asked them to do the same thing again (Barenboim, 1981). **Figure 9.1** shows the results for two of the categories used in the study's data analysis. A *behavioural comparison* was any description that involved comparing a child's behaviours or physical features with those of another child or with a norm—for example, "Billy runs a lot faster than Jason," or "She draws the best in our whole class." Any statement that involved some internal personality trait was referred to as a *psychological construct*, such as "Sarah is so kind," or "He's a real stubborn idiot!" You can see that behavioural comparisons peaked at around age 8 but psychological constructs increased steadily throughout middle childhood.

Before Going On

- How do Freud and Erikson characterize social and personality development in 6- to 12-year-olds?
- In what ways do children's descriptions of others change in middle childhood?

DIMENSIONS OF MORAL DEVELOPMENT

One of parents' and teachers' greatest concerns is helping children learn to be good people, to do the "right" thing according to the standards and values of their culture. Moral development is very complex. To understand it fully, we must take into account psychoanalytic, cognitive-developmental, and learning theories.

MORAL EMOTIONS

According to Freud, the child learns moral rules by identifying with the same-sex parent during the phallic stage (ages 3 to 6). In other words, boys learn moral rules from their fathers, and girls learn them from their mothers. The rules a child learns from the same-sex parent form the child's *superego,* or internal moral judge. Thus, Freud's theory claims that, by 6, a child has learned all she will ever know about moral rules.

According to Freud, the superego has two parts: a *conscience* and an *ego ideal.* The **conscience** is a list of things that "good boys" and "good girls" don't do, such as telling lies. The **ego ideal** is a list of things that "good boys" and "good girls" do, such as obeying parents. When a child disobeys her conscience, she feels guilt. When she fails to live up to the standards set by the ego ideal, she feels shame. Freud believed that the child learns to obey the rules of her conscience and ego ideal to avoid these uncomfortable feelings.

To better understand Freud's idea about how the superego works, think about a hungry 7-year-old at the grocery store. He can figure out how to take a candy bar without anyone noticing. However, his superego classifies this behaviour as stealing, and thinking about stealing a candy bar makes him feel guilty. This creates a conflict for him. If he steals the candy, he'll feel guilty. If he doesn't, he'll be hungry. If he has a healthy personality, Freud believed, he will obey his superego even though it will cause him to be hungry.

Erikson's views on moral development are similar to Freud's. However, Erikson believed that children learn moral rules from both parents. Erikson's theory also claims that pride is just as important to moral development as guilt and shame. For example, if the boy decides not to take the candy, he will not only avoid feeling guilty, but will also feel pride in his ability to resist temptation.

During the last decade, there has been a resurgence of interest in moral emotions among developmentalists (Eisenberg, 2000). Research has shown that, as Freud and Erikson predicted, feelings of guilt, shame, and pride develop before age 6 (Fung, 1999; Kochanska, Casey, & Fukumoto, 1995). Researchers infer that children are experiencing shame when they try to hide an act they know to be wrong. During the 6- to 12-year-old period, most children define "shame" as the emotion people experience when others find out that they have done something wrong (Levorato & Donati, 1999). Adolescents' understanding of shame, predictably, is more complex. They tell researchers that people experience shame when they fail to live up to their own standards of behaviour as well as when their wrongdoing is exposed to others.

Connections between moral emotions and moral behaviour may depend on cognitive development (Hoffman, 1988). Early in middle childhood, children connect moral feelings with adult observation. They seem to think that they should feel guilty or ashamed only if a parent or teacher sees them commit a violation of a moral rule. Thus, a 7-year-old candy thief is unlikely to feel guilty unless he gets caught in the act. Later, at about 10 or 11, when children better understand moral feelings, they are more likely to make behavioural choices based on how guilty, ashamed, or proud they think they will feel. For example, an older boy who wants candy at the grocery store will be more likely to choose not to take the candy because he knows resisting temptation will make him feel proud of himself.

conscience
the list of "don'ts" in the superego; violation of any of these rules leads to feelings of guilt

ego ideal
the list of "do's" in the superego; failure to live up to any of these leads to feelings of shame

Critical Thinking

Think about your own conscience and ego ideal. What kinds of prohibitions are contained in your conscience? How do you feel when you violate them? What are the standards of your ego ideal? Under what circumstances do you experience shame?

MORAL REASONING

Moral reasoning is the process of making judgments about the rightness or wrongness of specific acts. As you learned in **Chapter 7,** children learn to discriminate between intentional and unintentional acts between age 2 and age 6. However, using this understanding to make moral judgments is another matter. Piaget claimed that the ability to use reasoning about intentions to make judgments about the moral dimensions of behaviour appears to emerge along with concrete operational reasoning.

moral realism stage
the first of Piaget's stages of
moral development, in which
children believe rules are
inflexible

moral relativism stage
the second of Piaget's stages
of moral development, in which
children understand that many
rules can be changed through
social agreement

PIAGET'S MORAL REALISM AND MORAL RELATIVISM Piaget explained moral conduct by studying how cognitive and social factors act upon each other with reciprocal influence. For instance, he studied moral development by observing children playing games. As he watched them play, Piaget noticed that younger children seemed to have less understanding of the rules. Following up on these observations, Piaget questioned children of different ages about rules. Their answers led him to propose a two-stage theory of moral development (Piaget, 1932).

At the beginning of the middle childhood period, children are in what Piaget termed the **moral realism stage**. They believe that the rules of games can't be changed because they come from authorities, such as parents, government officials, or religious figures. For example, one 6-year-old told Piaget that the game of marbles was invented on Noah's ark. He went on to explain that the rules can't be changed because the "big ones," meaning adults and older children, wouldn't like it (Piaget, 1965, p. 60).

Moral realists also believe that all rule violations eventually result in punishment. For example, Piaget told children a story about a child who fell into a stream when he tried to use a rotten piece of wood as a bridge. Children younger than 8 told him that the child was being punished for something "naughty" he had done in the past.

After age 8, Piaget proposed, children move into the **moral relativism stage**, in which they learn that people can agree to change rules if they want to. They realize that the important thing about a game is that all the players follow the same rules, regardless of what those are. For example, 8- to 12-year-olds know that a group of children playing baseball can decide to give each batter four strikes rather than three. They understand that their agreement doesn't change the game of baseball and that it doesn't apply to other people who play the game. At the same time, children of this age get better at following the rules of games.

Eight- to 12-year-olds also know that you don't get punished for rule violations unless you get caught. As a result, they view events like the one in which the child fell into the stream as accidents. They understand that accidents are not caused by "naughty" behaviour. Children older than 8 also understand the relationship between punishment and intentions. For example, Piaget's research suggests that children over 8 can distinguish between a child who unintentionally left a store without paying for a candy bar and another who deliberately took it. Older children are likely to say that both children should return or pay for the candy, but only the one who intentionally stole it should be punished.

Research by University of Toronto psychologists Zelazo, Helwig, and Lau (1996) supports Piaget's claim that children over 8 give more weight to intentions than consequences when making moral judgments. However, although their thinking is more mature than that of preschoolers, 6- to 12-year-olds' moral reasoning is still highly egocentric. For example, every parent has heard the exclamation "It's not fair!" when a child fails to receive the same treat or privilege as a sibling. It is rare, if not completely unknown, for a 6- to 12-year-old to protest the fairness of receiving something that a sibling didn't. Thus, school-aged children still have a long way to go with respect to mature moral reasoning, and we will return to this topic in the chapters on adolescent development (see **The Real World**).

KOHLBERG'S THEORY OF MORAL DEVELOPMENT Building on and revising Piaget's ideas, Lawrence Kohlberg pioneered the practice of assessing moral development by presenting a series of dilemmas in story form, each of which highlighted a specific moral issue, such as the value of human life. One of the most famous of these stories is the dilemma of Heinz, a man whose wife is dying of a disease for which a new, expensive medicine has been developed. Heinz, who can't afford the medicine, must choose between stealing it or allowing his wife to die. After hearing this story, the child or young

The Real World
Parenting
Encouraging Moral Reasoning

In his book *Raising Good Children*, developmental psychologist Thomas Lickona reminds readers that the development of mature moral reasoning takes many years (Lickona, 1983). At the same time, he offers parents and teachers several suggestions that will help them help their 6- to 12-year-olds prepare for movement to more mature levels. Following are some of his suggestions:

• Require kids to give reasons for what they want.

• Play developmentally appropriate games with them.

• Praise them for observing social conventions such as saying "please" and "thank you."

• When punishment is necessary, provide them with an explanation, advice on how to avoid punishment in the future, and a way of repairing any damage their misbehaviour has caused.

• Teach them about reciprocity: "We do nice things for you, so you should be willing to help us."

• Give them meaningful chores so that they will think of themselves as important family and community members.

• Help and encourage them to base obedience on love and respect rather than fear.

• Teach them religious and philosophical values, including the idea that some actions are right and others are wrong, regardless of circumstances.

• Challenge their egocentrism by asking questions such as, "How would you feel if someone did that to you?" when they violate others' rights.

• Include them in charitable projects, such as food drives, to extend the idea of love and caring beyond their own families.

person is asked a series of questions—for example, "Should Heinz have stolen the drug? What if Heinz didn't love his wife, would that change anything?" On the basis of the answers to such questions about moral dilemmas, Kohlberg concluded that moral reasoning develops in six stages.

Because school-aged children seldom exhibit moral reasoning beyond Kohlberg's first stage, you won't read about his stages in detail until **Chapter 11**. However, at this point, it's important for you to know that Kohlberg and his colleagues carried out a significant number of longitudinal and cross-cultural studies. Taken together, these studies strongly supported the notion that moral reasoning develops in stages, just as both Piaget and Kohlberg believed, and that the stages are linked to progression through Piaget's concrete operational and formal operational stages (Colby, Kohlberg, Gibbs, & Lieberman, 1983; Nisan & Kohlberg, 1982; Snarey, Reimer, & Kohlberg, 1985; Walker, 1989).

MORAL BEHAVIOUR

Learning theorist B.F. Skinner proposed that consequences teach children to obey moral rules. According to Skinner, adults reward children with praise for morally acceptable behaviour and punish children for morally unacceptable behaviour. As a result, acceptable behaviour increases and unacceptable behaviour decreases as children get older. Consequences certainly do influence children's behaviour. However, both praise and punishment are more effective when they are combined with instruction, an approach called *inductive discipline* that you read about in **Chapter 7**.

Punishment may actually interfere with moral development (Hoffman, 1988). For example, if a child's parent spanks him in the grocery store parking lot for having stolen a candy bar, the parent hopes that the spanking will teach the child that stealing is wrong. However, the child may learn only that he can't steal when he's with the parent. Similarly, when punishment is severe or embarrassing, children may be distracted from making the connection between the behaviour and the punishment. A child who has stolen candy may be so angry at his parent for embarrassing him with a public spanking that he concentrates all his attention on his anger. As a result, he fails to realize that his choice to steal caused the spanking (Hoffman, 1988).

Upon discovering that a 7-year-old had stolen a candy bar, a parent who uses inductive discipline would respond by telling the child privately that it is wrong to take things that don't belong to you, even if you are very hungry. Next, the parent would require the child to correct the wrong done to the store by admitting his crime, apologizing to the cashier or manager, and paying for the candy. Finally, the 7-year-old would probably have to repay his parents in some way if he used their money to pay for the stolen candy. Such a process allows the child to learn both that it is wrong to steal and that, when a moral rule is broken, something must be done to set things right again (Zahn-Waxler, Radke-Yarrow, & King, 1979).

As you may recall from **Chapter 2**, social-learning theorist Albert Bandura claims that children learn more from observing others than from either rewards or punishments. His theory predicts that, when a child sees someone rewarded for a behaviour, she believes that she will also be rewarded if she behaves in the same way. Similarly, when she sees a model punished, she assumes that she will also experience punishment if she imitates the model's behaviour (Bandura, 1977a, 1989). For example, a story about a child who was praised by a parent for resisting the temptation to steal may teach the child who hears or reads it that resisting temptation is praiseworthy. Conversely, when a child is exposed to a story about a boy or girl who steals and doesn't get caught, she may learn that it's possible to steal without getting caught.

Before Going On

- What do psychoanalytic theorists emphasize in their explanations of moral development in middle childhood?

- How do cognitive-developmental theorists such as Piaget and Kohlberg explain 6- to 12-year-olds' moral development?

- According to learning theorists, what do reinforcement, punishment, and modelling contribute to moral development?

SOCIAL RELATIONSHIPS

School-aged children's growing ability to understand others changes their social relationships in important ways. Children continue to be attached to parents, but they are becoming more independent. Relationships with peers become more stable and many ripen into long-term friendships. In fact, the quality of 6- to 12-year-olds' peer relationships shapes their futures in many important ways.

FAMILY RELATIONSHIPS

Middle childhood is a period of increasing independence of child from family and is reflected in the declining amount of time that children spend with their parents.

University of Waterloo researcher Jiri Zuzanek (2000) reports that, after age six, parents spend less time looking after children's physical needs. He also found that the level of social and emotional support lessens considerably once children reach adolescence to the point where, on average, parents spend 11 minutes a day caring for their teens and only two minutes socializing with them. Yet, attachments to parents and relationships with siblings continue to be important.

One way that parents can remain connected with their children is by having family meals together. Recent studies have found that the single best predictor of better childhood outcomes, regardless of family structure, socioeconomic factors or time spent in school, church, playing sports, or involved in the arts, was having family meals together (five or more meals per week with a parent) (Council of Economic Advisers to the President, 2000; Hofferth, 2001). Children who had regular meals with a parent had significantly better academic success and fewer behavioural problems. Similarly, teens who ate dinner regularly with a parent had significantly better academic success and psychological adjustment, and lowered rates of smoking, drinking, drug use, early sexual activity, violence, and suicide attempts. As an added health bonus, children and teens who regularly ate dinners with their family had nutritionally superior diets (Gillman, et al., 2000).

THE CHILD'S UNDERSTANDING OF FAMILY ROLES AND PROCESSES As social-cognitive theory would predict, school-aged children understand family roles and relationships much better than younger children do. For example, psychologist Jenny Jenkins of the University of Toronto found that, by about age 9, children who live in two-parent homes understand that their parents' roles as parents are distinct from their roles as partners or spouses (Jenkins & Buccioni, 2000). Thus, a 9-year-old is better able than a 5-year-old to understand when divorcing parents say that their love for the child hasn't changed, even though their relationship with each other has ended. Emotionally, the divorce experience may be just as difficult, but school-aged children are more capable of understanding it cognitively.

School-aged children also know that marital conflict often arises when spouses have different goals (Jenkins & Buccioni, 2000). Moreover, while younger children seem to believe that the only solution for marital conflict is for one spouse to give in to the other, school-aged children appear to understand that spouses can compromise.

ATTACHMENT It would be a great mistake to assume that, because school-aged children are more independent than they were when younger, the parent–child attachment relationship has weakened. School-aged children continue to use their parents as a safe base; they continue to rely on their presence, support, and affection (Buhrmester, 1992). The quality of a school-aged child's attachment to his parents is also strongly related to his ability to maintain friendships with peers (Lieberman, Doyle, & Markiewicz, 1999). In addition, positive attitudes toward peers are related to quality of attachment in children of this age (Anan & Barnett, 1999).

What does change, though, is the agenda of issues between parent and child. When the child reaches elementary school, disciplinary interactions with parents decline. Key issues now include children's household responsibilities, whether they will receive allowances or be paid for chores, standards for school performance, and the like (Furnham, 1999; Maccoby, 1984): "Is it okay for Joe to stop off at his friend's house after school without asking ahead of time? How far from home may Diana ride her bike?" In many non-Western cultures, parents must also begin to teach children quite specific tasks, such as agricultural work and care of younger children or animals, all of which may be necessary for the survival of the family.

self-regulation
children's ability to conform to parental standards of behaviour without direct supervision

PARENTAL EXPECTATIONS The parent–child agenda changes because parents of 6- to 12-year-olds recognize their children's growing capacity for **self-regulation**, the ability to conform to parental standards of behaviour without direct supervision. Cultures differ to some degree in the specific age at which they expect this to occur. In general, though, most cultures expect 6- to 12-year-olds to be able to supervise their own behaviour at least part of the time.

Some studies suggest that there are sex differences in parents' expectations with respect to self-regulatory behaviour. For example, mothers make different kinds of demands on boys and girls. They appear to provide both with the same types of guidance, but are more likely to give boys more autonomy over their own behaviour than girls. Nevertheless, they are also more likely to hold daughters to a higher standard of accountability for failure than boys (Pomerantz & Ruble, 1998). Developmentalists speculate that this difference may lead to stronger standards of behaviour for girls in later developmental periods.

PARENTING FOR SELF-REGULATION Researchers have learned that there are several parenting variables that contribute to the development of self-regulation. First, the parents' own ability to self-regulate is important, perhaps because they are providing the child with models of good or poor self-regulation (Prinstein & La Greca, 1999). Also, the degree of self-regulation expected by parents influences the child's self-regulatory behaviour. Higher expectations, together with parental monitoring to make certain the expectations are met, are associated with greater self-regulatory competence (Rodrigo, Janssens, & Ceballos, 1999).

You should recall that such parental behaviours are associated with the authoritative style of parenting. Longitudinal research has demonstrated that school-aged children whose parents have been consistently authoritative since they were toddlers are the most socially competent (Baumrind, 1991). Children rated "competent" were seen as both assertive and responsible in their relationships; those rated "partially competent" typically lacked one of these skills; those rated "incompetent" showed neither. In Baumrind's (1991) study, the majority of children from authoritative families were rated as fully competent, while most of those from neglecting families were rated as incompetent.

A study of Canadian mothers and their children was conducted by Rosemary Mills of the University of Manitoba and Kenneth Rubin of the University of Maryland to see if maternal methods of control were related to childhood aggression and social withdrawal. They studied children in kindergarten and Grades 2 and 4 and found that mothers who were behaviourally overcontrolling (e.g., gave more compliance commands, punishment, criticism, or demonstrated greater devaluation of the child than other parents) had children who were socially withdrawn. In comparison, mothers of aggressive children were generally undercontrolling (e.g., were overly permissive and made fewer requests and were less responsive to a child's behaviour) (Mills & Rubin, 1998).

SIBLINGS AND ONLY CHILDREN As a general rule, sibling relationships seem to be less central to the lives of children in this age range than relationships with either friends or parents (Buhrmester, 1992). Elementary school children are less likely to turn to a sibling for affection than to parents and are less likely to turn to a brother or sister for companionship or intimacy than they are to a friend.

However, sibling relationships vary enormously. On the basis of direct studies of young children as well as retrospective reports by young adults about their sibling relationships when they were of school age, researchers have identified several patterns, or styles, of sibling relationships (Murphy, 1993; Stewart, Beilfuss, & Verbrugge, 1995):

- A *caregiver* relationship, in which one sibling serves as a kind of quasi-parent for the other (this pattern seems to be more common between an older sister and a younger brother than for any other combination)

- A *buddy* relationship, in which both members of the pair try to be like each other and take pleasure in being together

- A *critical,* or *conflictual,* relationship, which includes teasing, quarrelling, and attempts by one sibling to dominate the other

- A *rival* relationship, which contains many of the same elements as a critical relationship but is also low in any form of friendliness or support

- A *casual* relationship, in which the siblings have relatively little to do with one another

Rival or critical relationships seem to be more common when siblings differ in age by 4 years or less (Buhrmester & Furman, 1990). Caregiver or buddy relationships appear to be somewhat more common in pairs of sisters. Rivalry seems to be highest in boy–boy pairs (Buhrmester & Furman, 1990; Stewart et al., 1995).

People often speculate that only children, those without siblings, are deprived of an important developmental experience. Until recently, single-child families were fairly unusual. China's policy of encouraging families to have no more than one child has provided developmentalists with a unique opportunity to carry out research involving large numbers of only children. This research suggests that only children are no different from children with siblings in any important way (Wang et al., 2000). Research involving only children in other countries suggests that if any differences do exist, children without siblings seem to have the advantage. Only children tend to have higher achievement test scores, to be more obedient, and to experience better peer relationships than those who have siblings (Doh & Falbo, 1999; Falbo, 1992).

FRIENDSHIPS

The biggest shift in relationships during middle childhood is the increasing importance of peers, particularly close friends. Social-cognitive researcher Robert Selman was one of the first to study children's understanding of friendships. He found that if you ask preschoolers and young school-aged children how people make friends, the answer is usually that they "play together" or spend time physically near each other (Damon, 1977, 1983; Selman, 1980).

In the later years of middle childhood, at around age 10, this view of friendship gives way to one in which the key concept seems to be reciprocal trust (Chen, 1997). Older children see friends as special people who possess desired qualities other than mere proximity, who are generous with each other, who help and trust each other, and so on. **Figure 9.2** (page 296) is a 10-year-old boy's definition of a friend. His characterization of a friend as someone "you can trust," who "will always be there for you when you are feeling down in the dumps" and "always sits by you at lunch," illustrates the older child's understanding of dimensions of friendships such as trust, emotional support, and loyalty.

Evidence of the centrality of friends to social development in middle childhood also comes from studies of children's behaviour within friendships. Children are more open and more supportive when with their chums, smiling at, looking at, laughing with, and touching one another more than when they are with nonfriends; they talk more with friends and cooperate and help one another more. Pairs of friends are also more successful than nonfriends are in solving problems or performing some task together. Yet school-aged children are also more critical of friends and have more conflicts with them; they

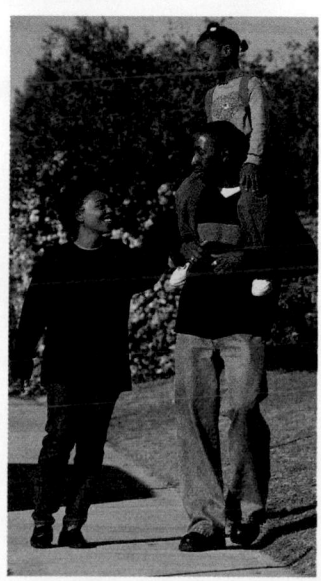

Research suggests that only children are just as well adjusted as those who have siblings.
(*Photo:* Michael Newman/PhotoEdit)

> My definition of a good friend is someone who you can trust. They will never turn their back on you. They will always be there for you. when you are feeling down in the dumps. They'll try to cheer you up, They will never forget about you.   They'll always sit next to you at lunch,

Figure 9.2

This essay on friendship written by a 10-year-old illustrates the way older school-aged children think about friends.

(Courtesy of Denise Boyd. Used with permission.)

are more polite with strangers (Hartup, 1996). At the same time, when conflicts with friends occur, children are more concerned about resolving them than they are about settling disagreements with nonfriends. Thus, friendship seems to represent an arena in which children can learn how to manage conflicts (Newcomb & Bagwell, 1995).

Canadian researchers have found that social competence is closely related to a reduction in both internalizing and externalizing behaviour problems in children (Craig, Peters, & Willms, 2002). Unfortunately, as peers begin to play a larger role in social development during late childhood, there are fewer opportunities for parents or educators to teach social skills to children who need them. Just as children are put into supervised activities in and out of school to develop their athletic and artistic skills, they also need opportunities to get involved with other children in enjoyable activities that support "skills in forming and maintaining positive relationships, dealing with conflict, and understanding their own feelings and behaviour" (Craig, Peters, & Willms, 2002, p. 326). In this way, as children develop their social skills, they become better equipped to build meaningful friendships, which would reduce their likelihood of having behaviour problems.

Critical Thinking

Do you still have any friends from your elementary school years? If not, why do you think those early friendships did not survive? If you do, what do you think differentiates an early friendship that survives from one that does not?

GENDER SEGREGATION

Possibly the most striking thing about peer group interactions in the elementary school years is how gender-segregated they are. This pattern seems to occur in every culture in the world and is frequently visible in children as young as 3 or 4. Boys play with boys and girls play with girls, each in their own areas and at their own kinds of games (Cairns & Cairns, 1994; Harkness & Super, 1985). In fact, gender seems to be more important than age, race, or any other categorical variable in 6- to 12-year-olds' selection of friends; in addition, the strength of children's preference for same-sex associates increases substantially across middle childhood (Graham, Cohen, Zbikowski, & Secrist, 1998). Moreover, gender segregation is unrelated to sex differences in parenting, suggesting that it is a feature of 6- to 12-year-olds' social relationships that they construct for reasons of their own (McHale, Crouter, & Tucker, 1999).

Shared interests and activities are a critical part of friendship in the early years of middle childhood. For example, rough-and-tumble play is common in boy–boy interactions but is typically avoided by girls. Thus, based on activity preferences, boys gravitate to other boys in social situations. In so doing, they learn how to socialize with other boys, but acquire few of the skills, such as self-disclosure, used by girls in their interactions (Phillipsen, 1999). Thus, boys establish stable peer groups with dominance hierarchies that are based on rough-and-tumble play skills (Pelligrini & Smith, 1998). A similar pattern exists for girls: Gender segregation begins with shared activity preferences but leads to the development of social skills that are more useful in interactions with other girls than in interactions with boys.

In middle childhood, boys play with boys and girls play with girls. In fact, children's play groups are more sex-segregated at this age than at any other.
(*Photos: top*, Jeffry W. Myers/Stock Boston; *bottom*, Mary Kate Denny/ PhotoEdit)

However, there are some ritualized "boundary violations" between boys' and girls' groups, such as chasing games. For example, in one universal series of interactions, a girl taunts a boy with a statement like "You can't catch me, nyah nyah." Next, a boy chases and catches her, to the delight of both of their fully supportive same-sex peer groups (Thorne, 1986). As soon as the brief cross-gender encounter ends, both girl and boy return to their respective groups. On the whole, however, girls and boys between the ages of 6 and 12 actively avoid interacting with one another and show strong favouritism toward their own gender and negative stereotyping of the opposite gender (Powlishta, 1995).

Gender segregation patterns are even more pronounced in friendships during middle childhood. For example, when researchers ask children to describe the kind of playmate a fictional child would prefer, school-aged children's predictions are largely gender-based (Halle, 1999). Girls' and boys' friendships also differ in quality in intriguing ways. Boys' friendship groups are larger and more accepting of newcomers than are girls'. Boys play more outdoors and roam over a larger area in their play. Girls are more likely to play in pairs or in small, fairly exclusive groups, and they spend more playtime indoors or near home or school (Benenson, 1994; Gottman, 1986).

Sex differences also characterize the interaction between a pair of friends, as you learned in **Chapter 7**. Boys' friendships appear to be focused more on competition and dominance than are girls' friendships (Maccoby, 1995). In fact, among school-aged boys, researchers see higher levels of competition between pairs of friends than between strangers—the opposite of what is observed among girls. Friendships between girls include more agreement, more compliance, and more self-disclosure than is true between boys. For example, "controlling" speech—a category that includes rejecting comments, ordering, manipulating, challenging, defiance, refutation, or resistance of another's attempts to control—is twice as common among pairs of 7- and 8-year-old male friends as among pairs of female friends of that age (Leaper, 1991). Among the 4- and 5-year-olds in Leaper's study, there were no sex differences in controlling speech, suggesting that these differences in interaction pattern arise during middle childhood.

None of this information should obscure the fact that the interactions of male and female friendship pairs have much in common. For example, collaborative and cooperative exchanges are the most common forms of communication in both boys' and girls' friendships in middle childhood. And it is not necessarily the case that boys' friendships are less important to them than girls' are to them. Nevertheless, it seems clear that there are gender differences in form and style that may well have enduring implications for patterns of friendship over the lifespan.

Furthermore, school-aged children appear to evaluate the role of gender in peer relationships in light of other variables. For example, when asked whether a fictitious boy would prefer to play with a boy who is a stranger or with a girl who has been his friend for a while, most school-aged children say the boy would prefer to play with the friend (Halle, 1999). Such results suggest that, even though gender is clearly important in school-aged children's peer relationships, they are beginning to understand that other factors may be more important. This is yet another example of how children's growing cognitive abilities—specifically, their ability to think about more than one variable at a time—influence their ideas about the social world.

A study of Canadian children shows that about three-quarters of children between Grades 6 and 10 say they have two or more close friends. The percentage of close friendships dips in Grade 9, probably because this is typically a transition year to secondary school and is associated with difficulty in establishing relationships with new fellow students. By age 13, about half of both boys and girls find it easier to talk to opposite-sex friends about more intimate topics (Health Canada, 2001g).

PATTERNS OF AGGRESSION

You may remember from **Chapter 7** that physical aggression declines over the preschool years, while verbal (indirect) aggression increases. Research on Canadian children shows that in middle childhood, physical aggression becomes even less common as children learn the cultural rules about when it is acceptable to display anger or aggression and how much of a display is acceptable (Tremblay, 2000; Tremblay et al., 1996). In contrast, boys at every age show more physical aggression and more assertiveness than do girls, both within friendship pairs and in general (Fabes, Knight, & Higgins, 1995; Tremblay, 2000). Furthermore, school-aged boys often express approval for the aggressive behaviour of peers (Rodkin, Farmer, Pearl, & Van Acker, 2000). **Table 9.1** gives representative data from a very large, carefully conducted Canadian survey, in which teachers completed checklists describing each child's behaviour (Offord, Boyle, & Racine, 1991). It is clear that boys are described as far more aggressive on all of this study's measures of physical aggressiveness.

Results like these have been so clear and so consistent that most psychologists have concluded that boys are simply "more aggressive." But that conclusion may turn out to be wrong. Instead, it begins to look as if girls simply express their aggressiveness in a different way, using what has recently been labelled *relational aggression,* instead of physical aggression. Physical aggression hurts others physically or poses a threat of such damage; **relational aggression** is aimed at damaging the other person's self-esteem or peer relationships, such as by ostracism or threats of ostracism ("I won't invite you to my birthday party if you do that"), cruel gossip, or facial expressions of disdain. Children are genuinely hurt by such indirect aggression, and they are likely to shun others who use this form of aggression a lot (Casas & Mosher, 1995; Cowan & Underwood, 1995; Crick & Grotpeter, 1995; Rys & Bear, 1997).

Girls are much more likely than boys to use relational aggression, especially toward other girls, a difference that begins as early as the preschool years and becomes very marked by Grade 4 or 5. For example, in one study of nearly 500 children in Grades 3 through 6, researchers found that 17.4% of the girls but only 2% of the boys were rated high in relational aggression—almost precisely the reverse of what is observed for physical aggression (Crick & Grotpeter, 1995). Researchers do not yet know whether this difference in form of aggression has some hormonal/biological basis or is learned at an

relational aggression
aggression aimed at damaging another person's self-esteem or peer relationships, such as by ostracism or threats of ostracism, cruel gossiping, or facial expressions of disdain

early age, or both. They do know that higher rates of physical aggression in males have been observed in every human society and in all varieties of primates. And scientists know that some link exists between rates of physical aggression and testosterone levels (e.g., Susman et al., 1987). But the origin of girls' apparent propensity toward relational aggression is still an open question.

Retaliatory aggression—aggression to get back at someone who has hurt you—increases among both boys and girls during the 6- to 12-year-old period (Astor, 1994). Its development is related to children's growing understanding of the difference between intentional and accidental actions. For example, if a child drops his pencil in the path of another child who is walking by and that child happens to kick the pencil across the floor, most 8-year-olds can identify this as an accident. Consequently, the child whose pencil was kicked feels no need to get back at the child who did the kicking. However, children over 8 view intentional harm differently. For example, let's say that one child intentionally takes another's pencil off her desk and throws it across the room. Most children over 8 will try to find a way to get back at a child who does something like this. In fact, children who don't try to retaliate in such situations are also more likely to be seen as socially incompetent and to be bullied by their peers in the future (Astor, 1994).

Peers may approve of retaliatory aggression, but most parents and teachers strive to teach children that, like other forms of intentional harm, such behaviour is unacceptable. Research suggests that children can learn nonaggressive techniques for managing the kinds of situations that lead to retaliatory aggression. In one program, called PeaceBuilders, psychologists have attempted to change individual behaviour by changing a school's overall emotional climate. In this approach, both children and teachers learn to use positive social strategies (Flannery et al., 2000). For example, both are urged to try to praise others more often than they criticize them. Research suggests that when such programs are integrated into students' classes every day for an entire school year or longer, aggression decreases and prosocial behaviour increases. Thus, aggressive interactions between elementary school children may be common, but they do not appear to be an inevitable aspect of development.

SOCIOECONOMIC STATUS (SES) AND FAMILIAL FACTORS OF AGGRESSION

Tremblay et al. (1996) found that there were social class and family differences in rates of aggression in children. In lower SES boys, for instance, the incidence of both physical and indirect forms of aggression was higher, appeared at an earlier age (preschool),

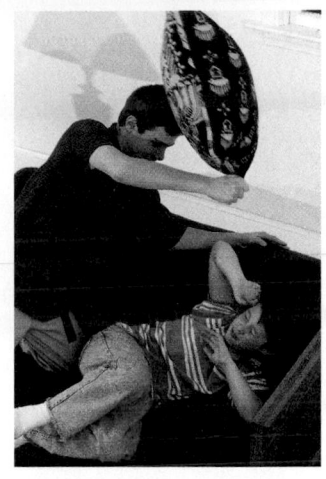

Why do you think competition is such a strong feature of friendship interactions among boys? Do you think this is true in every culture? (*Photo:* Vincent De Witt/Stock Boston)

retaliatory aggression
aggression to get back at someone who has hurt you

TABLE 9.1	Aggressive Behaviour in Boys and Girls Aged 4 to 11	
Percentages as Rated by Teachers		
Behaviour	**Boys**	**Girls**
Mean to others	21.8	9.6
Physically attacks people	18.1	4.4
Gets in many fights	30.9	9.8
Destroys own things	10.7	2.1
Destroys others' things	10.6	4.4
Threatens to hurt people	13.1	4.0

(*Source:* Offord, Boyle, Racine, 1991, from Table 2.3, p. 39.)

and persisted throughout childhood. The corresponding rates of aggression were proportionally less in boys who came from families with higher SES. Similarly, it was found that girls in lower SES families displayed both more physical and indirect aggression than girls from higher SES families.

Another strong predictor of aggression was family influence. Specifically, 38% of the variance in physical aggression and 43% of indirect aggression was found to be attributed to familial factors. The levels of aggressiveness among siblings were especially comparable in lower SES families. Moreover, physically aggressive boys were also more likely to have siblings who displayed both emotional disorders and hyperactivity. Aggressive girls were also more likely to have siblings who were more aggressive and had behavioural problems.

SOCIAL STATUS

social status

an individual child's classification as popular, rejected, or neglected

Developmentalists measure popularity and rejection by asking children to list peers they would not like to play with or by observing which children are sought out or avoided on the playground. These techniques allow researchers to group children according to the degree to which they are accepted by peers—a variable often called **social status**. Typically, researchers find three groups: *popular, rejected,* and *neglected.*

Some of the characteristics that differentiate popular children from those in the other two groups are things outside a child's control. In particular, attractive children and physically larger children are more likely to be popular. Conversely, being very different from her peers may cause a child to be neglected or rejected. For example, shy children usually have few friends (Fordham & Stevenson-Hinde, 1999). Similarly, highly creative children are often rejected, as are those who have difficulty controlling their emotions (Aranha, 1997; Maszk, Eisenberg, & Guthrie, 1999).

However, children's social behaviour seems to be more important than looks or temperament. Most studies show that popular children behave in positive, supporting, nonpunitive, and nonaggressive ways toward most other children. They explain things, take their playmates' wishes into consideration, take turns in conversation, and are able to regulate the expression of their strong emotions. In addition, popular children are usually good at regulating their own emotions and accurately assessing others' feelings (Underwood, 1997).

There are two types of rejected children. *Withdrawn/rejected* children realize that they are disliked by peers (Harrist, Zaia, Bates, Dodge, & Pettit, 1997). After repeated attempts to gain peer acceptance, these children eventually give up and become socially withdrawn. As a result, they often experience feelings of loneliness. *Aggressive/rejected* children are often disruptive and uncooperative and usually believe that their peers like them (Zakriski & Coie, 1996). Many appear to be unable to control the expression of strong feelings (Eisenberg et al., 1995; Pettit, Clawson, Dodge, & Bates, 1996). They interrupt their play partners more often and fail to take turns in a systematic way.

As you learned in **Chapter 7**, aggressive behaviour persists into adulthood in some individuals, and it is most likely to become a stable characteristic among children who are *both* aggressive and rejected by peers (see the **Research Report**). Of course, not all aggressive children are rejected. Among girls, aggression, whether physical or relational, seems to lead to peer rejection consistently. Among boys, however, aggression may result in either popularity or rejection (Rodkin et al., 2000; Xie, Cairns, & Cairns, 1999). For instance, Université Laval psychologists François Poulin and Michel Boivin have been studying the role of aggression in the formation and development of boys' friendships in Grades 4 through 6. They found that irrespective of aggressive boys' general popularity, their close friends tend to be aggressive as well. Furthermore, aggressiveness seems

Research Report

Long-Term Consequences of Childhood Aggression and Peer Rejection

As you learned in **Chapter 7**, early childhood aggression becomes a lifelong pattern of behaviour for some children. However, the correlations between childhood aggression and social difficulties in adulthood become even stronger once children reach middle childhood. Here are a few of the relevant research findings:

- Psychologist Leonard Eron, in an important 22-year longitudinal study, found a high level of aggressiveness toward peers at age 8 to be related to criminal behaviour at age 30 (Eron, 1987, p. 439).

- In the Concordia Project, in Canada, psychologists studied several thousand boys who were initially identified by their peers in Grade 1, 4, or 7 as either highly aggressive, withdrawn, or both (Serbin, Moskowitz, Schwartzman, & Ledingham, 1991). By adulthood, 45.5% of the aggressive men had appeared in court, compared with only 10.8% of the nonaggressive men.

- A longitudinal study of 400 working-class boys in England, which began when they were 8 and continued until they were in their 30s, found that those who were rated by their teachers as most aggressive at ages 8, 10, and 12 were twice as likely as their less aggressive peers to have committed a violent crime by age 32 (20.4% versus 9.8%) (Farrington, 1991).

- York University psychologists Robert Muller and Terry Diamond (1999) studied university students and their parents. They surveyed both groups to determine if there was a relationship between aggression and childhood physical abuse. First, they found that university students who had reported being physically abused by either their mother or father were more aggressive. The researchers also noted that spouses displayed equivalent levels of aggression, such that highly aggressive fathers were partnered with highly aggressive mothers. Second, high levels of aggression in both male and female university students was associated with having had parents who themselves had reported being physically abused as children. This cross-sectional study suggests that there is consistency in levels of aggression within families across generations.

The risk of future problems may be greatest for boys who are both aggressive and rejected. For example, in one important longitudinal study, psychologist John Coie and his colleagues followed a group of over a thousand children from Grades 3 to 10 (Coie, Terry, Lenox, Lochman, & Hyman, 1995). Among boys, those who were both aggressive and rejected in Grade 3 were far more likely to show delinquency or other behaviour problems in high school than were any other group of boys, including those who were aggressive but were not rejected by peers. Other researchers have produced similar findings with regard to aggressive boys who are either overtly rejected or who have more subtle types of problems maintaining peer relationships (Crick & Ladd, 1993; Woodward & Fergusson, 2000).

Remember, boys who are aggressive are very likely to misunderstand others' intentions and to perceive accidental acts as deliberate (Coie et al., 1999; Zakriski & Coie, 1996). Remember, too, that school-aged children tend to regard peers who do not retaliate against hostile acts as socially incompetent. Thus, psychologically and socially, aggressive/rejected children may be in a sort of double bind. Their immature social-cognitive skills predispose them to believe that others are hostile toward them, and their school-aged peers expect them to retaliate in response to acts of aggression. But because they can't discriminate well between situations that call for retaliation and those that do not, their acts of retaliation lead to rejection rather than peer approval. In this way, psychological factors and the unique social characteristics of middle childhood work together to shape these children's behaviour into a consistent pattern. Unfortunately, longitudinal research suggests that, for many of these boys, the pattern continues into adulthood.

to precede these relationships. In other words, boys who are aggressive seek out boys like themselves as friends, and being friends doesn't seem to make either member of the pair more aggressive (Poulin & Boivin, 2000). Research also suggests that children have more positive attitudes toward aggressive peers whose aggressive acts are seen as mostly retaliatory and toward those who engage in both prosocial and aggressive behaviour (Coie & Cillessen, 1993; Newcomb, Bukowski, & Pattee, 1993; Poulin & Boivin, 1999). Social approval may not increase aggressiveness, but it does seem to help maintain it; interventions to reduce aggressive behaviour typically have little effect on aggressive boys who are popular (Phillips, Schwean, & Saklofske, 1997).

Neglected children often do quite well in school, but they are more prone to depression and loneliness than are popular children (Cillessen, van IJzendoorn, van Lieshout, & Hartup, 1992; Rubin, Hymel, Mills, & Rose-Krasnor, 1991; Wentzel & Asher, 1995). This is especially true for girls, who seem to value popularity more than boys do (Oldenburg & Kerns, 1997). Neglect seems to be much less stable over time than rejection, and neglected children sometimes move to the popular category when they become part of a new peer group.

Before Going On

- Describe school-aged children's relationships with their parents.
- Describe the 6- to 12-year-old's understanding of friendship.
- What role does gender play in children's social behaviour and selection of friends?
- Describe the types of aggression most common in middle childhood.
- How do popular, rejected, and neglected children differ?

PERSONALITY AND SELF-CONCEPT

One key contributor to a school-aged child's social relationships is, of course, her own personality. A child's self-concept also has an impact on her social relationships, and the quality of her relationships contributes to her developing self-perceptions.

THE BIG FIVE PERSONALITY TRAITS

the Big Five
a set of five major dimensions of personality, including extraversion, agreeableness, conscientiousness, neuroticism, and openness/intellect

You'll recall from **Chapter 7** that many developmentalists today think of personality as being built on the foundation of the child's inborn temperament (Rothbart, Ahadi, & Evans, 2000). But just how can researchers describe personality? What are the key dimensions on which personalities differ? Over the past two decades, most personality researchers have reached a consensus that adult personality can be adequately described as a set of variations along five major dimensions, often referred to as **the Big Five** (see **Table 9.2**): *extraversion, agreeableness, conscientiousness, neuroticism,* and *openness/ intellect* (Digman, 1990; McCrae & John, 1992). To help you link this list of personality traits to the temperament dimensions described in **Chapter 5, Table 9.2** lists some of the possible connections between the two—although these links are still somewhat speculative (e.g., Ahadi & Rothbart, 1994; Digman, 1990).

TABLE 9.2	The Big Five Personality Traits	
Trait	Qualities of Individuals Who Show the Trait	Possible Temperament Components
Extraversion	Active, assertive, enthusiastic, outgoing	High activity level; sociability; positive emotionality; talkativeness
Agreeableness	Affectionate, forgiving, generous, kind, sympathetic, trusting	Perhaps high approach/positive emotionality; perhaps effortful control
Conscientiousness	Efficient, organized, prudent, reliable, responsible	Effortful control/task persistence
Neuroticism (also called emotional instability)	Anxious, self-pitying, tense, touchy, unstable, worrying	Negative emotionality; irritability
Openness/Intellect	Artistic, curious, imaginative, insightful, original, wide interests	Approach; low inhibition

(*Sources:* Ahadi & Rothbart, 1994; John, Caspi, Robins, Moffitt, & Stouthamer-Loeber, 1994, Table 1, p. 161, McCrae & Costa, 1990.)

The Big Five have been found in studies of adults in a variety of countries, including some non-Western cultures (Bond, Nakazato, & Shiraishi, 1975; Borkenau & Ostendorf, 1990). There is also evidence that they are stable traits; among adults, scores on these five personality dimensions have been shown to be stable over periods as long as a decade or more—a point you'll read more about in later chapters.

Research suggests that these five dimensions also describe children's and adolescents' personalities. For example, a large study of children and adolescents in the Netherlands found that the five clearest dimensions characterizing the young participants matched the Big Five very well (van Lieshout & Haselager, 1994). In this sample, agreeableness and neuroticism (emotional instability) were the two clearest dimensions, followed by conscientiousness, extraversion, and openness.

Moreover, in longitudinal studies, school-aged children's scores on these dimensions of personality have been found to strongly predict academic achievement and social skills in adolescence and early adulthood (Shiner, 2000). Measures of personality in middle childhood also predict antisocial behaviour, such as stealing, in adolescence and later (see **Figure 9.3**, page 284) (John et al., 1994; Shiner, 2000). Such longitudinal studies suggest that the Big Five are not only identifiable and stable in middle childhood, but are also extremely important. Thus, personality assessment in middle childhood may be a useful way to identify factors that are associated with criminal behaviour in children.

THE PSYCHOLOGICAL SELF

In earlier chapters, you read about the child's categorical, social, and emotional selves. During middle childhood, an additional component is added to the self-concept—the psychological self. The **psychological self** is a person's understanding of his or her enduring psychological characteristics, such as personality traits. During middle childhood, the psychological self becomes increasingly complex and abstract. For example, a 6-year-old might use simple psychological self-descriptors such as "smart" or "dumb." By 10, a child is more likely to use comparisons in self-descriptions: "I'm smarter than most other kids," or "I'm not as talented in art as my friend" (Rosenberg, 1986; Ruble, 1987).

psychological self
an understanding of one's stable, internal traits

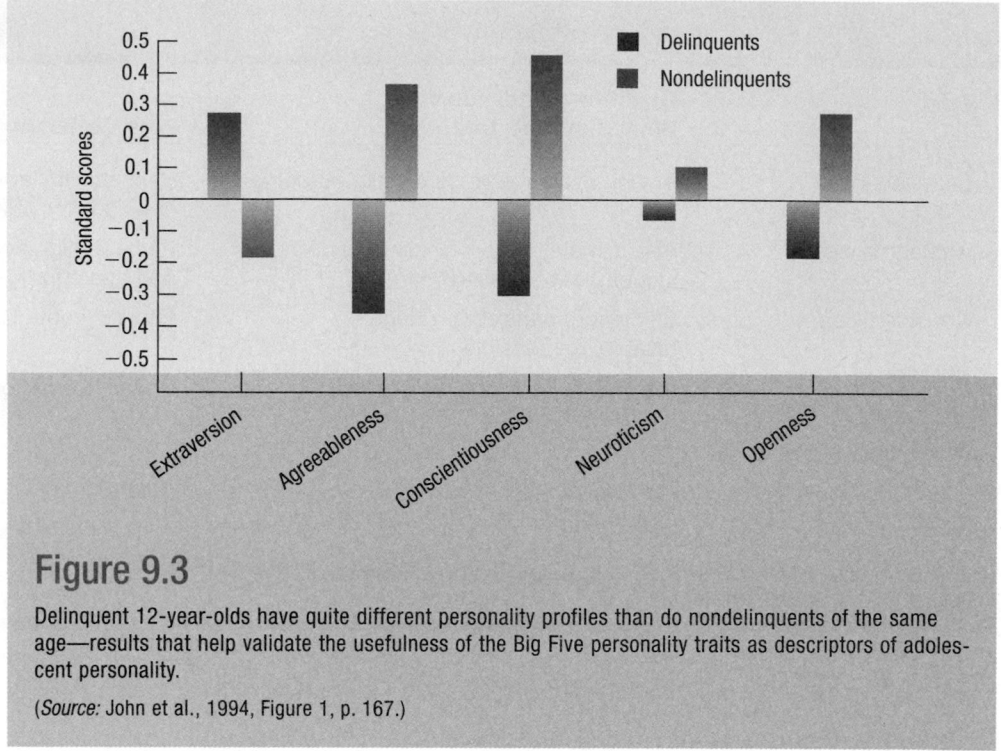

Figure 9.3

Delinquent 12-year-olds have quite different personality profiles than do nondelinquents of the same age—results that help validate the usefulness of the Big Five personality traits as descriptors of adolescent personality.

(*Source:* John et al., 1994, Figure 1, p. 167.)

This developmental trend was illustrated in the results of an older study of the self-concepts of 9- to 18-year-olds (Montemayor & Eisen, 1977). Children who participated were asked to give 20 answers to the question "Who am I?" The researchers found that the younger children were still using mostly surface qualities to describe themselves, as in this description by a 9-year-old:

> My name is Bruce C. I have brown eyes. I have brown hair. I have brown eyebrows. I am nine years old. I LOVE! Sports. I have seven people in my family. I have great! eye site. I have lots! of friends. I live on 1923 Pinecrest Dr. I am going on 10 in September. I'm a boy. I have an uncle that is almost 7 feet tall. My school is Pinecrest. My teacher is Mrs. V. I play Hockey! I'm almost the smartest boy in the class. I LOVE! food. I love fresh air. I LOVE school. (Montemayor & Eisen, 1977, p. 317)

In contrast, consider the self-description of this 11-year-old girl in Grade 6:

> My name is A. I'm a human being. I'm a girl. I'm a truthful person. I'm not very pretty. I do so-so in my studies. I'm a very good cellist. I'm a very good pianist. I'm a little bit tall for my age. I like several boys. I like several girls. I'm old-fashioned. I play tennis. I am a very good swimmer. I try to be helpful. I'm always ready to be friends with anybody. Mostly I'm good, but I lose my temper. I'm not well-liked by some girls and boys. I don't know if I'm liked by boys or not. (Montemayor & Eisen, 1977, pp. 317–318)

This girl, like the other 11-year-olds in the study, describes her external qualities, but she also emphasizes psychological factors such as personality traits.

Thus, as a child moves through the concrete operational period, her psychological self becomes more complex, more comparative, less tied to external features, and more centred on feelings and ideas.

A complex and understudied aspect of self-concept is the spiritual self. Most studies on the topic focus on the cognitive aspects of spirituality without considering the subjective and experiential elements (Bosacki, 2001a, 2001b). The little amount of spiritual education that preadolescents are exposed to commonly focused more on truisms and facts than on learning to trust one's intuition and emotions in the quest for a meaningful existence—attributes that are important in the formation of a complete and genuine preadolescent self-concept (Bosacki, 2001b). Educational strategies that may strengthen the development of the spiritual aspects of preadolescent self-concept include the use of experiential exercises, such as meditation and visualization, art therapy, and storytelling (Bosacki, 2001b, 2002).

Critical Thinking

Take a moment and write down your own 20 answers to the "Who am I?" question. Then compare your answers to the examples given in the text of children's answers. What types of descriptions did you include?

THE VALUED SELF

The self-concept of the 6- to 12-year-old also contains an evaluative aspect. Note, for example, the differences in tone in the two sets of answers to the "Who am I?" question. The 9-year-old makes a lot of positive statements about himself, while the 11-year-old gives a more mixed self-evaluation.

THE NATURE OF SELF-ESTEEM   A child's evaluative judgments have several interesting features. First of all, over the years of elementary school and high school, children's evaluations of their own abilities become increasingly differentiated, with quite separate judgments about academic or athletic skills, physical appearance, social acceptance, friendships, romantic appeal, and relationships with parents (Harter, 1990; Marsh, Craven, & Debus, 1999). Paradoxically, however, it is when they reach school age—around age 7—that children first develop a global self-evaluation. Seven- and eight-year-olds (but not younger children) readily answer questions about how well they like themselves as people, how happy they are, or how well they like the way they are leading their lives. It is this global evaluation of one's own worth that is usually referred to as **self-esteem**, and it is not merely the sum of all the separate assessments a child makes about his skills in different areas. Instead, each child's level of self-esteem is a product of two internal judgments (Harter, 1987, 1990).

self-esteem
a global evaluation of one's own worth

First, as children acquire more sophisticated information-processing skills, they are able to make mental comparisons of their ideal selves and their actual experiences to form experience-based self-esteem judgments. For example, social self-esteem, the assessment of one's own social skills, is higher in popular children than in those who are rejected by their peers (Jackson & Bracken, 1998). However, each component of self-esteem is valued differently by different children. Thus, a child who perceives herself to have poor social skills because she is unpopular may not necessarily have low self-esteem. The degree to which her social self-assessment affects her self-esteem is influenced by how much she values social skills and popularity. In addition, she may see herself as very competent in another area—such as academic skills—that balances her lack of social skills.

The key to self-esteem, then, is the amount of discrepancy between what the child desires and what the child thinks he has achieved. Thus, a child who values sports prowess but who isn't big enough or coordinated enough to be good at sports will have lower self-esteem than will an equally small or uncoordinated child who does not value sports skill so highly. Similarly, being good at something, such as singing or playing chess, won't raise a child's self-esteem unless the child values that particular skill.

The second major influence on a child's self-esteem is the overall support the child feels she is receiving from the important people around her, particularly parents and peers (Franco & Levitt, 1998). Apparently, to develop high self-esteem, children must first acquire the sense that they are liked and accepted in their families, by both parents

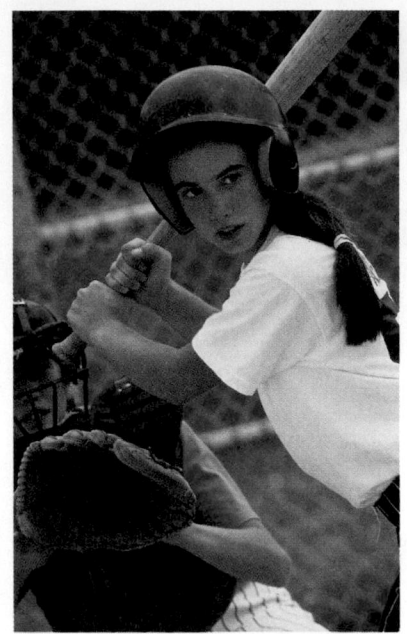

Hitting a home run will only raise this girl's self-esteem if she places a high value on being good at sports or at baseball specifically.
(*Photo:* Don Smetzer/Getty Images)

and siblings. Next, they need to be able to find friends with whom they can develop stable relationships. Since childhood friendships begin with shared interests and activities, children need to be in an environment in which they can find others who like the same things they do and are similarly skilled. Athletic children need other athletic children to associate with; those who are musically inclined need to meet peers who are also musical; and so on.

The separate influences of the perceived discrepancy between the ideal and actual self and the amount of social support are clear in the results of developmental psychologist Susan Harter's research on self-esteem. She asked children in Grades 3, 4, 5, and 6 how important it was to them to do well in each of five domains, and how well they thought they actually did in each. The total discrepancy between these sets of judgments constituted the discrepancy score. A high discrepancy score indicates that the child didn't feel he was doing well in areas that mattered to him. The social support score was based on children's replies to a set of questions about whether they thought others (parents and peers) liked them as they were, treated them as a person, or felt that they were important. **Figure 9.4** shows the results for children in Grades 3 and 4; the findings for the children in Grades 5 and 6 are virtually identical to these. Both sets of data support Harter's hypothesis, as does other research, including studies of African American children (Luster & McAdoo, 1995). Note that a low discrepancy score alone does not protect a child completely from low self-esteem if she lacks sufficient social support. Similarly, a loving and accepting family and peer group do not guarantee high self-esteem if the youngster does not feel that she is living up to her own standards.

CONSISTENCY OF SELF-ESTEEM OVER TIME How stable are self-esteem judgments? Is a Grade 3 child with low self-esteem doomed to feel less than worthy for the rest of his life? A number of longitudinal studies of elementary-school-aged children and teenagers show that self-esteem is quite stable in the short term but somewhat less so over periods of several years. The correlation between two self-esteem scores obtained a few months apart is generally about .60. Over several years, this correlation drops to about .40 (Alsaker & Olweus, 1992; Block & Robins, 1993). So, a child with high self-esteem at age 8 or 9 is likely to have high self-esteem at age 10 or 11. But it is also true that self-esteem is subject to a good deal of variation.

CONSEQUENCES OF VARIATIONS IN SELF-ESTEEM Harter and others have found that the child's level of self-esteem is strongly negatively correlated with depression in both middle childhood and adolescence; the lower the self-esteem score, the more depressed the child describes himself to be. The correlations in several of Harter's studies range from −.67 to −.80, which are remarkably strong correlations for research of this type (Harter, 1987; Renouf & Harter, 1990). Bear in mind, though, that this is still correlational evidence. These findings don't prove a causal connection between low self-esteem and depression. More persuasive is Harter's finding from her longitudinal studies that when a child's self-esteem score rises or falls, her depression score falls or rises accordingly.

Figure 9.4

For these Grade 3 and 4 children in Harter's studies, self-esteem was about equally influenced by the amount of support the children saw themselves receiving from parents and peers and the degree of discrepancy between the value the children placed on various domains and the skill they thought they had in each of those domains.

(*Source:* Harter, 1987, Figure 9.2, p. 227.)

ORIGINS OF DIFFERENCES IN SELF-ESTEEM Where do differences in self-esteem come from? There are at least three sources. First, of course, a child's own direct experience with success or failure in various arenas plays an obvious role. In elementary school, children become aware of their relative academic successes; they gain equally direct comparative information when they play sports, take music lessons, or try out for the school play.

Second, the value a child attaches to some skill or quality is obviously affected fairly directly by peers' and parents' attitudes and values. For example, peer (and general cultural) standards for appearance establish benchmarks for all children and teens. A child who is "too tall" or "too fat" or who deviates in some other way from the accepted norms is likely to feel a sense of inadequacy. Similarly, the degree of emphasis parents place on the child's performing well in some domain—whether it is school, athletics, or playing chess—is an important element in the child's formation of aspirations in that area.

Finally, labels and judgments from others play a highly significant role. To a very considerable extent, we come to think of ourselves as others think of us (Cole, 1991). A child who is repeatedly told that she is "smart," "a good athlete," or "pretty" is likely to have higher self-esteem than a child who is told that she is "dumb," "clumsy," or "a late bloomer." A child who brings home a report card with C's and B's on it and hears her parents say, "That's fine, honey. We don't expect you to get all A's" draws conclusions both about the parents' expectations and about their judgments of her abilities.

From all of these sources, the child fashions her ideas (her internal model) about what she should be and what she is. Like the internal model of attachment, self-esteem is not fixed in stone. It is responsive to changes in others' judgments as well as to changes in the child's own experience of success or failure. But once created, the model does tend to persist, both because the child tends to choose experiences that will confirm and support it and because the social environment—including the parents' evaluations of the child—tends to be at least moderately consistent.

Before Going On

- List and describe the Big Five personality traits.
- Characterize the psychological self-concepts of 6- to 12-year-olds.
- What is the valued self, and how does it develop?

INFLUENCES BEYOND FAMILY AND SCHOOL

The daily life of the school-aged child is shaped by more than the hours she spends in school. The circumstances in which a child lives also affect her. For example, some parents are at home when children come home from school; others are still at work. A child is also affected by her family's economic circumstances, by the neighbourhood she lives in, and by the TV programs she watches.

AFTER-SCHOOL CARE

self-care children
children who are at home by themselves after school for an hour or more each day

In Canada, many children are at home by themselves after school for an hour or more each weekday. They are often referred to as **self-care children**. Self-care arrangements differ so much from child to child that it is impossible to say whether, as a group, self-care children differ from others. For example, some self-care children are home alone but are closely monitored by neighbours or relatives, while others are completely without supervision of any kind (Brandon, 1999). Consequently, the global category "self-care children" isn't very useful in research. To compare self-care children with others and to make predictions, investigators have to focus on variables that may affect self-care—such as the crime rate of the neighbourhood in which self-care occurs. Thus, developmentalists have learned that the effects of self-care on a child's development depend on behavioural history, age, gender, the kind of neighbourhood the child lives in, and how well parents monitor the child during self-care periods (Posner & Vandell, 1994; Steinberg, 1986).

Research consistently demonstrates that self-care children are more poorly adjusted in terms of both peer relationships and school performance. They tend to be less socially skilled and to have a greater number of behaviour problems. However, some of these differences between self-care children and others arise from the effect of self-care on children who already have social and behavioural difficulties before self-care begins. Investigators have found that children who have such problems in the preschool years, before they experience any self-care, are the most negatively affected by the self-care experience (Pettit, Laird, Bates, & Dodge, 1997).

With respect to age, most developmentalists agree that children under the age of 9 or 10 should not care for themselves. The age at which children may be legally left to care for themselves and/or other children varies by province or territory from 10 to 12 years (Safety Canada Online, 2001). Before allowing their child to look after himself or other children, parents can find out what to consider by speaking to an intake worker either at their local Children's Aid Society or the government department in their province or territory that deals with family services.

From a developmental perspective, children younger than 9 do not have the cognitive abilities necessary to evaluate risks and deal with emergencies. Children who start self-care in the early elementary years are vulnerable to older self-care children in their neighbourhoods who may hurt or even sexually abuse them and are more likely to have adjustment difficulties in school (Pettit et al., 1997). High-quality after-school programs can help these younger children attain a higher level of achievement (Peterson, Ewigman, & Kivlahan, 1993; Zigler & Finn-Stevenson, 1993).

Children older than 9 may be cognitively able to manage self-care, but they, too, benefit from participation in well-supervised after-school programs. Even part-time participation in supervised activities after school seems to make a difference in the adjustment of self-care children (Pettit et al., 1997). Good programs provide children with opportunities to play, do homework, and get help from adults (Posner & Vandell, 1994).

There are no achievement differences between girls who experience self-care and those who do not. In fact, girls who must engage in self-care because their mothers are working often have more confidence and higher educational goals than girls whose mothers are at home with them after school (Richards & Duckett, 1994; Vandell & Ramanan, 1992; Williams & Radin, 1993). In contrast, boys do better in school if they have a parent at home with them after school. Most developmentalists attribute this finding to the fact that boys tend to have more behaviour and learning problems in school on average. Thus, they may have a greater need for the after-school tutoring and individual attention a parent can provide (Hoffman, 1989; Vandell & Ramanan, 1991).

Many Canadian children are at home by themselves after school for an hour or more each weekday. (*Photo:* David Young-Wolff/Getty Images)

Self-care has the most negative effects for children in low-income neighbourhoods with high crime rates (Marshall et al., 1997). Self-care children in such areas may use after-school time to "hang out" with socially deviant peers who may be involved in criminal activity or who have negative attitudes about school. Predictably, then, the positive effects of organized after-school programs on academic achievement are greater for children in low-income neighbourhoods (Posner & Vandell, 1994).

Taking everything into consideration, the most important factor in self-care seems to be parental monitoring. Many parents enlist the help of neighbours and relatives to keep an eye on their self-care children. Most require children to call them at work when they get home from school to talk about their school day and get instructions about homework and chores. For example, a working mother might tell her Grade 5 child, "By the time I get home at 5:00, you should be finished with your math and spelling. Don't work on your history project until I get home and can help you with it. As soon as you finish your math and spelling, start the dishwasher." Research suggests that children whose periods of self-care are monitored in this way are less likely to experience the potential negative effects of self-care (Galambos & Maggs, 1991).

TELEVISION

Another major influence on children, particularly in industrialized countries, is television. Nearly every Canadian home has at least one television set and most have access to cable (68%) or satellite (19%) channels (Statistics Canada, 2003a). Canadian children between the ages of 2 and 11 spend an average of about 14.6 hours a week watching television. This number has declined from a peak of 19.2 hours a week in 1990 (Statistics Canada, 2001d; 2003a). There are also large regional differences in the television viewing patterns of children across Canada. For instance, children in English speaking homes in Quebec watched the least television, averaging 11.9 hours per week, followed by British Columbia children at 13.1 hours. Children in the Atlantic provinces of Newfoundland and Labrador, New Brunswick, and Nova Scotia had the highest television viewing rates, ranging between 16.1 and 17 hours per week (Statistics Canada, 2003a).

POSITIVE EDUCATIONAL EFFECTS Programs specifically designed to be educational or to teach children moral values do indeed have demonstrable positive effects. This is particularly clear among preschoolers, for whom most such programming is designed. For example, children who regularly watch *Sesame Street* develop larger vocabularies than do children who do not watch or who watch less often (Rice, Huston, Truglio, & Wright, 1990). Moreover, those who watch programs that emphasize sharing, kindness, and helpfulness, such as *Mr. Rogers' Neighborhood* or *Sesame Street,* show more kind and helpful behaviour (Murray, 1980).

In addition, children can have learning experiences through TV viewing—such as witnessing the migration of whales—that they could never have otherwise. As you learned in **Chapter 8,** the advances in information-processing skills that children undergo between 6 and 12 enable them to remember more from such experiences. Moreover, previously acquired knowledge is important to each new learning experience. Thus, television can be an important means by which school-aged children acquire the kinds of expertise that can make them more efficient learners. A child who has seen a TV program about whale migration is likely to get more out of a school science lesson about whales than one who has no relevant knowledge.

In North America, children between 6 and 12 spend more time watching television than they do playing. (*Photo:* Myrleen Cate/PhotoEdit)

NEGATIVE EFFECTS OF TELEVISION ON COGNITIVE SKILLS Despite the potential positive effects of television on cognitive development, research has demonstrated that heavy TV viewing is associated with lower scores on achievement tests, including measures of such basic skills as reading, arithmetic, and writing. This is particularly clear in the results of an enormous study in California that included more than 500 000 children in Grades 6 and 12 (California Achievement Program, 1980). The researchers found that the more hours of television the students watched, the lower their scores were on standardized tests. This relationship was stronger among children from well-educated families, so it was not due to greater amounts of TV viewing by children in families with lower levels of education. Thus, television can help teach children things they do not already know, but, overall, TV viewing time appears to have a negative effect on school performance.

TELEVISION AND AGGRESSION   By far the largest body of research has focused on the potential impact of television on children's aggressiveness. The level of violence on television is remarkably high and has remained high over the past two decades. In prime-time programs, a violent act occurs 5 or 6 times per hour; in Saturday morning cartoons, the rate is 20 to 25 times per hour. The highest rates of violence are generally found in programs broadcast between 6:00 and 9:00 in the morning and between 2:00 and 5:00 in the afternoon—both times when young children are likely to be watching (Donnerstein, Slaby, & Eron, 1994). The fact that, now, almost 9 out of 10 Canadian homes have access to hundreds of television channels via cable and satellite (Statistics Canada, 2003a) adds to this diet of violence. However, does viewing televised violence cause higher rates of aggression or violence in children? Three types of research evidence argue strongly for the existence of a causal link.

First, there have been a few genuinely experimental studies in which one group of children was exposed to a few episodes of moderately violent TV programs while others watched neutral programs. Collectively, these studies show a significant short-term increase in aggression among those who watched the violent programs (Paik & Comstock, 1994). In a recent example of this type of study, a psychologist found that early elementary-school-aged children who were randomly assigned to watch episodes of the popular (and very violent) children's program *The Mighty Morphin Power Rangers* showed 7 times as many aggressive acts during subsequent free play with peers as did comparable children who had not just viewed the episodes (Boyatzis, Matillo, Nesbitt, & Cathey, 1995).

A second type of research involves comparing levels of aggression among children who vary in the amount of television they watch in their everyday lives. The almost universal finding is that those who watch more television are more aggressive than their peers who watch less. Of course, this leaves researchers with a problem of interpretation. In particular, children who already behave aggressively may choose to watch more television and more violent television. And families who watch a great deal of television may also be more likely to use patterns of discipline that foster aggressiveness in the child.

One partial solution to this dilemma is to study children longitudinally. In one 22-year-long longitudinal study, researchers found that the best predictor of young men's aggressiveness at age 19 was the violence of TV programs they watched when they were 8 (Eron, 1987). When investigators interviewed the men again when they were 30, they

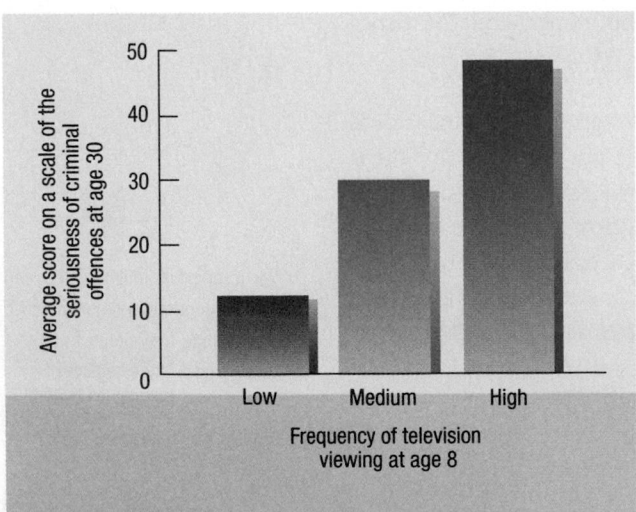

Figure 9.5

Eron finds a strong relationship between the amount of television a group of boys watched when they were 8 and the average severity of criminal offences they had committed by the age of 30. However, this finding alone does not prove there is a causal link between television and later violence.

(*Source:* Eron, 1987, Figure 9, p. 440.)

found that those who had had higher rates of TV viewing at age 8 were much more likely to have a record of serious criminal behaviour in adulthood, a set of results graphed in **Figure 9.5**. The pattern is the same for women, by the way, but the level of criminal offences is far lower, just as the level of aggression is lower among girls in childhood. In another important 15-year follow-up study, researchers found that the more television violence children were exposed to when they were aged 6 to 9 years, the higher the amount of direct physical aggression in adults of both genders and indirect aggression in adult females, regardless of how aggressive they were as children (Huesmann, Moise-Titus, Podolski, & Eron, 2003). Shorter-term longitudinal studies in Poland, Finland, Israel, and Australia have shown similar links between TV viewing and later high levels of aggression (Eron et al., 1991).

Another research strategy is to examine the conditions surrounding the emergence of a pattern of aggressive behaviour in several different countries, to see whether it is possible to identify common antecedents. For example, one researcher looked at changes in homicide rates in the whole population in Canada, and among whites in the United States and South Africa, as a function of the time since television was introduced into each country (Centerwall, 1989, 1992). Television was introduced in both the United States and Canada in about 1950; in South Africa, television became widely available about 25 years later. In each of these three countries, the homicide rate began to rise rapidly 10 to 15 years after TV viewing became widespread. That is, as soon as the first generation of children who had grown up watching television became adults, homicide rates soared. Moreover, statistical analyses showed that the rise in homicides could not be attributed to urbanization, civil unrest, alcohol use, availability of firearms, or any other social condition that had changed over the same period of time.

Other evidence suggests that repeated viewing of TV violence leads to emotional desensitization regarding violence, to a belief that aggression is a good way to solve problems, and to a reduction in prosocial behaviour (Donnerstein et al., 1994). Violent television is clearly not the only, or even the major, cause of aggressiveness among children or adults. Video games in which children commit violent acts vicariously, through characters whose weapons they choose and actions they direct, are also a concern. But television is a significant influence, both individually and at the broader cultural level.

For parents, the clear message from all the research on television is that it is an educational medium. Children learn from what they watch—vocabulary words, helpful behaviours, dietary preferences, and aggressive behaviours and attitudes. The overall content of television—violence and all—may indeed reflect general cultural values. But families can pick and choose among the various cultural messages by controlling what their children watch on television.

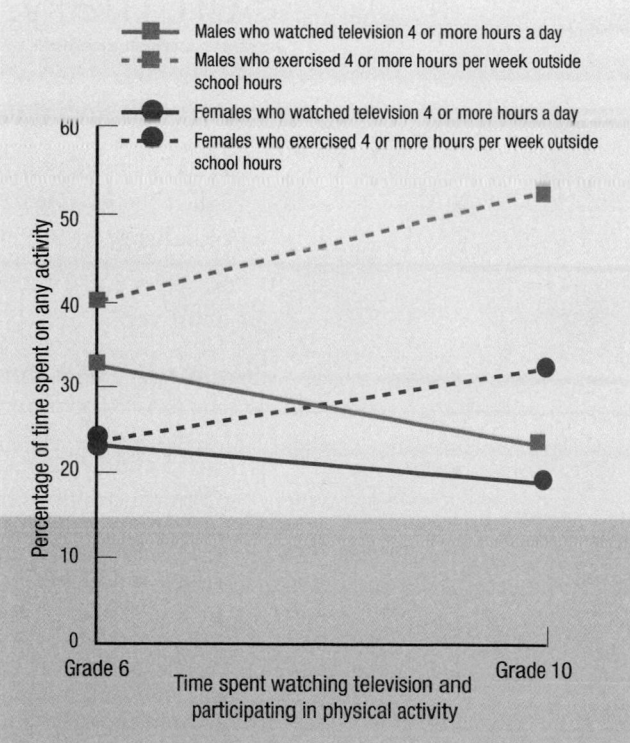

Figure 9.6

The percentage of males and females who watch television 4 or more hours per day decreased from Grades 6 to 10. In comparison, the percentage of males and females who exercised 4 or more hours per week outside school hours increased from Grades 6 to 10.

(*Source:* Adapted from Health Canada, 2001, from Figures 8.4 and 8.7, pp. 77 and 78.)

TELEVISION AND PHYSICAL ACTIVITY The amount of time that Canadian children spent viewing television per week decreased from 1990 to 1998, but gender and age differences persisted. For instance, boys in Grades 6 through 10 consistently watched more television than girls, and the rates of viewing for both boys and girls declined as the children grew older. Although most children watched some television, some children watched 4 or more hours a day, which is arguably unhealthy as those children lost the benefits of being physically active (Health Canada, 2001g). **Figure 9.6** on page 291 shows that the amount of time spent viewing television varied inversely with weekly physical activity levels.

Before Going On

- How does self-care affect girls' and boys' development?
- What are the risks associated with growing up in poverty? What types of variables protect children from the effects of poverty?
- How are televised violence and violent behaviour related?

Summary

Theories of Social and Personality Development

- Freud claimed that the libido is dormant between ages 6 and 12, a period he called the *latency stage*. Erikson theorized that 6- to 12-year-olds acquire a sense of industry by achieving educational goals determined by their cultures.

- Between 6 and 12, children's understanding of others' stable, internal traits improves.

Dimensions of Moral Development

- Psychoanalytic theory emphasizes emotions in explaining moral development. Freud and Erikson emphasized guilt, shame, and pride. More recent examinations of moral emotions have focused on delay of gratification and empathy.

- Cognitive-developmental theory focuses on moral reasoning. The theories of Piaget and Kohlberg claim that moral reasoning develops in sequential stages that are correlated with Piaget's cognitive-developmental stages.

- Behavioural theories assert that moral development is a function of reward, punishment, and modelling. Under some conditions, both punishment and modelling may interfere with moral development.

Social Relationships

- Relationships with parents become less overtly affectionate, with fewer attachment behaviours, in middle childhood. The strength of the attachment, however, appears to persist.

- Friendships become stable in middle childhood. Children's selection of friends depends on variables such as trustworthiness as well as overt characteristics such as play preferences and gender.

- Gender segregation of peer groups is at its peak in middle childhood and appears in every culture. Individual friendships also become more common and more enduring; boys' and girls' friendships appear to differ in specific ways.

- Physical aggression declines during middle childhood, although verbal aggression increases. Boys show markedly higher levels of physical and direct verbal aggression, and higher rates of conduct disorders, than girls. Girls show higher rates of relational aggression.

- Rejected children are most strongly characterized by high levels of aggression or bullying and low levels of agreeableness and helpfulness, but some aggressive children are very popular. Neglected children may suffer depression.

Personality and Self-Concept

- The Big Five personality traits are evident in 6- to 12-year-olds. Variations appear to be related to temperament in infancy and early childhood.

- Between 6 and 12, children construct a psychological self. As a result, their self-descriptions begin to include personality traits, such as intelligence and friendliness, along with physical characteristics.

- Self-esteem appears to be shaped by two factors: the degree of discrepancy a child experiences between goals and achievements, and the degree of perceived social support from peers and parents.

Influences Beyond Family and School

- Self-care is associated with several negative effects. Girls, children who live in safe neighbourhoods, and children whose parents closely monitor their activities after school are the least likely to be negatively affected by self-care.

- The average Canadian child watches about 14.6 hours of television per week. Preschoolers can learn vocabulary, prosocial behaviour, and other social skills. The more television school children watch, the lower their grades are and the less physically active they become. Experts agree that watching violence on television increases the level of personal aggression or violence shown by a child.

Key Terms

the Big Five (p. 282)	psychological self (p. 283)
conscience (p. 269)	relational aggression (p. 278)
ego ideal (p. 269)	retaliatory aggression (p. 279)
industry versus inferiority stage (p. 267)	self-care children (p. 288)
latency stage (p. 266)	self-esteem (p. 285)
moral realism stage (p. 270)	self-regulation (p. 274)
moral relativism stage (p. 270)	social status (p. 280)

Weblinks

"Kohlberg's Stages of Moral Development" by W.C. Crain
http://faculty.plts.edu/gpence/html/kohlberg.htm
Crain explores Kohlberg's six stages of moral judgment, the theoretical issues surrounding them, and their educational implications.

Media Awareness Network
www.media-awareness.ca/english/index.cfm
The Media Awareness Network (MNet) is a Canadian nonprofit organization and its website is home to one of the world's most comprehensive collections of media education and Internet literacy resources.

Childcare Resource and Research Unit
www.childcarecanada.org/index.shtml
The University of Toronto's Childcare Resource and Research Unit (CRRU) website provides support for a universal, high quality, publicly-funded, not-for-profit, inclusive early childhood education and care system in Canada.

National Child Day
www.hc-sc.gc.ca/dca-dea/ncd-jna/main_e.html
This Health Canada website promotes awareness of the "National Day of the Child" (November 20) in accordance with the United Nations Convention on the Rights of the Child (1991). Canada has made a commitment to support the basic human rights to which children (under the age of 18) everywhere are entitled.

Health4kids
www.hc-sc.gc.ca/english/for_you/health4kids/index.htm
This Health Canada website is designed for children. It contains a wide range of health and social tips and discusses issues of importance to children and youth.

Will and Deni McIntyre/Photo Researchers

CHAPTER 10

PHYSICAL AND COGNITIVE DEVELOPMENT IN ADOLESCENCE

When people think about adolescence, puberty is usually the first developmental milestone that comes to mind. However, the physical changes of puberty, as dramatic as they are, are only one component of this important period of transition from childhood to adulthood. For example, if you ask an 8-year-old what she wants to be when she grows up, she is likely to give you an answer like "a firefighter" or "a veterinarian." Ask a 15-year-old the same question, and you are likely to hear something like this: "Well, I'm thinking about several things. I know I want to go to college, but I don't know where, and I'm not sure what I want to study." Such differences reflect age-related changes in the overall quality of thought.

The second idea most people have about adolescence is that it is filled with problems. Mention teenagers and many people automatically think of shouting matches between parents and their teenaged children, or of high-risk behaviours such as drug use and unprotected sex. However, such stereotypical images stem from people's tendency to focus on the negative aspects of this period rather than on the enormous strides adolescents take toward maturity.

In this chapter, you will read about these strides as well as about the challenges of adolescence. For example, along with physical maturity come new health risks. You will also learn about advances in the cognitive domain that, by late adolescence, enable teenagers to function almost as well as adults. School experiences are also critical to adolescent development. As you read, keep the following questions in mind:

- How do the reproductive system, the brain, and other body systems change during adolescence?

- What are the major health concerns associated with adolescence?

- What are the characteristics of adolescents who develop substance abuse or mental health problems?

- What kind of thinking becomes possible in Piaget's formal operational stage, and how do adolescents' memory skills differ from those of younger children?

- How do schooling and employment influence adolescent development?

PHYSICAL CHANGES

When we think of the physical changes of adolescence, we usually give the greatest amount of attention to the reproductive system. Reproductive changes are important, as the text will point out. But momentous changes occur in other systems, and we will discuss those, as well.

THE ENDOCRINE AND REPRODUCTIVE SYSTEMS

endocrine glands
glands that secrete hormones governing growth and other aspects of physical development

pituitary gland
gland that triggers other glands to release hormones

The various **endocrine glands** in the body secrete hormones that govern pubertal growth and physical changes in several ways, as summarized in **Table 10.1**. The **pituitary gland** triggers the release of hormones from other glands; thus, it is sometimes called the *master gland*. For example, the thyroid gland secretes thyroxine only when it receives a signal in the form of a specific thyroid-stimulating hormone secreted by the pituitary.

The rate of growth is governed largely by thyroid hormone and pituitary growth hormone. Thyroid hormone is secreted in high quantities for the first 2 years of life, after which levels fall and remain steady until adolescence (Tanner, 1990). Secretions from the testes, ovaries, and adrenal gland are also at very low levels in the early years of childhood.

TABLE 10.1	Major Hormones That Contribute to Physical Growth and Development	
Gland	**Hormone(s)**	**Aspects of Growth Influenced**
Thyroid gland	Thyroxine	Normal brain development and overall rate of growth
Adrenal gland	Adrenal androgen	Some changes at puberty, particularly the development of secondary sex characteristics in girls
Tests (boys)	Testosterone	Crucial in the formation of male genitals prenatally; also triggers the sequence of changes in primary and secondary sex characteristics in the male
Ovaries (girls)	Estrogen (estradiol)	Development of the menstrual cycle and breasts in girls; has less to do with other secondary sex characteristics than testosterone does for boys
Pituitary gland	General growth hormone, thyroid stimulating hormone, and other activating hormones	Rate of physical maturation; signals other glands to secrete

This changes at age 7 or 8, when adrenal androgen begins to be secreted—the first signal of the changes of puberty (Shonkoff, 1984).

After the burst of androgen, there is a complex sequence of hormone changes that lasts for several years. The pituitary gland begins secreting increased levels of **gonadotrophic hormones** (two hormones in males, three in females), which are responsible for the development of the sex organs. These hormones also stimulate the testes and ovaries to secrete more of the so-called *sex hormones*—testosterone in boys and a form of estrogen called *estradiol* in girls. Hormonal changes are greater in males than in females. Over the course of puberty, testosterone levels increase 18-fold in boys, while levels of estradiol increase only 8-fold in girls (Biro, Lucky, Huster, & Morrison, 1995; Nottelmann et al., 1987).

The pituitary also secretes two other hormones, *thyroid stimulating hormone* and *general growth hormone*; these, along with adrenal androgen, interact with the specific sex hormones and affect growth. Adrenal androgen, which is chemically very similar to testosterone, plays a particularly important role for girls, triggering the growth spurt and affecting development of pubic hair. For boys, adrenal androgen is less significant, presumably because boys already have so much male hormone in the form of testosterone in their bloodstreams. These hormonal changes trigger two sets of body changes: development of the sex organs, and a much broader set of changes in the brain, bones, muscles, and other body organs.

The most obvious changes of puberty are those associated with sexual maturity. Changes in *primary sex characteristics* include growth of the testes and penis in the male and of the ovaries, uterus, and vagina in the female. Changes in *secondary sex characteristics* include breast development in girls, changing voice pitch and beard growth in boys, and the growth of body hair in both sexes. These physical developments occur in a defined sequence that is customarily divided into five stages, following a system originally suggested by J.M. Tanner (Tanner, 1990). Stage 1 is the preadolescent stage, stage 2 includes the first signs of pubertal change, stages 3 and 4 are the intermediate steps, and stage 5 encompasses the final development of adult characteristics.

gonadotrophic hormones
hormones responsible for the development of the sex organs

SEXUAL DEVELOPMENT IN GIRLS Studies of preteens and teens in both Europe and North America show that the various sequential changes are interlocked in a particular pattern in girls, which is shown schematically in the graph on the right in **Figure 10.1** (page 298) (Malina, 1990). The first steps are the early changes in breasts and pubic hair,

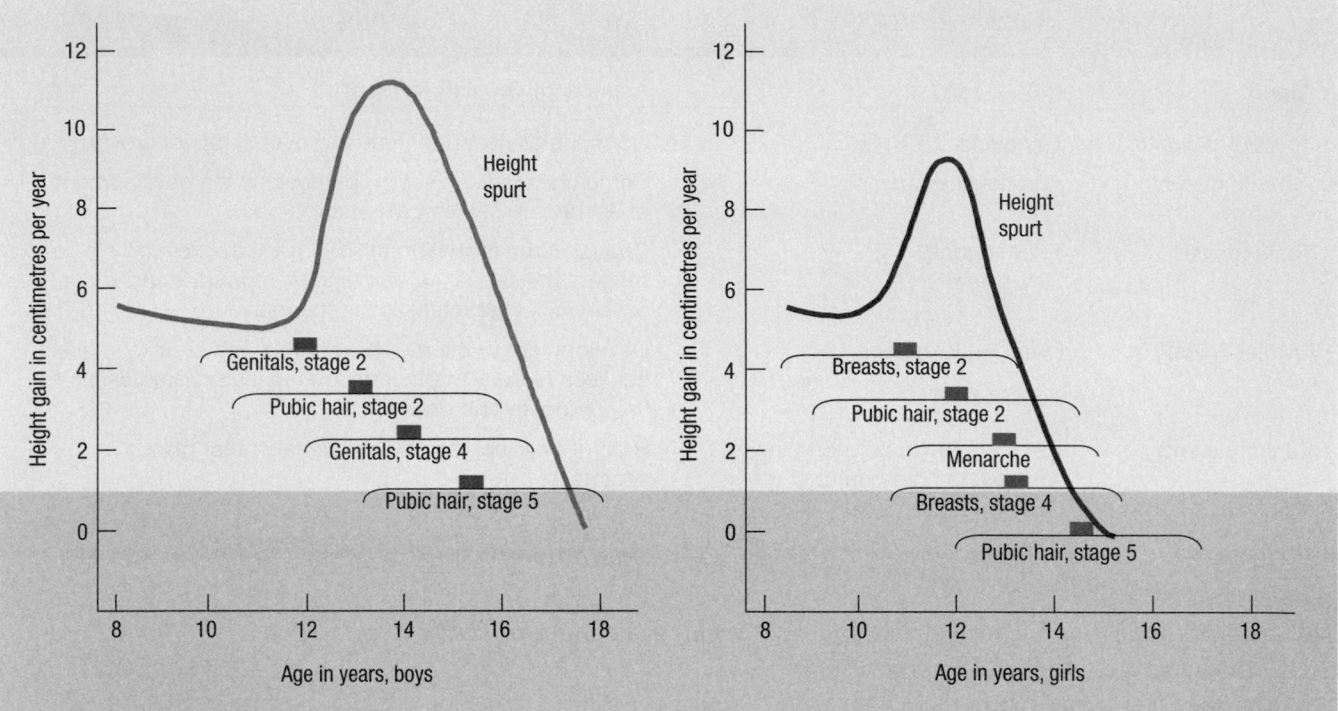

Figure 10.1

The typical sequence of pubertal development for boys (left) and girls (right). The lines show the gains in height at various ages. The coloured squares represent the average age at which each physical change occurs; braces show the range of normal times. Note the wide range of normality for all of these changes. Also, note how late in the sequence menarche occurs for girls, and that girls are about 2 years ahead of boys.

(*Sources:* Biro et al., 1995; Chumlea, 1982; Garn, 1980; Malina, 1990; Tanner, 1978.)

menarche

the beginning of menstrual cycles

secular trend

the decline in the average age of menarche, along with changes such as an increase in average height for both children and adults, that happened between the mid-19th and mid-20th centuries in Western countries and occurs in developing nations when nutrition and health improve

closely followed by the peak of the growth spurt and by the beginnings of stages 4 and 5, the development of breasts and pubic hair. First menstruation, an event called **menarche** (pronounced men-AR-kee), typically occurs 2 years after the beginning of other visible changes and is succeeded only by the final stages of breast and pubic hair development. Among girls in industrialized countries today, menarche occurs, on average, between $12\frac{1}{2}$ and $13\frac{1}{2}$; 95% of all girls experience this event between the ages of 11 and 15 (Malina, 1990).

Interestingly, the timing of menarche changed rather dramatically between the mid-19th and the mid-20th centuries. In 1840, the average age of menarche in Western industrialized countries was roughly 17; the average dropped steadily at a rate of about 3 to 4 months per decade until the 1950s. This steady drop among European populations is an example of what psychologists call a **secular trend.** The decline has levelled off in most industrialized countries, but is still happening in developing nations where women's diets and general health have been improving (Bagga & Kulkarni, 2000; Roche, 1979; Tanner, 1990). The change is most likely caused by significant changes in lifestyle and diet, particularly increases in protein and fat intake, along with reductions in physical exercise that resulted in an increase in the proportion of body fat in females.

It is possible to become pregnant shortly after menarche, but irregular menstrual cycles are the norm for some time. In as many as three-quarters of the cycles in the first year, and half the cycles in the second and third years after menarche, the girl's body produces no ovum (Vihko & Apter, 1980). Full adult fertility thus develops over a period of years. Such irregularity no doubt contributes to the widespread (but false) assumption among younger teenaged girls that they cannot get pregnant.

SEXUAL DEVELOPMENT IN BOYS In boys, as in girls, the peak of the growth spurt typically comes fairly late in the sequence of physical development, as you can see in the graph on the left in **Figure 10.1**. Studies suggest that, on average, a boy completes stages 2, 3, and 4 of genital development and stages 2 and 3 of pubic hair development before reaching the peak of the growth spurt (Malina, 1990). The development of a beard and the lowering of the voice occur near the end of the sequence. Precisely when in this sequence the boy begins to produce viable sperm is very difficult to determine, although current evidence places this event some time between ages 12 and 14, usually before the boy has reached the peak of the growth spurt (Brooks-Gunn & Reiter, 1990).

Although the order of physical developments in adolescence seems to be highly consistent, there is quite a lot of individual variability. **Figure 10.1** depicts the normative, or average, pattern, but individual teenagers often deviate from the norm. For instance, a girl might move through several stages of pubic hair development before experiencing the first clear breast changes, or experience menarche much earlier in the sequence than normal. It is important to keep this variation in mind if you are trying to make a prediction about an individual teenager.

TIMING OF PUBERTY In any random sample of 12- and 13-year-olds, you will find some who are already at stage 5, and others still at stage 1 in the steps of sexual maturation. The accumulated research suggests that each teenager has an internal model, or mental image, of "normal" or "right" timing for puberty (Faust, 1983; Lerner, 1987; Petersen, 1987). Each girl has an internal model about the "right age" to develop breasts or begin menstruation; each boy has an internal model about when it is normal to begin to grow a beard or to reach adult size.

A Canadian study based on NLSCY data determined that girls who are early developers (experience major body changes before age 10 or 11) showed no problems with self-esteem or academics and they had fewer behavioural problems than other girls their age (Japal, Tremblay, McDuff, & Willms, 2002). Although early maturing girls didn't smoke, drink alcohol, or do drugs any more or less than other girls their age, they did tend to belong to groups of older peers who displayed antisocial behaviours and who smoked, drank alcohol, and did drugs. Associating with older youths who get into trouble may set these early maturing girls up for sexual and school problems later on. Among boys, the earlier their development, the more positive their body image, the better they do in school, the less trouble they get into, and the more friends they have (Duke et al., 1982).

Critical Thinking

Do you remember whether you went through puberty very early, early, "on time," or late? Do you think that perception had any effect on your overall experience of adolescence?

OTHER BODY SYSTEMS

Changes in other body systems allow adolescents to acquire new cognitive and motor skills.

THE BRAIN There are two major brain growth spurts in the teenaged years. The first occurs between 13 and 15 (Spreen, Risser, & Edgell, 1995). During this spurt, the cerebral cortex becomes thicker, and the neuronal pathways become more efficient. In addition, more energy is produced and consumed by the brain during this spurt than in the years that precede and follow it (Fischer & Rose, 1994). For the most part, these growth and energy spurts take place in parts of the brain that control spatial perception and motor functions. Consequently, by the mid-teens, adolescents' abilities in these areas far exceed those of school-aged children.

Neuropsychologists Kurt Fischer and Samuel Rose believe that a qualitatively different neural network emerges during the brain growth spurt that occurs between ages 13 and 15, which enables teens to think abstractly and to reflect on their cognitive processes (Fischer & Rose, 1994). As evidence, these researchers cite numerous neurological and psychological studies revealing that major changes in brain organization show up between ages 13 and 15 and that qualitative shifts in cognitive functioning appear after age 15. They claim that the consistency of these research findings is too compelling to ignore.

The second brain growth spurt begins around age 17 and continues into early adulthood (Van der Molen & Molenaar, 1994). This time, the frontal lobes of the cerebral cortex are the focus of development (Davies & Rose, 1999). You may recall that this area of the brain controls logic and planning. Thus, it is not surprising that older teens differ from younger teens in terms of how they deal with problems that require these cognitive functions.

THE SKELETAL SYSTEM An adolescent may grow 5 to 13 centimetres a year for several years. After the growth spurt, teenagers add height and weight slowly until they reach their adult size. Girls attain most of their height by age 16, while boys continue to grow until they are 18 to 20 years old (Tanner, 1990).

The shape and proportions of the adolescent's body also go through a series of changes. During the growth spurt, the normal *cephalocaudal* and *proximodistal* patterns are reversed. Thus, a teenager's hands and feet are the first body parts to grow to full adult size, followed by the arms and legs; the trunk is usually the slowest part to grow. In fact, a good signal for a parent that a child is entering puberty is a rapid increase in the child's shoe size. Because of this asymmetry in the body parts, adolescents are often stereotyped as awkward or uncoordinated. However, adolescents may look awkward, but they are better coordinated than school-aged children (Malina, 1990).

The skeletal system goes through other changes as it increases in size. For example, during the elementary-school years, the size and shape of a child's jaw change when the permanent teeth come in. In adolescence, both jaws grow forward and the forehead becomes more prominent. This set of changes often gives teenagers' faces (especially boys') an angular, bony appearance.

Joint development enables adolescents to achieve levels of coordination that are close to those of adults. As they do at younger ages, boys continue to lag behind girls. You may remember from earlier chapters that boys' fine-motor skills are poorer than girls' because their wrists develop more slowly. In early adolescence, this sex difference is very large; girls achieve complete development of the wrist by their mid-teens (Tanner, 1990). A similar pattern of sex differences is evident in other joints as well, enabling early-adolescent girls to outperform boys of the same age on a variety of athletic skills that require coordination, such as pitching a softball. However, by the late teens, at age 17 or 18, boys finally catch up with girls in joint development and, on average, gain superiority over them in coordinated movement.

THE MUSCULAR SYSTEM Muscle fibres also go through a growth spurt at adolescence, becoming thicker and denser, and adolescents become quite a lot stronger in just a few years. Both boys and girls show this increase in strength, but it is much greater in boys. For example, in

Adolescent girls reach adult height sooner than boys because their bones grow and their joints develop more rapidly.
(*Photo:* Elena Rooraid/PhotoEdit)

a cross-sectional study in Canada involving 2673 children and teenagers, researchers measured strength by having each child hang from a bar, with eyes level with the bar, for as long as possible (Smoll & Schutz, 1990). Between age 9 and age 17, boys increased the average amount of time they could hang by 160%, while girls increased their time by only 37%. By age 17, the boys in this study were three times as strong as the girls. This substantial difference in strength reflects the underlying sex difference in muscle tissue that is accentuated at adolescence: Among adult men, about 40% of total body mass is muscle, compared with only about 24% in adult women.

This sex difference in muscle mass (and accompanying strength) seems to be largely a result of hormone differences. But sex differences in exercise patterns or activities may also be involved. For example, the sex difference in leg strength is much less than in arm strength. Some developmentalists hypothesize that the sex differences result from similar patterns of use of the legs in the sexes (walking, bicycling, and so on) and differential patterns of arm use. Boys are more likely than girls to use their arm muscles in various sports (Tanner, Hughes, & Whitehouse, 1981). Still, there does seem to be a basic hormonal difference as well, because researchers know that even very athletic girls and women are not as strong as very athletic boys and men.

Another major component of the body is fat, most of which is stored immediately under the skin. Canadian researchers have found that at birth, girls have slightly more fat tissue than boys do, and this discrepancy becomes gradually more marked during childhood and adolescence. Between ages 13 and 17, the percentage of body weight made up of fat rises from 21% to 24% among girls but drops from 16.1% to 14.0% among boys (Smoll & Schutz, 1990). So, during and after puberty, the proportion of fat rises among girls and declines among boys, while the proportion of weight that is muscle rises in boys and declines in girls of healthy weight. However, over the past few decades we have seen dramatic changes in the eating and physical activity patterns in youth, which has resulted in a doubling of the number of overweight young teens and a tripling in the rates of obesity. Now Canadian teen boys are about twice as likely as teen girls to be overweight (6%) or obese (17%) (Carrière, 2003; Dietitians of Canada, 2003).

THE HEART AND LUNGS During the teenaged years, the heart and lungs increase considerably in size, and the heart rate drops. Both of these changes are more marked in boys than in girls—another of the factors that make boys' capacity for sustained physical effort greater than that of girls. Before about age 12, boys and girls have similar endurance limits, although even at these earlier ages, when there is a difference, it is usually boys who have greater endurance, because of their lower levels of body fat. Canadian researchers Smoll and Schutz (1990) have determined that following puberty, boys have a clear advantage in endurance as well as in size, strength, and speed.

Before Going On

- How do patterns of hormone function change at adolescence, and what are the pubertal milestones for girls and boys?

- What are the consequences of early puberty for boys and girls?

- How are the brain and other body systems of adolescents different from those of younger children?

ADOLESCENT HEALTH

For most individuals, adolescence is one of the healthiest periods of life. However, as adolescents gain independence, they encounter numerous health risks.

HEALTH CARE ISSUES

Even though they get sick less often than children and infants, teenagers are frequent visitors to health care facilities. Many adolescents believe themselves to be less healthy than they actually are and may develop physical symptoms in response to perceived parental or peer rejection (Wickrama, Conger, Lorenz, & Elder, 1998). In contrast, teens who perceive their parents to be emotionally supportive think of themselves as healthier and experience fewer physical symptoms than peers whose parents seem to be less supportive (Wickrama, Lorenz, & Conger, 1997).

Teenagers also appear to have what many developmentalists describe as a heightened level of *sensation-seeking*, or a desire to experience increased levels of arousal such as those that accompany fast driving or the "highs" that are associated with drugs. Sensation-seeking leads to recklessness, which, in combination with lifestyle factors and inexperience, leads to increased rates of accidents and injuries in this age range. For example, adolescents drive faster and use seat belts less often than adults do (Canada Safety Online, 2000; Statistics Canada, 1999a). To reduce the number of accidents among teenaged drivers, six provinces have enacted laws establishing "graduated" driver's licences and two more have provisional or probationary licence systems (Canada Safety Online, 2000; Traffic Injury Research Foundation, 2001). Sixteen-year-olds can drive in most provinces (except Alberta, where 14-year-olds are eligible for a learner's permit), but they must remain alcohol-, accident-, and ticket-free for a certain period of time before they can have privileges such as driving at night. Other countermeasures include driver education programs and advertising campaigns to discourage risk-taking behaviour. Although road crashes remain the leading cause of death among teens aged 15 to 19, impressive progress has been achieved in reducing road crash death and injury in Canadian adolescents since 1980. After adjusting for population, the fatality rates have dropped by 55% and injuries have fallen by 38%. Alcohol-related deaths have also declined. In 1980 nearly 70% of teen drivers killed in motor vehicle accidents had been drinking. This figure has dropped to about 40% (Canada Safety Online, 2000).

Risky behaviours may be more common in adolescence than other periods because they help teenagers gain peer acceptance and establish autonomy with respect to parents and other authority figures (Jessor, 1992). In fact, researchers have found that teens who show high rates of reckless behaviours are likely to have been unsuccessful in school or to have experienced early rejection by peers, neglect at home, or some combination of these problems (Robins & McEvoy, 1990). In addition, adolescents who are not involved in extracurricular activities at school or to whom popularity is important are more likely than their peers who value popularity less to engage in risky behaviour (Carpenter, 2001; Stein, Roeser, & Markus, 1998).

The messages conveyed in the popular media about sex, violence, and drug and alcohol use may influence teens' risky behaviour. In North America, 12- to 17-year-olds spend more time watching television, listening to music, and playing video games than they do in school (The Vanier Institute of the Family, 2001). Surprisingly, though, most teenagers report that their parents have few, if any, rules regarding media use (Mediascope Press, 2000).

Sensation-seeking and risky behaviours may help teens achieve peer acceptance. Consequently, these behaviours are more likely to happen when adolescents are with peers than when they are alone or with family.
(*Photo:* Eyewire)

Prime-time television programs contain about five sexual incidents per hour, and only 4% of those impart information about the potential consequences of sex (Henry J. Kaiser Family Foundation, 1999). Drugs and alcohol are even more prevalent than sex in the popular media. One survey found that 98% of 200 movies surveyed portrayed characters using some kind of substance, and, in most cases, characters used more than one substance (Mediascope Press, 1999c). Another group of researchers found that 51% of films they surveyed depicted teenagers smoking (Mediascope Press, 1999c). In another 46%, teenagers were shown consuming alcohol, and 3% contained images of teens using illegal drugs. Again, references to the consequences of drug or alcohol use were rare; they occurred in only 13% of films surveyed.

SEXUAL BEHAVIOUR

Teens who date in early adolescence, as these two may be doing, are more likely to become sexually active while still in school than peers who begin dating later. (*Photo:* Omni Photo/MaXx Images Inc.)

Two percent of Canadian youth under the age of 14 are sexually active, but by age 17 about half of both males and females report having had sexual intercourse (Weidner, 2001). Females are more likely than males to report having sex without using a condom. Among students aged 15 to 19 who reported recent sexual activity, 51% of females and 29% of males said they had not used a condom in their recent sexual encounters (Galambos & Tilton-Weaver, 1998).

In the Canadian Contraceptive Study it was determined that condoms and oral contraceptives (OC) were the two main nonpermanent methods of birth control favoured by Canadian women. Although women prefer OC to condoms, the rate of use is about equal for sexually active women of all ages, 44% and 43% respectively. Of sexually active unmarried women aged 15 to 17 using contraception, about 67% use OC (Fisher, Boroditsky & Bridges, 1999). The higher use of OC in relationship to condom use in female youth reflects the finding that women are more concerned about controlling pregnancy than they are about contracting sexually transmitted disease (STD) (Health Canada, 1998e).

Although sexual activity among boys is somewhat correlated with the amount of testosterone in the blood, social factors are much better predictors than hormones of teenagers' sexual activity (Halpern, Udry, Campbell, & Suchindran, 1993; Udry & Campbell, 1994). In fact, cross-cultural evidence suggests that the same factors are related to sexual behaviour even in societies with very low rates of teenaged sexual activity, such as Taiwan (Wang & Chou, 1999). Those who begin sexual activity early are more likely to live in poor neighbourhoods in which young people are not well-monitored by adults. They come from poorer families or from families in which sexual activity is condoned and dating rules are lax. They are more likely to use alcohol. Many were abused and/or neglected in early childhood (Herrenkohl, Herrenkohl, Egolf, & Russo, 1998).

Critical Thinking

List all the reasons you can think of to explain why teenagers often do not use contraceptives.

Among girls, those who are sexually active are also more likely to have experienced early menarche, to have low interest in school, to have had their first date at a relatively early age, and to have a history of sexual abuse (Billy, Brewster, & Grady, 1994; Hovell et al., 1994; Miller et al., 1998; Small & Luster, 1994). In general, the greater the number of risk factors present in the life of an individual teenager, the greater the likelihood that he or she will be sexually active.

Adolescents' moral beliefs and the activities in which they participate also predict their sexual activity. For example, teenagers who believe that premarital sex is morally wrong and who attend religious services frequently are less likely than their peers to become sexually active before reaching adulthood (Miller et al., 1998). Rates of sexual activity are also lower among teens who are involved in sports or other after-school pursuits than they are among their peers who do not participate in such activities (Savage & Holcomb, 1999). Moreover, alcohol use is associated with 25–30% of adolescent sexual encounters; thus, teens who do not use alcohol are less likely to be sexually active than are their peers who drink (CDC, 2000d).

Even when they are knowledgeable about STDs, many teens may lack the assertiveness necessary to resist sexual pressure from a romantic partner or to discuss condom use. For example, although infection rates have declined in Canada since 1991, chlamydia, a disease that is preventable through condom use, continues to be the most commonly reported infectious disease in Canada (Health Canada, 1999j). Infection rates are highest among 15- to 19-year-old females, who have an infection rate of about 12 cases per 1000, six times higher than the incidence found in males (Health Canada, 2001i). Up until 1997, rates of Sexually Transmitted Infections (STI) were decreasing. However, the rate of decline in new HIV infections has stalled and the rates of chlamydia, gonorrhea, and syphilis have been increasing in youth aged 15 to 19 since 1997 (Patrick, Wong, & Jordan, 2000).

Public health experts estimate that 75% of females and 50% of males who suffer from chlamydia are symptomless (CDC, 2000). Thus, routine chlamydia screening of asymptomatic, sexually active teens and young adults is critical to reducing the prevalence of this disease. Left untreated, chlamydia can lead to pelvic inflammatory disease (PID), ectopic pregnancy, and infertility in females and a number of genital and urinary tract disorders in males (Health Canada, 1998e).

In addition to routine screening, many developmentalists and public health advocates say that more effective sex education programs are needed. Most suggest that programs that include training in social and decision-making skills, as well as information about STDs and pregnancy, are more likely than information-only approaches to reduce the prevalence of sexual activity and to increase the number of teens who protect themselves against disease and pregnancy when they do have sex. However, no clear consensus about the effectiveness of various approaches to sex education has emerged (Hovell et al., 1998).

Some adults object to sex education because they believe it will cause teenagers who are not sexually active to become so. Research suggests that such fears are unfounded (Berne & Huberman, 1996). There are also debates over the degree to which sex education programs should emphasize abstaining from sex or using contraceptives. There is no scientific research that shows that abstinence-only sex-education programs significantly increase the delay of first intercourse or reduce the prevalence of sexual behaviour in teens (Kirby, 2000; Thomas, 2000). Moreover, making condoms more readily available to teenagers does not increase their rate of sexual activity but does increase the use of condoms by teenagers who are already sexually active (Schuster, Bell, Berry, & Kanouse, 1998).

Health Canada's (1997b) *Canadian Guidelines for Sexual Health Education* emphasizes the importance of equipping youth with the information, motivation, and skills needed to make informed and responsible sexual decisions. Therefore the focus is on reducing specific risk-taking behaviour, which includes teaching them about proper use of contraceptives. In fact, the large majority of Canadian parents and teens believe that sex education that provides explicit information on a wide range of topics including reproduction, birth control, STD/AIDS prevention, relationships, sexual orientation, sexual abuse, and societal beliefs about sexual morals is vitally important and is best provided in our schools (Barret, 1994; McKay & Holowaty, 1997; McKay, Pietrusiak, & Holowaty, 1998).

TEENAGED PREGNANCY

Among the developed nations of the world, the rate of teenaged pregnancy is highest in the United States, where it is about 9 times higher than in Japan and the Netherlands and twice as high as the rate in Canada (Alan Guttmacher Institute, 1996). In Canada the rate of teenaged pregnancy has generally declined since 1974 (when it was 54 per 1000) to 42.7 per 1000 in 1997 for women aged 15 to 19 (Health Canada, 1999k; Statistics Canada, 2000b). A 1997 survey found that rates of teenaged pregnancy were much higher in the Northwest Territories (123.3/1000) and Yukon and Manitoba (both 60/1000), and lowest in the Atlantic provinces of Newfoundland and Labrador and New Brunswick (both 35/1000) (Statistics Canada, 2000b).

However, teenaged pregnancy statistics can be confusing because they usually refer to all pregnancies among women under age 20. To clarify the extent of the teen pregnancy problem, it is useful to break down the statistics by adolescent subgroups. For example, in Canada the annual pregnancy rate was 25.5 per 1000 among girls aged 15 to 17; and 68.8 per 1000 among girls aged 18 and 19 (Statistics Canada, 2000b). Looking at the numbers this way shows that teen pregnancy is far more frequent among older adolescents and, in fact, is most likely to happen after a girl leaves secondary school.

However, the age at which an adolescent becomes a parent is only one aspect of the teen pregnancy issue. Live birth rates among teenagers have actually dropped in Canada since 1974 when pregnancy statistics were first compiled. In 1997 the live birth rate for women aged 15 to 19 was 20.0/1000, down from the peak rate of 35.6/1000 in 1974 (Health Canada, 1999k; Statistics Canada, 2000b). During the same time abortion rates for women aged 15 to 19 continued to rise from 14/1000 in 1974 to about 22/1000 in 1997. The rate of abortion among 18- and 19-year-old women was higher at 33/1000, which reflects the higher pregnancy rate among older teenagers (Canadian Institute of Child Health [CICH], 2000; Statistics Canada, 2000b). In 1997 the percentage of pregnant women aged 15 to 19 ending their pregnancy in abortion (50.3%) surpassed the percentage of live births (46.8%) and miscarriage or stillbirths (2.9%) for the first time (Statistics Canada, 2000b) (see **Figure 10.2**).

Whether a girl becomes pregnant during her teenaged years depends on many of the same factors that predict sexual activity in general. The younger a girl is when she becomes

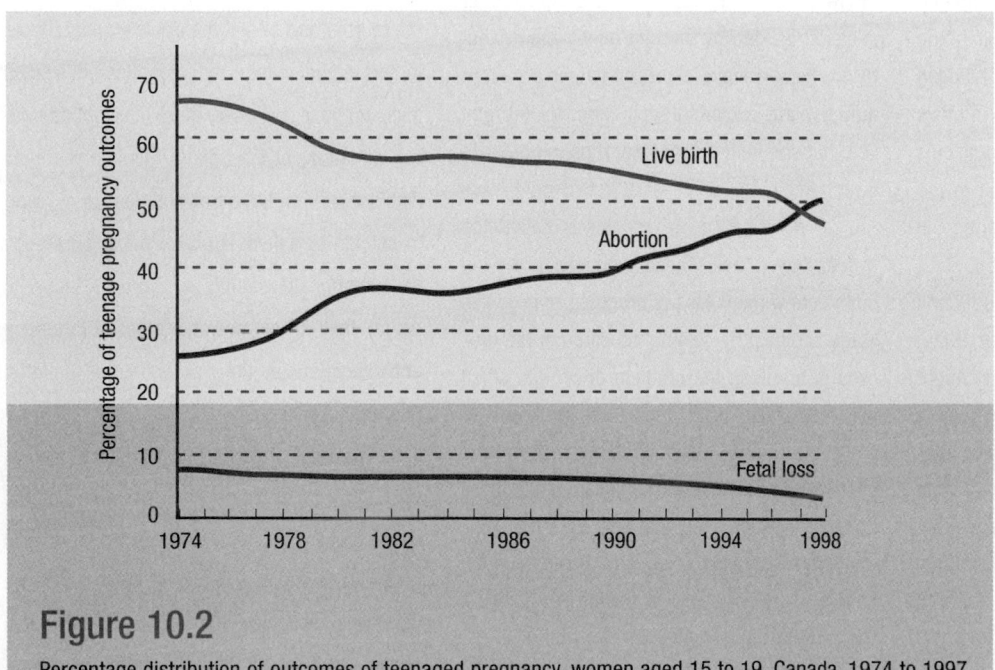

Figure 10.2

Percentage distribution of outcomes of teenaged pregnancy, women aged 15 to 19, Canada, 1974 to 1997.

(*Source:* Adapted from Statistics Canada, *Health Reports*, Cat. No. 82-003, Vol. 12, No.1, Chart 3, available at: http://www.statcan.ca/english/kits/preg/preg3.htm)

sexually active, the more likely she is to become pregnant. Among teenaged girls from poor families, from single-parent families, or from families with relatively uneducated parents, pregnancy rates are higher. Likewise, girls whose mothers became sexually active at an early age and who bore their first child early are likely to follow a similar path. Peer rejection also increases the likelihood that a girl will become pregnant, especially among girls who are high in aggressiveness (Underwood, Kupersmidt, & Coie, 1996).

In contrast, the likelihood of pregnancy is lower among teenaged girls who do well in school and have strong educational aspirations. Such girls are both less likely to be sexually active at an early age and more likely to use contraception if they are sexually active. Girls who have good communication about sex and contraception with their mothers are also less likely to get pregnant.

When teenaged girls become pregnant, in most cases they face the most momentous set of decisions they have encountered in their young lives (see **The Real World**). The

The Real World
Caregiving
Crisis Intervention for the Pregnant Teen

A crisis intervention model proposed more than three decades ago continues to be helpful to mental health professionals, teachers, and parents in understanding and dealing with teens in crisis (Caplan, 1964). The first stage in a crisis, called the *initial phase*, is characterized by anxiety and confusion. In fact, any teenager, male or female, who suddenly begins exhibiting such behaviour should be suspected of being in some sort of crisis. Thus, the first step in crisis intervention in many teenaged pregnancies often happens when a significant adult in the teenager's life recognizes a change in behaviour and questions the girl about it.

Mental health professionals recommend gentle confrontation during this phase (Blau, 1996). For example, a pregnant teenager might be reminded that it isn't possible to keep a pregnancy secret for very long. Pregnant adolescents may be more willing to accept help during the initial phase than in later stages, but this is clearly not the time to bombard them with questions such as "How are you going to support a baby? What about school? Are you going to go to college?"

The second stage of a crisis, the *escalation phase*, happens as the teenager begins to try to confront the crisis. In many cases, adolescents in this phase become convinced that they are unable to cope with the situation and may feel too overwhelmed to maintain daily functions such as getting to school and keeping track of homework. Teens in this phase may be responsive to helpers who simplify their decision-making by directly telling them what to do. For example, a pregnant teen's mother may make a doctor's appointment for her and see that she keeps it instead of nagging her to do it herself.

The third stage of a crisis is called the *redefinition phase*. Those who are providing emotional support for the pregnant teen in this stage can help by guiding her through the process of breaking the problem down into small pieces. For the teen who wants to raise her baby, counsellors or parents can divide the decisions to be made into financial and educational categories. They can help the teen identify short-term and long-term goals in each category and assist her in finding the answers to important questions. For example, in the financial category, the girl must find out how much financial support she can expect to receive from the baby's father. With respect to continuing her education, she must determine the available day-care options.

Teens who leave the redefinition phase with a realistic plan of action are typically no longer in a crisis mode. However, teens who fail to redefine their problem appropriately enter the fourth crisis stage, the *dysfunctional phase*. In this stage, either the pregnant adolescent gives up hope, believing there is no solution for her dilemma, or she goes into denial. Teens who see their situation as hopeless may resort to suicide or self-destructive behaviours such as intentionally failing in school. Those in denial may delay seeking medical attention until very late in their pregnancies (Gullotta, Adams, & Montemayor, 1993).

The goal of crisis intervention is to prevent either of the stage-four outcomes. Yet, the entire process probably depends on whether a pregnant teen has a sensitive adult in her life who will recognize the signs of the initial phase—just one more reason why teenagers, who may seem very grown up, still need warm, authoritative parenting.

children of teenaged mothers are more likely to grow up in poverty than children born to older mothers, with all the accompanying negative consequences for the child's optimum development (Osofsky, Hann, & Peebles, 1993). However, the children of teenaged mothers whose own parents help with child care, finances, and parenting skills are less likely to suffer such negative effects (Birch, 1998; Uno, Florsheim, & Uchino, 1998). Moreover, social programs that provide teenaged mothers with child care and the support they need to remain in school positively affect both these mothers and their babies. Such programs also improve outcomes for teenaged fathers (Kost, 1997).

Before Going On

- How does risky behaviour affect adolescent health?
- What are the patterns of adolescent sexual behaviour in Canada?
- What are the consequences of teenaged pregnancy, and which teenaged girls are most likely to get pregnant?

SUBSTANCE ABUSE AND MENTAL HEALTH PROBLEMS

Despite the stereotype of adolescence as a period of "storm and stress," most teenagers are well adjusted. For a few, however, serious substance abuse or mental health problems arise during this period.

DRUGS, ALCOHOL, AND TOBACCO

Drug use among Canadian youth had been steadily declining since the late 1970s. After a slight rebound in the late 1990s the use of cigarettes, hallucinogens, amphetamines, ecstasy, and barbiturates has been dropping. However, there are indications that the use of some drugs is on the rise again—marijuana, in particular (Adlaf & Paglia, 2003a; Health Canada, 1999i, 2001g). For example, the use of cannabis (i.e., marijuana and hashish) has been on the rise from 1990 onward and, after alcohol, is the substance most commonly used by students. The average age of first-time drug use (including alcohol intoxication) is 13 to 14 years (Hotton & Haans, 2004). The use of substances generally increases with age, with alcohol being the top choice of Canadian students followed, in order, by marijuana, cigarettes, hallucinogens (including LSD, PCP, and mescaline), cocaine/crack, and ecstasy (Adlaf & Paglia, 2003b; Health Canada, 2001g). **Figure 10.3** on page 308 shows the results of a recent annual survey of Ontario students (average rate of drug use, Grades 7 through 12).

As you can see, alcohol use is also very common among Canadian youth. For example, about two-thirds of children in Grade 6 have tried alcohol and by Grade 10 about 90% of students have consumed it (Health Canada, 2001g). Moreover, about one-third

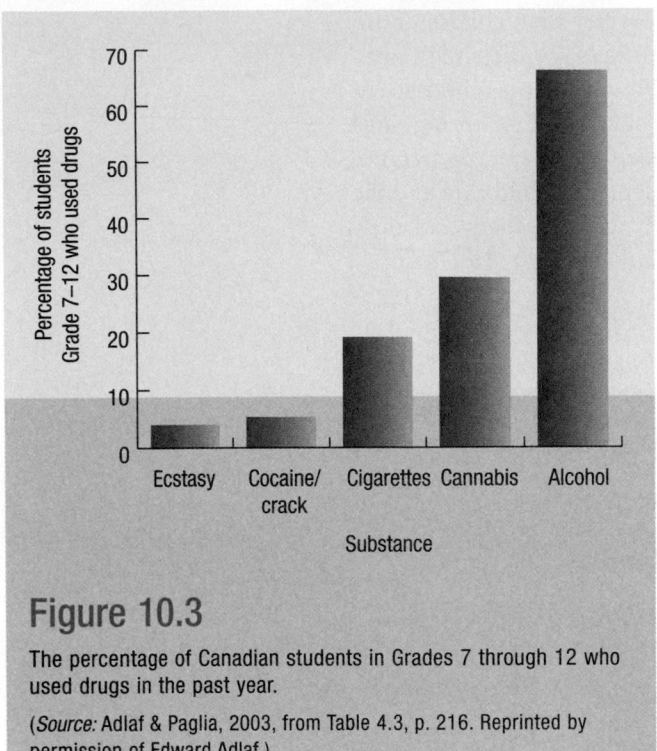

Figure 10.3

The percentage of Canadian students in Grades 7 through 12 who used drugs in the past year.

(*Source:* Adlaf & Paglia, 2003, from Table 4.3, p. 216. Reprinted by permission of Edward Adlaf.)

of young Canadian drinkers aged 15 to 19 are reportedly heavy drinkers (defined as consuming 5 or more drinks on a single occasion at least 12 times in the past year)—up from 18% in 1995 (Statistics Canada, 2001e). One serious consequence is that 15- to 19-year-old youth have had higher rates of drinking and driving than any other age group except 20- to 24-year-olds (CICH, 2000). On the positive side, even though the rate of drivers under the age of 21 with illegal levels of blood alcohol is still high, it has fallen by about 20% since 1977 (Health Canada, 1999i).

Teenagers who express the most interest in sensation-seeking are those who are most likely to use drugs and consume alcohol (Donohew et al., 1999). Indeed, researchers have found that individual levels of sensation seeking predict peer associations—that is, teens who are high sensation-seekers choose friends who are similar. Once such groups are formed, sensation seeking becomes a central feature of their activities. So, for example, if one member tries marijuana or alcohol, others do so as well.

Sensation seeking also interacts with parenting style to increase the likelihood of drug use. Authoritative parenting seems to provide high sensation-seeking teenagers with protection against their reckless tendencies (Pilgrim, Luo, Urberg, & Fang, 1999). Parents who have realistic perceptions of the prevalence of teenaged drinking are also less likely to have teenaged children who are drinkers. These parents, who are aware of the prevalence of alcohol use among adolescents, try to prevent their children from getting into situations, such as attending unsupervised social events, where drinking is likely to happen (Bogenschneider, Wu, Raffaelli, & Tsay, 1998).

Cigarette smoking by Canadian youth had generally declined since the 1970s, but saw a resurgence during the middle 1990s (Bondy, Cohen, & Rehm, 2000). Fortunately the rate has begun to fall again, and has hit its lowest point in decades—for the first time, the youth smoking rate is lower than it is for the general population (Health Canada, 2004a). Although more teen girls were daily smokers (19%) than teen boys (16%), girls smoked fewer cigarettes per day (10.8); teen boys who smoked averaged almost 14 cigarettes per day. The youth rates of smoking varied considerably across the provinces, however, from a low in Ontario of 13% to a high of 27% in Quebec (Health Canada, 2004a) (see **Figure 10.4**).

Some developmentalists speculate that teenagers begin smoking because they really don't understand its health consequences. Consequently, many antismoking campaigns emphasize health risks. However, teenagers seem to be well aware of these risks, including the link between smoking and lung cancer (Taylor et al., 1999). Further, many teens cite moral and ethical reasons for not smoking when asked about it by researchers. Thus, it seems that adolescents are very familiar with all the reasons they shouldn't smoke. So, why do they start smoking if they know they shouldn't?

Peer influences appear to outweigh perceptions of future health risks for many teenagers (Chopak, Vicary, & Crockett, 1998; West, Sweeting, & Ecob, 1999). In fact, some developmentalists advise parents that if their teenaged child's friends smoke, especially close friends with whom the child spends a lot of time, parents should probably assume that their child smokes as well (Urberg, Degirmencioglu, & Pilgrim, 1997). Moreover, the period between ages 15 and 17 seems to be the time during which a teenager is most susceptible to peer influences with regard to smoking (West, Sweeting,

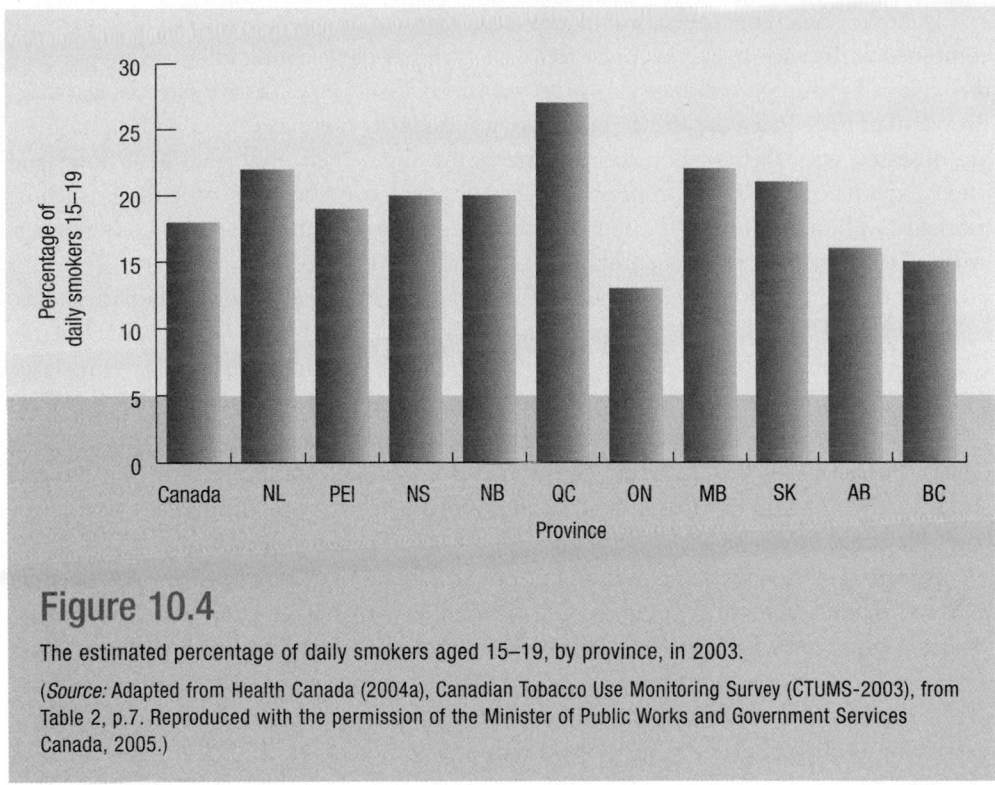

Figure 10.4

The estimated percentage of daily smokers aged 15–19, by province, in 2003.

(*Source:* Adapted from Health Canada (2004a), Canadian Tobacco Use Monitoring Survey (CTUMS-2003), from Table 2, p.7. Reproduced with the permission of the Minister of Public Works and Government Services Canada, 2005.)

& Ecob, 1999). Clearly, then, monitoring the friends of 15- to 17-year olds and discouraging these teens from associating with smokers may help parents prevent their smoking (Mott, Crowe, Richardson, & Flay, 1999).

Parental influence is important, too—a pattern that is especially clear for mothers and daughters (Kandel & Wu, 1995). When an adult stops smoking, the likelihood that her children will smoke decreases. Thus, another way to prevent teenaged smoking is to encourage parents to give up the habit. In addition, having a family rule against substance use—including drugs, alcohol, and tobacco—has a lot more influence on teenagers' decisions about using such substances than most parents think (Abdelrahman, Rodriguez, Ryan, French, & Weinbaum, 1998; Mott et al., 1999). Similarly, teens who view smoking as morally wrong are less likely to smoke than peers who do not think of smoking as a moral issue (Taylor et al., 1999). Thus, parents who think tobacco use is morally wrong should discuss their beliefs with their children.

EATING DISORDERS

Eating disorders, once considered rare in Canada, are among the most significant mental health problems during adolescence—hospitalization rates for young women with eating disorders increased by almost 40% between 1987 and 1999 (Health Canada, 2002e). Canadian sources indicate that these disorders typically develop during adolescence or early adulthood when the pressures to be thin are the strongest (Jilek, 2001; National Institute of Nutrition, 2001). As these social pressures have increased, so too have the rates of eating disorders. About 9 out of 10 cases occur in women, especially young women (Bitomsky, 2002; HealthyOntario.com, 2003). Rates of eating disorders among young Canadian males are much lower than in females, estimated at about 3 in 1000 (Woodside, Garfinkel et al., 2001).

bulimia
an eating disorder characterized by binge eating and purging

anorexia nervosa
an eating disorder characterized by self-starvation

When this anorexic 15-year-old looks at herself in the mirror, chances are she sees herself as "too fat," despite being obviously emaciated.
(*Photo:* Tony Freeman/PhotoEdit)

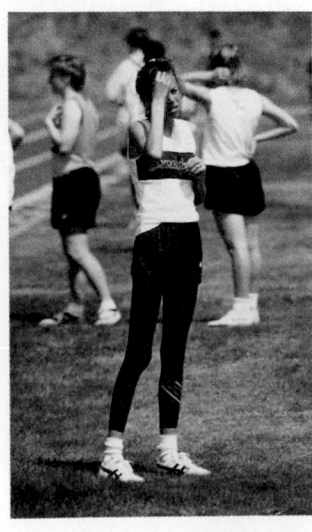

Bulimia (sometimes called *bulimia nervosa*) involves an intense concern about weight combined with twice-weekly or more frequent cycles of binge eating followed by purging, through self-induced vomiting, excessive use of laxatives, or excessive exercising (Attie, Brooks-Gunn, & Petersen, 1990). Bulimics are ordinarily not exceptionally thin, but they are obsessed with their weight, feel intense shame about their abnormal behaviour, and often experience significant depression. The physical consequences of bulimia include marked tooth decay (from repeated vomiting), stomach irritation, lowered body temperature, disturbances of body chemistry, and loss of hair (Palla & Litt, 1988).

It is difficult to estimate, but anywhere between 3% to 10% of Canadian adolescent girls and young adult women may experience the full syndrome of bulimia (Canadian Mental Health Association, 2003; Polivy & Herman, 2002). One large Ontario study found that as many as one-quarter of girls in high school show at least some bulimic behaviours, such as dieting along with occasional bingeing and purging (Jones, Bennett, Olmsted, Lawson, & Rodin, 2001). It's interesting to note that bulimia is essentially unheard of in countries where food is scarce or body thinness is not idealized (Pies, 2003; Mental Health Foundation of New Zealand, 2002).

Anorexia nervosa is less common but potentially more deadly. It is characterized by extreme dieting, intense fear of gaining weight, and obsessive exercising. In girls or women (who are by far the most common sufferers), the weight loss eventually produces a variety of physical symptoms associated with starvation: sleep disturbance, cessation of menstruation, insensitivity to pain, loss of hair on the head, low blood pressure, a variety of cardiovascular problems, and reduced body temperature. Estimates are that between 1% and 2% of female adolescents and young adults in Canada develop anorexia (Canadian Mental Health Association, 2003). Tragically, anywhere from 10% to 15% of anorexics literally starve themselves to death; and others die as a result of some type of cardiovascular dysfunction (Deter & Herzog, 1994).

Some theorists have proposed biological causes for eating disorders—for example, some kind of brain dysfunction in the case of bulimics, who often show abnormal brain waves. Others argue for a psychoanalytic explanation, such as a fear of growing up. The most promising explanation, however, may lie in the discrepancy between the young person's internal image of a desirable body and her (or his) perception of her (or his) own body (see the **Research Report**).

This explanation is supported by cross-cultural research demonstrating that adolescents in Western societies, who have the highest rates of eating disorders, are more likely to have negative body images than are adolescents in non-Western societies (Akiba, 1998). In addition, girls who participate in activities such as ballet and gymnastics, in which thinness is highly valued, are at greater risk of developing eating disorders (Picard, 1999; Stoutjesdyk & Jevne, 1993). However, a recent survey suggests that a fairly large proportion of the general population of teenaged girls may be at risk. When the eating habits of 1739 Ontario girls aged 12 to 18 years were examined, 27% were found to have what the authors described as "disordered eating attitudes and behaviours." Twenty-three percent were dieting to lose weight, and 7% of girls 12 to 14 years of age reported that they had used self-induced vomiting as a weight-loss method (Jones, Bennett, Olmsted, Lawson, & Rodin, 2001).

Some developmentalists suggest that an emphasis on thinness as a characteristic of attractive women, which is common in Western cultures, contributes to the prevalence of eating disorders. However, it is likely that family and individual variables determine the effect of cultural influences on teenagers. For example, one study suggested that mothers' beliefs about the desirability of thinness and their daughters' attractiveness may be just as important in the development of eating disorders as the daughters' own views (Hill & Franklin, 1998). In addition, images of extremely thin models seem to affect only those girls who are already dissatisfied with their bodies (Rabasca, 1999).

Research Report

An Australian

Study Illustrating

Sex Differences in

Body Image

Among

Adolescents

A study of Australian high school students illustrated that distortions in body image are not restricted to North American teenagers and showed how such distortions affect girls' attitudes and behaviour (Paxton et al., 1991). A total of 562 Australian teenagers in Grades 7 to 11 reported on their current weight and height and gave their judgment of themselves as either underweight, at a good weight, or overweight. They also responded to questions about the effect that being thinner might have on their lives and described their weight-control behaviours, including dieting and exercise.

Among teenagers whose weight was actually normal for their height, 30.1% of the girls but only 6.8% of the boys described themselves as overweight. Thus, just as research has found in North America, many of these Australian girls perceived themselves as too fat when they were actually normal. Furthermore, the majority of girls thought that being thinner would make them happier; and a few even thought that being thinner would make them more intelligent! Boys, in contrast, thought that being thinner would actually have some negative effects.

Not surprisingly, these differences in the perception of thinness were reflected in dieting behaviour in this sample. Twenty-three percent of the girls reported that they went on a crash diet at least occasionally, and 4% said that they did so once or twice a week. The comparable percentages for boys were 9% and 1%, respectively. More girls than boys also reported taking diet pills, using laxatives, and vomiting, although the rates of these behaviours were low for both sexes.

Certainly, having a distorted body image doesn't necessarily mean that a girl will become bulimic or anorexic. However, the potential impact of such distorted thinking on girls' general feelings about themselves and initiation of dangerous practices such as crash dieting should be cause for concern.

It is also important to note that a general tendency toward mental illness may also be a factor in eating disorders. In one longitudinal study, young women who had been anorexic in adolescence (94% of whom had recovered from their eating disorders) were found to be far more likely than the general population to suffer from a variety of mental disorders (Nilsson, Gillberg, Gillberg, & Rastam, 1999). *Obsessive-compulsive personality disorder*, a condition characterized by an excessive need for control of the environment, seemed to be especially prevalent in this group. The study's authors further stated that the young women's mental difficulties did not appear to be the result of having previously suffered from an eating disorder. Instead, both the adolescent eating disorders and the women's problems in adulthood seem to have been produced by a consistent tendency toward distorted perceptions.

Critical Thinking

If you had the power to change Canadian society to greatly reduce the rates of bulimia and anorexia, what changes would you want to make? Why and how?

DEPRESSION AND SUICIDE

A revealing study by Nancy Galambos and her colleagues at the University of Alberta found that 25% of young women and half as many young men aged 16 to 19 experienced at least one major depressive episode (MDE) (Galambos, Leadbeater, & Barker, 2004). This sex difference persists throughout adolescence and into adulthood and has been found in a number of industrialized countries (Nolen-Hoeksema & Girgus, 1994; Petersen et al., 1993; Roberts & Sobhan, 1992).

The search for developmental pathways leading to adolescent depression begins with the clear finding that children growing up with depressed parents are much more likely to develop depression than are those growing up with nondepressed parents (Merikangas & Angst, 1995). This could indicate that depression is determined to some extent by a genetic factor, a possibility supported by at least a few studies of twins and adopted children (Petersen et al., 1993). Or this link between parental and child depression could be explained in terms of the parenting behaviours of depressed parents, which you read about in earlier chapters. Furthermore, the contributions of a variety of family stressors to adolescent depression are just as clear among children whose parents are not depressed. Any combination of stresses—such as the parents' divorce, the death of a parent or another loved person, the primary caregiver's loss of job, a move, or a change of schools—increases the likelihood of depression or other kinds of emotional distress in the adolescent (Compas et al., 1993; D'Imperio, Dubow, & Ippolito, 2000). Even smoking has been linked to depression—teen smokers were 1.4 times more likely to develop an MDE (Galambos, Leadbeater, & Barker, 2004).

You'll remember from **Chapter 9** that low self-esteem is also part of the equation. Harter's studies reveal that a young person who feels she (or he) does not measure up to her (or his) own standards is much more likely to show symptoms of depression. A great many teenagers are convinced that they do not live up to culturally defined standards of physical appearance. Self-esteem thus drops in early adolescence, and depression rises.

Depression isn't simply an emotional "low" period. It can also hinder academic achievement, because it interferes with memory. For example, depressed adolescents are more likely to remember negative information than positive information (Neshat-Doost, Taghavi, Moradi, Yule, & Dalgleish, 1998). If a teacher says to a depressed adolescent, "You're going to fail algebra unless you start handing in your homework on time," the teenager is likely to remember the part about failing algebra and forget that the teacher also provided a remedy—getting homework done on time. Further, depressed adolescents seem to be less able than their nondepressed peers to store and retrieve verbal information (Horan, Pogge, Borgaro, & Stokes, 1997).

In some teenagers, sadly, the suicidal thoughts that often accompany depression lead to action. Although depression is more common among girls than boys, the likelihood of actually completing a suicide attempt is about $3^1/_2$ times higher for adolescent boys. Suicide is the second leading cause of death for Canadian young people aged 15 to 19, and the 1997 suicide rate was 5.1 per 100 000 for females and 19.6 per 100 000 for males (Statistics Canada, 1999b). In contrast, suicide attempts are estimated to be three times more common among girls than among boys based on hospital admissions for nonfatal self-inflicted injuries. Girls use methods that are less likely to succeed, such as self-poisoning. The major exception to this national trend is the disproportionately high rate of suicide among First Nations youth, young Aboriginal girls in particular (Health Canada, 1999l) (see **No Easy Answers**).

Although at least three neurobiological systems have been found to be involved in the neurobiology of suicidal behaviour (van Heeringen, 2003), most medical treatment has focused on the treatment of depression associated with suicidal behaviour. The most controversial of these treatments is the use of the newer antidepressant drugs known as *selective serotonin (and noradrenalin) reuptake inhibitors* (SSRIs/SNRIs). Recent disclosures about the outcomes of these drugs on children and adolescents have not only cast doubt on their effectiveness for treating depression, but revealed evidence that SSRIs/SNRIs can contribute to increased suicidal ideation, attempts and risk of suicide, and hostile aggression in these young populations (Garland, 2004; Herxheimer & Mintzes, 2004; Meek, 2004; Sibbald, 2004). In 2003, the United Kingdom banned the use of SSRIs/SNRIs, with the exception of fluoxetine (Prozac), for children and adolescents. In response, Health Canada issued a rare public warning that advised parents to

No Easy Answers

First Nations Youth

Suicide Crisis

The suicide rate for First Nations people in Canada is three to four times higher than for non-Aboriginal people. Even more alarming is the high rate of suicides among First Nation youth—suicide and self-inflicted injury is the leading cause of death (38%) for Aboriginal children 10 to 19 years of age (Health Canada, 2003c). The suicide rate for young First Nation females is 8 times higher than the national rate for same-aged female peers (Health Canada, 2001j; 2003c). In addition, there are some communities in which the incidence of suicide is unmatched in the rest of the world (Canadian Aboriginal, 1999). For example, the community of Pikangikum in Northwestern Ontario, with a population of about 1700, experienced 12 suicides in the 18 months prior to June 2001 (Kent, 2001). Of these, in the year 2000 alone, 8 were young girls and 5 of them were just 13 years old (Elliott, 2000; Barnsley, 2001). This represents a suicide rate of 470/100 000 compared with the Canadian average of 13/100 000 (Barnsley, 2001). Another small community, the Siksika Nation near Calgary, reported 8 suicides and 247 attempted suicides in 2000 (Barnsley, 2001).

Crisis support can be supplied in the short term, but a long-term prevention plan that involves significant change is the prime goal. British Columbia psychologists, led by Michael Chandler of UBC, have shown that factors that promote *cultural continuity* in aboriginal communities are related to significant suicide reduction in First Nations youth (Chandler & Lalonde, 1998; Chandler, Lalonde, Sokol, & Hallet, 2003). The six factors associated with *cultural continuity* are:

- local self-government (the single strongest factor)
- security over traditional lands
- band-controlled school systems
- band-controlled health services
- communal-use cultural facilities
- band-controlled police and fire services

The researchers found that suicide rates varied inversely with the number of indicators of cultural continuity that First Nations communities embraced to strengthen and preserve their cultural heritage. For example, British Columbia First Nation bands that had established all of the factors had no youth suicides. In comparison, bands that had none of the six factors had close to 140 youth suicides per 100 000—a rate that is about 100 times the provincial average. Sadly, in the face of nearly two generations of high suicide rates, the challenge of implementing a nation-wide strategy to assist First Nation communities reduce the risk of suicide is daunting.

consult with the primary care physician about the risks and benefits of prescribing these drugs for patients under the age of 18 (Health Canada, 2004b; Kondro, 2004).

It is obviously very difficult to uncover the contributing factors in completed suicides. Although we know that suicide is related to depression, other factors also play a role. Canadian teens diagnosed with personality disorders, such as antisocial, borderline, and narcissistic in particular, have been found to be at increased risk for suicide and suicidal behaviour (Links, Gould, & Ratnayake, 2003). Behaviour problems such as aggression are also common in the histories of those who complete suicides, as is a family history of psychiatric disorder or suicide or a pattern of drug or alcohol abuse (Garland & Zigler, 1993). In addition, psychologists suggest at least three other contributing factors (Shaffer, Garland, Gould, Fisher, & Trautman, 1988; Swedo et al., 1991):

- Some triggering stressful event. Studies of suicides suggest that this triggering event is often a disciplinary crisis with the parents or some rejection or humiliation, such as breaking up with a girlfriend or boyfriend or failing in a valued activity.

- An altered mental state. Such a state might be a sense of hopelessness, reduced inhibitions from alcohol consumption, or rage.

- An opportunity. A loaded gun in the house or a bottle of sleeping pills in the parents' medicine cabinet creates an opportunity for a teenager to carry out suicidal plans.

Suicide prevention efforts have focused on education—for example, providing training to teachers or to teenagers on how to identify students who are at risk for suicide, in the hope that vulnerable individuals might be reached before they attempt suicide. Special training in coping abilities has also been offered to teenaged students, so that they might be able to find a nonlethal solution to their problems. Unfortunately, most such programs appear to be ineffective in changing teenagers' attitudes or knowledge (Shaffer, Garland, Vieland, Underwood, & Busner, 1991). These discouraging results are not likely to change until psychologists know a great deal more about the developmental pathways that lead to this particular form of psychopathology.

Developmental Psychology in Your Career

Child and Youth (Care) Worker/Counsellor

Occupation	Child and Youth (Care) Worker/Counsellor
Description	• work with a wide array of psychosocial, medical and educational specialists, and families, in a variety of community settings and treatment centres • provide therapeutic services that help young people with emotional and behavioural troubles to maximize their physical, emotional, intellectual, and social development
Entry Credentials	• 3-year Child and Youth (Care) Worker/Counsellor diploma
Essential Lifespan Development Knowledge	• whole-person developmental principles and theories • disorders of childhood and signs of maltreatment • behavioural management and crisis intervention techniques for children and their families • Acts and codes that pertain to children and youth
Essential Lifespan Development Skills	• interview children and their families to obtain a case history • apply developmentally appropriate therapeutic services • organize and conduct individual and group treatment strategies and structured recreational and social activities appropriate for different age groups
Lifespan Development and Essential Professional Attitude	• likes to help young people with problems • is energetic and diligent about self-care and managing stress • has professional rapport with family and treatment team members • respects diversity and values personal development • is safety-conscious to protect self and others
Lifespan Development Career Profile: Sheila Arges, Coordinator, Child and Youth Worker Program, Confederation College	"Tackling challenges for youth is commonplace in this profession. For example, a youth sentenced to secure custody, whose life experience has inhibited his personal and social growth, is given an opportunity to make changes, invest in himself and his community, and become a well-functioning individual. We establish appropriate goals and develop effective, age-appropriate interventions. We deal with the whole child or adolescent in a manner that supports her growth and development." November 15, 2004

Before Going On

- Describe recent trends in adolescents' drug, alcohol, and tobacco use in Canada.
- What are the characteristics and causes of eating disorders?
- Which adolescents are at greatest risk of depression and suicide?

CHANGES IN THINKING AND MEMORY

At some point in adolescence, most people become capable of several types of thought that appear to be impossible at earlier ages. Piaget was the first psychologist to offer an explanation of this important developmental milestone.

PIAGET'S FORMAL OPERATIONAL STAGE

Piaget's observations led him to conclude that this new level of thinking—the **formal operational stage**—emerges fairly rapidly in early adolescence, between roughly age 12 and age 16. During this stage, teenagers learn to reason logically about abstract concepts. Instead of thinking only about real things and actual occurrences, as younger children do, teenagers can think about possible occurrences. Piaget called this kind of thinking hypothetico-deductive reasoning. **Hypothetico-deductive reasoning** is the ability to derive conclusions from hypothetical premises. For example, when a teenager imagines what her life will be like if she goes to college and then compares her imagined future with another possible future that doesn't involve college, she is engaging in hypothetico-deductive reasoning.

The development of hypothetico-deductive reasoning is part of a larger developmental trend: the emergence of the capacity for *deductive reasoning*. Deductive reasoning involves if-then relationships: "If all people are equal, then you and I must be equal." A great deal of the logic of science is deductive. Scientists begin with a theory and a prediction: "If this theory is correct, then I should observe such and such." Children as young as 4 or 5 can understand some such relationships if the premises given are factually true. But only at adolescence are young people able to understand and use the basic logical relationship implied by if-then statements (Ward & Overton, 1990). Consequently, it isn't surprising that adolescents learn all kinds of scientific processes more easily than elementary school children do.

Similarly, advances in logic enable adolescents to engage in **systematic problem-solving**, a process in which a problem-solver searches for a solution by testing hypotheses about single factors. To study this process, Piaget presented adolescents with complex tasks drawn mostly from the physical sciences. In one of these tasks, the participants were given varying lengths of string and a set of objects of various weights that could be tied to the strings to make a swinging pendulum (Inhelder & Piaget, 1958). They were shown how to start the pendulum by pushing the weight with differing amounts of force and by holding the weight at different heights. The task was to figure out which one factor or combination of factors (length of string, weight of object, force of push, or height of push) determined the *period* of the pendulum, which is the amount of time for one swing. (In case you have forgotten your high school physics, the answer is that only the length of the string affects the period of the pendulum.)

formal operational stage
the fourth of Piaget's stages, during which adolescents learn to reason logically about abstract concepts

hypothetico-deductive reasoning
the ability to derive conclusions from hypothetical premises

systematic problem solving
the process of finding a solution to a problem by testing single factors

High school science classes may be one of the first places where adolescents are required to use deductive logic—a skill Piaget did not think was developed until the period of formal operations.
(*Photo:* Bob Daemmrich/Stock Boston)

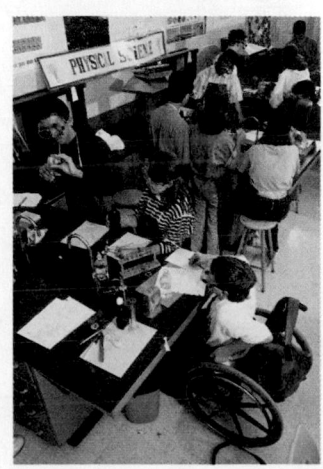

Critical Thinking

Think of a few real-life examples of tasks that demand systematic problem-solving.

An adolescent using a formal operational approach is likely to vary just one of the four factors at a time. She may try a heavy object with a short string, then with a medium string, then with a long one. After that, she might try a light object with the three lengths of string. By contrast, the concrete operational thinker (a younger child) will vary the factors in a haphazard way and, thus, never reach a solution.

DIRECT TESTS OF PIAGET'S VIEW

Developmentalist Edith Neimark has summarized the accumulated information on changes in adolescent thinking succinctly:

> An enormous amount of evidence from an assortment of tasks shows that adolescents and adults are capable of feats of reasoning not attained under normal circumstances by [younger] children, and that these abilities develop fairly rapidly during the ages of about 11 to 15. (Neimark, 1982, p. 493)

Some research illustrations will make the change clearer.

In an early cross-sectional study, researchers tested 20 girls in each of four grades (6, 8, 10, and 12) on 10 different tasks that required one or more of what Piaget called *formal operational skills* (Martorano, 1977). Indeed, many of the tasks the researchers used were those Piaget himself had devised. Results of performance on two of these tasks are graphed in **Figure 10.5**. The pendulum problem is the one described earlier in this section; the balance problem requires a youngster to predict whether two different weights, hung at varying distances on either side of a scale, will balance—a task similar to the balance scale problem Siegler used (recall **Figure 8.3** on page 245). To solve this problem using formal operations, the teenager must consider both weight and distance simultaneously. You can see from **Figure 10.5** that older students generally did better, with the biggest improvement in scores between Grades 8 and 10 (between ages 13 and 15).

Formal operational reasoning also seems to enable adolescents to understand figurative language, such as metaphors, to a greater degree. For example, one early study found that teenagers were much better than younger children at interpreting proverbs (Saltz, 1979). Statements such as "People who live in glass houses shouldn't throw stones" are usually interpreted literally by 6- to 11-year-olds. By 12 or 13, most adolescents can easily understand them, even though it isn't until much later that teenagers actually use such expressions in their everyday speech (Gibbs & Beitel, 1995).

In a more practical vein, developmentalists have shown that teenagers' new cognitive abilities alter the ways they make decisions. In one classic study, experimenters asked students in Grades 8, 10, and 12 to respond to a set of dilemmas that involved a person facing a difficult decision, such as whether to have an operation to repair a facial disfigurement (Lewis, 1981). Forty-two percent of the Grade 12 students, but only 11% of those in Grade 8, mentioned future possibilities in their comments on these dilemmas. For example, in answer to the cosmetic surgery dilemma, a Grade 12 student said,

Well, you have to look into the different things. . . that might be more important later on in your life. You should think

Figure 10.5

These are the results from two of the ten different formal operational tasks used in Martorano's cross-sectional study.

(*Source:* Martorano, 1977, p. 670. Copyright by the American Psychological Association.)

about, will it have any effect on your future and with, maybe, the people you meet. (Lewis, 1981, p. 541)

A Grade 8 student, in response to the same dilemma, said,

The different things I would think about in getting the operation is like if the girls turn you down on a date, or the money, or the kids teasing you at school. (Lewis, 1981, p. 542)

The Grade 8 student's answer focused on the here and now, on concrete things. By contrast, the Grade 12 student considered things that might happen in the future.

However, even among Grade 12 students, nearly three-fifths did not show this type of future orientation. And take another look at **Figure 10.5**: Only about 50–60% of the Grade 12 students solved the two formal operations problems, and only 2 of the 20 used formal operational logic on all 10 problems. Further, recent studies have found rates of formal operational thinking in high school students that are very similar to those found in studies conducted in the 1960s, 1970s, and 1980s (Bradmetz, 1999). The consistency of such findings over several cohorts of adolescents suggests that Piaget's predictions about adolescents' thinking abilities were overly optimistic—in contrast to his overly pessimistic estimates of young children's abilities, which you read about in earlier chapters.

In adulthood, rates of formal operational thinking increase with education. Generally, the better educated the adult participants in a study of formal operational thinking, the greater the percentage who display this kind of reasoning (Mwamwenda, 1999). Piaget's belief in the universality of formal operations may have resulted from his failure to appreciate the role of education in the development of advanced forms of thought. The current consensus among developmentalists is that all non–developmentally delayed teenagers and adults have the capacity for formal operational thinking, but they actually acquire it in response to specific demands, such as those imposed by higher levels of education. Thus, people whose life situations or cultures do not require formal operational thinking do not develop it.

Make the Connection

In what way might formal operational thinking influence decision-making about risky behaviour in adolescence?

ADVANCES IN INFORMATION-PROCESSING

Adolescents process information faster, use processing resources more efficiently, understand their own memory processes better, and have more knowledge than do elementary school children (Kail, 1990, 1997). As a result, they are much better at using strategies to help themselves remember things and can more easily understand and remember complex information, such as that presented in a textbook.

METACOGNITION, METAMEMORY, AND STRATEGY USE By age 14 or 15, the metacognitive and metamemory skills of adolescents far exceed those of younger children. For example, in one classic study, 10- and 14-year-olds were instructed to do a particular activity for exactly 30 minutes (Ceci & Bronfenbrenner, 1985). Experimenters provided them with a clock and instructed them to use it to determine when they should stop. Few of the 10-year-olds periodically checked the time to see if 30 minutes had elapsed, but most of the 14-year-olds did. As a result, less than half of the younger participants succeeded in stopping on time, but more than three-quarters of the teenagers did so.

Another early study of metamemory involved offering students in Grades 5 and 8 and in college the opportunity to earn money for remembering words (Cuvo, 1974). Researchers designated the words to be recalled as being worth either 1 cent or 10 cents. The Grade 5 students rehearsed 1-cent and 10-cent words equally. In contrast, the Grade 8 and college students put more effort into rehearsing the 10-cent words. At the end of the rehearsal period, the Grade 5 students recalled equal numbers of 1- and 10-cent words, while the older participants remembered more 10-cent words. Further, the college students outperformed those in Grade 8 in both rehearsal and recall. This finding suggests that the capacity to apply memory strategies selectively, based on the characteristics of a memory task, appears early in the teenaged years and continues to improve throughout adolescence.

Training studies, in which children and adolescents are taught to use a particular memory strategy, also suggest that metacognitive abilities enable teenagers to benefit more from training than younger children do. For example, researchers taught elementary school students and secondary school students a strategy for memorizing the manufacturing products associated with different cities (for example, Detroit—automobiles) (Pressley & Dennis-Rounds, 1980). Once participants had learned the strategy and were convinced of its effectiveness, researchers presented them with a similar task, memorizing Latin words and their English translations. Experimenters found that only the secondary school students made an effort to use the strategy they had just learned to accomplish the new memory task. The elementary school children used the new strategy only when researchers told them to and demonstrated how it could be applied to the new task. Secondary school students' success seemed to be due to their superior ability to recognize the similarity between the two tasks—an aspect of metamemory.

TEXT LEARNING Differences between younger children's and adolescents' processing of and memory for text are even more dramatic. In a classic study of text processing, experimenters asked 10-, 13-, 15-, and 18-year-olds to read and summarize a 500-word passage. The researchers hypothesized that participants would use four rules in writing summaries (Brown & Day, 1983). First, they would delete trivial information. Second, their summaries would show categorical organization—that is, they would use terms such as "animals" rather than specific names of animals mentioned in the text. Third, the summaries would use topic sentences from the text. Finally, the participants would invent topic sentences for paragraphs that didn't have them.

The results of the study suggested that participants of all ages used the first rule, because all the summaries included more general than detailed or trivial information about the passage. However, the 10-year-olds and 13-year-olds used the other rules far less frequently than did the 15- and 18-year-olds. There were also interesting differences between the two older groups. Fifteen-year-olds used categories about as frequently as 18-year-olds did, but the oldest group used topic sentences far more effectively. This pattern of age differences suggests that the ability to summarize a text improves gradually during the second half of adolescence.

Studies of text outlining reveal a similar pattern (Drum, 1985). Both elementary and secondary school students know that an outline should include the main ideas of a passage along with supporting details. However, research suggests that 17-year-olds generate much more complete outlines than 14-year-olds do. Moreover, 11-year-olds' outlines usually include only a few of the main ideas of a passage and provide little or no supporting details for those main ideas.

Before Going On

- What are the characteristics of thought in Piaget's formal operational stage?
- What are some major research findings regarding the formal operational stage?
- List the advances in information-processing capabilities that occur during adolescence.

SCHOOLING

School experiences are clearly formative in middle childhood, as you'll recall from **Chapter 8**, but school is no less central a force in the lives of adolescents.

TRANSITION TO SECONDARY SCHOOL

There are many places in the world, including Canada, where children attend elementary school for 8 years before moving on to a secondary school for 4 years. In Canada, the exceptions are British Columbia and Quebec, where students switch from elementary to secondary school after Grade 7 and Grade 6 respectively. Because students typically show achievement declines after entering secondary school, educators have developed a model that includes a transitional school—a junior high school or middle school—between elementary and secondary school. The junior high system typically includes 6 or 7 years of elementary school followed by 2 or 3 years of junior high and 3 or 4 years of secondary school. As a consequence, the organization and structure of instruction is most likely to vary for Grade 8 across Canada, whereas Grades 6 and 10 are relatively stable.

However, the junior high/middle school approach does not seem to have solved the transition problem. Students show losses in achievement and in self-esteem across both transition points in these systems. Further, students in both of these systems show greater losses during the transition to secondary school than those in standard elementary-secondary track systems (Alspaugh, 1998; Anderman, 1998). Consequently, educators and developmentalists are currently searching for explanations and practical remedies.

One potential explanation for transition-related achievement declines is that students' academic goals change once they enter junior high/middle school. Researchers classify such goals into two very broad categories: *task goals* and *ability goals*. **Task goals** are goals based on personal standards and a desire to become more competent at something. For example, a runner who wants to improve her time in the 100-metre dash has a task goal. An **ability goal** is one that defines success in competitive terms, being better than another person at something. For example, a runner who wants to be the fastest person on her team has an ability goal. Longitudinal research shows that most Grade 5 students have task goals, but by the time they have been in Grade 6 a few months, most children have shifted to ability goals (Anderman & Anderman, 1999; Anderman & Midgley, 1997).

A student's goal influences his behaviour in important ways. Task goals are associated with a greater sense of personal control and more positive attitudes about school (Anderman, 1999). A student who takes a task-goal approach to school work tends to set increasingly higher standards for his performance and attributes success and failure to his own efforts. For example, a task-goal-oriented student is likely to say he received an A in a class because he worked hard or because he wanted to improve his performance.

In contrast, students with ability goals adopt relative standards—that is, they view performance on a given academic task as good as long as it is better than someone else's. Consequently, such students are more strongly influenced by the group with which they identify than by internal standards that define good and bad academic performance. Ability-goal-oriented students are also more likely than others to attribute success

task goals

goals based on a desire for self-improvement

ability goals

goals based on a desire to be superior to others

Some developmentalists argue that the transition to middle school or junior high school is difficult for many young adolescents because they are not developmentally ready for the secondary-school model. Children who attend middle and junior high schools where close relationships between teachers and students are encouraged, as they are in elementary school, show smaller declines in achievement and self-esteem.
(*Photo:* Bob Rowan/Progressive Images/CORBIS)

and failure to forces outside themselves. For example, such a student might say he got an A in a class because it was easy or because the teacher liked him. Moreover, such students are likely to have a negative view of school (Anderman, 1999).

Because junior high/middle schools emphasize ability grouping more than elementary schools, it is likely that many middle school students change their beliefs about their own abilities during these years (Anderman, Maehr, & Midgley, 1999; Roeser & Eccles, 1998). Thus, high-achieving elementary students who maintain their levels of achievement across the Grade 6 transition gain confidence in their abilities (Pajares & Graham, 1999). In contrast, the changes in self-concept experienced by high achievers who fail to meet expectations in middle school as well as average and low-achieving students do probably lead to self-esteem losses for many of them. Once an ability-goal-oriented student adopts the belief that her academic ability is less than adequate, she is likely to stop putting effort into school work. In addition, such students are likely to use ineffective cognitive strategies when attempting to learn academic material (Young, 1997). Consequently, achievement suffers along with self-esteem.

Critical Thinking

What was your first year of high school like? Did your grades and self-esteem decline? What do you think teachers and administrators could do differently to make the transition easier for students?

Regardless of the type of school they attended previously, the early days of secondary school set a general pattern of success or failure for teenagers that continues into their adult years. For example, teenagers who fail one or more courses in the first year of secondary school are far less likely than their peers to graduate (Roderick & Camburn, 1999). It appears that minority students have a particularly difficult time recovering from early failure.

However, some psychologists emphasize the positive aspects of transition to secondary school, claiming that participation in activities that are usually offered only in secondary school allows students opportunities to develop psychological attributes that can't be acquired elsewhere. To demonstrate the point, a number of research studies had secondary school students use pagers to signal researchers whenever they were experiencing high levels of intrinsic motivation along with intense mental effort (Larson, 2000). The results showed that students experienced both states in elective classes and during extracurricular activities far more often than in academic classes (Larson, 2000). In other words, a student engaged in an art project or sports practice is more likely to experience this particular combination of states than one who is in a history class. Consequently, educators may be able to ease the transition to secondary school for many students by offering a wide variety of elective and extracurricular activities and encouraging students to participate.

GENDER AND ACADEMIC ACHIEVEMENT

Canadian girls generally obtain higher marks than boys in most subjects in school and outperform boys on some standard achievement measures (King & Peart, 1994; HRDC, 2001b). In particular, 13-year-old girls are 16 percentage points ahead of boys in basic-level reading, and by age 16 are 22 percentage points ahead. Research also shows that the gender gap is even wider among the more intellectually talented students. For example, 55% of 13-year-old girls were successful in advanced-level reading compared with only 33% of boys. Moreover, in the areas of math and science, Canadian Grade 8 girls have caught up to boys over the last decade and score equally well on international achievement measures (Robitaille, Taylor & Orpwood, 1996).

Not surprisingly, elementary school teachers have differing expectations for girls and boys. Teachers anticipate that 40% of elementary school girls will go on to complete a university degree but that only 33% of boys will do so (Fine, 2000a). Teachers' predictions have been somewhat fulfilled, as large differences have been found in the number of women graduating with Bachelor's degrees and first professional degrees in comparison with males. For instance, in the late 1990s, there were consistently around 40% more female than male graduates. As well, a slight but consistently higher number of females has been granted Master's degrees (Statistics Canada, 2000a). This reflects the trend of more women pursuing post-secondary education over the past two decades in Canada, although women are still the minority in the physical sciences, engineering, and mathematics (HRDC, 2001; Statistics Canada, 2000c).

There are a few curiosities surrounding students' actual achievement, their self-perception of their achievement, and perceived pressure from school. The percentage of students who experience a lot of pressure with school work increases from Grade 6 to Grade 8. In Grades 6 and 8, boys were more likely to say that they felt a great deal of pressure, but the trend was reversed in Grade 10, when girls reported that they felt more pressure from school (Health Canada, 2001g).

In addition, consistent relationships were found between a variety of factors and school achievement. Students who correctly perceived themselves as being higher achievers were more satisfied with school and had better relationships with both school and parents. In contrast, students who correctly perceived themselves as being lower achievers were moderately associated with high-risk behaviours such as smoking, drinking, and using marijuana. Another factor associated with lower achievement levels was skipping classes. Boys were only slightly more likely to skip classes than girls. In Grade 6 almost one-quarter of students skipped classes, but by Grade 10 over 40% of students were skipping classes. When students skip classes they are more likely to become involved with high-risk behaviours both during school hours and in the evenings. Consequently, skipping classes is associated with lower levels of academic achievement and strained relationship with parents (Health Canada, 2001g).

DROPPING OUT OF SECONDARY SCHOOL

The cumulative effect of success over many years of schooling fosters a greater sense of academic confidence among academically successful secondary school students. Those who achieve, especially those who achieve despite backgrounds that include poverty or other daunting obstacles, are likely to have parents who have high aspirations for them or an authoritative parenting style (Brooks-Gunn, Guo, & Furstenberg, 1993). Moreover, for Canadians, "completing high school is now widely considered as a minimal educational requirement for access to the labour market and lifelong learning" (Bushnik, Bar-Telford, & Bussière, 2004, p.5).

About 16% of 18- to 20-year-old Canadian youth do not have a secondary school diploma and are not currently enrolled in school. Among Aboriginal youth of the same age, the number is 40%. All the same, there is some reason to believe that the long-term trends are improving. For example, results from the School-Leavers Follow-Up Survey determined that a steep decline had occurred in dropout rates over time. Only 11.9% of young adults aged 20 to 24 had not completed their secondary school education in 1999 compared with 17.1% in 1990. The rates in 1999 were lower for females (9%) than for males (14.7%), and these rates are some of the lowest in the world (HRDC, 2000a).

Dropping out of secondary school, like academic success, results from a complex interaction of academic and social variables (Garnier, Stein, & Jacobs, 1997). Children growing up in poor families, especially poor families with a lone parent, are considerably more likely to drop out

Family interactive style predicts academic achievement in high school. Adolescents whose parents display authoritative parenting are more likely than those with authoritarian or permissive parents to achieve academic success in high school.
(*Photo:* Will and Deni McIntyre/Photo Researchers)

of secondary school than are those from more economically advantaged and/or intact families. Teenagers who are living alone, or come from families that do not provide psychological support for academic achievement, or have caregivers who have negative attitudes toward education or low levels of education are also more likely to drop out of school (HRDC, 2000). Plus, when a teenager's peer group puts a low value on achievement, the risk of dropping out is even higher (Takei & Dubas, 1993).

Longitudinal studies have found three strong predictors of dropping out: a history of academic failure, a pattern of aggressive behaviour, and poor decisions about risky behaviour (Bushnik, Bar-Telford, & Bussière, 2004; Garnier, Stein, & Jacobs, 1997; Jimerson, 1999). With respect to risky behaviour, decisions about sexual intercourse seem to be especially critical. For girls, giving birth and getting married are strongly linked to dropping out. Another risky behaviour, adolescent drug use, is also a strong predictor of dropping out (Garnier, Stein, & Jacobs, 1997). In fact, alcohol and drug use better predict a secondary school student's grades than do the student's grades in elementary or middle school. Consequently, decisions about such risky behaviours seem to be one factor that can cause a teen to deviate from a previously positive developmental pathway.

Peer influence may also be a factor in dropping out. Teens who quit school are likely to have friends who have dropped out or who are contemplating leaving school (Bushnik, Bar-Telford, & Bussière, 2004). Family variables are also linked to dropping out. For example, children whose families move a lot when they are in elementary or middle school are at increased risk for dropping out of secondary school (Worrell, 1997).

One group of University of Montreal researchers has compiled a general profile of students who are at risk for dropping out of secondary school. Their research has identified the type of secondary school student who is likely to drop out: one who is quiet, disengaged, low-achieving, and poorly adjusted (Janosz, Le Blanc, Boulerice, & Tremblay, 2000). This concurs with the outcomes of another Canadian study that reported that dropping out of school was linked with being less involved in social, extracurricular, and academic activities (Bushnik, Bar-Telford, & Bussière, 2004).

Whatever its cause, dropping out of secondary school is associated with a number of long-term consequences. For instance, unemployment is higher among adults who dropped out of secondary school than among those who graduated, and dropouts who do manage to find jobs earn lower wages than peers who graduate (Crystal, Shae, & Krishnaswami, 1992). Adults who dropped out of secondary school are also more likely to experience depression (Hagan, 1997). Furthermore, research suggests that staying in school may be an important protective factor for boys who have poor self-regulation skills. When boys who are poor self-regulators stay in school, they appear to be less likely than poor self-regulators who drop out to become involved in criminal activity in early adulthood (Henry et al., 1999).

WORKING TEENS

There is a trend toward staying in school longer because youth employment opportunities are relatively poor and most students are motivated to stay in school and get a better education in order to improve their chances of finding a better job. In fact, from age 16 it now takes students about eight years to complete the transition from high school to regular employment (Franke, 2003). Canadian researchers have found that students increase their hours of employment from ages 15 to 19 and are employed in mostly "entry-level" part-time and summer jobs. About one-third of full-time students were employed during the school term. Students who have some paid employment have better school performance, but employment beyond 15 to 20 hours per week can be detrimental to academic achievement (CCSD, 2001a, 1999b; Jackson & Schetagne, 2001).

Most teenagers with jobs have low-level, low-responsibility, low-paying ones. Some psychologists believe that the negative effects of employment in adolescence may be caused by the type of work teens do.
(*Photo:* David R. Frazier/Photo Researchers)

TABLE 10.2	High School Students with Paid Jobs Don't Cut Back on Study Time					
	Women			Men		
	No job	Job	Difference	No job	Job	Difference
	Average hours per day					
High School						
Time spent on:						
Personal care*	11.2	10.3	−0.9	10.9	10.5	−0.4
Leisure	6.8	6.5	−0.3	7.7	6.2	−1.5
Paid Work	0.2	0.7	0.5	0.1	1.9	1.8
Education	4.4	4.8	0.4	4.4	4.4	0.0
Unpaid work	1.4	1.7	0.3	0.9	1.1	0.2

*Includes sleeping, eating, and hygiene

(*Sources:* Adapted from Statistics Canada, General Social Survey, 1998.)

Some studies that consider the quality of the job as well as the number of hours worked find little or no correlation between the number of hours students work and their school grades or risk of problem behaviour (Mael, Morath, & McLellan, 1997; McNeal, 1997; Mortimer, Finch, Dennehy, Lee, & Beebe, 1995). It seems that students who have positive work experiences develop increased feelings of competence and efficacy.

Studies based on this more complex view of teenagers' employment have also shown that students who seem to benefit from work allocate their time differently from those who experience negative effects (Schoenhals, Tienda, & Schneider, 1998). For example, Canadian teens reduce the amount of time they devote to other activities in order to work—male students start to cut back on leisure activities, such as television and video games, whereas female students reduce their time sleeping (Franke, 2003). In addition, **Table 10.2** shows that male students continue to spend just as much time, and female students actually spend slightly more time, studying as they did before they were employed (when they work 15 hours or fewer per week).

Before Going On

- How might changes in students' academic goals explain declines in achievement and self-esteem at the middle school transition, and what are the negative and positive aspects of the transition to high school?

- How do male and female students differ with respect to academic achievement?

- What variables predict the likelihood of dropping out of secondary school?

- List the negative and positive effects of teenagers' employment.

Summary

Physical Changes

- Puberty is triggered by a complex set of hormonal changes, beginning at about age 7 or 8. Very large increases in gonadotrophic hormones are central to the process. In girls, sexual maturity is achieved as early as $12^1/_2$ or $13^1/_2$. Sexual maturity is achieved later in boys, with the growth spurt occurring a year or more after the start of genital changes.

- The brain continues to develop in adolescence. There are two major brain growth spurts: the first between ages 13 and 15, and the second between ages 17 and 19. Puberty is accompanied by a rapid growth spurt in height and an increase in muscle mass and fat. Boys add more muscle, and girls more fat.

Adolescent Health

- Adolescents have fewer acute illnesses than younger children but more injuries. In general, they show higher rates of various kinds of risky behaviour, including unprotected sex, drug use, and fast driving.

- Sexual activity among teenagers has increased in recent decades in Canada. Roughly half of all Canadian teens have had sexual intercourse by the time they reach their last year of secondary school.

- Every year, 5 out of every 100 teenage girls become pregnant. About half of them give birth.

- Long-term consequences for adolescent girls who bear children are generally negative, although a minority of such girls are able to overcome the disadvantages.

Substance Abuse and Mental Health Problems

- The use of alcohol and marijuana remains high among Canadian teenagers, although they are using most other drugs, including cigarettes, less frequently. Those most likely to use or abuse drugs are those who also show other forms of deviant or problem behaviour, including poor school achievement.

- Eating disorders such as bulimia and anorexia are more common among teenaged girls than among boys.

- Depression and suicide are other mental health problems that are common during adolescence, especially in young Aboriginal Canadians. Recent warnings have come out about treating depression with the newer antidepressant drugs.

Changes in Thinking and Memory

- Piaget proposed a fourth stage of cognitive development in adolescence. The formal operational stage is characterized by the ability to apply basic cognitive operations to ideas and possibilities, in addition to actual objects.

- Researchers have found clear evidence of such advanced forms of thinking in at least some adolescents. But formal operational thinking is not universal, nor is it consistently used by those who are able to do it.

- Memory function improves in adolescence as teens become more proficient in metacognition, metamemory, and strategy use.

Schooling

- The transition to middle school may be accompanied by changes in children's goal orientation that result in declines in achievement and self-esteem. The secondary school transition offers many teens more opportunities to pursue special interests and extracurricular activities.

- Canadian schoolgirls continue to surpass boys in literacy achievement and have recently become roughly equivalent in math and science achievement.

- Those who succeed academically in secondary school are typically from authoritative families. Those who drop out are less likely to find value in school life and education and more likely to be doing poorly in school.

- Adolescents who work more than 10 to 15 hours per week get lower grades and engage in more risky behaviour than those who work less. Work can be beneficial for students who have positive work experiences.

Key Terms

ability goals (p. 319)

anorexia nervosa (p. 310)

bulimia (p. 310)

endocrine glands (p. 296)

formal operational stage (p. 315)

gonadotrophic hormones (p. 297)

hypothetico-deductive reasoning (p. 315)

menarche (p. 298)

pituitary gland (p. 296)

secular trend (p. 298)

systematic problem-solving (p. 315)

task goals (p. 319)

Weblinks

Adolescence: Change and Continuity
http://inside.bard.edu/academic/specialproj/darling/adolesce.htm
This site details the biological, cognitive, and social transitions that occur during adolescence, the influence of family and peers, and issues such as school, work, leisure, sexuality, intimacy, and identity through a vast catalogue of informative articles.

Adolescent Development Resources
www.mhhe.com/socscience/devel/teen/devel-2.htm
This site contains links to hundreds of resources relating to adolescent physical, cognitive, and social development.

The Medicines and Healthcare products Regulatory Agency (MHRA)
www.mhra.gov.uk
This U.K. website provides information that helps to safeguard public health by ensuring that medicines, healthcare products, and medical equipment meet appropriate standards of safety, quality, performance, and effectiveness, and are used safely. It contains links that address the issue of SSRI (antidepressant drug) use in children.

Canadian Medical Association Journal—"Suicide: The Hidden Epidemic"
www.cmaj.ca/cgi/content/full/165/5/634
This article from the Canadian Medical Association Journal explores the history, management, and prevention of teen suicide.

The Aboriginal Youth Network
www.ayn.ca/AYNhome.aspx
The Aboriginal Youth Network website is designed by and for Aboriginal youth. Its purpose is to unite youth and bring cultural identity to Aboriginal youth across Canada by providing information that focuses on news, events, and getting youth to share ideas, ideals, values, beliefs, and cultures and traditions with each other.

It Stock/Firstlight.ca

CHAPTER 11

SOCIAL AND PERSONALITY DEVELOPMENT IN ADOLESCENCE

The change in status from child to adult is considered to be so important that many societies mark it with a *rite of passage*, a formal ritual representing an adolescent's initiation into adult culture. In some nonindustrialized societies, young adolescents begin working or sleeping separately from their families for the first time since birth, emphasizing the child's membership in the larger social group (Cohen, 1964). In other cultures, alterations of a teen's physical appearance or trials of endurance play a part in the rite of passage.

Adolescents in industrialized societies like Canada have no universally shared initiation rites. Social scientists speculate that this is one reason why adolescents in these cultures often emphasize their own separation and distinctness by such means as wearing unusual or even outlandish clothing or hairstyles, getting tattoos and/or body piercings, and using special mannerisms and language.

Nevertheless, all teens in industrialized countries share many changes in status. Graduation from secondary school is one such change. In Canada, young people can have a driver's licence at 16 (14 in Alberta) and can see R-rated movies at 18. At ages 14 to 17, depending on the crime, adolescents can be given adult sentences. At 18, teenagers can vote, and now have full adult privileges and legal responsibilities for their behaviour.

In this chapter, you will learn about the psychological and social aspects of this important transition. We will begin by examining the process of identity development. In the sections that follow, you will read about changes in adolescents' self-concepts and social relationships. Finally, we will examine the development of moral reasoning. While you read, keep the following questions in mind:

- How do Freud, Erikson, and Marcia view the adolescent years?
- How do teenagers' self-concepts change, and how does personality contribute to development in these years?
- In what ways do adolescents' relationships with parents and peers change?
- How do the views of Kohlberg and his critics differ with respect to moral development?

THEORIES OF SOCIAL AND PERSONALITY DEVELOPMENT

As you have learned in earlier chapters, psychoanalytic approaches to social and personality development emphasize conflicts between individual needs and societal demands. Psychoanalytic theories identify and clarify the major themes of social and personality development during adolescence, such as the teenager's acquiring a sense of who she is as an individual. Likewise, cultural perspectives derived from other disciplines can reveal the important role culture plays in the adolescent's transition from child to adult.

PSYCHOANALYTIC PERSPECTIVES

genital stage
in Freud's theory, the period during which people reach psychosexual maturity

According to Freud, the postpubertal years constitute the last stage of personality development; both adolescents and adults are in what Freud called the **genital stage**, the period during which psychosexual maturity is reached. Freud believed that puberty awakens the sexual drive that has lain dormant during the latency stage. Thus, for Freud, the primary developmental task of the genital stage is to channel the libido into a healthy sexual relationship.

Erikson, though not denying the importance of achieving sexual maturity, proposed a somewhat different way of conceptualizing adolescence. In his model, the central crisis of adolescence is **identity versus role confusion**. Erikson argued that the child's early sense of identity comes partly "unglued" in early adolescence because of the combination of rapid body growth and the sexual changes of puberty. Erikson claimed that during this period the adolescent's mind is in a kind of moratorium between childhood and adulthood. The old identity will no longer suffice; a new identity must be forged, one that will equip the young person for the myriad roles of adult life—occupational roles, sexual values, religious and political beliefs, and others.

Confusion about all these role choices is inevitable and leads to a pivotal transition Erikson called the *identity crisis*. The **identity crisis** is a period during which an adolescent is troubled by his lack of an identity. Erikson believed that adolescents' tendency to identify with peer groups is a defence against the emotional turmoil engendered by the identity crisis. In a sense, he claimed, teens protect themselves against the unpleasant emotions of the identity crisis by merging their individual identities with that of a group (Erikson, 1980a). The teenaged group thus forms a base of security from which the young person can move toward a unique solution of the identity crisis. Ultimately, however, each teenager must achieve an integrated view of himself, including his own pattern of beliefs, occupational goals, and relationships.

identity versus role confusion
in Erikson's theory, the stage during which adolescents attain a sense of who they are

identity crisis
Erikson's term for the psychological state of emotional turmoil that arises when an adolescent's sense of self becomes "unglued" so that a new, more mature sense of self can be achieved

MARCIA'S THEORY OF IDENTITY ACHIEVEMENT

Much of the research on the formation of adolescent identity is based on Simon Fraser University professor emeritus James Marcia's descriptions of *identity statuses*. Marcia's early studies confirmed Erikson's general conceptions of the adolescent identity process (Marcia, 1966, 1980, 2001; Schwartz, 2001). Expanding one of Erikson's ideas, Marcia argued that adolescent identity formation has two key parts: a crisis and a commitment. A *crisis*, according to Marcia, meant a period of decision-making when old values and old choices are re-examined. This may occur as an upheaval—the classic notion of a crisis—or it may occur gradually. The outcome of the re-evaluation is a *commitment* to some specific role, value, goal, or ideology. In sum, the achievement of an "ego identity refers to a sense of who one is, based on who one has been and who one can realistically imagine oneself to be in the future" (Marcia, 2002, p. 202).

Critical Thinking

The implication in Marcia's formulation is that foreclosure is a less developmentally mature status—that one must go through a crisis in order to achieve a mature identity. Does this make sense to you? What is your current identity status? Has it changed much over the past few years?

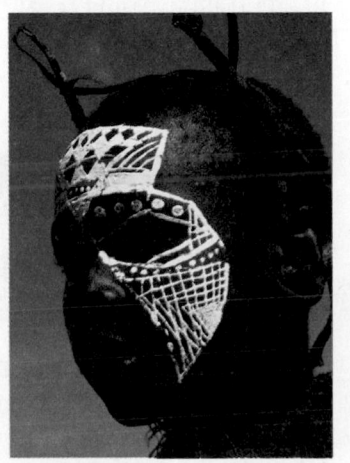

In the Jewish ceremony called bar mitzvah (for boys) or bat mitzvah (for girls), 12- or 13-year-olds read from the Torah in Hebrew and are admitted to full adult status in the congregation. The Tanzanian boy has had his face painted with white clay as part of an adolescent rite of passage.
(*Photos: left,* Bill Aron/PhotoEdit, *right,* The Purcell Team/CORBIS)

Figure 11.1

The four identity statuses proposed by Marcia, based on Erikson's theory. For a fully achieved identity, the young person must have both examined her values or goals and reached a firm commitment.

(*Source:* Marcia, 1980.)

If you put these two elements together, as shown in **Figure 11.1**, you can see that four different *identity statuses* are possible:

- **Identity achievement:** The person has been through a crisis and has reached a commitment to ideological, occupational, or other goals.

- **Moratorium:** A crisis is in progress, but no commitment has yet been made.

- **Foreclosure:** The person has made a commitment without having gone through a crisis. No reassessment of old positions has been made. Instead, the young person has simply accepted a parentally or culturally defined commitment.

- **Identity diffusion:** The young person is not in the midst of a crisis (although there may have been one in the past) and has not made a commitment. Diffusion may thus represent either an early stage in the process (before a crisis) or a failure to reach a commitment after a crisis.

identity achievement

in Marcia's theory, the identity status achieved by a person who has been through a crisis and reached a commitment to ideological or occupational goals

moratorium

in Marcia's theory, the identity status of a person who is in a crisis but who has made no commitment

foreclosure

in Marcia's theory, the identity status of a person who has made a commitment without having gone through a crisis; the person has simply accepted a parentally or culturally defined commitment

identity diffusion

in Marcia's theory, the identity status of a person who is not in the midst of a crisis and who has made no commitment

Most identity theorists agree that the quest for personal identity continues throughout the lifespan, with alternating periods of instability and stability (Marcia, 2002). For example, a person's sense of being "young" or "old" and the integration of that idea into a sense of belonging to a particular generation appears to change several times over the course of the adolescent and adult years (Sato, Shimonska, Nakazato, & Kawaai, 1997). Consequently, adolescence may be only one period of identity formation among several. What makes the formation of an identity during adolescence special is that all the essential elements for the formation of identity are present for the first time in a person's life. The person now possesses a sufficient level of physical, sexual, cognitive, and moral maturity. In conjunction with this, society encourages the individual to take on adult roles, such as worker, parent, and citizen (Marcia, 2002).

Finally, Marcia has suggested that there are two key reasons why adolescence is so important in the life cycle. For one, "it is the time during which a fourth personality structure, an *identity*, is added to the previous structures of ego, self, and superego" (Marcia, 2002, p. 201). For another, adolescence defines the period of transition from childhood to adulthood when "the consolidation of *identity* marks the end of childhood" (Marcia, 1993, p. 3).

Before Going On

- Describe Freud's genital stage and Erikson's stage of identity versus role confusion.

- How does Marcia explain identity development?

- What makes identity formation during adolescence distinct from subsequent identity development later in adulthood?

SELF-CONCEPT AND PERSONALITY

In **Chapter 10**, you read that thinking becomes more abstract in adolescence. Thus, you shouldn't be surprised to find that teenagers' self-concepts are a lot more complex than those of younger children.

SELF-UNDERSTANDING

You should remember that, through the elementary school years, the child's self-concept becomes more focused on enduring internal characteristics—the psychological self. This trend continues in adolescence, with self-definition becoming more abstract. You may remember the replies of a 9-year-old and an 11-year-old to the question "Who am I?" in Montemayor and Eisen's study, cited in **Chapter 9**.

By comparison, older adolescents' self-concept becomes even less tied to their physical characteristics or even their abilities than is evident in younger children. Older adolescents will use abstract traits or ideology to describe themselves. You can see the change very graphically in **Figure 11.2**, which is based on the answers of all 262 participants in Montemayor and Eisen's study. Each of the answers to the "Who am I?" question was categorized as either a reference to physical properties ("I am tall," "I have blue eyes") or to ideology ("I am an environmentalist," "I believe in God"). As you can see, appearance was a highly prominent dimension in the preteen and early teen years but became less dominant in late adolescence, a time when ideology and belief became more important. By late adolescence, most teenagers think of themselves in terms of enduring traits, beliefs, personal philosophy, and moral standards (Damon & Hart, 1988).

At the same time, adolescents' self-concept becomes more differentiated, as they come to see themselves somewhat differently in each of several roles: as a student, with friends, with parents, and in romantic relationships (Harter & Monsour, 1992). Once these self-concepts are formed, they begin to influence adolescents' behaviour. For example, a longitudinal study of Canadian teens found that a strong self-concept is important to the development of good mental and physical health (Park, 2003). Conversely, a weak self-concept during adolescence puts girls at risk for depression and poor self-perceived health and obesity, and boys at risk for obesity and inactivity in young adulthood.

Adolescents' academic self-concepts seem to come both from internal comparisons of their performance to a self-generated ideal and from external comparisons to peer performance (Bong, 1998). It also appears that perceived competency in one domain affects how a teenager feels about his ability in other areas. For example, if a high school student fails a math course, it is likely to affect his self-concept in other disciplines as well as in math. This suggests that teens' self-concepts are hierarchical in nature: Perceived competencies in various domains serve as building blocks for creating a global academic self-concept (Yeung, Chui, & Lau, 1999).

Social self-concepts also predict behaviour. For example, a teenager's family self-concept reflects his beliefs about the

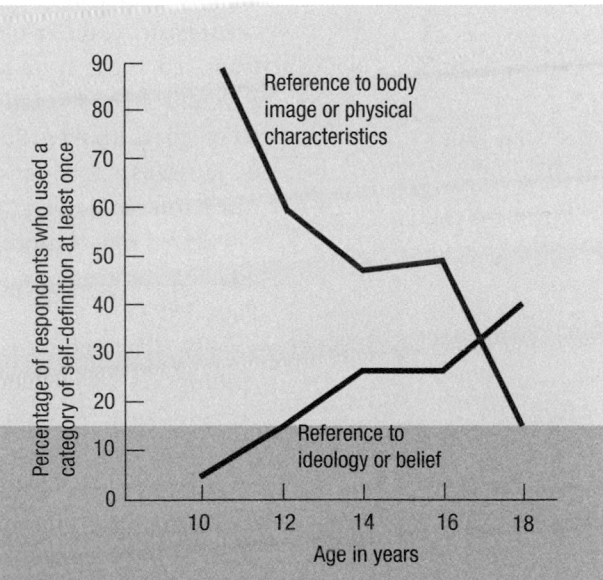

Figure 11.2

As they get older, children and adolescents define themselves less and less by what they look like and more and more by what they believe or feel.

(*Source:* Montemayor & Eisen, 1977, from Table 1, p. 316.)

likelihood of attaining and/or maintaining satisfactory relationships with family members. Developmentalists have found that adolescents who are estranged from their families, such as runaways, perceive themselves to be less competent in the give-and-take of family relations than teens who are close to parents and siblings (Swaim & Bracken, 1997). Indeed, the perceived lack of competency in family relations appears to be distinct from other components of self-concept.

Girls and boys also appear to construct the various components of self-concept somewhat differently. For example, a recent study of teens' evaluations of their own writing abilities found that boys and girls rated themselves as equally capable writers (Pajares & Valiante, 1999). However, the girls scored higher on objective tests of writing ability. In addition, the girls were more likely to describe themselves as being better writers than their peers of both genders. The boys, by contrast, seemed to perceive few ability differences in their peers. In other words, the boys believed they were good writers, but they also thought that their classmates were as good as they were.

Such findings are predictable, given the information in the previous section about girls being influenced by both internal and external comparisons while boys attend more to internal, self-defined standards. The findings also raise interesting questions about the degree to which self-concept development is influenced by cultural ideas about sex roles. Perhaps girls pay more attention to their own and others' writing skills because they know that girls are supposed to be better at language skills than boys.

SEX-ROLE IDENTITY

The links between gender and development in adolescence are partly a result of the physical changes of puberty, are undergirded by each individual teenager's understanding of gender itself, and are influenced by the social environment. For example, in **Chapter 10**, you learned that early-maturing teens differ in important ways. Also, in contrast to younger children, adolescents understand that sex roles are social conventions, so their attitudes toward them are more flexible (Katz & Ksansnak, 1994). Parental attitudes and parental behaviour become increasingly important in shaping teens' ideas about gender and sex roles (Castellino, Lerner, Lerner, & von Eye, 1998; Ex & Janssens, 1998; Jackson & Tein, 1998). In addition, concepts that were largely separate earlier in development, such as beliefs about sex roles and sexuality, seem to become integrated into a conceptual framework that teens use to formulate ideas about the significance of gender in personal identity and social relationships (Mallet, Apostolidis, & Paty, 1997).

By their mid-teens, most adolescents have also largely abandoned the automatic assumption that whatever their own gender does is better or preferable (Powlishta, Serbin, Doyle, & White, 1994). Indeed, a significant minority of teenagers include both masculine and feminine traits in their psychological self-concepts. Developmentalists use the term **sex-role identity** to refer to gender-related aspects of the psychological self.

In the early days of research on sex-role identity, psychologists conceived of masculinity and femininity as polar opposites. A person could be masculine or feminine, but couldn't be both. However, theories first advanced in the 1970s have resulted in a large body of research in support of the notion that masculinity and femininity are dimensions along a continuum and each may be found in varying quantities in the personalities of both men and women (Bem, 1974; Spence & Helmreich, 1978). A male or a female can be high or low on masculinity or femininity, or both. Indeed, if people are categorized as high or low on each of these two dimensions, based on their self-descriptions, four basic sex-role types emerge: *masculine, feminine, androgynous,* and *undifferentiated* (see **Figure 11.3**).

sex-role identity
the gender-related aspects of the psychological self

The masculine and feminine types are the traditional categories; a person in either of these categories sees himself or herself as high in one and low in the other. A "masculine" teenager or adult, according to this view, is thus one who perceives himself (or herself) as having many traditional masculine qualities and few traditional feminine qualities. A feminine teenager or adult shows the reverse pattern. In contrast, androgynous individuals see themselves as having both masculine and feminine traits; undifferentiated individuals describe themselves as lacking both. Several studies show that roughly 25–35% of junior high and high school students define themselves as androgynous (e.g., Boldizar, 1991; Rose & Montemayor, 1994). More girls than boys seem to show this pattern, and more girls fall into the masculine category than boys in the feminine category.

Figure 11.3

This diagram illustrates how the dimensions of masculinity and femininity interact to produce four types of sex-role orientation.

SELF-ESTEEM

Interestingly, research suggests that either an androgynous or a masculine sex-role identity is associated with higher self-esteem among both boys and girls (Boldizar, 1991; Burnett, Anderson, & Heppner, 1995; Rose & Montemayor, 1994). This finding makes sense in light of the existence of a "masculine bias" in North American and other Western societies, which causes both men and women to value traditionally masculine qualities such as independence and competitiveness more than many traditionally female qualities.

If such a bias exists—and there is good reason to think that it does—then the teenaged boy's task is simpler than the teenaged girl's. He can achieve high self-esteem and success with his peers by adopting a traditional masculine sex role. But a girl who adopts a traditional feminine sex role is adopting a less-valued role, with attendant risks of lower self-esteem and a reduced sense of competence (Rose & Montemayor, 1994). Findings like these suggest the possibility that although the creation of rigid rules, or schemas, for sex roles is a normal—even essential—process in young children, a blurring of those rules may be an important process in adolescence, particularly for girls, for whom a more masculine or androgynous self-concept is associated with more positive outcomes.

However, cross-cultural research suggests that adoption of an androgynous or masculine orientation by a girl can lead to lower self-esteem. For example, one study of Israeli girls found that preteens who were tomboys and who rated themselves high on masculine personality traits were less popular and had lower self-esteem than their more feminine peers (Lobel, Slone, & Winch, 1997). Consequently, when considering gender roles and sex-role identity, it is important to remember that both are very strongly tied to culture. A particular society may value the masculine role more highly but also actively discourage girls from adopting it. Thus, it may not be universally true that teens who adopt the more highly valued sex-role identity gain self-esteem.

Self-esteem shows other interesting shifts during the teenage years. The overall trend is a rise in self-esteem through the years of adolescence. The average 19- or 20-year-old has a considerably more positive sense of her global self-worth than she did at age 8 or 11 (Diehl, Vicary, & Deike, 1997; Harter, 1990; Wigfield, Eccles, MacIver, Reuman, & Midgley, 1991). However, the rise to higher self-esteem during adolescence is not steady (see **Figure 11.4** on page 334). The 1994–95 National Population Survey found that psychological well-being in general, and self-esteem in

Teenaged boys like these may have an easier time achieving high self-esteem than girls of the same age, because both boys and girls seem to place a higher value on certain traditionally "masculine" qualities than on traditionally "feminine" ones.
(*Photo:* Jeff Greenberg/PhotoEdit)

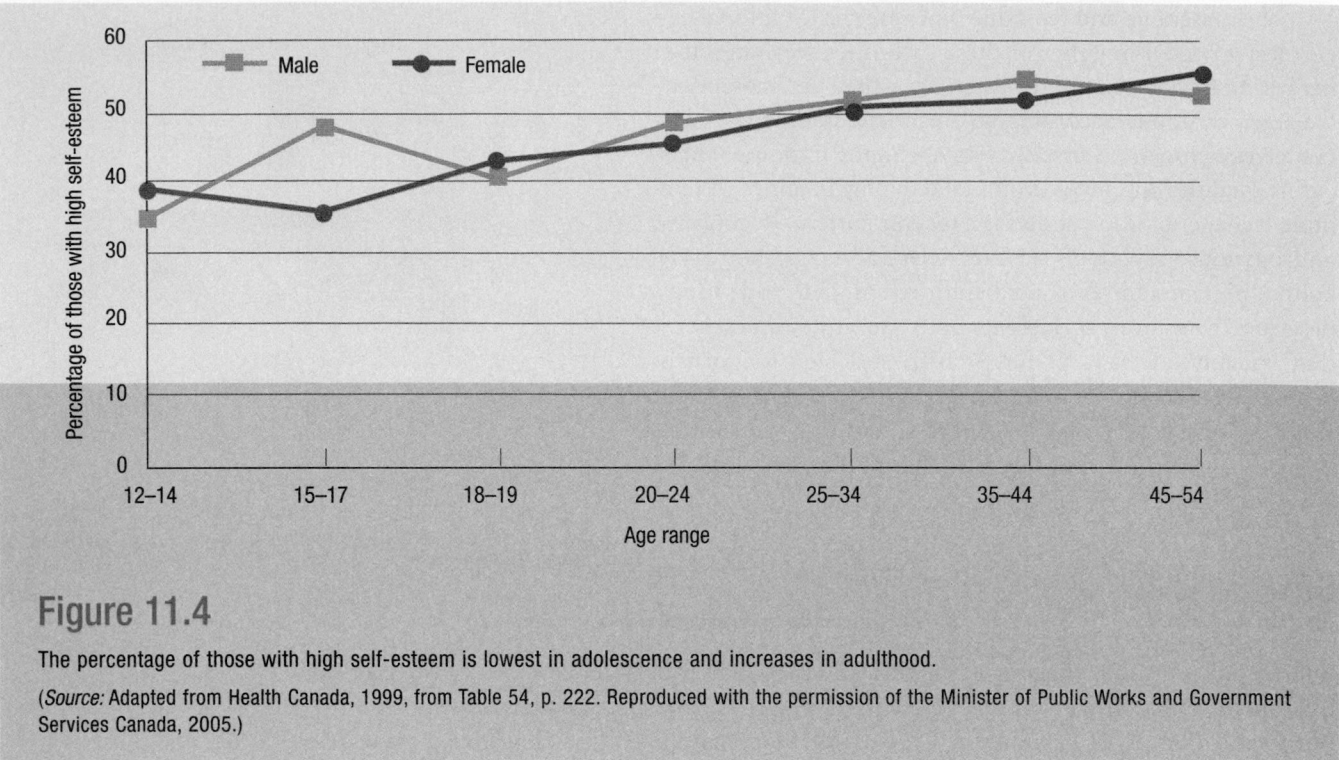

Figure 11.4

The percentage of those with high self-esteem is lowest in adolescence and increases in adulthood.

(*Source:* Adapted from Health Canada, 1999, from Table 54, p. 222. Reproduced with the permission of the Minister of Public Works and Government Services Canada, 2005.)

particular, were lowest in adolescent Canadians. For instance, Canadian adolescents not only reported the lowest rates of high self-esteem, but they also expressed the highest percentages of low-self esteem. Specifically, almost 20% of 12- to 19-year-olds had low self-esteem, which was the highest rate of all the age groups. The largest gender gap in levels of self-esteem was in 15- to 19-year-olds: 22% of females expressed low self-esteem compared with 13% of males (Health Canada, 1999e; Statistics Canada, 2001f).

To study the relationship of self-esteem to important developmental outcomes, such as school achievement, researchers often divide teens into four groups based on the stability of their self-esteem ratings across adolescence (Diehl, Vicary, & Deike, 1997; Zimmerman, Copeland, Shope, & Dielman, 1997). The largest group, about half in most studies, display consistently high self-esteem throughout adolescence. The self-esteem of those in the second group steadily increases, and the self-esteem ratings of those in the third group are consistently low. Teens in the fourth group enjoy moderate to high self-esteem at the beginning of the period, but it declines steadily as adolescence progresses. One finding of concern is that girls outnumber boys in the third and fourth groups (Zimmerman et al., 1997). In addition, several studies have found that high self-esteem is correlated with positive developmental outcomes. For example, teens with high self-esteem are better able to resist peer pressure and get higher grades in school. You may also remember from **Chapter 10** that such teens are less likely to become involved in substance abuse or early sexual intercourse.

ETHNIC IDENTITY

There are more than 70 distinct ethnic identities in Canada, and Canadian identities vary along linguistic, national, regional, racial, and religious groupings (Rummens, 2001). Minority teenagers, especially recent immigrant youth, face the task of creating two identities in adolescence. Like other teens, they must develop a sense of individual identity that they believe sets them apart from others. In addition, they must develop an **ethnic identity** that includes self-identification as a member of their specific group, commitment to that group and its values and attitudes, and some attitudes (positive or negative) about the group to which they belong (Phinney, Ferguson, & Tate, 1997). Moreover, the process of developing an ethnic identity can be at variance with a social environment that is dominated by the concerns of the majority (Phinney, Ong, & Madden, 2000). For example, immigrant parents' expectations about helping out with family obligations, obeying parents, and freedom to date or socialize can differ from the views of the adolescents who have been exposed to majority cultural values (Sodhi Kalsi, 2003). Furthermore, intergenerational differences tend to become more pronounced the longer the term of residency.

Ethic identity tends to strengthen with age (Phinney, Ferguson, & Tate, 1997) and progresses through phases. The first phase is typical of younger children who haven't paid attention to or haven't shown much interest in their ethnic identity. Next, as the young person is exposed to the media, or experiences racism or inequality in society, they may start to become acutely aware of the gulf that lies between the values and attitudes that exist within the larger culture and their own culture. Following a period of exploration of what it means to be a part of an ethnic group, adolescents may internalize their ethnic identity by developing a secure sense of membership and pride in and commitment to their own ethnic group (Phinney, 1990, 1993; Phinney & Alipuria, 1996; Phinney & Kohastu, 1997). Of course ethnic identity development does not always progress smoothly or completely and people may cycle through the phases at different times throughout their lives (Parham, 1989).

Adolescents who form strong and favourable ethnic identities have higher levels of self-esteem and optimism than their peers with weak ethnic identities (Phinney, Ferguson, & Tate, 1997). Moreover, adolescents who form a combined identity based on strong identification and participation in both their own ethnic culture and the larger culture have the highest self-esteem and the best outcomes. Teens who possess a **bicultural identity** not only feel more positive about their own ethnic group, but they have more favourable relationships with people from other ethnic groups as well (Phinney, Ferguson, & Tate, 1997; Phinney & Kohastu, 1997).

Recent-immigrant youth experience mixed feelings toward Canadian society. Although they enjoy the freedom associated with Canadian youth culture they feel "somewhat overwhelmed and alienated by what they perceive to be its rampant consumerism and superficiality" (**www.ccsd.ca/subsites/cd/docs/iy/hl.htm**). Those who speak neither English nor French face the extra challenge of learning a new language as well as overcoming social isolation when they arrive in Canada (CCSD, 2000b). A Canadian Council on Social Development report on cultural diversity (CCSD, 2000c) found that new arrivals have to contend with developing new relationships with friends in whom they can confide. More than one-quarter of immigrant youth aged 12 to 14 who have been in Canada less than 10 years reported that they do not have someone on whom they can rely during a crisis or when making important decisions. Consequently, immigrant youth often seek social support through formal social groups such as volunteer and religious organizations, and actively participate in religious organizations in part as a way to establish a social network.

However, once they have lived in Canada for at least a decade, immigrant youth adopt patterns of lifestyle behaviours similar to those of Canadian-born youth, especially in terms of changes in participation in religious activities, smoking, and alcohol consumption (CCSD, 2000c). Specifically, immigrant youth who have lived in Canada for more than 10 years have about as many friends in whom they can confide as

ethnic identity
a sense of belonging to an ethnic group

Critical Thinking

How do you think your own ethnicity affects your sense of identity? Do you ever think of yourself as being "bicultural"?

bicultural identity
personal identification and satisfaction with more than one culture

Young recent immigrants often develop two identities: a psychological sense of self and an ethnic identity. Those who succeed at both tasks often think of themselves as "bicultural" and have an easier time relating to peers of the same and other ethnicities.
(*Photos: top,* Yannis Kontos/Gamma/PONOPRESSE; *bottom,* Vicki Kasala/Getty Images)

locus of control
a set of beliefs about the causes of events

Canadian-born youth; are about as likely to never attend a religious service; have more friends who drink and smoke than do recent immigrants; and have somewhat increased their rates of smoking and alcohol consumption.

One organization that has provided an influential forum for dealing with youth concerns is The Students Commission, a not-for-profit organization that was established in 1991 to bring students together in order to discuss issues and direct public policy both nationally and internationally. Delegates of The Students Commission have made presentations to "the Prime Minister, the Governor General, cabinet ministers, provincial premiers, and business, education, community and labour leaders across Canada" (**http://collections.ic.gc.ca/sharing/history_e.html**) (Students Commission, 1995). Members have also had a voice at the tables of many prominent international organizations, such as the United Nations, the G-7 Summit, APEC, and UNESCO. In 1992, during the Canadian national unity debates, The Students Commission conference delegates discussed what it means to be "Canadian." The essence of the youth delegates' comments on Canadian "culture" and ethnic identity is as relevant today as it was then (see **The Real World**).

LOCUS OF CONTROL AND OTHER TRAITS

During adolescence, the Big Five personality traits coalesce with components of teens' understanding of themselves and others to form clusters that can be used to predict variables such as academic achievement and mental illness. One particularly important factor is a social and self-understanding variable known as **locus of control**, a set of beliefs about the causes of events (Rotter, 1990). Locus of control beliefs appear in middle childhood but become stable during the teenaged years, as adolescents' ability to think logically and to engage in complex information-processing improves.

Someone with an *external* locus of control attributes the causes of experiences such as school failure to factors outside himself. For example, an adolescent with an external locus of control might claim that he failed a class because the teacher didn't like him or because the class was too difficult. Someone with an *internal* locus of control views personal variables, such as ability and effort, as responsible for outcomes. A teen who believes either that she failed a class because she lacks ability or that she failed because she didn't try hard enough has an internal locus of control.

There are important correlations between locus of control and behaviour (Janssen & Carton, 1999). An external locus of control is associated with procrastination and poor academic performance. In contrast, both teens and adults with an internal locus of control are more likely to complete tasks and to succeed in school.

For most teens who have external locus of control, the trait is balanced by other more positive aspects of personality. However, researchers have found that an external locus of control is sometimes part of a cluster of personality variables that includes low self-esteem, along with the introversion and neuroticism dimensions of the Big Five (Beautrais, Joyce, & Mulder, 1999). (You'll recall that introversion is a preference for solitary rather than social activities; individuals who score high on tests of neuroticism are pessimistic, irritable, and worry a lot.) Developmentalists have found that teens across a variety of cultures who possess this particular combination of characteristics have a very negative outlook on life, resist efforts by parents and friends to help them, and are at greater risk for all kinds of adjustment problems than their peers. For instance, these adolescents are more likely to use *avoidant coping* when they face

The Real World
Empowered Youth
The Students Commission

When Canadians were hotly debating national unity in 1992, youth at The Students Commission Conference were focusing on accepting everyone no matter what their differences. One of the discussion topics revolved around the question "What does being Canadian mean?" Below are excerpts of some of their responses, which illustrate how Canadian life looked from their point of view:

- We cannot define Canada as only one culture. Canadian society is multicultural, multiracial, multifaith, and multilingual. Your identity is made up of what you value from various cultures that make up your ethnic background.

- Being of the first generation means that one has to keep [one's] cultural heritage and try to combine it with the Canadian lifestyle and values. At one extreme there is the uniqueness of the individual and at the other extreme [we are] all citizens of the earth; somewhere in the middle lies a Canadian identity.

- All Canadian cultures were at one point faced with conflict between their own cultural heritage/ethnic background and the culture of their new surroundings. Differences and adjustments are the things which make the transition to the new culture difficult. These include a change in language, food, value systems, and traditions. These may seem like easy things to change, but to an immigrant, a difficulty with these things could translate to a resentment of their new land. Someone who has lived in Canada for a long time might ask why there is such a big deal about blending two different cultures. Immigrants are faced with this difficult juggling act—a dilemma in which they feel they might have to compromise their traditions [in order] to fit in with the surrounding culture.

- Two [difficulties] facing immigrants have always been adjusting to the new culture and maintaining their own cultural heritage. Often the values and traditions of one ethnic culture get swallowed up by the surrounding environment.

- For many people, the feeling of being Canadian has somewhat erased the feeling of being an immigrant. This may be true for a large number of people in our society. However, we must never lose sight of the fact that we are all immigrants to this country and that our ancestors suffered and sacrificed to reach Canada. Some of our ancestors were escaping from famine, war, [or] religious, social, or political persecution. To escape these things they migrated to Canada just as people migrate today.

(Source: http://collections.ic.gc.ca/sharing/ B_C_e.html. Students Commission, 1992.)

problems (Gomez, Bounds, Holmberg, Fullarton, & Gomez, 1999; Gomez, Holmberg, Bounds, Fullarton, & Gomez, 1999; Medvedova, 1998). This means that they ignore problems or put off dealing with them. For example, a high school student with these traits who finds out he is failing a class may wait until it is too late to try to do anything about it. However, because he tends to blame others for his problems, he is unlikely to be able to learn from the experience.

Such teens get into these situations over and over again without ever seeming to be able to prevent them or to pull themselves out of trouble in any effective way. As a consequence of their negative outlook combined with their repeated experiences of disappointment and failure, these adolescents are prone to depression (del Barrio, Moreno-Rosset, Lopez-Martinez, & Olmedo, 1997; Ge & Conger, 1999). Once depressed, such teens are likely to attempt suicide (Beautrais, Joyce, & Mulder, 1999). Their emotional difficulties are compounded by the fact that most are rejected by peers (Young & Bradley, 1998).

Teens with these characteristics also seem to be, figuratively speaking, looking at the world through a different lens than their more optimistic peers. For example, they appear to think about themselves and their emotions a great deal more (Yarcheski,

Mahon, & Yarcheski, 1998). Girls with this cluster of traits tend to see greater distinctions between male and female roles and personality than other girls do (Wilcox & Francis, 1997). They are also more likely to be intolerant of people whose ethnicity or political beliefs are different from their own (Sotelo & Sangrador, 1997).

The outlook for teens with this set of characteristics is not good. Their beliefs about themselves and the social world are resistant to change and persist into adulthood (Offer, Kaiz, Howard, & Bennett, 1998). In addition, as adults, they continue to be subject to bouts of depression and a variety of occupational and relationship difficulties. Consequently, developmentalists are currently searching for assessment tools and intervention strategies that can be used to identify and help such individuals in middle childhood or early adolescence (Young & Bradley, 1998).

Before Going On

- In what ways does self-understanding in adolescence differ from that in childhood?

- What are the sex-role concepts of adolescents?

- How does self-esteem change across the teenaged years?

- How do minority teenagers develop an ethnic identity?

- How does the combination of external locus of control, low self-esteem, introversion, and neuroticism influence an adolescent's development?

SOCIAL RELATIONSHIPS

As you can see from the solutions for peer conflicts listed in **Table 11.1,** adolescents' ideas about other people and their understanding of social situations are more complex than those of children. These advances in interpersonal understanding lead to changes in family and peer relationships.

RELATIONSHIPS WITH PARENTS

Teenagers have two, apparently contradictory, tasks in their relationships with their parents: to establish autonomy from them and to maintain a sense of relatedness with them.

CONFLICTS WITH PARENTS The rise in conflict between parents and teenagers has been documented by a number of researchers (e.g., Flannery, Montemayor, & Eberly, 1994; Laursen, 1995; Steinberg, 1988). University of Lethbridge sociologist Reginald Bibby found that Canadian teens disagree with their parents most when it comes to issues such as chores around the house, school, their parents' reaction to the way they talk to them, and their parent's concern about their safety. These issues account for roughly half of the conflicts. It's interesting that there was less parent-teen conflict over issues such as who they are dating, drugs, their appearance (clothing and hairstyle), and sex (about one-fifth of the conflicts) (Bibby, 2001).

TABLE 11.1	Children's and Adolescents' Comments About How to Solve Disagreements Between Friends
Age	**Comments**
5-Year-Olds	Go away from her and come back later when you're not fighting.
	Punch her out.
8-Year-Olds	Around our way the guy who started it just says he's sorry.
	Well, if you say something and don't really mean it, then you have to mean it when you take it back.
14-Year-Olds	Sometimes you got to get away for a while. Calm down a bit so you won't be so angry. Then get back and try to talk it out.
	If you just settle up after a fight that is no good. You gotta really feel that you'd be happy the way things went if you were in your friend's shoes. You can just settle up with someone who is not a friend, but that's not what friendship is really about.
16-Year-Old	Well, you could talk it out, but it usually fades itself out. It usually takes care of itself. You don't have to explain everything. You do certain things and each of you knows what it means. But if not, then talk it out.

(*Source:* Selman, 1980, pp. 107–113.)

Although this increase in discord is widely observed, you should not assume that it signifies a major disruption of the quality of the parent–child relationships. For most Canadian teens, their families are still important to them, especially as a source of enjoyment and support (Bibby, 2001). Furthermore, parent–teen conflicts appear to cause more distress for parents than for adolescents (Dekovic, 1999).

Individual traits of teenagers themselves may contribute to conflicts with parents. The adolescent's temperament, for example, contributes to the amount of conflict. Those who have been difficult from early childhood are the most likely to experience high degrees of conflict with parents in adolescence (Dekovic, 1999). Teens' pubertal status may be a factor as well. Among girls, conflict seems to rise after menarche (Holmbeck & Hill, 1991). Moreover, as noted earlier, cultural factors affect both the degree of parent–teen conflict and perceptions of its meaning.

ATTACHMENT Teenagers' underlying emotional attachment to their parents remains strong on average. For example, a large study in the Netherlands suggests that the teenager's bond with her parents may weaken somewhat in the middle of adolescence (ages 15 and 16) and then return to former levels (van Wel, 1994). But virtually all the researchers who have explored this question find that a teenager's sense of well-being or happiness is more strongly correlated with the quality of her attachment to her parents than with the quality of her relationships with peers (e.g., Greenberg, Siegel, & Leitch, 1983; Raja, McGee, & Stanton, 1992). Moreover, research findings regarding the centrality of parent–teen relationships have been consistent across a variety of cultures (Claes, 1998; Okamoto & Uechi, 1999).

Research in several countries has also found that teens who remain closely attached to their parents are the most likely to be academically successful and to enjoy good peer relations (Black & McCartney, 1997; Claes, 1998; Kim, Hetherington, & Reiss, 1999;

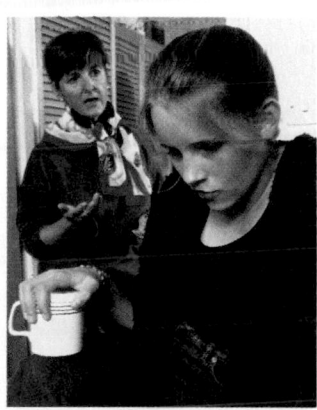

While it is true that the physical changes of puberty are often followed by an increase in the number of conflicts, it is a myth that conflict is the main feature of the parent–adolescent relationship.
(*Photo:* Penny Tweedie/Getty Images)

Mayseless, Wiseman, & Hai, 1998). They are also less likely than less securely attached teens to engage in antisocial behaviour (Ma, Shek, Cheung, & Oi Bun Lam, 2000). Further, the quality of attachment in early adolescence predicts drug use in later adolescence and early adulthood (Brook, Whiteman, Finch, & Cohen, 2000). Teens who are close to their parents are less likely to use drugs than peers whose bonds with parents are weaker. Thus, even while teenagers are becoming more autonomous, they need their parents to provide a psychological safe base.

PARENTING STYLES For adolescents, as for younger children, authoritative parenting is consistently associated with more positive outcomes. Research suggests that parenting style influences a teen's self-concept and other intrapersonal variables (Dekovic & Meeus, 1997). Internal locus of control, for example, is more common in teens who perceive their parents to be authoritative (McClun & Merrell, 1998). Parental acceptance also appears to be important in teens' development of realistic assessments of their academic abilities (Bornholt & Goodnow, 1999).

Parental involvement in education and extracurricular activities seems to be just as important for teenagers as it is for younger children. For example, lack of parental involvement in school and extracurricular activities is strongly related to conduct problems such as disruptive classroom behaviour (Frick, Christian, & Wooton, 1999). In addition, parental involvement in school-based organizations is related to secondary school students' postgraduation plans (Trusty, 1999). Those whose parents are most involved are the most likely to attend a post-secondary institution.

FAMILY STRUCTURE Family structure, too, continues to be an important factor in a teenager's life. Although the vast majority of Canadian youth aged 15 to 19 live with their families (93%) (see **Figure 11.5**), some live with spouses of their own, live common-law, or are lone parents (4%). Still others live on their own, or with relatives or non-relatives (3%) (Statistics Canada, 2002d).

Adolescents in households including a step-parent are, on average, somewhat less well-adjusted than those who live with two biological parents. These differences are evident even when teens have been living with a step-parent for several years (Hetherington et al., 1999). Among adolescents, girls show more distress when parents divorce, both when the girl lives with her single mother after the divorce and when there is a stepfather in the household (Amato, 1993; Hetherington & Clingempeel, 1992). Adolescent girls have more trouble interacting with a new stepfather than do their brothers, and they treat him more as an intruder. Girls in this situation are also likely to become depressed and are more likely than boys in the same situation to begin using drugs.

Why this pattern occurs is not so obvious. The adolescent girl may feel displaced from a special position in the family system that she held after her parents' divorce and before the mother's remarriage. In contrast, the teenaged boy may benefit from the addition of the stepfather, because he acquires a male role model. Whatever the explanation, findings like these are reminders that family systems are astonishingly complex.

RELATIONSHIPS WITH PEERS

Despite the importance of family relationships to adolescents, it is an undeniable fact that peer relationships become far more significant in adolescence than they have been at any earlier period, and perhaps than they will be at any time later in life.

FRIENDSHIPS Shared activities and interests continue to be important elements in the selection of friends in adolescence. However, similarity of psychological characteristics

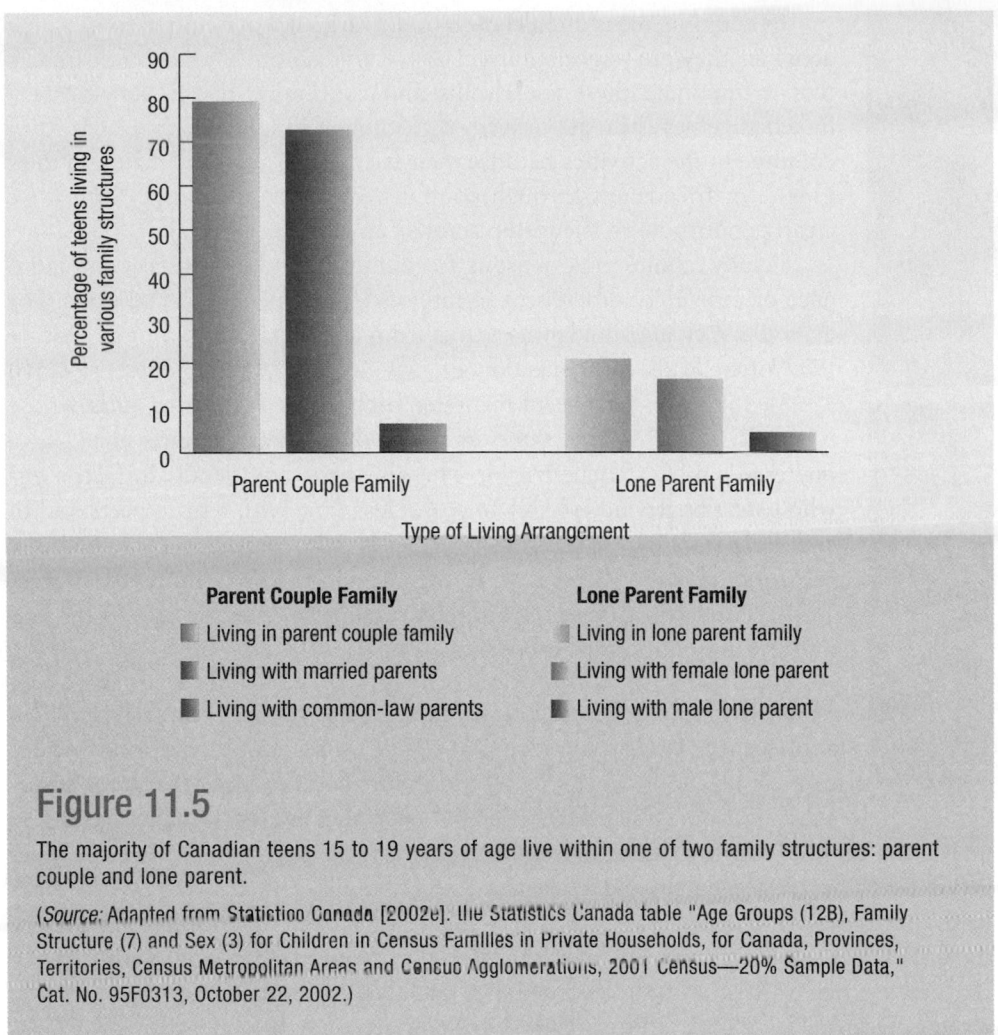

Figure 11.5

The majority of Canadian teens 15 to 19 years of age live within one of two family structures: parent couple and lone parent.

(*Source:* Adapted from Statistics Canada [2002e]. the Statistics Canada table "Age Groups (12B), Family Structure (7) and Sex (3) for Children in Census Families in Private Households, for Canada, Provinces, Territories, Census Metropolitan Areas and Census Agglomerations, 2001 Census—20% Sample Data," Cat. No. 95F0313, October 22, 2002.)

and attitudes takes on new significance during the teenaged years. For example, adolescents tend to choose friends who share their beliefs about smoking, drug use, sex, and the importance of academic achievement (Urdan, 1997).

Teens' friendships are increasingly intimate, in the sense that adolescent friends share more and more of their inner feelings and secrets and are more knowledgeable about each other's feelings. Loyalty and faithfulness become more valued characteristics of friendship. However, the ability to display intimacy, loyalty, and faithfulness in the context of a friendship doesn't come automatically with age. In fact, teens vary considerably in these interpersonal skills. The variation may be the result of individual differences in temperament and personality or of teens' experiences with family relationships (Updegraff & Obeidallah, 1999).

Adolescent friendships are also more stable than those of younger children (Degirmencioglu, Urberg, & Tolson, 1998). In one longitudinal study, researchers found that only about 20% of friendships among children in Grade 4 lasted as long as a year, whereas about 40% of friendships formed by these same youngsters when they were in Grade 10 were long-lasting (Cairns & Cairns, 1994). Friendship stability probably increases in adolescence because older teens work harder than younger teens and elementary school children at maintaining positive relationships with friends through negotiation of conflicts (Nagamine, 1999).

As adolescents age, the structures of their peer groups change. (*Photos: top,* David Young-Wolff/Getty Images; *bottom,* Tessa Codrington/Getty Images)

In addition, teens often choose friends who are committed to the same activities they are—sports, music, dance, and so on. They tell researchers that maintaining these friendships and continuing in the activities are linked together (Marsh, Craven, & Debus, 1999). In other words, they continue in the activities because their friends do, and they maintain their long-term friendships through continuation of the activities. Such links clearly contribute to friendship stability in adolescence.

Finally, adolescents' reasons for ending friendships reflect the influence of individual differences in rate of development of social skills. For example, a change in identity status from a less mature to a more mature level often leads to acquisition of new friends (Akers, Jones, & Coyl, 1998). Likewise, girls seem to prefer friendships with other girls whose romantic status is the same as their own—that is, girls who have boyfriends prefer female friends who also have boyfriends. In fact, a girl who gets a boyfriend is likely to spend less time with female peers and to end long-standing friendships with girls who haven't yet acquired a romantic partner (Benenson & Benarroch, 1998; Zimmer-Gembeck, 1999). For boys, differences in athletic achievements can lead to the end of previously important friendships.

PEER GROUPS Like friendships, peer groups become relatively stable in adolescence (Degirmencioglu et al., 1998). Peer group conformity seems to peak at about age 13 or 14 (at about the same time that adolescents show a drop in self-esteem) and then wanes as the teenager begins to arrive at a sense of identity that is more independent of the peer group. However, peer group pressures are less potent and less negative than popular cultural stereotypes might lead you to believe (Berndt, 1992). For one thing, remember that adolescents choose their friends and their crowd. And they are likely to choose to associate with a group that shares their values, attitudes, behaviours, and identity status (Akers et al., 1998; Urberg, Degirmencioglu, & Tolson, 1998). If the discrepancy between their own ideas and those of their friends becomes too great, teens are more likely to switch to a more compatible group of friends than to be persuaded to adopt the first group's values or behaviours. Furthermore, teenagers report that when explicit peer pressure is exerted, it is likely to be pressure toward positive activities, such as school involvement, and away from misconduct.

Only in so-called druggie-tough crowds does there seem to be explicit pressure toward misconduct or lawbreaking, and teens who appear to respond to such pressure may be motivated as much by a desire to prove "I'm as tough as you are" as by explicit pressure from peers (Berndt & Keefe, 1995b; Brown, Dolcini, & Leventhal, 1995). Thus, while Erikson appears to have been quite correct in saying that peers are a major force in shaping a child's identity development in adolescence, peer influence is neither all-powerful nor uniformly negative.

CHANGES IN PEER GROUP STRUCTURE The structure of the peer group also changes over the years of adolescence. The classic, widely quoted early study is that of Dunphy (1963) on the formation, dissolution, and interaction of teenaged groups in a high school in Sydney, Australia, between 1958 and 1960. Dunphy identified two important subvarieties of groups. The first type, which he called a **clique**, is made up of four to six young people who appear to be strongly attached to one another. Cliques have strong cohesiveness and high levels of intimate sharing.

In the early years of adolescence, cliques are almost entirely same-sex groups—a holdover from the preadolescent pattern. Gradually, however, the cliques combine into

clique

four to six young people who appear to be strongly attached to one another larger sets that Dunphy called crowds, which include both males and females. Finally, the crowd breaks down again into heterosexual cliques and then into loose associations of couples. In Dunphy's study, the period during which adolescents socialized in crowds was roughly between 13 and 15—the very years when they display the greatest conformity to peer pressure.

Contemporary researchers on adolescence have changed Dunphy's labels somewhat (Brown, 1990; Brown, Mory, & Kinney, 1994). They use the word *crowd* to refer to the *reputation-based group* with which a young person is identified, either by choice or by peer designation. In Canadian schools, these groups have labels such as "all stars," "jocks," "nerds," "skaters," "thugs," "goths," "stoners," "normals," "tech-ers," "preppies," and "loners." Studies in junior high and high schools make it clear that teenagers can readily identify each of the major crowds in their school and have quite stereotypical descriptions of them (e.g., "The partiers goof off a lot more than the jocks do, but they don't come to school stoned like the burnouts do") (Brown et al., 1994, p. 133). Each of these descriptions serves as what Brown calls an *identity prototype*: Labelling others and oneself as belonging to one or more of these groups helps to create or reinforce the adolescent's own identity (Brown et al., 1994). Such labelling also helps the adolescent identify potential friends or foes.

Within any given school, the various crowds are organized into a fairly clear, widely understood pecking order. In North American schools, the groups labelled as some variant of "populars," "jocks," or "normals" are typically at the top of the heap, with "brains" somewhere in the middle and "druggies," "loners," and "nerds" at the bottom (Brown et al., 1994).

Throughout the years of junior high and high school, the social system of crowds becomes increasingly differentiated, with more and more distinct groups (Kinney, 1993). Within (and sometimes between) these crowds, Kinney found, adolescents created smaller cliques. As Dunphy observed, social groups were almost entirely same-sex in early adolescence but, by late adolescence, they had become mixed in gender, often composed of groups of dating couples. Mutual friendships and dating pairs become more central to social interactions in later adolescence than are cliques or crowds (Urberg et al., 1995).

ROMANTIC RELATIONSHIPS Of all the changes in social relationships in adolescence, perhaps the most profound is the shift from the total dominance of same-sex friendships toward the inclusion of heterosexual relationships. The change happens gradually, but it seems to proceed at a somewhat more rapid pace in girls. At the beginning of adolescence, teens are still fairly rigid about their preferences for same-sex friends (Bukowski, Sippola, & Hoza, 1999). Over the next year or two, they become more open to opposite-sex friendships (Harton & Latane, 1997; Kuttler, LaGreca, & Prinstein, 1999). The skills they gain in relating to opposite-sex peers in such friendships and in mixed-gender groups prepare them for heterosexual romantic relationships (Feiring, 1999). Thus, although adults often assume that sexual desires are the basis of emergent romantic relationships, it appears that social factors are just as important. In fact, research suggests that social competence in a variety of relationships—with parents, peers, and friends—predicts the ease with which teens move from exclusive same-sex relationships to opposite-sex friendships and romantic relationships (Theriault, 1998).

Despite their social function, these new relationships are nevertheless clearly part of the preparation for assuming a full adult sexual identity. Physical sexuality is part of that role, but so are the skills of personal intimacy with the opposite sex, including flirting, communicating, and reading the social cues used by the other gender. In Western societies, these skills are learned first in larger crowds or cliques and then in dating pairs (Zani, 1993).

crowd
a combination of cliques, which includes both males and females

Critical Thinking

Think back to your own high school years and draw a diagram or map to describe the organization of crowds and cliques. Were those crowds or cliques more or less important in the last few years of high school than they had been earlier?

By 12 or 13, most adolescents have a basic conception of what it means to be "in love." Interestingly, even though the actual progression toward romantic relationships happens faster for girls, boys report having had the experience of falling in love for the first time at an earlier age. Moreover, by the end of adolescence, it appears that the average boy believes he has been in love several more times than the average girl (Montgomery & Sorel, 1998).

The sense of being in love is an important factor in adolescent dating patterns (Montgomery & Sorel, 1998). In other words, teenagers prefer to date those with whom they believe they are in love, and they view falling out of love as a reason for ending a dating relationship. In addition, for girls (but not for boys), romantic relationships are seen as a context for self-disclosure. Put another way, girls seem to want more psychological intimacy from these early relationships than their partners do (Feiring, 1999).

Early dating and early sexual activity are more common among the poor of every ethnic group and among those who experience relatively early puberty. Religious teachings and individual attitudes about the appropriate age for dating and sexual behaviour also make a difference, as does family structure. Girls with parents who are divorced or remarried, for example, report earlier dating and higher levels of sexual experience than do girls from intact families, and those with a strong religious identity report later dating and lower levels of sexuality (Bingham, Miller, & Adams, 1990; Miller & Moore, 1990). But for every group, these are years of experimentation with romantic relationships.

HOMOSEXUALITY

For the great majority of teens, the pathway through adolescence includes a progression in peer relationships, a movement from unisexual cliques to heterosexual groups and then to heterosexual pairs. For the subgroup of homosexual teens, the process is different. In a study of nearly 35 000 youths in Minnesota public schools, researchers found that about 1% of the adolescent boys and approximately 0.4% of the adolescent girls defined themselves as homosexual, but a much larger number said they were unsure of their sexual orientation (Remafedi, Resnick, Blum, & Harris, 1998). These figures are generally consistent with a Queen's University study of 5514 Canadian community college and university students. King et al. (1988) reported that 1% of students under the age of 25 were homosexual and 1% were bisexual. Furthermore, results from Statistics Canada's (first ever) survey question about sexual orientation found that 1% of Canadians aged 18 to 59 reported that they were homosexual and 0.7% bisexual. Slightly more younger Canadians (about 2% of 18- to 34-year olds) considered themselves either homosexual or bisexual than did older Canadians (Statistics Canada, 2004d).

Several twin studies show that when one identical twin is homosexual, the probability that the other twin will also be homosexual is 50–60%, whereas the concordance rate is only about 20% for fraternal twins and only about 11% among pairs of biologically unrelated boys adopted into the same family (Bailey & Pillard, 1991; Bailey, Pillard, Neale, & Agyei, 1993; Whitam, Diamond, & Martin, 1993). Family studies also suggest that male homosexuality runs in families—that is, the families of most gay men have a higher proportion of homosexual males than do the families of heterosexual men (Bailey et al., 1999). Such findings strengthen the hypothesis that biological factors play a role in the development of homosexuality (Gladue, 1994; Pillard & Bailey, 1995).

Additional studies suggest that prenatal hormone patterns may also be a causal factor in homosexuality. For example, women whose mothers took the drug diethylstilbestrol (DES, a synthetic estrogen) during pregnancy are more likely to be homosexual as adults than are women who were not exposed to DES in the womb (Meyer-Bahlburg et

Development in the Information Age

The Social Aspects of Electronic Communication

Canada's youth are among the most "wired" of all adolescents in the world (Bell Canada, 2001a; Media Awareness Network [MNet], 2001a, 2001b; Ellison & Clark, 2001). They are the first generation to be raised on cable and satellite television, cell phones and Internet communication. This means that the youth of today have instantaneous access to more information and more people than any other previous generation. The full impact of how this will affect the perception of this cohort of teenagers is yet to be realized, in part because the technology continues to become more subtle and user friendly, and thus commonplace, much like how their parents now view devices such as VCRs and microwave ovens.

Cell phones have helped strengthen the relationship between parents and teenagers. For example, the cell phone allows teens to keep parents informed about their activities away from home, while building a sense of connection and dialogue between the parents and children. Cell phones therefore afford teens more independence while providing increased reassurance to parents about their child's safety and whereabouts. A recent study of Ontario and Quebec 16- to 24-year-olds by Bell Canada (2001b) found that young people are high-volume users; half of the users spend 45 minutes or more on the phone per week. Although half of the youth surveyed use their cell phones to keep up to date with their friends, they also use their cells to talk with relatives, family members, and to a lesser extent their girlfriend or boyfriend. More than two-thirds use the cell phone for practical purposes and 11% use it for emergencies. Young people are less likely to call others just to casually chat. Having been raised with cell phone technology, adolescents tend to be sophisticated and mature users. They view the cell phone as a practical tool and as a way to keep in contact with significant others while enjoying greater freedom.

In addition to providing cell phones, most parents stated that they bought a home computer specifically for their children in order to help them keep up with their peers—about nine out of every ten 15-year-old students have and regularly use a computer in the home (Willms & Corbett, 2003). Not surprisingly, today's generation of youth, many of whom have had access to a computer since the age of 3 or 4, perceive computers and the Internet as being a natural and integral part of their daily routines—81% of youth have Internet access at home and 99% of Canadian youth aged 9 to 17 have used the Internet to some extent over the past 12 months (Industry Canada, 2000, MNet, 2004b). It is interesting to note that during the 1990s the amount of time teenagers spent watching television went down while the time they spent on the Internet went up (Statistics Canada, 2001g, 2001k). The recent MNet (2001a) survey found that about eight in ten youth spend an hour or more watching television daily while almost half of the youth said they spend an equivalent amount of time using the Internet.

MNet (2001a, 2004) surveys indicate that in addition to downloading music, playing games, and personal interest research, youth show significant use of the Internet for social purposes, such as instant messaging (IM), chat rooms, and e-mail messaging. Interestingly, the survey revealed some important differ-

ences between how parents thought their children were using the Internet and children's actual activity use (see **Figure 11.6**). Parents greatly underestimated the amount of time their children spent on all but one of the activities measured; the exception was the parents' overestimation of their children's use of the Internet to help with homework!

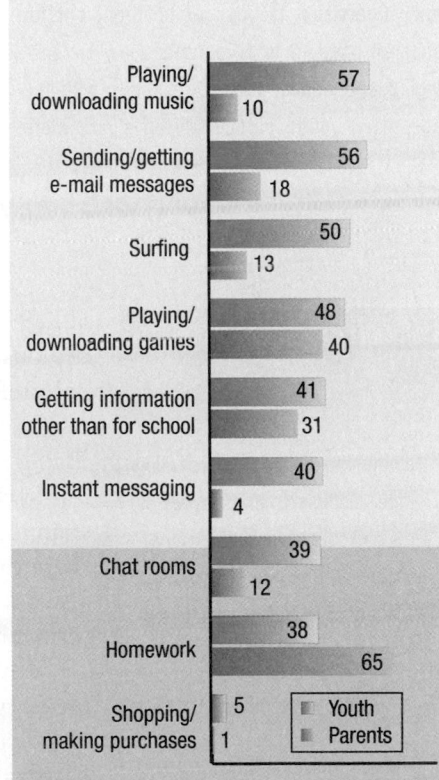

Figure 11.6

Comparison of what youth say they do on the Internet versus what parents think their children use the Internet for.

(*Source:* Environics Research/Media Awareness Network, 2001, from *Young Canadians in a Wired World*, Activities on the Net, p. 26.)

Secondary school students report that social factors are the most valuable aspect of using the Internet. Thirty-six percent of youth said that being able to communicate with people they know or making new friends is more important than easy access to information, entertainment, or education. There was a gender difference for secondary school students whereby girls were twice as likely as boys to place importance on the social benefits of communicating with people they know on the Internet. Boys were twice as likely as girls to value the entertainment benefits of the Internet (MNet, 2001a).

As is true with most technology, there are benefits as well as risks associated with its use (Clark, 2001). The MNet (2001a) survey found that parents provide more instruction and supervision of younger children, but for children aged 13 to 17 parents allow increasing independence. This corresponds with the age when youth, particularly boys, are more

likely to engage in risky Internet use (MNet, 2001b).

Some of the primary risks include:

- exploring private and adult-only chat rooms (58% of 11- to 12-year-olds and 70% of those aged 13 to 14 went into restricted chat rooms)

- meeting Internet acquaintances in person (one-quarter of youth said they had been asked to meet, and 15% actually did meet someone in person whom they had first met on the Internet)

- being exposed to sexually explicit and hateful material (53% of young users received pornographic junk mail and about half of students in secondary school received unwanted sexual comments. In addition, one-quarter were sent material that was hateful about others)

- sharing personal information (one in five youth said that they would provide both

their name and address over the Internet in order to win a prize)

Like many high-risk behaviours to which young people are exposed, parents should be concerned with equipping their children with the knowledge and skills necessary to prevent harm while at the same time not stifling the creative and beneficial use of electronic media. These are the tools of communication for this generation and they will likely increase in importance in the future. In fact, youth accept that exposure to violent and sexual content is unavoidable, but at the same time, they have learned to fend off offensive material. Accordingly, teens argue that it is a waste of time and resources trying to keep unsuitable material away from children. Rather, they suggest, children need to develop the critical thinking skills that will prepare them to make informed choices and decisions about what material to censor (MNet, 2004).

Make the Connection

Review the concept of reaction range discussed in **Chapter 6**. How can this view of the interaction of heredity and environment be used to explain the development of homosexuality?

al., 1995). Moreover, as you learned in **Chapter 7**, there is some evidence that boys who demonstrate strong cross-sex behaviour in early childhood are likely to show homosexual preferences when they reach adolescence. Like the twin and family studies, these results are consistent with the hypothesis that homosexuality is programmed in at birth (Bailey & Zucker, 1995).

Such evidence does not mean that environment plays no role in homosexuality. For example, when one of a pair of identical twins is homosexual, the other twin does *not* share that sexual orientation 40–50% of the time. Something beyond biology must be at work, although developmentalists do not yet know what environmental factors may be involved.

Whatever the cause of variations in sexual orientation, homosexual teenagers are a minority who face high levels of prejudice and stereotyping. Many are verbally attacked or ridiculed, and as many as a third are physically assaulted by their peers (Remafedi, Farrow, & Deisher, 1991; Savin-Williams, 1994). For these and other reasons, these young people are at high risk for a variety of problems. For example, homosexual adolescents are more likely than their heterosexual peers to be depressed and to attempt suicide (Remafedi, French, Story, Resnick, & Blum, 1998; Safren & Heimberg, 1999).

Homosexual teenagers must also cope with the decision about whether to "come out" about their homosexuality. Those who do come out are far more likely to tell peers than parents, although telling peers carries some risk. Some research suggests that as many as two-thirds of homosexual youth have not told their parents (Rotheram-Borus, Rosario, & Koopman, 1991).

While homosexual adolescents clearly face unique challenges, they share many of the same concerns as their heterosexual peers. For example, both homosexual and heterosexual girls are more likely than boys to be dissatisfied with their physical appearance (Saewyc, Bearinger, Heinz, Blum, & Resnick, 1998). Consequently, dieting is more common among both homosexual and heterosexual girls than among boys of either sexual orientation. Like their heterosexual counterparts, homosexual male adolescents drink alcohol more often and engage in more risky behaviour than do female teenagers.

The same factors predict successful identity and social development in homosexual and heterosexual teens. For example, attachment to parents appears to be just as important for homosexual teens as for their heterosexual peers. In fact, attachment to parents and the maintenance of good relations with them in adolescence seems to help homosexual teens in the coming-out process (Beaty, 1999; Floyd et al., 1999).

There is obviously much that researchers do not know about homosexual adolescents. But it is reasonable to hypothesize that the years of adolescence may be particularly stressful for this subgroup. Like teenagers from ethnic minorities, homosexual teens have an additional task facing them in forming a clear identity.

Before Going On

- Describe adolescents' family relationships in terms of conflict, attachment, parenting styles, and family structure.
- What are the characteristics of adolescents' friendships, peer groups, and romantic relationships?
- What are the unique challenges faced by teenagers who are homosexual?

MORAL DEVELOPMENT

As you read in **Chapter 9**, theorists representing various orientations think differently about moral development. However, the theorist whose work has had the most powerful impact has been psychologist Lawrence Kohlberg (Colby, Kohlberg, Gibbs, & Lieberman 1983; Kohlberg, 1976, 1981). Moreover, theories of moral reasoning have been important in explanations of adolescent antisocial behaviour.

KOHLBERG'S THEORY OF MORAL REASONING

You may recall from **Chapter 9** that Piaget proposed two stages in the development of moral reasoning. Working from Piaget's basic assumptions, Kohlberg devised a way of measuring moral reasoning based on research participants' responses to moral dilemmas such as the following:

> In Europe, a woman was near death from a special kind of cancer. There was one drug that the doctors thought might save her. It was a form of radium that a druggist in the same town had recently discovered. The drug was expensive to make, but the druggist was charging ten times what the drug cost him to make. He paid $200 for the radium and charged $2000 for a small dose of the drug. The sick woman's husband, Heinz, went to everyone he knew to borrow the money, but he could only get together about $1000.... He told the druggist that his wife was dying, and asked him to sell it cheaper or let him pay later. But the druggist said, "No, I discovered the drug and I'm going to

make money from it." So Heinz got desperate and broke into the man's store to steal the drug for his wife. (Kohlberg & Elfenbein, 1975, p. 621)

Critical Thinking

How would you respond to the Heinz dilemma? What does your response suggest about your level of moral reasoning?

Kohlberg analyzed participants' answers to questions about such dilemmas (for example, "Should Heinz have stolen the drug? Why?") and concluded that there were three levels of moral development, each made up of two substages, as summarized in **Table 11.2**.

The stages are correlated with age somewhat loosely. Very few children reason beyond stage 1 or 2, and stage 2 and stage 3 reasoning are the most common types found among adolescents (Walker, de Vries, & Trevethan, 1987). Among adults, stages 3 and 4 are the most common (Gibson, 1990). You can see the pattern of age changes in **Figure 11.7**, which shows the results from Kohlberg's longitudinal study of 58 boys, first interviewed when they were 10 and subsequently followed for more than 20 years (Colby et al., 1983).

preconventional morality
in Kohlberg's theory, the level of moral reasoning in which judgments are based on authorities outside the self

At level I, **preconventional morality**, the child's judgments are based on sources of authority who are close by and physically superior—usually the parents. Just as descriptions of others are largely external at this level, so the standards the child uses to judge rightness or wrongness are external rather than internal. In particular, it is the outcome

---

TABLE 11.2   Kohlberg's Stages of Moral Development

Level	Stages	Description
Level I: Preconventional	Stage 1: Punishment and Obedience Orientation	The child or teenager decides what is wrong on the basis of what is punished. Obedience is valued for its own sake, but the child obeys because the adults have superior power.
	Stage 2: Individualism, Instrumental Purpose, and Exchange	Children and teens follow rules when it is in their immediate interest. What is good is what brings pleasant results.
Level II: Conventional	Stage 3: Mutual Interpersonal Expectations, Relationships, and Interpersonal Conformity	Moral actions are those that live up to the expectations of the family or other significant group. "Being good" becomes important for its own sake.
	Stage 4: Social System and Conscience (Law and Order)	Moral actions are those so defined by larger social groups or the society as a whole. One should fulfill duties one has agreed to and uphold laws, except in extreme cases.
Level III: Postconventional	Stage 5: Social Contract or Utility and Individual Rights	This stage involves acting so as to achieve the "greatest good for the greatest number." The teenager or adult is aware that most values are relative and laws are changeable, although rules should be upheld in order to preserve the social order. Still, there are some basic absolute values, such as the importance of each person's life and liberty.
	Stage 6: Universal Ethical Principles	The small number of adults who reason at Stage 6 develop and follow self-chosen ethical principles in determining what is right. These ethical principles are part of an articulated, integrated, carefully thought-out, and consistently followed system of values and principles.

(*Sources:* Kohlberg, 1976; Lickona, 1978.)

or consequence of an action that determines the rightness or wrongness of the action.

In stage 1 of this level—*the punishment and obedience orientation*—the child relies on the physical consequences of some action to decide whether it is right or wrong. If he is punished, the behaviour was wrong; if he is not punished, it was right. He is obedient to adults because they are bigger and stronger.

In stage 2—*individualism, instrumental purpose, and exchange*—the child or adolescent operates on the principle that you should do things that are rewarded and avoid things that are punished. For this reason, the stage is sometimes called naive hedonism. If it feels good, or brings pleasant results, it is good. Some beginning of concern for other people is apparent during this stage, but only if that concern can be expressed as something that benefits the child or teenager himself as well. So he can enter into agreements such as "If you help me, I'll help you."

To illustrate, here are some responses to variations of the Heinz dilemma, drawn from studies of children and teenagers in a number of different cultures, all of whom were at stage 2:

> He should steal the food for his wife because if she dies he'll have to pay for the funeral, and that costs a lot. [Taiwan] [He should steal the drug because] he should protect the life of his wife so he doesn't have to stay alone in life. [Puerto Rico] (Snarey, 1985, p. 221)

At the next major level, the level of **conventional morality**, rules or norms of a group to which the individual belongs become the basis of moral judgments, whether that group is the family, the peer group, a church, or the nation. What the chosen reference group defines as right or good is right or good in the individual's view. Again, very few children exhibit conventional thinking, but many adolescents are capable of this kind of moral reasoning.

Stage 3 (the first stage of level II) is the stage of *mutual interpersonal expectations, relationships, and interpersonal conformity* (sometimes also called the *good boy/nice girl stage*). Regardless of age, individuals who reason at this stage believe that good behaviour is what pleases other people. They value trust, loyalty, respect, gratitude, and maintenance of mutual relationships. Andy, a boy Kohlberg interviewed who was at stage 3, said:

> I try to do things for my parents, they've always done things for you. I try to do everything my mother says, I try to please her. Like she wants me to be a doctor and I want to, too, and she's helping me get up there. (Kohlberg, 1964, p. 401)

Another mark of this third stage is that the individual makes judgments based on intentions as well as on outward behaviour. If someone "didn't mean to do it," the wrongdoing is seen as less serious than if the person did it "on purpose."

Stage 4, the second stage of the conventional morality level, incorporates the norms of a larger reference group into moral judgments. Kohlberg labelled this the stage of *social system and conscience*. It is also sometimes called the *law-and-order orientation*. People reasoning at this stage focus on doing their duty, respecting authority, and following rules and laws. The emphasis is less on what is pleasing to particular people (as

Figure 11.7

These findings are from Colby and Kohlberg's long-term longitudinal study of a group of boys who were asked about Kohlberg's moral dilemmas every few years from age 10 through early adulthood. As they got older, the stage or level of their answers changed, with conventional reasoning appearing fairly widely at high school age. Postconventional, or principled, reasoning was not very common at any age.

(*Source:* Colby et al., Figure 1, p. 46. © The Society for Research in Child Development.)

conventional morality
in Kohlberg's theory, the level of moral reasoning in which judgments are based on rules or norms of a group to which the person belongs

postconventional morality
in Kohlberg's theory, the level of moral reasoning in which judgments are based on an integration of individual rights and the needs of society

in stage 3) and more on adhering to a complex set of regulations. However, the regulations themselves are not questioned, and morality and legality are assumed to be equivalent. Therefore, for a person at stage 4, something that is legal is right, whereas something that is illegal is wrong. Consequently, changes in law can effect changes in the moral views of individuals who reason at stage 4.

The transition to level III, **postconventional morality**, is marked by several changes, the most important of which is a shift in the source of authority. Individuals who reason at level I see authority as totally outside of themselves; at level II, the judgments or rules of external authorities are internalized, but they are not questioned or analyzed; at level III, a new kind of personal authority emerges, in which an individual makes choices and judgments based on self-chosen principles or on principles that are assumed to transcend the needs and concerns of any individual or group. Postconventional thinkers represent only a minority of adults and an even smaller minority of adolescents.

In stage 5 at this level, which Kohlberg called the *social contract orientation*, such self-chosen principles begin to be evident. Rules, laws, and regulations are not seen as irrelevant; they are important ways of ensuring fairness. But people operating at this level also acknowledge that there are times when the rules, laws, and regulations need to be ignored or changed.

The American civil rights movement of the 1950s and 1960s is a good example of stage 5 reasoning in action. *Civil disobedience*—deliberately breaking laws that were believed to be immoral—arose as a way of protesting racial segregation. For example, African Americans intentionally took seats in restaurants that were reserved for whites. It is important to note that the practice of civil disobedience does not usually involve avoiding the penalties that accompany criminal behaviour. Indeed, some of the most effective and poignant images from that period of U.S. history are photographs of individuals who surrendered and were jailed for breaking segregation laws. This behaviour illustrates the stage 5 view that, as a general principle, upholding the law is important, even though a specific law that is deemed to be immoral can, or even should, be broken when breaking it will serve to promote the common good.

Civil disobedience involves intentionally breaking laws one believes to be immoral. For example, in the early years of the U.S. civil rights movement, African Americans broke laws that excluded them from certain sections of restaurants by "sitting in" at whites-only lunch counters. Practitioners of civil disobedience do not try to evade the consequences of their actions, because they believe in upholding the law as a general principle even though they may view some specific laws as immoral. Thus, the thinking that underlies acts of civil disobedience represents Kohlberg's postconventional level of moral reasoning.
(*Photo:* Bettman/CORBIS)

In his original writing about moral development, Kohlberg also included a sixth stage, *the universal ethical principles orientation*. People who reason at this level assume personal responsibility for their own actions, based on fundamental and universal principles such as justice and basic respect for persons. Kohlberg eventually concluded that such people are quite rare, but they do represent the logical end point to the sequence of stages.

It is important to understand that what determines the stage or level of a person's moral judgment is not any specific moral choice but the form of reasoning used to justify that choice. For example, either response to Kohlberg's dilemma—that Heinz should steal the drug or that he should not—could be justified with logic at any given stage.

Kohlberg argued that this sequence of reasoning is both universal and hierarchically organized. That is, each stage grows out of the preceding one. Kohlberg did not suggest that all individuals eventually progress through all six stages, or even that each stage is tied to specific ages. But he insisted that the order is invariant and universal. He also believed that the social environment determines how slowly or rapidly individuals move through the stages.

The evidence seems fairly strong that the stages follow one another in the sequence Kohlberg proposed. Long-term longitudinal studies of teenagers and young adults in the United States, Israel, and Turkey show that changes in participants' reasoning nearly always occur in the hypothesized order (Colby et al., 1983;

Nisan & Kohlberg, 1982; Snarey, Reimer, & Kohlberg, 1985; Walker, 1989). People do not skip stages, and movement down the sequence rather than up occurs only about 5–7% of the time.

Variations of Kohlberg's dilemmas have been used with children in a wide range of countries, including both Western and non-Western, industrialized and nonindustrialized (Snarey, 1985). In every culture, researchers find higher stages of reasoning among older children, but cultures differ in the highest level of reasoning observed. In urban cultures (both Western and non-Western), stage 5 is typically the highest stage observed; in agricultural societies and those in which there is little opportunity for formal education, stage 4 is typically the highest. Collectively, this evidence seems to provide quite strong support for the universality of Kohlberg's stage sequence.

CAUSES AND CONSEQUENCES OF MORAL DEVELOPMENT

The most obvious reason for the general correlations between Kohlberg's stages and chronological age is cognitive development. Specifically, it appears that children must have a firm grasp of concrete operational thinking before they can develop or use conventional moral reasoning. Likewise, formal operations appears to be necessary for advancement to the postconventional level.

To be more specific, Kohlberg and many other theorists suggest that the decline of egocentrism that occurs as an individual moves through Piaget's concrete and formal operational stages is the cognitive-developmental variable that matters most in moral reasoning. The idea is that the greater a child's or adolescent's ability to look at a situation from another person's perspective, the more advanced she is likely to be in moral reasoning. Psychologists use the term **role-taking** to refer to this ability (Selman, 1980). Research has provided strong support for the hypothesized link between role-taking and moral development (Kuhn, Kohlberg, Languer, & Haan, 1977; Walker, 1980).

Nevertheless, cognitive development isn't enough. Kohlberg thought that the development of moral reasoning also required support from the social environment. Specifically, he claimed that in order to foster mature moral reasoning, a child's or teenager's social environment must provide him with opportunities for meaningful, reciprocal dialogue about moral issues.

Longitudinal research relating parenting styles and family climate to levels of moral reasoning suggest that Kohlberg was right (Pratt, Arnold, & Pratt, 1999). Parents' ability to identify, understand, and respond to children's and adolescents' less mature forms of moral reasoning seems to be particularly important to the development of moral reasoning. This ability on the part of parents is important because people of all ages have difficulty understanding and remembering moral arguments that are more advanced than their own level (Narvaez, 1998). Thus, a parent who can express her own moral views in words that reflect her child's level of understanding is more likely to be able to influence the child's moral development.

As an individual's capacity for moral reasoning grows, so does her ability to think logically about issues in other domains. For example, the complexity of an individual's political reasoning is very similar to the complexity of her moral reasoning (Raaijmakers, Verbogt, & Vollebergh, 1998). Further, attitudes toward the acceptability of violence also vary with levels of moral reasoning. Individuals at lower levels are more tolerant of violence (Sotelo & Sangrador, 1999).

Perhaps most importantly, teenagers' level of moral reasoning appears to be positively correlated with prosocial behaviour and negatively related to antisocial behaviour (Schonert-Reichl, 1999). In other words, the highest levels of prosocial behaviour are

role-taking

the ability to look at a situation from another person's perspective found among teens at the highest levels of moral reasoning (compared with their peers). Alternatively, the highest levels of antisocial behaviour are found among adolescents at the lowest levels of moral reasoning.

CRITICISMS OF KOHLBERG'S THEORY

Criticisms of Kohlberg's theory have come from theorists representing different perspectives.

MORAL REASONING AND BEHAVIOUR
Although moral reasoning and moral behaviour are correlated, the relationship is far from perfect. To explain inconsistencies between reasoning and behaviour, learning theorists suggest that moral reasoning is situational rather than developmental. They point to a variety of studies to support this assertion.

First, neither adolescents nor adults reason at the same level in response to every hypothetical dilemma (Rique & Camino, 1997). An individual research participant might reason at the conventional level in response to one dilemma and at the postconventional level with respect to another. Second, the types of characters in moral dilemmas strongly influence research participants' responses to them, especially when the participants are adolescents. For example, hypothetical dilemmas involving celebrities as characters elicit much lower levels of moral reasoning from teenagers than those involving fictional characters such as Heinz (Einerson, 1998).

In addition, research participants show disparities in levels of moral reasoning in response to hypothetical dilemmas compared with real-life moral issues. For example, Israeli Jewish, Israeli Bedouin, and Palestinian youths living in Israel demonstrate different levels of moral reasoning when responding to hypothetical stories such as the Heinz dilemma than they exhibit in discussing the moral dimensions of the long-standing conflicts among their ethnic groups (Elbedour, Baker, & Charlesworth, 1997). Thus, as learning theorists predict, it appears that situational factors may be more important variables for decisions about actual moral behaviour than the level of moral reasoning exhibited in response to hypothetical dilemmas.

MORAL REASONING AND EMOTIONS
Some theorists criticize Kohlberg's failure to connect moral reasoning to moral emotions. Psychologist Nancy Eisenberg, for example, suggests that empathy, the ability to identify with others' emotions, is both a cause and a consequence of moral development (Eisenberg, 2000). Similarly, Eisenberg suggests that a complete explanation of moral development should include age-related and individual variations in the ability to regulate emotions (such as anger) that can motivate antisocial behaviour.

Likewise, Carol Gilligan claims that an ethic based on caring for others and on maintaining social relationships may be as important to moral reasoning as ideas about justice. Gilligan's theory argues that there are at least two distinct "moral orientations": justice and care (Gilligan, 1982; Gilligan & Wiggins, 1987). Each has its own central injunction—not to treat others unfairly (justice), and not to turn away from someone in need (caring). Research suggests that adolescents do exhibit a moral orientation based on care and that care-based reasoning about hypothetical moral dilemmas is related to reasoning about real-life dilemmas (Skoe et al., 1999). In response, Kohlberg acknowledged in his later writings that his theory

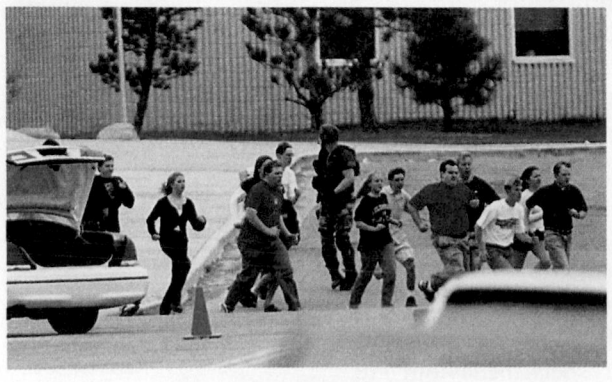

Incidents such as the Columbine High School shooting in April 1999 capture a great deal of public attention and often lead to increased security measures in schools. However, statistically speaking, schools are actually quite safe. Only 1% of all violent deaths among youths in the United States occur in schools (NCIPC, 2000).
(*Photo:* AFP/CORBIS)

deals specifically with development of reasoning about justice and does not claim to be a comprehensive account of moral development (Kohlberg, Levine, & Hewer, 1983).

Possible sex differences in moral reasoning are another focus of Gilligan's theory. According to Gilligan, boys and girls learn both the justice and care orientations, but girls are more likely to operate from the care orientation, whereas boys are more likely to operate from a justice orientation. Because of these differences, girls and boys tend to perceive moral dilemmas quite differently.

Given the emerging evidence on sex differences in styles of interaction and in friendship patterns, Gilligan's hypothesis makes some sense. Perhaps girls, focused more on intimacy in their relationships, judge moral dilemmas by different criteria. But, in fact, research on moral dilemmas has not consistently shown that boys are more likely to use justice reasoning or that girls more often use care reasoning. Several studies of adults do show such a pattern (e.g., Lyons, 1983; Wark & Krebs, 1996). However, studies of children and teenagers generally have not (Jadack, Hyde, Moore, & Keller, 1995; Smetana, Killen, & Turiel, 1991; Walker et al., 1987). Further, recent evidence suggests that such sex differences, if they exist, may be restricted to North American culture (Skoe et al., 1999).

MORAL DEVELOPMENT AND ANTISOCIAL BEHAVIOUR

The consistent finding of low levels of moral reasoning among adolescents who engage in serious forms of antisocial behaviour has been of particular interest to developmentalists (Aleixo & Norris, 2000; Gregg, Gibbs, & Basinger, 1994; Smetana, 1990). A young person who commits an offence (previously known as a delinquent or a young offender) is distinguished from other youth who engage in other forms of antisocial behaviour, such as bullying, on the basis of actual lawbreaking (**criminality**). To address youth criminality, Canada's new *Youth Criminal Justice Act* (YCJA) focuses in part on rehabilitation and reintegration of a young person into society. Thus the YCJA avoids the practice of labelling a youth as a criminal and instead focuses on the young person's offensive actions, which are malleable to change (see **No Easy Answers**).

Youth who commit offences appear to be behind their peers in moral reasoning because of deficits in role-taking skills. They seem to be unable to look at their crimes from their victims' perspectives or to assess hypothetical crimes from the victims' perspectives. Thus, programs aimed at helping youth who commit offences develop more mature levels of moral reasoning usually focus on heightening their awareness of the victim's point of view. However, few such programs have been successful (Moody, 1997; Putnins, 1997). Consequently, psychologists believe that there is far more to youth criminality than just a lack of role-taking and moral reasoning skills.

First, it appears that there are at least two important subvarieties of youth who commit offences, distinguished by the age at which the criminal behaviour begins. Childhood-onset problems are more serious and are more likely to persist into adulthood. Adolescent-onset problems are typically milder and more transitory, apparently more a reflection of peer-group processes or a testing of the limits of authority than a deeply ingrained behaviour problem.

The developmental pathway for early-onset youth criminality seems to be directed by factors inside the child, such as temperament and personality. In early life, these children throw tantrums and defy parents; they may also develop insecure attachments (Greenberg, Speltz, & DeKlyen, 1993). Once the defiance appears, if the parents are not up to the task of controlling the child, the child's behaviour worsens. He may begin to display overt aggression toward others, who then reject him, which aggravates the problem. The seriously aggressive child is pushed in the direction of other children with

criminality
antisocial behaviour that includes lawbreaking

No Easy Answers

Youth Criminal

Justice

In Canada there are some uneven trends in the incidence of youth crime. From 1991 the overall youth crime rate fell steadily, especially for property offences, theft, and break and enter, but then it levelled off in 2000 and rebounded slightly in 2003. Rates of violent youth crime, including homicide, assault, sexual assault, and robbery, increased until 1997, at which time the rates continued to rise, but more gradually (Statistics Canada, 2001i; Sudworth & deSouza, 2000; Wallace, 2003, 2004). Forty-one youth were charged with homicide in 2000, which is 11 fewer than the average since 1990 (Statistics Canada, 2001j).

Youth crime rates vary with location, age and sex. Demographic data shows that in 2002 Saskatchewan and Manitoba experienced the highest rates of youth crime, while Quebec, Prince Edward Island, and British Columbia experienced the lowest rates (Wallace, 2003). Canadian youth crime rates increase with age and peak at age 15 in females and age 17 in males. Further, males have higher crime rates at every age and account for about 8 out of 10 of all court cases; males 16 and 17 years of age account for slightly more than half of all youth court cases (Robinson, 2004). At all age groups youth are more likely to be victims of crimes committed by other youth than by adults. A disproportionately high number of youth are crime victims compared with adults, and girls are more likely to be victims of violent crime than boys (Statistics Canada, 2001i).

Two socializing factors that predict youth crime rates are peer influences and parenting style. The percentage of children engaging in high-risk behaviours such as smoking, fighting, and stealing was four to nine times higher than when children were not part of a group "doing bad things." Children who witnessed violence at home or who were raised by a parent who had either an ineffective or aversive parenting style were very often likely to exhibit conduct disorder behaviours (Statistics Canada, 2001i).

It is difficult to understand the motivations that underlie criminal activity, especially violent offences, but a new approach to youth crime has resulted in a major restructuring of our youth justice system. Canada's new *Youth Criminal Justice Act* is based on "the values, rights and responsibilities of both society and young people in relation to crime [and has three main objectives:] to prevent crime, rehabilitate and reintegrate offenders into society, and ensure meaningful consequences for offences committed by young people" (Department of Justice, 2001b, p. 1). All the same, it is not easy to balance what should be done to satisfy our need for justice for the suffering of victims of violence against the personal consequences of violent behaviour for the young perpetrators of these crimes, while at the same time reducing future violent offences. Intervention that would reduce future violence would require a considerable commitment of time and resources. Developmentalists play an important role by providing research-based guidance in the mental development factors of individuals as well as a broader perspective of the social factors associated with criminality.

similar problems, who then become the child's only supportive peer group (Shaw, Kennan, & Vondra, 1994).

By adolescence, these youngsters may exhibit serious disturbances in thinking (Aleixo & Norris, 2000). Canadian researchers have found that most have friends drawn almost exclusively from among other young people who commit crimes (Tremblay, Masse, Vitaro, & Dobkin, 1995). Of course, this situation is reinforced by frequent rejection by noncriminal peers (Brendgen, Vitaro, & Bukowski, 1998). Many of these adolescents have parents with histories of antisocial behaviour as well (Gainey, Catalano, Haggerty, & Hoppe, 1997). Youth who commit crimes at an early age are also highly likely to display a whole cluster of other problem behaviours, including drug and alcohol use, truancy or dropping out of school, and early and risky sexual behaviour, including having multiple sexual partners (Dishion, French, & Patterson, 1995).

For young people whose criminality appears first in adolescence, the pathway is different. They, too, have friends who commit crimes. However, associating with peers who commit crimes worsens their behaviour, while the behaviour of youth who commit crimes at an early age remains essentially the same, whether they have antisocial friends or are "loners" (Vitaro, Tremblay, Kerr, Pagani, & Bukowski, 1997). Moreover, the antisocial behaviour patterns of adolescent-onset youth who commit offences often change as their relationships change (Laird, Pettit, Dodge, & Bates, 1999). Consequently, peer influence seems to be the most important factor in the development of adolescent-onset youth criminality.

Parenting style and other relationship variables seem to be additional factors in this type of antisocial behaviour. Most of these teens have parents who do not monitor them sufficiently; their individual friendships are not very supportive or intimate; and they are drawn to a clique or crowd that includes some teens who are experimenting with drugs or mild law-breaking. After a period of months of hanging out with such a group of peers, previously noncriminal adolescents show some increase in risky or antisocial behaviours, such as increased drug-taking (Berndt & Keefe, 1995a; Dishion et al., 1995; Steinberg, Fletcher, & Darling, 1994). However, when parents do provide good monitoring and emotional support, their adolescent child is unlikely to get involved in criminal acts or drug use even if she hangs around with a tougher crowd or has a close friend who engages in such behaviour (Brown & Huang, 1995; Mounts & Steinberg, 1995).

Before Going On

- What are the features of moral reasoning at each of Kohlberg's stages?
- What are some important causes and effects in the development of moral reasoning?
- How has Kohlberg's theory been criticized?
- Describe the moral reasoning abilities and other characteristics of young people who commit criminal offences.

Summary

Theories of Social and Personality Development

- According to Freud, adolescents are in the genital stage, a period during which sexual maturity is reached. Erikson viewed adolescence as a period when a person faces a crisis of identity versus role confusion, out of which the teenager must develop a sense of who he is and where he belongs in his culture.

- Building on Erikson's notion of an adolescent identity crisis, Marcia identified four identity statuses.

Self-Concept and Personality

- Self-definitions become increasingly abstract at adolescence, with more emphasis on enduring, internal qualities and ideology.

- Teenagers also increasingly define themselves in terms that include both masculine and feminine traits. When both masculinity and femininity are present, the individual is described as androgynous. High levels of androgyny are associated with higher self-esteem in both male and female adolescents.

- Self-esteem drops somewhat at the beginning of adolescence and then rises steadily throughout the teenaged years.

- Young people in clearly identifiable minority groups have the additional task in adolescence of forming an ethnic identity, a process that appears to have several steps analogous to Marcia's model of identity formation.

- Teens who are introverted, neurotic, and pessimistic and who blame their problems on forces outside themselves encounter more difficulties than peers who have a more positive outlook.

Social Relationships

- Adolescent–parent interactions typically become somewhat more conflicted in early adolescence, an effect possibly linked to the physical changes of puberty.

- Strong attachments to parents remain so and are predictive of good peer relations. Authoritative parenting continues to be the optimal style to use with adolescents. The parents' remarriage during a child's adolescence appears to have a more negative effect on girls than on boys.

- Susceptibility to peer-group pressure appears to be at its peak at about age 13 or 14. Reputation-based groups, or *crowds,* as well as smaller groups, called *cliques,* are important parts of adolescent social relationships. By early adolescence, most teens have a concept of being "in love."

- Teens who are homosexual or who are unsure about their sexual orientation face many obstacles in the formation of an identity.

Moral Development

- Kohlberg proposed six stages of moral reasoning, organized into three levels. Preconventional moral reasoning includes reliance on external authority: What is punished is bad, and what feels good is good. Conventional morality is based on rules and norms provided by outside groups, such as the family, church, or society. Postconventional morality is based on self-chosen principles. Research evidence suggests that these levels and stages are loosely correlated with age, develop in a specified order, and appear in this same sequence in all cultures studied so far.

- The acquisition of cognitive role-taking skills is important to moral development, but the social environment is important as well. Specifically, to foster moral reasoning, adults must provide children with opportunities for discussion of moral issues. Moral reasoning and moral behaviour are correlated, though the relationship is far from perfect.

- Kohlberg's theory has been criticized by theorists who place more emphasis on learning moral behaviour and others who believe that moral reasoning may be based more on emotional factors than on ideas about justice and fairness.

- Youth who commit criminal offences are usually found to be far behind their peers in both role-taking and moral reasoning. However, other factors, such as parenting style, may be equally important in criminality.

Key Terms

bicultural identity (p. 335)

clique (p. 342)

conventional morality (p. 349)

criminality (p. 353)

Weblinks

Canadian Association for Adolescent Health
www.acsa-caah.ca/
This nonprofit multidisciplinary organization is of interest to adolescents as well
as clinicians, educators, community workers. The website provides "news,
upcoming scientific events, publication, research summaries, health facts,
description of programs and Associations in the field of adolescence, and state
of the art articles."

"Adolescence and Peer Pressure" by Herbert G. Lingren
http://ianrpubs.unl.edu/family/nf211.htm
This article examines peer relationships during adolescence, the impact of community, and effective strategies for coping with peer pressure.

The Great *Young Offenders Act* Debate
www.lawyers.ca/tgyad
This site outlines recent arguments for and against various issues relating to the
Young Offenders Act in Ontario thorough discussion forums.

The PACT Youth Crime Reduction Program
www.pactprogram.ca/
PACT (Participation, Acknowledgment, Commitment, and Transformation) is a
privately funded youth crime prevention and recidivism reduction organization that
provides an alternative to the court system.

Youthbet.net
www.youthbet.net/
The youth-designed website in association with the University of Toronto provides
information for youth aged 10 to 19, educators, and clinicians who want balanced
information about youth gambling, the gaming industry, and methods of preventing
gambling-related problems.

**McGill University's International Centre for Youth Gambling Problems and
High-Risk Behaviours**
www.education.mcgill.ca/gambling
McGill University's site seeks to define problem gambling behaviour in youth and
presents current research and potential treatments for this growing issue. It includes
several links to other addiction-related sites.

What Can Be Done About Gambling Among Canadian Youth?

Today's youth are the first generation of Canadians to live within a culture that views gambling as an everyday and acceptable form of entertainment. Recently, Canadian researchers have discovered some startling facts about the depth of the problem of gambling in Canadian youth. One factor is that gambling often begins at an earlier age than other high-risk behaviours such as alcohol or drug use. University of Windsor researchers Govoni, Rupcich, and Frisch (1996) found that the pattern of gambling behaviour can be established by age 14. In addition, McGill University researchers Gupta and Derevensky (1998a, 2000) found that "pathological gamblers" started serious gambling by age 10. Although most adult problem gamblers reported that their problem with gambling began in their youth, it is not clear if adolescent gambling leads to adult gambling problems or if gambling is related to an underlying propensity for thrill-seeking, risk-taking behaviour that persists into adulthood. The latter contention is supported by research that found adolescent problem gamblers to be more excitable, greater risk-takers, more extraverted, anxious, nonconforming, and lower in self-discipline and self-esteem than non–problem gambling youth (Derevensky & Gupta, 1998; Gupta & Derevensky, 2000).

Gambling and wagering are popular and on the rise among children and adolescents alike (Shaffer & Hall, 1996). The vast majority of adolescents surveyed by researchers from Laval University (Ladouceur, Boudreault, Jacques, & Vitaro, 1999) and Brock University (Lawrence, Yardley, Root, Canham, & McPhee, 2002) acknowledged that they have participated in gaming activities. For instance, studies show that roughly three-quarters or more of teenagers report that they have wagered money in the previous year and anywhere between 9% and 35% did so at least once a week (Derevensky & Gupta, 1998; Gupta & Derevensky, 1998a; Lawrence, et al., 2002). Of these youths, 55% are considered casual gamblers, 13% have some gambling problems, and 4–6% have serious problems with gambling.

Gambling, like many high-risk behaviours, is more prevalent in males than females, and boys are two to four times as likely as girls to have a serious gambling problem (Gupta & Derevensky, 2000; Ladouceur, et al., 1999; Lawrence, et al., 2002). Adolescents display a higher incidence of gambling problems than adults, and youth are two to four times more likely than adults to have a serious gambling problem (Derevensky, Gupta, & Winters, 2003; Gupta & Derevensky, 2000; Noonan, Turner, & Macdonald, 1999).

Older adolescents and adults prefer to wager money, and a significant number of underage youth engage in age-restricted gambling activities such as lotteries (72%), instant-win tickets (70%), pull-tabs (35%), and Pro-line (28%) (Lawrence, et al., 2002). In comparison, children wager valued possessions, e.g., Pogs (a picture-disk collector's game), marbles, and collector cards (Ladouceur, Dubé, & Bujold, 1995). Some youth activities such as Pogs and marbles may act as a bridge to gambling when played for "keepsies." This could be an ideal opportunity for parental intervention but, like many forms of gambling that are not seen as harmful, these activities are not usually checked by adult caregivers (Noonan et al., Turner, & Macdonald, 1999). Consequently, children are not informed about the inherent dangers of gambling as they are with smoking, drugs, and alcohol use (Derevensky & Gupta, 1998). On the contrary, children and adolescents often gamble with their parents or other family members, e.g., they go together to buy and play lottery tickets, play cards, or play bingo (Gupta & Derevensky, 1997).

Adolescents with gambling problems are twice as likely to have parents who gamble excessively as adolescents whose parents do not gamble excessively (Govoni et al., 1996). Bandura's social learning theory (1977a, 1989) can explain some of the effects that social role models have on gambling behaviour in youth. When children are exposed to family members, peers, neighbours, or celebrities who relish gambling, youth may acquire favourable expec-

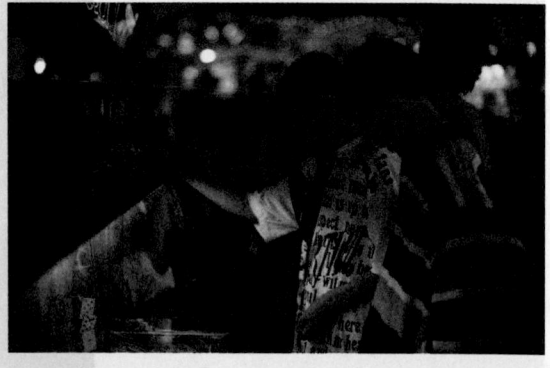

(*Photo:* Paul A. Souders/CORBIS/MAGMA)

tations about gambling (Gupta & Derevensky. 1997). Well-intentioned social groups such as schools and religious groups may inadvertently endorse gambling by sponsoring fundraising events such as bingo or casino nights that are supported by parents and the community (Derevensky & Gupta, 2000).

Cognitively, children and young adolescents are at a disadvantage because they lack an appreciation of what the odds of winning are and have an overly optimistic view of the probability of winning (Turner, Toneatto & Stanovich, 1999). Moreover, for most teens and adults (including parents and community leaders) gambling is perceived as a relatively benign activity. Even teens who are in treatment for gambling do not see themselves as having a gambling problem (Gupta & Derevensky, 1999, as reported in Derevensky & Gupta, 2000).

Like other addictive behaviours, gambling offers a way to temporarily escape problems, boredom, and stress. At the same time, these benefits are mixed with the excitement of winning. In fact, most adolescents do not gamble primarily for money but for the excitement and sensations of dissociation and escape (Derevensky & Gupta, 1998; Gupta & Derevensky, 1998b). Young problem gamblers have been found to dissociate more frequently when gambling compared with peers who do not have a gambling problem (Gupta & Derevensky, 2000). It has also been shown that when young problem gamblers are away from the gambling situation (a Video Lottery Terminal [VLT], for instance) they can experience withdrawal-like symptoms that make them more likely to want to play again in order to escape these undesirable sensations (Noonan et al., 1999). Not surprisingly, adolescents with serious gambling problems have an increased risk for the development of multiple addictions. They also have higher rates of depression, which

puts them at a heightened risk for suicidal thoughts and suicide attempts. Furthermore, within a social context, adolescents with gambling problems report having a support group, but old friends are often replaced by gambling associates (Gupta & Derevensky, 2000).

Derevensky and Gupta (1998, 2000, 2004) have reported that youth gambling treatment program research remains wanting. Although research into gambling prevention programs is in the formative stages of development, there are some practical measures that can be taken to help inoculate children against the risk of developing a gambling dependence. Parents and caregivers need to first become aware of the seriousness of the problem and then advise and instruct their children accordingly, just as they would with the dangers of other risk-taking behaviours such as smoking and alcohol use or unsafe sexual activity. In terms of social learning theory, "actions speak louder than words." Therefore, if parents believe that they are important role models against gambling, they need to act in ways that are consistent with what they say. Another preventive measure is teaching children about the nature of random events and statistical probability at a level that they can understand. Other cognitive preventive measures include giving a child facts that counter unrealistic expectations and changing inappropriate ideas a child may have concerning the roles of skill, luck, and the illusion of control in gambling activities. It should also be emphasized that gambling is not a method of making money; rather it is another way of spending money. The aim of discussion should be to help modify and change the attitude that gambling is a harmless behaviour.

The school system can provide another important venue for implementing prevention activities that increase knowledge about youth gambling problems. Indeed,

recent studies show that instructional videos can increase the level of accurate knowledge and reduce misconceived attitudes about gambling in students from Grades 6 to 8 (Ferland, Ladouceur, & Vitaro, 2002; Lavoie & Ladouceur, 2004). There is also a need to develop a protocol for the identification, assessment, and referral of students who are at risk of developing a serious gambling problem. Students need to be introduced to both alternative and effective ways of coping with problems and need to improve the skills that would prevent the development of problematic gambling. It would be appropriate for these school-based programs to be integrated into both the elementary and secondary school levels.

YOUR TURN

- Explain whether or not there is a relationship between the proliferation of gambling opportunities for adults, such as casinos and lottery ticket sales, and adolescent gambling.

- Describe the ways that problem gambling can be harmful to more than just the gambler.

- Explain why youth are more vulnerable to problem gambling than adults.

- Explain how gambling on a computer (no stakes) could help inoculate children against false beliefs they may have about the odds of winning.

- Some young problem gamblers are driven by the excitement and sensations of dissociation they experience when they gamble. What kinds of intervention would help them overcome their dependence on gambling?

- Where do youth get the money to gamble?

CHAPTER 12

David Barber/PhotoEdit

PHYSICAL AND COGNITIVE DEVELOPMENT IN EARLY ADULTHOOD

You probably know someone like one of the people in the following list. What do all of them have in common?

Devon, a 20-year-old second-year university student who is trying to choose between psychology and social work as his major

Cassie, a 22-year-old single mother of a 4-year-old who lives with her parents, works full-time, and attends community college classes part-time

Joe, a 25-year-old married computer programmer who attended a community college after 4 years of working in a computer store

Marta, a 30-year-old remarried mother of a preschooler who works as a registered nurse

Renée, a married 33-year-old mother of two school-aged children who has just started university

Marshall, a 35-year-old single man who has been a public school teacher for 12 years

Each member of this diverse group is a young adult. If you think about the people you know who are between the ages of 20 and 40, they probably make up just as varied a group.

Clearly, young adulthood is the period of life when individuals' developmental pathways begin to diverge significantly. For example, in contrast to younger individuals, the educational experiences of young adults are highly diverse. Some go on to college or university as soon as they graduate from high school. Others work and attend school part-time. Still others work for a while and then further their education.

Despite these variations, most social science researchers believe that it is still useful to divide the adult years into three roughly equal parts: early adulthood, from 20 to 40; middle adulthood, from 40 to about 65; and late adulthood, from 65 until death. This way of dividing adulthood reflects the fact that optimum physical and cognitive functioning, achieved in the 20s and 30s, begins to wane in some noticeable and measurable ways in the 40s and 50s. Moreover, several important role changes often occur when adults are in their 40s. Children begin to leave home, careers near their peak, and so on.

We will follow the common usage and define "young" or "early" adulthood as the period from age 20 to age 40. In this chapter, you will read about the changes that occur in early adulthood, along with a number of variables that are associated with variation from the "typical" pathway. As you read this chapter, keep the following questions in mind:

> ## Critical Thinking
>
> Before you read the rest of the chapter, think about how you might answer the following question for yourself: In what ways have your body and mind changed since you were younger? How do you expect them to change as you get older? How has attending post-secondary school affected your life, and what difference will it make in your future?

- How does physical functioning change in the years from 20 to 40?

- What are the major health issues during early adulthood?

- How do thinking and problem-solving improve in early adulthood?

- How does post-secondary education help shape young adults' development?

PHYSICAL FUNCTIONING

When developmentalists study children's development, they are looking at increases or improvements. When developmentalists study adults, especially adults' physical functioning, they begin to ask questions about loss of function, or decline.

primary aging
age-related physical changes that have a biological basis and are universally shared and inevitable

secondary aging
age-related changes that are due to social and environmental influences, poor health habits, or disease

Disability-Adjusted Life Years (DALY)
a measure of the gap between a population's ideal and actual levels of health. It is derived from the number of life-years lost to premature death, due to illness or injury, and the number of years living with a disability. It assumes a potential life limit of 82.5 years for women and 80 for men

Health-Adjusted Life Expectancy (HALE)
an estimate of life expectancy at birth. It is the number of years that a newborn can expect to live in full health given current rates of morbidity and mortality

Quality-Adjusted Life Years (QALY)
a measure of how much benefit is gained, and at what cost, for any particular physical or mental intervention. It provides an estimate of the time a person will live at different levels of health over their remaining years of life

Critical Thinking

Given that there is only so much money that can be spent on health care, what priorities would you recommend for Canadian society? How important is it for you to have a "good quality life" rather than just a "long life?" Would you be in agreement if the government were to reallocate some hospital funds to pay for illness prevention and health promotion programs?

PRIMARY AND SECONDARY AGING

Researchers distinguish between two types of aging. The basic, underlying, inevitable aging process is called **primary aging** by most developmentalists. To learn about its effects, they study adults who are disease-free and who have good health practices (Birren & Schroots, 1996).

Secondary aging, in contrast, is the product of social and environmental influences, health habits, or disease, and is neither inevitable nor experienced by all adults. Research on age differences in health and death rates reveals the expected pattern. For example, a minority of 20- to 34-year-olds die from disease; the majority of deaths are caused by unintentional injuries or suicide (Health Canada, 2000b). In addition, researchers have found that socioeconomic status (SES) factors are implicated in health and well-being, a pattern suggesting the influence of secondary aging.

For example, the relationship between an individual's income and measures of health, illness, and longevity is well established in nations worldwide (Hertzman, 1999). The income-status differences in health, where the rich are generally healthier and live longer than the poor, are very unlikely due to group variations in patterns of primary aging. Accordingly, most developmentalists believe that the differences represent secondary aging. In other words, the health differences result from cultural and economic factors such as diet, stress levels, and access to health care that are associated with social class as well as with disease (James, Keenan, & Browning, 1992).

A closer look at the differences in levels of health among developed nations reveals that it is not just a simple case that the wealthy members of a population are healthier than those who are less well off. Rather, as described in the **Research Report**, the degree of socioeconomic inequality of a country is related to the overall health of its citizens (Kawachi & Kennedy, 2002; United Nations Development Programme (UNDP), 2003). Prosperous nations with high levels of social inequality, most notably the United States, experience poorer overall health than less wealthy but more egalitarian societies, such as Costa Rica. By comparison, Canada distributes its social and economic resources fairly equitably among its citizens (e.g., public funding of, and relatively universal access to, health care and education) and as a consequence Canadians enjoy relatively good health (Ross, et al., 2000; UNDP, 2003).

The study of the factors associated with secondary aging can be viewed in relation to an individual, which we look at later in this chapter, and with respect to a population, an approach that looks at the health indicators that influence populations as a whole. Common indicators of the *population health approach* include mortality statistics and rates of hospitalization, although measures of morbidity are also important because morbidity measures tap into "a key health policy challenge facing Western industrialized nations: that some health interventions may be adding years of sickness to life, rather than years of health" (Chomik, 2001, p. 9). From this perspective it becomes important to measure the health status of populations by looking at *aggregate health indicators* that measure quality of life, such as **Disability-Adjusted Life Years (DALY)**, **Health-Adjusted Life Expectancy (HALE)**, and **Quality-Adjusted Life Years (QALY)**.

THE BRAIN AND NERVOUS SYSTEM

No matter what age an individual is, new synapses are forming, myelinization is occurring, and old connections are dying off. Further,

Research Report

The Distribution

of Wealth and

Health

Canadian researchers have published the first valid comparison of income to health and mortality rates between Canada and the United States (Ross, et al., 2000). The results were surprising. In the United States, as in other industrialized nations, a relationship exists between health and degree of income distribution (the spread between the rich and poor). In those U.S. states and urban centres where income inequality was the greatest, health outcomes were the poorest, and where relative income equality existed, health outcomes were the best. By contrast, most Canadian cities and provinces showed greater income equality, along with the associated good health and lower mortality rates, than their U.S. counterparts (see **Figure 12.1**).

University of British Columbia health researcher Clyde Hertzman reports that, regardless of the average income level, Americans who live in states that have greater income equality also have longer life expectancy. According to Hertzman, this pattern of income equality and greater longevity holds true in communities in developed nations worldwide. Even more notable is the finding that in jurisdictions where income disparity is greatest, e.g. the United Kingdom, the health status of the wealthy is lower than it is for the wealthy in communities and nations where income distribution is more equitable, e.g. Sweden (Hertzman, 1999).

In another first-of-its-kind study, the Joint Canada/United States Survey of Health, 2002–03, comparable precise data from both Canada and the U.S. was analyzed. Although the study found that there are many similarities between our two countries, there are also some significant differences in our health statuses (Sanmartin & Ng, 2004). The greatest disparity in

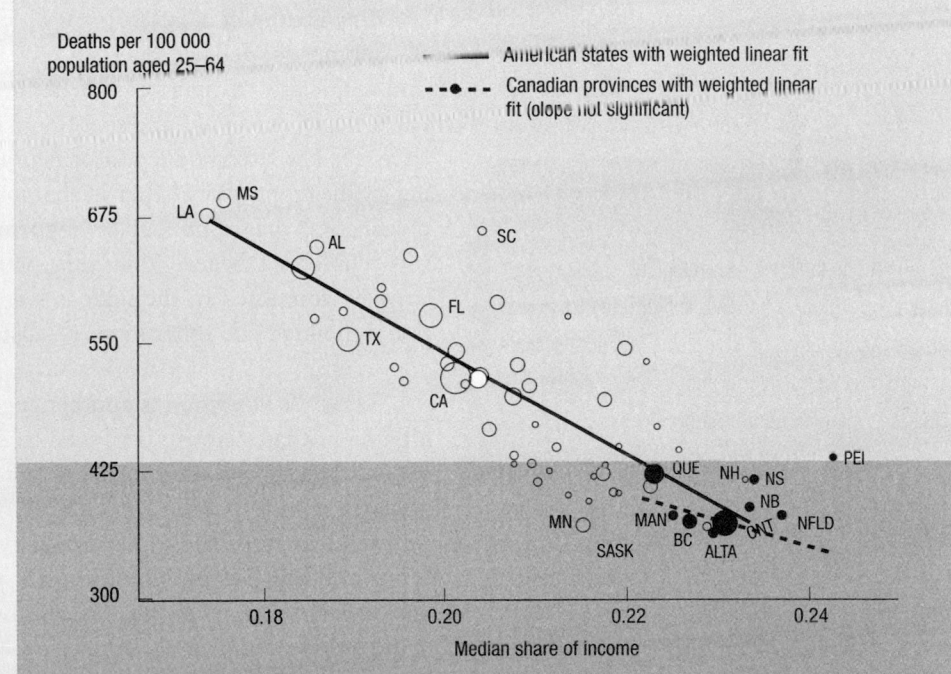

Figure 12.1

Mortality rates of the population aged 25 to 64 in Canadian provinces and American states, by percentage of total household income in province or state received by households with income below the median, 1991 (Canada) and 1990 (United States).

(*Sources:* Health Reports, 1999a, Chart 1, p. 80. 1991 Census of Canada; Canadian Vital Statistics Data Base; Centers for Disease Control, standardized to 1991 Canadian population.)

health is related to differences in income—Americans in the lowest income bracket experience significantly lower levels of health, higher obesity, and more severe mobility impairment than their Canadian counterparts. Across all other income ranges, both Canadians (88%) and Americans (85%) reported similar levels of good to excellent health. Those most poorly off in the U.S. also reported significantly more unmet health problems in addition to poorer health, especially Americans who lack any kind of medical insurance coverage. In line with what you might suspect, the top reason for unmet health care needs in Canada is waiting time, whereas cost was the most reported reason in the U.S.

Critical Thinking

What reasons can you think of to explain why a society's distribution of income makes such a difference to health and mortality?

there is recent evidence that, contrary to what neurologists have believed for a long time, some parts of the brain produce new neurons to replace those that die, even in the brains of older adults (Gould, Reeves, Graziano, & Gross, 1999). At some point in development, though, usually in the late teens, developmental processes reach a balance and the brain attains a stable size and weight. Similarly, by early adulthood, most functions have become localized in specific areas of the brain (Gaillard et al., 2000).

Neurologists have found that the pattern of peaks and valleys in the development of brain functions that begins during the fetal period continues into adulthood (see the **Research Report**). In fact, neuroscientists have now found evidence, based on MRI studies, that the human brain continues to mature throughout early adulthood (Giedd, et al., 1999; Gogtay, et al., 2004; Sowell, Thompson, Holmes, Jernigan, & Toga, 1999; Sowell, Thompson, Tessner, & Toga, 2001). As you may remember from **Chapter 10**, a second major growth spurt of the grey matter of frontal lobes—the area of the brain devoted to logic, planning, and emotional control—begins during preadolescence. The overproduction of neural tissue is followed by a maturing of the frontal lobes that is characterized by synaptic pruning and myelination that continues through to young adulthood. Many neuropsychologists believe that this pattern of neural development is strongly connected to the increases in the capacity for formal operational thinking and other kinds of abstract reasoning that occur in late adolescence.

Critical Thinking

If teenagers lack the neurological capacity to fully control their emotions, should they be held to the same level of culpability as adults for committing impulsive criminal acts, such as "knifing" someone during a brawl?

Response inhibition is another cognitive skill that emerges in early adulthood that seems to be linked to changes in the brain. For example, when you take a multiple-choice test, you need to be able to keep yourself from responding too quickly to the options in order to carefully weigh all of them. Response inhibition also helps you to "bite-your-tongue" in order to keep from putting your "foot in your mouth" as often as you did at a younger age. Neuropsychologists suggest that response inhibition may depend on the ability of the frontal lobes of the brain to regulate the **limbic system**, or the emotional part of the brain. Many scientists believe that the capacity to integrate various brain functions in this way does not become fully developed until early adulthood (Spreen, Risser, & Edgell, 1995).

limbic system
the part of the brain that regulates emotional responses

OTHER BODY SYSTEMS

Young adults perform better than do the middle-aged or old on virtually every physical measure. Compared with older adults, adults in their 20s and 30s have more muscle

Research Report

The Brain Matures into Adulthood

The brain contains two types of tissue: *grey matter* and *white matter*. Grey matter is made up of neuron cell bodies and axon and dendrite terminals that "connect" neurons to one another (look back at **Figure 3.3** on page 69); white matter is the myelinated axons. Normal brain development seems to follow a cyclical pattern of development. It starts with the rapid proliferation of grey matter and is followed by the simultaneous processes of *synaptic pruning*, and *myelination*. Synaptic pruning is a process that results in a decline in grey matter density as unused synapses—neural circuits—are discarded. Any unused neural cells and synaptic connections wither away while those that are used become stronger and more efficient with the help of myelination. During myelination, white matter density increases as a cholesterol-rich fatty substance coats the axons to improve neural transmission. A period of relative stability follows once this stage of brain maturation is reached, usually around the age of 30 (Sowell, et al., 2003).

Maturation of the brain does not happen all at once—the human brain matures in uneven patterns whereby specific regions of the brain develop at different times and rates than others (Gogtay, et al., 2004). For example, the first stage of grey matter proliferation occurs during the first 18 months of life in the parts of the brain that control basic somatosensory functions. The next major cycle of brain development begins just prior to puberty, when there is a surge in grey matter production in areas of the brain associated with higher mental processes, namely the frontal lobes (Giedd, et al., 1999; Gogtay, et al., 2004). In both instances, the surge in grey matter production is followed by synaptic pruning and myelination.

Selected slides from MRI scans that tracked brain maturation from ages 5 to 20 (a time-lapse movie can be viewed at **www.loni.ucla.edu/~thompson/DEVEL/dynamic.html**). Grey matter (red) diminishes as the brain matures because of synaptic pruning and myelination (blue). Notice that the region at the front of the brain (the prefrontal cortex that is associated with higher mental functioning) matures last.

(*Source:* Gogtay et al., 2004, Figure 3, p. 8178. Copyright 2004 National Academy of Sciences, U.S.A.)

The time-lapse MRI scans in the figure illustrate a part of this process—you can see that over time, grey matter recedes at the same time that white matter advances across the surface of the brain (Sowell et al., 2001).

The human brain seems to mature in the primitive areas first and in the newer parts of the brain last (Gogtay, et al., 2004). One exception to this pattern is the development of the areas of the brain that are associated with language and vocabulary. Although grey matter formation develops early in life in these brain regions, growth continues until a person reaches middle adulthood. This fits the research that shows that language skills improve continuously through to middle age (Sowell, et al., 2003).

A final cycle of brain development is associated with the overall natural degenerative process that occurs in later adulthood (Sowell, et al., 2003). This phase is characterized by a decline in grey matter density coupled with an end to white matter growth, resulting in an overall decline in brain volume. In this last stage of development, brain function begins to slow and becomes gradually less efficient, as you'll read later in **Chapters 14 and 16**.

tissue; maximum bone calcium; more brain mass; better eyesight, hearing, and sense of smell; greater oxygen capacity; and a more efficient immune system. The young adult is stronger, faster, and better able to recover from exercise or to adapt to changing conditions, such as alterations in temperature or light levels.

DECLINES IN PHYSICAL FUNCTIONING   After this early peak, there is a gradual decline in almost every measure of physical functioning through the years of adulthood. **Table 12.1** summarizes these changes. Most of the summary statements in the table are based on both longitudinal and cross-sectional data; many are based on studies in which both experimental and control groups consisted of participants in good health. So developmentalists can be reasonably confident that most of the age changes listed reflect primary aging and not secondary aging.

It's hard to draw a clear line between "early adulthood" and "middle adulthood" because the physical and mental changes are so gradual; even at 30, adults may find that it takes a bit more work to get into or stay in shape than it did at 20.
(*Photo:* Charles Gupton/Stock Boston)

The centre column of the table lists the approximate age at which the loss or decline reaches the point where it becomes fairly readily apparent. Virtually all these changes begin in early adulthood. But the early losses or declines are not typically noticeable in everyday physical functioning during these years, except when a person is attempting to operate at the absolute edge of physical ability. Among top athletes, for example, the very small losses of speed and strength that occur in the late 20s and 30s are highly significant, often dropping 25-year-olds or 30-year-olds out of the group of elite athletes (see **The Real World**). Nonathletes, though, typically notice little or no drop in everyday physical functioning until middle age.

Another way to think of this change is in terms of a balance between physical demand and physical capacity (Welford, 1993). In early adulthood, almost all of us have ample physical capacity to meet the physical demands we encounter in everyday life. We can read the fine print in the telephone book without bifocals; we can carry heavy boxes or furniture when we move; our immune systems are strong enough to fight off most illnesses, and we recover quickly from sickness. As we move into middle adulthood, the balance sheet changes. We find more and more arenas in which our physical capacities no longer quite meet the demands.

TABLE 12.1	A Summary of Age Changes in Physical Functioning	
Body Function	**Age at Which Change Begins to Be Clear or Measurable**	**Nature of Change**
Vision	Mid-40s	Lens of eye thickens and loses accommodative power, resulting in poorer near vision and more sensitivity to glare
Hearing	50 or 60	Loss of ability to hear very high and very low tones
Smell	About 40	Decline in ability to detect and discriminate among different smells
Taste	None	No apparent loss in taste discrimination ability
Muscles	About 50	Loss of muscle tissue, particularly in "fast twitch" fibres used for bursts of strength or speed
Bones	Mid-30s (women)	Loss of calcium in the bones, called osteoporosis; also wear and tear on bone in joints, called osteoarthritis, more marked after about 60
Heart and lungs	35 or 40	Most functions (such as aerobic capacity or cardiac output) do not show age changes at rest, but do show age changes during work or exercise
Nervous system	Probably gradual throughout adulthood	Some loss (but not clear how much) of neurons in the brain; gradual reduction in density of dendrites; gradual decline in total brain volume and weight
Immune system	Adolescence	Loss in size of thymus; reduction in number and maturity of T cells; not clear how much of this change is due to stress and how much is primary aging
Reproductive system	Mid-30s (women)	Increased reproductive risk and lowered fertility
	Early 40s (men)	Gradual decline in viable sperm beginning at about age 40; very gradual decline in testosterone from early adulthood
Cellular elasticity	Gradual	Gradual loss of elasticity in most cells, including skin, muscle, tendon, and blood vessel cells; faster deterioration in cells exposed to sunlight
Height	40	Compression of disks in the spine, with resulting loss of height of 1–2 inches by age 80
Weight	Nonlinear	In U.S. studies, weight reaches a maximum in middle adulthood and then gradually declines in old age
Skin	40	Increase in wrinkles, as a result of loss of elasticity; oil-secreting glands become less efficient
Hair	About 50	Becomes thinner and may grey

(*Sources:* Bartoshuk & Weiffenbach, 1990; Blatter et al., 1995; Braveman, 1987; Briggs, 1990; Brock, Guralnik, & Brody, 1990; Doty et al., 1984; Fiatarone & Evans, 1993; Fozard, 1990; Fozard, Metter, & Brant, 1990; Gray, Berlin, McKinlay, & Longcope, 1991; Hallfrisch, Muller, Drinkwater, Tobin, & Adres, 1990; Hayflick, 1994; Ivy, MacLeod, Petit, & Marcus, 1992; Kallman, Plato, & Tobi, 1990; Kline & Scialfa, 1996; Kozma, Stones, & Hannah, 1991; Lakatta, 1990; Lim, Zipursky, Watts, & Pfefferbaum, 1992; McFalls, 1990; Miller, 1990; Mundy, 1994; Scheibel, 1992, 1996; Shock et al., 1984; Weisse, 1992.)

HEART AND LUNGS The most common measure of overall aerobic fitness is **maximum oxygen uptake (VO$_2$ max)**, which reflects the ability of the body to take in and transport oxygen to various body organs. When VO$_2$ max is measured in a person at rest, scientists find only minimal decrements associated with age. But when they measure VO$_2$ max during exercise (such as during a treadmill test), it shows a systematic decline with age of about 1% per year, beginning between ages 35 and 40 (Goldberg, Dengel, & Hagberg, 1996). **Figure 12.2** on page 368 graphs some typical results from

maximum oxygen uptake (VO$_2$ max)

a measure of the body's ability to take in and transport oxygen to various body organs

Research on peak performance in various sports suggests that professional golfers do not perform at peak levels until they are in their early 30s. (*Photo:* Reuters NewMedia Inc./CORBIS)

both cross-sectional and longitudinal studies of women. Similar results are found with men (Kozma et al., 1991; Lakatta, 1990). Notice the slight decline in the years of early adulthood, followed by a somewhat more rapid drop in the middle years, a pattern that is highly typical of data on physical changes over adulthood. Similarly, under resting conditions, the quantity of blood flow from the heart (called *cardiac output*) does not decline with age; under exercise or work conditions, however, it declines significantly, dropping 30–40% between age 25 and age 65 (Lakatta, 1990; Rossman, 1980).

STRENGTH AND SPEED The collective effect of changes in muscles and cardiovascular fitness is a general loss of strength and speed with age—not just in top athletes, but in all of us. **Figure 12.3** shows both cross-sectional and 9-year longitudinal changes in grip strength in a group of men who participated in the Baltimore Longitudinal Studies of Aging (Kallman et al., 1990). Clearly, strength was at its peak in the men's 20s and early 30s and then declined steadily. Once again, though, such a difference might be the result of the fact that younger adults are more physically active or more likely to be engaged in activities or jobs that demand strength. Arguing against this conclusion, however, are studies of physically active older adults, who also show loss of muscle strength (e.g., Phillips, Bruce, Newton, & Woledge, 1992).

REPRODUCTIVE CAPACITY In **Chapter 3**, you read that the risk of miscarriage and other complications of pregnancy is higher in a woman's 30s than in her 20s. An equivalent change occurs in fertility—the ability to conceive—which is at its highest in the late teens and early 20s and drops steadily thereafter (McFalls, 1990; Mosher, 1987; Mosher & Pratt, 1987). Infertility is typically defined as the inability to conceive after 1 or more years of unprotected intercourse. Using this definition, one large American study found

Figure 12.2

The continuous line shows VO_2 max averages for cross-sectional comparisons; the arrows show changes on the same measure for groups of women studied longitudinally. The two sets of findings match remarkably. Note that the largest drop was between ages 40 and 50.

(*Source:* Plowman, Drinkwater, & Horvath, 1979, Figure 1, p. 514.)

Figure 12.3

These data, from the Baltimore Longitudinal Study of Aging, show both cross-sectional data (the dots) and longitudinal data (the lines) for grip strength among men. Once again, there is striking agreement between the two sets of information.

(*Source:* Kallman et al., 1990, Figure 2, p. M84.)

The Real World

Aging

Age   and   Peak   Sports   Performance

One of the most obvious ways to confirm whether human bodies are at their physical peak in early adulthood is to look at sports performance. Olympic athletes or other top performers in any sport push their bodies to the limit of their abilities. If early adulthood is really the period of peak physical ability, most world-record-holders and top performers should be in their 20s or perhaps early 30s. Another way to approach the same question is to look at the average performance of top athletes in each of several age groups, including those in "master" categories (athletes who are 35 or older). Both types of analysis lead inescapably to the same conclusion: Athletic performance peaks early in life, although the exact timing of the peak varies somewhat from one sport to another.

Swimmers, for example, reach their peak very early—at about age 17 for women and about age 19 for men. Golfers peak the latest, at about age 31 (Ericsson, 1990; Schulz &

Curnow, 1988; Stones & Kozma, 1996). Runners fall in between, with top performances in their early or middle 20s, although the longer the distance, the later the peak. You can see that pattern in the figure, which represents the average age at which each of a series of top male runners ran his fastest time.

Cross-sectional comparisons of the top performances of competitors of different ages

lead to the same conclusion. For example, Germany holds national swimming championships each year, giving awards to the top performers in each 5-year age range from 25 through 70. The best times drop steadily with age (Ericsson, 1990).

At the same time, it is also true that older athletes can perform far better than has been commonly thought. World records for master athletes have been repeatedly broken over the past several decades; in many sports, present-day 50-year-olds are performing at higher levels than did Olympic athletes 100 years ago. The human body, at any age, is more responsive to training than researchers even a decade ago had presumed. But it is still true that for those who achieve and maintain a high level of fitness throughout adult life, peak performance will come in early adulthood (Stones & Kozma, 1996).

that only 7% of women aged 20 to 24 were infertile, compared with 15% of those between 30 and 34, and 28% of those between 35 and 39 (McFalls, 1990). This does not mean, by the way, that 28% of women in their late 30s will be totally unable to conceive; it means that rapid conception is more likely in the early 20s, and that a significant minority of women who postpone childbearing into their late 30s or 40s will not conceive.

The reasons for this decline with age in women's fertility are multiple, including increased problems with ovulation, endometriosis, and a higher probability of having contracted at least one sexually transmitted disease because of more years of potential exposure (Garner, 1995). Sexually transmitted diseases increase the risk of **pelvic inflammatory disease,** which frequently results in a blockage of the fallopian tubes and thus prevents conception.

A man's capacity to impregnate does not appear to change over the years of early adulthood. Male fertility declines somewhat after age 40, but there is no equivalent of menopause among men, who commonly are able to impregnate well into late life. When men in early adulthood have infertility problems—and a significant minority do—it is because their bodies have produced an insufficient number of viable sperm ever since puberty, not because they have lost fertility they once had. In couples experiencing prob-

pelvic inflammatory disease
an infection of the female reproductive tract that may result from a sexually transmitted disease and can lead to infertility

lems conceiving, the problem is as likely to be with the man as the woman (Davajan & Israel, 1991).

IMMUNE SYSTEM FUNCTIONING The two key organs in the immune system are the thymus gland and the bone marrow. Between them, they create two types of cells, B cells and T cells, each of which plays a distinct role. B cells fight against external threats by producing antibodies against such disease organisms as viruses or bacteria; T cells defend against essentially internal threats, such as transplanted tissue, cancer cells, and viruses that live within the body's cells (Kiecolt-Glaser & Glaser, 1995). It is T cells that are most deficient in someone with AIDS and that decline most in number and efficiency with age (Miller, 1996).

Whereas the pituitary gland rules during adolescence, the thymus gland plays a larger role during adulthood. Changes in the thymus gland appear to be central to the aging process. This gland is largest in adolescence and declines dramatically thereafter in both size and mass. By age 45 or 50, the thymus has only about 5–10% of the cellular mass it had at puberty (Braveman, 1987; Hausman & Weksler, 1985). This smaller, less functional thymus is less able to turn the immature T cells produced by the bone marrow into fully "adult" cells. As a result, both of the basic protective mechanisms work less efficiently. Adults produce fewer antibodies than do children or teenagers. And T cells partially lose the ability to "recognize" a foreign cell, so that the body may fail to fight off some disease cells (cancer cells, for example). Thus, one of the key physical changes over the years of adulthood is an increasing susceptibility to disease.

But it is not entirely clear whether this susceptibility is due to primary or secondary aging. These changes in the immune system are found in healthy adults, which makes them look like part of primary aging. But there also is growing evidence that the functioning of the immune system is highly responsive to psychological stress and depression (Maier, Watkins, & Fleshner, 1994; Weisse, 1992). College and university students, for example, show lower levels of one variety of T cells ("natural killer" T cells) during exam periods than at other times (Glaser et al., 1992). And adults who have recently been widowed show a sharp drop in immune system functioning (Irwin & Pike, 1993). Chronic stress, too, has an effect on the immune system, initially stimulating an increase in immune efficiency, followed by a drop (Kiecolt-Glaser et al., 1987).

Collectively, this research points to the possibility that life experiences that demand high levels of change or adaptation will affect immune system functioning. Over a period of years and many stresses, the immune system may become less and less efficient. It may well be that the immune system changes with age in basic ways regardless of the level of stress. But it is also possible that what is thought of as normal aging of the immune system is a response to cumulative stress.

Before Going On

- Define primary and secondary aging.
- How does an equitable distribution of wealth affect a nation's health?
- What patterns of brain maturation have neuroscientists found leading up to early adulthood?
- Describe the various changes in other body systems that happen in early adulthood.

HEALTH PROMOTION AND WELLNESS

Early adulthood is a relatively healthy period of life, but risky behaviours—having multiple sex partners or engaging in substance use, for example—along with generally poor health habits can be problematic.

SEXUALLY TRANSMITTED INFECTIONS

In contrast to other types of disease, most sexually transmitted infections (STIs), including chlamydia (by far the most widespread), gonorrhea, and syphilis, are more common among young adults (aged 20 to 29) than in any other age group (Health Canada 2001i, 2001k, 2001l). After declining for two decades, the number of reported new cases of these infections has been increasing, especially for gonorrhea (Health Canada, 2003d, 2004c; Sarwal, Wong, Sevigny, & Ng, 2003). The occurrence of gonorrhea almost doubled between 1997 and 2001 and the increase has been most dramatic among men aged 30 to 39, jumping 68% (Hansen, Wong, & Perrin, 2003; Health Canada, 2003d). The other disease that is more common in young adults than in other age groups is HIV/AIDS.

The precise measurement of HIV infection in the Canadian population is difficult because it relies on individuals to come forward and be tested. This means that HIV infection may be present but remain undiagnosed. Another challenge in determining the levels of current and new HIV infections is that estimates are based upon data from major Canadian cities and therefore do not reflect local trends. Even so, we see some disturbing trends appearing from the data that is available.

Early in the Canadian HIV epidemic, those most affected were men who had sex with men (MSM) and to a lesser extent unsuspecting victims who received HIV-contaminated blood products in the 1980s. The rate of new infections for the MSM population has been increasing since the mid-1990s, following more than a decade of decline. In contrast, the rate of new HIV infection for another high-risk group, injection drug users (IDU), has declined after peaking in the mid-1990s, (see **Figure 12.4**). The HIV epidemic has recently invaded other segments of the population, with new infections on the rise in heterosexuals, women, and, to a disproportionately high level, in Aboriginals (5–8% of all reported cases) (Health Canada, 2004d).

Critical Thinking

After waning for two decades, what factors do you think have been contributing to the resurgence of STIs in Canada?

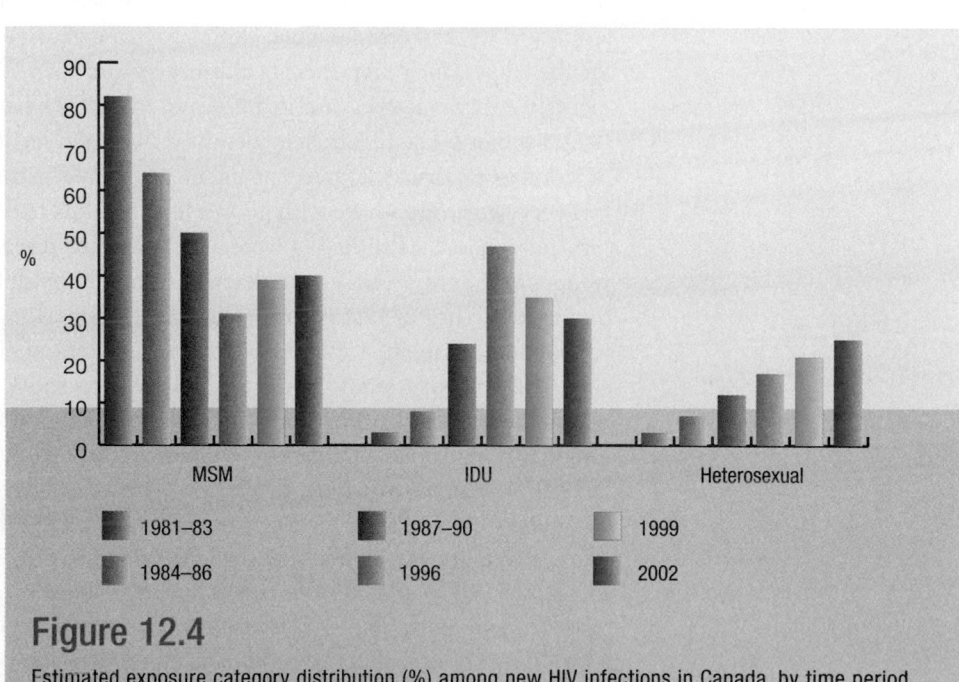

Figure 12.4

Estimated exposure category distribution (%) among new HIV infections in Canada, by time period.

(*Source:* Health Canada [2004d], May 2004. Reproduced with the permission of the Minister of Public Works and Government Services Canada, 2005.)

Sexually transmitted diseases are one of the most significant health risks of young adulthood. Casual sexual encounters with multiple partners carry with them a higher risk of contracting such diseases than do more careful relationship choices.
(*Photo:* Timothy Shonnard/ Getty Images)

It is estimated that 56 000 Canadians now live with HIV and/or AIDS, of which about 7600 are women. Almost half of the new HIV infections in women are due to heterosexual contact (53%), while the remainder is attributable to IDU (Health Canada, 2004b). Women are most likely to test positive for HIV between the ages of 20 and 39. In comparison, men are more than twice as likely to be diagnosed at ages 30 to 39 than at ages 20 to 29 (Health Canada, 2000c). The highest percentage of newly diagnosed AIDS cases in Canada occurs between the ages of 30 and 39 (Health Canada, 2000d). Age determinants are difficult to measure because of the lengthy delay between exposure and diagnosis. In many cases, the onset of AIDS occurs in individuals who were exposed to HIV infection in their early 20s.

Like adolescents, many young adults engage in high-risk behaviours that are specifically linked to STIs: having multiple sexual partners, having sex without adequate protection, and frequently using drugs or alcohol. However, for most young adults, STIs remain one of the taboo topics. Many young adults are unwilling to insist on the use of condoms; many do not seek medical attention when they develop symptoms and do not inform their partners of potential problems (Lewis, Malow, & Ireland, 1997; Schuster, 1997). And the risks of these behaviours are considerable, especially with the increase in drug-resistant strains of gonorrhea and syphilis. So take note: Safe sex practices—including knowledge of your partner's sexual history—are worth the effort.

HEALTH HABITS AND PERSONAL FACTORS

As you might expect, individual health habits, such as exercise, influence health in the early adult years and beyond. Social support networks and attitudes also affect health.

HEALTH HABITS The best evidence for the long-term effects of various health habits comes from the Alameda County Study, a major longitudinal epidemiological study conducted in one county in California (Berkman & Breslow, 1983; Breslow & Breslow, 1993; Kaplan, 1992). The study began in 1965, when a random sample of all residents of the county, a total of 6928 people, completed an extensive questionnaire about many aspects of their lives, including their health habits and their health and disability. These participants were contacted again in 1974 and in 1983, when they again described their health and disability. The researchers identified five good health habits: getting physical exercise, not smoking, drinking, over- or undereating, and getting regular sleep. They found that, in every age group, those with poorer health habits had a higher risk of mortality. Not surprisingly, poor health habits were also related to disease and disability rates over the 18 years of the study. Those who described poorer health habits in 1965 were more likely to report disability or disease symptoms in 1974 and in 1983 (Breslow & Breslow, 1993; Guralnik & Kaplan, 1989; Strawbridge, Camacho, Cohen, & Kaplan, 1993).

The Alameda study is not the only one to show these connections between health habits and mortality. For example, a 20-year longitudinal study in Sweden confirms the link between physical exercise and lower risk of death (Lissner, Bengtsson, Bjorkelund, & Wedel, 1996). In addition, the Nurses' Health Study, a longitudinal investigation that examined the health behaviours of more than 115 000 nurses in the United States for almost two decades, found that the lower a woman's initial Body-Mass Index (BMI) (BMI is the ratio of weight to height), the lower her likelihood of death (Manson et al., 1995).

These longitudinal studies suggest that the lifestyle choices of early adulthood have cumulative effects. For example, the effect of a high-fat diet coupled with a sedentary lifestyle appears to add up over time. However, a radical lowering of fat levels in the diet along with regular exercise can reduce the risk of heart disease and diabetes (Health Canada, 1999b). Thus, the long-term effects of lifestyle choice made in early adulthood may be either negative or positive (see No Easy Answers). So there is likely to be a pay-off for changing your health habits.

SOCIAL SUPPORT Abundant research shows that adults with adequate *social support* have lower risk of disease, death, and depression than do adults with weaker social networks or less supportive relationships (e.g., Berkman, 1985; Berkman & Breslow, 1983; Cohen, 1991). However, a person's perception of the adequacy of her social contacts and emotional support is more strongly related to physical and emotional health than is the actual number of such contacts (Feld & George, 1994; Sarason, Sarason, & Pierce, 1990). Thus, it is not the objective amount of contact with others that is important, but how that contact is understood or interpreted.

Critical Thinking

Think about your own less-than-ideal health habits. What rationalizations do you use to justify them to yourself?

The link between social support and health was revealed in some of the findings from the Alameda study. In this study, the *social network index* reflected an objective measurement: number of contacts with friends and relatives, marital status, and church and group membership. Even using this less-than-perfect measure of support, the relationship was vividly clear: Among both men and women in three different age groups (30 to 49, 50 to 59, and 60 to 69), those with the fewest social connections had higher death rates than those with more social connections. Since similar patterns have been

No Easy Answers

There Is No Fountain

of Youth

Spend a few hours watching television or leafing through magazines, and the advertisements will tell you something very significant about the adult population: Many of us appear to be looking for a quick and easy way to escape the ravages of age. A pill promises to cure a man's baldness. A cream is said to dissolve fat on women's thighs. As appealing as the idea of a fountain of youth is, the truth is that the best way to moderate the effects of primary aging on the body is to follow the hard road of behavioural change. The most significant barriers to remaining youthful are the result of secondary aging and are often preventable. Further, if you develop good habits while you are young, not only will it be easier to maintain those habits, but you will reap the benefits over many years.

These are the most important changes you can make:

- Don't smoke. If you smoke now, stop. If you don't smoke, don't start.

- Exercise, exercise, exercise. Take the stairs instead of the elevator; walk to the grocery store or on other errands; ride a bike to work; get at least 20 to 30 minutes of vigorous exercise at least three times a week (more than that is even better).

- Eat a lower-fat diet. High fat in the diet has been linked to increased risks of both cancer and heart disease, as well as to obesity. Canada's Nutrient Recommendations suggest that 30% of daily calories come from fat—well below the average Canadian diet (Health Canada, 2001d). But there is good evidence that a level of 15–20% of calories from fat would be even better. Achieving this level means eating much less meat and dairy products and a lot more vegetables, fruits, grains, and beans. (Goodbye, fast foods!)

- Get enough calcium. This is especially important for women, who lose more calcium from their bones than do men, especially after menopause. And once the calcium is lost, it is very hard—perhaps impossible—to regain it. So here is one place where prevention is critical. Weight-bearing exercise helps to retain calcium, but taking calcium supplements from early adulthood is also a good idea.

found in other countries, including Sweden and Japan, this link between social contact and physical hardiness is not restricted to the United States or to Western cultures (Orth-Gomér, Rosengren, & Wilhelmsen, 1993; Sugisawa, Liang, & Liu, 1994).

A SENSE OF CONTROL Another personal characteristic that affects health is an individual's level of what Rodin has called *perceived control* (Rodin, 1990). Recall from **Chapter 2** that psychologist Albert Bandura talks about this same characteristic but refers to it as **self-efficacy**, the belief in one's ability to perform some action or to control one's behaviour or environment, to reach some goal or to make something happen (Bandura, 1977b, 1986; 1997a, b). Such a belief is one aspect of the internal model of the self and is affected by one's experiences with mastering tasks and overcoming obstacles.

A similar idea comes from the work of Martin Seligman, who differentiates between positions of *optimism* and *helplessness* (Seligman, 1991). The pessimist, who feels helpless, believes that misfortune will last a long time, will undermine everything, and is his own fault. The optimist believes that setbacks are temporary and usually caused by circumstances. He is convinced that there is always some solution and that he will be able to work things out. Confronted by defeat, the optimist sees it as a challenge and tries harder, whereas the pessimist gives up. Both Bandura and Seligman propose that self-efficacy or optimism arise in childhood and adolescence, as a result of early experiences of effectiveness, success or failure, and frustration.

Research on the links between a sense of control and health shows that those with a more helpless attitude or with a low sense of self-efficacy are more likely to become depressed or physically ill ("Optimism can mean life," 1994; Seligman, 1991; Syme, 1990). The most striking demonstration of this connection is from a 35-year study of a group of Harvard men who were first interviewed in their freshman years, in 1938–1940. Researchers were able to use material from interviews with these men when they were 25 to assess their degree of pessimism. Their physical health from ages 30 to 60 was then rated by physicians who examined the men every 5 years. Pessimism was not related to health at 30, 35, or 40, but at every assessment from age 45 to age 60, those who had had a more pessimistic approach at age 25 had significantly poorer health, and this was true even after controlling statistically for physical and mental health at 25 (Peterson, Seligman, & Vaillant, 1988).

It is also possible to show that experimentally increasing the sense of control improves an adult's health, even immune function. On this point, there is cross-sectional, longitudinal, and experimental evidence (Welch & West, 1995). In the earliest and best-known study of this kind, researchers found that mortality rates of nursing home residents were lower among those who had been given control over even quite simple aspects of their daily lives, such as whether to have scrambled eggs or omelettes for breakfast or whether to sign up to attend a movie (Rodin & Langer, 1977).

INTIMATE PARTNER ABUSE

Researchers define **intimate partner abuse** as physical acts or other behaviour intended to cause physical, psychological or sexual harm to an intimate partner. Intimate partners are couples who are dating, cohabiting, engaged, or married, or who were formerly partners. The more common term, *domestic abuse,* refers only to incidents involving individuals who live in the same household.

PREVALENCE Throughout the world women are more likely than men to be victimized by intimate partners regardless of their social, economic, religious, or cultural background (Heise & Garcia-Moreno, 2002). And as **Figure 12.5** reveals, the rates of abuse

self-efficacy
the belief in one's own capacity to cause an intended event to occur or to perform a task

intimate partner abuse
physical acts or other behaviour intended to intimidate or harm an intimate partner

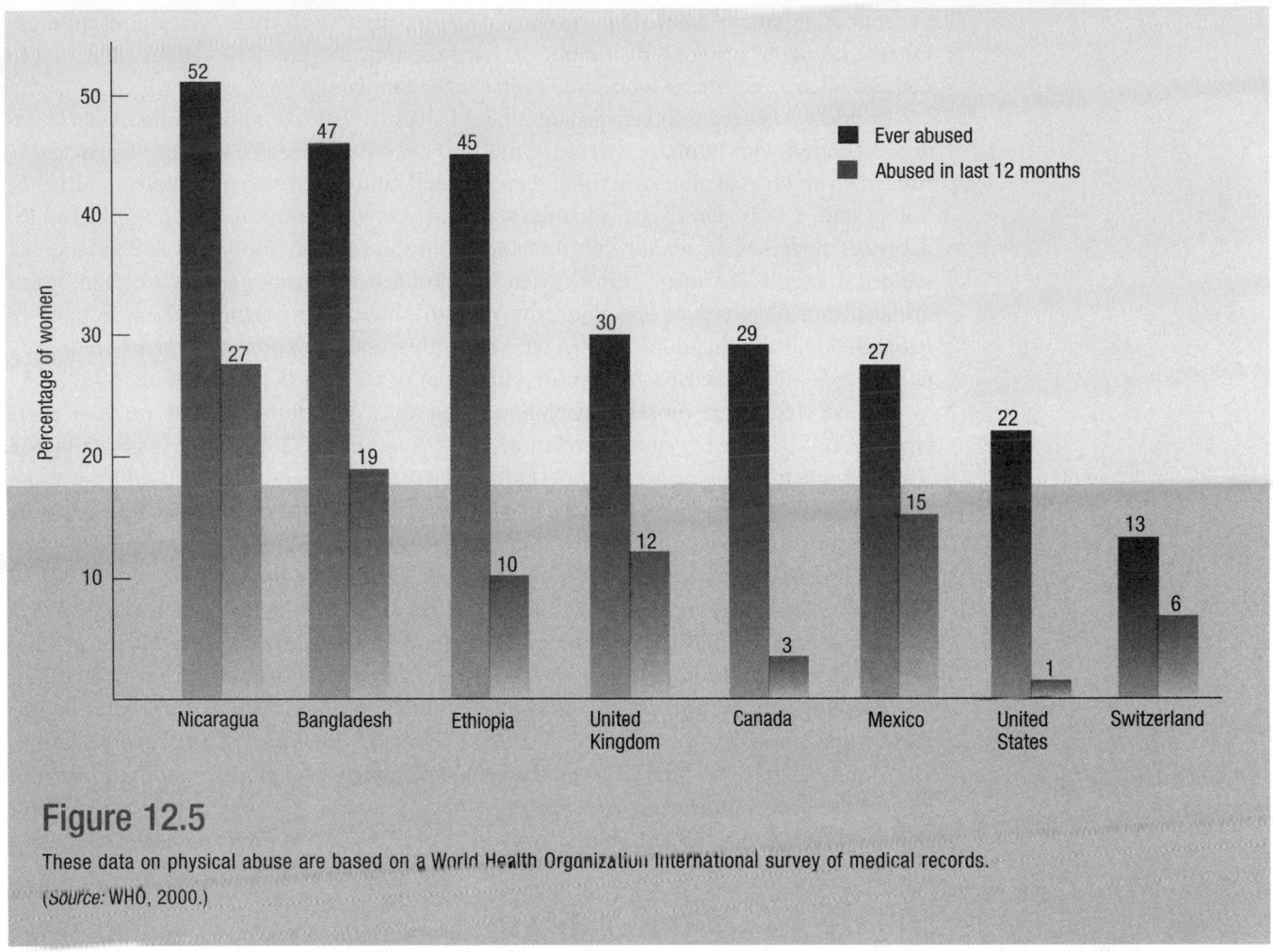

Figure 12.5

These data on physical abuse are based on a World Health Organization International survey of medical records. (*Source:* WHO, 2000.)

of women vary significantly around the world (World Health Organization [WHO], 2000). In Canada, a 1999 survey suggested that over a 5-year period about 8% of women had been physically abused by a spouse, compared with 7% of men. Spousal violence within the Aboriginal population is higher than average, with 25% of Aboriginal women and 13% of Aboriginal men being assaulted by their spouse (Statistics Canada, 2001k). In both Aboriginal and non-Aboriginal populations, persons living in common-law relationships are more likely to be victims of lethal and nonlethal spousal violence than those who are legally married (Hotton, 2001). Both women (28%) and men (22%) who had contact with an ex-marital or common-law partner reported violence committed by an ex-partner (Statistics Canada, 2001k). Moreover, violence by former partners is reportedly more severe and lethal than assault by a current partner (Statistics Canada, 2000d).

CAUSES OF PARTNER ABUSE Anthropologists believe that cultural attitudes contribute to rates of abuse (Hicks & Gwynne, 1996). Specifically, in many societies, women were regarded as property, and a man's "right" to beat his partner was at times protected by law. In fact, there was a time when, based on English common-law traditions, this was true in British-governed parts of North America.

Gender-role prescriptions may also contribute to abuse. For example, rates of abuse are particularly high among Japanese women, over 50% of whom claim to have been victimized (Kozu, 1999). Researchers attribute the prevalence of abuse to the cultural belief that Japanese husbands are absolute authorities over their wives and children. Further, to avoid bringing dishonour on her husband, the Japanese wife is obligated to conceal abusive incidents from those outside the family.

In addition to cultural beliefs, a number of characteristics of abusers and their victims are associated with intimate partner abuse. For example, the same cluster of personality traits contributes to abuse in both heterosexual and homosexual couples (Burke & Follingstad, 1999). The cluster includes a tendency toward irrational jealousy, a need for dependency in the partner and control in a relationship, sudden mood swings, and a quick temper (Landolt & Dutton, 1997). Men who are generally more aggressive than others are also more likely than less aggressive men to abuse their partners (Kane, Staiger, & Ricciardelli, 2000). In addition, men who are high school dropouts or who are frequently unemployed abuse their partners more often than other men (Kyriacou et al., 1999).

Abuse victims are more likely to have been abused as children than are their peers who are not involved in abusive relationships (Wyatt et al., 2000). Age is also a factor. Young women between the ages of 16 and 24 are more likely to be abused than those who are older (Buss, 1999; Duncan et al., 1999). This pattern of age differences may result from younger women's lesser ability to function independently from abusive partners. They may lack the education and/or work experience necessary to gain employment. Finally, younger women are more likely to be caring for infants and young children for whom they cannot obtain day care. As a result, many such women remain in abusive relationships, believing they have no other choice (Kaplan & Sadock, 1991).

Alcohol and drug problems are more common among both abusers and victims than among nonabusive partners (Kyriacou et al., 1999; Van Hightower & Gorton, 1998). One extensive study of more than 8000 intrafamily killings found that, in about half of spousal homicides, the perpetrator had been drinking alcohol or using drugs (Dawson & Langan, 1994). Similarly, in 50% of cases, the victim had been using alcohol or drugs.

EFFECTS OF ABUSE ON INDIVIDUALS Women who are abused are at heightened risk for physical injury, sexual and reproductive disorders, and homicide (Heise & Garcia-Moreno, 2002). They may develop feelings of anxiety, depression, and low self-esteem (Kaplan & Sadock, 1991). Such feelings are intensified when victims believe they cannot escape from the abusive relationship. Some become so despondent that they consider or attempt suicide as an escape (National Center for Injury Prevention and Control [NCIPC], 2000).

Witnessing abuse also influences children's development. One study involving 420 adults who had witnessed physical violence between their parents as children suggested that there are strong relationships between parental violence and a variety of negative developmental outcomes (McNeal & Amato, 1998). For one thing, many of these adults were found to have poor relationships with their own partners and children. Moreover, many had become perpetrators or victims of partner abuse themselves.

PREVENTION Vigorous law enforcement is one approach to prevention (Sacco & Kennedy, 1996). Advocates of this approach suggest that a stigma of arrest may force abusers to face the reality that they have a serious problem. Training programs for law enforcement officials and hospital emergency room personnel that teach them to recognize signs of abuse are also essential (Hamberger & Minsky, 2000). As a result of such training, advocates claim, perpetrators may be identified and prosecuted even when victims do not voluntarily report abusive incidents.

A different approach is to provide victims with problem-solving skills and temporary shelters that may prevent their revictimization (NCIPC, 2000). Further, community-wide and school-based approaches to prevention seek to educate the public about

Criminologists point out that intimate partner abuse happens most often in the context of arguments over long-standing disagreements that take place when partners are home from work in the evening, on holidays or weekends, and/or have been drinking or using drugs. (*Photo:* Jonathan Nourok/PhotoEdit)

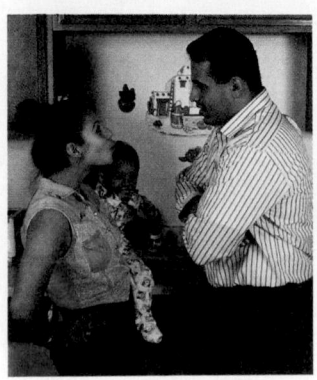

intimate partner abuse and to change attitudes about the acceptability of violence in intimate relationships, so that abuse will not happen in the first place.

SEXUAL ASSAULT

Sexual assault is any form of sexual activity with another person without his or her consent. Engaging in sex with a person who is incapable of consenting or of understanding what is happening to him or her because of a mental disability or a temporary altered state of consciousness is also defined as sexual assault.

Canadian law prescribes three levels of sexual assault: level 1—sexual assault (e.g., kissing, touching, oral or anal sex, intercourse or other forms of penetration); level 2—sexual assault with a weapon or resulting in bodily harm; and level 3—aggravated sexual assault (e.g., wounding, maiming, disfiguring, or endangering the life of the victim).

PREVALENCE The rate of reported sexual assault incidents was 86 per 100 000 in 2002 (see **Figure 12.6**), and of these, 88% were level 1 sexual assaults (Kong, Johnson, Beattie, & Cardillo, 2003). Six of 10 reported sexual assault victims were young—the majority were girls aged 11 to 19 and boys aged 3 to 14. Women are far more likely than men to be sexually victimized, accounting for 85% of all reported cases in 2002.

Most sexual violence occurs within the context of social or romantic relationships; fewer than half of all sexual assaults are committed by strangers. Eighty percent of the victims of reported cases in 2002 knew their assailants—10% were assaulted by a friend, 41% by an acquaintance, 28% by a family member (Kong, et al., 2003). Like sexual assault by men against women, male rape against males usually involves men who are acquaintances or who are intimate partners (Hodge & Canter, 1998).

Sexual assault rates are quite similar across cultures, with a few rather dramatic exceptions. For example, in an international survey of medical records, 48% of women in Peru were found to have reported being forced into a sexual act during the previous 12 months (WHO, 2000).

CAUSES Anthropologists hypothesize that rates of sexual assault are similar across nations because there is a prohibition against forced sex in almost all cultures (Hicks & Gwynne, 1996). Exceptionally high rates, such as those in Peru, are probably the result of a complex set of cultural beliefs. Sexual intercourse, even if it is obtained by force, may be seen as evidence of masculinity, one component of which in many cultures is the right and ability to dominate women. Thus, tolerance of sexual assault may be greater in societies that have a culture of "machismo," as a way of "reminding" men and women of their relative social positions.

Attitudes and behaviours intersect in subtle ways to influence the likelihood of sexual assault. For example, *date rape* is nonconsensual sex that takes place in the context of a date. Men's beliefs about women's sexual behaviour—namely, the idea that women say no when they really mean yes—are believed to contribute to date rape (Christopher, Madura, & Weaver, 1998). Frequently, alcohol and/or drugs, such as the so-called

sexual assault

any form of sexual activity with another person without his or her consent

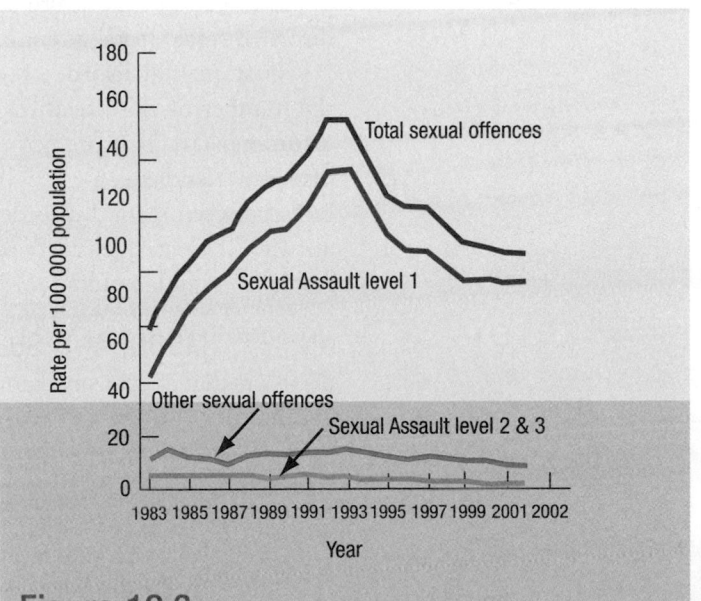

Figure 12.6

The rates of police-reported sexual offences peaked during the 1990s and then declined in Canada.

(*Source:* Adapted from Statistics Canada, [2003b], available at: http://www.statcan.ca/Daily/English/030725/d030725.pdf)

date rape drug Rohypnol, are used by the perpetrator to sedate or to loosen the inhibitions of the victim. Thus, prevention programs urge young women to avoid drinking or using drugs on dates, to confine dating to public places until they know a man very well, and to be as emphatic as possible when discouraging a man's sexual advances.

EFFECTS Sexual assault is associated with many of the same psychological effects as intimate partner abuse: depression, low self-esteem, and fear. Moreover, victims of sexual assault can develop post-traumatic stress disorder, and many have difficulties in their sex lives (Kaplan & Sadock, 1991). The effects of male rape are similar, but they also include fear of developing a homosexual orientation among victims who are heterosexual (Kaplan & Sadock, 1991).

MENTAL HEALTH PROBLEMS

Studies in a number of developed countries show that the risk of virtually every kind of emotional disturbance is higher in early adulthood than in middle age (Kessler, Foster, Webster, & House, 1992; Regier et al., 1988). In fact, survey research suggests that as many as 10% of younger adults, those aged 18 to 24, have seriously considered committing suicide (Brener, Hassan, & Barrios, 1999).

CAUSES OF MENTAL DISORDERS The most plausible explanation for the differing rates of mental disorder between young adults and middle-aged adults is that early adulthood is the period in which adults have both the highest expectations and the highest levels of role conflict and role strain. These are the years when each of us must learn a series of major new roles (spouse, parent, worker). If we fall short of our expectations, emotional difficulties such as anxiety and depression become more likely.

Some people respond very effectively to the challenges of young adulthood, while others do not. For example, the personal factors you read about in an earlier section are important to mental health as well as physical health. However, with respect to mental disorder, researchers' attention is becoming more focused on biological causes.

First, mental disorders tend to run in families, suggesting a hereditary factor. In fact, the number of close relatives a person has who suffer from depression or other mood disorders is the best predictor of the likelihood that the individual will develop a mood disorder (Kendler et al., 1995). In addition, an increasing number of studies demonstrate links between mental disorder and disturbances in specific brain functions (Drevets et al., 1997). Consequently, the current view of most psychologists is that mental disorders result from an interaction of biological, psychological, and sociocultural factors.

ANXIETY, MOOD, AND SUBSTANCE USE DISORDERS The most common mental disorders that affect Canadians are those that are associated with intense or prolonged fear and anxiety (Health Canada, 2002e). For example, anxiety disorders, such as *phobias*, *generalized anxiety disorder*, *obsessive-compulsive disorder*, and *panic disorder*, affect a reported 12% of the Canadian adult population in any given year. Anxiety disorders are of such severity as to interfere with normal daily functioning, and because they are so common they also contribute to lost productivity from both absenteeism and unemployment.

After anxiety disorders, problems associated with moods are the most common type of mental difficulty. Depression is the most frequent of these disorders, with the most debilitating type, called *major depression*, affecting between 4% and 5% of Canadians annually (Health Canada, 2002e). Rates of depression are higher in early adulthood than in either adolescence or middle age. Thus, paradoxically, the time of life in which people experience their peak of physical and intellectual functioning is also the time when they may be most prone to feelings of sadness. Depression rates may be higher in early adulthood because these are the years when people must create new attachment relationships while at the same time separating from parents (Erikson's task of *intimacy*). Consequently, brief periods during which a person is alone may result in feelings of loneliness and social failure that may lead to depression.

Rates of alcoholism and significant drug addiction also peak between ages 18 and 40, after which they decline gradually. The rates of addiction are higher for men than for women, but the age pattern is very similar in both genders (Anthony & Aboraya, 1992). One recent study found the rate of regular heavy drinking to be about 38% for young Canadian drinkers aged 20 to 24, compared with 23% among 25- to 34-year-olds, and 6% for those over 65. The greatest disparity between gender drinking rates was found for the age group 20 to 24, with 53% of male drinkers and 23% of female drinkers considered to be regular heavy drinkers (Statistics Canada, 2001e).

Binge drinking (usually defined as consuming five or more drinks on one occasion) is also particularly common among college and university students in Canada. Although most binge drinkers do not think of themselves as having a problem with alcohol, they clearly display a variety of problem behaviours, including substantially higher rates of unprotected sex, physical injury, driving while intoxicated, and trouble with the police (Wechsler, Davenport, Dowdall, Moeykens, & Castillo, 1994; Wechsler, Dowdall, Maenner, Gledhill-Hoyt, & Lee, 1998). Thus, alarmed by surveys showing that as many as 50% of post-secondary students engage in binge drinking, a growing number of colleges and universities are strictly enforcing rules against on-campus substance use (Wechsler et al., 1998). Many also provide students with treatment for alcohol and substance abuse problems.

PERSONALITY DISORDERS In a few cases, the stresses of young adulthood, presumably in combination with some type of biological factor, lead to serious disturbances in cognitive, emotional, and social functioning that are not easily treated. For example, a **personality disorder** is an inflexible pattern of behaviour that leads to difficulties in social, educational, and occupational functioning. In many cases, the problems that are associated with these disorders appear early in life. However, the behaviour pattern is usually not diagnosed as a mental disorder until late adolescence or early adulthood (American Psychiatric Association (APA), 2000). The five most common types of personality disorders are listed in **Table 12.2** on page 380.

Generally, to be diagnosed with any of the disorders in **Table 12.2**, a young adult has to have been exhibiting the associated behaviour since mid- or late adolescence. In addition, the person should demonstrate the behaviour consistently, across all kinds of situations. For example, a person who steals from an employer but generally respects the property rights of others outside the work environment would probably not be diagnosed with antisocial personality disorder. The individual's functioning at work, at school, or in social relationships also must be impaired to some degree. Psychological tests can be helpful in distinguishing whether an individual simply has a troublesome personality trait, such as suspiciousness, or a genuine mental disorder, such as paranoid personality disorder.

Some personality disorders, such as antisocial and borderline disorders, become less severe in their manifestations with age (APA, 2000). However, most of these disorders remain problematic throughout adult life. In addition, they are not easily treated. They often do not respond to psychotherapy, because those who suffer from them seem to believe their problems result from others' behaviour rather than their own.

SCHIZOPHRENIA One of the most serious mental disorders that is often first diagnosed in early adulthood is **schizophrenia**. This mental disorder affects an estimated 1% of

personality disorder
an inflexible pattern of behaviour that leads to difficulty in educational, occupational, and social functioning

schizophrenia
a serious mental disorder characterized by disturbances of thought such as delusions and hallucinations

TABLE 12.2	Personality Disorders
Type	**Characteristics**
Antisocial	Difficulty forming emotional attachments; lack of empathy; little regard for the rights of others; self-centred; willingness to violate the law or social rules to achieve a desired objective
Paranoid	Suspicious of others' behaviour and motives; emotionally guarded and highly sensitive to minor violations of personal space or perceived rights
Histrionic	Irrational, attention-seeking behaviour; inappropriate emotional responses; sexually seductive behaviour and clothing
Narcissistic	Exaggerated sense of self-importance; craves attention and approval; exploits others; lack of empathy
Borderline	Unstable moods, relationships; fear of abandonment; tendency to self-injury; highly dependent on others; impulsive and reckless behaviour

(*Source:* APA, 2000.)

Canadians and is characterized by confused thinking, false beliefs known as *delusions*, and false sensory experiences called *hallucinations*. Schizophrenia is related to impaired interpersonal relationships and problems in living (Health Canada, 2002e). For example, a first-year biology student who breaks into a laboratory on his university campus to work on a cure for cancer he has just thought of may suffer from a *delusion of grandeur*. Likewise, a young woman who hears voices that guide her behaviour is likely to be experiencing hallucinations.

For most schizophrenics, these disturbances of thought become so severe that they can no longer function at work, at school, or in social relationships. In fact, many engage in behaviour that endangers themselves or others. For example, a schizophrenic may believe that he can fly and may jump out of an upper-storey window. Consequently, schizophrenics are frequently hospitalized. Fortunately, powerful antipsychotic medications can help most schizophrenics regain some degree of normal functioning. Yet many continue to experience recurring episodes of disturbed thinking even when medication helps them to gain control over their behaviour.

Before Going On

- How are age, health habits, and stress related to illness?
- What habits are associated with good health?
- How do social support and a sense of control contribute to good health?
- What are the rates, causes, and effects of intimate partner abuse?
- What factors are involved in most cases of sexual assault, and what are its effects on victims?
- What are the characteristics of people who suffer from anxiety or mood disorders, substance abuse, personality disorders, or schizophrenia?

COGNITIVE CHANGES

Like most aspects of physical functioning, intellectual processes are at their peak in early adulthood. Indeed, it now seems clear that the intellectual peak lasts longer than many early researchers had thought, and that the rate of decline is quite slow. Current research also makes it clear that the rate and pattern of cognitive decline varies widely—differences that appear to be caused by a variety of environmental and lifestyle factors, as well as by heredity.

FORMAL OPERATIONS AND BEYOND

As you should recall from **Chapter 10,** Piaget's formal operational stage emerges in mid- to late adolescence but is not nearly so well developed then as his theory proposed. In fact, it appears that formal operational thinking is more characteristic of adults than of adolescents and is strongly tied to educational experiences. But some theorists dispute Piaget's hypothesis that formal operations is the last stage of cognitive development.

A number of theorists argue that Piaget's concept of formal operations simply doesn't capture many of the kinds of thinking that adults are called on to do. They propose, instead, that new structures, or new stages, of thinking occur in adulthood. One such theorist is Gisela Labouvie-Vief, who argues that formal operational thinking is useful in early adulthood, when the young person has some need to explore or examine many life options (Labouvie-Vief, 1980, 1990). But once an adult has made his initial choices, he no longer has much need for formal operations; instead, he needs thinking skills that are specialized and pragmatic. Adults learn how to solve the problems associated with the particular roles they occupy, or the particular jobs they hold. In the process, they trade the deductive thoroughness of formal operations for what Labouvie-Vief calls *contextual validity*. In her view, this trade-off does not reflect a regression or loss, but rather a necessary structural change.

Labouvie-Vief also makes the point that many young adults begin to turn away from a purely logical, analytic approach, toward a more open, perhaps deeper, mode of understanding that incorporates myth and metaphor and recognizes and accepts paradox and uncertainty. Michael Basseches calls this new adult type of thinking **dialectical thought** (Basseches, 1984, 1989). He suggests that whereas formal operational thought "involves the effort to find fundamental fixed realities—basic elements and immutable laws—[dialectical thought] attempts to describe fundamental processes of change and the dynamic relationships through which this change occurs" (1984, p. 24). According to this view, adults do not give up their ability to use formal reasoning. Instead, they acquire a new ability to deal with the fuzzier problems that make up the majority of the problems of adulthood—problems that do not have a single solution, or in which some critical pieces of information may be missing. Choosing what type of refrigerator to buy might be a decision aided by formal operational thought. But such forms of logical thought may not be helpful in making a decision about whether to adopt a child, or whether to place your aging parent in a nursing home. Basseches argues that such problems demand a different kind of thinking—not a "higher" kind of thinking, but a different one.

Still a third model of "postformal" thinking comes from Patricia Arlin, who argues that Piaget's stage of formal operations is a stage of problem-solving (Arlin, 1975, 1989, 1990). Some adults, Arlin proposes,

dialectical thought
a form of thought involving recognition and acceptance of paradox and uncertainty

What kind of thinking might this young couple be using to make a budget decision? Pragmatic, concrete, or formal operational? (*Photo:* Diana White/PhotoEdit)

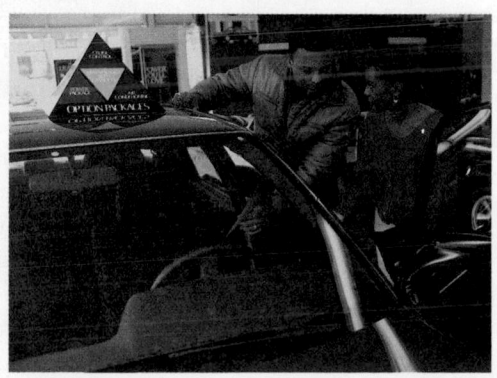

Critical Thinking

List two personal problems you have had to solve in the past 6 months. What kind of logic or thought process did you use to solve each one? Did your mode of thinking change in response to the nature of the problem?

develop a further stage characterized by problem *finding*. This new mode, which includes much of what is normally called *creativity,* is optimal for dealing with problems that have no clear solution or that have multiple solutions. A person operating at this stage is able to generate many possible solutions to ill-defined problems and to see old problems in new ways. Arlin argues that problem finding is a clear stage following formal operations, but that it is achieved by only a small number of adults, such as those involved in advanced science or the arts.

Many of these new theories of adult cognition are intriguing, but they remain highly speculative, with little empirical evidence to back them up. More generally, psychologists do not yet agree on whether these new types of thinking represent "higher" forms of thought, built on the stages Piaget described, or whether it is more appropriate simply to describe them as different forms of thinking that may or may not emerge in adulthood. What may be most important about such theories is the emphasis on the fact that the normal problems of adult life, with their inconsistencies and complexities, cannot always be addressed fruitfully using formal operational logic. It seems entirely plausible that adults are pushed toward more pragmatic, relativistic forms of thinking and use formal operational thinking only occasionally, if at all. Postformal theorists agree that this change should not be thought of as a loss or a deterioration, but rather as a reasonable adaptation to a different set of cognitive tasks.

INTELLIGENCE AND MEMORY

Examination of intelligence and memory in early adulthood suggests that both continuity and change characterize these components of cognitive functioning.

IQ SCORES IQ scores remain quite stable across middle childhood, adolescence, and early adulthood. For example, a study of Canadian army veterans, first tested when they were in their early 20s and then again in their early 60s, yielded similar results; there was a correlation of .78 between verbal IQ scores achieved at the two ages (Gold et al., 1995). Over shorter intervals, the correlations were even higher.

The best single source of evidence on the stability of IQ in adulthood is a remarkable 35-year study by Werner Schaie, referred to as the Seattle Longitudinal Study (1983, 1989, 1993, 1994, 1996; Schaie & Hertzog, 1983). Schaie began in 1956 with a set of cross-sectional samples; the participants in different samples were 7 years apart in age and ranged in age from 25 to 67. All participants took an IQ test at the outset of the study; a subset of the participants in each age group was then followed over 35 years and retested every 7 years. In 1963, another set of cross-sectional samples, covering the same age ranges, was tested, and a subset of these was retested 7, 14, 21, and 28 years later. Further samples were added in 1970, 1977, 1984, and 1991. This remarkable data-collection process enabled Schaie to look at IQ changes over 7-, 14-, 21-, and 28-year intervals for several sets of participants, each from a slightly different cohort. **Figure 12.7** graphs one set of cross-sectional comparisons made in 1977 as well as 14-year longitudinal results smoothed over the whole age range. The test involved in this case is a measure of global intelligence on which the average score is set at 50 points (equivalent to an IQ of 100 on most other tests).

You can see that the cross-sectional comparisons show a steady drop in IQ. But the longitudinal evidence suggests that overall intelligence test scores actually rise in early adulthood and then remain quite constant until perhaps age 60, when they begin to decline. Since this pattern has also been found by other researchers (e.g., Sands, Terry,

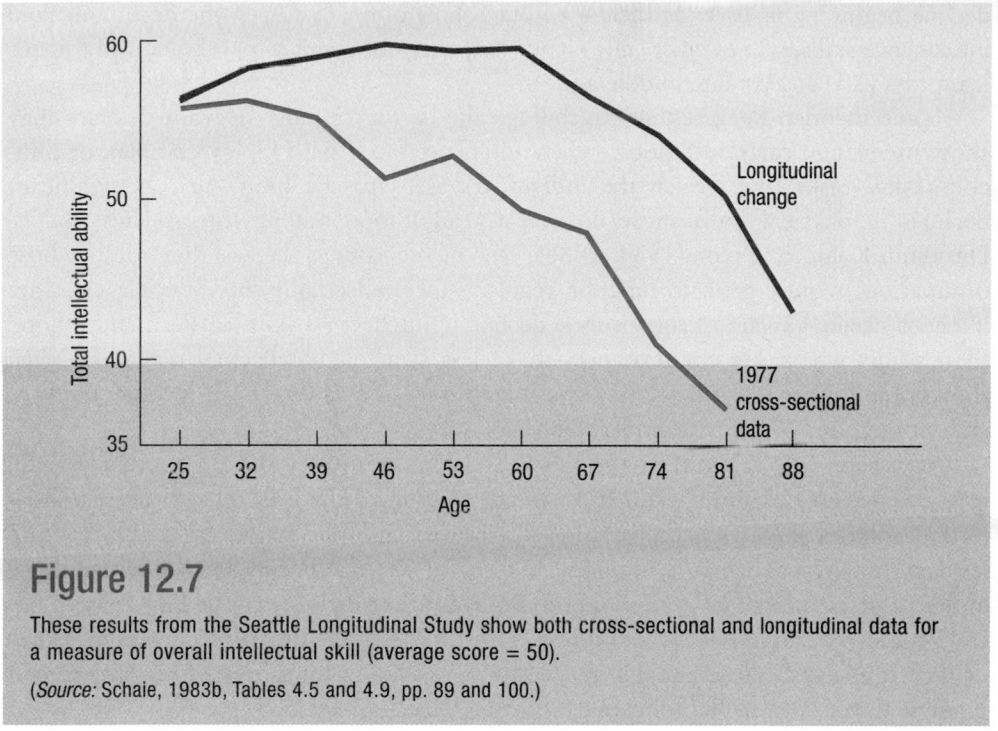

Figure 12.7

These results from the Seattle Longitudinal Study show both cross-sectional and longitudinal data for a measure of overall intellectual skill (average score = 50).

(*Source:* Schaie, 1983b, Tables 4.5 and 4.9, pp. 89 and 100.)

& Meredith, 1989; Siegler, 1983), there is good support for the temptingly optimistic view that intellectual ability remains essentially stable through most of adulthood.

CRYSTALLIZED AND FLUID INTELLIGENCE Looking at different components of intellectual ability gives a clearer picture of change and stability across the adult years. Theorists have suggested several ways to subdivide intellectual tasks. However, the most influential of these theories has been Raymond Cattell and John Horn's distinction between crystallized intelligence and fluid intelligence (Cattell, 1963; Horn, 1982; Horn & Donaldson, 1980).

Crystallized intelligence depends heavily on education and experiences. It consists of the set of skills and bits of knowledge that every adult learns as part of growing up in any given culture, such as vocabulary, the ability to read and understand the newspaper, and the ability to evaluate experience. Technical skills you may learn for your job or your life—balancing a cheque book, using a computer, making change, finding the mayonnaise in the grocery store—also represent crystallized intelligence.

Fluid intelligence, in contrast, involves more "basic" abilities—it is the aspect of intelligence that depends more on the efficient functioning of the central nervous system and less on specific experience. A common measure of fluid intelligence is a "letter series test," in which a participant is given a series of letters (for example, A C F J O) and must figure out what letter should go next. This problem demands abstract reasoning rather than reasoning about known or everyday events. Most tests of memory also measure fluid intelligence, as do many tests measuring response speed and those measuring higher-level or abstract mathematical skills. Schaie's results, and the results of many other investigators, suggest that adults maintain crystallized intelligence throughout early and middle adulthood, but that fluid intelligence declines fairly steadily over adulthood, beginning at perhaps age 35 or 40 (Horn & Donaldson, 1980; Schaie, 1994).

Do results like these mean that developmentalists must revise their generally optimistic conclusions about adult intelligence based on longitudinal studies of total IQ scores? On the face of it, yes: On some kinds of tests, adults appear to show some

crystallized intelligence
knowledge and judgment acquired through education and experience

fluid intelligence
the aspect of intelligence that reflects fundamental biological processes and does not depend on specific experiences

decline beginning as early as their 40s. But Schaie notes that even the decline in fluid intelligence skills, while statistically significant, may not result in psychologically significant loss until at least late middle age.

Some theorists suggest that psychologically or functionally relevant declines may show up even in early adulthood, when adults are faced with highly complex or difficult tasks—tasks that stretch the individual's skills to the limit—just as significant declines in physical skills show up in early adulthood among top athletes (Baltes, Dittmann-Kohli, & Dixon, 1984, 1986). One of the ironies, then, is that adults whose occupations require them to function regularly at intellectually more taxing levels are likely to become aware of some subtle decline in intellectual skills earlier in adulthood than adults whose life circumstances make less stringent intellectual demands—even though the former individuals may continue to function at very high absolute levels of skill throughout their early and middle years.

So where does this leave us in answering the question about intellectual maintenance or decline over adulthood? It seems safe to conclude, at least tentatively, that intellectual abilities show essentially no decline in early adulthood except at the very top levels of intellectual demand. In middle adulthood, though, declines in fluid intelligence abilities—those tasks that are thought to represent the efficiency of the basic physiological process—become evident (Salthouse, 1991). Indeed, the rate of decline in measures of fluid intelligence closely matches the rate of decline in total brain size, suggesting a possible direct link (Bigler, Johnson, Jackson, & Blatter, 1995).

MEMORY The pattern of results from studies of memory ability generally follows the pattern found in studies of fluid intelligence. Memory skills remain stable during early adulthood, decline somewhat during middle adulthood, and decline more noticeably in late adulthood. For example, measures of short-term memory—recalling something after only a short time, such as a phone number you've just looked up in the phone book—generally show a drop with age.

Age differences become more pronounced for measures of long-term memory—memory for items stored for longer periods, or permanently. Both the process of getting memories into this long-term storage (a process called *encoding* by memory theorists) and the process of retrieving them again seem to be impaired among older adults, as compared with young adults (Salthouse, 1991). With age, memory processes become both slower and less efficient.

Before Going On

- What are some theoretical proposals regarding a stage of cognitive development beyond Piaget's formal operational stage?

- How do the concepts of crystallized and fluid intelligence help explain age-related changes in IQ scores?

POST-SECONDARY EDUCATION

post-secondary education
any formal educational experience that follows high school

In today's high-tech, global economy, **post-secondary education**, any formal educational experience that follows high school, has become a necessity for virtually everyone (see **Development in the Information Age**). This helps to explain why the number of students enrolled in some level of post-secondary education in Canada has been on the rise. Moreover, a higher proportion of highly educated immigrants and recessionary labour markets have also encouraged young adults to further their studies (Clark, 2003a).

DEVELOPMENTAL IMPACT

Canada has the world's highest proportion of 25- to 64-year-old college and university graduates combined (41%)—higher than the U.S., Ireland, Japan, or Sweden. Additionally, for the first time, more Canadian women than men 25 to 34 years of age now possess a bachelor's degree (56%), or a master's degree (52%); although fewer women have doctoral degrees (37%) (Statistics Canada, 2003c). Only 15% of Canadians in this age range lack a high school diploma.

Development in the
Information Age
Distance Learning

One of the most promising technological innovations in recent years has been the remarkable increase in the availability of opportunities for distance learning. Distance learning is any mode of instruction in which teacher and students are at a distance from each other. Information technologies—television, computers, and so on—serve as mediators between the two.

Of course, distance learning in the form of correspondence courses has been around for a long time. Likewise, colleges have offered classes via television for several decades. However, widespread access to the Internet has opened the door to a new era in distance learning. Thanks to the Internet, students can enrol in institutions very far removed from their place of residence. They can also create a flexible schedule for themselves. For example, a student can download a professor's lecture at 4:00 a.m. if that is the hour that suits his particular needs. Thus, it isn't surprising that distance learning college and university students, especially nontraditional ones, report high levels of satisfaction with web-based courses (Wernet, Olliges, & Delicath, 2000).

The potential of the Internet to attract distance learning students and to allow them to register and pay for courses from a distance has led to the creation of new virtual universities, or universities that offer courses only on the Internet. Some are owned by nonprofit or governmental entities, but many are for-profit businesses. The stimulus for these new institutions is simple: North Americans currently spend more than $200 billion each year on distance learning (Bulkeley, 1998). Thus, traditional colleges and universities see distance learning as an avenue to much-needed additional funds, and entrepreneurs see a potentially profitable market.

However, distance learning students drop out at much higher rates than do on-campus students (Carr, 2000). Most likely, the higher dropout rate reflects the fact that nontraditional students enrol in distance courses at a higher rate than do traditional students. All the factors that make nontraditional students more likely to withdraw from on-campus courses probably affect their persistence in distance learning courses. In addition, weaker students may need the periodic contact with the instructor and other class members that on-campus courses can provide.

There are other concerns as well. Distance learning raises new questions about fraud and cheating (Kennedy, Nowak, Raghuraman, Thomas, & Davis, 2000). If a professor requires distance students to participate in online chats, how does she know if a student has someone substitute for him? Moreover, concerns about fraud make it almost impossible to use conventional tests in online courses unless students can physically come to a testing centre. Again, this raises questions about course quality and the equivalence of on-campus and online courses.

Predictions about the potential for distance learning to revolutionize post-secondary education are probably valid. However, like other information-age innovations, there are costs as well as benefits.

There is no longer any doubt about the economic value of post-secondary education, as **Figure 12.8** suggests. Further, although some post-secondary education is better than none, people who succeed in completing a degree have a clear income advantage. Those who graduated from university between 1980 and 1998 have enjoyed employment rates consistently above 85%, whereas those with only a high school education had about a 75% rate of employment (Bouchard & Zhao, 2000). Moreover, a review of the 1995 HRDC School Leavers Follow-up Survey found that workers with post-secondary qualifications rated themselves as "very satisfied" with their main job more often than non-post-secondary graduates (Marquardt, 1998). Interestingly, although there are sex differences in the earnings of men and women at all educational levels, the advantage of post-secondary education seems to be as great for women as for men. (We will return to the issue of sex differences in compensation in **Chapter 13**.)

College and university graduates earn more than nongraduates for a variety of reasons (Pascarella & Terenzi, 1991). First, graduates get more promotions and are far less likely than nongraduates to be unemployed for prolonged periods of time. In addition, college and university graduates have higher status. This means that they are more likely than nongraduates to get high-status managerial, technical, and professional positions, and they are viewed by those who make hiring decisions as more desirable employees than are nongraduates. This finding raises the question of whether graduates of post-secondary schools are really different from nongraduates or are simply perceived to be. However, longitudinal evidence suggests that the longer a person remains in a post-secondary school, the better her performance on Piaget's formal operational tasks and other measures of abstract reasoning (Lehman & Nisbett, 1990; Pascarella, 1999).

Make the Connection

Review Erikson's stage of industry versus inferiority, discussed in **Chapter 9**. What would his theory predict about the link between experiences in elementary school and obtaining a university degree or college diploma?

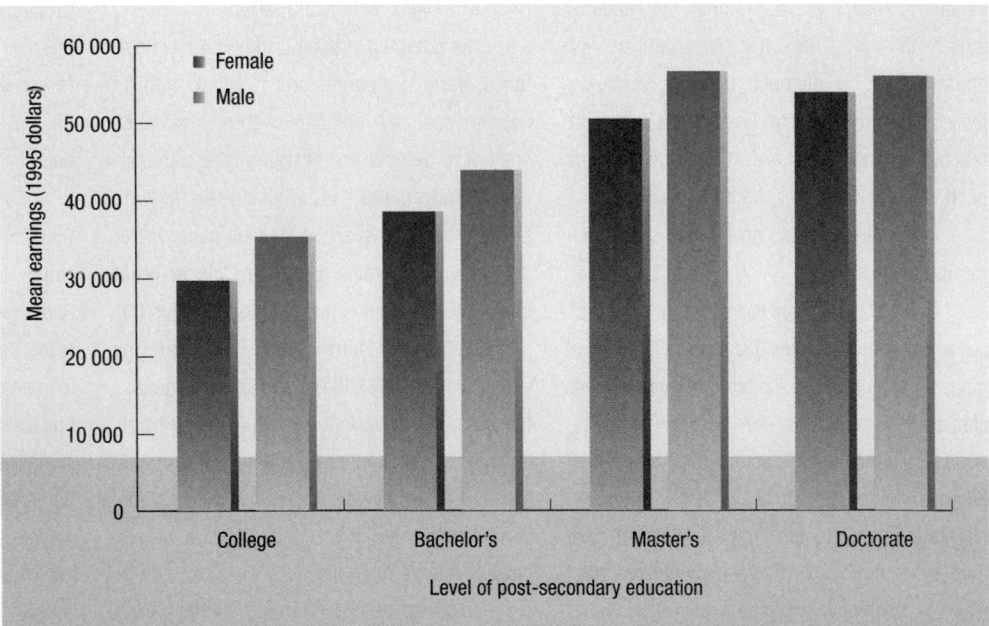

Figure 12.8

Mean earnings of post-secondary graduates in Canada (1990 cohort) 5 years after graduation (1995 dollars). Note: The calculations of the mean earnings omit individuals with reported earnings below $5000. Earnings have been truncated to $143 035.

(*Source:* Social Development Canada, Strategic Policy. Policy, Knowledge and Research Directorate, Gatineau, Quebec, © Her Majesty the Queen in Right of Canada, at: http://www.11.sdc.gc.ca/en/cs/sp/arb/publications/ : Finnie, [2000], Table 3, p. 21.)

There is also evidence that, during their years of post-secondary school enrolment, students' academic and vocational aspirations change (Pascarella & Terenzi, 1991). For example, a young woman may enter university with the goal of becoming a biology teacher but graduate with the intention of going on to medical school. What seems critical about post-secondary education for making such decisions is that college- and university-level classes enable students to make realistic assessments of their academic abilities. Thus, another student who may have intended to be a doctor when he began his first year may soon conclude that becoming a biology teacher is a more realistic, attainable goal, given his performance in university-level classes.

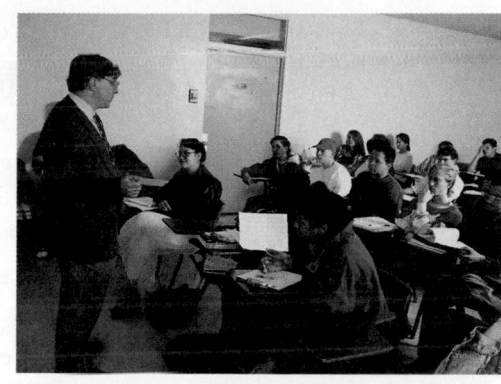

College and university attendance is associated with developmental advances in both the cognitive and social domains.
(*Photo:* Michael Newman/PhotoEdit)

In addition to cognitive and motivational benefits, going to college or university provides students with new socialization opportunities. Many students encounter people from racial or ethnic groups other than their own for the first time in a post-secondary school setting. Advances in moral and social reasoning, as well as increases in the capacity to empathize with others' feelings, are also linked to college or university attendance (Chickering & Reisser, 1993; Pascarella & Terenzi, 1991). However, the relationships among authoritative parenting, academic performance, and social adjustment you have read about so often in earlier chapters hold true for college and university students as well (Wintre & Yaffe, 2000). Thus, students' social experiences prior to entering post-secondary education seem to be critical to their ability to benefit fully from the college or university experience.

Before Going On

- Describe how post-secondary education influences employment.

- List some of the ways in which a post-secondary education affects individual development.

Summary

Physical Functioning

- It is important to distinguish between the unavoidable effects of primary aging and the preventable consequences of secondary aging.

- Developed nations that have an equitable distribution of wealth have the healthiest populations.

- The brain reaches a stable size and weight in early adulthood. There is strong evidence that the frontal lobes of the brain do not fully mature until young adulthood. This mirrors the development of cognitive abilities, such as abstract reasoning, logic, planning, and emotional control.

- It is clear that adults are at their peak both physically and cognitively between ages 20 and 40. In these years, a person has more muscle tissue, more calcium in the bones, better sensory acuity, greater aerobic capacity, and a more efficient immune system.

Health Promotion and Wellness

- In contrast to other diseases, sexually transmitted infections are more common among young adults than among older adults.

- The rate of loss of physical and cognitive abilities varies widely across individuals. Some of this difference seems to be explained by varying health habits. Adults with good health habits have lower risk of death and disease at any age.

- Social support and a sense of personal control also affect rates of disease and death.

- Intimate partner abuse is a significant global health problem. Causal factors include cultural beliefs about gender roles, as well as personal variables such as alcohol and drug use.

- Sexual assault usually involves individuals who are acquaintances or intimate partners. Its causes and effects are similar for both heterosexuals and homosexuals.

- Rates of mental disorder are higher in early adulthood than in middle adulthood; young adults are more likely to be depressed, anxious, or lonely than are the middle-aged. Early adulthood is the period during which personality disorders and schizophrenia are usually diagnosed.

Cognitive Changes

- There may be a change in cognitive structure in adult life, and theorists have suggested that cognitive development goes beyond Piaget's formal operational stage.

- Some studies of measures of intelligence show a decline with age, but the decline occurs quite late for well-exercised abilities (crystallized abilities) such as recall of vocabulary, everyday memory use, and normal problem-solving. A measurable decline occurs earlier for so-called fluid abilities. Memory differences between younger and older adults are usually restricted to tasks involving speed of processing.

Post-Secondary Education

- Post-secondary education has beneficial effects on both cognitive and social development, in addition to being associated with better career opportunities and benefits.

Key Terms

crystallized intelligence (p. 383)

Disability-Adjusted Life Years (DALY) (p. 362)

dialectical thought (p. 381)

fluid intelligence (p. 383)

Health-Adjusted Life Expectancy (HALE) (p. 362)

intimate partner abuse (p. 374)

limbic system (p. 364)

maximum oxygen uptake (VO$_2$ max) (p. 367)

pelvic inflammatory disease (p. 369)

personality disorder (p. 379)

Quality-Adjusted Life Years (QALY) (p. 362)

post-secondary education (p. 384)

primary aging (p. 362)

schizophrenia (p. 379)

secondary aging (p. 362)

self-efficacy (p. 374)

sexual assault (p. 377)

Weblinks

The Population Health Template: Key Elements and Actions That Define a Population Health Approach
www.hc-sc.gc.ca/hppb/phdd/pdf/discussion_paper.pdf
This ongoing Health Canada initiative describes the current knowledge and rationale for implementing a population health approach to health promotion and public health.

Neuro
www.mni.mcgill.ca/nm/neuro_m.html
The *Neuro* magazine is published by the Montreal Neurological Institute, an affiliate of McGill University. It carries informative articles and images from a Canadian neuroscience perspective.

The Mensa Canada Society
www.canada.mensa.org
The Mensa Canada Society is a part of Mensa International, an international high-IQ society. Their website offers IQ quizzes, information about the organization and its activities, and links to other IQ sites.

National Clearinghouse on Family Violence
www.hc-sc.gc.ca/hppb/familyviolence
This is a resource centre for those seeking information about violence within the family and looking for new resources being used to address it. The site provides comprehensive listings of book, video, and article resources, online bibliographic searching, a referral service, and a newsletter.

Health Canada
www.hc-sc.gc.ca/english/diseases/std.html
Health Canada's website on STIs provides links to Canadian research and statistics on the topic, as well as information on government programs and telephone help lines.

CHAPTER 13

Andy Sacks/Getty Images

SOCIAL AND PERSONALITY DEVELOPMENT IN EARLY ADULTHOOD

In early adulthood, individuals turn away from the preoccupation with self-definition that is characteristic of adolescence and take on a series of roles that involve new relationships with other people. For example, from their wedding day forward, newlyweds will be known both as individuals and as spouses. The bride is also now a daughter-in-law as well as a daughter; the groom has become a son-in-law in addition to continuing to be his parents' son. It is also likely that the two young adults have already taken on occupational roles, and they may also become parents within a few years.

The timing and content of the various adult roles obviously differ from one culture to another, from one cohort to another, and even from one individual to another. For example, the median age for first marriage among women in Canada rose from about 21 in the 1960s and 1970s to 28.2 by 2001. The median age of first marriage for men similarly rose from about 23 to 30.2 during the same time period (Beaujot & Kerr, 2004; Statistics Canada, 2003d). Marriage remains an important milestone of the young adult years, as evidenced by the fact that the percentage of women who have never married drops from 34% among 20- to 29-year-old females to 16% among 30- to 39-year-old females (Le Bourdais, Neill, & Turcotte, 2000); the trend in men is similar (Wu, 1998). In addition, most people become parents for the first time in early adulthood. Thus, regardless of variations in timing, adults' social connections become far more complex between the ages of 20 and 40—through marriage, divorce, parenthood, and career development.

In this chapter you will learn about how these role transitions affect young adults' development. As you read, keep the following questions in mind:

- How do theorists view social and personality development in early adulthood?

- How do young adults go about establishing intimate relationships?

- How do young adults manage the challenges of parenthood and other relationships?

- What factors contribute to career choice, job satisfaction, and sex differences in work patterns?

THEORIES OF SOCIAL AND PERSONALITY DEVELOPMENT

Psychoanalytic theories view adult development, like development at younger ages, as a result of a struggle between a person's inner thoughts, feelings, and motives and society's demands. Other perspectives provide different views of this period. Integrating ideas from all of them allows us to better understand early adult development.

ERIKSON'S STAGE OF INTIMACY VERSUS ISOLATION

For Erikson, the central crisis of early adulthood is **intimacy versus isolation**. The young adult must find a life partner, someone outside her own family with whom she can share her life, or face the prospect of being isolated from society. More specifically, **intimacy** is the capacity to engage in a supportive, affectionate relationship without losing one's own sense of self. Intimate partners can share their views and feelings with each other without fearing that the relationship will end. They can also allow each other some degree of independence without feeling threatened.

intimacy versus isolation
Erikson's early adulthood stage, in which an individual must find a life partner or supportive friends in order to avoid social isolation

intimacy
the capacity to engage in a supportive, affectionate relationship without losing one's own sense of self

Social scientists have not done very well at devising theories to explain lovely romantic moments like these. (*Photos: left*, David Young-Wolff/ PhotoEdit; *right*, Timothy Shonnard/ Getty Images)

Critical Thinking

Have you experienced periods of loneliness? If so, how do you think the state of your love life at the time contributed to your feelings?

As you might suspect, successful resolution of the intimacy versus isolation stage depends on a good resolution of the identity versus role confusion crisis you read about in **Chapter 11**. Erikson predicted that individuals who reached early adulthood without having established a sense of identity would be incapable of intimacy. That is, such young adults would be, in a sense, predestined to social isolation.

Still, a poor sense of identity is only one barrier to intimacy. Misunderstandings stemming from sex differences in styles of interaction can also get in the way. To women, intimacy is bound up with self-disclosure. Thus, women who are involved with a partner who does not reveal much that is personal perceive the relationship as lacking in intimacy. However, most men don't see self-disclosure as essential to intimacy. Consequently, many men are satisfied with relationships that their female partners see as inadequate.

Though many people involved in intimate relationships wish their relationships were better, most adults succeed in establishing some kind of close relationship. Not everyone marries, of course, but many adults develop affectionate, long-lasting friendships that are significant sources of support for them and may, in some cases, serve the same functions as an intimate life partner. For those who have no such relationships, Erikson's theory seems to be fairly accurate. These individuals experience more loneliness and depression than the average adult and suffer from a variety of mental health problems (Stack, 1998).

LEVINSON'S LIFE STRUCTURES

life structure
a key concept in Levinson's theory: the underlying pattern or design of a person's life at a given time, which includes roles, relationships, and behaviour patterns

Levinson's concept of *life structure* represents a different approach to adult development (Levinson, 1978, 1990). A **life structure** includes all the roles an individual occupies, all of his or her relationships, and the conflicts and balance that exist among them. **Figure 13.1** illustrates how life structures change over the course of adulthood.

Like Erikson, Levinson theorized that each of these periods presents adults with new developmental tasks and conflicts. He believed that individuals respond psychologically to these tasks and conflicts by creating new life structures. Consequently, adults cycle through periods of stability and instability.

As adults enter a period in which a new life structure is required, there is a period of adjustment, which Levinson called the *novice* phase. In the *mid-era* phase, adults become more competent at meeting the new challenges through reassessment and reorganization of the life structure they created during the novice phase. Stability returns in the *culmination* phase, when adults have succeeded in creating a life structure that allows them to manage the demands of the new developmental challenges with more confidence and less distress.

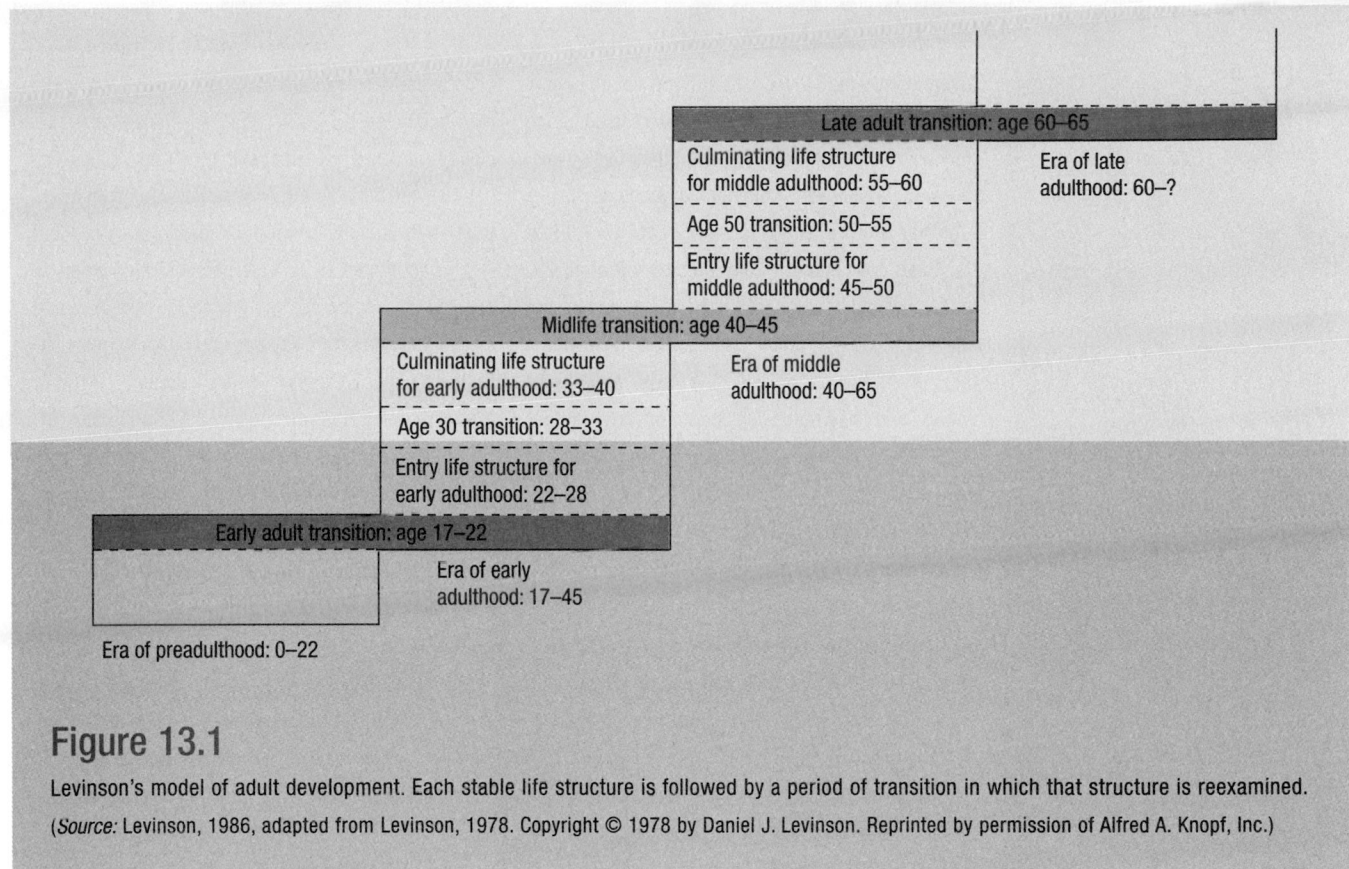

Figure 13.1

Levinson's model of adult development. Each stable life structure is followed by a period of transition in which that structure is reexamined.

(*Source:* Levinson, 1986, adapted from Levinson, 1978. Copyright © 1978 by Daniel J. Levinson. Reprinted by permission of Alfred A. Knopf, Inc.)

For example, marriage requires a new life structure. Even if the newlyweds have known each other for a very long time or have been living together, they have not known each other in the roles of husband and wife (see **No Easy Answers**). Moreover, they have never had in-laws. So, young adults who marry acquire a whole new set of relationships. At the same time, they face many new day-to-day, practical issues such as how finances will be managed, how housekeeping chores will be done, and whose family they will visit on which holidays. As Levinson's theory predicts, newlyweds usually go through a period of adjustment, during which they experience more conflict than before the wedding, and after which things are much calmer. The calm comes, as Levinson would put it, when each spouse has achieved a new life structure that is adapted to the demands of marriage.

Both Erikson and Levinson regard formation of an intimate relationship with another adult as a central developmental task of early adulthood. However, neither addresses the process of just how an adult goes about finding a suitable partner. However, other theorists focus specifically on the mating process.

EVOLUTIONARY THEORY AND MATE SELECTION

As you should remember from **Chapter 2**, evolutionary explanations of behaviour focus on survival value. Heterosexual relationships ensure the survival of the species, of course, because they are the context in which conception takes place. However, when choosing a mate, heterosexuals don't simply look for someone of the opposite sex. Instead, mating is a selective process, and evolutionary theorists often cite research on sex differences in mate preferences and mating behaviour in support of their views.

No Easy Answers

Does Cohabitation Help Couples Construct a Life Structure for Marriage?

Given today's high divorce rate, many young people want to be sure the person they marry is someone they want to be with for the rest of their lives. Thus, today it is relatively common for couples to live together before marriage. In fact, the latest Canadian census shows that almost half of all 20- to 29-year-old couples who lived together were not married (48%) (Turcotte, 2003). It was also found that, given the opportunity, the large majority of young adults would live common-law (Milan, 2003). Many such couples conceive of cohabitation as a final "filter," a sort of "test" before marriage: Can we really get along together? Are we sexually compatible? In Levinson's terms, they believe that cohabitation will lessen the likelihood of divorce because it will provide them with an opportunity to build a life structure they can use in adapting to marriage. Interestingly, the great bulk of the evidence shows exactly the opposite.

Studies in Canada, the United States, and European countries such as Sweden all show that those who cohabit before marriage are less satisfied with their subsequent marriages and more likely to divorce than are those who marry without cohabiting (Ambert, 2002; Hall & Zhao, 1995; Statistics Canada, 2002f). The most likely explanation of this surprising set of findings is twofold.

First, cohabiting leads to development of a life structure for cohabiting, not for marriage, because the two relationships are fundamentally different (Ambert, 2003b). For example, moving in together is seldom accompanied by the public announcements and celebratory fanfare that are associated with marriage (Lindsay, 2000). Further, cohabiting couples regard their relationships as ambiguous in nature—they may or may not be permanent. In contrast, marriage involves a public declaration of life-long commitment to another person. Thus, when a cohabiting couple marries, the social and psychological aspects of the relationship change, because of the deepened sense of commitment and the expectation that the relationship is permanent.

Second, adults who choose to live together before marriage are different, in key ways, from those who marry without cohabiting (Ambert, 2003b). For example, cohabiting couples are less homogamous (less similar) than married couples (Blackwell & Lichter, 2000). Couples in which partners are of different races, religions, educational levels, and socio-economic statuses, are more likely to cohabit prior to marriage. Moreover, a closer look reveals that cohabitators are more than twice as likely to have sexual affairs (Treas & Geisen, 2000), are more likely to be unhappy or depressed (Brown, 2000), and have an increased risk for domestic violence (Brownridge & Halli, 2001; Salari & Baldwin, 2002; Shackelford, 2001; Wilson, Daly, & Wright, 1993).

As appealing as the idea of a trial marriage might be, there appears to be no way to adjust to marriage before one is actually married. The best a couple can do is to examine their relationship in light of what researchers have discovered about the characteristics of stable marriages, which you will read about later in the chapter.

Cross-cultural studies conducted over a period of several decades suggest that men prefer physically attractive, younger women, while women look for men whose socioeconomic status is higher than their own, who offer earning potential and stability (Buss, 1999). Moreover, in the short run, men appear to be willing to lower their standards when forced to choose between a partner who meets their standards and no partner at all. Thus, availability strongly influences men's selection of short-term mates. In contrast, women seem to have little interest in short-term mating unless it will lead to a beneficial long-term relationship. For example, evolutionary theorists hypothesize that *mate-switching*—using an affair to lead to a long-term relationship with a higher-status man—is an important motive in women's extramarital affairs.

The reasons behind men's and women's divergent mating goals are explained by **parental investment theory** (Trivers, 1972). This theory proposes that men value health

parental investment theory
the theory that sex differences in mate preferences and mating behaviour are based on the different amounts of time and effort men and women must invest in child-rearing

and availability in their mates and are less selective because their minimum investment in parenting offspring—a single act of sexual intercourse—requires only a few minutes. In contrast, women's minimum investment in childbearing involves nurturing an unborn child in their own bodies for 9 months as well as enduring the potentially physically traumatic experience of giving birth. Given their minimum investments, men seek to maximize the likelihood of survival of the species by maximizing the number of their offspring; women seek to minimize them because their investment is so much greater. Further, evolutionary theorists argue that both men and women realize that a truly adaptive approach to child-rearing requires much more than a minimum investment (Buss, 1999). Human offspring cannot raise themselves. Therefore, men value health and youth in their mates not only because these traits suggest fertility but also because a young, healthy woman is likely to live long enough to raise the children. Moreover, men are willing to abandon their focus on short-term mating in order to gain continuing and exclusive sexual access to a desirable mate through committed, long-term relationships such as marriage. Making such a commitment ensures that any offspring the woman produces will be the man's own and that the children will have a mother to raise them.

Similarly, women realize that to be able to nurture children to adulthood, they must have an economic provider so that they will be able to invest the time needed to raise offspring. Consequently, they look for men who seem to be capable of fulfilling these requirements. Further, women's mating behaviour is affected by the higher costs they bear if a selected mate fails to fulfill expectations. Faced with the prospect of having to provide children with both economic support and physical nurturing if a mate fails to "bring home the bacon," women choose mates more carefully and more slowly than men; they prefer not to engage in sexual intercourse until they have tested a man's trustworthiness and reliability (Buss & Schmitt, 1993).

As mentioned above, consistent sex differences in mate preferences and mating behaviour have been found across many cultures, and evolutionary theorists suggest that this cross-cultural consistency is strong evidence for a genetic basis for the behaviour. However, these claims take us back to the basic nature-versus-nurture arguments we have examined so many times before. Certainly, these sex differences are consistent, but they could be the result of variations in gender roles that are passed on within cultures.

SOCIAL ROLE THEORY AND MATE SELECTION

Social role theory provides a different perspective on sex differences in mating (Eagly & Wood, 1999). According to this view, such sex differences are adaptations to gender roles that result from present-day social realities rather than from natural selection pressures that arose in a bygone evolutionary era. Social role theorists point out that gender-based divisions of labour in child-rearing are just as consistent across cultures as sex differences in mating. Men look for women who can perform domestic duties (healthy and young), and women look for men who will be good economic providers (higher socioeconomic status and good earning potential).

For example, one team of researchers found that post-secondary-educated women with high earning potential prefer to date and marry men whose income potential is higher than their own (Wiederman & Allgeier, 1992). In fact, the more a woman expects to earn herself, the higher are her income requirements in a prospective mate. This study was widely cited by evolutionary theorists as supporting their view that such preferences are genetic and are not influenced by cultural conditions.

However, a different perspective on the same study, proposed by social role theorists, led to a different conclusion (Eagly & Wood, 1999). These theorists suggest that

social role theory
the idea that sex differences in mate preferences and mating behaviour are adaptations to gender roles

today's high-income women desire to have and raise children almost as much as earlier generations of women. What is different about them, compared with their mothers and grandmothers, is that they want to be able to both pursue a career and raise a family. To meet both goals, most women plan to take time out from their careers to have and raise children (a pattern you will read more about later in this chapter). To be able to do so without lowering their standard of living substantially, these women require a mate who can earn a lot of money. Thus, social role theorists say, such research findings can be explained by social role theory just as well as by evolutionary theory.

In addition, social role theorists point out that high-income women desire high-income husbands because members of both sexes prefer mates who are like themselves. People are drawn to those who are of similar age, education, social class, ethnic group membership, religion, attitudes, interests, and temperament. Sociologists refer to this tendency as **assortative mating**, or **homogamy**. Further, partnerships based on homogamy are much more likely to endure than are those in which the partners differ markedly (Murstein, 1986).

In addition to the process of assortative mating, choosing a partner appears to involve some kind of exchange process. Each individual has certain assets to offer to a potential mate. Exchange theorists argue that people try for the best bargain, the best exchange, they can manage (Edwards, 1969). According to this model, women frequently exchange their sexual and domestic services for the economic support offered by a man (Schoen & Wooldredge, 1989). However, social role theorists suggest that, over the past few decades, women have improved their income-producing prospects considerably. As a result, if social role theory is correct, women today should be less concerned about a potential mate's earning potential than women were in the past.

To test this hypothesis, social role theorists reanalyzed a very large set of cross-cultural data, a data set produced and interpreted by evolutionary psychologist David Buss in support of parental investment theory (Buss et al., 1990). In their reanalysis, advocates of social role theory found that both men's and women's mate preferences changed as women gained economic power (Eagly & Wood, 1999): Women's emphasis on potential mates' earning power declined, and men's focus on potential mates' domestic skills decreased.

assortative mating (homogamy)
sociologists' term for the tendency to mate with someone who has traits similar to one's own

Before Going On

- What did Erikson mean when he described early adulthood as a crisis of intimacy versus isolation?

- What is a life structure? Why and how does it change?

- What types of research findings do evolutionary theorists cite to support their views on mate selection?

- How can social role theory contribute to an understanding of partner selection?

INTIMATE RELATIONSHIPS

Theories notwithstanding, everyday observations of adults reveal that an intimate relationship forms the secure base from which most young adults move out into the adult

Development in the
Information Age
Internet Relationships

In a survey of 235 Internet users aged 13 to 74, 93% reported that they had established a personal relationship of some kind online (Parks & Roberts, 1998). Most of these relationships were with people of the opposite sex, and one-third had resulted in face-to-face meetings. Internet dating has become so popular that there are websites devoted to matching cyber-daters with others who have similar interests. There is even an *Online Dating for Dummies* book available for individuals who want to learn how to start cyber-dating (Silverstein & Lasky, 2003).

The appeal of Internet dating for many seems to be its capacity to allow individuals to bypass conventional relationship "filters"— physical attractiveness, socioeconomic status, and age. Through e-mail, bulletin boards, and chat rooms, cyber-daters can get to know one another psychologically, without the distraction of characteristics that are easily discernible in face-to-face relationships. Cross-cultural research also suggests that interpersonal communication on the Internet is viewed as more pleasurable than in-person communication (Chou, Chou, & Tyang, 1998).

However, some psychologists speculate that, in contrast to conventional dating, Internet relationships may retard development of social skills in young people, because online relationships don't allow for the kind of immediate behavioural feedback, such as facial expressions, that face-to-face relationships typically provide (Schnarch, 1997). Further, the more time people spend on the Internet, the less time they spend in other kinds of social interactions where such feedback is available (Kraut et al., 1998).

Another major drawback to Internet dating is the possibility of being deceived. A recent poll found that although three-quarters of Canadians 25 to 34 years of age believe the Internet makes it easier to meet people, about 80% of Canadians agree that online dating is dangerous because you do not know who you are dealing with (Wyatt, 2004). For some, Internet relationships may be preferable in situations where deception is desirable. For example, married people who want to present themselves to potential partners as single can do so more easily online.

Not surprisingly, extramarital affairs that begin or are carried out exclusively on the Internet are a growing phenomenon. One Canadian website that caters to customers who want to have extramarital affairs boasts that it has 60 000 profiles of clients (Durbin, 2003). Historically, an affair has involved sexual contact. But online affairs often lack any face-to-face contact, sexual or otherwise. Still, sexual tension and stimulation are typically a large part of online affairs. While online, partners trade pictures, sometimes sexually provocative ones, and engage in flirtatious sexual banter. Consequently, marital counsellors now define an affair as a relationship that involves psychological intimacy, secrecy, and sexual chemistry, in order to help clients understand that marital fidelity involves something more than just sexual monogamy (Glass, 1998).

No doubt the phenomenon of Internet dating will continue to grow. Thus, there is a need for research that will lead to a better understanding of how online relationships develop and dissolve as well as how they affect individual development.

world. In many cases, marriage is the context in which such a relationship is created. However, as society has become more tolerant of nonmarital relationships—homosexual and lesbian partners, cohabiting heterosexual couples—behavioural scientists have had to expand research on intimacy to include these relationships as well. Further, Internet relationships have added a whole new dimension to courtship and dating (see **Development in the Information Age**).

PSYCHOLOGICAL FACTORS IN INTIMATE RELATIONSHIPS

In predicting the quality of relationships as well as who mates with whom, two psychological factors—attachment and love—seem to be of importance.

THE ROLE OF ATTACHMENT A number of theorists have suggested that internal working models of attachment play an important role in partner selection and relationship formation (e.g., Crowell & Waters, 1995; Feeney, 1994; Fuller & Fincham, 1995; Hazan & Shaver, 1987; Owens et al., 1995; Rothbard & Shaver, 1994). This does not mean that the security of the very first attachment in infancy is invariably carried forward, unaltered. In particular, some adults with insecure attachment histories are able to analyze and accept their childhood relationships and create new internal working models. But whether a young adult's internal working model is the product of redefinition or remains unchanged, it will still affect her expectations for a partner, the sort of partner she chooses, the way she behaves with her partner, and the stability of the relationship.

Research reveals that adults do indeed tend to create internal models of attachment to a prospective spouse that are similar to their attachment to their parents. For example, one study found that nearly two-thirds of a sample of about-to-be-married young people showed the same attachment category (secure, dismissing, or preoccupied) when they described their love relationship as when they described their relationship with their parents (Owens et al., 1995).

THE ROLE OF LOVE In the Western world, physical attraction and emotional affection are usually the starting points for intimate relationships. In other parts of the world, relationships are often arranged by parents. However, mutual love seems to be important no matter how a relationship begins (Hortacsu, 1999).

The most compelling theory of romantic love comes from Robert Sternberg, whose approach is much broader than models based on the concept of attachment. Sternberg argues that love has three key components: (1) *intimacy*, which includes feelings that promote closeness and connectedness; (2) *passion*, which includes a feeling of intense longing for union with the other person, including sexual union; and (3) *commitment to a particular other*, often over a long period of time (Sternberg, 1987). When these three components are combined in all possible ways, the result is eight subvarieties of love, as shown in **Figure 13.2**. (The eighth combination is mere acquaintanceship, with none of the elements of love present.) Sternberg's theory suggests that the characteristics of the emotional bond that holds a couple together influence the unique pattern of interaction that develops in each intimate relationship.

PARTNERSHIPS OVER TIME

In one important group of studies, researchers studied 168 couples in their first marriages (Huston & Chorost, 1994; Huston, McHale, & Crouter, 1986; MacDermid, Huston, & McHale, 1990). Each partner was given a lengthy interview within the first 3 months of the marriage, and then again after 1 year. In addition, in the weeks surrounding each of these interviews, each couple was called nine different times and asked to describe in detail what they had done over the

Figure 13.2

Sternberg's theory postulates three components of love: passion, intimacy, and commitment. Relationships can be classified according to which of the three components is present.

previous 24 hours. Thus, these researchers had information not only about feelings and attitudes but also about activities. They found that over the first year partners experienced a decrease in satisfaction with both the quantity and the quality of interaction. These couples reported lower levels of love for each other after 1 year, and that was true whether they had had a child or not. Furthermore, their activities had changed. In the early months, they spent a lot more of their leisure time together; after 1 year, when they did things together it was more likely to be "instrumental tasks" (grocery shopping, errands, housework, and the like). They also talked to each other less. Perhaps most importantly, the husbands and wives both described a sizeable drop in the frequency of positive interactions, a pattern illustrated in **Figure 13.3**. In Sternberg's terms, there was a decline in the intimacy aspect of love as well as in the passion aspect.

Such a decline in pleasing behaviours, accompanied by a drop in marital satisfaction, is entirely consistent with the results of research on the sources of stability and instability, satisfaction and dissatisfaction in marriages. In fact, a great deal of what developmentalists know about partnerships in early adulthood comes from studies of the causes of divorce (Gottman, 1994a).

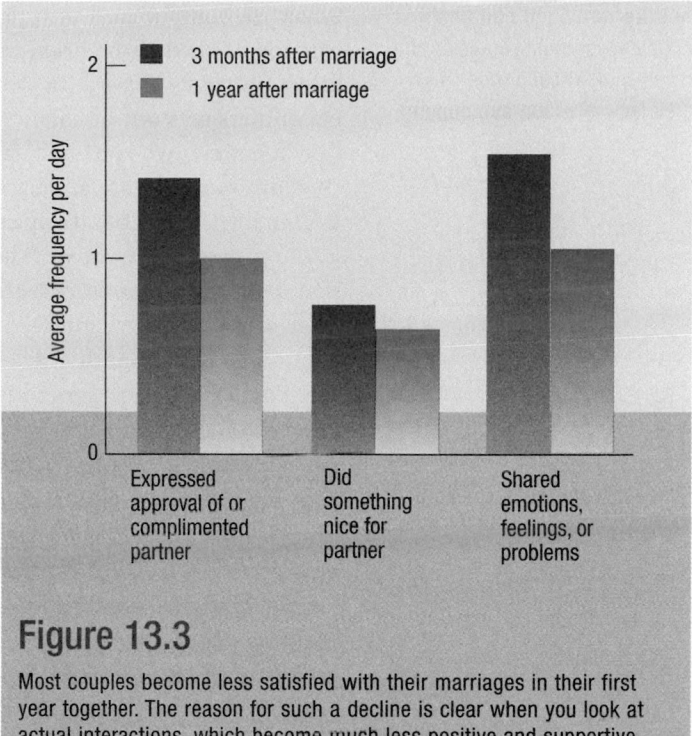

Figure 13.3

Most couples become less satisfied with their marriages in their first year together. The reason for such a decline is clear when you look at actual interactions, which become much less positive and supportive.

(*Source:* Huston et al., 1986, from Table 7.4, p. 124.)

Many powerful influences on marital success are established before a marriage even begins. Each partner brings to the relationship certain skills, resources, and traits that affect the emerging partnership system. The personality characteristics of the partners seem to be especially important (Arrindell & Luteijn, 2000). For example, a high degree of neuroticism in one or both partners usually leads to dissatisfaction and instability in the relationship (Robins et al., 2000). Likewise, attitudes toward divorce affect marital stability. Couples who have tolerant attitudes are less likely to be satisfied with their marriages than those who view divorce as highly undesirable (Amato & Rogers, 1999).

But a marriage or partnership is more than the sum of the characteristics of the two individuals. Equally important for the success of a marriage is the quality of the actual interactions between the couple. And in those interactions, the most crucial feature seems to be simply the relative proportion of "nice" to "nasty" everyday encounters. Couples who will eventually divorce can be identified years ahead of time by looking at the pattern of these positive and negative exchanges (Gottman, 1994a). When negative interactions—criticism, complaints, "yes, but" statements, putdowns, or the like—exceed the positive by too much, divorce becomes far more likely (Gottman, 1994a).

Of course, not all successful marriages are alike. Drawing on a large body of research, psychologists have identified three quite different types of stable or enduring marriages (Gottman, 1994b). **Validating couples** have disagreements, but the disagreements rarely escalate. Partners express mutual respect even when they disagree and listen well to one another. **Volatile couples** squabble a lot, disagree, and don't listen to each other very well when they argue. But they still have more positive than negative encounters and show high levels of laughter and affection. **Avoidant couples**, or "conflict minimizers," don't try to persuade each other—they simply agree to disagree, without apparent rancour, a pattern that is sometimes described as "devitalized."

Similarly, psychologists find two types of unsuccessful marriages. **Hostile/engaged couples**, like volatile couples, have frequent hot arguments, but they lack the balancing

validating couples
couples who express mutual respect even in disagreements and are good listeners

volatile couples
couples who argue a lot, don't listen well, but still have more positive than negative interactions

avoidant couples
couples who agree to disagree and who minimize conflict by avoiding each other

hostile/engaged couples
partners who have frequent arguments that lack the balancing effect of humour and affection

hostile/detached couples
couples who fight regularly and rarely look at each other; they also lack affection and support

effect of humour and affection. **Hostile/detached couples** fight regularly, though the arguments tend to be brief; such couples rarely look at each other, and they also lack affection and support. In both unsuccessful types, the ratio of negative to positive encounters gets out of balance, and the marriage spirals downward toward dissolution.

What can we conclude about causality here? Do couples become unhappy because they are more negative, or are they more negative because they are already unhappy? Both may happen, but it appears that it is more common for couples to become unhappy because they are negative. The best support for this conclusion comes from studies of therapeutic interventions with unhappy couples: Couples who are trained to increase their rate of positive interactions typically show increases in their marital satisfaction (e.g., O'Leary & Smith, 1991).

Finally, there appears to be a parallel between the qualities of a successful marriage and the qualities of a secure attachment. Adults in good marriages have a high level of the same kind of responsiveness to the other's signals that developmentalists see between securely attached infants and their parents. Satisfied partners take turns, read each other's cues, and respond positively. Whatever internal model of attachment each individual may bring to a marriage, the ability of the partners to create such a mutually interlocking and supportive interactive system seems to be critical to the survival of the marriage. Many of the same qualities characterize both homosexual and heterosexual couples (see the **Research Report**).

Research Report

Comparing Heterosexual and Homosexual Partnerships

Comparing heterosexual and homosexual partnerships is not as simple as it might seem. For one thing, it is important to compare apples to apples. Consequently, to find out whether relationship characteristics vary across sexual orientation, researchers must limit research samples to couples who are similar in commitment status—that is, to restrict themselves to comparisons of married heterosexuals, long-term cohabiting heterosexuals, and committed, monogamous homosexual couples. Therefore, any comparisons between married heterosexuals and cohabiting homosexuals, or child-free cohabiting heterosexuals for that matter, need to be interpreted with caution because the forces that hold them together are different—there are few legal and social incentives for unmarried couples to stay together (Ambert, 2003a). Furthermore, because same-sex marriages in Canada are such a new phenomenon, no long-term comparisons can be made with heterosexual marriages. Moreover, research must take into account possible differences between gay and lesbian couples.

The most recent census found that there are about 0.5% Canadian same-sex couples, although this is believed to be an underestimate of the actual figures (Statistics Canada, 2003e). Estimates vary, but perhaps 70% of lesbians are in committed relationships, most often monogamous ones. Among gay men, the percentages are somewhat lower. Between 40% and 60% are in long-term committed relationships, but only about one-fifth of these relationships are monogamous (compared with roughly four-fifths of heterosexual partnerships) (Blumstein & Schwartz, 1990; Kurdek, 1995b).

In Canada, a fairly large percentage of married heterosexuals remain together for many years. Nearly 90% of marriages last at least 10 years (Statistics Canada, 2004c), but only about 12% of common-law relationships last 10 years (Wu, 2000, p. 108). In comparison, the average length of lesbian partnerships is about 6 years ("National survey results," 1990). Although a large majority of gay men report that they prefer long-term to short-term relationships, such partnerships are less common among gay men than they are among lesbians

(Lever, 1994; "National survey results," 1990).

However, among couples who are committed and monogamous, gay men and lesbians are as likely as heterosexuals to be satisfied with their partner relationships. What does differentiate homosexual from heterosexual unions is the nature of the power relation between the couple. Homosexual couples seem to be more egalitarian than heterosexual couples, with less-specific role prescriptions. It is quite uncommon in homosexual couples for one partner to occupy a "male" role and the other a "female" role. Instead, power and tasks are more equally divided. However, this is more true of lesbian couples—among whom equality of roles is frequently a strong philosophical ideal—than of gay couples (Kurdek, 1995a).

In **Chapter 12**, you learned that, although rates of partner abuse differ across sexual orientation groups, the same factors contribute to abuse in heterosexual and homosexual couples. Likewise, many of the same variables that affect the success of heterosexual marriages seem to be important in the endurance of homosexual partnerships (Kurdek, 1998). For example, neuroticism in one or both partners is related to relationship quality and length (Kurdek, 1997, 2000). Like married heterosexuals, gay couples experience a drop in their relationship satisfaction in the early months of their partnership (Kurdek & Schmitt, 1986). They argue over similar things, and, like marriages, gay relationships are more likely to last if the two partners share similar backgrounds and are equally committed to the relationship (Krueger-Lebus & Rauchfleisch, 1999; Kurdek, 1997; Peplau, 1991).

In summary, it would be overstating the case to say that homosexual and heterosexual relationships function in exactly the same ways. The varying degrees of monogamy and the varying lengths of relationships, as well as the different rates of partner abuse, reveal that there are important differences among them. At the same time, however, research suggests that factors related to success or failure are highly consistent across the three types of relationships. Clearly, the most reliable conclusions that can be derived from the current state of research are (1) that homosexual relationships are similar to heterosexual relationships in some ways but differ from them in significant ways, and (2) that a great deal more research is needed to identify the sources of these differences.

DEVELOPMENTAL IMPACT OF INTIMATE RELATIONSHIPS

Married young adults are happier and healthier, live longer, and have lower rates of a variety of psychiatric problems than do young adults without committed partners (Coombs, 1991; Glenn & Weaver, 1988; Lee, Seccombe, & Shehan, 1991; Ross, 1995; Sorlie, Backlund, & Keller, 1995).

Men generally benefit more from marriage than do women on measures of physical and mental health. That is, married men are generally the healthiest and live the longest, while unmarried men are collectively the worst off. The two groups of women fall in between, with married women having a slight advantage over unmarried women. But unmarried women are considerably healthier and happier than are unmarried men.

One explanation of this pattern that has been offered is that some sort of self-selection is occurring. People who are healthy and happy are simply more likely to marry. Logical as it may sound, researchers have found little support for this explanation (Coombs, 1991; Waite, 1995). A second alternative is that married adults follow better health practices. For example, Dutch researchers find that married adults are less likely to smoke or drink to excess, and more likely to exercise than are unmarried adults (Joung, Stronks, van de Mheen, & Mackenbach, 1995).

However, developmentalists argue that it is not marital status per se that is the causal factor, but rather the *quality* of the relationship. For example, researchers in one large-scale study asked unmarried respondents whether they were living with a partner or had a partner who lived in a separate household (Ross, 1995). Each respondent who was in a relationship was asked to say how happy that relationship was. Those whose relationships were very happy were the least likely to report symptoms of depression, while those without a partner or those with unhappy partnerships were most likely to be depressed.

Other research has suggested that the link between relationship quality and an individual's subjective sense of well-being is physiological in nature. An interesting two-phase study of marital quality and health looked for a possible correlation between levels of a stress-related hormone called *cortisol* and the quality of a person's marriage (Kiecolt-Glaser, 2000). Researchers focused on cortisol because it is known to increase when individuals experience negative emotions, and is one of many stress hormones that are thought to impair immune system functioning. Thus, it may be an important mechanism through which relationship quality affects health.

Investigators measured newlyweds' cortisol levels after they had discussed issues involving conflict, such as in-law relationships or finances. As expected, both husbands' and wives' cortisol levels were somewhat elevated after these discussions. Next, researchers asked couples to tell the story of how they met. As expected, in the majority of both husbands and wives, cortisol levels dropped as they discussed the emotionally neutral topic of relationship history. However, cortisol levels dropped least in participants who were the most emotionally negative (as measured by the number of negative words used in describing their relationships). This component of the study demonstrated a direct link between stress hormones and marital negativity.

In addition, an important sex difference emerged. When couples described negative events in their relationships, wives' cortisol levels increased, while husbands' levels remained constant. This finding suggests that women may be more physiologically sensitive to relationship negativity than men. Thus, these results may help explain why marriage is a more consistently protective factor for men than for women.

Sex differences were also apparent in the study's second phase, during which researchers surveyed participants 8 to 12 years later to find out if they were still married. Remarkably, the researchers found that the higher the wife's cortisol response to emotional negativity in the first phase, the more likely the couple was to be divorced. Consequently, researchers hypothesized that women's physiological responses to marital quality are an important determinant of relationship stability.

Of course, research findings on the benefits of marriage do not mean that all single adults are unhappy and unhealthy. Many adults are single by preference and have found alternative sources of support. Never-married women, for example, are more likely to maintain very close contact with their parents and siblings, perhaps retaining that central attachment in a less intense form (Allen & Pickett, 1987; Campbell, Connidis, & Davies, 1999). They are also more likely than their married peers to have full-time, continuous careers and to be more successful and better paid as a result (Sørensen, 1983). However, single women are also likely to experience feelings of ambivalence about being single (Lewis & Moon, 1997). Many express feelings of loss or regret related to their unmarried status, while at the same time experiencing high levels of satisfaction with their lives.

Moreover, as you might suspect, there are differences between single adults who have never married and those who are divorced or widowed. Continuous singlehood is associated with greater individual autonomy and capacity for personal growth (Marks & Lambert, 1998). By contrast, the negative effects of the transitional state that accompanies divorce or loss of a spouse seem to hamper the subjective sense of well-being in adults who are single for these reasons.

DIVORCE

York University sociologist Anne-Marie Ambert (2002) describes how different ways of computing the divorce rate can distort our ideas about how frequently divorce happens. The figure usually cited, 50%, is the ratio of divorces to marriages in a given year. In other words, a divorce rate of 50% means that there is one divorce for every two marriages. However, when researchers followed married couples longitudinally, they found that the actual statistical likelihood is that roughly 38% of marriages in Canada will end in divorce within 30 years of marriage (Statistics Canada, 2004c). Men divorced at the average age of 43.1 years and women at the age of 40.5. Although the rate of divorce had peaked before the fifth wedding anniversary, the average marriage lasted 14.2 years.

PSYCHOLOGICAL EFFECTS At a psychological level, divorce is clearly a major stressor. It is associated with increases in both physical and emotional illness. Recently separated or divorced adults have more automobile accidents, are more likely to commit suicide, lose more days at work because of illness, and are more likely to become depressed (Bloom, White, & Asher, 1979; Menaghan & Lieberman, 1986; Stack, 1992a, 1992b; Stack & Wasserman, 1993). They also report strong feelings of failure and a loss of self-esteem, as well as loneliness (Chase-Lansdale & Hetherington, 1990). These negative effects are strongest in the first months after the separation or divorce, like the effects of parents' divorce on children, which are greatest during the first 12 to 24 months (Chase-Lansdale & Hetherington, 1990; Kitson, 1992).

Long-term effects vary far more. Some adults seem to grow from the experience of divorce and show better psychological functioning 5 or 10 years later than they had shown before the divorce. Others seem to be worse off psychologically, even 10 years later (Wallerstein, 1986). It appears that those who remarry are likely to be happier than those who remain single—yet another bit of evidence supporting the general conclusion that marriage (or a stable partnership) is linked to better mental and physical health. Yet for those whose second marriage ends in divorce, the negative consequences can be substantial (Spanier & Furstenberg, 1987). At the moment, the most that developmentalists can say is that adults are highly heterogeneous in their responses to divorce. And very little is known about the factors that might predict good or poor long-term reactions, except that those adults with adequate social support are less disrupted in the short term (Chase-Lansdale & Hetherington, 1990).

ECONOMIC EFFECTS The psychological effects of divorce are often significantly worsened by serious economic effects, particularly for women. Because most men have had continuous work histories, they commonly leave a marriage with far greater earning power than do women. Women not only typically lack high earning capacity, but also usually retain custody of any children, with attendant costs. Several longitudinal studies in Canada, the United States, and European countries show that divorced men slightly improve in their economic position, while divorced women are strongly adversely affected, with an average decline of 40–50% of household income (Ambert, 2002; Smock, 1993). Furthermore, this negative economic effect does not disappear quickly—and for some women, it doesn't disappear at all. Such a long-term economic loss from divorce is especially likely for working-class women or those with relatively low levels of education, especially if they do not remarry. Women who were earning above-average incomes before their divorce are more likely to recover financially, even if they do not remarry (Ambert, 2002; Holden & Smock, 1991).

EFFECTS ON LIFE PATHWAYS For many adults, divorce also affects the sequence and timing of family roles. Even though divorced women with children are less likely to remarry than those who are child-free, remarriage expands the number of years of child-rearing for many divorced women (Lampard & Peggs, 1999; Norton, 1983). The total number of years of child-rearing may also be significantly increased for divorced men, especially for those who remarry younger women with young children. One effect of this change in timing is to reduce the number of years a remarried couple may have between the departure of the last child and the time when their elder parents may need economic or physical assistance.

Divorce also brings on a whole new set of roles. For the custodial parent (usually the woman), divorce means taking on parenting roles previously filled by the now-departed spouse. A divorced woman is also likely to take on a greatly expanded job role.

Developmental Psychology in Your Career

Community/Social Service Worker

Occupation	Community/Social Service Worker
Description	• work with social workers, teachers, psychologists, physicians, and related professionals in settings such as schools, group homes, and health, correctional, and mental health treatment centres • provide psychosocial assessments and counselling and referral services that help individuals and families with personal, interpersonal, and social problems, such as: poverty, addictions, mental disorders, assault, and family dysfunction
Entry Credentials	• 2-year (Community) Social Service Worker diploma • 3-year Bachelor of Social Work degree
Essential Lifespan Development Knowledge	• principles and theories of sociology and diversity, developmental and abnormal psychology, health and wellness, and culture • biopsychosocial assessment tools and intervention techniques for the poor and unwell, young and old • Acts and codes that pertain to children, adults, and families
Essential Lifespan Development Skills	• interview children, family members, and adults to obtain a case history • apply developmentally appropriate advisement, crisis intervention, and referral services for individuals and families • as part of a health care team, organize and conduct age-appropriate programs for groups, such as life skills workshops and substance abuse treatment
Lifespan Development and Essential Professional Attitude	• has desire to promote social justice, equality, and well-being • has respect for diversity and values a person's right to privacy and self-determination • maintains a professional helping relationship with clients and family members • is safety-conscious to protect self and others
Lifespan Development Career Profile: Janice Duda-Kosar, Supportive Housing Coordinator, Canadian Mental Health Association	"My career has given me the privilege of supporting adults with serious mental illness. My community-based mental health agency provides opportunities for consumers to actively participate in a recovery process that emphasizes rehabilitation. I have worked in the mental health field for 23 years. There has been a lot to learn and a lot of change over time. The consumers have taught me so much; they have inspired me with their courage, determination, and resilience. It has been a rewarding and fulfilling career." December 14, 2004

Thus, it isn't surprising that divorced women who are custodial mothers experience feel-ings of anger and frustration for a longer period of time after divorce than do non-custodial fathers (Dreman, Pielberger, & Darzi, 1997).

Remarriage frequently brings with it the remarkably complex role of step-parent (Jube, 2003; Preece, 2003). If several sets of children are involved, stages may be added to the standard family role cycle. A woman with children in elementary school may now find herself also the parent of teenagers—a role that demands different skills. Each of these changes seems to be accompanied by a new period of adaptation, often with con-siderable upheaval. In Levinson's theoretical language, this means divorced and remar-ried adults have fewer opportunities to create stable life structures and have more periods of transition or crisis. Thus, divorce changes the rhythm of adult life, for good or ill.

Before Going On

- In what ways do attachment and love contribute to the formation and stability of relationships?
- How do partnerships change over time?
- How does divorce affect young adults, especially women?

PARENTHOOD AND OTHER RELATIONSHIPS

The second major new role typically acquired in early adulthood is that of parent. The transition into this new role brings with it unique stresses, and, to make matters more complicated, it usually happens at a time when most other social relationships are in transition as well.

PARENTHOOD

Most parents would agree that parenthood is a remarkably mixed emotional experience. On one hand, the desire to become a parent is, for many adults, extremely strong. Thus, fulfilling that desire is an emotional high point for most. On the other hand, parenthood results in a number of stressful changes.

THE DESIRE TO BECOME A PARENT In Canada, the vast majority of both young men and women expect to have at least one child; only about 7–8% of 20- to 34-year-olds report that they do not expect to have children (Stobert & Kemeny, 2003). Not surprisingly, a major Canadian survey found that most parents (92%) believe that par-enting is the most important thing they could do and most individuals enjoyed the role of being a parent (94%) (Oldershaw, 2002). The percentage of men who strongly feel they want to become parents and view parenting as a life-enriching experience is actu-ally greater than the percentage of women who feel this way (Horowitz, McLaughlin, & White, 1998; Muzi, 2000). Furthermore, most expectant fathers become emotionally attached to their unborn children during the third trimester of pregnancy and eagerly anticipate the birth (White, Wilson, Elander, & Persson, 1999).

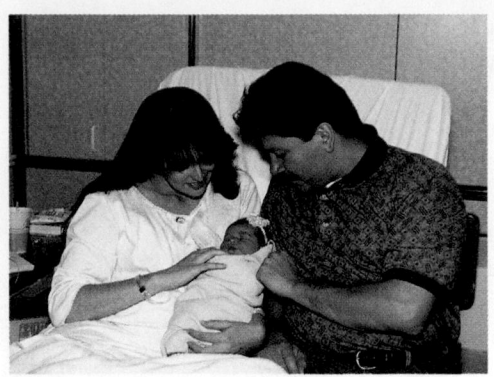

For most couples in long-term relationships, especially those who are married, having a child is an important goal.

(*Photo:* Michael Newman/PhotoEdit)

POSTPARTUM DEPRESSION Between 10% and 25% of new mothers experience a severe mood disturbance called *postpartum depression (PPD)*—a disorder found among mothers in Canada (Pearce, 1997) as well as in many countries around the world, including Australia, China, Sweden, Scotland, and the United States (Campbell, Cohn, Flanagan, Popper, & Meyers, 1992; Guo, 1993; Lundh & Gyllang, 1993; Webster, Thompson, Mitchell, & Werry, 1994). Women who develop PPD suffer from feelings of sadness for several weeks after the baby's birth. Most cases of PPD persist only a few weeks, but 1–2% of women suffer for a year or more.

Women whose bodies produce unusually high levels of steroid hormones toward the end of pregnancy are more likely to develop postpartum depression (Harris et al., 1994). The disorder is also more common in women whose pregnancies were unplanned, who were anxious about the pregnancy, or whose partner was unsupportive (Campbell et al., 1992; O'Hara, Schlechte, Lewis, & Varner, 1992). The presence of major life stressors during pregnancy or immediately after the baby's birth—such as a move to a new home, the death of someone close, or job loss—also increases the risk of PPD (Swendsen & Mazure, 2000).

However, the best predictor of postpartum depression is depression during pregnancy (Da Costa, Larouche, Dritsa, & Brender, 2000). Thus, many cases of PPD can probably be prevented by training health professionals to recognize depression in pregnant women. Similarly, family members of women with absent or unsupportive partners can help them locate agencies that provide material and social support.

THE TRANSITION EXPERIENCE Even when new mothers are emotionally healthy, the transition to parenthood can be very stressful. New parents may argue about child-rearing philosophy as well as how, when, where, and by whom child-care chores should be done (Reichle & Gefke, 1998). Both parents are usually also physically exhausted, perhaps even seriously sleep-deprived, because their newborn keeps them up for much of the night. Predictably, new parents report that they have much less time for each other—less time for conversation, for sex, for simple affection, or even for doing routine chores together (Belsky, Lang, & Rovine, 1985).

Some cultures have developed ritualized rites of passage for this important transition, which can help new parents manage stress. For example, in Hispanic cultures, *la cuarenta* is a period of 40 days following the birth of a child, during which fathers are expected to take on typically feminine tasks such as housework. Extended family members are also expected to help out. Researchers have found that Hispanic couples who observe *la cuarenta* adjust to parenthood more easily than those who do not (Niska, Snyder, & Lia-Hoagberg, 1998).

DEVELOPMENTAL IMPACT OF PARENTHOOD Despite its inherent stressfulness, the transition to parenthood is associated with positive behaviour change. Sensation-seeking and risky behaviour decline considerably when young adults become parents (Arnett, 1998). Despite these positive changes, marital satisfaction tends to decline after the birth of a child. The general pattern is that such satisfaction is at its peak before the birth of the first child, after which it drops and remains at a lower level until the last child leaves home.

In a review of all the research on this point, one psychologist concluded that this curvilinear pattern "is about as close to being certain as anything ever is in the social sciences" (Glenn, 1990, p. 853). **Figure 13.4** illustrates the pattern, based on results from an early and widely quoted study (Rollins & Feldman, 1970). The best-documented portion of this curvilinear pattern is the drop in marital satisfaction after the birth of the

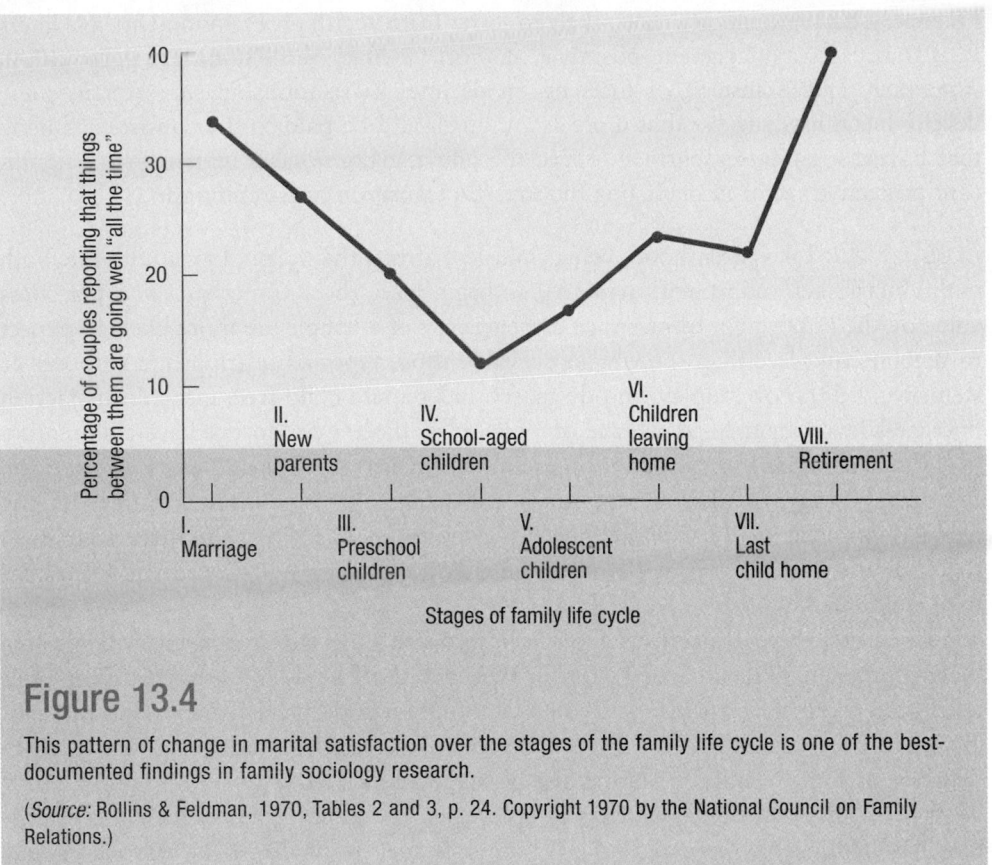

Figure 13.4

This pattern of change in marital satisfaction over the stages of the family life cycle is one of the best-documented findings in family sociology research.

(*Source:* Rollins & Feldman, 1970, Tables 2 and 3, p. 24. Copyright 1970 by the National Council on Family Relations.)

first child, for which there is both longitudinal and cross-sectional evidence. More recent studies suggest that the decline in marital satisfaction is characteristic of contemporary cohorts of new parents as well, and researchers have found a pattern of marital satisfaction similar to that reported by Rollins and Feldman across a variety of cultures (Ahmad & Najam, 1998; Gloger-Tippelt & Huerkamp, 1998).

A number of variables contribute to just how dissatisfied a couple becomes. One important factor is the division of labour. The more a partner feels that he or she is carrying an unfair proportion of the economic, household, or child-care workload, the greater his or her loss of satisfaction (Wicki, 1999). Support from extended family members is another variable that predicts maintenance or loss of satisfaction (Lee & Keith, 1999).

Some developmentalists suggest that the relative effectiveness of the coping strategies couples use to adjust to their new roles determines how their relationship satisfaction will be affected by the birth of a child (Belsky & Hsieh, 1998). For example, couples who have established effective conflict-resolution strategies before the birth of a child experience less loss of satisfaction (Cox, Paley, Burchinal, & Payne, 1999; Lindahl, Clements, & Markman, 1997). The quality of new parents' attachment to their own parents also predicts how much their relationship satisfaction declines after the birth of a child (Gloger-Tippelt & Huerkamp, 1998). In fact, young adults with anxious or avoidant attachments to their own parents expect the transition to parenthood to be a negative experience more often than do those whose attachments are secure (Rholes, Simpson, Blakely, Lanigan, & Allen, 1997).

It's important to keep in mind, though, that new parents who are married or cohabiting experience a much smaller decline in overall life satisfaction than new single parents, whose lives are far more complicated and stressful (Lee, Law, & Tam, 1999).

Likewise, single parents are more likely to suffer from health problems and are less likely to advance to management positions at work (Khlat, Sermet, & Le Pape, 2000; Tharenou, 1999). Instead of focusing on declines in relationship satisfaction, some developmentalists suggest that more attention should be paid to the consistent finding that having a parenting partner—especially one to whom one is married—is a significant protective factor in managing the stressful transition to parenthood.

CHILD-FREE   Like parenthood, being child-free affects the shape of an adult's life, both within marriages and in work patterns. To begin with, those Canadians who place less value on the importance of marriage or being part of a couple are more likely to expect to remain child-free than those who do value those types of relationships (Stobert & Kemeny, 2003). For couples who do marry and remain child-free, marital satisfaction fluctuates less over time. As is true of all couples, those who do not have children are likely to experience some drop in satisfaction in the first months and years of marriage. But over the range of adult life, the curve of marital satisfaction is much flatter than the one shown in **Figure 13.4** (Houseknecht, 1987; Somers, 1993). Child-free couples in their 20s and 30s consistently report higher cohesion in their marriages than do couples with children.

Being child-free also affects the role of worker, especially for women. Child-free married women, like unmarried women, are much more likely to have full-time continuous careers. However, a survey involving more than 2000 participants found that single, child-free women had no higher rates of managerial advancement than mothers (Tharenou, 1999). Thus, one of the disadvantages associated with being child-free may be that it is always socially a bit risky to be seen as "different" from others in any important way (Mueller & Yoder, 1999). Tharenou's survey's finding that married fathers whose wives were not employed were more likely to advance than workers of any marital or parental status also supports this conclusion.

SOCIAL NETWORKS

Critical Thinking

List all the people in your current social network. What is the relative importance of family and friends for you?

Creating a partnership may be the most central task of the process of achieving intimacy, but it is certainly not the only reflection of that basic process. In early adult life, each of us creates a social network made up of family and friends as well as our life partner.

FAMILY   If you ask children and adults "Who is the person you don't like to be away from?" or "Who is the person you know will always be there for you?" children and teenagers most often list their parents, while adults most often name their spouses or partners and almost never mention their parents (Hazan, Hutt, Sturgeon, & Bricker, 1991). However, most adults feel emotionally close to their parents and see or talk to them regularly (Campbell, Connidis, & Davies, 1999; Lawton, Silverstein, & Bengtson, 1994).

Not surprisingly, the amount and kind of contact an adult has with kin is strongly influenced by proximity. Adults who live within 2 hours of their parents and siblings see them far more often than those who live farther away. But distance does not prevent a parent or sibling from being part of an individual adult's social network. These relationships can provide support in times of need, even if physical contact is infrequent.

There are also important cultural differences in young adults' involvement with their families. For example, one study compared the development of social independence among Australian, Canadian, and Japanese children and adults (Takata, 1999).

In all three cultures, the sense of being independent from parents and family increased with age. However, Australian and Canadian participants appeared to develop self-perceptions of independence earlier in life. Consequently, Japanese young adults reported a greater sense of connectedness to their families of origin than either Australian or Canadian young adults.

FRIENDS

Friends, too, are important members of a social network. We choose our friends as we choose our partners, from among those who are similar to us in education, social class, interests, family background, or family life-cycle stage. Cross-sex friendships are more common among adults than they are among 10-year-olds, but they are still outnumbered by same-sex friendships. Young adults' friends are also overwhelmingly drawn from their own age group. Beyond this basic requirement of similarity, close friendship seems to rest on mutual openness and personal disclosure.

Because of the centrality of the task of intimacy in early adulthood, most researchers and theorists assume that young adults have more friends than do middle-aged or older adults. Research has offered some hints of support for this idea, but it has been a difficult assumption to test properly. Developmentalists lack longitudinal data and do not agree on definitions of friendship, which makes combining data across studies very difficult.

SEX DIFFERENCES IN RELATIONSHIP STYLES As in childhood, there are very striking sex differences in both the number and quality of friendships in the social network of young adults. Women have more close friends, and their friendships are more intimate, with more self-disclosure and more exchange of emotional support. Young men's friendships, like those of boys and older men, are more competitive. Male friends are less likely to agree with each other or to ask for or provide emotional support to one another (Dindia & Allen, 1992; Maccoby, 1990). Adult women friends talk to one another; adult men friends do things together.

Whether one sees the female pattern or the male pattern as "better" or "worse" obviously depends on one's gender and point of view. Theorists continue to argue the point (Antonucci, 1994). Most research shows men to be less satisfied with their friendships than women are (although the sexes are equally satisfied with their family relationships), and women clearly gain in quite specific ways from the buffering effect of their social network. But men also gain from their style of relationship. Women's style, for example, sometimes has the effect of burdening them too much with emotional obligations, whereas men are more able to focus on their work (Antonucci, 1994b). Setting aside value judgments, the important point remains: Men and women appear to create different kinds of relationships, and this difference permeates society.

Another facet of this difference is that women most often fill the role of **kin-keeper** (Moen, 1996). They write the letters, make the phone calls, arrange the gatherings of family and friends. (In later stages of adult life, it is also the women who are likely to take on the role of caring for aging parents—a pattern you'll learn more about in **Chapter 15**.)

Taken together, all this means that women have a much larger "relationship role" than men do. In virtually all cultures, it is part of the female role to be responsible for maintaining the emotional aspects of relationships—with a spouse, with friends, with family, and, of course, with children.

kin-keeper
a family role, usually occupied by a woman, which includes responsibility for maintaining family and friendship relationships

Before Going On

- Describe the transition to parenthood and the developmental effects of becoming a parent and remaining child-free.
- How are family and friends important to young adults?

THE ROLE OF WORKER

In addition to the roles of spouse or partner and parent, a large percentage of young adults are simultaneously filling yet another major and relatively new role, that of worker. Most young people need to take on this role to support themselves economically. But that is not the only reason for the centrality of this role. Satisfying work also seems to be an important ingredient in mental health and life satisfaction, for both men and women (Meeus, Dekovic, & Iedema, 1997; Tait, Padgett, & Baldwin, 1989). However, before looking at what developmentalists know about career steps and sequences in early adulthood, let's examine how young people choose an occupation.

CHOOSING AN OCCUPATION

As you might imagine, a multitude of factors influence a young person's choice of job or career: family background and values; intelligence and education; gender; and personality (in addition to other factors such as ethnic group, self-concept, and school performance).

FAMILY INFLUENCES Typically, young people tend to choose occupations at the same general social class level as those of their parents—although this is less true today than it was in decades past (Biblarz, Bengtson, & Bucur, 1996). In part, this effect operates through the medium of education. For example, parents who have higher-than-average levels of education themselves are more likely to encourage their children to go on to further education past high school (Statistics Canada, 2001l). Such added education, in turn, makes it more likely that the young person will qualify for middle-class jobs, for which a post-secondary education is frequently a required credential.

Families also influence job choices through their value systems. In particular, parents who value academic and professional achievement are far more likely to have children who attend a post-secondary school and choose professional-level jobs. This effect is not just social-class difference in disguise. Among working-class families, it is the children of those who place the strongest emphasis on achievement who are most likely to move up into middle-class jobs (Gustafson & Magnusson, 1991). Further, families whose career aspirations for their children are high tend to produce young adults who are more intrinsically motivated as employees (Cotton, Bynum, & Madhere, 1997).

Similarly, parental moral beliefs influence young adults' willingness to enter various occupations (Bregman & Killen, 1999). For example, young adults whose families believe that drinking alcohol is morally wrong are unlikely to choose alcohol-related occupations such as bartending, waiting tables in a restaurant where liquor is served, or working at a liquor store.

EDUCATION AND INTELLIGENCE Education and intelligence also interact very strongly to influence not just the specific job a young person chooses, but also career success over the long haul. You read about some of these links in **Chapter 10**, but they bear repeating: The higher your intelligence, the more years of education you are likely to complete; the more education you have, the higher the level at which you enter the job market; the higher the level of entry, the further you are likely to go over your lifetime (Brody, 1992; Kamo, Ries, Farmer, Nickinovich, & Borgatta, 1991).

Intelligence has direct effects on job choice and job success as well. Brighter students are more likely to choose technical or professional careers. And highly intelligent workers are more likely to advance, even if they enter the job market at a lower level than those who are less intelligent (Dreher & Bretz, 1991).

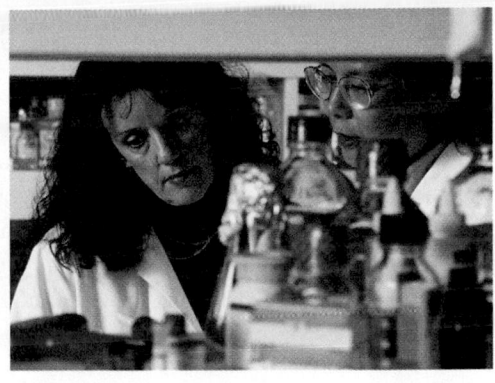

Parents who have higher-than-average levels of education themselves are more likely to encourage their children to pursue post-secondary studies.
(*Photo:* PhotoDisc)

GENDER   Canadian researchers Thiessen and Nickerson (2001) contend that "the nature and extent of women's and men's educational and labour market activities evolves continuously" (p. 10). Academically, for instance, there are now more women enrolled in all the major fields of study except for two: engineering/applied science and mathematics/physical sciences. Nonetheless, specific job selection remains strongly affected by gender. Despite the women's movement, and despite the vast increase in the proportion of women working, about 70% of women occupy traditionally female occupations, such as nursing, teaching, and clerical (Cooke-Reynolds & Zukewich, 2004; Statistics Canada, 2004e; Thiessen & Nickerson, 2001). However, the trend is shifting—Canadian women are increasing their presence in traditionally male-dominated jobs, such as doctors, dentists, and senior managers, as well as doubling their ranks in agriculture and manufacturing (see **Figure 13.5**) (Cooke-Reynolds & Zukewich, 2004). It is not surprising that women's income has been increasing steadily—in 2002 it was slightly more than four-fifths of men's wages over all.

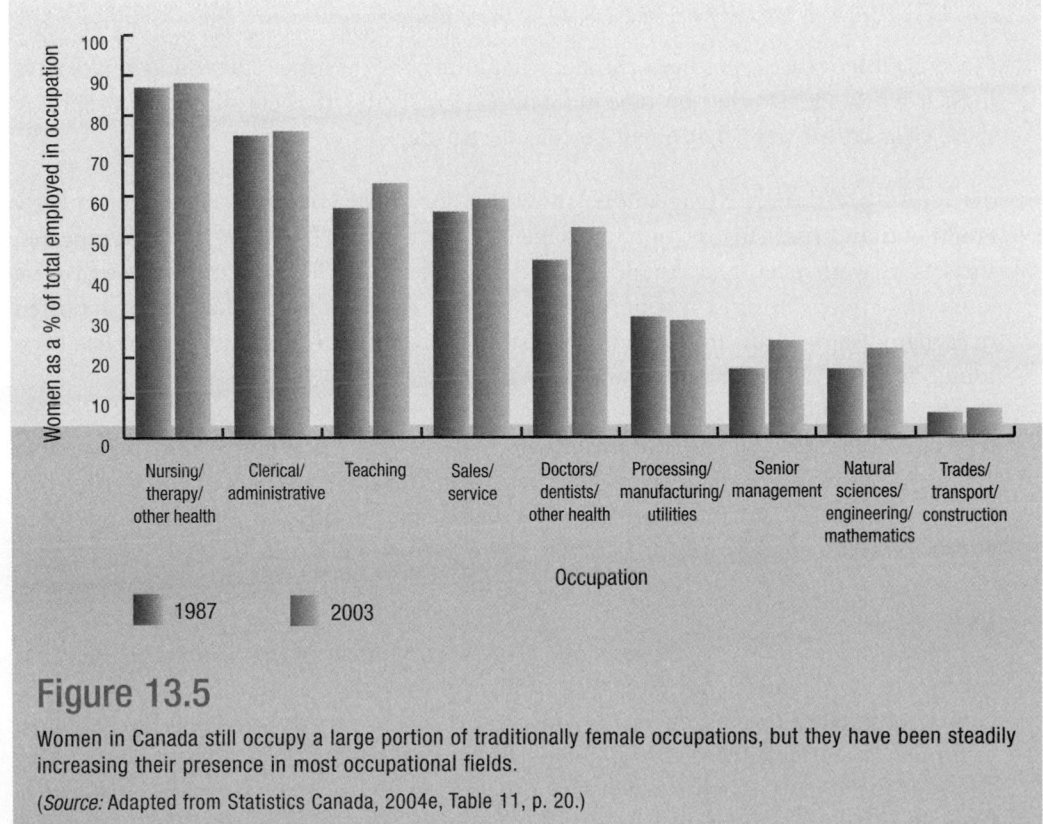

Figure 13.5

Women in Canada still occupy a large portion of traditionally female occupations, but they have been steadily increasing their presence in most occupational fields.

(*Source:* Adapted from Statistics Canada, 2004e, Table 11, p. 20.)

Children learn these cultural definitions of "appropriate" jobs for men and women in their early years, just as they learn all the other aspects of sex roles. So it is not surprising that most young women and men choose jobs that fit these sex-role designations. Nonstereotypical job choices are much more common among young people who see themselves as androgynous, or whose parents have less conventional occupations. For instance, young women who choose traditionally masculine careers are more likely to have a mother who has had a long-term career, and are more likely to define themselves either as androgynous or as masculine (Betz & Fitzgerald, 1987; Fitzpatrick & Silverman, 1989).

PERSONALITY A fourth important influence on job choice is the young adult's personality. John Holland, whose work has been the most influential in this area, proposes six basic personality types, summarized in **Table 13.1** (Holland, 1973, 1992). Holland's basic hypothesis is that each of us tends to choose, and be most successful at, an occupation that matches our personality.

Research in non-Western as well as Western cultures has generally supported Holland's proposal (e.g., Kahn, Alvi, Shaukat, Hussain, & Baig, 1990; Leong, Austin, Sekaran, & Komarraju, 1998; Tokar, Fischer, & Subich, 1998; Tracey & Rounds, 1993; Upperman & Church, 1995). Ministers, for example, generally score highest on Holland's social scale, engineers highest on the investigative scale, car salespeople on the enterprising scale, and career army officers on the realistic scale.

People whose personalities match their jobs are also more likely to be satisfied with their work. Moreover, obtaining a personality assessment prior to making an occupational choice is associated with greater feelings of confidence about the decision (Francis-Smythe & Smith, 1997).

JOBS OVER TIME

Once the job or career has been chosen, what kinds of experiences do young adults have in their work life? Do they become more or less satisfied with their work over time? Are there clear career steps that might be considered stages?

JOB SATISFACTION Many studies show that job satisfaction is at its lowest in early adulthood and rises steadily until retirement, a pattern that has been found in repeated surveys of both male and female respondents (Glenn & Weaver, 1985). Researchers know that this is not just a cohort effect, because similar findings have been reported over many years of research, and that it is not entirely culture-specific, since it has been found in many industrialized countries.

But what might cause the pattern? Some research points to the possibility that this pattern is the effect of time on job rather than age (e.g., Bedeian, Ferris, & Kacmar, 1992). Older workers are likely to have had their jobs longer, which may contribute to several sources of satisfaction, including better pay, more job security, and more authority. But there may be some genuine age effects at work, too. The jobs young people hold are likely to be dirtier, physically harder, and less complex and interesting (Spenner, 1988).

However, research also suggests that there are a number of important variables that contribute to job satisfaction in young adults. As with almost every life situation, individual personality traits such as neuroticism affect job satisfaction (Blustein, Phillips, Jobin-Davis, & Finkelberg, 1997; Judge, Bono, & Locke, 2000). In addition, young adults engaged in careers for which they prepared in high school or college have higher levels of satisfaction (Blustein et al., 1997). Ethnicity is also related to job satisfaction,

TABLE 13.1	Holland's Personality Types and Work Preferences
Type	**Personality and Work Preferences**
Realistic	Aggressive, masculine, physically strong, often with low verbal or interpersonal skills; prefer mechanical activities and tool use, choosing jobs such as mechanic, electrician, or surveyor
Investigative	Oriented toward thinking (particularly abstract thinking), organizing, and planning; prefer ambiguous, challenging tasks, but are low in social skills; are often scientists or engineers
Artistic	Asocial; prefer unstructured, highly individual activity; are often artists
Social	Extraverts; people-oriented, sociable, and need attention; avoid intellectual activity and dislike highly ordered activity; prefer to work with people and choose service jobs like nursing and education
Enterprising	Highly verbal and dominating; enjoy organizing and directing others; are persuasive and strong leaders, often choosing careers in sales
Conventional	Prefer structured activities and subordinate roles; like clear guidelines and see themselves as accurate and precise; may choose occupations such as bookkeeping or filing

(*Source*: Holland, 1973, 1992.)

with white workers reporting higher levels of satisfaction than ethnic minority workers (Weaver & Hinson, 2000).

In addition to personal factors, a number of workplace variables influence job satisfaction. For example, the degree to which a work setting encourages or discourages young employees makes a difference (Blustein et al., 1997). Encouragement may be part of a set of workplace variables that contribute to positive affect, or feelings of emotional contentment, among workers, which, in turn, lead to higher levels of job satisfaction. Research suggests that workers are most satisfied when they experience more pleasant than unpleasant emotions while working (Fisher, 2000).

CAREER LADDERS In most careers, workers tend to move from step to step through a series of milestones that make up a **career ladder**. In academic jobs, the sequence is from instructor to assistant professor to associate professor and then full professor. In an automobile plant, the ladder may go from assembly-line worker to foreman to general foreman to superintendent and on up. In the corporate world, there may be many rungs in a management career ladder.

career ladder
the milestones associated with a particular occupation

What kind of progress up the career ladder do young adults typically make? To answer such a question properly, of course, researchers need to conduct longitudinal studies. There have not been many of these, but fortunately there are a few, including a 20-year study of AT&T managers (Bray & Howard, 1983) and a 15-year study of workers in a large manufacturing company (Rosenbaum, 1984). This research suggests several generalizations about the developmental progression of work careers in early adulthood. First, post-secondary education makes a very large difference, as you should remember from **Chapter 12**. Even if the effects of differing intellectual ability are accounted for, research shows that those with post-secondary educations advance further and faster.

Second, early promotion is associated with greater advancement over the long haul. In the manufacturing company that Rosenbaum studied, 83% of those who were promoted within the first year eventually got as far as lower management, while only 33% of those who were first promoted after 3 years of employment got that far.

Third, and perhaps most important, most work advancement occurs early in a career path, after which a plateau is reached. The policy in the manufacturing company that Rosenbaum studied was for all workers—whether they had a college degree or not—to enter at the submanagement level. The first possible promotional step was to the job of foreman; promotion to lower management was the second possible step. The majority of promotions to either position occurred when workers were between the ages of 29 and 34; by age 40, virtually all the promotions that a person was going to receive had already happened. The same pattern is evident in other career paths as well, such as those of accountants and academics, so it is not unique to business career ladders (Spenner, 1988).

Such a pattern may be unique, however, to adults who enter a profession in their 20s and stay in it through most of their adult lives. There are at least a few hints from research with women—whose work histories are frequently much less continuous than men's—that time-in-career rather than age may be the critical variable for the timing of promotions. There may be a window of 10 to 15 years between the time you enter a profession and the time you reach a plateau. If you begin in your 20s, you are likely to have peaked by your mid-30s. But if you begin when you are 40, you may still have 15 years in which to advance.

SEX DIFFERENCES IN WORK PATTERNS

It is estimated that it now takes the average Canadian youth about seven years to make the transition from school to work—the point from which most young people are only attending school, through a period of school mixed with part-time work, to the point at which more than half of the average Canadian youths are working full-time (Beaujot, 2004). The transitional delay has meant that young men are economically worse off in comparison to men of previous generations. Young women, however, especially if they have continued to advance their education, are better off than women of earlier generations. From a couple's standpoint, the woman's greater financial contribution compensates for the man's losses, as most couples form a two-worker family. Overall, most studies show that it is advantageous to delay the transition into work, provided that you pursue an advanced education and put off building a family.

Some of what you have read so far about work patterns is as true for women as it is for men. For example, women's work satisfaction goes up with age (and with job tenure), just as men's does. But women's work experience in early adulthood differs from men's in one strikingly important respect: The great majority of women move in and out of the work force at least once, often many times (Drobnic, Blossfeld, & Rohwer, 1999).

This pattern has numerous repercussions for women's work roles. For example, Canadian women who work continuously or delay motherhood to keep working have higher salaries and achieve higher levels in their jobs than do those who have moved in and out of employment (Drolet, 2003). Among women who have not worked continuously, those who worked for several short bursts during their in-and-out stage do better economically than those who were unemployed for a single long stretch, even when the total months or years of employment are the same in the two groups (Gwartney-Gibbs, 1988). Very likely these short bursts of work allow the woman to keep up her work skills, especially if she works at the same type of job each time she re-enters the labour market. Part-time work also seems to serve the same function. Clearly, some strategies can help a woman maximize her work success while still allowing her to spend time with her family, but accomplishing both takes a good deal of thought and planning.

Women's work patterns and attitudes are obviously changing rapidly. For example, one Canadian study found that most of the high school girls the researchers interviewed

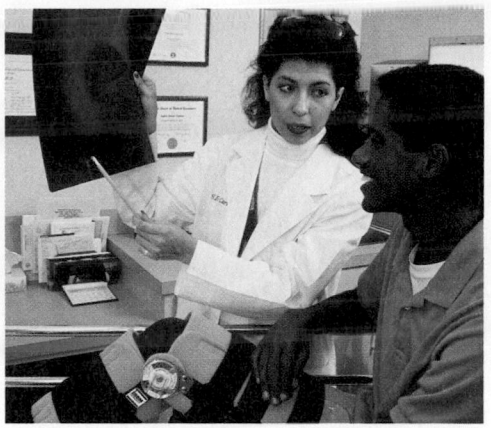

Women are working in larger and larger numbers, but fewer than a third work continuously during the early adult years.
(*Photos: left*, David Young-Wolff/Getty Images; *right*, Robert E. Daemmrich/ Getty Images)

in the early 1990s expected both to be continuously employed and to have a family in adulthood (Davey, 1998). However, when they were re-interviewed 4 years later, these young women had begun to think about potential conflicts between career and family goals. Most still expected to be continuously employed, but many indicated that they preferred to take time out from their careers to achieve family goals such as raising children. So although the cultural climate has changed drastically with regard to women's work patterns, the essential conflict women feel with regard to work and family, which is the driving force behind discontinuous patterns of employment, continues to be evident in current cohorts.

The evidence on women's patterns of discontinuous employment raises the more general question of how individuals and couples balance the roles of worker and parent and those of worker and spouse. It is an interesting testimony to the strength of cultural gender roles that people have no trouble thinking of a man as simultaneously a worker, a parent, and a spouse, but think it is problematic for a woman to be all three at once. Women do, in fact, feel more role conflict among these three roles than men do, for several clear reasons (Higgins, Duxbury, & Lee, 1994).

The most obvious reason is that if the hours spent in family work (child care, cleaning, cooking, shopping, etc.) and in paid employment are added together, employed women are working more hours a week than are their husbands or partners, as suggested by **Figure 13.6** on page 416—despite the fact that men whose wives are employed are doing more child care than men in previous generations did (Higgins et al., 1994). Further, unmarried men are as likely as their female counterparts to anticipate the need to balance work and family roles after marriage (Kerpelman & Schvaneveldt, 1999).

Kerry Daly (2000) of the University of Guelph found that young Canadian adults aged 25 to 44 experience the most time pressure of all age groups. Both single mothers and married parents who were employed full-time reported the highest levels of time-related stress. In addition, Daly determined that there was a curvilinear relationship between age and leisure time, whereby youth and late middle-aged adults had the highest proportion of leisure time per day and 35- to 44-year-olds reported the least amount of leisure time per day. Men in this latter age bracket averaged 4.8 hours and women averaged only 4.5 hours of leisure per day over a week. Of course parents with children had even less leisure time than average.

Women also feel more conflict between family and work roles because of the way sex roles are defined in most cultures. The woman's role is to be relationship-oriented, to care for others, to nurture. To the extent that a woman has internalized that role expectation—and most have—she will define herself, and judge herself, more by how well she performs such caring roles than by how well she performs her job role. Joseph Pleck argues that this means that the boundaries between work and family roles are therefore

Make the Connection

In **Chapter 7** you learned about gender schema theory. How would this theory explain women's responses to conflicts between work and family roles?

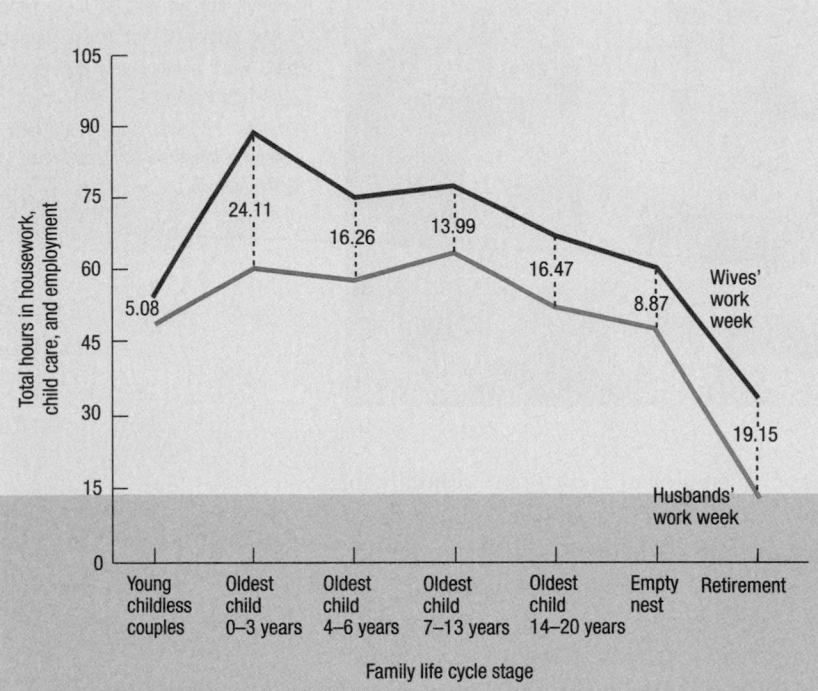

Figure 13.6

When both partners work full-time, women still do more housework and child care, so their total work week is many hours longer—contributing significantly to women's greater sense of conflict between work and family roles. Note that the gap is greatest right after the birth of the first child—perhaps a time when the man is most likely to be intensely committed to his career.

(*Source:* Rexroat & Shehan, 1987, Fig. 1, p. 746.)

"asymmetrically permeable" for the two sexes (Pleck, 1977). That is, for a woman, family roles spill over into work life. She not only takes time off from her job when children are born, but also stays home with a sick child, takes time off to go to a parent-teacher meeting, and thinks about her family tasks during her workday. Women view themselves as mothers and wives all day, even when they work. These simultaneous, competing demands are the very definition of role conflict. For men, work and family roles are more sequential than simultaneous. Men view themselves as workers during the day, husbands and fathers when they come home. If the two roles conflict for men, it is more likely to be the work role that spills over into family life than the other way around.

Not all the intersections of family and work roles are problematic for women. For example, working women have more power in their marriages or partnerships than do nonworking women (Blumstein & Schwartz, 1983; Spitze, 1988). The more equal the earnings of the partners, the more equality there is in decision-making and in household work. But it remains true that the most striking single fact about work and family roles in this age of high women's employment is that women struggle more than men do to resolve the conflict between the two. It is also clear that this conflict is vastly greater during early adulthood, when children are young and need constant care, than it is in middle or later adult life. In many respects, it is this complex intersection of spousal, parental, and work roles that is the defining feature of early adult life in industrialized societies (see **The Real World**).

Critical Thinking

What plans do you have to combine work and family? Might your planning, or your thinking, change as a result of what you have read so far?

Before Going On

- What factors influence a person's choice of occupation?

- How do the concepts of job satisfaction and the career ladder contribute to an understanding of how jobs change over time?

- Describe women's patterns of work and how they relate to on-the-job achievement and income. What are the potential conflicts among work and family roles, and how do they differ for men and women?

The Real World
Working
Strategies for Coping with Conflict Between Work and Family Life

The most helpful strategy overall is something psychologists call cognitive restructuring—recasting or reframing the situation for yourself in a way that identifies the positive elements. Cognitive restructuring might include reminding yourself that you had good reasons for choosing to have both a job and a family and recalling other times when you have coped successfully with similar problems (Paden & Buehler, 1995).

A related kind of restructuring involves redefining family roles. In several older studies, psychologists found that women who found ways to redistribute basic household tasks to other family members (husband and children), or who simply gave up doing some tasks, experienced less stress and conflict (Hall, 1972, 1975). You might make a list of all the household chores you and your partner do and go over the list together, eliminating whatever items you can and reassigning some of the others. Men can clean toilets; clutter can be dealt with less frequently (or not at all!); meals can perhaps be simpler. If economic resources are sufficient, help can also be hired.

You can also redefine the sex roles themselves. Where is it written that only women can stay home with a sick child? It is probably written in your internal model of yourself or in your gender schema. Many women find it difficult to give up such responsibilities, even when they cause severe role conflict, because such nurturing is part of their image of themselves. As one woman whose husband was very involved in the care of their infant said,

> I love seeing the closeness between him and the baby, especially since I didn't have that with my father, but if he does well at his work and his relationship with the baby, what's my special contribution? (Cowan & Cowan, 1987, p. 168)

It may be helpful to try to discover whether the current division of labour in your own household exists because others in the household don't do their share or because of your own inner resistance to changing your view of yourself and your basic contribution to the family unit.

Finally, you may find it helpful to take a class in time management. Research reveals that good planning can, in fact, reduce the sense of strain you feel (Paden & Buehler, 1995). You have probably already heard lots of advice about how to organize things better. Easier said than done! But there are techniques that can help, and many of these are taught in workshops and classes in most cities.

What does not help is simply trying harder to do it all yourself. Women who continue to try to fulfill several roles perfectly report maximum strain and stress. Something has to give, whether it is your standards for housework or your sense of your female role. Combining a number of roles is inherently full of opportunities for conflict. At best, you may manage a delicate balance. At worst, you will find yourself overwhelmed.

Summary

Theories of Social and Personality Development

- Erikson proposed that young adults face the crisis of intimacy versus isolation. Those who fail to establish a stable relationship with an intimate partner or a network of friends become socially isolated.

- Levinson hypothesized that adult development involves alternating periods of stability and instability, through which adults construct and refine life structures.

- Evolutionary theories of mate selection suggest that sex differences in mate preferences and mating behaviour are the result of natural selection.

- Social role theory emphasizes factors such as gender roles, similarity, and economic exchange in explaining sex differences in mating.

Intimate Relationships

- Internal models of attachment are related to assumptions about others and the quality of relationships created in early adulthood. Sternberg's model of love is also influential. He posited three elements: intimacy, passion, and commitment. These three may combine to produce eight varieties of love.

- The quality of a committed partnership—marriage or long-term cohabitation—tends to decline in the first year as the rate of positive interactions drops. Those who enter into a relationship with good resources (education, problem-solving ability, etc.) and who create positive communication strategies are more likely to enjoy enduring relationships and to avoid divorce or separation.

- Married adults are generally happier and healthier than singles. However, psychologists believe that it is relationship quality, rather than marriage itself, that is associated with both mental and physical health.

- Divorced young adults experience more loneliness and depression, and divorced women are more likely to be poor. Divorce and remarriage may also influence the developmental pathway of early adulthood by increasing the years devoted to child-rearing and complicating family roles.

Parenthood and Other Relationships

- Most men and women want to become parents, because they view raising children as a life-enriching experience.

- The transition to parenthood is stressful and leads to a decline in relationship satisfaction. Factors such as the division of labour between mother and father, individual personality traits, and the availability of help from extended family members contribute to relationship satisfaction.

- Young adults' relationships with their parents tend to be steady and supportive, even if less central than they were at earlier ages. The quality of attachment to parents continues to predict a number of important variables in early adulthood.

- Each young adult creates a network of relationships with friends as well as with a partner and family members.

The Role of Worker

- The specific job or career a young adult chooses is affected by his or her education, intelligence, family background and resources, family values, personality, and gender. The majority of adults choose jobs that fit the cultural norms for their social class and gender. More intelligent young people, and those with more education, are more upwardly mobile.

- Job satisfaction rises steadily throughout early adulthood, in part because the jobs typically available to young adults are less well paid, more repetitive, less creative, and allow the worker very little power or influence. The work role has two stages in early adulthood: a trial stage, in which alternative pathways are explored, and an establishment stage, in which the career path is established.

- For most women, the work role includes an additional "in-and-out" stage, in which periods of focusing on family responsibilities alternate with periods of employment. The more continuous a woman's work history, the more successful she is likely to be at her job.

- When both partners work, the family responsibilities are not equally divided: Women continue to perform more work in the home and feel more role conflict.

Key Terms

assortative mating (homogamy) (p. 396)

avoidant couples (p. 399)

career ladder (p. 413)

hostile/detached couples (p. 400)

hostile/engaged couples (p. 399)

intimacy (p. 391)

intimacy versus isolation (p. 391)

kin-keeper (p. 409)

life structure (p. 392)

parental investment theory (p. 394)

social role theory (p. 395)

validating couples (p. 399)

volatile couples (p. 399)

Weblinks

Realm Magazine
www.realm.net/index-e.cfm
Realm Magazine is a Canadian web-based publication devoted to the issue of working life in your 20s. The magazine profiles interesting career options and explores the pitfalls and highlights of working life at the beginning of your career.

No Kidding Society
www.nokidding.net
No Kidding Society, founded in Vancouver in 1984, is an all-volunteer, nonprofit social club for couples and singles who, for whatever reason, have never had children. The website provides information about the club's mandate and activities, as well as links to articles that have been written on the topic.

Postpartum Support International
www.postpartum.net
This website offers a clear introduction to the topic, a wealth of information on current news and research about postpartum depression, and links to support groups worldwide.

Job Futures
www.jobfutures.ca/en/home.shtml
This Government of Canada website is a career tool that will help you plan for your future. It provides useful information about 226 occupational groups. There are also Career Quizzes that are designed to help you find out about your work interests, styles, and preferences.

Kathy Ferguson/PhotoEdit

CHAPTER 14

PHYSICAL AND COGNITIVE DEVELOPMENT IN MIDDLE ADULTHOOD

The great baseball player Satchel Paige, who was still pitching in the major leagues at age 62, once said, "Age is mind over matter. If you don't mind, it doesn't matter."

It's a nice summary of the physical changes of the middle years. Yes, there are changes. Memory does get less efficient in some situations in mid-life; vision and hearing get worse; people slow down slightly and become somewhat weaker. But among adults who are otherwise healthy, the amount of loss is far less than folklore would have us believe. Further, along with obvious losses come important gains. Indeed, although early adulthood may be the physical high point of adulthood, there is a great deal of evidence that middle adulthood is the intellectual and creative peak.

In this chapter you will learn that, with advancing age, the story of human development seems to become more an account of differences than a description of universals. This happens because there are so many factors—behavioural choices, poor health, and so on—that determine the specific developmental pathway an adult follows. Most middle-aged adults are healthy, energetic, and intellectually productive, but others are in decline. Moreover, because developmental psychology has focused more on younger individuals, there simply isn't as much knowledge about universal changes in adulthood. As you read this chapter, keep the following questions in mind:

- How do the nervous system, reproductive system, and other body systems change between age 40 and age 60?

- What are the major issues of physical and mental health in middle adulthood?

- In what ways does cognitive function improve and/or decline?

PHYSICAL CHANGES

For a quick overview of the common physical changes of middle age, take another look at **Table 12.1** (page 367), which summarizes most of the evidence. Changes or declines in many physical functions occur very gradually through the 40s and 50s. For a few physical functions, however, change or decline is already substantial in the middle adult years.

THE BRAIN AND NERVOUS SYSTEM

Our knowledge of what happens to the normal, undamaged brain during middle adulthood has increased dramatically over the past few years because of the findings of recent MRI studies. One of the first studies of its kind, based at the UCLA Department of Neurology, compared brain development in a cross-sectional study of people ranging from the first to ninth decade of life (Sowell, et al., 2003). For example, **Figure 14.1** (page 422) shows significant changes in two main components of the brain. Broadly speaking, it shows that white matter volume crests during middle adulthood. However, grey matter volume continues its decline that began in childhood and does not level off until about age 60. The volume of *cerebrospinal fluid* (CSF) also increases steadily across the lifespan. It is important to note that new synapses are continuing to form in middle age. Earlier in life, though, new synapses form more rapidly or at the same rate as old connections are lost. In middle age, it appears, more synapses are lost than are formed; this net loss is associated with the cognitive declines seen in older adults.

As noted in **Chapter 12**, hidden within the global changes depicted in **Figure 14.1** are localized changes that occur in various parts of the brain at different times and rates. It is suspected that the decline in grey matter density that occurs after age 40 is

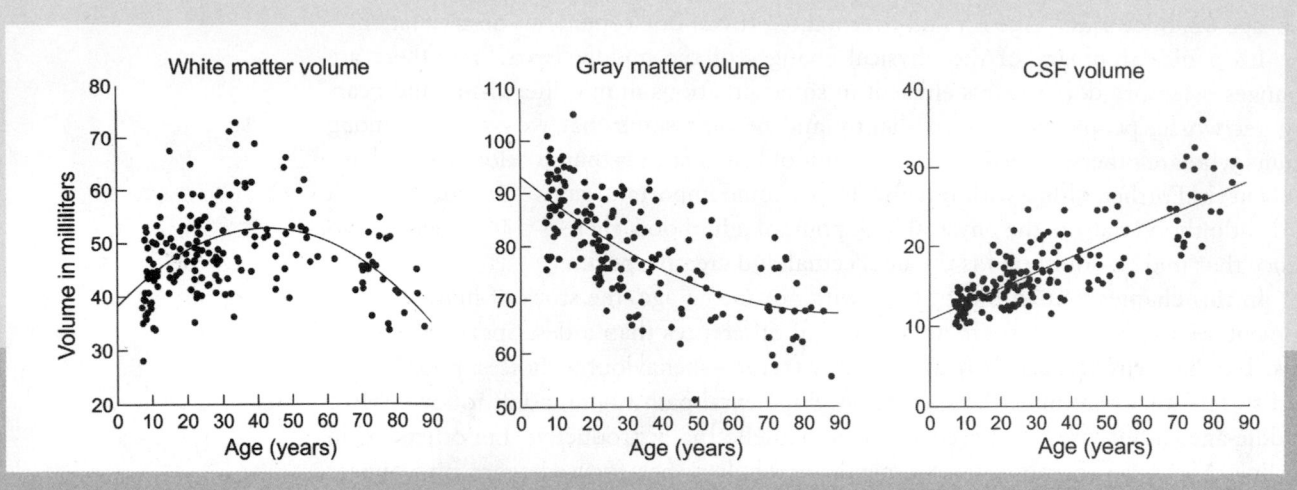

Figure 14.1

These graphs illustrate the changes that take place in the brain across the lifespan. White matter volume increases until middle adulthood and then declines. Grey matter volume declines from childhood and then levels off at the end of middle adulthood. Cerebrospinal fluid increases at a regular rate across the lifespan.

(*Source:* Image courtesy of Elizabeth R. Sowell, Ph.D., UCLA Laboratory of Neuro Imaging. From Sowell et al, 2003, Figure 6, p. 314.)

associated with subtle degenerative processes—this is the time when white matter growth peaks and total brain weight begins to decline (Sowell, et al., 2003; Sowell, Thompson, & Toga, 2004). With the exception of specific regions in the left temporal lobe that are associated with language comprehension skills, the general rule of brain maturation is that the areas of the brain that develop last are the ones that begin to decline first, namely areas located within the frontal and parietal lobes. You can read more about the associated changes in cognitive function later in the chapter.

In addition, developmentalists know that behavioural choices and mental health affect the adult brain. For example, alcoholics and nonalcoholics differ in the distribution of electrical activity in the brain (Duffy, 1994). The brains of depressed and non-depressed adults differ as well. Further, a number of serious mental illnesses, such as schizophrenia, are associated with structural variations in the brain. What researchers don't know yet is whether the brains of alcoholics, depressed persons, or schizophrenics were different from others before the onset of their difficulties. The longitudinal research necessary to answer such questions hasn't yet been done.

Besides studying the effects of trauma and disease, neuropsychologists are also involved in investigating a very important issue in the study of aging—whether declines in cognitive functions are caused by a loss of neurological processing resources. To find out, researchers examine how the brains of young and middle-aged people respond to cognitive tasks. Such studies have produced a rather complex set of findings.

One fairly consistent finding is that cognitive tasks activate a larger area of brain tissue in middle-aged adults than they do in younger adults (Gunter, Jackson, & Mulder, 1998). Of course, neuropsychologists don't know why, but they speculate that cognitive processing in middle-aged adults is less selective than it is in younger adults. It's as if the middle-aged brain has a more difficult time finding just the right neurological tool to carry out a particular function, and so it activates more tools than are necessary. This lack of selectivity could account for differences between age groups in the speed at which cognitive tasks are carried out.

One way of examining this hypothesis is to see if it explains individual differences as well as age variation. Typically, when middle-aged and young adults are compared, the range of individual differences within each age group is far greater than the average difference between the two age groups. Researchers find that in participants in both age groups who perform poorly on tasks such as remembering lists of associated words (*table–chair*) or nonassociated words (*knife–car*), larger areas of the brain are activated than in those who perform well.

In addition, the brains of high performers are more sensitive to different kinds of tasks. For example, recalling nonassociated words requires a larger area of activation (more neurological tools) than recalling associated words, because nonassociated words are more difficult to memorize. The more difficult task activates more of the brain than the easy one does in all adults. But in both young and middle-aged high performers, the difference in brain activation on difficult and easy tasks is much greater.

The brains of middle-aged and younger adults also respond differently to sensory stimuli. For example, patterns of brain waves in different areas vary across age groups when participants are presented with a simple auditory stimulus such as a musical tone (Yordanova, Kolev, & Basar, 1998). Research along this line has suggested that middle-aged adults may have less ability to control attention processes by inhibiting brain responses to irrelevant stimuli (Amenedo & Diaz, 1998, 1999). Their difficulty with attentional control could be another reason for the average difference in processing speed between young and middle-aged adults.

Such findings might lead you to conclude that, in everyday situations requiring intense concentration and rapid judgments, middle-aged adults would perform more poorly than their younger counterparts. Interestingly, though, recent research on lapses of concentration and poor decision-making among drivers shows just the opposite (Dobson, Brown, Ball, Powers, & McFadden, 1999). Younger drivers exhibit more lapses in attention and driving errors than middle-aged drivers. These lapses and errors, combined with younger drivers' greater likelihood of driving after drinking alcohol, help account for the different accident rates of young and middle-aged adults. Such findings, when considered with those on age differences in brain function, illustrate the difficulty researchers face in finding direct relationships between age-related brain differences and cross-age variations in behaviour.

THE REPRODUCTIVE SYSTEM

If you were asked to name a single significant physical change occurring in the years of middle adulthood, chances are you'd say *menopause*—especially if you're a woman. The more general term is the **climacteric**, which refers to the years of middle or late adulthood in both men and women during which reproductive capacity declines or is lost.

climacteric
the term used to describe the adult period during which reproductive capacity declines or is lost

MALE CLIMACTERIC In men, the climacteric is extremely gradual, with a slow loss of reproductive capacity, although the rate of change varies widely from one man to the next, and there are documented cases of men in their 90s fathering children. On average, the quantity of viable sperm produced declines slightly, beginning perhaps at about age 40. The testes also shrink very gradually, and the volume of seminal fluid declines after about age 60.

The causal factor is most likely a very slow drop in testosterone levels, beginning in early adulthood and continuing well into old age. There has been some disagreement among researchers about whether such a decline actually occurs; some longitudinal studies among healthy adults have shown no such decline (e.g., Harman & Tsitouras, 1980). But the weight of the evidence seems to point to a small, very gradual, average decline in testosterone over the adult years, with wide variation from one man to the next in normal hormone levels (Tsitouras & Bulat, 1995).

This decline in testosterone is implicated in the gradual loss of muscle tissue (and hence strength) that becomes evident in the middle and later years, as well as in the increased risk of heart disease in middle and old age. It also appears to affect sexual function. In particular, in the middle years, the incidence of erectile dysfunction (ED) begins to increase—although many things other than the slight decline in testosterone contribute to this change, including an increased incidence of poor health, especially heart disease, use of blood pressure medication (and other medications), alcohol abuse, and smoking.

The most complete information about ED in mid-life comes from a study in Boston involving 1290 men between the ages of 40 and 90 (Feldman, Goldstein, Hatzichristou, Krane, & McKinlay, 1994). Each man completed a questionnaire about the frequency and duration of his erections and rated himself as having no ED or minimal, moderate, or complete ED. Those describing themselves as having minimal ED reported some problems achieving and/or maintaining erections, although most of these men did still have active sex lives. Those describing themselves as having moderate ED had more significant difficulties, but most also reported that they had intercourse at least occasionally. Researchers noted an increase in both categories of ED during the middle years, a finding replicated in other studies (Keil, Sutherland, Knapp, Waid, & Gazes, 1992). Overall, though, a clear majority of men in the Boston study reported that they were experiencing either no ED or only a minimal degree of ED.

MENOPAUSE   Declines in key sex hormones are also clearly implicated in the set of changes in women called **menopause**, which means literally the cessation of the menses. You'll remember from **Chapter 10** that secretion of several forms of estrogen by the ovaries increases rapidly during puberty, triggering the onset of menstruation as well as stimulating the development of breasts and secondary sex characteristics. In the adult woman, estrogen levels are high during the first 14 days of the menstrual cycle, stimulating the release of an ovum and the preparation of the uterus for possible implantation. *Progesterone,* which is secreted by the ruptured ovarian follicle from which the ovum emerges, rises during the second half of the menstrual cycle and stimulates the sloughing off of accumulated material in the uterus each month if conception has not occurred.

The Society of Obstetricians and Gynaecologists of Canada (SOGC) (2001) regularly sponsors the annual National Menopause Awareness Month (October 15–November 15) in order to provide accurate information and tips for coping with symptoms of both perimenopause and menopause. About 4 million Canadian women are currently experiencing menopause. The transition phase of menopause, called *perimenopause,* can be expected to begin after age 40. Menopause usually occurs when a woman is between her late 40s and early 50s, and can last beyond age 55 (SOGC, 2001). About 1 woman in 12 experiences menopause before the age of 40, referred to by physicians as *premature menopause* (Wich & Carnes, 1995).

MENOPAUSAL PHASES   Menopause, like puberty, is often thought of as a single event. However, it actually occurs over several years, and researchers generally agree that it consists of three phases. First, during the **premenopausal phase**, estrogen levels begin to fluctuate and decline, typically in the late 30s or early 40s, producing irregular menstrual periods in many women. The ovaries are less sensitive to cyclical hormonal signals, and many women experience *anovulatory cycles,* or cycles in which no ovum is released. Even though no ovum is produced, estrogen levels are high enough in premenopausal women to produce periodic bleeding. However, the lack of ovulation results in a dramatic drop in progesterone. Thus, many experts believe that the menstrual

menopause
the cessation of monthly menstrual cycles in middle-aged women

premenopausal phase
the stage of menopause during which estrogen levels fall somewhat, menstrual periods are less regular, and anovulatory cycles begin to occur

irregularity associated with the premenopausal period is due to progesterone loss rather than estrogen loss (Lee, 1996).

During the **perimenopausal phase**, estrogen levels decrease and women experience more extreme variations in the timing of their menstrual cycles. In addition, about 75% of perimenopausal women experience *hot flashes,* sudden sensations of feeling hot. Of those who have hot flashes, 85% will have them for more than a year; a third or more will have them for 5 years or more (Kletzky & Borenstein, 1987). It is hypothesized that fluctuating levels of estrogen and other hormones cause a woman's blood vessels to expand and contract erratically, thus producing hot flashes (see **No Easy Answers**).

During a hot flash, the temperature of the skin can rise as much as 4°C in some parts of the body, although the core body temperature actually drops (Kronenberg, 1994). Hot flashes last, on average, about 3 minutes and may recur as seldom as daily or as often as three times per hour (Bellantoni & Blackman, 1996). Most women learn to manage these brief periods of discomfort if they occur during the day. However, hot flashes frequently disrupt women's sleep. When this happens, it sets in motion a series of changes that are actually due to sleep deprivation rather than menopause. For example, lack of sleep can lead to mental confusion, difficulty with everyday memory tasks, and emotional instability. Thus, perimenopausal women may have the subjective feeling that they are "going crazy" when the real problem is that hot flashes are preventing them from getting enough sleep. The general light-headedness and shakiness that accompany some women's hot flashes can add to this sensation.

Eventually, estrogen and progesterone drop to consistently low levels and menstruation ceases altogether. Once a women has ceased to menstruate for a year, she is in the **postmenopausal phase**. In postmenopausal women, estradiol and estrone, both types of estrogen, drop to about a quarter or less of their premenopausal levels. Progesterone decreases even more, as a result of the cessation of ovulation, although the adrenal glands continue to provide postmenopausal women with some progesterone.

The reduction in estrogen during the perimenopausal and postmenopausal phases also has effects on genital and other tissue. The breasts become less firm, the genitals and the uterus shrink somewhat, and the vagina becomes both shorter and smaller in diameter. The walls of the vagina also become somewhat thinner and less elastic and produce less lubrication during intercourse (McCoy, 1998; Wich & Carnes, 1995).

perimenopausal phase
the stage of menopause during which estrogen and progesterone levels are erratic, menstrual cycles may be very irregular, and women begin to experience symptoms such as hot flashes

postmenopausal phase
the last stage of menopause; a woman is postmenopausal when she has had no menstrual periods for a year or more

No Easy Answers

The Pros and Cons

of Hormone

Replacement Therapy

Most of the physical symptoms and effects of menopause—including hot flashes, thinning of the vaginal wall, and loss of vaginal lubrication—can be dramatically reduced by taking estrogen and progesterone. Moreover, hormone replacement is associated with a reduction in mood swings in menopausal women (Klaiber, Broverman, Vogel, Peterson, & Snyder, 1997). However, researchers have found that women are very poorly informed about both menopause itself and the potential risks and benefits of hormone replacement therapy. Apparently, unlike women in nonindustrialized societies, who rely on older women for information, women in the industri-alized world rely on drug manufacturers' advertise-ments on television and in women's magazines for information about menopause (Berg & Lipson, 1999; Clinkingbeard, Minton, Davis, & McDermott, 1999; Whittaker, 1998). Analyses of these sources of information have shown that they contain more misleading than helpful information (Gannon & Stevens, 1998). Thus, a woman who wants to make an informed decision about alternatives for dealing with the effects of menopause has to look beyond these information sources.

Hormone replacement therapy has had a somewhat checkered history. In the 1950s and

1960s, estrogen therapy became extremely common. In some surveys, as many as half of all post-menopausal women in the United States reported using replacement estrogen, many of them over periods of 10 years or more (Stadel & Weiss, 1975). In the 1970s, however, new evidence showed that the risk of endometrial cancer (cancer of the lining of the uterus) increased threefold to tenfold in women taking replacement estrogen (Nathanson & Lorenz, 1982). Not surprisingly, when this information became public, the use of estrogen therapy dropped dramatically.

The third act in this drama was the discovery that a combination of estrogen and progesterone, at quite low dosages, had the same benefits as estrogen alone and eliminated the increased risk of endometrial cancer. Furthermore, studies also made clear that the use of replacement estrogen it significantly retards the bone loss of osteoporosis (Barrett-Connor & Bush, 1991; Ross, Paganini-Hill, Mack, & Henderson, 1987). Research reveals that this benefit occurs with the newer estrogen-progesterone combinations as well as with estrogen alone (e.g., Cauley et al., 1995; Stampfer et al., 1991; Working Group for the PEPI Trial, 1995).

This sounds almost too good to be true, doesn't it? Why shouldn't every postmenopausal woman be on a program of hormone replacement? There are serious counterarguments: First, many women consider the process of aging, including the changes of menopause, to be natural physical processes with which they do not want to tinker. Second, although scientists have evidence that hormone replacement therapy is linked to slightly lower overall cancer risks, some studies have found that it is associated with somewhat higher rates of breast cancer and very slightly higher rates of ovarian cancer (Posthuma, Westendorp, & Vandenbroucke, 1994). In the Nurses' Health Study (which you read about in **Chapter 12**), researchers

found that for every woman diagnosed with breast cancer who did not take replacement hormones, there were roughly 1.4 cases of breast cancer diagnosed among women who did use hormone therapy (Colditz et al., 1995). The equivalent comparison for ovarian cancers, drawn from another study (Rodriguez et al., 1995), was 1.0 case of ovarian cancer in women who did not take hormones and 1.15 cases in women who did. Third, the latest milestone in this story is the NIH's Women's Health Initiative (2004) study of HRT. Findings included increased risk of heart attack, stroke, blood clots, dementia, and breast cancer. There was so much concern that certain parts of the study were stopped. Since the release of these findings, prescriptions of estrogen-progesterone for HRT have dropped off the charts.

How can an individual woman add up these various benefits and risks? Among other things, a woman should consider not only her present discomfort, but also her overall risk of heart disease and cancer (heart disease is actually the larger overall risk in the years of middle and late adulthood), which includes her family history of these diseases. Above all, a woman entering menopause should commit herself to seeking information beyond what can be learned from television and women's magazines. For example, Canadian experts (Blake, et al., 2002) advise that women should discuss their concerns with health care professionals in order to make an informed choice based on their unique medical history. Moreover, it is recommended that hormone replacement therapy should be used primarily for the treatment of menopausal symptoms rather than solely for the prevention of disease, especially among post-menopausal women in whom alternative lifestyle changes should be encouraged, including exercise, eating a healthy diet, smoking cessation, and the like (SOGC, 2002).

PSYCHOLOGICAL EFFECTS OF MENOPAUSE One other aspect of the climacteric in women deserves some mention. It has been part of folklore for a very long time that menopause involves major emotional upheaval as well as clear physical changes. Women were presumed to be emotionally volatile, angry, depressed, even shrewish during these mid-life years. Studies have shown that, in accordance with this myth, women are likely to view menopausal moods and behaviour as being beyond their control (Lawlor & Choi, 1998; Poole, 1998). However, the available evidence contradicts this myth.

Four relevant, well-designed longitudinal studies, three in the United States and one in Sweden, have examined this aspect of menopause. In the largest and most recent of these studies, researchers followed a group of 3049 women aged 40 to 60 over a 10-year period (Busch, Zonderman, & Costa, 1994). None of the studies reported any connection between menopausal status and a rise in depression or other psychological symptoms (Busch et al., 1994; Hallstrom & Samuelsson, 1985; Matthews et al., 1990; McKinlay, McKinlay, & Brambilla, 1987). Subsequent studies have produced similar findings (Slaven & Lee, 1998).

What does seem to be associated with moods and social functioning during menopause is, among other things, a woman's overall negativity and number of life stressors before entering menopause (Dennerstein, Lehert, Burger, & Dudley, 1999; Woods & Mitchell, 1997). In other words, a woman's negativity may be attributed to menopause when, in reality, it may be a long-standing component of her personality. Alternatively, she may have a particularly stressful life, and menopausal symptoms are just one more source of difficulty.

> ## Critical Thinking
>
> What is your own view of menopause? How much has your view been influenced by negative stereotypes of menopausal women in the media?

In addition, the actual level of symptoms women experience makes a difference. It isn't surprising that women who are most uncomfortable because of hot flashes and other physical changes, and whose symptoms last the longest, experience the most depression and negative mood. At any rate, research suggests that once they reach the postmenopausal phase, these women's dispositions change.

Cultural factors also influence the menopause experience. In contrast to our society's perspective, there are many societies in which menopause is viewed positively (McMaster, Pitts, & Poyah, 1997). For women in such cultures, pregnancy and childbearing continue to be major threats to health. Thus, with concerns about conception behind them, women in these societies report few menopausal symptoms and generally positive attitudes toward this change. In contrast, women in North America view menopause as a cardinal sign that one's youth has ended, and they often confuse symptoms of menopause with normal consequences of aging (Jones, 1997). For example, they may think that wrinkled skin is caused by menopause. Thus, research has demonstrated that the more women know about menopause, the less negatively they view it (Hunter & O'Dea, 1999; Liao & Hunter, 1998).

SEXUAL ACTIVITY Despite changes in the reproductive system, the great majority of middle-aged adults remain sexually active, although the frequency of sex declines somewhat during these years (Laumann, Gagnon, Michael, & Michaels, 1994; Michael, Gagnon, Laumann, & Kolata, 1994). It is unlikely that this decline during mid-life is due wholly or even largely to drops in sex hormone levels; women do not experience major estrogen declines until their late 40s, but the decline in sexual activity begins much sooner. And the drop in testosterone among men is so gradual and slight during these years that it cannot be the full explanation. An alternative explanation is that the demands of other roles are simply so pressing that middle-aged adults find it hard to find time for sex.

THE SKELETAL SYSTEM

Another change that begins to be quite significant in middle adulthood is a loss of calcium from the bones, resulting in reduced bone mass and more brittle and porous bones. This process is called **osteoporosis**. Bone loss begins at about age 30 for both men and women, but in women the process is accelerated by menopause. The major consequence

osteoporosis
loss of bone mass with age, resulting in more brittle and porous bones

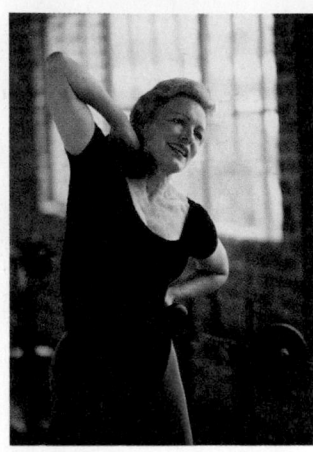

Any weight-bearing exercise—even walking—will help prevent osteoporosis.
(*Photo:* David Madison/Getty Images)

of this loss of bone density is a significantly increased risk of fractures, beginning as early as age 50 for women, and much later for men. In the United States, it is estimated that almost one in four women will experience a hip fracture before the age of 80 (Lindsay, 1985). Among older women (and men), such fractures can be a major cause of disability and reduced activity, so osteoporosis is not a trivial change. In fact, University of Toronto researchers found that with advancing age, there was an exponential increase in hip fractures, accompanying lengths of stay in the hospital, and death rates following the fracture for both men and women (Papadimitropoulos, Coyte, Josse, & Greenwood, 1997).

In women, it is clear that bone loss is linked quite directly to estrogen and progesterone levels. Researchers know that these hormones fall dramatically after menopause, and it is the timing of menopause rather than age that signals the increase in rate of bone loss. Researchers also know that the rate of bone loss drops to premenopausal levels among women who take replacement hormones, all of which makes the link quite clear (Duursma, Raymakers, Boereboom, & Scheven, 1991). While the overall pattern of bone loss seems to be a part of primary aging, the amount of such loss nonetheless varies quite a lot from one individual to another. **Table 14.1** lists the known risk factors for osteoporosis.

Aside from taking replacement hormones, women can help prevent osteoporosis by one or both of two strategies. First, they can get enough calcium during early adulthood, so that peak levels of bone mass are as robust as possible. Second, throughout adult life women can get regular exercise, particularly weight-bearing exercise such as walking or strength training. In one study, postmenopausal women who began a program of walking, jogging, or stair climbing for 1 hour three times a week showed an increase in bone mineral content of 5.2% within 9 months, compared with a loss of 1.4% in the nonexercising comparison group (Dalsky et al., 1988). But this benefit faded if the exercise was not maintained. In another study, a group of middle-aged or older women were randomly assigned to a strength-training program consisting of twice-weekly sessions for a

TABLE 14.1	Risk Factors for Osteoporosis
Risk Factor	**Explanation**
Race	Whites are at higher risk than other races.
Gender	Women have considerably higher risk than men.
Weight	Those who are underweight are at higher risk.
Timing of climacteric	Women who experience early menopause and those who have had their ovaries removed are at higher risk, presumably because their estrogen levels decline at earlier ages.
Family history	Those with a family history of osteoporosis are at higher risk.
Diet	A diet low in calcium during adolescence and early adulthood results in lower peak levels of bone mass, and hence greater risk of falling below critical levels later. Whether there is any benefit in increasing intake of calcium postmenopausally remains in debate. Diets high in either caffeine (especially black coffee) or alcohol are also linked to higher risk.
Exercise	Those with a sedentary lifestyle are at higher risk. Prolonged immobility, such as bed rest, also increases the rate of bone loss. Exercise reduces the rate of bone loss.

(*Sources:* Dalsky et al., 1988; Duursma et al., 1991; Gambert, Schultz, & Hamdy, 1995; Goldberg & Hagberg, 1990; Gordon & Vaughan, 1986; Lindsay, 1985; Morrison et al., 1994; Smith, 1982.)

year. They showed a gain in bone density over the year, whereas women in a control group without such weight training showed a loss (Nelson et al., 1994).

VISION AND HEARING

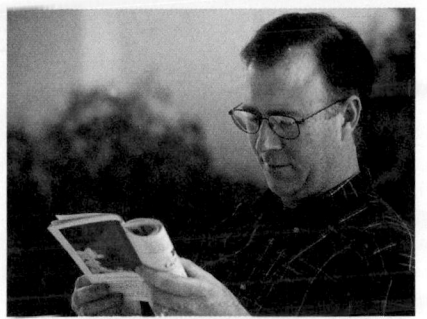

By age 45 or 50, nearly everyone needs glasses, especially for reading. (*Photo:* Myrleen Ferguson Cate/PhotoEdit)

One of the most noticeable physical changes occurring in the middle years is a loss of visual acuity. Most people find that they need reading glasses or bifocals by the time they are 45 or 50. Two changes in the eyes, collectively called **presbyopia**, are involved. First, the lens of the eye thickens. In a process that begins in childhood but produces noticeable effects only in middle adulthood, layer after layer of slightly pigmented material accumulates on the lens. Because light coming into the eye must pass through this thickened, slightly yellowed material, the total light reaching the retina decreases, which reduces a person's overall sensitivity to light waves, particularly to short wavelengths that are perceived as blue, blue-green, and violet (Fozard, 1990).

Because of this thickening of the lens, it is also harder and harder for the muscles surrounding the eye to change the shape of the lens to adjust the focus. In a young eye, the shape of the lens readily adjusts for distance, so no matter how near or far away some object may be, the light rays passing through the eye converge where they should, on the retina in the back of the eye, giving a sharp image. But as the thickening increases, the elasticity of the lens declines and it can no longer make these fine adjustments. Many images become blurry. In particular, the ability to focus clearly on near objects deteriorates rapidly in the 40s and early 50s. As a result, middle-aged adults often hold books and other items farther and farther away, because only in that way can they get a clear image. Finally, of course, they cannot read print at the distance at which they can focus, and they are forced to wear reading glasses or bifocals. These same changes also affect the ability to adapt quickly to variations in levels of light or glare, such as from passing headlights when driving at night or in the rain. So driving may become more stressful. All in all, these changes in the eyes, which appear to be a genuine part of primary aging, require both physical and psychological adjustment.

The equivalent process in hearing is called **presbycusis**. The auditory nerves and the structures of the inner ear gradually degenerate as a result of basic wear and tear, resulting primarily in losses in the ability to hear sounds of high and very low frequencies. But these changes do not accumulate to the level of significant hearing loss until somewhat later in life than is typical for presbyopia. Hearing loss is quite slow until about age 50, and only a small percentage of middle-aged adults require hearing aids (Fozard, 1990). After age 50 or 55, however, the rate of hearing loss accelerates. Such a pattern of loss also appears to be an aspect of primary aging. But some secondary aging processes are involved as well. In particular, the amount of hearing loss is considerably greater in adults who work or live in very noisy environments—or who listen regularly to very loud music (Baltes, Reese, & Nesselroade, 1977).

presbyopia
normal loss of visual acuity with aging, especially the ability to focus the eyes on near objects

presbycusis
normal loss of hearing with aging, especially of high-frequency tones

Before Going On

- What do researchers know about brain function in middle age?
- How does reproductive function change in men and women in middle age?
- What is osteoporosis, and what factors are associated with it?
- How do vision and hearing change in middle ages?

HEALTH PROMOTION AND WELLNESS

No single variable affects the quality of life in middle and late adulthood as much as health. A middle-aged person in good health often functions as well and has as much energy as much younger adults. However, mid-life is the era during which the poor health habits and risky behaviours of earlier years begin to catch up with us.

HEALTH TRENDS AT MID-LIFE

In general, middle-aged adults report that they experience annoying aches and pains with greater frequency than when they were younger (Helme, 1998). Moreover, many middle-aged adults, especially women, are unhappy with their bodies; most would prefer to be thinner (Allaz, Bernstein, Rouget, Archinard, & Morabia, 1998). In addition, the number of truly healthy adults declines in mid-life. Perhaps half of adults between 40 and 65 have either some diagnosed disease or disability or a significant but undiagnosed problem, such as the early stages of heart disease. Still, a 40-year-old's life expectancy is remarkably high, as you can see from **Figure 14.2**, and has been rising over the past few decades (Statistics Canada, 2000a). In addition, even though middle-aged adults have more chronic diseases and disabilities, such as diabetes and arthritis, than those who are younger, the risk of having chronic health problems is significantly lower now than it was in the 1970s (Crompton, 2000; Statistics Canada, 2000e). Similarly, disease-related death rates increase significantly in middle adulthood, as you can see in **Figure 14.3**. The two leading causes of death in middle age are heart disease and cancer.

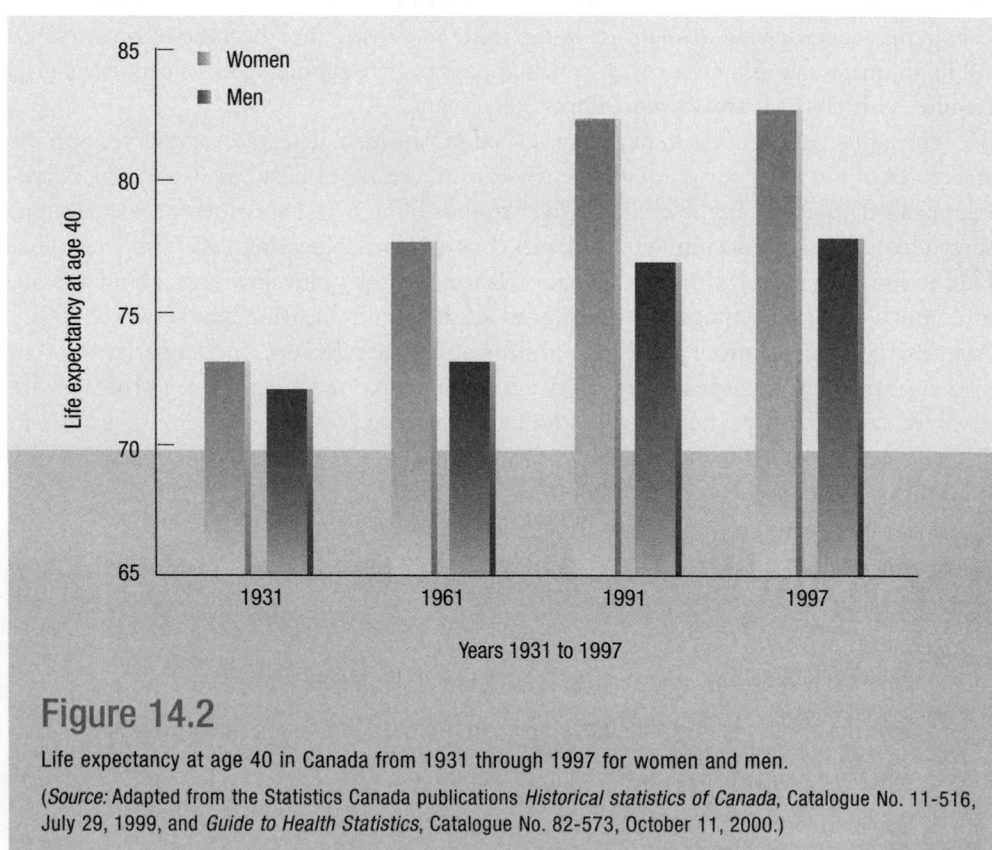

Figure 14.2

Life expectancy at age 40 in Canada from 1931 through 1997 for women and men.

(*Source:* Adapted from the Statistics Canada publications *Historical statistics of Canada*, Catalogue No. 11-516, July 29, 1999, and *Guide to Health Statistics*, Catalogue No. 82-573, October 11, 2000.)

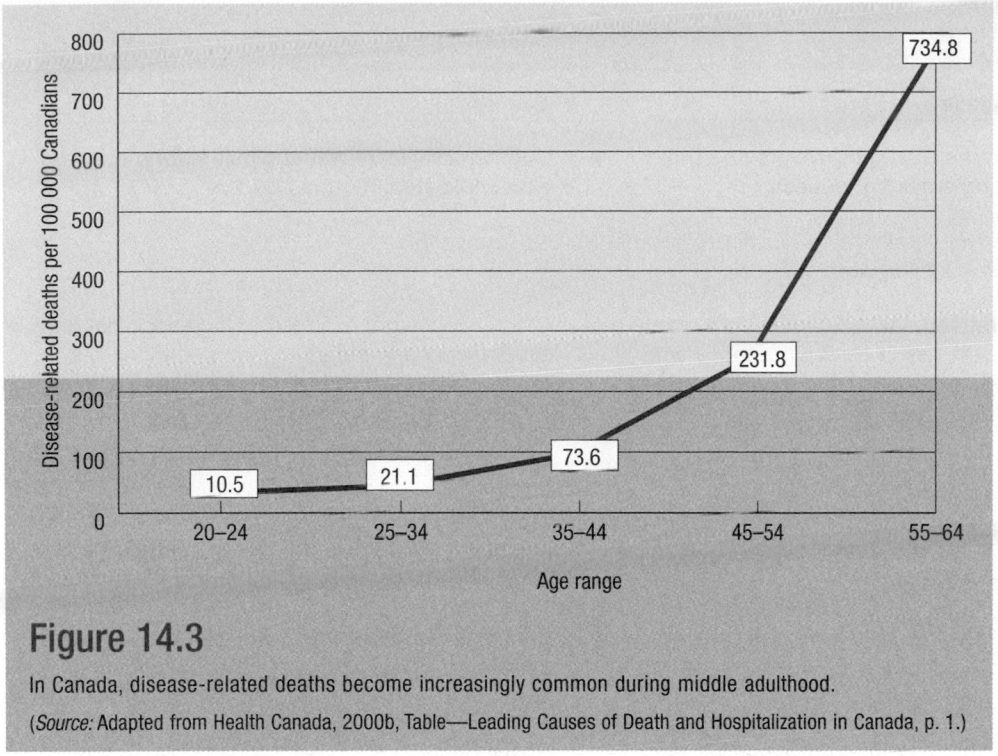

Figure 14.3

In Canada, disease-related deaths become increasingly common during middle adulthood.

(*Source:* Adapted from Health Canada, 2000b, Table—Leading Causes of Death and Hospitalization in Canada, p. 1.)

CARDIOVASCULAR DISEASE

The term **cardiovascular disease (CVD)** covers a variety of physical problems, but the key problem is in the arteries. In individuals suffering from CVD, the arteries become clogged with *plaque* (a fibrous or fatty substance), in a process called **atherosclerosis**. Eventually, vital arteries may become completely blocked, producing what laypeople call a heart attack (if the blockage is in the coronary arteries) or a stroke (if the blockage is in the brain). Atherosclerosis is not a normal part of aging. It is a disease, increasingly common with age, but not inevitable.

The rate of CVD has been dropping rapidly in Canada and in most other industrialized countries in recent years. Between 1985 and 1999, for example, it decreased by 45.8% among those aged 35 to 64 and dropped by 34.5% for those aged 65 to 84, fairly startling declines that have contributed greatly to the increased life expectancy among today's adults (Health Canada, 2002f). Yet CVD remains the leading cause of death among adults in Canada, accounting for 36% of all deaths in 1999: 35% of all deaths of men and 37% of all deaths of women (Health Canada, 2002f).

The best information about who is at risk for CVD comes from a number of long-term epidemiological studies, such as the Framingham study or the Nurses' Health Study, in which the health and habits of large numbers of individuals have been tracked over time. In the Framingham study, 5209 adults were first studied in 1948, when they were aged 30 to 59. Their health (and mortality) has since been assessed repeatedly, which makes it possible to identify characteristics that predict CVD (Anderson, Castelli, & Levy, 1987; Dawber, Kannel, & Lyell, 1963; Garrison, Gold, Wilson, & Kannel, 1993; Kannel & Gordon, 1980). More recent studies continue to suggest the same risk factors (Heart and Stroke Foundation of Canada, 1999). The left side of **Table 14.2** (page 432) lists the well-established risk factors that emerged from the Framingham study and similar studies, along with a few other risk factors that are more speculative.

cardiovascular disease (CVD)
a set of disease processes in the heart and circulatory system

atherosclerosis
narrowing of the arteries caused by deposits of a fatty substance called plaque

TABLE 14.2 Risk Factors for Heart Disease and Cancer

Risk	Heart Disease	Cancer
Smoking	Major risk; the more you smoke, the greater the risk. Quitting smoking reduces risk.	Substantially increases the risk of lung cancer; also implicated in other cancers.
Blood pressure	Systolic pressure above 140 or diastolic pressure above 90 linked to higher risk.	No known risk.
Weight	Some increased risk with any weight above the normal range; risk is greater for those with weight 20% or more above recommended amount.	Being overweight is linked to increased risk of several cancers, including breast cancer, but the risk is smaller than for heart disease.
Cholesterol	Clear risk with elevated levels of low-density lipoproteins.	No known risk.
Inactivity	Inactive adults have about twice the risk as those who exercise.	Inactivity is associated in some studies with higher rates of colon cancer.
Diet	High-fat, low-fibre diet increases risk; antioxidants, such as vitamin E, vitamin C, or beta-carotene, may decrease risk.	Results are still unclear; a high-fat diet is linked to risks of some cancers; high-fibre diets appear to be protective for some cancers.
Alcohol	Moderate intake of alcohol, especially wine, is linked to decreased CVD risk. Heavy drinking can weaken the heart muscle.	Heavy drinking is associated with cancers of the digestive system.
Heredity	Those with first-degree relatives with CVD have seven to ten times the risk; those who inherit a gene for a particular protein are up to twice as likely to have CVD.	Some genetic component with nearly every cancer.

(*Sources:* Centers for Disease Control, 1994; Gaziano & Hennekens, 1995; Hunter et al., 1996; Lee, Manson, Hennekens, & Paffenbarger, 1993; Manson et al., 1995; Morris, Kritchevsky, & Davis, 1994; Rich-Edwards, Manson, Hennekens, & Buring, 1995; Risch, Jain, Marrett, & Howe, 1994; Rose, 1993; Stampfer et al., 1993; Woodward & Tunstall-Pedoe, 1995.)

Because lists like the one in **Table 14.2** have appeared in numerous popular magazines and newspapers, there's not likely to be much that is news here, but there are still a few important points to be made. First, many Canadians have the risk factors listed in **Table 14.2**. In fact, surveys have shown that 41% of men and 33% of women aged 18 to 74 have two or more of the major CVD risk factors (smoking, high blood pressure, elevated cholesterol, physical inactivity, or obesity) (Heart and Stroke Foundation of Canada, 1999, p. 23). So, although rates of both smoking and high cholesterol have declined since the significance of these two risk factors became widely publicized, most Canadians could still do a much better job of reducing their heart disease risks (Heart and Stroke Foundation of Canada, 1999).

Second, it is important to understand that these risks are cumulative in the same way that the health habits investigated in the Alameda County study seem to be cumulative: The more high-risk behaviours or characteristics you have, the higher your risk of heart disease; the effect is not just additive. For example, high cholesterol is three times more serious in a heavy smoker than in a nonsmoker (Tunstall-Pedoe & Smith, 1990).

Critical Thinking

How many of the risk factors in **Table 14.2** apply to you?

Personality may also contribute to heart disease. The **type A personality pattern** was first described by two cardiologists, Meyer Friedman and Ray Rosenman (1974; Rosenman & Friedman, 1983). They were struck by the apparently consistent presence among patients who suffered from heart disease of several other characteristics, including competitive striving for achievement, a sense of time urgency, and hostility or aggressiveness. These people, whom Friedman and Rosenman named type A personalities, were perpetually comparing themselves with others, always wanting to win. They scheduled their lives tightly, timed themselves in routine activities, and often tried to do such tasks faster each time. They had frequent conflicts with their co-workers and family. Type B people, in contrast, were thought to be less hurried, more laid back, less competitive, and less hostile.

Early research by Friedman and Rosenman suggested that type A behaviour was linked to higher levels of cholesterol, and hence to increased risk of CVD, even among people who did not suffer from observable heart disease. Contradictory results from more extensive studies since then, however, have forced some modifications in the original hypothesis (e.g., Miller, Turner, Tindale, Posavac, & Dugoni, 1991; O'Connor, Manson, O'Connor, & Buring, 1995).

For one thing, not all facets of the type A personality, as originally described, seem to be equally significant for CVD. The most consistent link has been found between CVD and hostility; hard-driving competitiveness is less consistently linked to CVD. Time pressure is not consistently related to CVD at all (Friedman, Hawley, & Tucker, 1994; Miller, Smith, Turner, Guijarro, & Hallet, 1996).

What is more, for individuals who are already at high risk of CVD—because of smoking, high blood pressure, or the like—information about levels of hostility does not add to the accuracy of heart disease predictions. That is, if two adults each have high blood pressure and high cholesterol, they are both equally at risk of heart disease, even if one of them also displays high levels of hostility and the other does not. It is only among people who do not show other risk factors that measures of hostility add helpful information to the prediction. The effect is fairly small, but in large samples of otherwise low-risk adults, those who are hostile and competitive are slightly more likely to develop CVD than those who are more easygoing.

Most people who have analyzed this research would now agree that there is some kind of connection between personality and CVD. What is less clear is just which aspect(s) of personality are most strongly predictive. Some research suggests that measures of neuroticism or depression may be even better risk predictors than hostility (e.g., Cramer, 1991).

CANCER

The second leading cause of death in middle and old age (in industrialized countries, at least) is cancer. The lifetime probability of developing cancer is one chance in 2.3 for men and one chance in 2.6 for women. In addition, men have a 28.1% and women have a 23.4% lifetime probability of dying from cancer (National Cancer Institute of Canada (NCIC), 2004).

Lung cancer remains the number one cause of cancer deaths in Canada, killing 7.9% of men and 4.9% of women (NCIC, 2004). For men, the incidence of new cases of lung cancer peaked in the 1980s and has been dropping steadily; for women the bad news is that number of new cases of lung cancer has jumped nearly fourfold over the past 30 years. After lung cancer, the next leading cause of cancer deaths for Canadians is prostate cancer in men (3.8%) and breast cancer in women (3.7%). Colorectal cancer, the third major cause of cancer deaths for both genders in Canada, kills 3.6% of

type A personality pattern
a personality type associated with greater risk of coronary heart disease; it includes competitive achievement striving, a sense of time urgency, and, sometimes, hostility or aggressiveness

The Japanese, whose diet is very low in fat, have lower rates of some kinds of cancer than North Americans and Europeans. (*Photo:* Charles Gupton/Getty Images)

men and 3.2% of women (NCIC, 2003). As alarming as these figures sound, the Canadian Cancer Society (2004) warns that by 2010, cancer may replace CVD as the number one killer of Canadians as the baby boom generation moves into late adulthood.

Like heart disease, cancer does not strike in a totally random fashion. Indeed, as you can see in the right-hand column of **Table 14.2**, some of the same risk factors are implicated in both diseases. Most of these risk factors are at least partially under your own control. It helps to have established good health habits in early adulthood, but it is also clear from the research that improving your health habits in middle age can reduce your risks of both cancer and heart disease.

The most controversial item listed in **Table 14.2** is diet; in particular, scientists debate the role of dietary fat as a potential risk factor. The evidence linking high dietary fat and heart disease is increasingly clear; the data on dietary fat and cancer continue to be very confusing. Some experts estimate that as many as 35% of all cancer deaths can be attributed to diet (Bal & Foerster, 1991); others conclude that the effect is weak at best (e.g., Howe, 1994). This is definitely an area of active research. We can only hope that clearer conclusions—and thus clearer advice—will eventually emerge.

Animal studies demonstrate an obvious causal link between high-fat diets and cancer rates (e.g., Weisburger & Wynder, 1991). Of course, researchers can't experimentally manipulate human diets to find out if a high-fat diet causes cancer in humans. However, some of the strongest evidence for a link between diet and cancer comes from cross-national comparisons.

For example, the typical Japanese diet contains only about 15% fat; the typical North American diet is closer to 40% fat. Cancer is much less common in Japan. The possibility of a causal link between dietary fat and cancer is further strengthened by the observation that in those areas in Japan where Western dietary habits have been most extensively adopted, cancer rates have risen to nearer Western levels (Weisburger & Wynder, 1991).

Comparisons of diet and cancer rates in many nations show similar patterns. This is especially clear in results from a study of U.N. data (Kesteloot, Lesaffre, & Joossens, 1991). Researchers obtained two kinds of information for each of 36 countries: (1) the death rates from each of several types of cancer, and (2) the estimated per-person intake of fat from dairy products or lard. (Only dairy fat and lard are included because these are the major sources of saturated fats, thought to be more strongly implicated in disease.) **Figure 14.4** shows the relationship between deaths from rectal cancer and fat consumption, one of the clearest connections, by country; the average correlation between the two was .64. The average correlations for other types of cancer were .60 for breast cancer in women, .70 for prostate cancer in men, and .43 (in men) and .47 (in women) for colorectal cancer. For all cancers combined, the correlations were .58 in men and .65 in women.

The relationship among dietary fat, other risk factors, and cancer is obviously complex, and researchers have much yet to learn. For one thing, the typical diets in various countries differ widely in a great many other ways besides fat intake; any one of these differences might affect cancer rates. But cross-national comparisons of this type have generated highly useful hypotheses.

GENDER AND HEALTH

Figure 14.2 makes it clear that women's life expectancy is greater than men's. But what is not evident is an interesting paradox: Women live longer, but they have more diseases and disabilities. Women are more likely to describe their health as poor, to have more chronic conditions such as arthritis, and to be more limited in their daily activities. Such differences have been found in every country in which the pattern has been studied, including nonindustrialized countries (Rahman, Strauss, Gertler, Ashley, & Fox, 1994).

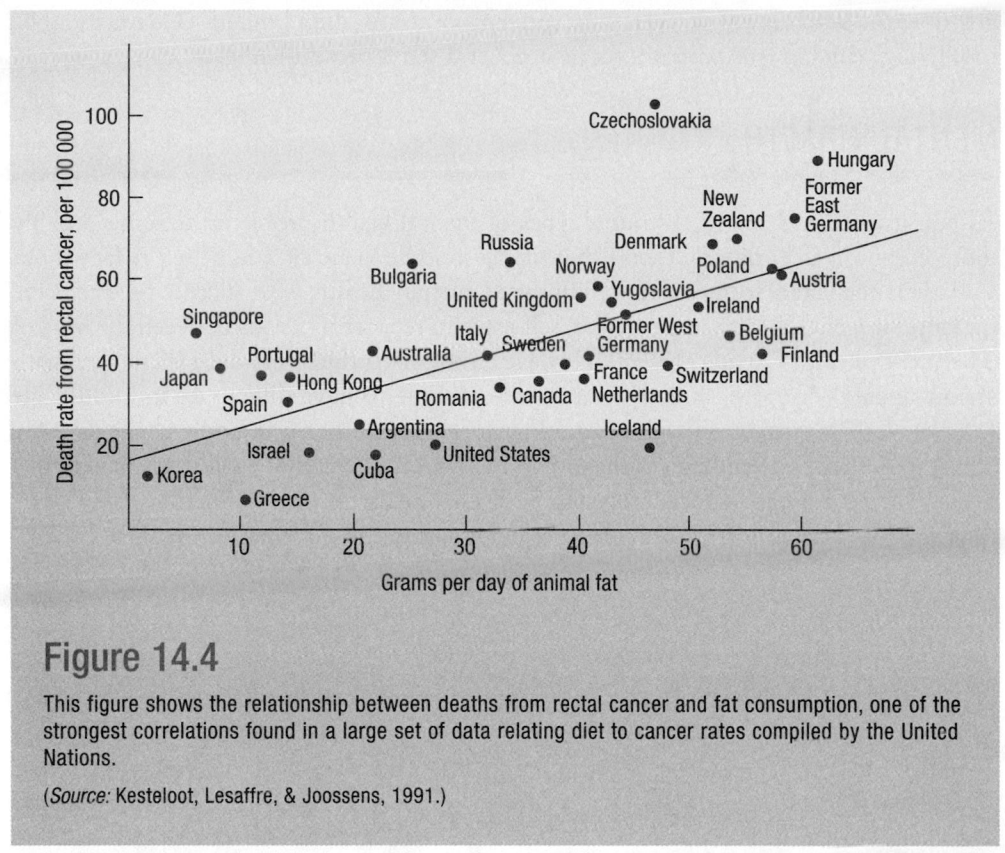

Figure 14.4

This figure shows the relationship between deaths from rectal cancer and fat consumption, one of the strongest correlations found in a large set of data relating diet to cancer rates compiled by the United Nations.

(*Source:* Kesteloot, Lesaffre, & Joossens, 1991.)

This difference is already present in early adulthood and grows larger with age. By old age, women are substantially more likely than men to be chronically ill (Guralnik, Land, Blazer, Fillenbaum, & Branch, 1993; Kunkel & Applebaum, 1992). In early adulthood, this gender difference in disease rate can be largely attributed to health problems associated with childbearing. At later ages, the difference cannot be explained in this same way.

How is it possible that men die younger but are healthier while they are alive? Researchers suggest that the apparent paradox can be resolved by considering sex differences in potentially fatal conditions such as cardiovascular disease (Verbrugge, 1989). In Canada, 101 of every 100 000 men between the ages of 45 and 54 die of heart disease annually, compared with only 35 of every 100 000 women (Health Canada, 2002f). This difference in rates of heart disease diminishes once women are past menopause, although it does not disappear totally even in late old age.

It isn't just that men have higher rates of CVD; they also are more likely to die from the disease once it has been acquired. One reason may be that the heart muscles of women who have CVD seem to be better able to adapt to stresses such as physical exertion (van Doornen, Snieder, & Boomsma, 1998). In addition, once they suffer a heart attack, women recover to a higher level of physical functioning than men do (Bosworth et al., 2000). Sex differences in health habits also seem to contribute to women's greater ability to recover from CVD. For example, women are more likely to get regular checkups and to seek help earlier in an illness than men are (Verbrugge & Wingard, 1987).

By contrast, women are more likely than men to suffer from nonfatal chronic ailments such as arthritis. Because chronic pain is characteristic of

Chances are this man will die before his wife does, but she will be more troubled by chronic illnesses in her middle and later years. (*Photo:* Eyewire)

arthritis, the activities of women who suffer from it are often limited. Understandably, too, living with chronic pain affects their general sense of well-being.

MENTAL HEALTH

As you learned in **Chapter 12,** most types of mental health problems are considerably more common in early adulthood than in the middle years of adult life. In fact, both Canadian men and women report improved mental health with increasing age. One measure of mental health in particular, self-esteem, reportedly peaks between the ages of 35 and 54 (Health Canada, 1999e). However, about two-thirds of adults diagnosed with serious mental disorders in early adulthood continue to have difficulties in middle age (Meeks, 1997). Further, though most addictive disorders begin in adolescence or early adulthood, they frequently go undiagnosed until the middle adulthood years, when they begin to have dramatic effects on health and other areas of functioning that sufferers or their families can no longer deny (see **Development in the Information Age**).

Development in the
Information Age
Is the Internet Addictive?

Although new technologies are usually associated with the young, surveys suggest that middle-aged and even older adults spend more time "surfing the net" than those who are younger (Hinden, 2000; Miller, 1996). Recently, some mental health professionals have raised concerns about the amount of time some individuals spend online. Some claim to have discovered a new disorder they call Internet Addictive Disorder, or IAD (Griffiths, 1999). The criteria for the disorder are the same as for other addictions. Specifically, to be diagnosed with IAD, a person must demonstrate a pattern of Internet use that interferes with normal educational, occupational, and social functioning.

To be sure, there are individuals who spend a great deal of time online and who admit that Internet use often interferes with other activities (Brenner, 1997). However, to justify the use of the term addiction in relation to a specific activity, the activity itself must have some addictive power. For example, alco-

hol induces an altered state of consciousness that users find desirable. The altered state reinforces the behaviour of consuming alcohol. Thus, those who propose that IAD exists are, by implication, saying that the experience of being online has the capacity to induce some kind of reinforcing state in users.

Some Internet users report that online communication is more pleasurable than face-to-face social encounters (Chou, Chou, & Tyang, 1998). But is this sense of pleasure enough to bring about an addiction, or is socializing on the Internet nothing more than an easy way to escape the usual pressures of social interaction? Similarly, use of online pornography for sexual gratification is clearly a problem for some people (Cooper, Putnam, Planchon, & Boies, 1999). However, is it any different from the use of conventional sources of pornography such as adult magazines and videos?

In fact, research has suggested that excessive Internet use may be part of a

behaviour pattern that is consistent across several media (Greenberg, Lewis, & Dodd, 1999). Those who are "addicted" to the Internet also spend inordinate amounts of time watching television and playing video games. They are also more likely to be addicted to alcohol and other substances.

Thus, rather than being a distinct addictive disorder, what seems more likely is that Internet use is a new means by which people can escape from everyday problems. As such, it is no different from books, television, movies, or even drugs. The Internet may simply provide people who have some kind of tendency toward a specific addictive problem with an additional avenue through which to express this tendency. Thus, mental health professionals who oppose the idea of Internet addiction suggest that excessive time online either is a symptom of another disorder or may simply reflect fascination with a new medium (Griffiths, 1999; Grohol, 1999).

For example, **alcoholism**, which is the physical and psychological dependence on alcohol, is frequently diagnosed in the middle adulthood years. Regular heavy drinking puts people at risk for developing the harmful outcomes associated with alcohol dependence. The Statistical Report on the Health of Canadians (Health Canada, 1999e) found that Canadian men are more likely to be regular heavy drinkers than women, which means that they consumed five or more drinks at least once a month on average. For instance, 9% of men versus 3% of women reported drinking heavily on more than 52 occasions in the previous year. The rate of heavy regular drinking peaks during the young adult years, with more than half of young adults drinking heavily at least some of the time. The rates begin to decline at ages 34 to 44, and continue to decline thereafter.

The strongest risk factor for alcoholism in both men and women is a family history of problem drinking (Curran et al., 1999; Sher & Gotham, 1999). This suggests a genetic basis for the disease, and twin studies also suggest that heritability may be a factor, as the concordance rate for alcoholism in identical twins is about 50% (Kendler, Neale, Heath, Kessler, & Eaves, 1994; McGue, Pickens, & Svikis, 1992). However, variables such as socioeconomic status, personality, attitudes toward drinking, amount of time spent socializing with drinkers, and cultural attitudes that endorse drinking as a means of dealing with life's problems also contribute to alcoholism (Curran et al., 1999; Pacheco, 1999; Sher & Gotham, 1999).

The individual costs of alcoholism are high as well. In one longitudinal study, researchers found that about one-third of participants who had been hospitalized for alcoholism in their late 20s or early 30s were still abusing alcohol 10 years later (Powell et al., 1998). Another third abstained from alcohol, but the remaining third had died—a rather remarkable rate of mortality for such a young group. Of course, age-related mortality patterns suggest that many of these young men died from accidents or homicides, not from the physical effects of alcohol. However, alcohol is frequently a factor in fatal automobile accidents and is often associated with homicide. Alcoholics are also more likely to attempt suicide, both in early adulthood and in middle adulthood (Rossow, Romelsjoe, & Leifman, 1999). Thus, the reason why rates of alcoholism decline from early to middle adulthood may be the extraordinarily high mortality rate of young alcoholics.

Among alcoholics who survive to middle age, the natural declines associated with primary aging interact with the effects of long-term heavy drinking. For example, some parts of the brains of middle-aged alcoholics are smaller and are less responsive to stimuli than the brains of nonalcoholics (Laakso et al., 2000; Polo, Escera, Gual, & Grau, 1999). Functional deficits among alcoholics include problems with memory and language. Cardiovascular disease is more prevalent among alcoholics as well, because long-term exposure to alcohol weakens the muscles of the heart along with the valves and walls of the body's blood vessels. Further, long-term heavy drinking damages the digestive system, impairs the immune system, and contributes to losses in muscle strength (Laso et al., 1999; Tarter et al., 1997). In women, alcoholism is associated with a delay in the course of the phases of menopause (Torgerson, Thomas, Campbell, & Reid, 1997).

The result of this interaction between aging and alcohol abuse is that alcoholics face an increased risk of health problems and death (Dawson, 2000). A longitudinal study involving more than 40 000 males in Norway found that the rate of death prior to age 60 was significantly higher among alcoholics than among nonalcoholics (Rossow & Amundsen, 1997). Not surprising, perhaps, is the finding that alcoholics were three times as likely to die in automobile accidents as their nonalcoholic peers. However, alcoholics were also almost three times as likely to die of heart disease and had twice the rate of deaths from cancer.

Many of the effects of long-term heavy alcohol use are reversible if a person stops drinking. To do so, most alcoholics need help. For example, there is evidence that recovering alcoholics for whom religious faith and participation in a supportive faith

alcoholism
physical and psychological dependence on alcohol

community are important are more optimistic about the recovery process and have less anxiety than others (Plante & Pardini, 2000). Thus, some mental health professionals believe that these positive effects of religious faith may increase the likelihood of recovery from alcoholism.

For most alcoholics, a multiple treatment approach is called for (Kaplan & Saddock, 1991). Alcoholics require medical attention to deal with alcohol's physical effects. Medications may be helpful in managing withdrawal from alcohol and depression. In addition, most mental health professionals recommend self-help programs, such as Alcoholics Anonymous, where alcoholics instruct and support each other through the process of recovery.

Before Going On

- What are the major trends in health during middle adulthood?
- How does coronary heart disease develop?
- What factors contribute to cancer?
- What are some important differences in the health of middle-aged men and women?
- What are some of the consequences of alcoholism for middle-aged adults?

COGNITIVE FUNCTIONING

In the middle adult years, some cognitive abilities improve, while others slow down a bit. Still, many adults have acquired large bodies of knowledge and skill that help them compensate for losses and solve problems within their areas of expertise more efficiently than younger adults do.

A MODEL OF PHYSICAL AND COGNITIVE AGING

Many of the various bits and pieces of information you've encountered so far about physical and cognitive changes in adulthood can be combined in a single model, suggested by Nancy Denney and illustrated in **Figure 14.5** (Denney 1982, 1984). Denney proposed that, on nearly any measure of physical or cognitive functioning, age-related changes follow a typical curve, like those shown in the figure. But she also argued that the height of this curve varies depending on the amount an individual exercises some ability or skill. Denney used the word *exercise* very broadly, to refer not only to physical exercise but also to mental exercise and to the extent some specific task may have been performed before. Unexercised abilities generally have a lower peak level of performance; exercised abilities generally have a higher peak.

Many laboratory tests of memory, for example, such as memorizing lists of names, tap unexercised abilities. Everyday memory tasks, such as recalling details from a newspaper column, tap much more exercised abilities. The distinction is somewhat similar to the distinction between crystallized and fluid abilities (see **Chapter 12**). Most crystallized abilities are at least moderately exercised, whereas

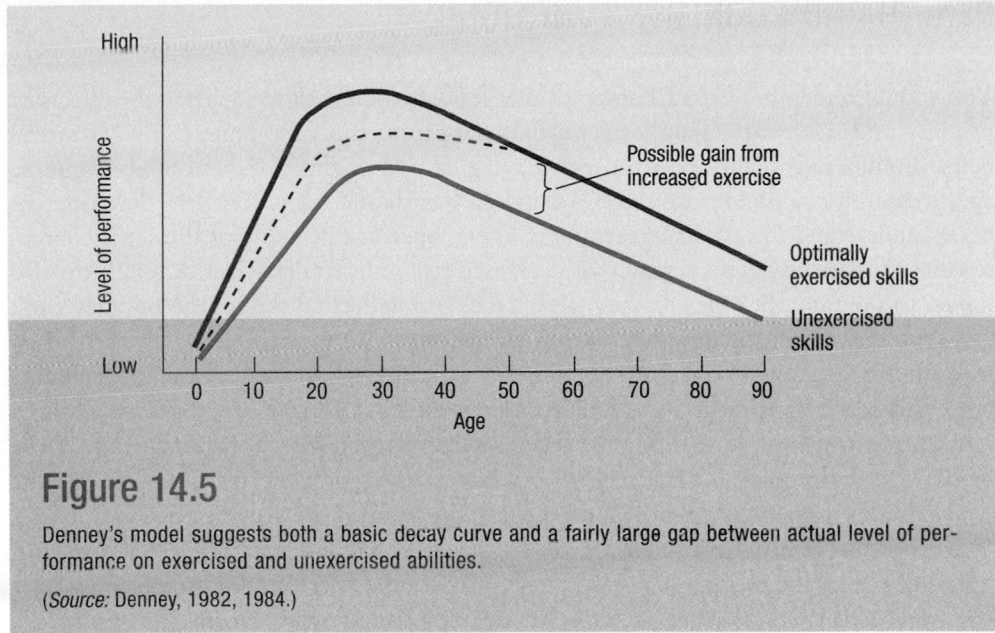

Figure 14.5

Denney's model suggests both a basic decay curve and a fairly large gap between actual level of performance on exercised and unexercised abilities.

(*Source:* Denney, 1982, 1984.)

many fluid abilities are relatively unexercised. But Denney was making a more general point: Whether abilities are crystallized or fluid, those that are more fully exercised will have a higher peak.

The gap between the curve for unexercised abilities and the curve for maximally exercised abilities represents the degree of improvement that would be possible for any given skill. Any skill that is not fully exercised can be improved if the individual begins to exercise that ability. There is clear evidence, for example, that aerobic capacity (VO_2 max) can be increased at any age if a person begins a program of physical exercise (e.g., Blumenthal et al., 1991; Buchner, Beresford, Larson, LaCroix, & Wagner, 1992). Nonetheless, in Denney's model, the maximum level an adult will be able to achieve, even with optimum exercise, will decline with age, just as performance of top athletes declines, even with optimum training regimens. One implication of this is that young adults are more likely to be able to get away with laziness or poor study habits and still perform well; as adults age, this becomes less and less true, because they are fighting against the basic decay curve of aging.

The dashed line in **Figure 14.5** represents a hypothetical curve for a skill that is not optimally exercised but is still used fairly regularly. Many verbal skills fall into this category, as do problem-solving skills. Because skills like these are demanded in a great many jobs, they are well exercised in most adults in their 20s, 30s, 40s, and 50s and are therefore well maintained, creating a flat-topped curve. But if Denney is correct, then at some point even optimum exercise will no longer maintain these abilities at that same level, and some decline will occur.

This model does not take into account all the facts. In particular, Denney's model does not easily handle the wide degree of variation from one individual to the next in the pattern of skill maintenance or decline over age, variation revealed clearly in Schaie's longitudinal study (Schaie, 1990). But what Denney's model does do is emphasize that there is an underlying decay curve. Those in middle adulthood may perform as well or better than the average young adult in areas in which they regularly exercise their skills. However, with increasing age, this high level of function requires more and more effort, until eventually every adult reaches a point at which even maximum effort will no longer maintain peak function.

HEALTH AND COGNITIVE FUNCTIONING

You should remember from **Chapter 12** that it is often difficult to separate the effects of primary and secondary aging, because they happen at the same time. Denney's model helps illuminate the links between primary aging and cognitive functioning in middle age. Research examining correlations between health and cognition help developmentalists understand the effects of secondary aging. Specifically, many of the same characteristics that are linked to increased or decreased risk of heart disease and cancer are also linked to the rate of change or the maintenance of intellectual skill in the middle years.

One illustration of this relationship comes from Walter Schaie's analysis of data from the Seattle Longitudinal Study (1983a). He found that those research participants who had some kind of cardiovascular disease (either coronary heart disease or high blood pressure) showed earlier and larger declines on intellectual tests than did those who were disease-free. Other researchers have found similar linkages. Even adults whose blood pressure is controlled by medication seem to show earlier declines (Sands & Meredith, 1992; Schultz, Elias, Robbins, Streeten, & Blakeman, 1986). Schaie cautions against taking these findings too far. The size of the effect is quite small, and it may operate indirectly rather than directly. For example, adults with cardiovascular disease may become physically less active as a response to their disease. The lower level of activity, in turn, may affect the rate of intellectual decline. This raises the possibility that exercise may be one of the critical factors in determining an individual person's overall physical health and cognitive performance during middle adulthood. A growing amount of information confirms such an effect.

One particularly large and well-designed study of the effects of exercise on physical health involved 17 321 Harvard alumni who had been students between 1916 and 1950. In 1962 or 1966, when the men were in their 30s, 40s, or 50s, each man provided detailed information about his daily levels of physical activity (Lee, Hsieh, & Paffenbarger, 1995). (The measures of physical activity were quite detailed. Each man reported how many blocks he normally walked each day, how often he climbed stairs, the amount of time per week he normally engaged in various sports, and so on. All the answers were then converted into estimates of calories expended per week. For example, walking 1 mile on level ground uses roughly 100 calories; climbing one flight of stairs uses about 17.) The researchers tracked all these men until 1988 to identify who had died and of what cause. The link between the level of physical activity and death rates over the succeeding 25 years is shown clearly in **Figure 14.6**: The more exercise a man reported, the lower his mortality risk.

Researchers were careful to exclude from the study any man who was known to suffer from heart disease or other disease at the outset of the study, in the 1960s. Furthermore, the groups differed *only* in level of energy expenditure; they did not differ in age, or whether they smoked, had high blood pressure, were overweight, or had a family history of early death—which makes the effect of exercise even clearer. To be sure, because the level of exercise was each man's own choice, there may have been other differences that separated the various exercise groups that could account for the different death rates. But the pattern, which has been replicated in other groups of both men and women, is so substantial and striking that alternative explanations are hard to come by (e.g., Blair et al., 1995; Lissner, Bengtsson, Bjorkelund, & Wedel, 1996). By far the most likely explanation is that there is a causal connection between longevity and level of physical activity.

Physical exercise also seems to help maintain cognitive abilities in the middle adult years, very likely because it helps to maintain cardiovascular fitness (Rogers, Meyer, & Mortel, 1990). Among physically healthy middle-aged and older adults, those who are

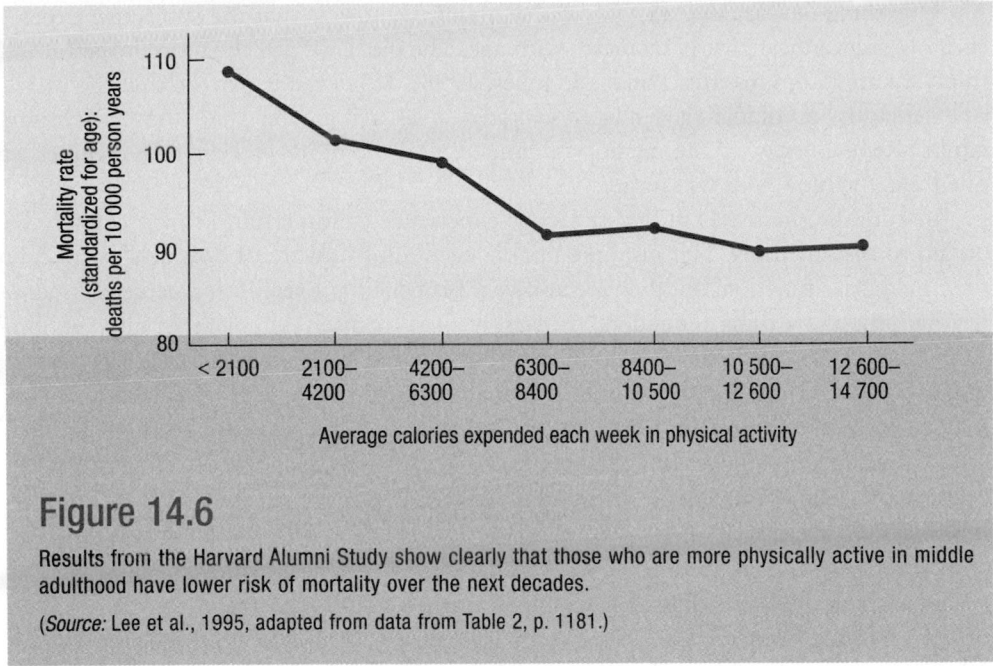

Figure 14.6

Results from the Harvard Alumni Study show clearly that those who are more physically active in middle adulthood have lower risk of mortality over the next decades.

(*Source:* Lee et al., 1995, adapted from data from Table 2, p. 1181.)

more physically active—doing gardening, heavy housework, or aerobic exercise such as walking, running, or swimming—score higher on tests of reasoning, reaction time, and short-term memory (Van Boxtel et al., 1997).

A different approach to studying exercise and cognitive functioning would involve randomly assigning some people to an exercise program and some to a nonexercise control group, and then seeing whether the two groups differed in their cognitive functioning after a period of exercise. The results of the small number of studies of this type have been quite mixed. Every study finds that exercise increases measures of physical functioning, such as VO$_2$ max, even in very elderly adults. Some—but not all—such studies also show that exercise improves thinking (Hawkins, Kramer, & Capaldi, 1992; Hill, Storandt, & Malley, 1993). Other studies do not come to that conclusion (e.g., Buchner et al., 1992; Emery & Gatz, 1990). In most cases, the experimental exercise program lasts only a few months, and that may not be sufficient to make any difference in mental functioning. Still, because researchers already know that exercise is linked to lower levels of disease and greater longevity, prudence alone would argue for including it in your life.

CHANGES IN MEMORY AND COGNITION

When developmentalists study changes in cognitive functioning in middle age, they find almost precisely what Denney's model and Schaie's longitudinal study suggest. That is, lack of mental exercise tends to be correlated with declines in memory and cognitive skills, but major deficits are not found until after ages 60 to 65.

MEMORY FUNCTION Drawing conclusions about memory function in middle age is difficult, because studies of age differences in adult memory rarely include middle-aged people. Typically, researchers compare very young adults, such as college students, to adults in their 60s and 70s. When the two groups are found to differ, psychologists often infer that middle-aged adults' performance falls somewhere between the two. In other words, they assume that memory function declines steadily, in linear fashion, across the adult years—an assumption that may not be true.

Make the Connection

Look back at the information on cross-sectional and longitudinal research designs in **Chapter 1**. How might cohort differences affect the results of studies comparing cognitive functioning of middle-aged adults to that of both younger and older adults? What kind of design would minimize such cohort effects? If such a study were begun today, how long would it be before researchers could derive useful conclusions from the data?

One thing developmentalists do know about memory is that the subjective experience of forgetfulness clearly increases with age. The older we get, the more forgetful we think we are (Commissaris, Ponds, & Jolles, 1998). However, it may be that the memory demands of middle-aged adults' everyday lives are greater than those of young adults. Remember, working memory is limited, and the more you try to remember at one time, the more you will forget.

In addition, increases in the subjective experience of forgetfulness may actually be an aid to metamemory. Not only are middle-aged adults aware of how well or poorly their memories function, but they are also very proficient at overcoming perceived memory limitations by using reminders, or *cues,* to help themselves remember information. Thus, the middle-aged person who knows that she may forget where her car is parked makes a point of noting nearby landmarks that will help her remember its location. This may be because middle-aged adults, in contrast to those who are older, continue to have a high sense of self-efficacy with respect to memory (Lineweaver & Hertzog, 1998). In other words, they believe their efforts will make a difference, so they actively work to improve their memories.

Nevertheless, there seem to be some real differences in the memory performance of young and middle-aged adults. For example, visual memory, the ability to remember an object you have seen for just a few seconds, declines in middle age (Fahle & Daum, 1997; Giambra, Arenberg, Zonderman, Kawas, & Costa, 1995). Further, the more complex the visual stimulus and the longer the interval between presentation and recall, the greater the difference. By contrast, memory for auditory stimuli seems to remain stable throughout adulthood.

Performance on more complex memory tasks, such as remembering lists of words and passages of text, also declines with age, but usually not until after about age 55. In contrast, recognition of words and texts appears to remain stable throughout adulthood (Zelinski & Burnight, 1997). Such findings suggest that there are age differences in working memory. Research examining short-term memory capacity at various ages shows that it remains very stable throughout early, middle, and late adulthood. What changes, apparently, is the ability to make efficient use of available capacity (Lincourt, Rybash, & Hoyer, 1998).

SEMANTIC AND EPISODIC MEMORIES Researchers can gain additional insight into age-related memory changes by studying how well young and middle-aged adults encode different kinds of memories. In the 1960s at the University of Toronto, Endel Tulving (1972, 2004) was the first to distinguish between two important types of memory: **Episodic memories** have to do with the ability to re-experience personal events or episodes (Tulving, 1999); and **semantic memories** represent our general knowledge of the world, facts, and the meaning of words. For example, a person's memories of a vacation in Newfoundland and Labrador are episodic, and her knowledge that Newfoundland became the last Canadian province in 1949 is semantic.

Researchers find that young and middle-aged adults differ more with respect to new episodic memories than they do with respect to semantic memories (Maylor, 1998; Nilsson, Baeckman, Erngrund, & Nyberg, 1997). For example, a middle-aged person attending a hockey game may forget where he parked his car (episodic memory). However, he is unlikely to forget the basic rules of the game (semantic memory).

Yet, it is too simplistic to say that episodic encoding is better in younger than in older adults. The difference is a bit more complex than that. Research examining the memories of adults for highly memorable episodes, often called *flashbulb memories,* has demonstrated that age has no effect on our ability to recall such events. For example, in one study, researchers asked young, middle-aged, and older adults to recount where they were and what they were doing when they heard about the verdict in the O.J. Simpson

episodic memories
recollections of personal events

semantic memories
general knowledge, facts and word meanings

trial (Bluck, Levine, & Laulhere, 1999). Respondents of all ages remembered the event with equal clarity. Younger respondents were somewhat more likely to report details. However, other research on such memories suggests that memory for details surrounding such episodes is subject to suggestion and overconfidence (Neisser & Harsch, 1992). So, the younger participants may have thought they remembered details when, in reality, their minds were simply filling in gaps in their memories with assumed details.

PRACTISED AND UNPRACTISED SKILLS In general, most adults maintain or even gain in skill on any task that they practise often or that is based on specific learning. For example, verbal abilities increase in middle age (Giambra et al., 1995). It appears that vocabulary—or, more precisely, performance on vocabulary tests—doesn't begin to decline until about age 65.

Similarly, expertise in a particular field helps to compensate for age-related deficits in cognitive functioning (Colonia-Willner, 1999; Tsang, 1998). For example, in one study, researchers examined 17- to 79-year-old participants' ability to recognize melodies performed at varying tempos (Andrews, Dowling, Bartlett, & Halpern, 1998). Some tunes were played very rapidly and then slowed until participants could recognize them. Both age and years of musical training predicted participants' ability to recognize melodies presented in this way, but the relationship between age and recognition was much weaker than the relationship between recognition and musical training. Other melodies were played too slowly to be recognized at the beginning and then speeded up. Interestingly, only musical training correlated with recognition of tunes played this way; there was no association with age whatsoever.

When researchers examine middle-aged adults' performance on unfamiliar or unpractised skills, such as a timed arithmetic test or a three-dimensional spatial task, the effects of aging are apparent. In particular, mental processes get steadily slower with age (Salthouse, 1991). Still, longitudinal research suggests that, even in these unfamiliar domains, the actual losses for most adults in this age range are small (Giambra et al., 1995). Major declines seem to happen after about age 60. Such results support conclusions such as that expressed by psychologist Walter Schaie:

> It is my general conclusion that reliably replicable age changes in psychometric abilities of more than trivial magnitude cannot be demonstrated prior to age 60, but that reliable decrements can be shown to have occurred for all abilities by age 74. (Schaie, 1983a, p. 127)

NEW LEARNING When it comes to acquiring new knowledge, middle-aged adults seem to be just as capable as younger adults of learning and remembering new information. In fact, middle-aged college students tend to be more academically successful than their younger peers (Burley, Turner, & Vitulli, 1999). Psychologists hypothesize that this difference is due both to motivational differences and the greater amount of background knowledge and experience possessed by older students.

Interestingly, too, surveys suggest that employers believe young adults to be more capable of learning new job skills than those who are older. However, research seems to show that there are few, if any, differences in the rates at which young and middle-aged adults learn new job skills (Forte & Hansvick, 1999). Particularly with regard to computer skills, once the skills have been acquired, there are no age-related differences in performance.

SCHEMATIC PROCESSING The literature on memory change with age also offers support for Labouvie-Vief's view that what happens to cognition in adulthood involves not only decline but also changes in emphasis, or structure. Labouvie-Vief, as you may recall from **Chapter 12**, suggests that middle adults tend to shift away from the logical or formal-operational approach that dominates thinking in adolescence and young adulthood, to a more pragmatic approach aimed at solving everyday problems—a process some developmentalists call *schematic processing* (Labouvie-Vief, 1990). In other words, a middle-aged adult may use schemas to process information that are qualitatively different from those used earlier in life. Such a schematic difference might lead middle-aged adults to pay more attention to overarching themes than to details. In memory, this difference in schematic processing might be reflected in a decline in memory for surface detail, accompanied by an increase in memory for themes and meanings.

A study in which researchers asked adults of various ages to read a story and then to recall it immediately afterward, in writing, yielded support for this hypothesis (Adams, 1991). Younger adults were more likely to report specific events or actions in the story, while middle-aged adults recalled more of the psychological motivations of the characters and offered more interpretations of the story in their recall. What this may mean is that, along with a shift in schematic processing, the encoding process changes as we get older. We may not attempt to encode as much detail, but may store more summarizing information.

CREATIVITY

A somewhat different question about cognitive functioning in the middle years of adulthood—one that may have more direct relevance for one's work life—has to do with creativity and productivity (see **The Real World**). Some widely quoted early research suggested that peak creativity, like peak physical functioning, occurs in early adulthood (Lehman, 1953). The technique used in this study involved identifying a series of major scientific discoveries of the past several hundred years and finding out how old each scientist was at the time of that discovery. Most were quite young, especially those who worked in more theoretical sciences and in mathematics. The classic example is Einstein, who was 26 when he developed the theory of relativity. These are interesting patterns, but this approach may be going at the question backwards. The alternative is to study scientists or other problem-solvers throughout their working lives and see whether the average person (someone who *isn't* an Einstein) is more productive and creative in early or middle adult life.

More recently, one psychologist has moved a step in this direction by looking at the lifetime creativity and productivity of thousands of notable scientists from the 19th century and earlier (Simonton, 1991, 2000). Simonton identified the age at which these individuals (nearly all men) published their first significant work, their best work, and their last work. In every scientific discipline represented, the thinkers produced their best work at about age 40, on average. But most of them were publishing significant, even outstanding, research through their 40s and into their 50s. In fact, researchers propose that the reason that people tend to do their best work at about 40 is not that the mind works better at that age, but that productivity is at its highest at that time. Chance alone suggests that the best work will come during the time when the most work is being done.

Lifetime creative output of modern-day scientists follows a similar pattern. Mathematicians, psychologists, physicists, and other scientists born in the 20th century have consistently shown their maximum productivity (usually measured by the number of papers published in a single year) when they were about 40. But research quality (as measured by the number of times each research paper is cited by peers) remains high through age 50 or even 60 (Horner, Rushton, & Vernon, 1986; Simonton, 1988).

Among musicians or other artists, peak creativity may occur later or be maintained far longer. For example, in one study, researchers asked judges to rate the aesthetic

The Real World

Working

Maintaining the Creative "Edge" in Mid-Life and Beyond

In a fascinating set of interviews, a number of highly successful and creative people described how they viewed creativity ("The creators," 2000). Interviewees ranged in age from 50 (musician Bobby McFerrin) to 93 (architect Phillip Johnson). Interestingly, all reported that they viewed themselves as more creative than they had been when they were younger. Their comments suggested that the creative process is a highly individualized intellectual activity. However, what was remarkable was that, by middle age, all had arrived at firm conclusions about what did and did not work for them. So, some part of the maintenance of creativity included acceptance of their own creative idiosyncrasies. Some, for example, expressed the need for external motivation,

such as a deadline. Guitarist B.B. King, 74, said, "If you want me to be creative, give me the line to cross and when I have to cross it" (p. 44). Others were more motivated by self-imposed standards than by externals. For example, writer Isabel Allende, 57, reported that she always begins a new work on January 8, because the date is a personally meaningful anniversary for her. Advertising writer Stan Freberg, 73, claimed that when he needs an idea, he takes a shower, because he often gets inspiration while in the shower.

A second theme pervaded these reports. Each creative person, in one way or another, recognized the value of accumulated knowledge and experience. They also tended to acknowledge important sources of this knowl-

edge, such as parents, spouses, and friends. Consequently, these people saw their creative work not only as the product of their own abilities but also as the result of a complex network of influential individuals, life experiences, and their own capacity to reflect on their lives.

We can learn two important things about maintaining creativity and productivity in the middle and late adult years from these extraordinary individuals: First, being consciously aware of one's own creative process—and accepting its boundaries—seems to be critical. Second, some degree of humility, a sense of indebtedness to those who have contributed to and supported one's creative development, appears to be associated with continuing productivity in the middle and late adult years.

---

qualities of musical compositions by the 172 composers whose works are most often performed (Simonton, 1988). Works created late in life ("swan songs") were most likely to be evaluated as masterpieces by the judges.

It is also possible to approach the question of how age is related to creativity or professional effectiveness experimentally. One such study broadened examination of adult creativity beyond the realm of scientific research by focusing on business executives (Streufert, Pogash, Piasecki, & Post, 1990). The researchers created four-person decision-making teams, made up of mid-level managers from state and federal government and private industry. On 15 of the teams, the participants were all between ages 28 and 35. Members of another 15 teams were middle-aged (aged 45 to 55), and another 15 teams included only older adults (aged 65 to 75). Each team was given a wonderfully complex simulated task: They were asked to manage an imaginary developing country called Shamba. They were given packets of information about Shamba ahead of time and could request additional information during their group work, done via a computer—which was of course programmed to make the experience of the different groups as much alike as possible, although the participants did not know that. Every team faced a crisis in Shamba at about the same time in their work.

Researchers recorded all the questions, suggestions, and plans generated by each team, from which they created a series of measures of activity rate, speed of response, depth of analysis, diversity of suggestions, and strategic excellence of each group's performance. The teams of young and middle-aged participants differed significantly on only 3 of the 16 measures: The younger teams did more things (made more decisions and took more actions); they asked for more additional information (often excessively, to the point of creating information overload); they suggested a greater diversity of actions. Middle-aged teams asked for just about the right amount of information—not too much to overload the system, but enough to make good decisions—and used the information effectively. On most of the measures the researchers devised, there were no differences between the young and middle-aged. In contrast, the oldest teams performed less well on virtually every measure. These findings suggest that the ability to apply creative thinking efficiently to complex problems may, indeed, be at its peak in the middle adult years.

Before Going On

- How does Denney's model explain the relationships among exercise, physical health, and cognitive functioning in middle adulthood?

- What does research reveal about the link between health and cognitive functioning?

- Describe differences between young and middle-aged adults in cognition and memory function.

- What does research evidence suggest about age-related changes in creativity?

Summary

Physical Changes

- Brain volume peaks during the middle adult years. Middle-aged adults often out-perform younger adults on everyday tasks that require concentration and rapid judgments, such as driving.

- The loss of reproductive capacity, called the *climacteric* in both men and women, occurs very gradually in men, but more rapidly in women. Menopause is a three-phase process that results from a series of hormonal changes.

- Bone mass declines significantly beginning at about age 30; accelerated declines in women at menopause are linked to decreased levels of estrogen and progesterone. Faster bone loss occurs in women who experience early menopause, who are underweight, who exercise little, or who have low-calcium diets.

- Thickening of the lens of the eye, with accompanying loss of elasticity, reduces visual acuity noticeably in the 40s or 50s. Hearing loss is more gradual.

Health Promotion and Wellness

- The rate of illness and death rises noticeably toward the end of middle adulthood. Young adults have more acute illnesses; middle-aged adults have more chronic illnesses. The two major causes of death in middle adulthood are heart disease and cancer.

- Cardiovascular disease is not a normal part of aging; it is a disease for which there are known risk factors, including smoking, high blood pressure, high blood cholesterol, obesity, and a high-fat diet.

- Cancer, too, has known risk factors, including smoking, obesity, and an inactive lifestyle. The role of a high-fat diet has been debated, but most evidence supports the hypothesis that such a diet contributes to the risk.

- Women tend to live longer than men but are more likely to suffer from chronic illnesses.

- Middle-aged adults have lower rates of mental health problems of virtually every kind than young adults. Alcoholism usually starts at younger ages but often remains undiagnosed until middle age.

Cognitive Functioning

- Denney's model of aging suggests that exercising either physical or cognitive abilities can improve performance at any age, but the upper limit on improvement declines with increasing age.

- Some studies suggest that differences in health contribute to variations in cognitive functioning among middle-aged adults. Exercise clearly affects the physical health of middle-aged adults, but research is less conclusive with regard to its effects on cognitive functioning.

- Verbal abilities continue to grow in middle age. Some loss of memory speed and skill occurs, but by most measures the loss is quite small until fairly late in the middle adult years. Expertise helps middle-aged adults compensate for losses in processing speed.

- Creative productivity also appears to remain high during middle adulthood, at least for adults in challenging jobs (the category of adults on whom most of this research has focused).

Key Terms

alcoholism (p. 437)

atherosclerosis (p. 431)

cardiovascular disease (CVD) (p. 431)

climacteric (p. 423)

episodic memories (p. 442)

menopause (p. 424)

osteoporosis (p. 427)

perimenopausal phase (p. 425)

postmenopausal phase (p. 425)

premenopausal phase (p. 424)

presbycusis (p. 429)

presbyopia (p. 429)

semantic memories (p. 442)

type A personality pattern (p. 433)

Weblinks

Statistical Report on the Health of Canadians
www.statcan.ca/english/freepub/82-570-XIE/82-570-XIE.pdf
Health Canada's *Statistical Report on the Health of Canadians* (1999) provides detailed statistics on over 80 health topics. The entire report is available online, along with an overview and information on the report's approach and implementation.

The Osteoporosis Society of Canada
www.osteoporosis.ca
The Osteoporosis Society of Canada's website provides an introduction to the topic of osteoporosis, information on prevention, diagnosis, and treatment options, as well as tools to help you calculate risk factors.

Heart and Stroke Foundation of Canada
ww1.heartandstroke.ca
The Heart and Stroke Foundation of Canada has an excellent and comprehensive website with healthy living information and tools, research links, statistics, a keyword search, recipes, and more.

The Canadian Cancer Society
www.cancer.ca/
The Canadian Cancer Society is a national, community-based organization of volunteers whose mission is the eradication of cancer and the enhancement of the quality of life of people living with cancer. It is Canada's largest charitable fundraiser for cancer research, an advocate for health reforms, cancer prevention, and healthy lifestyle choices, and a source of reliable and current research information. It provides support programs for caregivers, family, and friends.

The Mental Health Website at Health Canada
www.hc-sc.gc.ca/hppb/mentalhealth/
This Mental Health website provides convenient access to a range of online materials related to the promotion of mental health, the planning, delivery, cost, and evaluation of mental health programs and services in Canada, and the mental health issues, problems, and disorders encountered by Canadians.

Jeff Greenberg/PhotoEdit

CHAPTER 15

SOCIAL AND PERSONALITY DEVELOPMENT IN MIDDLE ADULTHOOD

When is the best time for a man to be at the peak of his career? What is the best age for a woman to initiate a new business venture? When is the best time to complete an advanced university degree? When is the best age to retire? People within any given society carry general social expectations about how a person's life should progress and unfold, and these expectations are closely associated with a person's age. Most often, expectations reflect cultural beliefs about the social clock. Middle adulthood is commonly seen as the time when people are best able, developmentally, to manage the weighty demands associated with positions of authority and responsibility.

Such beliefs and expectations are not entirely unfounded. When middle-aged adults get together with acquaintances, friends, or relatives at events such as high school or family reunions, they find most of their agemates to be in the most powerful positions of their lives. Most have higher incomes than they ever had before or ever will again, and a greater proportion of them hold positions of authority in business, education, and government than was true when they were younger.

The social clock is evident in family relationships as well. The middle-aged cohort of any family tends to have the most responsibility. They are "sandwiched" between adolescent or young adult children and aging parents. When a younger or older family member requires help, the middle-aged members are expected to respond.

What seems most striking about everyday life in middle age, however, is how much less constricting social roles feel. Most middle-aged adults are married, parents, and workers, but by age 40 or 50, these roles have changed in important ways. Children begin to leave home, which dramatically alters and reduces the intensity of the parental role; job promotions have usually reached their limit, so workers have less need to learn new work skills. And when both parenting and work are less demanding, partners can find more time for themselves and for each other. As you read this chapter, keep the following questions in mind:

- How does Erikson view social and personality development in middle adulthood, and what evidence exists to support the "crisis" view of mid-life?

- How do family roles and relationships change in middle adulthood?

- What are the major career issues facing middle-aged adults?

- How do individual personalities and life pathways influence development in middle adulthood?

THEORIES OF SOCIAL AND PERSONALITY DEVELOPMENT

generativity versus stagnation stage
the seventh of Erikson's stages, in which middle-aged adults find meaning in contributing to the development of younger individuals

generativity
a sense that one is making a valuable contribution to society by bringing up children or mentoring younger people in some way

You should remember from **Chapter 2** that Erik Erikson viewed middle age as a period when attention turns to creation of a legacy. Adults do this by influencing the lives of those in younger generations. Yet, many have characterized middle age less positively, suggesting that it is a period of intense crisis.

ERIKSON'S GENERATIVITY VERSUS STAGNATION STAGE

Middle-aged adults are in Erikson's **generativity versus stagnation stage**. Their developmental task is to acquire a sense of **generativity**, which involves an interest in establishing and guiding the next generation. Generativity is expressed not only in bearing or rearing one's own children, but through teaching, serving as mentor, or taking on leadership roles in various civic, religious, or charitable organizations. Merely having children is not enough for developing generativity in Erikson's terms. The optimum expression of generativity requires turning outward from a preoccupation with self, a kind of psychological expansion toward caring for others. Those who fail to develop generativity often suffer from a "pervading sense of stagnation and personal impoverishment [and indulge themselves] as if they were their own one and only child" (Erikson, 1963, p. 267).

Research has produced hints of such a developmental stage, but the findings are much less clear than data on changes in earlier years. One hint comes from the Berkeley/Oakland longitudinal studies, which found that assertiveness peaks in the 40s and then drops. The same studies found that a measure of outgoingness also peaks in the 40s among women and then drops, as did the measure the Berkeley researchers called "cognitively committed," which includes aspects of ambition, valuing independence, and valuing intellect. In this sample, then, there are signs of a major change around age 50, after which assertiveness, ambition, and outgoingness seem to decline.

Erikson's theory also raises questions about the impact of childlessness on adult development. One very interesting analysis comes from a 40-year longitudinal study of a group of inner-city, nondelinquent boys who had originally served as a comparison group in a study of delinquent boys (Snarey, Son, Kuehne, Hauser, & Vaillant, 1987). Of the 343 married men who were still part of this sample in their late 40s, 29 had fathered no children. Researchers found that the way a man had responded earlier to his childlessness was predictive of his psychological health at age 47. At that age, each man was rated on his degree of generativity. A man was considered to be "generative" if he had participated in some kind of mentoring or other teaching or supervising of children or younger adults. Among those with no children, those who were rated as most generative were likely to have responded to their childlessness by finding another child to nurture. They adopted a child, became Big Brothers, or helped with the rearing of someone else's child, such as a niece or nephew. Those childless men rated as nongenerative were more likely to have chosen a pet as a child substitute.

Critical Thinking

Make a list of ways to express generativity other than by bringing up your own children and helping them get a start in life.

Such findings raise the possibility that some aspects of psychological growth in early adulthood may depend on bearing and rearing one's own children or another child who calls forth one's nurturing and caring qualities—just as Erikson proposed. However, critics have suggested that studies of generativity have focused on well-educated, white, middle-aged adults. Researchers who have examined the issue of generativity in other groups have found that generativity is somewhat related to education (McAdams, Hart, & Maruna, 1998). Still, researchers have found consistent patterns of generativity-related behaviours and attitudes among poor as well as middle-class adults and across a variety of ethnic groups (McAdams et al., 1998; Schulz, 1998). Thus, expressions of generativity appear to be normal middle-aged experiences that are relatively independent of ethnicity and economic factors.

MID-LIFE CRISIS: FACT OR FICTION?

Jaques (1965) popularized the term "mid-life crisis" in the 1960s, an era when the occurrence of major events along the timeline of life was relatively lockstep and predictable, especially for men. The landmarks of life (particularly in industrialized countries like Canada) included finishing school, going to work, retiring, and ultimately, dying. Midway between completing school and death there was a change in a person's time perspective that shifted from "time since birth" to "time left till death." At this point, any perceived gap between what one had accomplished thus far in life and where one had expected to be, coupled with the realization that only so much time was left to close the gap, was therefore thought to be responsible for creating a sense of urgency, a sense of having just one last chance at a fulfilled life. The realization of the inevitability of death, along with other tangible indicators of time passing, such as noticeable body aging, children leaving home, or elderly or deceased parents, seemed to be a universal phenomenon that hit people during their 40s.

Decades later, of course, the timing and nature of major life events have changed dramatically. The progression from formal secondary schooling to late adulthood is much less predictable than it was in the 1960s and it is certainly not a universal, worldwide experience as thought previously. In Canada, for instance, both women and men engage in life-long learning, have different family living arrangements at various times in their lives, and generally hit the major milestones later in life. By the 1980s, the concept of a mid-life crisis was being challenged. For example, using a mid-life crisis scale, including items about inner turmoil, marital or job dissatisfaction, and a sense of declining power, researchers compared the responses of over 500 participants in a cross-sectional study of men ranging in age from 35 to 70 (Costa & McCrae, 1980b; McCrae & Costa, 1984). The researchers could find no distinct ages at which measures of "mid-life crisis" occurred.

Epidemiological studies also do not show any clear rise in mid-life of such likely signs of crisis as divorce, alcoholism, or depression in men (Hunter & Sundel, 1989). In addition, other researchers who have conducted longitudinal studies do not lend much support to the idea of a mid-life crisis. For example, researchers found no indication that any kind of crisis was common at mid-life among the participants in the Berkeley/Oakland longitudinal study (Haan, 1981). Finally, in a study of 724 adults, 28 to 78 years of age, it was found that only about one-quarter of the men and women reported having had a "mid-life crisis" (Wethington, 2000). However, a closer analysis revealed that the definitions that respondents used to describe their "crises" were very broadly defined—they were more likely to be describing stressful life events than turmoil associated with the awareness of aging or the inevitability of death. Moreover, most of the stressful events reportedly happened before or after the middle adulthood range of 39 through 50 years of age, leading to the conclusion that the so-called mid-life crisis is more an exception than the rule and by no means a universal experience of adult life.

Clearly, there are stresses and tasks that are unique to this period of life. But few signs show that stresses and tasks are more likely to overwhelm an adult's coping resources at this age than at any other (Gallagher, 1993; McCrae & Costa, 1990). A better term may be "mid-life transition," with a focus on growth rather than stress (Wethington, Cooper, & Holmes, 1997).

ROLE TRANSITIONS

The concept of *role* provides a different perspective on adjustment to the various transitions of adulthood. This important idea, which developmentalists borrowed from sociology, has been discussed in several previous chapters. Any social system can be thought of as being made up of interlocking positions (also called *statuses*) such as "employer," "worker," "teacher," "student," "retired person," and "widow." A *role* is the content of a social position—the behaviours and characteristics expected of a person filling that position (Marshall, 1996). Thus, a role is a kind of job description.

Several aspects of the concept of a role are important for an understanding of development. First, roles are at least partially culture- and cohort-specific. "Teacher," for example, may be a different role (a different set of expected behaviours) in one culture than in another, or in the same culture from one time to another.

Second, each of us must occupy multiple roles at the same time, and this inevitably produces frictions of various kinds. For example, a woman can be a member of a profession (say, a psychologist) while simultaneously occupying the roles of wife, mother, stepmother, grandmother, daughter, sister, sister-in-law, aunt, niece, friend, author, board member, singer, and volunteer. There will certainly be times when all these roles don't fit together tidily.

Sociologists use the term **role conflict** to describe any situation in which two or more roles are at least partially incompatible, either because they call for different behaviours or because their separate demands add up to more hours than there are in the day. Role conflict happens, for example, when a middle-aged father must choose between helping his aging parents with financial or health problems and attending his teenaged son's football games. A person experiences **role strain** when her own qualities or skills do not measure up to the demands of some role. For example, a 40-year-old worker who is forced to return to college to acquire new skills after a job layoff and who feels anxious about her ability to succeed is experiencing role strain.

The concept of roles can also help explain changes in adult life, because certain roles shift predictably with age. Each age level has accompanying roles. Even more conspicuously, family roles change in predictable ways, and one could argue that adult life marches to the rhythm of these shifts in family roles.

Evelyn Duvall described a sequence of eight family life stages, listed in **Table 15.1**. Each stage involves either adding or deleting some role or changing the content of a central role (Duvall, 1962). Duvall's idea has served as an organizing model for a great deal of sociological research on adulthood. Instead of comparing adults of different ages, researchers have compared adults in different life-cycle stages, creating a variant of the cross-sectional design. The basic idea, obviously, is that an individual's behaviour and attitudes are shaped by the roles he occupies. And since these roles change with age in systematic and predictable ways, adults will also change systematically and predictably. Knowing that a person has a new infant tells you something about his life. If you knew that another person's youngest child had just gone off to college, you would quite correctly infer very different things about her daily existence.

But the idea of family life stages, helpful as it has been, has two major flaws. First, the model totally omits a number of important roles, such as the role of grandparent

role conflict
any situation in which two or more roles are at least partially incompatible, either because they call for different behaviours or because their separate demands add up to more hours than there are in the day

role strain
the strain experienced by an individual whose own qualities or skills do not measure up to the demands of some role

TABLE 15.1	Duvall's Stages of the Family Life Cycle
Stage	**Description**
1	Adult is newly married, with no children; the person assumes the spousal role.
2	First child is born; role of parent is added.
3	Oldest child is between 2 and 6; role of parent changes.
4	Oldest child is in school; parental role changes again.
5	Oldest child is an adolescent; parental role changes again.
6	Oldest child leaves home; parental role involves helping child become independent.
7	All children have left home; sometimes called the postparental stage.
8	One or both spouses has retired; worker role ends.

(*Source:* Duvall, 1962.)

and that of caregiver to one's own aging parents. The model also does not reflect the years beyond age 65; it is as if the model assumes that no further changes in roles or life patterns occur after retirement. Yet it is increasingly clear that substantial variations in life patterns and roles exist among those over 60. Indeed, gerontologists today customarily divide the later adult years into three periods: the young old (60 to about 75), the old old (from 75 to about 85), and the oldest old (those over 85).

An even more telling problem with Duvall's simple model of family life stages is that in modern industrialized societies, a great many people simply don't move through this sequence of roles in the listed order. Increasing numbers of today's adults do not marry or do not have children; many divorce and move through complex cycles or combinations of family roles.

Yet the concept of the family life cycle has important elements that both sociologists and psychologists would like to retain. Although the sequence and timing may vary, the particular family life cycle an individual experiences clearly has an important effect on his or her life pattern (Aldous, 1996). And in any given culture or cohort, some role shifts are likely to be shared, such as retirement in one's 60s in most industrialized countries. One sociologist suggests that the life course should be thought of as containing a number of transitions, defined as "changes in status that are discrete and bounded in duration," such as shifting from being single to being married or from working to being retired (George, 1993, p. 358). Transitions that are highly predictable and widely shared in any given culture or cohort are called *life course markers*. In recent cohorts in industrialized countries, many of the family life transitions that used to be concentrated in early adulthood—such as marriage and first parenthood—have become less predictable, with highly variable timing and sequence. At the same time, some transitions in middle and late adulthood—such as the death of a parent while one is in middle age or voluntary retirement in one's 60s—have become more prevalent and predictable. Sociologists believe that some aspects of Duvall's basic theoretical perspective remain useful, despite the fact that family life stages are not precisely the same for all adults (e.g., Caspi & Elder, 1988). The specific sequence of roles, or the timing of those roles, may change from one cohort to the next, from one culture to the next, or even between different subgroups within a given culture, but dealing with some sequence of roles is the very stuff of adult life.

Before Going On

- Briefly describe Erikson's generativity versus stagnation stage and the evidence that supports his theory.

- What does research suggest about the existence of a universal mid-life crisis?

- What do the concepts of role conflict and role strain add to an understanding of middle adulthood?

CHANGES IN RELATIONSHIPS

As suggested previously, family roles are still an important part of life in middle age. However, these roles change significantly during this period of life.

PARTNERSHIPS

Several lines of evidence suggest that, on average, marital stability and satisfaction increase in mid-life as conflicts over child-rearing and other matters decline (Swensen, Eskew, & Kohlhepp, 1981; Veroff, Douvan, & Kulka, 1981; Wu & Penning, 1997). Indeed, only a quarter of divorces involve couples over the age of 40 (Uhlenberg, Cooney, & Boyd, 1990). So, despite considerable diversity among mid-life marriages or partnerships, overall, they are less conflicted than those of young adults.

Improvements in marital satisfaction may derive from middle-aged adults' increased sense of control—a kind of marital self-efficacy (Lachman & Weaver, 1998). It is likely that middle-aged partners' identification of successful problem-solving strategies contributes to the sense that they have control over their relationship. Research has provided useful illustrations of this point. For example, researchers typically find that marital problem themes among middle-aged couples are remarkably similar to those of younger adults. Wives complain of an unjust division of labour; husbands express dissatisfaction with limits on their freedom. Yet, relationship stability among middle-aged couples is maintained through the practice of what one researcher called "skilled diplomacy," an approach to solving problems that involves confrontation of the spouse about an issue, followed by a period during which the confronting spouse works to restore harmony (Perho & Korhonen, 1999). Skilled diplomacy is practised more often by wives than by husbands, but it appears to be an effective technique for marital problem solving no matter which spouse uses it.

CHILDREN AND PARENTS

The discussion of the relationship between young adults and their families in **Chapter 13** focused almost entirely on connections *up* the chain of family generations—that is, relationships between the young adults and their own middle-aged parents. When looking at family relationships from the perspective of middle age, we have to look in both directions: down the generational chain to relationships with grown children, and up the chain to relationships with aging parents.

One of the striking effects of increased life expectancy in developed countries is that adults are likely to spend many more years focusing on both older and younger generations in their families. For example, in 1800, a woman in North America could expect both of her parents to be dead by the time she was 37 (Watkins, Menken, & Bongaarts, 1987). Early in the 21st century, the average woman can expect to have at least one parent still living until she is in her late 50s, and this pattern will only become more prevalent as projected life expectancy increases still further (Health Reports, 2001).

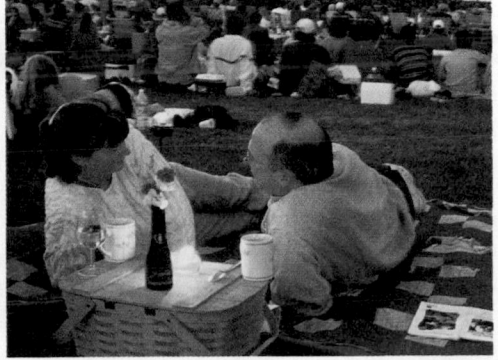

Once the children are grown and gone, many couples find it easier to spend time together—perhaps one of the reasons that marital satisfaction generally rises in middle age. (*Photo:* Jeff Greenberg/PhotoEdit)

Each of the positions in a family's generational chain has certain role prescriptions, and people expect to move in an orderly way through those roles (Hagestad, 1986, 1990). In middle adulthood, for current age cohorts at least, the family role involves not only giving assistance in both directions in the generational chain, but also shouldering the primary responsibility for maintaining affectional bonds. These responsibilities produce what is sometimes called the mid-life "squeeze," and those being squeezed form the "sandwich generation."

Such a squeeze was illustrated in the results of interviews with over 13 000 American adults in one frequently cited survey. Among many other things, respondents were asked about the amount of help of various kinds—financial, child care, household assistance, and so forth—they gave to and received from both adult children and aging parents (Bumpass & Aquilino, 1995). The results, graphed in **Figure 15.1**, make it clear that those between ages 40 and 65 give help more than they receive help in both directions within the family—to adult children and to aging parents. This pattern was confirmed in a variety of other studies in the United States (e.g., Gallagher, 1994), as well as within the Canadian population by gerontology researchers John Hirdes of the University of Waterloo and Laurel Strain of the University of Manitoba (Hirdes & Strain, 1995).

Whether most middle-aged adults experience this combination of responsibilities as a burden is not clear from the available information (Bengtson, Rosenthal, & Burton, 1996). Doubtless some do and some do not, depending on the degree of infirmity of the aging parents, the nature of the relationship the middle-aged adult has with those aging parents, and the degree of help required by the young adult children. A 50-year-old whose divorced daughter has returned with young grandchildren to live at home or one who has a parent living nearby and suffering from the early stages of Alzheimer's is far more likely to experience major role strain than is someone of the same age who babysits the grandchildren from time to time and helps her aging parents by doing occasional shopping, snow shovelling, or housecleaning. But, on average, it is clear that middle adulthood is likely to be a time when more help is given than is received.

A quite different look at patterns of family interaction among middle-aged adults is taken in sociologist Gunhild Hagestad's fascinating three-generation family study (Hagestad, 1984). Hagestad was interested not so much in patterns of aid, but in attempts to influence other generations in the family. Middle-aged adults in this sample of 148 families typically expended more effort trying to influence their children than their parents, but both kinds of effort occurred fairly regularly. Their most successful efforts to influence their aging parents came in the form of practical advice about where to live or how to manage the household and money. Attempts to change their parents' views about social issues or family dynamics largely fell on deaf ears. Influence attempts directed at their young adult children were aimed mostly at shaping the children's

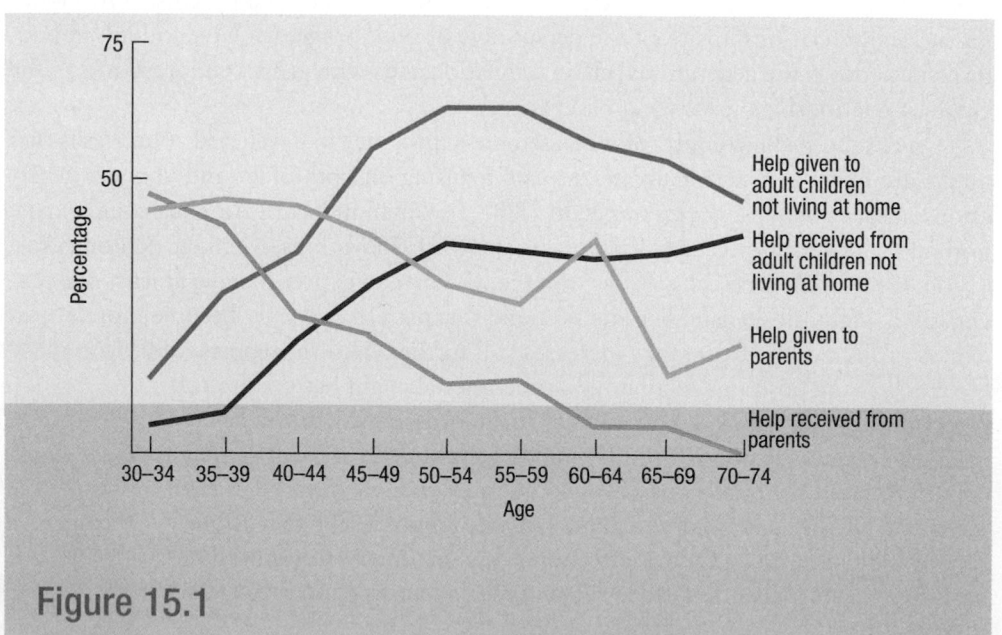

Figure 15.1

The midlife "squeeze," or "sandwich generation," is illustrated in this graph of data from a national survey of adults. Middle-aged adults give more help to both their adult children and their own parents than they receive.

(*Source:* Bumpass & Aquilino, 1995, data from Tables 11, 12, 25, and 26.)

transition into key adult roles. So, for example, the older adults talked about educational choices, work, money, and personal lifestyle.

Influence attempts did not radiate exclusively from the middle-aged generation. Both the young adult children and the aging parents in this study tried to influence the middle-aged generation, with varying success. Hagestad found that parents, whatever their age, kept trying to influence their children, and that children, whatever their age, continued to resist such influence and advice. Advice from child to parent was much more likely to be successful. Only about a third of the influence attempts from parents to children were effective, whereas about 70% of the influence attempts in the other direction were received positively.

Hagestad also found that each family seemed to have a particular agenda, or set of themes, that cropped up again and again in their descriptions of interactions across the generations. Some families spent a lot of time talking about money; others never mentioned this subject. Some focused on family dynamics or on health issues. Themes like this were particularly clear in the all-male or all-female lineage. In more than half of the families Hagestad studied, the three generations of women regularly talked about some aspect of interpersonal relationships, particularly family dynamics, while such themes never surfaced in the male lineage. Grandfathers, fathers, and grown sons were more likely to talk about work, education, or money with one another.

Critical Thinking

What do men and women talk about at multi-generational gatherings of your own family?

Other studies of multigenerational families confirm these patterns. When women family members have conflicts, it is most likely to be over how members of the family ought to relate to one another. When fathers, sons, and grandsons have conflicts, they are likely to be about nonfamily issues, such as politics or social issues (e.g., Hagestad, 1985; Lehr, 1982).

Hagestad's research gives a glimpse into the complex workings of family relationships across several generations. But further understanding of family relationships for middle-aged adults can be gained by considering specific aspects of their situation. Research on the "empty nest," on grandparenthood, and on care of aging parents creates a more complete picture of this sandwich generation.

EMPTYING THE NEST

The timing of the "empty nest" stage in the family life cycle obviously depends on a person's (or couple's) age when the last child is born. In conjunction with women delaying childbearing, men are delaying parenting, which pushes the empty nest stage to a later age, in a pattern typical of today's Canadian adults. This is quite different from the historical parenting trends in Canada. For example, McMaster University researchers Carolyn Rosenthal and James Gladstone have been studying trends in contemporary families. They reported that women born in the mid-1800s had their last child, on average, when they were about 40 (Rosenthal & Gladstone, 2000). If we assume that this last child left home when he or she was between 20 and 25, then women in this cohort were roughly 60 when the last child left. Since the life expectancy for women during the first decades of the 1900s was less than 60 years (Health Reports, 2001), there was little possibility for women to experience what we now call the empty nest stage. By comparison, women born during the 1930s and later were only about 30 when they bore their last child, and were in their 50s when the last child left home (Beaujot & Ravanera, 2001). Their life expectancy was somewhat beyond 60 years. Thus, there was greater likelihood that they would experience the empty nest stage. This stage is likely be prolonged even more in the near future due to a number of other factors associated with

Contrary to popular belief, when this woman's daughter leaves the nest in a few years, it will be a joyful experience.
(*Photo:* Courtesy of Drs. Booker and Madeline Wright. Used with permission.)

women born in the late 1940s and 1950s because these women started having fewer, more closely spaced babies at an earlier age (Rosenthal & Gladstone, 2000). This cohort also enjoys a much longer projected lifespan, which increases the likelihood of living well beyond the time when the youngest child leaves home.

A study by University of Western Ontario researchers Ravanera and Rajulton (1998) found that male parenting in Canada parallels the female pattern, whereby male parenting patterns in the later half of the 20th century have been more variable than prior to that time—both men and women experience nontraditional family patterns, including sole-parenting and step-parenting. Moreover, on average, Canadian men end parenting at just over age 56, and since they are living longer, they too experience the empty nest. Ravanera and Rajulton also reported two other interesting trends in male parenting. First, men of lower status start parenting younger but end parenting at an older age. Second, men in the Atlantic provinces have the longest parenting duration, whereas men from Ontario have the shortest.

The role of parent does not cease when the child leaves home. Support and advice continue to be expected and offered. But the content of the parental role in this "post-parental" phase is clearly quite different from what it was when the children were still living at home. The child does not need daily care or supervision. As a result, adults have much more time for their spousal roles, a change that undoubtedly contributes to the higher reported marital satisfaction in this stage of family life.

Folklore in Western cultures predicts that some or even most women become depressed or upset once the "nest" is empty, because they are losing the central role of mother. Of course, it is possible that such a pattern exists in some cultures, but it seems not to be true of Canadian society, at least not for the great majority of middle-aged women. Suicide rates do go up for women in mid-life, but the rise begins between the ages of 35 and 54, when children are still at home, and then drops for women past their mid-50s, which is when the empty nest typically occurs. Similarly, high rates of depression among mid-life women are apparent until after the mid-40s, also before the children have left home. Furthermore, high levels of chronic stress also peak after age 44 and decline thereafter (Health Canada, 1999e).

More to the point, when women are asked specifically about positive and negative transitions in their lives, those who list the departure of the last child are more likely to describe this event as positive rather than negative. In one study of 60 women between the ages of 45 and 60, researchers found that only a third of the participants described any significant transition point when the last child left home (Harris, Ellicott, & Holmes, 1986). Of these, 25% reported that the transition involved a distinct "mellowing," increased marital satisfaction, or increased inner stability; 17% reported that the transition involved an adjustment to the departure of the children. Those few women who do experience some distress in this role transition appear to be those whose sense of self-identity has been heavily focused on the role of mother. In contrast, women in this age range who are in the labour force are much more likely to experience the empty nest as positive.

GRANDPARENTING

Middle-aged adults typically move into several new roles, such as becoming in-laws as their children marry (see **The Real World**). In addition, more than half of Canadian adults become grandparents by the end of middle adulthood (Milan & Hamm, 2003) (see **Figure 15.2**). In Canada, there are about 5.7 million grandparents and almost five grandchildren for each grandparent. Nearly half a million grandchildren share the same

The Real World

Parenting

Me, a Mother-in-Law?

Most middle-aged adults are happy to see their adult children marry and form their own families. However, somewhere in the midst of the excitement a middle-aged woman experiences when an adult child gets married comes the realization that she is going to acquire one of the most maligned social roles there is: that of mother-in-law. Mother-in-law jokes abound in films and TV shows, and relationships between mothers-in-law and their children's spouses are regularly characterized as full of tension and conflict. Typically, it is the relationship between the mother-in-law and the daughter-in-law that is depicted most negatively. Thus, it isn't surprising that most middle-aged women don't look forward to becoming mothers-in-law. But is the negative stereotyping of mothers-in-law justified?

Research in some societies suggests that the stereotype is somewhat accurate. In these societies, the mother-in-law has a well-defined social role. Newlyweds usually reside with the husband's parents, and the mother-in-law is the supervisor of the young wife and is responsible for socializing her into the family. In such

cultures, wives remain under the authority of their mothers-in-law for many years, usually until the older woman is no longer physically able to fulfill her role's requirements.

Despite the cultural reinforcement of the relationship between mother-in-law and daughter-in-law in traditional societies, these relationships are often high in conflict (Chiapin, DeAraujo, & Wagner, 1998). Most such conflicts involve the husband: The daughter-in-law thinks her husband is too loyal to his mother, or the mother-in-law thinks her son's wife is trying to undermine her relationship with him. Some mothers-in-law go so far as to physically abuse their daughters-in-law, and abusive husbands sometimes receive praise from their mothers for keeping young wives in line (Fernandez, 1997).

However, some mothers-in-law may be treated poorly by daughters-in-law. For example, in rural China, a daughter-in-law is expected to care for her elderly mother-in-law. Research suggests that many daughters-in-law fail to live up to this cultural obligation (Yang & Chandler, 1992). This is especially devastating

for the mother-in-law, because, in China, the elderly are completely dependent on their adult children for economic support.

Parallels to these situations exist in more industrialized societies like Canada. Mothers-in-law are perceived as interfering in the marital relationship; daughters-in-law are accused of trying to turn their husbands against their mothers. Consequently, family therapists have devised recommendations to help middle-aged women adjust to the mother-in-law role and to forestall conflict (Greider, 2000). Here are a few such recommendations:

- Don't give unsolicited advice or make unannounced visits.

- When asked for your advice, share your experience in a nonjudgmental way.

- Don't criticize your daughters- or sons-in-law behind their backs.

- Don't insist on being visited every weekend or holiday.

- Respect your children's wishes regarding how grandchildren are to be cared for.

---

household with their grandparents, although a relatively small number (25 200) live with only their grandparents.

Most grandparents—92% in one study—express high levels of satisfaction with this role (Peterson, 1999). A majority see or talk to their grandchildren regularly. They may write, call, or visit as often as every couple of weeks, and most describe their relationships as warm and loving. Likewise, many studies have demonstrated the positive impact of warm relationships with grandparents on children's development (Adkins, 1999).

Grandparents seem to be an especially important source of stability in the lives of children of divorced parents. However, in most cases, grandparents in Canada have privileges, as does any interested third party, but not rights of access to their grandchildren. With the exception of Quebec, Alberta, and B.C., there is a lack of provincial legislation that provides grandparents with a legal basis for matters such as visitation or access to their grandchildren (Kruk, 1995).

Figure 15.2

The likelihood of being a grandparent increases with age. Two-thirds of women and over one-half of men 55 to 64 years of age are grandparents in Canada.

(*Source:* Adapted from Statistics Canada, 2003, *Canadian Social Trends Winter* (71), 2–7, Catalogue No. 11-008 [Milan & Hamm, 2003].)

remote relationships
relationships in which grandparents do not see their grandchildren often

companionate relationships
relationships in which grandparents have frequent contact and warm interactions with grandchildren

involved relationships
relationships in which grandparents are directly involved in the everyday care of grandchildren or have close emotional ties with them

Fortunately, most parents welcome the involvement of their own parents in their children's lives, and surveys suggest that grandparents and grandchildren engage in many of the same activities—watching television, shopping, attending religious services—that parents and children share (Waggoner, 2000). However, while parenthood clearly involves full-time responsibility, there are many degrees of being a grandparent.

Most behavioural scientists place grandparents in one of several categories derived from a study in which researchers interviewed a nationally representative sample of over 500 grandparents (Cherlin & Furstenberg, 1986). Twenty-nine percent of grandparents in the study had **remote relationships**; they saw their grandchildren relatively infrequently and had little direct influence over their grandchildren's lives. The most common reason for this remoteness was physical distance.

By contrast, this statement by one of the grandmothers in the study illustrates a different kind of relationship, for which researchers used the term **companionate relationship**:

When you have grandchildren, you have more love to spare. Because the discipline goes to the parents and whoever's in charge. But you just have extra love and you will tend to spoil them a little bit. And you know, you give. (Cherlin & Furstenberg, 1986, p. 55)

Just over half of the survey's participants exhibited such attitudes toward their grandchildren and responded that they had very warm, pleasurable relationships with them. Yet these grandparents also said that they were glad they no longer had the day-to-day responsibility. They could love the grandchildren and then send them home.

The third, and least common (16%), type of relationship was exhibited by grandparents who had **involved relationships** with their grandchildren. These grandparents were everyday participants in the rearing of their grandchildren. Some of them lived in three-generation households with one or more children and grandchildren; some had nearly full-time care of the grandchildren. But involved relationships also occurred in some cases in which the grandparent had no daily responsibility for the grandchildren's care but created an unusually close link.

Gerontologists Joan Norris and Joseph Tindale (1994) of the University of Guelph determined that grandparents commonly help their children and grandchildren with child care, although most grandparents prefer to avoid full-time child care arrangements. Full-time grandparent care is especially likely when the grandchild's mother is unmarried. In such cases, the grandmother frequently takes on child-care responsibilities so that her daughter can continue in school or hold down a job. That such assistance is indeed helpful is indicated by the fact that teenaged mothers who have such help from their own mothers complete more years of education and have more successful work careers in adulthood (Taylor, Chatters, Tucker, & Lewis, 1990).

Gender is related to grandparenting as well. Among all ethnic groups, the role of grandmother is likely to be both broader and more intimate than that of grandfather (Hagestad, 1985). In addition, young grandparents, those in their 40s, have less day-to-day contact with grandchildren than those who are older, perhaps because most are still working (Watson, 1997). As a result, they know less about and are less involved in their grandchildren's everyday lives than older grandparents are.

The role of grandparent obviously brings many middle-aged and older adults a good deal of pleasure and satisfaction. However, grandparents who see their grandchildren more often do not describe themselves as happier than those who see theirs less often (Palmore, 1981). Thus, for most adults in middle age, grandparenthood is not central to their lives, to their sense of self, or to their overall morale.

This girl seems delighted with her grandmother, with whom she seems to have what Cherlin and Furstenberg would call a "companionate" relationship.
(*Photo:* Jack Monnier/Getty Images)

CARING FOR AGING PARENTS

Another role that may be added at mid-life, and that *does* have a powerful effect on overall life satisfaction, is that of major caregiver for aging parents (see **No Easy Answers**). The great majority of adults, in virtually every culture, feel a strong sense of filial responsibility. When their parents need assistance, they endeavour to provide it (Ogawa & Retherford, 1993; Wolfson, Handfield-Jones, Glass, McClaran, & Keyserlingk, 1993). Interestingly, young adults seem to feel a stronger sense of obligation than those who are middle-aged (Stein et al., 1998). This may be because their parents are still healthy and fairly young and they have not yet had to face the prospect of caring for them. In contrast, for middle-aged people, the day-to-day problem of how to care for aging parents is more of a present reality. However, just how many adults actually take on this role is surprisingly unclear.

Just what impact does caregiving have on the middle-aged adult? First off, we know that about one in five Canadians provides care to a senior family member or friend (Cranswick, 2003). We also know that about one-quarter of Canadians aged 45 to 54 provided the greatest proportion of unpaid care for elderly parents (Canadian Council on Social Development, 1999b; Cranswick, 2003). As you can see from **Figure 15.3**, informal caregiving can take time away from other social and recreational activities. Caregivers can incur additional costs as well, such as extra expenses or poor health (Cranswick, 2003).

Not surprisingly, this demanding caregiver role takes its toll. Caregivers who provide a high level of assistance to the daily needs of a parent (or spouse) who is disabled, frail, or demented are more depressed

Daughters, far more than sons, are likely to take on the role of significant caregiver for a disabled or demented parent, as this daughter has done, now that her mother is suffering from Alzheimer's disease.
(*Photo:* Michael Newman/PhotoEdit)

and have lower marital satisfaction than people in comparison groups of similar age and social class (Hoyert & Seltzer, 1992; Jutras & Lavoie, 1995; Schulz, Visintainer, &

No Easy Answers

Who Cares for Aging

Parents in Canada?

One of the most difficult dilemmas of mid-life arises when elderly parents become incapable of caring for themselves. Inevitably, the issue of who will care for them creates conflict. Following some form of needs assessment, the caregiver must choose between several care options, each of which carries its own unique blend of quality, convenience, and cost. Options in Canada include in-home care (private and publicly funded); independent-supportive living, e.g., full-service residences or apartments, retirement homes; nursing homes and homes for the aged; and palliative care and hospice care facilities. Some caregivers feel a sense of moral obligation, or have a desire to care for their parents directly. In fact, Canada's 2001 census data shows that 13% of men and 12% of women aged 65 and over who had adult children now live with one of those children (Statistics Canada, 2002h). Ultimately, even if elders move to long-term care facilities, someone has to take primary responsibility for overseeing their care.

Families typically negotiate the caregiving task along a number of dimensions, including each family member's competing demands and availability of resources. Within a group of siblings, the one most likely to take on the task of caregiving is the one who has no children still at home, is not working, not married, and lives closest to the aging parent (Brody, Litvin, Albert, & Hoffman, 1994; Stoller, Forster, & Duniho, 1992). The child with the strongest attachment to the parent is also most likely to provide help, although distance and time factors often override this effect (Whitbeck, Simons, & Conger, 1991).

Anne Martin-Matthews (2001), a University of British Columbia gerontologist, points out that Canadian women are the ones most likely to be actively involved in the caregiving of their elderly parents and, in their later years, an elderly spouse. Moreover, women have traditionally married older men, and since men have a shorter life expectancy, proportionally more women than men will outlive their spouse. This means that, if they require care,

these women will be dependent upon alternative (rather than spousal) sources of care in their senior years. These factors combine to make a daughter or daughter-in-law the most likely candidate for the role of caregiver. But it makes a difference whether the frail elder is a mother or a father. Daughters are four times as likely as sons to help an older mother, but only 40% more likely than sons are to help a frail father (Lee, Dwyer, & Coward, 1993). Because women (mothers) live longer than men and are thus more likely to require help, this tendency for children to provide relatively more help to the same-sex parent means that women have a much higher probability of providing such care.

Another factor that increases daughters' involvement in parental care is simple proximity. Perhaps because of greater emotional closeness to their parents or their socialization for the role of kinkeeping, daughters are more likely to live near their parents. And parents, when they approach their later years, are more likely to move to be close to a daughter than to a son.

Yet sons are quite often involved in the care of an elder. If a son is unmarried, he is more likely to take on the caregiving role than is a married sister (Stoller et al., 1992). And if both a son and a daughter are involved, the two often divide the responsibilities, with sons providing more financial assistance or instrumental support (mowing the lawn, home repairs, perhaps shopping) and daughters more often providing help with physical activities of daily living, such as dressing, cleaning, and cooking.

But despite these complexities, the inescapable conclusion is that women are far more likely than men to take on the role of caregiver of an aging parent, just as women are more likely to take on the role of caregiver with children. Whether this will change in the next few decades, as many more middle-aged women enter or remain in the labour force, remains to be seen.

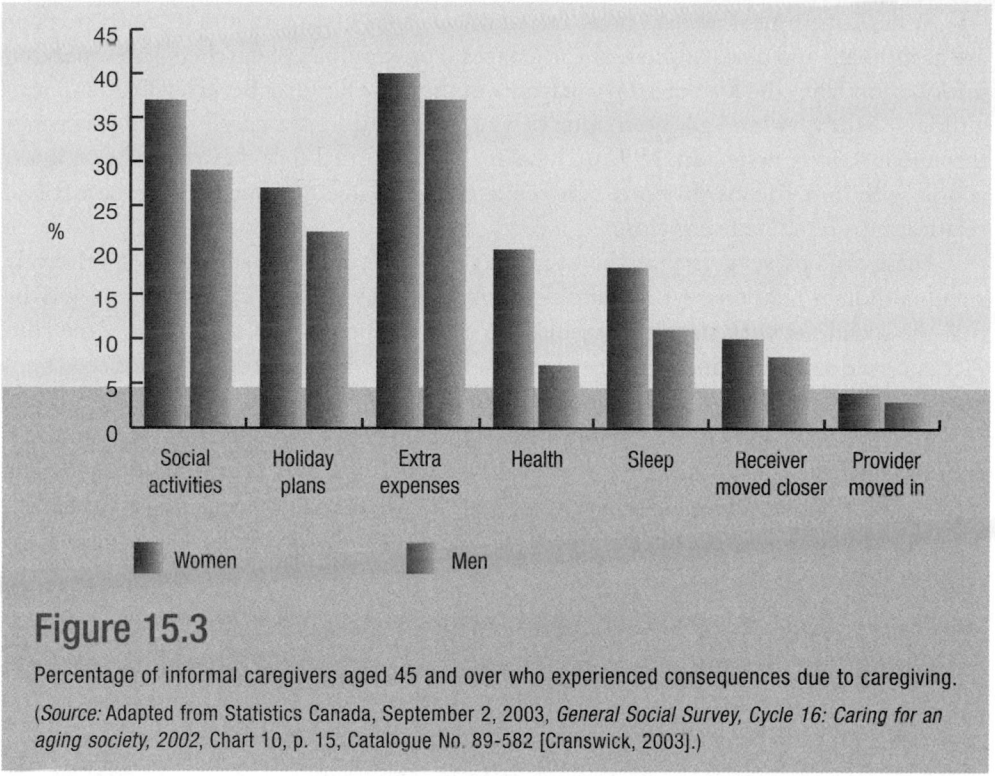

Figure 15.3

Percentage of informal caregivers aged 45 and over who experienced consequences due to caregiving.

(*Source:* Adapted from Statistics Canada, September 2, 2003, *General Social Survey, Cycle 16: Caring for an aging society, 2002*, Chart 10, p. 15, Catalogue No. 89-582 [Cranswick, 2003].)

Williamson, 1990). Some research also suggests those who care for demented or frail elders are often more ill themselves or have some reduced efficiency of immune system function (Dura & Kiecolt-Glaser, 1991; Hoyert & Seltzer, 1992; Kiecolt-Glaser et al., 1987). Collectively, these effects are often termed **caregiver burden.** However, it is clear that certain factors can significantly lessen the burden, even for those with major caregiving responsibilities. Those individuals who have good support networks (including a supportive spouse), as well as help from other caregivers, experience fewer negative consequences (Brody, Litvin, Hoffman, & Kleban, 1992; Pearlin, Aneshensel, Mullan, & Whitlatch, 1996; Schulz & Williamson, 1991).

For the majority of mid-life adults, the relationship with aging parents is far more positive. Most give more assistance to their parents than they did before, but they also continue to see them regularly for ceremonial and celebratory occasions and to feel affection as well as filial responsibility (Stein et al., 1998). Parents are also symbolically important to middle-aged adults, because as long as they are alive, they occupy the role of elder in the family lineage. When they are gone, each generation moves up a notch in the sequence: Those in the middle generation must come to terms with the fact that they have now become the elders and are confronted directly with their own mortality.

caregiver burden
a term for the cumulative negative effects of caring for an elderly or disabled person

FRIENDS

The scant research on friendships in middle adulthood suggests that the total number of friendships is lower in these years than in young adulthood. For example, in one small American study, researchers interviewed three generations of women in each of 53 families (Levitt, Weber, & Guacci, 1993). Each woman was asked to describe her close relationships. Among both groups, the young adult women had more friends in their social networks than did their middle-aged mothers.

At the same time, there are other bits of research suggesting that mid-life friendships are as intimate and close as those at earlier ages. For example, researchers have analyzed information from the files of 50 participants in the now-familiar Berkeley/Oakland longitudinal study, who had been interviewed or tested repeatedly from adolescence through age 50 (Carstensen, 1992). These analyses revealed that the frequency of interaction with best friends dropped between age 17 and age 50, but that the best-friend relationships remained very close.

These studies suggest that the social network of middle-aged adults is relatively small, although relationships are just as intimate as they were at earlier ages. It may be that the social network shrinks as adults age because there is less need for it. Role conflict and role strain decline significantly in middle age, and the need for emotional support from a social network outside the family seems to decrease accordingly (Due, Holstein, Lund, Modvig, & Avlund, 1999). Yet, because the relationships that do endure are close, the social network is available when needed. Friendship depends less on frequent contact than on a sense that friends are there to provide support as needed. Thus, the nature of friendship itself may be different in middle age.

Before Going On

- What contributes to the "mellowing" of marital relationships in middle age?
- What is the family role of middle-aged adults with respect to older and younger generations?
- What is the evidence regarding the existence of an "empty nest syndrome"?
- How does the grandparent role affect middle-aged adults?
- How might caregiver burden affect a middle-aged adult's life?
- How do social networks change during middle adulthood?

MID-LIFE CAREER ISSUES

Work in mid-life is characterized by two paradoxes: First, work satisfaction is at its peak in these years, despite the fact that most adults receive few work promotions in middle age. Second, the quality of work performance remains high, despite declines in some cognitive or physical skills.

WORK SATISFACTION

Despite the plateau in promotions that occurs for most adults in the middle years, job satisfaction is typically at its peak, as is a sense of power or job clout. Still, patterns of work and work satisfaction do vary between men and women in middle adulthood.

A cross-sectional study of a nationally representative sample of men suggested that, for them, work satisfaction increases in middle age because the issue of work is less central to their lives (Tamir, 1982). Among young adult men (aged 25 to 39) in this study, job satisfaction was strongly correlated with various measures of personal satisfaction; for the middle-aged men (aged 40 to 65), it was not. Middle-aged men, in other words, have begun to disengage from their work as a primary source of personal fulfillment or satisfaction, even though they are likely to be more pleased with the work itself.

Whether the same is true of women workers at mid-life is not so clear. For women who begin to work steadily only in their 30s or 40s, the middle adult years may be the time of most rapid work advancement rather than simple maintenance of previous gains. For such women, work satisfaction might have as strong a correlation with overall life satisfaction as it does for young adult men.

Interestingly, though, a shift to full-time employment once the nest is empty is not a very common pattern for women, at least in current cohorts. Longitudinal data from the 10-year Michigan Panel Study of Income Dynamics suggest that most middle-aged women began paid employment while their children were still at home (Moen, 1991). Few began work for the first time after their last child left home. When women did return to full-time work in middle adulthood, the most likely reasons were divorce or widowhood, not the final departure of children.

Moreover, patterns of work satisfaction among middle-aged women may be more complex than those of men. For example, men's satisfaction is generally linked to objective measures of achievement such as promotions and salary history (Allen, Poteet, & Russell, 1998). In contrast, even among very successful women, work satisfaction often depends on how they view the career decisions they made in early adulthood. Many in one study believed that they had given family concerns too high a priority in deciding what kind of career to pursue, and claimed that they should have given less primacy to marital and family responsibilities and chosen a different career field (Stewart & Ostrove, 1998). For such women, work satisfaction tends to be low. However, many respond by making mid-life career changes or pursuing additional education.

Cross-gender variations in patterns of work and job satisfaction are accompanied by sex differences in coping style at work (Perho & Korhonen, 1999). Men and women cite the same sources of work dissatisfaction in middle age: time pressure, difficult co-workers, boring tasks, and fear of losing one's job. However, they cope with these challenges differently. Men are more likely to negotiate with supervisors and co-workers directly to effect change. In contrast, women tend to withdraw and to engage in collective complaining with female co-workers. Still, women are better able than men to balance their dissatisfactions with areas of contentment. Consequently, a statement such as "I don't like the boss, but the hours fit my needs" is more likely to come from a woman than a man. Because of their different coping styles, men are more likely to improve their level of satisfaction in situations where change is possible. By contrast, women are probably better able to cope with work settings where they must adjust to dissatisfaction because the situation can't be changed.

Despite their differences, both men and women in mid life have a greater sense of control over their work lives than younger adults do (Lachman & Weaver, 1998). One reason for the increased feeling of control may be that social-cognitive skills improve from early to middle adulthood (Blanchard-Fields, Chen, Schocke, & Hertzog, 1998; Hess, Bolstad, Woodburn, & Auman, 1999). Middle-aged adults are better than they were when younger at "sizing up" people, relationships, and situations. At the same time, by middle age, they have become proficient at directing their own behaviour in ways that allow them to maintain levels of personal satisfaction even in unpleasant circumstances.

JOB PERFORMANCE

In the great majority of occupations, job performance remains high throughout middle adulthood (McEvoy & Cascio, 1989). The few exceptions are those occupations in which physical strength or speedy reaction time is a critical element; some examples are longshoreman, air traffic controller, truck driver, professional athlete, and the like. In these jobs, performance begins to decline at mid-life or earlier, just as you would expect (Sparrow & Davies, 1988). In fact, many adults in such occupations change jobs at mid-life in anticipation of, or because of, such declines. But in most occupations that demand high levels of cognitive skill, performance remains at essentially the same level throughout middle adulthood (Salthouse & Maurer, 1996).

Researchers Paul and Margaret Baltes argue that maintaining high job productivity or performance is possible because adults, faced with small but noticeable erosions of cognitive or physical skill, engage in a process the Balteses call "selective optimization with compensation" (Baltes & Baltes, 1990a). Three subprocesses are involved:

- *Selection*. Workers narrow their range of activities—for example, by focusing on only the most central tasks, delegating more responsibilities to others, or giving up or reducing peripheral job activities.

- *Optimization*. Workers deliberately "exercise" crucial abilities—such as by taking added training or polishing rusty skills—so as to remain as close to maximum skill levels as possible.

- *Compensation*. Workers adopt pragmatic strategies for overcoming specific obstacles—for example, getting stronger glasses or hearing aids, making lists to reduce memory loads, or even carefully emphasizing strengths and minimizing weaknesses when talking to co-workers or bosses.

Researchers have tested this model in a study of 224 working adults aged 40 to 69 (Abraham & Hansson, 1995). Measuring each of the three aspects of the proposed compensatory process as well as job competence, they found that the link between the use of selection, optimization, and compensation on the one hand and the quality of work performance on the other got stronger with increasing age. That is, the older the worker, the more it mattered whether she used helpful compensatory practices. In the older groups (primarily those in their 50s and early 60s), those who used the most selection, optimization, and compensation had the highest work performance. But among the younger workers in this sample (those in their early 40s), the same relationship did not hold. This is obviously only one study, but the results provide some support for the idea that job performance remains high during middle age at least in part because adults take deliberate compensatory actions.

UNEMPLOYMENT AND CAREER TRANSITIONS

In today's rapidly changing job market, it is not unusual for men and women to change occupations. However, career transitions can be more difficult in middle age than earlier in adulthood. For one thing, as you learned in **Chapter 14**, potential employers tend to believe that young adults are more capable of learning a new job than middle-aged applicants, even though research suggests that this generalization is untrue (Forte & Hansvick, 1999). Employers give middle-aged applicants higher ratings on variables such as dependability, but they tend to think that younger applicants will be able to acquire new skills (especially computer skills) more rapidly. Thus, mid-life career changers must often overcome ageism in obtaining new employment.

Career counsellors also point out that to understand mid-life career changes, it is useful to categorize workers on the basis of their reasons for changing occupations (Zunker, 1994). They suggest that people change careers for either external or internal reasons and can thus be classified as either *involuntary* or *voluntary* career changers.

INVOLUNTARY CAREER CHANGERS Involuntary career changers are people who are in transition due to external reasons: their skills have become obsolete, their jobs have been eliminated through organizational restructuring, or they have been laid off because of shifting economic conditions. They experience heightened levels of mental health disorders such as anxiety, depression, and substance abuse and are at higher risk of physical illness in the months after the job loss (Avison, 1997; Canadian Mental Health Association, 1995; Kessler, Turner, & House, 1988; Liem & Liem, 1988; Price, 1992). William Avison (1997), a University of Western Ontario sociologist, also reported higher levels of mortality associated with unemployment, whereby the longer the period of unemployment the higher the mortality rate. Avison also noted that negative health effects are heightened during economic recessions. Such effects are not unique to workers in Canada and the United States. Similar results have been found in studies in England, Denmark, and other Western developed countries (e.g., Iversen & Sabroe, 1988; Warr, Jackson, & Banks, 1988). You can see an example of this effect in **Figure 15.4**, which shows results from a study comparing 146 unemployed and 184 employed men and women (Kessler et al., 1988). Interestingly, just as remarriage alleviates many of the stresses associated with divorce, re-employment seems to restore health, emotional stability, and a sense of well-being quite rapidly.

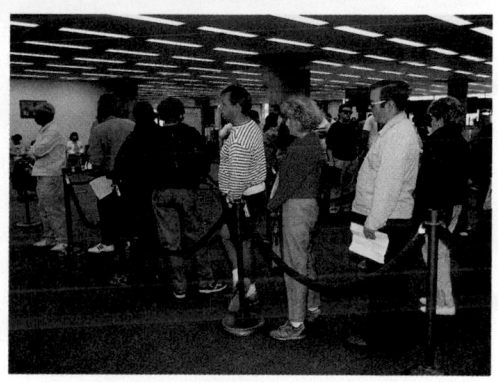

Involuntary career changers must confront a series of stressful situations, such as applying for Employment Insurance (EI) benefits. (*Photo:* Rob Crandall/Stock Boston)

The causal link between job loss and emotional or physical distress is both direct and indirect. The financial strain of job loss is itself a major contributor to heightened levels of anxiety and depression. When job loss does not create significant financial strain—such as when a spouse continues to work at a well-paying job or the family has other resources—the negative effect of job loss is only about half as great (Kessler et al., 1988).

The indirect effects of job loss include changes in family relationships and loss of self-esteem. Most strikingly, marital relationships deteriorate rapidly after one or the other spouse has been laid off. The number of hostile or negative interactions increases, and the number of warm and supportive interactions declines—which means that the crucial ratio of positive to negative interactions spirals downward. Separation and divorce become much more common as a result (Conger, Patterson, & Ge, 1995; Crouter & McHale, 1993; Elder & Caspi, 1988; McLoyd, Jayaratne, Ceballo, & Borquez, 1994).

These negative effects of unemployment are seen in both young and middle-aged adults, but those aged 30 to 60 seem to show the largest effects—the greatest increases in physical illness and the biggest declines in mental health (Warr et al., 1988). This pattern makes some sense in terms of the stages of men's work lives you read about in **Chapter 13**. During the trial stage, young adults between 18 and 29 may interpret periods of unemployment as a normal part of the trial-and-error process of finding the right job. But workers in the stabilization stage may interpret job loss quite differently—either as a sign of personal failure or as an unrecoverable loss of security. Younger workers are also more likely to be unmarried, with fewer economic responsibilities, and they may be able to return to live with their parents during a period of unemployment. For them, the stress is therefore less pronounced.

Predictably, the Big Five personality dimensions, especially neuroticism and openness to experience, affect mental health during involuntary career transitions across all racial and ethnic groups

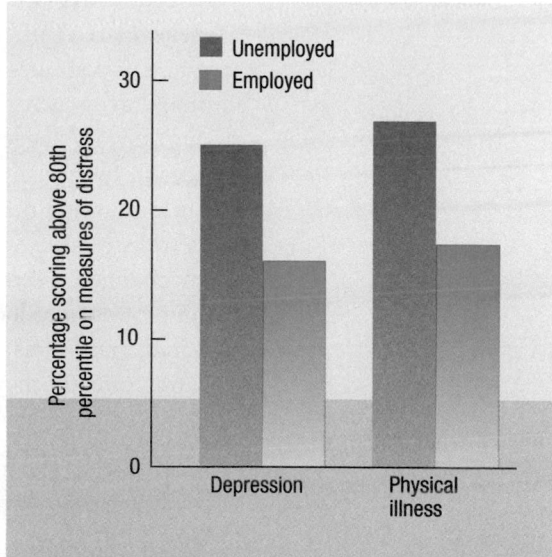

Figure 15.4

Adults who are involuntarily unemployed report more distress on nearly every measure, including both depression and physical illness, as shown by the results of a study in Michigan.

(*Source:* Kessler et al., 1988, from Table 2, p. 74.)

(Heppner, Fuller, & Multon, 1998). Nevertheless, mental health professionals suggest that the impact of an involuntary career change on an individual's life may be more directly affected by his or her coping skills (Zunker, 1994). For example, the person must be able to assess the situation realistically. If new work skills are needed, then the person must be able to formulate and carry out a plan for obtaining such skills. Researchers have found that mid-life career changers who have good coping skills and use them to manage involuntary transitions are less likely to become depressed (Cook & Heppner, 1997).

As with all types of stress, the effects of unemployment can be partially buffered by having adequate social support (Vinokur & van Ryn, 1993). Further, involuntary career changers benefit from career counselling that addresses both their occupational needs and their psychosocial development (Schadt, 1997). Counsellors can help people who are forced to change jobs learn to think of the transition as an opportunity to re-examine goals and priorities—to treat the crisis as an opportunity (Zunker, 1994).

Counsellors also urge involuntary career changers to avoid acting impulsively. They suggest viewing the transition as a process of stages that begins with a review of the individual's work history, interests, skills, and values. Based on the information gathered, the career changer should formulate an occupational goal and a plan for obtaining training, if needed. Finally, the person should develop a strategy to reduce the likelihood of another involuntary transition in the future, such as an educational plan for keeping work skills up-to-date.

VOLUNTARY CAREER CHANGERS Voluntary career changers leave one career to pursue another for a variety of internal reasons (Allen, Dreves, & Ruhe, 1999). For example, they may believe that the new job will be more fulfilling. One pattern occurs when workers look at the next step on the career ladder and decide they don't want to pursue further advancement in their current occupation. For example, both male and female certified public accountants are more likely to leave their profession for this reason than for any other (Greenhaus, Collins, Singh, & Parasuraman, 1997). Others change careers in order to be able to express aspects of their personalities that they believe aren't utilized in their present jobs (Young & Rodgers, 1997).

Twin studies suggest that the tendency to change careers voluntarily in adulthood may have a genetic basis (McCall, Cavanaugh, Arvey, & Taubman, 1997). These findings further suggest that such transitions are a by-product of personality. Whatever the reason for the transition, voluntary career changers have a better sense of control over their situation than do people whose job changes are forced on them, but the transition is still stressful. Spouses and family members may not understand why the person wants to change careers. Moreover, changing careers can involve periods of unemployment and, often, a reduction in income. Thus, voluntary career changers manifest many of the same symptoms of anxiety and depression seen in involuntary career changers. Consequently they, too, benefit from social support and career counselling.

PREPARING FOR RETIREMENT

Many middle-aged adults begin to prepare for retirement as early as 15 years before their anticipated retirement date. One aspect of such preparation is a gradual reduction in workload. For example, the peak participation rate in the Canadian labour force is between the ages of 25 and 54 for both men and women. However, the participation rates for Canadians aged 55 to 65 drops by about one-third for men and about half for women. This pattern of reduced participation after age 55 is common to many industrialized nations such as the United States, Japan, Sweden, and the United Kingdom (Statistics Canada, 2001m). One random national sample of 1339 American adults

Make the Connection

How might a middle-aged adult use the postformal thinking you learned about in **Chapter 12** to cope with an involuntary career transition?

found that not only do participation rates decline during middle adulthood, but so do the hours worked per year for both men and women (see **Figure 15.5**) (Herzog, House, & Morgan, 1991). You can see that the percentage of men and women working very long hours (2500 hours per year or more, which averages out to 48 hours a week) drops among those aged 55 to 64.

As they get nearer to the standard time for retirement, middle-aged adults also increase both formal and informal preparations (Evans, Ekerdt, & Bossé, 1985). They talk with their spouse and with friends or co-workers about retirement options and read more articles about retirement in the popular press. Some also undertake such formal preparations as attending financial planning seminars, determining how much Canada Pension Plan income they can expect upon retirement, investigating their pension plan at work in more detail, or seeking guidance from a professional retirement planner.

Such preparations are more likely among workers who are looking forward to retirement, who are dissatisfied with their work, or who have a retired friend (Evans et al., 1985). Those who dread retirement do the least planning, but even in this group, the level of informal planning increases as the time of retirement approaches.

However, it may be too early to form conclusions about how people prepare for retirement. After all, the notion of retirement is relatively new and tends to be exclusive to industrialized cultures. Even among the most prosperous nations, the idea of a period of leisure following many years of work did not exist prior to the mid-20th century. Thus, all our notions about preparation for retirement are based on a small number of cohorts, all of whose members were born in the first half of the 20th century. Comparisons of their behaviour with that of the current generation of middle-aged adults suggest that ideas about preparing for retirement have changed.

The retirement preparations of the Baby Boom cohort, who are all now middle-aged, are quite different from those of their parents (Monroy, 2000). For one thing,

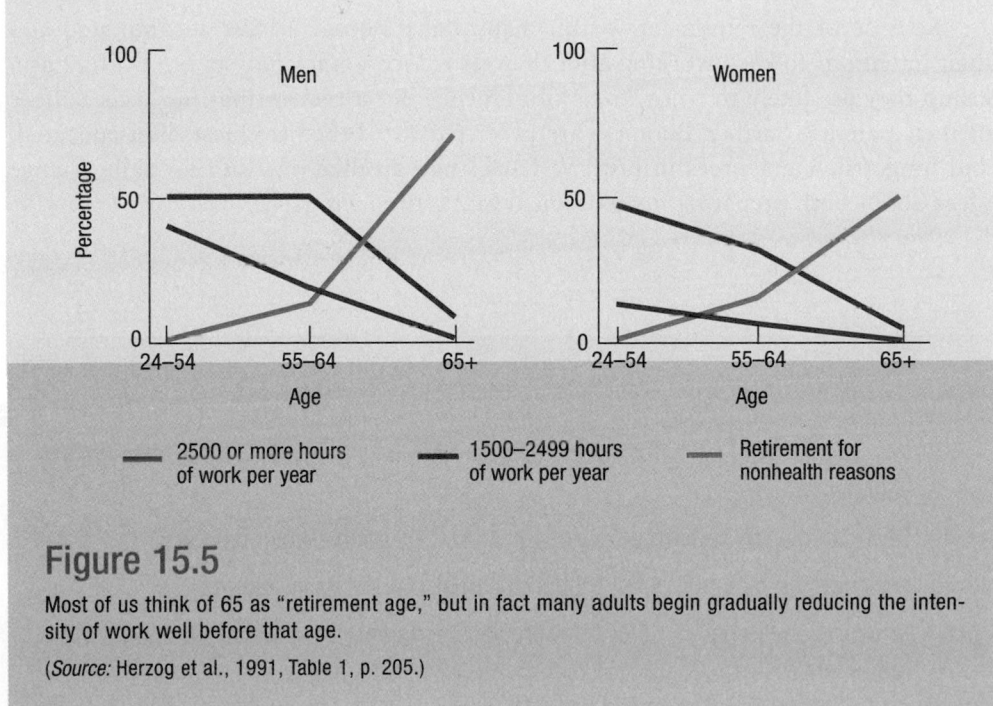

Figure 15.5

Most of us think of 65 as "retirement age," but in fact many adults begin gradually reducing the intensity of work well before that age.

(*Source:* Herzog et al., 1991, Table 1, p. 205.)

One difference between Baby Boomers and earlier cohorts is that more women are involved in retirement planning.
(*Photo:* Bob Daemmrich/Stock Boston)

among their parents, retirement planning was primarily a male responsibility. In contrast, Baby Boom women are also doing retirement planning, sometimes together with their husbands, but sometimes independently (Glass & Kilpatrick, 1998). Further, retirement-minded Boomers are largely responsible for the growth of electronic financial services, because of their enthusiastic response to the availability of such services on the Internet.

Most Baby Boomers expect to die in their mid-80s or later but expect to retire fairly early, in their early 60s (Monroy, 2000). This means that their expected length of retirement is 20 years or more longer than that of earlier generations. Moreover, Baby Boomers believe that they need higher retirement incomes than their parents. Most have enjoyed a comfortable standard of living compared with earlier generations, in part because of the proliferation of the two-income family. They expect some decline in income after their retirement, but generally much less change in their standard of living. Further, most do not expect that Old Age Security and Canada Pension Plan benefits will be adequate to meet their desired lifestyle needs.

Because of their expected length of retirement and income requirements, traditional ideas about preparation for retirement don't seem to fit the Baby Boomers. For example, earlier cohorts tended to put funds they expected to use for retirement into very safe investments (certificates of deposit, government bonds, and the like). However, many Baby Boomers have put their retirement nest eggs into the stock market. Further, they have borrowed rather than saved to achieve their investment objectives. Consequently, financial analysts claim that many individual Boomers may be in precarious situations when they reach retirement age because they are not saving enough money and have substantial debts (Glass & Kilpatrick, 1998; Monroy, 2000). In addition, while their parents' generation tended to think of retirement exclusively in terms of leisure time, most Boomers expect to work at least part-time during their retirement years. In fact, many Boomers look forward to retirement as a time when they can try out occupations that interest them but that they haven't had time to pursue earlier in life.

Because of the retirement wealth many Baby Boomers have accumulated and their intentions to keep working after they retire, economic analysts predict that as a group they are likely to enjoy levels of affluence in retirement that far exceed those of their parents. Further, Boomers are projected to be the healthiest, best-educated, and longest-living retirees in history. Thus, they are likely to substantially change ideas about both preparing for retirement and retirement itself.

Before Going On

- Why are levels of job satisfaction higher among middle-aged workers than among younger workers?
- Describe the job performance strategies used by middle-aged workers.
- What are the factors that contribute to career transitions in mid-life?
- How do Baby Boomers differ from previous cohorts with respect to preparation for retirement?

INDIVIDUAL DIFFERENCES

There are many individual differences in life experiences during middle adulthood. The pathway an adult follows, or the degree of movement along any one pathway, is affected by a whole range of factors, including individual family history and personality. By mid-life, many people have also encountered specific crises, such as divorce, poor health, early widowhood, or losing a job. As you've learned in earlier chapters, the timing of major life crises and transitions can also make a difference.

CONTINUITY AND CHANGE IN PERSONALITY

Can developmentalists tell what kind of person someone will be in middle adulthood, based on what is known about his childhood, adolescence, or early adult life? As you should remember, the Big Five personality traits are relatively stable across adolescence and adulthood. Similarly, masculinity and androgyny are correlated with self-esteem and social adjustment in adults of all ages (Shimonaka, Nakazato, Kawaai, & Sato, 1997).

Despite the evidence for continuity, most people believe that personality changes with age, and most expect themselves to change. In one study, researchers examined 26- to 67-year-olds' current perceptions of their own personalities in terms of the Big Five (Fleeson & Heckhausen, 1997). They also asked them to describe themselves when they were 20 to 25 years old and to speculate about how their personalities might change by the time they reach age 70. Further, they were asked to describe an ideal personality they would like to have. All respondents believed that their personalities had changed since they were younger and that they would change in the future. Their ideas about the kinds of changes that would take place included both gaining and losing some traits. The researchers pointed out that these respondents per-ceived much more change in personality than is shown by longitu-dinal studies of the Big Five traits. Apparently, we believe we change much more than we actually do.

However, there is some evidence of real change in personality in adulthood. For example, most observers agree that during the years from 40 to 65, most adults decline in achievement striving, independence, assertiveness, and individualism, which tend to peak at about mid-life. In fact, several studies suggest that people become more prosocial and less individualistic in middle and late adulthood (e.g., Van Lange, DeBruin, Otten, & Joireman, 1997). Interestingly, though, this change seems to be linked to secure attachment in infancy and childhood, so it has elements of both conti-nuity and change.

Studies of negative and positive emotionality suggest a similar pattern. Even though negative emotionality in early adulthood is moderately to strongly correlated with neg-ative emotionality in middle adulthood, longitudinal studies show that many individu-als become *less* negative over time (Helson & Klohnen, 1998). Apparently, then, when researchers consider large groups—which they must to correlate variables such as per-sonality factors—they find that personality is fairly stable over time. However, the cor-relations can mask a number of individual cases in which there is a great deal of change. Consequently, the best conclusion to draw is that stability is the general pattern, but the increased individual variability in personality that is typically found among middle-aged and older adults suggests that change is clearly possible and may even be common (Nelson & Dannefer, 1992).

Critical Thinking

Has your personality changed since you were younger? In what ways? How do you expect it to change as you get older?

Cohort differences must also be kept in mind when interpreting research results. For example, one recent study found that middle-aged women from the Baby Boom generation, most of whom have worked outside the home for a large proportion of their adult lives, may possess characteristics that have not been found in research on earlier cohorts (Stewart & Ostrove, 1998). Historically, researchers consistently found that menopause and the empty nest were the primary landmarks middle-aged women used to characterize their lives. Baby Boom women, however, seem to be more likely to engage in the sort of comprehensive life review that previously was more characteristic of middle-aged men. Physical and family changes appear to continue to be important for these women at mid-life, but career issues and the potential for reshaping their lives as they age seem also to be crucial.

Cross-sectional studies suggest the mechanism behind personality change in middle adulthood may be an increasing ability to maintain control of one's emotions in a variety of situations (Gross et al., 1997). Supporting this hypothesis are the findings from a recent Internet survey of 132 515 American and Canadian adults aged 21 to 60 (Srivastava, John, Gosling & Potter, 2003). The massive cross-sectional study revealed that personality continues to change across adulthood, but at different rates and directions depending on which Big Five personality traits are being measured. For example, *contentiousness* increased significantly up to age 30 and then continued to increase, but at a slower rate; *agreeableness* showed a dramatic increase between ages 30 and 60; *neuroticism* declined significantly across adulthood, but only in women; both men and women decreased in *openness* after age 30; and on the fifth trait, *extraversion*, women showed a significant decrease after age 30 whereas men showed an increase.

Another possible cause of change is growth in personal flexibility. Researchers have examined the tendency of adults to either remain committed to difficult goals or adjust their goals when an objective seems to be impossible to achieve (Brandtstädter & Baltes-Götz, 1990; Brandtstädter & Greve, 1994). An individual high in **tenacious goal pursuit** would agree with statements like these (Brandtstädter & Baltes-Götz, 1990, p. 216):

> The harder a goal is to achieve, the more desirable it often appears to me. Even if everything seems hopeless, I still look for a way to master the situation.

Someone high in **flexible goal adjustment** would agree with the following (pp. 215–216):

> I can adapt quite easily to changes in a situation. In general, I'm not upset very long about an opportunity passed up. I usually recognize quite easily my own limitations.

Tenacious goal pursuit tends to decrease in middle adulthood, while flexible goal adjustment rises, suggesting a kind of "mellowing" of personality in the middle years.

tenacious goal pursuit
a behaviour pattern in which middle-aged adults remain committed to goals that are difficult, and may be impossible, for them to achieve

flexible goal adjustment
a behaviour pattern in which middle-aged adults adjust goals in order to enhance the likelihood of success

THE EFFECTS OF TIMING

As in earlier periods, the timing of major life events in middle adulthood affects individual developmental pathways. For example, early menopause seems to be particularly stressful. Women who are peri- or postmenopausal in their late 30s or early 40s manifest negative reactions simply to the word *menopause* (Singer & Hunter, 1999). Many react to discovering that they are menopausal with shock and denial. When they realize that the physical transition is unavoidable, many respond with anger and feel a sense of loss of control. Long-term consequences of early menopause are predicted by a woman's developmental history, material circumstances, and the way in which she fits early menopause into her own autobiography and sense of self.

In another variation on the timing theme, middle-aged adults are likely to feel extra strain, even a sense of failure, if children do not leave home by the time they are about 25 (Hagestad, 1986). Moreover, conflicts between parents and resident adult children are common (Muzi, 2000). Both parents and children feel that they have inadequate privacy. Middle-aged parents' sense of obligation to their children may cause them to feel that they can't pursue their own goals until they have helped their late-blooming children to become self-sufficient. As a child's departure is further and further delayed, frustrations can accumulate.

Research suggests that middle-aged women are more resilient than younger women in managing transitions such as divorce.
(*Photo:* David Young-Wolff/PhotoEdit)

The percentage of adult children living with their middle-aged parents is increasing. Gerontologist Barbara Mitchell (2000) of Simon Fraser University reported that 20- to 34-year-olds are staying at home longer (about half are still living with their parents). Many others leave home and then return (about 27% of 19- to 35-year-olds are part of this so-called *boomerang generation*). Financial difficulties associated with unemployment and/or extended post-secondary schooling, delayed marriage, and a rise in the divorce rate probably explain this increase (Baker, 1996; Muzi, 2000; Schwartz & Scott, 2000).

Research suggests that, even though conflict occurs, more than half of parents with adult resident children manage to work out good systems for handling the potential stresses and say that they are satisfied with their arrangement (Aquilino & Supple, 1991). In fact, some parents enjoy greater social support from their resident children than from their children who live away from home (Umberson, 1992). But there is little doubt that such an arrangement brings a new set of tasks and roles, and that it is linked to somewhat higher stress levels in many families.

Similarly, adults who become grandparents unusually early seem to be less comfortable with the role (see the **Research Report**) (Burton & Bengtson, 1985; Troll, 1985, Watson, 1997). Likewise, those whose parents die early find themselves unexpectedly thrust into the role of family "elders" before they are ready for it. As one 40-year-old man whose parents had both just died said, "I'm too young to be next in line!" (Hagestad, 1986).

Research Report

Early Grandparenthood

McMaster University researchers Rosenthal and Gladstone (2000) reported that despite the fact that Canadian adults are now putting off childbearing until later in life, grandparenthood is occurring at an earlier age than in the past. Mothers of the Baby Boom cohort had their first child at a historically young age and this contributes to the early grandmotherhood trend, although this trend may be reversed with the next generation. On an individual level, the dominant factor that affects early grandparenthood is the rate of teenage pregnancy. Although the rates of teenage pregnancy have been declining in Canada, when a teenager does have a baby, it leads to early grandparenthood for the teenagers' parents.

What is striking is how different the experience of grandmotherhood can be for those who became grandmothers early as opposed to those who were in line with current patterns (Burton & Bengtson, 1985). Early grandmothers reported far more strain and distress. In part, this occurred because these young grandmothers were still in early adulthood themselves, with all of the role conflict and role overload of that period. Many of these early grandmothers still had young children of their own at home to rear. They were distressed to have the role of grandparent added to the list, especially if they expected to have to take on some of the task of rearing the grandchild.

But the early timing of the role change also seemed to be disturbing in itself. These women associated grandparenthood with being "old," and they did not want to feel old. According to a 28-year-old grandmother,

I could break my daughter's neck for having this baby. I just got a new boyfriend. Now he will think I'm too old. It was bad enough being a mother so young—now a grandmother too! (Burton & Bengtson, 1985, p. 61)

Another woman who became a grandmother at 27 said, "I'm too young to be a grandmother. You made this baby, you take care of it" (p. 61). Many of these very early grandmothers did end up helping to rear their new grandchildren, but clearly they did so reluctantly. In contrast, women in this study who became grandmothers at the standard time were much more willing to participate in the new child's care and much more pleased about becoming grandmothers.

Many factors are clearly involved here. Very early grandmothers must, of necessity, have been early mothers themselves, and this fact sets them apart from other women in some ways. Further, when grandparents have more material resources than their unmarried children who become parents, the experience of early grandparenting is often mingled with that of parenting a live-in teenaged or young adult mother and her child. In such situations, it is difficult to separate the effects of timing and family stress (Gordon, Chase-Lansdale, Matjasko, & Brooks-Gunn, 1997). But these results are consistent with researchers' general knowledge about the impact of being on-time or off-time in major life transitions.

By contrast, divorce, which is typically an early adulthood event, appears to be less traumatic for middle-aged women than for younger women (Marks & Lambert, 1998). Perhaps the "mellowing" of personality you read about earlier in this chapter renders the middle-aged woman more resilient to such traumatic events. So, timing may be important only when events that are perceived to signal movement into the late adult years—menopause and grandparenthood—occur earlier than expected.

Before Going On

- What is the evidence for continuity in personality throughout adulthood?
- What does research suggest about the possibility of adult personality changes?
- In what way does the timing of adult role transitions affect a middle-aged individual's sense of well-being?

Summary

Theories of Social and Personality Development

- Erikson proposed that the primary developmental task of middle adulthood is to acquire a sense of generativity through mentoring younger individuals.

- Many different models of the "mid-life crisis" in middle adulthood have been proposed, but none has been strongly supported by research.

- Sociologists explain adult development in terms of role transitions. Duvall's stage theory of role transitions has provided a framework for research, but it is not comprehensive enough to explain adult development.

Changes in Relationships

- Marital satisfaction is typically higher at mid-life than it is earlier. This higher level of satisfaction appears to be due primarily to a decline in problems and conflicts.

- Middle-aged adults have significant family interactions both up and down the generational chain. The two-way responsibilities can create a mid-life "squeeze" or a "sandwich generation." Middle adults provide more assistance in both directions and attempt to influence both preceding and succeeding generations.

- There is little sign that middle-aged parents experience negative reactions to the "empty nest" when the last child leaves home. On the contrary, the reduction in role demands may contribute to the rise in life satisfaction at this age.

- Most adults become grandparents in middle age. The majority have warm, affectionate relationships with their grandchildren, although there are also many remote relationships. A minority of grandparents are involved in day-to-day care of grandchildren.

- Almost one-quarter of middle-aged adults take on the role of caregiver for an aging parent. Those who do report feeling a considerable burden and suffer increased depression, particularly if the parent being cared for suffers from some form of dementia. Women are two to four times as likely as men to fill the role of caregiver to a frail elder.

- Friendships appear to be somewhat less numerous in middle adulthood, although they appear to be as intimate and central to the individual.

Mid-Life Career Issues

- Job satisfaction is at its peak in middle adulthood, and productivity remains high. But the centrality of the work role appears to wane somewhat, and job satisfaction is less clearly linked to overall life satisfaction than at earlier ages. Research suggests that patterns of work and satisfaction are different for men and women in middle age.

- Levels of job performance in middle adulthood are consistent with those at earlier ages, with the exception of work that involves physical strength or reaction time.

- Involuntary career changes are associated with anxiety and depression. Even many middle-aged adults who make voluntary career transitions experience negative emotions.

- Middle-aged adults prepare for retirement in several ways, not only by specific planning but also by reducing the number of hours they work.

Individual Differences

- The Big Five personality traits and other aspects of personality are correlated across early and middle adulthood. There is evidence for personality change in middle age as well. There are some signs of "mellowing," a lowering of intensity and striving, but middle-aged adults vary more in personality traits than do younger adults.

- Any role change or crisis that is not timed according to expectations for a given cohort or culture is associated with higher levels of stress. Such events include very early grandparenthood, early death of one's parents, and late departure of grown children from the home.

Key Terms

caregiver burden (p. 463)

companionate relationships (p. 460)

flexible goal adjustment (p. 472)

generativity (p. 450)

generativity versus stagnation stage (p. 450)

involved relationships (p. 460)

remote relationships (p. 460)

role conflict (p. 453)

role strain (p. 453)

tenacious goal pursuit (p. 472)

Weblinks

Caring for Aging Parents
www.warrenshepell.com/articles/caring.asp
This article, from the HealthQuest newsletter on mental health issues, provides a useful overview of the difficulties associated with caring for aging parents.

Cangrands
www.cangrands.com/
This not-for-profit organization offers insights, statistics, and useful links about grandparenting in Canada today.

Canada's Retirement Income System: What's In It for You?"
www.sdc.gc.ca/asp/gateway.asp?hr=/en/isp/common/ris/ristoc.shtml&hs=cpr
This Social Development Canada website is provided to help you learn more about the retirement income system in Canada.

Egale Canada
www.egale.ca/
Egale was founded to advance equality for lesbian, gay, bisexual, and transgendered people and their families across Canada. The website promotes public education and awareness.

Equal Marriage for Same-Sex Couples
www.samesexmarriage.ca
Two well-known married gay activists produced this website to help raise awareness about and advocate for same-sex marriage and rights.

What Is the Changing Status of Canadian Couples?

During the sexual revolution of the 1960s and early 1970s, young adults often referred to marriage as "just a piece of paper." The real bond between intimate partners was psychological, many asserted, and need not be validated by a government licence. This view became the driving force behind a movement away from marriage and toward cohabitation. At the same time, gay rights advocates began to suggest that, if being a couple is essentially a psychological union, then sexual orientation should be irrelevant. That is, they argued, homosexuals are capable of establishing the same kinds of interpersonal relationships as heterosexuals. Therefore, heterosexual unions should not be seen as superior in any way simply because they are legally sanctioned by society.

Behavioural scientists are interested in the question of how and to what degree the legal status of a relationship alters its impact on partners' interactions with each other and on their individual development. One interesting point is that changing ideas about relationships, instead of causing marriage to disappear, have led to an increase in the number of legal options available to intimate partners. Thus, it seems that both heterosexual and homosexual couples, rather than regarding a licence as "just a piece of paper," continue to want to have their relationships recognized by society in some official way. This common motivation to enter into legally sanctioned relationships has led to a number of changes in social policy.

MARRIAGE AND DIVORCE REFORM

The institution of marriage is currently undergoing a wave of reforms. The first reform stems from the right-to-marry movement among homosexuals. Court challenges to Canada's marriage laws were initially brought forth in Ontario, British Columbia, and Quebec after same-sex couples petitioned the provinces to register their marriages. The provincial courts relented, stating that the federal common law that defines marriage strictly as a legal relationship between a man and a woman is discriminatory. The same-sex marriage issue has been debated in several countries for many years. At the time of writing, the Netherlands and Belgium have

legally sanctioned same-sex marriage, as have most of Canada's provinces and the Yukon; the next section gives more details of recent developments in Canada.

Another set of marriage reforms is aimed at reducing divorce. For example, in Canada and in many U.S. states, efforts are underway to require couples to undergo premarital counselling. Advocates of mandatory premarital counselling cite research suggesting that couples who go through this counselling experience higher levels of marital satisfaction and are less likely to divorce (e.g., Sayers, Kohn, & Heavey, 1998; Schumm, Resnick, Silliman, & Bell, 1998). Opponents of such requirements point to studies that indicate that couples who go through premarital

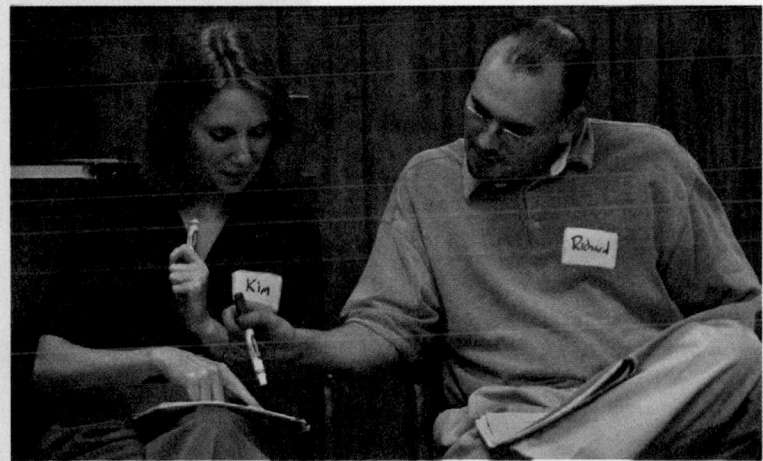

In the hope of reducing divorce rates, efforts are under way in both Canada and the United States to make premarital counselling a requirement. However, there is a great deal of debate about whether such measures really are effective, or whether couples who are likely to seek premarital counselling are already morally opposed to the idea of divorce in the first place.
(*Photo:* John Bazemore/CP Photo Archive)

counselling are no less likely to divorce than others (e.g., Sullivan & Bradbury, 1997). Moreover, couples who participate in pre-marital counselling are typically more religious than couples who don't go through counselling—and religion itself is a factor that predisposes against divorce. Thus, opponents claim, positive effects associated with premarital counselling are actually self-selection effects: Those who are least likely to divorce are the most likely to obtain premarital counselling.

Similarly, proposed changes in divorce laws include one requiring a couple to undergo marriage counselling before they can divorce. Most studies suggest that marital therapy usually results in short-term improvements in relationship quality. However, findings regarding long-term effectiveness of therapy in preventing divorce are inconsistent (Bodenmann, Widmer, & Cina, 1999; Christensen & Heavey, 1999).

STATUS OF SAME-SEX COUPLES IN CANADA

In May 1999, the Supreme Court of Canada ruled that all provinces must provide same-sex couples with benefits that are equal to those provided to common-law, heterosexual couples. Following the ruling, the federal parliament passed the *Modernization of Benefits and Obligations Act* (MBOA) in June 2000. The MBOA ensures that same-sex common-law partners have the same benefits and obligations as opposite-sex common-law partners. Initially, the provinces and territories developed a variety of ways to accommodate the act. For instance, Nova Scotia allowed both same-sex and opposite-sex couples to apply for registered domestic partnerships once they satisfy the requirements for the legal definition of "common-law partner." Once a couple makes a "domestic-partner declaration," they have

most of the same rights as married heterosexual couples. Quebec's response was similar to the Nova Scotia model, whereby same-sex couples would be allowed to enter into a civil union and would thus be governed by the same rules that apply to marriages (e.g., those registered under the civil union would have the same tax, health insurance, and pension rules and responsibilities as married couples).

As other provinces and territories struggled to find a solution, everything suddenly changed. In 2002 the Supreme Court of Ontario ruled that the federal law that limits marriage to the "union of one man and one woman to the exclusion of all others" was discriminatory and unconstitutional. The ruling effectively allowed legal same-sex marriages to take place in Ontario and, over the next two years, British Columbia, Quebec, and the Yukon followed suit. Soon after, Nunavut, Manitoba, Nova Scotia, Saskatchewan, and Newfoundland and Labrador judiciaries declared they would not contest the legality of same-sex marriages. By December 2004, the Supreme Court of Canada had ruled that the federal government had the right to sanction same-sex marriages. This ruling gave Parliament the

go-ahead to pass legislation allowing those marriages.

Typically, opposition to same-sex marriage comes from religious groups that believe homosexuality to be immoral (Tettamanzi, 1998). Proponents argue that homosexual couples who want to legally affirm their relationship should do so irrespective of others' views of the morality of their sexual orientation. Advocates also suggest that homosexuals need a legal means by which to make employee health benefits or survivor pensions and benefits available immediately to their partners. Similarly, in the absence of a legal relationship, homosexuals have no right to authorize or terminate medical treatment for an ailing or injured partner.

THE IMPACT OF LEGAL STATUS ON RELATIONSHIPS AND INDIVIDUALS

The number of legal options available to couples is growing. Researchers interested in individual development and the effects of legal status on intimate partners' relationships are faced with a much more complex

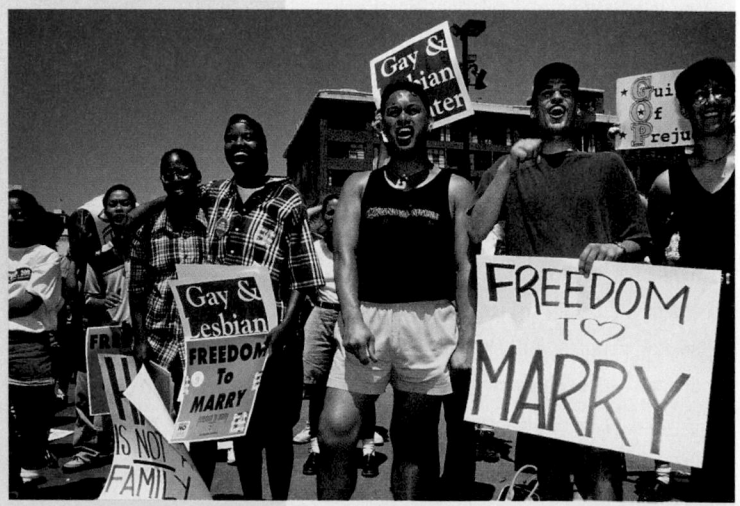

Most jurisdictions in Canada's provinces and territories now legally recognize same-sex marriages. (*Photo:* Jonathan Nourok/Getty Images)

In January 2001, two same-sex couples were married at Metropolitan Community Church in Toronto, the first formal same-sex weddings in the country. Banns had been read in church, a Christian tradition recognized in Ontario law. When the Registrar-General refused to register the marriage documents, the church successfully took the government to court.

(*Photo:* Kevin Frayer/CP Photo Archive)

task compared to when a "couple" consisted of a man and a woman who were either married or living together. Until recently, examination of the correlations among relationship legal status, sexual orientation, relationship quality, and individual development has not been possible because the social recognition of the homosexual union is such a recent occurrence (Ambert, 2003a). However, we can expect the homosexual union will likely become an active area of research over the next several decades. To be most useful, such research would have to take into account other variables, such as whether or not people have had prior heterosexual relationships, whether they have children, gay versus lesbian couples, the partners' cultural backgrounds, their personalities, their ages, and so on. Preferably, the various groups will be studied longitudinally. Currently, researchers can say there are qualitative differences between legally married and cohabiting heterosexuals (see **Chapter 13**). Likewise, despite some similarities, there are a few important differences between heterosexual and homosexual relationships (see **Chapter 13**). Thus, both legal status and sexual orientation seem to matter in relationships, but as yet there is no reliable evidence about how the two factors might interact.

YOUR TURN

- What kinds of marriage and divorce reform efforts are currently underway in your province or territory?

- Consult a gay-rights website (such as **www.egale.ca**) to find out the current status of same-sex marriages across Canada.

- Describe some of the practical benefits and potential problems with mandatory premarital and predivorce counselling.

- Find out whether your province or territory has a domestic partnership law. If so, does the law have separate rules for domestic partnership and for legal marriages?

- How will the change in the definition of marriage affect parenting, religious practices, and other traditional social customs? Explain.

CHAPTER 16

R.W. Jones/CORBIS

PHYSICAL AND COGNITIVE DEVELOPMENT IN LATE ADULTHOOD

In an earlier book, Helen Bee wrote about her 81-year-old father's tendency to use the term "my brains" to refer to a notebook in which he kept information such as frequently used phone numbers, appointments, birthdays, and the like. He developed this behaviour in response to his self-observed increasing forgetfulness, and the substitute "brains" enabled him to get through each day without having to rely on his own brain. As this anecdote illustrates, for many older adults, the experience of aging is a process of learning to offset weaknesses, such as increasing forgetfulness, with strengths, such as practicality and inventiveness.

As the example of Helen Bee's father illustrates, older adults often find ingenious ways of managing age-related changes. Thus, one of the most striking characteristics of old age is the degree to which the experience of growing old varies from one individual to another. In this chapter we will examine this variability, along with changes that appear to affect almost everyone. As you read, keep the following questions in mind:

- How variable are the elderly?

- What physical changes are associated with late adulthood, how do theorists explain them, and how do they affect the lives of older adults?

- What are the major mental health concerns of late adulthood?

- How does aging affect memory, and what theories have psychologists formed regarding the development of wisdom and creativity in old age?

VARIABILITY IN LATE ADULTHOOD

The scientific study of aging is known as **gerontology**. For many years, gerontologists thought about old age almost exclusively in terms of decline and loss. However, perspectives on the later years are rapidly changing, and late adulthood is now thought of as a period of tremendous individual variability rather than one of universal decline (Weaver, 1999).

gerontology
the scientific study of aging

CHARACTERISTICS OF THE ELDERLY POPULATION

Stereotypes of the elderly abound—they are the stuff of jokes and fairy tales, and today they are reinforced in the media. But real people often belie the stereotypes.

LIFE EXPECTANCY You might be surprised to learn that life expectancy increases as adults get older. For example, in Canada, the average 65-year-old man lives to just over age 82, but once a man reaches his early 80s, he is likely to live to be 90 (Health Canada, 1999e; Statistics Canada, 2004f). Life expectancy among women is even longer. The average 65-year-old woman is likely to live to the age of 87, and the women who make it to their mid-80s can expect to live to over 92. Because of this sex difference in life expectancy, there are more elderly women than men. However, the gender gap has been narrowing in Canada since 1981, at which time women outlived men by 7.1 years (Statistics Canada, 2001n). Interestingly enough, the most recent estimates indicate that a male baby born in 2001 can expect to live to be 77 and a female baby may live to age 82.1, a difference of only 5.1 years (Statistics Canada (2004f).

SUBGROUPS Gerontologists point out that there are important differences among the *young old* (aged 60 to 75), the *old old* (aged 75 to 85), and the *oldest old* (aged 85 and over). The oldest old are the fastest-growing segment of the population in Canada, which means that terms such as *octogenarian* (a person in his or her 80s) and *centenarian* (a person over 100 years of age) will be used far more often than in the past. From 1981 to 2000, the over-65 population in Canada increased by about two-thirds, from about 10% to 13% of the total population (Health Canada, 2003e). The over-85 population almost tripled during the same time frame, and it is estimated that by 2051 the over-85 population will grow to almost five times the current figure of 400 000-plus (Health Canada, 2003f). Furthermore, every industrialized country in the world is experiencing this same kind of growth in the elderly population (Century Foundation, 1998).

The oldest old are more likely to suffer from significant physical and mental impairments than are the young old or old old. Consequently, the increase in their numbers means that the population of **frail elderly**, older adults who cannot care for themselves, is also likely to grow significantly. Consequently, demographers and economists have become concerned about the ability of young and middle-aged adults to support the growing number of elderly (see **No Easy Answers**).

frail elderly

older adults whose physical and/or mental impairments are so extensive that they cannot care for themselves

HEALTH As **Figure 16.1** indicates, a majority of older adults across all three age subgroups regard their health as good to excellent (Statistics Canada, 2004g). These data contradict stereotypes of old age as a period of illness. However, the proportion of elderly with fair or poor health is a great deal higher than the equivalent proportions for young and middle-aged adults. For instance, the proportion of fair or poor self-rated health scores jumped from 5% in Canadians aged 25 to 34 up to 32% in elders aged 75 and older. Thus, as you might suspect, health is the single largest factor determining the trajectory of an adult's physical or mental status over the years beyond age 65. As you read more about the prevalence of disability and disease among older adults, keep **Figure 16.1** in mind. You will see that these data are a testimony to the emotional resilience of older adults, a majority of whom are able to maintain an optimistic view of themselves and their lives in the face of growing physical challenges.

Those who are already suffering from one or more chronic diseases at 65 show far more rapid declines than do those who begin late adulthood with no disease symptoms. In part, of course, this is an effect of the disease processes themselves. Cardiovascular disease results, among other things, in restricted blood flow to many organs, including the brain, with predictable effects on an adult's ability to learn or remember. Analyses from an American investigation, the Seattle Longitudinal Study, show that adults with this disease experience earlier declines in all mental abilities (Schaie, 1996). And, of course, those suffering from the early stages of Alzheimer's disease or another disease that causes dementia will experience far more rapid declines in mental abilities than will those who do not have such diseases.

COGNITIVE FUNCTIONING Christopher Patterson, professor of geriatric medicine at McMaster University, states that, as the prevalence of dementia increases in Canadian elderly, so does the rate of cognitive impairment. Alzheimer's disease, an irreversible degenerative condition, is the most common cause of dementia. Other sources of mental confusion include "intercurrent illnesses, infections, metabolic disturbances and drug intoxications" (Patterson, 1994, p. 902). Little of the cognitive impairment associated with the later cluster of disorders is reversible. For instance, Patterson

Figure 16.1

Most Canadian elders rated their health as good to excellent.

(*Source:* Adapted from Statistics Canada, June 2004, *Health Indicators, 2004*(1), Chart—Self-rated health, by age group and sex, household population aged 12 and over, Canada, 2003, Catalogue No. 82-221 [Statistics Canada 2004g].)

No Easy Answers

The Coming

Demographic Crisis

in Canada

Every industrialized nation in the world, including Canada, will face a demographic crisis in the near future. Within the next decade, the elderly population will increase dramatically. As a result, there will be fewer young and middle-aged adult workers for every retired person (Century Foundation, 1998). Consequently, Canadians are concerned that the various levels of government may lack sufficient tax revenues to pay for the many benefits they have guaranteed to senior citizens.

With respect to pension plans, the two public sources, the Old Age Security (OAS) program (28%) and Canada and Quebec Pension Plan (C/QPP) (21%), combined to make up half of the income for seniors (Health Canada, 2003g). The other half of seniors' income came from private sources, including retirement pensions and RRSP investments (29%), investments other than RRSPs (13%), and employment income (5%).

The reliance on the C/QPP, OAS, and work-related pensions as the major sources of retirement income has been increasing steadily since the early 1980s, but this will likely change as today's workers reach retirement. First, fewer Canadians are enrolled in company or private retirement pension plans, which now stand at 40% (HRDC, 2001c). Second, Canadian workers are worried that the C/QPP will run out of money before they will be eligible to collect from the plan. Not having a secure, predictable retirement income source puts more pressure on individuals to rely on risk-laden personal investment strategies (RRSPs and non-RRSP investments) and/or the prospect of working past retirement age.

Voters in Canada overwhelmingly oppose reducing benefits for the current cohort of retired people and are only slightly less opposed to reducing benefits for future retirees. At the same time, most workers believe that their C/QPP payroll deductions are already too high but do not want the government to use other funds, such as those generated by income taxes, to pay for pension benefits. Consequently, lawmakers face a dilemma: A solution must be found or governments may go bankrupt trying to fulfill their obligations to future elderly citizens. However, any solution politicians impose on voters is likely to be unpopular.

For these reasons, policy makers are looking for ways to make elderly entitlement reform more palatable to voters. For example, one proposal involves workers taking responsibility for their own retirement income by directing how their government pension funds are to be invested. The appeal of this option is that it offers workers more autonomy. However, unlike the current system, it would not include a guaranteed retirement income. Those who invest wisely will enjoy a comfortable retirement; those who are less astute may be left with little or nothing.

The federal government has recently made pension reforms designed to ensure that you have income security when you reach retirement. In 1997 the CPP Investment Board was created by an Act of Parliament to invest funds not required by the Canada Pension Plan (CPP) for paying current pensions. The resultant assets, and the income earned on them, will be available to the CCP to pay future pensions. The CPP Investment Board is governed by a qualified board of directors who are independent from governments in making investment decisions. As for long-term pension security, the federal Chief Actuary has projected that CPP contributions will exceed benefits until 2021. After that, contributions plus investment income will pay benefits. This is important in helping to pay the pensions of younger workers who are decades away from retirement (Canada Pension Plan Investment Board, 2001).

As more Canadians age, future retirees are more likely to have to rely on personal retirement savings rather than CPP, QPP, or OAS as a source of income in later life. If their retirement savings are insufficient, some elderly people may need to continue working beyond the age of 65. (*Photo:* ImageState/Firstlight.ca)

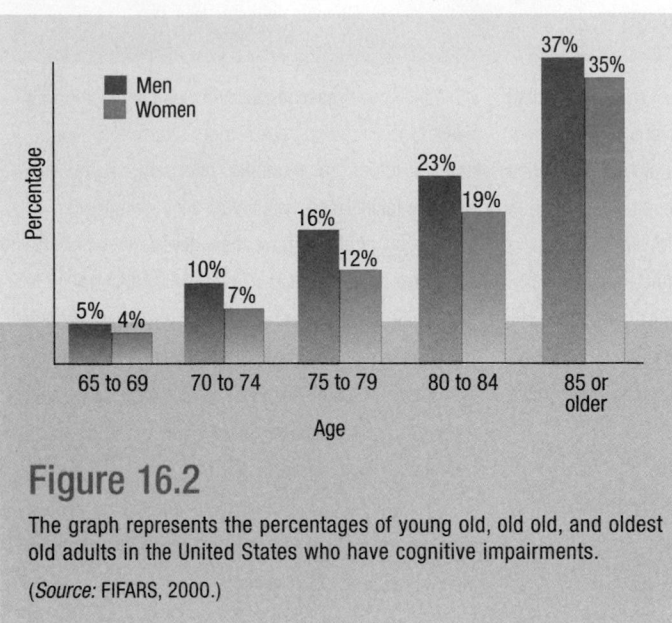

Figure 16.2

The graph represents the percentages of young old, old old, and oldest old adults in the United States who have cognitive impairments.

(*Source:* FIFARS, 2000.)

(1994) reported that only 11% of dementing disorders were partially (8%) or completely (3%) cleared up.

The prevalence of mild and severe forms of dementia, which both contribute to cognitive deficits, has been found to be relatively consistent in Canada, Europe, and the United States (Patterson, 1994). Researchers found a great deal of variability in a 7-year longitudinal study of the cognitive abilities of 102 older adults, first tested when they were between ages 62 and 86 (Willis, Jay, Diehl, & Marsiske, 1992). Over the ensuing 7 years, when most of the participants shifted from being young old to being old old, 62% of the group either remained at their original level of competence or showed improvement in competence on everyday intellectual tasks, while the remaining 38% showed decline (Willis et al., 1992). These results are supported by the graph in **Figure 16.2**, which illustrates that a majority of elderly adults, even among those who are over 85, do not suffer from cognitive impairments.

MENTAL EXERCISE Can mental exercise improve mental functioning, just as physical exercise improves physical functioning? Studies with rats show that older rats placed in very rich, interesting environments experience growth in brain tissue, whereas rats placed in neutral or boring environments experience a decrease in brain mass (Cotman & Neeper, 1996). Neurophysiologists involved in this animal research are convinced that something analogous occurs among humans—that older adults who continue to challenge themselves with complex mental activities can delay, or even reverse, the normal decline in brain mass that is part of primary aging.

Correlational evidence supports this argument. For example, in one study, researchers found that older adults who played bridge regularly had higher scores on tests of both memory and reasoning than did non–bridge players. The two groups did not differ in education, health, exercise levels, or life satisfaction or on measures of physical and cognitive functioning that have little relationship to bridge playing, such as reaction time and vocabulary size (Clarkson-Smith & Hartley, 1990).

The difficulties inherent in this research are obvious: Most strikingly, such research suffers from a serious self-selection problem. People who strive to remain mentally active are doubtless different to begin with from those who make less effort. And teasing out the unique effect of mental activity from the role of education, social class, and health is clearly very difficult. But it seems reasonable that some—perhaps significant—enhancement or better maintenance of intellectual skills results from an "engaged" and intellectually active lifestyle (Gold et al., 1995).

functional status

a measure of an individual's ability to perform certain roles and tasks, particularly self-help tasks and other chores of daily living (Havens & Finlayson, 1999)

activities of daily living (ADLs)

self-help tasks such as bathing, dressing, and using the toilet

instrumental activities of daily living (IADLs)

more complex daily living tasks such as doing housework, cooking, and managing money

LIMITATIONS ON ACTIVITIES University of Manitoba health care researchers Betty Havens and Marcia Finlayson (1999) define **functional status** as a measure of an individual's ability to perform certain roles and tasks, particularly self-help tasks and other chores of daily living. Daily living tasks are grouped into two categories: **Activities of daily living (ADLs)** include bathing, dressing, using the toilet, and so forth. **Instrumental activities of daily living (IADLs)** include doing housework, cooking, and managing money.

As you might expect, the proportion of older adults with disabilities rises with age. Haven and Finlayson (1999) reported that roughly one-third of Canadians over the age of 65 and 44% of those over the age of 85 experienced at least some level of difficulty performing some basic daily life activities. But this means that over half of these oldest old do *not* have such problems. Even more encouraging is the finding that the rate of disability among Canadians 75 years and older declined from 46.4% to 42.4% between 1994/95 and 1998/99 (Statistics Canada, 2001o), perhaps because of better health care or better health habits.

As you can see from **Figure 16.3**, the physical problems or diseases that are most likely to contribute to some functional disability in late adulthood are arthritis and hypertension. Not everyone with these problems is disabled. But the risk of some kind of functional disability is two to three times higher among elders who suffer from these diseases than among those who do not (Verbrugge, Lepkowski, & Konkol, 1991).

You can also see from **Figure 16.3** that arthritis is very common in both genders. However, women aged 65 or higher are considerably more likely than men to suffer from arthritis, so they are also more often limited in their ability to carry out the various movements and tasks necessary for independent life (Brock, Guralnik, & Brody, 1990; Wilkins & Park, 1996). Since women are more likely to be widowed and thus to lack a partner who can assist with these daily living tasks, it is not surprising that more women than men live with their children or in nursing homes.

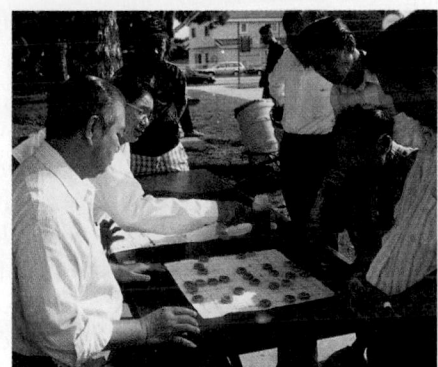

Use it or lose it? These men keep their minds sharp by playing games that require complex memory and strategy skills.
(*Photo:* A. Ramey/PhotoEdit)

LONGEVITY

Part of the shift in thinking about old age is evident in the fact that gerontologists have begun to devote a great deal of attention to studying why some people live to the age of 100 and beyond. By this time, you've learned enough about development to predict that, like most other developmental variables, longevity appears to result from interactions among heredity, environment, and behavioural choices.

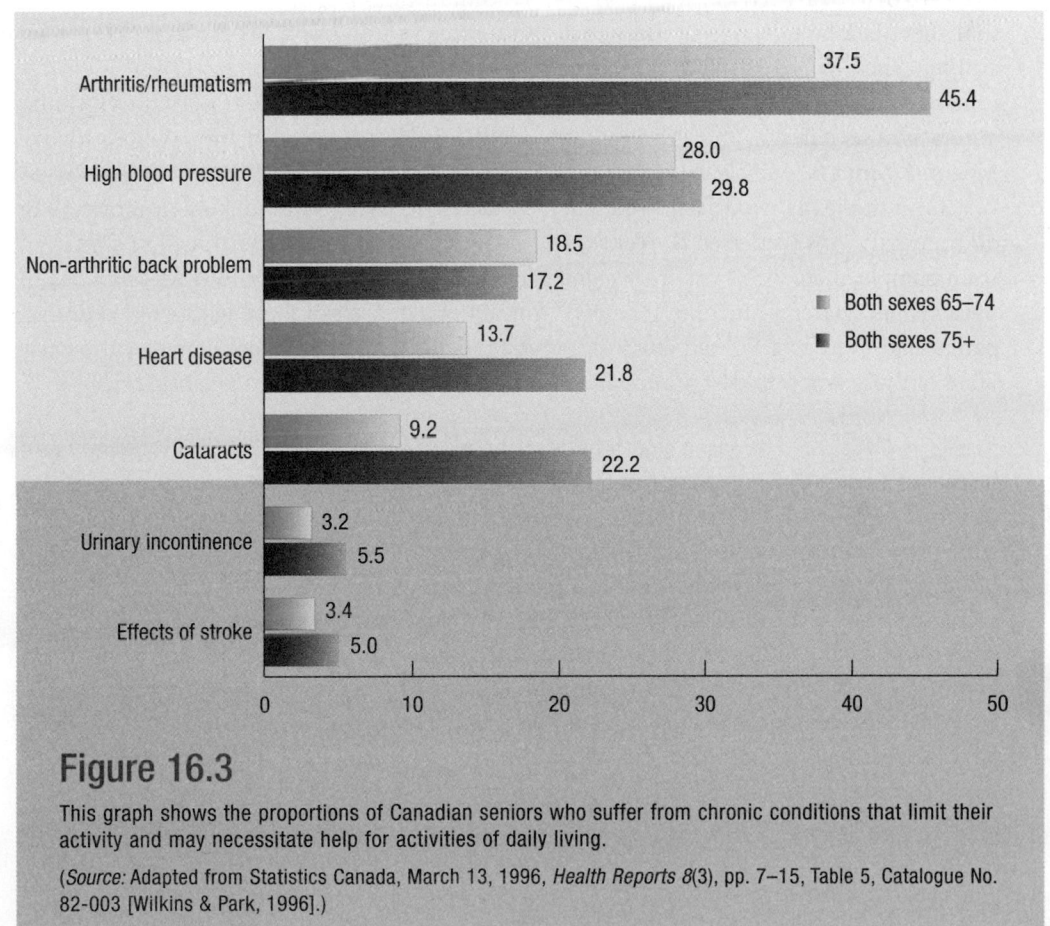

Figure 16.3

This graph shows the proportions of Canadian seniors who suffer from chronic conditions that limit their activity and may necessitate help for activities of daily living.

(*Source:* Adapted from Statistics Canada, March 13, 1996, *Health Reports 8*(3), pp. 7–15, Table 5, Catalogue No. 82-003 [Wilkins & Park, 1996].)

Hayflick limit

the theoretical proposal that each species is subject to a genetically programmed time limit after which cells no longer have any capacity to replicate themselves accurately

telomere

string of repetitive DNA at the tip of each chromosome in the body that appears to serve as a kind of timekeeping mechanism

THE MAXIMUM LIFESPAN For humans, the maximum lifespan seems to be about 110 or 120 years, although relatively few people attain the status of centenarian (see the **Research Report**). For turtles, the lifespan is far longer, and for chickens, far less. Such differences among species have persuaded some biologists that there may be some universal genetic process that limits lifespan (e.g., Hayflick, 1977, 1987).

Advocates of this view support their argument with research demonstrating that cells taken from the embryos of different species and placed in nutrient solution double only a fixed number of times, after which the cell colony degenerates. Human embryo cells double about 50 times; those from the Galapagos tortoise double roughly 100 times; chicken cells double only about 25 times. Furthermore, cells taken from human adults double only about 20 times, as if they had already "used up" some of their genetic capacity. The theoretical proposal that emerges from such observations is that each species is subject to a time limit, known as the **Hayflick limit** (because it was proposed by biologist Leonard Hayflick), beyond which cells simply lose their capacity to replicate themselves (Norwood, Smith, & Stein, 1990).

The genetic limits argument has been strengthened by the recent discovery that each chromosome in the human body (and presumably in other species, too) has, at its tip, a string of repetitive DNA called a **telomere** (Angier, 1992; Campisi, Dimri, & Hara, 1996). Among other functions, telomeres appear to serve as a kind of timekeeping mechanism for the organism. Researchers have found that the number of telomeres is reduced slightly each time a cell divides, so that the number remaining in a 70-year-old is much lower than what is found in a child. This raises the possibility that there may be a crucial minimum number of telomeres; when the total falls below that number, then disease or death comes fairly quickly.

INDIVIDUAL HEREDITY Whatever the maximum possible human lifespan, it is clear that there is a large range of individual differences in how long people live. Some general tendency to "live long and prosper" (to quote Mr. Spock from *Star Trek*) is clearly inherited. Identical twins are more similar in length of life than are fraternal twins, and adults whose parents and grandparents were long-lived are also more likely to live longer (Plomin & McClearn, 1990).

Twin studies in Sweden showed that identical twins have more similar illness rates than do fraternal twins (Pedersen & Harris, 1990). Similarly, for the Harvard men in the Grant study sample, there was a small but significant correlation between the longevity and health of each man's parents and grandparents. Only about a quarter of those whose oldest grandparent had lived past 90 had any kind of chronic illness at age 65, compared with nearly 70% of those whose oldest grandparent had died at 78 or younger (Vaillant, 1991).

HEALTH HABITS The same health habits that are important predictors of longevity and health in early adulthood continue to be significant predictors in late adulthood. For example, a 17-year follow-up of participants in the Alameda County epidemiological study, who were 60 or over at the start of the study, showed that smoking, low levels of physical activity, and being significantly underweight or overweight were linked to increased risk of death over the succeeding 17 years (Kaplan, 1992). Many other large epidemiological studies confirm such connections (e.g., Brody, 1996; Paffenbarger, Hyde, Wing, & Hsieh, 1987). A recent Canadian study of smokers found significant differences between smokers and nonsmokers (Statistics Canada, 2001a). For example, a 65-year-old male smoker can expect to live six years less than a nonsmoker, and for female smokers the difference is even greater at 8.5 years. Not only do smokers have shorter lifespans, they are also more likely to suffer disease-related disabilities—by age 65 more than half of all smokers will have a disability, whereas only one-third of nonsmokers can expect to be disabled.

Research Report

The New England

Centenarian Study

You might be surprised to learn that throughout the industrialized world, including Canada, the subgroup of the elderly who are 100 years old or older is growing at a more rapid rate than any other segment of the population. In 2001 there were 3795 Canadian centenarians, and demographers project that by 2010 the centenarian population will quadruple (Statistics Canada, 2002h; Perls, Silver, & Lauerman, 1998). As in all periods of older adulthood, the overwhelming majority of these 100-year-olds will be women.

Many researchers have turned their attention to the over-100 group to discover the causes of extreme longevity. Among the most important of these studies is the New England Centenarian Study, which is currently underway at Harvard Medical School. This study has made a number of interesting findings.

For one thing, researchers have found that reports of specific geographic locations where many people are said to live to the age of 150 are either complete fabrications or gross exaggerations. For example, several years ago a TV commercial advertising a certain brand of yogurt claimed that Russians who live in the Caucasus remain healthy into their mid-100s because of the amount of yogurt they consume. After thorough investigation, researchers determined that the group cited did include many individuals who were old, but their cultural traditions involved assuming the identities of their ancestors and adding the age at death of these forebears to their own ages (Perls, 1999). Thus, their self-reported ages were far older than their actual chronological ages. Still, researchers continue to investigate any region where large numbers of people live to be 100 to determine if these places have any characteristics that foster longevity. For example, researchers are currently focusing on a region that extends from Minnesota to Nova Scotia because a remarkable number of centenarians live there.

It turns out that the oldest documented person in recorded history was 122 years old at her death in 1997. Family studies suggest that longevity tends to run in families; that is, centenarians are more likely than others to have parents and siblings who survived past the age of 100. Surprisingly, most centenarians have large numbers of siblings. For example, researchers compared a current group of centenarians with members of the same cohort who died in their 70s during the late 1960s. They found that the centenarians averaged 4.5 siblings, whereas those who died in their 70s averaged only 3.2 brothers and sisters. Researchers hypothesize that the greater number of siblings may reflect a genetic predisposition to better general health, but as yet little or no evidence exists to support this notion.

Interesting, too, is the association between late motherhood and centenarian status. Among the 100-year-old women in the New England Centenarian Study, 20% gave birth to a child after age 40. In contrast, only 5% of members of their cohort who died in their 70s delivered a child in middle age. Researchers hypothesize an association between longevity and general health or between longevity and late menopause to be responsible for this correlation. However, evidence has yet to confirm either view.

Whatever the cause of extreme longevity, the increasing number of centenarians is likely to change developmentalists' understanding of old age. Perhaps future lifespan development textbooks will include chapters specifically devoted to these super-elders.

Another crucial variable is physical exercise, which has been clearly linked not only to greater longevity but also to lower rates of diseases such as heart disease, cancer, osteoporosis, diabetes, gastrointestinal problems, and arthritis (Brody, 1995; Deeg, Kardaun, & Fozard, 1996). Good evidence on this point comes from a longitudinal study of nearly 7000 participants who were all 70 or older when they were first tested

There are many ways to maintain physical fitness in old age. In China, elderly people can often be found practising Tai Chi in the early morning.

(*Photo:* A. Ramey/Stock Boston)

in 1984 (Wolinsky, Stump, & Clark, 1995). They were then retested every 2 years until 1990. Those who reported in 1984 that they had a regular exercise routine or walked a mile or more at least once a week maintained better physical functioning over the succeeding years, were less likely to die, and were less likely to be in a nursing home by 1990. These outcomes remained likely even when the variations in health in 1984 were factored out—that is, it isn't just that healthy adults are more likely to exercise, but that exercise keeps people healthier.

This point is reinforced by studies in which older adults have been assigned randomly to exercise and nonexercise groups (e.g., Blumenthal et al., 1991). In these studies, too, those who exercised had better scores on various measures of physical functioning. One such experiment, with a group of adults who were all over age 80, found that muscular strength increased and motor skills improved after only 12 weeks of exercise (Carmeli, Reznick, Coleman, & Carmeli, 2000).

Physical exercise also seems to help maintain higher levels of cognitive performance among the elderly (Albert et al., 1995). Studies with rats, for example, show that older rats who exercise regularly on treadmills have higher levels of a nerve growth factor that keeps neurons healthy (Cotman & Neeper, 1996). Studies of humans, naturally enough, provide less direct evidence, but nonetheless point in the same direction. Some particularly clear evidence comes from a study in which researchers followed a group of 85 men from age 65 through age 69. All the men were well-educated and were in good health at the start of the study, with no symptoms of heart disease or dementia (Rogers, Meyer, & Mortel, 1990). In the succeeding 4 years, a third of the men chose to continue working, mostly at fairly high-level jobs. Another third retired but remained physically active, while the remaining third retired and became physically (and mentally) inactive. The inactive participants showed progressive declines on a measure of blood flow to the brain and performed significantly less well than either the active retired men or the still-working men on a battery of cognitive tests.

Critical Thinking

In what ways would better health habits lower the incidence of disabilities in older adults?

If anything, physical exercise seems to be even more important in the later years than at earlier ages. For example, one investigation used medical records and self-reports of exercise to examine the degree to which physical activity influenced height loss in the elderly (Sagiv, Vogelaere, Soudry, & Shrsam, 2000). They found that study participants who had exercised regularly lost significantly less height over a 30-year period than those who had not exercised. Further, exercise after age 40 seemed to be especially important in preventing height loss.

Some authors have suggested that as much as half of the decline in various aspects of physical (and perhaps cognitive) functioning in late adulthood could be prevented through an improved lifestyle, particularly exercise. For instance, Statistics Canada (2000f), reporting on the 1998/99 National Population Health Survey, found that just over 52% of Canadians over the age of 65 engaged in a minimum of 15 minutes of vigorous activity, three or more times a week. Yet only 27% of older adults in Canada are active enough to achieve the desired health benefits associated with exercise, so it would seem that this amount of exercise is not enough (Canadian Fitness and Lifestyle Research Institute [CFLRI], 2001).

One of the reasons for the discrepancy may be a lack of understanding of how much physical activity older adults should engage in. Although more than one-third of adults over age 65 are generally aware of the guidelines for physical activity, roughly half lack a clear understanding of the requirements (CFLRI, 2001). It is worth mentioning that physical activity should be done 30 to 60 minutes per day, but this can be *accumulated* in segments throughout the day.

Of those Canadians above age 65, only 34% of males and 22% of females engage in vigorous exercise (CFLRI, 2001). People give many reasons for not exercising, including poor health, arthritic pain, time demands of caring for an ailing spouse, culturally based assumptions about appropriate behaviour for older persons, embarrassment about exposing an aging body to others in an exercise program, lack of fitness facilities or lack of transportation to such facilities, fears of various kinds, and plain lethargy.

One important part of a strategy to increase the fitness levels of inactive seniors was the development of *Canada's Physical Activity Guide to Healthy Active Living for Older Adults* (see **Figure 16.4**). This guide, modelled after the successful *Canada's Food*

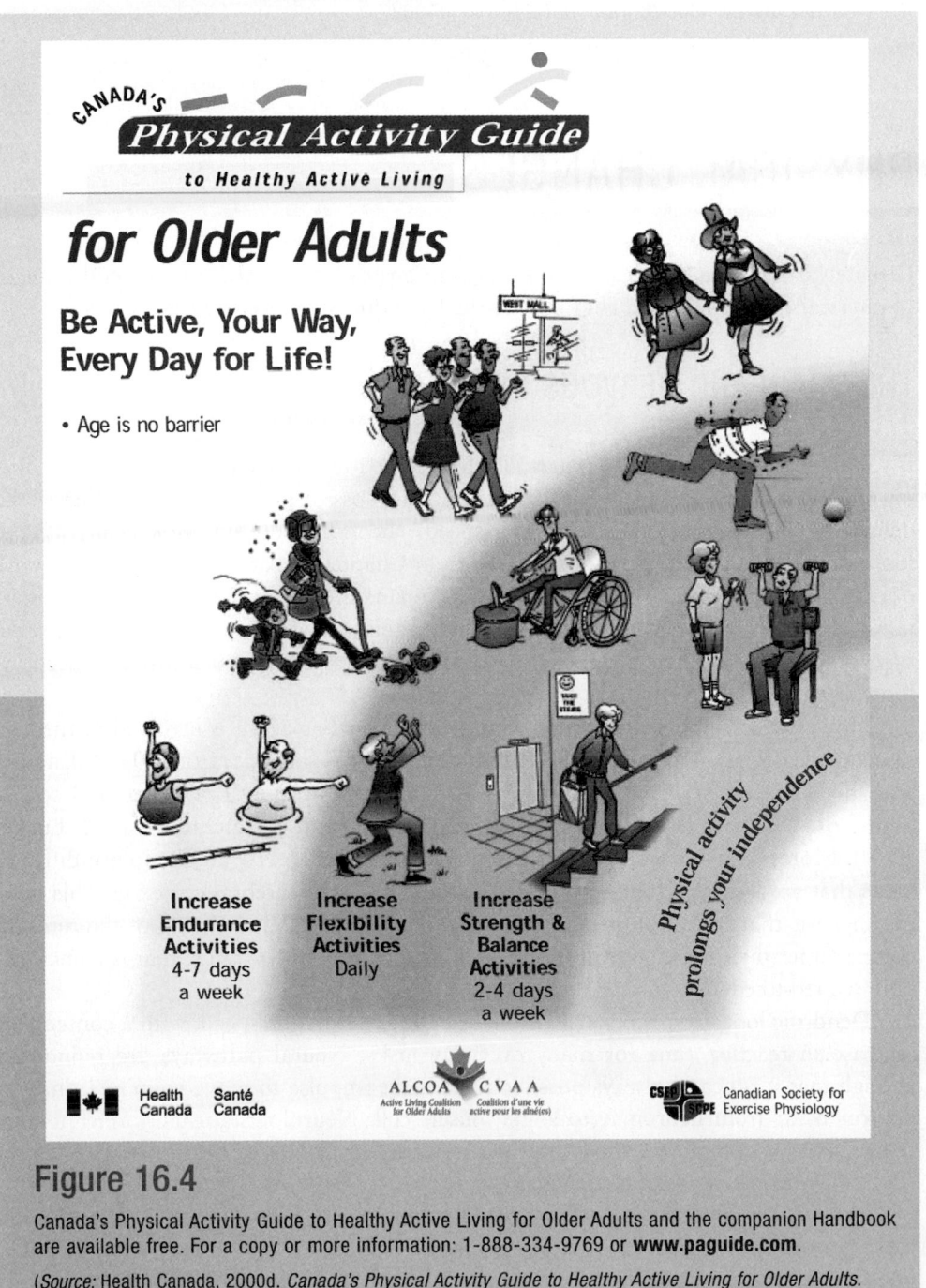

Figure 16.4

Canada's Physical Activity Guide to Healthy Active Living for Older Adults and the companion Handbook are available free. For a copy or more information: 1-888-334-9769 or **www.paguide.com**.

(*Source:* Health Canada, 2000d. *Canada's Physical Activity Guide to Healthy Active Living for Older Adults.* Reproduced with permission of the Minister of Public Works and Government Services Canada, 2005.)

Guide to Healthy Eating, is a readily available, practical handbook for overcoming misconceptions and excuses for inactivity. It promotes the perception that physical activity for health can be easily built into a person's daily routine regardless of his or her current level of activity.

Before Going On

- In what ways do older adults vary across age groups and individually?
- What are the factors that contribute to longevity?

PHYSICAL CHANGES

Despite variability in health and functioning among the elderly, there are several changes in physical functioning that characterize the late adult years for almost everyone.

THE BRAIN AND NERVOUS SYSTEM

If you look back at **Table 12.1** (page 367), you'll see four main changes in the brain during the adult years: a reduction of brain weight, a loss of grey matter, a decline in the density of dendrites, and slower synaptic speed. The most central of these changes is the loss of dendritic density. You'll remember from **Chapter 4** that dendrites are "pruned" during the first few years after birth, so that redundant or unused pathways are eliminated. The loss of dendrites in middle and late adulthood does not seem to be the same type of pruning. Rather, it appears to be a decrease in useful dendritic connections (Sowell, et al., 2003).

However, research suggests that experience as well as aging is involved in the loss of dendritic density. Neurologists have found that, across the years from 60 to 90, adults with higher levels of education show significantly less atrophy of the cerebral cortex than those who have fewer years of schooling (Coffey, Saxton, Ratcliff, Bryan, & Lucke, 1999). Moreover, the brains of well and poorly educated elderly adults do not differ in areas that are less involved in academic learning than the cerebral cortex is. This finding suggests that education itself is the cause of the reduced atrophying of the cerebral cortex rather than some general factor, such as socioeconomic status, that is coincidentally related to education.

Dendritic loss also results in a gradual slowing of synaptic speed, with a consequent increase in reaction time for many everyday tasks. Neural pathways are redundant enough that it is nearly always possible for a nerve impulse to move from neuron A to neuron B, or from neuron A to some muscle cell. Neurologists usually refer to this redundancy as **synaptic plasticity**. But with the increasing loss of dendrites, the shortest route may be lost, so plasticity decreases and reaction time increases.

One final change in the nervous system, about which physiologists disagree, is the loss of neurons themselves. For many years, it was believed that an adult lost 100 000 neurons every day. It now appears that this conclusion, like many such conclusions about primary aging, was based on cross-sectional comparisons that included many older adults who had diseases known to affect brain composition and functioning.

synaptic plasticity
the redundancy in the nervous system that ensures that it is nearly always possible for a nerve impulse to move from one neuron to another or from a neuron to another type of cell (e.g., a muscle cell)

Researchers have not yet reached a consensus on just how much loss occurs among healthy aging adults, but most agree that 100 000 neurons per day is a considerable overestimation (e.g., Ivy, MacLeod, Petit, & Marcus, 1992; Scheibel, 1996).

In addition, current estimates are that the brain has perhaps 1 trillion neurons (Morgan, 1992). A loss of 100 000 per day, even if it began at birth and lasted for a lifespan of 100 years, would only be about 4 billion neurons, leaving the vast majority (over 99%) still intact. It is only when the brain loses a significant amount of interconnectivity, which occurs as dendrites decrease in number, that "computational power" declines and symptoms of old age appear (Scheibel, 1992, p. 168). In addition, as you learned in **Chapter 12**, scientists have only recently discovered that new neurons are produced in some parts of the brain even in adulthood, although the effect of this neuron regeneration is not yet known (Gould, Reeves, Graziano, & Gross, 1999).

THE SENSES AND OTHER BODY SYSTEMS

In **Chapter 14**, you read about declines in sensory and other physical functions that occur in middle age. Such deficits become larger in late adulthood, and several more serious threats to the health of these systems arise.

VISION In addition to presbyopia (farsightedness), late adulthood can bring other vision defects due to body changes. For example, blood flow to the eye decreases (perhaps as a side effect of atherosclerosis), which results in an enlarged "blind spot" on the retina and thus a reduced field of vision. The pupil does not widen or narrow as much or as quickly as it previously did, which means that the older adult has more difficulty seeing at night and responding to rapid changes in brightness (Kline & Scialfa, 1996).

In addition, a significant minority of older adults suffer from diseases of the eye, such as cataracts or glaucoma, that further diminish visual acuity and adaptability. For example, among Canadians aged 65 to 74, 9.2% have cataracts and 3.4% have glaucoma. For those 75 years and older the corresponding rates increase to 22.2% and 6.8% respectively (Wilkins & Park, 1996). Thus, many older adults must adapt to significant impairments of vision, and the process of adaptation doesn't always go smoothly. Researchers have found that middle-aged adults adjust more easily than older adults to the difficulties associated with living with a serious vision impairment (Lindo & Nordholm, 1999). Moreover, vision loss has a greater negative effect on an elderly adult's sense of well-being.

HEARING You'll recall from **Chapter 14** that wear and tear on the auditory system results in some hearing loss (*presbycusis*) beginning in middle adulthood, but these gradual losses don't typically add up to functionally significant loss until late adulthood. Auditory problems, unlike many other disabilities of old age, are more likely to be experienced by men than by women. This sex difference is normally attributed to differential exposure to noise: More men have worked in environments with high levels of noise (at least in current cohorts of older adults in developed countries).

Hearing difficulties in late adulthood have several components: First, there is the loss of ability to hear high-frequency sounds. Both cross-sectional and longitudinal studies suggest that, for the range of sounds used in normal human speech, the loss after age 60 is such that a given sound has to be about 1 to 2 decibels louder each year for the individual to report that he hears it (Fozard, 1990; Kline & Scialfa, 1996).

Critical Thinking

How do you think a hearing impairment is likely to affect the life of an older adult? Aside from wearing a hearing aid, how could a person with a moderate hearing impairment adapt his life so as to reduce the impact of the disability?

Second, most older adults develop difficulties with word discrimination. Even when the sound is loud enough, older adults have more difficulty identifying individual words they have just heard (Schieber, 1992). In addition, many adults over the age of 60 have problems hearing under noisy conditions. The loss of ability to discriminate individual words is even greater in such situations, so large gatherings become increasingly difficult for older adults.

tinnitus
persistent ringing in the ears

Tinnitus, a persistent ringing in the ears, also increases in incidence with age, although this problem appears to be independent of the other changes just described. The Tinnitus Association of Canada (2001) reports that 360 000 Canadians experience tinnitus and that 150 000 have an impaired quality of life because of it. It is believed that tinnitus may be caused by exposure to noise, although this cause is not well established.

Even mild hearing loss can pose communication problems in some situations. Those with such problems may also be perceived by others as disoriented or suffering from poor memory, especially if the person with the hearing loss is unwilling to admit the problem and ask for a comment or instruction to be repeated. Nonetheless, the older adult with a hearing impairment is *not* necessarily socially isolated or unhappy. Mild and moderate hearing losses, even if uncorrected with a hearing aid, are simply not correlated with measures of general social, emotional, or psychological health among elderly adults. It is only severe hearing loss that is associated with an increase in social or psychological problems, including heightened rates of depression (Corso, 1987; Schieber, 1992).

Presbycusis and the other changes in hearing seem to result from gradual degeneration of virtually every part of the auditory system. Older adults secrete more ear wax, which may block the ear canal; the bones of the middle ear become calcified and less elastic; the cochlear membranes of the inner ear become less flexible and less responsive; and the nerve pathways to the brain show some degeneration (Schieber, 1992).

TASTE, SMELL, AND TOUCH The ability to taste the four basic flavours (salty, bitter, sweet, and sour) does not seem to decline over the years of adulthood. Taste receptor cells (taste buds) have short lives and are constantly replaced (Bornstein, 1992). But other changes in the taste system affect older adults, such as the secretion of somewhat less saliva, producing a sensation of "woolly mouth" for some. Many elders also report that flavours seem blander than in earlier years, leading them to prefer more intense concentrations of flavours, particularly sweetness (de Graaf, Polet, & van Staveren, 1994). But it may well be that this perception of flavour blandness is largely due to a loss of the sense of smell.

The sense of smell clearly deteriorates in old age. The best information comes from a cross-sectional study in which researchers tested nearly 2000 children and adults on their ability to identify 40 different smells—everything from pizza to gasoline (Doty et al., 1984). As **Figure 16.5** reveals, young and middle-aged adults had equally good scores on this smell identification test, but scores declined rapidly after age 60. However, the loss of sensitivity to odours is far greater among elderly men than women (Morgan, Covington, Geisler, Polich, & Murphy, 1997).

Interestingly, like hearing loss, the loss of the sense of smell seems to have an environmental component.

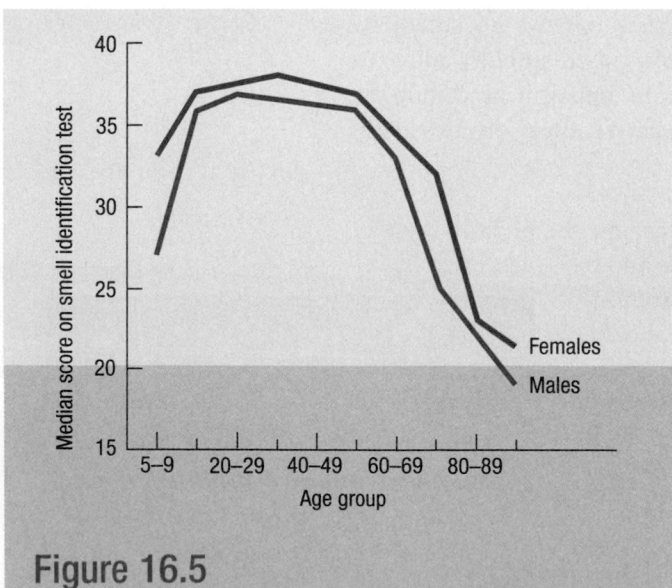

Figure 16.5

Doty's data show a very rapid drop in late adulthood in the ability to identify smells.

(*Source:* Doty et al., 1984.)

Specifically, both men and women who worked in factories (where, presumably, they were exposed to more pollutants) show much greater losses of sense of smell in old age than do those who worked in offices (Corwin, Loury, & Gilbert, 1995).

These changes in taste and smell can reduce many pleasures in life. But they can also have practical health consequences. Smells enhance the pleasure of food, so as the sense of smell becomes less acute, elders are less motivated to prepare tasty food. In some cases, this can result in inadequate nutrition or significant dietary imbalances.

Similarly, loss of sensitivity to touch can lead to significant declines in the quality of life. For example, the skin of elderly adults is less responsive to cold and heat (Stevens & Choo, 1998). Research suggests that the loss of sensitivity occurs in a pattern that is a reversal of the proximodistal principle of growth you learned about in **Chapter 3**. In other words, the extremities, usually the feet, are the first body parts that decline in sensitivity. Consequently, elderly people are less able to benefit from the potential comforts associated with physical stimuli. For example, for an elderly person to be able to feel a warm bath, the water temperature may have to be so high that it will burn the skin.

THEORIES OF BIOLOGICAL AGING

What are the basic causes of aging? Current theorists agree that the most likely explanation lies in basic cellular processes, which appear to change with age in specific ways that reduce the efficiency of cellular functioning. A number of theoretical variations on this theme have been proposed.

GENETICALLY PROGRAMMED SENESCENCE
Senescence is the gradual deterioration of body systems that happen as organisms age. **Programmed senescence theory** suggests that age-related physical declines result from species-specific genes for aging. Evolutionary theorists argue that programmed senescence prevents older, presumably less fit, individuals from becoming parents at an age when they are unlikely to be able to raise offspring to maturity (Buss, 1999). The idea is that these aging genes are equipped with some kind of built-in clock that prevents the genes from having an effect when humans are in their reproductive years but switches them on once the reproductive peak has passed.

REPAIR OF GENETIC MATERIAL AND CROSS-LINKING
Another theory of aging focuses on the cells' ability to repair breaks in DNA. Breaks in DNA strands are common events, resulting from unknown metabolic processes. Because the organism is apparently unable to repair all the damage, the theory proposes, the accumulation of unrepaired breaks results over time in a loss of cellular function, and the organism ages (Tice & Setlow, 1985).

A related theory focuses on another cellular process called cross-linking, which occurs more often in cell proteins of older than in those of younger adults. **Cross-linking** occurs when undesirable chemical bonds form between proteins or fats. In skin and connective tissue, for example, two proteins called *collagen* and *elastin* form cross-linkages, either between their molecules or within a given molecule. The resulting molecules cannot assume the correct shape for proper function, leading to effects such as wrinkling of the skin and arterial rigidity. (An equivalent process, by the way, occurs in old rubber, which explains why windshield wipers become stiffer over time.)

FREE RADICALS
A third type of cellular process that may contribute to aging relates to the body's ability to deal with free radicals. **Free radicals**, which are molecules or atoms that possess an unpaired electron, are a normal by-product of body metabolism and also

senescence
physical changes and declines associated with aging

programmed senescence theory
the view that age-related declines are the result of species-specific genes for aging

cross-linking
the formation of undesirable bonds between proteins or fats

free radicals
molecules or atoms that possess an unpaired electron

arise as a result of exposure to certain substances in foods, sunlight, X-rays, or air pollution. These radicals, especially the subgroup called *oxygen free radicals,* enter into many potentially harmful chemical reactions, resulting in irreparable cellular damage that accumulates with age. For example, oxidation reactions caused by free radicals can damage cell membranes, thereby reducing the cell's protection against toxins and carcinogens. Oxygen free radicals are also implicated in the body's reaction to cholesterol: Oxidation helps to transform some types of cholesterol into a form that adheres to artery walls, narrowing them and increasing the risk of heart attack and stroke (Brody, 1994).

A different line of evidence for this theory comes from research in which scientists genetically engineered a group of fruit flies to enhance the flies' built-in capacity to defend against free radicals (Orr & Sohal, 1994). These altered flies lived roughly one-third longer than normal fruit flies did—a result that raises the possibility that scientists might eventually be able to alter the limit of the human lifespan via genetic engineering.

Research on diet variations also points to the possibility that some foods, especially those high in fat and/or food additives such as preservatives, promote the formation of oxygen free radicals, whereas others, referred to as *antioxidants,* inhibit the formation of these radicals or promote chemical processes that help the body defend against them. Foods high in vitamins C and E and beta carotene (vitamin A) all belong in the latter group (Ornish, 1993). Several large epidemiological studies show that people who eat diets higher in antioxidants or who take regular supplements of vitamin E or beta carotene live somewhat longer and have lower rates of heart disease (Blumberg, 1996).

Furthermore, recent research on dietary supplementation suggests that some kinds of vision loss in old age may be reversed when elders increase their intake of antioxidants. Researchers at Johns Hopkins University gave patients who suffered from various kinds of retinal degeneration large doses of an antioxidant called *lutein,* a yellow pigment found in egg yolks and in some vegetables (Dgnelie, Zorge, & McDonald, 2000). They found that participants' visual acuity began to improve within just 2 weeks and continued to get better for several months.

Such findings do not mean that age-related problems such as heart disease and vision loss are *caused* by antioxidant deficiencies. Moreover, not all studies of antioxidant supplementation show positive effects (e.g., Alpha-Tocopherol Beta Carotene Cancer Prevention Study Group, 1994). However, studies that do demonstrate such benefits add support to the general notion that many of the effects of aging are modifiable and perhaps even preventable.

TERMINAL DROP Some theorists claim that physical and mental declines in old age are actually part of the dying process. For example, the **terminal drop hypothesis** asserts that all adults retain excellent physical and mental function until just a few years before death, at which time there are significant declines in all functions (Kleemeier, 1962). However, longitudinal research suggests that declines in most functions are gradual across late adulthood (Berg, 1996; Birren & Schroots, 1996). Only changes in IQ scores seem to fit the terminal drop pattern (Palmore & Cleveland, 1976).

terminal drop hypothesis
the hypothesis that mental and physical functioning decline drastically only in the few years immediately preceding death

BEHAVIOURAL EFFECTS OF PHYSICAL CHANGES

The great majority of older adults cope effectively with most everyday tasks—buying groceries, managing their finances, reading bus schedules, planning their lives, and so on—despite changes in vision, hearing, and other physical functions (Willis, 1996). Thus, in addition to knowing what these changes are and how they might be explained, it's important to know just how they affect older adults' daily lives.

GENERAL SLOWING The biggest single behavioural effect of age-related physical changes is a general slowing down. Dendritic loss at the neuronal level clearly contributes substantially to this general slowing, but other factors are also involved, including arthritic changes in the joints and loss of elasticity in the muscles. Everything takes longer—writing things down, tying one's shoes, and adapting to changes in temperature or changes in light conditions (Schaie & Willis, 1991). Even tasks that involve word skills, which tend to decline very little in accuracy with age, nonetheless are done more slowly (Lima, Hale, & Myerson, 1991; Madden, 1992).

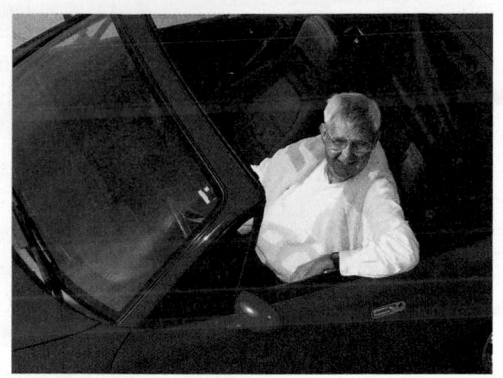

This older man has bought himself a very sporty car and doubtless thinks of himself as still a skilful driver. But it is nonetheless true that many of the physical changes associated with aging will make it harder for him to respond quickly, to see clearly in glare, and to adapt rapidly to changing driving conditions. (*Photo:* Tom Prettyman/PhotoEdit)

Further, many developmentalists believe that the decline in the speed of nerve impulses is responsible for age-related difficulties in translating thoughts into action. For example, neurologists sometimes assess nervous system functioning by having patients demonstrate a physical action involving a tool, such as hammering. Demonstrating an appropriate hand posture and moving the arm in an appropriate way are taken as indicators of neurological health. Developmentalists have found that healthy individuals in late adulthood make more initial errors than younger adults in trying to carry out such activities (Peigneux & van der Linden, 1999). However, they correct their errors just as quickly as those who are younger. Consequently, neuropsychologists think that general slowing of brain activity interferes with older adults' retrieval of the knowledge they need to accomplish the task and that they use behavioural feedback to compensate for mistakes.

Age-related physical changes add up to really significant differences in functioning in a complex motor activity such as driving. Young adults have more auto accidents than any other age group, primarily because they drive too fast. But older adults have more accidents per miles driven (Bianchi, 1993). Of course, other physical changes beyond general slowing contribute to driving problems in old age. Changes in the eyes mean that older adults have more trouble reading signs at night and adjusting to the glare of oncoming headlights. In addition, reduced range of motion in the neck, which often accompanies arthritis, may contribute to automobile accidents involving elderly drivers. Older adults also say that they have more trouble judging their own speed and that the instrument panel is too dim to see (Kline et al., 1992). Similarly, they seem to be less able to judge the speed of oncoming traffic when trying to execute turns and carry out other driving manoeuvres (Keskinen, Ota, & Katila, 1998). And the general increase in reaction time affects elders' ability to switch attention from one thing to the next or to react quickly and appropriately when a vehicle or obstacle appears unexpectedly.

Changes in temperature sensitivity, together with general slowing, lead to increases in accidental burns. For example, the elderly are more likely to burn themselves when they mistakenly pick up a hot pan while cooking. The neurological message "Put down this pan because it's going to burn your skin" moves from the hand to the brain almost instantaneously in a young or middle-aged adult. Among older adults, however, a greater amount of heat is required to initiate the message, the message itself travels to the brain more slowly, and the response from the brain that signals the hand to let go of the pan travels more slowly as well. Consequently, burns are far more common in late adulthood than earlier.

SLEEPING AND EATING PATTERNS Another common effect of physical change is a shift in sleep patterns in old age, which occurs among both healthy and less healthy elders. Adults older than 65 typically wake up more frequently in the night and show decreases in rapid eye movement (REM) sleep, the lighter sleep state in which dreaming occurs. Older adults are also more likely to wake early in the morning and go to bed early at night. They become "morning people" instead of "night people" (Hoch, Buysse, Monk, & Reynolds, 1992; Richardson, 1990). And because their night sleep is more

satiety
the feeling of fullness that follows a meal

often interrupted, older adults also nap more during the day in order to accumulate the needed amount of sleep. These changes in sleep and activity patterns are presumed to be related to changes in nervous system functioning.

The ability of the brain to regulate appetite also changes with advancing age. When you eat, your blood sugar rises, resulting in a chemical message to the brain that creates a sensation called **satiety**, the sense of being full. The feeling of satiety continues until your blood sugar drops, at which time another chemical message is sent to the brain that causes you to feel hunger. In older adults, the satiety part of the pattern seems to be impaired (Keene, Hope, Rogers, & Elliman, 1998). As a result, older adults may feel hungry all the time and may overeat. To compensate, they come to rely more on habits such as taking their meals at certain times and eating the same foods every day. Thus, they may seem to be unnecessarily rigid to those who are younger when, in reality, their adherence to a particular eating regime is simply a (perhaps unconscious) way of coping with a physiological change.

MOTOR FUNCTIONS The various physical changes associated with aging also combine to produce a reduction in stamina, dexterity, and balance. The loss of stamina clearly arises in large part from the changes in the cardiovascular system, as well as from changes in muscles. Dexterity is lost primarily as a result of arthritic changes in the joints.

Another significant change, one with particularly clear practical ramifications, is a gradual loss of the sense of balance (Guralnik et al., 1994; Simoneau & Liebowitz, 1996; Slobounov, Moss, Slobounova, & Newell, 1998). Older adults, who may be quite mobile in their home environments, are likely to have greater difficulty handling an uneven sidewalk or adapting their bodies to a swaying bus. Such situations require the ability to adjust rapidly to changing body cues and the muscular strength to maintain body position, both of which decline in old age. So older adults fall more often. About one-quarter of the young old and more than a third of the old old interviewed for one study reported having fallen in the previous year (Hornbrook, Stevens, & Wingfield, 1994). Because of osteoporosis, such falls more often result in a fracture in old age, which can be a very serious health complication for an older adult.

Critical Thinking

How might age-related changes in facial muscles contribute to stereotypes about "grumpiness" in the elderly?

Older adults also have more problems with fine-motor movements (Smith et al., 1999). Such losses are small and gradual with respect to well-practised skills such as handwriting. However, research suggests that some fine-motor activities, especially those that require learning a new pattern of movement, may be extremely difficult for elderly people. For example, older adults take far longer than young and middle-aged adults do to learn complex computer mouse skills such as clicking and dragging objects across the screen (Smith, Sharit, & Czaja, 1999).

SEXUAL ACTIVITY Another behaviour that is affected by the cumulative physical changes of aging is sexual behaviour. You read in **Chapter 14** that the frequency of sexual activity declines gradually in middle adulthood. Both cross-sectional and longitudinal data suggest that this trend continues in late adulthood (Marsiglio & Donnelly, 1991; Palmore, 1981).

The decline in the frequency of sexual activity in late adulthood doubtless has many causes (National Institute on Aging [NIA], 2000b). The continuing decline in testosterone levels among men clearly plays some role. The state of one's overall health plays an increasingly larger role with advancing age. For example, blood pressure medication sometimes produces impotence as a side effect; chronic pain may also affect sexual desire. Stereotypes that portray old age as an essentially asexual period of life may also have some effect.

Despite declining frequency, though, more than 70% of adults continue to be sexually active in old age (Bartlik & Goldstein, 2000). Moreover, the physiological capacity to respond to sexual stimulation, unlike other aspects of functioning, appears not to diminish with age. Indeed, some studies suggest that older adults, especially women, are more sexually adventurous; that is, they appear to be more willing to engage in sexual experimentation than young and middle-aged adults (Purnine & Carey, 1998).

Before Going On

- How does the brain change in late adulthood?
- What changes happen in other body systems of older adults?
- How do theories explain biological aging?
- What are the behavioural effects of changes in the various body systems of older adults?

MENTAL HEALTH

The best-known mental health problems of old age are the **dementias**, a group of neurological disorders involving problems with memory and thinking that affect an individual's emotional, social, and physical functioning. Dementia is the leading cause of institutionalization of the elderly in Canada, especially women (Hill, Forbes, Berthelot, Lindsay, & McDowell, 1996) (see **The Real World**). However, depression is also a concern in the late adult years.

dementia
a neurological disorder involving problems with memory and thinking that affect an individual's emotional, social, and physical functioning

ALZHEIMER'S DISEASE AND OTHER DEMENTIAS

Alzheimer's disease (technically known as *dementia of the Alzheimer's type*) is a very severe form of dementia. The early stages of Alzheimer's disease usually become evident very slowly, beginning with subtle memory difficulties, repetitive conversation, and disorientation in unfamiliar settings. Then, memory for recent events begins to go. Memory for long-ago events or for well-rehearsed daily routines is often retained until late in the illness, presumably because these memories can be accessed through many alternative neural pathways. Eventually, however, an individual with Alzheimer's disease may fail to recognize family members and may be unable to remember the names of common objects or how to perform such routine activities as brushing her teeth or dressing.

Those afflicted with Alzheimer's suffer declines in the ability to communicate and to carry out daily self-care routines. The changes in appetite regulation you read about earlier in this chapter are particularly problematic for those with Alzheimer's, because they can't rely on habit to regulate their eating behaviour, as healthy older people do. Left to their own devices, Alzheimer's victims may consume as many as three or four complete meals at one sitting without realizing how much they have eaten. Consequently, their eating behaviour must be closely supervised.

Some Alzheimer's patients also have angry outbursts. Others exhibit an increased level of dependency and clinginess toward family or friends (Raskind & Peskind, 1992).

Alzheimer's disease
a very severe form of dementia, the cause of which is unknown

The Real World

Caregiving

Institutionalization Among the Canadian Elderly

Research results such as those graphed in **Figure 16.3** suggest that the average older adult will spend at least a few years with some kind of disability or chronic disease. How often do such problems require nursing home care? There are several answers to that question, depending on what statistics you look at.

In Canada, roughly the same number of women (2.3%) and men (2.1%) aged 65 to 74 were in any kind of institutional care in 2001 (Cranswick, 2003). However, when we look at the oldest old, far more women (35.4%) than men (22.6%) were living in institutions. Still, these numbers may be lower than you would have guessed.

Another important piece of information examines key questions about the likelihood of institutionalization and what factors most strongly predict that a senior in Canada will live in an institution. The 1998/99 National Population Health Survey was used to provide some answers (Health Reports, 1999b). It was determined that four factors are most closely associated with institutionalization. First, and not surprisingly, age was one strong predictor of institutionalization, whereby the odds of living in an institution increase directly with age. Compared with those who were 65 to 74,

75- to 84-year-olds were five times as likely and those 85+ were 10 times as likely to be institutionalized. Second, two health conditions were also found to be predictive: Those seniors with a serious cognitive impairment were 3.2 times and those with uncorrected visual impairment were 3.0 times as likely to be institutionalized. Third, seniors with low or lower-middle household income had more than a twofold chance of being institutionalized compared with the higher income groups. And fourth, the odds of being institutionalized for those seniors who perceived themselves as having only fair or poor health were 2.6 times higher than for seniors who had good to excellent self-perceived health status.

The actual experiences of those in nursing homes paint both rosy and gloomy pictures. It is true that placement in a nursing home is often followed by death within a relatively short time. But it is not true that nursing home care necessarily shortens a person's life. Only when an older adult has been placed in an institution (or any other living situation) involuntarily is there evidence that the move itself is a causal factor in rapid decline and death. Involuntarily institutionalized elders show much higher

death rates in the ensuing months and years than do equivalently disabled elders who remain at home, although even this effect is not inevitable (Lawton, 1985, 1990). When the institution itself offers residents high levels of warmth, individuation, and opportunity for choice and control, even an involuntary move need not accelerate the process of physical or mental decline (Fields, 1992).

In Canada there is a growing need to create alternatives to institutionalization as the number of seniors increases over the next several decades. One of the solutions to controlling the number of seniors who need institutional care is to provide community support such as home care. Unfortunately, the existing national home care strategy needs much improvement. To this end, the Canadian Association of Retired Persons (CARP) released the Report Card on Home Care in Canada 2001, an evaluation of home care that is the first of its kind in Canada. The highest grade given was a "B" grade for "knowledge about home care." Funding achieved a "C" grade, and all other key areas of home care, such as strategic direction, human resources, and service delivery, received unsatisfactory grades (CARP, 2001).

In addition, research suggests that the incidence of depression among elders with Alzheimer's disease may be as high as 40% (Harwood et al., 2000).

CAUSES OF ALZHEIMER'S DISEASE Scientists do not yet fully understand the normal aging processes, which makes it extremely difficult to determine the causes of Alzheimer's disease. Genetic factors seem to be important in some, but not all, cases of Alzheimer's. Researchers have now found three separate genes that appear to be implicated. The most common is a gene on chromosome 19 that controls the production of a particular protein (Rose, 1995). When errors in the production of this protein occur, the dendrites and axons of neurons in the brain become tangled and, as a result, do not function as efficiently.

Genes found on chromosome 21 may also be involved in Alzheimer's disease. You should recall from **Chapter 3** that trisomy 21, or the presence of three copies of chromosome 21, causes Down syndrome. Alzheimer's disease is more prevalent among adults with Down syndrome than among other groups. In fact, as many as 40% of 30- to 39-year-olds with Down syndrome may also suffer from Alzheimer's disease (Holland, Hon, Huppert, Stevens, & Watson, 1998). Scientists speculate that the development of Alzheimer's disease follows a similar pattern for adults with Down syndrome and normal adults; the process is simply accelerated among those with trisomy 21. Thus, the incidence of the disease reaches 40–50% in the fourth decade of life among Down syndrome victims but does not reach this level until the eighth or ninth decade among normal individuals.

Brain-imaging studies show that patterns of neurological activity may also be genetically linked to Alzheimer's disease. Many relatives of Alzheimer's victims show patterns of neurological activity that differ from those of adults who have no Alzheimer's sufferers in their families (Ponomareva, Fokin, Selesneva, & Voskresenskaea, 1998). Neurologists are currently investigating the degree to which brain-imaging techniques, such as CT scans, may be used to predict future onset of Alzheimer's disease among middle-aged adults who have family histories of the disease.

Even in families with very high prevalences of Alzheimer's disease, ages of onset are highly variable. In one family study, age of onset ranged from 44 to 67 years (Axelman, Basun, & Lannfelt, 1998). Morever, there were wide variations in the severity of the disease's behavioural effects and in the length of time the victims lived once they developed Alzheimer's.

Newer models of Alzheimer's disease suggest that it is the breakdown of the myelin tissue (the fatty-substance that insulates axons and facilitates neural transmission) during the fifth decade that sets in motion a cascading series of neurological changes that eventually leads to the devastating effects seen in Alzheimer's patients (Bartzokis, 2004; Bartzokis, et al, 2004). Ironically, the last areas of the brain to develop—the regions where myelination continues into adulthood—are the first to be affected. As the cholesterol levels associated with myelination continue to rise, toxic proteins are released that foster a breakdown of the myelin and cause the plaques and tangles associated with Alzheimer's disease. Although genetics seem to play a role in Alzheimer's disease, there are preventive measures worth considering. For example, some preventative techniques include cholesterol and iron reduction through changes in diet and exercise, or with medications, a regime of anti-inflammatory medications, and for women, hormone replacement therapy. Importantly, it seems the time to prevent this destructive chain of neurological events is in middle adulthood—by the time the symptoms are obvious in older adults, the damage has been done and is probably not reversible.

OTHER TYPES OF DEMENTIA Strictly speaking, dementia is a symptom and not a disease, and neurological research indicates that Alzheimer's and non-Alzheimer's dementias involve very different disease processes (Fokin, Ponomareva, Androsova, & Gavrilova, 1997). For example, signs of dementia frequently appear after a person suffers multiple small strokes; in this case, the condition is called **multi-infarct dementia**. The brain damage caused by such strokes is irreversible. However, in contrast to most cases of Alzheimer's disease, various forms of therapy—occupational, recreational, and physical—can improve victims' functioning (see **Development in the Information Age**).

In addition, dementia can be caused by depression, metabolic disturbances, drug intoxication, Parkinson's disease, hypothyroidism, multiple blows to the head (frequent among boxers), a single head trauma, some kinds of tumours, vitamin B_{12} deficiency, anemia, or alcohol abuse (Anthony & Aboraya, 1992). Clearly, many of these causes are treatable; indeed, roughly 10% of all patients who are evaluated for dementia turn

multi-infarct dementia
a form of dementia caused by one or more strokes

Development in the
Information Age
Computers and Dementia

Computers are becoming increasingly important in the treatment of various neurological disorders affecting the elderly. For example, neuropsychologists use computers to test stroke and dementia victims to determine how their cognitive functioning has been affected. Computerization of standard neuropsychological tests allows psychologists to tailor the presentation of test stimuli more precisely to an individual examinee (McKitrick, Friedman, Thompson, Gray, & Yesavage, 1997).

For example, a common assessment task involves presenting test-takers with a series of digits and asking them to add the numbers two at a time. A computer can present a sample problem to determine how long an individual examinee takes to respond. After making that determination, the computer can then present problems at a rate that will allow the examinee

sufficient time to respond. Certainly, human examiners can do the same thing, but they are less precise.

Neuropsychologists also use computers in rehabilitation programs. For example, many stroke victims have problems with comprehending speech and/or speaking themselves. Researchers have found that computerized speech rehabilitation programs are highly effective at improving the language skills of such people (Katz & Wertz, 1997; Waller, Dennis, Brodie, & Cairns, 1998).

Dementia sufferers benefit from computerized rehabilitation as well. For example, one such program trains those with Alzheimer's and other types of dementia to remember routes from one place to another by guiding them through a virtual apartment. Neuropsychologists

report that practising route-learning in the virtual environment improves these patients' ability to remember such routes in their own living environments (Schreiber, Lutz, Schweizer, Kalveram, & Jaencke, 1998; Schreiber, Schweizer, Lutz, Kalveram, & Jaencke, 1999).

(*Photo:* Bob Daemmrich/Stock Boston)

out to have some reversible problem. So, when an older person shows signs of dementia, it is critical to arrange for a careful diagnosis.

INCIDENCE OF ALZHEIMER'S AND OTHER DEMENTIAS Evidence from research in Canada, China, Sweden, France, Great Britain, Italy, the United States, and Japan indicates that somewhere between 2% and 8% of all adults over age 65 show significant symptoms of some kind of dementia, and that about half of those with dementia have Alzheimer's disease (Corrada, Brookmeyer, & Kawas, 1995; Gurland et al., 1999; Rockwood & Stadnyk, 1994). Experts also agree that the rates of all kinds of dementias, including Alzheimer's disease, rise rapidly among people in their 70s and 80s. For example, a large, careful study in Canada showed that 11.1% of adults over 75 and 26.0% of those over 85 suffered from moderate to severe symptoms of dementia (Rockwood & Stadnyk, 1994).

DEPRESSION

The earliest studies of age differences in depression suggested that older adults were at higher risk for this disorder than any other age group, which contributed to a widespread cultural stereotype of the inevitably depressed elder. Certainly, suicide statistics suggest that depression increases in old age in Canadian males (see **Figure 16.6**). However, the full story on depression in late adulthood is complex.

DIAGNOSIS, DEFINITIONS, AND PREVALENCE Ageism can influence the diagnosis of depression in the elderly. Signs of depression in older adults may be dismissed as old-age "grumpiness" by family members (NIA, 2000a). Alternatively, as noted earlier, depression may be mistaken for dementia because it can cause confusion and memory loss.

Furthermore, standard questionnaires used to assess depression usually include questions about physical symptoms that commonly accompany that disorder, such as loss of appetite, sleep disturbances, and lack of energy. Older adults are more likely to report such symptoms no matter what their emotional state, and so are more likely to wind up with high scores on these standardized depression scales. As a result, elders may be diagnosed with depression when they are not actually depressed.

It is also important to distinguish between depressed mood and full-fledged clinical depression. The latter involves problems (e.g., feelings of hopelessness, insomnia, lack of appetite, loss of interest in social activities) that are of long duration and are severe enough to interfere with a person's ability to carry out normal activities (APA, 2000). By contrast, chronic depressed mood among the elderly, known as **geriatric dysthymia**, typically does not progress to clinical depression and has been found to be related to life stresses (Kocsis, 1998).

geriatric dysthymia
chronic depressed mood in older adults

Although four times as many Canadian men as women commit suicide, about twice as many women are depressed (Health Canada, 2002e). More than 11% of Canadian women aged 20 to 44 have a probable risk of depression, but the rate declines steadily to 3.6% after age 75 (Statistics Canada, 2002i). The trend is reversed for the duration of depressive episodes. Depressive episodes are briefest (about 5 weeks on average) for the youngest age group, whereas the duration of depression lasts an average of 10.3 weeks at age 75 and beyond (Health Canada, 1999e). These findings fit with other evidence that suggests that true clinical depression is, if anything, less common among older adults than among younger adults, while dysthymia increases somewhat in frequency in late old age (Beekman, Copeland, & Prince, 1999; Gatz, Kasl-Godley, & Karel, 1996). In fact, health professor Scott Patten of the University of Calgary reported that the prevalence of major depression in Canadians for both sexes is highest in 12- to 24-year-olds and then drops with every successive age group to 3.1% in females and a nominal level in males age 65 and above (Patten, 2000).

RISK FACTORS The risk factors for depression and dysthymia among the elderly are not difficult to identify: inadequate social support, inadequate income, emotional loss (such as following the deaths of spouse, family, or friends), and nagging health problems. However, the strongest predictor appears to be health status. Across all ethnic and socioeconomic groups, the more disabling conditions older adults have, the more depressive symptoms they have (Black, Markides, &

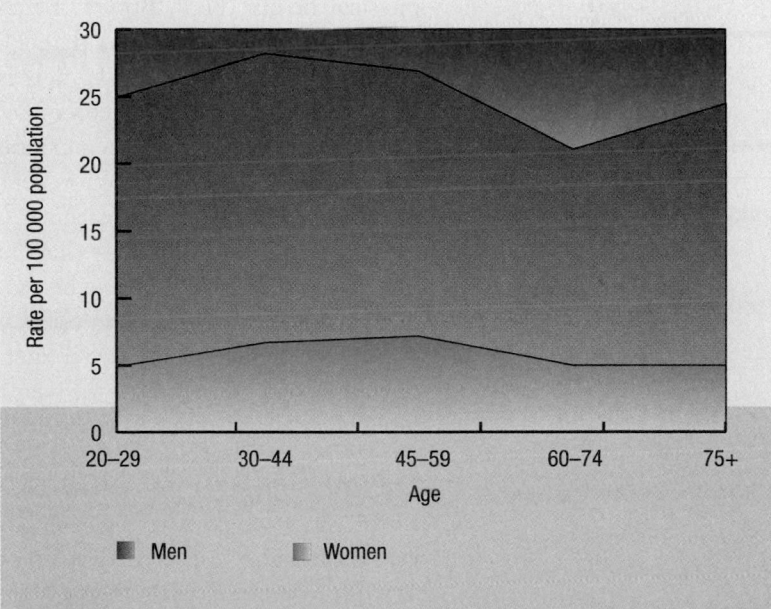

Figure 16.6

Suicide rates in Canada are four times higher for males than females. The difference is five times higher for males aged 65-plus than females.

(*Source:* Adapted from Statistics Canada, 2001, *Health Reports 13*(2), Table 2, p. 15, Catalogue No. 82-003 [Langlois & Morrison, 2002].)

Miller, 1998; Curyto, Chapleski, & Lichtenberg, 1999; FIFARS, 2000; Lam, Pacala, & Smith, 1997; Okwumabua, Baker, Wong, & Pilgram, 1997).

Gender is also a risk factor; in Canada, depressed women outnumber men two to one among the elderly, just as they do at younger ages (Statistics Canada, 2002i). However, sorting out the causes of this difference is difficult. For one thing, women appear to be more resilient in response to many life stressors. The death of a spouse, for example, is more likely to lead to depression in a man than in a woman (Byrne & Raphael, 1999; Chen et al., 1999). Such findings suggest that depression in women may more often be the result of an accumulation of everyday stresses, while traumatic events are more likely to bring on feelings of depression in men. Another possible explanation is that women are more willing to seek help for depression and, as a result, are more often diagnosed.

There is also a fair amount of consistency in findings that elders living in poverty are at higher risk for depression than others (Beekman et al., 1999). Education is also independently related to depression; that is, poorly educated older adults are more likely to be depressed (Gallagher-Thompson, Tazeau, & Basilio, 1997; Miech & Shanahan, 2000). The association between education and depression exists among elderly adults at all levels of income and in all racial and ethnic groups.

SUICIDE Suicide rates per 100 000 for all age groups of Canadians have increased almost 75% since the 1950s. Historically, elderly Canadians have had higher than average rates of suicide until the late 1980s. Since that time the suicide rate for the elderly has declined to a level slightly below the national average (Suicide Information & Education Centre, 1998). Despite higher rates of depression among women in Canada, elderly men are more than five times as likely to commit suicide, as illustrated in **Figure 16.6** on the previous page (Langlois & Morrison, 2002).

The reasons for this dramatic sex difference are not entirely clear. It's important to note, though, that suicide at all ages is predicted by the same factors: a sense of hopelessness, unemployment, psychological disorders, alcoholism, social isolation, and poor physical health (Beck, Brown, Berchick, Stewart, & Steer, 1990; Kaplan & Sadock, 1991). Some theorists believe that elderly men are at higher risk for suicide, even though elderly women are more often depressed, because men are more likely than women to have several of these risk factors in combination (Kaplan & Sadock, 1991).

In addition, loss of economic status through retirement may be more troubling for men than for women in present cohorts of the elderly, because traditional socialization patterns may have led men to equate earnings with self-worth (Mooney, Knox, & Schacht, 2000b). Similarly, declining health may cause an elderly man to view himself as a burden on others. The death of a spouse may also be a factor in many male suicides because, as you will learn in **Chapter 18**, men do not adjust as well as women do to the death of a spouse (Stroebe & Stroebe, 1993). Finally, as is true of younger people, older women attempt suicide more often than older men do, but the men complete the act more often, mostly because they are more likely than women to choose violent methods such as firearms.

THERAPY AND MEDICATION Therapies for depression are the same for older adults as for those who are younger. Psychotherapy is often recommended, especially interventions that help sufferers develop optimistic thought patterns (NIA, 2000a). However, as with younger adults, therapy appears to be most effective when combined with antidepressant medications ("Depressed elderly," 1999).

Longitudinal studies suggest that the use of antidepressant medications increases rather dramatically with age. One study involving more than 4000 elderly white and African Americans tracked their medication use for 10 years, beginning in the mid-1980s. At the beginning of the study, approximately 5% of white Americans and 2% of African Americans were taking antidepressant medicines. Remarkably, by 1996, 14%

of white participants and 5% of the African Americans were taking such medications (Blazer et al., 2000).

Experts point out that appropriate use of antidepressant medications among the elderly is critical. For one thing, antidepressants may reduce the effectiveness of the life-sustaining drugs some older adults take (NIA, 2000a). In addition, antidepressants are linked to an increased incidence of falls among the institutionalized elderly. One study found a remarkable 80% increase in falls in a group of more than 2000 nursing home residents who began taking antidepressants (Bender, 1999).

PREVENTION Given that poor overall health status predicts depression in the elderly, one important aspect of preventing depression is to help older adults improve their health. For example, arthritis limits the activities of more elderly Canadians than any other chronic condition (Wilkins & Park, 1996). There are many new and effective treatments for arthritis, of which older adults may be unaware. So, one indirect way of preventing depression is to educate older adults and their health care providers about such treatments and to encourage the elderly to get help. One cost-effective strategy that can reduce the risk of depression is a program of regular exercise, as prescribed in *Canada's Physical Activity Guide to Healthy Active Living for Older Adults* (Health Canada, 2000d) (see **Figure 16.4**).

Social involvement may also be important in preventing depression in the elderly. For example, in one study, researchers in Mexico examined how participation in activities with children, such as attending children's plays or helping plan children's parties, might affect nursing home residents' emotions (Saavedra, Ramirez, & Contreras, 1997). Researchers found that such activities significantly improved participants' emotional states. So, periodic involvement with children might be an effective way to prevent depression in institutionalized elders.

In addition, research on the connection between religion and depression suggests that caretakers can help elders avoid depression by supporting their spiritual needs. Many older adults need help getting to religious services; those who live in institutions may need to have services brought to them. Declines in vision may mean that an elderly person can no longer read religious books and may deeply appreciate having someone read to him or provide him with recordings. Helping elders maintain religious faith and practice in these ways may be an important key to reducing depression rates.

Interacting with children may help prevent depression in late adulthood.
(*Photo:* Alvin Smith)

Before Going On

- What is Alzheimer's disease, and how does it differ from other dementias?
- What does research suggest about depression among older adults?

COGNITIVE CHANGES

Among the young old (aged 65 to 75), cognitive changes are still fairly small, and these older adults show little or no average decline on a few measures, such as vocabulary knowledge. But the old old and the oldest old show average declines on virtually all measures of intellectual skill, with the largest declines evident on any measures that involve speed or unexercised abilities (Cunningham & Haman, 1992; Giambra,

Arenberg, Zonderman, Kawas, & Costa, 1995). Recall Schaie's comment, quoted in **Chapter 14**, that "reliable decrement can be shown to have occurred for all abilities by age 74" (Schaie, 1983, p. 127). By the 80s, the declines are substantial on most abilities (Schaie, 1993).

MEMORY

As you learned in **Chapter 14**, forgetfulness becomes more frequent with age (Ponds, Commissaris, & Jolles, 1997). However, it's important to remember that the same basic rules seem to apply to memory processes among both older and younger adults. For both groups, for example, recognition is easier than recall, and tasks that require speed are more difficult. Further, metamemory and metacognition skills are just as important to memory function in old age as they are earlier in life (Olin & Zelinski, 1997).

SHORT-TERM MEMORY FUNCTION One area in which researchers see significant late adulthood changes is in short-term, or working, memory capacity (Jenkins, Myerson, Hale, & Fry, 1999). You should remember from earlier chapters that there is a limitation on the number of items a person can retain in her memory at once. The more pieces of information she has to handle, the more she forgets, and the poorer her performance on memory and other kinds of cognitive tasks. Thus, the more any given cognitive task makes demands on working memory, the larger the decline with age.

A good illustration comes from a study involving a familiar, everyday task—remembering telephone numbers (West & Crook, 1990). Participants were shown a series of seven-digit or ten-digit telephone numbers on a computer screen, one at a time. The participant said each number as it appeared; then the number disappeared from the screen and the participant had to dial the number she had just seen on a push-button phone attached to the computer. On some trials, the participants got a busy signal when they first dialled and then had to dial the number over again. **Figure 16.7** shows the relationship between age and the correct recall of the phone numbers under these four conditions.

Notice that there is essentially no decline with age in immediate recall of a normal seven-digit telephone number (the equivalent of what you do when you look a number up in the phone book, say it to yourself as you read it, and then dial it immediately). When the length of the number increases to the ten digits used for long-distance numbers, however, a decline with age becomes evident, beginning at about age 60. And with even a brief delay between saying the number and dialling it, the decline occurs earlier.

Patterns of age differences are not identical for all memory tasks. For example, older adults outperform younger adults on *prospective* memory tasks in a natural setting, such as their home (Rendell & Thomson, 1999). Prospective tasks require a person to remember an event into the future—for example, remembering to take their medication, show up for a doctor's appointment, or pay a bill. However, University of Victoria memory researchers have found the elderly generally underperform young and middle-aged adults on such tasks when in a controlled laboratory setting where there are

Figure 16.7

The graph shows the results from West and Crook's study of memory for telephone numbers. Notice that there is no loss of memory in middle adulthood for the most common condition: a seven-digit number dialled immediately. But if the number of digits increases, or if you have to remember the number a bit longer, some decline in memory begins around age 50 or 60.

(*Source:* West & Crook, 1990, from Table 3, p. 524.)

no external memory cues, such as a calendar or reminder note (Cohen, Dixon, Lindsay, & Masson, 2003).

STRATEGY LEARNING A study of older adults in Germany provides a good example of research findings on strategy learning and memory in older adults (Baltes & Kliegl, 1992; Kliegl, Smith, & Baltes, 1990). Researchers tested 18 college students and 19 old, but physically healthy, adults who ranged in age from 65 to 80, with an average age of 71.7 years. Participants were shown sets of pictures of 30 familiar buildings in Berlin and asked to use the pictures to create associations that would help them remember a list of 30 words. For example, a castle might be paired with the word "bicycle." A typical association would be to imagine someone riding a bicycle in front of a castle. The pictures in each set were displayed for different amounts of time, ranging from 20 seconds each to 1 second each. After participants attempted to learn each list of words, the experimenters asked what images they had used and suggested possible improvements. Training sessions were interspersed with test sessions to check on the participants' progress.

Figure 16.8 shows the results for pictures and words presented at 5-second intervals. You can see that the older adults showed improvement after training, but their performance was poorer than that of younger adults. These findings suggest that the learning process simply takes longer for older adults—longer to create the mental image, and longer to link that image up with the word in the list. However, when allowed more time to associate each picture and word, older adults' performance was more similar to that of younger participants.

EVERYDAY MEMORY One common argument from those who take a more optimistic view of the effects of aging on cognitive functioning is that older adults may be able to remember just as well as younger adults, but they are simply less motivated to memorize lists of unrelated words given to them by researchers in a laboratory. However, on virtually all everyday tasks—remembering the main points of a story or a newspaper article; recalling movies, conversations, grocery lists, or recipes; recalling the information from a medicine label; remembering whether they did something ("Did I turn off the stove before I left the house?"); or remembering where they heard something (called *source memory*)—older adults perform less well than younger adults (Brown, Jones, & Davis, 1995; Light, 1991; Mäntylä, 1994; Maylor, 1993; Salthouse, 1991; Verhaeghen & Marcoen, 1993; Verhaeghen, Marcoen, & Goossens, 1993). These results have been found in longitudinal as well as cross-sectional studies, particularly after age 70 (Arenberg, 1983; Hultsch, Hertzog, Small, McDonald-Miszczak, & Dixon, 1992; Zelinski, Gilewski, & Schaie, 1993).

Still, task-specific knowledge seems to make a difference among the elderly. For example, older adults who have larger vocabularies outperform peers who know fewer words on tasks involving rapid recognition of words (Kitzan, Ferraro, Petros, & Ludorf, 1999). Researchers know that prior knowledge is the critical factor in such findings, because elders with large vocabularies perform just as poorly as their less knowledgeable peers on tasks involving nonsense words.

PRELIMINARY EXPLANATIONS How do researchers account for these changes in memory? Extensive statistical

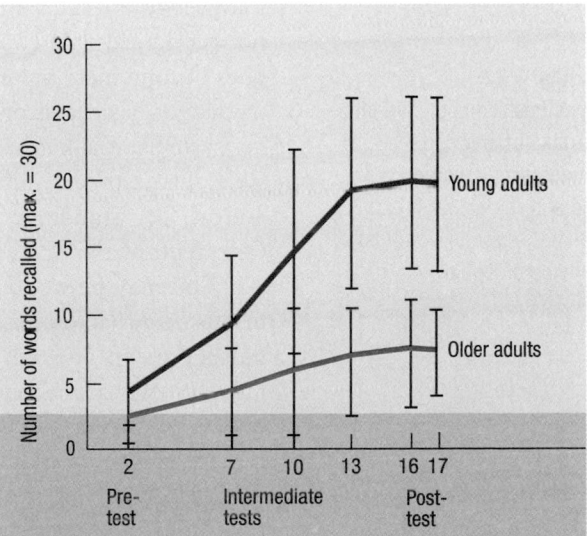

Figure 16.8

These results from Kliegl's study show that older adults can learn complex information-processing skills and improve their performance after training, but that they don't gain as much as younger adults do. However, this study also suggested that, given enough time, older adults can learn new strategies.

(*Source:* Kliegl et al., 1990, adapted from Figure, p. 899.)

analyses of memory function suggest that only a few variables may account for all of the age differences in memory so far identified (Salthouse, 1998; Salthouse & Czaja, 2000; Verhaeghen & Salthouse, 1997). However, exactly what those variables are remains unclear.

One likely candidate appears to be the speed of the whole memory process. Older adults take longer to register some new piece of information, encode it, and retrieve it. Some of the clearest evidence of the important role of speed in memory decline in old age comes from an extensive series of studies by Timothy Salthouse (e.g., Salthouse, 1991, 1993, 1996).

Salthouse has tested both basic reaction speed and memory or other cognitive skills in adults of various ages. According to him, a very large portion of the age decline in memory can be accounted for simply by slower reaction times in older adults. He is convinced that the loss of speed occurs at the level of the central nervous system and not in the peripheral nerves. So physiological changes in neurons and the accompanying loss of nerve conductance speed may be the root causes of these changes in memory.

Virtually all experts now agree with Salthouse that loss of speed is a key aspect of the process of memory decline, and studies have shown that quantitative losses in speed of information-processing very strongly predict qualitative changes in memory function (Byrne, 1998; Maylor, Vousden, & Brown, 1999). But most also believe that speed is not the entire explanation. There appear to be other factors as well, such as changes in attention strategies that lead to less effective processing of information (Gottlob & Madden, 1999).

WISDOM AND CREATIVITY

Theorists who study cognition in older adults have also recently begun to ask whether elders might have some advantages over the young because of their accumulation of knowledge and skills. In other words, older adults might be more wise. Researchers have not yet agreed on a common definition of wisdom, but most authors emphasize that it goes beyond mere accumulations of facts. **Wisdom** reflects understanding of "universal truths" or basic laws or patterns; it is knowledge that is blended with values and meaning systems; it is knowledge based on the understanding that clarity is not always possible, that unpredictability and uncertainty are part of life (Baltes & Smith, 1990; Baltes, Smith, & Staudinger, 1992; Baltes, Staudinger, Maercker, & Smith, 1995; Csikszentmihalyi & Rathunde, 1990; Sternberg, 1990).

You may be wondering how researchers measure wisdom. The leading researcher in this field, Paul Baltes, has devised one useful technique (Baltes & Staudinger, 2000). Baltes presents research participants with stories about fictional characters who are trying to make some major life decision. For example, one dilemma Baltes has used involves a 15-year-old girl who wants to get married. Participants' responses to the stories are judged according to five criteria Baltes hypothesizes to be central to wisdom as it relates to solving practical life problems: factual knowledge, procedural knowledge, understanding of relevance of context, understanding of relevance of values, and recognition that it is impossible to know in advance how any decision will ultimately affect one's life. A person would be judged to be low in wisdom if her response to the 15-year-old's desire to marry were something like "A 15-year-old getting married? That's stupid. I would tell the girl to forget about it until she's older." The answer of a person judged to be high in wisdom would be more complex. A wise person might point out that "There are circumstances when marriage at such a young age might be a good decision. Is she

wisdom
a hypothesized cognitive characteristic of older adults that includes accumulated knowledge and the ability to apply that knowledge to practical problems of living

Critical Thinking

Make a list of the people you think of as wise. How old are they? Is old age necessary for wisdom? If not, how do you think wisdom is acquired?

Developmental Psychology in Your Career

Gerontological specialists

Occupation	**Gerontological specialists** (Note: Colleges/universities offer programs related to aging or gerontology and courses in specific departments.)
Description	• may work within health or human services • help seniors attain or maintain independence and physical and mental well-being • promote healthy aging to minimize risks of later-life disease and disability • often work with a multidisciplinary team in nursing homes, hospitals and other institutional settings, public health offices, or senior citizen centres • may provide support for seniors and their families by utilizing community and governmental resources
Entry Credentials	• college or university certificate • college diploma • Bachelor's degree or postdegree certificate
Essential Lifespan Development Knowledge	• physical, psychological, sociological, cultural, political, and economic aspects of adult aging • characteristics and effects of normal and pathological aging processes • changing needs of the elderly, such as metabolic, sensorial, mobility, pharmacological, cognitive, interpersonal, sexual, and other activities of daily living • principloo of palliative care, grlef, and bereavement
Essential Lifespan Development Skills	• interview, assess, and communicate with and intervene on behalf of seniors and their families • implement strategies that encourage optimal functioning and self-determination • inform, guide, and train individuals or groups of other professionals, family members, and volunteers how to work with seniors
Lifespan Development and Essential Professional Attitude	• enjoy working with older people • respect, protect, and provide for the autonomy of older adults with regard to their physical or mental capacities • uphold basic human rights, and be considerate of guardianship issues, mental incompetence, the right to refuse treatment, age and gender discrimination, and financial security • advocate for the rights of, and make ethical decisions on behalf of, seniors who are deemed mentally incompetent • show compassionate care around issues of death and dying
Lifespan Development Career Profile: Dr. Georgina Fysh, RN, BScN, MA, EdD, Gerontological Nurse Educator, Grant MacEwan College	"The opportunity as a professional nurse to work with an aging population has provided me with a challenging and rewarding career. Older persons are a special group. Each one is unique, and within the group is a wide diversity of lived experiences and interest. Most are healthy and vigorous. There is also a vulnerable population—those that require care, concern, and knowledgeable nursing. The range of experience for nurses to work with older persons includes health promotion, community health, caring for persons with dementia, acute care, emergency care, and family care, and more roles continue to emerge. The opportunities for interested nurses are boundless. As a nurse educator, I have been fortunate to enter the lives of older persons in many ways. The experience of working to maintain and improve the quality of life in a person's last years and to enter the intimacy of dying and death requires creativity, empathy, and listening. Challenging, but so rewarding. To share with an individual their lived experience, to hear their stories, to listen to their wisdom is a rare privilege which I hold dear."

November 5, 2004

(continued)

Lifespan Development Career Profile: Dr. Colleen MacQuarrie, Assistant Professor, Psychology Department, University of Prince Edward Island

"I am a developmental health psychologist whose research with older adults has highlighted some of the challenges to aging well within our communities. My program of research is directed to better understand the multifaceted nature of health and wellness across the lifespan and within diverse community settings. My research examines a range of content areas including change processes for health behaviours as well as transitions following diagnosis of specific diseases such as Alzheimer's Disease. I have been working with population health interventions to better understand how environments support individuals' and families' health choices. Research in this area examines how people understand their role in prevention within a social ecological model. The projects have examined the impacts of social marketing on cervical cancer screening and diabetes lifestyle interventions. Current projects are focused on exploring primary prevention of chronic illnesses."

November 10, 2004

motivated by a desire to make a home for a child she is expecting? Also, the girl might come from a culture where marriage at 15 is quite common. You have to consider people's motivations and their backgrounds to understand their decisions. You also have to know how the person involved views the situation to be able to give advice."

Virtually all theorists who have written about wisdom assume that it is more likely to be found in the middle-aged and the elderly. However, Baltes has found that younger adults perform as well as older adults in response to the fictional dilemma task. In fact, Baltes has found that, rather than age, intelligence and professional experience are correlated with responses to the dilemma task. So, Baltes's research seems to suggest that the popular idea that age and wisdom are associated is probably not true. Wisdom does not appear to be a characteristic of the elderly that distinguishes them from other subgroups of adults.

Critics have suggested that Baltes is simply measuring general cognitive ability rather than what is usually thought of as wisdom. Nevertheless, Baltes's research has produced an important finding about wisdom and old age: In contrast to performance on information-processing tasks such as memorizing nonsense words, performance on wisdom tasks does not decline with age (Baltes & Staudinger, 2000). Moreover, the speed of accessing wisdom-related knowledge remains constant across adulthood, unlike speed of information-processing in other domains. In addition, other researchers (e.g., Orwoll & Perlmutter, 1990) have found that those older adults singled out by their peers as wise are more likely to rank high in what Erikson called ego integrity and are more likely to show concern for humanity as a whole.

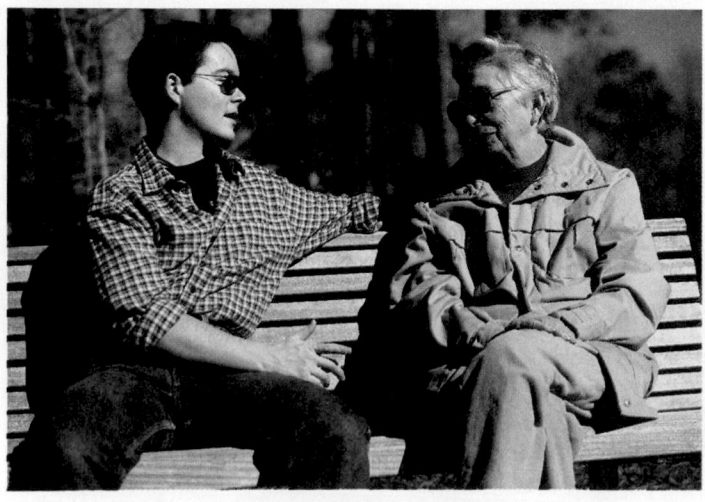

Seeking advice from an elder who is presumed to be wise is one way young adults act on the belief that those who are older have accumulated knowledge and information that can benefit them.
(*Photo:* Vincent DeWitt/Stock Boston)

Enhanced creativity may also be an element of cognition in older adults. As you learned in **Chapter 14**, some highly creative individuals, especially composers and artists, reach their peak in late adulthood. To describe the potential for creative work in the later years, a leading gerontologist, Gene Cohen, has developed a four-stage theory of mid- to late-life creativity (Cohen, 2000). Cohen believes that these phases apply to ordinary people who are more creative than others in their everyday lives as well as to "professional creators" such as composers and artists.

Cohen proposes that at around age 50, creative individuals enter a *re-evaluation phase,* during which they reflect on past accomplishments and formulate new goals. The re-evaluation process, along with an increasing sense of time limitations, leads to an intensification of the desire to create and produce. During the next stage, the *liberation phase,* individuals in their 60s become freer to create, because most have retired from everyday work. Most are also more tolerant of their own failures, and thus are willing to take risks that they would not have taken at earlier ages. In the *summing-up phase,* creative people in their 70s have a desire to knit their accomplishments together into a cohesive, meaningful story. They begin to view their early accomplishments in terms of how those accomplishments prefigured later achievements. Finally, in the *encore phase,* during the 80s and beyond, there is a desire to complete unfinished works or to fulfill desires that have been put aside in the past.

Make the Connection

Look back at the discussion of theories of postformal operational thought in **Chapter 12**. How would these theories explain abrupt opinion change in the elderly?

Before Going On

- Describe memory differences that distinguish older and younger adults, and suggest some possible explanations for these age differences.

- What do theory and research on wisdom and creativity reveal about cognitive functioning in late adulthood?

Summary

Variability in Late Adulthood

- Developmentalists group the elderly into three subgroups: the young old (60 to 75), the old old (75 to 85), and the oldest old (85 and older). The oldest old are the fastest-growing group of the elderly in Canada. There are vast individual differences in the timing and pace of all the physical and mental changes associated with aging.

- Heredity, overall health, current and prior health habits (particularly exercise), and availability of adequate social support all influence functioning and longevity. Skills that are not used regularly show more rapid decline.

Physical Changes

- Changes in the brain associated with aging include, most centrally, a loss of dendritic density of neurons, which has the effect of slowing reaction time for almost all tasks.

- Older adults have more difficulty adapting to darkness and light. Loss of hearing is more common and more noticeable after 65 than at earlier ages; many older adults experience loss of hearing for high sounds, some loss of ability to discriminate words, and greater difficulty hearing under noisy conditions. Taste discrimination remains largely unchanged with age, but ability to discriminate smells declines substantially in late adulthood.

- Theories of biological aging emphasize the possible existence of genetic limiting mechanisms and/or the cumulative effects of malfunctions within cells.

- General slowing alters behaviour in old age and makes tasks such as driving more dangerous. Older adults also change their sleeping and eating patterns. Motor abilities decline, causing more accidents due to falls. Sexual activity also decreases in frequency, although most older adults continue to be sexually active.

Mental Health

- Dementia is rare before late adulthood, becoming steadily more common with advancing age. The most common cause of dementia is Alzheimer's disease. Its causes are not fully understood, but several specific genetic patterns clearly contribute.

- Mild or moderate depression appears to rise in frequency after age 70 or 75. Serious clinical depression, however, appears not to become more common in old age.

Cognitive Changes

- The elderly experience difficulties in a variety of mental processes, which appear to reflect both the general slowing in the nervous system and perhaps a loss of working-memory capacity.

- Wisdom and creativity may be important aspects of cognitive functioning in old age.

Key Terms

activities of daily living (ADLs) (p. 484)

Alzheimer's disease (p. 497)

cross-linking (p. 493)

dementia (p. 497)

frail elderly (p. 482)

free radicals (p. 493)

functional status (p. 484)

geriatric dysthymia (p. 501)

gerontology (p. 481)

Hayflick limit (p. 486)

instrumental activities of daily living (IADLs) (p. 484)

multi-infarct dementia (p. 499)

programmed senescence theory (p. 493)

satiety (p. 496)

senescence (p. 493)

synaptic plasticity (p. 490)

telomere (p. 486)

terminal drop hypothesis (p. 494)

tinnitus (p. 492)

wisdom (p. 506)

 # Weblinks

Eat Well to Age Well
www.hc-sc.gc.ca/seniors-aines/naca/expression/17-3/pdf/exp17-3_e.pdf
This issue of the Bulletin of the National Advisory Council on Aging discusses what to eat, reading labels, nutrition and chronic conditions, and other items of interest for the dietary needs of seniors.

In an autobiography written when he was in his late 60s, comedian Groucho Marx, who died at 87, said, "Age is not a particularly interesting subject. Anyone can get old. All you have to do is live long enough" (Marx, 1987). Marx's observation implies that there is little value in regarding the attainment of old age as the only thing about oneself that is interesting or remarkable. Indeed, an important part of maintaining a sense of self in late adulthood is recognizing whatever it is about one's life that could not have been done by anyone else. But maintaining a sense of personal uniqueness can be especially challenging for older adults, who are often stereotyped by others as sick, disabled, or incompetent.

As you learned in **Chapter 16**, the biological clock ticks far more loudly in late adulthood. But the experiences of these years, as in every period of life, extend far beyond the physical domain. Indeed, as you will learn in this chapter, changes in roles and relationships are perhaps just as significant as physical ones. And for many older adults, these changes are not perceived as losses but as opportunities to create new roles and to make old age a time of personal and social gains. As you read this chapter, keep the following questions in mind:

- How do theorists describe the important aspects of social and personality development in late life?

- What factors predict successful aging, and how does religious coping affect older adults' physical and mental health?

- In what ways do social relationships change in late adulthood?

- How do retirement and continued work affect the lives of older adults?

THEORIES OF SOCIAL AND PERSONALITY DEVELOPMENT

If the social and personality changes of young adulthood can be described as "individuation" and those of middle adulthood can be described (more tentatively) as "mellowing," how might the changes of late adulthood be described? Several theorists have hypothesized specific forms of change, but there is little agreement among them and very little information supporting any of their theories.

ERIKSON'S STAGE OF EGO INTEGRITY VERSUS DESPAIR

Erikson termed the last of his eight life crises the **ego integrity versus despair stage**. He thought that the task of achieving **ego integrity**, the sense that one has lived a useful life, began in middle adulthood but was most central in late adulthood. To achieve ego integrity, the older adult must come to terms with who she is and has been, how her life has been lived, the choices that she made, the opportunities gained and lost. The process also involves coming to terms with death and accepting its imminence. Erikson hypothesized that failure to achieve ego integrity in late adulthood would result in feelings of hopelessness and despair because there would be too little time to make changes before death.

Developmentalists have essentially no longitudinal or even cross-sectional data to suggest whether older adults are more likely than younger or middle-aged adults to achieve such self-acceptance. What they have instead are a few bits of information

ego integrity versus despair stage
the last of Erikson's psychosocial stages, in which older adults must achieve a sense of satisfaction with their lives

ego integrity
the feeling that one's life has been worthwhile

suggesting that adults become more reflective and somewhat more philosophical in orientation as they move through the late adulthood years (Prager, 1998). Moreover, those who use their growing capacity for philosophical reflection to achieve a degree of self-satisfaction are less fearful of death. There is also some evidence that older adults are more likely than young and middle-aged adults to respond to thwarted personal goals with feelings of sadness—a hint that the kind of despair Erikson talked about may be more common in old age than earlier in life (Levine & Bluck, 1997).

One aspect of Erikson's theory that has received a great deal of attention from researchers is the notion that the process of **reminiscence**, thinking about the past, is a necessary and healthy part of achieving ego integrity, and thus an important aspect of old age and preparation for death. However, few developmentalists today would say that the only, or even the most important, purpose of these processes is to help an individual prepare for death. Instead, recent research has examined the link between reminiscence and health.

First, it's important to note that adults of all ages engage in reminiscence. In fact, young adults reminisce more often than middle-aged or older adults (Parker, 1999). Moreover, the emotional effects of reminiscence are correlated with age. For younger adults, reminiscence often evokes negative emotions, whereas it is generally a positive activity for elders.

Developmentalists hypothesize that young and older adults feel differently about reminiscence because they use it for different purposes (Webster & McCall, 1999). Young adults often use reminiscence to search for tried and true methods of solving problems ("How did I handle this the last time it happened?"). For older adults, reminiscence is more often seen as a way of communicating their experiences to younger individuals. In fact, elders who do not have this intergenerational view of reminiscence do not engage in reminiscence as much as peers who do (Muthesius, 1997).

Research suggesting that reminiscence is a positive emotional experience for older adults has led to the development of a wide variety of interventions for use with these adults. Experimental studies comparing reminiscence therapy with other approaches has shown that structured reminiscence increases life satisfaction among nursing home residents (Cook, 1998). In addition, structured reminiscence therapy has been found to be helpful in treating depression in elderly adults (Watt & Cappeliez, 2000). Developmentalists have found that, in general, elders are eager to participate in reminiscence interventions (Atkinson, Kim, Ruelas, & Lin, 1999). In fact, it may be this very eagerness that accounts for the positive effects observed with many of these programs. And as compelling as these research results may seem, they don't indicate whether Erikson was right about the *necessity* of reminiscence in old age.

ACTIVITY THEORY AND DISENGAGEMENT THEORY

Another theoretical perspective on old age focuses on the question of whether it is normal, necessary, or healthy for older adults to remain active as long as possible, or whether the more typical and healthy pattern is some kind of gradual turning inward. The perspective typically referred to as **activity theory** argues that the psychologically and physically healthiest response to old age is to maintain the greatest possible level of activity and involvement in the greatest possible number of roles.

Activity theorists often cite research demonstrating that the most active older adults report slightly greater satisfaction with themselves or their lives, are healthiest, and have the highest morale (Adelmann, 1994; Bryant & Rakowski, 1992; George, 1990; McIntosh & Danigelis, 1995). The effect is not large, but its direction is consistently positive: More social involvement is linked to better outcomes, even among elders who

reminiscence
reflecting on past experience

activity theory
the idea that it is normal and healthy for older adults to try to remain as active as possible for as long as possible

suffer from disabilities such as arthritis, for whom active social participation may be physically painful (Zimmer, Hickey, & Searle, 1995). Yet it is also true that every in-depth study of lifestyles of older adults identifies at least a few who lead socially isolated lives but remain contented, sometimes because they are engaged in an all-consuming hobby (e.g., Maas & Kuypers, 1974; Rubinstein, 1986).

An alternative theory of social and personality development in old age is disengagement theory, first proposed as a formulation of the central psychological process for older adults (Cumming, 1975; Cumming & Henry, 1961). In its current form, **disengagement theory** proposes that aging has three aspects:

Some older adults are quite content with solitary lives, but disengagement from social contacts is neither a typical nor optimal choice for most elders.
(*Photo:* Frank Siteman/Getty Images)

* *Shrinkage of life space:* As people age, they interact with fewer and fewer others and fill fewer and fewer roles.

* *Increased individuality:* In the roles and relationships that remain, the older individual is much less governed by strict rules or expectations.

* *Acceptance of these changes:* The healthy older adult actively disengages from roles and relationships, turning increasingly inward and away from interactions with others.

disengagement theory
the theory that it is normal and healthy for older adults to scale down their social lives and to separate themselves from others to a certain degree

The first two of these aspects seem largely beyond dispute. What has been controversial about disengagement theory is the third aspect. Advocates argue that the normal and healthy response to the shrinkage of roles and relationships is for the older adult to step back still further, to stop seeking new roles, to spend more time alone, to turn inward. In essence, they propose a kind of personality change, not just a decline in involvement.

Clearly, it is possible to choose a highly disengaged lifestyle in late adulthood and to find satisfaction in it. But such disengagement is neither normal for the majority of older adults nor necessary for overall mental health in the later years. For most elders, some level of social involvement is both a sign—and probably a cause—of higher morale and lower levels of depression and other psychiatric symptoms. Roles and relationships may rule our lives less in late adulthood than at earlier ages, but they still seem to be essential ingredients for emotional balance, at least for most of us.

Critical Thinking

Think about the oldest person in your family. Which do you think describes him or her better—activity theory or disengagement theory?

Before Going On

* Does research support the existence of Erikson's stage of ego integrity versus despair?

* What are the main ideas of activity theory and disengagement theory?

INDIVIDUAL DIFFERENCES

Individual differences continue to make substantial contributions to the experiences of older men and women. In fact, research suggests that differences in a variety of behaviours are related to overall quality of life as well as to longevity. Similarly, individual differences in reliance on religious beliefs and institutions as sources of support are also correlated with well-being in late adulthood.

THE SUCCESSFUL AGING PARADIGM

successful aging
the term gerontologists use to describe maintaining one's physical health, mental abilities, social competence, and overall satisfaction with one's life as one ages

In recent years, one of the dominant themes in gerontology literature has been the concept of successful aging. As defined by authors John Rowe and Robert Kahn, **successful aging** has three components: good physical health, retention of cognitive abilities, and continuing engagement in social and productive activities (Rowe & Kahn, 1997, 1998). An additional aspect of successful aging is an individual's subjective sense of life satisfaction. The idea of successful aging is part of the overall trend in gerontology (which you read about in **Chapter 16**) toward viewing old age in terms of variability rather than universal decline. In addition, the concept attempts to integrate physical, social, and personality development in order to create a comprehensive picture of what it means to age successfully.

The three dimensions of successful aging described by Rowe and Kahn are, of course, not entirely independent. For example, good health makes it more likely that an older adult will retain her mental abilities, and better mental functioning enables her to remain socially active. The concept of successful aging is referred to as a *paradigm* because it presents patterns for or examples of such aging. Rather than stating a theory of development, the paradigm of successful aging offers a way of thinking about late adulthood and about how earlier decisions and patterns of behaviour contribute to quality of life at later ages.

STAYING HEALTHY AND ABLE By now, you should be familiar with the factors that predict health and physical functioning across the lifespan: diet, exercise, avoidance of tobacco, and so on. In a sense, older people reap the consequences of the behavioural choices they made when younger. However, there are also aspects to staying healthy and able that most of us never face until old age.

For example, when an older adult suffers a stroke or fractures a bone, his willingness to engage in the sometimes painful process of rehabilitation significantly affects his degree of recovery. Researchers have found that older adults vary considerably in their willingness to comply with physicians and therapists who supervise their rehabilitations after such events. An individual's willingness to adopt recovery goals suggested by rehabilitation professionals is related to recovery prospects (Ushikubo, 1998). Those who believe they can reach the suggested goals appear to be the most willing to do the work required for optimal recovery of functioning. Not surprisingly, these individuals gain the most from rehabilitation. So, life-long health habits contribute to successful aging, but individuals' responses to the health crises of old age also matter.

RETAINING COGNITIVE ABILITIES The degree to which elders maintain cognitive functioning seems to be linked to education. As you learned in **Chapter 16**, those who are the best educated show the least cognitive decline. Moreover, researchers who have examined correlations between cognitive functioning and the other two dimensions of successful aging—physical health and social engagement—have found that verbal intelligence and education are related to both (Jorm et al., 1998). Cross-cultural research has found relationships among cognitive functioning, health, and social involvement in Taiwanese and North American elders, as well as in both Mexican Americans and white Americans (Hazuda, Wood, Lichtenstein, & Espino, 1998; Ofstedal, Zimmer, & Lin, 1999).

In addition to education, the complexity of the cognitive challenges older adults are willing to take on also influences their cognitive functioning. For example, older adults are sometimes reluctant to use new technologies such as automatic teller machines (Echt, Morrell, & Park, 1998). Psychologists suggest that self-stereotyping contributes to this reluctance; older people may believe that they can't learn as well as younger people can, and so they stick to established routines. However, neuropsychologists suggest that such avoidance of learning may actually contribute to cognitive decline (Volz, 2000). New learning, these scientists hypothesize, helps to establish new connections between neurons, connections that may protect the aging brain against deterioration. Thus, what might be called *cognitive adventurousness,* a willingness to learn new things, appears to be a key component of successful aging.

SOCIAL ENGAGEMENT Social connectedness and participation in productive activities are clearly important to successful aging. For example, nursing home residents report greater satisfaction with their lives when they have frequent contact with family and friends (Guse & Masesar, 1999). Similarly, among elders with disabilities, frequency of contact with family and friends is associated with reduced feelings of loneliness (Bondevik & Skogstad, 1998).

However, social support does not mean dependence on others. In fact, rehabilitation professionals have found that elderly adults who expect to have someone help them with daily living activities are less likely to recover fully from strokes or other potentially debilitating medical conditions than peers who have no one to help them (Ushikubo, 1998). Moreover, one study of recovering cardiac patients found that social support contributed to mental well-being but was negatively correlated with physical recovery, especially among women (Bosworth et al., 2000).

Research on dependency suggests that the past thinking of behavioural scientists about the role of social support may have been too simplistic. It seems that social support contributes to successful aging because it provides opportunities for older adults to *give* support as well as to receive it. For example, research involving elderly Mexican immigrants to the United States suggests that those who have better functional integration into a community—that is, those who are fulfilling some kind of purposeful role—exhibit higher levels of physical and emotional functioning than those who are socially isolated (Hazuda et al., 1998).

Similarly, researchers studying Japanese elders found that a majority of them say that helping others contributes to their own health and personal sense of well-being (Krause, Ingersoll-Dayton, Liang, & Sugisawa, 1999). In addition, researchers have found that elderly residents of Israeli *kibbutzim* (collective communities) display exceptionally high levels of functioning compared with Israeli elders who do not live in *kibbutzim* (Leviatan, 1999). The key to this successful aging, developmentalists believe, is that the social structure of the *kibbutz* offers older adults many opportunities to occupy meaningful roles, to remain socially connected to peers, and to contribute to the development of younger community members.

Of course, you might argue that elders who are the healthiest are naturally going to be the best able to make a social contribution. However, developmentalists have found correlations between feeling useful and having a sense of well-being even among older adults who are very unhealthy. For example, when researchers asked nursing home residents to rate various quality-of-life factors, the researchers found that the residents often gave high ratings to "opportunities to help others" (Guse & Masesar, 1999). Thus, even when elderly adults have significant disabilities, many are still oriented toward helping others and feel more satisfied with their lives when they can do so.

PRODUCTIVITY Contributing to a social network may be one important way of remaining productive, especially for older adults who are retired. **Volunteerism,** performing unpaid work for altruistic reasons, has been linked to successful aging. Neena

volunteerism
performance of unpaid work for altruistic motives

For some elders, remaining productive means venturing into new hobbies such as painting, sculpting, or other artistic pursuits.

(*Photo:* Stacy Pick/Stock Boston)

Make the Connection

Look back at the discussions of post-secondary education in **Chapter 12** and career selection in **Chapter 13**. Formulate a model that explains how the experiences of early adulthood contribute to successful aging.

Chappell, director of the University of Victoria Centre on Aging, conducted an extensive review of the literature on volunteerism in North America and concluded that people who volunteer, especially with helping others, are happier and healthier in their elder years. The social interaction aspect in particular has a beneficial impact upon both quality of life and mortality. This may not be surprising, since the elderly indicate that their relationships with others are what they value the most in life (Chappell, 1999).

Remarkably, a California study involving nearly 2000 older adults found that mortality rates were 60% lower among volunteers than among nonvolunteers (Oman, Thoresen, & McMahon, 1999). Studies have also shown that volunteerism improves older adults' overall life satisfaction (Glass & Jolly, 1997). Moreover, volunteers appear to be healthier than nonvolunteers (Krause et al., 1999). As noted earlier, however, selection effects may account for some of these observed effects—that is, the healthiest elders may volunteer the most.

Results from the 2000 National Survey of Giving, Volunteering and Participating show that the percentage of Canadians volunteering has declined in all age groups, including the elderly. However, those aged 65 to 74 clocked the highest number of annual volunteer hours of any age group (272 hours) and those 75 and older came in a close second (265 hours) (Canadian Centre for Philanthropy, 2003). So, it seems the volunteer activities of older adults have the potential to benefit society as well as enhance the volunteers' own physical and mental health (Warburton, Le Brocque, & Rosenman, 1998).

Some older adults remain productive by venturing into new pursuits, such as taking music lessons, attending college classes, or learning to paint or sculpt. Researchers conducting a study of 36 artists over age 60 asked them to explain how artistic productivity contributed to their successful aging (Fisher & Specht, 1999). Their responses contained several themes: producing art gave them a purpose in life, opportunities to interact with like-minded peers, and a sense of competence. These responses are perhaps not surprising, and they probably vary little from those that might be offered by younger artists. However, the older artists also claimed that creating art helped them stay healthy. Thus, creative productivity may help older adults maintain an optimistic outlook, which, as you have learned, contributes to physical health.

LIFE SATISFACTION *Life satisfaction,* or a sense of personal well-being, is also an important component of successful aging. Many of the factors that predict life satisfaction are very similar to the variables that you have already learned are predictive of successful aging. For example, one characteristic linking successful aging to life satisfaction is a sense of control, which you read about in **Chapter 12** (Rodin, 1986). Even life events that could be highly stressful, such as financial problems, may have little negative effect if the individual feels he has some choice (Krause, Jay, & Liang, 1991). Thus, involuntary retirement or involuntary institutionalization typically has negative effects, whereas planned and chosen retirement or a voluntary move to a nursing home does not.

What is critical to life satisfaction in almost all cases is an individual's perception of her own situation, which seems to be more important than objective measures. Perceived adequacy of social support and perceived adequacy of income are critical. Moreover, self-ratings of health, rather than objective measures of health, may be the most significant predictors of life satisfaction and morale (Draper, Gething, Fethney, & Winfield, 1999).

Research also suggests that social comparisons—how well an older adult thinks he is doing compared with others his age—are just as important to these perceptions as the older adult's awareness of the changes he has undergone since his younger years (Robinson-Whelen & Kiecolt-Glaser, 1997). A majority of older adults, no matter what their personal circumstances, believe that most others their age are worse off than they are (Heckhausen & Brim, 1997). Developmentalists speculate that the tendency to see others as having more problems is an important self-protective psychological device employed by those who are aging successfully.

CRITICISMS OF THE SUCCESSFUL AGING PARADIGM   Critics of the successful aging paradigm suggest that the concept can be misleading. For one thing, they say, the paradigm has the potential to become a new kind of ageist stereotype, one that portrays older adults who suffer from disabilities as incompetent (Scheidt, Humpherys, & Yorgason, 1999). Such critics point out that, for many elderly adults, no amount of optimism, willingness to rehabilitate, social support, or involvement in intellectually demanding activities can moderate their physical limitations. For example, studies of performance on reading comprehension tests that compared university professors over age 70 and graduate students show that some degree of age-based cognitive decline can be expected, even among very bright, highly experienced, and productive adults (Christensen, Henderson, Griffiths, & Levings, 1997). Thus, these critics claim, the danger of the successful aging paradigm is that it can give the erroneous impression that all the effects of aging are under one's control.

Another danger, some critics say, in shifting the focus of gerontology research from disease and decline to quality of life is that medical research still has enormous potential for discovering cures for many of the diseases of old age (Portnoi, 1999). Critics fear that emphasis on successful aging may cause public and institutional support for disease-related research to decline. These critics point out that there is good reason to believe that many conditions that are now thought to be part of "normal" aging are actually disease processes for which medical science can find effective treatments (Portnoi, 1999).

Nevertheless, critics concede that the successful aging paradigm has broadened gerontologists' approaches to studying old age. Thus, they agree that its influence has been largely positive. Still, keeping their criticisms in mind can help balance the optimism of the successful aging paradigm against the realities of life in late adulthood and the need to continue to encourage researchers to search for treatments for age-related diseases such as Alzheimer's.

RELIGIOUS COPING

Religion appears to be one factor contributing to individual differences in life satisfaction. Psychologists use the term **religious coping** to refer to the tendency to turn to religious beliefs and institutions in times of stress or trouble. People of all ages use religious coping. However, many developmentalists suggest that religious coping may be particularly important in the later years because of the high number of life stressors—including deaths of loved ones, chronic illnesses, and declining sensory abilities. And elders themselves often cite religious coping as their primary means of managing stress (Barusch, 1999).

religious coping
the tendency to turn to religious beliefs and institutions for support in times of difficulty

SEX DIFFERENCES   Canadian data suggest that women make more use of religious coping than men do (Bibby, 2001; Clark, 2000). Most developmentalists attribute this finding to sex differences in social behaviour that are observed across the lifespan. However, it's important to keep in mind that, even though the frequency with which religious coping is used may differ according to ethnicity and gender, its effects seem to be similar in all racial and ethnic groups and for both women and men. These effects can be best examined by separating the psychological and social components of religious coping.

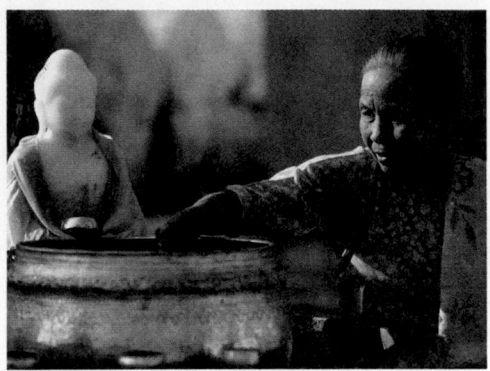

Strong religious beliefs appear to be positively associated with elders' health and well-being.
(*Photo:* Asia Images/Getty Images)

RELIGIOUS BELIEFS The psychological component of religious coping involves people's beliefs and attitudes. A number of investigators have examined links between religious beliefs and various measures of well-being among the elderly. Typically, researchers distinguish between positive and negative religious coping (Pargament, Smith, Koenig, & Perez, 1998). *Positive religious coping* involves a reliance on the belief that there is a divine purpose in one's difficulties and that one can trust in the divine purpose even when circumstances are grim. *Negative religious coping* is manifested by abandoning or doubting one's religious beliefs because of adversity, believing that one's problems are divine punishment, or attributing adverse events to an evil, all-powerful being. As you might suspect, researchers have found that elders who use positive religious coping are both physically and mentally healthier than those who use negative religious coping or no religious coping at all (Meisenhelder & Chandler, 2000; Pargament, Koenig, & Perez, 2000).

Of course, positive religious coping may be the result of good health rather than the cause of it. But some indication of the direction of causality can be gained from longitudinal studies. In one investigation, researchers in the Netherlands periodically studied symptoms of depression in a group of older adults over a year (Braam, Beekman, Deeg, Smit, & van Tilburg, 1997). Interestingly, they found that depressive symptoms occurred just as often in participants for whom religious beliefs were an important component of coping as they did in other participants. However, religious participants recovered from their depressive symptoms more rapidly and completely than did the participants for whom religious faith was less important. These results suggest that positive religious coping may indeed be a cause of better mental health.

Correlations between religious coping and anxiety have also been found. Elders who place a great deal of emphasis on religious faith worry much less than those who do not (Tapanya, Nicki, & Jarusawad, 1997). Moreover, associations between religious faith and physical and mental health have been found among older adults of diverse faiths—Christians, Buddhists, Muslims, Hindus, and Sikhs—and from a variety of cultures and ethnic groups (Krause et al., 1999; Mehta, 1997; Meisenhelder & Chandler, 2000; Tapanya et al., 1997).

The positive effects of religious coping seem to arise from its influence on how elders think about their lives. For example, older adults who rate their religious beliefs as highly important to them are more likely than others to think that their lives serve an important purpose (Gerwood, LeBlanc, & Piazza, 1998). In addition, religious faith seems to provide older adults with a theme that integrates the various periods of their lives (Mehta, 1999). As a result, religious elders are more likely than their nonreligious peers to view old age as a chapter in an ongoing story rather than as primarily a period of loss of capacities. Further, among low-income elders, divine power is viewed as a resource on which those who have little social power in the material world can rely (Barusch, 1999).

Critical Thinking

Do the people you know who use religious coping do so positively or negatively? How do you think their use of such coping affects these individuals' attitudes and behaviour?

ATTENDANCE AT RELIGIOUS SERVICES The social aspect of religious coping most often examined by researchers is attendance at religious services. Regular religious attendance dips during young adulthood, but rises steadily once Canadians reach their mid-30s. It is highest in seniors, with more than half attending at least once a month (Clark, 2000; 2003). Research suggests that Canadian adults who regularly attend such services are more optimistic, physically healthier, live longer, feel very satisfied with their lives, and have less stressful lives than their nonattending peers (Clark, 1998). These findings correspond with recent research on religious people that emphasizes the connection between a sense of belonging and a sense of well-being. As well, there seems to be a causal connection between a person's level of health and of belonging. Religious seniors who regularly attend religious services live healthier lives, and this is associated with a strong sense of connectedness to their community and a better personal support network (Clark, 2000). Interestingly, longitudinal studies suggest that patterns of attendance change little even if elders become ill or disabled (Idler & Kasl, 1997b).

Longitudinal studies also suggest that the mortality rate is lower among religious participants. In one study, researchers examined the association between religious attendance and mortality in nearly 2000 older adults over a 5-year period (Oman & Reed, 1998). Researchers compared participants who were associated with other kinds of organizations to those who were involved with religious institutions. They found that the mortality rate during the 5-year period was lower among the religious older adults, even when the amount of organizational involvement and the size of the organizational social networks were the same as for the nonreligious older adults (Oman & Reed, 1998).

Elders themselves cite a number of reasons for the benefits of religious involvement. For example, many say that religious institutions provide them with opportunities to help others (Krause et al., 1999). Intergenerational involvement is another aspect of religious participation often mentioned by older adults. For many, religious institutions provide a structure within which they can pass on their knowledge and beliefs to younger individuals (Mehta, 1999).

ALTERNATIVE EXPLANATIONS As noted throughout this discussion, researchers must always consider selection effects when examining links between variables such as religious coping and health. There are other possible confounding factors as well. For example, religious and nonreligious elders may differ in personality traits. It seems likely that those with higher levels of extraversion would be the most comfortable in religious social environments—and scientists know that extraversion is correlated with successful aging. Thus, the connection between religious coping and health in old age may be a manifestation of personality rather than an independent effect of religion.

In addition, research on the association between religious faith and health focuses on the personal relevance of spirituality rather than on intellectual acceptance of a set of doctrines. So, it may be the intensity and the personal nature of these beliefs, rather than the fact that they have a religious focus, that are responsible for the correlations. In addition, in most research studies, the participants have had long-standing belief and attendance patterns. Thus, these elders may persist in religious faith and involvement, even when they are ill or disabled, because it helps them achieve a sense of continuity of identity. That is, religious involvement may allow an older adult to feel that, despite physical losses, she is still the same person. So, it may be that the sense of personal integration that religion provides is responsible for the correlations. Whatever the reasons, the research evidence suggests that supporting the spiritual needs of the elderly may be just as important to maintaining their health and functioning as meeting their physical and material needs.

Before Going On

- Describe the successful aging paradigm, noting the ways in which it is manifested in the lives of older adults.
- How does religious coping influence physical and mental health in late adulthood?

SOCIAL RELATIONSHIPS

The social roles older adults occupy are usually different from those they held at younger ages. In addition, both consistency and change characterize social relationships during this period.

SOCIAL ROLES

Clearly, role changes are inevitable in old age, and physical and cognitive changes are responsible for many of them. Some, however, are the result of ageism. Appearance cues—wrinkles and grey hair and the like—are often the basis for judgments about the competence of those who are older (Hummert, Garstka, & Shaner, 1997). The older people look, the more negatively others stereotype them, and negative stereotypes are more often applied to older women than to older men. Consequently, older adults may be unjustly forced out of roles by younger adults.

Surprisingly, though, elderly adults are just as likely as their younger peers to hold ageist stereotypes. In fact, some data suggest that older adults are actually *more* likely than younger adults to be prejudiced against their elderly peers (Hummert et al., 1997). Thus, an older adult's beliefs about his own competence or attractiveness may be as important to his decisions about role transitions as the prejudices of others.

Moreover, sociologists point out that the roles that older adults do retain have far less content—that is, far fewer duties or expectations (Rosow, 1985). For example, most older adults continue to occupy the role of parent, but this role typically becomes far less demanding. Unless she had children very late in life, or her children encountered unusual difficulties in getting established in their own lives, by the time an individual reaches age 65, her last child is long since fully independent. Similarly, in other arenas, elders may occupy roles that have titles, but fewer duties. A retired university professor, for instance, may have the title of Emeritus Professor, a position that carries a few benefits but essentially no obligations. In other organizations, an older individual may be given the title of Honorary Chairman.

In a practical sense, the decline in role content means that the daily routines of many older adults are no longer structured by specific roles. But is this good or bad? Some developmentalists see this loss of role definition as carrying with it a significant risk of isolation or alienation. Others see distinct advantages to this "roleless" time in late life. One such advantage is a greater "license for eccentricity" (Bond & Coleman, 1990, p. 78). Because they do not have to fit into the sometimes tight confines of role expectations, older adults feel far freer to express their own individuality—in dress, language, and personal preferences. This change may begin even earlier than late adulthood; the gradual assertion of individuality seems to be characteristic of middle adulthood for many. But certainly older adults benefit from a kind of institutionalized acceptance of eccentricity.

LIVING ARRANGEMENTS

As you learned in **The Real World: Caregiving** feature in **Chapter 16**, only about 9% of women and 5% of men over age 65 reside in long-term care institutions, although the percentage increases substantially in seniors who are aged 85 and older (Cranswick, 2003). Most of the seniors who are not institutionalized live alone. The most common living arrangement for middle-aged adults is living with a spouse or partner, but this arrangement becomes much less common in late adulthood.

Figure 17.1 shows the marital status of the old and oldest old in Canada. Because men typically marry younger women and because women live longer than men, a man can normally expect to have a spouse or intimate partner until he dies. The normal expectation for a woman is that she will eventually be without such a partner, often for many years. Clearly, the percentages in **Figure 17.1** support these expectations, and it is hard to exaggerate the importance of that difference for the experience of late adulthood for men and women.

The difference is also clearly reflected in **Figure 17.2**, which shows the living arrangements of elders in Canada. As you can see, older women are more likely to live alone than older men. This pattern is typical in other industrialized countries as well.

In Canada and in many other Western industrialized countries, living alone is not only the most common but also the most desired living arrangement among unmarried elders, even among those whose health has declined. A particularly intriguing set of data comes from a study in which researchers interviewed more than 2000 unmarried men and women over 70 (Worobey & Angel, 1990). Each of the participants was contacted twice, once in 1984 and once in 1986, so it was possible for investigators to look at changes in living arrangements for those whose health stayed the same, improved, or declined. Of those who lived alone at the start of the study and whose health declined over the next 2 years, 81% of the men and 76% of the women still lived alone.

That does not mean that health has no impact on living arrangements. Older adults with significant health problems are more likely to live with their children or with other relatives than are those who are more healthy (Choi, 1991; Stinner, Byun, & Paita, 1990). But most elders with mild or moderate disabilities or health problems do not live with relatives. Most appear to prefer to live alone and do so as long as possible. In other cultures, the pattern is often quite different. In Japan, for example, only 7% of adults over 60 live alone, and only 29% live with a spouse only. Over half live with a child (Tsuya & Martin, 1992).

Besides health, several other factors affect the probability that an unattached older adult will live with a child or with other relatives:

- *Income.* Those with lower incomes are more likely to live with family members, although this difference is not large (Choi, 1991). Many elders with marginal or below-poverty incomes live alone.

- *Number of daughters and sons.* The more children an elder has, the more likely he or she is to live

Figure 17.1

This graph shows the marital status of Canadian seniors. For married seniors, the likelihood of living with a spouse declines with age, especially among older women.

(*Source:* Adapted from Havens & Finlayson, 1999, Table 2.6—Distribution of Marital Status Among Men and Women, 65+ and 85+, p. 10. Reproduced with permission of the Minister of Public Works and Government Services Canada, 2005.)

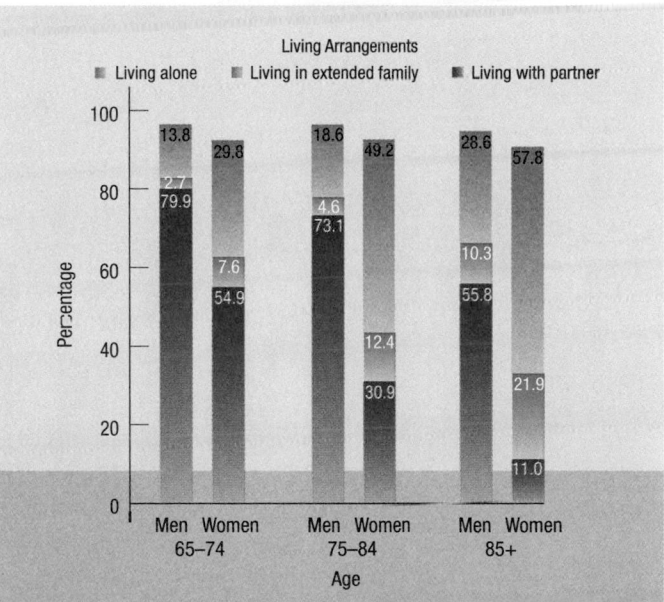

Figure 17.2

This graph shows the living arrangements of Canadian seniors. You can see that for those seniors who were not living with a spouse, living alone was the most common alternative, followed by living with extended families.

(*Sources:* Adapted from Health Canada, 2000e, figures from Statistical Snapshots: Most Live at Home, No. 6; Living with Extended Families, No. 7; and Most Living at Home, No. 8. Reproduced with permission of the Minister of Public Works and Government Services Canada, 2005.)

with one of them, but this is more true of daughters than of sons. That is, elders with more daughters are more likely to live with a grown child than are those with few daughters, but having more sons does not increase the likelihood of living with an adult child (Soldo, Wolf, & Agree, 1990).

What do all these statistics suggest about the roles and relationships of older adults? First and foremost, of course, they point to a sharp divergence of experience for men and women in the later years. They also indicate that developmentalists need to look beyond the spousal or partnership relationship if they are to understand the patterns of social interactions that are central to the aging individual.

As you can see from **Figure 17.3**, older adults in Canada are very socially active. The greatest proportion of their social activities involve contacts with family and friends. For widowed or unmarried elders, relationships with adult children and other family members may become more central in late adulthood than they were in earlier years. But an elder who is no longer able to live alone may be reluctant to live with an adult child with whom she has long-standing disagreements or whom she does not trust (see **The Real World**).

PARTNERSHIPS

Cross-sectional comparisons show that marital satisfaction is higher in the late adult years than when children are still at home. But this high marital satisfaction may have a somewhat different basis than that of the early years of marriage. In late adulthood, marriages tend to be based less on passion and mutual disclosure and more on loyalty,

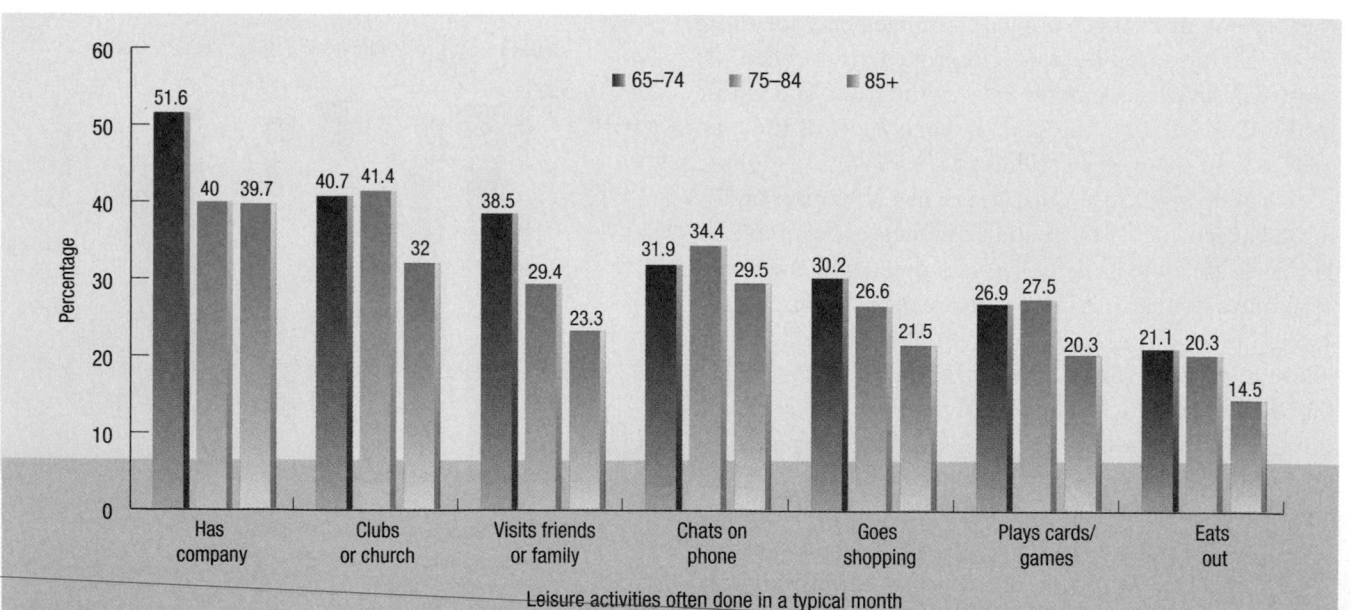

Figure 17.3

Participants in the Survey of Aging and Independence were asked what leisure activities they had engaged in within a typical month and the extent to which they participated in these pastimes. As this figure suggests, older adults are very socially active. Participation in social activities declines with age, yet overall remains fairly robust.

(*Source:* Adapted from Havens & Finlayson, 1999, Table 7.5—Participation in Selected Leisure Activities Typically Done at Home by Age Group, p. 54, and Table 7.6—Participation in Selected Leisure Activities Typically Done Outside of Home, by Age Group, p. 55. Reproduced with permission of the Minister of Public Works and Government Services Canada, 2005.)

The Real World
Caregiving
Elder Abuse in Canada

One extreme manifestation of conflict and strain between elders and their spouse or children is abuse and neglect of elders. In recent years, the maltreatment of elders has occasionally received a great deal of media coverage, but it is a largely hidden and growing problem in Canada and worldwide (Dauvergne, 2003; World Health Organization, 2002). Recent surveys show that 7% of Canadian elders reported emotional abuse, such as yelling, insulting, threatening, or ignoring. In addition, 1% reported financial exploitation and 1% reported being physically or sexually violated. Male abusers are more likely to commit physical abuse, whereas female abusers are more likely to fail to provide needed aid (neglect) (Swanson, 1999). Two-thirds of all the reported instances of elder abuse involve a non–family member and 6% an unknown person (Dauvergne, 2003). The remaining 28% of abuse cases entail family violence and, of these cases, 43% of elderly men reported abuse by their adult children, and elderly women reported being victimized equally often by their adult children (37%) as by their spouse (36%).

Researchers have identified several risk factors for elder abuse, including mental illness or alcoholism in the abuser, financial dependency of the abuser on the victim, social isolation, and external stresses (Pillemer & Suitor, 1990, 1992; Swanson, 1999). A likely victim of abuse is an elderly widow sharing her household with a dependent son who has a mental disorder or a drug or alcohol problem; the mother is typically too dependent on her son to kick him out and too ashamed of the abuse to tell others about it (Bengtson et al., 1996). Abuse is also more likely when the elder with dementia is physically violent and when a husband has physically abused his wife throughout their adult lives and simply continues to do so in old age.

The existence of such destructive forms of interaction is a clear reminder that older adults' relationships with their kin are not all sweetness and light. But it is also important to remember that these highly negative patterns are the exception rather than the rule. For most elders, relationships with children and other kin may be a mixture of positive and negative, but the scale most often tips toward the positive.

familiarity, and mutual investment in the relationship (Bengtson, Rosenthal, & Burton, 1990). In Sternberg's terms (look back at **Figure 13.2**, page 398), late adult marriages are more likely to reflect companionate love than romantic or even consummate love.

Of course, this does not mean that the marriages of older adults are necessarily devitalized or neutral. That may well be true of some marriages, but there is evidence to the contrary for many. You'll recall from **Chapter 16** that the majority of older adult couples are still sexually active and may be somewhat more sexually adventurous than younger adults. Collectively, older couples also report higher levels of pleasure and lower levels of conflict in their relationships than do middle-aged couples. When older couples do have conflicts, they resolve them in more affectionate and less negative ways (Carstensen, Gottman, & Levenson, 1995; Levenson, Carstensen, & Gottman, 1993). Older couples also spend more time with each other than with family or friends, and although much of this time is spent in passive or basic maintenance activities—watching TV, doing housework, running errands—it is also true that those married elders who spend more time with their spouses report high levels of happiness (Larson, Mannell, & Zuzanek, 1986).

Further evidence of the deep bond that continues to exist in late-life marriages is the remarkable degree of care and assistance older spouses give each other when one or the other is disabled. For married elders with some kind of disability, by far the largest source of assistance is the spouse, not children or friends. Many husbands and wives continue to care for spouses who are ill or who suffer from dementia for very long periods of time. And even when both spouses suffer from significant

Affection between married partners and pleasure in each other's company clearly do not disappear in old age.
(*Photo:* Jay Silverman Productions/ Getty Images)

Elderly newlyweds report higher levels of personal happiness than either long-married or single peers. (*Photo:* Myrleen Ferguson Cate/PhotoEdit)

disabilities, they nonetheless continue to care for each other "until death do us part." Marriages may thus be less romantic or less emotionally intense in late adulthood than they were in earlier years, but they are typically satisfying and highly committed.

Researchers have found similar characteristics and effects in long-term gay and lesbian relationships (Grossman, Daugelli, & Hershberger, 2000). Like heterosexuals, elderly homosexuals who have a long-term partner typically identify the partner as their most important source of emotional support. In addition, those who live with a partner report less loneliness and better physical and mental health.

It is the loss of the marriage or partnership relationship through the death of the spouse or partner that alters this pattern for so many older adults. The gender difference in marital status among elders illustrated in **Figure 17.1** is further increased by a higher rate of remarriage for men than for women, a pattern found among both the widowed and the divorced at every age. In Canada, 15% of unattached men over 65 remarry, compared with only 6% of women (Norris, 1994). Older unmarried men are also more likely to date and more likely to live with someone (Bulcroft & Bulcroft, 1991). By contrast, research suggests that widows have little interest in dating or remarriage (Talbott, 1998). Despite older women's reluctance to remarry, studies of the emotional impact of remarriage in late adulthood suggest that both men and women benefit emotionally (Winter, Lawton, Casten, & Sando, 2000). When researchers examine self-ratings of life satisfaction, elderly newlyweds rate their personal happiness more highly than do either long-married or unattached peers.

Married older adults, like married adults of any age, have certain distinct advantages: They have higher life satisfaction, better health, and lower rates of institutionalization. Such differential advantages are generally greater for married older men than for married older women (again, this is also true among younger adults). This difference might be interpreted as indicating that marriage affords more benefits to men than to women or that men rely more on their marriage relationship for social support and are thus more affected by its loss. Whatever the explanation, it seems clear that, for older women, marital status is less strongly connected to health or life satisfaction, but still strongly connected to financial security.

FAMILY RELATIONSHIPS

Folklore and descriptions of late adulthood in the popular press suggest that family, particularly children and grandchildren, form the core of the social life of older adults, perhaps especially those who are widowed. Older adults do describe intergenerational bonds as strong and important; most report a significant sense of family solidarity and support (Bengtson et al., 1996). These bonds are reflected, among other things, in regular contact between elders and family members.

CONTACTS WITH ADULT CHILDREN Canadian studies show that between two-thirds and three-quarters of older parents said their children see them at least once a week (Connidis, 1989; Rosenthal, 1987). The distance between where an elder parent and adult child live has an effect on the frequency of visitation. University of Alberta sociologist Susan McDaniel (1994) reported that of those Canadians who lived within 10 kilometres of one of their parents, 80% visited daily or at least once a week. Of those who lived between 11 and 50 kilometres away, 52% visited daily or weekly, but the rate of regular visitations dropped to 23% when a senior's child lived 51 to 100 kilometres away. For those children who do not visit frequently, close family ties are maintained with telephone calls, letters, and e-mail. In addition, it is important to emphasize that the frequency of contact is not the only measure of the closeness of family relationships.

Perhaps more important than the frequency of visitation is the satisfaction seniors experience with family contacts. Havens and Finlayson (1999) reported that seniors do not need to have frequent contact with family members in order to feel close to them. Regardless of frequency of visitation, 88% of seniors report that they feel close to family members. Moreover, about three-quarters of seniors aged 65 and above are very satisfied with the level of family contact, while fewer than 4% are less than satisfied with the level of contact with family members.

Part of the regular contact between the elderly and their adult children, of course, involves giving aid to or receiving it from the elder person—a pattern you learned about in **Chapter 15**. Havens and Finlayson (1999) found that aging parents in Canada are most likely to need support with activities that involve physical activity (e.g. lifting, bending). Young seniors are most likely to need help with housework, emotional support, grocery shopping, yard work, and transportation. The oldest old need assistance, in priority order, with transportation, housework, groceries, meals, and yard work. When older adults need help that cannot be provided by a spouse, it is most often provided by other family members, principally children. With advancing age, a spouse is less likely to be able to assist, and the rate of spousal help drops from a high of 57% in the young old down to about 23% in the oldest old. Conversely, as parents age, children provide an increasingly larger portion of the care. For parents aged 65 to 74, 29% of sons and more than 35% of daughters provide assistance. The rates of help for parents aged 85 and over increases by about 5% for sons and 7% for daughters.

EFFECTS OF RELATIONSHIPS WITH ADULT CHILDREN Some studies indicate that when relationships between elders and adult children are warm and close, they are more important to elders' sense of well-being than any other kind of social relationship (Pinquart & Soerensen, 2000). By contrast, other researchers have found that elders who see their children more often or report more positive interactions with their children do not describe themselves as happier or healthier overall than do those who have less frequent or less positive relationships with their children (e.g., Mullins & Mushel, 1992). Moreover, such results have been obtained in very different cultural settings, for example in India and among Mexican Americans (Lawrence, Bennett, & Markides, 1992; Venkatraman, 1995). In all these studies, the older adults reported regular contact with their children and said that they enjoyed it, but these relationships did not seem to enhance happiness or health. Moreover, research has shown that childless elders are just as happy and well adjusted as those who have children (Connidis & McMullin, 1993). Many developmentalists have concluded that good relationships and regular contact with adult children can add to an elderly adult's quality of life, but are not necessary for it.

One possible explanation for this inconsistency in findings is that the relationship with one's children is still governed by role prescriptions, even in old age. It may be friendly, but it is not chosen in the same way that a relationship with a friend is. With your friend, you feel free to be yourself and feel accepted as who you are. With your children, you may feel the need to live up to their demands and expectations.

Several studies support this explanation. For instance, one researcher interviewed 55 older widows at length about their relationships with their children (Talbott, 1990). These women said many positive things about those relationships, but they described certain negatives as well: Some felt neglected by their children, some felt unappreciated, and some were afraid of bothering or burdening their children.

GRANDCHILDREN AND SIBLINGS As you learned in **Chapter 15**, interactions between grandchildren and middle-aged grandparents are beneficial to both. However, in late adulthood, contact between grandchildren and grandparents declines as the

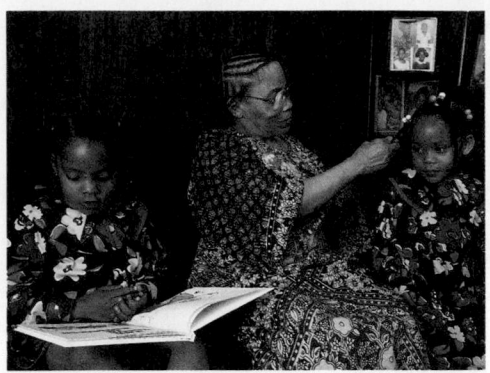

Most elders enjoy maintaining relationships with younger family members. However, research suggests that such connections are not essential to life satisfaction in old age.
(*Photo:* Michael Newman/PhotoEdit)

grandchildren become adults themselves (Silverstein & Long, 1998). Nonetheless, McDaniel (1994) reported that 39% of adult grandchildren visited their grandparents more than once a month and 41% less than once a month but at least some time in the previous 12 months. In addition, more than a third of adult grandchildren had daily, weekly, or monthly contact by telephone or letter.

Interestingly, though, it appears that relationships with siblings may become more important in late adulthood, especially after both parents have died (Bedford, 1995; Gold, 1996). Siblings seldom provide much practical assistance to one another in old age, but they can and often do serve two other important functions. First, siblings can provide a unique kind of emotional support for one another, based on shared reminiscences and companionship. Once parents are gone, no one else knows all the old stories, all the family jokes, the names and history of former friends and neighbours. Second, many elders see their siblings as a kind of "insurance policy" in old age, a source of support of last resort (Connidis, 1994).

FRIENDSHIPS

Critical Thinking

Why do you think most older adults' friends are long-standing ones? What social or psychological barriers might there be to creating new friendships in old age?

Because older adults' friends generally come from the same cohort and have been their friends for a number of years, they can provide the same sense of generational solidarity that siblings may provide. The small amount of research on late-life friendships supports the hypothesis that the number of friendships may diminish gradually from age 65 onward (e.g., Blieszner & Adams, 1992; Levitt, Weber, & Guacci, 1993). However, friendships gain importance in the lives of elders, even as they diminish in number.

Mounting evidence suggests that contact with friends has a significant impact on overall life satisfaction, on self-esteem, and on the amount of loneliness reported by older adults (Antonucci, 1990; Hartup & Stevens, 1999; Jerrome, 1990). Moreover, for those elders whose families are unavailable, friendships seem to provide an equally effective support network (Takahashi, Tamura, & Tokoro, 1997). This is particularly true of unmarried elders, but is at least somewhat true for married ones as well.

Friends meet different kinds of needs for older adults than do family members. For one thing, relationships with friends are likely to be more reciprocal or equitable, and developmentalists know that equitable relationships are more valued and less stressful. Friends provide companionship, opportunities for laughter, and shared activities. In one Canadian study, for example, friends were second only to spouses as sources of companionship among those over 65 (Connidis & Davies, 1992). Friends may also provide assistance with daily tasks, such as shopping or housework, although they typically provide less help of this kind than do family members.

Friends seem to play an important role in late adulthood, perhaps because they share the same background and memories—like favourite old tunes and dances.
(*Photo:* Michael L. Abramson/Woodfin Camp and Associates)

GENDER DIFFERENCES IN SOCIAL NETWORKS

As at earlier ages, women and men in late adulthood appear to form different kinds of social networks, with men's friendships involving less disclosure and less intimacy than women's. In addition, older women's networks tend to be larger and closer than those of older men.

Developmentalists attribute these findings to a continuation of a pattern evident across most of the lifespan (Barker, Morrow, & Mitteness, 1998). Thus, if you think back on what you learned about sex differences in the chapters on childhood, adolescence, early adulthood, and middle adulthood, sex differences in late adulthood social networks should not be surprising.

However, it would be a mistake to assume that, because men have smaller social networks, their relationships are unimportant to them. Some developmentalists suggest that research on social networks may be biased in such a way that women will always be found to have stronger networks. This bias, critics say, originates from the fact that research emphasizes shared activities and frequency of contact more than the quality of the relationships. Indeed, when quality of relationships is considered, research shows that men's social networks are just as important to them and provide them with the same kinds of emotional support as women's networks do, even though men's networks tend to be smaller (Riggs, 1997).

Before Going On

- How do social roles change in late adulthood?
- What are the living arrangements of most elderly people in Canada and other industrialized countries?
- How do intimate partnerships contribute to development in late adulthood?
- What is the significance for older adults of family relationships?
- How do friends affect elders' life satisfaction?
- What are some gender differences in older adults' social networks?

CAREER ISSUES IN LATE LIFE

A remarkable capacity for adaptation marks the transition from work to retirement. Although this transition certainly brings the loss of a major role, virtually all the folklore about the negative effects of this particular role loss turns out to be wrong, at least for current older cohorts in developed countries. Developmentalists' knowledge about the process of retirement has been greatly enhanced by a series of excellent longitudinal studies, each following a group of men or women from before retirement into the years past retirement. In one particularly helpful analysis, Erdman Palmore and his colleagues combined the results of seven such studies, yielding a sample of over 7000 adults, each interviewed at least twice and often many more times than that (Palmore, Burchett, Fillenbaum, George, & Wallman, 1985). Although these data are not completely current, they make up by far the most comprehensive set of longitudinal data available.

TIMING OF RETIREMENT

The normal retirement age is 65 in Canada, but there has been pressure to raise the age of retirement to 67 to alleviate some of the expected demand on pension plans and

Critical Thinking

Think about your own attitudes toward retirement. Do you expect this life change to be positive and enjoyable, or do you anticipate it with dread or some anxiety? What do you think has shaped your attitudes?

health care caused by the retiring Baby Boomers. Ironically, results from a recent survey of employed Canadians under the age of 40 found that only 18% were willing to postpone their retirement (Langlois, 2004). Furthermore the average age of retirement has been declining in most industrialized countries; in Canada, the average age of retirement dropped from age 64.9 twenty-five years ago to 61 years of age by the year 2000 (Statistics Canada, 2001p). There are also differences in the median retirement age by industry categories. For example, between 1996 and 2000, half of those in the public sector retired at age 58, half of the private sector employees retired at age 62, and half of those who were self-employed did not retire before the age of 65 (Rathje, 2003).

REASONS FOR RETIREMENT

Research suggests that financial incentives are only one reason for retiring. Studies point to a collection of "pushes" and "pulls" that combine to influence each person's decision to retire (Kohli, 1994; Quadagno & Hardy, 1996).

AGE Age itself is obviously an important ingredient in the retirement equation. Internal models play an important role here. If a person's "expected life history" includes retirement at age 55 or 65, he will be strongly inclined to retire at that age, regardless of other factors.

HEALTH Poor health provides a particularly strong push toward early retirement (Schulz, 1995). Poor health lowers the average age of retirement by 1 to 3 years, and is commonly found in industrialized countries (Hayward, Friedman, & Chen, 1996; McDonald & Wanner, 1990; Sammartino, 1987; Stanford, Happersett, Morton, Molgaard, & Peddecord, 1991). However, among those who retire at 65 or later, health is a less powerful factor, presumably because most of these later retirees are in good health.

FAMILY CONSIDERATIONS Family composition is important in the decision to retire. Those who are still supporting minor children retire later than do those in the postparental stage. Thus, men and women who bear their children very late, those who acquire a second and younger family in a second marriage, and those rearing grandchildren are likely to continue to work until these children have left home.

FINANCIAL SUPPORT Equally important in the timing of retirement is the availability of adequate financial support for retirement. Those who anticipate receiving pension support in addition to C/QPP pension benefits, or who have personal savings to draw on, retire earlier than do those who have no such financial backup.

Anticipated pension and health frequently work in opposite directions, because many working-class men and women who have worked in unskilled jobs can expect little supplementary retirement income and are in poor health. In general, working-class adults retire earlier than do middle-class and upper-class adults, often as a result of ill health and social norms, but many poor and working-class adults continue to work well past the normal retirement age in order to supplement their incomes.

On the other end of the social class scale, health and the adequacy of pensions work against each other in the opposite way. Adults in higher socioeconomic groups generally have both better health and better pensions; they also tend to have more interesting jobs. The three factors combine to produce somewhat later retirement for this group.

WORK CHARACTERISTICS Those who like their work and are highly committed to it, including many self-employed adults, retire later—often quite a lot later—than do those who are less gratified by their work. Those in challenging and interesting jobs are likely to postpone retirement until they are pushed by ill health or attracted by some extra financial inducement. For them, availability of a normal pension is less of an influence (Hayward & Hardy, 1985).

The ranks of Canadian seniors who were employed has been on the rise since 1996, and the average age of these generally better educated workers has also increased (Duchesne, 2004). In 2002, 8.4% of seniors were employed. Of these working seniors, the majority were involved with farming and, to a lesser extent, jobs in the retail trade. The largest number of elder professionals included accountants, general practitioners, and religious ministers.

SEX DIFFERENCES Except for age, none of the reasons for retirement is as significant for women as it is for men (Palmore et al., 1985). In Canada, the median age at which women retire is about two years before men (Statistics Canada, 2004h), but retirement benefits, health, or job characteristics do not predict when women will retire. The most reliable predictor of retirement for a woman is whether her husband has retired (Weaver, 1994). An opposing force that tends to keep women in the labour force is the lure of higher earnings that will augment future C/QPP pension benefits—a factor that may be especially important for current cohorts of women nearing retirement, many of whom entered the labour force only in middle adulthood.

By contrast, the factors that lead to positive views of retirement are very similar for men and women. For example, one study found that health was the most important predictor of quality of life in retirement for both sexes (Quick & Moen, 1998). However, extensive preretirement planning seemed to be more important for men. Moreover, almost all of the study's male participants had worked continuously until retirement. Among the retired women, though, some had worked continuously, but others had spent a significant number of years in the home or in part-time employment. The researchers found that those who had worked continuously expressed more satisfaction with the quality of their retirement.

EFFECTS OF RETIREMENT

There are a number of shifts that take place at retirement, some positive and some negative. But, overall, retirement seems to have positive effects on the lives of older adults.

INCOME One potentially significant change that occurs at retirement is related to the availability of alternative sources of income. Human Resources Development Canada (HRDC) (2001c) suggests that retired adults have several potential sources of income: government pensions, such as Old Age Security (OAS) and the Canada and Quebec Pension Plans (C/QPP); other pensions, such as those offered through an employer; income from savings, such as Registered Retirement Savings Plans (RRSPs), or other assets; and earnings from continued work. For most elderly in Canada, nongovernment sources now provide the largest portion of retirement income (Health Canada, 2003g). This means that young workers need to plan well ahead to ensure that they will have enough retirement income to meet their retirement lifestyle expectations. A common estimation is that you will need about 70% of your current pretax earnings to maintain your standard of living in retirement; for example, if you are earning $50 000 before you retire, you can expect to need $35 000 of annual income once you retire (HRDC, 2001c).

In Canada, as in many developed countries, many retired adults own their own homes and have no mortgage payments, and their children are self-reliant. Additionally, retirees are eligible for provincial health care benefits as well as for many special Senior Citizen benefits and discounts. When these factors are taken into consideration, on average, retired adults in most developed countries have incomes that are equivalent to 85–100% of preretirement levels (Smeeding, 1990).

POVERTY It used to be that postretirement income losses resulted in high poverty rates among the elderly. However, over the past several decades, poverty rates among the elderly have declined substantially. Health Canada (2003h) reported that after adjusting for inflation, senior men's income rose 21% and senior women's by 22% between 1981 and 1998. Accordingly, the incidence of seniors who were living below Statistics Canada's Low Income Cut-offs (LICOs) has fallen sharply since the early 1980s, from 34% to 20% in 1998 (Health Canada 2003i).

A variety of factors are responsible for declining poverty rates among the elderly. For one thing, there have been significant improvements in work-related pensions. As well, there have been moderate improvements in C/QPP and regular cost-of-living increases for pension incomes (Health Canada, 2003g). Equivalent progress has been made in reducing the rates of poverty among the elderly in many other countries. These improvements have meant that the relative financial position of the elderly has improved more than that of any other age group in the population. In fact, most elderly adults today had better jobs and earned a great deal more money before retirement than did members of previous generations. As a result, today's elders have more savings and better retirement benefits.

However, the recent trend toward a lower incidence of seniors living below the LICOs (a measure of poverty) obscures much higher rates in two subgroups. **Figure 17.4** shows declines in the elderly poverty rates of senior men and women who either live in families or are unattached. Although rates declined in all groups over the past two decades, large disparities across groups remained. Unattached older adults in particular continue to be more likely to be poor than their peers who live in families, and among the older unattached, women are more likely to be poor than men (48% versus 35%, respectively) (Health Canada, 2003j). Varying poverty rates for elderly unattached men and women arise from a number of differences in adult life experiences. At present, older women are much less likely than their male peers to have had paid employment, are less likely to have earned retirement benefits even if they did work, and generally worked for lower wages (Hardy & Hazelrigg, 1993). As a result, many older widows rely entirely on C/QPP and OAS income. Younger women are more likely to have been employed and to have participated in a retirement plan, but, as you learned in earlier chapters, gender differences in work patterns still exist. Thus, there are likely to be gender differences in poverty rates in future cohorts of retirees, though these will probably shrink a bit.

HEALTH, ATTITUDES, AND EMOTIONS Longitudinal studies indicate quite clearly that health simply does not change, for better or worse, because of retirement. When ill health accompanies retirement, the causal sequence is nearly always that the individual retired because of poor health. Among those in good health at retirement age, retirement itself has little or no effect on health status over the succeeding years (Palmore et al., 1985). This clear set of research results is interesting because it suggests that retirement is not a highly stressful life change for the vast majority of adults.

Similarly, the bulk of the evidence suggests that retirement has essentially no impact on overall life satisfaction or subjective well-being. Longitudinal studies that have included measures of such attitudes show little difference in scores before and after retirement, and those recently retired show little sign of any increase in depression (Palmore et al., 1985). For most, retirement is not perceived as a stressor at all.

One set of data that makes this point particularly clearly comes from a study of a group of more than 1500 men over a period of years (Bossé, Aldwin, Levenson, & Workman-Daniels, 1991). In the most recent interviews, participants were asked to indicate which of 31 possibly stressful life events they had experienced in the past year and to rate the overall stressfulness of each of these events. Retirement was ranked 30th out of 31 in overall stressfulness, below even such items as "move to a less desirable residence" or "decrease in responsibilities or hours at work or where you volunteer." Of those who had retired in the previous year, seven out of ten said that they found retirement either not stressful at all or only a little stressful. Among the 30% of retired men in this study who did list some problems with retirement, poor health and poor family finances were the most likely causes. Those with marital problems were also likely to report more daily hassles in their retired lives.

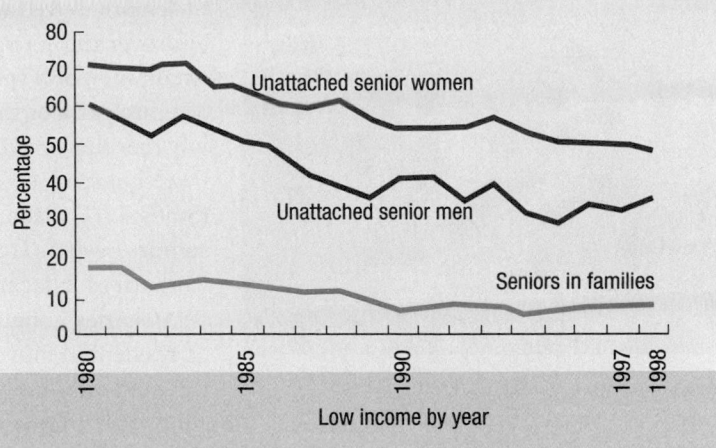

Figure 17.4

This graph illustrates how unattached older adults, in particular, continue to be poorer than their peers who live in families. Among the unattached seniors, women are more likely to be poor than men.

(*Source:* Adapted from Health Canada, 2001m, 2001n, figures from Statistical Snapshots: Gender Differences in Low Income, No. 15; and Low Income and Family Status, No. 16. Reproduced with permission of the Minister of Public Works and Government Services Canada, 2005.)

Other evidence suggests that those who respond least well to retirement are those who had the least control over the decision. For example, those who go into retirement because of a late-career job loss show declines in physical and mental health (Gallo, Bradley, Siegel, & Kasl, 2000). Similarly, those who are forced to retire by poor health typically adjust more poorly to retirement (Hardy & Quadagno, 1995). Even workers who accept special early retirement offers from their employers are likely to report lower satisfaction and higher levels of stress than do those who feel they had more control over the retirement decision (Herzog, House, & Morgan, 1991). Retirement is also likely to be more stressful for those whose economic situation is poor, or for those who must simultaneously cope with both retirement and other major life changes, such as widowhood (Stull & Hatch, 1984). But for those for whom retirement is anticipated and on time, this role loss is not stressful.

It appears that what predicts life satisfaction in late adulthood is not whether a person has retired but whether he was satisfied with life in earlier adulthood. We take ourselves with us through the years: Grumpy, negative young people tend to be grumpy, negative old people, and satisfied young adults find satisfaction in retirement as well. The consistency of this finding is quite striking and provides very good support for continuity theories of adulthood. Work does shape daily life for 40 years or more of adulthood, but a person's happiness or unhappiness with life, her growth or stagnation, seems less a function of the specifics of the work experience than a function of the attitudes and qualities she brings to the process.

GEOGRAPHIC MOBILITY For many adults, retirement brings an increase in choices about where to live. When your job or your spouse's job no longer ties you to a specific place, you can choose to move to sunnier climes or to live nearer one of your children. Surprisingly, however, most retirees stay fairly close to the place they have called home for many years (Burkhauser, Butrica, & Wasylenko, 1995; De Jong, Wilmoth, Angel, & Cornwell, 1995). In fact, Havens and Finlayson (1999) reported that only about 20%

Elders who have moved to resort communities specifically designed for retired people have made what social scientists call an amenity move.
(*Photo:* Frank Fournier/Woodfin Camp and Associates)

amenity move

postretirement move away from kin to a location that has some desirable feature, such as year-round warm weather

compensatory (kinship) migration

a move to a location near family or friends that happens when an elder requires frequent help because of a disability or disease

institutional migration

a move to an institution such as a nursing home that is necessitated by a disability

of seniors moved within a 5-year period. Moreover, when seniors aged 65 and over did move, most did so because their house was too big or too small; they or a spouse retired; there was a decline in the health of self or a spouse; and/or they wanted access to recreation or leisure. Regardless of whether they moved or remained where they lived before retirement, over three-quarters of all seniors lived in a Canadian urban area in 2001 (Statistics Canada, 2002h). The cities with the highest concentration of seniors were Trois-Rivières, Quebec, Victoria, B.C., and the St. Catharines–Niagara area of Ontario.

Charles Longino, who has been one of the most diligent investigators of residential moves among the elderly, suggests that elderly adults make three types of moves (Jackson, Longino, Zimmerman, & Bradsher, 1991; Litwak & Longino, 1987; Longino, 1990; Longino, Jackson, Zimmerman, & Bradsher, 1991). The first type, which he calls an amenity move, is the one most of us probably think of when we think of older adults changing residences. If an older adult makes such a move, it is almost always right around the time of retirement. Most typically, an **amenity move** is in a direction away from the older person's children, frequently to a warmer climate. The Department of Foreign Affairs and International Trade (DFAIT) (2001) suggests that Florida and Arizona are popular destinations for amenity moves to the United States. Other popular international destinations include Mexico, Latin American countries, and islands in the Caribbean, especially where there is a Canadian expatriate community. In Canada, amenity moves are most often westward, particularly to British Columbia. It's not surprising that Victoria, B.C., is among communities with the most seniors per capita (Health Canada, 2003k).

Those who make amenity moves are likely to be still married and relatively healthy and to have adequate or good retirement income (De Jong et al., 1995; Hazelrigg & Hardy, 1995). Often the relocating couple has vacationed in the new location; many have planned the move carefully over a number of years (Cuba & Longino, 1991). Most report higher levels of life satisfaction or morale after such a move, although some move back to where they came from because they find themselves too isolated from family and friends.

Another kind of amenity move is to move seasonally rather than making a permanent move to a new location. Some elders, often called "snowbirds," spend the winter months in sunnier areas and the summer months at home, nearer their families. Both permanent movers away from Canada and seasonal retirees (the so-called snowbirds) have to contend with many essential issues when they leave the country, namely immigration and citizenship, taxation, health care, and real estate matters (DFAIT, 2001).

The second type of move, which Longino calls **compensatory (kinship) migration**, occurs when the older adult—most often, a widow living alone—develops such a level of chronic disability that she has serious difficulty managing an independent household. When a move of this type occurs, it is nearly always a shift to be closer to a daughter, son, or some other relative who can provide regular assistance. In some cases, this means moving in with that daughter or son, but often the move is to an apartment or house nearby or into a retirement community in which the individual can live independently but has supportive services available.

The final type of move in late adulthood is what Longino calls **institutional migration**, to nursing home care (see **No Easy Answers**).

Of course, very few older adults actually move three times. Longino's point is that these are three very different kinds of moves, made by quite different subsets of the population of elderly, and at different times in the late adult years. Amenity moves usually occur early, kinship or compensatory migration is likely to occur in middle to late old age, and institutional migration clearly occurs late in life. Only the first of these types of moves reflects the increase in options that may result from retirement.

No Easy Answers

Deciding on

Long-Term Care

in Canada

In **Chapter 16** you read about the numbers of older adults living in long-term care institutions. Who are those institutionalized elders? And how do they and their families decide that a long-term care home is the best form of care?

A long-term care home in Canada usually denotes either not-for-profit homes for the aged or not-for-profit and for-profit nursing homes. One reason the decision to place an elderly parent or relative in a long-term care home is so difficult is that long-term institutional care is widely perceived as impersonal care that deprives elders of dignity and personal control (Biedenharn & Normoyle, 1991). The economics of long-term institutional care also make it unattractive for many older adults. Such care in Canada now costs anywhere from a minimum of about $1000 up to thousands of dollars per month, costs only partially covered by government or most health insurance plans. A stay of as long as a year is likely to exhaust the disposable assets of the majority of older adults. To be eligible for government subsidization for such care, a person must first use all of his own disposable assets, which may leave a surviving spouse in very difficult financial straits. Most Canadian jurisdictions permit ownership of certain assets, such as a home, to be transferred to a surviving spouse, so that this asset need not be disposed of before the partner in the long-term care institution is eligible for government subsidy—an alternative that leaves the surviving spouse in somewhat better financial condition. But the spouse may still suffer significant impoverishment.

Not surprisingly, the likelihood of placement into long-term care varies considerably from one cultural subgroup to another. Studies in Canada, the United States, and European countries show that the most likely candidate for institutional care is an unmarried white woman over the age of 75 with few or no children (in particular, with no daughters),

significant disability or dementia, and few economic resources (Carrière & Pelletier, 1995; Montgomery & Kosloski, 1994; Steinbach, 1992; Wolinsky, Calahan, Fitzgerald, & Johnson, 1993). Married elders are about half as likely as unattached ones to spend any time in a long-term care institution, and those with at least one daughter are about one-quarter as likely (Freedman, 1996). Long-term institutional care is especially likely if the elder is no longer able to use the toilet without help or to feed herself, although even among those who are disabled to this extent, home care rather than institutional care is still the most common arrangement.

The problem for individual families is balancing the older adult's need for independence and control against the needs of younger family members who have lives of their own to lead. What often tips the balance, one way or the other, is whether any family member is able or willing to provide assistance, and whether other community services are available. For some families, Meals on Wheels, visiting nurses, adult day-care services, and other help may make it possible to continue to care for a frail or demented elder at home. An intermediate alternative, which is becoming more available, is some kind of "supportive housing," where the older person can have an individual apartment and thus live independently but has nursing and meal services available in the building or complex (Pynoos & Golant, 1996).

Certainly, if average long-term facility care were of much higher quality than it is now, with built-in opportunities for personal control, challenging activities, and first-rate medical care, and if such care were covered by government funding or other national health insurance, choosing such an option might be less difficult. But until that better day arrives, the choice of long-term facility care—for oneself or for an aging parent—is likely to continue to be wrenching and painful.

CHOOSING NOT TO RETIRE

A small number of adults continue working past the typical retirement age. In 1999, 9.8% of men and 3.4% of women over age 65 were employed in Canada (Statistics Canada, 2001m). This subgroup actually includes two types of people: those who have

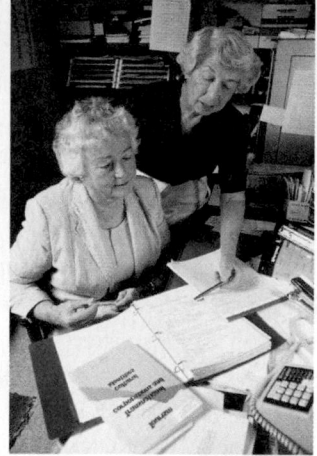

Only 9.8% of men and 3.4% of women over age 65 are employed in Canada. However, a fairly high proportion of middle-aged people say they plan to work at least part-time after retirement. Consequently, employers are eager to learn how best to train older workers.
(*Photos: left,* Don Smetzer/Stone; *right,* David Weintraub, Stock Boston)

Research suggests that older adults respond to computer training very much the way younger adults do. Most get over any anxieties they have about using computers after receiving training. In addition, they can become as proficient as younger adults, although they may require slower-paced training.
(*Photo:* Barbara Alper/Stock Boston)

never retired from their long-time occupations and those who retired from their regular occupations and ventured into new lines of work, often part-time.

CONTINUING IN A LIFE-LONG OCCUPATION

Developmentalists know almost nothing about women who choose not to retire, but they do know something about men who shun retirement. Some are men with very limited education, poor retirement benefits, and thus very low incomes. Many of these men continue working out of economic necessity.

A larger fraction of those who shun retirement are highly educated, healthy, highly work-committed professionals, whose wives often are also still working (Parnes & Sommers, 1994). Many of them have been highly work-committed all their adult lives. For example, men in the American National Longitudinal Surveys sample, a group that has been studied over a period of 25 years, were asked in their 50s whether they would continue working if they suddenly found themselves with enough money to live comfortably. Those who said they would continue working are much more likely to shun retirement and to be still working in their 70s and 80s (Parnes & Sommers, 1994). For these men, work continues to provide more satisfaction than they expect retirement to offer.

LEARNING NEW JOB SKILLS

Perhaps the greatest obstacle to employment for older adults is that many potential employers express concerns about older adults' ability to learn new job skills (Forte & Hansvick, 1999). However, studies of age differences in learning demonstrate that the learning process itself does not change with age. The same factors—interest, anxiety, motivation, quality of instruction, self-efficacy, and so on—predict learning success in both older and younger adults (Chasseigne, Grau, Mullet, & Cama, 1999; Gardiner, Luszcz, & Bryan, 1997; Mead & Fisk, 1998; Plaud, Plaud, & von Duvillard, 1999; Truluck & Courtenay, 1999). Thus, it seems reasonable that many aspects of effective training programs designed for younger workers, such as financial incentives for accomplishment of training goals, should also apply to older employees.

Moreover, an extensive body of research shows that, with appropriately paced training, older adults can significantly improve their performance on many cognitive tasks that are relevant to the workplace (Baltes & Kliegl, 1992; Dittmann-Kohli, Lachman, Kliegl, & Baltes, 1991; Kliegl, Smith, & Baltes, 1989, 1990; Verhaeghen, Marcoen, & Goossens, 1992). Pacing is important, because these studies do suggest that learning new skills sometimes takes longer for older adults. However, even training in the use of new technologies usually results in similar or identical skill levels among younger and older adults (see **Development in the Information Age**).

WORKPLACE FUNCTIONING

With respect to aspects of job functioning other than learning of new skills, supervisors typically give older adults higher ratings than younger adults (Forte & Hansvick, 1999). For example, they view older employees as more reliable. In addition, managers typically report that, although younger workers produce a greater quantity of work, the quality of older employees' work is better (Rao & Rao, 1997). Consequently, many employers view older adults as desirable employees.

Development in the
Information Age
Older Canadians in a Technical World

Canadians age 60 and older constitute the fastest growing segment of Internet users in the country. Statistics Canada's Cynthia Silver (2001) reported that, in 2000, 17% of senior men and 9% of senior women were Internet users who used the Internet mostly to surf for information about products, news, and health and medicine. In addition, most seniors who used the Internet regularly used e-mail (92%) to communicate with family (84%) and friends (77%).

In general though, older adults are somewhat more anxious about learning computer skills than those who are younger (Czaja & Sharit, 1998). However, knowledge and training reduce their anxiety, often to levels that are comparable to those of young and middle-aged adults (Dyck, Gee, & Smither, 1998; Ellis &

Allaire, 1999). Moreover, among elders, anxiety does not appear to interfere with skill learning (Laguna & Babcock, 1997).

Productivity studies suggest that older workers can be just as productive as younger employees in jobs involving computer usage. In fact, at least one study found that workers over the age of 60 made fewer data-entry mistakes (Czaja, Sharit, Nair, & Rubert, 1998). The study's authors suggested that employers can expect an equal amount of work output from older and younger computer workers because older employees' lower error rate compensates for their slower speed.

Older adults seem to benefit most from training that is specially designed to take into account their motor difficulties and slower speed of cognitive processing. In some cases,

training programs have been specifically tailored to the different needs of the young old and the old old (Mead & Fisk, 1998). For example, researchers used repetition strategies to train young old and old old adults to use automated teller machines (ATMs). They found that both groups benefited more from action training than from verbal explanations of how to use the machine. However, the old old group made more errors and required more repetitions of the various steps involved in ATM use. Studies involving other kinds of technology skills have also shown that the old old take longer to learn new skills than the young old (Echt et al., 1998). However, ultimately, the old old seem to be no less able to learn new skills than young old, middle-aged, and young adults.

Before Going On

- At what age do most men and women retire in Canada?
- What are the factors that influence the decision to retire?
- How does retirement affect income, health, attitudes, emotions, and mobility?
- What does research suggest about the decision not to retire?

Summary

Theories of Social and Personality Development

- Erikson's concept of ego integrity has been influential, but research does not indicate that the development of ego integrity is necessary to adjustment in old age. The notion of reminiscence has been helpful in researchers' attempts to understand development in late adulthood. However, research does not provide strong support for the hypothesis that reminiscence is necessary to successful aging.

- Similarly, disengagement has been found not to be essential in old age; high life satisfaction and good mental health are found most often among elders who disengage the least.

Individual Differences

- Successful aging is defined as maintenance of health along with cognitive and social functioning. Productivity and life satisfaction are also elements of successful aging.

- Religious coping has psychological and social components. It is associated with a lower mortality rate as well as with better physical and mental health.

Social Relationships

- Late adulthood is a time when people discard some roles. Remaining roles also have less content. Having fewer roles may offer greater licence for individuality.

- Among unmarried elders in Canada, living alone is the most common and preferred living arrangement.

- Marriages in late adulthood are, on average, highly satisfying for both spouses, who exhibit strong loyalty and mutual affection. If one spouse is disabled, the healthier spouse is likely to provide care. Married elders, as a group, are somewhat healthier and more satisfied with their lives than are single elders; this difference is larger among men than women.

- The majority of elders have at least one living child, and most take pleasure in seeing their children regularly. There is some indication that relationships with siblings may become more significant in late adulthood than at earlier ages.

- Degree of contact with friends is correlated with overall life satisfaction among older adults.

- Women in this age group continue to have larger social networks than men do.

Career Issues in Late Life

- The typical age of retirement is closer to 61 than 65 in Canada and in most Western developed countries.

- Time of retirement is affected by health, family responsibilities, adequacy of anticipated pension income, and satisfaction with one's job.

- Income typically decreases with retirement, but income adequacy does not decline very much. Among elders, women are most likely to live in poverty.

- Retirement appears not to be a stressful life change for the great majority of people. It is not the cause of deterioration in physical or mental health. The minority of older adults who find retirement stressful are likely to be those who feel they have least control over the decision to retire.

- Those who choose not to retire do so for economic reasons or because of particularly strong commitments to work. Research indicates that older adults can learn new job skills but may do so at slower rates than younger workers.

Key Terms

activity theory (p. 514)

amenity move (p. 534)

compensatory (kinship) migration (p. 534)

disengagement theory (p. 515)

ego integrity (p. 513)

ego integrity versus despair stage (p. 513)

institutional migration (p. 534)

religious coping (p. 519)

reminiscence (p. 514)

successful aging (p. 516)

volunteerism (p. 517)

Weblinks

Elder Abuse FAQs
www.law-faqs.org/elder/index.htm
Sponsored by the Department of Justice, this website offers a clear, concise guide to the issue of elder abuse, with definitions for what constitutes different forms of abuse and neglect. The question-and-answer format addresses Canadians' most common concerns.

Expression—Newsletter of the National Advisory Council on Aging
www.hc-sc.gc.ca/seniors-aines/naca/expression/8-4/exp_8-4_e.htm
Aging and the meaning of life: Special topic from The Division of Aging and Seniors, Health Canada.

National Survey of Giving, Volunteering and Participating
www.statcan.ca/english/freepub/71-542-XIE/71-542-XIE00001.pdf
Statistics Canada's 2000 National Survey of Giving, Volunteering and Participating is available in its entirety online. The survey results are also available as highlights, and are searchable by keyword or subject.

University of Victoria Centre on Aging
www.coag.uvic.ca
The University of Victoria Centre on Aging conducts research in partnership with seniors, their families, and organizations, health care providers and the government. The centre's website offers information on current and completed research, a newsletter, programs, and links to other relevant websites.

Canadian Association of Retired Persons (CARP)
www.50plus.com/carp/about/main.cfm
CARP is a 400 000 member nonprofit organization that promotes the rights and quality of life of Canadians who are 50 years or older.

Vic Bider/MaXx Images Inc.

CHAPTER 18

DEATH, DYING, AND BEREAVEMENT

We began our study of the human lifespan with an examination of birth and went on to consider the multitude of changes in the physical, cognitive, and social domains from infancy to late adulthood. Now we turn to the end of life. A particularly eloquent expression of the inevitability of death came from Stewart Alsop, a writer who kept a diary of the last years of his life, as he was dying of leukemia. In one of the very late entries in this journal, he said, "A dying man needs to die as a sleepy man needs to sleep, and there comes a time when it is wrong, as well as useless, to resist" (Alsop, 1973, p. 299). Alsop's statement calls to mind one of the important individual variables you have read about often in earlier chapters—the timing of a universal developmental event in a particular individual's life.

Like Alsop, many people contract fatal diseases and consciously face the inevitability of impending death for a period of months or years. Sometimes an unexpected event—perhaps an accident or a crime—ends a child's or young adult's life prematurely. For most of us, though, death comes in late adulthood and results from the subtle interplay between primary and secondary aging. Consequently, a good deal of what you will learn about dying and death will concern older adults. But the story must begin earlier, with an examination of people's understanding of and attitudes toward dying and death.

In this chapter you will learn about the physical, psychological, and social aspects of death. You will also learn how children's and teens' understanding of death differs from that of adults. The chapter also discusses individuals' responses to their own impending deaths and to the deaths of loved ones. As you read, keep the following questions in mind:

- What are three definitions of death, and how does where a person dies affect the experience of dying?
- How does the meaning of death change over the lifespan?
- How did Elisabeth Kübler-Ross and her critics think about the process of dying?
- In what ways do people experience the psychological process of grieving?
- How do psychoanalytic and attachment theorists explain grieving, and what theories do their critics propose?

THE EXPERIENCE OF DEATH

Most of us use the word *death* as if it described a simple phenomenon. You are either alive or dead. But, in fact, death is a process as well as a state, and physicians have different labels for different aspects of this process. Moreover, for both the deceased and the bereaved, the experience of death is shaped by the circumstances surrounding the end of life.

DEATH ITSELF

The term **clinical death** refers to the few minutes after the heart has stopped pumping, when breathing has stopped and there is no evident brain function, but during which resuscitation is still possible. Heart attack patients are sometimes brought back from clinical death; presumably those who report near-death experiences were in a state of clinical death.

clinical death
a period during which vital signs are absent but resuscitation is still possible

brain death

absence of vital signs, including brain activity; resuscitation is no longer possible

Brain death describes a state in which the person no longer has reflexes or any response to vigorous external stimuli and shows no electrical activity in the brain. When the cortex, but not the brain stem, is affected, the person may still be able to breathe without assistance and may survive for long periods in a vegetative state or on life-support systems. When the brain stem is also dead, no body functioning can occur independently, and the individual is said to be legally dead (Detchant, 1995). Brain death most often occurs after a period of 8 to 10 minutes of clinical death, but there are cases in which brain death has occurred because of brain injury, as in an auto accident, and other body functions can still be maintained artificially. In such cases, other body organs, such as the heart and kidneys, can be used for organ donation, as long as they are removed without delay.

social death

the point at which family members and medical personnel treat the deceased person as a corpse

Social death occurs at the point when the deceased person is treated like a corpse by others; for instance, someone may close the eyes or sign a death certificate. Once social death has been acknowledged, family and friends must begin to deal with the loss.

WHERE DEATH OCCURS

In Canada and other industrialized countries, the great majority of adults die in hospitals, rather than at home or even in nursing homes. Naturally, there is a great deal of variation, depending on such factors as age and type of disease or injury. Among the old old, for example, death in a nursing home is quite common. Among younger adults, in contrast, hospital death is the norm. Similarly, adults with progressive diseases, such as cancer or AIDS, are typically in and out of the hospital for months or years before death; at the other end of the continuum are many who are hospitalized with an acute problem, such as a heart attack or pneumonia, and who die soon thereafter, having had no prior hospitalization. In between fall those who may have experienced several different types of care in their final weeks or months, including hospitalization, home health care, and nursing home care. Despite such diversity, it is still true that the majority of deaths, particularly among the elderly, are preceded by some weeks of hospitalization (Merrill & Mor, 1993). In Canada, three-quarters of all deaths occur in a hospital or in long-term care facilities (Carstairs & Beaudoin, 2000).

hospice care

a holistic approach to care for the terminally ill that emphasizes individual and family control of the process of dying

In recent years, however, an alternative form of terminal care that has become common is **hospice care**, a holistic approach to caring for the dying that emphasizes individual and family control of the process. The hospice movement was given a boost by the writings of Elisabeth Kübler-Ross, who emphasized the importance of a "good death," or a "death with dignity," in which the patient and the patient's family have more control over the entire process (Kübler-Ross, 1974). Many health care professionals, particularly in England, Canada, and the United States, believe that such a good death is more likely if the dying person remains at home, or in a homelike setting in which contact with family and other friends can be part of daily experience.

Hospice care emerged in England in the late 1960s and in Canada in the mid-1970s (van Bommel, 2002). There are now more than 650 hospice palliative care organizations in Canada, serving thousands of terminally ill patients and their families. And yet, just over half of Canadians have never heard of hospice palliative care (Gardner, 2001).

The philosophy that underlies this alternative approach to the dying patient has several aspects (van Bommel, 2002):

• Death should be viewed as normal, not to be avoided but to be faced and accepted.

• The patient and family should be encouraged to prepare for the death by examining their feelings, planning for after the death, and talking openly about the death.

- The family should be involved in the patient's care as much as is physically possible, not only because this gives the patient the emotional support of loved ones, but because it allows each family member to come to some resolution of her or his relationship with the dying person.

- Control over the patient's care should be in the hands of the patient and the family. They decide what types of medical treatment they will ask for or accept; they decide whether the patient will remain at home or be hospitalized.

- Care should be aimed at satisfying the physical, emotional, spiritual, and psychosocial needs of a person with a life-threatening or terminal condition and his family.

- Medical care should be primarily **palliative care** rather than curative. The emphasis is on controlling pain and maximizing comfort, not on invasive or life-prolonging measures.

palliative care
a form of care for the terminally ill that focuses on relieving patients' pain, rather than curing their diseases

Three somewhat different types of hospice programs have been developed following these general guidelines. The most common hospice programs are home-based programs, in which one family caregiver—most frequently, the dying person's spouse—provides constant care for the dying person with the support and assistance of specially trained nurses or other staff who visit regularly, provide medication, and help the family deal psychologically with the impending death. A second type of program is the special hospice centre, where a small number of patients in the last stages of a terminal disease are cared for in a homelike setting. Finally, hospital-based hospice programs provide palliative care according to the basic hospice philosophy, with daily involvement of family members in the patient's care. It is interesting that these three options parallel so closely the basic birth options now available: home delivery, birthing centres, and hospital-based birthing rooms. The fourth choice, both at birth and at death, is traditional hospital care.

> ## Critical Thinking
>
> Given what you have just read and your own philosophical assumptions, do you think you would choose hospice care for yourself or urge it on a spouse or parent in the last stages of a terminal illness? Why or why not?

The choice of traditional hospital care versus hospice care is most often made on philosophical rather than medical grounds. But it is still worth asking how the two types of care compare in terms of patients' and caregivers' experiences. Two large comparison studies suggest that the differences are small, although the results indicate that patients and caregivers may prefer hospice care slightly.

The National Hospice Study analyzed the experiences of 1754 terminally ill cancer patients who were treated in 40 different hospices and 14 conventional hospitals (Greer et al., 1986; Mor, Greer, & Kastenbaum, 1988). Half of the hospice programs were home-based, half were hospital-based. The patients were not assigned randomly to hospice or conventional hospital care, but chose their own form of care.

In comparing the two forms of care, the researchers looked at the patient's reported pain and satisfaction with care and at the main caregiver's quality of life and satisfaction. What is remarkable is how similar the experiences of the hospital patients and those of the hospice patients were. There were no differences in patients' reported pain, length of survival, or satisfaction with care. The major finding of the study was that family members were most satisfied with hospital-based hospice care, while those whose loved one chose home-based hospice care reported feeling a greater sense of burden.

In a smaller study, researchers assigned participants randomly to either hospice care or normal hospital care (Kane, Klein, Bernstein, Rothenberg, & Wales, 1985; Kane, Wales, Bernstein, Leibowitz, & Kaplan, 1984). The hospice care in this case was a combination of home-based and hospital-based. Most hospice patients remained at home

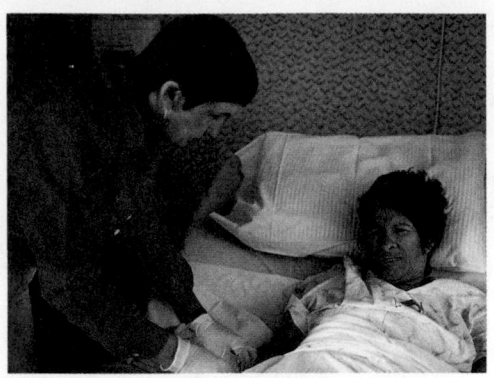

This woman, who is dying of cancer, has chosen to stay at home during her last months, supported by regular visits from hospice nurses. (*Photo:* Bill Aron/PhotoEdit)

but spent brief periods in the hospital's hospice ward, either when the family needed a break or when the patient's care become too complex to be handled at home. As in the National Hospice Study, investigators found no differences between these two groups in reports of pain or in length of survival. But they did find that patients in the hospice group were more consistently satisfied with the quality of care they received and with their degree of control over their own care. Similarly, the family members in the hospice group in Kane's study were more satisfied with their own involvement with the patient's care and had lower levels of anxiety than did family members in the hospital-treatment group.

Taken together, these two studies, as well as more recent research, suggest that based on purely objective measures, such as control of pain or survival duration, these two types of terminal care do not differ in effectiveness (Bretscher et al., 1999). Where differences exist, it is on measures of attitudes or feelings. On some—but not all—of such measures, those in hospice care and their families are slightly more satisfied. In addition, terminally ill patients who are cared for at home through hospice arrangements are admitted to the hospital less often in the last 6 months of life than those who do not receive home-based care (Stewart, Pearson, Luke, & Horowitz, 1998). Thus, the economic costs of death are reduced by hospice care. At the same time, both studies make it clear that home-based hospice care is a considerable burden, especially on the central caregiver, who may spend as many as 19 hours a day in physical care.

However, both patients and caregivers express concerns about hospice care. For example, both sometimes have more faith in hospital personnel when it comes to providing pain relief. Consequently, patients and their caregivers want assurances that the medical care they will receive in a hospice arrangement will be equivalent in quality to that of a hospital (Vachon, 1998).

In addition, hospice care providers must recognize that caregivers have needs as well (Health Canada, 2003l). In fact, caring for a dying loved one, particularly someone with dementia, induces a grief response (Lindgren, Connelly, & Gaspar, 1999; Rudd, Viney, & Preston, 1999). Consequently, another important element of hospice care is grief support for the primary caregiver, support that includes both psychosocial and educational components (Meredith & Rassa, 1999; Murphy, Hanrahan, & Luchins, 1997). Similarly, hospice care providers themselves also often require support services because of the emotional strain involved in caring for patients who are terminally ill.

Health Canada (2002g) launched a web-based Canadian Virtual Hospice to help support hospice care providers and their patients, the patient's family, and researchers across Canada. One of the main goals is to provide "Canadians with expert palliative care at home" (Health Canada, 2001o). The Canadian Virtual Hospice will enable physicians and other health care professionals to interact directly with informal caregivers, provide access to a wide range of palliative care service, and bring medical expertise to the home and to rural and remote areas of Canada.

Before Going On

- Define clinical death, brain death, and social death.
- How do hospice and hospital care differ with respect to their effects on terminally ill patients?

THE MEANING OF DEATH ACROSS THE LIFESPAN

Life teaches us how to survive, while death teaches us how to live. Life is a taskmaster, while death is a master teacher. We cannot learn how to appreciate the preciousness of life without coming to grips with the reality of death. (Wong, 2000, p. 27)

As an adult, you understand that death is irreversible, that it comes to everyone, and that it means a cessation of all function. But do children and teenagers understand these aspects of death? And what does death mean to adults of different ages?

CHILDREN'S AND ADOLESCENTS' UNDERSTANDING OF DEATH

Results from a variety of studies suggest that preschool-aged children typically understand none of these aspects of death. They believe that death can be reversed, for instance, through prayer, magic, or wishful thinking; they believe that dead persons can still feel or breathe. They also believe that at least some people—those who are clever or lucky, or members of their own families—can avoid death (Lansdown & Benjamin, 1985; Speece & Brent, 1984, 1992).

By the time they start school, just about the time Piaget described as the beginning of concrete operations, most children seem to understand both the permanence and the universality of death. This understanding is clear from children's own comments. In one study, children were told a story about two children who used to go into a candy store kept by an old lady who had recently died (Lansdown & Benjamin, 1985). After they heard the story, the participants were asked some questions about the old lady, and about what it meant that she was dead.

> A 5-year-old: "Someone came into the shop to kill her. She'll see them again and she'll die again. She can try to get up." A 7-year-old: "They never come alive again. You can't move because your heart has stopped. People wish you can come alive but you can't. Children can't die because they start at one and go to 100." A 9-year-old: "Their heart can't take it any longer and they die. Babies can die of cancer, kidney problems. Heaven is much nicer than down here." (Lansdown & Benjamin, 1985, p. 20)

The first of these children did not yet understand the permanence of death; the second did not understand its universality; but the third seems to have grasped all three.

Some investigators have found that children who understand conservation are also more likely to understand the permanence and universality of death, but not everyone has found such a link (Speece & Brent, 1984). Instead, as is true of so many other milestones of this age range, the child's specific experience seems to make a good deal of difference. Four- and five-year-olds who have had direct experience with the death of a family member are more likely to understand the permanence of death than are those who have had no such personal experience (Stambrook & Parker, 1987).

Adolescents understand the finality of death better than children do. Moreover, in an abstract sense, they understand that death is inevitable. However, psychologist David Elkind proposed that, as teens enter Piaget's formal operational stage, they construct a set of beliefs he called the **personal fable**, a hypothetical life story that tends to portray adolescents'

personal fable
a hypothetical life story created for himself or herself by an adolescent

These children being comforted by an adult at a loved one's grave are likely to have far more mature concepts of death than others their age who have not encountered death firsthand.
(*Photo:* Mark Gibson/MaXx Images Inc.)

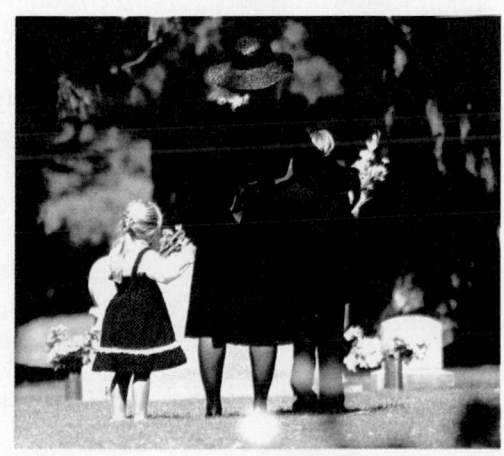

future lives in overly optimistic terms (Elkind, 1967). Elkind claimed that the personal fable leads most teens to believe that death will not happen to them because they do not imagine it happening. Thus, Elkind and others believe that the personal fable contributes to the frequency of teenagers' potentially fatal risky behaviours—fast driving, drug use, and so on—which you read about in **Chapter 10** (Arnett, 1990).

Similarly, unrealistic beliefs about personal death appear to contribute to adolescent suicide. Typically, teens who attempt suicide claim to understand that death is final, but many tell researchers and counsellors that the purpose of their suicidal behaviour was to achieve a temporary escape from a stressful personal problem (Blau, 1996). Further, researchers have found that some teenagers who attempt suicide believe that death is a pleasurable experience for most people who die (Gothelf et al., 1998). Certainly, such distorted beliefs may be the result of the powerful emotions that lead teens to attempt suicide, rather than the product of adolescent thinking. However, suicidal adults typically think of death, even when it is desired, as painful and unpleasant. So, there may be a developmental difference between suicidal adolescents' and suicidal adults' understanding of death.

Like those of children, adolescents' ideas about death are affected by their personal experiences. Experiencing the death of a family member or friend, especially someone who is near the teenager's own age, tends to shake an adolescent's confidence in her own immortality. In fact, research suggests that the loss of someone close, such as a sibling, may lead an adolescent to re-examine critically her ideas about death—both as a general concept and as something that is inevitable for herself (Batten & Oltjenbruns, 1999).

THE MEANING OF DEATH FOR ADULTS

Adults' ideas about death vary with age. Death seems remote to most young adults. The notion of personal mortality is a more common focus of thought in middle age, and by the later years, the idea of death becomes very personally relevant for most adults.

unique invulnerability
the belief that bad things, including death, only happen to others

EARLY ADULTHOOD In recent years, research examining young adults' views on death has been guided by a theoretical concept similar to the personal fable. Psychologists point out that young adults have a sense of **unique invulnerability**—a belief that bad things, including death, happen to others but not to themselves. Although young adults are more realistic about personal mortality than adolescents are, researchers find that many believe that they possess unique personal characteristics that somehow protect them against death. For example, researchers often ask participants of various ages to use life-expectancy statistics and risk-factor self-ratings to predict the age at which they will die. Such studies usually find that young adults overestimate their own life expectancy (Snyder, 1997). Moreover, young adults are more likely than those who are middle-aged or older to show increased fear of death following open discussions of the process of dying (Abengozar, Bueno, & Vega, 1999).

Here again, actual experience with death makes a difference. For example, nursing students display less fear of death than college students pursuing other careers, and their anxieties about death lessen with each additional year of training (Sharma, Monsen, & Gary, 1997). Moreover, the sudden loss of a loved one appears to shake a young adult's belief in unique invulnerability and, as a result, is often more traumatic for younger than for older adults. In fact, such losses frequently lead to suicidal thoughts in young adults. Young adults who have recently lost a loved one in an accident or to a homicide or suicide are about five times as likely to formulate a suicide plan as young adults who have not had such a loss, although most never follow through with their plans (Prigerson et al., 1999).

Analyses of public reactions to the deaths of relatively young celebrities, such as Princess Diana and 23-year-old Michel Trudeau, son of the late Prime Minister Trudeau, who drowned when an avalanche swept him into Kokanee Lake, provide additional insight into young adults' ideas about death. As you may have noticed, perceptions of public figures often change dramatically after their deaths, and they are given heroic status (Bourreille, 1999). Psychologists hypothesize that such early deaths challenge young people's beliefs in unique invulnerability and, therefore, provoke defensive reactions that cause them to place those who die young in a special category. In other words, to maintain belief in their own unique invulnerability, young people must come up with reasons why death came early to Michel Trudeau but will not happen to them. As a result, they elevate such figures to near-sainthood.

After the tragic death of Michel Trudeau there was a collective outpouring of empathy for his family. Ordinary Canadians flooded the former prime minister and his ex-wife Margaret Kemper with calls, flowers, and letters. Out of the desire to show they shared in the family's loss, two charitable organizations—the Kokanee Glacier Alpine Campaign and the Canadian Avalanche Foundation—were formed to raise awareness of avalanche risk and promote backcountry safety. (*Photo:* Ryan Remiorz/CP Photo Archive)

MIDDLE AND LATE ADULTHOOD In middle and late adulthood, an understanding of death goes well beyond the simple acceptance of finality, inevitability, and universality. A death changes the roles and relationships of everyone else in a family. For example, when an elder dies, everyone else in that particular lineage "moves up" in the generational system. As you learned in **Chapter 15**, the death of a parent can be particularly unsettling for a middle-aged adult if the adult does not yet consider himself ready to assume the elder role.

An individual's death also affects the roles of people beyond the family, such as younger adults in a business organization, who then can take on new and perhaps more significant roles. Retirement serves some of the same function, as an older adult steps aside for a younger one. But death brings many permanent changes in families and social systems.

At an individual level, the prospect of death may shape one's view of time (Kalish, 1985). In middle age, most people exhibit a shift in their thinking about time, thinking less about "time since birth" and being more aware of "time till death," a transition clearly reflected in the comment of this middle-aged adult:

> Before I was 35, the future just stretched forth. There would be time to do and see and carry out all the plans I had. . . . Now I keep thinking, will I have time enough to finish off some of the things I want to do? (Neugarten, 1970, p. 78)

Such an "awareness of finitude" is not a part of every middle-aged or older adult's view of death (Marshall, 1975). One study of a group of adults aged 72 and older found that only about half thought in terms of "time remaining" (Keith, 1981/1982). Interestingly, those who did think of death in these terms had less fear of death than did those who thought of their lives as "time lived." Other research confirms this: Middle-aged and older adults who continue to be preoccupied with the past are more likely to be fearful and anxious about death (Pollack, 1979/1980).

Critical Thinking

When you think of your own age, do you think of time since birth, or time till death, or both? If you think in terms of time till death, can you remember when you switched to this view?

FEAR OF DEATH

Paul T.P. Wong, an existentialist researcher with Trinity Western University in British Columbia, discusses the nature of death anxiety thus:

> Death is the only certainty in life. All living organisms die; there is no exception. However, human beings alone are burdened with the cognitive capacity to be aware of their own inevitable mortality and to fear what may come afterwards. Furthermore,

their capacity to reflect on the meaning of life and death creates additional existential anxiety. (Wong, 2003. n.p.)

Wong goes on to suggest that our fear of death stems from six existential uncertainties as described in **Table 18.1**.

Researchers have typically tried to measure fear of death with questionnaires. For example, one strategy is to ask participants to indicate, on a 5-point scale, how disturbed or anxious they feel when thinking about various aspects of death or dying, such as "the shortness of life" or "never thinking or experiencing anything again" or "your lack of control over the process of dying" (Lester, 1990). Another approach asks participants to respond to statements such as "I fear dying a painful death" or "Coffins make me anxious" or "I am worried about what happens to us after we die" (Thorson & Powell, 1992).

FEAR OF DEATH ACROSS ADULTHOOD Although you might think that those closest to death would fear it the most, research suggests that middle-aged adults are most fearful of death. For young adults, the sense of unique invulnerability probably prevents intense fears of death. In middle age, though, belief in one's own immortality begins to break down, resulting in increasing anxiety about the end of life. However, by late life, the inevitability of death has been accepted, and anxieties are focused on how death will actually come about.

The difference between the middle-aged and the aged is especially clear from a study in which researchers interviewed a sample of adults, aged 45 to 74, chosen to represent the population of Los Angeles (Bengtson, Cuellar, & Ragan, 1977). **Figure 18.1** shows the percentages of people in each age group who said they were "very afraid" or "somewhat afraid" of death. The fact that the shape of the curve is so remarkably similar for all three ethnic groups makes the results even more persuasive. And although these are cross-sectional results, similar patterns have emerged from cross-sectional comparisons done in the 1960s and the 1980s, which makes the conclusion that much more credible (e.g., Gesser, Wong, & Reker, 1987/1988).

TABLE 18.1 Sources of Fear of Death

Aspects of Death	Implications
The finality of death	There is no reversal, no remedy, no more tomorrow. Therefore, death signifies the cessation of all hope with respect to this world.
The uncertainty of what follows	Socrates has made the case that, since we really don't know what will happen, we should not fear. But uncertainty coupled with finality can create a potential for terror.
Annihilation anxiety or fear of non-existence	The concept of non-being can be very threatening, because it seems to go against a strong and innate conviction that life should not be reduced to non-being.
The ultimate loss	When death occurs, we are forced to lose everything we have ever valued. Those with the strongest attachments towards things of this world are likely to fear death most. Loss of control over affairs in the world and loss of the ability to care for dependents also contribute to death anxiety.
Fear of the pain and loneliness in dying	Many are afraid that they will die alone or die in pain, without any family or friends around them.
Fear of failing to complete life work	According to Goodman's (1981) interviews with eminent artists and scientists, many people are more afraid of a meaningless existence than death itself; their fear of death stems from fear of not being able to complete their mission or calling in life.

(*Source:* Wong, P.T.P. [2003]. From Death Anxiety to Death Acceptance: A meaning management model. Langley, BC: International Network on Personal Meaning. Retrieved September 9, 2004 from http://www.meaning.ca/articles/death_acceptance.htm Courtesy of Paul T.P. Wong, Graduate Program in Counselling Psychology, Trinity Western University.)

However, older adults do not become less pre-occupied with death. On the contrary, the elderly think and talk more about death than do those at any other age. Predictably, these discussions lead to less fear and anxiety about death among older adults (Abengozar et al., 1999). Thus, to an older person, death is highly important, but it is apparently not as frightening as it was at mid-life. Older adults are more likely to fear the period of uncertainty before death than they are to fear death itself (Sullivan, Ormel, Kempen, & Tymstra, 1998). They are anxious about where they may die, who will care for them until they do, and whether they will be able to cope with the pain and loss of control and independence that may be part of the last months or years of life (Marshall & Levy, 1990).

RELIGIOUS BELIEFS   Researchers typically find that adults who are deeply religious or who go to church regularly are less afraid of death than those who describe themselves as less religious or who participate less regularly in religious activities (Kalish, 1985; Thorson & Powell, 1990). In some instances, however, researchers have found that both those who are deeply religious and those who are totally irreligious report less fear of death. Thus, the most fearful may be those who are uncertain about or uncommitted to any religious or philosophical tradition.

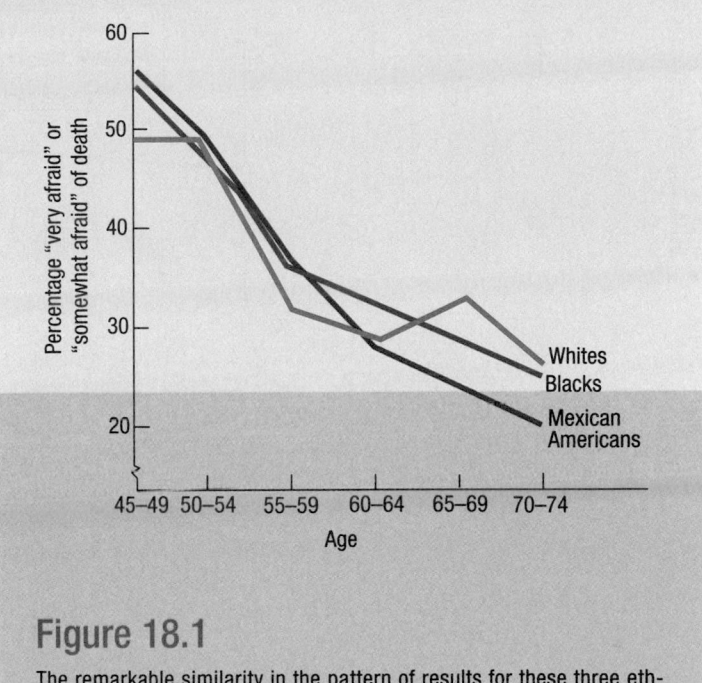

Figure 18.1

The remarkable similarity in the pattern of results for these three ethnic groups lends support to the generalization that older adults are less afraid of death than are the middle-aged.

(*Source:* Bengtson et al., 1977, Figure 1, p. 80.)

Religious beliefs may moderate fears of death because religious people tend to view death as a transition from one form of life to another, from physical life to some kind of immortality. Sociologist Reginald Bibby of the University of Lethbridge has been tracking the attitudes of thousands of Canadians of all ages since 1975. His survey in 2000 revealed some curious intergenerational differences in conventional and less conventional religious beliefs (see **Figure 18.2**). For one, the belief that God exists increases with each age group, from 73% of teens to 85% of grandparents. Yet, at the same time, belief in life after death decreases with age, from a high of 78% in teens to a low of 64% in grandparents (Bibby, 2001). This suggests that although youth may be somewhat less eager to participate in an organized set of religious practices, they do have a strong sense of spirituality. Two pioneers of hospice care in Canada, Dorothy Ley and Harry van Bommel, remind us that the spiritual search for meaning in our lives is often intensified by the reality of death. This spiritual struggle is arguably an important philosophical cornerstone of the dying process and thus an important factor behind providing palliative care (Ley & van Bommel, 1994).

In addition to framing death as a transition rather than an end, religious beliefs provide adults with death stories that help them cope with both their own deaths and those of loved ones (Winter, 1999). For example, Jewish scriptures, the Christian Bible, and the Moslem Quran all contain many stories that convey the idea that death comes when one's purpose in life has been fulfilled. Many such stories also teach that each individual life is part of a larger, multigenerational story. In this larger context, death is portrayed as a necessary part of the transfer of responsibility from one generation to another. This kind of philosophical approach to death leads believers to focus on the contributions to family and community that they have made during their lives rather than on the losses they will experience at their deaths.

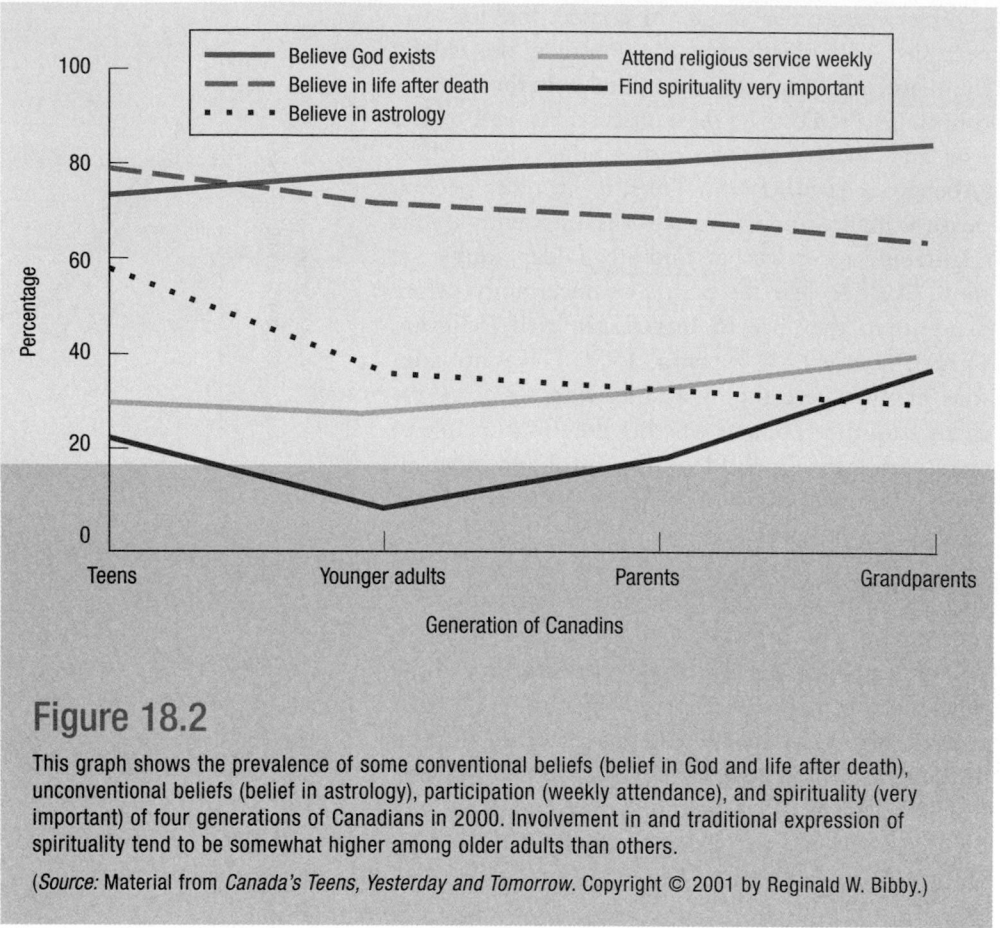

Figure 18.2

This graph shows the prevalence of some conventional beliefs (belief in God and life after death), unconventional beliefs (belief in astrology), participation (weekly attendance), and spirituality (very important) of four generations of Canadians in 2000. Involvement in and traditional expression of spirituality tend to be somewhat higher among older adults than others.

(*Source:* Material from *Canada's Teens, Yesterday and Tomorrow.* Copyright © 2001 by Reginald W. Bibby.)

PERSONAL WORTH Feelings about death are also linked to one's sense of personal worth or competence. Adults who feel that they have achieved the goals they set out to achieve, or who believe that they have become the person they wanted to be, are less anxious about death than are those who are disappointed in themselves (Neimeyer & Chapman, 1980/1981). Adults who believe that their lives have had some purpose or meaning also appear to be less fearful of death, as do those who have some sense of personal competence (Durlak, 1972; Pollack, 1979/1980).

Such findings suggest the possibility that adults who have successfully completed the major tasks of adult life, who have adequately fulfilled the demands of the roles they occupied, and who have developed inwardly are able to face death with greater equanimity. Adults who have not been able to resolve the various tasks and dilemmas of adulthood face their late adult years more anxiously, even with what Erikson described as despair. Fear of death may be merely one facet of such despair.

PREPARATION FOR DEATH

Preparation for death occurs on a number of levels (see **No Easy Answers**). At a practical level, a person can obtain life insurance or make out a will. Such preparations become more common as people enter late adulthood and become more accepting of the inevitability of death. Thus, older adults are more likely than younger ones to have completed a will and to have made arrangements for their own funeral or burial (Kalish & Reynolds, 1976).

No Easy Answers

Saying Goodbye

The Kaliai, a small Melanesian society in Papua New Guinea, believe that all deaths are caused by a person or spirit whom the dying person has offended in some way (Counts, 1976/1977). Any person who feels that he is near death moves from his house into a temporary shelter, where he attempts to appease whichever person or spirit he thinks he may have offended. He also attempts to thwart death through the use of various medicines and cures. When death becomes imminent, family members and friends return items borrowed from the dying person and pay debts they owe him. Likewise, the dying person returns borrowed items and repays debts owed to family and friends. The Kaliai believe that this process of bringing relationships into balance prepares the dying person for an afterlife in which he will become a powerful superhuman being.

But how do you say goodbye to a dying loved one, or how does a dying person say goodbye to loved ones, in a culture where discussions of death are largely taboo? Research suggests that, in our Western culture, even physicians who routinely treat terminally ill patients are reluctant to state directly that a patient is going to die (Lutfey & Maynard, 1998). Moreover, the sufferer and her loved ones may avoid discussions of death because admitting that death is approaching may be seen as rejection of the possibility of recovery. Family members may believe that discussing death will undermine the terminally ill patient's optimism and ability to fight the disease. Likewise, those who are dying may not want to make their loved ones feel bad. Still, most people in these situations feel that they must balance the need for closure against fears of fostering pessimism. Consequently, many terminally ill adults and their families create indirect methods of saying farewell.

A study in Australia gives a glimpse of the variety of such goodbyes devised by the dying (Kellehear & Lewin, 1988/1989). Researchers interviewed 90 terminally ill cancer patients, all of whom expected to die within a year. Most had known of their cancer diagnosis for at least a year prior to the interview but had only recently been given a short-term prognosis. As part of the interview, these 90 people were asked if they had already said farewell to anyone, and to describe any plans they had for future farewells. To whom did they want to say goodbye, and how would they say it?

About one-fifth of these people planned no farewells. Another three-fifths thought it was important to say goodbye, but wanted to put it off until very near the end so as to distress family and friends as little as possible. They hoped that there would then be time for a few final words with spouses, children, and close friends. The remaining fifth began their farewells much earlier and used many different avenues. In a particularly touching farewell gesture, one woman who had two grown daughters but no grandchildren knitted a set of baby clothes for each daughter, for the grandchildren she would never see.

Kellehear and Lewin make the important point that such farewells are a kind of gift. They signal that the dying person feels that someone is worthy of a last goodbye. Such farewells may also represent a balancing of the relationship slate just as important as the balancing of material possessions is among the Kaliai.

Farewells also may allow the dying person to disengage more readily when death comes closer, and to warn others that death is indeed approaching. Hearing someone say farewell may thus help the living to begin a kind of anticipatory grieving, and in this way prepare better for the loss.

At a somewhat deeper level, adults may prepare for death through some process of reminiscence. Deeper still, there may be unconscious changes that occur in the years just before death, which might be thought of as a type of preparation. You read about the physical and mental changes associated with terminal drop in **Chapter 16**. Research has pointed to the possibility that there may be terminal psychological changes as well.

For example, in a still influential study, researchers studied a group of older adults longitudinally, interviewing and testing each participant regularly over a period of 3 years (Lieberman, 1965; Lieberman & Coplan, 1970). After the testing, investigators kept track of the participants and noted when they died. They were able to identify one group of 40 participants who had all died within 1 year of the end of the interviewing and to compare them with another group of 40, matched to the first group by age, sex, and marital status, who had survived at least 3 years after the end of the testing. By comparing the psychological test scores obtained by those in these two groups during the course of the 3 years of testing, researchers could detect changes that occurred near death.

The study's results revealed that those nearer death not only showed terminal drop on tests of memory and learning, but also became less emotional, introspective, and aggressive or assertive and more conventional, docile, dependent, and warm. In those near death, all these characteristics increased over the 3 years of interviewing, a pattern that did not occur among those of the same age who were further from death. Thus, conventional, docile, dependent, and nonintrospective adults did not die sooner; rather, these qualities became accentuated in those who were close to death.

This is only a single study. As always in such cases, it's important to be careful about drawing sweeping conclusions from limited evidence. But the results are intriguing and suggestive. They paint a picture of a kind of psychological preparation for death—conscious or unconscious—in which an individual "gives up the fight," becomes less active physically and psychologically. Thus, near death, individuals do not necessarily become less involved with other people, but they do seem to show some kind of disengagement.

Before Going On

- What are the characteristics of children's and adolescent's ideas about death?
- How do young, middle-aged, and older adults think about death?
- What factors are related to fear of death in adults?
- How do adults prepare for death?

THE PROCESS OF DYING

Elisabeth Kübler-Ross was a Swiss-American psychiatrist who studied the experiences of the dying and their loved ones. In the 1960s, she formulated a model that asserted that those who are dying go through a series of psychological stages. These stages of dying, which were formulated on the basis of interviews with approximately 200 adults who were dying of cancer, continue to be highly influential, although Kübler-Ross's model has many critics. In addition, research suggests that individual differences affect the process of dying in important ways. (Kübler-Ross herself died in August 2004 at the age of 78.)

KÜBLER-ROSS'S STAGES OF DYING

In Kübler-Ross's early writings, she proposed that those who know they are dying move through a series of steps, or stages, arriving finally at the stage she called *acceptance*.

Kübler-Ross's ideas and her terminology are still widely used. In fact, surveys of death education programs suggest that Kübler-Ross's model is the only systematic approach to the dying process to which health professionals-in-training are exposed (Downe-Wamboldt & Tamlyn, 1997). Thus, you should at least be familiar with the stages she proposed.

Kübler-Ross's model predicts that most people who are confronted with a terminal diagnosis react with some variant of "Not me!" "It must be a mistake," "I'll get another opinion," or "I don't feel sick." All of these are forms of *denial*, a psychological defence that may be highly useful in the early hours and days after such a diagnosis. Denial of this kind may be helpful in insulating a person's emotions from the trauma of hearing such news. Keeping emotions in check in this way may help an individual formulate a rational plan of action based on "What if it's true?" Having a plan of action may help moderate the effects of acknowledging the reality of the diagnosis. Kübler-Ross thought that these extreme forms of denial would fade within a few days, to be replaced by *anger*.

The model further suggests that anger among the dying expresses itself in thoughts like "It's not fair!" but a dying person may also express anger toward God, the doctor who made the diagnosis, nurses, or family members. The anger seems to be a response not only to the diagnosis itself but also to the sense of loss of control and helplessness that many patients feel in impersonal medical settings.

Bargaining follows anger in the Kübler-Ross model. This is a form of defence in which the patient tries to make "deals" with doctors, nurses, family, or God: "If I do everything you tell me, then I'll live till spring." Kübler-Ross gave a particularly compelling example of this defence reaction: A patient with terminal cancer wanted to live long enough to attend the wedding of her eldest son. The hospital staff, to help her try to reach this goal, taught her self-hypnosis to deal with her pain and she was able to attend the wedding. Kübler-Ross reported, "I will never forget the moment when she returned to the hospital. She looked tired and somewhat exhausted and—before I could say hello—said, 'Now don't forget, I have another son!'" (1969, p. 83).

Bargaining may be successful as a defence for a while, but the model predicts that, eventually, bargaining breaks down in the face of signs of declining health. At this point, Kübler-Ross's theory predicts, the patient enters the stage of *depression*. According to Kübler-Ross, depression, or despair, is a necessary preparation for the final stage of *acceptance*. In order to reach acceptance, the dying person must grieve for all that will be lost with death.

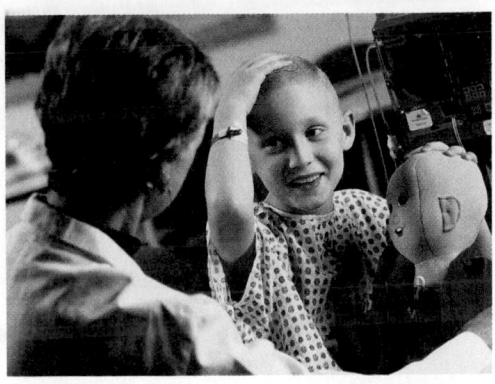

Children use some of the same defences to deal with impending death as adults. Young cancer patients may deny or bargain—for instance, "If I take my medicine I'll be able to go back to school in the fall."
(*Photo:* Zigy Kaluzny/Getty Images)

CRITICISMS AND ALTERNATIVE VIEWS

Kübler-Ross's model has provided a common language for those who work with dying patients, and her highly compassionate descriptions have, without doubt, sensitized health care workers and families to the complexities of the process of dying. At some moments, what the patient needs is cheering up; at other moments, he simply needs someone to listen to him. There are times to hold his hand quietly and times to provide encouragement or hope. Many new programs for terminally ill patients are clearly outgrowths of this greater sensitivity to the dying process.

These are all worthwhile changes. But Kübler-Ross's basic thesis—that the dying process necessarily involves these specific five stages, in this specific order—has been widely criticized, for several good reasons.

METHODOLOGICAL PROBLEMS Kübler-Ross's hypothesized sequence was initially based on clinical observation of 200 patients, and she did not provide information about how frequently she talked to them or over how long a period she continued to assess them. She also did not report the ages of the patients she studied, although it is clear that many were middle-aged or young adults, for whom a terminal illness was obviously "off time." Nearly all were apparently cancer patients. Would the same processes be evident in those dying of other diseases, for which it is much less common to have a specific diagnosis or a short-term prognosis? In other words, Kübler-Ross's observations might be correct, but only for a small subset of dying individuals.

CULTURAL SPECIFICITY A related question has to do with whether reactions to dying are culture-specific or universal. Kübler-Ross wrote as if the five stages of dying were universal human processes. But most social scientists agree that reactions to dying are strongly culturally conditioned.

For example, you have already read about the influence of religious beliefs on adults' ideas about death. Believing that death is a transition to immortality implies that one should face death with a sense of joy. Exhibitions of denial, anger, and bargaining may seem to indicate a lack of faith and, as a result, may be actively avoided by dying people who are religious. Thus, Kübler-Ross's model may fail to predict reactions to impending death by the religious.

Like religion, cultural traditions can also affect the individual process of dying. For example, in some Native North American cultures, death is to be faced and accepted with composure. Because it is part of nature's cycle, it is not to be feared or fought (DeSpelder & Strickland, 1983). And, in Mexican culture, death is seen as a mirror of the person's life. Thus, your way of dying tells much about what kind of person you have been. Furthermore, in Mexican culture, death is discussed frequently, even celebrated in a national feast day, the Day of the Dead (DeSpelder & Strickland, 1983). Would it be reasonable to expect denial, anger, bargaining, and so on, in the context of such cultural expectations?

THE STAGE CONCEPT The most potent criticism of Kübler-Ross's model, however, centres on the issue of stages. Many clinicians and researchers who have attempted to study the process systematically have found that not all dying patients exhibit these five emotions, let alone in a specific order. Of the five, only depression seems to be common among Western patients. Further, neither Kübler-Ross's acceptance nor Cumming and Henry's disengagement (discussed in **Chapter 17**) appears to be a common end point of the dying process (Baugher, Burger, Smith, & Wallston, 1989/1990). Some patients display acceptance, others remain as active and engaged as possible right up to the end. Edwin Shneidman (1980, 1983), a major theorist and clinician in the field of **thanatology** (the scientific study of death and dying), puts it this way:

thanatology
the scientific study of death and dying

> I reject the notion that human beings, as they die, are somehow marched in lock step through a series of stages of the dying process. On the contrary, in working with dying persons, I see a wide [array] of human feelings and emotions, of various human needs, and a broad selection of psychological defenses and maneuvers—a few of these in some people, dozens in others—experienced in an impressive variety of ways. (1980, p. 110)

Instead of stages, Shneidman suggests that the dying process has many "themes" that can appear, disappear, and reappear in any one patient in the process of dealing with death. These themes include terror, pervasive uncertainty, fantasies of being rescued, incredulity, feelings of unfairness, a concern with reputation after death, fear of pain, and so forth.

Another alternative to Kübler-Ross's model is a "task-based" approach suggested by Charles Corr (1991/1992). In his view, coping with dying is like coping with any other problem or dilemma: You need to take care of certain specific tasks. He suggests four such tasks for the dying person:

- Satisfying bodily needs and minimizing physical stress
- Maximizing psychological security, autonomy, and richness of life
- Sustaining and enhancing significant interpersonal attachments
- Identifying, developing, or reaffirming sources of spiritual energy, and thereby fostering hope

Corr does not deny the importance of the various emotional themes described by Shneidman. Rather, he argues that, for health professionals who deal with dying individuals, it is more helpful to think in terms of the patient's tasks, because the dying person may need help in performing some or all of them.

Whichever model one uses, what is clear is that there are no common patterns that typify most or all reactions to impending death. Common themes exist, but they are blended together in quite different patterns by each person who faces this last task.

RESPONSES TO IMPENDING DEATH

Individual variations in responding to imminent death have themselves been the subject of a good deal of research interest in the past few decades. The question that researchers have begun to ask is whether specific variations in patients' emotional responses to impending death have any effect at all on the physical process of dying.

The majority of research on individual adaptations to dying involves studies of patients with terminal cancer. Not only is cancer a clear diagnosis, but many forms of it progress quite rapidly, and the patient usually knows when her chances of survival are low. By contrast, heart disease, which is the leading cause of death in middle and old age in industrialized countries, may be present for a long period without the patient knowing that she has the disease. Also, the prognosis with this disease is highly variable. Researchers simply do not know whether any of the conclusions drawn from studies of cancer patients can be applied to adults dying less rapidly or less predictably. Still, the research is quite fascinating.

The most influential research on responses to impending death has been the work of Steven Greer and his colleagues (Greer, 1991; Greer, Morris, & Pettingale, 1979; Pettingale, Morris, Greer, & Haybittle, 1985). They followed a group of 62 women diagnosed in the 1970s with early stages of breast cancer. Three months after the original diagnosis, each woman was interviewed at some length and her reaction to the diagnosis and to her treatment was classed in one of five groups:

- *Denial (positive avoidance).* The person rejects evidence about diagnosis; she insists that surgery was just precautionary.
- *Fighting spirit.* The person maintains an optimistic attitude and searches for more information about the disease. These patients often see their disease as a challenge, and plan to fight it with every method available.
- *Stoic acceptance (fatalism).* The person acknowledges the diagnosis but makes no effort to seek any further information; or, the person ignores the diagnosis and carries on normal life as much as possible.
- *Helplessness/hopelessness.* The person acts overwhelmed by diagnosis; she sees herself as dying or gravely ill and as devoid of hope.
- *Anxious preoccupation.* Women in this category had originally been included in the helplessness group, but they were separated out later. The category includes those whose response to the diagnosis is strong and persistent anxiety. If they seek

information, they interpret it pessimistically; they monitor their body sensations carefully, interpreting each ache or pain as a possible recurrence.

Greer then checked on the survival rates of these five groups after 5, 10, and 15 years. **Table 18.2** shows the 15-year survival rates. Only 35% of those whose initial reaction had been either denial or fighting spirit had died of cancer 15 years later, compared with 76% of those whose initial reaction had been stoic acceptance, anxious preoccupation, or helplessness/hopelessness. Because those in the five groups did not differ initially in the stage of their disease or in their treatment, these results support the hypothesis that psychological responses contribute to disease progress—just as coping strategies more generally affect the likelihood of disease in the first place.

Similar results have emerged from studies of patients with melanoma (a form of skin cancer) as well as other cancers and from several studies of AIDS patients (Reed, Kemeny, Taylor, Wang, & Visscher, 1994; Solano et al., 1993; Temoshok, 1987). And at least one study of coronary bypass patients showed that men who had a more optimistic attitude before the surgery recovered more quickly in the 6 months after surgery and returned more fully to their presurgery pattern of life (Scheier et al., 1989). In general, individuals who report less hostility, who express more stoic acceptance and more helplessness, and who fail to express negative feelings die sooner (O'Leary, 1990). Those who struggle the most, who fight the hardest, who express their anger and hostility openly, and who also find some sources of joy in their lives live longer. In some ways, the data suggest that "good patients"—those who are obedient and who do not question or fight with their doctors or make life difficult for those around them—are in fact likely to die sooner. Difficult patients, who question and challenge those around them, last longer.

Furthermore, a few studies have linked these psychological differences to immune system functioning. A particular subset of immune cells, called NK cells and thought to form an important defence against cancer, have been found in lower counts among patients who report less distress and who seem better adjusted to their illness (O'Leary, 1990). And one study of AIDS patients showed that T-cell counts declined more rapidly among those who responded to their disease with repression (similar to the stoic acceptance or helplessness groups in the Greer study), while those who showed a fighting spirit had slower loss of T cells (Solano et al., 1993).

TABLE 18.2	15-Year Outcomes Among Women Cancer Patients			
	Outcome 15 Years Later			
Psychological Attitude 3 Months after Surgery	**Alive and Well**	**Died from Cancer**	**Died from Other Causes**	**Total**
Denial	5	5	0	10
Fighting spirit	4	2	4	10
Stoic acceptance	6	24	3	33
Anxious preoccupation	0	3	0	3
Helplessness/hopelessness	1	5	0	6
Total	16	39	7	62

(*Source:* Greer, 1991, from Table 1, p. 45.)

Despite the consistency of these results, two important cautions are in order before you leap to the conclusion that a fighting spirit is the optimum response to any disease. First, some careful studies find no link between depression, stoic acceptance, or helplessness and more rapid death from cancer (e.g., Cassileth, Walsh, & Lusk, 1988; Richardson, Zarnegar, Bisno, & Levine, 1990). Second, it is not clear that the same psychological response is necessarily appropriate for every disease. Consider heart disease, for example. There is a certain irony in the fact that many of the responses to cancer that appear to be optimum could be considered as reflections of a type A personality. Because having a type A personality constitutes a risk factor for heart disease, a "fighting spirit" response to a diagnosis of advanced heart disease might not be the most desirable. The growing body of research on responses to diseases does confirm, though, that there are connections between psychological defences or ways of coping and physical functioning, even in the last stages of life.

Another important ingredient in an individual's response to imminent death is the amount of social support he has. Those with positive and supportive relationships describe lower levels of pain and less depression during their final months of illness (Carey, 1974; Hinton, 1975). Such well-supported patients also live longer. For example, one American study found that both African American and white American heart attack patients who live alone are more likely to have a second heart attack than are those who live with someone else. Similarly, those with significant levels of atherosclerosis live longer if they have a confidant than if they do not (Case, Moss, Case, McDermott, & Eberly, 1992; Williams, 1992).

This link between social support and length of survival has also been found in experimental studies in which patients with equivalent diagnoses and equivalent medical care have been randomly assigned either to an experimental group in which they participate in regular support group sessions or to a control group in which they have no such support system. In one study of a group of 86 women with metastatic breast cancer (that is, cancer that had spread beyond the original site), researchers found that the average length of survival was 36.6 months for those who had access to the support group compared with 18.9 months for those in the control group (Spiegel, Bloom, Kraemer, & Gottheil, 1989). Thus, just as social support helps to buffer children and adults from some of the negative effects of many kinds of nonlethal stress, so does it seem to perform a similar function for those facing death.

Before Going On

- Describe Kübler-Ross's stages of dying.
- What are some other views of the process of dying?
- How do people vary in the ways they adapt to impending death?

THE EXPERIENCE OF GRIEVING

In virtually every culture, the immediate response to a death is some kind of funeral ritual. However, a death ritual is only the first step in the process of **grieving**—the emotional response to a death—which may take months or years to complete.

PSYCHOSOCIAL FUNCTIONS OF DEATH RITUALS

Funerals, wakes, and other death rituals help family members and friends manage their grief by giving them a specific set of roles to play. Like all roles, these include both expected behaviours and prohibited or discouraged behaviours. The content of these roles differs markedly from one culture to the next, but their clarity in most cases provides a shape to the days or weeks immediately following the death of a loved person. In Canadian society, the rituals prescribe what one should wear, who should be called, who should be fed, what demeanour one should show, and far more. Depending on one's ethnic or religious background, one may gather family and friends for a wake or to "sit shiva," a traditional Jewish 7-day period of mourning during which family members stay in the same home and formally mourn a deceased loved one. One may be expected to respond stoically or to wail and tear one's hair. Friends and acquaintances, too, have guiding rules, at least for those first few days. They may bring food, write letters of condolence, offer help, and attend wakes and funerals.

Critical Thinking

Do the various funerals or death rituals you have participated in seem to have served the purposes described in the text?

Death rituals also bring family members together as no other occasion does (with the possible exception of weddings). Frequently, cousins and other distant relatives see one another for the first time in many years at funerals. Such occasions typically inspire shared reminiscences and renew family relationships that have been inactive for a long time. In this way, death rituals can strengthen family ties, clarify the new lines of influence or authority within a family, and "pass the torch" in some way to the next generation. Likewise, funerals help establish deaths as shared milestones for family members—"that was before Grandpa died" or "the last time I saw her was at Grandpa's funeral." A death can become an important organizer of experience that separates the past from the present. Dividing time in this way seems to help survivors cope with grief (Katz & Bartone, 1998).

Death rituals are also designed to help the survivors understand the meaning of death itself, in part by emphasizing the meaning of the life of the person who has died. It is not accidental that most death rituals include testimonials, biographies, and witnessing. By telling the story of a person's life and describing that life's value and meaning, others can more readily accept the person's death.

Finally, death rituals may give some transcendent meaning to death itself by placing it in a philosophical or religious context. In this way, they provide comfort to the bereaved by offering answers to that inevitable question "Why?"

Each culture has its own death rituals. The customarily quiet graveside service in Canada would seem strange to people in many other societies.
(*Photos: left*, Steve/Mary Skjold/MaXx Images Inc.; *right*, A. Ramey/Stock Boston)

THE PROCESS OF GRIEVING

The ritual of a funeral, in whatever form it occurs, can provide structure and comfort in the days immediately following a death. But what happens when that structure is gone? How do people handle the sense of loss? Answering that question requires a look at a number of factors associated with grief.

AGE OF THE BEREAVED   Children express feelings of grief very much the way teens and adults do. Like adults, children demonstrate grief through sad facial expressions, crying, loss of appetite, and age-appropriate displays of anger such as temper tantrums (Oatley & Jenkins, 1996).

Funerals seem to serve the same adaptive function for children as for adults, and most children resolve their feelings of grief within the first year after the loss. In addition, knowing that a loved one or even a pet is ill and in danger of death helps children cope with the loss in advance, just as it does for those who are older (Jarolmen, 1998).

Although the behavioural aspects of adolescents' grief responses vary little from those of adults, teens may be more likely to experience prolonged grief than children or adults. One study found that more than 20% of a group of high school students who had a friend killed in an accident continued to experience intense feelings of grief 9 months after the death (Dyregrov, Gjestad, Bie Wikander, & Vigerust, 1999). Other research suggests that adolescent girls whose mothers have died run a particularly high risk of developing long-term, grief-related problems (Lenhardt & McCourt, 2000). Teenagers may also be more likely than adults to experience grief responses to the deaths of celebrities or to idealize peers' suicides (see **Development in the Information Age**).

Development in the Information Age
"Copycat" Suicides

In Shakespeare's Romeo and Juliet, the teenaged hero takes his own life because he believes that his beloved has already done so. When Juliet revives and discovers Romeo's body, she commits suicide as well. Many believe that Shakespeare's characterization is a realistic portrayal of an emotionally distressed adolescent's typical reaction to suicide—imitation, or a "copycat" suicide. Based on this belief, many observers have raised concerns about the potential effects of emotion-provoking suicide stories in both fiction and the news media (Samaritans, 1998).

In general, research suggests that concerns about fictional suicides are unfounded. For example, a few years ago, the British public responded with outrage to a TV program that depicted a 15-year-old girl's attempted suicide with a drug overdose. These concerns were based on the fear that teenaged viewers who were experiencing emotional problems might be likely to imitate the character's behaviour. Yet surveys that followed the airing

of the program found no increase in frequency of suicide attempts among teenagers. Moreover, few of those who did attempt suicide had seen the program (Simkin, Hawton, Whitehead, Fagg, & Eagle, 1995). Follow-up studies of other suicide-related programs on television have produced similar findings.

News accounts of suicides are a different matter. However, news stories about suicides influence adults' behaviour more often than that of teens. Research suggests that, when the news media present sensational coverage of a particular mode of suicide, the number of people who attempt and complete suicides using that method increases. The number of individuals who attempted suicide by setting themselves ablaze, for instance, increased dramatically in Great Britain after several news programs carried reports, including graphic film footage, of a single self-immolation suicide (Ashton & Donnan, 1981). Likewise, suicide attempts involving throwing oneself in front of a subway train became so frequent in

Vienna after sensational news reports of such incidents that members of the press agreed among themselves to no longer report them (Sonneck, Etzersdorfer, & Nagel-Kuess, 1992).

Despite inconsistencies in research examining the phenomenon of copycat suicide, mental health professionals believe that fictional or journalistic accounts of suicide may influence behaviour in individual cases. They suggest that a 15-year-old girl who has already been thinking about taking a drug overdose may become more likely to do so after viewing a television program in which a character carries out a similar suicide plan. Similarly, an individual who wants to add drama to a planned suicide attempt may be inspired by news reports of an unusual method of suicide. Thus, mental health professionals warn that news and entertainment media should avoid romanticizing and sensationalizing suicide (Samaritans, 1998).

Adolescents' grief responses are probably related to their general cognitive characteristics. You should remember from **Chapters 10 and 11** that adolescents often judge the real world by idealized images. Consequently, a teenager may become caught up in fantasizing about how the world would be different if a friend or loved one had not died. In addition, prolonged grieving among adolescents may be rooted in their tendency to engage in "what if" thinking. This kind of thinking may lead teens to believe that they could have prevented the death and, thus, cause them to develop irrational guilt feelings (Cunningham, 1996).

MODE OF DEATH How an individual dies also contributes to the grief process of those who are in mourning. For example, widows who have cared for spouses during a period of illness prior to death are less likely to become depressed after the death than those whose spouses die suddenly (Carnelley, Wortman, & Kessler, 1999). Grief-related depression seems to emerge during the spouse's illness rather than after the death. The spouse's death is thought of as an escape from suffering for the one who dies and a release from grieving for the caregiver. Similarly, a death that has intrinsic meaning, such as that of a young soldier who dies defending his country, is not necessarily easier to cope with but does provide the bereaved with a sense that the death has not been without purpose (Malkinson & Bar-Tur, 1999). Consequently, mourners have a built-in cognitive coping device—a rational explanation for the death—that allows them to grieve but also protects them from long-term depression.

However, sudden and violent deaths evoke more intense grief responses. One study found that 36% of widows and widowers whose spouses had died in accidents or by suicide were suffering from post-traumatic stress symptoms (e.g., nightmares) 2 months after the death, compared with only 10% of widows and widowers whose spouses had died of natural causes (Zisook, Chentsova-Dutton, & Shuchter, 1998). Moreover, almost all of those whose spouses had died unnaturally and who had PTSD symptoms were also depressed.

Furthermore, suicide is associated with a unique pattern of responses among survivors (Bailley, Kral, & Dunham, 1999). In general, family and close friends of someone who commits suicide experience feelings of rejection and anger. Moreover, their grief over the loss of the loved one is complicated by the feeling that they could or should have done something to prevent the suicide. They are also less likely to discuss the loss with other family members or with friends because of their sense that a suicide in the family is a source of shame. For these reasons, suicide survivors may be more likely than others who have lost loved ones to experience long-term negative effects.

WIDOWHOOD

The relationship between the deceased and those who are in mourning also affects the grieving process. For example, bereaved parents often report that their health is poorer than before a child's death, and many continue to experience intense feelings of sadness for several years (Arbuckle & De Vries, 1995; Malkinson & Bar-Tur, 1999) (see **The Real World**). As a general rule, the most difficult death to recover from is that of a spouse.

WIDOWHOOD AND PHYSICAL HEALTH The experience of widowhood (a term that applies to both men and women) appears to have both immediate and longer-term effects on the immune system (Beem et al., 1999; Gallagher-Thompson, Futterman, Farberow, Thompson, & Peterson, 1993; Irwin & Pike, 1993). In one Norwegian study, researchers measured immune functioning in widows twice, shortly after their husbands'

The Real World
Caregiving
When an Infant Dies

Many parents grieving for a lost infant do not receive adequate support from either their social networks or health professionals (Vaeisaenen, 1998). It is important for those who are in a position to support grieving parents to understand that the grief that follows the death of an infant is no less intense than any other kind of bereavement. In fact, it may be more complex.

When an older child dies, parents have a relationship history and an intimate knowledge of the child's personality on which to build reminiscences. Such cognitive devices help them reorganize their attachment to the lost child so that they are able to release the child psychologically. But with an infant, there is little or no relationship history to draw on. The parents, of course, feel deep emotions of attachment, but the cognitive elements that help parents cope with the loss of a child are absent. For these reasons, bereaved parents of a dead infant often have a greater need for support from family, friends, and health professionals than even they themselves realize (Vaeisaenen, 1998).

Well-intentioned friends or family may pressure the couple to cope with their loss by simply replacing the infant with another one. However, research suggests that starting another pregnancy soon after the loss of an infant doesn't necessarily end either a mother's or a father's grief, although it does tend to protect both against long-term negative effects such as depression (Franche & Bulow, 1999). Moreover, parents may fear that a subsequent child will also die in infancy and may try to avoid becoming emotionally attached to a newborn (Wong, 1993). This could have adverse effects on the whole family.

Health professionals have compiled a few guidelines that can be useful to family members or friends in supporting parents who have lost an infant (Wong, 1993):

- Don't try to force bereaved parents to talk about their grief or the infant if they don't want to.
- Always refer to the deceased infant by name.
- Express your own feelings of loss for the infant, if they are sincere.
- Follow the parents' lead in engaging in reminiscences about the baby's looks or personality.
- Discourage the parents from resorting to drugs or alcohol to manage grief.
- Assure grieving parents that their responses are normal and that it will take time to resolve the emotions associated with losing an infant.
- Don't pressure the parents to "replace" the baby with another one.
- Don't offer rationalizations (e.g., "Your baby's an angel now") that may offend the parents.
- Do offer support for the parents' own rationalizations.
- Be aware that the infant's siblings, even those who are very young, are likely to experience some degree of grief.

deaths and 1 year later (Lindstrom, 1997). Investigators found that the widows' immune systems were suppressed somewhat immediately after the death but had returned to normal a year later, in most cases.

Similarly, a study comparing widows with married women in the Netherlands found that widows' immune responses continued to differ from those of married participants 7 months after the spouses' deaths (Beem et al., 1999). Interestingly, 7 months after the spouses' deaths, psychological differences (such as feelings of sadness) between the two groups had disappeared, though the immune function differences persisted. Thus, the bereaved may continue to suffer at a biochemical level even after obvious signs of grieving have subsided. Moreover, the association between death of a spouse and ensuing illness in a surviving partner may be the result of the effects of grief on the body's defences against disease agents such as viruses and bacteria.

WIDOWHOOD AND MENTAL HEALTH In the year following bereavement, the incidence of depression among widows and widowers rises substantially, though rates of

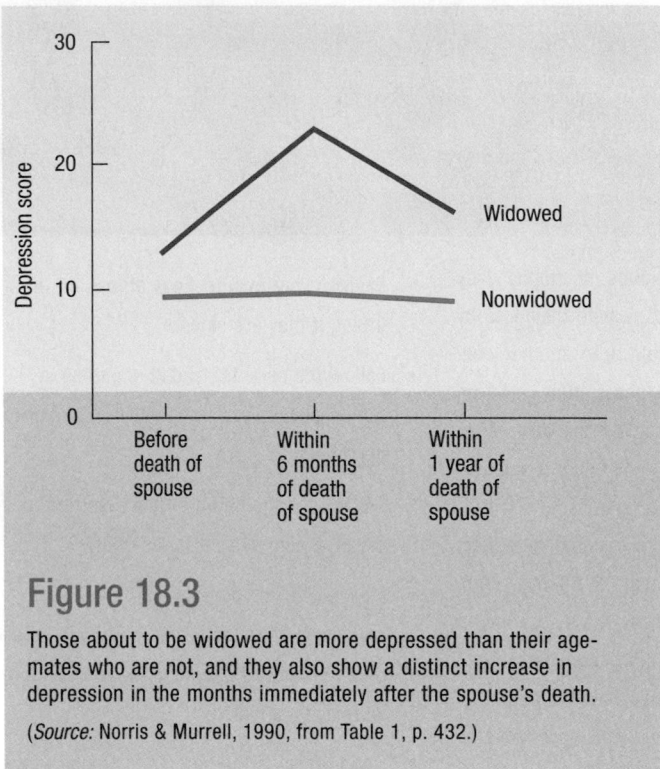

Figure 18.3

Those about to be widowed are more depressed than their age-mates who are not, and they also show a distinct increase in depression in the months immediately after the spouse's death.

(*Source:* Norris & Murrell, 1990, from Table 1, p. 432.)

death and disease rise only slightly (Reich, Zautra, & Guarnaccia, 1989; Stroebe, W. & Stroebe, M., 1993). In one important longitudinal study, researchers repeatedly interviewed a sample of 3000 adults, all age 55 or older at the beginning of the study (Norris & Murrell, 1990). Forty-eight of these adults were widowed during the $2^{1}/_{2}$ years of the study, which allowed investigators to look at depression and health status before and immediately after bereavement. They found no differences in physical health between widowed and nonwidowed participants, but they did note a rise in depression among the widowed immediately following the loss and then a decline within a year after bereavement, a set of results illustrated in **Figure 18.3**.

However, other researchers have found that older adults whose spouses have died differ in mental health for several years following the death from peers whose spouses are still alive (Bennett, 1997). So, it appears that declines in physical and mental health follow bereavement fairly consistently, but how long such effects last may be highly variable. Several factors contribute to this variability.

One such factor is mental health history. Older adults who enter widowhood with a history of depression are more likely to experience depression after the death of their spouse (Zisook, Paulus, Shuchter, & Judd 1997). Lack of social support, both actual and perceived, also contributes to variability in depression among widows and widowers (Reed, 1998; Tomita et al., 1997). Moreover, the quality of the relationship of the widow or widower to the deceased spouse is related to depressive symptoms. Perhaps surprisingly, relationships characterized by emotional distance and conflict are *more* likely to lead to depression than those that were warm (van Doorn, Kasl, Beery, Jacobs, & Prigerson, 1998).

Economic changes accompany the loss of a spouse and add to the overall stress involved in the transition to widowhood. Women typically suffer greater economic losses after the death of a spouse than men do, usually because they lose their husbands' income or pension (Zick & Holden, 2000). However, the household incomes of both widows and widowers are lower than those of married elders (Federal Interagency Forum on Aging-Related Statistics [FIFARS], 2000). Thus, the degree to which an individual's economic status changes as a result of a spouse's death is probably another factor that contributes to individual differences in the long-term effects of bereavement.

pathological grief
symptoms of depression brought on by death of a loved one

PATHOLOGICAL GRIEF Some psychologists argue that **pathological grief**, depression-like symptoms following death of a loved one, should be thought of as a separate disorder from depression (Stroebe, M., et al., 2000). They suggest that individuals who continue to experience grief symptoms such as loss of appetite more than 2 months following loss of a loved one may be developing pathological grief.

Diagnosis and treatment of pathological grief may be important for preventing problems in both mental and physical health among widows and widowers. Researchers have found that survivors whose grief symptoms continue for 6 months or longer are more likely to suffer long-term depression as well as physical ailments such as cancer and heart disease (Prigerson et al., 1997). Moreover, they continue to show important differences in physical and mental functioning for up to 2 years after their spouse's death.

However, it's important to keep in mind that many aspects of grief are culturally determined. Beliefs about how long mourning should last and how the bereaved should behave vary widely from one culture to another (Braun & Nichols, 1997; Rubin & Schechter, 1997). For example, Orthodox Jewish men traditionally do not shave or trim their beards for 30 days after the death of a family member. Furthermore, mourning traditions among Orthodox Jews require abstaining from entertainment such as attending the theatre or seeing movies for an entire year after the death of someone close (Bial, 1971).

Since inattention to grooming and lack of interest in social activities are also sometimes signs of depression, observers who are unfamiliar with Orthodox Jewish mourning practices might conclude that those who follow them are exhibiting pathological rather than normal **grieving**. Thus, mental health professionals are advised to learn about an individual's cultural beliefs before forming conclusions about grief-related behaviour. Likewise, friends, neighbours, and co-workers of someone who is mourning the death of a spouse or other close family member should also be careful to interpret any grief-related behaviours within the context of the person's cultural background.

grieving
the emotional response to a death

SEX DIFFERENCES The death of a spouse appears to be a more negative experience for men than for women, despite the fact that there seem to be no sex differences in the actual grieving process following such a loss (Quigley & Schatz, 1999). The risk of death from either natural causes or suicide in the months immediately after widowhood is significantly greater among men than among women (Stroebe & Stroebe, 1993). Depression and suicidal thoughts are also more common in widowers than in widows (Byrne & Raphael, 1999; Chen et al., 1999). Further, men seem to have a more difficult time than women do in returning to the levels of emotional functioning they exhibited before the spouse's death (van Grootheest, Beckman, van Groenou, & Deeg, 1999).

These differences are most often interpreted as yet another sign of the importance of social support. Social activities are very important in the lives of widows. In contrast, researchers have found that widowers withdraw from social activities to a far greater degree than widows do in the months immediately following bereavement (Bennett, 1998).

However, some developmentalists have suggested that activities-oriented studies have led to a stereotype that characterizes widowers as lonely and isolated. In fact, research involving in-depth examinations of widowers' friendships, rather than of just their social activities, suggests that social relationships are very important in the lives of men who have lost a spouse (Riggs, 1997). Thus, differences in social involvement may be part of the explanation for sex differences in health and depressions following the death of a spouse, but they do not appear to tell the whole story.

The results of a carefully designed longitudinal study of Australian widowers and married men over age 65 suggest that alcohol use may play a role in the greater prevalence of depression among widowers (Byrne, Raphael, & Arnold, 1999). Researchers found that more than twice as many widowers as married men (19% versus 8%) consumed five or more alcoholic drinks per day. Although alcohol may temporarily relieve unpleasant feelings of grief, it is a central nervous system depressant, and prolonged heavy drinking can lead to depression.

PREVENTING LONG-TERM PROBLEMS Some research suggests that the "talk-it-out" approach to managing grief can be helpful in preventing grief-related depression, especially when feelings are shared with others who have had similar experiences, in the context of a support group (Francis, 1997). Research also indicates that developing a coherent personal narrative of the events surrounding the spouse's death helps widows and widowers manage grief (van den Hoonaard, 1999). Participating in support groups, or even jointly recalling relevant events with close family members, can facilitate the formation of such stories.

Clearly, this kind of psychosocial management of grief requires time. Mental health professionals advise employers that providing bereaved employees (especially those whose spouses have died) with sufficient time off to grieve may be critical to their physical and mental health. In the long run, illness and depression among bereaved workers who return to their jobs too soon may be more costly to employers than providing additional time off (Eyetsemitan, 1998).

Before Going On

- How do funerals and ceremonies help survivors cope with grief?
- How do the age of the bereaved and the mode of death affect the grieving process?
- How does grief affect the physical and mental health of widows and widowers?

THEORETICAL PERSPECTIVES ON GRIEVING

There are a number of ways of looking at the emotion of grief, but the two that have had the greatest influence on the way psychologists think about grief are Freud's psychoanalytic theory and Bowlby's attachment theory.

FREUD'S PSYCHOANALYTIC THEORY

From the psychoanalytic perspective, the death of a loved one is an emotional trauma. As with any trauma, the ego, or mind, tries to insulate itself from the unpleasant emotions such losses induce through the use of defence mechanisms, including denial and repression. However, Freud believed that defence mechanisms were only temporary devices for dealing with negative emotions. Eventually, he thought, the individual must examine the emotions and their source directly. Otherwise, such emotions lead to the development of physical symptoms and, perhaps, mental illnesses.

Freud's view has been very influential in grief counselling and in popular notions about the necessity of "working through" grief in order to avoid its long-term negative effects. It is generally accepted that bereaved individuals need to talk openly about their loss. Thus, grief counsellors often recommend that friends of a bereaved person encourage the person to cry or express grief in other ways.

Psychoanalytically based grief therapy for children often emphasizes the use of defence mechanisms other than denial and repression to cope with grief. Following this approach, therapists sometimes encourage children to express their feelings through art. The idea is that this kind of defence mechanism, known as *sublimation,* will lead to better health outcomes than avoidance of emotions through more negative defence mechanisms (Glazer, 1998). Similarly, some therapists advocate encouraging children to use another defence mechanism, *identification,* to manage their grief. This goal can be accomplished by having the child watch popular films depicting children's grief, such as *The Lion King,* discuss the young characters' feelings, and compare the characters' emotions to their own (Sedney, 1999).

In addition, the psychoanalytic perspective has shaped grief research by characterizing the loss of a loved one as a trauma. An important concept in such research is that the more traumatic the death, the more likely it is to be followed by physical or mental problems. In fact, researchers have found that people who lose loved ones in sudden, tragic ways, such as to a drunk-driving accident or a murder, are more likely to display symptoms of post-traumatic stress disorder (Murphy et al., 1999; Sprang & McNeil, 1998).

BOWLBY'S ATTACHMENT THEORY

John Bowlby and other attachment theorists argue that intense grief reactions are likely to occur at the loss of any person to whom one is attached, whether a partner, a parent, or a child (Bowlby, 1980; Sanders, 1989). Moreover, their theories predict that the quality of attachment to the loved one should be related in some way to the experience of grief. Research seems to confirm this aspect of their view. The stronger the attachment between a mourner and a lost loved one, the deeper and more prolonged the grief response (van Doorn et al., 1998). By contrast, the death of someone who is part of one's social network but not an intimate confidant or an attachment figure is less likely to trigger an intense emotional reaction (Murrell & Himmelfarb, 1989).

Bowlby proposed four stages of grief, and Catherine Sanders, another attachment theorist, has proposed five stages, but as you can see in **Table 18.3**, the two systems overlap a great deal. In the first period, that of shock or numbness, people say things that reveal their state of mind:

I feel so vague. I can't keep my mind on anything for very long. (Bowlby, 1980, p. 47)

I'm afraid I'm losing my mind. I can't seem to think clearly. (Bowlby, 1980, p. 48)

It was so strange. I was putting on my makeup, combing my hair, and all the time it was as if I were standing by the door watching myself go through these motions. (Sanders, 1989, p. 56).

TABLE 18.3   Stages of Grief

Stage	Bowlby's Label	Sanders's Label	General Description
1	Numbness	Shock	Characteristic of the first few days after the death of the loved one, and occasionally longer; mourner experiences disbelief, confusion, restlessness, feelings of unreality, a sense of helplessness
2	Yearning	Awareness	The bereaved person tries to recover the lost person; may actively search, or wander as if searching; may report that he sees the dead person; mourner feels full of anger, anxiety, guilt, fear, frustration; may sleep poorly and weep often.
3	Disorganization and despair	Conservation/ withdrawal	Searching ceases and the loss is accepted, but acceptance of loss brings depression and despair, or a sense of helplessness; this stage is often accompanied by great fatigue and a desire to sleep all the time.
4	Reorganization	Healing and renewal	Sanders views this as two periods, Bowlby as only one. Both see this as the period when the individual takes control again. Some forgetting occurs and some sense of hope emerges, along with increased energy, better health, better sleep patterns, and reduced depression.

(*Sources:* Bowlby, 1980; Sanders, 1989.)

In the stage of awareness of loss, or yearning, when anger is a common ingredient, people say things such as "His boss should have known better than to ask him to work so hard." Bowlby also suggested that this period is equivalent to what is observed in young children who have been temporarily separated from their closest attachment figures and who go from room to room in search of this favoured person. Adults who are widowed do some of the same searching—sometimes physically, sometimes mentally.

In the stage of disorganization and despair, the restlessness of the previous period disappears and is replaced by a great lethargy. One 45-year-old whose child had just died described her feelings:

> I can't understand the way I feel. Up to now, I had been feeling restless. I couldn't sleep. I paced and ranted. Now, I have an opposite reaction. I sleep a lot. I feel fatigued and worn out. I don't even want to see the friends who have kept me going. I sit and stare, too exhausted to move. . . . Just when I thought I should be feeling better, I am feeling worse. (Sanders, 1989, p. 73)

Finally, the resolution of the grieving process comes in Bowlby's stage of reorganization. Sanders hypothesized that this stage comprises two separate periods: healing and renewal. The outcome, from both Bowlby's and Sanders's perspectives, is that the grieving person begins to be able to maintain control. Sleep patterns return to normal, and a more optimistic outlook is typical.

These descriptions of the grieving process are highly evocative and can be useful in counselling grieving individuals. Discussion of the stages helps those who are grieving communicate with therapists about how they are feeling and describe the kinds of symptoms they are experiencing. Stage approaches also help survivors realize that their emotions and physical symptoms are normal and that the grieving process is complex.

However, as with the concept of stages of dying, there are two important questions about these proposed stages of grieving:

(1) Do they really occur in fixed stages?
(2) Does everyone feel all these feelings, in whatever sequence? The answer to both questions, as you'll see, seems to be no.

Critical Thinking

Think about a loss in your own life. (Even losing a pet causes grief.) Do Bowlby's and Sanders's stages seem to fit your experience?

ALTERNATIVE PERSPECTIVES

A growing set of "revisionist" views of grieving give a rather different picture from that of either Freud or the attachment theorists. First, research suggests that, contrary to psychoanalytic hypotheses, avoiding expressions of grief neither prolongs the experience of grief nor leads inevitably to physical or mental health problems. In fact, at least one study suggests that bereaved individuals who avoid talking about the deceased or their feelings of loss actually experience milder grief and are less likely to suffer long-term effects (Bonanno, Znoj, Siddique, & Horowitz, 1999).

Second, many researchers and theorists find that grieving simply does not occur in fixed stages, with everyone following the same pattern (Wortman & Silver, 1990). There may be common themes, such as anger, guilt, depression, and restlessness, but these do not seem to appear in a fixed order.

One compromise model suggests that each of the key themes in the grieving process may have a likely trajectory, as suggested in **Figure 18.4** (Jacobs et al., 1987/1988). For example, numbness may be most prominent in the days immediately following the loved one's death. After a few months, the grieving person may feel numb at times, but depression may be a more dominant theme. The basic idea, obviously, is that many themes are present at the same time, but that one or another may dominate, in an approximate sequence. Thus, it may well be that disbelief is highest immediately after the death, and that depression peaks some months later—which makes the process look stage-like, although in fact both elements are present throughout. Some bereaved people might move more quickly and others more slowly through these various emotions.

In contrast, other revisionist theorists and researchers contend that for some adults, grieving simply does not include all these elements. Psychologists Camille Wortman and Roxane Silver have amassed an impressive amount of evidence to support such a view (Wortman & Silver, 1989, 1990, 1992; Wortman, Silver, & Kessler, 1993). They dispute the traditional view of grieving expressed in both Freud's and Bowlby's theories. First, Wortman and Silver do not agree that distress is an inevitable response to loss. Second, their research challenges the notion that failure to experience distress is a sign that the individual has not grieved "properly."

Based on their findings, Wortman and Silver conclude that there are at least four distinct patterns of grieving (Wortman & Silver, 1990):

- *Normal.* The person feels great distress immediately following the loss, with relatively rapid recovery.
- *Chronic.* The person's distress continues at a high level over several years.
- *Delayed.* The grieving person feels little distress in the first few months but high levels of distress some months or years later.
- *Absent.* The person feels no notable level of distress either immediately or at any later time.

Contrary to the predictions of stage theories of grief, it turns out that the pattern of absent grief is remarkably common. In Wortman and Silver's own first study, 26% of bereaved participants showed essentially no distress, either immediately after the death or several years later, a pattern confirmed in other research (Levy, Martinkowski, & Derby, 1994; Wortman & Silver, 1990). The least common pattern is delayed grief. Only 1–5% of adults appear to show such a response to loss, while as many as a third show chronic grief. Thus, Wortman and Silver find little support for either aspect of the traditional view: High levels of distress are neither an inevitable nor a necessary aspect of the grieving process. Many adults seem to handle the death of a spouse, a child, or a parent without significant psychological dislocation—although it remains true that on average, bereaved persons have more depression, less life satisfaction, and a greater risk of illness than the nonbereaved.

As yet, developmentalists know relatively little about the characteristics of individuals who react to bereavement in the very different ways outlined by Wortman and Silver, although their research gives a few hints (Wortman et al., 1993). In their studies, widows who had had the best marriages showed the most persistent grief reactions. More surprisingly, Wortman and Silver found that those widows who had had the

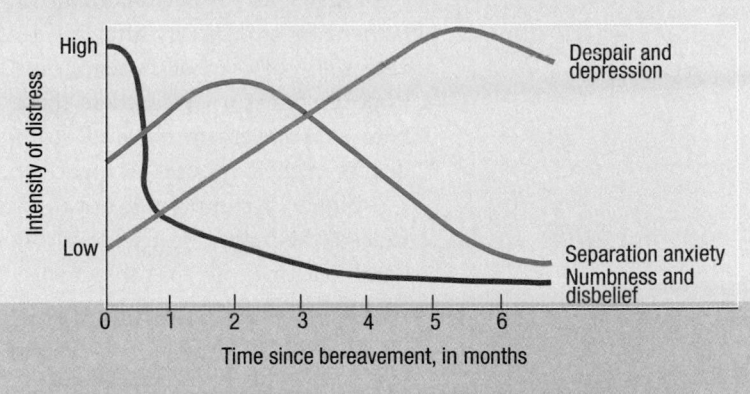

Figure 18.4

Jacobs offers this model as an alternative to strict stage theories of grieving. At any given moment, many different emotions or themes may be apparent, but each may have a typical trajectory.

(*Source:* Jacobs et al., 1987/1988, Figure 1, p. 43.)

strongest sense of personal control, self-esteem, or mastery prior to the spouse's death had the most difficulty after his death, as if the loss of the spouse had undermined this very sense of control. Research in Germany suggests that neuroticism may be another important factor; researchers there found that widows who were high in neuroticism before bereavement showed stronger and more persistent negative effects after the deaths of their spouses (Stroebe, W., & Stroebe, M., 1993).

Finally, it's important not to lose sight of the fact that loss can also lead to growth. Indeed, the majority of widows say not only that they changed as a result of their husbands' deaths, but that the change was toward greater independence and greater skill (Wortman & Silver, 1990). Like all crises and all major life changes, bereavement can be an opportunity as well as, or instead of, a disabling experience. Which way a person responds is likely to depend very heavily on the patterns established from early childhood: in temperament or personality, in internal working models of attachment and self, in intellectual skills, and in social networks. Ultimately, we respond to death—our own or someone else's—as we have responded to life.

Before Going On

- How does Freud's psychoanalytic theory view grief?
- What do Bowlby and Sanders suggest about the connection between attachment and grief, and what stages of grieving have they proposed?
- How have more recent theorists criticized the psychoanalytic and attachment theories of the grief process, and what alternative perspectives do they propose?

Summary

The Experience of Death

- *Death* is a somewhat nonspecific term. Medical personnel refer to *clinical death* and *brain death; social death* occurs when the deceased person is treated like a corpse by those around the person.
- The great majority of adults in industrialized countries die in hospitals. Hospice care emphasizes patient and family control of the dying process and palliative care rather than curative treatment. Some studies suggest that patients and families are more satisfied with hospice care than hospital care.

The Meaning of Death Across the Lifespan

- Until about age 6 or 7, children do not understand that death is permanent and inevitable and involves loss of function. Teens understand the physical aspects of death much better than children do, but they sometimes have distorted ideas about it, especially their own mortality.
- Many young adults believe they possess unique characteristics that protect them from death. For middle-aged and older adults, death has many possible meanings: a signal of changes in family roles, a transition to another state (such as a life after

death), and a loss of opportunity and relationships. Awareness of death may also help a person organize her remaining time.

- Fear of death appears to peak in mid-life, after which it drops rather sharply. Older adults talk more about death but are less afraid of it. Deeply religious adults are typically less afraid of death.

- Many adults prepare for death in practical ways, such as by buying life insurance or writing a will. Reminiscence may also serve as preparation. There are also some signs of deeper personality changes immediately before death, including more dependence and docility and less emotionality and assertiveness.

The Process of Dying

- Kübler-Ross suggested five stages of dying: denial, anger, bargaining, depression, and acceptance. Research fails to support the hypothesis that all dying adults go through all five stages or that the stages necessarily occur in this order. The emotion most commonly observed is depression.

- Critics of Kübler-Ross suggest that her findings may be culture-specific. They also argue that the process of dying is less stage-like than her theory claims.

- Research with cancer and AIDS patients suggests that those who are most pessimistic and docile in response to diagnosis and treatment have shorter life expectancies. Those who fight hardest, and even display anger, live longer. Dying adults who have better social support, either from family and friends or through specially created support groups, also live longer than those who lack such support.

The Experience of Grieving

- Funerals and other rituals after death serve important functions, including defining roles for the bereaved, bringing family together, and giving meaning to the deceased's life and death.

- Grief responses depend on a number of variables. The age of the bereaved and the mode of death shape the grief process.

- In general, the death of a spouse evokes the most intense and long-lasting grief. Widows and widowers show high levels of illness and death in the months immediately after the death of a spouse, perhaps as a result of the effects of grief on the immune system. Widowers appear to have a more difficult time managing grief than widows.

Theoretical Perspectives on Grieving

- Freud's psychoanalytic theory emphasizes loss as an emotional trauma, the effects of defence mechanisms, and the need to work through feelings of grief.

- Bowlby's attachment theory views grief as a natural response to the loss of an attachment figure. Attachment theorists suggest that the grief process involves several stages.

- Alternative views suggest that neither Freud's nor Bowlby's theory accurately characterizes the grief experience. Responses are more individual than either theory might suggest.

Key Terms

brain death (p. 542)

clinical death (p. 541)

grieving (p. 563)

hospice care (p. 542)

palliative care (p. 543)

pathological grief (p. 562)

personal fable (p. 545)

social death (p. 542)

thanatology (p. 554)

unique invulnerability (p. 546)

Weblinks

Canadian Virtual Hospice
www.hc-sc.gc.ca/english/media/releases/2001/2001_121ebk1.htm
Health Canada's website provides information on McMaster University's upcoming
Canadian Virtual Hospice website.

The Canadian Hospice Palliative Care Association
www.chpca.net/home.htm
The website for the Canadian Hospice Palliative Care Association is an informative
resource on palliative care issues in Canada. The association provides a useful definition of palliative care, their mission statement, press releases, and links to provincial resources.

*Hospice Care Handbook: The Fundamentals of Patient and Family Care for
Health Care Professionals, Volunteers and Students*
www.legacies.ca/Free%20Books%20Songs%20Home.htm
Fundamentals of patient and family physical, emotional, spiritual and informational
needs are presented in this e-book written by hospice care pioneer Harry van
Bommel. Issues of hospice care and euthanasia in Canada are also addressed.

Copycat Suicides
www.annenbergpublicpolicycenter.org
The Annenberg Public Policy Center of the University of Pennsylvania published a
report in 2001 that addresses the issue of the media's role in copycat suicides. A
national panel of experts in behavioural science, suicide, and the media developed
specific recommendations for the media on how to report acts of suicide.

Do People Have a Right to Die?

One element of having greater control over the process of dying might be the ability to choose the timing of death—a highly controversial topic. Today, most medical ethicists distinguish between two forms of euthanasia (also known as "mercy killing"). Passive euthanasia occurs when a person (typically, a physician) hastens a death by not using life support systems or medication that would prolong the life or by withdrawing life support or other treatment that may be keeping a patient alive. Active euthanasia (also called assisted suicide) occurs when a physician or other individual (at a patient's request) hastens the patient's death by active means, such as by administering a fatal dose of a drug.

LIVING WILLS

There is little controversy about passive euthanasia. Most people agree that individuals should be able to determine the degree to which life-support technology will be used to delay their own deaths. Thus, an increasing number of adults have made living wills specifying that life-support systems or resuscitation should not be used in case of their clinical death or near death. Such living wills essentially ask physicians to participate in passive euthanasia.

All Canadian provinces, except for New Brunswick, have legislation that recognizes the directives expressed in living wills. In Canada, living wills have several formats depending upon which province or territory you live in. These living wills are, and may be known variously as, an

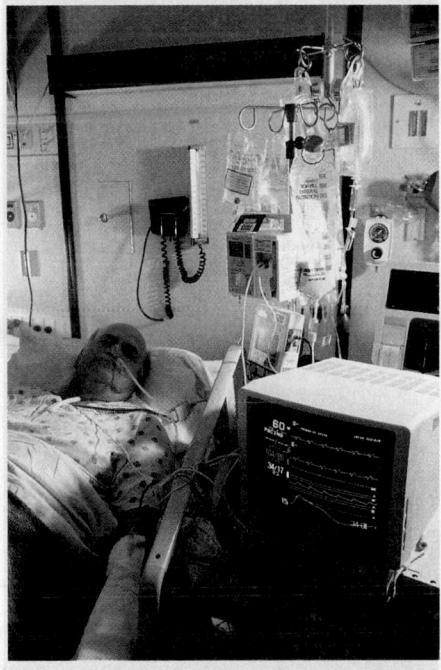

Many hospitals now specifically ask terminal patients during the admission process how they want to be treated in the event that they become mentally incapacitated.
(*Photo:* Blair Seitz/Photo Researchers)

advanced directive, a health care directive, or powers of attorney for personal care. A living will generally contains two essential elements: a *proxy directive*, which specifies who you deem to be responsible to make health care decisions on your behalf if you are no longer able to make your wishes known to others; and an *instruction directive*, which specifies the health care or other personal care choices that can be fulfilled by you or someone else (your designated proxy) on your behalf. The living will can include any combination of consent or refusal to consent to a diagnostic, therapeutic, preventative, or palliative treatment.

THE ASSISTED SUICIDE DEBATE

By contrast, assisted suicide (or any other form of active euthanasia) is far less common and much more controversial. The debate over physician-assisted suicide has been brought to public attention in North America by the actions of Dr. Jack Kevorkian, a physician who has helped several terminally ill or severely handicapped individuals end their own lives. A 1997 Ipsos-Reid poll found that three-quarters (76%) of Canadians surveyed support the notion of the patient's "right to die" and 21% were opposed. Although widespread support of euthanasia for the terminally ill exists, support is highest among those under the age of 35 (81%) and somewhat

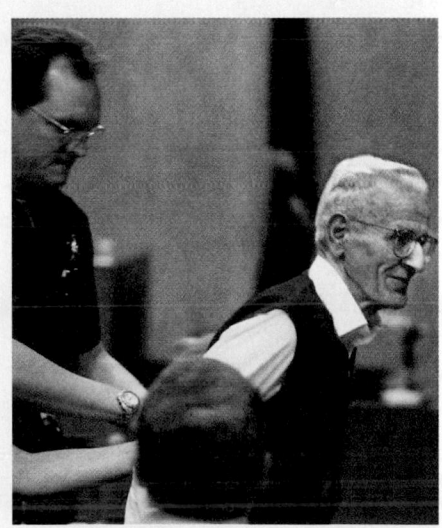

In 1999, Dr. Jack Kevorkian, who had lost his licence to practise medicine several years earlier, was convicted of murder by a Michigan jury. He is currently in prison.
(*Photo:* AFP/CORBIS)

less among those who are 55 and older (69%). Nonetheless, euthanasia and assisted suicide are still illegal in Canada. Doctors also have a legal obligation to prevent patients from harming themselves in a case where there is a risk of suicide.

The only place in the world where assisted suicide is fully and explicitly legal is in the Netherlands. A law passed in 2001 legalized the long-standing Dutch custom of providing terminally ill patients with lethal doses of pain-killing drugs ("Dutch Senate OKs Doctor-Assisted Suicide," 2001). Individuals who wish to die must be terminally ill and have no hope of recovery, and must obtain the approval of two physicians. Children under 12 are prohibited from requesting to die, and those between 12 and 15 must have parental consent. The parents of a 16- or 17-year-old must be notified of the child's request but do not have the right to prevent the assisted suicide from being carried out.

Many of those who oppose active euthanasia believe that each individual life is sacred. Therefore, they believe, decisions about when to end life should be subject only to divine authority. These critics also view assisted suicide as just another form of suicide—a practice they consider to be immoral.

Other opponents argue against active euthanasia on the grounds that it might be extremely difficult to set limits on the process, even with strict guidelines—a position often labelled "the slippery slope argument" (Twycross, 1996). Advocates for the disabled have been particularly vocal in putting forward this point of view. They claim that once assisted suicide becomes widely viewed as morally acceptable, society may come to the point where those who are infirm or severely disabled will be subtly (or not so subtly) encouraged to end their own lives in order to relieve others of the burden of their care. Such critics even fear that

things might reach a point where physicians administer fatal drugs without the patient's consent.

A third argument against any form of active euthanasia is that modern pain management techniques allow even those with extremely painful terminal illnesses to be comfortable in the last days or weeks of their lives. Thus, it is not necessary to hasten death in order to prevent pain. Over a decade ago, long-time Canadian hospice care advocate Harry van Bommel reasoned that it's not only the fear of death, but the fear of dying alone or in pain or of creating hardship for others that had helped to feed the pro-euthanasia movement. He suggested that the real fears about the quality of life that a dying person holds could be assuaged with an alternative form of care; namely, a Canadian style of palliative hospice care that meets the full range of human needs in which the patient and family are the primary decision-makers. Further, he warned of the danger that if palliative care and home care initiatives were not supported formally within the Canadian health care policy, then euthanasia would be seen as the only viable alternative (van Bommel, 1992, 2002).

For these reasons, as well as the personal religious beliefs of some, about three-quarters of a sample of 3000 oncologists (physicians who specialize in treating cancer) in a survey carried out by the National Institutes of Health were found to oppose active euthanasia of any kind (Emanuel et al., 2000). Instead, they advocate palliative-care education for all physicians to make them aware of the benefits of hospice care as well as the most effective ways of relieving patients' pain. They also suggest that physicians treating terminal patients engage their patients in frank discussions about pain

relief as early in the course of their illness as possible. Through such discussions, doctors and patients can decide together what pain relief measures will be taken.

Studies involving patients who refuse treatments such as chemotherapy suggest that such individuals often want to live as long as possible. However, they do not want to go through the difficulties associated with the treatments (Abrams, 1998). Such findings suggest that observers should be cautious about jumping to the conclusion that a person who doesn't want medical treatment is also interested in hastening death.

Opponents of assisted suicide also question terminally ill patients' psychological fitness for making the decision to end their lives. Some fear that such patients may be depressed and that a request to hasten death is really no different from any other kind of suicide attempt. In other words, it is an act born of emotional despair, not rationality. The distinction is important, they say, because the philosophical rationale of assisted suicide laws is that choosing to die involves a rational decision-making process.

To address this concern, assisted suicide legislation would have to include a mandatory waiting period between a

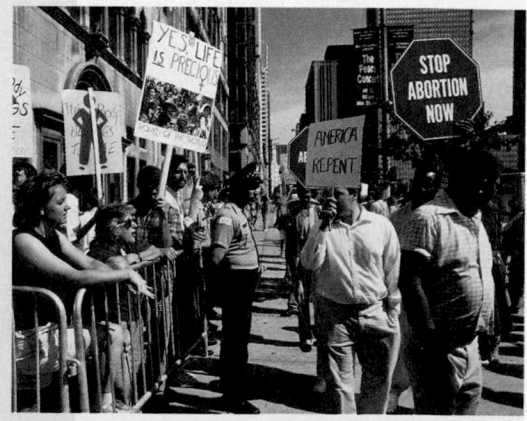

Pro-life groups oppose physician-assisted suicide as well as abortion.
(*Photo:* Robert Kusel/Getty Images)

request for death and the fulfilment of the request. During the waiting period, a psychologist or psychiatrist would be responsible for assessing the mental state of the patient to determine whether he or she is competent to make the life-ending decision. University of Calgary psychologists Kim Galbraith and Keith Dobson (2000) suggest that in the event that assisted suicide or euthanasia were legalized in Canada, psychologists would play a vital and prominent role in helping patients with end-of-life decisions and with determining the competency of the terminally ill patient to make an informed rational decision.

Those who favour assisted suicide legislation note that modern medical technology has increasingly made it possible to prolong life well past the point at which death, in earlier decades, would naturally have occurred. Further, proponents of assisted suicide argue that many terminal patients are unable to carry out their own suicides, and therefore require the help of a physician. However, opponents counter that asking another person to help with a suicide is a far cry from giving a person "death with dignity." As one German physician who opposes assisted suicide expressed it, "Everyone has the right to a dignified death, but nobody has the right to be killed" (Cohen, 2001).

YOUR TURN

- Find out from a local medical association or health unit whether hospitals and physicians in your area generally honour living wills. Does your province or territory require medical personnel to ask all hospitalized people whether they have a living will?

- The medical association or health unit should also be able to tell you whether your province or territory allows family members to authorize health professionals to terminate aspects of care such as tube feeding in cases where a terminally ill or seriously injured individual can't speak for himself.

- Has anyone in your province or territory ever been prosecuted for helping a dying person hasten death? If so, what were the circumstances and outcome of the case(s)?

- Are there efforts underway in your province or territory to legalize assisted suicide? If so, what do opinion polls suggest about public support for such laws?

GLOSSARY

ability goals goals based on a desire to be superior to others *319*

accommodation changing a scheme as a result of some new information *40*

achievement test a test designed to assess specific information learned in school *250*

activities of daily living (ADLs) self-help tasks such as bathing, dressing, and using the toilet *484*

activity theory the idea that it is normal and healthy for older adults to try to remain as active as possible for as long as possible *514*

adaptive reflexes reflexes such as sucking that help newborns survive; some adaptive reflexes persist throughout life *98*

affectional bond the emotional tie to an infant experienced by a parent *132*

ageism a prejudicial view of older adults that characterizes them in negative ways *12*

aggression behaviour intended to harm another person or an object *213*

alcoholism physical and psychological dependence on alcohol *437*

Alzheimer's disease a very severe form of dementia, the cause of which is unknown *497*

ambivalent attachment a pattern of attachment in which the infant shows little exploratory behaviour, is greatly upset when separated from the mother, and is not reassured by her return or efforts to comfort him *137*

amenity move postretirement move away from kin to a location that has some desirable feature, such as year-round warm weather *534*

amnion fluid-filled sac in which the fetus floats until just before it is born *66*

amygdala an almond-shaped brain structure that plays a key role in the regulation of defensive emotions like fear and anger *166*

anorexia nervosa an eating disorder characterized by self-starvation *310*

anoxia oxygen deprivation experienced by a fetus during labour and/or delivery *86*

assessment formal and informal methods of gathering information that can be used for programming to improve student learning. There are no grades or marks associated with assessment. *250*

assimilation the process of using a scheme to make sense of an event or experience *40*

assisted human reproduction (AHR) "any activity undertaken for the purpose of facilitating human reproduction" (Health Canada, 2001b) *58*

association areas parts of the brain where sensory, motor, and intellectual functions are linked *237*

assortative mating (homogamy) sociologists' term for the tendency to mate with someone who has traits similar to one's own *396*

atherosclerosis narrowing of the arteries caused by deposits of a fatty substance called plaque *431*

attachment the emotional tie to a parent experienced by an infant, from which the child derives security *132*

attachment theory the view that the ability and need to form an attachment relationship early in life are genetic characteristics of all human beings *131*

attention-deficit hyperactivity disorder (ADHD) a mental disorder that causes children to have difficulty attending to and completing tasks *257*

atypical development development that deviates from the typical developmental pathway in a way that is harmful to the individual *14*

authoritarian parenting style a style of parenting that is low in nurturance and communication, but high in control and maturity demands *200*

authoritative parenting style a style of parenting that is high in nurturance, maturity demands, control, and communication *200*

automaticity the ability to recall information from long-term memory without using short-term memory capacity *245*

avoidant attachment a pattern of attachment in which an infant avoids contact with the parent and shows no preference for the parent over other people *137*

avoidant couples couples who agree to disagree and who minimize conflict by avoiding each other *399*

behaviour genetics the study of the role of heredity in individual differences *46*

behaviourism the view that defines development in terms of behaviour changes caused by environmental influences *6*

bicultural identity personal identification and satisfaction with more than one culture *335*

Big Five, the a set of five major dimensions of personality, including extraversion, agreeableness, conscientiousness, neuroticism, and openness/intellect 282

bilingual education an approach to second-language education in which children receive instruction in two different languages 260

bioecological systems theory Bronfenbrenner's theory that explains development in terms of relationships between individuals and their environments, or interconnected contexts 48

body mass index (BMI) a body composition ratio of weight to height that is an estimate of under- or over-weight 78

brain death absence of vital signs, including brain activity; resuscitation is no longer possible 542

bulimia an eating disorder characterized by binge eating and purging 310

Canada's Food Guide to Healthy Eating guidelines for a balanced and healthy diet based on the four major food groups: grain products, vegetables and fruits, milk products, and meat and alternatives 105

cardiovascular disease (CVD) a set of disease processes in the heart and circulatory system 431

career ladder the milestones associated with a particular occupation 413

caregiver burden a term for the cumulative negative effects of caring for an elderly or disabled person 463

case study an in-depth examination of a single individual 19

cephalocaudal pattern growth that proceeds from the head downward 66

chromosomes strings of genetic material in the nuclei of cells 57

class inclusion the understanding that subordinate classes are included in larger, superordinate classes 243

classical conditioning learning that results from the association of stimuli 33

climacteric the term used to describe the adult period during which reproductive capacity declines or is lost 423

clinical death a period during which vital signs are absent but resuscitation is still possible 541

clique four to six young people who appear to be strongly attached to one another 342

cognitive theories theories that emphasize mental processes in development, such as logic and memory 39

cohort a group of individuals who share the same historical experiences at the same times in their lives 12

colic an infant behaviour pattern involving intense daily bouts of crying, totalling 3 or more hours a day 100

companionate relationships relationships in which grandparents have frequent contact and warm interactions with grandchildren 460

compensatory (kinship) migration a move to a location near family or friends that happens when an elder requires frequent help because of a disability or disease 534

concrete operations a set of mental schemes, including reversibility, addition, subtraction, multiplication, division, and serial ordering, that enable children to understand relations among objects 242

congenital anomaly an abnormality present at birth 72

conscience the list of "don'ts" in the superego; violation of any of these rules leads to feelings of guilt 269

conservation the understanding that matter can change in appearance without changing in quantity 169

contingent responsiveness being sensitive to the child's verbal and nonverbal cues and responding appropriately 137

control group a group in an experiment that receives either no special treatment or a neutral treatment 21

conventional morality in Kohlberg's theory, the level of moral reasoning in which judgments are based on rules or norms of a group to which the person belongs 349

corpus callosum the membrane that connects the right and left hemispheres of the cerebral cortex 162

correlation a relationship between two variables that can be expressed as a number ranging from −1.00 to +1.00 20

criminality antisocial behaviour that includes law-breaking 353

critical period a specific period in development when an organism is especially sensitive to the presence (or absence) of some particular kind of experience 13

cross-gender behaviour behaviour that is atypical for one's own sex but typical for the opposite sex 226

cross-linking the formation of undesirable bonds between proteins or fats 493

cross-modal perception transfer of information from one sense to another, as when an infant can recognize by feel a toy he has seen but never felt before 109

cross-sectional design a research design in which groups of different ages are compared *16*

crowd a combination of cliques, which includes both males and females *343*

crystallized intelligence knowledge and judgment acquired through education and experience *383*

deductive logic a type of reasoning based on hypothetical premises that requires predicting a specific outcome from a general principle *242*

defence mechanisms strategies for reducing anxiety, such as repression, denial, or projection, proposed by Freud *28*

deferred imitation imitation by an infant of an action seen earlier *111*

dementia a neurological disorder involving problems with memory and thinking that affect an individual's emotional, social, and physical functioning *497*

deoxyribonucleic acid (DNA) chemical material that makes up chromosomes and genes *58*

dependent variable the characteristic or behaviour that is expected to be affected by the independent variable *21*

depth perception ability to judge the relative distances of objects *108*

developmental psychology the scientific study of age-related changes in our bodies, behaviour, thinking, emotions, social relationships, and personalities *2*

dialectical thought a form of thought involving recognition and acceptance of paradox and uncertainty *381*

difficult temperament These active babies have uneven routines and adapt reluctantly to new experiences. They react with intensity and often negatively, and once upset, they are difficult to soothe. *141*

Disability-Adjusted Life Years (DALY) a measure of the gap between a population's ideal and actual levels of health. It is derived from the number of life-years lost to premature death, due to illness or injury, and the number of years living with a disability. It assumes a potential life limit of 82.5 years for women and 80 for men. *362*

discipline training, whether physical, mental, or moral, that develops self-control, moral character, and proper conduct *202*

disengagement theory the theory that it is normal and healthy for older adults to scale down their social lives and to separate themselves from others to a certain degree *515*

dishabituation learning to respond to a familiar stimulus as if it were new *113*

disorganized/disoriented attachment a pattern of attachment in which an infant seems confused or apprehensive and shows contradictory behaviour, such as moving toward the mother while looking away from her *137*

dominant-recessive pattern pattern of inheritance in which a single dominant gene influences a person's phenotype but two recessive genes are necessary to produce an associated trait *60*

dyslexia problems in reading or the inability to read *257*

easy temperament These babies have predictable routines and they approach and adjust quickly and easily to new experiences. They react mildly to discomfort and are generally cheerful. *141*

ego according to Freud, the thinking element of personality *27*

ego ideal the list of "do's" in the superego; failure to live up to any of these leads to feelings of shame *269*

ego integrity the feeling that one's life has been worthwhile *513*

ego integrity versus despair stage the last of Erikson's psychosocial stages, in which older adults must achieve a sense of satisfaction with their lives *513*

egocentrism the young child's belief that everyone sees and experiences the world the way she does *168*

embryonic stage the second stage of prenatal development, from week 2 through week 8, during which the embryo's organ systems form *66*

endocrine glands glands that secrete hormones governing growth and other aspects of physical development *296*

English-as-a-second-language (ESL) program an approach to second-language education in which children attend English classes for part of the day and receive most of their academic instruction in English *260*

episodic memories recollections of personal events *442*

equilibration the process of balancing assimilation and accommodation to create schemes that fit the environment *40*

ethnic identity a sense of belonging to an ethnic group *335*

ethnography a detailed description of a single culture or context *22*

ethology a perspective on development that emphasizes genetically determined survival behaviours presumed to have evolved through natural selection *45*

evaluation the process of assigning a grade or mark to a student's performance, representing the student's highest, most consistent level of achievement over time *250*

evolutionary developmental psychology the view that genetically inherited cognitive and social characteristics that promote survival and adaptation appear at different times across the lifespan *47*

evolutionary psychology the view that genetically inherited cognitive and social characteristics have evolved through natural selection *46*

exceptional child a child who has special learning needs; the term refers to students with disabilities as well as gifted students *255*

executive processes information-processing skills that involve devising and carrying out strategies for remembering and solving problems *246*

experiment a study that tests a causal hypothesis *21*

experimental group the group in an experiment that receives the treatment the experimenter thinks will produce a particular effect *21*

expressive language the ability to produce spoken language *120*

expressive vocabulary the words whose meaning is used correctly when speaking *181*

extended family a social network of grandparents, aunts, uncles, cousins, and so on *210*

extinction the gradual elimination of a behaviour through repeated nonreinforcement *35*

false belief principle an understanding that enables a child to look at a situation from another person's point of view and determine what kind of information will cause that person to have a false belief *170*

fetal stage the third stage of prenatal development, from week 9 to birth, during which growth and organ refinement take place *68*

flexible goal adjustment a behaviour pattern in which middle-aged adults adjust goals in order to enhance the likelihood of success *472*

fluid intelligence the aspect of intelligence that reflects fundamental biological processes and does not depend on specific experiences *383*

fluid reasoning ability to manipulate and use information in a reasoning process *186*

foreclosure in Marcia's theory, the identity status of a person who has made a commitment without having gone through a crisis; the person has simply accepted a parentally or culturally defined commitment *330*

formal operational stage the fourth of Piaget's stages, during which adolescents learn to reason logically about abstract concepts *315*

frail elderly older adults whose physical and/or mental impairments are so extensive that they cannot care for themselves *482*

free radicals molecules or atoms that possess an unpaired electron *493*

functional magnetic resonance imaging (fMRI) is a form of *Magnetic Resonance Imaging* (MRI) that records what regions of the brain are active during specific mental activities *166*

functional status a measure of an individual's ability to perform certain roles and tasks, particularly self-help tasks and other chores of daily living (Havens & Finlayson, 1999) *484*

gametes cells that unite at conception (ova in females; sperm in males) *57*

gender concept understanding of gender, gender-related behaviour, and sex roles *221*

gender constancy the understanding that gender is a component of the self that is not altered by external appearance *222*

gender constancy theory Kohlberg's assertion that children must understand that gender is a permanent characteristic before they can adopt appropriate sex roles *222*

gender identity the ability to correctly label oneself and others as male or female *223*

gender schema theory an information-processing approach to gender concept development that asserts that people use a schema for each gender to process information about themselves and others *222*

gender stability the understanding that gender is a stable, life-long characteristic *223*

generativity a sense that one is making a valuable contribution to society by bringing up children or mentoring younger people in some way *450*

generativity versus stagnation stage the seventh of Erikson's stages, in which middle-aged adults find meaning in contributing to the development of younger individuals *450*

genes pieces of genetic material that control or influence traits *58*

genital stage in Freud's theory, the period during which people reach psychosexual maturity *328*

genotype the unique genetic blueprint of each individual *60*

geriatric dysthymia chronic depressed mood in older adults *501*

germinal stage the first stage of prenatal development, beginning at conception and ending at implantation (approximately 2 weeks) *66*

gerontology the scientific study of aging *481*

glial cells specialized cells in the brain that support neurons *68*

gonadotrophic hormones hormones responsible for the development of the sex organs *297*

gonads sex glands (ovaries in females; testes in males) *68*

goodness of fit the degree to which an infant's temperament is adaptable to his or her environment, and vice versa *144*

grammatical words words that pertain to the rules of language and proper sentence construction, such as articles, prepositions, and auxiliaries *118*

grieving the emotional response to a death *563*

habituate to decrease one's attention because a stimulus has become familiar *108*

handedness a strong preference for using one hand or the other that develops between 3 and 5 years of age *163*

Hayflick limit the theoretical proposal that each species is subject to a genetically programmed time limit after which cells no longer have any capacity to replicate themselves accurately *486*

Health-Adjusted Life Expectancy (HALE) an estimate of life expectancy at birth. It is the number of years that a newborn can expect to live in full health given current rates of morbidity and mortality *362*

hippocampus a seahorse-shaped brain structure that is essential for the formation of memories *163*

holism the view that the whole is greater than the sum of its parts *48*

holophrases "phrases" or "sentences" consisting of words and gestures, used by infants in the second year of life *120*

hospice care a holistic approach to care for the terminally ill that emphasizes individual and family control of the process of dying *542*

hostile aggression aggression used to hurt another person physically or emotionally *214*

hostile/detached couples couples who fight regularly and rarely look at each other; they also lack affection and support *400*

hostile/engaged couples partners who have frequent arguments that lack the balancing effect of humour and affection *399*

hypothetico-deductive reasoning the ability to derive conclusions from hypothetical premises *315*

id in Freud's theory, the part of the personality that comprises a person's basic sexual and aggressive impulses; it contains the libido and motivates a person to seek pleasure and avoid pain *27*

identity achievement in Marcia's theory, the identity status achieved by a person who has been through a crisis and reached a commitment to ideological or occupational goals *330*

identity crisis Erikson's term for the psychological state of emotional turmoil that arises when an adolescent's sense of self becomes "unglued" so that a new, more mature sense of self can be achieved *329*

identity diffusion in Marcia's theory, the identity status of a person who is not in the midst of a crisis and who has made no commitment *330*

identity versus role confusion in Erikson's theory, the stage during which adolescents attain a sense of who they are *329*

independent variable the presumed causal element in an experiment *21*

Individual Education Plan (IEP) a written document containing learning and behavioural objectives for the exceptional student, a description of how the objectives will be achieved, and how the objectives will be evaluated *255*

inductive discipline a discipline strategy in which parents explain to children why a punished behaviour is wrong *202*

inductive logic a type of reasoning in which general principles are inferred from specific experiences *242*

industry versus inferiority stage the fourth of Erikson's psychosocial stages, during which children develop a sense of their own competence through mastery of culturally defined learning tasks *267*

infantile amnesia the inability of adults and older children to remember more than a few events that took place before 3 years of age *176*

inflections grammatical markers attached to words to indicate tense, gender, number, and the like, such as the use of the ending *-ed* to mark the past tense of a verb in English *176*

information-processing theory theoretical perspectives that use the computer as a model to explain how the mind manages information *41*

institutional migration a move to an institution such as a nursing home that is necessitated by a disability *534*

instrumental activities of daily living (IADLs) more complex daily living tasks such as doing housework, cooking, and managing money *484*

instrumental aggression aggression used to gain an advantage or control of objects, territory, or rights *214* intelligence quotient (IQ) the ratio of mental age to chronological age; also, a general term for any kind of score derived from an intelligence test *185*

interactionist model the theory that development results from complex reciprocal interactions between multiple personal and environment factors *9*

intersensory integration coordination of information from two or more senses, such as knowing which mouth movements go with which sounds *108*

intimacy the capacity to engage in a supportive, affectionate relationship without losing one's own sense of self *391*

intimacy versus isolation Erikson's early adulthood stage, in which an individual must find a life partner or supportive friends in order to avoid social isolation *391*

intimate partner abuse physical acts or other behaviour intended to intimidate or harm an intimate partner *374*

invented spelling a strategy young children with good phonological awareness skills use when they write *180*

involved relationships relationships in which grandparents are directly involved in the everyday care of grandchildren or have close emotional ties with them *460*

joint attention when two people are focusing their attention on an object and each is aware that the other is attending to that same object *146*

kin-keeper a family role, usually occupied by a woman, which includes responsibility for maintaining family and friendship relationships *409*

language acquisition device (LAD) an innate language processor, theorized by Chomsky, that contains the basic grammatical structure of all human language *115*

latency stage the fourth of Freud's psychosexual stages, during which 6- to 12-year-olds' libido is dormant while they establish relationships with same-sex peers *266*

lateralization the process through which brain functions are divided between the two hemispheres of the cerebral cortex *162*

learning disability a disorder in which a child has difficulty mastering a specific academic skill, even though she possesses normal intelligence and no physical or sensory handicaps *254*

learning theories theories that assert that development results from an accumulation of experiences *33*

lexical words words with a high level of meaning, such as nouns, verbs, adjectives, and adverbs *118*

libido in Freud's theory, an instinctual drive for physical pleasure present at birth and forming the motivating force behind virtually all human behaviour *27*

life structure a key concept in Levinson's theory: the underlying pattern or design of a person's life at a given time, which includes roles, relationships, and behaviour patterns *392*

lifespan perspective the current view of developmentalists that changes happen throughout the entire human lifespan and that changes must be interpreted in light of the culture and context in which they occur; thus, interdisciplinary research is critical to understanding human development *14*

limbic system the part of the brain that regulates emotional responses *364*

locus of control a set of beliefs about the causes of events *336*

longitudinal design a research design in which people in a single group are studied at different times in their lives *16*

low birth weight (LBW) newborn weight below 2500 grams *88*

macronutrients large amounts of carbohydrates, fats, and proteins that are needed for energy and for body- and brain-building elements *103*

maturation the gradual unfolding of genetically programmed sequential patterns of changes *6*

maximum oxygen uptake (VO$_2$ max) a measure of the body's ability to take in and transport oxygen to various body organs *367*

memory strategies learned methods for remembering information *246*

menarche the beginning of menstrual cycles *298*

menopause the cessation of monthly menstrual cycles in middle-aged women *424*

metacognition knowledge about how the mind thinks and the ability to control and reflect on one's own thought processes *174*

metamemory knowledge about how memory works and the ability to control and reflect on one's own memory function *174*

micronutrients essential vitamins and minerals that are needed in small amounts to regulate physical and mental processes *104*

modified program changes in the curriculum so that the modified outcomes differ from those of the standard curriculum *255*

moral realism stage the first of Piaget's stages of moral development, in which children believe rules are inflexible *270*

moral relativism stage the second of Piaget's stages of moral development, in which children understand that many rules can be changed through social agreement 270

moratorium in Marcia's theory, the identity status of a person who is in a crisis but who has made no commitment 330

multifactorial inheritance inheritance affected by both genes and the environment 63

multi-infarct dementia a form of dementia caused by one or more strokes 499

mutagens agents that damage cellular DNA 80

myelinization a process in the development of neurons in which sheaths of a substance called myelin gradually cover individual axons and electrically insulate them from one another, which improves the conductivity of the nerve 98

naming explosion a period between 16 and 24 months of age when most children rapidly begin to add new words to their vocabularies 120

nativism the view that human beings possess unique genetic traits that will be manifested in all members of the species, regardless of differences in environments 45

naturalistic observation the process of studying people in their normal environments 19

nature–nurture controversy the debate about the relative contributions of biological process and experiential factors to development 9

neonate baby between birth and 1 month of age 86

neo-Piagetian theory an approach that uses information-processing principles to explain the developmental stages identified by Piaget 43

neurons specialized cells of the nervous system 66

niche-picking the process of selecting experiences on the basis of temperament 142

norms average ages at which developmental milestones are reached 4

obese having an excessive amount of body fat in relation to lean body mass 240

object permanence the understanding that objects continue to exist when they can't be seen 111

objective (categorical) self the toddler's understanding that she or he is defined by various categories such as gender or qualities such as shyness 144

observational learning, or modelling learning that results from seeing a model reinforced or punished for a behaviour 35

operant conditioning learning to repeat or stop behaviours because of their consequences 34

operational efficiency a neo-Piagetian term that refers to the maximum number of schemes that can be processed in working memory at one time 173

organogenesis process of organ development 68

osteoporosis loss of bone mass with age, resulting in more brittle and porous bones 427

overregularization attachment of regular inflections to irregular words, such as the substitution of *goed* for *went* 179

overweight having increased body weight in relation to height, as compared to a standard of desirable weight 240

palliative care a form of care for the terminally ill that focuses on relieving patients' pain, rather than curing their diseases 543

parental investment theory the theory that sex differences in mate preferences and mating behaviour are based on the different amounts of time and effort men and women must invest in child-rearing 394

pathological grief symptoms of depression brought on by death of a loved one 562

pelvic inflammatory disease an infection of the female reproductive tract that may result from a sexually transmitted disease and can lead to infertility 369

perimenopausal phase the stage of menopause during which estrogen and progesterone levels are erratic, menstrual cycles may be very irregular, and women begin to experience symptoms such as hot flashes 425

permissive parenting style a style of parenting that is high in nurturance and low in maturity demands, control, and communication 200

person perception the ability to classify others according to categories such as age and gender 195

personal fable a hypothetical life story created for himself or herself by an adolescent 545

personality a pattern of responding to people and objects in the environment 140

personality disorder an inflexible pattern of behaviour that leads to difficulty in educational, occupational, and social functioning 379

phenotype an individual's particular set of observed characteristics 60

phonological awareness children's understanding of the sound patterns of the language they are acquiring 180

pituitary gland gland that triggers other glands to release hormones 296

placenta specialized organ that allows substances to be transferred from mother to embryo and from embryo to mother, without their blood mixing 66 plasticity ability of the brain to reorganize neural pathways and connections 97

polygenic inheritance pattern of inheritance in which many genes influence a trait 62

postconventional morality in Kohlberg's theory, the level of moral reasoning in which judgments are based on an integration of individual rights and the needs of society 350

postmenopausal phase the last stage of menopause; a woman is postmenopausal when she has had no menstrual periods for a year or more 425

post-secondary education any formal educational experience that follows high school 384

preconventional morality in Kohlberg's theory, the level of moral reasoning in which judgments are based on authorities outside the self 348

premenopausal phase the stage of menopause during which estrogen levels fall somewhat, menstrual periods are less regular, and anovulatory cycles begin to occur 424

preoperational stage Piaget's second stage of cognitive development, during which children become proficient in the use of symbols in thinking and communicating but still have difficulty thinking logically 167

presbycusis normal loss of hearing with aging, especially of high-frequency tones 429

presbyopia normal loss of visual acuity with aging, especially the ability to focus the eyes on near objects 429

primary aging age-related physical changes that have a biological basis and are universally shared and inevitable 362

primitive reflexes reflexes controlled by primitive parts of the brain; these reflexes disappear by about 6 months of age 98

processing efficiency the ability to make efficient use of short-term memory capacity 245

program accommodation the adjustment of teaching methods in order to help the child who has special needs achieve the outcomes of the standard curriculum 255

programmed senescence theory the view that age-related declines are the result of species-specific genes for aging 493

prosocial behaviour behaviour intended to help another person 216

proximodistal pattern growth that proceeds from the middle of the body outward 66

psychoanalytic theories theories proposing that developmental change happens because of the influence of internal drives and emotions on behaviour 27

psychological self an understanding of one's stable, internal traits 283

psychosexual stages Freud's five stages of personality development through which children move in a fixed sequence determined by maturation; the libido is centred in a different body part in each stage 28

psychosocial stages Erikson's eight stages, or crises, of personality development in which inner instincts interact with outer cultural and social demands to shape personality 29

punishment any immediate consequence that follows a behaviour and decreases the likelihood that the behaviour will be repeated 34

Quality-Adjusted Life Years (QALY) a measure of how much benefit is gained, and at what cost, for any particular physical or mental intervention. It provides an estimate of the time a person will live at different levels of health over their remaining years of life 362

reaction range a range between upper and lower boundaries for traits such as intelligence, which is established by one's genes; one's environment determines where, within those limits, one will be 190

reactive attachment disorder a disorder that appears to prevent a child from forming close social relationships 132

receptive language the ability to understand spoken language 118

receptive vocabulary the words that are understood when heard 181

reciprocal determinism a process of human development based upon the interaction of personal, behavioural, and environmental factors 37

reinforcement any immediate consequence that follows a behaviour and increases the likelihood that the behaviour will be repeated 34

relational aggression aggression aimed at damaging another person's self-esteem or peer relationships, such as by ostracism or threats of ostracism, cruel gossiping, or facial expressions of disdain 278

relative right-left orientation the ability to identify right and left from multiple perspectives 238

religious coping the tendency to turn to religious beliefs and institutions for support in times of difficulty 519

reminiscence reflecting on past experience 514

remote relationships relationships in which grandparents do not see their grandchildren often 460

research ethics the guidelines researchers follow to protect the rights of animals used in research and people who participate in studies 22

retaliatory aggression aggression to get back at someone who has hurt you *279*

reticular formation the part of the brain that regulates attention *98*

role conflict any situation in which two or more roles are at least partially incompatible, either because they call for different behaviours or because their separate demands add up to more hours than there are in the day *453*

role-taking the ability to look at a situation from another person's perspective *351*

role strain the strain experienced by an individual whose own qualities or skills do not measure up to the demands of some role *453*

satiety the feeling of fullness that follows a meal *496*

scaffolding a process in which the learning of new cognitive skills is guided by someone who is more skilled *43*

schematic learning organization of experiences into expectancies, called schemas, which enable infants to distinguish between familiar and unfamiliar stimuli *113*

scheme in Piaget's theory, an internal cognitive structure that provides an individual with a procedure to use in a specific circumstance *40*

schizophrenia a serious mental disorder characterized by disturbances of thought such as delusions and hallucinations *379*

secondary aging age-related changes that are due to social and environmental influences, poor health habits, or disease *362*

secular trend the decline in the average age of menarche, along with changes such as an increase in average height for both children and adults, that happened between the mid-19th and mid-20th centuries in Western countries and occurs in developing nations when nutrition and health improve *298*

secure attachment a pattern of attachment in which an infant readily separates from the parent, seeks proximity when stressed, and uses the parent as a safe base for exploration *137*

selective attention the ability to focus cognitive activity on the important elements of a problem or situation *237*

self-care children children who are at home by themselves after school for an hour or more each day *288*

self-efficacy the belief in one's own capacity to cause an intended event to occur or to perform a task *37, 374*

self-esteem a global evaluation of one's own worth *285*

self-fulfilling prophecy when an expectation or belief causes a person to act in a way that is consistent with the expectations *251*

self-regulation children's ability to conform to parental standards of behaviour without direct supervision *274*

semantic memories general knowledge, facts, and word meanings *442*

senescence physical changes and declines associated with aging *493*

sensitive period a span of months or years during which a child may be particularly responsive to specific forms of experience or particularly influenced by their absence *13*

sensorimotor stage Piaget's first stage of development, in which infants use information from their senses and motor actions to learn about the world *109*

separation anxiety expressions of discomfort, such as crying, when separated from an attachment figure *136*

sequential design a research design that combines cross-sectional and longitudinal examinations of development *16*

sex-role identity the gender-related aspects of the psychological self *332*

sex roles behaviour expected for males and females in a given culture *221*

sex-typed behaviour different patterns of behaviour exhibited by boys and girls *224*

sex-typing the manifestation or adoption of culturally defined sex-appropriate behaviour *155*

sexual assault any form of sexual activity with another person without his or her consent *377*

shaping the reinforcement of intermediate steps until an individual learns a complex behaviour *35*

short-term storage space (STSS) neo-Piagetian theorist Robbie Case's term for the working memory *173*

slow-to-warm-up temperament These inactive babies turn away from and adjust slowly to unfamiliar people and new experiences. They display mild signs of negativity and discomfort. *141*

social clock a set of age norms that defines a sequence of life experiences that is considered normal in a given culture and that all individuals in that culture are expected to follow *12*

social-cognitive theory the theoretical perspective that asserts that social and personality development in early childhood are related to improvements in the cognitive domain *195* social death the point at which family members and medical personnel treat the deceased person as a corpse 542

social referencing an infant's use of others' facial expressions as a guide to his or her own emotions 136

social role theory the idea that sex differences in mate preferences and mating behaviour are adaptations to gender roles 395

social skills a set of behaviours that usually lead to being accepted as a play partner or friend by peers 212

social status an individual child's classification as popular, rejected, or neglected 280

sociobiology the study of society using the methods and concepts of biology; when used by developmentalists, an approach that emphasizes genes that aid group survival 46

sociocultural theory Vygotsky's view that complex forms of thinking have their origins in social interactions rather than in an individual's private explorations 43

spatial cognition the ability to infer rules from and make predictions about the movement of objects in space 238

spatial perception the ability to identify and act on relationships between objects in space 238

states of consciousness different states of sleep and wakefulness in infants 99

stranger anxiety expressions of discomfort, such as clinging to the mother, in the presence of strangers 136

subjective self an infant's awareness that she or he is a separate person who endures through time and space and can act on the environment 144

successful aging the term gerontologists use to describe maintaining one's physical health, mental abilities, social competence, and overall satisfaction with one's life as one ages 516

sudden infant death syndrome (SIDS) the sudden and unexpected death of an apparently healthy infant 106

superego Freud's term for the part of personality that is the moral judge 28

synapses connections between neurons 96

synaptic plasticity the redundancy in the nervous system that ensures that it is nearly always possible for a nerve impulse to move from one neuron to another or from a neuron to another type of cell (e.g., a muscle cell) 490

synaptic pruning process by which unused or unnecessary neural pathways and connections are eliminated 97

synchrony a mutual, interlocking pattern of attachment behaviours shared by a parent and child 134

systematic problem-solving the process of finding a solution to a problem by testing single factors 315

systems approach the view that personal factors together with external factors form a dynamic integrated system 48

task goals goals based on a desire for self-improvement 319

telomere string of repetitive DNA at the tip of each chromosome in the body that appears to serve as a kind of timekeeping mechanism 486

temperament inborn predispositions such as activity level that form the foundations of personality 140

tenacious goal pursuit a behaviour pattern in which middle-aged adults remain committed to goals that are difficult, and may be impossible, for them to achieve 472

teratogens substances such as viruses and drugs that can cause birth defects 74

terminal drop hypothesis the hypothesis that mental and physical functioning decline drastically only in the few years immediately preceding death 494

thanatology the scientific study of death and dying 554

theory of mind a set of ideas constructed by a child or adult to explain other people's ideas, beliefs, desires, and behaviour 171

time-out removing the child from the situation and from attention and rewards for a short period of time, typically one minute for every year of the child's age, in order to stop unwanted behaviour 202

tinnitus persistent ringing in the ears 492

true sleep the number of minutes of sleep time excluding all periods of wakefulness, which can be distinguished by electroencephalograph (EEG) activity 258

type A personality pattern a personality type associated with greater risk of coronary heart disease; it includes competitive achievement striving, a sense of time urgency, and, sometimes, hostility or aggressiveness 433

umbilical cord organ that connects the embryo to the placenta 66

uninvolved parenting style a style of parenting that is low in nurturance, maturity demands, control, and communication 201

unique invulnerability the belief that bad things, including death, only happen to others *546*

validating couples couples who express mutual respect even in disagreements and are good listeners *399*

viability ability of the fetus to survive outside the womb *69*

visual acuity the ability to see details at a distance *99*

volatile couples couples who argue a lot, don't listen well, but still have more positive than negative interactions *399*

volunteerism performance of unpaid work for altruistic motives *517*

wellness a measure of holistic optimal health *48*

wisdom a hypothesized cognitive characteristic of older adults that includes accumulated knowledge and the ability to apply that knowledge to practical problems of living *506*

zone of proximal development signifies tasks that are too hard for a child to do alone but that can be managed with guidance *43*

zygote single cell created when sperm and ovum unite *58*

REFERENCES

Abdelrahman, A., Rodriguez, G., Ryan, J., French, J., & Weinbaum, D. (1998). The epidemiology of substance use among middle school students: The impact of school, familial, community and individual risk factors. *Journal of Child & Adolescent Substance Abuse, 8,* 55–75.

Abengozar, C., Bueno, B., & Vega, J. (1999). Intervention on attitudes toward death along the life span. *Educational Gerontology, 25,* 435–447.

Abraham, J.D., & Hansson, R.O. (1995). Successful aging at work: An applied study of selection, optimization, and compensation through impression management. *Journals of Gerontology: Psychological Sciences, 50B,* P94–P103.

Abrams, E.J., Matheson, P.B., Thomas, P.A., Thea, D.M., Krasinski, K., Lambert, G., Shaffer, N., Bamji, M., Hutson, D., Grimm, K., Kaul, A., Bateman, D., Rogers, M., & New York City Perinatal HIV Transmission Collaborative Study Group (1995). Neonatal predictors of infection status and early death among 332 infants at risk of HIV-1 infection monitored prospectively from birth. *Pediatrics, 96,* 451–458.

Abrams, R. (1998). Physician-assisted suicide and euthanasia's impact on the frail elderly: Something to think about. *Journal of Long Term Home Health Care: The Pride Institute Journal, 17,* 19–27.

Accardo, P., Tomazic, T., Fete, T., Heaney, M., Lindsay, R., & Whitman, B. (1997). Maternally reported fetal activity levels and developmental diagnoses. *Clinical Pediatrics, 36,* 279–283.

Adams, C. (1991). Qualitative age differences in memory for text: A life-span developmental perspective. *Psychology and Aging, 6,* 323–336.

Adams, M.J. (1990). *Beginning to read: Thinking and learning about print.* Cambridge, MA: The MIT Press.

Adams, M., & Henry, M. (1997). Myths and realities about words and literacy. *School Psychology Review, 26,* 425–436.

Adelmann, P.K. (1994). Multiple roles and physical health among older adults: Gender and ethnic comparisons. *Research on Aging, 16,* 142–166.

Adesman, A.R. (1996). Fragile X syndrome. In A.J. Capute & P.J. Accardo (Eds.), *Developmental disabilities in infancy and childhood:* Vol. II. *The spectrum of developmental disabilities* (2nd ed., pp. 255–269). Baltimore: Paul H. Brookes.

Adkins, V. (1999). Grandparents as a national asset: A brief note. *Activities, Adaptation, & Aging, 24,* 13–18.

Adlaf, E.M., & Paglia, A. (2003a). *Drug use among Ontario students 1977–2003: OSDUS highlights (CAMH Research Document Series, No. 13).* Toronto: Centre for Addiction and Mental Health. Retrieved July 10, 2004 from http://www.camh.net/pdf/OSDUS03_Drug_Report_highlights.pdf

Adlaf, E.M., & Paglia, A. (2003b). *Drug use among Ontario students 1977–2003: Detailed OSDUS findings (CAMH Research Document Series, No. 13).* Toronto: Centre for Addiction and Mental Health. Retrieved July 10, 2004 from http://www.camh.net/pdf/OSDUS03-drugdetail-final.pdf

Ahadi, S.A., & Rothbart, M.K. (1994). Temperament, development, and the Big Five. In C.F. Halverson, Jr., G.A. Kohnstamm, & R.P. Martin (Eds.), *The developing structure of temperament and personality from infancy to adulthood* (pp. 189–207). Hillsdale, NJ: Erlbaum.

Ahmad, G., & Najam, N. (1998). A study of marital adjustment during first transition to parenthood. *Journal of Behavioural Sciences, 9,* 67–86.

Ainsworth, M.D.S. (1989). Attachments beyond infancy. *American Psychologist, 44,* 709–716.

Ainsworth, M.D.S., Blehar, M., Waters, E., & Wall, S. (1978). *Patterns of attachment.* Hillsdale, NJ: Erlbaum.

Ainsworth, M.D.S., & Marvin, R.S. (1995). On the shaping of attachment theory and research: An interview with Mary D.S. Ainsworth (Fall 1994). *Monographs of the Society for Research in Child Development, 60* (244, Nos. 2–3), 3–21.

Akers, J., Jones, R., & Coyl, D. (1998). Adolescent friendship pairs: Similarities in identity status development, behaviors, attitudes, and interests. *Journal of Adolescent Research, 13,* 178–201.

Akiba, D. (1998). Cultural variations in body esteem: How young adults in Iran and the United States view their own appearances. *The Journal of Social Psychology, 138,* 539–540.

Albert, M.S., Jones, K., Savage, C.R., Berkman, L., Seeman, T., Blazer, D., & Rowe, J.W. (1995). Predictors of cognitive change in older persons: MacArthur studies of successful aging. *Psychology and Aging, 10,* 578–589.

Aldous, J. (1996). *Family careers: Rethinking the developmental perspective.* Thousand Oaks, CA: Sage.

Aleixo, P., & Norris, C. (2000). Personality and moral reasoning in young offenders. *Personality & Individual Differences, 28,* 609–623.

Alexander, G., & Hines, M. (1994). Gender labels and play styles: Their relative contribution to children's selection of playmates. *Child Development, 65,* 869–879.

Allan Guttmacher Institute (The) (1996). *Facts in brief: Teen sex and pregnancy.* New York: The Allan Guttmacher Institute.

Allaz, A., Bernstein, M., Rouget, P., Archinard, M., & Morabia, A. (1998). Body weight preoccupation in middle-aged and ageing women: A general population survey. *International Journal of Eating Disorders, 23,* 287–294.

Allen, C., & Kisilevsky, B. (1999). Fetal behavior in diabetic and nondiabetic pregnant women: An exploratory study. *Developmental Psychobiology, 35,* 69–80.

Allen, K.R., & Pickett, R.S. (1987). Forgotten streams in the family life course: Utilization of qualitative retrospective interviews in the analysis of lifelong single women's family careers. *Journal of Marriage and the Family, 49,* 517–526.

Allen, M. (2004). Minority language school systems: A profile of students, schools and communities. *Education Quarterly Review, 9*(4), 9–29.

Allen, T., Poteet, M., & Russell, J. (1998). Attitudes of managers who are more or less career plateaued. *Career Development Quarterly, 47,* 159–172.

Allen, W., Dreves, R., & Ruhe, J. (1999). Reasons why college-educated women change employment. *Journal of Business & Psychology, 14,* 77–93.

The Alpha-Tocopherol Beta Carotene Cancer Prevention Study Group (1994). The effect of vitamin E and beta carotene on the incidence of lung cancer and other cancers in male smokers. *New England Journal of Medicine, 330,* 1029–1035.

Alsaker, F.D., & Olweus, D. (1992). Stability of global self-evaluations in early adolescence: A cohort longitudinal study. *Journal of Research on Adolescence, 2,* 123–145.

Alsop, S. (1973). *Stay of execution.* New York: Lippincott.

Alspaugh, J. (1998). Achievement loss associated with the transition to middle school and high school. *Journal of Educational Research, 92,* 20–25.

Amato, P.R. (1993). Children's adjustment to divorce: Theories, hypotheses, and empirical support. *Journal of Marriage and the Family, 55,* 23–38.

Amato, P., & Rogers, S. (1999). Do attitudes toward divorce affect marital quality? *Journal of Family Issues, 20,* 69–86.

Amato, S. (1998). Human genetics and dysmorphy. In R. Behrman & R. Kliegman (Eds.), *Nelson essentials of pediatrics* (3rd ed., pp. 129–146). Philadelphia: W.B. Saunders.

Ambert, A. (2002). *Divorce: Facts, causes, and consequences.* Ottawa, ON: The Vanier Institute of the Family. Retrieved July 10, 2004 from http://www.vifamily.ca/library/cft/divorce.pdf

Ambert, A. (2003a). *Same-sex couples and same-sex-parent families: Relationships, parenting, and issues of marriage. (Online writings).* Ottawa, ON: Vanier Institute of the Family. Retrieved August 14, 2004 from http://www.vifamily.ca/library/cft/samesex.pdf

Ambert, A. (2003b). *Cohabitation and marriage: Are they equivalent?* Ottawa, ON: The Vanier Institute of the Family. August 14, 2004 from http://www.arts.yorku.ca/soci/ambert/writings/cohabitation.html

Amenedo, E., & Diaz, F. (1998). Aging-related changes in processing of non-target and target stimuli during an auditory oddball task. *Biological Psychology, 48,* 235–267.

Amenedo, E., & Diaz, F. (1999). Aging-related changes in the processing of attended and unattended standard stimuli. *Neuroreport: For Rapid Communication of Neuroscience Research, 10,* 2383–2388.

American Association of Family Physicians. (1998). *Epilepsy and pregnancy: What you should know* [Online patient brochure]. Retrieved March 6, 2001 from http://www.aafp.org/afp/ 971015ap/971015c.html

American Psychiatric Association. (2000). *Diagnostic and statistical manual of mental disorders* (4th ed., text revision). Washington, DC: Author.

Ames, E.W. (1997). *The development of Romanian orphanage children adopted to Canada: Final report.* Ottawa, ON: National Welfare Grants Program, Human Resources Development Canada.

Anan, R., & Barnett, D. (1999). Perceived social support mediates between prior attachment and subsequent adjustment: A study of urban African American children. *Developmental Psychology, 35,* 1210–1222.

Anderman, E. (1998). The middle school experience: Effects on the math and science achievement of adolescents with LD. *Journal of Learning Disabilities, 31,* 128–138.

Anderman, E., Maehr, M., & Midgley, C. (1999). Declining motivation after the transition to middle school: Schools can make a difference. *Journal of Research & Development in Education, 32,* 131–147.

Anderman, E., & Midgley, C. (1997). Changes in achievement goal orientations, perceived academic competence, and grades across the transition to middle-level schools. *Contemporary Educational Psychology, 22,* 269–298.

Anderman, L. (1999). Classroom goal orientation, school belonging and social goals as predictors of students' positive and negative affect following the transition to middle school. *Journal of Research & Development in Education, 32,* 89–103.

Anderman, L., & Anderman, E. (1999). Social predictors of changes in students' achievement goal orientations. *Contemporary Educational Psychology, 24,* 21–37.

Andersen, R.E. (2000). The spread of the childhood obesity epidemic. *Canadian Medical Association Journal, 163*(11), 1461–1462.

Anderson, C.A. (2004). An update on the effects of violent video games. *Journal of Adolescence, 27*(1), 113–122.

Anderson, C.A., & Bushman, B.J. (2001). Effects of violent video games on aggressive behavior, aggressive cognition, aggressive affect, physiological arousal, and prosocial behavior: A meta-analytic review of the scientific literature. *Psychological Science, 12*(5), 353–359.

Anderson, C.A., Carnagey, N.L., Flanagan, M., Benjamin, A.J., Eubanks, J., & Valentine, J.C. (in press). Violent video games: Specific effects of violent content on aggressive thoughts and behavior. In M. Zanna (Ed.), *Advances in experimental social psychology, Vol. 36.* New York: Elsevier.

Anderson, C.A., & Dill, K. (2000). Video games and aggressive thoughts, feelings, and behavior in the laboratory and in life. *Journal of Personality and Social Psychology, 78,* 772–790.

Anderson, K.M., Castelli, W.P., & Levy, D. (1987). Cholesterol and mortality: 30 years of follow-up from the Framingham study. *Journal of the American Medical Association, 257,* 2176–2180.

Anderson, R. (1998). Examining language loss in bilingual children. *Electronic Multicultural Journal of Communication Disorders, 1.*

Andersson, B. (1989). Effects of public day-care: A longitudinal study. *Child Development, 60,* 857–886.

Andersson, B. (1992). Effects of day-care on cognitive and socioemotional competence of thirteen-year-old Swedish schoolchildren. *Child Development, 63,* 20–36.

Andersson, H., & Sommerfelt, K. (1999). Infant temperamental factors of problem behavior and IQ at age 5 years: Interactional effects of biological and social risk factors. *Child Study Journal, 29,* 207–226.

Andersson, N., Sonnander, K., & Sommerfelt, K. (1998). Gender and its contribution to the prediction of cognitive abilities at 5 years. *Scandinavian Journal of Psychology, 39,* 257–274.

Andrews, M., Dowling, W., Bartlett, J., & Halpern, A. (1998). Identification of speeded and slowed familiar melodies by younger, middle-aged, and older musicians and nonmusicians. *Psychology & Aging, 13,* 462–471.

Angier, N. (1992, June 9). Clue to longevity found at chromosome tip. *New York Times,* pp. B5, B9.

Anglin, J.M. (1993). Vocabulary development: A morphological analysis. *Monographs of the Society for Research in Child Development, 58* (Serial No. 238).

Anglin, J.M. (1995, March). *Word learning and the growth of potentially knowable vocabulary.* Paper presented at the biennial meetings of the Society for Research in Child Development, Indianapolis, IN.

Anisfeld, M. (1991). Neonatal imitation. *Developmental Review, 11,* 60–97.

Antonucci, T.C. (1990). Social supports and social relationships. In R.H. Binstock & L.K. George (Eds.), *Handbook of aging and the social sciences* (3rd ed., pp. 205–226). San Diego, CA: Academic Press.

Antonucci, T.C. (1994). A life-span view of women's social relations. In B.F. Turner & L.E. Troll (Eds.), *Women growing older: Psychological perspectives* (pp. 239–269). Thousand Oaks, CA: Sage.

Antrop, I., Roeyers, H., Van Oost, P., & Buysse, A. (2000). Stimulation seeking and hyperactivity in children with ADHD. *Journal of Child Psychology, Psychiatry & Allied Disciplines, 41,* 225–231.

Apgar, V.A. (1953). A proposal for a new method of evaluation of the newborn infant. *Current Research in Anesthesia and Analgesia, 32,* 260–267.

Aquilino, W.S., & Supple, K.R. (1991). Parent-child relations and parent's satisfaction with living arrangements when adult children live at home. *Journal of Marriage and the Family, 53,* 13–27.

Aranha, M. (1997). Creativity in students and its relation to intelligence and peer perception. *Revista Interamericana de Psicologia, 31,* 309–313.

Arbuckle, N.W., & De Vries, B. (1995). The long-term effects of later life spousal and parental bereavement on personal functioning. *The Gerontologist, 35,* 637–647.

Arenberg, D. (1983). Memory and learning do decline late in life. In J.E. Birren, J.M.A. Munnichs, H. Thomae, & M. Marios (Eds.), *Aging: A challenge to science and society: Vol. 3. Behavioral sciences and conclusions* (pp. 312–322). New York: Oxford University Press.

Arlin, P.K. (1975). Cognitive development in adulthood: A fifth stage? *Developmental Psychology, 11,* 602–606.

Arlin, P.K. (1989). Problem solving and problem finding in young artists and young scientists. In M.L. Commons, J.D. Sinnott, F.A. Richards, & C. Armon (Eds.), *Adult Development: Vol. 1. Comparisons and applications of developmental models* (pp. 197–216). New York: Praeger.

Arlin, P.K. (1990). Wisdom: The art of problem finding. In R.J. Sternberg (Ed.), *Wisdom. Its nature, origins, and development* (pp. 230–243). New York: Cambridge University Press.

Arnett, J. (1990). Contraceptive use, sensation seeking, and adolescent egocentrism. *Journal of Youth and Adolescence, 19,* 171–180.

Arnett, J. (1998). Risk behavior and family role transitions during the twenties. *Journal of Youth & Adolescence, 27,* 301–320.

Arnold, D.H., Lonigan, C.J., Whitehurst, G.J., & Epstein, J.N. (1994). Accelerating language development through picture book reading: Replication and extention to a videotape training format. *Journal of Educational Psychology, 86(2),* 235–243.

Aronen, E.T., Paavonen, E., Fjäällberg, J., Soininen, M., & Törrönen, J. (2000). Sleep and psychiatric symptoms in school-age children. *Journal of the American Academy of Child & Adolescent Psychiatry, 39(4),* 502–508.

Arrindell, W., & Luteijn, F. (2000). Similarity between intimate partners for personality traits as related to individual levels of satisfaction with life. *Personality & Individual Differences, 28,* 629–637.

Asendorpf, J.B., Warkentin, V., & Baudonnière, P. (1996). Self-awareness and other-awareness. II: Mirror self-recognition, social contingency awareness, and synchronic imitation. *Developmental Psychology, 32,* 313–321.

Ashton, J., & Donnan, S. (1981). Suicide by burning as an epidemic phenomenon: An analysis of 82 deaths and inquests in England and Wales in 1978–1979. *Psychological Medicine, 11,* 735–739.

Astington, J.W., & Gopnik, A. (1991). Theoretical explanations of children's understanding of the mind. In G.E. Butterworth, P.L. Harris, A.M. Leslie, & H.M. Wellman (Eds.), *Perspectives on the child's theory of mind* (pp. 7–31). New York: Oxford University Press.

Astington, J., & Jenkins, J. (1999). A longitudinal study of the relation between language and theory-of-mind development. *Developmental Psychology, 35,* 1311–1320.

Astington, J.W., & Jenkins, J.M. (1995, March). *Language and theory of mind: A theoretical review and a longitudinal study.* Paper presented at the biennial meetings of the Society for Research in Child Development, Indianapolis, IN.

Astor, R. (1994). Children's moral reasoning about family and peer violence: The role of provocation and retribution. *Child Development, 65,* 1054–1067.

Atkinson, D., Kim, A., Ruelas, S., & Lin, A. (1999). Ethnicity and attitudes toward facilitated reminiscence. *Journal of Mental Health Counseling, 21,* 66–81.

Attie, I., Brooks-Gunn, J., & Petersen, A. (1990). A developmental perspective on eating disorders and eating problems. In M. Lewis & S.M. Miller (Eds.), *Handbook of developmental psychopathology* (pp. 409–420). New York: Plenum.

Atwood, S. (2004, June). Education Arcade: MIT researchers are creating academically driven computer games that rival commercial products and make learning fun. *Technology Review.* Cambridge, MA: MIT Retrieved July 1, 2004 from http://www.technologyreview.com/articles/atwood0604.asp

Auerback, S. (1998). *Dr. Toy's smart play: How to raise a child with a high PQ.* New York, NY: St. Martin's Press.

Avison, W.R. (1997). *National Forum on Health: Summary of the health consequences of unemployment.* Ottawa, ON: Health Canada. Retrieved December 21, 2001 from http://www.nfh.hc-sc.gc.ca/publicat/execsumm/avison.htm

Axelman, K., Basun, H., & Lannfelt, L. (1998). Wide range of disease onset in a family with Alzheimer disease and a His163Tyr mutation in the presenilin-l gene. *Archives of Neurology, 55,* 698–702.

Bagga, A., & Kulkarni, S. (2000). Age at menarche and secular trend in Maharashtrian (Indian) girls. *Acta Biologica Szegediensis, 44(1–4),* 53–57.

Bahrick, L., & Lickliter, R. (2000). Intersensory redundancy guides attentional selectivity and perceptual learning in infancy. *Developmental Psychology, 36,* 190–201.

Bailey, J., Brobow, D., Wolfe, M., & Mikach, S. (1995). Sexual orientation of adult sons of gay fathers. *Developmental Psychology, 31,* 124–129.

Bailey, J.M., & Pillard, R.C. (1991). A genetic study of male sexual orientation. *Archives of General Psychiatry, 48,* 1089–1096.

Bailey, J., Pillard, R., Dawood, K., Miller, M., Farrer, L., Trivedi, S., & Murphy, R. (1999). A family history study of male sexual orientation using three independent samples. *Behavior Genetics, 29,* 7986.

Bailey, J.M., Pillard, R.C., Neale, M.C., & Agyei, Y. (1993). Heritable factors influence sexual orientation in women. *Archives of General Psychiatry, 50,* 217–223.

Baillargeon, R. (1987). Object permanence in very young infants. *Developmental Psychology, 23,* 655–664.

Baillargeon, R. (1994). How do infants learn about the physical world? *Current Directions in Psychological Science, 3,* 133–140.

Baillargeon, R., & DeVos, J. (1991). Object permanence in young infants: Further evidence. *Child Development, 62,* 1227–1246.

Baillargeon, R., Spelke, E.S., & Wasserman, S. (1985). Object permanence in five-month-old infants. *Cognition, 20,* 191–208.

Baillargeon, R., Tremblay, R., & Willms, J.D. (2002). Physical aggression among toddlers. In J.D. Willms (Ed.), *Vulnerable children* (pp. 71–102). Edmonton, AB: The University of Alberta Press.

Bailley, S., Kral, M., & Dunham, K. (1999). Survivors of suicide do grieve differently: Empirical support for a common sense proposition. *Suicide and Life-Threatening Behavior, 29,* 256–271.

Baird, P.A., Sadovnick, A.D., & Yee, I.M.L. (1991). Maternal age and birth defects: A population study. *Lancet, 337,* 527–530.

Baker, M. (1996). The future of family life. In M. Baker (Ed.), *Families: Changing Trends in Canada* (pp. 1–34). Toronto: McGraw-Hill Ryerson Limited.

Bal, D., & Foerster, S.B. (1991). Changing the American diet. *Cancer, 67,* 2671–2680.

Balaban, M.T. (1995). Affective influences on startle in five-month-old infants: Reactions to facial expressions of emotion. *Child Development, 66,* 28–36.

Baldwin, D.A. (1995, March). *Understanding relations between constraints and a socio-pragmatic account of meaning acquisition.* Paper presented at the biennial meetings of the Society for Research in Child Development, Indianapolis, IN.

Ball, E. (1997). Phonological awareness: Implications for whole language and emergent literacy programs. *Topics in Language Disorders, 17,* 14–26.

Baltes, P.B., & Baltes, M.M. (1990). Psychological perspectives on successful aging: The model of selective optimization with compensation. In P.B. Baltes & M.M. Baltes (Eds.), *Successful aging* (pp. 1–34). Cambridge, England: Cambridge University Press.

Baltes, P.B., Dittmann-Kohli, F., & Dixon, R.A. (1984). New perspectives on the development of intelligence in adulthood: Toward a dual-process conception and a model of selective optimization with compensation. In P.B. Baltes & O.G. Brim, Jr. (Eds.), *Life-span development and behavior* (pp. 34–77). New York: Academic Press.

Baltes, P.B., Dittmann-Kohli, F., & Dixon, R.A. (1986). Multidisciplinary propositions on the development of intelligence during adulthood and old age. In A.B. Sørensen, F.E. Weinert, & L.R. Sherrod (Eds.), *Human development and the life course: Multidisciplinary perspectives* (pp. 467–508). Hillsdale, NJ: Erlbaum.

Baltes, P.B., & Kliegl, R. (1992). Further testing of limits of cognitive plasticity: Negative age differences in a mnemonic skill are robust. *Developmental Psychology, 28,* 121–125.

Baltes, P.B., Reese, H.W., & Lipsitt, L.P. (1980). Life-span developmental psychology. *Annual Review of Psychology, 31,* 65–10.

Baltes, P.B., Reese, H.W., & Nesselroade, J.R. (1977). *Life-span developmental psychology: Introduction to research methods.* Monterey, CA: Books/Cole.

Baltes, P.B., & Smith, J. (1990). Toward a psychology of wisdom and its ontogenesis. In R.J. Sternberg (Ed.), *Wisdom: Its nature, origins, and development* (pp. 87–120). Cambridge, England: Cambridge University Press.

Baltes, P.B., Smith, J., & Staudinger, U.M. (1992). Wisdom and successful aging. In T.B. Sonderegger (Ed.), *Nebraska Symposium on Motivation, 1991* (pp. 123–168). Lincoln: University of Nebraska Press.

Baltes, P., & Staudinger, U. (2000). Wisdom: A metaheuristic (pragmatic) to orchestrate mind and virtue toward excellence. *American Psychologist, 55,* 122–136.

Baltes, P.B., Staudinger, U.M., Maercker, A., & Smith, J. (1995). People nominated as wise: A comparative study of wisdom-related knowledge. *Psychology and Aging, 10,* 155–166.

Bambang, S., Spencer, N., Logan, S., & Gill, L. (2000). Cause-specific perinatal death rates, birth weight and deprivation in the West Midlands, 1991–1993. *Child: Care, Health & Development, 26,* 73–82.

Bamford, F.N., Bannister, R.P., Benjamin, C.M., Hillier, V.F., Ward, B.S., & Moore, W.M.O. (1990). Sleep in the first year of life. *Developmental Medicine and Child Neurology, 32,* 718–724.

Bandura, A. (1977a). *Social learning theory.* Englewood Cliffs, NJ: Prentice-Hall.

Bandura, A. (1977b). Self-efficacy: Toward a unifying theory of behavioral change. *Psychological Review, 84,* 91–125.

Bandura, A. (1982a). The psychology of chance encounters and life paths. *American Psychologist, 37,* 747–755.

Bandura, A. (1982b). Self-efficacy mechanism in human agency. *American Psychologist, 37,* 122–147.

Bandura, A. (1986). *Social foundations of thought and action: A social cognitive theory.* Englewood Cliffs, NJ: Prentice-Hall.

Bandura, A. (1989). Social cognitive theory. *Annals of Child Development, 6,* 1–60.

Bandura, A. (1991). Self-regulation of motivation through anticipatory and self-regulatory mechanisms. In R.A. Dienstbier (Ed.), *Perspectives on motivation: Nebraska symposium on motivation* (Vol. 38, pp. 69–164). Lincoln: University of Nebraska Press.

Bandura, A. (1997a). *Self-efficacy: The exercise of control.* New York: W.H. Freeman.

Bandura, A. (1997b). Self-efficacy. *Harvard Mental Health Letter, 13*(9), 4–6.

Bandura, A. (2001). Social cognitive theory: An agentic perspective. *Annual Review of Psychology, 52,* 1–26.

Bandura, A., Ross, D., & Ross, S.A. (1961). Transmission of aggression through imitation of aggressive models. *Journal of Abnormal and Social Psychology, 63,* 575–582.

Bandura, A., Ross, D., & Ross, S.A. (1963). Imitation of film-mediated aggressive models. *Journal of Abnormal and Social Psychology, 66,* 3–11.

Bandura, A. & Schunk, D.H. (1981). Cultivating competence, self-efficacy, and intrinsic interest through proximal self-motivation. *Journal of Personality and Social Psychology, 41,* 586–598.

Barenboim, C. (1981). The development of person perception in childhood and adolescence: From behavioral comparisons to psychological constructs to psychological comparisons. *Child Development, 52,* 129–144.

Barker, J., Morrow, J., & Mitteness, L. (1998). Gender, informal social support networks, and elderly urban African Americans. *Journal of Aging Studies, 12,* 199–222.

Barkley, R. (1990). *Attention-deficit hyperactivity disorder.* New York: Guilford Press.

Barlow, J., & Lewandowski, L. (2000, August). *Ten-year longitudinal study of preterm infants: Outcomes and predictors.* Paper presented at the annual meeting of the American Psychological Association, Washington, DC.

Barnard, K.E., Hammond, M.A., Booth, C.L., Bee, H.L., Mitchell, S.K., & Spieker, S.J. (1989). Measurement and meaning of parent-child interaction. In J.J. Morrison, C. Lord, & D.P. Keating (Eds.), *Applied developmental psychology* (Vol. 3, pp. 40–81). San Diego, CA: Academic Press.

Barnsley, P. (2001). Native youth remain in distress. *Windspeaker News.* Retrieved October 22, 2001, from http://www.ammsa.com/windspeaker/children/JAN2001-youthindistress.html

Barrett, M. (1994). Sexuality education in Canadian schools: An overview in 1994. *The Canadian Journal of Human Sexuality, 3,* 199–208.

Barrett-Connor, E., & Bush, T.L. (1991). Estrogen and coronary heart disease in women. *Journal of the American Medical Association, 265,* 1861–1867.

Bartlik, B., & Goldstein, M. (2000, June). Maintaining sexual health after menopause. *Psychiatric Services Journal, 51,* 751–753.

Bartoshuk, L.M., & Weiffenbach, J.M. (1990). Chemical senses and aging. In E.L. Schneider & J.W. Rowe (Eds.), *Handbook of the biology of aging* (3rd ed., pp. 429–444). San Diego, CA: Academic Press.

Bartzokis, G. (2004). Age-related myelin breakdown: A developmental model of cognitive decline and Alzheimer's disease. *Neurobiology of Aging, 25*(1), 5–18.

Bartzokis, G., Sultzer, D., Lu, P.H., Nuechterlein, K.H., Mintz, J., & Cummings, J.L. (2004). Heterogeneous age-related breakdown of white matter structural integrity: implications for cortical "disconnection" in aging and Alzheimer's disease. *Neurobiology of Aging, 25*(7), 843–851.

Barusch, A. (1999). Religion, adversity and age: Religious experiences of low-income elderly women. *Journal of Sociology & Social Welfare, 26,* 125–142.

Basseches, M. (1984). *Dialectical thinking and adult development.* Norwood, NJ: Ablex.

Basseches, M. (1989). Dialectical thinking as an organized whole: Comments on Irwin and Kramer. In M.L. Commons, J.D. Sinnott, F.A. Richards, & C. Armon (Eds.), *Adult development: Vol. 1. Comparisons and applications of developmental models* (pp. 161–178). New York: Praeger.

Bates, E. (1993). Commentary: Comprehension and production in early language development. *Monographs of the Society for Research in Child Development, 58* (3–4, Serial No. 233), 222–242.

Bates, E., O'Connell, B., & Shore, C. (1987). Language and communication in infancy. In J.D. Osofsky (Ed.), *Handbook of infant development* (2nd ed., pp. 149–203). New York: Wiley.

Bates, J.E. (1989). Applications of temperament concepts. In G.A. Kohnstamm, J.E. Bates, & M.K. Rothbart (Eds.), *Temperament in childhood* (pp. 321–356). Chichester, England: Wiley.

Bates, J.E., Marvinney, D., Kelly, T., Dodge, K.A., Bennett, D.S., & Pettit, G.S. (1994). Child-care history and kindergarten adjustment. *Developmental Psychology, 30,* 690–700.

Batten, M., & Oltjenbruns, K. (1999). Adolescent sibling bereavement as a catalyst for spiritual development: A model for understanding. *Death Studies, 23,* 529–546.

Bauer, P., Schwade, J., Wewerka, S., & Delaney, K. (1999). Planning ahead: Goal-directed problem solving by 2-year-olds. *Developmental Psychology, 35,* 1321–1337.

Baugher, R.J., Burger, C., Smith, R., & Wallston, K. (1989/1990). A comparison of terminally ill persons at various time periods to death. *Omega, 20,* 103–115.

Bauminger, N., & Kasari, C. (1999). Brief report: Theory of mind in high-functioning children with autism. *Journal of Autism & Developmental Disorders, 29,* 81–86.

Baumrind, D. (1967). Child care practices anteceding three patterns of preschool behavior. *Genetic Psychology Monographs, 75,* 43–88.

Baumrind, D. (1971). Current patterns of parental authority. *Developmental Psychology Monograph, 4* (1, Part 2).

Baumrind, D. (1972). Socialization and instrumental competence in young children. In W.W. Hartup (Ed.), *The young child: Reviews of research* (Vol. 2, pp. 202–224). Washington, DC: National Association for the Education of Young Children.

Baumrind, D. (1991). Effective parenting during the early adolescent transition. In P.A. Cowan & M. Hetherington (Eds.), *Family transitions* (pp. 111–163). Hillsdale, NJ: Erlbaum.

Baumrind, D. (2003, March). *When are causal inferences justified in the debate about physical discipline "effects"?* Paper presented at the Institute of Human Development University of California, Berkeley, CA.

Baumrind, D., Larzelere, R.E., & Cowan, P.A. (2002). Ordinary physical punishment: Is it harmful? Comment on Gershoff (2002). *Psychological Bulletin, 128*(4), 580–589.

Bayley, N. (1969). *Bayley scales of infant development.* New York: Psychological Corporation.

BC Stats. (1998). Special feature: A tale of three immigrant cities. Victoria, BC: Author. Retrieved October 6, 2001 from http://www.bcstats.gov.bc.ca/pubs/immig/imm973sf.pdf

Beaton, G.H., Martorell, R., L'Abbe, K.A., Edmonston, B., McCabe, G., Ross, A.C. & Harvey, B. (1993). Effectiveness of Vitamin A supplementation in the control of young child morbidity and mortality in developing countries. *Final report to the Canadian International Development Agency (CIDA).* Toronto: University of Toronto.

Beaty, L. (1999). Identity development of homosexual youth and parental and familial influences on the coming out process. *Adolescence, 34,* 597–601.

Beaujot, R. (2004). *Delayed life transitions: Trends and implications.* Ottawa, ON: The Vanier Institute of the Family. Retrieved July 10, 2004 from http://www.vifamily.ca/library/cft/delayed_life.pdf

Beaujot, R., & Kerr, D. (2004). *Population change in Canada.* Toronto: Oxford University Press.

Beautrais, A., Joyce, P., & Mulder, R. (1999). Personality traits and cognitive styles as risk factors for serious suicide attempts among young people. *Suicide & Life-Threatening Behavior, 29,* 37–47.

Beck, A., Brown, G., Berchick, R., Stewart, B., & Steer, R. (1990). Relationship between hopelessness and ultimate suicide: A replication with psychiatric outpatients. *American Journal of Psychiatry, 147,* 190–195.

Bedeian, A.G., Ferris, G.R., & Kacmar, K.M. (1992). Age, tenure, and job satisfaction: A tale of two perspectives. *Journal of Vocational Behavior, 40,* 33–48.

Bedford, V. (1995). Sibling relationships in middle and old age. In R. Blieszner & V.H. Bedford (Eds.), *Handbook of aging and the family.* Westport, CT: Greenwood Press.

Beekman, A., Copeland, J., & Prince, M. (1999). Review of community prevalence of depression in later life. *British Journal of Psychiatry, 174,* 307–311.

Beem, E., Hooijkaas, H., Cleriren, M., Schut, H., Garssen, B., Croon, M., Jabaaij, L., Goodkin, K., Wind, H., & de Vries, M. (1999). The immunological and psychological effects of bereavement: Does grief counseling really make a difference? A pilot study. *Psychiatry Research, 85,* 81–93.

Bell, L.G., & Bell, D.C. (1982). Family climate and the role of the female adolescent: Determinants of adolescent functioning. *Family Relations, 31,* 519–527.

Bell Canada (2001, 11a). Students move their mouse before they move house. Bell Canada Press Releases (August 22). Retrieved November 18, 2001 from http://www.bell.ca/en/about/press/release/2001/pr_20010822.asp

Bell Canada (2001, 11b). Young people show mature attitude toward cell phone use. Bell Canada Press Releases (August 16). Retrieved November 18, 2001 from http://www.bell.ca/en/about/press/release/2001/pr_20010816.asp

Bellantoni, M.F., & Blackman, M.R. (1996). Menopause and its consequences. In E.L. Schneider & J.W. Rowe (Eds.), *Handbook of the biology of aging* (4th ed., pp. 415–430). San Diego, CA: Academic Press.

Belsky, J. (1985). Prepared statement on the effects of day care. In Select Committee on Children, Youth, and Families, House of Representatives, 98th Congress, Second Session, *Improving child care services: What can be done?* Washington, DC: U.S. Government Printing Office.

Belsky, J. (1992). Consequences of child care for children's development: A deconstructionist view. In A. Booth (Ed.), *Child care in the 1990s: Trends and consequences* (pp. 83–94). Hillsdale, NJ: Erlbaum.

Belsky, J., & Hsieh, K. (1998). Patterns of marital change during the early childhood years: Parent personality, coparenting, and division-of-labor correlates. *Journal of Family Psychology, 12,* 511–528.

Belsky, J., Hsieh, K., & Crnic, K. (1996). Infant positive and negative emotionality: One dimension or two? *Developmental Psychology, 32,* 289–298.

Belsky, J., Lang, M.E., & Rovine, M. (1985). Stability and change in marriage across the transition to parenthood: A second study. *Journal of Marriage and the Family, 47,* 855–865.

Belsky, J., & Rovine, M. (1988). Nonmaternal care in the first year of life and the security of infant-parent attachment. *Child Development, 59,* 157–167.

Bem, S.L. (1974). The measurement of psychological androgyny. *Journal of Consulting and Clinical Psychology, 42,* 155–162.

Bender, B.G., Harmon, R.J., Linden, M.G., & Robinson, A. (1995). Psychosocial adaptation of 39 adolescents with sex chromosome abnormalities. *Pediatrics, 96,* 302–308.

Bender, K. (1999). Assessing antidepressant safety in the elderly. *Psychiatric Times, 16* [Online archives]. Retrieved February 7, 2001 from http://www.mhsource. com/pt/ p990151.html

Bendersky, M., & Lewis, M. (1994). Environmental risk, biological risk, and developmental outcome. *Developmental Psychology, 30,* 484–494.

Benenson, J.F. (1994). Ages four to six years: Changes in the structures of play networks of girls and boys. *Merrill-Palmer Quarterly, 40,* 478–487.

Benenson, J., & Benarroch, D. (1998). Gender differences in responses to friends' hypothetical greater success. *Journal of Early Adolescence, 18,* 192–208.

Bengtson, V.L., Cuellar, J.B., & Ragan, P.K. (1977). Stratum contrasts and similarities in attitudes toward death. *Journal of Gerontology, 32,* 76–88.

Bengtson, V., Rosenthal, C., & Burton, L. (1990). Families and aging: Diversity and heterogeneity. In R.H. Binstock & L.K. George (Eds.), *Handbook of aging and the social sciences* (3rd ed., pp. 263–287). San Diego, CA: Academic Press.

Bengtson, V., Rosenthal, C., & Burton, L. (1996). Paradoxes of families and aging. In R.H. Binstock & L.K. George (Eds.), *Handbook of aging and the social sciences* (4th ed., pp. 253–282). San Diego, CA: Academic Press.

Benn, P.A., & Egan, J.F.X. (2000). Letters to the Editor: Survival of Down syndrome in utero. *Prenatal Diagnosis, 20*(5), 432–433.

Bennett, M. (1997). A longitudinal study of wellbeing in widowed women. *International Journal of Geriatric Psychiatry, 12,* 61–66.

Bennett, M. (1998). Longitudinal changes in mental and physical health among elderly, recently widowed men. *Mortality, 3,* 265–273.

Benoit, D., & Parker, K.C.H. (1994). Stability and transmission of attachment across three generations. *Child Development, 65,* 1444–1456.

Berg, J., & Lipson, J. (1999). Information sources, menopause beliefs, and health complaints of midlife Filipinas. *Health, 20,* 81–92.

Berg, S. (1996). Aging, behavior, and terminal decline. In J.E. Birren & K.W. Schaie (Eds.), *Handbook of the psychology of aging* (4th ed., pp. 323–337). San Diego, CA: Academic Press.

Bergeson, T., & Trehub, S. (1999). Mothers' singing to infants and preschool children. *Infant Behavior & Development, 22,* 53–64.

Berkman, L.F. (1985). The relationship of social networks and social support to morbidity and mortality. In S. Coen & S.L. Syme (Eds.), *Social support and health* (pp. 241–262). Orlando, FL: Academic Press.

Berkman, L.F., & Breslow, L. (1983). *Health and ways of living: The Alameda County Study.* New York: Oxford University Press.

Berkowitz, G.S., & Papiernik, E. (1993). Epidemiology of preterm birth. *Epidemiological Review, 15,* 414–443.

Berkowitz, S., Skovron, M.L., Lapinski, R.H., & Berkowitz, R.L. (1990). Delayed childbearing and the outcome of pregnancy. *New England Journal of Medicine, 322,* 659–664.

Berndt, T.J. (1992). Friendship and friends' influence in adolescence. *Current Directions in Psychological Science, 1,* 156–159.

Berndt, T.J., & Keefe, K. (1995a). Friends' influence on adolescents' adjustment to school. *Child Development, 66,* 1312–1329.

Berndt, T.J., & Keefe, K. (1995b, March). *Friends' influence on school adjustment: A motivational analysis.* Paper presented at the biennial meetings of the Society for Research in Child Development, Indianapolis, IN.

Berne, L., & Huberman, B. (1996, February). Sexuality education works: Here's proof. *Education Digest,* 25–29.

Berninger, V., Abbott, R., Zook, D., Ogier, S., et al. (1999). Early intervention for reading disabilities: Teaching the alphabet principle in a connectionist framework. *Journal of Learning Disabilities, 32,* 491–503.

Bertenthal, B.I., & Campos, J.J. (1987). New directions in the study of early experience. *Child Development, 58,* 560–567.

Betancourt, H., & Lopez, S.R. (1993). The study of culture, ethnicity, and race in American psychology. *American Psychologist, 48,* 629–637.

Betancourt, L., Fischer, R., Gianetta, J., Malmud, E., Brodsky, N. & Hurt, H. (1999). Problem-solving ability of inner-city children with and without in utero cocaine exposure. *Journal of Developmental Disabilities, 20,* 418–424.

Betz, N.E., & Fitzgerald, L.F. (1987). *The career psychology of women.* Orlando, FL: Academic Press.

Bhatt, R.S., & Rovee-Collier, C. (1996). Infants' forgetting of correlated attributes and object recognition. *Child Development, 67,* 172–187.

Bial, M. (1971). *Liberal Judaism at home.* New York: Union of American Hebrew Congregations.

Bialystok, E. (1997). Effects of bilingualism and biliteracy on children's emerging concepts of print. *Developmental Psychology, 33.*

Bialystok, E. (1999). Cognitive complexity and attentional control in the bilingual mind. *Child Development, 70,* 636–644.

Bialystok, E., & Majumder, S. (1998). The relationship between bilingualism and the development of cognitive processes in problem solving. *Applied Psycholinguistics, 19,* 69–85.

Bialystok, E., Shenfield, T., & Codd, J. (2000). Languages, scripts, and the environment: Factors in developing concepts of print. *Developmental Psychology, 36,* 66–76.

Bianchi, A. (1993, January–February). Older drivers: The good, the bad, and the iffy. *Harvard Magazine,* pp. 12–13.

Bibby, R.W. (2001). *Canada's teens: Today, yesterday and tomorrow.* Toronto: Stoddart Publishing Co. Limited.

Biblarz, T.J., Bengtson, V.L., & Bucur, A. (1996). Social mobility across three generations. *Journal of Marriage and the Family, 58,* 188–200.

Biedenharn, P.J., & Normoyle, J.B. (1991). Elderly community residents' reactions to the nursing home: An analysis of nursing home-related beliefs. *The Gerontologist, 31,* 107–115.

Bigler, E.D., Johnson, S.C., Jackson, C., & Blatter, D.D. (1995). Aging, brain size, and IQ. *Intelligence, 21,* 109–119.

Billy, J.O.G., Brewster, K.L., & Grady, W.R. (1994). Contextual effects on the sexual behavior of adolescent women. *Journal of Marriage and the Family, 56,* 387–404.

Binet, A., & Simon, T. (1905). Méthodes nouvelles pour le diagnostic du niveau intellectuel des anormaux [New methods for diagnosing the intellectual level of the abnormal]. *L'Anée Psychologique, 11,* 191–244.

Bingham, C.R., Miller, B.C., & Adams, G.R. (1990). Correlates of age at first sexual intercourse in a national sample of young women. *Journal of Adolescent Research, 5,* 18–33.

Birch, D. (1998). The adolescent parent: A fifteen-year longitudinal study of school-age mothers and their children. *International Journal of Adolescent Medicine & Health, 19,* 141–153.

Birch, E., Garfield, S., Hoffman, D., Uauy, R., & Birch, D. (2000). A randomized controlled trial of early dietary supply of longchain polyunsaturated fatty acids and mental development in term infants. *Developmental Medicine & Child Neurology, 42,* 174–181.

Biringen, Z. (2000). Emotional availability: Conceptualization and research findings. *American Journal of Orthopsychiatry, 70,* 104–114.

Biro, F.M., Lucky, A.W., Huster, G.A., & Morrison, J.A. (1995). Pubertal staging in boys. *Journal of Pediatrics, 127,* 100–102.

Birren, J.E., & Schroots, J.J.F. (1996). History, concepts, and theory in the psychology of aging. In J.R. Birren & K.W. Schaie (Eds.), *Handbook of the psychology of aging* (4th ed., pp. 3–23). San Diego, CA: Academic Press.

Biswas, M.K., & Craigo, S.D. (1994). The course and conduct of normal labor and delivery. In A.H. DeCherney & M.L. Pernoll (Eds.), *Current obstetric and gynecologic diagnosis & treatment* (pp. 202–227). Norwalk, CT: Appleton & Lange.

Bitomsky, M. (2002). Men often untreated for eating disorders. *The Medical Post, 38*(37), 53.

Bittner, S., & Newberger, E. (1981). Pediatric understanding of child abuse and neglect. *Pediatric Review, 2,* 198.

Bjorklund, D.F., & Pellegrini, A.D. (2002). *The origins of human nature: Evolutionary developmental psychology.* Washington, DC: American Psychological Association.

Black, K., & McCartney, K. (1997). Adolescent females' security with parents predicts the quality of peer interactions. *Social Development, 6,* 91–110.

Black, K.A., & McCartney, K. (1995, March). *Associations between adolescent attachment to parents and peer interactions.* Paper presented at the biennial meetings of the Society for Research in Child Development, Indianapolis, IN.

Black, S., Markides, K., & Miller, T. (1998). Correlates of depressive symptomatology among older community-dwelling Mexican Americans: The hispanic EPESE. *Journals of Gerontology: Series B: Psychological Sciences & Social Sciences, 53B,* S198–S208.

Blackwell, D., & Lichter, D. (2000). Mate selection among married and cohabiting couples. *Journal of Family Issues, 21,* 275–302.

Blair, S.N., Kohl, H.W., III, Barlow, C.E., Paffenbarger, R.S., Gibbons, L.W., & Macera, C.A. (1995). Changes in physical fitness and all-cause mortality. *Journal of the American Medical Association, 273,* 1093–1098.

Blake, I.K. (1994). Language development and socialization in young African-American children. In P.M. Greenfield & R.R. Cocking (Eds.), *Cross-cultural roots of minority child development* (pp. 167–195). Hillsdale, NJ: Erlbaum.

Blake, J.M., Collins, J.A., Reid, R.L., Fedorkow, D.M., & Lalonde, A.B. (2002). The SOGC statement on the WHI report on estrogen and progestin use in postmenopausal women. *The Journal of Obstetrics and Gynaecology Canada, 24*(10), 783–787.

Blakemore, J., LaRue, A., Olejnik, A. (1979). Sex-appropriate toy preference and the ability to conceptualize toys as sex-role related. *Developmental Psychology, 15,* 339–340.

Blanchard-Fields, F., Chen, Y., Schocke, M., & Hertzog, C. (1998). Evidence for content-specificity of causal attributions across the adult life span. *Aging, Neuropsychology, & Cognition, 5,* 241–263.

Blatter, D.D., Bigler, E.D., Gale, S.D., Johnson, S.C., Anderson, C.V., Burnett, B.M., Parker, N., Kurth, S., & Horn, S. (1995). Quantitative volumetric analysis of brain MR: Normative database spanning five decades (16–65). *American Journal of Neuroradiology, 16,* 241–251.

Blau, G. (1996). Adolescent depression and suicide. In G. Blau & T. Gullotta (Eds.), *Adolescent dysfunctional behavior: Causes, interventions, and prevention* (pp. 187–205). Newbury Park, CA: Sage.

Blazer, D., Hybels, C., Simonsick, E., & Hanlon, J. (2000). Marked differences in antidepressant use by race in an elderly community sample: 1986–1996. *American Journal of Psychiatry, 157,* 1089–1094.

Blieszner, R., & Adams, R.G. (1992). *Adult friendship.* Newbury Park, CA: Sage.

Block, J., & Robins, R.W. (1993). A longitudinal study of consistency and change in self-esteem from early adolescence to early adulthood. *Child Development, 64,* 909–923.

Bloom, B.L., White, S.W., & Asher, S.J. (1979). Marital disruption as a stressful life event. In C. Levinger & O.C. Moles (Eds.), *Divorce and separation: Context, causes, and consequences* (pp. 184–200). New York: Basic Books.

Bloom, L. (1973). *One word at a time.* The Hague: Mouton.

Bloom, L. (1991). *Language development from two to three.* Cambridge, England: Cambridge University Press.

Bloom, L. (1993). *The transition from infancy to language: Acquiring the power of expression.* Cambridge, England: Cambridge University Press.

Bluck, S., Levine, L., & Laulhere, T. (1999). Autobiographical remembering and hypermnesia: A comparison of older and younger adults. *Psychology & Aging, 14,* 671–682.

Blumberg, J.B. (1996). Status and functional impact of nutrition in older adults. In E.L. Schneider & J.W. Rowe (Eds.), *Handbook of the biology of aging* (4th ed., pp. 393–414). San Diego, CA: Academic Press.

Blumenthal, J.A., Emery, C.F., Madden, D.J., Schniebolk, S., Walsh-Riddle, M., George, L.K., McKee, D.C., Higginbotham, M.B., Cobb, R.R., & Coleman, R.E. (1991). Long-term effects of exercise on physiological functioning in older men and women. *Journals of Gerontology: Psychological Sciences, 46,* P352–361.

Blumstein, P., & Schwartz, P. (1990). Intimate relationships and the creation of sexuality. In D. McWhirter, S. Sanders, and J. Reinisch (Eds.), *Homosexuality/heterosexuality: Concepts of sexual orientation* (pp. 96–109). New York: Oxford University Press.

Blustein, D., Phillips, S., Jobin-Davis, K., & Finkelberg, S. (1997). A theory-building investigation of the school-to-work transition. *Counseling Psychology, 25,* 364–402.

Bodenmann, G., Widmer, K., & Cina, A. (1999). The Couples Coping Enhancement Training (CCET): Subjective appraisal of changes within 6 months. *Verhaltenstherapie, 9,* 87–94.

Bogenschneider, K., Wu, M., Raffaelli, M., & Tsay, J. (1998). "Other teens drink, but not my kid": Does parental awareness of adolescent alcohol use protect adolescents from risky consequences? *Journal of Marriage & the Family, 60,* 356–373.

Bohman, M., & Sigvardsson, S. (1990). Outcome in adoption: Lessons from longitudinal studies. In D.M. Brodzinsky (Ed.), *The psychology of adoption* (pp. 93–106). New York: Oxford University Press.

Boldizar, J. (1991). Assessing sex typing and androgyny in children. *Developmental Psychology, 27,* 506–535.

Bonanno, G., Znoj, H., Siddique, H., & Horowitz, M. (1999). Verbal-autonomic dissociation and adaptation to midlife conjugal loss: A follow-up at 25 months.*Cognitive Therapy & Research, 23,* 605–624.

Bond, J., & Coleman, P. (Eds.). (1990). *Aging in society.* London: Sage.

Bond, M.H., Nakazato, H., & Shiraishi, D. (1975). Universality and distinctiveness in dimensions of Japanese person perception. *Journal of Cross-Cultural Psychology, 6,* 346–357.

Bondevik, M., & Skogstad, A. (1998). The oldest old, ADL, social network, and loneliness. *Western Journal of Nursing Research, 20,* 325–343.

Bondy, S.J., Cohen, J.E. & Rehm, J.T. (2000). Past trends in tobacco use and some thoughts on future trends. In R. Ferrence, J. Slade, R. Room & M. Pope (Eds.), *Nicotine and public health* (pp. 311–342). Washington: Public Health Association.

Bong, M. (1998). Tests of the internal/external frames of reference model with subject-specific academic self-efficacy and frame-specific academic self-concepts. *Journal of Educational Psychology, 90,* 102–110.

Boone, R., Higgins, K., Notari, A., & Stump, C. (1996). Hypermedia pre-reading lessons: Learner-centered software for kindergarten. *Journal of Computing in Childhood Education, 7,* 39–70.

Borkenau, P., & Ostendorf, F. (1990). Comparing exploratory and confirmatory factor analysis: A study on the five-factor model of personality. *Personality and Individual Differences, 11,* 515–524.

Bornholt, L., & Goodnow, J. (1999). Cross-generation perceptions of academic competence: Parental expectations and adolescent self-disclosure. *Journal of Adolescent Research, 14,* 427–447.

Bornstein, M.H. (1992). Perception across the life span. In M.H. Bornstein & M.E. Lamb (Eds.), *Developmental psychology: An advanced textbook* (3rd ed., pp. 155–210). Hillsdale, NJ: Erlbaum.

Bosacki, S. (2001a). "Theory of mind" or "theory of the soul"? The role of spirituality in children's understanding of minds and emotions. In J. Erricker, C. Ota, & C. Erricker (Eds.), *Spiritual Education: Cultural, Religious and Social Differences* (pp. 156–169). Portland OR: Sussex Academic Press.

Bosacki, S.L. (2001b). Spirituality, gendered subjectivities, and education in preadolescents: Canadian preadolescents' reflections on gender-roles and their sense of self. *International Journal of Children's Spirituality, 6(20),* 207–221.

Bosacki, S.L. (2002). Spirituality and self in preadolescents: Implications for a connected curriculum. *Journal of Beliefs & Values, 23(1),* 55–67.

Bosacki, S.L., & Moore, C. (in press). Preschoolers' understanding of simple and complex emotions: Links with gender and language. *Sex Roles: A Journal of Research.*

Bossé, R., Aldwin, C.M., Levenson, M.R., & Workman-Daniels, K. (1991). How stressful is retirement? Findings from the normative aging study. *Journals of Gerontology: Psychological Sciences, 46,* P9–14.

Bosworth, H., Siegler, I., Brummett, B., Barefoot, J., Williams, R., Clapp-Channing, N., & Mark, D. (2000, August). *Health-related quality of life in a coronary artery sample.* Paper presented at the annual meeting of the American Psychological Association. Washington, DC.

Bouchard, B. & Zhao, J. (2000). University education: Recent trends in participation, accessibility and returns. *Education Quarterly Review, 6(4),* 24–32. Retrieved December 10, 2001 from http://www.statcan.ca/english/indepth/81-003/feature/eqar2000006004s2a02.pdf

Bouchard, T.J., Jr., & McGue, M. (1981). Familial studies of intelligence: A review. *Science, 212,* 1055–1059.

Bourreille, C. (1999). Diana/Diana. *Cahiers Jungiens de Psychanalyse, 96,* 75–76.

Bowlby, J. (1969). *Attachment and loss: Vol. 1. Attachment.* New York: Basic Books.

Bowlby, J. (1973). *Attachment and loss: Vol. 2. Separation, anxiety, and anger.* New York: Basic Books.

Bowlby, J. (1980). *Attachment and loss: Vol. 3. Loss, sadness, and depression.* New York: Basic Books.

Bowlby, J. (1988a). Developmental psychiatry comes of age. *American Journal of Psychiatry, 145,* 1–10.

Bowlby, J. (1988b). *A secure base.* New York: Basic Books.

Bowler, D., Briskman, J., & Grice, S. (1999). Experimenter effects on children's understanding of false drawings and false beliefs. *Journal of Genetic Psychology, 160,* 443–460.

Boyatzis, C.J., Matillo, G., Nesbitt, K., & Cathey, G. (1995, March). *Effects of "The Mighty Morphin Power Rangers" on children's aggression and prosocial behavior.* Paper presented at the biennial meetings of the Society for Research in Child Development, Indianapolis, IN.

Braam, A., Beekman, A., Deeg, D., Smit, J., & van Tilburg, W. (1997). Religiosity as a protective or prognostic factor of depression in later life: Results from a community survey in the Netherlands. *Longitudinal Aging Study, 96,* 199–205.

Bradley, R.H., Caldwell, B.M., Rock, S.L., Barnard, K.E., Gray, C., Hammond, M.A., Mitchell, S., Siegel, L., Ramey, C.D., Gottfried, A.W., & Johnson, D.L. (1989). Home environment and cognitive development in the first 3 years of life: A collaborative study involving six sites and three ethnic groups in North America. *Developmental Psychology, 25,* 217–235.

Bradmetz, J. (1999). Precursors of formal thought: A longitudinal study. *British Journal of Developmental Psychology, 17,* 61–81.

Brand, A., & Brinich, P. (1999). Behavior problems and mental health contacts in adopted, foster, and nonadopted children. *Journal of Child Psychology & Psychiatry & Allied Disciplines, 40,* 1221–1229.

Brandon, P. (1999). Determinants of self-care arrangements among school-age children. *Children & Youth Services Review, 21,* 497–520.

Brandtstädter, J., & Baltes-Götz, B. (1990). Personal control over development and quality of life perspectives in adulthood. In P.

Baltes & M.M. Baltes (Eds.), *Successful aging* (pp. 197–224). Cambridge, England: Cambridge University Press.

Brandtstädter, J., & Greve, W. (1994). The aging self: Stabilizing and protective processes. *Developmental Review, 14,* 52–80.

Braun, K., & Nichols, R. (1997). Death and dying in four Asian American cultures: A descriptive study. *Death Studies, 21,* 327–359.

Braveman, N.S. (1987). Immunity and aging immunologic and behavioral perspectives. In M.W. Riley, J.D. Matarazzo, & A. Baum (Eds.), *Perspectives in behavioral medicine: The aging dimension* (pp. 94–124). Hillsdale, NJ: Erlbaum.

Bray, D.W., & Howard, A. (1983). The AT&T longitudinal studies of managers. In K.W. Schaie (Ed.), *Longitudinal studies of adult psychological development* (pp. 266–312). New York: Guilford Press.

Brazelton, T.B., & Nugent, J.K. (1995). *Neonatal Behavioral Assessment Scale.* London: MacKeith Press.

Bregman, G., & Killen, M. (1999). Adolescents' and young adults' reasoning about career choice and the role of parental influence. *Journal of Research on Adolescence, 9,* 253–275.

Brendgen, M., Vitaro, F., & Bukowski, W. (1998). Affiliation with delinquent friends: Contributions of parents, self-esteem, delinquent behavior, and rejection by peers. *Journal of Early Adolescence, 18,* 244–265.

Brener, N., Hassan, S., & Barrios, L. (1999). Suicidal ideation among college students in the United States. *Journal of Consulting & Clinical Psychology, 67,* 1004–1008.

Brennan, F., & Ireson, J. (1997). Training phonological awareness: A study to evaluate the effects of a program of metalinguistic games in kindergarten. *Reading & Writing, 9,* 241–263.

Brenner, V. (1997). Psychology of computer use: XLVII. Parameters of Internet use. *Psychological Reports, 80,* 879–882.

Breslau, N., & Chilcoat, H. (2000). Psychiatric sequelae of low birth weight at 11 years of age. *Biological Psychiatry, 47,* 1005–1011.

Breslau, N., DelDotto, J.E., Brown, G.G., Kumar, S., Ezhuthachan, S., Hufnagle, K.G., & Peterson, E.L. (1994). A gradient relationship between low birth weight and IQ at age 6 years. *Archives of Pediatric and Adolescent Medicine, 2148,* 377–383.

Breslow, L., & Breslow, N. (1993). Health practices and disability: Some evidence from Alameda County. *Preventive Medicine, 22,* 86–95.

Bretscher, M., Rummans, T., Sloan, J., Kaur, J., Bartlett, A., Borkenhagen, L., & Loprinzi, C. (1999). Quality of life in hospice patients: A pilot study. *Psychosomatics, 40,* 309–313.

Briggs, R. (1990). Biological aging. In J. Bond & P. Coleman (Eds.), *Aging in society* (pp. 48–61). London: Sage.

British Association of Toy Retailers. (n.d.). *LEGO is toy of the century.* Retrieved March 7, 2004, from http://www.batr.co.uk/totc/totc20.htm

British Columbia Ministry of Education. (2001). English as a second language. Victoria, BC: Author. Retrieved October 6, 2001 from http://www.bced.gov. bc.ca/esl/policy/introduction.htm

Brock, D.B., Guralnik, J.M., & Brody, J.A. (1990). Demography and the epidemiology of aging in the United States. In E.L. Schneider & J.W. Rowe (Eds.), *Handbook of the biology of aging* (3rd ed., pp. 3–23). San Diego, CA: Academic Press.

Brockington, I. (1996). *Motherhood and mental health.* Oxford, England: Oxford University Press.

Brody, E.M., Litvin, S.J., Albert, S.M., & Hoffman, C.J. (1994). Marital status of daughters and patterns of parent care. *Journals of Gerontology: Social Sciences, 49,* S95–103.

Brody, E.M., Litvin, S.J., Hoffman, C., & Kleban, M.H. (1992). Differential effects of daughters' marital status on their parent care experiences. *The Gerontologist, 32,* 58–67.

Brody, G.H., Stoneman, Z., & Flor, D. (1995). Linking family processes and academic competence among rural African American youths. *Journal of Marriage and the Family, 47,* 567–579.

Brody, J.E. (1994, April 20). Making a strong case for antioxidants. *New York Times,* p. B9.

Brody, J.E. (1995, October 4). Personal health. *New York Times,* p. B7.

Brody, J.E. (1996, February 28). Good habits outweigh genes as key to a healthy old age. *New York Times,* p. B9.

Brody, N. (1992). *Intelligence* (2nd ed.). San Diego, CA: Academic Press.

Bronfenbrenner, U. (1979). *The ecology of human development.* Cambridge, MA: Harvard University Press.

Bronfenbrenner, U. (1989). Ecological systems theory. *Annals of Child Development, 6,* 187–249.

Bronfenbrenner, U. (1993). The ecology of cognitive development: Research models and fugitive findings. In R.H. Wozniak and K.W. Fischer (Eds.), *Development in context: Acting and thinking in specific environments.* Hillsdale, NJ: Erlbaum.

Brook, J., Whiteman, M., Finch, S., & Cohen, P. (2000). Longitudinally foretelling drug use in the late twenties: Adolescent personality and social-environmental antecedents. *Journal of Genetic Psychology, 161,* 37–51.

Brooks-Gunn, J. (1995). Children in families in communities: Risk and intervention in the Bronfenbrenner tradition. In P. Moen, G.H. Elder, Jr., & K. Lüscher (Eds.), *Examining lives in context: Perspectives on the ecology of human development* (pp. 467–519). Washington, DC: American Psychological Association.

Brooks-Gunn, J., Guo, G., & Furstenberg, F.F., Jr. (1993). Who drops out of and who continues beyond high school? A 20-year follow-up of black urban youth. *Journal of Research on Adolescence, 3,* 271–294.

Brooks-Gunn, J., Klebanov, P., Liaw, F., & Spiler, D. (1993). Enhancing the development of low birthweight, premature infants: Changes in cognition and behavior over the first three years. *Child Development, 64,* 736–753.

Brooks-Gunn, J., & Reiter, E.O. (1990). The role of pubertal processes. In S.S. Feldman & G.R. Elliott (Eds.), *At the threshold: The developing adolescent* (pp. 16–53). Cambridge, MA: Harvard University Press.

Brown, A., & Day, J. (1983). Macrorules for summarizing text: The development of expertise. *Journal of Verbal Learning and Verbal Behavior, 22,* 1–14.

Brown, A.S., Jones, E.M., & Davis, T.L. (1995). Age differences in conversational source monitoring. *Psychology and Aging, 10,* 111–122.

Brown, B.B. (1990). Peer groups and peer cultures. In S.S. Feldman & G.R. Elliott (Eds.), *At the threshold: The developing adolescent* (pp. 171–196). Cambridge, MA: Harvard University Press.

Brown, B.B., Dolcini, M.M., & Leventhal, A. (1995, March). *The emergence of peer crowds: Friend or foe to adolescent health?* Paper presented at the biennial meetings of the Society for Research in Child Development, Indianapolis, IN.

Brown, B.B., & Huang, B. (1995). Examining parenting practices in different peer contexts: Implications for adolescent trajectories. In L.J. Crockett & A.C. Crouter (Eds.), *Pathways through adolescence* (pp. 151–174). Mahwah, NJ: Erlbaum.

Brown, B.B., Mory, M.S., & Kinney, D. (1994). Casting adolescent crowds in a relational perspective: Caricature, channel, and context. In R. Montemayor, G.R. Adams, & T.P. Gullotta (Eds.), *Personal relationships during adolescence* (pp. 123–167). Thousand Oaks, CA: Sage.

Brown, G., & Dixson, A. (2000). The development of behavioral sex differences in infant rhesus macaques. *Primates, 41,* 63–77.

Brown, I., & Fudge Schormans, A. (2004). *Maltreatment rates in children with developmental delay.* CECW Information Sheet #9E. Toronto: Faculty of Social Work, University of Toronto. Retrieved June 21, 2004 from http://www.cecw-cepb.ca/DocsEng/DDMaltreatmentRates9E.pdf

Brown, J., Bakeman, R., Coles, C., Sexson, W., & Demi, A. (1998). Maternal drug use during pregnancy: Are preterm and full-term infants affected differently? *Developmental Psychology, 34,* 540–554.

Brown, R. (1973). *A first language: The early stages.* Cambridge, MA: Harvard University Press.

Brown, S.L. (2000). The effect of union type on psychological well-being: Depression among cohabitors versus marrieds. *Journal of Health and Social Behavior, 41*(3), 241–255.

Brownell, C.A. (1990). Peer social skills in toddlers: Competencies and constraints illustrated by same-age and mixed-age interaction. *Child Development, 61,* 836–848.

Brownridge, D.A., & Halli, S.S. (2001). Marital status as differentiating factor in Canadian women's coping with partner violence. *Journal of Comparative Family Studies, 32*(1), 117–125.

Bruer, J. (1999). *The myth of the first three years.* New York: Free Press.

Bryant, P., MacLean, M., & Bradley, L. (1990). Rhyme, language, and children's reading. *Applied Psycholinguistics, 11,* 237–252.

Bryant, P.E., MacLean, M., Bradley, L.L., & Crossland, J. (1990). Rhyme and alliteration, phoneme detection, and learning to read. *Developmental Psychology, 26,* 429–438.

Bryant, S., & Rakowski, W. (1992). Predictors of mortality among elderly African-Americans. *Research on Aging, 14,* 50–67.

Buchanan, C.M., Maccoby, E.E., & Dornbusch, S.M. (1991). Caught between parents: Adolescents' experience in divorced homes. *Child Development, 62,* 1008–1029.

Buchner, D.M., Beresford, S.A.A., Larson, E.B., LaCroix, A.Z., & Wagner, E.H. (1992). Effects of physical activity on health status in older adults II: Intervention studies. *Annual Review of Public Health, 13,* 469–488.

Buhrmester, D. (1992). The developmental courses of sibling and peer relationships. In F. Boer & J. Dunn (Eds.), *Children's sibling relationships: Developmental and clinical issues.* Hillsdale, NJ: Erlbaum.

Buhrmester, D., & Furman, W. (1990). Perceptions of sibling relationships during middle childhood and adolescence. *Child Development, 61,* 1387–1398.

Bukowski, W., Sippola, L., & Hoza, B. (1999). Same and other: Interdependency between participation in same- and other-sex friendships. *Journal of Youth & Adolescence, 28,* 439–459.

Bulcroft, R.A., & Bulcroft, K.A. (1991). The nature and functions of dating in later life. *Research on Aging, 13,* 244–260.

Bulkeley, W. (1998, September 16). Education: Kaplan plans a law school via the Web. *Wall Street Journal,* B1.

Bullock, M., & Lütkenhaus, P. (1990). Who am I? Self-understanding in toddlers. *Merrill-Palmer Quarterly, 36,* 217–238.

Bumpass, L.L., & Aquilino, W.S. (1995). *A social map of midlife: Family and work over the middle life course.* Report of the MacArthur Foundation research network on successful midlife development, Vero Beach, FL.

Burgess, S. (1997). The role of shared reading in the development of phonological awareness: A longitudinal study of middle to upper class children. *Early Child Development & Care, 127/128,* 191–199.

Buriel, R., Perez, W., DeMent, T., Chavez, D., & Moran, V. (1998). The relationship of language brokering to academic performance, biculturalism, and self-efficacy among Latino adolescents. *Hispanic Journal of Behavioral Sciences, 20,* 283–297.

Burke, L., & Follingstad, D. (1999). Violence in lesbian and gay relationships: Theory, prevalence, and correlational factors. *Clinical Psychology Review, 19,* 487–512.

Burkhauser, R.V., Butrica, B.A., & Wasylenko, M.J. (1995). Mobility patterns of older home owners. *Research on Aging, 17,* 363–384.

Burley, R., Turner, L., & Vitulli, W. (1999). The relationship between goal orientation and age among adolescents and adults. *Journal of Genetic Psychology, 160,* 84–88.

Burnett, J.W., Anderson, W.P., & Heppner, P.P. (1995). Gender roles and self-esteem: A consideration of environmental factors. *Journal of Counseling and Development, 73,* 323–326.

Burton, L. (1992). Black grandparents rearing children of drug-addicted parents: Stressors, outcomes, and social service needs. *Gerontologist, 31,* 744–751.

Burton, L.M., & Bengtson, V.L. (1985). Black grandmothers: Issues of timing and continuity of roles. In V.L. Bengtson & J.F. Robertson (Eds.), *Grandparenthood* (pp. 61–78). Beverly Hills, CA: Sage.

Bus, A., & van IJzendoorn, M. (1999). Phonological awareness and early reading: A meta-analysis of experimental training studies. *Journal of Educational Psychology, 91,* 403–414.

Busch, C.M., Zonderman, A.B., & Costa, P.T., Jr. (1994). Menopausal transition and psychological distress in a nationally representative sample: Is menopause associated with psychological distress? *Journal of Aging and Health, 6,* 209–228.

Bushnik, T., Bar-Telford, L., & Bussière, P. (2004). *In and out of school: First results from the second cycle of Youth in Transition Survey, 2002* (Catalogue No. 81-595). Ottawa, ON: Statistics Canada.

Buss, A. (1989). Temperaments as personality traits. In G.A. Kohnstamm, J.E. Bates, & M.K. Rothbart (Eds.), *Temperament in childhood* (pp. 49–58). Chichester, England: Wiley.

Buss, A.H., & Plomin, R. (1984). *Temperament: Early developing personality traits.* Hillsdale, NJ: Erlbaum.

Buss, A.H., & Plomin, R. (1986). The EAS approach to temperament. In R. Plomin & J. Dunn (Eds.), *The study of temperament: Changes, continuities and challenges* (pp. 67–80). Hillsdale, NJ: Erlbaum.

Buss, D.M. (1999). *Evolutionary psychology: The new science of the mind.* Boston: Allyn & Bacon.

Buss, D., Abbott, M., Algleitner, A., Ahserian, A., Biaggio, A., et al. (1990). International preferences in selecting mates: A study of 37 cultures. *Journal of Cross-Cultural Psychology, 21,* 5–47.

Buss, D., & Schmitt, D. (1993). Sexual strategies theory: An evolutionary perspective on human mating. *Psychological Review, 100,* 204–232.

Bussey, K., Bandura, A. (1992). Self-regulation mechanisms governing gender development. *Child Development, 63,* 1236–1250.

Byrne, G., & Raphael, B. (1999). Depressive symptoms and depressive episodes in recently widowed older men. *International Psychogeriatrics, 11,* 67–74.

Byrne, G., Raphael, G., & Arnold, E. (1999). Alcohol consumption and psychological distress in recently widowed older men. *Australian & New Zealand Journal of Psychiatry, 33,* 740–747.

Byrne, M. (1998). Taking a computational approach to aging: The SPAN theory of working memory. *Psychology & Aging, 13,* 309–322.

Cahn, D., Marcotte, A., Stern, R., Arruda, J., Akshoomoff, N., & Leshko, I. (1966). The Boston Qualitative Scoring System for the Rey-Osterrieth Complex Figure: A study of children with attention deficit hyperactivity disorder. *Clinical Neuropsychologist, 10,* 397–406.

Cairns, B.D., & Cairns, R.B. (1994). *Lifelines and risks: Pathways of youth in our time.* Cambridge, England: Cambridge University Press.

California Achievement Program (1980). *Student achievement in California schools: 1979–1980 annual report: Television and student achievement.* Sacramento: California State Department of Education.

Callaghan, T. (1999). Early understanding and production of graphic symbols. *Child Development, 70,* 1314–1324.

Campbell, D.W., Eaton, W.O., & McKeen, N.A. (2002). Motor activity level and behavioural control in young children. *International Journal of Behavioral Development, 26*(4), 289–296.

Campbell, F.A., & Ramey, C.T. (1994). Effects of early intervention on intellectual and academic achievement: A follow-up study of children from low-income families. *Child Development, 65,* 684–698.

Campbell, L., Connidis, I., & Davies, L. (1999). Sibling ties in later life: A social network analysis. *Journal of Family Issues, 20,* 114–148.

Campbell, S.B., Cohn, J.F., Flanagan, C., Popper, S., & Meyers, T. (1992). Course and correlates of postpartum depression during the transition to parenthood. *Development and Psychopathology, 4,* 29–47.

Campisi, J., Dimri, G., & Hara, E. (1996). Control of replicative senescence. In E.L. Schneider & J.W. Rowe (Eds.), *Handbook of the biology of aging* (4th ed., pp. 121–149). San Diego, CA: Academic Press.

Canada Pension Plan Investment Board. (2001). *2001 Annual Report*. Toronto: Author. Retrieved December 28, 2001 from http://www.cppib.ca

Canadian Aboriginal. (1999). Federal paternalism angers Pikangikum. *Canadian Aboriginal News*. Retrieved October 24, 2001 from http://www.canadianaboriginal.com/news/ news131a.htm

Canadian Association of Retired Persons. (2001). *Homecare by Default, Not by Design*. Toronto: Author. Retrieved December 29, 2001 from http://www. 50plus.com/ArticleFullPrint.cfm?objec-tid=BA84FDAB-C103-44AB-AD2865C309853605

Canadian Cancer Society. (2004). *Cancer is number one cause of early death in Canada—Number of new cancer cases increasing—National coordinated strategy key to fighting Canada's cancer crisis*. Toronto: Author. Retrieved August 17, 2004 from http://www.cancer.ca/ccs/internet/mediareleaselist/ 0,3208,3172_210504871_192699993_langId-en,00.html

Canadian Centre for Philanthropy. (2003). *The giving and volunteering of seniors*. Toronto: Author. Retrieved August 31, 2004 from http://www.givingandvolunteering.ca/pdf/factsheets/ 2000_CA_Giving_and_volunteering_in_Seniors.pdf

Canadian Child Care Federation. (1998). *Our child care workforce: From recognition to remuneration: More than a labour of love: Executive summary* (Catalogue No. C98-900578-XE). Ottawa, ON: Author. Retrieved November 21, 2001 from http://www.childcarecanada.org/policy/polstudies/ccworkforce/ english.pdf

Canadian Child Care Federation. (2001). Toy safety. Retrieved March 7, 2004, from: http://www.cfc-efc.ca/docs/cccf/rs026_en.htm

Canadian Council on Social Development. (1999a). *Immigrant youth in Canada: Arriving in Canada*. Ottawa, ON: Author. Retrieved October 6, 2001 from http://www.ccsd.ca/subsites/cd/docs/ iy/arriving.htm

Canadian Council on Social Development. (1999b). Work, family and community: Key issues and directions for future research (3.2 Social trends). Ottawa, ON: Author. Retrieved December 23, 2001 from http://labour.hrdc-drhc.gc.ca/worklife/CCSD-CCDS/ c32-en.html

Canadian Council on Social Development. (2000a). *Time to debate social Canada*. Ottawa, ON: Author. Retrieved September 22, 2001 from http://www.ccsd.ca/pr/oped00ml.htm

Canadian Council on Social Development. (2000b). Immigrant youth in Canada: Highlights. In *Cultural diversity: A CCSD research program*. Ottawa, ON: Author. Retrieved November 18, 2001 from http://www.ccsd.ca/subsites/cd/docs/iy/hl.htm

Canadian Council on Social Development. (2000c). Immigrant youth in Canada: Lifestyle patterns of immigrant youth. In *Cultural Diversity: A CCSD research program*. Ottawa, ON: Author. Retrieved November 18, 2001 from http://www.ccsd.ca/subsites/ cd/docs/iy/lifestyl.htm

Canadian Council on Social Development. (2001a). *Highlights: The progress of Canada's Children 2001*. Ottawa, ON: Author. Retrieved September 22, 2001 from http://www.ccsd.ca/pubs/2001/ pcc2001/hl.htm

Canadian Council on Social Development. (2003a). *Census shows growing polarization of income in Canada*. Ottawa, ON: Author. Retrieved April 30, 2004 from http://www.ccsd.ca/pr/2003/ censusincome.htm

Canadian Council on Social Development. (2003b). *Aboriginal Children in Poverty in Urban Communities: Social exclusion and the growing racialization of poverty in Canada*. Ottawa, ON: Author. Retrieved July 9, 2004 from http://www.ccsd.ca/pr/2003/ aboriginal.htm

Canadian Fitness and Lifestyle Research Institute. (2001). *2000 physical activity monitor*. Ottawa, ON: Author. Retrieved December 28, 2001 from http://www.cflri.ca/pdf/e/2000pamrep.pdf

Canadian Heritage. (1999). *Second Language Education*, 2. Second Language Learning: A chance to become bilingual. Ottawa, ON: Author [Online information kit]. Retrieved October 6, 2001 from http://www.pch.gc.ca/offlangoff/publications/kit/ EF02b.htm

Canadian Heritage. (2001a). *Multiculturalism: Strength through diversity*. Ottawa, ON: Author. Retrieved November 19, 2001 from http://www.pch.gc.ca/multi/reports/ ann98-99/multic_e.shtml

Canadian Heritage. (2001b). *Bilingualism in Canada*. Ottawa, ON: Author. Retrieved August 16, 2001 from http://www.pch.gc.ca/ offlangoff/publications/facts/bilingualism.html

Canadian Hospitals Injury Reporting and Prevention Program. (2001). Injuries associated with unpowered scooters. Ottawa, ON: Health Canada. Retrieved October 3, 2001 from http://www.hc-sc.gc.ca/pphb-dgspsp/injury-bles/chirpp/ injrep-rapbles/scoot_e.html

Canadian Institute of Child Health. (2000). *The health of Canada's children: A CICH profile* (3rd ed.). Ottawa, ON: Canadian Institute of Child Health.

Canadian International Development Agency. (2000). *Micronutrient malnutrition*. Author. Retrieved November 12, 2001 from http://www.acdi-cida. gc.ca/cida_ind.nsf/vLUallDocByIDEn/ D1509FA7EF751EDF8525686C006D06B8?OpenDocument

Canadian Medical Association. (2001, August 3). *Dr. James Fraser Mustard to receive the CMA's highest honour*. Ottawa, ON: Author. Retrieved September 22, 2001 from http://www.cma.ca/ cma/common/displayPage.do?pageId=/staticContent/HTML/N0/l2/ MedPost/JamesFraserMustard.htm

Canadian Mental Health Association. (1995). *CMHA policies: Mental health and unemployment*. Toronto: Author. Retrieved December 23, 2001 from http://www.cmha.ca/english/about/ policies/unemployment.htm

Canadian Mental Health Association. (2003). *Eating disorders*. Toronto: Author. Retrieved July 31, 2003, from http://www.cmha.ca/ english/info_centre/mh_pamphlets/mh_pamphlet_ed.pdf

Canadian Paediatric Society. (2004a). Effective discipline for children. *Paediatrics & Child Health, 9*(1), 37–41.

Canadian Paediatric Society. (2004b). Weaning from the breast. *Paediatrics & Child Health, 9*(4), 249–253.

Canadian Parents for French. (2001). *The state of French second language in Canada 2001*. Ottawa, ON: Author. Retrieved October 7, 2001 from http://www.cpf.ca/English/resources/ FSL%202001%20Report/ stateoffsl2001.htm

Canadian Psychological Association. (2000). *Canadian Code of Ethics for Psychologists* (3rd ed.). Ottawa, ON: Canadian Psychological Association.

Canadian Psychological Association. (2004). Policy statement on *physical punishment of children and youth*. Ottawa, ON: Author. Retrieved June 12, 2004 from http://www.cpa.ca/documents/ policy.html

Canadian Toy Testing Council. (2004). *Welcome to the Canadian Toy Testing Council website!* Retrieved March 6, 2004, from http://www.toy-testing.org/CTTCmm.htm

Canadian Toy Testing Council. (n.d.). *Learn to play, play to learn*. Retrieved March 6, 2004, from http://www.cfc-efc.ca/docs/toytc/ 00001_en.htm

Capendale, J.E.M. & Lewis, C. (in press). Constructing an understanding of mind: The development of children's understanding of mind within social interaction. *Behavioral and Brain Sciences*.

Caplan, G. (1964). *Principles of preventive psychiatry*. New York: Basic Books.

Capron, C., & Duyme, M. (1989). Assessment of effects of socioeconomic status on IQ in a full cross-fostering study. *Nature, 340*, 552–554.

Capute, A.J., Palmer, F.B., Shapiro, B.K., Wachtel, R.C., Ross, A., & Accardo, P.J. (1984). Primitive reflex profile: A quantification of primitive reflexes in infancy. *Developmental Medicine and Child Neurology, 26*, 375–383.

Carey, R.G. (1974). Living until death: A program of service and research for the terminally ill. *Hospital Progress*. (Reprinted in E. Kübler-Ross [Ed.], *Death. The final stage of growth*. Englewood Cliffs, NJ: Prentice-Hall, 1975.)

Carlson, E.A., & Sroufe, L.A. (1995). Contribution of attachment theory to developmental psychopathology. In D. Cicchetti & D.J. Conen (Eds.), *Developmental psychopathology: Vol. 1. Theory and methods* (pp. 581–617). New York: Wiley.

Carmeli, E., Reznick, A., Coleman, R., & Carmeli, V. (2000). Muscle strength and mass of lower extremities in relation to functional abilities in elderly adults. *Gerontology, 46,* 249–257.

Carnelley, K., Wortman, C., & Kessler, R. (1999). The impact of widowhood on depression: Findings from a prospective survey. *Psychological Medicine, 29,* 1111–1123.

Caron, A.J., & Caron, R.F. (1981). Processing of relational information as an index of infant risk. In S. Friedman & M. Sigman (Eds.), *Preterm birth and psychological development* (pp. 219–240). New York: Academic Press.

Carpenter, S. (2001). Teens' risky behavior is about more than race and family resources. *APA Monitor, 32,* 22–23.

Carr, S. (2000). As distance education comes of age, the challenge is keeping the students. *Chronicle of Higher Education, 46,* A39–A41.

Carrière, G. (2003). Parent and child factors associated with obesity (Statistics Canada, Catalogue No. 82-003). *Health Reports, 14*(Supplement), 29–39.

Carrière, Y., & Pelletier, L. (1995). Factors underlying the institutionalization of elderly persons in Canada. *Journals of Gerontology: Social Sciences, 50B,* S164–S172.

Carson, D., Klee, T. & Perry, C. (1998). Comparisons of children with delayed and normal language at 24 months of age on measures of behavioral difficulties, social and cognitive development. *Infant Mental Health Journal, 19,* 59–75.

Carstairs, S., & Beaudoin, G.A. (2000). *Quality end-of-life care: The right of every Canadian* (Subcommittee to update "Of Life and Death" of the Standing Senate Committee on Social Affairs, Science and Technology: Final report). Ottawa, ON: Standing Senate Committee on Social Affairs. Retrieved September 8, 2004 from http://www.parl.gc.ca/36/2/parlbus/commbus/senate/com-e/upda-e/rep-e/repfinjun00-e.htm

Carstensen, L.L. (1992). Social and emotional patterns in adulthood: Support for socioemotional selectivity theory. *Psychology and Aging, 7,* 331–338.

Carstensen, L.L., Gottman, J.M., & Levenson, R.W. (1995). Emotional behavior in long-term marriage. *Psychology and Aging, 10,* 140–149.

Carver, R.P. (1990). Intelligence and reading ability in grades 2–12. *Intelligence, 14,* 449–455.

Casas, J.F., & Mosher, M. (1995, March). *Relational and overt aggression in preschool: "You can't come to my birthday party unless..."* Paper presented at the biennial meeting of the Society for Research in Child Development, Indianapolis, IN.

Casasola, M., & Cohen, L. (2000). Infants' association of linguistic labels with causal actions. *Developmental Psychology, 36,* 155–168.

Case, R. (1985). *Intellectual development: Birth to adulthood.* New York: Academic Press.

Case, R. (1991). Stages in the development of the young child's first sense of self. *Developmental Review, 11,* 210–230.

Case, R. (1992). *The mind's staircase: Exploring thought and knowledge.* Hillsdale, NJ: Erlbaum.

Case, R.B., Moss, A.J., Case, N., McDermott, M., & Eberly, S. (1992). Living alone after myocardial infarction: Impact on prognosis. *Journal of the American Medical Association, 267,* 515–519.

Caspi, A. (1998). Personality development across the life course. In N. Eisenberg (Ed.), *Handbook of child psychology: Vol. 3. Social, emotional, and personality development* (5th ed., pp. 311–388). New York: Wiley.

Caspi, A. (2000). The child is father of the man: Personality continuities from childhood to adulthood. *Journal of Personality & Social Psychology, 78,* 158–172.

Caspi, A., Henry, B., McGee, R.O., Moffitt, T.E., & Silva, P.A. (1995). Temperamental origins of child and adolescent behavior problems: From age three to age fifteen. *Child Development, 66,* 55–68.

Cassidy, J., & Berlin, L.J. (1994). The insecure/ambivalent pattern of attachment: Theory and research. *Child Development, 65,* 971–991.

Cassileth, B.R., Walsh, W.P., & Lusk, E.J. (1988). Psychosocial correlates of cancer survival: A subsequent report 3 to 8 years after cancer diagnosis. *Journal of Clinical Oncology, 6,* 1753–1759.

Castellino, D., Lerner, J., Lerner, R., & von Eye, A. (1998). Maternal employment and education: Predictors of young adolescent career trajectories. *Applied Developmental Science, 2,* 114–126.

Castle, J., Groothues, C., Bredenkamp, D., Beckett, C., et al. (1999). Effects of qualities of early institutional care on cognitive attainment. *American Journal of Orthopsychiatry, 69,* 424–437.

Cattell, R.B. (1963). Theory of fluid and crystallized intelligence: A critical experiment. *Journal of Educational Psychology, 54,* 1–22.

Cauley, J.A., Seeley, D.G., Ensrud, K., Ettinger, B., Black, D., & Cummings, S.R. (1995). Estrogen replacement therapy and fractures in older women. *Annals of Internal Medicine, 122,* 9–16.

Ceci, S., & Bronfenbrenner, U. (1985). "Don't forget to take the cupcakes out of the oven": Prospective memory, strategic time-monitoring, and context. *Child Development, 56,* 152–164.

Centers for Disease Control. (1994). Prevalence of adults with no known major risk factors for coronary heart disease—behavioral risk factor surveillance system, 1992. *Morbidity and Mortality Weekly Report, 43,* 61–69.

Centers for Disease Control. (1999a). AIDS Surveillance Report. *Morbidity and Mortality Weekly Report,* 11.

Centers for Disease Control. (1999b). Syphilis fact sheet [Online report]. Retrieved September 1, 2000 from http://www.cdc.gov

Centers for Disease Control. (2000a). The burden of prostate cancer [Online at-a-glance factsheet]. Retrieved October 4, 2000 from http://www.cdc.gov

Centers for Disease Control. (2000b). Some facts about genital herpes [Online report]. Retrieved September 1, 2000 from http://www.cdc.gov

Centers for Disease Control. (2000c). *STD facts: Gonorrhea* [Online report]. Retrieved September 1, 2000 from http://www.cdc.gov

Centers for Disease Control. (2000d). Youth risk behavior surveillance—United States, 1999. *Morbidity and Mortality Weekly Report, 49,* 1–96.

Centers for Disease Control. National Immunization Program. (1999, April 2). Achievements in public health, 1900–1999: Impact of vaccines universally recommended for children. *Morbidity & Mortality Weekly Report, 48* (12), 243–248.

Centerwall, B.S. (1989). Exposure to television as a cause of violence. In G. Comstock (Ed.), *Public communication and behavior* (pp. 1–58). San Diego, CA: Academic Press.

Centerwall, B.S. (1992). Television and violence. The scale of the problem and where to go from here. *Journal of the American Medical Association, 267*(22), 3059–3063.

Century Foundation. (1998). *Social security reform: A Century Foundation guide to the issues* [Online version]. Retrieved February 22, 2001 from www.tcf.org/publications/Basics

Cernoch, J.M., & Porter, R.H. (1985). Recognition of maternal axillary odors by infants. *Child Development, 56,* 1593–1598.

Chadwick, O., Taylor, E., Taylor, A., Heptinstall, E. et al., (1999). Hyperactivity and reading disability: A longitudinal study of the nature of the association. *Journal of Child Psychology & Psychiatry, 40,* 1039–1050.

Chan, R., Raboy, B., & Patterson, C. (1998). Psychosocial adjustment among children conceived via donor insemination by lesbian and heterosexual mothers. *Child Development, 69,* 443–457.

Chandler, M.J., & Lalonde, C. (1998). Cultural continuity as a hedge against suicide in Canada's First Nations. *Transcultural Psychiatry, 35*(2), 193–211.

Chandler, M.J., Lalonde, C.E., Sokol, B., & Hallett, D. (2003). Personal persistence, identity development, and suicide: A study of native and non-native North American adolescents. *Monographs of the Society for Research in Child Development, 68*(2), 1–130.

Chao, R. (1994). Beyond parental control and authoritarian parenting style: Understanding Chinese parenting through the cultural notion of training. *Child Development, 65,* 1111–1119.

Chao, R.K., & Willms, J.D. (1998). Do parenting practices make a difference? (Catalogue No. W-98-32Es). Ottawa, ON: Human

Resources Development Canada. Retrieved September 22, 2001 from http://www.hrdc-drhc.gc.ca/stratpol/arb/conferences/nlscyconf/chao-e.shtml

Chapman, J., & Tunmer, W. (1997). A longitudinal study of beginning reading achievement and reading self-concept. *British Journal of Educational Psychology, 67,* 279–291.

Chaptman, D. (2004, January 24). Education Arcade aims for video-game literacy, markets. *Wisconsin Week.* Madison, WI: University of Wisconsin Retrieved July 1, 2004 from http://www.news.wisc.edu/9333.html

Chappell, N. (1999). *Volunteering and healthy aging: What we know.* Ottawa, ON: Volunteer Canada. Retrieved December 29, 2001 from http://www.volunteer.ca/volunteer/canada_adults_report_printable.htm

Charlesworth, W.R. (1992). Darwin and developmental psychology: Past and present. *Developmental Psychology, 28,* 5–16.

Chase-Lansdale, P.L., Cherlin, A.J., & Kiernan, K.E. (1995). The long-term effects of parental divorce on the mental health of young adults: A developmental perspective. *Child Development, 66,* 1614–1634.

Chase-Lansdale, P.L., & Hetherington, E.M. (1990). The impact of divorce on life-span development: Short and long term effects. In P.B. Baltes, D.L. Featherman, & R.M. Lerner (Eds.), *Life-span development and behavior* (Vol. 10, pp. 107–151). Hillsdale, NJ: Erlbaum.

Chasseigne, G., Grau, S., Mullet, E., & Cama, V. (1999). How well do elderly people cope with uncertainty in a learning task? *Acta Psychologica, 103,* 229–238.

Chatlos, J. (1997). Substance use and abuse and the impact on academic difficulties. *Child & Adolescent Clinics of North America, 6,* 545–568.

Chen, C.Y., & Carvell, T. (1999, November 22). Products of the Century. *Fortune, 134–136.*

Chen, J., Bierhals, A., Prigerson, H., Kasl, S., Mazure, C., & Jacobs, S. (1999). Gender differences in the effects of bereavement-related psychological distress in health outcomes. *Psychological Medicine, 29,* 367–380.

Chen, S. (1997). Child's understanding of secret and friendship development. *Psychological Science (China), 20,* 565–545.

Chen, Z. (1999). Ethnic similarities and differences in the association of emotional autonomy and adolescent outcomes: Comparing Euro-American and Asian-American adolescents. *Psychological Reports, 84,* 501–516.

Chen-Hafteck, L. (1997). Music and language development in early childhood: Integrating past research in the two domains. *Early Child Development & Care, 130,* 85–97.

Cherlin, A., Chase-Lansdale, P., & McRae, C. (1998). Effects of parental divorce on mental health throughout the life course. *American Sociological Review, 63,* 239–249.

Cherlin, A., & Furstenberg, F.F. (1986). *The new American grandparent.* New York: Basic Books.

Chess, S., & Thomas, A. (1984). *Origins and evolution of behavior disorders: Infancy to early adult life.* New York: Brunner/Mazel.

Chi, M.T. (1978). Knowledge structure and memory development. In R.S. Siegler (Ed.), *Children's thinking: What develops?* (pp. 73–96). Hillsdale, NJ: Erlbaum.

Chiapin, G., DeAraujo, G., & Wagner, A. (1998). Mother-in-law and daughter-in-law: How is the relationship between these two women? *Psicologia: Reflexao e Critica, 11,* 541–550.

Chiappe, P., & Siegel, L. (1999). Phonological awareness and reading acquisition in English- and Punjabi-speaking Canadian children. *Journal of Educational Psychology, 91,* 20–28.

Chickering, A., & Reisser, L. (1993). *Education and identity* (2nd ed.). San Francisco: Jossey-Bass.

Children's Hospital of Eastern Ontario. (2003). *Joint statement on physical punishment of children and youth.* Ottawa, ON: Author. Retrieved June 24, 2004 from http://www.cheo.on.ca/english/pdf/joint_statement_e.pdf

Chincotta, D., & Underwood, G. (1997). Estimates, language of schooling and bilingual digit span. *European Journal of Cognitive Psychology, 9,* 325–348.

Choa, R.K., & Willms, J.D. (2002). The effects of parenting practices on children's outcomes. In J.D. Willms (Ed.), *Vulnerable children* (pp. 71–102). Edmonton, AB: The University of Alberta Press.

Choi, N.G. (1991). Racial differences in the determinants of living arrangements of widowed and divorced elderly women. *The Gerontologist, 31,* 496–504.

Choi, S. (2000). Caregiver input in English and Korean: Use of nouns and verbs in book-reading and toy-play contexts. *Journal of Children's Language, 27,* 69–96.

Chomsky, N. (1959). A review of B.F. Skinner's *Verbal Behavior. Language, 35,* 26–129.

Chomik, T.A. (2001). *The population health template.* Ottawa, ON: Health Canada. Retrieved August 7, 2004 from http://www.hc-sc.gc.ca/hppb/phdd/pdf/discussion_paper.pdf

Chopak, J., Vicary, J., & Crockett, L. (1998). Predicting alcohol and tobacco use in a sample of rural adolescents. *American Journal of Health Behavior, 22,* 334–341.

Chou, C., Chou, J., & Tyang, N. (1998, February 18–22). *An exploratory study of Internet addiction, usage, and communication pleasure.* Paper presented at the annual meeting of the Association for Educational Communications and Technology. St. Louis, MO. (ERIC No. ED 416 838).

Christensen, A., & Heavey, C. (1999). Interventions for couples. *Annual Review of Psychology, 50,* 165–190.

Christensen, C. (1997). Onset, rhymes, and phonemes in learning to read. *Scientific Studies of Reading, 1,* 341–358.

Christensen, H., Henderson, A., Griffiths, K., & Levings, C. (1997). Does aging inevitably lead to declines in cognitive performance? A longitudinal study of elite academics. *Personality & Individual Differences, 23,* 67–78.

Christopher, F., Madura, M., & Weaver, L. (1998). Premarital sexual aggressors: A multivariate analysis of social, relational, and individual variables. *Journal of Marriage and the Family, 60,* 56–69.

Chumlea, W.C. (1982). Physical growth in adolescence. In B.B. Wolman (Ed.), *Handbook of developmental psychology* (pp. 471–485). Englewood Cliffs, NJ: Prentice-Hall.

Church, M., Eldis, F., Blakley, B., & Bawle, E. Hearing, language, speech, vestibular, and dento-facial disorders in fetal alcohol syndrome. *Alcoholism: Clinical & Experimental Research, 21,* 227–237.

Ciancio, D., Sadovsky, A., Malabonga, V., Trueblood, L., et al. (1999). Teaching classification and seriation to preschoolers. *Child Study Journal, 29,* 193–205.

Cillessen, A.H.N., van IJzendoorn, H.W., van Lieshout, C.F.M., & Hartup, W.W. (1992). Heterogeneity among peer-rejected boys: Subtypes and stabilities. *Child Development, 63,* 893–905.

Claes, M. (1998). Adolescents' closeness with parents, siblings, and friends in three countries: Canada, Belgium, and Italy. *Journal of Youth & Adolescence, 27,* 165–184.

Clark, S., & Miles, M. (1999). Conflicting responses: The experiences of fathers of infants diagnosed with severe congenital heart disease. *Journal of the Society of Pediatric Nurses, 4,* 7–14.

Clark, W. (1998). Religious observance: Marriage and family (Catalogue No. 11-008-XPE). *Canadian Social Trends, Autumn(50),* 2–7.

Clark, W. (2000). Patterns of religious attendance (Catalogue No. 11-008-XPE). *Canadian Social Trends, Winter(59),* 23–27.

Clark, W. (2001, 11b). Kids and teens on the net. *Canadian Social Trends, 62,* 6–10.

Clark, W. (2003). Update on Education. *Canadian Social Trends, Winter(71),* 19–22.

Clark, W. (2003). Pockets of belief: Religious attendance patterns in Canada (Catalogue No. 11-008-XPE). *Canadian Social Trends, Spring(68),* 2–5.

Clarke-Stewart, K.A., Gruber, C.P., & Fitzgerald, L.M. (1994). *Children at home and in day care.* Hillsdale, NJ: Erlbaum.

Clarkson-Smith, L., & Hartley, A.A. (1990). The game of bridge as an exercise in working memory and reasoning. *Journals of Gerontology: Psychological Sciences, 45,* P233–238.

Cleveland, G., & Hyatt, D. (1997). *Using the NLSCY to study the effects of child care on child development: Final report* (Catalogue

No. T-97-6E). Ottawa, ON: Human Resources Development Canada. Retrieved November 21, 2001 from http://www.hrdc-drhc.gc.ca/arb/publications/research/1999docs/t-97-6e.pdf

Clifford, T.J., Campbell, M.K., Speechley, K.N., & Gorodzinsky, F. (2002). Empirical evidence of the absence of an association with source of early infant nutrition. *Archives of Pediatrics & Adolescent Medicine, 156*(11), 1123–1128.

Clinkingbeard, C., Minton, B., Davis, J., & McDermott, K. (1999). Women's knowledge about menopause, hormone replacement therapy (HRT), and interactions with healthcare providers: An exploratory study. *Journal of Women's Health & Gender-Based Medicine, 8,* 1097–1102.

Cnattingius, S., Berendes, H.W., & Forman, M.R. (1993). Do delayed childbearers face increased risks of adverse pregnancy outcomes after the first birth? *Obstetrics and Gynecology, 81,* 512–516.

Coffey, C., Saxton, J., Ratcliff, G., Bryan, R., & Lucke, J. (1999). Relation of education to brain size in normal aging: Implications for the reserve hypothesis. *Neurology, 53,* 189–196.

Cohen, A.-L., Dixon, R.A., Lindsay, D.S., Masson, M.E.J. (2003). The effect of perceptual distinctiveness on the prospective and retrospective. *Canadian Journal of Experimental Psychology, 57*(4), 274–289.

Cohen, G. (2000). *The creative age: Awakening human potential in the second half of life.* New York: Avon Books.

Cohen, R. (2000, April 11). Horror expressed in Germany over Dutch euthanasia. *New York Times Online.* Retrieved April 17, 2001 from www.nytimes.com

Cohen, S. (1991). Social supports and physical health: Symptoms, health behaviors, and infectious disease. In E.M. Cummings, A.L. Greene, & K.H. Karraker (Eds.), *Life-span developmental psychology: Perspectives on stress and coping* (pp. 213–234). Hillsdale, NJ: Erlbaum.

Cohen, Y.A. (1964). *The transition from childhood to adolescence.* Chicago: Aldine.

Co-ordinated Access for Child Care (2001). *Choosing quality child care.* The Regional Municipality of Hamilton-Wentworth: Author. Retrieved November 13, 2001 from http://www.cafcc.on.ca/quality.htm

Coie, J.D., & Cillessen, A.H.N. (1993). Peer rejection: Origins and effects on children's development. *Current Directions in Psychological Science, 2,* 89–92.

Coie, J., Cillessen, A., Dodge, K., Hubbard, J., et al., (1999). It takes two to fight: A test of relational factors and a method for assessing aggressive dyads. *Developmental Psychology, 35,* 1179–1188.

Coie, J., Terry, R., Lenox, K., Lochman, J., & Hyman, C. (1995). Childhood peer rejection and aggression as predictors of stable patterns of adolescent disorder. *Development and Psychopathology, 7,* 697–713.

Coiro, M.J. (1995, March). *Child behavior problems as a function of marital conflict and parenting.* Paper presented at the biennial meetings of the Society for Research in Child Development, Indianapolis, IN.

Colby, A., Kohlberg, L., Gibbs, J., & Lieberman, M. (1983). A longitudinal study of moral judgment. *Monographs of the Society for Research in Child Development, 48*(1–2, Serial No. 200).

Colditz, G.A., Hankinson, S.E., Hunter, D.J., Willett, W.C., Manson, J.E., Stampfer, M.J., Hennekens, C., Rosner, B., & Speizer, F.E. (1995). The use of estrogens and progestins and the risk of breast cancer in postmenopausal women. *New England Journal of Medicine, 332,* 1589–1593.

Cole, D.A. (1991). Change in self-perceived competence as a function of peer and teacher evaluation. *Developmental Psychology, 27,* 682–688.

Cole, M. (1992). Culture in development. In M.H. Bornstein & M.E. Lamb (Eds.), *Developmental psychology: An advanced textbook* (pp. 731–789). Hillsdale, NJ: Erlbaum.

Coleman, J., Pratt, R., Stoddard, R., Gerstmann, D., & Abel, H. (1997). The effects of the male and female singing and speaking voices on selected physiological and behavioral measures of pre-

mature infants in the intensive care unit. *International Journal of Arts Medicine, 5,* 4–11.

Coley, R., & Chase-Lansdale, L. (1998). Adolescent pregnancy and parenthood: Recent evidence and future directions. *American Psychologist, 53,* 152–166.

Collaer, M.L., & Hines, M. (1995). Human behavioral sex differences: A role for gonadal hormones during early development? *Psychological Bulletin, 118,* 55–107.

Collet, J.P., Burtin, P., Gillet, J., Bossard, N., Ducruet, T., & Durr, F. (1994). Risk of infectious diseases in children attending different types of day-care setting. Epicreche Research Group. *Respiration, 61,* 16–19.

Colombo, J. (1993). *Infant cognition: Predicting later intellectual functioning.* Newbury Park, CA: Sage.

Colonia-Willner, R. (1999). Investing in practical intelligence: Ageing and cognitive efficiency among executives. *International Journal of Behavioral Development, 23,* 591–614.

Colton, M., Buss, K., Mangelsdorf, S., Brooks, C., Sorenson, D., Stansbury, K., Harris, M., & Gunnar, M. (1992). *Relations between toddler coping strategies, temperament, attachment and adrenocortical stress responses.* Poster presented at the 8th International Conference on Infant Studies, Miami, FL.

Comley, L., & Mousmanis, P. (2004). *Improving the odds: Healthy child development.* Toronto: Ontario College of Physicians. Retrieved June 22, 2004 from http://www.beststart.org/resources/hlthy_chld_dev/pdf/HCD_complete.pdf

Commissaris, C., Ponds, R., & Jolles, J. (1998). Subjective forgetfulness in a normal Dutch population: Possibilities of health education and other interventions. *Patient Education & Counseling, 34,* 25–32.

Common, R.W. & Frost, L.G. (1998). The implications of the mismeasurement of native students' intelligence through the use of standardized intelligence tests. *Canadian Journal of Native Education, 15*(1), 18–30.

Communication Canada (2004). *Statutes of Canada 2004 Chapter 2: An Act respecting assisted human reproduction and related research Bill C-6.* Retrieved April 16, 2004 from http://www.hc-sc.gc.ca/english/pdf/protection/ahr/C-6_4_RA.pdf

Compas, B.E., Ey, S., & Grant, K.E. (1993). Taxonomy, assessment, and diagnosis of depression during adolescence. *Psychological Bulletin, 114,* 323–344.

Condry, J., & Condry, S. (1976). Sex differences: A study in the eye of the beholder. *Child Development, 47,* 812–819.

Conger, R.D., Patterson, G.R., & Ge, X. (1995). It takes two to replicate: A mediational model for the impact of parents' stress on adolescent adjustment. *Child Development, 66,* 80–97.

Conner, S., & Brink, S. (1999). The impacts of non-parental care on child development. Ottawa, ON: Human Resources Development Canada (W-00-2E). Retrieved November 13, 2001 from http://www.hrdc-drhc.gc.ca/stratpol/arb/publications/research/2000docs/abw-00 2c.shtml

Connidis, I.A. (1989). *Family Ties Later in Life.* Toronto & Vancouver: Butterworths.

Connidis, I.A. (1994). Sibling support in older age. *Journals of Gerontology: Social Sciences, 49,* S309–317.

Connidis, I.A., & Davies, L. (1992). Confidants and companions: Choices in later life. *Journals of Gerontology: Social Sciences, 47,* S115–122.

Connidis, I.A., & McMullin, J.A. (1993). To have or have not: Parent status and the subjective well-being of older men and women. *The Gerontologist, 33,* 630–636.

Connolly, K., & Dalgleish, M. (1989). The emergence of a tool-using skill in infancy. *Developmental Psychology, 25,* 894–912.

Connor, S.K, McIntyre, L. (1998). *How Tobacco and Alcohol Affect Newborn Children* (W-98-34Es). Ottawa, ON: Human Resources Development Canada. Retrieved November 19, 2001 from http://www.hrdc-drhc.gc.ca/arb/nlscy-elnej/w-98-34es-e.pdf

Cook, E. (1998). Effects of reminiscence on life satisfaction of elderly female nursing home residents. *Health Care for Women International, 19,* 109–118.

Cook, S., & Heppner, P. (1997). Coping control, problem-solving appraisal, and depressive symptoms during a farm crisis. *Journal of Mental Health Counseling, 19,* 64–77.

Cooke-Reynolds, M., & Zukewich, N. (2004). The feminization of work (Catalogue No. 11-008). *Canadian Social Trends, Spring*(72), 24–29.

Coombs, R.H. (1991). Marital status and personal well-being: A literature review. *Family Relations, 40,* 97–102.

Cooper, A., Putnam, D., Planchon, L., & Boies, S. (1999). Online sexual compulsivity: Getting tangled in the net. *Sexual Addiction & Compulsivity, 6,* 79–104.

Coplan, R.J., & Armer, M. (in press). 'Talking yourself out of being shy': Shyness, expressive vocabulary, and adjustment in preschool. *Merrill-Palmer Quarterly.*

Coplan, R.J., & Prakash, K. (2003). Spending time with teacher: Characteristics of preschoolers who frequently elicit versus initiate interactions with teachers. *Early Childhood Research Quarterly, 18*(1), 143–158.

Coplan, R.J., Prakash, K., O'Neil, K., & Armer, M. (2004). Do you 'want' to play? Distinguishing between conflicted-shyness and social disinterest in early childhood. *Developmental Psychology, 40*(2), 244–258.

Corbet, A., Long, W., Schumacher, R., Gerdes, J., & Cotton, R. (1995). Double-blind developmental evaluation at 1-year corrected age of 597 premature infants with birth weights from 500 to 1350 grams enrolled in three placebo-controlled trials of prophylactic synthetic surfactant. *Journal of Pediatrics, 126,* S5–12.

Corkum, P., Moldofsky, H., Hogg-Johnson, S., Humphries, T. & Tannock, R. (1999). Sleep problems in children with attention-deficit/hyperactivity disorder: Impact of subtype, comorbidity, and stimulant medication. *Journal of the American Academy of Child and Adolescent Psychiatry, 38*(10), 1285–1293.

Corkum, P., Tannock, R. & Moldofsky, H. (1998). Sleep disturbances in children with attention-deficit/hyperactivity disorder. *Journal of the American Academy of Child and Adolescent Psychiatry, 37*(6), 637–646.

Corr, C.A. (1991/1992). A task-based approach to coping with dying. *Omega, 24,* 81–94.

Corrada, M., Brookmeyer, R., & Kawas, C. (1995). Sources of variability in prevalence rates of Alzheimer's disease. *International Journal of Epidemiology, 24,* 1000–1005.

Corso, J.F. (1987). Sensory-perceptual processes and aging. In K.W. Schaie (Ed.), *Annual Review of Gerontology and Geriatrics* (Vol. 7, pp. 29–56). New York: Springer.

Corwin, J., Loury, M., & Gilbert, A.N. (1995). Workplace, age, and sex as mediators of olfactory function: Data from the National Geographic smell survey. *Journals of Gerontology: Psychological Sciences, 50B,* P179–186.

Cosmides, L., & Tooby, J. (2000). Evolutionary Psychology and the Emotions. In M. Lewis & J. Haviland-Jones (Eds.), *Handbook of Emotions* (2nd ed.). New York: Guilford.

Cossette, L., Malcuit, G., & Pomerleau, A. (1991). Sex differences in motor activity during early infancy. *Infant Behavior and Development, 14,* 175–186.

Costa, P.T., & McCrae, R.R. (1980a). Influence of extraversion and neuroticism on subjective well-being: Happy and unhappy people. *Journal of Personality and Social Psychology, 38,* 668–678.

Costa, P.T., Jr., & McCrae, R.R. (1980b). Still stable after all these years: Personality as a key to some issues in adulthood and old age. In P.B. Baltes & O.G. Brim, Jr. (Eds.), *Life-span development and behavior* (pp. 65–102). New York: Academic Press.

Cotman, C.W., & Neeper, S. (1996). Activity-dependent plasticity and the aging brain. In E.L. Schneider & J.W. Rowe (Eds.), *Handbook of the biology of aging* (4th ed., pp. 284–299). San Diego, CA: Academic Press.

Cotton, L., Bynum, D., & Madhere, S. (1997). Socialization forces and the stability of work values from late adolescence to early adulthood. *Psychological Reports, 80,* 115–124.

Coulton, C.J., Korbin, J.E., Su, M., & Chow, J. (1995). Community level factors and child maltreatment rates. *Child Development, 66,* 1262–1276.

Council of Economic Advisers to the President. (2000). Teens and their parents in the 21st century: An examination of trends in teen behavior and the role of parental involvement. Washington, DC: Author. Retrieved July 7, 2004 from http://clinton4.nara.gov/media/pdf/CEAreport.pdf

Counts, D.R. (1976/1977). The good death in Kaliai: Preparation for death in western New Britain. *Omega, 7,* 367–372.

Cowan, B.R., & Underwood, M.K. (1995, March). *Sugar and spice and everything nice? A developmental investigation of social aggression among girls.* Paper presented at the biennial meetings of the Society for Research in Child Development, Indianapolis, IN.

Cowan, C.P., & Cowan, P.A. (1987). Men's involvement in parenthood: Identifying the antecedents and understanding the barriers. In P.W. Berman & F.A. Pedersen (Eds.), *Men's transitions to parenthood: Longitudinal studies of early family experience* (pp. 145–174). Hillsdale, NJ: Erlbaum.

Cox, M., Paley, B., Burchinal, M., & Payne, C. (1999). Marital perceptions and interactions across the transition to parenthood. *Journal of Marriage & the Family, 61,* 611–625.

Craig, W.M., Peters, R.D., & Konarski, R. (1998). *Bullying and Victimization Among Canadian School Children* (Catalogue No. W-98-28E). Ottawa, ON: Human Resources Development Canada. Retrieved November 15, 2001 from http://www.hrdc-drhc.gc.ca/stratpol/arb/conferences/nlscyconf/craig-e.shtml

Craig, W.M., Peters, R.D., & Willms, J.D. (2002). The role of peer group in pre-adolescent behaviour. In J.D. Willms (Ed.), *Vulnerable children* (pp. 71–102). Edmonton, AB: The University of Alberta Press.

Cramer, D. (1991). Type A behavior pattern, extraversion, neuroticism and psychological distress. *British Journal of Medical Psychology, 64,* 73–83.

Cramer, P. (2000). Defense mechanisms in psychology today. *American Psychologist, 55,* 637–646.

Cranswick, K. (2003). *General Social Survey—Cycle 16: Caring for an aging society, 2002* (Catalogue No. 89-582-XIE). Ottawa, ON: Statistics Canada. Retrieved August 25, 2004 from http://erl.bibliocentre.ca:2067/english/freepub/89-582-XIE/pdf/89-582-XIE03001.pdf

Crawley, A., Anderson, D., Wilder, A., Williams, M., & Santomero, A. (1999). Effects of repeated exposures to a single episode of the television program *Blue's Clues* on the viewing behaviors and comprehension of preschool children. *Educational Psychology, 91,* 630–638.

The creators. (2000, March/April). *Modern Maturity,* 38–44.

Crick, N., & Dodge, K. (1994). A review and reformulation of social information processing mechanisms in children's social adjustment. *Psychological Bulletin,115,* 74–101.

Crick, N., & Dodge, K. (1996). Social information-processing mechanisms in reactive and proactive aggression. *Child Development, 67,* 993–1002.

Crick, N.R., & Grotpeter, J.K. (1995). Relational aggression, gender, and social-psychological adjustment. *Child Development, 66,* 710–722.

Crick, N., & Ladd, G. (1993). Children's perceptions of their peer experiences: Attributions, loneliness, social anxiety, and social avoidance. *Developmental Psychology, 29,* 244–254.

Crittenden, P.M. (1992). Quality of attachment in the preschool years. *Development and Psychopathology, 4,* 209–241.

Crittenden, P.M., Partridge, M.F., & Claussen, A.H. (1991). Family patterns of relationship in normative and dysfunctional families. *Development and Psychopathology, 3,* 491–512.

Crompton, S. (2000). Health (Catalogue No. 11-008-XPE). *Canadian Social Trends, Winter*(59), 12–17.

Crone, D., & Whitehurst, G. (1999). Age and schooling effects on emergent literacy and early reading skills. *Journal of Educational Psychology, 91,* 594–603.

Crouter, A.C., & McHale, S.M. (1993). Familial economic circumstances: Implications for adjustment and development in early adolescence. In R.M. Lerner (Ed.), *Early adolescence: Perspectives on research, policy, and intervention* (pp. 71–91). Hillsdale, NJ: Erlbaum.

Crowell, J.A., & Feldman, S.S. (1988). Mothers' internal models of relationships and children's behavioral and developmental status: A study of mother-child interaction. *Child Development, 50,* 1273–1285.

Crowell, J.A., & Waters, E. (1995, March). *Is the parent–child relationship a prototype of later love relationships? Studies of attachment and working models of attachment.* Paper presented at the biennial meeting of the Society for Research in Child Development, Indianapolis, IN.

Crystal, S., Shae, D., & Krishnaswami, S. (1992). Educational attainment, occupational history, and stratification: Determinants of later-life economic outcomes. *Journals of Gerontology: Social Sciences, 47,* S213–221.

Csikszentmihalyi, M., & Rathunde, K. (1990). The psychology of wisdom: An evolutionary interpretation. In R. Sternberg (Ed.), *Wisdom: Its nature, origins, and development* (pp. 25–51). Cambridge, England: Cambridge University Press.

Cuba, L., & Longino, C.F., Jr. (1991). Regional retirement migration: The case of Cape Cod. *Journals of Gerontology: Social Sciences, 46,* S33–42.

Culp, A., Culp, R., Blankemeyer, M., & Passmark, L. (1998). Parent Education Home Visitation Program: Adolescent and nonadolescent mother comparison after six months of intervention. *Infant Mental Health Journal, 19,* 111–123.

Cumming, E. (1975). Engagement with an old theory. *International Journal of Aging and Human Development, 6,* 187–191.

Cumming, E., & Henry, W.E. (1961). *Growing old.* New York: Basic Books.

Cummings, E.M., & Davies, P.T. (1994). Maternal depression and child development. *Journal of Child Psychology and Psychiatry, 35,* 73–112.

Cunningham, A.S., Jelliffe, D.B., & Jelliffe, E.F.P. (1991). Breast-feeding and health in the 1980s: A global epidemiologic review. *Journal of Pediatrics, 118,* 659–666.

Cunningham, L. (1996). *Grief and the adolescent.* Newhall, CA: TeenAge Grief, Inc.

Cunningham, W.R., & Haman, K.L. (1992). Intellectual functioning in relation to mental health. In J.E. Birren, R.B. Sloane, & G.D. Cohen (Eds.), *Handbook of mental health and aging* (2nd ed., pp. 340–355). San Diego, CA: Academic Press.

Curran, G., Stoltenberg, S., Hill, E., Mudd, S., Blow, F., & Zucker, R. (1999). Gender differences in the relationship among SES, family history of alcohol disorders and alcohol dependence. *Journal of Studies on Alcohol, 60,* 825–832.

Curyto, K., Chapleski, E., & Lichtenberg, P. (1999). Prediction of the presence and stability of depression in the Great Lakes Native American elderly. *Journal of Mental Health & Aging, 5,* 323–340.

Cushner, K., McClelland, A., & Safford, P. (1992). *Human diversity in education.* New York: McGraw-Hill.

Cuvo, A. (1974). Incentive level influence on overt rehearsal and free recall as a function of age. *Journal of Experimental Child Psychology, 18,* 167–181.

Czaja, S., & Sharit, J. (1998). Age differences in attitudes toward computers. *Journals of Gerontology: Series B: Psychological Sciences & Social Sciences, 53B,* P329–P340.

Czaja, S., Sharit, J., Nair, S., & Rubert, M. (1998). Understanding sources of user variability in computer-based data entry performance. *Behaviour & Information Technology, 17,* 282–293.

Da Costa, D., Larouche, J., Dritsa, M., & Brender, W. (2000). Psychosocial correlates of prepartum and postpartum depressed mood. *Journal of Affective Disorders, 59,* 31–40.

Dalsky, G.P., Stocke, K.S., Ehsani, A.I., Slatopolsky, E., Lee, W., & Birge, S.J. (1988). Weight-bearing exercise training and lumbar bone mineral content in post-menopausal women. *Annals of Internal Medicine, 108,* 824–828.

D'Alton, M.E., & DeCherney, A.H. (1993). Prenatal diagnosis. *New England Journal of Medicine, 328,* 114–118.

Daly, K. (2000). *It keeps getting faster: Changing patterns of time in families.* Ottawa, ON: The Vanier Institute of the Family. Retrieved December 13, 2001 from http://www.vifamily.ca/cft/daly/dalye.htm

Daly, L.E., Kirke, P.N., Molloy, A., Weir, D.G., & Scott, J.M. (1995). Folate levels and neural tube defects: Implications for prevention. *Journal of the American Medical Association, 274,* 1698–1702.

Daly, M., & Wilson, M. (1996). Violence against stepchildren. *Current Directions in Psychological Science, 5,* 77–81.

Daly, S., & Glenwick, D. (2000). Personal adjustment and perceptions of grandchild behavior in custodial grandmothers. *Journal of Clinical Child Psychology, 29,* 108–118.

Damon, W. (1977). *The social world of the child.* San Francisco: Jossey-Bass.

Damon, W. (1983). The nature of social-cognitive change in the developing child. In W.F. Overton (Ed.), *The relationship between social and cognitive development* (pp. 103–142). Hillsdale, NJ: Erlbaum.

Damon, W., & Hart, D. (1988). *Self understanding in childhood and adolescence.* New York: Cambridge University Press.

Danby, S., & Baker, C. (1998). How to be masculine in the block area. *Childhood: A Global Journal of Child Research, 5,* 151–175.

Darou, W.G. (1992). Native Canadians and intelligence testing. *Canadian Journal of Counselling, 26(2),* 96–99.

Dauvergne, M. (2003). Family violence against seniors (Catalogue No. 11-008-XPE). *Canadian Social Trends, Spring(68),* 10–14.

Davajan, V., & Israel, R. (1991). Diagnosis and medical treatment of infertility. In A.L. Stanton & C. Dunkel-Schetter (Eds.), *Infertility: Perspectives from stress and coping research* (pp. 17–28). New York: Plenum.

Davey, F. (1998). Young women's expected and preferred patterns of employment and child care. *Sex Roles, 38,* 95–102.

Davidson, R. (1994). Temperament, affective style, and frontal lobe asymmetry. In G. Dawson & K. Fischer (Eds.), *Human behavior and the developing brain.* New York: Guilford Press.

Davies, P., & Rose, J. (1999). Assessment of cognitive development in adolescents by means of neuropsychological tasks. *Developmental Neuropsychology, 15,* 227–248.

Dawber, T.R., Kannel, W.B., & Lyell, L.P. (1963). An approach to longitudinal studies in a community: The Framingham study. *Annals of the New York Academy of Science, 107,* 539–556.

Dawson, D. (2000). Alcohol consumption, alcohol dependence, and all-cause mortality. *Alcoholism: Clinical & Experimental Research, 24,* 72–81.

Dawson, J., & Langan, P. (1994). *Murder in families.* Washington, DC: U.S. Department of Justice.

DeAngelis, T. (1997). When children don't bond with parents. *Monitor of the American Psychological Association, 28(6),* 10–12.

DeCasper, A.J., Lecaneut, J., Busnel, M., Granier-Deferre, C., & Maugeais, R. (1994). Fetal reactions to recurrent maternal speech. *Infant Behavior and Development, 17,* 159–164.

DeCasper, A.J., & Spence, M.J. (1986). Prenatal maternal speech influences newborns' perception of speech sounds. *Infant Behavior and Development, 9,* 133–150.

Deeg, D.J.H., Kardaun, W.P.F., & Fozard, J.L. (1996). Health, behavior, and aging. In J.E. Birren & K.W. Schaie (Eds.), *Handbook of the psychology of aging* (4th ed., pp. 129–149). San Diego, CA: Academic Press.

Degirmencioglu, S., Urberg, K., & Tolson, J. (1998). Adolescent friendship networks: Continuity and change over the school year. *Merrill-Palmer Quarterly, 44,* 313–337.

de Graaf, C., Polet, P., & van Staveren, W.A. (1994). Sensory perception and pleasantness of food flavors in elderly subjects. *Journals of Gerontology: Psychological Sciences, 49,* P93–99.

de Haan, M., Luciana, M., Maslone, S.M., Matheny, L.S., & Richards, M.L.M. (1994). Development, plasticity, and risk: Commentary on Huttenlocher, Pollit and Gorman, and Gottesman and Goldsmith. In C.A. Nelson (Ed.), *The Minnesota*

Symposia on Child Psychology (Vol. 27, pp. 161–178). Hillsdale, NJ: Erlbaum.

De Jong, G.F., Wilmoth, J.M., Angel, J.L., & Cornwell, G.T. (1995). Motives and the geographic mobility of very old Americans. *Journals of Gerontology: Social Sciences, 50B,* S395–404.

Dekovic, M. (1999). Parent-adolescent conflict: Possible determinants and consequences. *International Journal of Behavioral Development, 23,* 977–1000.

Dekovic, M., & Meeus, W. (1997). Peer relations in adolescence: Effects of parenting and adolescents' self-concept. *Journal of Adolescence, 20,* 163–176.

de Lacoste, M., Horvath, D., & Woodward, J. (1991). Possible sex differences in the developing human fetal brain. *Journal of Clinical and Experimental Neuropsychology, 13,* 831.

del Barrio, V., Moreno-Rosset, C., Lopez-Martinez, R., & Olmedo, M. (1997). Anxiety, depression and personality structure. *Personality & Individual Differences, 23,* 327–335.

DeLoache, J.S. (1995). Early understanding and use of symbols: The model model. *Current Directions in Psychological Science, 4,* 109–113.

DeMeis, D.K., Hock, E., & McBride, S.L. (1986). The balance of employment and motherhood: Longitudinal study of mothers' feelings about separation from their first-born infants. *Developmental Psychology, 22,* 627–632.

DeMulder, E., Denham, S., Schmidt, M., & Mitchell, J. (2000). Q-sort assessment of attachment security during the preschool years: Links from home to school. *Developmental Psycholgy, 36,* 274–282.

Dennerstein, L., Lehert, P., Burger, H., & Dudley, E. (1999). Mood and the menopausal transition. *Journal of Nervous & Mental Disease, 187,* 685–691.

Denney, N.W. (1982). Aging and cognitive changes. In B.B. Wolman (Ed.), *Handbook of developmental psychology* (pp. 807–827). Englewood Cliffs, NJ: Prentice-Hall.

Denney, N.W. (1984). Model of cognitive development across the life span. *Developmental Review, 4,* 171–191.

Dennis, W. (1960). Causes of retardation among institutional children: Iran. *Journal of Genetic Psychology, 96,* 47–59.

Den Ouden, L., Rijken, M., Brand, R., Verloove-Vanhorick, S.P., & Ruys, J.H. (1991). Is it correct to correct? Developmental milestones in 555 "normal" preterm infants compared with term infants. *Journal of Pediatrics, 118,* 399–404.

D'Entremont, B. (2000). A perceptual-attentional explanation of gaze following in 3- and 6-month-olds. *Developmental Science, 3,* 302–311.

D'Entremont, B., Hains, S.M.J., & Muir, D.W. (1997). A demonstration of gaze following in 3- to 6-month-olds. *Infant Behavior and Development, 20,* 560–572.

D'Entremont, B. & Hartung, C. (2003). *A longitudinal investigation of joint attention, emotion regulation and attachment.* Poster presented at the Society for Research in Child Development, Tampa, FL.

Department of Foreign Affairs and International Trade (2001). *Retirement abroad: Seeing the sunsets.* Ottawa, ON: Author, Consular Affairs. Retrieved December 31, 2001 from http://www.voyage.gc.ca/Consular-e/Publications/ retirement_abroad-e.htm

Department of Justice Canada. (2001a). *Criminal Code. R.S., c. C-34, s. 1.* Ottawa, ON: Author. Retrieved November 19, 2001 from http://lois.justice.gc.ca/en/C-46/text.html

Department of Justice Canada. (2001b). *Backgrounder: Youth Criminal Justice Act.* Ottawa, ON: Author. Retrieved November 18, 2001 from http://canada.justice.gc.ca/en/news/nr/2001/doc_25948.html

Department of Justice Canada. (2004). *Fact sheet—Section 43 of the Criminal Code (Corporal Punishment): The Canadian Foundation for Children, Youth and the Law v. The Attorney General of Canada.* Ottawa, ON: Author. Retrieved June 24, 2004 from http://canada.justice.gc.ca/en/news/fs/2004/doc_31114.html

Depressed elderly react best to a mix of drugs and psychotherapy. (1999, March). *APA Monitor Online* [Archives]. Retrieved February 7, 2001 from www.apa.org/monitor/mar99/depress.html

Derevensky, J.L. & Gupta, R. (1998). Youth gambling: Lack of public awareness is contributing to the increasing number. *Psynopsis,* Fall. Retrieved October 25, 2001 from http://www.cpa.ca/Psynopsis/ Gambling.html

Derevensky, J.L., & Gupta, R. (2004, February). Adolescents with gambling problems: A synopsis of our current knowledge. *eGambling: The Electronic Journal of Gambling Issues, 10,* 1–22. Retrieved February 21, 2004 from http://www.camh.net/egambling/ issue10/ejgi_10_derevensky_gupta.html

Derevensky, J.L., Gupta, R., & Winters, K. (2003). Prevalence rates of youth gambling problems: Are the current rates inflated? *Journal of Gambling Studies, 19*(4), 405–425.

DeSpelder, L.A., & Strickland, A.L. (1983). *The last dance: Encountering death and dying.* Palo Alto, CA: Mayfield.

Dessens, A., Cohen-Kettenis, P., Mellenbergh, G., van de Poll, N., Koppe, J., & Boer, K. (1999). Prenatal exposure to anticonvulsants and psychosexual development. *Archives of Sexual Behavior, 28,* 31–44.

Detchant, Lord Walton. (1995). Dilemmas of life and death: Part one. *Journal of the Royal Society of Medicine, 88,* 311–315.

Deter, H., & Herzog, W. (1994). Anorexia nervosa in a long-term perspective: Results of the Heidelberg-Mannheim study. *Psychosomatic Medicine, 56,* 20–27.

de Villiers, P.A., & de Villiers, J.G. (1992). Language development. In M.H. Bornstein & M.E. Lamb (Eds.), *Developmental psychology: An advanced textbook* (3rd ed., pp. 337–418). Hillsdale, NJ: Erlbaum.

Dgnelie, G., Zorge, I., & McDonald, T. (2000). Lutein improves visual function in some patients with retinal degeneration: A pilot study via the Internet. *Journal of the American Optometric Association, 71,* 147–164.

The Diagram Group (1977). *Child's body.* New York: Paddington.

Diamond, A. (1991). Neuropsychological insights into the meaning of object concept development. In S. Carey & R. Gelman (Eds.), *The epigenesis of mind: Essays on biology and cognition* (pp. 67–110). Hillsdale, NJ: Erlbaum.

Diehl, L., Vicary, J., & Deike, R. (1997). Longitudinal trajectories of self-esteem from early to middle adolescence and related psychosocial variables among rural adolescents. *Journal of Research on Adolescence, 7,* 393–411.

Dietitians of Canada. (2003). *Eating, physical activity and body weight trends in Canadian children and youth.* Toronto: Author. Retrieved July 12, 2004 from http://www.dietitians.ca/child/ pdf/backgrounder.pdf

Digman, J.M. (1990). Personality structure: Emergence of the five-factor model. *Annual Review of Psychology, 41,* 417–440.

D'Imperio, R., Dubow, E., & Ippolito, M. (2000). Resilient and stress-affected adolescents in an urban setting. *Journal of Clinical Child Psychology, 29,* 129–142.

Dindia, K., & Allen, M. (1992). Sex differences in self-disclosure: A meta-analysis. *Psychological Bulletin, 112,* 106–124.

DiPietro, J., Hodgson, D., Costigan, K., Hilton, S., & Johnson, T. (1996). Fetal neurobehavioral development. *Child Development, 67,* 2553–2567.

DiPietro, J., Hodgson, D., Costigan, K., & Johnson, T. (1996). Fetal antecedents of infant temperament. *Child Development, 67,* 2568–2583.

Dishion, T.J., French, D.C., & Patterson, G.R. (1995). The development and ecology of antisocial behavior. In D. Cicchetti & D.J. Cohen (Eds.), *Developmental psychopathology: Vol. 2. Risk, disorder, and adaptation* (pp. 421–471). New York: Wiley.

Dishion, T.J., Patterson, G.R., Stoolmiller, M., & Skinner, M.L. (1991). Family, school, and behavioral antecedents to early adolescent involvement with antisocial peers. *Developmental Psychology, 27,* 172–180.

Dittmann-Kohli, F., Lachman, M.E., Kliegl, R., & Baltes, P.B. (1991). Effects of cognitive training and testing on intellectual efficacy beliefs in elderly adults. *The Journals of Gerontology: Psychological Sciences, 46,* P162–164.

Divgi, V. (2000). What about sleep? *Archives of Pediatrics & Adolescent Medicine, 154*(6), 636.

Dobson, A., Brown, W., Ball, J., Powers, J., & McFadden, M. (1999). Women drivers' behaviour, socio-demographic characteristics and accidents. *Accident Analysis & Prevention, 31,* 525–535.

Dockett, S., & Smith, I. (1995, March). *Children's theories of mind and their involvement in complex shared pretense.* Paper presented at the biennial meetings of the Society for Research in Child Development, Indianapolis, IN.

Doctoroff, S. (1997). Sociodramatic script training and peer role prompting: Two tactics to promote sociodramatic play and peer interaction. *Early Child Development & Care, 136,* 27–43.

Dodge, K. (1993). Social-cognitive mechanisms in the development of conduct disorder and depression. *Annual Review of Psychology, 44,* 559–584.

Dodge, K.A., Pettit, G.S., & Bates, J.E. (1994). Socialization mediators of the relation between socioeconomic status and child conduct problems. *Child Development, 65,* 649–665.

Doh, H., & Falbo, T. (1999). Social competence, maternal attentiveness, and overprotectiveness: Only children in Korea. *International Journal of Behavioral Development, 23,* 149–162.

Dollard, J., Doob, L.W., Miller, N.E., Mowrer, O.H., & Sears, R.R. (1939). *Frustration and aggression.* New Haven, CT: Yale University Press.

Donnerstein, E., Slaby, R.G., & Eron, L.D. (1994). The mass media and youth aggression. In L.D. Eron, J.H. Gentry, & P. Schlegel (Eds.), *Reason to hope: A psychosocial perspective on violence and youth* (pp. 219–250). Washington, DC: American Psychological Association.

Donohew, R., Hoyle, R., Clayton, R., Skinner, W., Colon, S., & Rice, R. (1999). Sensation seeking and drug use by adolescents and their friends: Models for marijuana and alcohol. *Journal of Studies on Alcohol, 60,* 622–631.

Doty, R.L., Shaman, P., Applebaum, S.L., Bigerson, R., Sikorski, L., & Rosenberg, L. (1984). Smell identification ability: Changes with age. *Science, 226,* 1441–1443.

Downe-Wamboldt, B., & Tamlyn, D. (1997). An international survey of death education trends in faculties of nursing and medicine. *Death Studies, 21,* 177–188.

Draper, B., Gething, L., Fethney, J., & Winfield, S. (1999). The Senior Psychiatrist Survey III: Attitudes towards personal ageing, life experiences and psychiatric practice. *Australian & New Zealand Journal of Psychiatry, 33,* 717–722.

Dreher, G.F., & Bretz, R.D., Jr. (1991). Cognitive ability and career attainment: Moderating effects of early career success. *Journal of Applied Psychology, 76,* 392–397.

Dreman, S., Pielberger, C., & Darzi, O. (1997). The relation of state-anger to self-esteem, perceptions of family structure and attributions of responsibility for divorce of custodial mothers in the stabilization phase of the divorce process. *Journal of Divorce & Remarriage, 28,* 157–170.

Drevets, W., Price, J., Simpson, J., Todd, R., Reich, T., Vannier, M., & Raichle, M. (1997). Subgenual prefrontal cortex abnormalities in mood disorders. *Nature, 386,* 824–827.

Driscoll, A., & Nagel, N. (1999). *Early childhood education: Birth–8.* Needham Heights, MA: Allyn & Bacon.

Drobnic, S., Blossfeld, H., & Rohwer, G. (1999). Dynamics of women's employment patterns over the family life course: A comparison of the United States and Germany. *Journal of Marriage & the Family, 61,* 133–146.

Droege, K., & Stipek, D. (1993). Children's use of dispositions to predict classmates' behavior. *Developmental Psychology, 29,* 646–654.

Drolet, M. (2003). Motherhood and paycheques (Catalogue No. 11-008). *Canadian Social Trends, Spring*(68), 7–10.

Drum, P. (1985). Retention of text information by grade, ability and study. *Discourse Processes, 8,* 21–52.

Duchesne, D. (2004). More seniors at work (Catalogue No. 75-001). *Perspectives on Labour and Income, 5*(2). Retrieved August 31, 2004 from http://www.statcan.ca/english/studies/75-001/10204/high-1.htm

Due, P., Holstein, B., Lund, R., Modvig, J., & Avlund, K. (1999). Social relations: Network, support and relational strain. *Social Science & Medicine, 48,* 661–673.

Duffy, F. (1994). The role of quantified electroencephalography in psychological research. In K. Fischer & G. Dawson (Eds.), *Human behavior and the developing brain* (pp. 93–136). New York: Guilford Press.

Duke, P.M., Carlsmith, J.M., Jennings, D., Martin, J.A., Dornbusch, S.M., Gross, R.T., & Siegel-Gorelick, B. (1982). Educational correlates of early and late sexual maturation in adolescence. *Journal of Pediatrics, 100,* 633–637.

Duncan, M., Stayton, C., & Hall, C. (1999). Police reports on domestic incidents involving intimate partners: Injuries and medical help-seeking. *Women & Health, 30,* 1–13.

Dunn, J. (1994). Experience and understanding of emotions, relationships, and membership in a particular culture. In P. Ekman & R.J. Davidson (Eds.), *The nature of emotion: Fundamental questions* (pp. 352–355). New York: Oxford University Press.

Dunphy, D.C. (1963). The social structure of urban adolescent peer groups. *Sociometry, 26,* 230–246.

Dura, J.R., & Kiecolt-Glaser, J.K. (1991). Family transitions, stress, and health. In P.A. Cowan & M. Hetherington (Eds.), *Family transitions* (pp. 59–76). Hillsdale, NJ: Erlbaum.

Durbin, J. (2003, October 6). Internet sex unzipped. *Maclean's,* 18–22.

Durlak, J.A. (1972). Relationship between attitudes toward life and death among elderly women. *Developmental Psychology, 8,* 146.

Durrant, J. (2004). Distinguishing physical punishment from physical abuse: Implications for professionals. *Ontario Association of Children's Aid Societies Journal, 48*(2), 15–20.

Durrant, J., & Ensom, R. (2004). *Physical punishment of children.* CECW Information Sheet #7F. Ottawa, ON: Child Welfare League of Canada. Retrieved June 21, 2004 from http://www.cecw-cepb.ca/DocsEng/PhysPun7E.pdf

Dutch Senate OKs doctor-assisted suicide. (2001, April 11). *Houston Chronicle,* p. 16A.

Duursma, S.A., Raymakers, J.A., Boereboom, F.T.J., & Scheven, B.A.A. (1991). Estrogen and bone metabolism. *Obstetrical and Gynecological Survey, 47,* 38–44.

Duvall, E.M. (1962). *Family development.* New York: Lippincott.

Dwyer, T., & Ponsonby, A.L. (1992). Sudden infant death syndrome—Insights from epidemiological research. *Journal of Epidemiological and Community Health, 46,* 98–102.

Dyack, S. (2004). Expanding newborn screening: Lessons learned from MCAD deficiency. *Paediatrics & Child Health, 9*(4), 241–243.

Dyck, J., Gee, N., & Smither, J. (1998). The changing construct of computer anxiety for younger and older adults. *Computers in Human Behavior, 14,* 61–77.

Dyregrov, A., Gjestad, R., Bie Wikander, A., & Vigerust, S. (1999). Reactions following the sudden death of a classmate. *Scandinavian Journal of Psychology, 40,* 167–176.

Eagly, A., & Wood, W. (1999). The origins of sex differences in human behavior: Evolved dispositions versus social roles. *American Psychologist, 54,* 408–423.

Eaton, W.O. (1994). Temperament, development, and the five factor model: Lessons from activity level. In C.F. Halverson, G.A. Kohnstamm, & R.P. Martin (Eds.), *The developing structure of temperament and personality from infancy to adulthood* (pp. 173–187). Hillsdale, NJ: Erlbaum.

Eaton, W. (2003, Fall). *Infant milestones newsletter.* Winnipeg, MB: University of Manitoba Milestone Study. Retrieved May 1, 2004, from http://www.umanitoba.ca/outreach/milestones/fallnewsletter2003.shtml

Eaton, W.O., McKeen, N.A., & Campbell, D.W. (2001). The waxing and waning of movement: Implications for psychological development. *Developmental Review, 21*(2), 205–223.

Echt, K., Morrell, R., & Park, D. (1998). Effects of age and training formats on basic computer skill acquisition in older adults. *Educational Gerontology, 24,* 3–25.

Edwards, G. (n.d.). *Health and environmental issues linked to the nuclear fuel chain: Health effects* (Section B). Montreal: Canadian Coalition for Nuclear Responsibility. Retrieved April 24, 2004, from http://www.ccnr.org/ceac_B.html#b.14

Edwards, J.N. (1969). Familial behavior as social exchange. *Journal of Marriage and the Family, 31,* 518–526.

Einerson, M. (1998). Fame, fortune, and failure: Young girls' moral language surrounding popular culture. *Youth & Society, 30,* 241–257.

Eisenberg, N. (1992). *The caring child.* Cambridge, MA: Harvard University Press.

Eisenberg, N. (2000). Emotion, regulation, and moral development. *Annual Review of Psychology, 51,* 665–697.

Eisenberg, N., Fabes, R.A., Murphy, B., Karbon, M., Smith, M., & Maszk, P. (1996). The relations of children's dispositional empathy-related responding to their emotionality, regulation, and social functioning. *Developmental Psychology, 32,* 195–209.

Eisenberg, N., Fabes, R.A., Murphy, B., Maszk, P., Smith, M., & Karbon, M. (1995). The role of emotionality and regulation in children's social functioning: A longitudinal study. *Child Development, 66,* 1360–1384.

Eisenberg, N., Guthrie, I., Murphy, B., Shepard, S., et al. (1999). Consistency and development of prosocial dispositions: A longitudinal study. *Child Development, 70,* 1360–1372.

Elbedour, S., Baker, A., & Charlesworth, W. (1997). The impact of political violence on moral reasoning in children. *Child Abuse & Neglect, 21,* 1053–1066.

Elder, G.H., Jr. (1974). *Children of the Great Depression.* Chicago: University of Chicago Press.

Elder, G.H., Jr., & Caspi, A. (1988). Economic stress in lives: Developmental perspectives. *Journal of Social Issues, 44,* 25–45.

Elder, G.H., Jr., Liker, J.K., & Cross, C.E. (1984). Parent-child behavior in the Great Depression: Life course and intergenerational influences. In P.B. Baltes & O.G. Brim, Jr. (Eds.), *Life-span development and behavior* (Vol. 6, pp. 111–159). New York: Academic Press.

Elkind, D. (1967). Egocentrism in adolescence. *Child Development, 38,* 1025–1033.

Elliot, A., & Hall, N. (1997). The impact of self-regulatory teaching strategies on "at-risk" preschoolers' mathematical learning in a computer-mediated environment. *Journal of Computing in Childhood Education, 8,* 187–198.

Elliott, L. (2000). Aboriginal girls taking their lives in record numbers across Ontario's north. *Canadian Aboriginal News.* Retrieved October 24, 2001 from http://www.canadianaboriginal.com/health/health15b.htm

Ellis R., & Allaire, J. (1999). Modeling computer interest in older adults: The role of age, education, computer knowledge, and computer anxiety. *Human Factors, 41,* 345–355.

Ellison, J. & Clark, W. (2001). Net shopping. *Canadian Social Trends, 60,* 6–9.

Emanuel, E., Fairclough, D., Clarridge, B., Blum, D., Bruera, E., Penley, W., Schnipper, L., & Mayer, R. (2000). Attitudes and practices of U.S. oncologists regarding euthanasia and physician-assisted suicide. *Annals of Internal Medicine, 133,* 527–532.

Emde, R.N. (1992). Individual meaning and increasing complexity: Contributions of Sigmund Freud and Rene Spitz to developmental psychology. *Developmental Psychology, 28,* 347–359.

Emde, R.N., Plomin, R., Robinson, J., Corley, R., DeFries, J., Fulker, D.W., Reznick, J.S., Campos, J., Kagan, J., & Zahn-Waxler, C. (1992). Temperament, emotion, and cognition at fourteen months: The MacArthur longitudinal twin study. *Child Development, 63,* 1437–1455.

Emery, C.F., & Gatz, M. (1990). Psychological and cognitive effects of an exercise program for community-residing older adults. *The Gerontologist, 30,* 184–192.

Emery, R., & Laumann-Billings, L. (1998). An overview of the nature, causes, and consequences of abusive family relationships: Toward differentiating maltreatment and violence. *American Psychologist, 53,* 121–135.

Ensign, J. (1998). *Defying the stereotypes of special education: Homeschool students.* Paper presented at the annual meeting of the American Education Research Association, San Diego, CA.

Entwisle, D.R., & Alexander, K.L. (1990). Beginning school math competence: Minority and majority comparisons. *Child Development, 61,* 454–471.

Ericsson, K.A. (1990). Peak performance and age: An examination of peak performance in sports. In P. Baltes & M.M. Baltes (Eds.), *Successful aging* (pp. 164–196). Cambridge, MA: Cambridge University Press.

Ericsson, K.A., & Crutcher, R.J. (1990). The nature of exceptional performance. In P.B. Baltes, D.L. Featherman, & R.M. Lerner (Eds.), *Life-span development and behavior* (Vol. 10, pp. 188–218). Hillsdale, NJ: Erlbaum.

Erikson, E.H. (1950). *Childhood and society.* New York: Norton.

Erikson, E.H. (1959). *Identity and the life cycle.* New York: Norton. (Reissued, 1980.)

Erikson, E.H. (1963). *Childhood and society* (2nd ed.). New York: Norton.

Erikson, E.H. (1980a). *Identity and the life cycle.* New York: Norton. (Originally published 1959.)

Erikson, E.H. (1980b). Themes of adulthood in the Freud-Jung correspondence. In N.J. Smelser & E. Erikson (Eds.), *Themes of work and love in adulthood* (pp. 43–76). Cambridge, MA: Harvard University Press.

Erikson, E.H. (1982). *The life cycle completed.* New York: Norton.

Erikson, E.H., Erikson, J.M., & Kivnick, H.Q. (1986). *Vital involvement in old age.* New York: Norton.

Eron, L.D. (1987). The development of aggressive behavior from the perspective of a developing behaviorism. *American Psychologist, 42,* 435–442.

Eron, L.D., Huesmann, L.R., & Zelli, A. (1991). The role of parental variables in the learning of aggression. In D.J. Pepler & K.H. Rubin (Eds.), *The development and treatment of childhood aggression* (pp. 169–188). Hillsdale, NJ: Erlbaum.

Eskes, T.K.A.B. (1992). Home deliveries in the Netherlands—perinatal mortality and morbidity. *International Journal of Gynecology and Obstetrics, 38,* 161–169.

Etaugh, C., & Liss, M. (1992). Home, school, and playroom: Training grounds for adult gender roles. *Sex Roles, 26,* 129–147.

Eugster, A., & Vingerhoets, A. (1999). Psychological aspects of in vitro fertilization: A review. *Social Science & Medicine, 48,* 575–589.

Evans, D.A., Funkenstein, H.H., Albert, M.S., Scherr, P.A., Cook, N.R., Chown, M.J., Hebert, L.E., Hennekens, C.H., & Taylor, J.O. (1989). Prevalence of Alzheimer's disease in a community population of older persons. *Journal of the American Medical Association, 262,* 2551–2556.

Evans, L., Ekerdt, D.J., & Bossé, R. (1985). Proximity to retirement and anticipatory involvement: Findings from the Normative Aging Study. *Journal of Gerontology, 40,* 368–374.

Evans, R.I. (1969). *Dialogue with Erik Erikson.* New York: Dutton.

Ex, C., & Janssens, J. (1998). Maternal influences on daughters' gender role attitudes. *Sex Roles, 38,* 171–186.

Eyetsemitan, F. (1998). Stifled grief in the workplace. *Death Studies, 22,* 469–479.

Fabes, R.A., Knight, G.P., & Higgins, D.A. (1995, March). *Gender differences in aggression: A meta-analytic reexamination of time and age effects.* Paper presented at the biennial meetings of the Society for Research in Child Development, Indianapolis, IN.

Fagard, J., & Jacquet, A. (1989). Onset of bimanual coordination and symmetry versus asymmetry of movement. *Infant Behavior and Development, 12,* 229–235.

Fagot, B.I., & Hagan, R. (1991). Observations of parent reactions to sex-stereotyped behaviors: Age and sex effects. *Child Development, 62,* 617–628.

Fagot, B.I., & Leinbach, M.D. (1989). The young child's gender schema: Environmental input, internal organization. *Child Development, 60,* 663–672.

Fagot, B.I., & Leinbach, M.D. (1993). Gender-role development in young children: From discrimination to labeling. *Developmental Review, 13*, 205–224.

Fagot, B.I., Leinbach, M.D., & O'Boyle, C. (1992). Gender labeling, gender stereotyping, and parenting behaviors. *Developmental Psychology, 28*, 225–230.

Fahle, M., & Daum, I. (1997). Visual learning and memory as functions of age. *Neuropsychologia, 35*, 1583–1589.

Fahrenfort, J., Jacobs, E., Miedema, S., & Schweizer, A. (1996). Signs of emotional disturbance three years after early hospitalization. *Journal of Pediatric Psychology, 21*, 353–366.

Falbo, T. (1992). Social norms and one-child family: Clinical and policy limitations. In F. Boer & J. Dunn (Eds.), Children's sibling relationships (pp. 71–82). Hillsdale, NJ: Erlbaum.

Fantuzzo, J., Coolahan, K., & Mendez, J. (1998). Contextually relevant validation of peer play constructs with African American Head Start children: Penn Interactive Peer Play Scale. *Early Childhood Research Quarterly, 13*, 411–431.

Farnham-Diggory, S. (1992). *The learning disabled child.* Cambridge, MA: Harvard University Press.

Farrington, D.P. (1991). Childhood aggression and adult violence: Early precursors and later life outcomes. In D.J. Pepler & K.H. Rubin (Eds.), *The development and treatment of childhood aggression* (pp. 5–30). Hillsdale, NJ: Erlbaum.

Farver, J. (1996). Aggressive behavior in preschoolers' social networks: Do birds of a feather flock together? *Early Childhood Research Quarterly, 11*, 333–350.

Faust, M.S. (1983). Alternative constructions of adolescent growth. In J. Brooks-Gunn & A.C. Petersen (Eds.), *Girls at puberty: Biological and psychosocial perspectives* (pp. 105–126). New York: Plenum.

Federal Interagency Forum on Aging-Related Statistics (FIFARS). (2000). *Older Americans 2000: Key indicators of well-being.* Retrieved February 7, 2001 from http://www.agingstats.gov/chartbook2000

Feeney, J.A. (1994). Attachment style, communication patterns, and satisfaction across the life cycle of marriage. *Personal Relationships, 1*, 333–348.

Feiring, C. (1999). Other-sex friendship networks and the development of romantic relationships in adolescence. *Journal of Youth & Adolescence, 28*, 495–512.

Feld, S., & George, L.K. (1994). Moderating effects of prior social resources on the hospitalizations of elders who become widowed. *Aging and Health, 6*, 275–295.

Feldman, H.A., Goldstein, I., Hatzichristou, D.G., Krane, R.J., & McKinlay, J.B. (1994). Impotence and its medical and psychosocial correlates: Results of the Massachusetts male aging study. *The Journal of Urology, 151*, 54–61.

Feldman, R., Weller, A., Leckman, J., Kuint, J., & Eidelman, A. (1999). The nature of the mother's tie to her infant: Maternal bonding under conditions of proximity, separation, and potential loss. *Journal of Child Psychology & Psychiatry & Allied Disciplines, 40*, 929–939.

Fenson, L., Dale, P.S., Reznick, J.S., Bates, E., Thal, D.J., & Pethick, S.J. (1994). Variability in early communicative development. *Monographs of the Society for Research in Child Development, 59*(5, Serial No. 242).

Ferguson, G.A. (1993). Psychology in Canada 1939–1945. *Canadian Psychology, 33*(2), Abstract.

Ferland, F., Ladouceur, R. & Vitaro, F. (2002). Prevention of problem gambling: Modifying misconception and increasing knowledge. *Journal of Gambling Studies, 18*(10), 19–29.

Fernald, A., & Kuhl, P. (1987). Acoustic determinants of infant preference for motherese speech. *Infant Behavior and Development, 10*, 279–293.

Fernandez, M. (1997). Domestic violence by extended family members in India. *Journal of Interpersonal Violence, 12*, 433–455.

Fiatarone, M.A., & Evans, W.J. (1993). The etiology and reversibility of muscle dysfunction in the aged. *The Journals of Gerontology, 48*(Special Issue), 77–83.

Fiedorowicz, C. (1999). *Neurobiological basis of learning disabilities: An overview.* Linking Research to Practice: Second Canadian Forum Proceedings Report, Canadian Child Care Federation Symposium (pp. 64–67). Ottawa, ON: Canadian Child Care Federation.

Fiedorowicz, C., Benezra, E., MacDonald, W., McElgunn, B., & Wilson, A. (1999). *Neurobiological Basis of Learning Disabilities.* Ottawa, ON: Learning Disabilities Association of Canada.

Fiedorowicz, C., Benezra, E., MacDonald, W., McElgunn, B., Wilson, A., & Kaplan, B. (2002). The neurobiological basis of learning disabilities: An update. *Learning Disabilities: A Multidisciplinary Focus, 11*(2), 61–73.

Field, T.M. (1991). Quality infant day-care and grade school behavior and performance. *Child Development, 62*, 863–870.

Field, T. (1995). Psychologically depressed parents. In M.H. Bornstein (Ed.), *Handbook of parenting: Vol. 4. Applied and practical parenting* (pp. 85–99). Mahwah, NJ: Erlbaum.

Fields, R.B. (1992). Psychosocial response to environment change. In V.B. Van Hasselt & M. Hersen (Eds.), *Handbook of social development: A lifespan perspective* (pp. 503–544). New York: Plenum.

Fine, S. (2000a, September 5). Are the schools failing boys? *The Globe and Mail*, pp. A1, A9.

Fine, S. (2000b, November 3). Ontario students score poorly. *The Globe and Mail*, p. A3.

Finnie, R. (2000). *Earnings of post-secondary graduates in Canada: Holding their own* (Catalogue No. MP 32-29/99-12-1E). Ottawa, ON: Human Resources Development Canada. Retrieved December 10, 2001 from http://www.hrdc-drhc.gc.ca/arb/publications/research/1999docs/r-99-12ea.pdf

Fischer, K.W., & Bidell, T. (1991). Constraining nativist inferences about cognitive capacities. In S. Carey & R. Gelman (Eds.), *The epigenesis of mind: Essays on biology and cognition* (pp. 199–236). Hillsdale, NJ: Erlbaum.

Fish, M., Stifter, C.A., & Belsky, J. (1991). Conditions of continuity and discontinuity in infant negative emotionality: Newborn to five months. *Child Development, 62*, 1525–1537.

Fisher, B., & Specht, D. (1999). Successful aging and creativity in later life. *Journal of Aging Studies, 13*, 457–472.

Fisher, C. (2000). Mood and emotions while working: Missing pieces of job satisfaction? *Journal of Organizational Behavior, 21*, 185–202.

Fisher, W.A., Boroditsky, R. & Bridges, M. (1999). The 1998 Canadian contraception study: Part 2. *The Canadian Journal of Sexuality, 8*(3), 167–174.

Fitzgerald, B. (1999). Children of lesbian and gay parents: A review of the literature. *Marriage & Family Review, 29*, 57–75.

Fitzpatrick, J.L., & Silverman, T. (1989). Women's selection of careers in engineering: Do traditional-nontraditional differences still exist? *Journal of Vocational Behavior, 34*, 266–278.

Flannery, D.J., Montemayor, R., & Eberly, M.B. (1994). The influence of parent negative emotional expression on adolescents' perceptions of their relationships with their parents. *Personal Relationships, 1*, 259–274.

Flannery, D., Vazsonyi, A., Embry, D., Powell, K., Atha, H., Vesterdal, W., & Shenyang, G. (2000, August). *Longitudinal effectiveness of the PeaceBuilders' universal school-based violence prevention program.* Paper presented at the annual meeting of the American Psychological Association, Washington, DC.

Flavell, J.H. (1986). The development of children's knowledge about the appearance-reality distinction. *American Psychologist, 41*, 418–425.

Flavell, J.H. (1993). Young children's understanding of thinking and consciousness. *Current Directions in Psychological Science, 2*, 40–43.

Flavell, J.H., Everett, B.A., Croft, K., & Flavell, E.R. (1981). Young children's knowledge about visual perception: Further evidence for the Level 1–Level 2 distinction. *Developmental Psychology, 17*, 99–103.

Flavell, J.H., Green, F.L., & Flavell, E.R. (1989). Young children's ability to differentiate appearance-reality and level 2 perspectives in the tactile modality. *Child Development, 60,* 201–213.

Flavell, J.H., Green, F.L., & Flavell, E.R. (1990). Developmental changes in young children's knowledge about the mind. *Cognitive Development, 5,* 1–27.

Flavell, J.H., Green, F.L., Wahl, K.E., & Flavell, E.R. (1987). The effects of question clarification and memory aids on young children's performance on appearance-reality tasks. *Cognitive Development, 2,* 127–144.

Fleeson, W., & Heckhausen, J. (1997). More or less "me" in past, present, and future: Perceived lifetime personality during adulthood. *Psychology & Aging, 12,* 125–136.

Fleming, P.J., Blair, P.S., Bacon, C., Bensley, D., Smith, I., Taylor, E., Berry, J., Golding, J., & Tripp, J. (1996). Environment of infants during sleep and risk of the sudden infant death syndrome: Results of 1993–5 case-control study for confidential inquiry into stillbirths and deaths in infancy. *British Medical Journal, 313,* 191–195.

Floyd, F., Stein, T., Harter, K., Allison, A., et al. (1999). Gay, lesbian, and bisexual youths: Separation-individuation, parental attitudes, identity consolidation, and well-being. *Journal of Youth & Adolescence, 28,* 705–717.

Floyd, R.L., Rimer, B.K., Giovino, G.A., Mullen, P.D., & Sullivan, S.E. (1993). A review of smoking in pregnancy: Effects on pregnancy outcomes and cessation efforts. *Annual Review of Public Health, 14,* 379–411.

Focus on the Family Canada. (2002). *Canadian attitudes on the family.* Vancouver: Author. Retrieved June 24, 2004 from http://www.fotf.ca/familyfacts/attitudes/report.pdf

Fokin, V., Ponomareva, N., Androsova, L., & Gavrilova, S. (1997). Interhemispheric asymmetry and neuroimmune modulation in normal aging and Alzheimer's dementias. *Human Physiology, 23,* 284–288.

Folk, K.F., & Yi, Y. (1994). Piecing together child care with multiple arrangements: Crazy quilt or preferred pattern for employed parents of preschool children? *Journal of Marriage and the Family, 56,* 669–680.

Folven, R.J., & Bonvillian, J.D. (1991). The transition from nonreferential to referential language in children acquiring American Sign Language. *Developmental Psychology, 27,* 806–816.

Forbes, J.C, Money, D.M, Remple, V.P, et al. (2000). Effect of antiretroviral use on HIV vertical transmission rate and injection drug use on adherence in British Columbia. As reported in Health Canada (2001c). *Perinatal Transmission of HIV.* Ottawa, ON: Author. Retrieved November 19, 2001 from http://www.hc-sc.gc.ca/hpb/lcdc/bah/epi/peri_e.html

Fordham, K., & Stevenson-Hinde, J. (1999). Shyness, friendship quality, and adjustment during middle childhood. *Journal of Child Psychology & Psychiatry & Allied Disciplines, 40,* 757–768.

Forte, C., & Hansvick, C. (1999). Applicant age as a subjective employability factor: A study of workers over and under age fifty. *Journal of Employment Counseling, 36,* 24–34.

Fourn, L., Ducic, S., & Seguin, L. (1999). Smoking and intrauterine growth retardation in the Republic of Benin. *Journal of Epidemiology & Community Health, 53,* 432–433.

Fox, N.A., Kimmerly, N.L., & Schafer, W.D. (1991). Attachment to mother/attachment to father: A meta-analysis. *Child Development, 62,* 210–225.

Fozard, J.L. (1990). Vision and hearing in aging. In J.E. Birren & K.W. Schaie (Eds.), *Handbook of the psychology of aging* (3rd ed., pp. 150–171). San Diego, CA: Academic Press.

Fozard, J.L., Metter, E.J., & Brant, L.J. (1990). Next steps in describing aging and disease in longitudinal studies. *Journals of Gerontology: Psychological Sciences, 45,* P116–127.

Franche, R., & Bulow, C. (1999). The impact of a subsequent pregnancy on grief and emotional adjustment following a perinatal loss. *Infant Mental Health Journal, 20,* 175–187.

Francis, L. (1997). Ideology and interpersonal emotion management: Redefining identity in two support groups. *Social Psychology Quarterly, 60,* 153–171.

Francis, P.L., Self, P.A., & Horowitz, F.D. (1987). The behavioral assessment of the neonate: An overview. In J.D. Osofsky (Ed.), *Handbook of infant development* (2nd ed., pp. 723–779). New York: Wiley-Interscience.

Francis-Smythe, J., & Smith, P. (1997). The psychological impact of assessment in a development center. *Human Relations, 50,* 149–167.

Franco, N., & Levitt, M. (1998). The social ecology of middle childhood: Family support, friendship quality, and self-esteem. *Family Relations: Interdisciplinary Journal of Applied Family Studies, 47,* 315–321.

Franke, S. (2003). Studying and working: The busy lives of students with paid employment (Catalogue No. 11-008). *Canadian Social Trends, Spring*(68), 22–25.

Freedman, V.A. (1996). Family structure and the risk of nursing home admission. *Journals of Gerontology: Social Sciences, 51B,* S61–69.

Frey, K.S., & Ruble, D.N. (1992). Gender constancy and the "cost" of sex-typed behavior: A test of the conflict hypothesis. *Developmental Psychology, 28,* 714–721.

Frick, P., Christian, R., & Wooton, J. (1999). Age trends in association between parenting practices and conduct problems. *Behavior Modification, 23,* 106–128.

Friedman, H.S., Hawley, P.H., & Tucker, J.S. (1994). Personality, health, and longevity. *Current Directions in Psychological Science, 3,* 37–41.

Friedman, M., & Rosenman, R.H. (1974). *Type A behavior and your heart.* New York: Knopf.

Fuller, T.L., & Fincham, F.D. (1995). Attachment style in married couples: Relation to current marital functioning, stability over time, and method of assessment. *Personal Relationships, 2,* 17–34.

Fung, H. (1999). Becoming a moral child: The socialization of shame among young Chinese children. *Ethos, 27,* 180–209.

Funk, J., & Buchman, D. (1999). Playing violent video and computer games and adolescent self-concept. *Journal of Communication, 46,* 19–32.

Funk, J.B., Buchman, D.D., Jenks, J., & Bechtoldt, H. (2002). An evidence-based approach to examining the impact of playing violent video and computer games. *Studies in Media & Information Literacy Education, 2*(4). Retrieved June 30, 2004 from http://www.utpjournals.com/jour.ihtml?lp=simile/issue8/funkfulltext.html

Funk, J., Buchman, D., Myers, B., & Jenks, J. (2000, August). *Asking the right questions in research on violent electronic games.* Paper presented at the annual meeting of the American Psychological Association, Washington, DC.

Furnham, A. (1999). Economic socialization: A study of adults' perceptions and uses of allowances (pocket money) to educate children. *British Journal of Developmental Psychology, 17,* 585–604.

Furstenberg, F.F., Jr., & Cherlin, A.J. (1991). *Divided families: What happens to children when parents part.* Cambridge, MA: Harvard University Press.

Gaillard, W., Hertz-Pannier, L., Mott, S., Barnett, A., LeBihan, D., & Theodore, W. (2000). Functional anatomy of cognitive development: fMRI of verbal fluency in children and adults. *Neurology, 54,* 180–185.

Gailbraith, K.M., & Dobson, K.S. (2000). The role of the psychologist in determining competence for assisted suicide/euthanasia in the terminally ill. *Canadian Psychology, 41*(3), 174–183.

Gainey, R., Catalano, R., Haggerty, K., & Hoppe, M. (1997). Deviance among the children of heroin addicts in treatment: Impact of parents and peers. *Deviant Behavior, 18,* 143–159.

Galambos, N.L., Leadbeater, B.J., & Barker, E.T. (2004). Gender differences in and risk factors for depression in adolescence: A 4-year longitudinal study. *International Journal of Behavioral Development, 28*(1), 16–25.

Galambos, N., & Maggs, J. (1991). Out-of-school care of young adolescents and self-reported behavior. *Developmental Psychology, 27*, 644–655.

Galambos, N.L. & Tilton-Weaver, L.C. (1998, Autumn). Multiple-risk behaviour in adolescents and young adults, *Health Reports, 10*(2), 9–20.

Gallagher, A., Frith, U., & Snowling, M. (2000). Precursors of literacy delay among children at genetic risk of dyslexia. *Journal of Child Psychology & Psychiatry & Allied Disciplines, 41*, 202–213.

Gallagher, S.K. (1994). Doing their share: Comparing patterns of help given by older and younger adults. *Journal of Marriage and the Family, 56*, 567–578.

Gallagher, W. (1993, May). Midlife myths. *The Atlantic Monthly*, pp. 51–68.

Gallagher-Thompson, D., Futterman, A., Farberow, N., Thompson, L.W., & Peterson, J. (1993). The impact of spousal bereavement on older widows and widowers. In M.S. Stroebe, W. Stroebe, & R.O. Hansson (Eds.), *Handbook of bereavement: Theory, research, and intervention* (pp. 227–239). Cambridge, England: Cambridge University Press.

Gallagher-Thompson, D., Tazeau, Y., & Basilio L. (1997). The relationships of dimensions of acculturation to self-reported depression in older Mexican-American women. *Journal of Clinical Geropsychology, 3*, 123–137.

Gallo, W., Bradley, E., Siegel, M., & Kasl, S. (2000). Health effects of involuntary job loss among older workers: Findings from the health and retirement survey. *Journals of Gerontology: Series B: Psychological Sciences & Social Sciences, 55B*, S131–S140.

Gambert, S.R., Schultz, B.M., & Hamdy, R.C. (1995). Osteoporosis: Clinical features, prevention, and treatment. *Endocrinology and Metabolism Clinics of North America, 24*, 317–371.

Gannon, L., & Stevens, J. (1998). Portraits of menopause in the mass media. *Women & Health, 27*, 1–15.

Garbarino, J., & Sherman, D. (1980). High-risk neighborhoods and high-risk families: The human ecology of child maltreatment. *Child Development, 51*, 188–198.

Gardiner, M., Luszcz, M., & Bryan, J. (1997). The manipulation and measurement of task-specific memory self-efficacy in younger and older adults. *International Journal of Behavioral Development, 21*, 209–227.

Gardner, E. (2001). Making every day count: Hospice palliative care in Canada. *Transition Magazine, 31*(1). Ottawa, ON: The Vanier Institute of the Family. Retrieved January 4, 2002 from http://www.vifamily.ca/tm/311/1.htm

Gardner, H. (1983). *Frames of mind: The theory of multiple intelligence*. New York: Basic Books.

Gardner, R., Friedman, B., & Jackson, N. (1999). Body size estimations, body dissatisfaction, and ideal size preferences in children six through thirteen. *Journal of Youth & Adolescence, 28*, 603–618.

Garland, A.F., & Zigler, E. (1993). Adolescent suicide prevention: Current research and social policy implications. *American Psychologist, 48*, 169–182.

Garland, E.J. (2004). Facing the evidence: Antidepressant treatment in children and adolescents. *Canadian Medical Association Journal, 170*(4), 489–491.

Garmezy, N. (1993). Vulnerability and resilience. In D.C. Funder, R.D. Parke, C. Tomlinson-Keasey, & K. Widaman (Eds.), *Studying lives through time: Personality and development* (pp. 377–398). Washington, DC: American Psychological Association.

Garn, S.M. (1980). Continuities and change in maturational timing. In O.G. Brim, Jr. & J. Kagan (Eds.), *Constancy and change in human development* (pp. 113–162). Cambridge, MA: Harvard University Press.

Garner, C. (1995). Infertility. In C.I. Fogel & N.F. Woods (Eds.), *Women's health care* (pp. 611–628). Thousand Oaks, CA: Sage.

Garnier, H., Stein, J., & Jacobs, J. (1997). The process of dropping out of high school: A 19-year perspective. *American Educational Research Journal, 34*, 395–419.

Garrison, R.J., Gold, R.S., Wilson, P.W.F., & Kannel, W.B. (1993). Educational attainment and coronary heart disease risk: The Framingham offspring study. *Preventive Medicine, 22*, 54–64.

Gatz, M., Kasl-Godley, J.E., & Karel, M.J. (1996). Aging and mental disorders. In J.E. Birren & K.W. Schaie (Eds.), *Handbook of the psychology of aging* (4th ed., pp. 365–381). San Diego, CA: Academic Press.

Gaziano, J.M., & Hennekens, C.H. (1995). Dietary fat and risk of prostate cancer. *Journal of the National Cancer Institute, 87*, 1427–1428.

Ge, X., & Conger, R. (1999). Adjustment problems and emerging personality characteristics from early to late adolescence. *American Journal of Community Psychology, 27*, 429–459.

Gelman, R. (1972). Logical capacity of very young children: Number invariance rules. *Child Development, 43*, 75–90.

Gentile, D.A. & Anderson, C.A. (2003). Violent video games: The newest media violence hazard. In D.A. Gentile (Ed.), *Media violence and children* (pp. 131–152). Westport, CT: Praeger Publishing.

Gentile, D.A., Lynch, P.J., Linder, J.R., & Walsh, D.A. (2004). The effects of violent video game habits on adolescent aggressive attitudes and behaviors. *Journal of Adolescence, 27*(1), 5–22.

Gentile, D.A., Walsh, D.A., Ellison, P.R., Fox, M., & Cameron, J. (2004, May). *Media violence as a risk factor for children: A longitudinal study*. Paper presented at the American Psychological Society 16th Annual Convention, Chicago, IL.

George, L.K. (1990). Social structure, social processes, and social-psychological states. In R.H. Binstock & L.K. George (Eds.), *Handbook of aging and the social sciences* (3rd ed., pp. 186–204). San Diego, CA: Academic Press.

George, L.K. (1993). Sociological perspectives on life transitions. *Annual Review of Sociology, 19*, 353–373.

Gerhardstein, P., Liu, J., & Rovee-Collier, C. (1998). Perceptual constraints on infant memory retrieval. *Journal of Experimental Child Psychology, 69*, 109–131.

Gershoff, E.T. (2002). Corporal punishment by parents and associated child behaviors and experiences: A meta-analytic and theoretical review. *Psychological Bulletin, 128*(4), 539–579.

Gerwood, J., LeBlanc, M., & Piazza, N. (1998). The Purpose-in-Life Test and religious denomination: Protestant and Catholic scores in an elderly population. *Journal of Clinical Psychology, 54*, 49–53.

Gesell, A. (1925). *The mental growth of the preschool child*. New York: Macmillan.

Gesser, G., Wong, P.T.P., & Reker, G.T. (1987/1988). Death attitudes across the life-span: The development and validation of the death attitude profile (DAP). *Omega, 18*, 113–128.

Giambra, L.M., Arenberg, D., Zonderman, A.B., Kawas, C., & Costa, P.T., Jr. (1995). Adult life span changes in immediate visual memory and verbal intelligence. *Psychology and Aging, 10*, 123–139.

Gibbs, R., & Beitel, D. (1995). What proverb understanding reveals about how people think. *Psychological Bulletin, 118*, 133–154.

Gibson, D.R. (1990). Relation of socioeconomic status to logical and sociomoral judgment of middle-aged men. *Psychology and Aging, 5*, 510–513.

Giedd, J.N., Blumenthal, J., Jeffries, N.O., Castellanos, F.X., Liu, H., Zijdenbos, A., Paus, T., Evans, A.C., & Rapoport, J.L. (1999). Brain development during childhood and adolescence: A longitudinal MRI study. *Nature Neuroscience, 2*(10), 861–863.

Gilbertson, M., & Bramlett, R. (1998). Phonological awareness screening to identify at-risk readers: Implications for practitioners. *Language, Speech, & Hearing Services in Schools, 29*, 109–116.

Gilligan, C. (1982). *In a different voice: Psychological theory and women's development*. Cambridge, MA: Harvard University Press.

Gilligan, C., & Wiggins, G. (1987). The origins of morality in early childhood relationships. In J. Kagan & S. Lamb (Eds.), *The emergence of morality in young children* (pp. 277–307). Chicago: University of Chicago Press.

Gillman, M.W., Rifas-Shiman, S.L., Frazier, L.A., Rockett, H.R.H., Camargo, C.A., Field, A.E., Berkey, C.S., & Colditz, G.A. (2000). Family dinner and diet quality among older children and adolescents. *Archives of Family Medicine, 9*(3), 235–240.

Girard, D.L. (2004). Social determinants of initiation, duration and exclusivity of breast feeding at the population level: The results of the Longitudinal Study of Child Development in Quebec (ELDEQ 1998–2002). *Canadian Journal of Public Health, 94*(4), 300–305.

Gladue, B.A. (1994). The biopsychology of sexual orientation. *Current Directions in Psychological Science, 3,* 150–154.

Glaser, D. (2000). Child abuse and neglect and the brain—a review. *Journal of Child Psychology & Psychiatry & Allied Disciplines, 41,* 97–116.

Glaser, R., Kiecolt-Glaser, J.K., Bonneau, R.H., Malarkey, W., Kennedy, S., & Hughes, J. (1992). Stress-induced modulation of the immune response to recombinant hepatitis B vaccine. *Psychosomatic Medicine, 54,* 22–29.

Glass, J., & Jolly, G. (1997). Satisfaction in later life among women 60 or over. *Educational Gerontology, 23,* 297–314.

Glass, J., & Kilpatrick, B. (1998). Gender comparisons of baby boomers and financial preparation for retirement. *Educational Gerontology, 24,* 719–745.

Glass, S. (1998). Shared vows. *Psychology Today, 31,* 34.

Glazer, H. (1998). Expressions of children's grief: A qualitative study. *International Journal of Play Therapy, 7,* 51–65.

Gleitman, L.R., & Gleitman, H. (1992). A picture is worth a thousand words, but that's the problem: The role of syntax in vocabulary acquisition. *Current Directions in Psychological Science, 1,* 31–35.

Glenn, N.D. (1990). Quantitative research on marital quality in the 1980s: A critical review. *Journal of Marriage and the Family, 52,* 818–831.

Glenn, N.D., & Weaver, C.N. (1985). Age, cohort, and reported job satisfaction in the United States. In A.S. Blau (Ed.), *Current perspectives on aging and the life cycle. A research annual: Vol. 1. Work, retirement and social policy* (pp. 89–110). Greenwich, CT.

Glenn, N.D., & Weaver, C.N. (1988). The changing relationship of marital status to reported happiness. *Journal of Marriage and the Family, 50,* 317–324.

Gloger-Tippelt, G., & Huerkamp, M. (1998). Relationship change at the transition to parenthood and security of infant-mother attachment. *International Journal of Behavioral Development, 23,* 633–655.

Gnepp, J., & Chilamkurti, C. (1988). Children's use of personality attributions to predict other people's emotional and behavioral reactions. *Child Development, 50,* 743–754.

Gogtay, N., Giedd, J.N., Lusk, L., Hayashi, K.M., Greenstein, D., Vaituzis, A.C., Nugent, T.F. 3rd, Herman, D.H., Clasen, L.S., Togam, A.W., Rapoport, J.L., & Thompson, P.M. (2004). Dynamic mapping of human cortical development during childhood through early adulthood. *Proceedings of the National Academy of Sciences of the United States of America, 101*(21), 8174–8179.

Gold, D. (1996). Continuities and discontinuities in sibling relationships across the life span. In V.I. Bengtson (Ed.), *Adulthood and aging: Research on continuities and discontinuities.* New York: Springer.

Gold, D.P., Andres, D., Etezadi, J., Arbuckle, T., Schwartzman, A., & Chaikelson, J. (1995). Structural equation model of intellectual change and continuity and predictors of intelligence in older men. *Psychology and Aging, 10,* 294–303.

Goldberg, A.P., Dengel, D.R., & Hagberg, J.M. (1996). Exercise physiology and aging. In E.L. Schneider & J.W. Rowe (Eds.), *Handbook of the biology of aging* (4th ed., pp. 331–354). San Diego, CA: Academic Press.

Goldberg, A.P., & Hagberg, J.M. (1990). Physical exercise in the elderly. In E.R. Schneider & J.W. Rowe (Eds.), *Handbook of the biology of aging* (3rd ed., pp. 407–428). San Diego, CA: Academic Press.

Goldberg, W.A. (1990). Marital quality, parental personality, and spousal agreement about perceptions and expectations for children. *Merrill-Palmer Quarterly, 36,* 531–556.

Goldfield, B.A., & Reznick, J.S. (1990). Early lexical acquisition: Rate, content, and the vocabulary spurt. *Journal of Child Language, 17,* 171–183.

Goldsmith, H., & Alansky, J. (1987). Maternal and infant temperamental predictors of attachment: A meta-analytic review. *Journal of Consulting and Clinical Psychology, 55,* 805–806.

Goldsmith, H.H., Lemery, K.S., Buss, K.A., & Campos, J.J. (1999). Genetic analyses of focal aspects of infant temperament. *Developmental Psychology, 35*(4), 972–985.

Goleman, D. (1995). *Emotional intelligence.* New York: Bantam.

Golinkoff, R.M., Mervis, C.V., & Hirsh-Pasek, K. (1994). Early object labels: The case for a developmental lexical principles framework. *Journal of Child Language, 21,* 125–155. Also in K. Perera (Ed.), *Growing points in child language.* Cambridge, MA: Cambridge University Press.

Golombok, S., & Fivush, R. (1994). *Gender development.* Cambridge, England: Cambridge University Press.

Golombok, S., & Tasker, F. (1996). Do parents influence the sexual orientation of their children? Findings from a longitudinal study of lesbian families. *Developmental Psychology, 32,* 3–11.

Gomez, R., Bounds, J., Holmberg, K., Fullarton, C., & Gomez, A. (1999). Effects of neuroticism and avoidant coping style on maladjustment during early adolescence. *Personality & Individual Differences, 26,* 305–319.

Gomez, R., Holmberg, K., Bounds, J., Fullarton, C., & Gomez, A. (1999). Neuroticism and extraversion as predictors of coping styles during early adolescence. *Personality & Individual Differences, 27,* 3–17.

Gonzalez, J., & Valle, I. (2000). Word identification and reading disorders in the Spanish language. *Journal of Learning Disabilities, 33,* 44–60.

Good, T.L., & Weinstein, R.S. (1986). Schools make a difference: Evidence, criticisms, and new directions. *American Psychologist, 41,* 1090–1097.

Goodman, L.M. (1981). *Death and the creative life: Conversations with eminent artists and scientists as they reflect on life and death.* New York: Springer Publishing Company.

Goodsitt, J.V., Morse, P.A., Ver Hoeve, J.N., & Cowan, N. (1984). Infant speech recognition in multisyllabic contexts. *Child Development, 55,* 903–910.

Goossens, R., & van IJzendoorn, M. (1990). Quality of infants' attachments to professional caregivers: Relation to infant-parent attachment and day-care characteristics. *Child Development, 61,* 832–837.

Gopnik, A., & Astington, J.W. (1988). Children's understanding of representational change and its relation to the understanding of false belief and the appearance-reality distinction. *Child Development, 59,* 26–37.

Gopnik, A., & Wellman, H.M. (1994). The theory theory. In L.A. Hirschfeld & S.A. Gelman (Eds.), *Mapping the mind* (pp. 257–293). Cambridge, England: Cambridge University Press.

Gordon, G.S., & Vaughan, C. (1986). Calcium and osteoporosis. *Journal of Nutrition, 116,* 319–322.

Gordon, R., Chase-Lansdale, P., Matjasko, J., & Brooks-Gunn, J. (1997). Young mothers living with grandmothers and living apart: How neighborhood and household contexts relate to multigenerational coresidence in African American families. *Applied Developmental Science, 1,* 89–106.

Gothelf, D., Apter, A., Brand-Gothelf, A., Offer, N., Ofek, H., Tyano, S., & Pfeffer, C. (1998). Death concepts in suicidal adolescents. *Journal of the American Academy of Child & Adolescent Psychiatry, 37,* 1279–1286.

Gottlob, L., & Madden, D. (1999). Age differences in the strategic allocation of visual attention. *Journals of Gerontology: Series B: Psychological Sciences & Social Sciences, 54B,* P165–P172.

Gottman, J.M. (1986). The world of coordinated play: Same- and cross-sex friendship in young children. In J.M. Gottman & J.G. Parker (Eds.), *Conversations of friends: Speculations on affective development* (pp. 139–191). Cambridge, England: Cambridge University Press.

Gottman, J.M. (1994a). *What predicts divorce? The relationship between marital processes and marital outcomes.* Hillsdale, NJ: Erlbaum.

Gottman, J.M. (1994b). *Why marriages succeed or fail.* New York: Simon & Schuster.

Gould, E., Reeves, A., Graziano, M., & Gross, C. (1999). Neurogenesis in the neocortex of adult primates. *Science, 286,* 548–552.

Govoni, R., Rupcich, N. & Frisch, G.R. (1996). Gambling behavior of adolescent gamblers. *Journal of Gambling Studies, 12,* 305–317.

Graham, J., Cohen, R., Zbikowski, S., & Secrist, M. (1998). A longitudinal investigation of race and sex as factors in children's classroom friendship choices. *Child Study Journal, 28,* 245–266.

Graham, S., & Harris, K. (1997). It can be taught, but it does not develop naturally: Myths and realities in writing instruction. *School Psychology Review, 26,* 414–424.

Gralinski, J.H., & Kopp, C.B. (1993). Everyday rules for behavior: Mothers' requests to young children. *Developmental Psychology, 29,* 573–584.

Greenberg, J., Lewis, S., & Dodd, D. (1999). Overlapping addictions and self-esteem among college men and women. *Addictive Behaviors, 24,* 565–571.

Greenberg, M.T., Siegel, J.M., & Leitch, C.J. (1983). The nature and importance of attachment relationships to parents and peers during adolescence. *Journal of Youth and Adolescence, 12,* 373–386.

Greenberg, M.T., Speltz, M.L., & DeKlyen, M. (1993). The role of attachment in the early development of disruptive behavior problems. *Development and Psychopathology, 5,* 191–213.

Greenberger, E., & Goldberg, W.A. (1989). Work, parenting, and the socialization of children. *Developmental Psychology, 25,* 22–35.

Greenfield, P. (1994). Video games as cultural artifacts. *Journal of Applied Developmental Psychology, 15,* 3–12.

Greenfield, P., Brannon, C., & Lohr, D. (1994). Two-dimensional representation of movement through three-dimensional space: The role of video game expertise. *Journal of Applied Developmental Psychology, 15,* 87–104.

Greenhaus, J., Collins, K., Singh, R., & Parasuraman, S. (1997). Work and family influences on departure from public accounting. *Journal of Vocational Behavior, 50,* 249–270.

Greenough, W.T., Black, J.E., & Wallace, C.S. (1987). Experience and brain development. *Child Development, 58,* 539–559.

Greer, D.S., Mor, V., Morris, J.N., Sherwood, S., Kidder, D., & Birnbaum, H. (1986). An alternative in terminal care: Results of the National Hospice Study. *Journal of Chronic Diseases, 39,* 9–26.

Greer, S. (1991). Psychological response to cancer and survival. *Psychological Medicine, 21,* 43–49.

Greer, S., Morris, T., & Pettingale, K.W. (1979). Psychological response to breast cancer: Effect on outcome. *Lancet,* 785–787.

Gregg, V., Gibbs, J.C., & Basinger, K.S. (1994). Patterns of developmental delay in moral judgment by male and female delinquents. *Merrill-Palmer Quarterly, 40,* 538–553.

Greider, L. (2000, March/April). How not to be a monster-in-law. *Modern Maturity, 43*(2), 56–59, 81.

Griffith, J. (1998). The relation of school structure and social environment to parent involvement in elementary schools. *Elementary School Journal, 99,* 53–80.

Griffiths, M. (1999). Internet addiction: Fact or fiction? *Psychologist, 12,* 246–250.

Grohol, J. (1999). *Internet Addiction Guide* [Online brochure]. Retrieved February 3, 2000 from http://www.psychcentral.com/netaddiction

Grolnick, W.S., & Slowiaczek, M.L. (1994). Parents' involvement in children's schooling: A multidimensional conceptualization and motivational model. *Child Development, 65,* 237–252.

Groome, L., Mooney, D., Holland, S., Smith, L., Atterbury, J., & Dykman, R. (1999). Behavioral state affects heart rate response to low-intensity sound in human fetuses. *Early Human Development, 54,* 39–54.

Grossman, A., Daugelli, A., & Hershberger, S. (2000). Social support networks of lesbian, gay, and bisexual adults 60 years of age and older. *Journals of Gerontology: Series B: Psychological Sciences & Social Sciences, 55B,* P171–P179.

Grouios, G., Sakadami, N., Poderi, A., & Alevriadou, A. (1999). Excess of non-right-handedness among individuals with intellectual disability: Experimental evidence and possible explanations. *Journal of Intellectual Disability Research, 43,* 306–313.

Gruber, R., Sadeh, A., & Raviv, A. (2000). Instability of sleep patterns in children with attention-deficit/hyperactivity disorder. *Journal of the American Academy of Child and Adolescent Psychiatry, 379*(4), 495–501.

Guerin, D.W., & Gottfried, A.W. (1994a). Developmental stability and change in parent reports of temperament: A ten-year longitudinal investigation from infancy through preadolescence. *Merrill-Palmer Quarterly, 40,* 334–355.

Guerin, D.W., & Gottfried, A.W. (1994b). Temperamental consequences of infant difficultness. *Infant Behavior and Development, 17,* 413–421.

Guesry, P. (1998). The role of nutrition in brain development. *Preventive Medicine, 27,* 189–194.

Gullotta, T., Adams, G., & Montemayor, R. (1993). *Adolescent sexuality.* Newbury Park, CA: Sage.

Gunnar, M.R. (1994). Psychoendocrine studies of temperament and stress in early childhood: Expanding current models. In J.E. Bates & T.D. Wachs (Eds.), *Temperament: Individual differences at the interface of biology and behavior* (pp. 175–198). Washington, DC: American Psychological Association.

Gunter, T., Jackson, J., & Mulder, G. (1998). Priming and aging: An electrophysiological investigation of N400 and recall. *Brain & Language, 65,* 333–355.

Guo, S.F. (1993). Postpartum depression. *Chung-Hua Fu Chan Ko Tsa Chi, 28,* 532–533, 569.

Gupta, R. & Derevensky, J.L. (1997). Familial and social influences on juvenile gambling. *Journal of Gambling Studies, 13,* 179–192.

Gupta, R. & Derevensky, J.L. (1998a). Adolescent gambling behaviour: A prevalence study and examination of the correlates associated with excessive gambling. *Journal of Gambling Studies, 14,* 227–244.

Gupta, R. & Derevensky, J.L. (1998b). An empirical examination of Jacob's General Theory of Addictions: Do adolescent gamblers fit the theory? *Journal of Gambling Studies, 14,* 17–49.

Gupta, R. & Derevensky, J.L. (2000). Adolescents with gambling problems: From research to treatment. *Journal of Gambling Studies, 16*(2–3), 315–342.

Guralnik, J.M., & Kaplan, G.A. (1989). Predictors of healthy aging: Prospective evidence from the Alameda County Study. *American Journal of Public Health, 79,* 703–708.

Guralnik, J.M., Land, K.C., Blazer, D., Fillenbaum, G.G., & Branch, L.G. (1993). Educational status and active life expectancy among older blacks and whites. *New England Journal of Medicine, 329,* 110–116.

Guralnik, J.M., & Paul-Brown, D. (1984). Communicative adjustments during behavior-request episodes among children at different developmental levels. *Child Development, 55,* 911–919.

Guralnik, J.M., Simonsick, E.M., Ferrucci, L., Glynn, R.J., Berkman, L.F., Blazer, D.G., Scherr, P.A., & Wallace, R.B. (1994). A short physical performance battery assessing lower extremity function: Association with self-reported disability and prediction of mortality and nursing home admission. *Journals of Gerontology: Medical Sciences, 49,* M85–94.

Gurland, B., Wilder, D., Lantiga, R., Stern, Y., Chen, J., Killeffer, E., & Mayeux, R. (1999). Rates of dementia in three ethnoracial groups. *International Journal of Geriatric Psychiatry, 14,* 481–493.

Guse, L., & Masesar, M. (1999). Quality of life and successful aging in long-term care: Perceptions of residents. *Issues in Mental Health Nursing, 20,* 527–539.

Gustafson, S.B., & Magnusson, D. (1991). *Female life careers: A pattern approach.* Hillsdale, NJ: Erlbaum.

Gwartney-Gibbs, P.A. (1988). Women's work experience and the "rusty skills" hypothesis: A reconceptualization and reevaluation of the evidence. In B.A. Gutek, A.H. Stromberg, & L. Larwood (Eds.), *Women and work: An annual review* (Vol. 3, pp. 169–188). Newbury Park, CA: Sage.

Gzesh, S.M., & Surber, C.F. (1985). Visual perspective-taking skills in children. *Child Development, 56,* 1204–1213.

Haan, N. (1981). Common dimensions of personality development: Early adolescence to middle life. In D.H. Eichorn, J.A. Clausen, N. Haan, M.P. Honzik, & P.H. Mussen (Eds.), *Present and past in middle life.* New York: Academic Press.

Hack, M., Taylor, C.B.H., Klein, N., Eiben, R., Schatschneider, C., & Mercuri-Minich, N. (1994). School-age outcomes in children with birth weights under 750 g. *New England Journal of Medicine, 331,* 753–759.

Hagan, J. (1997). Defiance and despair: Subcultural and structural linkages between delinquency and despair in the life course. *Social Forces, 76,* 119–134.

Hagestad, G.O. (1984). The continuous bond: A dynamic, multigenerational perspective on parent-child relations between adults. In M. Perlmutter (Ed.), *Minnesota Symposia on Child Psychology* (pp. 129–158). Hillsdale, NJ: Erlbaum.

Hagestad, G.O. (1985). Continuity and connectedness. In V.L. Bengtson (Ed.), *Grandparenthood* (pp. 31–38). Beverly Hills, CA: Sage.

Hagestad, G.O. (1986). Dimensions of time and the family. *American Behavioral Scientist, 29,* 679–694.

Hagestad, G.O. (1990). Social perspectives on the life course. In R.H. Binstock & L.K. George (Eds.), *Handbook of aging and the social sciences* (3rd ed., pp. 151–168). San Diego, CA: Academic Press.

Haier, R.J., Chueh, D., Touchette, P., Lott, I., Buchsbaum, M.S., MacMillan, D., Sandman, C., LaCasse, L., & Sosa, E. (1995). Brain size and cerebral glucose metabolic rate in nonspecific mental retardation and Down syndrome. *Intelligence, 20,* 191–210.

Haight, W., Wang, X., Fung, H., Williams, K., et al. (1999). Universal, developmental, and variable aspects of young children's play. *Child Development, 70,* 1477–1488.

Haith, M.M. (1980). *Rules that babies look by.* Hillsdale, NJ: Erlbaum.

Hale, T.W. (2004). *Medications and Mothers' Milk* (11th ed.). Amarillo, TX: Pharmasoft Medical Pub.

Halford, G.S., Maybery, M.T., O'Hare, A.W., & Grant, P. (1994). The development of memory and processing capacity. *Child Development, 65,* 1338–1356.

Hall, D.R., & Zhao, J.Z. (1995). Cohabitation and divorce in Canada: Testing the selectivity hypothesis. *Journal of Marriage and the Family, 57,* 421–427.

Hall, D.T. (1972). A model of coping with role conflict: The role behavior of college educated women. *Administrative Science Quarterly, 17,* 471–486.

Hall, D.T. (1975). Pressures from work, self, and home in the life stages of married women. *Journal of Vocational Behavior, 6,* 121–132.

Halle, T. (1999). Implicit theories of social interactions: Children's reasoning about the relative importance of gender and friendship in social partner choices. *Merrill-Palmer Quarterly, 45,* 445–467.

Hallstrom, T., & Samuelsson, S. (1985). Mental health in the climacteric: The longitudinal study of women in Gothenberg. *Acta Obstetricia et Gynecologica Scandinavica, 130*(Suppl), 13–18.

Halpern, C.T., Udry, J.R., Campbell, B., & Suchindran, C. (1993). Testosterone and pubertal development as predictors of sexual activity: A panel analysis of adolescent males. *Psychosomatic Medicine, 55,* 436–447.

Halpern, D.F. (1986). *Sex differences in cognitive abilities.* Hillsdale, NJ: Erlbaum.

Halpern, D. (1997). Sex differences in intelligence: Implications for education. *American Psychologist, 52,* 1091–1102.

Hamberger, K., & Minsky, D. (2000, August). *Evaluation of domestic violence training programs for health care professionals.* Paper presented at the annual meeting of the American Psychological Association. Washington, DC.

Hamilton, C.E. (1995, March). *Continuity and discontinuity of attachment from infancy through adolescence.* Paper presented at the biennial meetings of the Society for Research in Child Development, Indianapolis, IN.

Hammond, M., Landry, S., Swank, P., & Smith, K. (2000). Relation of mothers' affective development history and parenting behavior: Effects on infant medical risk. *American Journal of Orthopsychiatry, 70,* 95–103.

Handley-Derry, M., Low, J., Burke, S., Waurick, M., Killen, H., Derrick, E. (1997). Intrapartum fetal asphyxia and the occurrence of minor deficits in 4- to 8-year-old children. *Developmental Medicine & Child Neurology, 39,* 508–514.

Hanna, E., & Meltzoff, A.N. (1993). Peer imitation by toddlers in laboratory, home, and day-care contexts: Implications for social learning and memory. *Developmental Psychology, 29,* 701–710.

Hansen, L., Wong, T., & Perrin, M. (2003). Gonorrhoea resurgence in Canada. *International Journal of STD & AIDS, 14*(11), 727–31.

Hardy, M.A., & Hazelrigg, L.E. (1993). The gender of poverty in an aging population. *Research on Aging, 15,* 243–278.

Hargrave, A.C. & Sénéchal, M. (2000). Book reading interventions with language-delayed preschool children: The benefits of regular reading and dialogic reading. *Early Childhood Research Quarterly, 15*(1), 75–90.

Harkness, S. (1998). Time for families. *Anthropology Newsletter, 39,* 1, 4.

Harkness, S., & Super, C.M. (1985). The cultural context of gender segregation in children's peer groups. *Child Development, 56,* 219–224.

Harley, B. & Jean, G. (1999). Vocabulary skills of French immersion students in their second language. *Zeitschrift für Interkulturellen Fremdsprachenunterricht* [online], 4(2), 19. Retrieved November 16, 2001 from http://www.ualberta.ca/~german/ejournal/harley2.htm

Harlow, H., & Zimmerman, R. (1959). Affectional responses in the infant monkey. *Science, 130,* 421–432.

Harman, S.M., & Tsitouras, P.D. (1980). Reproductive hormones in aging men: I. Measurement of sex steroids, basal luteinizing hormone, and Leydig cell response to human chorionic gonadotropin. *Journal of Clinical Endocrinology and Metabolism, 51,* 35–40.

Harris, B., Lovett, L., Newcombe, R.G., Read, G.F., Walker, R., & Riad-Fahmy, D. (1994). Maternity blues and major endocrine changes: Cardiff puerperal mood and hormone study II. *British Medical Journal, 308,* 949–953.

Harris, P.L. (1989). *Children and emotion: The development of psychological understanding.* Oxford: Blackwell.

Harris, R.L., Ellicott, A.M., & Holmes, D.S. (1986). The timing of psychosocial transitions and changes in women's lives: An examination of women aged 45 to 60. *Journal of Personality and Social Psychology, 51,* 409–416.

Harrison, M.J., Magill-Evans, J., & Benzies, K. (1999). Fathers' scores on the nursing child assessment teaching scale: Are they different from those of mothers? *Journal of Pediatric Nursing, 14,* 1–8.

Harrist, A., Zaia, A., Bates, J., Dodge, K., & Pettit, G. (1997). Subtypes of social withdrawal in early childhood: Sociometric status and social-cognitive differences across four years. *Child Development, 68,* 278–294.

Hart, B., & Risley, T.R. (1995). *Meaningful differences in the everyday experience of young American children.* Baltimore: Paul H. Brookes.

Hart, C., Olsen, S., Robinson, C., & Mandleco, B. (1997). The development of social and communicative competence in childhood: Review and a model of personal, familial, and extrafamilial processes. *Communication Yearbook, 20,* 305–373.

Hart, S., Jones, N., Field, T., & Lundy, B. (1999). One-year-old infants of intrusive and withdrawn depressed mothers. *Child Psychiatry & Human Development, 30,* 111–120.

Harter, S. (1987). The determinations and mediational role of global self-worth in children. In N. Eisenberg (Ed.), *Contemporary topics in developmental psychology* (pp. 219–242). New York: Wiley-Interscience.

Harter, S. (1990). Processes underlying adolescent self-concept formation. In R. Montemayor, G.R. Adams, & T.P. Gullotta (Eds.), *From childhood to adolescence: A transitional period?* (pp. 205–239). Newbury Park, CA: Sage.

Harter, S., & Monsour, A. (1992). Developmental analysis of conflict caused by opposing attributes in the adolescent self-portrait. *Developmental Psychology, 28,* 251–260.

Harton, H., & Latane, B. (1997). Social influence and adolescent lifestyle attitudes. *Journal of Research on Adolescence, 7,* 197–220.

Hartup, W.W. (1996). The company they keep: Friendships and their developmental significance. *Child Development, 67,* 1–13.

Harwood, D., Barker, W., Ownby, R., Bravo, M., Aguero, H., & Duara, R. (2000). Depressive symptoms in Alzheimer's disease: An examination among community-dwelling Cuban American patients. *American Journal of Geriatric Psychiatry, 8,* 84–91.

Hashima, P.Y., & Amato, P.R. (1994). Poverty, social support, and parental behavior. *Child Development, 65,* 394–403.

Hauge, M.R., & Gentile, D.A. (2003, April). *Video game addiction among adolescents: Associations with academic performance and aggression.* Paper presented at the Society for Research in Child Development Conference, Tampa, FL.

Hausman, P.B., & Weksler, M.E. (1985). Changes in the immune response with age. In C.E. Finch & E.L. Schneider (Eds.), *Handbook of the biology of aging* (2nd ed., pp. 414–432). New York: Van Nostrand Reinhold.

Haviland, J.M., & Lelwica, M. (1987). The induced affect response: 10-week-old infants' responses to three emotional expressions. *Developmental Psychology, 23,* 97–104.

Hawkins, H.L., Kramer, A.F., & Capaldi, D. (1992). Aging, exercise, and attention. *Psychology and Aging, 7,* 643–653.

Hayflick, L. (1977). The cellular basis for biological aging. In C.E. Finch & L. Hayflick (Eds.), *Handbook of the biology of aging* (pp. 159–186). New York: Van Nostrand Reinhold.

Hayflick, L. (1987). Origins of longevity. In H.R. Warner, R.N. Butler, R.L. Sprott, & E.L. Schneider (Eds.), *Aging: Vol. 31. Modern biological theories of aging* (pp. 21–34). New York: Raven Press.

Hayne, H., & Rovee-Collier, C. (1995). The organization of reactivated memory in infancy. *Child Development, 66,* 893–906.

Hayward, M.D., Friedman, S., & Chen, H. (1996). Race inequities in men's retirement. *Journals of Gerontology: Social Sciences, 51B,* S1–10.

Hayward, M.D., & Hardy, M.A. (1985). Early retirement processes among older men: Occupational differences. *Research on Aging, 7,* 491–518.

Hazan, C., Hutt, M., Sturgeon, J., & Bricker, T. (1991, April). *The process of relinquishing parents as attachment figures.* Paper presented at the biennial meetings of the Society for Research in Child Development, Seattle, WA.

Hazan, C., & Shaver, P. (1987). Romantic love conceptualized as an attachment process. *Journal of Personality and Social Psychology, 52,* 511–524.

Hazelrigg, L.E., & Hardy, M.A. (1995). Older adult migration to the sunbelt: Assessing income and related characteristics of recent migrants. *Research on Aging, 17,* 109–234.

Hazuda, H., Wood, R., Lichtenstein, M., & Espino, D. (1998). Sociocultural status, psychosocial factors, and cognitive functional limitation in elderly Mexican Americans: Findings from the San Antonio Longitudinal Study of Aging. *Journal of Gerontological Social Work, 30,* 99–121.

Health Canada. (1997a). *A multicultural perspective of breastfeeding in Canada.* (Catalogue No. H39-386/1997E). Ottawa, ON: Author.Retrieved November 20, 2001 from http://www.hc-sc.gc.ca/hppb/enfancejeunesse/cyfh/ pdf/multicultural.pdf

Health Canada. (1997b). *Canadian guidelines for sexual health education: Framework for sexual education.* Ottawa, ON: Author.

Retrieved October 20, 2001 from http://www.hc-sc.gc.ca/hpb/lcdc/ publicat/sheguide/framew_e.html

Health Canada. (1998a). *Canadian Perinatal Health Surveillance System: Alcohol and Pregnancy.* Ottawa, ON: Author. Retrieved July 11, 2001 from http://www.hc-sc.gc.ca/hpb/lcdc/brch/factshts/ alcprg_e.html

Health Canada. (1998b). *Regulations amending the food and drug regulations* (1066). Ottawa, ON: Author. Retrieved November 19, 2001 from http://www.hc-sc.gc.ca/foodaliment/english/subjects/ dietary_reference_intakes/1066eng.pdf

Health Canada. (1998c). *Canadian Perinatal Health Surveillance System: Infant mortality* Ottawa, ON: Author. Retrieved July 11, 2001 from http://www.hc-sc.gc.ca/hpb/lcdc/brch/factshts/mort_e.html

Health Canada. (1998d). *Canadian Perinatal Health Surveillance System: Breastfeeding.* Ottawa, ON: Author. Retrieved August 8, 2001 from http://www.hc-sc.gc.ca/hpb/lcdc/brch/factshts/brstfd_e.html

Health Canada. (1998e). *Oral contraceptive and condom use.* Ottawa, ON: Author. Retrieved November 17, 2001 from http://www.hc-sc.gc.ca/hpb/lcdc/bah/epi/std511_e.html

Health Canada. (1999a). *The Aboriginal Diabetes Initiative.* Ottawa, ON: Author. Retrieved July 7, 2001 from http://www.hc-sc.gc.ca/ english/archives/releases/1999/99135ebk2.htm

Health Canada. (1999b). *Weight control and heart disease: How to control your weight and reduce your risk of heart disease.* Ottawa, ON: Author. Retrieved April 24, 2004 from http:// www.hc-sc.gc.ca/pphb-dgspsp/ccdpc-cpcmc/hhk-tcs/english/pdf_e/ weig_eng.pdf

Health Canada. (1999c). *The Addition of Vitamins and Minerals to Foods Policy Recommendations.* Ottawa, ON: Author. Retrieved November 12, 2001 from http://www.hc-sc.gc.ca/food-aliment/ english/subjects/dietary_reference_intakes/review_of_hc_policies/ q_a.html

Health Canada. (1999d). *Canadian Perinatal Health Surveillance System: Sudden Infant Death Syndrome.* Ottawa, ON: Author. Retrieved July 11, 2001 from http://www.hc-sc.gc.ca/hpb/lcdc/ brch/factshts/sids_c.html

Health Canada. (1999e). Positive mental health. In *Statistical report on the health of Canadians* (Catalogue No. H39-467/1999E.) (pp. 220-222). Ottawa, ON: Author. Retrieved November 21, 2001 from http://www.hc-sc.ca/hppb/phdd/report/stat/pdf/english/ all_english/pdf

Health Canada. (1999f). *Toward a healthy future: Second report on the health of Canadians* (Catalogue No. H39-468/1999E). Ottawa, ON: Minister of Public Works and Government Services Canada. Retrieved November 22, 2001 from http://www.hc-sc.gc.ca/ hppb/phdd/report/toward/pdf/english/toward_a_healthy_english.PDF

Health Canada. (1999g). *Injury mortality.* Ottawa, ON: Author. Retrieved October 2, 2001 from http://www.hc-sc.gc.ca/hpb/lcdc/ brch/measuring/mu_w_e.html

Health Canada. (1999h). *For the safety of Canadian children and youth.* Ottawa, ON: Author. Retrieved October 2, 2001 from http://www.hc-sc.gc.ca/hpb/lcdc/brch/chirrpbk/ch1_e.html

Health Canada. (1999i). *Healthy development of children and youth: The role of the determinants of health.* (Catalogue No. H39-501/1999E). Ottawa, ON: Author. Retrieved November 22, 2001 from http://www.hc-sc.gc.ca/hppb/childhood-youth/spsc/pdf/ child&yo.pdf

Health Canada. (1999j). *Genital chlamydia in Canada.* Ottawa, ON: Author. Retrieved November 17, 2001 from http://www.hc-sc.gc.ca/ hpb/lcdc/bah/epi/chla_e.html

Health Canada. (1999k). *Teen pregnancy.* Ottawa, ON: Author. Retrieved October 20, 2001 from http://www.hc-sc.gc.ca/hpb/lcdc/ brch/measuring/mu_ee_e.html

Health Canada. (1999l). *Suicide.* Ottawa, ON: Author. Retrieved October 22, 2001 from http://www.hc-sc.gc.ca/hpb/lcdc/brch/ measuring/mu_y_e.html

Health Canada. (2000a). *Perinatal health indicators for Canada* (H49-135/2000E). Ottawa, ON: Minister of Public Works and Government Services Canada.

Health Canada. (2000b). *Leading causes of death and hospitalization in Canada.* Ottawa, ON: Author. Retrieved June 3, 2004 from

http://www.hc-sc.gc.ca/pphb-dgspsp/publicat/lcd-pcd97/pdf/
hos_mrt_e.pdf

Health Canada. (2000c). *Positive HIV test reports in Canada.*
Ottawa, ON: Author. Retrieved December 8, 2001 from
http://www.hc-sc.gc.ca/hpb/lcdc/bah/epi/poshiv_e.html

Health Canada. (2000d). *AIDS and HIV in Canada.* Ottawa, ON:
Author. Retrieved December 8, 2001 from http://
www.hc-sc.gc.ca/hpb/lcdc/bah/epi/ahcan_e.html

Health Canada. (2000e). *Statistical snapshots of Canada's seniors*
(Nos. 6, 7, and 8). Ottawa, ON: Health Canada, Division of
Aging and Seniors. Retrieved December 29, 2001 from
http://www.hc-sc.gc.ca/seniors-aines/seniors/english/resrc2_e.htm

Health Canada. (2001a). *No. 2—Canada's oldest seniors.* Ottawa,
ON: Author. Retrieved November 19, 2001 from http://
www.hc-sc.gc.ca/seniors-aines/pubs/factoids_2001/no02_e.htm

Health Canada. (2001b). *Proposal for legislation governing assisted
human reproduction: An overview.* Ottawa, ON: Author.
Retrieved November 19, 2001 from http://www.hc-sc.gc.ca/english/
archives/releases/2001/2001_44ebk1.htm

Health Canada. (2001c). *Perinatal transmission of HIV.* Ottawa,
ON: Author. Retrieved November 19, 2001 from http://
www.hc-sc.gc.ca/hpb/lcdc/bah/epi/peri_e.html

Health Canada. (2001d). *Canada's food guide to healthy eating.*
Ottawa, ON: Author. Retrieved November 20, 2001 from
http://www.hc-sc.gc.ca/hppb/nutrition/pube/foodguid/e_guideb.html

Health Canada. (2001e). *About us—child maltreatment division—
LCDC—Health Canada.* Ottawa, ON: Author. Retrieved
November 14, 2001 from http://www.hc-sc.gc.ca/hpb/lcdc/brch/
maltreat/about_e.html

Health Canada. (2001f). *At a glance... the Canadian incidence study
of reported child abuse and neglect.* Ottawa, ON: Author.
Retrieved September 15, 2001 from http://www.hc-sc.gc.ca/hpb/lcdc/
brch/maltreat/cishl01/index.html

Health Canada. (2001g). Coping with life. *Trends in the health of
Canadian youth.* Ottawa, ON: Author. Retrieved September 20,
2001 from http://www.hc-sc.gc.ca/hppb/childhood-youth/spsc/
e_trends.html

Health Canada. (2001h). Health Canada and Transport Canada
advise Canadians about scooter safety (2001–99). Ottawa, ON:
Author. Retrieved October 3, 2001 from http://www.hc-sc.gc.ca/
english/archives/warnings/2001/2001_99e.htm

Health Canada. (2001i). STD data tables July 2001: Appendix 1.1.
Ottawa, ON: Author. Retrieved October 21, 2001 from
http://www.hc-sc.gc.ca/pphb-dgspsp/std-mts/stddata0701/ tabl-1_e.html

Health Canada. (2001j). *National Report—Canada: Ten-year review
of the world summit for children.* Ottawa, ON: Author. Retrieved
November 23, 2001 from http://www.hc-sc.gc.ca/hppb/
childhood-youth/spsc/pdf/WSC10FinalEnglish.pdf

Health Canada. (2001k). *STD Data Tables: Reported gonorrhea
cases and rates in Canada by age group and sex, 1980–2000.*
Ottawa, ON: Author. Retrieved December 8, 2001 from
http://www.hc-sc.gc.ca/pphb-dgspsp/std-mts/stddata0701/tab2-2_e.html

Health Canada. (2001l). *STD Data Tables: Reported infectious
syphilis cases and rates in Canada by age group and sex,
1993–2000.* Ottawa, ON: Author. Retrieved December 8, 2001
from http://www.hc-sc.gc.ca/pphb-dgspsp/std-mts/stddata0701/
tab3-1_e.html

Health Canada. (2001m). *Canada's seniors: No. 15—Gender differences in low income.* Ottawa, ON: Author. Retrieved December
29, 2001 from http://www.hc-sc.gc.ca/seniors-aines/pubs/factoids_2001//
no15_3.htm

Health Canada. (2001n). *Canada's seniors: No. 16—Low income
and family status.* Ottawa, ON: Author. Retrieved December 29,
2001 from http://www.hc-sc.gc.ca/seniors-aines/pubs/factoids_2001/
no16_e.htm

Health Canada. (2001o). *News release: Health Minister Allan Rock
and Minister with Special Responsibility for Palliative Care
Sharon Carstairs announce funding for Canadian Virtual
Hospice.* Ottawa, ON: Health Canada, Online. Retrieved January
4, 2002 from http://www.hc-sc.gc.ca/english/media/releases/
2001/2001_121e.htm

Health Canada. (2002a). *Congenital anomalies in Canada—A perinatal health report, 2002* (H39-641/2002E). Ottawa, ON:
Minister of Public Works and Government Services Canada.

Health Canada. (2002b). *Nutrition for a healthy pregnancy—
National guidelines for the childbearing years.* Retrieved April 15,
2004, from http://www.hc-sc.gc.ca/hpfb-dgpsa/onpp-bppn/
national_guidelines_entire_e.html

Health Canada. (2002c). *ECD strategy for Aboriginal children:
Expansion of Aboriginal Head Start (AHS).* Ottawa, ON: Author.
Retrieved November 11, 2004 from http://www.hc-sc.gc.ca/fnihb/cp/
publications/ecd_ahs.htm

Health Canada. (2002d). *Canadian immunization guide* (6th ed.)
(H49-8/2002E). Ottawa, ON: Minister of Public Works and
Government Services Canada.

Health Canada. (2002e). *A Report on Mental Illnesses in Canada*
(Catalogue No. 0-662-32817-5). Ottawa, ON: Health Canada
Editorial Board Mental Illnesses in Canada. Retrieved January 31,
2003, from http://www.hc-sc.gc.ca/pphb-dgspsp/publicat/miic-mmac/
pdf/men_ill_e.pdf

Health Canada. (2002f). *Cardiovascular disease surveillance on-line:
Mortality by age group.* Ottawa, ON: Author. Retrieved August
17, 2004 from http://dsol-smed.hc-sc.gc.ca/dsol-smed/cvd/c_age_e.html

Health Canada. (2002g). *Needs assessment for the Canadian virtual
hospice: Final report.* Ottawa, ON: Author, Applied Research
Initiative Program. Retrieved September 8, 2004 from
http://www.hc-sc.gc.ca/ohih-bsi/pubs/kdec/on_virt_rpt_e.html

Health Canada. (2003a). *Toy safety.* Retrieved March 7, 2004, from
http://www.hc-sc.gc.ca/english/pdf/iyh/toys_e.pdf

Health Canada. (2003b). *Canadian perinatal health report* (H49-
142/2003E). Ottawa, ON: Minister of Public Works and
Government Services Canada.

Health Canada. (2003c). *A Statistical Profile on the Health of First
Nations in Canada.* Ottawa, ON: Author. Retrieved July 12,
2004 from http://www.hc-sc.gc.ca/fnihb-dgspni/fnihb/sppa/hia/
publications/statistical_profile.pdf

Health Canada. (2003d). *Sexual health and sexually transmitted
infections: Gonorrhea resurgence in Canada.* Ottawa, ON:
Author. Retrieved August 6, 2004 from http://www.hc-sc.gc.ca/
pphb-dgspsp/std-mts/gono_e.html

Health Canada. (2003e). *Canada's seniors: No. 2—Canada's oldest
seniors.* Ottawa, ON: Author. Retrieved August 27, 2004 from
http://www.hc-sc.gc.ca/seniors-aines/pubs/factoids/2001/no02_e.htm

Health Canada. (2003f). *Canada's seniors: No. 1—A growing population.* Ottawa, ON: Author. Retrieved August 27, 2004 from
http://www.hc-sc.gc.ca/seniors-aines/pubs/factoids/2001/no01_e.htm

Health Canada. (2003g). *Canada's seniors: No. 19—Private retirement pensions largest source of income.* Ottawa, ON: Author,
Division of Aging and Seniors. Retrieved August 31, 2004 from
http://www.hc-sc.gc.ca/seniors-aines/pubs/factoids/2001/no19_e.htm

Health Canada. (2003h). *Canada's seniors: No. 13—Gender differences in income.* Ottawa, ON: Author, Division of Aging and
Seniors. Retrieved August 31, 2004 from http://www.hc-sc.gc.ca/
seniors-aines/pubs/factoids/2001/no13_e.htm

Health Canada. (2003i). *Canada's seniors: No. 14—The incidence of
low income falling.* Ottawa, ON: Author, Division of Aging and
Seniors. Retrieved August 31, 2004 from http://www.hc-sc.gc.ca/
seniors-aines/pubs/factoids/2001/no14_e.htm

Health Canada. (2003j). *Canada's seniors: No. 15—Gender differences in low income.* Ottawa, ON: Author, Division of Aging and
Seniors. Retrieved August 31, 2004 from http://www.hc-sc.gc.ca/
seniors-aines/pubs/factoids/2001/no15_e.htm

Health Canada. (2003k). *Canada's seniors: No. 6—In cities, towns
and elsewhere.* Ottawa, ON: Author. Retrieved August 31, 2004
from http://www.hc-sc.gc.ca/seniors-aines/pubs/factoids/2001/
no06_e.htm

Health Canada. (2003l). Palliative care: Info sheets for seniors.
Ottawa, ON: Author. Retrieved September 8, 2004 from
http://www.hc-sc.gc.ca/seniors-aines/pubs/info_sheets/palliative_care/
pall_e.htm

Health Canada. (2004a). *Canadian Tobacco Use Monitoring Survey
(CTUMS).* Ottawa, ON: Author. Retrieved March 6, 2004 from

http://www.hc-sc.gc.ca/hecs-sesc/tobacco/research/atums/index.html#prevalence

Health Canada. (2004b). *Health Canada advises Canadians under the age of 18 to consult physicians if they are being treated with newer anti-depressants.* Ottawa, ON: Author. Retrieved February 8, 2004 from http://www.hc-sc.gc.ca/english/protection/warnings/2004/2004_02.htm

Health Canada. (2004c). *Reported cases and rates of notifiable STI from January 1 to December 31, 2003 and January 1 to December 31, 2002.* Ottawa, ON: Author. Retrieved August 6, 2004 from http://www.hc-sc.gc.ca/pphb-dgspsp/std-mts/stdcases-casmts/index.html

Health Reports. (1999a). Income inequality and mortality among working-age people in Canada and the U.S. *Health Reports, 11*(3), 77–82.

Health Reports. (1999b). Health among older adults (Catalogue No. 82-003-XPB). *Health Reports, 11*(3), 47–61.

Health Reports. (2001). Death—shifting trends (Catalogue No. 82-003-XPE). *Health Reports, 12*(3), 41–47.

HealthyOntario.com. (2003). *Eating disorders: The facts.* Toronto: Ministry of Health and Long-Term Care. Retrieved July 31, 2003, from http://www.healthyontario.com/english/printVersion.asp?which=features&text_id=91&channel_id=0

Heart and Stroke Foundation of Canada. (1999). *The changing face of heart disease and stroke in Canada.* Author: Ottawa. Retrieved December 17, 2001 from http://www. hc-sc.gc.ca/hpb/lcdc/bcrdd/hdsc2000/pdf/card2ke.pdf

Heckhausen, J., & Brim, O. (1997). Perceived problems for self and others: Self-protection by social downgrading throughout adulthood. *Psychology & Aging, 12*, 610–619.

Heidt-Kozisek, E., Pipp-Siegel, S., Easterbrooks, M., & Harmon, R. (1997). Knowledge of self, mother, and father in preterm and full-term toddlers. *Infant Behavior & Development, 20*, 311–324.

Heinicke, C., Goorsky, M., Moscov, S., Dudley, K., Gordon, J., Schneider, C., & Guthrie, D. (2000). Relationship-based intervention with at-risk mothers: Factors affecting variations in outcome. *Infant Mental Health Journal, 21*, 133–155.

Heise, L. & Garcia-Moreno, C. (2002). Violence by intimate partners. In E.G. Krug, L.L. Dahlberg, J.A. Mercy, A.B. Zwi, & R. Lozano (eds.), *World report on violence and health* (pp. 87–121). Geneva: World Health Organization. Retrieved August 7, 2004 from http://www.who.int/violence_injury_prevention/violence/world_report/en/full_en.pdf

Helgele, R.A, Cao, H, Harris, S.B, Hanley, A.J.G & Zinman, B. (1999) The hepatic nuclear factor—1% G319S variant is associated with early-onset type 2 diabetes in Canadian Oji-Cree. *The Journal of Clinical Endocrinology and Metabolism, 84*(3), 1007–1082.

Hellinghausen, M. (1999, April 29). Miracle birth: Nurses recount unforgettable arrival of the Houston octuplets. *Nurse Week/Health Week.* Retrieved March 6, 2001 from http://www.nurseweek.com

Helme, R. (1998). Pain in the elderly. *Australasian Journal on Aging, 17*, 33–35.

Helson, R., & Klohnen, D. (1998). Affective coloring of personality from young adulthood to midlife. *Personality & Social Psychology Bulletin, 24*, 241–252.

Helson, R., Mitchell, V., & Moane, G. (1984). Personality and patterns of adherence and nonadherence to the social clock. *Journal of Personality and Social Psychology, 46*, 1079–1096.

Henderson-Smart, D.J., Ponsonby, A., & Murphy, E. (1998). Reducing the risk of sudden infant death syndrome (SIDS): A review of the scientific literature. *Journal of Paediatrics and Child Health, 34*, 213–219.

Henry J. Kaiser Family Foundation. (1999). *Sex on TV.* Washington, DC: Author.

Henry, B., Caspi, A., Moffitt, T., Harrington, H., et al. (1999). Staying in school protects boys with poor self-regulation in childhood from later crime: A longitudinal study. *International Journal of Behavioral Development, 23*, 1049–1073.

Henry, B., Caspi, A., Moffitt, T., & Silva, P. (1996). Temperamental and familial predictors of violent and nonviolent criminal convictions: Age 3 to age 18. *Developmental Psychology, 32*, 614–623.

Heppner, M., Fuller, B., & Multon, K. (1998). Adults in involuntary career transition: An analysis of the relationship between the psychological and career domains. *Journal of Career Assessment, 6*, 329–346.

Hernandez, S., Camacho-Rosales, J., Nieto, A., & Barroso, J. (1997). Cerebral asymmetry and reading performance: Effect of language lateralization and hand preference. *Child Neuropsychology, 3*, 206–225.

Herrenkohl, E., Herrenkohl, R., Egolf, B., & Russo, M. (1998). The relationship between early maltreatment and teenage parenthood. *Journal of Adolescence, 21*, 291–303.

Hertzman, C. (1999). Population health and human development. In D.P. Keating & C. Hertzman (Eds.) *Developmental health and the wealth of nations: Social, Biological, and Educational Dynamics* (pp. 21–40). New York: Guilford Press.

Herxheimer, A., & Mintzes, B. (2004). Antidepressants and adverse effects in young patients: Uncovering the evidence. *Canadian Medical Association Journal, 170*(4), 487–488.

Herzog, A.R., House, J.S., & Morgan, J.N. (1991). Relation of work and retirement to health and well-being in older age. *Psychology and Aging, 6*, 202–211.

Hess, E.H. (1972). "Imprinting" in a natural laboratory. *Scientific American, 227*, 24–31.

Hess, T., Bolstad, C., Woodburn, S., & Auman, C. (1999). Trait diagnosticity versus behavioral consistency as determinants of impression change in adulthood. *Psychology & Aging, 14*, 77–89.

Hetherington, E.M. (1991a). Presidential address: Families, lies, and videotapes. *Journal of Research on Adolescence, 1*, 323–348.

Hetherington, E.M. (1991b). The role of individual differences and family relationships in children's coping with divorce and remarriage. In P.A. Cowen & M. Hetherington (Eds.), *Family transitions* (pp. 165–194). Hillsdale, NJ: Erlbaum.

Hetherington, E., Bridges, M., & Insabella, G. (1998). What matters? What does not?: Five perspectives on the association between marital transitions and children's adjustment. *American Psychologist, 53*, 167–184.

Hetherington, E.M., & Clingempeel, W.G. (1992). Coping with marital transitions: A family systems perspective. *Monographs of the Society for Research in Child Development, 57*(2–3, Serial No. 227).

Hetherington, E., Henderson, S., Reiss, D., Anderson, E., et al. (1999). Adolescent siblings in stepfamilies: Family functioning and adolescent adjustment. *Monographs of the Society for Research in Child Development, 64*, 222.

Hetherington, E.M., & Stanley-Hagan, M.M. (1995). Parenting in divorced and remarried families. In M.H. Bornstein (Ed.), *Handbook of parenting: Vol. 3. Status and social conditions of parenting* (pp. 233–254). Mahwah, NJ: Erlbaum.

Hicks, D., & Gwynne, M. (1996). *Cultural anthropology.* New York: HarperCollins.

Higgins, C., Duxbury, L., & Lee, C. (1994). Impact of life-cycle stage and gender on the ability to balance work and family responsibilities. *Family Relations, 43*, 144–150.

Hilder, L., Costeloe, K., & Thilaganathan, B. (1998). Prolonged pregnancy: Evaluating gestation-specific risks of fetal and infant mortality. *British Journal of Obstetric Gynacology, 105*, 169–173.

Hill, A., & Franklin, J. (1998). Mothers, daughters, and dieting: Investigating the transmission of weight control. *British Journal of Clinical Psychology, 37*, 3–13.

Hill, G., Forbes, W., Berthelot, J., Lindsay, J., & McDowell, I. (1996). Dementia among seniors (Catalogue No. 82-003-XPB). *Health Reports, 8*(2), 7–10.

Hill, R.D., Storandt, M., & Malley, M. (1993). The impact of long-term exercise training on psychological function in older adults. *Journals of Gerontology: Psychological Sciences, 48*, P12–17.

Hincks-Dellcrest Institute Foundation (2001). What is TLC3? Toronto: Author. Retrieved July 11, 2001 from http://www.hincksdellcrest.org/tlc3/institute-about.html

Hinde, R.A., Titmus, G., Easton, D., & Tamplin, A. (1985). Incidence of "friendship" and behavior toward strong associates versus nonassociates in preschoolers. *Child Development, 56,* 234–245.

Hinden, S. (2000). Computer age brings wide new world to golden age. *Washington Post Online.* Retrieved March 19, 2000 from www.washingtonpost.com

Hinton, J. (1975). The influence of previous personality on reactions to having terminal cancer. *Omega, 6,* 95–111.

Hirdes, J.P., & Strain, L.A. (1995). The balance of exchange in instrumental support with network members outside the household. *Journals of Gerontology: Social Sciences, 50B,* S134–142.

Ho, C., & Bryant, P. (1997). Learning to read Chinese beyond the logographic phase. *Reading Research Quarterly, 32,* 276–289.

Hoch, C.C., Buysse, D.J., Monk, T.H., & Reynolds, C.F.I. (1992). Sleep disorders and aging. In J.E. Birren, R.B. Sloane, & G.D. Cohen (Eds.), *Handbook of mental health and aging* (2nd ed., pp. 557–582). San Diego, CA: Academic Press.

Hobbs, J., & Ferth, P. (1993). *The Bounty pregnancy guide.* New York: Bounty Health Care Publishing.

Hodge, S., & Canter, D. (1998). Victims and perpetrators of male sexual assault. *Journal of Interpersonal Violence, 13,* 222–239.

Hoff, T.L. (1992). Psychology in Canada one hundred years ago: James Mark Baldwin at the University of Toronto. *Canadian Psychology, 33*(2), Abstract.

Hofferth, S.L. (2001). How American children spend their time. *Journal of Marriage and the Family, 63*(2), 295–308.

Hoffman, H.J., & Hillman, L.S. (1992). Epidemiology of the sudden infant death syndrome: Maternal, neonatal, and postneonatal risk factors. *Clinics in Perinatology, 19*(4), 717–737.

Hoffman, L. (1989). Effects of maternal employment in the two-parent family. *American Psychologist, 44,* 283–292.

Hoffman, M. (1970). Moral Development. In P. Mussen (Ed.), *Carmichael's manual of child psychology* (Vol. 2). New York: Wiley.

Hoffman, M. (1988). Moral development. In M. Bornstein & M. Lamb (Eds.), *Developmental psychology: An advanced textbook* (2nd ed., pp. 497–548). Hillsdale, NJ: Erlbaum.

Holden, K.C., & Smock, P.J. (1991). The economic costs of marital dissolution: Why do women bear a disproportionate cost? *Annual Review of Sociology, 17,* 51–78.

Holland, A., Hon, J., Huppert, F., Stevens, F., & Watson, P. (1998). Population-based study of the prevalence and presentation of dementia in adults with Down syndrome. *British Journal of Psychiatry, 172,* 493–498.

Holland, J.L. (1973). *Making vocational choices: A theory of careers.* Englewood Cliffs, NJ: Prentice-Hall.

Holland, J.L. (1992). *Making vocational choices: A theory of vocational personalities and work environments* (2nd ed.). Odessa, FL: Psychological Assessment Resources.

Holmbeck, G.N., & Hill, J.P. (1991). Conflictive engagement, positive affect, and menarche in families with seventh-grade girls. *Child Development, 62,* 1030–1048.

Holobow, N., Genesee, F., & Lambert, W. (1991). The effectiveness of a foreign language immersion program for children from different ethnic and social class backgrounds: Report 2. *Applied Psycholinguistics, 12,* 179–198.

Holowka, S., & Petitto, L.A. (2002). Left hemisphere cerebral specialization for babies while babbling. *Science, 297*(5586), 1515.

Honzik, M.P. (1986). The role of the family in the development of mental abilities: A 50-year study. In N. Datan, A.L. Greene, & H.W. Reese (Eds.), *Life-span developmental psychology: Intergenerational relations* (pp. 185–210). Hillsdale, NJ: Erlbaum.

Horan, W., Pogge, D., Borgaro, S., & Stokes, J. (1997). Learning and memory in adolescent psychiatric inpatients with major depression: A normative study of the California Verbal Learning Test. *Archives of Clinical Neuropsychology, 12,* 575–584.

Horn, J.L. (1982). The aging of human abilities. In B.B. Wolman (Ed.), *Handbook of developmental psychology* (pp. 847–870). Englewood Cliffs, NJ: Prentice-Hall.

Horn, J.L., & Donaldson, G. (1980). Cognitive development in adulthood. In O.G. Brim, Jr. & J. Kagan (Eds.), *Constancy and change in human development* (pp. 415–529). Cambridge, MA: Harvard University Press.

Hornbrook, M.C., Stevens, V.J., & Wingfield, D.J. (1994). Preventing falls among community-dwelling older persons: Results from a randomized trial. *The Gerontologist, 34,* 16–23.

Horner, K.W., Rushton, J.P., & Vernon, P.A. (1986). Relation between aging and research productivity of academic psychologists. *Psychology and Aging, 1,* 319–324.

Horowitz, A., McLaughlin, J., & White, H. (1998). How the negative and positive aspects of partner relationships affect the mental health of young married people. *Journal of Health & Social Behavior, 39,* 124–136.

Hortacsu, N. (1999). The first year of family- and couple-initiated marriages of a Turkish sample: A longitudinal investigation. *International Journal of Psychology, 34,* 29–41.

Hotton, T. (2001). Spousal violence after marital separation (Catalogue No. 85-002). *Juristat 21*(7), 2–18.

Hotton, T., & Haans, D. (2004). Alcohol and drug use in early adolescence. *Health Reports, 15*(3), 9–19.

Houseknecht, S.K. (1987). Voluntary childlessness. In M.B. Sussman & S.K. Steinmetz (Eds.), *Handbook of marriage and the family* (pp. 369–395). New York: Plenum.

Hovell, M., Blumberg, E., Sipan, C., Hofstetter, C., Burkham, S., Atkins, C., & Felice, M. (1998). Skills training for pregnancy and AIDS prevention in Anglo and Latino youth. *Journal of Adolescent Health, 23,* 139–149.

Hovell, M., Sipan, C., Blumberg, E., Atkins, C., Hofstetter, C.R., & Kreitner, S. (1994). Family influences on Latino and Anglo adolescents' sexual behavior. *Journal of Marriage and the Family, 56,* 973–986.

Howe, G.R. (1994). Dietary fat and breast cancer risks: An epidemiologic perspective. *Cancer, 74*(3 Suppl.), 1078–1084.

Howes, C. (1983). Patterns of friendship. *Child Development, 54,* 1041–1053.

Howes, C. (1987). Social competence with peers in young children: Developmental sequences. *Developmental Review, 7,* 252–272.

Howes, C., & Matheson, C.C. (1992). Sequences in the development of competent play with peers: Social and pretend play. *Developmental Psychology, 28,* 961–974.

Hoyert, D.L., & Seltzer, M.M. (1992). Factors related to the well-being and life activities of family caregivers. *Family Relations, 41,* 74–81.

Huang, H., & Hanley, J. (1997). A longitudinal study of phonological awareness, visual skills, and Chinese reading acquisition among first-graders in Taiwan. *International Journal of Behavioral Development, 20,* 249–268.

Huesmann, L.R., Moise-Titus, J., Podolski, C.L., & Eron, L.D. (2003). Longitudinal relations between children's exposure to TV violence and their aggressive and violent behaviour in young adulthood: 1977—1992. *Developmental Psychology, 39*(2), 201–221.

Hultsch, D.F., Hertzog, C., Small, B.J., McDonald-Miszczak, L., & Dixon, R.A. (1992). Short-term longitudinal change in cognitive performance in later life. *Psychology and Aging, 7,* 571–584.

Human Resources Development Canada. (1996a). *National Longitudinal Survey of Children and Youth (NLSCY).* (Catalogue No. SP-AH036E-10-96). Ottawa, ON: Author. Retrieved November 19, 2001 from http://www11.hrdc-drhc.gc.ca/edd/NLSCY_172000.htm

Human Resources Development Canada. (2001a). *Does parental separation affect children's behaviour?* Ottawa, ON: Author. Retrieved September 20, 2001 from http://www.hrdc-drhc.gc.ca/stratpol/arb/publications/bulletin/child_dev/chi_dev2.shtml

Human Resources Development Canada. (2001b). *Canadian gender trends in education and work* (Catalogue No. MP32-30/00-4E). Ottawa, ON: Author. Retrieved November 23, 2001 from http://www.hrdc-drhc.gc.ca/stratpol/arb/publications/research/2000docs/t-00-4e.pdf

Human Resources Development Canada. (2001c). *Canada's retirement income system—simply stated*. Ottawa, ON: Author. Retrieved December 28, 2001 from http://www.hrdc-drhc.gc.ca/isp/ris/cris_e.shtml

Human Resources Development Canada. (2003). *A new generation of Canadian families raising young children* (Catalogue No. SP-579-09-03E). Retrieved May 15, 2004 from http://www11.sdc.gc.ca/en/cs/sp/arb/publications/research/2003-001330/2003-001330.pdf

Human Resources Development Canada. (2004). *Leave and benefits (workplace programs, policies and practices)*. Retrieved May 15, 2004 from http://www.hrsdc.gc.ca/en/lp/spila/wlb/wppp/02leave_benefits.shtml

Human Resources Development Canada and Statistics Canada. (1996). *Growing up in Canada 1994/95* (Catalogue No. 89-550-MPE). Ottawa, ON: Author.

Hummert, M., Garstka, T., & Shaner, J. (1997). Stereotyping of older adults: The role of target facial cues and perceiver characteristics. *Psychology & Aging, 21,* 107–114.

Humphreys, A., & Smith, P. (1987). Rough and tumble, friendship, and dominance in school children: Evidence for continuity and change with age. *Child Development, 58,* 201–212.

Hunfeld, J., Tempels, A., Passchier, J., Hazebroek, F., et al. (1999). Parental burden and grief one year after the birth of a child with a congenital anomaly. *Journal of Pediatric Psychology, 24,* 515–520.

Hunter, D.J., Spiegelman, D., Adami, H., Beeson, L., van den Brandt, P.A., Folsom, A.R., Fraser, G.E., Goldbohm, A., Graham, S., Howe, G.R., Kushi, L.H., Marshall, J.R., McDermott, A., Miller, A.B., Speizer, F.E., Wolk, A., Yuan, S., & Willett, W. (1996). Cohort studies of fat intake and the risk of breast cancer—a pooled analysis. *New England Journal of Medicine, 334,* 356–361.

Hunter, M., & O'Dea, I. (1999). An evaluation of a health education intervention for mid-aged women: Five-year follow-up of effects upon knowledge, impact of menopause and health. *Patient Education & Counseling, 38,* 249–255.

Hunter, S., & Sundel, M. (1989). *Midlife myths: Issues, findings, and practice implications.* Newbury Park, CA: Sage.

Huntington Society of Canada. (2001). *Huntington disease (HD) is a hereditary brain disorder with devastating effects on both mind and body.* Kitchener, ON: Author. Retrieved November 19, 2001 from http://www.hsc-ca.org/english/about_hd.shtml

Hurwitz, E., Gunn, W.J., Pinsky, P.F., & Schonberger, L.B. (1991). Risk of respiratory illness associated with day-care attendance: A nationwide study. *Pediatrics, 87,* 62–69.

Huston, T.L., & Chorost, A.F. (1994). Behavioral buffers on the effect of negativity on marital satisfaction: A longitudinal study. *Personal Relationships, 1,* 223–239.

Huston, T.L., McHale, S.M., & Crouter, A.C. (1986). When the honeymoon's over: Changes in the marriage relationship over the first year. In R. Gilmour & S. Duck (Eds.), *The emerging field of personal relationships* (pp. 109–132). Hillsdale, NJ: Erlbaum.

Hutt, S.J., Lenard, H.G., & Prechtl, H.F.R. (1969). Psychophysiological studies in newborn infants. In L.P. Lipsitt & H.W. Reese (Eds.), *Advances in child development and behavior* (Vol. 4, pp. 128–173). New York: Academic Press.

Idler, E., & Kasl, S. (1997a). Religion among disabled and nondisabled persons I: Cross-sectional patterns in health practices, social activities, and well-being. *Journals of Gerontology: Series B: Psychological Sciences & Social Sciences, 52B,* S294–S305.

Idler, E., & Kasl, S. (1997b). Religion among disabled and nondisabled persons II: Attendance at religious services as a predictor of the course of disability. *Journals of Gerontology: Series B: Psychological Sciences & Social Sciences, 52B,* S306–S316.

Industry Canada (2000). *Canada's children in a wired world: The parents' view.* Ottawa, ON: Author. Retrieved November 18, 2001 from http://strategis.ic.gc.ca/pics/sf/finalreporteng.pdf

Ingoldsby, E., Shaw, D., Owens, E., & Winslow, E. (1999). A longitudinal study of interparental conflict, emotional and behavioral reactivity, and preschoolers' adjustment problems among low-income families. *Journal of Abnormal Child Psychology, 27,* 343–356.

Ingram, D. (1981). Early patterns of grammatical development. In R.E. Stark (Ed.), *Language behavior in infancy and early childhood* (pp. 327–358). New York: Elsevier North-Holland.

Inhelder, B., & Piaget, J. (1958). *The growth of logical thinking from childhood to adolescence.* New York: Basic Books.

Insabella, G.M. (1995, March). *Varying levels of exposure to marital conflict: Prediction of adolescent adjustment across intact families and stepfamilies.* Paper presented at the biennial meetings of the Society for Research in Child Development, Indianapolis, IN.

Ipsos-Reid/CTV/*Globe and Mail.* (1999). *Canadians overwhelmingly believe that spanking should not be made a criminal offence.* Toronto: Author. Retrieved June 24, 2004 from http://www.ipsos-na.com/news/pressrelease.cfm?id=866&content=full

Irwin, M., & Pike, J. (1993). Bereavement, depressive symptoms, and immune function. In M.S. Stroebe, W. Stroebe, & R.O. Hansson (Eds.), *Handbook of bereavement: Theory, research, and intervention* (pp. 160–171). Cambridge, England: Cambridge University Press.

Isabella, R.A. (1995). The origins of infant-mother attachment: Maternal behavior and infant development. *Annals of Child Development, 10,* 57–81.

Iversen, L., & Sabroe, S. (1988). Psychological well-being among unemployed and employed people after a company closedown: A longitudinal study. *Journal of Social Issues, 44,* 141–152.

Ivy, G.O., MacLeod, C.M., Petit, T.L., & Marcus, E.J. (1992). A physiological framework for perceptual and cognitive changes in aging. In F.I.M. Craik & T.A. Salthouse (Eds.), *The handbook of aging and cognition* (pp. 273–314). Hillsdale, NJ: Erlbaum.

Izard, C.E., Fantauzzo, C.A., Castle, J.M., Haynes, O.M., Rayias, M.F., & Putnam, P.H. (1995). The ontogeny and significance of infants' facial expressions in the first 9 months of life. *Developmental Psychology, 31,* 997–1013.

Izard, C.E., & Harris, P. (1995). Emotional development and developmental psychopathology. In D. Cicchetti & D.J. Cohen (Eds.), *Developmental psychopathology: Vol. 1. Theory and methods* (pp. 467–503). New York: Wiley.

Jackson, A. (2001). *The incidence and depth of child poverty in recession and recovery: Some preliminary lessons on child benefits.* Ottawa, ON: Canadian Council on Social Development. Retrieved September 15, 2001 from http://www.ccsd.ca/pubs/2001/ajncb.htm

Jackson, A. & Schetagne, S. (2001). *Still struggling: An update on teenagers at work.* Ottawa, ON: Canadian Council on Social Development. Retrieved October 24, 2001 from http://www.ccsd.ca/pubs/2001/pcc2001/employ.htm

Jackson, D.J., Longino, C.F., Jr., Zimmerman, R.S., & Bradsher, J.E. (1991). Environmental adjustments to declining functional ability: Residential mobility and living arrangements. *Research on Aging, 13,* 289–309.

Jackson, D., & Tein, J. (1998). Adolescents' conceptualization of adult roles: Relationships with age, gender, work goal, and maternal employment. *Sex Roles, 38,* 987–1008.

Jackson, L., & Bracken, B. (1998). Relationship between students' social status and global and domain-specific self-concepts. *Journal of School Psychology, 36,* 233–246.

Jacobs, S.C., Kosten, T.R., Kasl, S.V., Ostfeld, A.M., Berkman, L., & Charpentier, P. (1987/1988). Attachment theory and multiple dimensions of grief. *Omega, 18,* 41–52.

Jacobsen, T., & Hofmann, V. (1997). Children's attachment representations: Longitudinal relations to school behavior, and academic competency in middle childhood and adolescence. *Developmental Psychology, 33,* 703–710.

Jacobsen, T., Husa, M., Fendrich, M., Kruesi, M., & Ziegenhain, U. (1997). Children's ability to delay gratification: Longitudinal relations to mother-child attachment. *Journal of Genetic Psychology, 158,* 411–426.

Jacques, E. (1965). Death and the mid-life crisis. *International Journal of Psychoanalysis, 46*(4), 502–514.

Jacques, S., & Zelazo, P.D. (2001). The Flexible Item Selection Task (FIST): A measure of executive function in preschoolers. *Developmental Neuropsychology, 20*(3), 573–591.

Jadack, R.A., Hyde, J.S., Moore, C.F., & Keller, M.L. (1995). Moral reasoning about sexually transmitted diseases. *Child Development, 66,* 167–177.

James, S.A., Keenan, N.L., & Browning, S. (1992). Socioeconomic status, health behaviors, and health status among blacks. In K.W. Schaie, D. Blazer, & J.M. House (Eds.), *Aging, health behaviors, and health outcomes* (pp. 39–57). Hillsdale, NJ: Erlbaum.

Janosz, M., Le Blanc, M., Boulerice, B., & Tremblay, R. (2000). Predicting different types of school dropouts: A typological approach with two longitudinal samples. *Journal of Educational Psychology, 92,* 171–190.

Janssen, T., & Carton, J. (1999). The effects of locus of control and task difficulty on procrastination. *Journal of Genetic Psychology, 160,* 436–442.

Japal, C., Tremblay, R., McDuff, P., & Willms, J.D. (2002). Pre-adolescent girls and the onset of puberty. In J.D. Willms (Ed.), *Vulnerable children* (pp. 305–316). Edmonton, AB: The University of Alberta Press.

Jarolmen, J. (1998). A comparison of the grief reaction of children and adults: Focusing on pet loss and bereavement. *Omega: Journal of Death & Dying, 37,* 133–150.

Jendrek, M. (1993). Grandparents who parent their grandchildren: Effects on lifestyle. *Journal of Marriage and the Family, 55,* 609–621.

Jenkins, J.M., & Astington, J.W. (1996). Cognitive factors and family structure associated with theory of mind development in young children. *Developmental Psychology, 32,* 70–78.

Jenkins, J. & Buccioni, J. (2000). Children's understanding of marital conflict and the marital relationship. *Journal of Child Psychology & Psychiatry & Allied Disciplines, 41,* 161–168.

Jenkins, L., Myerson, J., Hale, S., & Fry, A. (1999). Individual and developmental differences in working memory across the life span. *Psychonomic Bulletin & Review, 6,* 28–40.

Jensen, A., & Whang, P. (1994). Speed of accessing arithmetic facts in long-term memory: A comparison of Chinese-American and Anglo-American children. *Contemporary Educational Psychology, 19,* 1–12.

Jerrome, D. (1990). Intimate relationships. In J. Bond & P. Coleman (Eds.), *Aging in society* (pp. 181–208). London: Sage.

Jessor, R. (1992). Risk behavior in adolescence: A psychosocial framework for understanding and action. *Developmental Review, 12,* 374–390.

Jilek, W.G. (2001). *Anorexia nervosa: Cultural factors in psychiatric disorders.* Paper presented at the 26th Congress of the World Federation for Mental Health, July, 2001. Retrieved July 31, 2003, from http://www.mentalhealth.com/mag1/wolfgangex.html

Jimerson, S. (1999). On the failure of failure: Examining the association between early grade retention and educational and employment outcomes during late adolescence. *Journal of School Psychology, 37,* 243–272.

John, O.P., Caspi, A., Robins, R.W., Moffitt, T.E., & Stouthamer-Loeber, M. (1994). The "little five": Exploring the nomological network of the five-factor model of personality in adolescent boys. *Child Development, 65,* 160–178.

Johnson, E., & Breslau, N. (2000). Increased risk of learning disabilities in low birth weight boys at age 11 years. *Biological Psychiatry, 47,* 490–500.

Johnson, H., Nusbaum, B., Bejarano, A., & Rosen, T. (1999). An ecological approach to development in children with prenatal drug exposure. *American Journal of Orthopsychiatry, 69,* 448–456.

Johnson, K.L., Lero, D.S., & Rooney, J.A. (2001). *Work-life compendium 2001: 150 Canadian statistics on work, family and wellbeing* (ISBN 0-88955-517-6). Guelph, ON: Centre for Families, Work and Well-Being, University of Guelph. Retrieved May 15, 2004 from http://www11.sdc.gc.ca/en/cs/sp/sac/gap/publications/2001-000031/2001-000031.pdf

Johnson, M.H. (1998). The neural basis of cognitive development. In D. Kuhn & R.S. Siegler (Eds.), *Handbook of child psychology: Vol. 2. Cognition, perception, and language* (5th ed., pp. 1–49). New York: Wiley.

Johnson, M.H. (2001). Functional brain development during infancy. In G. Bremner & A. Fogel (Eds.), *Blackwell handbook of infant development* (pp. 169–190). Oxford, UK: Blackwell Publishers Inc.

Johnson, N., & Cremo, E. (1995). Socialization and the native family. In K. Covell (Ed.), *Readings in child development.* Toronto: Nelson.

Johnston, C. (1996). Interactive storybook software: Effects on verbal development in kindergarten children. *Early Child Development & Care, 132,* 33–44.

Jones, J. (1997). Representations of menopause and their health care implications: A qualitative study. *American Journal of Preventive Medicine, 13,* 58–65.

Jones, J.M., Bennett, S., Olmsted, M.P., Lawson, M.L., & Rodin, G. (2001). Disordered eating attitudes and behaviours in teenaged girls: A school-based study. *Canadian Medical Association Journal, 165*(5), 547–552.

Jones, M.C. (1924). A laboratory study of fear: The case of Peter. *Pedagogical Seminary, 31,* 308–315.

Jorgenson, S. (1993). Adolescent pregnancy and parenting. In T. Gullotta, G. Adams, & R. Montemayor (Eds.), *Adolescent sexuality* (pp. 103–140). Thousand Oaks, CA: Sage Publications.

Jorm, A., Christensen, H., Henderson, A., Jacomb, P., Korten, A., & Mackinnon, A. (1998). Factors associated with successful aging. *Journal of Ageing, 17,* 33–37.

Joseph, R. (2000). Fetal brain behavior and cognitive development. *Developmental Review, 20,* 81–98.

Josephson, W.L. (1995). Television violence: A review of the effects on children of different ages. Ottawa, ON: Department of Canadian Heritage.

Joung, I.M.A., Stronks, K., van de Mheen, H., & Mackenbach, J.P. (1995). Health behaviours explain part of the differences in self reported health associated with partner/marital status in The Netherlands. *Journal of Epidemiology and Community Health, 49,* 482–488.

Jube, H. (2003). Yours, mine, and ours: New boundaries for the modern stepfamily. *Transition, 33*(4), 3–6.

Judge, T., Bono, J., & Locke, E. (2000). Personality and job satisfaction: The mediating role of job characteristics. *Journal of Applied Psychology, 85,* 237–249.

Juffer, F., Hoksbergen, R., Riksen-Walraven, J., & Kohnstamm, G. (1997). Early intervention in adoptive families: Supporting maternal sensitive responsiveness, infant-mother attachment, and infant competence. *Journal of Child Psychology & Psychiatry & Allied Disciplines, 38,* 1039–1050.

Juffer, F., & Rosenboom, L., (1997). Infant mother attachment of internationally adopted children in the Netherlands. *International Journal of Behavioral Development, 20,* 93–107.

Jusczyk, P. (1995). Language acquisition: Speech sounds and phonological development. In J. Miler & P. Eimas (Eds.), *Handbook of perception and cognition: Vol. 11. Speech, language, and communication* (pp. 263–301). Orlando, FL: Academic Press.

Jusczyk, P., & Hohne, E. (1997). Infants' memory for spoken words. *Science, 277.*

Jusczyk, P., Houston, D., & Newsome, M. (1999). The beginnings of word segmentation in English-learning infants. *Cognitive Psychology, 39,* 159–207.

Jutras, S., & Lavoie, J. (1995). Living with an impaired elderly person: The informal caregiver's physical and mental health. *Journal of Aging and Health, 7,* 46–73.

Kagan, J. (1989). *Unstable ideas: Temperament, cognition, and self.* Cambridge, MA: Harvard University Press.

Kagan, J. (1994). *Galen's prophecy.* New York: Basic Books.

Kagan, J., Reznick, J.S., & Snidman, N. (1990). The temperamental qualities of inhibition and lack of inhibition. In M. Lewis & S.M. Miller (Eds.), *Handbook of developmental psychopathology* (pp. 219–226). New York: Plenum.

Kagan, J., Snidman, N., & Arcus, D. (1993). On the temperamental categories of inhibited and uninhibited children. In K.H. Rubin & J.B. Asendorpf (Eds.), *Social withdrawal, inhibition, and shyness in childhood* (pp. 19–28). Hillsdale, NJ: Erlbaum.

Kahn, S.B., Alvi, S., Shaukat, N., Hussain, M.A., & Baig, T. (1990). A study of the validity of Holland's theory in a non-Western culture. *Journal of Vocational Behavior, 36,* 132–146.

Kail, R. (1990). *The development of memory in children* (3rd ed.). New York: Freeman.

Kail, R. (1991). Processing time declines exponentially during childhood and adolescence. *Developmental Psychology, 27,* 259–266.

Kail, R. (1997). Processing time, imagery, and spatial memory. *Journal of Experimental Child Psychology, 64,* 67–78.

Kail, R., & Hall, L.K. (1994). Processing speed, naming speed, and reading. *Developmental Psychology, 30,* 949–954.

Kalish, R.A. (1985). The social context of death and dying. In R.H. Binstock & E. Shanas (Eds.), *Handbook of aging and the social sciences* (2nd ed., pp. 149–170). New York: Van Nostrand Reinhold.

Kalish, R.A., & Reynolds, D.K. (1976). *Death and ethnicity: A psychocultural study.* Los Angeles: University of Southern California Press. (Reprinted 1981, Baywood Publishing Co, Farmingdale, NJ.)

Kallman, D.A., Plato, C.C., & Tobin, J.D. (1990). The role of muscle loss in the age-related decline of grip strength: Cross-sectional and longitudinal perspectives. *Journals of Gerontology: Medical Sciences, 45,* M82–88.

Kamo, Y., Ries, L.M., Farmer, Y.M., Nickinovich, D.G., & Borgatta, E.F. (1991). Status attainment revisited. The National Survey of Families and Households. *Research on Aging, 13,* 124–143.

Kandel, D.B., & Wu, P. (1995). The contributions of mothers and fathers to the intergenerational transmission of cigarette smoking in adolescence. *Journal of Research on Adolescence, 5,* 225–252.

Kane, R.L., Klein, S.J., Bernstein, L., Rothenberg, R., & Wales, J. (1985). Hospice role in alleviating the emotional stress of terminal patients and their families. *Medical Care, 23,* 189–197.

Kane, R.L., Wales, J., Bernstein, L., Leibowitz, A., & Kaplan, S. (1984). A randomized controlled trial of hospice care. *Lancet,* 890–894.

Kane, T., Staiger, P., & Ricciardelli, L. (2000). Male domestic violence: Attitudes, aggression and interpersonal dependency. *Journal of Interpersonal Violence, 15,* 16–29.

Kannel, W.B., & Gordon, T. (1980). Cardiovascular risk factors in the aged: The Framingham study. In S.G. Haynes & M. Feinleib (Eds.), *Second conference on the epidemiology of aging.* U.S. Department of Health and Human Services, NIH Publication No. 80–969 (pp. 65–89). Washington, DC: U.S. Government Printing Office.

Kaplan, G.A. (1992). Health and aging in the Alameda County study. In K.W. Schaie, D. Blazer, & J.M. House (Eds.), *Aging, health behaviors, and health outcomes* (pp. 69–88). Hillsdale, NJ: Erlbaum.

Kaplan, H., & Sadock, B. (1991). *Synopsis of psychiatry* (6th ed.). Baltimore, MD: Williams & Wilkins.

Karmiloff-Smith, A. (1991). Beyond modularity: Innate constraints and developmental change. In S. Carey & R. Gelman (Eds.), *The epigenesis of mind: Essays on biology and cognition* (pp. 171–197). Hillsdale, NJ: Erlbaum.

Katz, P., & Bartone, P. (1998). Mourning, ritual and recovery after an airline tragedy. *Omega: Journal of Death & Dying, 36,* 193–200.

Katz, P.A., & Ksansnak, K.R. (1994). Developmental aspects of gender role flexibility and traditionality in middle childhood and adolescence. *Developmental Psychology, 30,* 272–282.

Katz, R., & Wertz, R. (1997). The efficacy of computer-provided reading treatment for chronic aphasic adults. *Journal of Speech & Hearing Research, 40,* 493–507.

Kaufman, M. (1997). The teratogenic effects of alcohol following exposure during pregnancy, and its influence on the chromosome constitution of the pre-ovulatory egg. *Alcohol & Alcoholism, 32,* 113–128.

Kawachi, I., & Kennedy, B.P. (2002). *The health of nations: Why inequality is harmful to your health.* New York: The New Press.

Kaye, K.L., & Bower, T.G.R. (1994). Learning and intermodal transfer of information in newborns. *Psychological Science, 5,* 286–288.

Kazdin, A.E., & Benjet, C. (2003). Spanking children: Evidence and issues. *Current Directions in Psychological Science, 12*(3), 99–103.

Keene, J., Hope, T., Rogers, P., & Elliman, N. (1998). An investigation of satiety in ageing, dementia, and hyperphagia. *International Journal of Eating Disorders, 23,* 409–418.

Keep Kids Healthy (2003). Choosing toys for your kids. Retrieved March 6, 2004, from http://www.keepkidshealthy.com/development/choosing_toys.html

Keil, J.E., Sutherland, S.E., Knapp, R.G., Waid, L.R., & Gazes, P.C. (1992). Self-reported sexual functioning in elderly blacks and whites. *Journal of Aging and Health, 4,* 112–125.

Keith, P.M. (1981/1982). Perception of time remaining and distance from death. *Omega, 12,* 307–318.

Kellehear, A., & Lewin, T. (1988/1989). Farewells by the dying: A sociological study. *Omega, 19,* 275–292.

Kelley, M.L., Sanches-Hucles, J., & Walker, R.R. (1993). Correlates of disciplinary practices in working- to middle-class African-American mothers. *Merrill-Palmer Quarterly, 39,* 252–264.

Kendler, K., Kessler, R., Walters, E., MacLean, C., Neale, M., Heath, A., & Eaves, L. (1995). Stressful life events, genetic liability, and onset of an episode of major depression in women. *American Journal of Psychiatry, 152,* 833–842.

Kendler, K., Neale, M., Heath, A., Kessler, R., & Eaves, L. (1994). A twin-family study of alcoholism in women. *American Journal of Psychiatry, 49,* 707–715.

Kennedy, K., Nowak, S., Raghuraman, R., Thomas, J., & Davis, S. (2000). Academic dishonesty and distance learning: Student and faculty views. *College Student Journal, 34,* 309–314.

Kent, H. (2001). Eighteen months, 12 suicides. *Canadian Medical Association Journal, 164*(13), 1940.

Kercsmar, C. (1998). The respiratory system. In R. Behrman & R. Kliegman (Eds.), *Nelson essentials of pediatrics* (3rd ed.). Philadelphia: W.B. Saunders.

Kerpelman, J., & Schvaneveldt, P. (1999). Young adults' anticipated identity importance of career, marital, and parental roles: Comparisons of men and women with different role balance orientations. *Sex Roles, 41,* 189–217.

Keskinen, E., Ota, H., & Katila, A. (1998). Older drivers fail in intersections: Speed discrepancies between older and younger male drivers. *Accident Analysis & Prevention, 30,* 323–330.

Kessler, R.C., Foster, C., Webster, P.S., & House, J.S. (1992). The relationship between age and depressive symptoms in two national surveys. *Psychology and Aging, 7,* 119–126.

Kessler, R.C., Turner, J.B., & House, J.S. (1988). Effects of unemployment on health in a community survey: Main, modifying, and mediating effects. *Journal of Social Issues, 44,* 69–85.

Kesteloot, H., Lesaffre, E., & Joossens, J.V. (1991). Dairy fat, saturated animal fat, and cancer risk. *Preventive Medicine, 20,* 226–236.

Khlat, M., Sermet, C., & Le Pape, A. (2000). Women's health in relation with their family and work roles: France in the early 1990s. *Social Science & Medicine, 50,* 1807–1825.

Kiecolt-Glaser, J. (2000, August). *Friends, lovers, relaxation, and immunity: How behavior modifies health. Cortisol and the language of love: Text analysis of newlyweds' relationship stories.* Paper presented at the annual meeting of the American Psychological Association. Washington, DC.

Kiecolt-Glaser, J.K., & Glaser, R. (1995). Measurement of immune response. In S. Cohen, R.C. Kessler, & L.U. Gordon (Eds.), *Measuring stress: A guide for health and social scientists* (pp. 213–229). New York: Oxford University Press.

Kiecolt-Glaser, J.K., Glaser, R., Suttleworth, E.E., Dyer, C.S., Ogrocki, P., & Speicher, C.E. (1987). Chronic stress and immunity in family caregivers of Alzheimer's disease patients. *Psychosomatic Medicine, 49,* 523–535.

Kilbride, H., Castor, C., Hoffman, E., & Fuger, K. (2000). Thirty-six month outcome of prenatal cocaine exposure for term or near-term infants: Impact of early case management. *Journal of Developmental Pediatrics, 21,* 19–26.

Kilpatrick, S.J., & Laros, R.K. (1989). Characteristics of normal labor. *Obstetrics and Gynecology, 74,* 85–87.

Kim, J., Hetherington, E., & Reiss, D. (1999). Associations among family relationships, antisocial peers, and adolescents' externalizing behaviors: Gender and family type differences. *Child Development, 70,* 1209–1230.

Kim, S. (1997). Relationships between young children's day care experience and their attachment relationships with parents and socioemotional behavior problems. *Korean Journal of Child Studies, 18,* 5–18.

King, A., Beazley, R., Warren, W., Hankins, C., Robertson, A., & Radford, J. (1988). *Canada Youth and AIDS study: Report of the Social Program Evaluation Group.* Kingston, ON: Queen's University.

King, A.J.C. & Peart, M.J. (1994). *The numbers game: A study of evaluation and achievement in Ontario schools.* Toronto: Ontario Secondary School Teachers' Federation.

King, S.M, Singer, J., Forbes, J., et al. (2000) Trends in antiretroviral therapy (ART) in pregnant women in Canada 1994–1998. *Canadian Journal of Infectious Disease,* 11(75B), Abstract. As reported in Health Canada (2001c). *Perinatal Transmission of HIV.* Ottawa, ON: Author. Retrieved November 19, 2001 from http://www.hc-sc.gc.ca/hpb/lcdc/bah/epi/peri_e.html

Kinney, D.A. (1993). From "nerds" to "normals": Adolescent identity recovery within a changing social system. *Sociology of Education, 66,* 21–40.

Kinzl, J., Mangweth, B., Traweger, C., & Biebl, W. (1996). Sexual dysfunction in males: Significance of adverse childhood experiences. *Child Abuse & Neglect, 20,* 759–766.

Kirkby, D. (2000). School-based interventions to prevent unprotected sex and HIV among adolescents. In J. Peterson & D. Diclemente (Eds.), *Handbook of HIV prevention* (pp. 83–97). New York: Plenum Publishers.

Kirkness, V.J. (1999). The critical state of aboriginal languages in Canada. *Canadian Journal of Native Education, 22,* 1–15.

Kisilevsky, B.S., Hains, S.M.J., Lee, K., Xie, X., Huang, H., Ye, H.-H., Zang, K. & Wang, Z. (2003). Effects of experience on fetal voice recognition. *Psychological Sicence, 14,* 220–224.

Kitson, G.C. (1992). *Portrait of divorce: Adjustment to marital breakdown.* New York: Guilford Press.

Kitzan, L., Ferraro, F., Petros, T., & Ludorf, M. (1999). The role of vocabulary ability during visual word recognition in younger and older adults. *Journal of General Psychology, 126,* 6–16.

Klahr, D. (1992). Information-processing approaches to cognitive development. In M.H. Bernstein & M.E. Lamb (Eds.), *Developmental psychology: An advanced textbook* (3rd ed., pp. 273–335). Hillsdale, NJ: Erlbaum.

Klaiber, E., Broverman, D., Vogel, W., Peterson, L., & Snyder, M. (1997). Relationships of serum estradiol levels, menopausal duration, and mood during hormonal replacement therapy. *Psychoneuroendocrinology, 22,* 549–558.

Klebanov, P.K., Brooks-Gunn, J., Hofferth, S., & Duncan, G.J. (1995, March). *Neighborhood resources, social support and maternal competence.* Paper presented at the biennial meetings of the Society for Research in Child Development, Indianapolis, IN.

Kleemeier, R.W. (1962). Intellectual changes in the senium. *Proceedings of the Social Statistics Section of the American Statistics Association, 1,* 290–295.

Klein, A., & Swartz, S. (1996). *Reading Recovery in California: Program overview.* San Francisco: San Francisco Unified School District.

Klein, J.S., & Bisanz, J. (2000). Preschoolers doing arithmetic: The concepts are willing but the working memory is weak. *Canadian Journal of Experimental Psychology,* 54(2), 105–115.

Klerman, L.V. (1991). The health of poor children: Problems and programs. In A.C. Huston (Ed.), *Children in poverty: Child devel-*

opment and public policy (pp. 136–157). Cambridge, England: Cambridge University Press.

Kletzky, O.A., & Borenstein, R. (1987). Vasomotor instability of the menopause. In D.R. Mishell, Jr. (Ed.), *Menopause: Physiology and pharmacology.* (pp. 53–66). Chicago: Year Book Medical Publishers.

Kliegl, R., Smith, J., & Baltes, P.B. (1989). Testing-the-limits and the study of adult age differences in cognitive plasticity of a mnemonic skill. *Developmental Psychology, 25,* 247–256.

Kliegl, R., Smith, J., & Baltes, P.B. (1990). On the locus and process of magnification of age differences during mnemonic training. *Developmental Psychology, 26,* 894–904.

Kliegman, R. (1998). Fetal and neonatal medicine. In R. Behrman & R. Kliegman (Eds.), *Nelson essentials of pediatrics* (3rd ed., pp. 167–225). Philadelphia: W.B. Saunders.

Kline, D.W., Kline, T.J.B., Fozard, J.L., Kosnik, W., Schieber, F., & Sekuler, R. (1992). Vision, aging, and driving: The problem of older drivers. *Journals of Gerontology: Psychological Sciences,* 47, P27–34.

Kline, D.W., & Scialfa, C.T. (1996). Visual and auditory aging. In J.E. Birren & K.W. Schaie (Eds.), *Handbook of the psychology of aging* (4th ed., pp. 181–203). San Diego, CA: Academic Press.

Kline, S. (1998). *Video Game Culture: Leisure and play preferences of BC teens.* Vancouver: Simon Fraser University Media Analysis Laboratory.

Kline, S. (2002). *Moral panics and video games.* Vancouver: Simon Fraser University Media Analysis Laboratory. Retrieved June 30, 2004 from http://www2.sfu.ca/media-lab/

Kline, S. (2003). *Media consumption as a health and safety risk factor.* Vancouver: Simon Fraser University Media Analysis Laboratory. Retrieved June 30, 2004 from http://www2.sfu.ca/media-lab/risk/docs/kline_media_risk_reduction5.doc

Klonoff-Cohen, H.D., Edelstein, S.L., Lefkowitz, E.S., Srinivasan, I.P., Kaegi, D., Chang, J.C., & Wiley, K.J. (1995). The effect of passive smoking and tobacco exposure through breast milk on sudden infant death syndrome. *Journal of the American Medical Association, 273,* 795–798.

Kochanska, G. (1997a). Multiple pathways to conscience for children with different temperaments: From toddlerhood to age 5. *Developmental Psychology, 33,* 228–240.

Kochanska, G. (1997b). Mutually responsive orientation between mothers and their young: Implications for early socialization. *Child Development, 68,* 94–112.

Kochanska, G., Casey, R., & Fukumoto, A. (1995). Toddlers' sensitivity to standard violations. *Child Development, 66,* 643–656.

Kochanska, G., Murray, K., & Coy, K. (1997). Inhibitory control as a contributor to conscience in childhood: From toddler to early school age. *Child Development, 68,* 263–277.

Kochanska, G., Murray, K., Jacques, T., Koenig, A., Vandegeest, K. (1996). Inhibitory control in young children and its role in emerging internalization. *Child Development, 67,* 490–507.

Kocsis, J. (1998). Geriatric dysthymia. *Journal of Clinical Psychiatry,* 59, 13–15.

Kohen, D., & Hertzman, C. (1998). The importance of quality child care. In J. Douglas Willms (Ed.). *Vulnerable Children.* Edmonton: University of Alberta Press.

Kohlberg, L. (1964). Development of moral character and moral ideology. In M.L. Hoffman & L.W. Hoffman (Eds.), *Review of child development research* (Vol. 1, pp. 283–332). New York: Russell Sage Foundation.

Kohlberg, L. (1966). A cognitive-developmental analysis of children's sex-role concepts and attitudes. In E.E. Maccoby (Ed.), *The development of sex differences* (pp. 82–172). Stanford, CA: Stanford University Press.

Kohlberg, L. (1976). Moral stages and moralization: The cognitive developmental approach. In T. Lickona (Ed.), *Moral development and behavior: Theory, research, and social issues* (pp. 31–53). New York: Holt.

Kohlberg, L. (1981). *Essays on moral development: Vol. 1. The philosophy of moral development.* New York: Harper & Row.

Kohlberg, L., & Elfenbein, D. (1975). The development of moral judgments concerning capital punishment. *American Journal of Orthopsychiatry, 54,* 614–640.

Kohlberg, L., Levine, C., & Hewer, A. (1983). *Moral stages: A current formulation and a response to critics.* Basel, Switzerland: S. Karger.

Kohlberg, L., & Ullian, D.Z. (1974). Stages in the development of psychosexual concepts and attitudes. In R.C. Friedman, R.M. Richart, & R.L. Vande Wiele (Eds.), *Sex differences in behavior* (pp. 209–222). New York: Wiley.

Kohli, M. (1994). Work and retirement: A comparative perspective. In M.W. Riley, R.L. Kahn, & A. Foner (Eds.), *Age and structural lag* (pp. 80–106). New York: Wiley-Interscience.

Kondro, W. (2004). UK bans, Health Canada warns about antidepressants. *Canadian Medical Association Journal, 170*(4), 23.

Kong, R., Johnson, H., Beattie, S., & Cardillo, A. (2003). Sexual offences in Canada (Catalogue No. 85-002-XPE). Ottawa, ON: Statistics Canada.

Koskinen, P., Blum, I., Bisson, S., Phillips, S., et al. (2000). Book access, shared reading, and audio models: The effects of supporting the literacy learning of linguistically diverse students in school and at home. *Journal of Educational Psychology, 92,* 23–36.

Kost, K. (1997). The effects of support on the economic well-being of young fathers. *Families in Society, 78,* 370–382.

Kostanski, M., & Gullone, E. (1999). Dieting and body image in the child's world: Conceptualization and behavior. *Journal of Genetic Psychology, 160,* 488–499.

Kozma, A., Stones, M.J., & Hannah, T.E. (1991). Age, activity, and physical performance: An evaluation of performance models. *Psychology and Aging, 6,* 43–49.

Kozu, J. (1999). Domestic violence in Japan. *American Psychologist, 54,* 50–54.

Krause, N., Ingersoll-Dayton, B., Liang, J., & Sugisawa, H. (1999). Religion, social support, and health among the Japanese elderly. *Journal of Health Behavior & Health Education, 40,* 405–421.

Krause, N., Jay, G., & Liang, J. (1991). Financial strain and psychological well-being among the American and Japanese elderly. *Psychology and Aging, 6,* 170–181.

Krause, N., Liang, J., & Keith, V. (1990). Personality, social support, and psychological distress in later life. *Psychology and Aging, 5,* 315–326.

Kraut, R., Patterson, M., Lundmark, V., Kiesler, S., Mukophadhyay, T., & Schertis, W. (1998). Internet paradox: A social technology that reduces social involvement and psychological well-being? *American Psychologist, 53,* 1017–1031.

Kronenberg, F. (1994). Hot flashes: Phenomenology, quality of life, and search for treatment options. *Experimental Gerontology, 29,* 319–336.

Krueger-Lebus, S., & Rauchfleisch, U. (1999). Level of contentment in lesbian partnerships with and without children. *System Familie, 12,* 74–79.

Kruk, E. (1995). Grandparent-grandchild contact loss: Findings from a study of "grandparent rights" members. *Canadian Journal on Aging, 14*(4), 737–754.

Kübler-Ross, E. (1969). *On death and dying.* New York: Macmillan.

Kübler-Ross, E. (1974). *Questions and answers on death and dying.* New York: Macmillan.

Kuebli, J., Butler, S., & Fivush, R. (1995). Mother-child talk about past emotions: Relationships of maternal language and child gender over time. *Cognition and Emotion, 9,* 265–283.

Kuhn, D. (1992). Cognitive development. In M.H. Bornstein & M.E. Lamb (Eds.), *Developmental psychology: An advanced textbook* (3rd ed., pp. 211–272). Hillsdale, NJ: Erlbaum.

Kuhn, D., Kohlberg, L., Languer, J., & Haan, N. (1977). The development of formal operations in logical and moral judgment. *Genetic Psychology Monographs, 95,* 97–188.

Kunkel, S.R., & Applebaum, R.A. (1992). Estimating the prevalence of long-term disability for an aging society. *Journals of Gerontology: Social Sciences, 47,* S253–260.

Kupersmidt, J.B., Griesler, P.C., DeRosier, M.E., Patterson, C.J., & Davis, P.W. (1995). Childhood aggression and peer relations in the context of family and neighborhood factors. *Child Development, 66,* 360–375.

Kurdek, L.A. (1995a). Developmental changes in relationship quality in gay and lesbian cohabiting couples. *Developmental Psychology, 31,* 86–94.

Kurdek, L.A. (1995b). Lesbian and gay couples. In A.R. D'Augelli & C.J. Patterson (Eds.), *Lesbian, gay, and bisexual identities over the lifespan: Psychological perspectives* (pp. 243–261). New York: Oxford University Press.Kurdek, L. (1997). Relation between neuroticism and dimensions of relationship commitment: evidence from gay, lesbian, and heterosexual couples. *Journal of Family Psychology, 11,* 109–124.

Kurdek, L. (1998). Relationship outcomes and their predictors: Longitudinal evidence from heterosexual married, gay cohabiting, and lesbian cohabiting couples. *Journal of Marriage & the Family, 60,* 553–568.

Kurdek, L. (2000). The link between sociotropy/autonomy and dimensions of relationship commitment: Evidence from gay and lesbian couples. *Personal Relationships, 7,* 153–164.

Kurdek, L.A., & Schmitt, J.P. (1986). Early development of relationship quality in heterosexual married, heterosexual cohabiting, gay, and lesbian couples. *Developmental Psychology, 22,* 305–309.

Kurtler, A., LaGreca, A., & Prinstein, M. (1999). Friendship qualities and social-emotional functioning of adolescents with close, cross-sex friendships. *Journal of Research on Adolescence, 9,* 339–366.

Kyriacou, D., Anglin, D., Taliaferro, E., Stone, S., Tubb, T., Linden, J., Muelleman, R., Barton, E., & Kraus, J. (1999). Risk factors for injury to women from domestic violence. *New England Journal of Medicine, 341,* 1892–1898.

Laakso, M., Vaurio, O., Savolainen, L., Repo, E., Soininen, H., Aronen, H., & Tiihonen, J. (2000). A volumetric MRI study of the hippocampus in type 1 and 2 alcoholism. *Behavioral Brain Research, 109,* 177–186.

Labouvie-Vief, G. (1980). Beyond formal operations: Uses and limits of pure logic in life-span development. *Human Development, 23,* 141–161.

Labouvie-Vief, G. (1990). Modes of knowledge and the organization of development. In M.L. Commons, C. Armon, L. Kohlberg, F.A. Richards, T.A. Grotzer, & J.D. Sinnott (Eds.), *Adult development: Vol. 2. Models and methods in the study of adolescent and adult thought* (pp. 43–62). New York: Praeger.

Lachman, M., & Weaver, S. (1998). Sociodemographic variations in the sense of control by domain: Findings from the MacArthur studies of midlife. *Psychology & Aging, 13,* 553–562.

Lacroix, V., Pomerleau, A., Malcuit, G., Séguin, R., & Lamarre, G. (2001). Développement langagier et cognitif de l'enfant durant les trois premières années en relation avec la durée des vocalisations maternelles et jouets présents dans l'environnement: Étude longitudinale auprès de populations à risque. *Canadian Journal of Behavioural Science, 33*(2), 65–76.

Ladouceur, R., Boudreault, N., Jacques, C., and Vitaro, F. (1999). Pathological gambling and related problems among adolescents. *Journal of Child and Adolescent Substance Abuse, 8,* 55–68.

Ladouceur, R., Dubé, D., & Bujold, A. (1995). Gambling among primary school students. In E. Eadington (Ed.), *Gambling behavior and gambling problem.* Reno: University of Nevada Press.

Lafuente, M., Grifol, R., Segarra, J., Soriano, J., Gorba, M., & Montesinos, A. (1997). Effects of the Firstart method of prenatal stimulation on psychomotor development: The first six months. *Pre- & Peri-Natal Psychology Journal, 11,* 151–162.

Laguna, K., & Babcock, R. (1997). Computer anxiety in young and older adults: Implications for human-computer interactions in older populations. *Computers in Human Behavior, 13,* 317–326.

Laird, R., Pettit, G., Dodge, K., & Bates, J. (1999). Best friendships, group relationships, and antisocial behavior in early adolescence. *Journal of Early Adolescence, 19,* 413–437.

Lakatta, E.G. (1990). Heart and circulation. In E.L. Schneider & J.W. Rowe (Eds.), *Handbook of the biology of aging* (3rd ed., pp. 181–217). San Diego, CA: Academic Press.

Lam, R., Pacala, J., & Smith, S. (1997). Factors related to depressive symptoms in an elderly Chinese American sample. *Gerontologist, 17*, 57–70.

Lamb, M.E. (1981). The development of father-infant relationships. In M.E. Lamb (Ed.), *The role of the father in child development* (2nd ed., pp. 459–488). New York: Wiley.

Lambert, W. & Tucker, G.R. (1972). *Bilingual education of children: The St. Lambert experiment.* Rowley, MA: Newbury House.

Lampard, R., & Peggs, K. (1999). Repartnering: The relevance of parenthood and gender to cohabitation and remarriage among the formerly married. *British Journal of Sociology, 50*, 443–465.

Landolt, M., & Dutton, D. (1997). Power and personality: An analysis of gay male intimate abuse. *Sex Roles, 37*, 335–359.

Landry, S.H., Garner, P.W., Swank, P.R., & Baldwin, C.D. (1996). Effects of maternal scaffolding during joint toy play with preterm and full-term infants. *Merrill-Palmer Quarterly, 42*, 177–199.

Landy, S., & Tam, K.K. (1996). "Yes, parenting does make a difference to the development of children in Canada." In *Growing up in Canada: National longitudinal survey of children and youth.* Ottawa, ON: Human Resources Development Canada and Statistics Canada.

Landy, S., & Tam, K.K. (1998). Understanding the contribution of multiple risk factors on child development at various ages (Catalogue No. W-98-22E). Ottawa, ON: Human Resources Development Canada.

Langlois, A. (2004, May). Retiring on the instalment plan. *CAmagazine.com.* Retrieved September 2, 2004 from http://www.camagazine.com/index.cfm/ci_id/20901/la_id/1/camagazine/1/print/true.htm

Langlois, J.H., Ritter, J.M., Roggman, L.A., & Vaughn, L.S. (1991). Facial diversity and infant preferences for attractive faces. *Developmental Psychology, 27*, 79–84.

Langlois, J.H., Roggman, L.A., Casey, R.J., Ritter, J.M., Rieser-Danner, L.A., & Jenkins, V.Y. (1987). Infant preferences for attractive faces: Rudiments of a stereotype? *Developmental Psychology, 23*, 363–369.

Langlois, S. & Morrison, P. (2002). Suicide deaths and suicide attempts (Catalogue No. 82-003). *Health Reports, 13*(2), 9–22.

Lanius, R.A., Williamson, P.C., Densmore, M., Boksman, K., Neufeld, R.W., Gati, J.S., & Menon, R.S. (2004). The nature of traumatic memories: A 4-T fMRI functional connectivity analysis. *American Journal of Psychiatry, 161*(1), 36–44.

Lanius, R.A., Williamson, P.C., Hopper, J., Densmore, M., Boksman, K., Gupta, M.A., Neufeld, R.W.J., Gati, J.S., & Menon, R.S. (2003). Recall of emotional states in posttraumatic stress disorder: An fMRI investigation. *Biological Psychiatry, 53*(3), 204–210.

Lansdown, R., & Benjamin, G. (1985). The development of the concept of death in children aged 5–9 years. *Child Care, Health and Development, 11*, 13–30.

Larroque, B., & Kaminski, M. (1998). Prenatal alcohol exposure and development at preschool age: Main results of a French study. *Alcoholism: Clinical & Experimental Research, 22*, 295–303.

Larson, R. (2000). Toward a psychology of positive youth development. *American Psychologist, 55*, 170–183.

Larson, R., Mannell, R., & Zuzanek, J. (1986). Daily well-being of older adults with friends and family. *Psychology and Aging, 1*, 117–126.

Larzelere, R.E. (2000). Child outcomes of non-abusive and customary physical punishment by parents: An updated literature review. *Clinical Child and Family Psychology Review, 3*(4), 199–221.

Larzelere, R.E. (2003, April). *A meta-analysis comparing the effect sizes and correlates of corporal punishment with alternative disciplinary tactics.* Paper presented at the Society for Research in Child Development, Tampa, FL.

Larzelere, R.E., Kuhn, B.R., & Johnson, B. (2004). The intervention selection bias: An underrecognized confound in intervention research. *Psychological Bulletin, 130*(2), 289–303.

Laso, F., Iglesias-Osma, C., Ciudad, J., Lopez, A., Pastor, I., & Orfao, A. (1999). Chronic alcoholism is associated with an imbalanced production of the Th-a/Th-2 cytokines by peripheral blood T cells. *Alcoholism: Clinical & Experimental Research, 23*, 1306–1311.

Laumann, E.O., Gagnon, J.H., Michael, R.T., & Michaels, S. (1994). *The social organization of sexuality: Sexual practices in the United States.* Chicago: University of Chicago Press.

Laursen, B. (1995). Conflict and social interaction in adolescent relationships. *Journal of Research on Adolescence, 5*, 55–70.

Lavoie, M., & Ladouceur, R. (2004, February). Prevention of gambling among youth: Increasing knowledge and modifying attitudes towards gambling. *eGambling: The Electronic Journal of Gambling Issues, 10*, 1–10. Retrieved February, 21, 2004 from http://www.camh.net/egambling/issue10/ejgi_10_lavoie_ladouceur.html

Lawlor, S., & Choi, P. (1998). The generation gap in menstrual cycle attributions. *British Journal of Health Psychology, 3*, 257–263.

Lawrence, K., Yardley, J., Root, L., Canham, B., & McPhee, J. (2002). *Report on adolescent gambling: Attitudes and behaviours of Niagara Region youth.* St. Catharines, ON: Brock University. Retrieved August 3, 2004 from http://www.gamblingresearch.org/download.sz/037%20Report%20web%20version.pdf?docid=5372

Lawrence, R.H., Bennett, J.M., & Markides, K.S. (1992). Perceived intergenerational solidarity and psychological distress among older Mexican Americans. *Journals of Gerontology: Social Sciences, 47*, S55–65.

Lawton, L., Silverstein, M., & Bengtson, V. (1994). Affection, social contact, and geographic distance between adult children and their parents. *Journal of Marriage and the Family, 56*, 57–68.

Lawton, M.P. (1985). Housing and living environments of older people. In R.H. Binstock & E. Shanas (Eds.), *Aging and the social sciences* (2nd ed., pp. 450–478). New York: Van Nostrand Reinhold.

Lawton, M.P. (1990). Residential environment and self-directedness among older people. *American Psychologist, 45*, 638–640.

Layton, L., Deeny, K., Tall, G., & Upton, G. (1996). Researching and promoting phonological awareness in the nursery class. *Journal of Research in Reading, 19*, 1–13.

Leaper, C. (1991). Influence and involvement in children's discourse: Age, gender, and partner effects. *Child Development, 62*, 797–811.

Learning Disabilities Association of Canada (2002). *Official definition of learning disabilities.* Ottawa, ON: Author. Retrieved January 25, 2003, from http://www.ldac-taac.ca/english/defined/jan02eng.pdf

Le Bourdais, C., Neill, G., & Turcotte, P. (2000). The changing face of conjugal relationships (Catalogue No. 11-008). *Canadian Social Trends, Spring*(56), 14–17.

Lee C. (2004). Physical punishment of children: A psychological perspective. *Canadian Clinical Psychologist, 14*(2), 4–5.

Lee, G.R., Dwyer, J.W., & Coward, R.T. (1993). Gender differences in parent care: Demographic factors and same-gender preferences. *Journals of Gerontology: Social Sciences, 48*, S9–16.

Lee, G.R., Seccombe, K., & Shehan, C.L. (1991). Marital status and personal happiness: An analysis of trend data. *Journal of Marriage and the Family, 53*, 839–844.

Lee, I., Manson, J.E., Hennekens, C.H., & Paffenbarger, R.S., Jr. (1993). Body weight and mortality: A 27-year follow-up of middle-aged men. *Journal of the American Medical Association, 270*, 2823–2828.

Lee, I.-M., Hsieh, C., & Paffenbarger, R.S. (1995). Exercise intensity and longevity in men. *Journal of the American Medical Association, 273*, 1179–1184.

Lee, M., Law, C., & Tam, K. (1999). Parenthood and life satisfaction: A comparison of single and dual-parent families in Hong Kong. *International Social Work, 42*, 139–162.

Lee, S. & Keith, P. (1999). The transition to motherhood of Korean women. *Journal of Comparative Family Studies, 30*, 453–470.

Lee, V.E., Burkham, D.T., Zimiles, H., & Ladewski, B. (1994). Family structure and its effect on behavioral and emotional problems in young adolescents. *Journal of Research on Adolescence, 4*, 405–437.

Leger Marketing (2002). *Child abuse report.* Montreal. Author. Retrieved June 24, 2004 from http://www.legermarketing.com/documents/spclm/020211cng.pdf

Legerstee, M., Anderson, D., & Schaffer, A. (1998). Five- and eight-month-old infants recognize their faces and voices as familiar and social stimuli. *Child Development, 69,* 37–50.

Legerstee, M., Pomerleau, A., Malcuit, G., & Feider, H. (1987). The development of infants' response to people and a doll: Implications for research communication. *Infant Behavior and Development, 10,* 82–95.

Le Grand, R., Mondloch, C., Maurer, D., & Brent, H.P. (2001). Early visual experience and face processing. *Nature, 410*(6831), 890.

Lehman, D., & Nisbett, R. (1990). A longitudinal study of the effects of undergraduate training on reasoning. *Developmental Psychology, 26,* 952–960.

Lehman, H.C. (1953). *Age and achievement.* Princeton, NJ: Princeton University Press.

Lehr, U. (1982). Hat die Grosfamilie heute noch eine Chance? [Does the extended family have a chance these days?]. *Der Deutsche Artz, 18* Sonderdruck.

Le Mare, L., Fernyhough, L., & Warford, L. (2001, April 19–22). *Intellectual and academic performance of Romanian orphans 10 years after being adopted to Canada.* Poster presented at the Biennial Meeting of the Society for Research in Child Development, Minneapolis, MN.

Le Mare, L., Warford, L., & Fernyhough, L. (2001, April 19–22). *Peer relationships of Romanian orphans 10 years after being adopted to Canada.* Poster presented at the Biennial Meeting of the Society for Research in Child Development, Minneapolis, MN.

Lenhardt, A., & McCourt, B. (2000). Adolescent unresolved grief in response to the death of a mother. *Professional School Counseling, 3,* 189–196.

Leong, F., Austin, J., Sekaran, U., & Komarraju, M. (1998). An evaluation of the cross-cultural validity of Holland's theory: Career choices by workers in India. *Journal of Vocational Behavior, 52,* 441–455.

Lerner, R.M. (1987). A life-span perspective for early adolescence. In R.M. Lerner & T.T. Foch (Eds.), *Biological-psychosocial interactions in early adolescence* (pp. 9–34). Hillsdale, NJ: Erlbaum.

Lester, B., Hoffman, J., & Brazelton, T. (1985). The rhythmic structure of mother-infant interactions in term and preterm infants. *Child Development, 56,* 15–27.

Lester, D. (1990). The Collett-Lester fear of death scale: The original version and a revision. *Death Studies, 14,* 451–468.

Levenson, R.W., Carstensen, L.L., & Gottman, J.M. (1993). Long-term marriage: Age, gender, and satisfaction. *Psychology and Aging, 8,* 301–313.

Lever, J. (1994, August 23). The 1994 Advocate survey of sexuality and relationships: The men. *Advocate,* 16–24.

Leviatan, U. (1999). Contribution of social arrangements to the attainment of successful aging: The experience of the Israeli kibbutz. *Journals of Gerontology: Series B: Psychological Sciences & Social Sciences, 54B,* P205–P213.

Levine, L., & Bluck, S. (1997). Experienced and remembered emotional intensity in older adults. *Psychology of Aging, 12,* 514–523.

Levinson, D.J. (1978). *The seasons of a man's life.* New York: Knopf.

Levinson, D.J. (1986). A conception of adult development. *American Psychologist, 41,* 3–13.

Levinson, D.J. (1990). A theory of life structure development in adulthood. In C.N. Alexander & E.J. Langer (Eds.), *Higher stages of human development* (pp. 35–54). New York: Oxford University Press.

Levitt, M.J., Weber, R.A., & Guacci, N. (1993). Convoys of social support: An intergenerational analysis. *Psychology and Aging, 8,* 323–326.

Levorato, M., & Donati, V. (1999). Conceptual and lexical knowledge of shame in Italian children and adolescents. *International Journal of Behavioral Development, 23,* 873–898.

Levy, G.D., & Fivush, R. (1993). Scripts and gender: A new approach for examining gender-role development. *Developmental Review, 13,* 126–146.

Levy, L.H., Martinkowski, K.S., & Derby, J.F. (1994). Differences in patterns of adaptation in conjugal bereavement: Their sources and potential significance. *Omega, 29,* 71–87.

Levy-Shiff, R., Vakil, E., Dimitrovsky, L., Abramovitz, M., Shahar, N., Har-Even, D., Gross, S., Lerman, M., Levy, I., Sirota, L., & Fish, B. (1998). Medical, cognitive, emotional, and behavioral outcomes in school-age children conceived by in-vitro fertilization. *Journal of Clinical Child Psychology, 27,* 320–329.

Lewis, C.C. (1981). How adolescents approach decisions: Changes over grades seven to twelve and policy implications. *Child Development, 52,* 538–544.

Lewis, J., Malow, R., & Ireland, S. (1997). HIV/AIDS in heterosexual college students: A review of a decade of literature. *Journal of American College Health, 45,* 147–158.

Lewis, K., & Moon, S. (1997). Always single and single-again women: A qualitative study. *Journal of Marital & Family Therapy, 23,* 115–134.

Lewis, M. (1990). Social knowledge and social development. *Merrill-Palmer Quarterly, 36,* 93–116.

Lewis, M. (1991). Ways of knowing: Objective self-awareness of consciousness. *Developmental Review, 11,* 231–243.

Lewis, M.D. (1993). Early socioemotional predictors of cognitive competence at 4 years. *Developmental Psychology, 29,* 1036–1045. Lewis, M., Allesandri, S.M., & Sullivan, M.W. (1992). Differences in shame and pride as a function of children's gender and task difficulty. *Child Development, 63,* 630–638.

Lewis, M., & Brooks, J. (1978). Self-knowledge and emotional development. In M. Lewis & L.A. Rosenblum (Eds.), *The development of affect* (pp. 205–226). New York: Plenum.

Lewis, M., Sullivan, M.W., Stanger, C., & Weiss, M. (1989). Self development and self-conscious emotions. *Child Development, 60,* 146–156.

Lewis, T.L., Ellemberg, D., Maurer, D., Wilkinson, F., Wilson, H.R., Dirks, M., & Brent, H.P. (2002). Sensitivity to global form in glass patterns after early visual deprivation in humans. *Vision Research, 42*(8), 939–948.

Lewkowicz, D.J. (1994). Limitations on infants' response to rate-based auditory-visual relations. *Developmental Psychology, 30,* 880–892.

Ley, D.C.H., & van Bommel, H. (1994). *The heart of hospice.* Toronto: NC Press Limited.

Liao, K., & Hunter, M. (1998). Preparation for menopause: Prospective evaluation of a health education intervention for mid-aged women. *Maturitas, 29,* 215–224.

Liberal Party of Canada. (2004). *Moving Canada forward: Foundations—An early learning and child care program.* Ottawa, ON: Author. Retrieved July 9, 2004 from http://www.liberal.ca/news_e.aspx?site=news&news=596

Lickona, T. (1983). *Raising good children.* New York: Bantam Books.

Lieberman, D.A. (1997). Interactive video games for health promotion: Effects on knowledge, self-efficacy, social support, and health. In R.L. Street, W.R. Gold, & T. Manning (Eds.), *Health promotion and interactive technology: Theoretical applications and future directions* (pp. 103–120). Mahwah, NJ: Erlbaum.

Lieberman, M., Doyle, A., & Markiewicz, D. (1995, March). *Attachment to mother and father: Links to peer relations in children.* Paper presented at the biennial meetings of the Society for Research in Child Development, Indianapolis, IN.

Lieberman, M., Doyle, A., & Markiewicz, D. (1999). Developmental patterns in security of attachment to mother and father in late childhood and early adolescence: Associations with peer relations. *Child Development, 70,* 202–213.

Lieberman, M.A. (1965). Psychological correlates of impending death: Some preliminary observations. *Journal of Gerontology, 20,* 182–190.

Lieberman, M.A., & Coplan, A.S. (1970). Distance from death as a variable in the study of aging. *Developmental Psychology, 2,* 71–84.

Liem, R., & Liem, J.H. (1988). Psychological effects of unemployment on workers and their families. *Journal of Social Issues, 44,* 87–105.

Light, L.L. (1991). Memory and aging: Four hypotheses in search of data. *Annual Review of Psychology, 42,* 333–376.

Lima, S.D., Hale, S., & Myerson, J. (1991). How general is general slowing? Evidence from the lexical domain. *Psychology and Aging, 6,* 416–425.

Lin, C., Hsiao, C., & Chen, W. (1999). Development of sustained attention assessed using the Continuous Performance Test among children 6–15 years of age. *Journal of Abnormal Child Psychology, 27,* 403–412.

Lincourt, A., Rybash, J., & Hoyer, W. (1998). Aging, working memory, and the development of instance-based retrieval. *Brain & Cognition, 37,* 100–102.

Lindahl, K., Clements, M., & Markman, H. (1997). Predicting marital and parent functioning in dyads and triads: A longitudinal investigation of marital processes. *Journal of Family Psychology, 11,* 139–151.

Lindahl, L. & Heimann, M. (1997). Social proximity in early mother-infant interactions: Implications for gender differences? *Early Development & Parenting, 6,* 83–88.

Lindgren, C., Connelly, C., & Gaspar, H. (1999). Grief in spouse and children caregivers of dementia patients. *Western Journal of Nursing Research, 21,* 521–537.

Lindo, G., & Nordholm, L. (1999). Adaptation strategies, well-being, and activities of daily living among people with low vision. *Journal of Visual Impairment & Blindness, 93,* 434–446.

Lindsay, J. (2000). An ambiguous commitment: Moving in to a cohabiting relationship. *Journal of Family Studies, 6,* 120–134.

Lindsay, R. (1985). The aging skeleton. In M.R. Haug, A.B. Ford, & M. Sheafor (Eds.), *The physical and mental health of aged women* (pp. 65–82). New York: Springer.

Lindstrom, T. (1997). Immunity and somatic health in bereavement. A prospective study of 39 Norwegian widows. *Omega: Journal of Death & Dying, 35,* 231–241.

Lineweaver, T., & Hertzog, C. (1998). Adults' efficacy and control beliefs regarding memory and aging: Separating general from personal beliefs. *Aging, Neuropsychology, & Cognition, 5,* 264–296.

Links, P.S., Gould, B., & Ratnayake, R. (2003). Assessing suicidal youth with antisocial, borderline, or narcissistic personality disorder. *Canadian Journal of Psychiatry, 48(5),* 301–310.

Lissner, L., Bengtsson, C., Björkelund, C., & Wedel, H. (1996). Physical activity levels and changes in relation to longevity: A prospective study of Swedish women. *American Journal of Epidemiology, 143,* 54–62.

Litwak, E., & Longino, C.F., Jr. (1987). Migration patterns among the elderly: A developmental perspective. *The Gerontologist, 27,* 266–272.

Livesley, W.J., & Bromley, D.B. (1973). *Person perception in childhood and adolescence.* London: Wiley.

Lobel, T., Slone, M., & Winch, G. (1997). Masculinity, popularity, and self-esteem among Israeli preadolescent girls. *Sex Roles, 36,* 395–408.

Loehlin, J.C., Horn, J.M., & Willerman, L. (1994). Differential inheritance of mental abilities in the Texas Adoption Project. *Intelligence, 19,* 325–336.

Lofti, M. (2001). *Experiences and issues in controlling micronutrient malnutrition.* Ottawa, ON: International Development Research Centre.

Longino, C.F., Jr. (1990). Geographical distribution and migration. In R.H. Binstock & L.K. George (Eds.), *Handbook of aging and the social sciences* (3rd ed., pp. 45–63). San Diego, CA: Academic Press.

Longino, C.F., Jr., Jackson, D.J., Zimmerman, R.S., & Bradsher, J.E. (1991). The second move: Health and geographic mobility. *Journals of Gerontology: Social Sciences, 46,* S218–224.

Lundh, W., & Gyllang, C. (1993). Use of the Edinburgh Postnatal Depression Scale in some Swedish child health care centres. *Scandinavian Journal of Caring Sciences, 7,* 149–154.

Luster, T., Boger, R., & Hannan, K. (1993). Infant affect and home environment. *Journal of Marriage and the Family, 55,* 651–661.

Luster, T., & McAdoo, H.P. (1995). Factors related to self-esteem among African American youths: A secondary analysis of the High/Scope Perry Preschool data. *Journal of Research on Adolescence, 5,* 451–467.

Luster, T., & McAdoo, H. (1996). Family and child influences on educational attainment: A secondary analysis of the High/Scope Perry Preschool data. *Developmental Psychology, 32,* 26–39.

Lutfey, K., & Maynard, D. (1998). Bad news in oncology: How physician and patient talk about death and dying without using those words. *Social Psychology Quarterly, 61,* 321–341.

Lyons, N.P. (1983). Two perspectives: On self, relationships, and morality. *Harvard Educational Review, 53,* 125–145.

Lytton, H., & Romney, D.M. (1991). Parents' differential socialization of boys and girls: A meta-analysis. *Psychological Bulletin, 109,* 267–296.

Ma, H., Shek, D., Cheung, P., & Oi Bun Lam, C. (2000). Parental, peer and teacher influences on the social behavior of Hong Kong Chinese adolescents. *Journal of Genetic Psychology, 161,* 65–78.

Maas, H.S., & Kuypers, J.A. (1974). *From thirty to seventy.* San Francisco: Jossey-Bass.

Maccoby, E.E. (1980). *Social development: Psychological growth and the parent-child relationship.* New York: Harcourt Brace Jovanovich.

Maccoby, E.E. (1984). Middle childhood in the context of the family. In W.A. Collins (Ed.), *Development during middle childhood: The years from six to twelve* (pp. 184–239). Washington, DC: National Academy Press.

Maccoby, E.E. (1988). Gender as a social category. *Developmental Psychology, 24,* 755–765.

Maccoby, E.E. (1990). Gender and relationships: A developmental account. *American Psychologist, 45,* 513–520.

Maccoby, E.E. (1995). The two sexes and their social systems. In P. Moen, G.H. Elder, Jr., & K. Lüscher (Eds.), *Examining lives in context: Perspectives on the ecology of human development* (pp. 347–364). Washington, DC: American Psychological Association.

Maccoby, E., & Jacklin, C. (1974). *The psychology of sex differences.* Stanford, CA: Stanford University Press.

Maccoby, E.E., & Jacklin, C.N. (1987). Gender segregation in childhood. In H.W. Reese (Ed.), *Advances in child development and behavior* (Vol. 20, pp. 239–288). Orlando, FL: Academic Press.

Maccoby, E.E., & Martin, J.A. (1983). Socialization in the context of the family: Parent-child interaction. In E.M. Hetherington (Ed.), *Handbook of child psychology: Socialization, personality, and social development* (Vol. 4, pp. 1–102). New York: Wiley.

MacDermid, S.M., Huston, T.L., & McHale, S.M. (1990). Changes in marriage associated with the transition to parenthood: Individual differences as a function of sex-role attitudes and changes in the division of household labor. *Journal of Marriage and the Family, 52,* 475–486.

MacDorman, M., & Atkinson, J. (1999, July 30). Infant mortality statistics from the 1997 period. Linked birth/infant death data set. *National Vital Statistics Reports, 47(23),* 1–24.

MacIver, D.J., Reuman, D.A., & Main, S.R. (1995). Social structuring of the school: Studying what is, illuminating what could be. *Annual Review of Psychology, 46,* 375–400.

MacMillan, H.L., Boyle, M.H., Wong, M.Y.Y., Duku, E.K., Fleming, J.E., & Walsh, C.A. (1999). Slapping and spanking in childhood and its association with lifetime prevalence of psychiatric disorders in a general population sample. *Canadian Medical Association Journal, 161(7),* 805–809.

Macrae, C., & Bodenhausen, G. (2000). Social cognition: Thinking categorically about others. *Annual Review of Psychology, 51,* 93–120.

Madden, D.J. (1992). Four to ten milliseconds per year: Age-related slowing of visual word identification. *Journals of Gerontology: Psychological Sciences, 47,* P59–68.

Madison, C., Johnson, J., Seikel, J., Arnold, M., & Schultheis, L. (1998). Comparative study of the phonology of preschool children prenatally exposed to cocaine and multiple drugs and nonexposed children. *Journal of Communication Disorders, 31,* 231–244.

Mael, F., Morath, R., & McLellan, J. (1997). Dimensions of adolescent employment. *Career Development Quarterly, 45,* 351–368.

Maguire, M., & Dunn, J. (1997). Friendships in early childhood and social understanding. *International Journal of Behavioral Development, 21,* 669–686.

Maier, S.F., Watkins, L.R., & Fleshner, M. (1994). The interface between behavior, brain, and immunity. *American Psychologist, 49,* 1004–1017.

Main, M., & Hesse, E. (1990). Parents' unresolved traumatic experiences are related to infant disorganized attachment status: Is frightened and/or frightening parental behavior the linking mechanism? In M.T. Greenberg, D. Cicchetti, & E.M. Cummings (Eds.), *Attachment in the preschool years: Theory, research, and intervention* (pp. 161–182). Chicago: University of Chicago Press.

Main, M., & Solomon, J. (1990). Procedures for identifying infants as disorganized/disoriented during the Ainsworth Strange Situation. In M.T. Greenberg, D. Cicchetti, & E.M. Cummings (Eds.), *Attachment in the preschool years: Theory, research, and intervention* (pp. 121–160). Chicago: University of Chicago Press.

Mainemer, H., Gilman, L., & Ames, E. (1998). Parenting stress in families adopting children from Romanian orphanages. *Journal of Family Issues, 19,* 164–180.

Maitel, S., Dromi, E., Sagi, A., & Bornstein, M. (2000). The Hebrew Communicative Development Inventory: Language-specific properties and cross-linguistic generalizations. *Journal of Child Language, 27,* 43–67.

Malina, R.M. (1982). Motor development in the early years. In S.G. Moore & C.R. Cooper (Eds.), *The young child: Reviews of research* (Vol. 3, pp. 211–232). Washington, DC: National Association for the Education of Young Children.

Malina, R.M. (1990). Physical growth and performance during the transition years. In R. Montemayor, G.R. Adams, & T.P. Gullotta (Eds.), *From childhood to adolescence: A transitional period?* (pp. 41–62). Newbury Park, CA: Sage.

Malinosky-Rummell, R., & Hansen, D. (1993). Long-term consequences of childhood physical abuse. *Psychological Bulletin, 114,* 68–79.

Malkinson, R., & Bar-Tur, L., (1999). The aging of grief in Israel: A perspective of bereaved parents. *Death Studies, 23,* 413–431.

Mallet, P., Apostolidis, T., & Paty, B. (1997). The development of gender schemata about heterosexual and homosexual others during adolescence. *Journal of General Psychology, 124,* 91–104.

Mangelsdorf, S., Plunkett, J., Dedrick, C., Berlin, M., Meiseis, S., McHale, J., & Dichtellmiller, M. (1996). Attachment security in very low birthweight infants. *Developmental Psychology, 32,* 914–920.

Manson, J.E., Willett, W.C., Stampfer, M.J., Colditz, G.A., Hunter, D.J., Hankinson, S.E., Hennekens, C.H., & Speizer, F.E. (1995). Body weight and mortality among women. *New England Journal of Medicine, 333,* 677–685.

Mäntylä, T. (1994). Remembering to remember: Adult age differences in prospective memory. *Journals of Gerontology: Psychological Sciences, 49,* P276–282.

Maratsos, M. (2000). More overregularizations after all: New data and discussion on Marcus, Pinker, Ullman, Hollander, Rosen & Xu. *Journal of Child Language, 27,* 183–212.

Marcia, J.E. (1966). Development and validation of ego identity status. *Journal of Personality and Social Psychology, 3,* 551–558.

Marcia, J.E. (1980). Identity in adolescence. In J. Adelson (Ed.), *Handbook of adolescent psychology* (pp. 159–187). New York: Wiley.

Marcia, J.E. (1993). The ego identity status approach to ego identity. In J.E. Marcia, A.S. Waterman, D.R. Matteson, S.L. Archer, & J.L. Orlofsky (Eds.), *Ego identity: A handbook for psychosocial research* (pp. 1–21). New York: Springer-Verlag.

Marcia, J.E. (2001). A commentary on Seth Schwartz's review of identity theory and research. *Identity: An International Journal of Theory and Research, 1*(1), 59–65.

Marcia, J.E. (2002). Adolescence, identity, and the Bernardone family. *Identity: An International Journal of Theory and Research, 2*(3), 199–209.

Marcus, D.E., & Overton, W.F. (1978). The development of cognitive gender constancy and sex role preferences. *Child Development, 49,* 434–444.

Marcus, R.F. (1986). Naturalistic observation of cooperation, helping, and sharing and their association with empathy and affect. In C. Zahn-Waxler, E.M. Cummings, & R. Iannotti (Eds.), *Altruism and aggression: Biological and social origins* (pp. 256–279). Cambridge, England: Cambridge University Press.

Marean, G.C., Werner, L.A., & Kuhl, P.K. (1992). Vowel categorization by very young infants. *Developmental Psychology, 28,* 396–405.

Margolin, G., & Gordis, E. (2000). The effects of family and community violence on children. *Annual Review of Psychology, 51,* 445–479.

Markman, E.M. (1992). Constraints on word learning: Speculations about their nature, origins, and domain specificity. In M.R. Gunnar & M. Maratsos (Eds.), *Minnesota Symposia on Child Psychology* (Vol. 25, pp. 59–101). Hillsdale, NJ: Erlbaum.

Marks, N., & Lamberg, J. (1998). Marital status continuity and change among young and midlife adults. *Journal of Family Issues, 19,* 652–686.

Marquardt, R.(1998). Quality of youth employment. In: Human Resources Development Canada, *High school may not be enough: An analysis of results from the school leavers follow-up survey, 1995* (Catalogue No. MP43-380/1998E). Ottawa, ON: Author. Retrieved December 10, 2001 from http://www.hrdc-drhc.gc.ca/arb/publications/books/notenough/c5_e.shtml#anchor1533972

Marsh, H., Craven, R., & Debus, R. (1999). Separation of competency and affect components of multiple dimensions of academic self-concept: A developmental perspective. *Merrill-Palmer Quarterly, 45,* 567–601.

Marshall, N., Coll, C., Marx, F., McCartney, K., Keefe, N., & Ruh, J. (1997). After-school time and children's behavioral adjustment. *Merrill-Palmer Quarterly, 43,* 497–514.

Marshall, V.W. (1975). Age and awareness of finitude in developmental gerontology. *Omega, 6,* 113–129.

Marshall, V.W. (1996). The state of theory in aging and the social sciences. In R.H. Binstock & L.K. George (Eds.), *Handbook of aging and the social sciences* (4th ed., pp. 12–30). San Diego, CA: Academic Press.

Marshall, V.W., & Levy, J.A. (1990). Aging and dying. In R.H. Binstock & L.K. George (Eds.), *Handbook of aging and the social sciences* (3rd ed., pp. 245–260). San Diego, CA: Academic Press.

Marsiglio, W., & Donnelly, D. (1991). Sexual relations in later life: A national study of married persons. *Journals of Gerontology: Social Sciences, 46,* S338–344.

Martin, C.L. (1991). The role of cognition in understanding gender effects. In H.W. Reese (Ed.), *Advances in child development and behavior* (Vol. 23, pp. 113–150). San Diego, CA: Academic Press.

Martin, C.L. (1993). New directions for investigating children's gender knowledge. *Developmental Review, 13,* 184–204.

Martin, C.L., & Halverson, C.F., Jr. (1981). A schematic processing model of sex typing and stereotyping in children. *Child Development, 52,* 1119–1134.

Martin, C.L., & Little, J.K. (1990). The relation of gender understanding to children's sex-typed preferences and gender stereotypes. *Child Development, 61,* 1427–1439.

Martin, C.L., Wood, C.H., & Little, J.K. (1990). The development of gender stereotype components. *Child Development, 61,* 1891–1904.

Martin, J.L., & Ross, H.S. (1995). The development of aggression within sibling conflict. *Early Education and Development, 6,* 335–358.

Martin, R.P., Wisenbaker, J., & Huttunen, M. (1994). Review of factor analytic studies of temperament measures based on the

Thomas-Chess structural model: Implications for the Big Five. In C.F. Halverson, Jr., G.A. Kohnstamm, & R.P. Martin (Eds.), *The developing structure of temperament and personality from infancy to adulthood* (pp. 157–172). Hillsdale, NJ: Erlbaum.

Martinez, L. (2002). Teratogen hot topic: Anticoagulants. *The Genetic Drift 20*(4), Retrieved April 23, 2004, from http://www.mostgene.org/gd/gdvol20e.htm

Martini, T.S., Root, C.A., & Jenkins, J.M. (in press). Low and middle income mothers' regulation of negative emotion: Effects of children's temperament and situational emotional responses. *Social Development.*

Martin-Matthews, A.E. (2001). *The ties that bind aging families: Caregiving roles and relationships.* Ottawa, ON: Vanier Institute of the Family. Retrieved December 23, 2001 from http://www.vifamily.ca/cft/aging/caregiving.htm

Martorano, S.C. (1977). A developmental analysis of performance on Piaget's formal operations tasks. *Developmental Psychology, 13*, 666–672.

Marx, G. (1987). *Groucho and me.* New York: AMS Press.

Masataka, N. (1999). Preference for infant-directed singing in 2-day-old hearing infants of deaf parents. *Developmental Psychology, 35*, 1001–1005.

Mascolo, M.F., & Fischer, K.W. (1995). Developmental transformations in appraisals for pride, shame, and guilt. In J.P. Tangney & K.W. Fischer (Eds.), *Self-conscious emotions: The psychology of shame, guilt, embarrassment, and pride* (pp. 64–113). New York: Guilford Press.

Masi, R. (1988). Multiculturalism, medicine and health, Part I: Multicultural healthcare. *Médecin de Famille Canadien, 34.*

Maslow, A.H. (1968). *Toward a psychology of being* (2nd ed.). New York: Van Nostrand Reinhold.

Maslow, A.H. (1970a). *Motivation and personality* (2nd ed.). New York: Harper & Row.

Maslow, A.H. (1970b). *Religions, values, and peak-experiences.* New York: Viking. (Original work published 1964.)

Maslow, A.H. (1971). *The farther reaches of human nature.* New York: Viking.

Masten, A.S., Best, K.M., & Garmezy, N. (1990). Resilience and development: Contributions from the study of children who overcome adversity. *Development and Psychopathology, 2*, 425–444.

Masur, E., & Rodemaker, J. (1999). Mothers' and infants' spontaneous vocal, verbal, and action imitation during the second year. *Merrill-Palmer Quarterly, 45*, 392–412.

Maszk, P., Eisenberg, N., & Guthrie, I. (1999). Relations of children's social status to their emotionality and regulation: A short-term longitudinal study. *Merrill-Palmer Quarterly, 454*, 468–492.

Mather, P.L., & Black, K.N. (1984). Heredity and environmental influences on preschool twins' language skills. *Developmental Psychology, 20*, 303–308.

Mathew, A., & Cook, M. (1990). The control of reaching movements by young infants. *Child Development, 61*, 1238–1257.

Matthews, K.A., Wing, R.R., Kuller, L.H., Meilahn, E.N., Kelsey, S.F., Costello, E.J., & Caggiula, A.W. (1990). Influences of natural menopause on psychological characteristics and symptoms of middle-aged healthy women. *Journal of Consulting and Clinical Psychology, 58*, 345–351.

Mattson, S., & Riley, E. (1999). Implicit and explicit memory functioning in children with heavy prenatal alcohol exposure. *Journal of the International Neuropsychological Society, 5*, 462–471.

Mattson, S., Riley, E., Gramling, L., Delis, D. & Jones, K. (1998). Neuropsychological comparison of alcohol-exposed children with or without physical features of fetal alcohol syndrome. *Neuropsychology, 12*, 146–153.

Maughan, B., Pickles, A., & Quinton, D. (1995). Parental hostility, childhood behavior, and adult social functioning. In J. McCord (Ed.), *Coercion and punishment in long-term perspectives* (pp. 34–58). Cambridge, England: Cambridge University Press.

Maurer, D. & Lewis, T.L. (1993). Visual outcomes after infantile cataract. In K. Simons (Ed.) *Early visual development: Normal and abnormal.* Oxford: Oxford University Press.

Maurer, D., & Lewis, T.L. (2001). Visual acuity: The role of visual input in inducing postnatal change. *Clinical Neuroscience Research, 1*(4), 239–247.

Maurer, D., & Maurer, C. (1988). *The world of the newborn.* New York: Basic Books.

Maylor, D., Vousden, J., & Brown, D. (1999). Adult age differences in short-term memory for serial order: Data and a model. *Psychology & Aging, 14*, 572–594.

Maylor, E.A. (1993). Aging and forgetting in prospective and retrospective memory tasks. *Psychology and Aging, 8*, 420–428.

Maylor, E. (1998). Changes in event-based prospective memory across adulthood. *Aging, Neuropsychology, & Cognition, 5*, 107–128.

Mayringer, H., & Wimmer, H. (2000). Pseudoname learning by German-speaking children with dyslexia: Evidence for a phonological learning deficit. *Journal of Experimental Child Psychology, 75*, 116–133.

Mayseless, O., Wiseman, H., & Hai, I. (1998). Adolescents' relationships with father, mother, and same-gender friend. *Journal of Adolescent Research, 13*, 101–123.

McAdams, D., Hart, H., & Maruna, S. (1998). The anatomy of generativity. In D.P. McAdams & E. de St. Aubin (Eds.), *Generativity and adult development: How and why we care about the next generation* (pp. 7–44). Washington, DC: American Psychological Association.

McAllister, D., Kaplan, B., Edworthy, S., Martin, L., et al. (1997). The influence of systemic lupus erythematosus on fetal development: Cognitive, behavioral, and health trends. *Journal of the International Neurological Society, 3*, 370–376.

McBride-Chang, C. (1998). The development of invented spelling. *Early Education & Development, 9*, 147–160.

McBride-Chang, C., & Ho, C. (2000). Developmental issues in Chinese children's character acquisition. *Journal of Educational Psychology, 92*, 50–55.

McCain, M., & Mustard, F. (1999). *Early years study: Reversing the real brain drain.* Toronto: Ontario Children's Secretariat.

McCain, M.N., & Mustard, J.F. (2002). *The early years study three years later.* Toronto: The Founders' Network.

McCall, B., Cavanaugh, M., Arvey, R., & Taubman, P. (1997). Genetic influences on job and occupational switching. *Journal of Vocational Behavior, 50*, 60–77.

McCall, R.B. (1993). Developmental functions for general mental performance. In D.K. Detterman (Ed.), *Current topics in human intelligence: Vol. 3. Individual differences and cognition* (pp. 3–30). Norwood, NJ: Ablex.

McCarton, C., Brooks-Gunn, J., Wallace, I., Bauer, C., Benett, F., Bernbaum, J., Broyles, S., Casey, P., McCormick, M., Scott, D., Tyson, J., Tonascia, J., & Mainhart, C. (1997). Results at age 8 years of early intervention for low-birth-weight premature infants. *Journal of the American Medical Association, 277*, 126–132.

McClelland, S. (2001, September 17). Child poverty. *Maclean's, 114*(38), 18–23.

McClun, L., & Merrell, K. (1998). Relationship of perceived parenting styles, locus of control orientation, and self-concept among junior high age students. *Psychology in the Schools, 35*, 381–390.

McClure, E. (2000). A meta-analytic review of sex differences in facial expression processing and their development in infants, children, and adolescents. *Psychological Bulletin, 126*, 242–453.

McCoy, N. (1998). Methodological problems in the study of sexuality and the menopause. *Maturitas, 29*, 51–60.

McCrae, R.R., & Costa, P.T., Jr. (1984). *Emerging lives, enduring dispositions: Personality in adulthood.* Boston: Little, Brown.

McCrae, R., & Costa, P. (1990). *Personality in adulthood.* New York: Guilford.

McCrae, R., Costa, P., Ostendord, F., & Angleitner, A. (2000). Nature over nurture: Temperament, personality, and life span development. *Journal of Personality & Social Psychology, 78*, 173–186.

McCrae, R.R., & John, O.P. (1992). An introduction to the Five-Factor Model and its applications. *Journal of Personality, 60*, 175–215.

McCullough, M. (1998, December 22). Birth of octuplets worries infertility specialists. *Seattle Times* [Online edition archives]. Retrieved March 6, 2001 from http://www.seattletimes.com

McDaniel, S. (1994). *Family and friends: General Social Survey analysis series* (Catalogue No. 11-612E—No. 9). Ottawa, ON: Statistics Canada.

McDonald, P.L., & Wanner, R.A. (1990). *Retirement in Canada.* Toronto: Butterworths.

McEvoy, G.M., & Cascio, W.F. (1989). Cumulative evidence of the relationship between employee age and job performance. *Journal of Applied Psychology, 74*, 11–17.

McFadden, D. (1998). Sex differences in the auditory system. *Developmental Neuropsychology,14*, 261–298.

McFalls, J.A., Jr. (1990). The risks of reproductive impairment in the later years of childbearing. *Annual Review of Sociology, 16*, 491–519.

McFayden-Ketchumm, S., Bates, J., Dodge, K., & Pettit, G. (1996). Patterns of change in early childhood aggressive-disruptive behavior: Gender differences in predictions from early coercive and affectionate mother-child interactions. *Child Development, 67*, 2417–2433.

McGue, M., Pickens, R., & Svikis, D. (1992). Sex and age effects on the inheritance of alcohol problems: A twin study. *Journal of Abnormal Psychology, 101*, 3–17.

McHale, S., Crouter, A., & Tucker, C. (1999). Family context and gender role socialization in middle childhood: Comparing girls to boys and sisters to brothers. *Child Development, 70*, 990–1004.

McIntosh, B.R., & Danigelis, N.L. (1995). Race, gender, and the relevance of productive activity for elders' affect. *Journals of Gerontology: Social Sciences, 50B*, S229–239.

McIntyre, L., Walsh, G., & Conner, S.K. (2001). A follow-up study on child hunger in Canada (Catalogue No. W-01-1-2E). Ottawa, ON: Human Resources Development Canada. Retrieved September 20, 2001 from http://www.hrdc-drhc.gc.ca/stratpol/arb/publications/research/2001docs/abw-01-1-2e.shtml

McKay, A. & Holowaty, P. (1997). Sexual health education: A study of adolescents' opinions, self-perceived needs, and current and preferred sources of information. *The Canadian Journal of Human Sexuality, 6*, 29–38.

McKay, A., Pietrusiak, M.A., & Holowaty, P. (1998). Parents' opinion and attitudes towards sexuality education in the schools. *The Canadian Journal of Human Sexuality, 7*, 139–146.

McKim, M.K., Cramer, K.M., Stuart, B., & O'Connor, D.L. (1999). Infant care decisions and attachment security: The Canadian transition to child care study. *Canadian Journal of Behavioural Science, 31*(2), 92–106.

McKinlay, J.B., McKinlay, S.M., & Brambilla, D.J. (1987). Health status and utilization behavior associated with menopause. *American Journal of Epidemiology, 125*, 110–121.

McKitrick, L., Friedman, L., Thompson, L., Gray, C., & Yesavage, J. (1997). Feasibility and psychometric description of a paced auditory serial addition task adapted for older adults. *Journal of Clinical Geropsychology, 3*, 57–71.

McLanahan, S., & Sandefur, G. (1994). *Growing up with a single parent: What hurts, what helps.* Cambridge, MA: Harvard University Press.

McLoyd, V. (1998). Socioeconomic disadvantage and child development. *American Psychologist, 53*, 185–204.

McLoyd, V.C., Jayaratne, T.E., Ceballo, R., & Borquez, J. (1994). Unemployment and work interruption among African American single mothers: Effects on parenting and adolescent socioemotional functioning. *Child Development, 65*, 562–589.

McLoyd, V., & Wilson, L. (1991). The strain of living poor: Parenting, social support, and child mental health. In A.C. Huston (Ed.), *Children in poverty: Child development and public policy* (pp. 105–135). Cambridge, England: Cambridge University Press.

McMaster, J., Pitts, M., & Poyah, G. (1997). The menopausal experiences of women in a developing country: "There is a time for everything: to be a teenager, a mother and a granny." *Women & Health, 26*, 1–13.

McNally, E., Hendricks, S., & Horowitz, I. (1985). A look at breast-feeding trends in Canada (1963–1982). *Canadian Journal of Public Health, 76*, 101–107.

McNeal, C., & Amato, P. (1998). Parents' marital violence: Long-term consequences for children. *Journal of Family Issues, 19*, 123–139.

McNeal, R. (1997). Are students being pulled out of high school? The effect of adolescent employment on dropping out. *Sociology of Education, 70*, 206–220.

Mead, S., & Fisk, A. (1998). Measuring skill acquisition and retention with an ATM simulator: The need for age-specific training. *Human Factors, 40*, 516–523.

Media Awareness Network. (2001a). Young Canadians in a wired world: The students' view. Media Awareness Network. Retrieved November 18, 2001 from http://www.media-awareness.ca/eng/webaware/netsurvey/pdf/reportoct.pdf

Media Awareness Network. (2001b). Young Canadians in a wired world: The students' view—key findings. Media Awareness Network. Retrieved November 18, 2001 from http://www.media-awareness.ca/eng/webaware/netsurvey/students/keyfindingsoct.htm

Media Awareness Network. (2004a). *Video games.* Retrieved June 30, 2004 from http://www.media-awareness.ca/english/parents/video_games/index.cfm

Media Awareness Network. (2004b). Young Canadians in a wired world—Phase II: A qualitative research report. Media Awareness Network. Ottawa, ON: Author. Retrieved August 3, 2004 from http://www.media-awareness.ca/english/special_initiatives/surveys/phase_two/index.cfm

Mediascope, Inc. (1999). *The social effects of electronic interactive games: An annotated bibliography.* Studio City, CA: Mediascope Press.

Mediascope Press. (2000). *Teens, sex and the media/Issue Brief Series.* Studio City, CA: Mediascope Inc.

Medvedova, L. (1998). Personality dimensions—"little five"—and their relationships with coping strategies in early adolescence. *Studia Psychologica, 40*, 261–265.

Meek, C. (2004). UK psychiatrists question SSRI warnings for under-18s. *Canadian Medical Association Journal, 170*(4), 455.

Meeks, S. (1997). Illnesses in late life: Short-term course of mental illness in middle age and late life. *International Psychogeriatrics, 9*, 343–358.

Meeus, W., Dekovic, M., & Iedema, J. (1997). Unemployment and identity in adolescence: A social comparison perspective. *Career Development Quarterly, 45*, 369–380.

Mehta, K. (1997). The impact of religious beliefs and practices on aging: A cross-cultural comparison. *Journal of Aging Studies, 11*, 101–114.

Meisenhelder, J., & Chandler, E. (2000). Faith, prayer, and health outcomes in elderly Native Americans. *Clinical Nursing Research, 9*, 191–203.

Melot, A., & Houde, O. (1998). Categorization and theories of mind: The case of the appearance/reality distinction. *Cahiers de Psychologie Cognitive/Current Psychology of Cognition, 17*, 71–93.

Melson, G., Peet, S., & Sparks, C. (1991). Children's attachments to their pets: Links to socioemotional development. *Children's Environmental Quarterly, 8*, 55–65.

Meltzoff, A.N. (1988). Infant imitation and memory: Nine-month-olds in immediate and deferred tasks. *Child Development, 59*, 217–225.

Meltzoff, A.N. (1995). Understanding the intentions of others: Re-enactment of intended acts by 18-month-old children. *Developmental Psychology, 31*, 838–850.

Menaghan, E.G., & Lieberman, M.A. (1986). Changes in depression following divorce: A panel study. *Journal of Marriage and the Family, 48*, 319–328.

Mental Health Foundation of New Zealand. (2002). *Bulimia Nervosa.* Auckland, NZ: Author. Retrieved July 14, 2004 from http://www.mentalhealth.org.nz/conditions/docs/pdf8.pdf

Meredith, K., & Rassa, G. (1999). Aligning the levels of awareness with the stages of grieving. *Journal of Cognitive Rehabilitation, 17,* 10–12.

Merikangas, K.R., & Angst, J. (1995). The challenge of depressive disorders in adolescence. In M. Rutter (Ed.), *Psychosocial disturbances in young people: Challenges for prevention* (pp. 131–165). Cambridge, England: Cambridge University Press.

Merrill, D.M., & Mor, V. (1993). Pathways to hospital death among the oldest old. *Journal of Aging and Health, 5,* 516–535.

Meyer, M. (1998). Perceptual differences in fetal alcohol syndrome affect boys performing a modeling task. *Perceptual & Motor Skills, 87,* 784–786.

Meyer-Bahlburg, H.F.L., Ehrhardt, A.A., Rosen, L.R., Gruen, R.S., Veridiano, N.P., Vann, F.H., & Neuwalder, H.F. (1995). Prenatal estrogens and the development of homosexual orientation. *Developmental Psychology, 31,* 12–21.

Michael, R.T., Gagnon, J.H., Laumann, E.O., & Kolata, G. (1994). *Sex in America.* Boston: Little, Brown.

Miech, R., & Shanahan, M. (2000). Socioeconomic status and depression over the life course. *Journal of Health & Social Behavior, 41,* 162–176.

Milan, A. (2003). Would you live common-law? (Catalogue No. 11-008). *Canadian Social Trends, Autumn*(70), 2–6.

Milan, A., & Hamm, B. (2003). Across the generations: Grandparents and grandchildren (Catalogue No. 11-008). *Canadian Social Trends, Winter*(71), 2–7.

Miller, B.C., & Moore, K.A. (1990). Adolescent sexual behavior, pregnancy, and parenting: Research through the 1980s. *Journal of Marriage and the Family, 52,* 1025–1044.

Miller, B., Norton, M., Curtis, T., Hill, E., Schvaneveldt, P., & Young, M. (1998). The timing of sexual intercourse among adolescents: Family, peer, and other antecedents: Erratum. *Youth & Society, 29,* 390.

Miller, F., Jenkins, J., & Keating, D. (2002). Parenting and children's behaviour problems. In J.D. Willms (Ed.), *Vulnerable children* (pp. 71–102). Edmonton, AB: The University of Alberta Press.

Miller, P., Eisenberg, N., Fabes, R., & Shell, R. (1996). Relations of moral reasoning and vicarious emotion to young children's prosocial behavior toward peers and adults. *Developmental Psychology, 29,* 3–18.

Miller, R.A. (1996). Aging and the immune response. In E.L. Schneider & J.W. Rowe (Eds.), *Handbook of the biology of aging* (4th ed., pp. 355–392). San Diego, CA: Academic Press.

Miller, T. (1996, July). Segmenting the Internet. *American Demographics.* Retrieved March 21, 2000 from www.americandemographics.com

Miller, T.Q., Smith, T.W., Turner, C.W., Guijarro, M.L., & Hallet, A.J. (1996). A meta-analytic review of research on hostility and physical health. *Psychological Bulletin, 119,* 322–348.

Miller, T.Q., Turner, C.W., Tindale, R.S., Posavac, E.J., & Dugoni, B.L. (1991). Reasons for the trend toward null findings in research on Type A behavior. *Psychological Bulletin, 110,* 469–495.

Mills, D., Coffey-Corina, S., & Neville, H. (1994). Variability in cerebral organization during primary language acquisition. In G. Dawson & K. Fischer (Eds.) *Human behavior and the developing brain.* New York: Guilford Press.

Mills, R.S.L. & Rubin, K.H. (1998). Are behavioural and psychological control both differentially associated with childhood aggression and social withdrawal? *Canadian Journal of Behavioural Science, 30*(2), 132–136.

Minty, B. (1999). Outcomes in long-term foster family care. *Journal of Child Psychology & Psychiatry & Allied Disciplines, 40,* 991–999.

Mischel, W. (1966). A social learning view of sex differences in behavior. In E.E. Maccoby (Ed.), *The development of sex differences* (pp. 56–81). Stanford, CA: Stanford University Press.

Mischel, W. (1970). Sex typing and socialization. In P.H. Mussen (Ed.), *Carmichael's manual of child psychology* (Vol. 2, pp. 3–72). New York: Wiley.

Mishra, R.C. (1997). Cognition and cognitive development. In J. Berry, P. Dasen, & T. Sarswathi (Eds.), *Handbook of cross-cultural psychology* (Vol. 2). Boston: Allyn & Bacon.

Mitchell, B.A. (2000). The refilled "nest": Debunking the myth of families-in-crisis. In E.M. Gee & G. Gutman (eds.), *The overselling of population aging: Apocalyptic demography and intergenerational challenges* (pp. 80–99). Toronto: Oxford University Press.

Mitchell, P.R., & Kent, R.D. (1990). Phonetic variation in multisyllable babbling. *Journal of Child Language, 17,* 247–265.

Moehn, D., & Rossetti, L. (1996). The effects of neonatal intensive care on parental emotions and attachment. *Infant-Toddler Intervention, 6,* 229–246.

Moen, P. (1991). Transitions in mid-life: Women's work and family roles in the 1970s. *Journal of Marriage and the Family, 53,* 135–150.

Moen, P. (1996). Gender, age, and the life course. In R.H. Binstock & L.K. George (Eds.), *Handbook of aging and the social sciences* (4th ed., pp. 171–187). San Diego, CA: Academic Press.

Moen, P., & Erickson, M.A. (1995). Linked lives: A transgenerational approach to resilience. In P. Moen, G.H. Elder, Jr., & K. Lüscher (Eds.), *Examining lives in context: Perspectives on the ecology of human development* (pp. 169–210). Washington, DC: American Psychological Association.

Mohanty, A. & Perregaux, C. (1997). Language acquisition and bilingualism. In J. Berry, P. Dasen, & T. Saraswath (Eds.), *Handbook of cross-cultural psychology* (Vol. 2). Boston: Allyn & Bacon.

Monroy, T. (2000, March 15). Boomers alter economics. *Interactive Week.* Retrieved March 21, 2000 from www.ZDNet.com

Montemayor, R., & Eisen, M. (1977). The development of self-conceptions from childhood to adolescence. *Developmental Psychology, 13,* 314–319.

Montgomery, M., & Sorel, G. (1998). Love and dating experience in early and middle adolescence: Grade and gender comparisons. *Journal of Adolescence, 21,* 677–689.

Montgomery, R.J.V., & Kosloski, K. (1994). A longitudinal analysis of nursing home placement for dependent elders cared for by spouses vs adult children. *Journals of Gerontology: Social Sciences, 49,* S62–74.

Moody, E. (1997). Lessons from pair counseling with incarcerated juvenile delinquents. *Journal of Addictions & Offender Counseling, 18,* 10–25.

Moon, C., & Fifer, W.P. (1990). Syllables as signals for 2-day-old infants. *Infant Behavior and Development, 13,* 377–390.

Mooney, L., Knox, D., & Schacht, C. (2000a). *Social problems.* Belmont, CA: Wadsworth.

Mooney, L., Knox, D., & Schacht, C. (2000b). *Understanding social problems* (2nd ed.). Thousand Oaks, CA: Wadsworth.

Moore, C., Barresi, J., & Thompson, C. (1998). The cognitive basis of future-oriented prosocial behavior. *Social Development, 7,* 198–218.

Moore, C. & D'Entremont, B. (2001). Developmental changes in pointing as a function of attentional focus. *Journal of Cognition and Development, 2,* 109–129.

Moore, K.L., & Persaud, T.V.N. (1993). *The developing human: Clinically oriented embryology* (5th ed.). Philadelphia: Saunders.

Mor, V., Greer, D.S., & Kastenbaum, R. (Eds.). (1988). *The hospice experiment.* Baltimore, MD: Johns Hopkins University Press.

Morgan, C., Covington, J., Geisler, M., Polich, J., & Murphy, C. (1997). Olfactory event-related potentials: Older males demonstrate the greatest deficits. *Electroencephalography & Clinical Neurophysiology, 104,* 351–358.

Morgan, D.G. (1992). Neurochemical changes with aging: Predisposition towards age-related mental disorders. In J.E. Birren, R.B. Sloane, & G.D. Cohen (Eds.), *Handbook of mental health and aging* (2nd ed., pp. 175–200). San Diego, CA: Academic Press.

Morris, D.L., Kritchevsky, S.B., & Davis, C.E. (1994). Serum carotenoids and coronary heart disease. The Lipid Research

Clinics Coronary Primary Prevention Trial and Follow-up Study. *Journal of the American Medical Association, 272,* 1439–1441.

Morrison, D.R., & Cherlin, A.J. (1995). The divorce process and young children's well-being: A prospective analysis. *Journal of Marriage and the Family, 57,* 800–812.

Morrison, N.A., Qi, J.C., Tokita, A., Kelly, P.J., Crofts, L., Nguyen, T.V., Sambrook, P.N., & Eisman, J.A. (1994). Prediction of bone density from vitamin D receptor alleles. *Nature, 367,* 284–287.

Morrissette, P. (1999). Post-traumatic stress disorder in child sexual abuse: Diagnostic and treatment considerations. *Child & Youth Care Forum, 28,* 205–219.

Morrongiello, B.A., & Dawber, T. (1999). Parental influences on toddlers' injury-risk behaviors: Are sons and daughters socialized differently? *Journal of Applied Developmental Psychology, 20,* 227–251.

Morrongiello, B.A., & House, K. (2004). Measuring parent attributes and supervision behaviors relevant to child injury risk: Examining the usefulness of questionnaire measures. *Injury Prevention, 10*(2), 114–119.

Morrongiello, B.A., & Kiriakou, S. (2004). Mothers' home-safety practices for preventing six types of childhood injuries: What do they do, and why? *Journal of Pediatric Psychology, 29*(4), 285–297.

Morrongiello, B.A., Midgett, C., & Shields, R. (2001). Don't run with scissors: Young children's knowledge of home safety rules. *Journal of Pediatric Psychology, 26,* 105–115.

Morrongiello, B.A., & Rennie, H. (1998). Why do boys engage in more risk taking than girls? The role of attributions, beliefs, and risk appraisal. *Journal of Pediatric Psychology, 23,* 33–44.

Morse, P.A., & Cowan, N. (1982). Infant auditory and speech perception. In T.M. Field, A. Houston, H.C. Quay, L. Troll, & G.E. Finley (Eds.), *Review of human development* (pp. 32–61). New York: Wiley.

Mortimer, J.T., Finch, M.D., Dennehy, K., Lee, C., & Beebe, T. (1995, March). *Work experience in adolescence.* Paper presented at the biennial meetings of the Society for Research in Child Development, Indianapolis, IN.

Mosher, W.D. (1987, June). Infertility: Why business is booming. *American Demography,* 42–43.

Mosher, W.D., & Pratt, W.F. (1987). *Fecundity, infertility, and reproductive health in the United States, 1982: Vital Health Statistics, Series 23, No. 14. National Center for Health Statistics, U.S. Public Health Service.* Washington, DC: USGPO.

Moss, E., St-Laurent, D., Rousseau, D., Parent, S., Gosselin, C., & Saintange, J., (1999). L'attachement à l'âge scolaire et le développement des troubles de comportement. *Canadian Journal of Behavioural Science, 31*(2), 107–118.

Mott, J., Crowe, P., Richardson, J., & Flay, B. (1999). After-school supervision and adolescent cigarette smoking: Contributions of the setting and intensity of after-school self-care. *Journal of Behavioral Medicine, 22,* 35–58.

Mounts, N.S., & Steinberg, L. (1995). An ecological analysis of peer influence on adolescent grade point average and drug use. *Developmental Psychology, 31,* 915–922.

Mueller, K., & Yoder, J. (1999). Stigmatization of non-normative family size status. *Sex Roles, 41,* 901–919.

Muller, R.T. & Diamond, T. (1999). Father and mother physical abuse and child aggressive behaviour in two generations. *Canadian Journal of Behavioural Science, 31*(4), 221–228.

Mullins, L.C., & Mushel, M. (1992). The existence and emotional closeness of relationships with children, friends, and spouses. The effect on loneliness among older persons. *Research on Aging, 14,* 448–470.

Munroe, R.H., Shimmin, H.S., & Munroe, R.L. (1984). Gender understanding and sex role preference in four cultures. *Developmental Psychology, 20,* 673–682.

Munsch, R. (1985). *Thomas' Snowsuit.* Toronto: Annick Press Ltd.

Murphy, K., Hanrahan, P., & Luchins, D. (1997). A survey of grief and bereavement in nursing homes: The importance of hospice grief and bereavement for the end-stage Alzheimer's disease patient and family. *Journal of the American Geriatrics Society, 45,* 1104–1107.

Murphy, S., Braun, T., Tillery, L., Cain, K., Johnson, L., & Beaton, R. (1999). PTSD among bereaved parents following the violent deaths of their 12- to 28-year-old children: A longitudinal prospective analysis. *Journal of Traumatic Stress, 12,* 273–291.

Murphy, S.O. (1993, April). *The family context and the transition to siblinghood: Strategies parents use to influence sibling-infant relationships.* Paper presented at the biennial meetings of the Society for Research in Child Development, New Orleans, LA.

Murray, J.P. (1980). *Television and youth: 25 years of research and controversy.* Stanford, CA: The Boys Town Center for the Study of Youth Development.

Murray, L., Sinclair, D., Cooper, P., Ducournau, P., et al. (1999). The socioemotional development of 5-year-old children of postnatally depressed mothers. *Journal of Child Psychology & Psychiatry & Allied Disciplines, 40,* 1259–1271.

Murrell, S.A., & Himmelfarb, S. (1989). Effects of attachment bereavement and pre-event conditions on subsequent depressive symptoms in older adults. *Psychology and Aging, 4,* 166–172.

Murrell, S.A., & Norris, F.H. (1991). Differential social support and life change as contributors to the social class–distress relationship in old age. *Psychology and Aging, 6,* 223–231.

Murstein, B.I. (1986). *Paths to marriage.* Beverly Hills, CA: Sage.

Mutagens. (1995, Spring). *Genetic Drift, 12.* Retrieved April 22, 2004, from http://www.mostgene.org/gd/gdvol12f.htm

Mutch, L., Leyland, A., & McGee, A. (1993). Patterns of neuropsychological function in a low-birth-weight population. *Developmental Medicine & Child Neurology, 35,* 943–956.

Muthesius, D. (1997). Reminiscence and the relationship between young and old. *Zeitschrift fuer Gerontologie und Geriatrie, 30,* 354–361.

Muzi, M. (2000). *The experience of parenting.* Upper Saddle River, NJ: Prentice Hall.

Mwamwenda, T. (1999). Undergraduate and graduate students' combinatorial reasoning and formal operations. *Journal of Genetic Psychology, 160,* 503–506.

Myerowitz, R & Hogikyan, N.D. (1987). A deletion involving Alu sequences in the beta-hexosaminidase alpha-chain gene of French Canadians with Tay-Sachs disease. *Journal of Biological Chemistry, 15:262*(32), 15396–15399.

Nachmias, M. (1993, April). *Maternal personality relations with toddler's attachment classification, use of coping strategies, and adrenocortical stress response.* Paper presented at the biennial meetings of the Society for Research in Child Development, New Orleans, LA.

Nagamine, S. (1999). Interpersonal conflict situations: Adolescents' negotiation processes using an interpersonal negotiation strategy model: Adolescents' relations with their parents and friends. *Japanese Journal of Educational Psychology, 47,* 218–228.

Narvaez, D. (1998). The influence of moral schemas on the reconstruction of moral narratives in eighth graders and college students. *Journal of Educational Psychology, 90,* 13–24.

Nathanson, C.A., & Lorenz, G. (1982). Women and health: The social dimensions of biomedical data. In J.Z. Giele (Ed.), *Women in the middle years* (pp. 37–88). New York: Wiley.

National Cancer Institute of Canada. (2003). *Review of trends in colorectal cancer: Incidence and mortality patterns.* Toronto: Author. Retrieved August 17, 2004 from http://www.ncic.cancer.ca/ncic/internet/standard/ 0,3621,84658243_85787780_91035926_langId-en,00.html#table8_1

National Cancer Institute of Canada. (2004). *Canadian Cancer Statistics 2001.* Toronto: Author. Retrieved August 17, 2004 from http://www.ncic.cancer.ca/vgn/images/portal/cit_86751114/14/35/ 195991821ncic_stats2004_en.pdf

National Center for Chronic Disease Prevention and Health Promotion. (2000). *Obesity epidemic increases dramatically in the United States* [Online press release]. Retrieved August 23, 2000 from http://www.cdc.gov

National Center for Educational Statistics (NCES). (1997a). *Condition of Education/1997.* Washington, DC: U.S. Department of Education.

National Center for Educational Statistics. (1997b). *National Assessment of Educational Progress: 1996 Long-Term Trend Assessment.* Washington, DC: U.S. Department of Education.

National Center for Health Statistics (NCHS). (1996). Guidelines for school health programs to promote lifelong healthy eating. *Morbidity and Mortality Weekly Report, 45,* 1–33.

National Center for Health Statistics. (1999a, September 14). Trends in twin and triplet births: 1980–1997. *National Vital Statistics Reports.*

National Center for Health Statistics. (1999b). Surveillance for injuries and violence among older adults. *Morbidity and Mortality Weekly Report, 48,* 27–50.

National Health and Welfare. (1979). *The Canadian Mother and Child* (4th ed.). Ottawa, ON: Author.

National Institute of Child Health & Human Development (NICHD) Early Child Care Research Network. (1999). Chronicity of maternal depressive symptoms, maternal sensitivity, and child functioning at 36 months. *Developmental Psychology, 35,* 1297–1310.

National Institute of Nutrition. (2001). *Giving adolescents a fighting chance against eating disorders.* Retrieved July 31, 2003, from http://www.nin.ca/public_html/Publications/HealthyBites/hb4_93en.html

National Institute on Aging. (2000a) *Depression: A serious but treatable illness* [Online "Age Page"]. Retrieved February 7, 2001 from http://www.nih.gov/nia

National Institute on Aging. (2000b). *Sexuality in later life* [Online "Age Page"]. Retrieved February 7, 2001 from http://www.nih.gov/nia

National survey results of gay couples in long-lasting relationships. (1990, May/June). *Partners: Newsletter for Gay and Lesbian Couples,* 1–16.

Neill, M. (1998). *High stakes tests do not improve student learning* [Online report]. Retrieved October 21, 1998 from http://www.fairtest.org

Neimark, E.D. (1982). Adolescent thought: Transition to formal operations. In B.B. Wolman (Ed.), *Handbook of developmental psychology* (pp. 486–502). Englewood Cliffs, NJ: Prentice-Hall.

Neimeyer, R.A., & Chapman, K.M. (1980/1981). Self/ideal discrepancy and fear of death: The test of an existential hypothesis. *Omega, 11,* 233–239.

Neisser, U., Boodoo, G., Bouchard, T.J., Jr., Boykin, A.W., Brody, N., Ceci, S.J., Halpern, D.F., Loehlin, J.C., Perloff, R., Sternberg, R.J., & Urbina, S. (1996). Intelligence: Knowns and unknowns. *American Psychologist, 51,* 77–101.

Neisser, U., & Harsch, N. (1992). Phantom flashbulbs: False recollections of hearing the news about Challenger. In E. Winograd & U. Neisser (Eds.), *Affect and accuracy in recall: Studies of "flashbulb" memories.* (pp. 9–31). New York: Cambridge University Press.

Nelson, E.A., & Dannefer, D. (1992). Aged heterogeneity: Fact or fiction? The fate of diversity in gerontological research. *The Gerontologist, 32,* 17–23.

Nelson, K. (1973). Structure and strategy in learning to talk. *Monographs of the Society for Research in Child Development, 38*(Serial No. 149).

Nelson, M.E., Fiatarone, M.A., Morganti, C.M., Trice, I., Greenberg, R.A., & Evans, W.J. (1994). Effects of high-intensity strength training on multiple risk factors for osteoporotic fractures. *Journal of the American Medical Association, 272,* 1909–1914.

Nelson, S. (1980). Factors influencing young children's use of motives and outcomes as moral criteria. *Child Development, 51,* 823–829.

Neshat-Doost, H., Taghavi, M., Moradi, A., Yule, W., & Dalgleish, T. (1998). Memory for emotional trait adjectives in clinically depressed youth. *Journal of Abnormal Psychology, 107,* 642–650.

Neugarten, B.L. (1970). Dynamics of transition of middle age to old age. *Journal of Geriatric Psychiatry, 4,* 71–87.

Neugarten, B.L. (1979). Time, age, and the life cycle. *American Journal of Psychiatry, 136,* 887–894.

Neugebauer, R., Hoek, H., & Susser, E. (1999). Prenatal exposure to wartime famine and development of antisocial personal disorder in early adulthood. *Journal of the American Medical Association, 282,* 455–462.

Newcomb, A.F., & Bagwell, C.L. (1995). Children's friendship relations: A meta-analytic review. *Psychological Bulletin, 117,* 306–347.

Newcomb, A.F., Bukowski, W.M., & Pattee, L. (1993). Children's peer relations: A meta-analytic review of popular, rejected, neglected, controversial, and average sociometric status. *Psychological Bulletin, 113,* 99–128.

Newman, D., Caspi, A., Moffitt, T., & Silva, P. (1997). Antecedents of adult interpersonal functioning: Effects of individual differences in age 3 temperament. *Developmental Psychology, 33,* 206–217.

Newman, J., & Pittman, T. (2003). *Dr. Jack Newman's guide to breastfeeding* (revised ed.). Toronto, ON: Harper Collins Canada.

Ni, Y. (1998). Cognitive structure, content knowledge, and classificatory reasoning. *Journal of Genetic Psychology, 159,* 280–296.

Nicholson, J. (1998). Inborn errors of metabolism. In R. Behrman & R. Kliegman (Eds.), *Nelson essentials of pediatrics* (3rd ed., pp. 147–166). Philadelphia: W.B. Saunders.

Nicoladis, E., & Genesee, F. (1996). A longitudinal study of pragmatic differentiation in young bilingual children. *Language Learning, 46,* 439–464.

Nicoladis, E., & Genesee, F. (1997). Language development in preschool bilingual children. *Journal of Speech-Language Pathology and Audiology, 21*(4), 258–270.

Nilsson, E., Gillberg, C., Gillberg, I., & Rastam, M. (1999). Ten-year follow-up of adolescent-onset anorexia nervosa: Personality disorders. *Journal of the American Academy of Child & Adolescent Psychiatry, 38,* 1389–1395.

Nilsson, L., Baeckman, L., Erngrund, K., & Nyberg, L. (1997). The Betula prospective cohort study: Memory, health, and aging. *Aging, Neuropsychology, & Cognition, 4,* 1–32.

Nilsson, L., & Hamberger, L. (1990). *A child is born.* New York: Delacorte.

Nisan, M., & Kohlberg, L. (1982). Universality and variation in moral judgment: A longitudinal and cross-sectional study in Turkey. *Child Development, 53,* 865–876.

Niska, K., Snyder, M., & Lia-Hoagberg, B. (1998). Family ritual facilitates adaptation to parenthood. *Public Health Nursing, 15,* 329–337.

Nolen-Hoeksema, S., & Girgus, J.S. (1994). The emergence of gender differences in depression during adolescence. *Psychological Bulletin, 115,* 424–443.

Noonan, G., Turner, N.E., & Macdonald, J. (1999). *Gambling and problem gambling amongst students in grades 5 to 11.* Centre for Addiction and Mental Health, May, 1–22. Retrieved November 18, 2001 from http://www.cfcg.org/search/ documents/ Gambling_and_problem_gambling_amongst_students_ in_grades_5_ to_11-14_02_2000-15_11_09.pdf

Norboru, T. (1997). A developmental study of wordplay in preschool children: The Japanese game of "Shiritori." *Japanese Journal of Developmental Psychology, 8,* 42–52.

Norris, F.H., & Murrell, S.A. (1990). Social support, life events, and stress as modifiers of adjustment to bereavement by older adults. *Psychology and Aging, 5,* 429–436.

Norton, A.J. (1983). Family life cycle: 1980. *Journal of Marriage and the Family, 45,* 267–275.

Norris, J.E. (1994). Widowhood in later life. In *Writings in gerontology, (14) Late-life marital disruptions* (pp. 34–45). Ottawa, ON: National Advisory Council on Aging.

Norris, J.E., & Tindale, J.A. (1994). *Among generations: The cycle of adult relationships.* New York: W.H. Freeman.

Norwood, T.H., Smith, J.R., & Stein, G.H. (1990). Aging at the cellular level: The human fibroblastlike cell model. In E.R. Schneider & J.W. Rowe (Eds.), *Handbook of the biology of aging* (3rd ed., pp. 131–154). San Diego, CA: Academic Press.

Nottelmann, E.D., Susman, E.J., Blue, J.H., Inoff-Germain, G., Dorn, L.D., Loriaux, D.L., Cutler, G.B., Jr., & Chrousos, G.P. (1987).

Gonadal and adrenal hormone correlates of adjustment in early adolescence. In R.M. Lerner & T.T. Foch (Eds.), *Biological-psychosocial interactions in early adolescence* (pp. 303–324). Hillsdale, NJ: Erlbaum.

Novosad, C., & Thoman, E. (1999). Stability of temperament over the childhood years. *American Journal of Orthopsychiatry, 69,* 457–474.

Nowakowski, R.S. (1987). Basic concepts of CNS development. *Child Development, 58,* 568–595.

Nucci, L., & Smetana, J. (1996). Mothers' concepts of young children's areas of personal freedom. *Child Development, 67,* 1870–1886.

Nutter, J. (1997). Middle school students' attitudes and use of anabolic steroids. *Journal of Strength Conditioning Research, 11,* 35–39.

Oates, J. (1998). Risk factors for infant attrition and low engagement in experiments and free-play. *Infant Behavior & Development, 21,* 555–569.

Oatley, K., & Jenkins, J. (1996). *Understanding emotions.* Cambridge, MA: Blackwell Publishers.

O'Beirne, H., & Moore, C. (1995, March). *Attachment and sexual behavior in adolescence.* Paper presented at the biennial meetings of the Society for Research in Child Development, Indianapolis, IN.

O'Brien, M. (1992). Gender identity and sex roles. In V.B. Van Hasselt & M. Hersen (Eds.), *Handbook of social development: A lifespan perspective* (pp. 325–345). New York: Plenum.

O'Conner, T.G., & Jenkins, J.M. (2000). *Marital transitions and children's adjustment* (Catalogue No. W-00-1-3E). Ottawa, ON: Human Resources Development Canada. Retrieved September 20, 2001 from http://www.hrdc-drhc.gc.ca/stratpol/arb/publications/research/2001docs/w-01-1-3e.pdf

O'Connor, N.J., Manson, J.E., O'Connor, G.T., & Buring, J.E. (1995). Psychosocial risk factors and nonfatal myocardial infarction. *Circulation, 92,* 1458–1464.

Offer, D., Kaiz, M., Howard, K., & Bennett, E. (1998). Emotional variables in adolescence and their stability and contribution to the mental health of adult men: Implications for early intervention strategies. *Journal of Youth & Adolescence, 27,* 675–690.

Offord, D.R., Boyle, M.H., & Racine, Y.A. (1991). The epidemiology of antisocial behavior in childhood and adolescence. In D.J. Pepler & K.H. Rubin (Eds.), *The development and treatment of childhood aggression* (pp. 31–54). Hillsdale, NJ: Erlbaum.

Ofstedal, M., Zimmer, Z., & Lin, H. (1999). A comparison of correlates of cognitive functioning in older persons in Taiwan and the United States. *Journals of Gerontology: Series B: Psychological Sciences & Social Sciences. 54B,* S291–S301.

Ogawa, N., & Retherford, R.D. (1993). Care of the elderly in Japan: Changing norms and expectations. *Journal of Marriage and the Family, 55,* 585–597.

O'Hara, M.W., Schlechte, J.A., Lewis, D.A., & Varner, M.W. (1992). Controlled prospective study of postpartum mood disorders: Psychological, environmental, and hormonal variables. *Journal of Abnormal Psychology, 100,* 63–73.

Okamoto, K., & Uechi, Y. (1999). Adolescents' relations with parents and friends in the second individuation process. *Japanese Journal of Educational Psychology, 47,* 248–258.

Okwumabua, J., Baker, F., Wong, S., & Pilgram, B. (1997). Characteristics of depressive symptoms in elderly urban and rural African Americans. *Journal of Gerontology, 52A,* M241–M246.

Oldenburg, C., & Kerns, K. (1997). Associations between peer relationships and depressive symptoms: Testing moderator effects of gender and age. *Journal of Early Adolescence, 17,* 319–337.

Oldershaw, L. (2002). *A national survey of parents of young children.* Toronto: Invest in Kids. Retrieved July 10, 2004 from http://www.investinkids.ca/content/documents/parent_poll_10_29_02.pdf

O'Leary, A. (1990). Stress, emotion, and human immune function. *Psychological Bulletin, 108,* 363–382.

O'Leary, K.D., & Smith, D.A. (1991). Marital interactions. *Annual Review of Psychology, 42,* 191–212.

O'Leary, S., Slep, A.S., & Reid, M. (1999). A longitudinal study of mothers' overreactive discipline and toddlers' externalizing behavior. *Journal of Abnormal Child Psychology, 27,* 331–341.

Olin, J., & Zelinski, E. (1997). Age differences in calibration of comprehension. *Educational Gerontology, 23,* 67–77.

Oller, D.K. (1981). Infant vocalizations: Exploration and reflectivity. In R.E. Stark (Ed.), *Language behavior in infancy and early childhood* (pp. 85–104). New York: Elsevier North-Holland.

Oller, D., Cobo-Lewis, A., & Eilers, R. (1998). Phonological translation in bilingual and monolingual children. *Applied Psycholinguistics, 19,* 259–278.

Olson, H.C., Sampson, P.D., Barr, H., Streissguth, A.P., & Bookstein, F.L. (1992). Prenatal exposure to alcohol and school problems in late childhood: A longitudinal prospective study. *Development and Psychopathology, 4,* 341–359.

Olson, J.M., Vernon, P.A., Aitken Harris, J., & Jang, K.L. (2001). The heritability of attitudes: A study of twins. *Journal of Personality and Social Psychology, 80*(6), 845–860.

Olson, S.L., Bates, J.E., & Kaskie, B. (1992). Caregiver-infant interaction antecedents of children's school-age cognitive ability. *Merrill-Palmer Quarterly, 38,* 309–330.

Oman, D., & Reed, D. (1998). Religion and mortality among the community-dwelling elderly. *American Journal of Public Health, 88,* 1469–1475.

Oman, D., Thoresen, C., & McMahon, K. (1999). Volunteerism and mortality among the community-dwelling elderly. *Journal of Health Psychology, 4,* 301–316.

O'Neill, D.K., Astington, J.W., & Flavell, J.H. (1992). Young children's understanding of the role that sensory experiences play in knowledge acquisition. *Child Development, 63,* 474–490.

Onyskiw, J.E., Harrison, M.J., & Magill-Evans, J.E. (1997). Past childhood experiences and current parent-infant interactions. *Western Journal of Nursing Research, 19,* 501–518.

Optimism can mean life for heart patients and pessimism death, study says (1994a, April 16). *New York Times,* p. 12.

Orr, W.C., & Sohal, R.S. (1994). Extension of life-span by overexpression of superoxide dismutase and catalase in *Drosophila melanogaster. Science, 263,* 1128–1130.

Orth-Gomér, K., Rosengren, A., & Wilhelmsen, L. (1993). Lack of social support and incidence of coronary heart disease in middle-aged Swedish men. *Psychosomatic Medicine, 55,* 37–43.

Orwoll, L., & Perlmutter, M. (1990). The study of wise persons: Integrating a personality perspective. In R.J. Sternberg (Ed.), *Wisdom: Its nature, origins, and development* (pp. 160–180). Cambridge, England: Cambridge University Press.

Ostoja, E., McCrone, E., Lehn, L., Reed, T., & Sroufe, L.A. (1995, March). *Representations of close relationships in adolescence: Longitudinal antecedents from infancy through childhood.* Paper presented at the biennial meetings of the Society for Research in Child Development, Indianapolis, IN.

Owens, G., Crowell, J.A., Pan, H., Treboux, D., O'Connor, E., & Waters, E. (1995). The prototype hypothesis and the origins of attachment working models: Adult relationships with parents and romantic partners. *Monographs of the Society for Research in Child Development, 60*(244, No. 2–3), 216–233.

Ozman, H.A., & Craver, S.M. (1986). *Philosophical foundations of education.* Columbus, OH: Merrill.

Paarlberg, K., Vingerhoets, A.J., Passchier, J., Dekker, G., & van Geign, H. (1995). Psychosocial factors and pregnancy outcome: A review with emphasis on methodological issues. *Journal of Psychosomatic Research, 39,* 563–595.

Pacheco, C. (1999). Alcoholism and work: Representations of masculinity. *PSICO, 30,* 185–204.

Paden, S.L., & Buehler, C. (1995). Coping with the dual-income lifestyle. *Journal of Marriage and the Family, 57,* 101–110.

Paediatrics & Child Health (1999). Reducing the risk of sudden infant death in Canada (Reference No. CPS98-01). *Paediatrics & Child Health, 4*(3), 223–224.

Paffenbarger, R.S., Hyde, R.T., Wing, A.L., & Hsieh, C. (1987). Physical activity, all-cause mortality, and longevity of college alumni. *New England Journal of Medicine, 314,* 605–613.

Pagani, L., Boulerice, B., Tremblay, R., & Vitaro, F. (1997). Behavioural development in children of divorce and remarriage. *Journal of Child Psychology & Psychiatry & Allied Disciplines, 38,* 769–781.

Paik, H., & Comstock, G. (1994). The effects of television violence on antisocial behavior: A meta-analysis. *Communication Research, 21,* 516–546.

Painter, M., & Bergman, I. (1998). Neurology. In R. Behrman & R. Kliegman (Eds.), *Nelson essentials of pediatrics* (3rd ed., pp. 694–745). Philadelphia: W.B. Saunders.

Pajares, F., & Graham, L. (1999). Self-efficacy, motivation constructs, and mathematics performance of entering middle school students. *Contemporary Educational Psychology, 24,* 124–139.

Pajares, F., & Valiante, G. (1999). Grade level and gender differences in the writing self-beliefs of middle school students. *Contemporary Educational Psychology, 24,* 390–405.

Paley, V. (1986). *Mollie is three: Growing up in school.* Chicago: University of Chicago Press.

Palla, B., & Litt, I.R. (1988). Medical complications of eating disorders in adolescents. *Pediatrics, 81,* 613–623.

Palmore, E. (1981). *Social patterns in normal aging: Findings from the Duke Longitudinal Study.* Durham, NC: Duke University Press.

Palmore, E.B. (1990). *Ageism: Negative and positive.* New York: Springer.

Palmore, E.B., Burchett, B.M., Fillenbaum, G.G., George, L.K., & Wallman, L.M. (1985). *Retirement. Causes and consequences.* New York: Springer.

Palmore, E.B., & Cleveland, W. (1976). Aging, terminal decline, and terminal drop. *Journal of Gerontology, 31,* 76–81.

Papadimitropoulos, E.A., Coyte, P.C., Josse, R.G., & Greenwood, C.E. (1997). Current and projected rates of hip fracture in Canada. *Canadian Medical Association Journal, 157*(10), 1357–1363.

Papousek, H., & Papousek, M. (1991). Innate and cultural guidance of infants' integrative competencies: China, the United States, and Germany. In M.H. Bornstein (Ed.), *Cultural approaches to parenting* (pp. 23–44). Hillsdale, NJ: Erlbaum.

Parault, S., & Schwanenflugel, P. (2000). The development of conceptual categories of attention during the elementary school years. *Journal of Experimental Child Psychology, 75,* 245–262.

Pargament, K., Koenig, H., & Perez, L. (2000). The many methods of religious coping: Development and initial validation of the RCOPE. *Journal of Clinical Psychology, 56,* 519–543.

Pargament, K., Smith, B., Koenig, H., & Perez, L. (1998). Patterns of positive and negative religious coping with major life stressors. *Journal for the Scientific Study of Religion, 37,* 710–724.

Parham, T. (1989). Cycles of psychological Nigrescence. *The Counseling Psychologist, 17*(2), 187–226.

Park, J. (2003). Adolescent self-concept and health into adulthood (Catalogue No. 82-003). *Health Reports, 14*(Supplement), 41–52.

Parke, R.D., & Tinsley, B.R. (1981). The father's role in infancy: Determinants of involvement in caregiving and play. In M.E. Lamb (Ed.), *The role of the father in child development* (2nd ed., pp. 429–458). New York: Wiley.

Parker, R. (1999). Reminiscence as continuity: Comparison of young and older adults. *Journal of Clinical Geropsychology, 5,* 147–157.

Parks, M., & Roberts, L. (1998). "Making MOOsic": The development of personal relationships on line and a comparison to their off-line counterparts. *Journal of Social & Personal Relationships, 15,* 517–537.

Parmelee, A.H., Jr., Wenner, W.H., & Schulz, H.R. (1964). Infant sleep patterns from birth to 16 weeks of age. *Journal of Pediatrics, 65,* 576–582.

Parnes, H.S., & Sommers, D.G. (1994). Shunning retirement: Work experience of men in their seventies and early eighties. *Journals of Gerontology: Social Sciences, 49,* S117–124.

Pascarella, E. (1999). The development of critical thinking: Does college make a difference? *Journal of College Student Development, 40,* 562–569.

Pascarella, E., & Terenzi, P. (1991). *How college affects students: Findings and insights from twenty years of research.* San Francisco: Jossey-Bass.

Pascual-Leone, J. (1987). Organismic processes for Neo-Piagetian theories: A dialectical causal account of cognitive development. *International Journal of Psychology, 22,* 531–570.

Patrick, D.M., Wong, T., & Jordan, R.I. (2000). Sexually transmitted infections in Canada: Recent resurgence threatens national goals. *The Canadian Journal of Sexuality, 9*(3), 149–168.

Patten, S.B. (2000). Incidence of major depression in Canada. *Canadian Medical Association Journal, 163*(6), 714–715.

Patterson, C. (1994). Screening for cognitive impairment in the elderly. In Health Canada, *The Canadian guide to clinical preventive health care* (Section 11, Chapter 75). Ottawa, ON: Health Canada. Retrieved December 27, 2001 from http://www.hc-sc.gc.ca/hppb/healthcare/pubs/clinical_preventive/pdf/s11c75e.pdf

Patterson, C. (1997). Children of lesbian and gay parents. *Advances in Clinical Child Psychology, 19,* 235–282.

Patterson, G.R., Capaldi, D., & Bank, L. (1991). An early starter model for predicting delinquency. In D.J. Pepler & K.H. Rubin (Eds.), *The development and treatment of childhood aggression* (pp. 139–168). Hillsdale, NJ: Erlbaum.

Patterson, G.R., DeBarsyshe, B.D., & Ramsey, E. (1989). A developmental perspective on antisocial behavior. *American Psychologist, 44,* 329–335.

Patterson, M. & Werker, J.F. (1999). Matching phonetic information in face and voice is robust in 4.5-month old infants. *Infant Behavior and Development, 22*(2), 237–247.

Pauen, S. (2000). Early differentiation within the animate domain: Are humans something special? *Journal of Experimental Child Psychology, 75,* 134–151.

Paxton, S.J., Wertheim, E.H., Gibbons, K., Szmukler, G.I., Hillier, L., & Petrovich, J.L. (1991). Body image satisfaction, dieting beliefs, and weight loss behaviors in adolescent girls and boys. *Journal of Youth and Adolescence, 20,* 361–379.

Pearce, P. (1997). Postpartum depression more than "the blues." *Canadian Journal of Continuing Medical Education, 9*(2), 31–5.

Pearlin, L.I., Aneshensel, C.S., Mullan, J., & Whitlatch, C.J. (1996). Caregiving and its social support. In R.H. Binstock & L.K. George (Eds.), *Handbook of aging and the social sciences* (4th ed., pp. 283–302). San Diego, CA: Academic Press.

Pease-Alvarez, L. (1993). *Moving in and out of bilingualism: Investigating native language maintenance and shift in Mexican-descent children.* Research Report. Washington, DC: National Council on Bilingual Education.

Pedersen, N.L., & Harris, J.R. (1990). Developmental behavioral genetics and successful aging. In P.B. Baltes & M.M. Baltes (Eds.), *Successful aging* (pp. 359–380). Cambridge, England: Cambridge University Press.

Pederson, D.R., Gleason, K.E., Moran, G., & Bento, S. (1998). Maternal attachment representations, maternal sensitivity, and the infant-mother attachment relationship. *Developmental Psychology, 34,* 925–933.

Pederson, D.R., & Moran, G. (1995). A categorical description of infant-mother relationships in the home and its relation to Q-sort measures of infant-mother interaction. *Monographs of the Society for Research in Child Development, 60*(244, Nos. 2–3), 111–132.

Pederson, D., & Moran, G. (1996). Expressions of the attachment relationship outside of the Strange Situation. *Child Development, 67,* 915–927.

Pederson, D.R., Moran, G., Sitko, C., Campbell, K., Ghesquire, K., & Acton, H. (1990). Maternal sensitivity and the security of infant-mother attachment: A Q-sort study. *Child Development, 61,* 1974–1983.

Pedlow, R., Sanson, A., Prior, M., & Oberklaid, F. (1993). Stability of maternally reported temperament from infancy to 8 years. *Developmental Psychology, 29,* 998–1007.

Peigneux, P., & van der Linden, M. (1999). Influence of ageing and educational level on the prevalence of body-part-as-objects in normal subjects. *Journal of Clinical & Experimental Neuropsychology, 21,* 547–552.

Peisner-Feinberg, E.S. (1995, March). *Developmental outcomes and the relationship to quality of child care experiences.* Paper presented at the biennial meetings of the Society for Research in Child Development, Indianapolis, IN.

Pelligrini, A., & Smith, P. (1998). Physical activity play: The nature and function of a neglected aspect of play. *Child Development, 69,* 577–598.

Peplau, L.A. (1991). Lesbian and gay relationships. In J.C. Gonsiorek & J.D. Weinrich (Eds.), *Homosexuality: Research implications for public policy* (pp. 177–196). Newbury Park, CA: Sage.

Pepler, D.J. & Craig, W.M. (1995). A peek behind the fence: Naturalistic observations of aggressive children with remote audiovisual recording. *Developmental Psychology, 31(4),* 548–553.

Pérez, C.E. (2003). Children who become active. *Supplement to Health Reports, 2003* (Catalogue No. 82-003). Ottawa, ON: Statistics Canada.

Perho, H., & Korhonen, M. (1999). Coping in work and marriage at the onset of middle age. *Psykologia, 34,* 115–127.

Perlman, M., & Ross, H.S. (1997). The benefits of parent intervention in children's disputes: An examination of concurrent changes in children's fighting styles. *Child Development, 64,* 690–700.

Perls, T. (1999). *The New England Centenarian Study.* Harvard Medical School [Online article]. Retrieved February 7, 2001 from http://www.med.harvard.edu/programs/nccs/studies.html

Perls, T., Silver, M., and Lauerman, J. (1998). *Living to 100: Lessons in living to your maximum potential at any age.* Cambridge, MA: Harvard University Press.

Perry, B.D. (2001). The neuroarcheology of childhood maltreatment: The neurodevelopmental costs of adverse childhood events In K. Franey, R. Geffner, & R. Falconer (Eds), *The cost of maltreatment: Who pays? We all do* (pp. 15–37). San Diego, CA: Family Violence and Sexual Assault Institute.

Perry, B.D. (2002). Stress, trauma and post-traumatic stress disorders in children: An introduction. Houston, TX: ChildTrauma Academy. Retrieved February 7, 2004, from http://www.childtrauma.org/CTAMATERIALS/PTSDfn_03_v2.pdf

Perry, B.D., Pollard, R., Blakely, T., Baker, W., & Vigilante, D. (1995). Childhood trauma, the neurobiology of adaptation and 'use-dependent' development of the brain: How "states" become "traits." *Infant Mental Health Journal, 16(4),* 271–291.

Peskin, J. (1992). Ruse and representations: On children's ability to conceal information. *Developmental Psychology, 28(1),* 84–89.

Petersen, A.C. (1987). The nature of biological-psychosocial interactions: The sample case of early adolescence. In R.M. Lerner & T.T. Foch (Eds.), *Biological-psychosocial interactions in early adolescence* (pp. 35–62). Hillsdale, NJ: Erlbaum.

Petersen, A.C., Compas, B.E., Brooks-Gunn, J., Stemmler, M., Ey, S., & Grant, K.E. (1993). Depression in adolescence. *American Psychologist, 48,* 155–168.

Peterson, C. (1999). Grandfathers' and grandmothers' satisfaction with the grandparenting role: Seeking new answers to old questions. *International Journal of Aging & Human Development, 49,* 61–78.

Peterson, C. (2002). Children's long-term memory for autobiographical events. *Developmental Review, 22(3),* 370–402.

Peterson, C., & Biggs, M. (1997). Interviewing children about trauma: Problems with "specific" questions. *Journal of Traumatic Stress, 10(2),* 279–290.

Peterson, C., Dowden, C., & Tobin, J. (1999). Interviewing preschoolers: Comparisons of yes/no and wh- questions. *Law and Human Behavior, 23(5),* 539–555.

Peterson, C., & Grant, M. (2001). Forced-choice: Are forensic interviewers asking the right questions? *Canadian Journal of Behavioural Science, 33(2),* 118–127.

Peterson, C., Moores, L., & White, G. (2001). Recounting the same events again and again: Children's consistency across multiple interviews. *Applied Cognitive Psychology, 15(4),* 353–371.

Peterson, C., & Parsons, B. (in press). Across the preverbal to verbal memory gap: Can former one-year-olds recall medical emergencies five years later?

Peterson, C., & Rideout, R. (1998). Memory for medical emergencies experienced by 1- and 2-year-olds. *Developmental Psychology, 34(5),* 1059–1072.

Peterson, C., Seligman, M.E.P., & Vaillant, G.E. (1988). Pessimistic explanatory style is a risk factor for physical illness: A thirty-five-year longitudinal study. *Journal of Personality and Social Psychology, 55,* 23–27.

Peterson, C.C., & Siegal, M. (1995). Deafness, conversation and theory of mind. *Journal of Child Psychology and Psychiatry, 36,* 459–474.

Peterson, C., & Siegal, M. (1999). Representing inner worlds: Theory of mind in autistic, deaf, and normal hearing children. *Psychological Science, 10,* 126–129.

Peterson, C., & Whalen, N. (2001). Five years later: Children's memory for medical emergencies. *Applied Cognitive Psychology, 15(7),* 7–24.

Peterson, L., Ewigman, B., & Kivlahan, C. (1993). Judgments regarding appropriate child supervision to prevent injury: The role of environmental risk and child age. *Child Development, 64,* 934–950.

Petitto, L.A. (1988). "Language" in the prelinguistic child. In F.S. Kessell (Ed.), *The development of language and language researchers: Essays in honor of Roger Brown* (pp. 187–222). Hillsdale, NJ: Erlbaum.

Pettito, L.A., & Holowka, S. (2002). Evaluating attributions of delay and confusion in young bilinguals: Special insights from infants acquiring a signed and spoken language. *Sign Language Studies, 3(1),* 4–34.

Petitto, L.A., Holowka, S., Sergio, L.E., Levy, B., & Ostry, D. (2004). Baby hands that move to the rhythm of language: Hearing babies acquiring sign languages babble silently on the hands. *Cognition, 93(1),* 43–73.

Petitto, L.A., & Marentette, P (1991). Babbling in the manual mode: Evidence for the ontology of language. *Science 251,* 1483–1496.

Pettingale, K.W., Morris, T., Greer, S., & Haybittle, J.L. (1985). Mental attitudes to cancer: An additional prognostic factor. *Lancet, 85.*

Pettit, G.S., Clawson, M.A., Dodge, K.A., & Bates, J.E. (1996). Stability and change in peer-rejected status: The role of child behavior, parenting, and family ecology. *Merrill-Palmer Quarterly, 42,* 295–318.

Pettit, G., Laird, R., Bates, J., & Dodge, K. (1997). Patterns of after-school care in middle childhood: Risk factors and developmental outcomes. *Merrill-Palmer Quarterly, 43,* 515–538.

Phelps, L., Wallace, N., & Bontrager, A. (1997). Risk factors in early child development: Is prenatal cocaine/polydrug exposure a key variable? *Psychology in the Schools, 34,* 245–252.

Phillips, D., Schwean, V., & Saklofske, D. (1997). Treatment effect of a school-based cognitive-behavioral program for aggressive children. *Canadian Journal of School Psychology, 13,* 60–67.

Phillips, S.K., Bruce, S.A., Newton, D., & Woledge, R.C. (1992). The weakness of old age is not due to failure of muscle activation. *Journals of Gerontology: Medical Sciences, 47,* M45–49.

Phillipsen, L. (1999). Associations between age, gender, and group acceptance and three components of friendship quality. *Journal of Early Adolescence, 19,* 438–464.

Phinney, J. (1993). A three stage model of ethnic identity development in adolescents. In M.E. Bernal & G.P. Knight (Eds.), *Ethnic identity: Formation and transmission among Hispanic and other minorities* (pp. 61–80). Albany, NY: State University of New York Press.

Phinney, J.S., & Alipuria, L.L. (1996). At the interface of cultures: Multi-ethnic/multiracial high school and college students. *Journal of Social Psychology, 136(2),* 139–158.

Phinney, J.S., Ferguson, D.L., & Tate, J.D. (1997). Intergroup attitudes among ethnic minority adolescents: A causal model. *Child Development, 68(5),* 955–969.

Phinney, J.S., & Kohatsu, E.L. (1997). Ethnic and racial identity development and mental health. In J. Schulenberg, J.L. Maggs, & K. Hurrelmann (eds.), *Health risks and developmental transitions during adolescence* (pp. 420–443). Cambridge, UK: Cambridge University Press.

Phinney, J.S., Ong, A., & Madden, T. (2000). Cultural values and intergenerational value discrepancies in immigrant and non-immigrant families. *Child Development, 71*(2), 528–539.

Piaget, J. (1932). *The moral judgment of the child.* New York: Macmillan.

Piaget, J. (1952). *The origins of intelligence in children.* New York: International Universities Press.

Piaget, J. (1954). *The construction of reality in the child.* New York: Basic Books. (Originally published 1937.)

Piaget, J. (1965). *The moral judgment of the child.* New York: Free Press.

Piaget, J. (1970). Piaget's theory. In P.H. Mussen (Ed.), *Carmichael's manual of child psychology* (Vol. 1, 3rd ed., pp. 703–732). New York: Wiley.

Piaget, J. (1977). *The development of thought: Equilibration of cognitive structures.* New York: Viking.

Piaget, J., & Inhelder, B. (1959). *La gènese des structures logiques élémentaires: Classifications et sériations [The origin of elementary logical structures: Classification and seriation].* Neuchâtel, Switzerland: Delachaux et Niestlé.

Piaget, J., & Inhelder, B. (1969). *The psychology of the child.* New York: Basic Books.

Pianta, R.C., & Egeland, B. (1994). Predictors of instability in children's mental test performance at 24, 48, and 96 months. *Intelligence, 18,* 145–163.

Pianta, R., Egeland, B., & Erickson, M.F. (1989). The antecedents of maltreatment: Results of the Mother-Child Interaction Research Project. In D. Cicchetti & V. Carlson (Eds.), *Child maltreatment* (pp. 203–253). Cambridge, England: Cambridge University Press.

Pianta, R.C., Steinberg, M.S., & Rollins, K.B. (1995). Teacher-child relationships and deflections in children's classroom adjustment. *Development and Psychopathology, 7,* 295–312.

Picard, C. (1999). The level of competition as a factor for the development of eating disorders in female collegiate athletes. *Journal of Youth and Adolescence, 28,* 583–594.

Pies, R. (2003). *Body image.* Irvine, CA: Continuing Medical Education. Inc. Retrieved July 12, 2004 from http://www.mhsource.com/expert/exp1090803c.html

Pilgrim, C., Luo, Q., Urberg, K., & Fang, X. (1999). Influence of peers, parents, and individual characteristics on adolescent drug use in two cultures. *Merrill-Palmer Quarterly, 45,* 85–107.

Pillard, R.C., & Bailey, J.M. (1995). A biologic perspective on sexual orientation. *The Psychiatric Clinics of North America, 18*(1), 71–84.

Pillemer, K., & Suitor, J.J. (1990). Prevention of elder abuse. In R. Ammerman & M. Hersen (Eds.), *Treatment of family violence: A sourcebook* (pp. 406–422). New York: Wiley.

Pillemer, K., & Suitor, J.J. (1992). Violence and violent feelings: What causes them among family caregivers? *Journals of Gerontology: Social Sciences, 47,* S165–172.

Pillow, B. (1999). Children's understanding of inferential knowledge. *Journal of Genetic Psychology, 160,* 419–428.

Pinker, S. (1994). *The language instinct: How the mind creates language.* New York: Morrow.

Pinker, S. (1997). *How the mind works.* New York: Norton.

Pinker, S. (2002). *The blank slate: The modern denial of human nature.* New York: Viking.

Pinquart, M., & Soerensen, S. (2000). Influences of socioeconomic status, social network, and competence on subjective well-being in later life: A meta-analysis. *Psychology & Aging, 15,* 187–224.

Plante, T., & Pardini, D. (2000, August). *Religious denomination affiliation and psychological health: Results from a substance abuse population.* Paper presented at the annual meeting of the American Psychological Association. Washington, DC.

Plaud, J., Plaud, D., & von Duvillard, S. (1999). Human behavioral momentum in a sample of older adults. *Journal of General Psychology, 126,* 165–175.

Pleck, J. (1977). The work-family role system. *Social Problems, 24,* 417–427.

Pless, B. & Millar, W. (2000). *Unintentional injuries in childhood: Results from Canadian health surveys* (Catalogue No. H39-523/2000E). Ottawa, ON: Health Canada. Retrieved November 22, 2001 from http://www.hc-sc.gc.ca/hppb/childhood-youth/cyfh/safe_and_supportive/resources/Unintentional_E.pdf

Plomin, R. (1990). *Nature and nurture: An introduction to behavior genetics.* Pacific Grove, CA: Brooks/Cole.

Plomin, R., & DeFries, J.C. (1985). *Origins of individual differences in infancy: The Colorado Adoption Project.* Orlando, FL: Academic Press.

Plomin, R., Emde, R.N., Braungart, J.M., Campos, J., Corley, R., Fulker, D.W., Kagan, J., Reznick, J.S., Robinson, J., Zahn-Waxler, C., & DeFries, J.C. (1993). Genetic change and continuity from fourteen to twenty months: The MacArthur longitudinal twin study. *Child Development, 64,* 1354–1376.

Plomin, R., & McClearn, G.E. (1990). Human behavioral genetics of aging. In J.E. Birren & K.W. Schaie (Eds.), *Handbook of the psychology of aging* (3rd ed., pp. 67–79). San Diego, CA: Academic Press.

Plomin, R., & Rende, R. (1991). Human behavioral genetics. *Annual Review of Psychology, 42,* 161–190.

Plowman, S.A., Drinkwater, B.L., & Horvath, S.M. (1979). Age and aerobic power in women: A longitudinal study. *Journal of Gerontology, 34,* 512–520.

Polivy, J., & Herman, P. (2002). Causes of eating disorders. *Annual Review of Psychology, 53,* 187–213.

Polka, L., & Werker, J.F. (1994). Developmental changes in perception of nonnative vowel contrasts. *Journal of Experimental Psychology: Human Perception and Performance, 20,* 421–435.

Pollack, J.M. (1979/1980). Correlates of death anxiety: A review of empirical studies. *Omega, 10,* 97–121.

Pollitt, E., & Gorman, K.S. (1994). Nutritional deficiencies as developmental risk factors. In C.A. Nelson (Ed.), *The Minnesota Symposia on Child Development* (Vol. 27, pp. 121–144). Hillsdale, NJ: Erlbaum.

Polo, M., Escera, D., Gual, A., & Grau, C. (1999). Mismatch negativity and auditory sensory memory in chronic alcoholics. *Clinical & Experimental Research, 23,* 1744–1750.

Pomerantz, E., & Ruble, D. (1998). The role of maternal control in the development of sex differences in child self-evaluative factors. *Child Development, 69,* 458–478.

Pomerleau, A., Malcuit, G., Turgeon, L., & Cossette, L. (1997). Effects of labelled gender on vocal communication of young women with 4-month-old infants. *International Journal of Psychology, 32,* 65–72.

Ponds, R., Commissaris, K., & Jolles, J. (1997). Prevalence and covariates of subjective forgetfulness in a normal population in the Netherlands. *International Journal of Aging and Human Development, 45,* 207–221.

Ponomareva, N., Fokin, V., Selesneva, N., & Voskresenskaea, N. (1998). Possible neurophysiological markers of genetic predisposition to Alzheimer's disease. *Dementia & Geriatric Cognitive Disorders, 9,* 267–273.

Poole, L. (1998). Attributions of responsibility for depression of menopausal women. *TCA Journal, 26,* 115–122.

Porter, R., Making, J., Davis, L., & Christensen, K. (1992). Breast-fed infants respond to olfactory clues from their own mother and unfamiliar lactating females. *Infant Behavior and Development, 15,* 85–93.

Portnoi, V. (1999). Progressing from disease prevention to health promotion. *Journal of the American Medical Association, 282,* 1813.

Posner, J., & Vandell, D. (1994). Low-income children's after-school care: Are there beneficial effects of after-school programs? *Child Development, 65,* 440–456.

Posthuma, W.F.M., Westendorp, R.G.J., & Vandenbroucke, J.P. (1994). Cardioprotective effect of hormone replacement therapy in postmenopausal women: Is the evidence biased? *British Medical Journal, 308,* 1268–1269.

Poulin, F., & Boivin, M. (1999). Proactive and reactive aggression and boys' friendship quality in mainstream classrooms. *Journal of Emotional & Behavioral Disorders, 7,* 168–177.

Poulin, F., & Boivin, M. (2000). The role of proactive and reactive aggression in the formation and development of boys' friendships. *Developmental Psychology, 36,* 233–240.

Poulson, C.L., Nunes, L.R.D., & Warren, S.F. (1989). Imitation in infancy: A critical review. In H.W. Reese (Ed.), *Advances in child development and behavior* (Vol. 22, pp. 272–298). San Diego, CA: Academic Press.

Powell, B., Landon, J., Cantrell, P., Penick, E., Nickel, E., Liskow, B., Coddington, T., Campbell, J., Dale, T., Vance, M., & Rice, A. (1998). Prediction of drinking outcomes for male alcoholics after 10 to 14 years. *Alcoholism: Clinical & Experimental Research, 22,* 559–566.

Powlishta, K.K. (1995). Intergroup processes in childhood: Social categorization and sex role development. *Developmental Psychology, 31,* 781–788.

Powlishta, K.K., Serbin, L.A., Doyle, A., & White, D.R. (1994). Gender, ethnic, and body type biases: The generality of prejudice in childhood. *Developmental Psychologym, 30,* 526–536.

Prager, E. (1998). Men and meaning in later life. *Journal of Clinical Geropsychology, 4,* 191–203.

Prasad, K.N., Cole, W.C., & Hasse, G.M. (2004). Health risks of low dose ionizing radiation in humans: A review. *Experimental Biology and Medicine, 229*(5), 378–382.

Prat-Sala, M., Shillcock, R., & Sorace, A. (2000). Animacy effects on the production of object-dislocated descriptions by Catalan-speaking children. *Journal of Child Language, 27,* 97–117.

Pratt, M., Arnold, M., & Pratt, A. (1999). Predicting adolescent moral reasoning from family climate: A longitudinal study. *Journal of Early Adolescence, 19,* 148–175.

Prechtl, H.F.R., & Beintema, D.J. (1964). *The neurological examination of the full-term newborn infant: Clinics in Developmental Medicine, 12.* London: Heinemann.

Preece, M. (2003). When lone parents marry: The challenge of step-family relationships. *Transition, 33*(4), 7–10.

Prentice, A. (1994). Extended breast-feeding and growth in rural China. *Nutrition Reviews, 52,* 144–146.

Pressley, M., & Dennis-Rounds, J. (1980). Transfer of a mnemonic keyword strategy at two age levels. *Journal of Educational Psychology, 72,* 575–582.

Pressley, M., & Wharton-McDonald, R. (1997). Skilled comprehension and its development through instruction. *School Psychology Review, 26,* 448–466.

Pressman, E., DiPietro, J., Costigan, K., Shupe, A., & Johnson, T. (1998). Fetal neurobehavioral development: Associations with socioeconomic class and fetal sex. *Developmental Psychobiology, 33,* 79–91.

Price, R.H. (1992). Psychosocial impact of job loss on individuals and families. *Current Directions in Psychological Science, 1,* 9–11.

Prigerson, H., Bierhals, A., Kasl, S., Reynolds, C., et al. (1997). Traumatic grief as a risk factor for mental and physical morbidity. *American Journal of Psychiatry, 154,* 616–623.

Prigerson, H., Bridge, J., Maciejewski, P., Beery, L., Rosenheck, R., Jacobs, S., Bierhals, A., Kupfer, D., & Brent, D. (1999). Influence of traumatic grief on suicidal ideation among young adults. *American Journal of Psychiatry, 156,* 1994–1995.

Prince, A. (1998). Infectious diseases. In R. Behrman & R. Kliegman (Eds.), *Nelson essentials of pediatrics* (3rd ed., pp. 315–418). Philadelphia: W.B. Saunders.

Prinstein, M., & La Greca, A. (1999). Links between mothers' and children's social competence and associations with maternal adjustment. *Journal of Clinical Child Psychology, 28,* 197–210.

Pujol, J., Deus, J., Losilla, J., & Capdevila, A. (1999). Cerebral lateralization of language in normal left-handed people: Studies by functional MRI. *Neurology, 52,* 1038–1043.

Purnine, D., & Carey, M. (1998). Age and gender differences in sexual behavior preferences: A follow-up report. *Journal of Sex & Marital Therapy, 24,* 93–102.

Putnins, A. (1997). Victim awareness programs for delinquent youths: Effects on moral reasoning maturity. *Adolescence, 32,* 709–714.

Pynoos, J., & Golant, S. (1996). Housing and living arrangements for the elderly. In R.H. Binstock & L.K. George (Eds.), *Handbook of aging and the social sciences* (4th ed., pp. 303–324). San Diego, CA: Academic Press.

Quadagno, J., & Hardy, M.A. (1996). Work and retirement. In R.H. Binstock & L.K. George (Eds.), *Handbook of aging and the social sciences* (4th ed., pp. 325–345). San Diego, CA: Academic Press.

Quick, H., & Moen, P. (1998). Gender, employment and retirement quality: A life course approach to the differential experiences of men and women. *Journal of Occupational Health Psychology, 3,* 44–64.

Quigley, D., & Schatz, M. (1999). Men and women and their responses in spousal bereavement. *Hospice Journal, 14,* 65–78.

Raaijmakers, Q., Verbogt, T., & Vollebergh, W. (1998). Moral reasoning and political beliefs of Dutch adolescents and young adults. *Journal of Social Issues, 54,* 531–546.

Rabasca, L. (1999, October). Ultra-thin magazine models found to have little negative effect on adolescent girls. *APA Monitor Online, 30.* Retrieved January 16, 2001 from http://www.apa.org/monitor/oct99

Ragnarsdottir, H., Simonsen, H., & Plunkett, K. (1999). The acquisition of past tense morphology in Icelandic and Norwegian children: An experimental study. *Journal of Child Language, 26,* 577–618.

Rahman, O., Strauss, J., Gertler, P., Ashley, D., & Fox, K. (1994). Gender differences in adult health: An international comparison. *The Gerontologist, 34,* 463–469.

Raja, S.N., McGee, R., & Stanton, W.R. (1992). Perceived attachments to parents and peers and psychological well-being in adolescence. *Journal of Youth and Adolescence, 21,* 471–485.

Ramey, C.T. (1992). High-risk children and IQ: Altering intergenerational patterns. *Intelligence, 16,* 239–256.

Ramey, C.T. (1993). A rejoinder to Spitz's critique of the Abecedarian experiment. *Intelligence, 17,* 25–30.

Ramey, C.T., & Campbell, F.A. (1987). The Carolina Abecedarian Project: An educational experiment concerning human malleability. In J.J. Gallagher & C.T. Ramey (Eds.), *The malleability of children* (pp. 127–140). Baltimore: Paul H. Brookes.

Ramey, C., & Ramey, S. (1998). Early intervention and early experience. *American Psychologist, 53,* 109–120.

Rao G., & Rao, S. (1997). Sector and age differences in productivity. *Social Science International, 13,* 51–56.

Raskind, M.A., & Peskind, E.R. (1992). Alzheimer's disease and other dementing disorders. In J.E. Birren, R.B. Sloane, & G.D. Cohen (Eds.), *Handbook of mental health and aging* (2nd ed., pp. 478–515). San Diego, CA: Academic Press.

Rathje, K. (2003). Retirement trends in Canada. *Economica Ltd.; The Expert Witness Newsletter, 8*(1). Retrieved September 2, 2004 from http://www.economica.ca/ew81p2.htm

Ravanera, Z.R., & Rajulton, F. (1998, April 2–4). *Variations in the length of male parenting: Evidence from the 1995 GSS Canada* (Discussion Paper No. 98-6). Paper presented at the Annual Meeting of the Population Association of America, Chicago, IL. Retrieved December 21, 2001 from http://www.ssc.uwo.ca/sociology/popstudies/dp/dp98-6.pdf

Ray, B. (1999). *Home schooling on the threshold: A survey of research at the dawn of the new millennium.* Washington, DC: Home Education Research Institute.

Reed, G.M., Kemeny, M.E., Taylor, S.E., Wang, H.J., & Visscher, B.R. (1994). Realistic acceptance as a predictor of decreased survival time in gay men with AIDS. *Health Psychology, 13,* 299–307.

Reed, M. (1998). Predicting grief symptomatology among the suddenly bereaved. *Suicide & Life-Threatening Behavior, 28,* 285–301.

Regier, D.A., Boyd, J.H., Burke, J.D., Rae, D.S., Myers, J.K., Kramer, M., Robins, L.N., George, L.K., Karno, M., & Locke, B.Z.

(1988). One-month prevalence of mental disorders in the United States. *Archives of General Psychiatry, 45,* 977–986.

Reich, J.W., Zautra, A.J., & Guarnaccia, C.A. (1989). Effects of disability and bereavement on the mental health and recovery of older adults. *Psychology and Aging, 4,* 57–65.

Reichle, B., & Gefke, M. (1998). Justice of conjugal divisions of labor—you can't always get what you want. *Social Justice Research, 11,* 271–287.

Remafedi, G., Farrow, J.A., & Deisher, R.W. (1991). Risk factors for attempted suicide in gay and bisexual youth. *Pediatrics, 87,* 869–875.

Remafedi, G., French, S., Story, M., Resnick, M., & Blum, R. (1998). The relationship between suicide risk and sexual orientation: Results of a population-based study. *American Journal of Public Health, 88,* 57–60.

Remafedi, G., Resnick, M., Blum, R., & Harris, L. (1998). Demography of sexual orientation in adolescents. *Pediatrics, 89,* 714–721.

Rendell, P., & Thomson, D. (1999). Aging and prospective memory: Differences between naturalistic and laboratory tasks. *Journals of Gerontology, 54B,* P256–P269.

Renouf, A.G., & Harter, S. (1990). Low self-worth and anger as components of the depressive experience in young adolescents. *Development and Psychopathology, 2,* 293–310.

Rexroat, C., & Shehan, C. (1987). The family life cycle and spouses' time in housework. *Journal of Marriage and the Family, 49,* 737–750.

Reynolds, A.J., & Bezruczko, N. (1993). School adjustment of children at risk through fourth grade. *Merrill-Palmer Quarterly, 39,* 457–480.

Reynolds, D. (1992). School effectiveness and school improvement: An updated review of the British literature. In D. Reynolds & P. Cuttance (Eds.), *School effectiveness: Research, policy, and prejudice.* London: Cassell.

Rholes, W.S., & Ruble, D.N. (1984). Children's understanding of dispositional characteristics of others. *Child Development, 55,* 550–560.

Rholes, W., Simpson, J., Blakely, B., Lanigan, L., & Allen, D. (1997). Adult attachment styles, the desire to have children, and working models of parenthood. *Journal of Personality, 65,* 357–385.

Rice, M.L., Huston, A.C., Truglio, R., & Wright, J. (1990). Words from "Sesame Street": Learning vocabulary while viewing. *Developmental Psychology, 26,* 421–428.

Richards, M.H., & Duckett, E. (1994). The relationship of maternal employment to early adolescent daily experience with and without parents. *Child Development, 65,* 225–236.

Richardson, G.S. (1990). Circadian rhythms and aging. In E.R. Scheider & J.W. Rowe (Eds.), *Handbook of the biology of aging* (3rd ed., pp. 275–305). San Diego, CA: Academic Press.

Richardson, G., Conroy, M., & Day, N. (1996). Prenatal cocaine exposure: Effects on the development of school-aged children. *Neurotoxicology & Teratology, 18,* 627–634.

Richardson, J.L., Zarnegar, Z., Bisno, B., & Levine, A. (1990). Psychosocial status at initiation of cancer treatment and survival. *Journal of Psychosomatic Research, 34,* 189–201.

Rich-Edwards, J.W., Manson, J.E., Hennekens, C.H., & Buring, J.E. (1995). The primary prevention of coronary heart disease in women. *New England Journal of Medicine, 332,* 1758–1766.

Riggs, A. (1997). Men, friends, and widowhood: Towards successful aging. *Australian Journal on Ageing, 16,* 182–185.

Righetti, P. (1996). The emotional experience of the fetus: A preliminary report. *Pre- & Peri-Natal Psychology Journal, 11,* 55–65.

Rique, J., & Camino, C. (1997). Consistency and inconsistency in adolescents' moral reasoning. *International Journal of Behavioral Development, 21,* 813–836.

Risch, H.A., Jain, M., Marrett, L.D., & Howe, G.R. (1994). Dietary fat intake and risk of epithelial ovarian cancer. *Journal of the National Cancer Institute, 86,* 1409–1415.

Roberts, R.E., & Sobhan, M. (1992). Symptoms of depression in adolescence: A comparison of Anglo, African, and Hispanic Americans. *Journal of Youth and Adolescence, 21,* 639–651.

Roberts, W., & Strayer, J. (1996). Empathy, emotional expressiveness, and prosocial behavior. *Child Development, 67,* 449–470.

Robins, L.N., & McEvoy, L. (1990). Conduct problems as predictors of substance abuse. In L.N. Robins & M. Rutter (Eds.), *Straight and devious pathways from childhood to adulthood* (pp. 182–204). Cambridge, England: Cambridge University Press.

Robins, R., Caspi, A., & Moffitt, T. (2000). Two personalities, one relationship: Both partners' personality traits shape the quality of their relationship. *Journal of Personality & Social Psychology, 79,* 251–259.

Robinson, P. (2004). Youth court statistics, 2002/03 (Catalogue No. 85-002-XPE). *Juristat, 24*(2), 1–20.

Robinson-Whelen, S., & Kiecolt-Glaser, N. (1997). The importance of social versus temporal comparison appraisals among older adults. *Journal of Applied Social Psychology, 27,* 959–966.

Robitaille, D.F., Taylor, A.R., & Orpwood, G. (1996). *TIMSS-Canada report.* (Vol. 1: Grade 8). Vancouver: University of British Columbia, Department of Curriculum Studies.

Roche, A.F. (1979). Secular trends in human growth, maturation, and development. *Monographs of the Society for Research in Child Development, 44*(3–4, Serial No. 179).

Rock, A., Trainor, L., & Addison, T. (1999). Distinctive messages in infant-directed lullabies and play songs. *Developmental Psychology, 35,* 527–534.

Rockwood, K., & Stadnyk, K. (1994). The prevalence of dementia in the elderly: A review. *Canadian Journal of Psychiatry, 29,* 253–257.

Roderick, M., & Camburn, E. (1999). Risk and recovery from course failure in the early years of high school. *American Educational Research Journal, 36,* 303–343.

Rodin, J. (1986). Aging and health: Effects of the sense of control. *Science, 233,* 1271–1275.

Rodin, J. (1990). Control by any other name: Definitions, concepts, and processes. In J. Rodin, C. Schooler, & K.W. Schaie (Eds.), *Self-directedness: Cause and effects throughout the life course* (pp. 1–17). Hillsdale, NJ: Erlbaum.

Rodin, J., & Langer, E.J. (1977). Long-term effects of a control-relevant intervention with the institutionalized aged. *Journal of Personality and Social Psychology, 35,* 897–902.

Rodkin, P., Farmer, T., Pearl, R., & Van Acker, R. (2000). Heterogeneity of popular boys: Antisocial and prosocial configurations. *Developmental Psychology, 36,* 14–24.

Rodrigo, M., Janssens, J., & Ceballos, E. (1999). Do children's perceptions and attributions mediate the effects of mothers' child rearing actions? *Journal of Family Psychology, 13,* 508–522.

Rodriguez, C., Calle, E.E., Coates, R.J., Miracle-McMahil, H.L., Thun, M.J., & Heath, C.W., Jr. (1995). Estrogen replacement therapy and fatal ovarian cancer. *American Journal of Epidemiology, 141,* 828–835.

Roeser, R., & Eccles J. (1998). Adolescents' perceptions of middle school: Relation to longitudinal changes in academic and psychological adjustment. *Journal of Research on Adolescence, 8,* 123–158.

Rogers, C.R. (1961). *On becoming a person.* Boston: Houghton Mifflin.

Rogers, J.L., Rowe, D.C., & May, K. (1994). DF analysis of NLSY IQ/Achievement data: Nonshared environmental influences. *Intelligence, 19,* 157–177.

Rogers, R.L., Meyer, J.S., & Mortel, K.F. (1990). After reaching retirement age physical activity sustains cerebral perfusion and cognition. *Journal of the American Geriatric Society, 38,* 123–128.

Roggman, L.A., Langlois, J.H., Hubbs-Tait, L., & Rieser-Danner, L.A. (1994). Infant day-care, attachment, and the "file drawer problem." *Child Development, 65,* 1429–1443.

Rogoff, B. (1990). *Apprenticeship in thinking: Cognitive development in social contexts.* New York: Oxford University Press.

Rogosch, F., Cicchetti, D., & Aber, J. (1995). The role of child maltreatment in early deviations in cognitive and affective processing abilities and later peer relationship problems. *Development and Psychopathology, 7,* 591–609.

Rollins, B.C., & Feldman, H. (1970). Marital satisfaction over the family life cycle. *Journal of Marriage and the Family, 32,* 20–27.

Rolls, E. (2000). Memory systems in the brain. *Annual Review of Psychology, 51,* 599–630.

Romano, E., Baillargeon, R.H., & Tremblay, R.E. (2002). *Prevalence of hyperactivity-impulsivity and inattention among Canadian children: Findings from the first data collection cycle (1994–1995) of the National Longitudinal Survey of Children and Youth* (Catalogue No. RH63-1/561-01-03E). Ottawa, ON: Human Resources Development Canada.

Rose, A.J., & Montemayor, R. (1994). The relationship between gender role orientation and perceived self-competence in male and female adolescents. *Sex Roles, 31,* 579–595.

Rose, D.P. (1993). Diet, hormones, and cancer. *Annual Review of Public Health, 14,* 1–17.

Rose, R.J. (1995). Genes and human behavior. *Annual Review of Psychology, 56,* 625–654.

Rose, S.A., & Feldman, J.F. (1995). Prediction of IQ and specific cognitive abilities at 11 years from infancy measures. *Developmental Psychology, 31,* 685–696.

Rose, S.A., Feldman, J.F., & Janowsky, J.J. (2001). Attention and recognition memory in the 1st year of life: A longitudinal study of preterm and full-term infants. *Developmental Psychology, 37*(1), 135–151.

Rosenbaum, J.E. (1984). *Career mobility in a corporate hierarchy.* New York: Academic Press.

Rosenberg, M. (1986). Self-concept from middle childhood through adolescence. In J. Suls & A.G. Greenwald (Eds.), *Psychological perspectives on the self* (Vol. 3, pp. 107–136). Hillsdale, NJ: Erlbaum.

Rosenblith, J.F. (1992). *In the beginning* (2nd ed.). Thousand Oaks, CA: Sage.

Rosenman, R.H., & Friedman, M. (1983). Relationship of Type A behavior pattern to coronary heart disease. In H. Selye (Ed.), *Selye's guide to stress research* (Vol. 2, pp. 47–106). New York: Scientific and Academic Editions.

Rosenthal, C.J. (1987). Aging and intergenerational relations in Canada. In V.W. Marshall (Ed.). *Aging in Canada: Social perspectives* (2nd ed., Chapter 17, pp. 311–342). Markam, ON: Fitzhenry and Whiteside.

Rosenthal, C.J., & Gladstone, J. (2000). *Grandparenthood in Canada.* Ottawa, ON: The Vanier Institute of the Family. Retrieved December 21, 2001 from http://www.vifamily.ca/cft/grandpt/CONTEXT.HTM

Rosenthal, R. (1994). Interpersonal expectancy effects: A 30-year perspective. *Current Directions in Psychological Science, 3,* 176–179.

Rosow, I. (1985). Status and role change through the life cycle. In R.H. Binstock & E. Shanas (Eds.), *Handbook of aging and the social sciences* (2nd ed., pp. 62–93). New York: Van Nostrand Reinhold.

Ross, C.E. (1995). Reconceptualizing marital status as a continuum of social attachment. *Journal of Marriage and the Family, 57,* 129–140.

Ross, D. (1998a). *Child poverty in Canada: Recasting the issue.* Ottawa, ON: Canadian Council on Social Development. Retrieved September 22, 2001 from http://www.ccsd.ca/pubs/recastin.htm

Ross, D.P. (1998b). *Rethinking child poverty. Perception, 22*(1), Insight #8. Retrieved November 16, 2001 from http://www.ccsd.ca/perception/insite8.htm

Ross, D.P., Roberts, P.A., & Scott, K. (1998). *Mediating factors in child development outcomes: Children in lone-parent families* (Catalogue No. W-98-8E). Ottawa, ON: Human Resources Development Canada.

Ross, R.K., Paganini-Hill, A., Mack, T.M., & Henderson, B.E. (1987). Estrogen use and cardiovascular disease. In D.R. Mishell, Jr. (Ed.), *Menopause: Physiology and pharmacology* (pp. 209–224). Chicago: Year Book Medical Publishers.

Rossman, I. (1980). Bodily changes with aging. In E.W. Busse & D.G. Blazer (Eds.), *Handbook of geriatric psychiatry* (pp. 125–146). New York: Van Nostrand Reinhold.

Rossow, I., & Amundsen, A. (1997). Alcohol abuse and mortality: A 40-year prospective study of Norwegian conscripts. *Social Science & Medicine, 44,* 261–267.

Rossow, I., Romelsjoe, A., & Leifman, H. (1999). Alcohol abuse and suicidal behaviour in young and middle aged men: Differentiating between attempted and completed suicide. *Addiction, 94,* 1199–1207.

Rothbard, J.C., & Shaver, P.R. (1994). Continuity of attachment across the life span. In M.B. Sperling & W.H. Berman (Eds.), *Attachment in adults. Clinical and developmental perspectives* (pp. 31–71). New York: Guilford Press.

Rothbart, M., Ahadi, S., & Evans, D. (2000). Temperament and personality: Origins and outcomes. *Journal of Personality & Social Psychology, 78,* 122–135.

Rothbart, M.K., Derryberry, D., & Posner, M.I. (1994). A psychobiological approach to the development of temperament. In J.E. Bates & T.D. Wachs (Eds.), *Temperament: Individual differences at the interface of biology and behavior* (pp. 83–116). Washington, DC: American Psychological Association.

Rotheram-Borus, M.J., Rosario, M., & Koopman, C. (1991). Minority youths at high risk: Gay males and runaways. In M.E. Colten & S. Gore (Eds.), *Adolescent stress: Causes and consequences* (pp. 181–200). New York: Aldine de Gruyter.

Rotter, J. (1990). Internal versus external control of reinforcement: A case history of a variable. *American Psychologist, 45,* 489–493.

Roumeliotis, P. (2001). Colic and the newborn. Dr. Paul—Children's Health and Wellness info site. Retrieved November 12, 2001 from http://www.drpaul.com/newborn/colic.html

Rovee-Collier, C. (1993). The capacity for long-term memory in infancy. *Current Directions in Psychological Science, 2,* 130–135.

Rowe, J., & Kahn, R. (1997). Successful aging. *Gerontologist, 37,* 133–440.

Rowe, J., & Kahn, R. (1998). *Successful aging.* New York: Pantheon.

Ruben, K., Nelson, L., Hastings, P., & Asendorpt, J. (1999). The transaction between parents' perception of their children's shyness and their parenting styles. *International Journal of Behavioral Development, 23,* 937–958.

Rubin, K.H., Hymel, S., Mills, R.S.L., & Rose-Krasnor, L. (1991). Conceptualizing different developmental pathways to and from social isolation in childhood. In D. Cicchetti & S.L. Toth (Eds.), *Internalizing and externalizing expressions of dysfunction: Rochester Symposium on Developmental Psychopathology* (Vol. 2, pp. 91–122). Hillsdale, NJ: Erlbaum.

Rubin, S., & Schechter, N. (1997). Exploring the social construction of bereavement: Perceptions of adjustment and recovery in bereaved men. *American Journal of Orthopsychiatry, 67,* 279–289.

Rubinstein, R.L. (1986). *Singular paths: Old men living alone.* New York: Columbia University Press.

Ruble, D.N. (1987). The acquisition of self-knowledge: A self-socialization perspective. In N. Eisenberg (Ed.), *Contemporary topics in developmental psychology* (pp. 243–270). New York: Wiley-Interscience.

Ruble, D., & Dweck, C. (1995). Self-conceptions, person conceptions, and their development. In N. Eisenberg (Ed.), *Social development.* Thousand Oaks, CA: Sage.

Rudd, M., Viney, L., & Preston, C. (1999). The grief experienced by spousal caregivers of dementia patients: The role of place of care of patient and gender of caregiver. *International Journal of Aging & Human Development, 48,* 217–240.

Rummens, J. (2001). *Canadian identities: An interdisciplinary overview of Canadian research on identity. Commissioned by the Department of Canadian Heritage for the Ethnocultural, Racial, Religious, and Linguistic Diversity and Identity Seminar Halifax, Nova Scotia November 1–2, 2001.* Retrieved July 15, 2004 from http://canada.metropolis.net/events/ethnocultural/publications/identity_e.pdf

Rutter, M. (1983). School effects on pupil progress: Research findings and policy implications. *Child Development, 54*, 1–29.

Rutter, M. (1993). Resilience: Some conceptual considerations. *Journal of Adolescent Health Care, 14*(8), 626–631.

Rys, G., & Bear, G. (1997). Relational aggression and peer relations: Gender and developmental issues. *Merrill-Palmer Quarterly, 43*, 87–106.

Saavedra, M., Ramirez, A., & Contreras, C. (1997). Interactive interviews between elders and children: A possible procedure for improving affective state in the elderly. *Acta Psiquiatrica y Psicologica de America Latina, 43*, 63–66.

Sacco, V., & Kennedy, L. (1996). *The criminal event.* Belmont, CA: Wadsworth.

Sack, W.H., Mason, R., & Higgins, J.E. (1985). The single parent family and abusive child punishment. *American Journal of Orthopsychiatry, 55*, 252–259.

Saewyc, E., Bearinger, L., Heinz, P., Blum, R., & Resnick, M. (1998). Gender differences in health and risk behaviors among bisexual and homosexual adolescents. *Journal of Adolescent Health, 23*, 181–188.

Safety Canada Online (2001a). *Preparation and communication the key for children home alone.* Ottawa, ON: Canada Safety Council. Retrieved October 11, 2001 from http://www.safety-council.org/index.html

Safren, S., & Heimberg, R. (1999). Depression, hopelessness, suicidality, and related factors in sexual minority and heterosexual adolescents. *Journal of Consulting & Clinical Psychology, 67*, 859–866.

Safty, A. (1995). French immersion and the making of a bilingual society: A critical review and discussion. In L.W. Roberts & R.A. Clifton (eds.), *Contemporary Canadian educational issues.* Toronto: Nelson.

Sagiv, M., Vogelaere, P., Soudry, M., & Shrsam, R. (2000). Role of physical activity training in attenuation of height loss. *Gerontology, 46*, 266–270.

St. James-Roberts, I., Bowyer, J., Varghese, S., & Sawdon, J. (1994). Infant crying patterns in Manila and London. *Child: Care, Health and Development, 20*, 323–337.

Salari, S.M., & Baldwin, B.M. (2002). Verbal, physical and injurious aggression among intimate couples over time. *Journal of Family Issues, 23*(4), 523–550.

Saltaris, C., Serbin, L.A., Stack, D.M., Karp, J.A., Schwartzman, A.E., & Ledingham, J.E. (2004). Nurturing cognitive competence in preschoolers: A longitudinal study of intergenerational continuity and risk. *International Journal of Behavioral Development, 28*(20), 105–115.

Salthouse, T.A. (1991). *Theoretical perspectives on cognitive aging.* Hillsdale, NJ: Erlbaum.

Salthouse, T.A. (1996). General and specific speed mediation of adult age differences in memory. *Journals of Gerontology: Psychological Sciences, 51B*, P30–42.

Salthouse, T. (1998). Independence of age-related influences on cognitive abilities across the life span. *Developmental Psychology, 34*, 851–864.

Salthouse, T., & Czaja, S. (2000). Structural constraints on process explanations in cognitive aging. *Psychology & Aging, 15*, 44–55.

Salthouse, T.A., & Maurer, T.J. (1996). Aging, job performance, and career development. In J.E. Birren & K.W. Schaie (Eds.), *Handbook of the psychology of aging* (4th ed., pp. 353–364). San Diego, CA: Academic Press.

Saltz, R. (1979). Children's interpretation of proverbs. *Language Arts, 56*, 508–514.

Saluja, G., Brenner, R., Morrongiello, B.A., Haynie, D., Rivera, M., Cheng, T.L. (2004). The role of supervision in child injury risk: Definition, conceptual and measurement issues. *Injury Control & Safety Promotion, 11*(1), 17–23.

Samaritans. (1998). *Media guidelines on portrayals of suicide* [Online booklet]. Retrieved February 16, 2001 from http://www.mentalhelp.net/samaritans/medreport.htm

Sammartino, F.J. (1987). The effect of health on retirement. *Social Security Bulletin, 50*(2), 31–47.

Sampson, P., Kerr, B., Olson, H., Streissguth, A., Hunt, E., Barr, H., Bookstein, F., & Thiede, K. (1997). The effects of prenatal alcohol exposure on adolescent cognitive processing: A speed-accuracy tradeoff. *Intelligence, 24*, 329–353.

Sampson, R.J., & Laub, J.H. (1994). Urban poverty and the family context of delinquency: A new look at structure and process in a classic study. *Child Development, 65*, 523–540.

Samuels, S., & Flor, R. (1997). The importance of automaticity for developing expertise in reading. *Reading & Writing Quarterly: Overcoming Learning Difficulties, 13*, 107–121.

Sanders, C.M. (1989). *Grief: The mourning after.* New York: Wiley-Interscience.

Sandman, C., Wadhwa, P., Chicz-DeMet, A., Porto, M., & Garite, T. (1999). Maternal corticotropin-releasing hormone and habituation in the human fetus. *Developmental Psychobiology, 34*, 163–173.

Sandman, C., Wadhwa, P., Hetrick, W., Porto, M., & Peeke, H. (1997). Human fetal heart rate dishabituation between thirty and thirty-two weeks. *Child Development, 68*, 1031–1040.

Sandnabba, N., & Ahlberg, C. (1999). Parents' attitudes and expectations about children's cross-gender behavior. *Sex Roles, 40*, 249–263.

Sands, L.P., & Meredith, W. (1992). Blood pressure and intellectual functioning in late midlife. *Journals of Gerontology: Psychological Sciences, 47*, P81–84.

Sands, L.P., Terry, H., & Meredith, W. (1989). Change and stability in adult intellectual functioning assessed by Wechsler item responses. *Psychology and Aging, 4*, 79–87.

Sandson, T., Bachna, K., & Morin, M. (2000). Right hemisphere dysfunction in ADHD: Visual hemispatial inattention and clinical subtype. *Journal of Learning Disabilities, 33*, 83–90.

Sanmartin, C., & Ng, E. (2004). Joint Canada/United States survey of health, 2002–3 (Catalogue No. 82M0022XIE). Ottawa, ON: Statistics Canada. Retrieved August 6, 2004 from http://www.statcan.ca/english/freepub/82M0022XIE/2003001/pdf/82M0022XIE2003001.pdf

Sanson, A., Pedlow, R., Cann, W., Prior, M., et al. (1996). Shyness ratings: Stability and correlates in early childhood. *International Journal of Behavioral Development, 19*, 705–724.

Sarason, B.R., Sarason, I.G., & Pierce, G.R. (1990). Traditional views of social support and their impact on assessment. In B.R. Sarason, I.G. Sarason, & G.R. Pierce (Eds.), *Social support: An interactional view* (pp. 9–25). New York: Wiley.

Sarwal, S., Wong, T., Sevigny, C., & Ng, L.K. (2003). Increasing incidence of ciprofloxacin-resistant Neisseria gonorrhoeae infection in Canada. *Canadian Medical Association Journal, 168*(7), 872–873.

Sato, S., Shimonaka, Y., Nakazato, K., & Kawaai, C. (1997). A life-span developmental study of age identity: Cohort and gender differences. *Japanese Journal of Developmental Psychology, 8*, 88–97.

Saugstad, L. (1997). Optimal foetal growth in the reduction of learning and behavior disorder and prevention of sudden infant death (SIDS) after the first month. *International Journal of Psychophysiology, 27*, 107–121.

Savage, M., & Holcomb, D. (1999). Adolescent female athletes' sexual risk-taking behaviors. *Journal of Youth and Adolescence, 28*, 583–594.

Savin-Williams, R.C. (1994). Verbal and physical abuse as stressors in the lives of lesbian, gay male, and bisexual youths: Associations with school problems, running away, substance abuse, prostitution, and suicide. *Journal of Consulting and Clinical Psychology, 62*, 261–269.

Saxon, T., Colombo, J., Robinson, E., & Frick, J. (2000). Dyadic interaction profiles in infancy and preschool intelligence. *Journal of School Psychology, 38*, 9–25.

Sayers, S., Kohn, C., & Heavey, C. (1998). Prevention of marital dysfunction: Behavioral approaches and beyond. *Clinical Psychology Review, 18*, 713–744.

Scarr, S. (1997). Why child care has little impact on most children's development. *Current Directions in Psychological Science, 6,* 143–147.

Scarr, S., & Eisenberg, M. (1993). Child care research: Issues, perspectives, and results. *Annual Review of Psychology, 44,* 613–644.

Scarr, S., & McCartney, K. (1983). How people make their own environments: A theory of genotype/environment effects. *Child Development, 54,* 424–435.

Scarr, S., Weinberg, R.A., & Waldman, I.D. (1993). IQ correlations in transracial adoptive families. *Intelligence, 17,* 541–555.

Schaal, B., Marlier, L., & Soussignan, R. (1998). Olfactory function in the human fetus: Evidence from selective neonatal responsiveness to the odor of amniotic fluid. *Behavioral Neuroscience, 112,* 1438–1449.

Schachter, H.M., Pham, B., King, J., Langford, S., & Moher, D. (2001). How efficacious and safe is short-acting methylphenidate for the treatment of attention-deficit disorder in children and adolescents? A meta-analysis. *Canadian Medical Association Journal, 165*(11), 1475–1488.

Schadt, D. (1997). The relationship of type to developmental issues of midlife women: Implications for counseling. *Journal of Psychological Type, 43,* 12–21.

Schaffer, H., & Emerson, P. (1964). The development of social attachments in infancy. *Monographs of the Society for Research in Child Development, 29*(3, Serial No. 94).

Schaie, K.W. (1983). The Seattle longitudinal study: A 21-year exploration of psychometric intelligence in adulthood. In K.W. Schaie (Ed.), *Longitudinal studies of adult psychological development* (pp. 64–135). New York: Guilford Press.

Schaie, K.W. (1989). The hazards of cognitive aging. *The Gerontologist, 29,* 484–493.

Schaie, K.W. (1990). Intellectual development in adulthood. In J.E. Birren & K.W. Schaie (Eds.), *Handbook of the psychology of aging* (3rd ed., pp. 291–309). San Diego, CA: Academic Press.

Schaie, K.W. (1993). The Seattle Longitudinal Studies of adult intelligence. *Current Directions in Psychological Science, 2,* 171–175.

Schaie, K.W. (1994). The course of adult intellectual development. *American Psychologist, 49,* 304–313.

Schaie, K.W. (1996). Intellectual development in adulthood. In J.E. Birren & K.W. Schaie (Eds.), *Handbook of the psychology of aging* (4th ed., pp. 266–286). San Diego, CA: Academic Press.

Schaie, K.W., & Hertzog, C. (1983). Fourteen-year cohort-sequential analyses of adult intellectual development. *Developmental Psychology, 19,* 531–543.

Schaie, K.W., & Willis, S.L. (1991). Adult personality and psychomotor performance: Cross-sectional and longitudinal analyses. *Journals of Gerontology: Psychological Sciences, 46,* P275–284.

Schatschneider, C., Francis, D., Foorman, B., Fletcher, J., & Mehta, P. (1999). The dimensionality of phonological awareness: An application of item response theory. *Journal of Educational Psychology, 91,* 439–449.

Scheibel, A.B. (1992). Structural changes in the aging brain. In J.E. Birren, R.B. Sloane, & G.D. Cohen (Eds.), *Handbook of mental health and aging* (2nd ed., pp. 147–174). San Diego, CA: Academic Press.

Scheibel, A.B. (1996). Structural and functional changes in the aging brain. In J.E. Birren & K.W. Schaie (Eds.), *Handbook of the psychology of aging* (4th ed., pp. 105–128). San Diego, CA: Academic Press.

Scheidt, R., Humpherys, D., & Yorgason, J. (1999). Successful aging: What's not to like? *Journal of Applied Gerontology, 18,* 277–282.

Scheier, M.F., Matthews, K.A., Owens, J.F., Magovern, G.J., Lefebvre, S., Abbott, R.A., & Carver, C.S. (1989). Dispositional optimism and recovery from coronary artery bypass surgery: The beneficial effects on physical and psychological well-being. *Journal of Personality and Social Psychology, 57,* 1024–1040.

Schieber, F. (1992). Aging and the senses. In J.E. Birren, R.B. Sloane, & G.D. Cohen (Eds.), *Handbook of mental health and aging* (2nd ed., pp. 252–306). San Diego, CA: Academic Press.

Schieve, L., Peterson, H., Meikle, S., Jeng, G., Danel, I., Burnett, N., & Wilcox, L. (1999). Birth rates and multiple-birth risk using in vitro fertilization. *Journal of the American Medical Association, 282,* 1832–1838.

Schliemann, A., Carraher, D., & Ceci, S. (1997). Everyday cognition. In J. Berry, P. Dasen, & T. Saraswathi (Eds.), *Handbook of cross-cultural psychology. Vol. 2: Basic processes and human development.* Needham Heights, MA: Allyn & Bacon.

Schmitz, S., Fulker, D., Plomin, R., Zahn-Waxler, C., Emde, R., & DeFries, J. (1999). Temperament and problem behavior during early childhood. *International Journal of Behavioral Development, 23,* 333–355.

Schnarch, D. (1997). Sex, intimacy, and the Internet. *Journal of Sex Education & Therapy, 22,* 15–20.

Schoen, R., & Wooldredge, J. (1989). Marriage choices in North Carolina and Virginia, 1969–71 and 1979–81. *Journal of Marriage and the Family, 51,* 465–481.

Schoendorf, K.C., & Kiely, J.L. (1992). Relationship of Sudden Infant Death Syndrome to maternal smoking during and after pregnancy. *Pediatrics, 90,* 905–908.

Schoenhals, M., Tienda, M., & Schneider, B. (1998). The educational and personal consequences of adolescent employment. *Social Forces, 77,* 723–762.

Schonert-Reichl, K. (1999). Relations of peer acceptance, friendship adjustment, and social behavior to moral reasoning during early adolescence. *Journal of Early Adolescence, 19,* 249–279.

Schonert-Reichl, K.A. (2000). *Children and youth at risk: Some conceptual considerations.* Ottawa, ON: Council of Ministers of Education, Canada (CMEC). Retrieved March 7, 2004, from: http://www.cmec.ca/stats/pcera/symposium2000/schonert.en.pdf

Schothorst, P., & van Engeland, H. (1996). Long-term behavioral sequelae of prematurity. *Journal of the American Academy of Child & Adolescent Psychiatry, 35,* 175–183.

Schreiber, M., Lutz, K., Schweizer, A., Kalveram, K., & Jaencke, L., (1998). Development and evaluation of an interactive computer-based training as a rehabilitation tool for dementia. *Psychologische Beitraege, 40,* 85–102.

Schreiber, M., Schweizer, A., Lutz, K., Kalveram, K., & Jaencke, L. (1999). Potential of an interactive computer-based training in the rehabilitation of dementia. An initial study. *Neuropsychological Rehabilitation, 9,* 155–167.

Schuler, M., & Nair, P. (1999). Frequency of maternal cocaine use during pregnancy and infant neurobehavioral outcome. *Journal of Pediatric Psychology, 24,* 511–514.

Schultz, N.R., Jr., Elias, M.F., Robbins, M.A., Streeten, D.H.P., & Blakeman, N. (1986). A longitudinal comparison of hypertensives and normotensives on the Wechsler Adult Intelligence Scale: Initial findings. *Journal of Gerontology, 41,* 169–175.

Schulz, A. (1998). Navajo women and the politics of identities. *Social Problems, 45,* 336–355.

Schulz, J.H. (1995). *The economics of aging* (6th ed.). Westport, CT: Auburn House.

Schulz, R., & Curnow, C. (1988). Peak performance and age among superathletes: Track and field, swimming, baseball, tennis, and golf. *Journals of Gerontology: Psychological Sciences, 43,* P113–120.

Schulz, R., Visintainer, P., & Williamson, G.M. (1990). Psychiatric and physical morbidity effects of caregiving. *Journals of Gerontology: Psychological Sciences, 45,* 181–191.

Schulz, R., & Williamson, G.M. (1991). A 2-year longitudinal study of depression among Alzheimer's caregivers. *Psychology and Aging, 6,* 569–578.

Schumm, W., Resnick, G., Silliman, B., & Bell, D. (1998). Premarital counseling and marital satisfaction among civilian wives of military service members. *Journal of Sex & Marital Therapy, 24,* 21–28.

Schunk, D.H. (1983). Reward contingencies and the development of children's skills and self-efficacy. *Educational Psychologist, 75,* 511–518.

Schuster, C. (1997). Condom use behavior: An assessment of United States college students' health education needs. *International Quarterly of Community Health Education, 17,* 237–254.

Schuster, M., Bell, R., Berry, S., & Kanouse, D. (1998). Impact of a high school condom availability program on sexual attitudes and behaviors. *Family Planning Perspectives, 30,* 67–72.

Schwartz, C., Snidman, N., & Kagan, J. (1996). Early childhood temperament as a determinant of externalizing behavior in adolescence. *Development & Psychopathology, 8,* 527–537.

Schwartz, M.A., & Scott, B.M. (2000). *Marriages and families: Diversity and change* (3rd ed.). Upper Saddle River, NJ: Prentice Hall.

Schwartz, R.M., Anastasia, M.L., Scanlon, J.W., & Kellogg, R.J. (1994). Effect of surfactant on morbidity, mortality, and resource use in newborn infants weighing 500 to 1500 g. *New England Journal of Medicine, 330,* 1476–1480.

Schwartz, S.J. (2001). The evolution of Eriksonian and Neo-Eriksonian identity theory and research: A review and integration. *Identity: An International Journal of Theory and Research, 1*(1), 7–58.

Schwebel, D., Rosen, C., & Singer, J. (1999). Preschoolers' pretend play and theory of mind: The role of jointly constructed pretence. *British Journal of Developmental Psychology, 17,* 333–348.

Schweinhart, L.J. (2003, April). *Benefits, costs, and explanation of the High/Scope Perry Preschool Program.* Paper presented at the Meeting of the Society for Research in Child Development, Tampa, FL. Retrieved November 22, 2004 from http://www.highscope.org/Research/PerryProject/Perry-SRCD-2003.pdf

Scott, J. (1998). Hematology. In R. Behrman & R. Kliegman (Eds.), *Nelson essentials of pediatrics* (3rd ed., pp. 545–582). Philadelphia: W.B. Saunders.

Sedney, M. (1999). Children's grief narratives in popular films. *Omega: Journal of Death & Dying, 39,* 314–324.

Séguin, L., Xu, Q., Potvin, L., Zunzunegui, M.V., & Frohlich, K.L. (2003). Effects of low income on infant health. *Canadian Medical Association Journal, 168*(12), 1533–1538.

Seifer, R., Schiller, M., Sameroff, A.J., Resnick, S., & Riordan, K. (1996). Attachment, maternal sensitivity, and infant temperament during the first year of life. *Developmental Psychology, 32,* 12–25.

Seligman, M.E.P. (1991). *Learned optimism.* New York: Knopf.

Selman, R.L. (1980). *The growth of interpersonal understanding.* New York: Academic Press.

Semrud-Clikeman, M., Nielsen, K., Clinton, A., Sylvester, L., et al. (1999). An intervention approach for children with teacher- and parent-identified attentional difficulties. *Journal of Learning Disabilities, 32,* 581–590.

Sénéchal, M. (1997). The differential effect of storybook reading on preschooler's expressive and receptive vocabulary acquisition. *Journal of Child Language, 24,* 123–138.

Sénéchal, M., & Cornell, E.H. (1993). Vocabulary acquisition through shared reading experiences. *Reading Research Quarterly, 28,* 360–374.

Sénéchal, M., Cornell, E.H., & Broda, L.S. (1995). Age-related differences in the organization of parent-infant interactions during picture-book reading. *Early Childhood Research Quarterly, 10,* 317–337.

Sénéchal, M., & LeFevre, J. (1998). *Long-term consequences of early home literacy experiences.* Paper presented at the annual meeting of the Canadian Psychological Conference, Edmonton, AB.

Sénéchal, M., & LeFevre, J. (2002). Parental involvement in the development of children's reading skill: A 5-year longitudinal study. *Child Development, 73*(2), 445–460.

Sénéchal, M., LeFevre, J., Thomas, E., & Daley, K. (1998). Differential effects of home literacy experiences on the development of oral and written language. *Reading Research Quarterly, 32,* 96–116.

Sénéchal, M., Thomas, E., & Monker, J. (1995). Individual differences in 4-year-old children's acquisition of vocabulary during storybook reading. *Journal of Educational Psychology, 87,* 218–229.

Serbin, L.A, Cooperman, J.M, Peters, P.L, Lehoux, P.M, Stack, D.M & Schwartzman A.E. (1998). Intergenerational transfer of psychosocial risk in women with childhood histories of aggression, withdrawal. *Developmental Psychology, 34*(6), 1246–1262.

Serbin, L., Moskowitz, D.S., Schwartzman, A.E., & Ledingham, J.E. (1991). Aggressive, withdrawn, and aggressive/withdrawn children in adolescence: Into the next generation. In D.J. Pepler & K.H. Rubin (Eds.), *The development and treatment of childhood aggression* (pp. 55–70). Hillsdale, NJ: Erlbaum.

Serbin, L.A., Poulin-Dubois, D., & Eichstedt, J.A. (2002). Infants' responses to gender-inconsistent events. *Infancy, 3*(4), 531–542.

Serbin, L.A., Powlishta, K.K., & Gulko, J. (1993). The development of sex typing in middle childhood. *Monographs of the Society for Research in Child Development, 58*(2, Serial No. 232).

Serdula, M.K., Ivery, D., Coates, R.J., Freedman, D.S., Williamson, D.F., & Byers, T. (1993). Do obese children become obese adults? A review of the literature. *Preventive Medicine, 22,* 167–177.

Settlement.org (2001). First-language literacy and heritage: Heritage language programs. Retrieved November 16, 2001 from http://www.settlement.org/site/LL/firstlanguage_heritage.asp

Shackelford, T.K. (2001). Cohabitation, marriage and murder. *Aggressive Behavior, 27*(4), 284–291.

Shaffer, D., Garland, A., Gould, M., Fisher, P., & Trautman, P. (1988). Preventing teenage suicide: A critical review. *Journal of the American Academy of Child and Adolescent Psychiatry, 27,* 675–687.

Shaffer, D., Garland, A., Vieland, V., Underwood, M., & Busner, C. (1991). The impact of curriculum-based suicide prevention programs for teenagers. *Journal of the American Academy of Child and Adolescent Psychiatry, 30,* 588–596.

Shaffer, H.J. & Hall, M.N. (1996). Estimating prevalence of adolescent gambling disorders: A quantitative synthesis and guide toward standard gambling nomenclature. *Journal of Gambling Studies, 142,* 193–214.

Sharma, S., Monsen, R., & Gary, B. (1997). Comparison of attitudes toward death and dying among nursing majors and other college students. *Omega: Journal of Death & Dying, 34,* 219–232.

Shaw, D.S., Kennan, K., & Vondra, J.I. (1994). Developmental precursors of externalizing behavior: Ages 1 to 3. *Developmental Psychology, 30,* 355–364.

Shaw, R., Ryst, E., & Steiner, H. (1996). Temperament as a correlate of adolescent defense mechanisms. *Child Psychiatry & Human Development, 27,* 105–114.

Shea, S.E., Gordon, K., Hawkins, A., Kawchuk, J., & Smith, D. (2001). Pathology in the Hundred Acre Wood: A neurodevelopmental perspective on A.A. Milne. *Canadian Medical Association Journal, 163*(12), 1557–1559.

Sher, K., & Gotham, H. (1999). Pathological alcohol involvement: A developmental disorder of young adulthood. *Development & Psychopathology, 11,* 933–956.

Shi, R., & Werker, J.F. (2001). Six-month-old infants' preference for lexical over grammatical words. *Psychological Science, 12*(1), 70–75.

Shi, R., Werker, J.F., & Morgan, J.L. (1999). Newborn infants' sensitivity to perceptual cues to lexical and grammatical words. *Cognition, 72,* B11–B12.

Shimonaka, Y., Nakazato, K., Kawaai, C., & Sato, S. (1997). Androgyny and successful adaptation across the life span among Japanese adults. *Journal of Genetic Psychology, 158,* 389–400.

Shiner, R. (2000). Linking childhood personality with adaptation: Evidence for continuity and change across time into late adolescence. *Journal of Personality & Social Psychology, 78,* 310–325.

Shneidman, E.S. (1980). *Voices of death.* New York: Harper & Row.

Shneidman, E.S. (1983). *Deaths of man.* New York: Jason Aronson.

Shock, N.W., Greulich, R.C., Andres, R., Arenberg, D., Costa, P.T., Jr., Lakatta, E.G., & Tobin, J.D. (1984). *Normal human aging: The Baltimore Longitudinal Study of Aging.* NIH Publication No. 84–2450, U.S. Department of Health and Human Services, National Institute on Aging. Washington, DC: U.S. Government Printing Office.

Shoda, Y., Mischel, W. & Peake, P. (1990). Predicting adolescent cognitive and self-regulatory competencies from preschool delay of gratification. *Developmental Psychology, 26,* 978–986.

Shonkoff, J.P. (1984). The biological substrate and physical health in middle childhood. In W.A. Collins (Ed.), *Development during middle childhood: The years from six to twelve* (pp. 24–69). Washington, DC: National Academy Press.

Shore, C.M. (1995). *Individual differences in language development.* Thousand Oaks, CA: Sage.

Shu, H., Anderson, R., & Wu, N. (2000). Phonetic awareness: Knowledge of orthography-phonology relationships in the character acquisition of Chinese children. *Journal of Educational Psychology, 92,* 56–62.

Sibbald, B. (2004). Legal action against GSK over SSRI data. *Canadian Medical Association Journal, 170*(4), 23.

Sicotte, C., & Stemberger, R. (1999). Do children with PDDNOS have a theory of mind? *Journal of Autism & Developmental Disorders, 29,* 225–233.

Siegal, M. (1987). Are sons and daughters treated more differently by fathers than by mothers? *Developmental Review, 7,* 183–209.

Siegler, I.C. (1983). Psychological aspects of the Duke Longitudinal Studies. In K.W. Schaie (Ed.), *Longitudinal studies of adult psychological development* (pp. 136–190). New York: Guilford Press.

Siegler, R.S. (1976). Three aspects of cognitive development. *Cognitive Psychology, 8,* 431–520.

Siegler, R.S. (1978). The origins of scientific reasoning. In R.S. Siegler (Ed.), *Children's thinking: What develops?* (pp. 109–150). Hillsdale, NJ: Erlbaum.

Siegler, R.S. (1981). Developmental sequences within and between concepts. *Monographs of the Society for Research in Child Development, 46*(2, Serial No. 189).

Siegler, R.S. (1994). Cognitive variability: A key to understanding cognitive development. *Current Directions in Psychological Science, 3,* 1–5.

Sigman, M., Neumann, C., Carter, E., Cattle, D.J., D'Souza, S., & Bwibo, N. (1988). Home interactions and the development of Embu toddlers in Kenya. *Child Development, 59,* 1251–1261.

Silver, C. (2001). *Connectedness Series: Internet use among older Canadians* (Catalogue No. 56F0004MIE, No. 4). Ottawa, ON: Statistics Canada. Retrieved December 31, 2001 from http://www.statcan.ca/english/research/56F0004MIE/56F0004MIE01004.pdf

Silverstein, J., & Lasky, M. (2003). *Online Dating For Dummies.* Mississauga, ON: Wiley Canada.

Silverstein, M., & Long, J. (1998). Trajectories of grandparents' perceived solidarity with adult grandchildren: A growth curve analysis over 23 years. *Journal of Marriage & the Family, 60,* 912–923.

Simkin, S., Hawton, K., Whitehead, L., Fagg, J., & Eagle, M. (1995). A study of the effects of television drama portrayal of paracetamol self-poisoning. *British Journal of Psychiatry, 167,* 754–759.

Simoneau, G.G., & Liebowitz, H.W. (1996). Posture, gait, and falls. In J.E. Birren & K.W. Schaie (Eds.), *Handbook of the psychology of aging* (4th ed., pp. 204–217). San Diego, CA: Academic Press.

Simons, R.L., Robertson, J.F., & Downs, W.R. (1989). The nature of the association between parental rejection and delinquent behavior. *Journal of Youth and Adolescence, 18,* 297–309.

Simonton, D.K. (1988). Age and outstanding achievement: What do we know after a century of research? *Psychological Bulletin, 104,* 251–267.

Simonton, D.K. (1991). Career landmarks in science: Individual differences and interdisciplinary contrasts. *Developmental Psychology, 27,* 119–130.

Simonton, D. (2000). Creativity: Cognitive, personal, developmental, and social aspects. *American Psychologist, 55,* 151–158.

Sims, M., Hutchins, T., & Taylor, M. (1997). Conflict as social interaction: Building relationship skills in child care settings. *Child & Youth Care Forum, 26,* 247–260.

Singer, D., & Hunter, M. (1999). The experience of premature menopause: A thematic discourse analysis. *Journal of Reproductive & Infant Psychology, 17,* 63–81.

Skaalvik, E., & Valas, H. (1999). Relations among achievement, self-concept and motivation in mathematics and language arts: A longitudinal study. *Journal of Experimental Education, 67,* 135–149.

Skinner, B.F. (1953). *Science and human behavior.* New York: Macmillan.

Skinner, B.F. (1980). The experimental analysis of operant behavior: A history. In R.W. Riebes & K. Salzinger (Eds.), *Psychology: Theoretical-historical perspectives.* New York: Academic Press.

Skoe, E., Hansen, K., Morch, W., Bakke, I., Hoffman, T., Larsen, B., & Aasheim, M. (1999). Care-based moral reasoning in Norwegian and Canadian early adolescents: A cross-national comparison. *Journal of Early Adolescence, 19,* 280–291.

Slaby, R.G., & Frey, K.S. (1975). Development of gender constancy and selective attention to same-sex models. *Child Development, 46,* 849–856.

Slater, A. (1995). Individual differences in infancy and later IQ. *Journal of Child Psychology and Psychiatry, 36,* 69–112.

Slaven, L., & Lee, C. (1998). A cross-sectional survey of menopausal status, symptoms and psychological distress in a community sample of Australian women. *Journal of Health Psychology, 3,* 117–123.

Slobin, D.I. (1985). Introduction: Why study acquisition crosslinguistically? In D.I. Slobin (Ed.), *The crosslinguistic study of language acquisition: Vol. 1. The data* (pp. 3–24). Hillsdale, NJ: Erlbaum.

Slobounov, S., Moss, S., Slobounova, E., & Newell, K. (1998). Aging and time to instability in posture. *Journals of Gerontology: Series A: Biological Sciences & Medical Sciences, 53A,* B71–B78.

Small, S.A., & Luster, T. (1994). Adolescent sexual activity: An ecological, risk-factor approach. *Journal of Marriage and the Family, 56,* 181–192.

Smeeding, T.M. (1990). Economic status of the elderly. In R.H. Binstock & L.K. George (Eds.), *Handbook of aging and the social sciences* (3rd ed., pp. 362–381). San Diego, CA: Academic Press.

Smetana, J.G. (1990). Morality and conduct disorders. In M. Lewis & S.M. Miller (Eds.), *Handbook of developmental psychopathology* (pp. 157–180). New York: Plenum.

Smetana, J.G., Killen, M., & Turiel, E. (1991). Children's reasoning about interpersonal and moral conflicts. *Child Development, 62,* 629–644.

Smetana, J., Schlagman, N., & Adams, P. (1993). Preschool children's judgments about hypothetical and actual transgressions. *Child Development, 64,* 202–214.

Smith, C., Umberger, G., Manning, E., Sleven, J., Wekstein, D., Schmitt, F., Markesbery, W., & Zhang, Z. (1999). Critical decline in fine motor hand movements in human aging. *Neurology, 53,* 1458–1461.

Smith, E.L. (1982). Exercise for prevention of osteoporosis: A review. *Physician and Sportsmedicine, 10,* 72–83.

Smith, M., Sharit, J., & Czaja, S. (1999). Aging, motor control, and the performance of computer mouse tasks. *Human Factors, 41,* 389–396.

Smock, P.J. (1993). The economic costs of marital disruption for young women over the past two decades. *Demography, 30,* 353–371.

Smoll, F.L., & Schutz, R.W. (1990). Quantifying gender differences in physical performance: A developmental perspective. *Developmental Psychology, 26,* 360–369.

Snarey, J.R. (1985). Cross-cultural universality of social-moral development: A critical review of Kohlbergian research. *Psychological Bulletin, 97,* 202–232.

Snarey, J.R., Reimer, J., & Kohlberg, L. (1985). Development of social-moral reasoning among kibbutz adolescents: A longitudinal cross-sectional study. *Developmental Psychology, 21,* 3–17.

Snarey, J., Son, L., Kuehne, V.S., Hauser, S., & Vaillant, G. (1987). The role of parenting in men's psychosocial development: A longitudinal study of early adulthood infertility and midlife generativity. *Developmental Psychology, 23,* 593–603.

Snyder, C. (1997). Unique invulnerability: A classroom demonstration in estimating personal mortality. *Teaching of Psychology, 24,* 197–199.

Society of Obstetricians and Gynaecologists of Canada. (2001). The Society of Obstetricians and Gynaecologists of Canada dispels myths and misconceptions about change of life. Ottawa, ON: Author. Retrieved December 14, 2001 from http://www.sogc.org/SOGCnet/sogc_docs/press/releases2001/ oct12_01_e.htm

Society of Obstetricians and Gynaecologists of Canada. (2002). *The SOGC statement on the WHI report on estrogen and progestin use in postmenopausal women: Appendix: Revisions to recommendations: Canadian consensus conference on menopause and osteoporosis.* Ottawa, ON: Author. Retrieved August 17, 2004 from http://sogc.medical.org/sogcnet/pdfs/rev_recommend.pdf

Society of Obstetricians and Gynaecologists of Canada. (2004). C-sections on demand—SOGC's position. *SOGC Advisory* (March 10, 2004). Retrieved November 24, 2004 from http://www.sogc/org/sogcnet/sogc%5Fdocs/press/releases2004/pdfs/electivecaesareanspart%20ii.pdf

Sodhi Kalsi, P. (2003). *"The best of both worlds": Bicultural identity formation of Punjabi women living in Canada.* Canadian Association for the Study of Adult Education—Online Proceedings 2003. University of Toronto. Retrieved July 16, 2003 from http://www.oise.utoronto.ca/CASAE/cnf2003/2003_papers/psodhiCAS03.pdf

Soken, N., & Pick, A. (1999). Infants' perception of dynamic affective expressions: Do infants distinguish specific expressions? *Child Development, 70,* 1275–1282.

Solano, L., Costa, M., Salvati, S., Coda, R., Aiuti, F., Mezzaroma, I., & Bertini, M. (1993). Psychosocial factors and clinical evolution in HIV–1 infection: A longitudinal study. *Journal of Psychosomatic Research, 37,* 39–51.

Soldo, B.J., Wolf, D.A., & Agree, E.M. (1990). Family, households, and care arrangements of frail older women: A structural analysis. *Journals of Gerontology: Social Sciences, 45,* S238–249.

Somers, M.D. (1993). A comparison of voluntarily childfree adults and parents. *Journal of Marriage and the Family, 55,* 643–650.

Sonneck, G., Etzersdorfer, E., & Nagel-Kuess, S. (1992). Subway suicide in Vienna (1980–1990): A contribution to the imitation effect in suicidal behavior. In P. Crepet, G. Ferrari, S. Platt, & M. Bellini (Eds.), *Suicidal behavior in Europe: Recent research findings.* Rome: Libbey.

Sophian, C. (1995). Representation and reasoning in early numerical development: Counting, conservation, and comparisons between sets. *Child Development, 66,* 559–577.

Sørensen, A. (1983). Women's employment patterns after marriage. *Journal of Marriage and the Family, 45,* 311–321.

Sorlie, P.D., Backlund, E., & Keller, J.B. (1995). U.S. mortality by economic, demographic, and social characteristics: The National Longitudinal Mortality Study. *American Journal of Public Health, 85,* 949–956.

Sotelo, M., & Sangrador, J. (1997). Psychological aspects of political tolerance among adolescents. *Psychological Reports, 81,* 1279–1288.

Sotelo, M., & Sangrador, J. (1999). Correlations of self-ratings of attitude towards violent groups with measures of personality, self-esteem, and moral reasoning. *Psychological Reports, 84,* 558–560.

Sowell, E.R., Peterson, B.S., Thompson, P.M., Welcome, S.E., Henkenius, A.L., & Toga, A.W. (2003). Mapping cortical change across the human life span. *Nature Neuroscience, 6*(3), 309–315.

Sowell, E.R., Thompson, P.M., Holmes, C.J., Jernigan, T.L., & Toga, A.W. (1999). *In vivo* evidence for post-adolescent brain maturation in frontal and striatal regions. *Nature Neuroscience, 2*(10), 859–861.

Sowell, E.R., Thompson, P.M., Tessner, K.D., & Toga, A.W. (2001). Mapping continued brain growth and gray matter density reduction in dorsal frontal cortex: Inverse relationships during post-adolescent brain maturation. *The Journal of Neuroscience, 21*(22), 8819–8829.

Sowell, E.R., Thompson, P.M., & Toga, A.W. (2004). Mapping changes in the human cortex throughout the span of life. *Neuroscientist, 10*(4), 372–392.

Spanier, G.B., & Furstenberg, F.F., Jr. (1987). Remarriage and reconstituted families. In M.B. Sussman & S.K. Steinmetz (Eds.), *Handbook of marriage and the family* (pp. 419–434). New York: Plenum.

Sparrow, P.R., & Davies, D.R. (1988). Effects of age, tenure, training, and job complexity on technical performance. *Psychology and Aging, 3,* 307–314.

Speece, M.W., & Brent, S.B. (1984). Children's understanding of death: A review of three components of a death concept. *Child Development, 55,* 1671–1686.

Speece, M.W., & Brent, S.B. (1992). The acquisition of a mature understanding of three components of the concept of death. *Death Studies, 16,* 211–229.

Spelke, E.S. (1991). Physical knowledge in infancy: Reflections on Piaget's theory. In S. Carey & R. Gelman (Eds.), *The epigenesis of mind. Essays on biology and cognition* (pp. 133–169). Hillsdale, NJ: Erlbaum.

Spence, J.T., & Helmreich, R.L. (1978). *Masculinity and femininity.* Austin: University of Texas Press.

Spenner, K.I. (1988). Occupations, work settings and the course of adult development: Tracing the implications of select historical changes. In P.B. Baltes, D.L. Featherman, & R.M. Lerner (Eds.), *Life-span development and behavior* (Vol. 9, pp. 244–288). Hillsdale, NJ: Erlbaum.

Spiegel, D., Bloom, J.R., Kraemer, H.C., & Gottheil, E. (1989, October 14). Effect of psychosocial treatment on survival of patients with metastatic breast cancer. *Lancet,* 888–901.

Spitze, G. (1988). Women's employment and family relations: A review. *Journal of Marriage and the Family, 50,* 595–618.

Sprang, G., & McNeil, J. (1998). Post-homicide reactions: Grief, mourning and post-traumatic stress disorder following a drunk driving fatality. *Omega: Journal of Death & Dying, 37,* 41–58.

Spreen, O., Risser, A., & Edgell, D. (1995). *Developmental neuropsychology.* New York: Oxford University Press.

Srivastava, S., John, O.P., Gosling, S.D., & Potter, J. (2003). Development of personality in early and middle adulthood: Set like plaster or persistent change? *Journal of Personality and Social Psychology, 84*(5), 1041–1053.

Sroufe, L.A., Carlson, E., & Schulman, S. (1993). Individuals in relationships: Development from infancy through adolescence. In D.C. Funder, R.D. Parke, C. Tomlinson-Keasey, & K. Widaman (Eds.), *Studying lives through time: Personality and development* (pp. 315–342). Washington, DC: American Psychological Association.

Stack, S. (1992a). The effect of divorce on suicide in Finland: A time series analysis. *Journal of Marriage and the Family, 54,* 636–642.

Stack, S. (1992b). The effect of divorce on suicide in Japan: A time series analysis, 1950–1980. *Journal of Marriage and the Family, 54,* 327–334.

Stack, S., & Wasserman, I. (1993). Marital status, alcohol consumption, and suicide: An analysis of national data. *Journal of Marriage and the Family, 55,* 1018–1024.

Stadel, B.V., & Weiss, N.S. (1975). Characteristics of menopausal women: A survey of King and Pierce Counties in Washington, 1973–74. *American Journal of Epidemiology, 102,* 209–216.

Stager, C.L., & Werker, J.F. (1997). Infants listen for more phonetic detail in speech perception than in word learning tasks. *Nature, 388,* 381–382.

Stambrook, M., & Parker, K.C.H. (1987). The development of the concept of death in childhood: A review of the literature. *Merrill-Palmer Quarterly, 33,* 133–158.

Stampfer, M.J., Colditz, G.A., Willett, W.C., Manson, J.E. Rosner, B., Speizer, F.E., & Hennekens, C.H. (1991). Postmenopausal estrogen therapy and cardiovascular disease: Ten-year follow-up from the Nurses' Health Study. *New England Journal of Medicine, 325,* 756–762.

Stampfer, M.J., Hennekins, C.H., Manson, J.E., Colditz, G.A., Rosner, B., & Willett, W.C. (1993). Vitamin E consumption and the risk of coronary disease in women. *New England Journal of Medicine, 328,* 1444–1449.

Stanford, E.P., Happersett, C.J., Morton, D.J., Molgaard, C.A., & Peddecord, K.M. (1991). Early retirement and functional impairment from a multiethnic perspective. *Research on Aging, 13,* 5–38.

Statistics Canada. (1994a). *1993 General Social Survey—Cycle 9 Personal Risk. Public Microdata File Documentation and User's Guide.* Ottawa, ON: Statistics Canada.

Statistics Canada. (1995a). *National Population Health Survey Overview 1994–95.* (Catalogue No. 82-567). Ottawa, ON: Minister of Industry.

Statistics Canada. (1998a). *The Daily* (October 28). National Longitudinal Survey of Children and Youth, Cycle 2, 1996. Ottawa, ON: Author. Retrieved September 23, 2001 from http://www.statcan.ca:80/Daily/English/981028/d981028.htm

Statistics Canada. (1999a). *The Daily* (September 1). Employment after childbirth. Ottawa, ON: Author. Retrieved November 13, 2001 from http://www.statcan.ca/Daily/English/990901/d990901a.htm

Statistics Canada. (1999b). *Statistical report on the health of Canadians* (Catalogue No. 82-570-XIE). Ottawa, ON: Author. Retrieved November 23, 2001 from http://www.statcan.ca/english/freepub/82-570-XIE/82-570-XIE.pdf

Statistics Canada. (2000a). *Canada at a Glance* (2nd ed.). (Catalogue No. 12-581-XPE.) Ottawa, ON: Communications Division. Retrieved November 19, 2001 from http://www.statcan.ca/english/freepub/12-581-XIE/12-581-XIE.pdf

Statistics Canada. (2000b). *The Daily* (October 20). Teenage pregnancy. Ottawa, ON: Author. Retrieved October 21, 2001 from http://www.statcan.ca/Daily/English/001020/d001020b.htm

Statistics Canada. (2000c). *The Daily* (September 14). Women in Canada. Ottawa, ON: Author. Retrieved November 23, 2001 from http://www.statcan.ca/Daily/English/000914/d000914c.htm

Statistics Canada. (2000d). *The Daily* (July 25, 2000). Family violence. Ottawa, ON: Author. Retrieved December 8, 2001 from http://www.statcan.ca/Daily/English/000725/d000725b.htm

Statistics Canada. (2000e). *The Daily* (March 31, 2000). Health Reports: How healthy are Canadians? Ottawa, ON: Author. Retrieved December 16, 20001 from http://www.statcan.ca/Daily/English/000331/d000331a.htm

Statistics Canada. (2000f). *Exercise frequency.* Ottawa, ON: Author. Retrieved December 28, 2001 from http://www.statcan.ca/english/Pgdb/People/Health/health19b.htm

Statistics Canada. (2001a). *The Daily* (June 22). Impact of smoking on life expectancy and disability. Ottawa, ON: Author. Retrieved August 18, 2004 from http://www.statcan.ca/Daily/English/010622/d010622a.htm

Statistics Canada. (2001b). *The Daily* (June 28). Family violence: Focus on child abuse and children at risk. Ottawa, ON: Author. Retrieved November 15, 2001 from http://www.statcan.ca/Daily/English/010628/d010628b.htm

Statistics Canada. (2001c). *The Daily* (May 30). National Longitudinal Survey of children and Youth: Participation in activities 1998/99. Ottawa, ON: Author. Retrieved November 16, 2001 from http://www.statcan.ca/Daily/English/010530/d010530a.htm

Statistics Canada. (2001d). *The Daily* (January 25). Television viewing. Ottawa, ON: Author. Retrieved November 17, 2001 from http://www.statcan.ca/Daily/English/010125/ d010125a.htm

Statistics Canada. (2001e). Frequency of heavy drinking. In *Health Indicators* (June 2001. Catalogue No. 82-221-XIE). Ottawa, ON: Author. Retrieved November 17, 2001 from http://www.statcan.ca/english/freepub/82-221-XIE/00601/high/drink/htm

Statistics Canada. (2001f). Self-esteem. In *Health Indicators* (June 2001, Catalogue No. 82-221-XIE). Ottawa, ON: Author. Retrieved November 17, 2001 from http://www. statcan.ca/english/freepub/82-221-XIE/00601/high/esteem.htm

Statistics Canada. (2001g). *The Daily* (March 26). General Social Survey: Internet use 2000. Ottawa, ON: Author. Retrieved October 2, 2001 from http://www.statcan.ca/Daily/English/010326/d010326a.htm

Statistics Canada. (2001h). *The Daily* (January 25). Television viewing, Fall 1999. Ottawa, ON: Author. Retrieved August 17, 2001 from http://www.statcan.ca/Daily/English/010125/d010125a.htm

Statistics Canada. (2001i). *Children and Youth in Canada* (Catalogue No. 85F0033MIE-01005). Ottawa, ON: Author. Retrieved November 23, 2001 from http://www.statcan.ca/english/freepub/85F0033MIE/85F0033MIE01005.pdf

Statistics Canada. (2001j). *The Daily* (October 31). Homicide statistics, 2000. Ottawa, ON: Author. Retrieved November 18, 2001 from http://www.statcan.ca/Daily/English/011031/d011031b.htm

Statistics Canada. (2001k). *Family violence in Canada: A statistical profile* (Catalogue No. 85-224-XIE). Ottawa, ON: Author. Retrieved December 8, 2001 from http://www.statcan.ca/english/freepub/85-224-XIE/0100085-224-XIE.pdf

Statistics Canada. (2001l). *The Daily* (April 10). Survey of approaches to educational planning. Ottawa, ON: Author. Retrieved December 12, 2001 from http://www.statcan.ca/Daily/English/010410/d010410a.htm

Statistics Canada. (2001m). Participation rates and unemployment rates by age and sex, Canada and selected countries (Canadian Statistics: Labour, employment and unemployment—Participation, employment and unemployment). Ottawa, ON: Author. Retrieved December 23, 2001 from http://www.statcan.ca/english/Pgdb/People/Labour/labor23a.htm

Statistics Canada. (2001n). *The Daily* (May 23). Deaths, 1998. Ottawa, ON: Author. Retrieved December 12, 2001 from http://www.statcan.ca/Daily/English/010523/d010523e.htm

Statistics Canada. (2001o). *Activity limitation or handicap, by age group and sex, household population aged 4 and over, Canada excluding territories, 1994/95–1998/99.*

Statistics Canada. (2001p). Retirement by sex, class of worker, Canada, annual average (File No. CDIT28AN). *Labour Force Survey, 2000–2001* (CD-ROM, Catalogue No. 71F0004XCB). Ottawa, ON: Author.

Statistics Canada. (2002a). *2001 Census: Analysis series.* Profile of languages in Canada: English, French and many others (96F0030XIE2001005). Ottawa, ON: Ministry of Industry. Retrieved May 1, 2004, from http://www12.statcan.ca/english/census01/products/analytic/companion/lang/pdf/96F0030XIE2001005.pdf

Statistics Canada. (2002b). *Statistics Canada, 2001 Census. More children living with common-law parents* (Table—Distribution of children aged 0 to 14 by family structure, Canada, provinces and territories, 2001). Retrieved June 26, 2004 from http://www12.statcan.ca/english/census01/products/analytic/companion/fam/children

Statistics Canada. (2002c). *General Social Survey—Cycle 15: Changing conjugal life in Canada* (Catalogue No. 89-576-XIE). Ottawa, ON: Author. Retrieved June 26, 2004 from http://www.statcan.ca/english/freepub/89-576-XIE/89-576-XIE2001001.pdf

Statistics Canada. (2002d). Household Living Arrangements (10), Age Groups (17A) and Sex (3) for Population in Private Households, for Canada, Provinces, Territories, Census Metropolitan Areas and Census Agglomerations, 2001 Census—20% Sample Data (Catalogue No. 95F0315XCB01004). Ottawa, ON: Author. Retrieved August 3, 2004 from http://www12.statcan.ca/english/census01/products/standard/themes/index.cfm

Statistics Canada. (2002e). 2001 Census. Families and Household Living Arrangements: Age Groups (12B), Family Structure (7) and Sex (3) for Children in Census Families in Private Households, for Canada, Provinces, Territories, Census Metropolitan Areas and Census Agglomerations, 2001 Census—20% Sample Data (Catalogue No. 95F0313XCB01004) October 22, 2002. Ottawa, ON: Author. Retrieved August 3, 2004 from http://www12.statcan.ca/english/census01/products/standard/themes/index.cfm

Statistics Canada. (2002f). *General Social Survey—Cycle 15: Changing conjugal life in Canada* (Catalogue No. 89-576-XIE). Retrieved August 14, 2004 from http://erl.bibliocentre.ca:2067/english/ freepub/89-576-XIE/89-576-XIE2001001.pdf

Statistics Canada. (2002g). *2001 Census: Families and household profile: Canada.* Ottawa, ON: Author. Retrieved August 25, 2004 from http://www12.statcan.ca/english/census01/Products/Analytic/companion/fam/canada.cfm#seniors

Statistics Canada. (2002h). *Profile of the Canadian population by age and sex: Canada ages* (Catalogue No. 96F0030XIE2001002). Ottawa, ON: Author. Retrieved August 31, 2004 from http://www12.statcan.ca/english/census01/Products/Analytic/companion/age/images/96F0030XIE2001002.pdf

Statistics Canada. (2002i). *Risk of depression, by age group and sex, household population aged 12 and over, Canada, 2000/01*(Health indicators Catalogue No. 82-221). Ottawa, ON: Author. Retrieved August 28, 2004 from (see next page) http://www.statcan.ca/english/freepub/82-221-XIE/00604/tables/pdf/1295.pdf

Statistics Canada. (2003a). *The Daily* (November 21). Television viewing. Ottawa, ON: Author. Retrieved July 8, 2004 from http://www.statcan.ca/Daily/English/031121/d031121a.htm

Statistics Canada. (2003b). *The Daily*, (July 25). Sexual offences. (Catalogue No. 11-001.) Ottawa, ON: Author. Retrieved August 8, 2004 from http://www.statcan.ca/Daily/English/030725/d030725.pdf

Statistics Canada. (2003c). *2001 Census: Analysis series. Education in Canada: Raising the standard* (Catalogue No. 96F0030XIE2001012). Ottawa, ON: Author. Retrieved August 9, 2004 from http://www12.statcan.ca/english/census01/Products/Analytic/companion/educ/pdf/96F0030XIE2001012.pdf

Statistics Canada. (2003d). *Marriages, 2001* (Catalogue No. 84F0212XPB). Ottawa, ON: Author.

Statistics Canada. (2004a). *The Daily*, September 27: Deaths, 2002. Ottawa, ON: Author. Retrieved September 28, 2004 from http://www.statcan.ca/Daily/English/040927/d040927a.htm

Statistics Canada. (2004b). *National Longitudinal Survey of Children and Youth*. Retrieved March 11, 2004 from http://www.statcan.ca/english/sdds/4450.htm

Statistics Canada. (2004c). *The Daily*, May 4, 2004: Divorces. Ottawa, ON: Author. Retrieved May 19, 2004 from http://www.statcan.ca/Daily/English/040504/d040504.pdf

Statistics Canada. (2004d). *The Daily*, June 15, 2004: Canadian Community Health Survey (Catalogue No. 82-221). Ottawa, ON: Author. Retrieved August 3, 2004 from http://www.statcan.ca/Daily/English/040615/d040615b.htm

Statistics Canada. (2004e). *Women in Canada: Work chapters updates, 2003* (Catalogue No. 89F0133XIE), March 25. Ottawa, ON: Author. Retrieved August 15, 2004 from http://www.statcan.ca/english/freepub/89F0133XIE/89F0133XIE2003000.pdf

Statistics Canada. (2004f). Table 102-0511—Life expectancy—abridged life table, at birth and at age 65, by sex, Canada, provinces and territories, annual (years). Ottawa, ON: Author. Retrieved August 27, 2004 from http://cansim2.statcan.ca/cgi-win/CNSMCGI.EXE?Lang=E&ArrayId=01020511&Array_Pick=1&Detail=1&ResultTemplate=CII/CII___&RootDir=CII/&TblDetail=1&C2SUB=HEALTH

Statistics Canada. (2004g). *Self-rated health, by age group and sex, household population aged 12 and over, Canada, 2003* (Health Indicators Catalogue No. 82-221). Ottawa, ON: Author. Retrieved August 28, 2004 from http://www.statcan.ca/english/freepub/82-221-XIE/00604/tables/pdf/1117_03.pdf

Statistics Canada. (2004h). Fact-sheet on retirement (Catalogue No. 75-001). *Perspectives on Labour and Income, 5*(2), 1–7. Retrieved August 31, 2004 from http://www.statcan.ca/english/studies/75-001/10204/200402_04.pdf

Steele, J., & Mayes, S. (1995). Handedness and directional asymmetry in the long bones of the human upper limb. *International Journal of Osteoarchaeology, 5*, 39–49.

Stein, C., Wemmerus, V., Ward, M., Gaines, M., Freeberg, A., & Jewell, T. (1998). "Because they're my parents": An intergenerational study of felt obligation and parental caregiving. *Journal of Marriage & the Family, 60*, 611–622.

Stein, K., Roeser, R., & Markus, H. (1998). Self-schemas and possible selves as predictors and outcomes of risky behaviors in adolescents. *Nursing Research, 47*, 96–106.

Steinbach, U. (1992). Social networks, institutionalization, and mortality among elderly people in the United States. *Journals of Gerontology: Social Sciences, 47*, S183–190.

Steinberg, L. (1986). Latchkey children and susceptibility to peer pressure: An ecological analysis. *Developmental Psychology, 22*, 433–439.

Steinberg, L. (1988). Reciprocal relation between parent-child distance and pubertal maturation. *Developmental Psychology, 24*, 122–128.

Steinberg, L., Fletcher, A., & Darling, N. (1994). Parental monitoring and peer influences on adolescent substance use. *Pediatrics, 93*, 1060–1064.

Sternberg, R.J. (1987). Liking versus loving: A comparative evaluation of theories. *Psychological Bulletin, 102*, 331–345.

Sternberg, R. (1988). *The triarchic mind: A new theory of intelligence.* New York: Viking Press.

Sternberg, R.J. (1990). Wisdom and its relations to intelligence and creativity. In R.J. Sternberg (Ed.), *Wisdom: Its nature, origins, and development* (pp. 142–159). Cambridge, England: Cambridge University Press.

Sternberg, R.J., & Wagner, R.K. (1993). The g-ocentric view of intelligence and job performance is wrong. *Current Directions in Psychological Science, 2*, 1–5.

Sternberg, R., Wagner, R., Williams, W., & Horvath, J. (1995). Testing common sense. *American Psychologist, 50*, 912–927.

Stevens, J., & Choo, K. (1998). Temperature sensitivity of the body surface over the life span. *Somatosensory & Motor Research, 15*, 13–28.

Stewart, A., & Ostrove, J. (1998). Women's personality in middle age: Gender, history, and midcourse corrections. *American Psychologist, 53*, 1185–1194.

Stewart, R.B., Beilfuss, M.L., & Verbrugge, K.M. (1995, March). *That was then, this is now: An empirical typology of adult sibling relationships.* Paper presented at the biennial meetings of the Society for Research in Child Development, Indianapolis, IN.

Stewart, S., Pearson, S., Luke, C., & Horowitz, J. (1998). Effects of home-based intervention on unplanned readmissions and out-of-hospital deaths. *Journal of the American Geriatrics Society, 46*, 174–180.

Stinner, W.F., Byun, Y., & Paita, L. (1990). Disability and living arrangements among elderly American men. *Research on Aging, 12*, 339–363.

Stipek, D., Gralinski, J., & Kopp, C. (1990). Self-concept development in the toddler years. *Developmental Psychology, 26*, 972–977.

Stobert, S. & Kemeny, A. (2003). Childfree by choice (Catalogue No. 11-008). *Canadian Social Trends, Summer*(69), 7–10.

Stockman, K., & Budd, K. (1997). Directions for intervention with adolescent mothers in substitute care. *Families in Society, 78*, 617–623.

Stoller, E.P., Forster, L.E., & Duniho, T.S. (1992). Systems of parent care within sibling networks. *Research on Aging, 14*, 28–49.

Stones, M.J., & Kozma, A. (1996). Activity, exercise, and behavior. In J.E. Birren & K.W. Schaie (Eds.), *Handbook of the psychology of aging* (4th ed., pp. 338–352). San Diego, CA: Academic Press.

Stormshak, E., Bierman, K., McMahon, R., Lengua, L., et al. (2000). Parenting practices and child disruptive behavior problems in early elementary school. *Journal of Clinical Child Psychology, 29*, 17–29.

Stoutjesdyk, D., & Jevne, R. (1993). Eating disorders among high performance athletes. *Journal of Youth and Adolescence, 22*, 271–282.

Strawbridge, W.J., Camacho, T.C., Cohen, R.D., & Kaplan, G.A. (1993). Gender differences in factors associated with change in physical functioning in old age: A 6-year longitudinal study. *The Gerontologist, 33*, 603–609.

Strayer, F.F. (1980). Social ecology of the preschool peer group. In A. Collins (Ed.), *Minnesota symposia on child psychology* (Vol. 13, pp. 165–196). Hillsdale, NJ: Erlbaum.

Strayer, J., & Roberts, W. (1997). Children's personal distance and their empathy: Indices of interpersonal closeness. *International Journal of Behavioral Development, 20*(3), 385–403.

Strayer, J., & Roberts, W. (2004). Children's anger, emotional expressiveness, and empathy: Relations with parents' empathy, emotional expressiveness, and parenting practices. *Social Development, 13*(2), 229–254.

Streissguth, A.P., Barr, H.M., & Sampson, P.D. (1990). Moderate prenatal alcohol exposure: Effects on child IQ and learning problems at age 7 1/2 years. *Alcoholism. Clinical and Experimental Research, 14*, 662–669.

Streufert, S., Pogash, R., Piasecki, M., & Post, G.M. (1990). Age and management team performance. *Psychology and Aging, 5*, 551–559.

Striano, T., & Rochat, P. (1999). Developmental link between dyadic and triadic social competence in infancy. *British Journal of Developmental Psychology, 17*, 551–562.

Stroebe, M.S., & Stroebe, W. (1993). The mortality of bereavement: A review. In M.S. Stroebe, W. Stroebe, & R.O. Hansson (Eds.), *Handbook of bereavement: Theory, research, and intervention* (pp. 175–195). Cambridge, England: Cambridge University Press.

Stroebe, M., van Son, M., Stroebe, W., Kleber, R., Schut, H., & van den Bout, J. (2000). On the classification and diagnosis of pathological grief. *Clinical Psychology Review, 20*, 57–75.

Stroebe, W., & Stroebe, M.S. (1993). Determinants of adjustment to bereavement in younger widows and widowers. In M.S. Stroebe, W. Stroebe, & R.O. Hansson (Eds.), *Handbook of bereavement. Theory, research, and intervention* (pp. 208–226). Cambridge, England: Cambridge University Press.

Struthers, J. (2000). *The 2000 Canadian Encyclopedia National Edition* [Computer Software]. Toronto: McClelland & Stewart.

Students Commission. (1992). Being Canadian: Culture, heritage, and identity. Students Commission. Retrieved November 18, 2001 from http://collections.ic.gc.ca/sharing/B_C_e.html

Students Commission. (1995). History. Students commission. Retrieved November 18, 2001 from http://collections.ic.gc.ca/sharing/history_e.html

Stull, D.E., & Hatch, L.R. (1984). Unravelling the effects of multiple life changes. *Research on Aging, 6*, 560–571.

Stunkard, A.J., Harris, J.R., Pedersen, N.L., & McClearn, G.E. (1990). The body-mass index of twins who have been reared apart. *New England Journal of Medicine, 322*, 1483–1487.

Sudworth, M. & deSouza, P. (2000). *Youth court statistics, 1999/00* (Vol. 21, No. 3). (Catalogue No. 85-002-XPE). Ottawa, ON: Statistics Canada. Retrieved November 18, 2001 from http://www.statcan.ca/english/previews/85-002-XIE/P0030185-002-XIE.pdf

Sugisawa, H., Liang, J., & Liu, X. (1994). Social networks, social support, and mortality among older people in Japan. *Journals of Gerontology: Social Sciences, 49*, S3–13.

Suicide Information & Education Centre. (1998). *SIEC Alert: Trends in Canadian suicide.* Calgary: Author. Retrieved December 28, 2001 from http://www.suicideinfo.ca/library/alert/alert30.pdf

Sullivan, K., & Bradbury, T. (1997). Are premarital prevention programs reaching couples at risk for marital dysfunction? *Journal of Consulting & Clinical Psychology, 65*, 24–30.

Sullivan, K., Zaitchik, D., & Tager-Flusberg, H. (1994). Preschoolers can attribute second-order beliefs. *Developmental Psychology, 30*, 395–402.

Sullivan, M., Ormel, J., Kempen, G., & Tymstra, T. (1998). Beliefs concerning death, dying, and hastening death among older, functionally impaired Dutch adults: A one-year longitudinal study. *Journal of the American Geriatrics Society, 46*, 1251–1257.

Susman, E.J., Inoff-Germain, G., Nottelmann, E.D., Loriaux, D.L., Cutler, G.B., Jr., & Chrousos, G.P. (1987). Hormones, emotional dispositions, and aggressive attributes in young adolescents. *Child Development, 58*, 1114–1134.

Susser, E., & Lin, S. (1992). Schizophrenia after prenatal exposure to the Dutch hunger winter of 1944–45. *Archives of General Psychiatry, 49*, 983–988.

Svrakic, N., Svrakic, D., & Cloninger, C. (1996). A general quantitative theory of personality development: Fundamentals of a self-organizing psychobiological complex. *Development & Psychopathology, 8*, 247–272.

Swaim, K., & Bracken, B. (1997). Global and domain-specific self-concepts of a matched sample of adolescent runaways and non-runaways. *Journal of Clinical Child Psychology, 26*, 37–403.

Swanson, S.M. (1999). *Abuse and neglect of older adults.* Ottawa, ON: Health Canada, The National Clearinghouse on Family Violence. Retrieved December 30, 2001 from http://www.hc-sc.gc.ca/hppb/familyviolence/pdfs/abuseneg98en.pdf

Swedo, S.E., Rettew, D.C., Kuppenheimer, M., Lum, D., Dolan, S., & Goldberger, E. (1991). Can adolescent suicide attempters be distinguished from at-risk adolescents? *Pediatrics, 88*, 620–629.

Swendsen, J., & Mazure, C. (2000). Life stress as a risk factor for postpartum depression: Current research and methodological issues. *Clinical Psychology, 7*, 17–31.

Swensen, C.H., Eskew, R.W., & Kohlhepp, K.A. (1981). Stage of family life cycle, ego development, and the marriage relationship. *Journal of Marriage and the Family, 43*, 841–853.

Syme, S.L. (1990). Control and health: An epidemiological perspective. In J. Rodin, C. Schooler, & K.W. Schaie (Eds.), *Self directedness: Cause and effects throughout the life course* (pp. 213–229). Hillsdale, NJ: Erlbaum.

Symons, D.K. (1998). Post-partum employment patterns, family-based care arrangements, and the mother-infant relationship at age two. *Canadian Journal of Behavioural Sciences, 30*(2), 121–131.

Tait, M., Padgett, M.Y., & Baldwin, T.T. (1989). Job and life satisfaction: A reevaluation of the strength of the relationship and gender effects as a function of the date of the study. *Journal of Applied Psychology, 74*, 502–507.

Takahashi, K., Tamura, J., & Tokoro, M. (1997). Patterns of social relationships and psychological well-being among the elderly. *International Journal of Behavioral Development, 21*, 417–430.

Takata, T. (1999). Development process of independent and interdependent self-construal in Japanese culture: Cross-cultural and cross-sectional analyses. *Japanese Journal of Educational Psychology, 47*, 480–489.

Takei, Y., & Dubas, J.S. (1993). Academic achievement among early adolescents: Social and cultural diversity. In R.M. Lerner (Ed.), *Early adolescence: Perspectives on research, policy, and intervention* (pp. 175–190). Hillsdale, NJ: Erlbaum.

Talan, J. (1998, October 28). Possible genetic link found for right-handedness, not for left. *Seattle Times.*

Talbott, M. (1998). Older widows' attitudes towards men and remarriage. *Journal of Aging Studies, 12*, 429–449.

Tanner, J. (1978). *Fetus into man: Physical growth from conception to maturity.* Cambridge, MA: Harvard University Press.

Tanner, J.M. (1990). *Foetus into man: Physical growth from conception to maturity* (2nd ed.). Cambridge, MA: Harvard University Press.

Tanner, J.M., Hughes, P.C.R., & Whitehouse, R.H. (1981). Radiographically determined widths of bone, muscle and fat in the upper arm and calf from 3–18 years. *Annals of Human Biology, 8*, 495–517.

Tan-Niam, C., Wood, D., & O'Malley, C. (1998). A cross-cultural perspective on children's theories of mind and social interaction. *Early Child Development & Care, 144*, 55–67.

Tapanya, S., Nicki, R., & Jarusawad, O. (1997). Worry and intrinsic/extrinsic religious orientation among Buddhist (Thai) and Christian (Canadian) elderly persons. *International Journal of Aging and Human Development, 44*, 73–83.

Tarter, R., Panzak, G., Switala, J., Lu, S., et al. (1997). Isokinetic muscle strength and its association with neuropsychological capacity in cirrhotic alcoholics. *Alcoholism: Clinical & Experimental Research, 21*, 191–196.

Taylor, J.A., & Danderson, M. (1995). A reexamination of the risk factors for the sudden infant death syndrome. *Journal of Pediatrics, 126*, 887–891.

Taylor, M., Cartwright, B.S., & Carlson, S.M. (1993). A developmental investigation of children's imaginary companions. *Developmental Psychology, 29,* 276–285.

Taylor, R.D., & Roberts, D. (1995). Kinship support and maternal and adolescent well-being in economically disadvantaged African-American families. *Child Development, 66,* 1585–1597.

Taylor, R.J., Chatters, L.M., Tucker, M.B., & Lewis, E. (1990). Developments in research on black families: A decade review. *Journal of Marriage and the Family, 52,* 993–1014.

Taylor, W., Ayars, C., Gladney, A., Peters, R., Roy, J., Prokhorov, A., Chamberlain, R., & Gritz, E. (1999). Beliefs about smoking among adolescents: Gender and ethnic differences. *Journal of Child & Adolescent Substance Abuse, 8,* 37–54.

Teicher, M.H. (2002). Scars that won't heal: The neurobiology of child abuse. *Scientific American, 286*(3), 68–75.

Temoshok, L. (1987). Personality, coping style, emotion and cancer: Towards an integrative model. *Cancer Surveys, 6,* 545–567.

Terman, L. (1916). *The measurement of intelligence.* Boston: Houghton Mifflin.

Terman, L., & Merrill, M.A. (1937). *Measuring intelligence: A guide to the administration of the new revised Stanford-Binet tests.* Boston: Houghton Mifflin.

Tershakovec, A. & Stallings, V. (1998). Pediatric nutrition and nutritional disorders. In R. Behrman & R. Kliegman (Eds.), *Nelson essentials of pediatrics* (3rd ed.). Philadelphia: W.B. Saunders.

Teti, D.M., Gelfand, D.M., Messinger, D.S., & Isabella, R. (1995). Maternal depression and the quality of early attachment: An examination of infants, preschoolers, and their mothers. *Developmental Psychology, 31,* 364–376.

Tettamanzi, D. (1998, September 30). Anthropological and ethical thoughts on whether domestic partnerships should have same legal status as the family. *L'Osservatore Romano/English Edition,* p. 9.

Thagard, P. (1996). *Mind: Introduction to cognitive science.* Cambridge, MA: MIT Press/Bradford Books.

Thagard, P. (2002). Cognitive science. In *The Stanford Encyclopedia of Philosophy* (Winter 2002 Edition), Edward N. Zalta (Ed.). Retrieved March 21, 2004, from http://plato.stanford.edu/archives/win2002/entries/cognitive-science/

Thal, D., & Bates, E. (1990). Continuity and variation in early language development. In J. Colombo & J. Fagen (Eds.), *Individual differences in infancy: Reliability, stability, prediction* (pp. 359–385). Hillsdale, NJ: Erlbaum.

Tharenou, P. (1999). Is there a link between family structures and women's and men's managerial career advancement? *Journal of Organizational Behavior, 20,* 837–863.

Tharp, R.G., & Gallimore, R. (1988). *Rousing minds to life.* New York: Cambridge University Press.

Thelen, E. (1995). Motor development: A new synthesis. *American Psychologist, 50,* 79–95.

Thelen, E., & Adolph, K.E. (1992). Arnold L. Gesell: The paradox of nature and nurture. *Developmental Psychology, 28,* 368–380.

Theriault, J. (1998). Assessing intimacy with the best friend and the sexual partner during adolescence: The PAIR-M inventory. *Journal of Psychology, 132,* 493–506.

Thiessen, V., & Nickerson, C. (2001). *Canadian gender trends in education and work* (Catalogue No. MP32-30/00-4E). Ottawa, ON: Human Resources Development Canada. Retrieved December 12, 2001 from http://www.hrdc-drhc.gc.ca/arb/publications/research/2000docs/t-00-4e.pdf

Thomas, A., & Chess, S. (1977). *Temperament and development.* New York: Brunner/Mazel.

Thomas, E.M. (2004). *Aggressive behaviour outcomes for young children: Change in parenting environment predicts change in behaviour* (Catalogue No. 89-599-MIE2004001). Ottawa, ON: Statistics Canada.

Thomas, J., Yan, J., & Stelmach, G. (2000). Movement substructures change as a function of practice in children and adults. *Journal of Experimental Child Psychology, 75,* 228–244.

Thomas, M. (1996). *Comparing theories of child development* (4th ed.). New York: Norton.

Thomas, M.H. (2000). Abstinence-based programs for prevention of adolescent pregnancies: A review. *Journal of Adolescent Health, 26,* 5–17.

Thomas, R.M. (Ed.). (1990a). *The encyclopedia of human development and education: Theory, research, and studies.* Oxford, England: Pergamon Press.

Thorn, A., & Gathercole, S. (1999). Language-specific knowledge and short-term memory in bilingual and non-bilingual children. *Quarterly Journal of Experimental Psychology: Human Experimental Psychology, 52A,* 303–324.

Thorne, B. (1986). Girls and boys together... but mostly apart: Gender arrangements in elementary schools. In W.W. Hartup & Z. Rubin (Eds.), *Relationships and development* (pp. 167–184). Hillsdale, NJ: Erlbaum.

Thorson, J.A., & Powell, F.C. (1990). Meanings of death and intrinsic religiosity. *Journal of Clinical Psychology, 46,* 379–390.

Thorson, J.A., & Powell, F.C. (1992). A revised death anxiety scale. *Death Studies, 16,* 507–521.

Tice, R.R., & Setlow, R.B. (1985). DNA repair and replication in aging organisms and cells. In C.E. Finch & E.L. Schneider (Eds.), *Handbook of the biology of aging* (2nd ed., pp. 173–224). New York: Van Nostrand Reinhold.

Tinnitis Association of Canada. (2001). *Questions & Answers.* Toronto: Author. Retrieved December 28, 2001 from http://www.kadis.com/ta/faq.htm

Todd, R.D., Swarzenski, B., Rossi, P.G., & Visconti, P. (1995). Structural and functional development of the human brain. In D. Cicchetti & D.J. Cohen (Eds.), *Developmental psychopathology: Vol. 1. Theory and methods* (pp. 161–194). New York: Wiley.

Tokar, D., Fischer, A., & Subich, L. (1998). Personality and vocational behavior: A selective review of the literature, 1993–1997. *Journal of Vocational Behavior, 53,* 115–153.

Tomita, T., Ohta, Y., Ogawa, K., Sugiyama, H., Kagami, N., & Agari, I. (1997). Grief process and strategies of psychological helping: A review. *Japanese Journal of Counseling Science, 30,* 49–67.

Tomlinson-Keasey, C., Eisert, D.C., Kahle, L.R., Hardy-Brown, K., & Keasey, B. (1979). The structure of concrete operational thought. *Child Development, 50,* 1153–1163.

Torgerson, D., Thomas, R., Campbell, M., & Reid, D. (1997). Alcohol consumption and age of maternal menopause are associated with menopause onset. *Maturitas, 26,* 21–25.

Torgesen, J., Wagner, R., Rashotte, C., Rose, E., et al. (1999). Preventing reading failure in young children with phonological processing disabilities: Group and individual responses to instruction. *Journal of Educational Psychology, 91,* 594–603.

Toronto District School Board (2001). *Facts and figures about the TDSB.* Toronto: Author. Retrieved October 6, 2001 from http://www.tdsb.on.ca/communications/TDSBFacts.html

Torrey, E. (1992). *Freudian fraud: The malignant effect of Freud's theory on American thought and culture.* New York: HarperCollins.

Tortora, G., & Grabowski, S. (1993). *Principles of anatomy and physiology.* New York: HarperCollins.

Tracey, T.J., & Rounds, J. (1993). Evaluating Holland's and Gati's vocational-interest models: A structural meta-analysis. *Psychological Bulletin, 113,* 229–246.

Traffic Injury Research Foundation (2001). *Graduated licensing: A blueprint for North America.* Ottawa, ON: Author.

Trainor, L., Clark, E., Huntley, A., & Adams, B. (1997). The acoustic basis of preferences for infant-directed singing. *Infant Behavior & Development, 20,* 383–396.

Treas, J. & Giesen, D. (2000). Sexual infidelity among married and cohabiting Americans. *Journal of Marriage & the Family, 62*(1), 48–60.

Trehub, S., Hill, D., & Kamenetsky, S. (1997). Parents' sung performances for infants. *Canadian Journal of Experimental Psychology, 51,* 385–396.

Trehub, S., Unyk, A., Kamenetsky, S., Hill, D., et al. (1997). Mothers' and fathers' singing to infants. *Developmental Psychology, 33,* 500–507.

Tremblay, M.S. & Willms, J.D. (2000). Secular trends in the body mass index of Canadian children. *Canadian Medical Association Journal, 163*(11), 1429–1433.

Tremblay, R.F. (2000). The origins of youth violence. *Isuma, 1*(2), 19–24.

Tremblay, R.E., Boulerice, B., Harden, P.W., McDuff, P., Perusse, D., Pihl, R.O., & Zoccolillo, M. (1996). Do children in Canada become more aggressive as they approach adolescence? In Human Resources Development Canada & Statistics Canada, *Growing up in Canada: National longitudinal survey of children and youth*. Ottawa, ON: Author.

Triggs-Raine, B., Richard, M., Wasel, N., Prence, E.M & Natowicz, M.R. (1995) Mutational analyses of Tay-Sachs disease: studies on Tay-Sachs carriers of French Canadian background living in New England. *American Journal of Human Genetics, 56*(4), 870–879.

Trivers, R. (1972). Parental investment and sexual selection. In B. Campbell (Ed.), *Sexual selection and the descent of man: 1871–1971* (pp. 136–179). Chicago: Aldine.

Trocmé, N., Durrant, J., Ensom, R., & Marwah, I. (2004). *Physical abuse of children in the context of punishment*. CECW Information Sheet #8E. Toronto, Canada: Faculty of Social Work, University of Toronto. Retrieved June 21, 2004 from http://www.cecwcepb.ca/DocsEng/PhysAbuse&Punishment8E.pdf

Troll, L.E. (1985). The contingencies of grandparenting. In V.L. Bengtson & J.F. Robertson (Eds.), *Grandparenthood* (pp. 135–150). Beverly Hills, CA: Sage.

Trovato, F. (1991). Early childhood mortality 1926–1986. *Canadian Social Trends (Summer)*, 6–10. Ottawa, ON: Statistics Canada.

Truluck, J., & Courtenay, B. (1999). Learning style preferences among older adults. *Educational Gerontology, 25*, 221–236.

Trusty, J. (1999). Effects of eighth-grade parental involvement on late adolescents' educational expectations. *Journal of Research & Development in Education, 32*, 224–233.

Tsang, P. (1998). Age, attention, expertise, and time-sharing performance. *Psychology & Aging, 13*, 323–347.

Tsitouras, P.D., & Bulat, T. (1995). The aging male reproductive system. *Endocrinology and Metabolism Clinics of North America, 24*, 297–315.

Tsuya, N.O., & Martin, L.G. (1992). Living arrangements of elderly Japanese and attitudes toward inheritance. *Journals of Gerontology: Social Sciences, 47*, S45–54.

Tulving, E. (1972). Episodic and semantic memory. In E. Tulving & W. Donaldson (Eds.), *Organization of memory* (pp. 381–403). New York: Academic Press.

Tulving, E. (1999). *What is episodic memory and why is it unique?* Bauer Colloquium Series. Toronto: University of Toronto. Retrieved August 18, 2004 from http://www.bio.brandeis.edu/news/bauer/1999/tulving.html

Tulving, E. (2004). Episodic memory: from mind to brain. *Revue Neurologique (Paris), 160*(4), 9–23.

Tunstall-Pedoe, H., & Smith, W.C.S. (1990). Cholesterol as a risk factor for coronary heart disease. *British Medical Bulletin, 46*, 1075–1087.

Turcotte, P. (2003). Update on families (Catalogue No. 11-008-XPE). *Canadian Social Trends, Summer*(69), 11–13.

Turiel, E. (1983). *The development of social knowledge: Morality and convention*. New York: Cambridge University Press.

Turner, N.E., Toneatto, T., & Stanovich, K. (1999, February). Cognitive Biases in Problem Gamblers. *New Directions in Gambling Research Conference of the National Centre for Responsible Gaming*.

Twycross, R.G. (1996). Euthanasia: Going Dutch? *Journal of the Royal Society of Medicine, 89*, 61–63.

Udry, J.R., & Campbell, B.C. (1994). Getting started on sexual behavior. In A.S. Rossi (Ed.), *Sexuality across the life course* (pp. 187–208). Chicago: University of Chicago Press.

Uecker, A., & Nadel, L. (1996). Spatial locations gone awry: Object and spatial memory deficits in children with fetal alcohol syndrome. *Neuropsychologia, 34*, 209–223.

Uhlenberg, P., Cooney, T., & Boyd, R. (1990). Divorce for women after midlife. *Journals of Gerontology: Social Sciences, 45*, S3–11.

Umberson, D. (1992). Relationships between adult children and their parents: Psychological consequences for both generations. *Journal of Marriage and the Family, 54*, 664–674.

Underwood, M. (1997). Peer social status and children's understanding of the expression and control of positive and negative emotions. *Merrill-Palmer Quarterly, 43*, 610–634.

Underwood, M.K., Kupersmidt, J.B., & Coie, J.D. (1996). Childhood peer sociometric status and aggression as predictors of adolescent childbearing. *Journal of Research on Adolescence, 6*, 201–224.

United Nations Development Programme. (2003). *Human development index*. Retrieved August 10, 2004 from http://www.undp.org/hdr2003/indicator/pdf/hdr03_table_1.pdf

Uno, D., Florsheim, P., & Uchino, B. (1998). Psychosocial mechanisms underlying quality of parenting among Mexican-American and White adolescent mothers. *Journal of Youth & Adolescence, 27*, 585–605.

Updegraff, K., & Obeidallah, D. (1999). Young adolescents' patterns of involvement with siblings and friends. *Social Development, 8*, 52–69.

Upperman, P.U., & Church, A.T. (1995). Investigating Holland's typological theory with army occupational specialties. *Journal of Vocational Behavior, 47*, 61–75.

Urban, J., Carlson, E., Egeland, B., & Sroufe, L A. (1991). Patterns of individual adaptation across childhood. *Development and Psychopathology, 3*, 445–460.

Urberg, K., Degirmencioglu, S., & Pilgrim, C. (1997). Close friend and group influence on adolescent cigarette smoking and alcohol use. *Developmental Psychology, 33*, 834–844.

Urberg, K., Degirmencioglu, S., & Tolson, J. (1998). Adolescent friendship selection and termination: The role of similarity. *Journal of Social & Personal Relationships, 15*, 703–710.

Urberg, K.A., Degirmencioglu, S.M., Tolson, J.M., & Halliday-Scher, K. (1995). The structure of adolescent peer networks. *Developmental Psychology, 31*, 540–547.

Urdan, T. (1997). Examining the relations among early adolescent students' goals and friends' orientation toward effort and achievement in school. *Contemporary Educational Psychology, 22*, 165–191.

Ushikubo, M. (1998). A study of factors facilitating and inhibiting the willingness of the institutionalized disabled elderly for rehabilitation: A United States–Japanese comparison. *Journal of Cross-Cultural Gerontology, 13*, 127–157.

Uttl, B., Graf, P., & Richter, L.K. (2002). Verbal Paired Associates tests limits on validity and reliability. *Archives of Clinical Neuropsychology, 17*(6), 567–581.

Vachon, M. (1998). Psychosocial needs of patients and families. *Journal of Palliative Care, 14*, 49–56.

Vaeisaenen, L. (1998). Family grief and recovery process when a baby dies. *Psychiatria Fennica, 29*, 163–174.

Vaillant, G.E. (1991). The association of ancestral longevity with successful aging. *Journals of Gerontology: Psychological Sciences, 46*, P292–298.

van Balen, F. (1998). Development of IVF children. *Developmental Review, 18*, 30–46.

van Bommel, H. (1992). *Dying for care: Hospice care or euthanasia*. Toronto: NC Press Limited.

van Bommel, H. (2002). *Family hospice care: Pre-planning and care guide* (16th Anniversary Edition). Scarborough, ON: Resources Supporting Family and Community Legacies Inc. Retrieved September 8, 2004 from http://www.legacies.ca/Family_Hospice_Care%20Index.htm

Van Boxtel, M., Paas, F., Houx, P., Adam, J., Teeken, J., & Jolles, J. (1997). Aerobic capacity and cognitive performance in a cross-sectional aging study. *Medicine & Science in Sports & Exercise, 29*, 1357–1365.

Vandell, D., & Ramanan, J. (1991). Children of the National Longitudinal Survey of Youth: Choices in after-school care and child development. *Developmental Psychology, 27*, 637–643.

Vandell, D., & Ramanan, J. (1992). Effects of early and recent maternal employment of children from low-income families. *Child Development, 63*, 938–949.

van den Boom, D.C. (1994). The influence of temperament and mothering on attachment and exploration: An experimental manipulation of sensitive responsiveness among lower-class mothers with irritable infants. *Child Development, 65,* 1457–1477.

van den Boom, D. (1995). Do first-year intervention effects endure? Follow-up during toddlerhood of a sample of Dutch irritable infants. *Child Development, 66,* 1798–1816.

van den Hoonaard, D. (1999). "No regrets": Widows' stories about the last days of their husbands' lives. *Journal of Aging Studies, 13,* 59–72.

van der Molen, M., Molenaar, P. (1994). Cognitive psychophysiology: A window to cognitive development and brain maturation. In G. Dawson & K. Fischer (Eds.), *Human behavior and the developing brain* (pp. 456–492). New York: Guilford Press.

Van Doorn, C., Kasl, S., Beery, L., Jacobs, S., & Prigerson, H. (1998). The influence of marital quality and attachment styles on traumatic grief and depressive symptoms. *Journal of Nervous & Mental Disease, 186,* 566–573.

van Doornen, L., Snieder, H., & Boomsma, D. (1998). Serum lipids and cardiovascular reactivity to stress. *Biological Psychology, 47,* 279–297.

van Grootheest, D., Beekman, A., van Groenou, M., & Deeg, D. (1999). Sex differences in depression after widowhood: Do men suffer more? *Social Psychiatry & Psychiatric Epidemiology, 34,* 391–398.

van Heeringen, K. (2003). The neurobiology of suicide and suicidality. *Canadian Journal of Psychiatry, 48*(5), 292–300.

Van Hightower, N., & Gorton, J. (1998). Domestic violence among patients at two rural health care clinics: Prevalence and social correlates. *Public Health Nursing, 15,* 355–362.

van IJzendoorn, M.H. (1995). Adult attachment representations, parental responsiveness, and infant attachment: A meta-analysis on the predictive validity of the Adult Attachment Interview. *Psychological Bulletin, 117,* 387–403.

van IJzendoorn, M.H., Goldberg, S., Kroonenberg, P.M., & Frenkel, O.J. (1992). The relative effects of maternal and child problems on the quality of attachment: A meta-analysis of attachment in clinical samples. *Child Development, 63,* 840–858.

Vanier Institute of the Family (2001). Did you know? How much time do Canadians spend watching television? Ottawa, ON: Author. Retrieved November 17, 2001 from http://www.vifamily.ca/faqs/didyouknow.htm

Van Lange, P., DeBruin, E., Otten, W., & Joireman, J. (1997). Development of prosocial, individualistic, and competitive orientations: Theory and preliminary evidence. *Journal of Personality & Social Psychology, 73,* 733–746.

van Lieshout, C.F.M., & Haselager, G.J.T. (1994). The big five personality factors in Q-sort descriptions of children and adolescents. In C.F. Halverson, Jr., G.A. Kohnstamm, & R.P. Martin (Eds.), *The developing structure of temperament and personality from infancy to adulthood* (pp. 293–318). Hillsdale, NJ: Erlbaum.

van Wel, F. (1994). "I count my parents among my best friends": Youths' bonds with parents and friends in the Netherlands. *Journal of Marriage and the Family, 56,* 835–843.

Vaughn, B., Stevenson-Hinde, J., Waters, E., Kotsaftis, A., Lefever, G., Shouldice, A., Trudel, M., & Belsky, J. (1992). Attachment security and temperament in infancy and early childhood: Some conceptual clarification. *Developmental Psychology, 28,* 463–473.

Venkatraman, M.M. (1995). A cross-cultural study of the subjective well-being of married elderly persons in the United States and India. *Journals of Gerontology: Social Sciences, 50B,* S35–44.

Verbrugge, L.M. (1989). Gender, aging, and health. In K.S. Markides (Ed.), *Aging and health* (pp. 23–78). Newbury Park, CA: Sage.

Verbrugge, L.M., Lepkowski, J.M., & Konkol, L.L. (1991). Levels of disability among U.S. adults with arthritis. *Journals of Gerontology: Social Sciences, 46,* S71–83.

Verbrugge, L.M., & Wingard, D.L. (1987). Sex differentials in health and mortality. *Women and Health, 12,* 103–145.

Verhaeghen, P., & Marcoen, A. (1993). Memory aging as a general phenomenon: Episodic recall of older adults is a function of episodic recall of young adults. *Psychology and Aging, 8,* 380–388.

Verhaeghen, P., Marcoen, A., & Goossens, L. (1992). Improving memory performance in the aged through mnemonic training: A meta-analytic study. *Psychology and Aging, 7,* 242–251.

Verhaeghen, P., Marcoen, A., & Goossens, L. (1993). Facts and fiction about memory aging: A quantitative integration of research findings. *Journals of Gerontology: Psychological Sciences, 48,* P157–171.

Verhaeghen, P., & Salthouse, T. (1997). Meta-analyses of age-cognition relations in adulthood: Estimates of linear and nonlinear age effects and structural models. *Psychological Bulletin, 122,* 231–249.

Veroff, J., Douvan, E., & Kulka, R.A. (1981). *The inner American: A self-portrait from 1957 to 1976.* New York: Basic Books.

Vihko, R., & Apter, D. (1980). The role of androgens in adolescent cycles. *Journal of Steroid Biochemistry, 12,* 369–373.

Vinokur, A.D., & van Ryn, M. (1993). Social support and undermining in close relationships: Their independent effects on the mental health of unemployed persons. *Journal of Personality and Social Psychology, 65,* 350–359.

Vitaro, F., Tremblay, R., Kerr, M., Pagani, L., & Bukowski, W. (1997). Disruptiveness, friends' characteristics, and delinquency in early adolescence: A test of two competing models of development. *Child Development, 68,* 676–689.

Volz, J. (2000). Successful aging: The second 50. *Monitor, 31,* 24–28.

Vouloumanos, A. & Werker, J.F. (in press). Tuned to the signal: The privileged status of speech for young infants. *Developmental Science.*

Voyer, D., Voyer, S., & Bryden, M.P. (1995). Magnitude of sex differences in spatial abilities: A meta-analysis and consideration of critical variables. *Psychological Bulletin, 117,* 250–270.

Vuchinich, S., Bank, L., & Patterson, G.R. (1992). Parenting, peers, and the stability of antisocial behavior in preadolescent boys. *Developmental Psychology, 28,* 510–521.

Vuorenkoski, L., Kuure, O., Moilanen, I., & Peninkilampi, V. (2000). Bilingualism, school achievement, and mental wellbeing: A follow-up study of return migrant children. *Journal of Child Psychology & Psychiatry & Allied Disciplines, 41,* 261–266.

Vygotsky, L.S. (1978). *Mind and society: The development of higher mental processes.* Cambridge, MA: Harvard University Press. (Original works published 1930, 1933, and 1935.)

Waggoner, G. (2000). The new grandparents: What they buy, what they think. *Modern Maturity, 43,* 85, 91.

Waite, L.J. (1995). *Does marriage matter?* Presidential address to the Population Association of America, Chicago.

Walden, T.A. (1991). Infant social referencing. In J. Garber & K.A. Dodge (Eds.), *The development of emotion regulation and dysregulation* (pp. 69–88). Cambridge, England: Cambridge University Press.

Walker, H., Messinger, D., Fogel, A., & Karns, J. (1992). Social and communicative development in infancy. In V.B.V. Hasselt & M. Hersen (Eds.), *Handbook of social development: A lifespan perspective* (pp. 157–181). New York: Plenum.

Walker, L. (1980). Cognitive and perspective-taking prerequisites for moral development. *Child Development, 51,* 131–139.

Walker, L.J. (1989). A longitudinal study of moral reasoning. *Child Development, 60,* 157–160.

Walker, L.J., de Vries, B., & Trevethan, S.D. (1987). Moral stages and moral orientations in real-life and hypothetical dilemmas. *Child Development, 58,* 842–858.

Walker-Andrews, A., & Kahana-Kalman, R. (1999). The understanding of pretence across the second year of life. *British Journal of Developmental Psychology, 17,* 523–536.

Walker-Andrews, A.S., & Lennon, E. (1991). Infants' discrimination of vocal expressions: Contributions of auditory and visual information. *Infant Behavior and Development, 14,* 131–142.

Wallace, M. (2003). Crime statistics in Canada, 2002. (Catalogue No. 85-002-XPE). *Juristat, 23*(5), np.

Wallace, M. (2004). Crime statistics in Canada, 2003. (Catalogue No. 85-002-XPE). *Juristat, 24*(6), np.

Waller, A., Dennis, F., Brodie, J., & Cairns, A. (1998). Evaluating the use of TalksBac, a predictive communication device for nonfluent adults with aphasia. *International Journal of Language and Communication Disorders, 33*, 45–70.

Wallerstein, J.S. (1986). Women after divorce: Preliminary report from a ten-year-follow-up. *American Journal of Orthopsychiatry, 56*, 65–77.

Wallerstein, J., & Lewis, J. (1998). The long-term impact of divorce on children: A first report from a 25-year study. *Family & Conciliation Courts Review, 36*, 368–383.

Walton, G.E., Bower, N.J.A., & Bower, T.G.R. (1992). Recognition of familiar faces by newborns. *Infant Behavior and Development, 15*, 265–269.

Wang, C., & Chou, P. (1999). Risk factors for adolescent primigravida in Kaohsium County, Taiwan. *American Journal of Preventive Medicine, 17*, 43–47.

Wang, C., & Phinney, J. (1998). Differences in child rearing attitudes between immigrant Chinese mothers and Anglo-American mothers. *Early Development & Parenting, 7*, 181–189.

Wang, D., Kato, N., Inaba, Y., Tango, T., et al. (2000). Physical and personality traits of preschool children in Fuzhou, China: Only child vs. sibling. *Child: Care, Health & Development, 26*, 49–60.

Warburton, J., Le Brocque, R., & Rosenman, L. (1998). Older people: the reserve army of volunteers? An analysis of volunteerism among older Australians. *International Journal of Aging & Human Development, 46*, 229–245.

Ward, S.L., & Overton, W.F. (1990). Semantic familiarity, relevance, and the development of deductive reasoning. *Developmental Psychology, 26*, 488–493.

Wark, G.R., & Krebs, D.L. (1996). Gender and dilemma differences in real-life moral judgment. *Developmental Psychology, 32*, 220–230.

Warr, P., Jackson, P., & Banks, M. (1988). Unemployment and mental health: Some British studies. *Journal of Social Issues, 44*, 47–68.

Wartner, U.D., Grossman, K., Fremmer-Bombik, E., & Suess, G. (1994). Attachment patterns at age six in south Germany: Predictability from infancy and implications for preschool behavior. *Child Development, 65*, 1014–1027.

Waters, E., Treboux, D., Crowell, J., Merrick, S., & Albersheim, L. (1995, March). *From the Strange Situation to the Adult Attachment Interview: A 20-year longitudinal study of attachment security in infancy and early adulthood.* Paper presented at the biennial meetings of the Society for Research in Child Development, Indianapolis, IN.

Watkins, S.C., Menken, J.A., & Bongaarts, J. (1987). Demographic foundations of family change. *American Sociological Review, 52*, 346–358.

Watson, A., Nixon, C., Wilson, A., & Capage, L. (1999). Social interaction skills and theory of mind in young children. *Developmental Psychology, 35*, 386–391.

Watson, J. (1997). Grandmothering across the lifespan. *Journal of Gerontological Social Work, 28*, 45–62.

Watson, J.B. (1913). Psychology as the behaviorist views it. *Psychological Review, 20*, 158–177.

Watson, J.B. (1928). *Psychological care of the infant and child.* New York: Norton.

Watson, J.B. (1930). *Behaviorism.* New York: Norton.

Watson, J.B., & Rayner, R. (1920). Conditioned emotional reactions. *Journal of Experimental Psychology, 3*, 1–14.

Watt, L., & Cappeliez, P. (2000). Integrative and instrumental reminiscence therapies for depression in older adults: Intervention strategies and treatment effectiveness. *Aging & Mental Health, 4*, 166–177.

Waxman, S.R., & Kosowski, T.D. (1990). Nouns mark category relations: Toddlers' and preschoolers' word-learning biases. *Child Development, 61*, 1461–1473.

Weaver, C., & Hinson, S. (2000). Job satisfaction of Asian Americans. *Psychological Reports, 86*, 586–594.

Weaver, D.A. (1994). The work and retirement decisions of older women: A literature review. *Social Security Bulletin, 57*, 3–24.

Weaver, J. (1999). Gerontology education: A new paradigm for the 21st century. *Educational Gerontology, 25*, 479–490.

Weaver, S., Clifford, E., Hay, D., & Robinson, J. (1997). Psychosocial adjustment to unsuccessful IVF and GIFT treatment. *Patient Education & Counseling, 31*, 7–18.

Weber, K. (1993). *Special Education in Ontario Schools.* Thornhill, ON: Highland Press.

Webster, J., & McCall, M. (1999). Reminiscence functions across adulthood: A replication and extension. *Journal of Adult Development, 6*, 73–85.

Webster, M.L., Thompson, J.M., Mitchell, E.A., & Werry, J.S. (1994). Postnatal depression in a community cohort. *Australian & New Zealand Journal of Psychiatry, 28*, 42–49.

Webster, P.S., & Herzog, A.R. (1995). Effects of parental divorce and memories of family problems on relationships between adult children and their parents. *Journals of Gerontology: Social Sciences, 50B*, S24–34.

Wechsler, D. (2003). *Wechsler Intelligence Scale for Children— Fourth Edition.* San Antonio, TX: Harcourt Assessment, Inc.

Wechsler, H., Davenport, A., Dowdall, G., Moeykens, B., & Castillo, S. (1994). Health and behavioral consequences of binge drinking in college. *Journal of the American Medical Association, 272*, 1672–1677.

Wechsler, H., Dowdall, G., Maenner, G., Gledhill-Hoyt, J., & Lee, H. (1998). Changes in binge drinking and related problems among American college students between 1993 and 1997. *Journal of American College Health, 47*, 57–68.

Weidner, J. (2001, June 21). Few kids have sex before 16, expert says. *The Kitchener-Waterloo Record.* Retrieved November 17, 2001 from http://www.therecord.com/cgi-bin/PFP.cgi?doc=news/news_0106219126.html

Weinberg, R.A. (1989). Intelligence and IQ: Landmark issues and great debates. *American Psychologist, 44*, 98–104.

Weinberger, J. (1996). A longitudinal study of children's early literacy experiences at home and later literacy development at home and school. *Journal of Research in Reading, 19*, 14–24.

Weinstock, L. (1999). Gender differences in the presentation and management of social anxiety disorder. *Journal of Clinical Psychiatry, 60*, 9–13.

Weisburger, J.H., & Wynder, E.L. (1991). Dietary fat intake and cancer. *Hematology/Oncology Clinics of North America, 5*, 7–23.

Weisner, T., & Wilson-Mitchell, J. (1990). Nonconventional family lifestyles and sex typing in six-year olds. *Child Development, 62*, 1915–1933.

Weiss, M. (1998). Conditions of mothering: The bio-politics of falling in love with your child. *Social Science Journal, 35*, 87–105.

Weisse, C.S. (1992). Depression and immunocompetence: A review of the literature. *Psychological Bulletin, 111*, 475–489.

Welch, D.C., & West, R.L. (1995). Self-efficacy and mastery: Its application to issues of environmental control, cognition, and aging. *Developmental Review, 15*, 150–171.

Welch-Ross, M. (1997). Mother-child participation in conversation about the past: Relationships to preschoolers' theory of mind. *Developmental Psychology, 33*, 618–629.

Welford, A.T. (1993). The gerontological balance sheet. In J. Cerella, J. Rybash, W. Hoyer, & M.L. Commons (Eds.), *Adult information processing: Limits on loss* (pp. 3–10). San Diego, CA: Academic Press.

Wellman, H.M. (1982). The foundations of knowledge: Concept development in the young child. In S.G. Moore & C.C. Cooper (Eds.), *The young child: Reviews of research* (Vol. 3, pp. 115–134). Washington, DC: National Association for the Education of Young Children.

Wen, S.W., Goldenberg, R.L., Cutter, G.R., Hoffman, H.J., Cliver, S.P., Davis, R.O., & DuBard, M.D. (1990). Smoking, maternal age, fetal growth, and gestational age at delivery. *American Journal of Obstetrics and Gynecology, 162*, 53–58.

Wentzel, K.R., & Asher, S.R. (1995). The academic lives of neglected, rejected, popular, and controversial children. *Child Development, 66*, 754–763.

Werker, J.F. (1989). Becoming a native listener: A developmental perspective on human speech perception. *American Scientist, 77*(1), 54–59.

Werker, J.F. (1995). Exploring developmental changes in cross-language speech perception. In D.N. Osherson (Ed.), *An invitation to cognitive science: Language* (Vol. 1). Cambridge, MA: MIT Press.

Werker, J.F., Cohen, L.B., Lloyd, V., Cassosola, M., & Stager, C. (1998). Acquisition of word-object associations by 14-month-old infants. *Developmental Psychology, 34*(6), 1289–1309.

Werker, J.F., & Tees, R.C. (1984). Phonemic and phonetic factors in adult cross-language speech perception. *Journal of the Acoustical Society of America, 75*(6), 1866–1878.

Werner, E.E. (1995). Resilience in development. *Current Directions in Psychological Science, 4,* 81–85.

Wernet, S., Olliges, R., & Delicath, T. (2000). Postcourse evaluations of WebCT (web course tools) classes by social work students. *Research on Social Work Practice, 10,* 387–504.

West, P., Sweeting, H., & Ecob, R. (1999). Family and friends' influences on the uptake of regular smoking from mid-adolescence to early adulthood. *Addiction, 97,* 1397–1411.

West, R.L., & Crook, T.H. (1990). Age differences in everyday memory: Laboratory analogues of telephone number recall. *Psychology and Aging, 5,* 520–529.

Wethington, E. (2000). Expecting stress: Americans and the "midlife crisis." *Motivation and Emotion, 24*(2), 85–103.

Wethington, E., Cooper, H., & Holmes, C.S. (1997). Turning points in midlife. In I.H. Gotlib & B. Wheaton (Eds.), *Stress and adversity across the life course: Trajectories and turning points* (pp. 215–231). New York: Cambridge University Press.

Whitam, F.L., Diamond, M., & Martin, J. (1993). Homosexual orientation in twins: A report on 61 pairs and three triplet sets. *Archives of Sexual Behavior, 22,* 187–206.

Whitbeck, L.B., Simons, R.L., & Conger, R.D. (1991). The effects of early family relationships on contemporary relationships and assistance patterns between adult children and their parents. *Journals of Gerontology: Social Sciences, 46,* S330–337.

White, M., Wilson, M., Elander, G., & Persson, B. (1999). The Swedish family: Transition to parenthood. *Scandinavian Journal of Caring Sciences, 13,* 171–176.

White, W.H. (1992). G. Stanley Hall: From philosophy to developmental psychology. *Developmental Psychology, 28,* 25–34.

Whitehurst, G.J., Arnold, D.S., & Lonigan, C.J. (1990). *Dialogic reading: The hear-say method.* A video workshop. Stony Brook, NY: Acorn Films.

Whiting, B., & Edwards, C. (1988). *Children of different worlds.* Cambridge, MA: Harvard University Press.

Whitney, M.P., & Thoman, E.B. (1994). Sleep in premature and full-term infants from 24-hour home recordings. *Infant Behavior and Development, 17,* 223–234.

Whittaker, R. (1998). Re-framing the representation of women in advertisements for hormone replacement therapy. *Nursing Inquiry, 5,* 77–86.

Wich, B.K., & Carnes, M. (1995). Menopause and the aging female reproductive system. *Endocrinology and Metabolism Clinics of North America, 24,* 273–295.

Wicki, W. (1999). The impact of family resources and satisfaction with division of labour on coping and worries after the birth of the first child. *International Journal of Behavioral Development, 23,* 431–456.

Wickrama, K., Conger, R., Lorenz, F., & Elder, G. (1998). Parental education and adolescent self-reported physical health. *Journal of Marriage & the Family, 60,* 967–978.

Wickrama, K., Lorenz, F., & Conger, R. (1997). Parental support and adolescent physical health status: A latent growth-curve analysis. *Journal of Health & Social Behavior, 38,* 149–163.

Wiederman, M., & Allgeier, E. (1992). Gender differences in mate selection criteria: Sociobiological or socioeconomic explanation? *Ethology and Sociobiology, 13,* 115–124.

Wigfield, A., Eccles, J.S., MacIver, D., Reuman, D.A., & Midgley, C. (1991). Transitions during early adolescence: Changes in children's domain-specific self-perceptions and general self-esteem across the transition to junior high school. *Developmental Psychology, 27,* 552–565.

Wilcox, C., & Francis, L. (1997). The relationship between neuroticism and the perceived social desirability of feminine characteristics among 16–19-year-old females. *Social Behavior & Personality, 25,* 291–294.

Wilkins, K., & Park, E. (1996). Chronic conditions, physical limitations and dependency among seniors living in the community (Catalogue No. 82-003-XPB). *Health Reports, 8*(3), 7–15.

Wilkins, R., Houle, C., Berthelot, J., & Ross, N. (2000). The changing health status of Canada's children. *Isuma, 1*(2), 57–63.

Williams, C. (2001). Family disruptions and childhood happiness (Catalogue No. 11-008-XPE). *Canadian Social Trends, Autumn,* 2–4.

Williams, D.R. (1992). Social structure and the health behaviors of blacks. In K.W. Schaie, D. Blazer, & J.S. House (Eds.), *Aging, health behaviors, and health outcomes* (pp. 59–64). Hillsdale, NJ: Erlbaum.

Williams, E., & Radin, N. (1993). Parental involvement, maternal employment, and adolescents' academic achievement: An 11-year follow-up. *American Journal of Orthopsychiatry, 63,* 306–312.

Williams, J.E., & Best, D.L. (1990). *Measuring sex stereotypes: A multination study* (rev. ed.). Newbury Park, CA: Sage.

Willis, S.L. (1996). Everyday problem solving. In J.E. Birren & K.W. Schaie (Eds.), *Handbook of the psychology of aging* (4th ed., pp. 287–307). San Diego, CA: Academic Press.

Willis, S.L., Jay, G.M., Diehl, M., & Marsiske, M. (1992). Longitudinal change and prediction of everyday task competence in the elderly. *Research on Aging, 14,* 68–91.

Willms, J.D. (2002a). Research findings bearing on Canadian social policy. In J.D. Willms (Ed.), *Vulnerable children* (pp. 331–358). Edmonton, AB: The University of Alberta Press.

Willms, J.D. (2002b). Socioeconomic gradients for childhood vulnerability. In J.D. Willms (Ed.), *Vulnerable children* (pp. 71–102). Edmonton, AB: The University of Alberta Press.

Willms, J.D., & Corbett, B.A. (2003). Tech and teens: Access and use. *Canadian Social Trends, Summer*(69), 15–20.

Wilson, M., Daly, M., & Wright, C. (1993). Uxoricide in Canada: Demographic risk patterns. *Canadian Journal of Criminology, 35,* 263–291.

Wilson, W.J. (1995). Jobless ghettos and the social outcome of youngsters. In P. Moen, G.H. Elder, Jr., & K. Lüscher (Eds.), *Examining lives in context: Perspectives on the ecology of human development* (pp. 527–543). Washington, DC: American Psychological Association.

Wimmer, H., Mayringer, H., & Landerl, K. (1998). Poor reading: A deficit in skill-automatization or a phonological deficit? *Scientific Studies of Reading, 2,* 321–340.

Winter, L., Lawton, M., Casten, R., & Sando, R. (2000). The relationship between external events and affect states in older people. *International Journal of Aging & Human Development, 50,* 85–96.

Winter, R. (1999). A Biblical and theological view of grief and bereavement. *Journal of Psychology & Christianity, 18,* 367–379.

Wintgens, A., Lepine, S., Lefebvre, F., Glorieux, J., Gauthier, Y., & Robaey, P. (1998). Attachment, self-esteem, and psychomotor development in extremely premature children at preschool age. *Infant Mental Health Journal, 19,* 394–408.

Wintre, M., & Yaffe, M. (2000). First-year students' adjustment to university life as a function of relationships with parents. *Journal of Adolescent Research, 15,* 9–37.

Winzer, M. (1993). *Children with exceptionalities* (3rd ed.). Scarborough, ON: Prentice-Hall Canada.

Wolfson, C., Handfield-Jones, R., Glass, K.C., McClaran, J., & Keyserlingk, E. (1993). Adult children's perceptions of their responsibility to provide care for dependent elderly parents. *The Gerontologist, 33,* 315–323.

Wolinsky, F.D., Calahan, C.M., Fitzgerald, J.F., & Johnson, R.J. (1993). Changes in functional status and the risks of subsequent nursing home placement and death. *Journals of Gerontology: Social Sciences, 48*, S93–101.

Wolinsky, F.D., Stump, T.E., & Clark, D. (1995). Antecedents and consequences of physical activity and exercise among older adults. *The Gerontologist, 35,* 451–462.

Wong, D. (1993). *Whaley & Wong's essentials of pediatric nursing.* St. Louis, MO: Mosby-Yearbook, Inc.

Wong, P.T.P. (2000). Meaning in life and meaning in death in successful aging. In A. Tomer (Ed.), *Death Attitudes and the Older Adult: Theories, Concepts, and Applications* (pp. 23–36). Philadelphia, PA: Brunner/Mazel.

Wong, P.T.P. (2003). *From death anxiety to death acceptance: A meaning management model.* Langley, BC: International Network on Personal Meaning. Retrieved September 9, 2004 from http://www.meaning.ca/articles/death_acceptance.htm

Wood, C., & Terrell, C. (1998). Pre-school phonological awareness and subsequent literacy development. *Educational Psychology, 18,* 253–274.

Woods, N., & Mitchell, E. (1997). Pathways to depressed mood for midlife women: Observations from the Seattle Midlife Women's Health Study. *Research in Nursing & Health, 20,* 119–129.

Woodside, D.B., Garfinkel, P.E., Lin, E., Goering, P., Kaplan, A.S., Goldbloom, D.S., & Kennedy, S.H. (2001). Comparisons of men with full or partial eating disorders, men without eating disorders, and women with eating disorders in the community. *American Journal of Psychiatry, 158*(4), 570–574.

Woodward, L., & Fergusson, D. (2000). Childhood peer relationship problems and later risks of educational under-achievement and unemployment. *Journal of Child Psychology & Psychiatry & Allied Disciplines, 41,* 191–201.

Woodward, M., & Tunstall-Pedoe, H. (1995). Alcohol consumption, diet, coronary risk factors, and prevalent coronary heart disease in men and women in the Scottish heart health study. *Journal of Epidemiology and Community Health, 49,* 354–362.

The Working Group for the PEPI Trial (1995). Effects of estrogen or estrogen/progestin regimens on heart disease risk factors in postmenopausal women: The Postmenopausal Estrogen/Progestin Interventions (PEPI) Trial. *Journal of the American Medical Association, 273,* 199–208.

World Health Organization. (2000). *Violence against women* [Online report]. Retrieved September 1, 2000 from http://www.who.int

World Health Organization. (2002). Abuse of the elderly (Chapter 5). In E.G. Krug, L.L. Dahlberg, J.A. Mercy, A.B. Zwi, & R. Lozano (Eds.), *World report on violence and health* (pp. 123–145). Retrieved August 31, 2004 from http://www.who.int/violence_injury_prevention/violence/world_report/en/full_en.pdf

Worobey, J.L., & Angel, R.J. (1990). Functional capacity and living arrangements of unmarried elderly persons. *Journals of Gerontology: Social Sciences, 45,* S95–101.

Worrell, F. (1997). Predicting successful or non-successful at-risk status using demographic risk factors. *High School Journal, 81,* 46–53.

Wortman, C.B., & Silver, R.C. (1989). The myths of coping with loss. *Journal of Consulting and Clinical Psychology, 57,* 349–357.

Wortman, C.B., & Silver, R.C. (1990). Successful mastery of bereavement and widowhood: A life course perspective. In P.B. Baltes & M.M. Baltes (Eds.), *Successful aging: Perspectives from the behavioral sciences* (pp. 225–264). New York: Cambridge University Press.

Wortman, C.B., & Silver, R.C. (1992). Reconsidering assumptions about coping with loss: An overview of current research. In L. Montada, S. Filipp, & M.J. Lerner (Eds.), *Life crises and experiences of loss in adulthood* (pp. 341–365). Hillsdale, NJ: Erlbaum.

Wortman, C.B., Silver, R.C., & Kessler, R.C. (1993). The meaning of loss and adjustment to bereavement. In M.S. Stroebe, W. Stroebe, & R.O. Hansson (Eds.), *Handbook of bereavement* (pp. 349–366). Cambridge, England: Cambridge University Press.

Wright, C., & Birks, E. (2000). Risk factors for failure to thrive: A population-based survey. *Child: Care, Health & Development, 26,* 5–16.

Wright, M.J. (1993). Women groundbreakers in Canadian psychology: World War II and its aftermath. *Canadian Psychology, 33*(2), Abstract.

Wright, M.J, & Myers, C. (1982). *History of academic psychology in Canada.* Toronto: C.J. Hogrefe, Inc.

Wright, S., Taylor, D., & Macarthur, J. (2000). Subtractive bilingualism and the survival of the Inuit language: Heritage versus second-language education. *Journal of Educational Psychology, 92,* 63–84.

Wu, Z. (1998). Recent trends in marriage patterns in Canada. *Policy Options, September,* 3–6. Retrieved December 11, 2001 from http://www.irpp.org/po/archives/sep98/wu.pd

Wu, Z. 2000. *Cohabitation: An alternative form of family living.* Toronto: Oxford University Press.

Wu, Z., & Penning, M. (1997). Marital instability after midlife. *Journal of Family Issues, 18,* 459–478.

Wyatt, G., Axelrod, J., Chin, D., Carmona, J., & Loeb, T. (2000). Examining patterns of vulnerability to domestic violence among African American women. *Violence Against Women, 6,* 495–514.

Wyatt, N. (2004, August 8). Survey: Online dating dangerous. *CNEWS.* Retrieved August 14, 2004 from http://cnews.canoe.ca/CNEWS/Canada/2004/08/08/pf-575064.html

Xie, H., Cairns, R., & Cairns, B. (1999). Social networks and configurations in inner-city schools: Aggression, popularity, and implications for students with EBD. *Journal of Emotional & Behavioral Disorders, 7,* 147–155.

Yang, H., & Chandler, D. (1992). Intergenerational relations: Grievances of the elderly in rural China. *Journal of Comparative Family Studies, 23,* 431–453.

Yarcheski, A., Mahon, N., & Yarcheski, T. (1998). A study of introspectiveness in adolescents and young adults. *Western Journal of Nursing Research, 20,* 312–324.

Yeung, A., Chui, H., & Lau, I. (1999). Hierarchical and multidimensional academic self-concept of commercial students. *Contemporary Educational Psychology, 24,* 376–389.

Yirmiya, N., Eriel, O., Shaked, M., & Solomonica-Levi, D. (1998). Meta-analyses comparing theory of mind abilities of individuals with autism, individuals with mental retardation, and normally developing individuals. *Psychological Bulletin, 124,* 283–307.

Yirmiya, N., & Shulman, C. (1996). Seriation, conservation, and theory of mind abilities in individuals with autism, individuals with mental retardation, and normally developing children. *Child Development, 67,* 2045–2059.

Yirmiya, N., Solomonica-Levi, D., Shulman, C., & Pilowsky, T. (1996). Theory of mind abilities in individuals with autism, Down syndrome, and mental retardation of unknown etiology: The role of age and intelligence. *Journal of Child Psychology & Psychiatry & Allied Disciplines, 37,* 1003–1014.

Yonas, A., & Owsley, C. (1987). Development of visual space perception. In P. Salpatek & L. Cohen (Eds.), *Handbook of infant perception: Vol. 2. From perception to cognition* (pp. 80–122). Orlando, FL: Academic Press.

Yordanova, J., Kolev, V., & Basar, E. (1998). EEG theta and frontal alpha oscillations during auditory processing change with aging. *Electroencephalography & Clinical Neurophysiology: Evoked Potentials, 108,* 497–505.

Young, A. (1997). I think, therefore I'm motivated: The relations among cognitive strategy use, motivational orientation and classroom perceptions over time. *Learning & Individual Differences, 9,* 249–283.

Young, J., & Rodgers, R. (1997). A model of radical career change in the context of psychosocial development. *Journal of Career Assessment, 5,* 167–182.

Young, M., & Bradley, M. (1998). Social withdrawal: Self-efficacy, happiness, and popularity in introverted and extroverted adolescents. *Canadian Journal of School Psychology, 14,* 21–35.

Young, S., Fox, N., & Zahn-Waxler, C. (1999). The relations between temperament and empathy in 2-year-olds. *Developmental Psychology, 35,* 1189–1197.

Young, T.K, Reading, J., Elias, B. & O'Neil, J.D. (2000). Type 2 diabetes mellitus in Canada's First Nations: Status of an epidemic in progress. *Canadian Medical Association Journal, 163*(5), 561–566.

Yuill, N. (1997). English children as personality theorists: Accounts of the modifiability, development, and origin of traits. *Genetic, Social & General Psychology Monographs, 123,* 5–26.

Yuji, H. (1996). Computer games and information-processing skills. *Perceptual & Motor Skills, 83,* 643–647.

Zahn-Waxler, C., & Radke-Yarrow, M. (1982). The development of altruism: Alternative research strategies. In N. Eisenberg (Ed.), *The development of prosocial behavior* (pp. 109–138). New York: Academic Press.

Zahn-Waxler, C., Radke-Yarrow, M., & King, R. (1979). Child rearing and children's prosocial initiations toward victims of distress. *Child Development, 50,* 319–330.

Zahn-Waxler, C., Radke-Yarrow, M., Wagner, E., & Chapman, M. (1992). Development of concern for others. *Developmental Psychology, 28,* 126–136.

Zakriski, A., & Coie, J. (1996). A comparison of aggressive-rejected and nonaggressive-rejected children's interpretation of self-directed and other-directed rejection. *Child Development, 67,* 1048–1070.

Zani, B. (1993). Dating and interpersonal relationships in adolescence. In S. Jackson & H. Rodrigues-Tomé (Eds.), *Adolescence and its social worlds* (pp. 95–119). Hove, England: Erlbaum.

Zelazo, N.A., Zelazo, P.R., Cohen, K.M., & Zelazo, P.D. (1993). Specificity of practice effects on elementary neuromotor patterns. *Developmental Psychology, 29,* 686–691.

Zelazo, P.D., & Boseovski, J.J. (2001). Video reminders in a representational change task: Memory for cues but not beliefs or statements. *Journal of Experimental Child Psychology, 78,* 107–129.

Zelazo, P., Helwig, C., & Lau, A. (1996). Intention, act, and outcome in behavioral prediction and moral judgment. *Child Development, 67,* 2478–2492.

Zelazo, P.R., Zelazo, N.A., & Kolb, S. (1972). "Walking" in the newborn. *Science, 176,* 314–315.

Zelinski, E., & Burnight, K. (1997). Sixteen-year longitudinal and time lag changes in memory and cognition in older adults. *Psychology & Aging, 12,* 503–513.

Zelinski, E.M., Gilewski, M.J., & Schaie, K.W. (1993). Individual differences in cross-sectional and 3-year longitudinal memory performance across the adult life span. *Psychology and Aging, 8,* 176–186.

Zick, C., & Holden, K. (2000). An assessment of the wealth holdings of recent widows. *Journal of Gerontology, 55B,* S90–S97.

Zigler, E., & Finn-Stevenson, M. (1993). *Children in a changing world: Developmental and social issues.* Pacific Grove, CA: Brooks/Cole.

Zigler, E., & Hodapp, R.M. (1991). Behavioral functioning in individuals with mental retardation. *Annual Review of Psychology, 42,* 29–50.

Zigler, E., & Styfco, S.J. (1993). Using research and theory to justify and inform Head Start expansion. *Social Policy Report, Society for Research in Child Development, VII*(2), 1–21.

Zimmer, Z., Hickey, T., & Searle, M.S. (1995). Activity participation and well-being among older people with arthritis. *The Gerontologist, 35,* 463–471.

Zimmer-Gembeck, M. (1999). Stability, change and individual differences in involvement with friends and romantic partners among adolescent females. *Journal of Youth & Adolescence, 28,* 419–438.

Zimmerman, C. (2000). The development of scientific reasoning skills. *Developmental Review, 20,* 99–149.

Zimmerman, M., Copeland, L., Shope, J., & Dielman, T. (1997). A longitudinal study of self-esteem: Implications for adolescent development. *Journal of Youth & Adolescence, 26,* 117–141.

Zisook, S., Chentsova-Dutton, Y., & Shuchter, S. (1998). PTSD following bereavement. *Annals of Clinical Psychiatry, 10,* 157–163.

Zisook, S., Paulus, M., Shuchter, S., & Judd, L. (1997). The many faces of depression following spousal bereavement. *Journal of Affective Disorders, 45,* 85–94.

Zunker, V. (1994). *Career counseling.* Pacific Grove, CA: Brooks/Cole.

Zuzanek, J. (2000). *The effects of time use and time pressure on child-parent relationships.* Waterloo: Otium Publications. Retrieved July 7, 2004 from http://www.hc-sc.gc.ca/dca-dea/publications/pdf/timepcr-tempsrpe_e.pdf

NAME INDEX

SUBJECT INDEX

June 25/08